Second Edition

ECONOMETRIC MODELS, TECHNIQUES, AND APPLICATIONS

MICHAEL D. INTRILIGATOR
University of California, Los Angeles

RONALD G. BODKIN
University of Ottawa

CHENG HSIAO
University of Southern California

Prentice Hall, Upper Saddle River, NJ 07458

Library of Congress Cataloging-in-Publication Data

Intriligator, Michael D.
Econometric models, techniques, and applications / Michael D. Intriligator, Ronald G. Bodkin, Cheng Hsiao, — 2bd ed,
p. cm.
Includes bibliographical references and index.
ISBN 0-13-224775-5
1. Econometrics. 2. Econometric models. I. Bodkin, Ronald G. II. Hsiao, Cheng.
HB139.I57 1996
330'.01'5195—dc20 95-26103
CIP

Acquisitions editor *Leah Jewell*
Production manager *Maureen Wilson*
Associate editor *Teresa Cohan*
Buyer *Marie McNamara*
Marketing manager *Susan McLaughlin*
Cover designer *Jayne Conte*
Cover art *Michael Schneps, The Image Bank*

A Pearson Education Co.
Upper Saddle River, NJ 07458

Printed in the United States of America

10 9 8 7 6 5 4 3 2 1

ISBN 0-13-224775-5

Prentice-Hall International (UK) Limited, London
Prentice-Hall of Australia Pty. Limited, Sydney
Prentice-Hall Canada Inc., Toronto
Prentice-Hall Hispanoamericana, S.A., Mexico
Prentice-Hall of India Private Limited, New Delhi
Prentice-Hall of Japan, Inc., Tokyo
Pearson Education Asia Pte. Ltd., Singapore
Editora Prentice-Hall do Brasil, Ltda., Rio de Janeiro

Michael D. Intriligator wishes to dedicate his portion of this book to his sons, Kenneth, James, William and Robert;
Ronald G. Bodkin, to his wife Brenda;
and Cheng Hsiao, to his wife Amy Mei-Yun

CONTENTS

Preface xiii

PART I INTRODUCTION: OVERVIEW, MODELS, AND DATA

Chapter 1 The Econometric Approach 1

1.1 *What is econometrics?* 1
1.2 *The nature of the econometric approach* 2
1.3 *The purposes of econometrics* 4
1.4 *An example: The demand curve and the price elasticity of demand* 5
1.5 *Second example: The consumption function* 7
1.6 *Third example: The growth of science* 8
1.7 *Traditional econometrics under criticism* 9
1.8 *Learning by doing in econometrics* 11
Bibliography 11

Chapter 2 Models, Economic Models, and Econometric Models 13

2.1 *What is a model?* 13
2.2 *Types of models: Verbal/logical, physical, and geometric* 15
2.3 *Algebraic models* 17
2.4 *Econometric models* 19
2.5 *The prototype micro model* 24
2.6 *The prototype macro model* 29
2.7 *Related approaches to econometric modeling* 33
2.8 *The general econometric model: Structural form and reduced form* 35

2.9 *The final form* 40
2.10 *Identification of the general econometric model; concluding remarks* 42
Problems 45
Bibliography 47

Chapter 3 Data and Refined Data 50

3.1 *What are data?* 50
3.2 *Quantitative versus qualitative data; dummy variables* 51
3.3 *Time-series versus cross-section data; pooling; microdata* 54
3.4 *Nonexperimental versus experimental data: Social experimentation* 57
3.5 *Problems with the data* 58
3.6 *Refining the data* 59
3.7 *Accuracy of economic data* 62
3.8 *Sources of economic data* 64
Problems 64
Bibliography 68

PART II SINGLE-EQUATION ESTIMATION

Chapter 4 The Basic Linear Regression Model 70

4.1 *Introduction* 70
4.2 *The linear regression model* 70
4.3 *Estimation using the method of least squares* 74
4.4 *The Gauss–Markov theorem and properties of the least squares estimator* 79
4.5 *Maximum likelihood and the method of moments estimators* 84
4.6 *Linear restrictions on the coefficients* 86
4.7 *Statistical inference* 88
4.8 *Prediction* 98
4.9 *Examples* 99
4.10 *Nonnested hypothesis testing and model selection criteria* 104
4.11 *Bayesian analysis of the linear regression model* 109
Problems 117
Bibliography 122

Chapter 5 Extensions of the Simple Linear Regression Model 125

5.1 *Problems: Their diagnosis and treatment* 125
5.2 *Multicollinearity* 126
5.3 *Generalized least squares method and seemingly unrelated regression models* 133
5.4 *Heteroskedasticity* 136
5.5 *Serial correlation* 139
5.6 *Error components models* 146
5.7 *Specification error* 151
5.8 *Errors in variables and the method of instrumental variables* 155
5.9 *Nonlinear least squares estimator: Gauss–Newton and Newton–Raphson methods for solving nonlinear equations* 159

5.10 *Discrete response models: Linear probability, probit, and logit models* 161
5.11 *Censored or truncated regression models* 164
5.12 *Robust methods* 167
5.13 *Parametric and semiparametric estimation* 169
5.14 *Approaches to analyzing economic data* 174
Problems 176
Bibliography 181

Chapter 6 Introduction to Time-Series Analysis and Dynamic Specification 187

6.1 *Introduction* 187
6.2 *Some basic tools* 189
6.3 *Stationary processes* 191
6.4 *Box–Jenkins procedure for building linear (stationary) time-series models* 198
6.5 *Nonstationary time series* 207
6.6 *Example* 216
6.7 *Minimum mean square error forecast* 219
6.8 *Transfer function models* 222
Problems 232
Bibliography 235

PART III APPLICATIONS OF SINGLE-EQUATION ESTIMATION

Chapter 7 Application to Households; Demand Analysis 238

7.1 *Introduction* 238
7.2 *The theory of the household* 239
7.3 *Single demand equations versus systems of demand equations* 248
7.4 *Single demand equations* 249
7.5 *Systems of demand equations* 254
7.6 *Identification* 258
7.7 *Aggregation* 261
7.8 *Dynamic demand analysis* 263
Problems 268
Bibliography 273

Chapter 8 Applications to Firms; Production Functions and Cost Functions 275

8.1 *Introduction* 275
8.2 *The theory of the firm* 275
8.3 *Estimation of production functions* 284
8.4 *Estimation of cost curves and cost functions* 299
8.5 *Estimation of factor demand equations* 302
8.6 *Technical change* 306
Problems 309
Bibliography 313

PART IV SIMULTANEOUS EQUATIONS AND DYNAMIC SYSTEMS

Chapter 9 The Simultaneous-Equations System and Its Identification 318

9.1 *The simultaneous-equations system* 318
9.2 *The problem of identification* 323
9.3 *Identification by zero restrictions in the nonstochastic case* 326
9.4 *Identification by general linear restrictions* 332
9.5 *Recursive systems* 336
9.6 *Identification of nonlinear models* 339
Problems 341
Bibliography 345

Chapter 10 Estimation of Simultaneous-Equations Systems 347

10.1 *Introduction* 347
10.2 *Naive, limited-information, and full-information approaches* 351
10.3 *Ordinary least squares and least squares bias* 353
10.4 *Indirect least squares* 356
10.5 *Two-stage least squares and* k*-class estimators* 360
10.6 *Instrumental variables* 369
10.7 *Three-stage least squares* 374
10.8 *Full-information maximum likelihood* 382
10.9 *Monte Carlo studies of small-sample properties of estimators* 386
10.10 *Nonlinear simultaneous equations models* 390
Problems 393
Bibliography 396

Chapter 11 Dynamic Systems 400

11.1 *Introduction* 400
11.2 *Dynamic simultaneous-equations models* 400
11.3 *Modeling unrestricted multiple time series: The approach of Tiao and Box* 403
11.4 *Granger causality* 409
11.5 *Cointegration* 412
11.6 *Relations between time-series models and structural econometric models* 421
Problems 425
Bibliography 426

PART V APPLICATIONS OF SIMULTANEOUS-EQUATIONS ESTIMATION

Chapter 12 Applications to Macroeconometric Models 430

12.1 *The nature of macroeconometric models* 430
12.2 *The Klein interwar model* 432
12.3 *The Klein–Goldberger model* 436

12.4 *The Wharton model* 438
12.5 *The MPS model* 441
12.6 *The DRI model* 443
12.7 *Survey of some macroeconometric models of the U.S. economy* 447
12.8 *Some international experience; the CANDIDE model of the Canadian economy* 453
12.9 *Trends in macroeconometric model construction* 456
Problems 458
Bibliography 460

Chapter 13 Other Applications of Simultaneous-Equations Estimation 465

13.1 *Introduction* 465
13.2 *Simultaneous-equations model of money demand and supply* 466
13.3 *Simultaneous-equations model of industrial-organization relationships* 470
13.4 *Simultaneous-equations model in labor economics* 474
13.5 *Simultaneous-equations model of the health system* 475
13.6 *Simultaneous-equations model of alcoholism* 479
13.7 *Economic history; cliometrics* 483
Problems 484
Bibliography 486

PART VI THE USES AND EVALUATION OF ECONOMETRIC MODELS

Chapter 14 Structural Analysis 490

14.1 *The uses of econometric models* 490
14.2 *The nature of structural analysis* 491
14.3 *Comparative statics* 492
14.4 *Elasticities* 495
14.5 *Multipliers: Impact, interim, and long-run (the linear case)* 498
14.6 *Multipliers: Impact, interim, and long-run (the nonlinear case)* 500
14.7 *Example of multiplier analysis: The Suits study* 502
14.8 *Second example of multiplier analysis: The Goldberger study* 504
14.9 *Third example of multiplier analysis: Study of comparative multipliers of U.S. macroeconometric models from a models comparisons project* 505
14.10 *Fourth example of multiplier analysis: Comparative interim multipliers with Canadian macroeconometric models* 507
14.11 *Final example of multiplier analysis: The DRI model of the early 1980s* 508
Problems 510
Bibliography 511

Chapter 15 Forecasting 513

15.1 *The nature of forecasting* 513
15.2 *Alternative approaches to forecasting* 515
15.3 *The econometric approach to forecasting; short-term forecasts* 518
15.4 *Long-term forecasts* 523
15.5 *Forecast accuracy* 523
15.6 *Forecasting experience with macroeconometric models: Specific studies* 527
15.7 *Forecasting experience with macroeconometric models: General lessons* 532

15.8 *Combining forecasts and forecasting methods* 535
Problems 537
Bibliography 540

Chapter 16 Policy Evaluation 545

16.1 *The nature of policy evaluation* 545
16.2 *Alternative approaches to policy evaluation* 546
16.3 *Policy evaluation using an econometric model* 548
16.4 *The instruments-targets approach* 549
16.5 *The social-welfare-function approach; optimal control* 551
16.6 *The simulation approach* 555
16.7 *The options for Canadian policymakers at the beginning of the 1980s and two other examples* 559
16.8 *The econometric approach to policy evaluation* 562
Problems 564
Bibliography 565

Chapter 17 Validation of Econometric Models and Managerial Aspects of the Uses of Econometric Models 569

17.1 *Introduction* 569
17.2 *Are the a priori constraints respected?* 570
17.3 *Parametric tests prior to the release of the model* 572
17.4 *Parametric tests after release* 574
17.5 *Nonparametric tests of an econometric model* 576
17.6 *The model as a system or gestalt* 578
17.7 *The problem of a possible break in structure; the "Lucas critique"* 579
17.8 *Managerial aspects of model uses: Four examples* 580
17.9 *Model management and the role of judgment* 582
Problems 583
Bibliography 584

Appendix A An Econometric Project 586

A.1 *The nature of the econometric project* 586
A.2 *The model* 586
A.3 *The data* 589
A.4 *Estimation of the model* 591
A.5 *What to include in the write-up* 591
A.6 *A bibliography of econometric applications* 593

Appendix B Matrices 599

B.1 *Basic definitions and examples* 599
B.2 *Some special matrices* 600
B.3 *Matrix relations and operations* 602
B.4 *Scalar-valued functions defined on matrices* 607
B.5 *Inverse and generalized inverse matrices* 610
B.6 *Systems of linear equations; solutions and least squares fits* 612
B.7 *Linear transformations and characteristic roots and vectors* 616

B.8 *Quadratic forms* 618
B.9 *Matrix derivatives* 619
B.10 *Mathematical programming* 621
Bibliography 624

Appendix C Probability and Statistics 625

C.1 *Probability* 625
C.2 *Random variables; distribution and density functions* 627
C.3 *Mean, variance, covariance, and other moments; sample measures* 632
C.4 *Some specific distributions* 635
C.5 *Additional results on distribution theory* 639
Bibliography 639

Indexes 641

PREFACE

Econometrics has come of age. It has produced a solid body of theory and, of equal importance, a host of applications both in economics and in other social sciences. In economics, econometrics has traditionally been applied to macroeconomics, but in recent years it has been applied to virtually every other field of economics, including microeconomics, industrial organization, public economics, international economics, labor economics, economic history, economic development, health economics, monetary economics, and urban and regional economics. Among the other social sciences, applications of econometric methods have been utilized in political science, sociology (including criminology), anthropology, psychology, geography, and history. Applications have been made in such diverse areas as education, law, health, crime, international finance, and transportation. As a consequence, there has been a tremendous growth of interest in econometrics on the part of both students and professional workers in economics and other social sciences.

THIS SECOND EDITION

While the organization and level of this second edition of *Econometric Models, Techniques, and Applications* are similar to those of the first edition, written by Michael D. Intriligator and published in 1978, we cover in this edition more recent developments in all three components of the book's focus: econometric models, econometric techniques, and econometric applications. Accordingly, this second edition is intended as both an up-to-date textbook for graduate and advanced undergraduate students and a reference work for professionals who want to learn more about the field of econometrics. This edition has several new and important features that distinguish it from the first edition. In the first place, the second edition has three entirely new chapters, one on time-series methods in econometrics (Chapter 6), another on dynamic systems (Chapter 11), and a third on validation and managerial experience with econometric models (Chapter 17). The chapters dealing with econometric theory have been largely rewritten, generally to include some recent developments in this burgeoning field. Other chapters, while not altered so greatly, have been updated, including discussions of and references to current literature.

PURPOSE

This book introduces and surveys the approach, techniques, and applications of econometrics. Its motivation arose largely from the observation that at least 80 percent of the material in most of the existing textbooks in econometrics focuses purely on econometric techniques. By contrast, practicing econometricians—or economists or social scientists performing econometric studies—typically spend 20 percent or less of their time and effort on econometric techniques per se; the remainder is spent on other aspects of the study, particularly on the construction of a relevant econometric model and the development of appropriate data before estimation and on the interpretation of results after estimation. The distinctive feature of this book is its balance between the econometric techniques per se—the model-building and data-collection areas—and the applications and uses of econometrics. It does not slight the techniques; rather it presents them in a logical, understandable, and usable fashion. It does, however, stress those aspects of econometrics of major importance to students and researchers interested in performing or evaluating econometric studies.

The book should enable the reader to understand and to evaluate existing econometric studies in a variety of areas. To a large extent, econometrics is not a science, defined by a narrow set of theorems, but rather an approach that can be appreciated and understood only by use. Indeed, the reader's comprehension of econometrics in practice will not be complete until he or she has performed an original econometric study, preparation for which is one of this book's basic objectives.

The book can be used as a textbook in first-year graduate or advanced undergraduate courses in econometrics. It can also be utilized as a supplementary text for courses in economic theory, economic statistics, sociometrics, engineering, public administration, policy sciences, system sciences, or other social sciences. It should also be of interest to economists, statisticians, engineers, and operations research analysts.

LEVEL AND PREREQUISITES

With regard to the level of the book, we have retained the same general level as the first edition in the firm belief that the only way to learn and to do econometrics is in the language of econometricians, namely with matrix notation and with the use of multivariate statistics. These topics are reviewed in a summary fashion in Appendices B and C respectively. In courses using this book as a text we would recommend that these materials be covered by digressions from the econometrics topics in order to review, when appropriate, the nature of, for example, matrix addition and multiplication and the nature of a multivariate random variable. As these appendices are not intended as text materials, references to introductory books on these subjects are also given at the beginning of each appendix. In addition, we assume an elementary knowledge of the basic concepts of multivariate calculus.

ORGANIZATION

The book now consists of six major parts. *Part I* introduces the nature of econometrics and the econometric approach. It discusses some of the important objectives of econometrics in order to motivate the student by specifically indicating what the study of econometrics may provide. It also treats models and data, particularly econometric models and economic data. It provides examples of relevant models, including two prototype models, the prototype micro model and the prototype macro model, which not only illustrate various aspects of model building but also represent a bridge to the later discussions of the applications of econometrics. The discussion of data, their nature and their limitations, and their sources should facilitate an understanding of this essential part of any applied econometric study. *Part II* concerns the estimation of single-equation models, including discussions of multiple linear regression and problems in and extensions of the basic linear regression model. We have completely rewritten Chapters 4 and 5 and added a new chapter, 6, on time-series problems. *Part III* covers applications of the techniques developed in Part II, including applications to the household (demand functions) and to the firm (production and cost functions). *Part IV* concerns the estimation of simultaneous-equations systems, including discussions of the identification problem and of limited-information and full-information estimation techniques. In line with current research we have added a chapter, 11, on dynamic systems. *Part V* discusses applications of these techniques to macroeconometric models and to other areas. Finally, *Part VI* provides a discussion of the three major uses of an estimated econometric model—structural analysis, forecasting, and policy evaluation—and of the validation or evaluation of econometric models. We have added a new final chapter, 17, "Validation of Econometric Models and Managerial Aspects of the Use of Econometric Models." In it we discuss some criteria for model evaluation and also consider some of the experience with the use of econometric models for managerial forecasting and for policy evaluation.

Appendix A outlines an econometric project, which students and other readers of this book are encouraged to perform as a way of learning econometrics by doing econometrics. *Appendix B* summarizes important definitions and theorems concerning matrices. Finally, *Appendix C* presents summary results concerning probability and statistics as used in this book.

DISTINCTIVE FEATURES

The distinctive features of this book are primarily the materials covered in Parts I, III, V, and VI.

Part I discusses those aspects of econometrics that are logically prior to estimation, namely the specification of the model and the development of data for its estimation. Remarkably enough, these aspects are still generally not treated in most current econometric textbooks, although the situation is better than it was a decade ago.

Parts III and V provide case studies of the applications of econometrics to a wide array of areas. They include traditional areas such as the estimation of demand functions and production functions, as illustrative of single-equation estimation, and macroeconometric models, which are illustrative of simultaneous-equation estimation. In this second edition we have included several newer econometric models not with the goal of exhaustively covering all such models but with the objective of conveying the nature of these models. At the same time we have retained many of the classical macroeconometric models summarized in the first edition, which continue to be the basis for newer developments. Readers, particularly student readers, should find these models valuable as guides to the development of their own econometric models. The applications surveyed, however, also include some newer areas in which both single-equation and simultaneous-equations methods are employed, such as monetary economics, labor economics, industrial organization, and health economics. Again, our purpose is not to be exhaustive, but rather to select several studies illustrating the application of econometric techniques to each area and to provide references to other such studies. (See, in particular, the Bibliography for Appendix A.) After having seen econometric methods applied to several areas, the reader, especially the student, should be able to carry out his or her own econometric project, including the specification of the model; the development of the data; the estimation of the model; and the use of the estimated model for purposes of structural analysis, forecasting, and policy evaluation, as outlined in Appendix A.

Part VI discusses the various uses to which an estimated econometric model may be put, as well as some managerial techniques for "auditing" an existing model, so that it retains its validity (as far as possible). An estimated econometric model is a very valuable product, not to be admired as an *objet d'art*, but rather to be put to use for the purposes discussed in Part VI, i.e., structural analysis, forecasting, and policy evaluation. This elementary but important message appears largely to have been omitted in most existing econometrics textbooks.

Finally, we note that a more complete and generally more advanced treatment of all three major topics of this book—econometric models, techniques, and applications—may be found in the *Handbook of Econometrics*, Zvi Griliches and Michael D. Intriligator, Eds. (Vol. 1, 1983; Vol. 2, 1984; Vol. 3, 1986; North-Holland Publishing Co., Amsterdam); and the *Handbook of Econometrics*, Vol. 4 (1994), Robert F. Engle and Daniel L. McFadden, Eds. (North-Holland Publishing Co., Amsterdam). These four volumes could be used as a supplement to this book for advanced students/readers or as a follow-on reference.

THE NATURE OF THE PROBLEMS

Another distinctive feature of this book remains the inclusion of problems in most chapters. We continue to believe that the problems play an important role in learning econometrics, in starting to speak the language of econometrics, and in diagnosing whether the text material has been fully comprehended. In particular, these problems should challenge the reader to enlarge upon the basic knowledge contained in the chapter by proving further results or by developing extensions. The intent is to provide the student of econometrics with a challenge somewhat comparable to the laboratory problem facing a student in the natural sciences. The problems have been updated, and, in many chapters, their number has been increased in this edition.

ACKNOWLEDGMENTS

This book is based on courses that the authors have given separately over many years, Intriligator's courses having been given at the University of California, Los Angeles, the University of Southern California, and the California Institute of Technology; Bodkin's courses having been given at the University of Ottawa, Carleton University (in Ottawa), and the University of Western Ontario; and Hsiao's courses having been given at the University of Southern California, the University of Toronto, and the University of California, Irvine. Our major acknowledgment is to the many students who have given us the benefit of their suggestions and comments, and so helped to teach us while we were "teaching" them. For the first edition, helpful comments and suggestions were received from William Barger, David Belsley, Christopher Bliss, Murray Brown, Jeffrey Conner, Camilo Dagum, the late Otto Eckstein, Arthur Goldberger, Stephen Goldfeld, Jay Helms, Bruce Herrick, the late Leif Johansen, Dale Jorgenson, Linda Kleiger, Robert McKnown, Jeffrey Perloff, Inga Rynell-Heller, Herman Stekler, Jack Tawil, and Victor Zarnowitz. For the second edition, we have had similarly helpful suggestions and comments from Herman Bierens, Andrew Buck, Siddhartha Chib, Fred Floss, Alan Kessler, Leonard Lardaro, Elizabeth Landaw, Stephen K. McNees, Peter Phillips, Tom Wansbeek, Andrew Weiss, and Arnold Zellner. In particular, we wish to acknowledge invaluable assistance from DRI–McGraw-Hill and from Cynthia Stevens, Roger Brinner, David Kelly, and Joyce Yanchar in particular, with regard to Section 12.6. For permission to reprint published materials, we should like to thank the scholarly journals: *Journal of the American Statistical Association*, *Journal of Econometrics*, and *Econometric Theory*. For partial support of Hsiao's contribution to this book, we wish to thank the National Science Foundation (of the United States). Finally, we wish to acknowledge heartily the encouragement and assistance of present and former Economics Editors at Prentice Hall, especially Bill Webber, Whitney Blake, Steve Dietrich, and Leah Jewell, as well as to our Production Manager, Maureen Wilson. To all of the above, we express warm gratitude.

MICHAEL D. INTRILIGATOR
RONALD G. BODKIN
CHENG HSIAO

1

THE ECONOMETRIC APPROACH

1.1 WHAT IS ECONOMETRICS?

To start with a definition, *econometrics* is the branch of economics concerned with the empirical estimation of economic relationships. The "metric" part of the word signifies *measurement*; and econometrics is concerned primarily with measuring economic relationships. Econometrics utilizes economic theory, as embodied in an *econometric model*; facts, as summarized by *relevant data*; and statistical theory, as refined into *econometric techniques*, to measure and to test empirically certain relationships among economic variables, thereby giving empirical content to economic reasoning. Although this definition is oriented to economics, the econometric approach is not confined exclusively to economics; it can be applied to other disciplines, especially other social sciences, such as history, political science, sociology, and psychology. It can also be applied to areas of public policy, including health, education, transportation, housing, and environmental protection.

When the term *econometrics* was first used, in the 1930s, it conveyed both the development of pure theory from a mathematical viewpoint and the empirical estimation of economic relationships. Now it signifies primarily the latter; the mathematical development of economic theory is now called *mathematical economics*.[1]

A distinction might also be drawn between econometrics and economic statistics. *Economic statistics* is concerned with descriptive statistics, including developing and refining economic data such as the national income accounts and index numbers, while econo-

[1]For presentations of mathematical economics, see Intriligator (1971a), Arrow and Intriligator (1981, 1982, 1985), and Hildenbrand and Sonnenschein (1991). The theory developed in mathematical economics is often a guide to the specification of an econometric model, as will be seen in Chapters 7 and 8, which include the applications of econometrics to the estimation of demand functions and production functions, respectively.

metrics utilizes these data to estimate quantitative economic relationships and to test hypotheses about them.[2]

1.2 THE NATURE OF THE ECONOMETRIC APPROACH

Figure 1.1 summarizes the econometric approach.[3] There are two basic ingredients in any econometric study—theory and facts. Indeed, a major accomplishment of econometrics is simply that of combining these two ingredients. By contrast, a considerable amount of work in economics emphasizes one of them to the exclusion of the other. The "theory-only" school is concerned solely with purely deductive implications of certain postulate systems involving economic phenomena. Examples from mathematical economics include the neoclassical theories of demand, production, and general equilibrium. The "facts-only" school, by contrast, is concerned solely with developing and improving data on the economy. Examples from economic statistics include the collection of data at the macro level, such as the national income accounts, or at the micro level, such as individual lifetime work and income histories. Either of these extreme positions would be difficult to defend. As to the theory-only school, pure theory, by itself, has little empirical content. Furthermore, rival theories can often be developed, and the proper way to choose between them is on the basis of evidence in the form of facts, with facts guiding the development of theory. As to the facts-only school, the facts do not "speak for themselves," and to use them effectively they typically

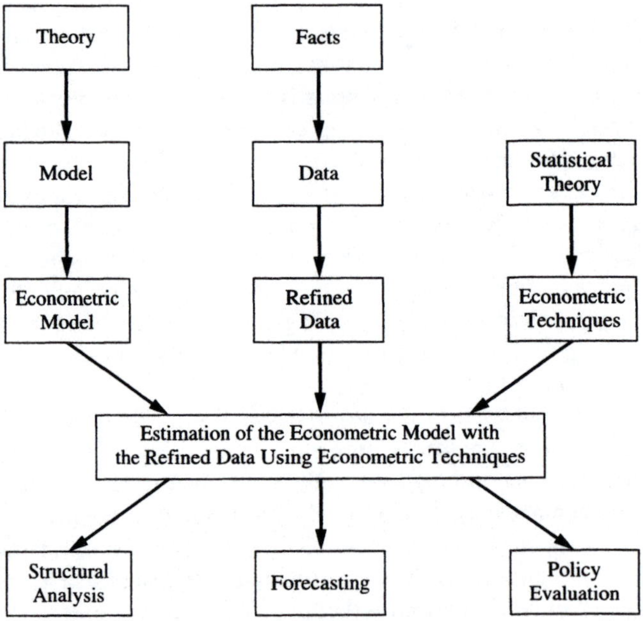

Figure 1.1 Econometric Approach

[2]See Chapter 3 for a discussion of data used in econometric studies.

[3]For a related diagram, see Stone (1965) and Intriligator (1971b). For a similar point of view, see Solari (1979).

must be interpreted in terms of an underlying structure, embodied in a theory. Econometrics utilizes both theory and facts, combining them, using statistical techniques, to estimate economic relationships.

Theory is one of the basic ingredients in any econometric study, but it must be developed in a usable form. The most usable form for the purposes of econometrics, as shown in Figure 1.1, is typically that of a *model*, in particular an *econometric model*. The model summarizes the theory relevant to the system under consideration, and it is the most convenient way of summarizing this theory for empirical measurement and testing. An important aspect of econometrics and an essential part of any econometric study is the *specification* of the model—that is, the construction and elaboration of a model that appropriately represents the phenomena to be studied. In later sections of this chapter we give a few simple examples of models, and in Chapter 2 we discuss models in general and in Chapter 12 and 13, econometric models in particular. Chapters 7, 8, 12, and 13—the "applications" chapters of this book—include many specific models that have been used in econometric studies. They should assist the reader in carrying out an original econometric study, as outlined in Appendix A.

The other basic ingredient in an econometric study is a set of *facts*, referring to events in the real world relating to the phenomena under investigation.[4] These facts lead to a set of *data*, representing observations of relevant facts. In general, however, the data have to be *refined*, or "massaged," in a variety of ways to make them suitable for use in an econometric study. This refinement includes various adjustments such as seasonal or cyclical adjustments, extrapolation, interpolation, merging of different data sources, and in general, the use of other information to adjust the data. The result is a set of *refined data*. These subjects are taken up in Chapter 3, which includes a table of data sources that should be useful in generating data for the original econometric study.

The theory has been developed in the form of an econometric model, and the facts into a set of refined data; the next and central step in the econometric approach combines these two basic ingredients. That step—the estimation of the econometric model using the refined data—requires the use of a set of *econometric techniques*. These are extensions of classical methods of statistics, particularly statistical inference (the use of sample information to infer certain characteristics of a population). Extensions of the classical methods are needed to account for certain special problems encountered in estimating an econometric model. These techniques, discussed at length in Chapters 4, 5, 6, 9, 10, and 11—the "techniques" chapters of this book—should be used in the original econometric study.

The result of this process is an estimated econometric model, in which certain magnitudes, known as *parameters*, are estimated on the basis of relevant data. The estimated model provides a way of measuring and testing relationships suggested by economic theory. In the applications chapters we provide examples of estimated models from a variety of areas.

The econometric approach thus combines theory and facts in a particular way. From the viewpoint of theory, econometrics can be considered the application of real-world data to economic theory. Conversely, from the viewpoint of the facts, econometrics can be considered a systematic way of studying economic history.[5]

[4]See Section 3.1 for a discussion of quantitative representations of qualitative facts.

[5]A new approach to economic history, which uses the tools of econometrics to study such issues as the role of railroads in the economic development of the United States or the role of slavery in the antebellum South, has emerged in recent years. Called *cliometrics*, it is discussed in Section 13.7.

1.3 THE PURPOSES OF ECONOMETRICS

Figure 1.1 also shows the three principal purposes of econometrics: structural analysis, forecasting, and policy evaluation. Any econometric study may have one, two, or all of these purposes, which represent the "end products" of econometrics, just as "theory" and "facts" represent its "raw materials." In this sense Figure 1.1 can be thought of as a flow diagram showing schematically how the different parts of an econometric study are combined and eventually utilized.

Structural analysis is the use of an estimated econometric model for the quantitative measurement of economic relationships. It also facilitates the comparison of rival theories of the same phenomena. Structural analysis represents what might be considered the "scientific" purpose of econometrics—that of understanding real-world phenomena by quantitatively measuring, testing, and validating economic relationships. One result of this analysis may be a "feedback" influence on theory. For example, a measured relationship between the rate of inflation and the rate of unemployment, the Phillips curve, has led to various developments in the theory of unemployment.[6]

Forecasting is the use of an estimated econometric model to predict quantitative values of certain variables outside the sample of data actually observed. Forecasts may be the basis for action; for example, the purchase of raw materials and employment of additional workers in a firm may be based on a forecast that sales will increase over the subsequent two quarters.

Policy evaluation is the use of an estimated econometric model to choose between alternative policies. One approach is to introduce explicitly an objective function to be maximized by choice of policies and to regard the estimated model as a constraint in this optimization process. Another approach, often more useful to policymakers, is to simulate alternative policies and to make conditional forecasts of the future values of relevant variables under each alternative. The selection of a most desired alternative among the various possible "candidate futures" would indicate which policy should be pursued. In either case, the selection of a particular policy, combined with the effects of those outside events that have an influence on the system, leads to specific outcomes. The outcomes, in turn, lead to another feedback relationship connecting policy evaluation with the facts of future experience.

These three principal purposes of econometrics are closely related. The structure determined by structural analysis is used in forecasting using an econometric model, while policy evaluation using an econometric model is a type of conditional forecast. The uses and their interrelationships are discussed at greater length below, particularly in Chapters 14, 15, and 16, the "uses" chapters of this book. These discussions should guide the reader in completing an original econometric study. The book concludes with a discussion in Chapter 17 of various managerial aspects of the use of econometric models. An important managerial aspect is the evaluation, including a self-evaluation, of the quality of an econometric model, and in Chapter 17 we discuss some criteria for model evaluation.

[6]The study that brought this measured relationship dramatically to the attention of economists was Phillips (1958), although a virtually identical relationship appeared in Klein (1950) as an alternative specification in his most detailed econometric model. Examples of the theoretical developments inspired in part by this measured relationship appear in Phelps (1970). For a discussion of the iterative approach to modeling, with feedback from estimation to theory, see Hamilton et al. (1969).

1.4 AN EXAMPLE: THE DEMAND CURVE AND THE PRICE ELASTICITY OF DEMAND

An example of an econometric study is the estimation of a demand curve for a particular commodity, say gasoline. The demand curve for an individual consumer, illustrated in Figure 1.2, gives the quantity that he or she demands, q, in gallons per month, as a function of the price, p, in dollars per gallon[7]

$$q = q(p). \qquad *(1.4.1)$$

The concept of a demand curve, which is the model in this example, should be familiar, it is basic to the microeconomic theory of demand and is relevant both for the individual consumer and, in the aggregate, for the market as a whole. It is also a basic component of the prototype micro model discussed in Chapter 2, and it is fundamental to the discussion of applications of econometrics to households in Chapter 7.

Two points are shown on the hypothetical individual consumer demand curve of Figure 1.2. The first, A, indicates that at a price of \$1.20 per gallon, the particular consumer whose demand curve is represented by *dd* would buy 50 gallons of gasoline per month. The second, B, indicates that if everything else is the same but the price goes up to \$1.32 per gallon, he or she would buy 49 gallons of gasoline per month.

A useful measure of the responsiveness of the quantity demanded of a particular product to its price is the *price elasticity of demand*, ε, defined as the ratio of the relative change in quantity demanded to the relative change in price. Since the relative change in any variable z is the ratio of a change in z, say Δz, to the base level of z, that is, $\Delta z/z$, the price elasticity of demand can be written[8]

$$\varepsilon = \frac{\Delta q/q}{\Delta p/p} = \frac{p}{q}\frac{\Delta q}{\Delta p}. \qquad *(1.4.2)$$

The elasticity of demand defined this way is an *arc elasticity* of demand, and it is generally negative.[9] With the data shown in Figure 1.2, the price elasticity of demand at A is approximately[10]

$$\varepsilon = \frac{\Delta q/q}{\Delta p/p} = \frac{(49-50)/50}{(1.32-1.20)/1.20} = \frac{-0.02}{0.10} = -0.2. \qquad (1.4.3)$$

Thus, at A, a 10% increase in price would reduce the quantity demanded by approximately 2%, while a 5% decrease in price would increase the quantity demanded by approximately 1%.

The estimation of price elasticities of demand for particular goods or services is an example of an econometric study. It combines theory, here represented by the demand curve

[7]Note that following a long-standing convention, the independent variable, price, is shown on the *vertical* axis, while the dependent variable, quantity demanded, is shown on the *horizontal* axis, reversing the usual mathematical convention. Also note that equations are numbered according to the section in which they appear. Thus equation (1.4.1) is the first equation in Section 1.4. An asterisk (*) preceding an equation number, as here, indicates an important equation.

[8]Section 7.2 provides a discussion of elasticity in the context of the theory of demand.

[9]Since the demand curve is downward sloping, Δp and Δq are of opposite sign.

[10]In general, the elasticity varies along the demand curve. The estimate, (1.4.3), approximates its value at A. The approximation becomes better the closer point B is to A.

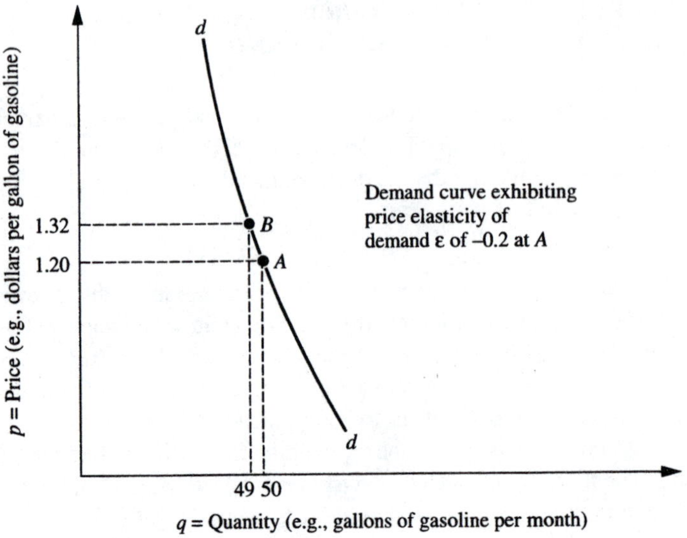

Figure 1.2 Demand Curve (e.g., for Gasoline)

model, with facts, here represented by only two price–quantity pairs.[11] The technique of estimation is the arc elasticity formula (1.4.3). The resulting numerical measures of the responsiveness of quantity demanded to price are of considerable interest for purposes of structural analysis. They are also useful for purposes of forecasting and policy evaluation (e.g., to predict next year's imports of petroleum or to set appropriate taxes on gasoline).

Table 1.1 gives some estimates of price elasticities of demand for some basic food items from the study by Stone of consumer behavior in the United Kingdom, 1920–1938.[12] According to these results, the demand for condensed milk is highly responsive to price, whereas the demand for margarine is insensitive to price. This study was an important one for both forecasting and policy evaluation purposes. In particular, the estimated elasticities were used to forecast the demands for various products after wartime rationing was elimi-

TABLE 1.1 Estimated Price Elasticities of Demand, United Kingdom, 1920–1938

Commodity	Price Elasticity of Demand
Fresh milk	–0.49
Condensed milk	–1.23
Butter	–0.41
Margarine	0.01
Tea	–0.26

Source Stone (1954), as reported in Table 7.5.

[11]Note that A and B were assumed to be points on the demand curve. (In general, observed price–quantity pairs from a marketplace do *not* represent points on a single demand curve; for example, the demand curve may have shifted as a result of changes in income or prices of other goods.) Rather they represent points of intersection of demand and supply curves. This point is developed in detail in Chapters 2, 7, and 9.

[12]See Stone (1954). These results are discussed in Section 7.4.

nated and thus to evaluate the policy of eliminating such wartime controls. The estimation of such elasticities is discussed in Chapter 7.

1.5 SECOND EXAMPLE: THE CONSUMPTION FUNCTION

A second example of an econometric study is the estimation of a consumption function, a basic component of virtually all macroeconomic models, which determines total consumption for the national economy as a function of total income. This concept is utilized in Chapter 2 in the development of a prototype macro model and in Chapter 12 on macroeconometric models.

Figure 1.3 illustrates a linear consumption function, giving the dollar value of total consumption expenditure C as a function of the dollar value of national income, Y (e.g., gross national product). The consumption function is, in general, a rising curve but has a slope less than unity (i.e., added income leads to added consumption but also leads to added savings). The slope of the curve is called the *marginal propensity to consume* (MPC), and it is therefore assumed positive but less than unity. Thus in this case of a linear consumption function

$$C = a + bY, \qquad 0 < b \equiv \text{MPC} < 1. \qquad *(1.5.1)$$

From the two points shown on Figure 1.3, the MPC can be estimated to be

$$\frac{\Delta C}{\Delta Y} = \frac{616 - 600}{820 - 800} = 0.8, \qquad (1.5.2)$$

implying that 80 cents of each dollar of added income is spent on consumption.

Measurement of the MPC exemplifies an econometric study, combining theory (of the consumption function) and data (on aggregate consumption and income) with econometric techniques [e.g., the estimate defined in (1.5.2)]. Such a measurement is important in understanding the structure of the macro economy, in forecasting future levels of aggre-

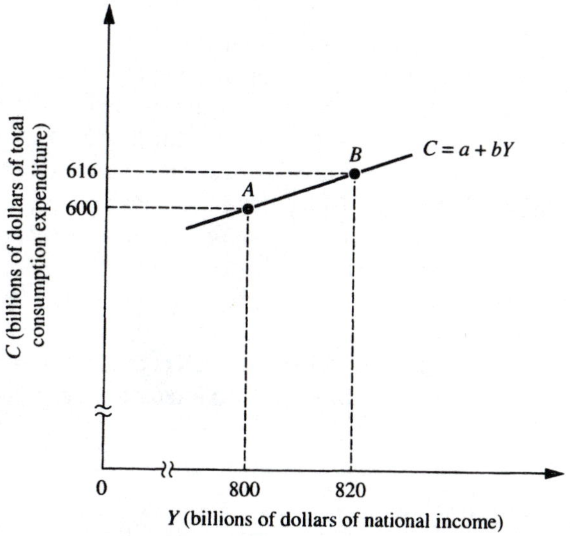

Figure 1.3 Linear Consumption Function

gate income (and employment), and in analyzing policy proposals, such as monetary and fiscal policy alternatives. Estimation of MPC and other macroeconomic parameters is discussed in Chapter 12, and the use of macroeconometric models in policy evaluation is treated in Chapter 16.

1.6 THIRD EXAMPLE: THE GROWTH OF SCIENCE

A final example of an econometric study comes from a field other than economics, illustrating the fact that the econometric approach is by no means confined to economics. Historians of science have performed quantitative studies in which science is measured by variables such as the number of scientists and the number of papers published in scientific journals.[13] These quantitative studies have generally found that most measures of science grow at a constant proportionate rate. Letting N_t be the measure (e.g., numbers of scientists) in year t, it is found that the change in N_t from one year to the next, given as $\Delta N_t = N_{t+1} - N_t$, relative to the total N_t, is approximately constant. Thus

$$\frac{\Delta N_t}{N_t} = \text{constant} = \alpha \tag{1.6.1}$$

(e.g., growth of 10% per year, where $\alpha = 0.1$). Consideration of the related differential equation

$$\frac{1}{N}\frac{dN}{dt} = \alpha \tag{1.6.2}$$

leads to the exponential relationship

$$N = N_0 e^{\alpha t}, \tag{1.6.3}$$

where t is time and N_0 is the base number of the measure of science at time $t = 0$. This relationship is the basic hypothesis. Taking logs of (1.6.3)[14] leads to the model

$$\ln N = \ln N_0 + \alpha t, \tag{1.6.4}$$

expressing a simple linear relationship between $\ln N$ and time, t. The slope coefficient α gives the rate of growth of N, while the intercept is the log of N_0, the base number at $t = 0$. This relationship is shown in Figure 1.4, where the horizontal axis, for time, is an arithmetic scale, but the vertical axis, for N, is a logarithmic scale. Figure 1.4 is a convenient one for studying the growth of science. It is a particularly simple example of the econometric approach: the simple hypothesis that there is a constant growth rate of science is combined with the values taken by the measure of science at different points in time in order to study the structure of the process, here embodied in the estimation of the growth rate α. The estimate of α can be utilized to forecast the future levels of science, assuming that the future will be like the past.

It may be recalled that forecasting refers to the determination of values of variables outside the sample of observed data. Thus forecasting can refer to past as well as future lev-

[13] See Price (1961, 1963).

[14] Base e logs are used here and elsewhere, and "ln" means natural logarithm (i.e., log with the base e = 2.718 . . .).

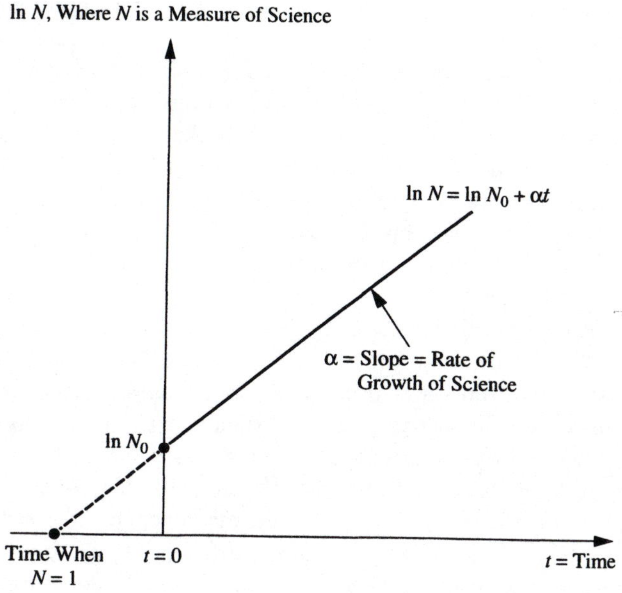

Figure 1.4 Growth of Science

els of science. One study performed in this framework considered the number of electrical engineers in the United States, measured by personnel employed in electrical engineering. As was anticipated, the growth rate was almost constant, so that plotting numbers of electrical engineers N as a function of time, t, on semilog graph paper yielded a set of points that fell very close to a straight line. This line was then projected back in time, as on Figure 1.4, to determine the time at which it hit the axis. This point is interpreted as being the time when there existed exactly *one* electrical engineer. The result of this forecast was amazingly "accurate": it turned out to be the year 1752, the year in which Benjamin Franklin flew his kite experiment!

1.7 TRADITIONAL ECONOMETRICS UNDER CRITICISM

During the 1980s, econometrics, particularly applied econometrics in the form of econometric modeling, has been the subject of a number of criticisms, some rather violent in nature. In the view of the authors, applied econometrics has weathered these storms rather well; indeed, it has probably emerged stronger as a result of the fundamental reevaluation of the subject that has resulted from these attacks.

One such criticism has been the tendency, in classical econometrics, for the researcher to take a very conservative stance in advance of estimation (or hypothesis testing), assuming (almost literally) that nothing was known about numerical values of the parameters of a model. Often this was a gross oversimplification, and classical statisticians and econometricians have rightly been criticized (by a school of thought that may be called "Bayesian"; see the bibliography in Chapter 17) on the grounds that they (the classical econometricians) really knew a lot more than they somewhat disingenuously pretended to know, on the basis of their methodology.[15]

A related critique is that of Hendry (1980), who argues that many past econometric studies have been flawed by imperfect test procedures. (For example, a number of then-current macroeconometric models "broke down" in the face of the oil price and availability shocks of 1973–1974, which he argues would not have happened had the "best practice" econometric technique that he recommends been followed.) The good news is that these defects are remediable, and in Chapter 5 we examine some concrete suggestions, which place a heavy emphasis on testing, particularly within the sample period, made by Hendry.[16]

Another criticism has been the *Lucas critique*, based on the writings of Robert E. Lucas, Jr. (1976) of the University of Chicago. The Lucas critique, based in part on the hypothesis of "rational expectations" in economics, argues that the proximate parameters of most econometric models (particularly macroeconometric models) will display extreme instability in general and, in particular, that changes in policy regimes will almost certainly produce shifts in the values of structural parameters of the models.[17] If true (*and important*), such objections to macroeconometric models would be fatal to their usefulness, at least for purposes of important policy decisions.[18] This criticism, while it represents a possible theoretical caveat, may well not be important enough to be taken as a major qualification to the econometric approach; see the argument presented in Chapter 17.[19]

[15]More generally, the role of *judgment* in econometrics and its applications is a very important qualification to mechanistic applications of econometric procedures, even including modeling. This important subject is discussed briefly in the concluding chapter, in Section 17.9. Leamer's suggestion of careful specification searches through nonexperimental data (1978) would certainly be an instance of the exercise of such judgment.

[16]In this regard, mention might be made of a technical criticism by Sims (1980). Sims raises the point that the theoretical knowledge of econometricians is imperfect, and that some of the zero restrictions imposed to *identify* econometric models may in practice be invalid. (The subject of identification is discussed in Chapters 2 and 9.) In the judgment of the authors, this controversial assertion quickly reduces to a philosophical debate. If one is not willing to assume anything, no progress can be made, so the issue would appear to come down to whether Sims's assumptions or those that are traditionally made are the more plausible (or, a cynic might say, the less implausible).

[17]While it is true that the *fundamental* parameters of the "true" structural model will probably be invariant to changes in expectations and hence to shifts in public policy, the problem from the model builder's point of view is that these fundamental parameters (being generally microeconomic in nature) are generally not observable with the aggregative data available to macroeconometric model builders.

[18]Lucas and his followers might grudgingly concede that macroeconometric models estimated over a period of an unchanging policy regime might have some relevance for purposes of pure historical description, but they would claim that the numerical values of the parameters would change (in unpredictable ways) when such a system is subjected to a change in policy regime. Thus it would become impossible to use such a system to *predict* the effects of varying economic policy, to obtain better functioning of the economy.

[19]In addition, it may be noted that econometricians have developed techniques both to identify econometric models suitably and to estimate their parameters consistently, in the face of the rational expectations hypothesis. The seminal work in this area is Wallis (1980). For macroeconometric practice, the rational-expectations hypothesis has been interpreted as one with "model-consistent" expectations, in which the representative economic agent's expectations for a typical economic variable are those that the dynamic solution of the model produces as the evolution of the time path of the variable in question. It may be noted that for more complicated variables, this solution time path need not be unique.

1.8 LEARNING BY DOING IN ECONOMETRICS

As in the case of many other subjects, econometrics is best learned by doing an applied econometric study, and all readers of this book (particularly students) are encouraged to perform such a study. Appendix A provides a guide on how to do such a study and includes an overview of the literature using econometric methods. From this bibliography the reader will see how extensively econometrics is used not only in many fields of economics but also in several other social sciences. The bibliography should also be of help to those doing research papers, both in suggesting topics for such papers and in providing references. For example, these references could be used as the starting point in a search in the *Social Science Citation Index* (see the bibliography below, under ISI).

BIBLIOGRAPHY

ARROW, K. J., and M. D. INTRILIGATOR, Eds. (1981, 1982, 1985). *Handbook of Mathematical Economics*, Vols. 1–3. Amsterdam: North-Holland Publishing Company.

HAMILTON, H. R., S. E. GOLDSTONE, J. W. MILLIMAN, A. L. PUGH, E. R. ROBERTS, and A. ZELLNER (1969). *Systems Simulation for Regional Analysis: An Application to River Basin Planning*. Cambridge, Mass.: MIT Press.

HENDRY, D. F. (1980). "Econometrics—Alchemy or Science?" *Economica*, 47: 387–406.

HILDENBRAND, W., and H. SONNENSCHEIN, Eds. (1991). *Handbook of Mathematical Economics*, Vol. 4. Amsterdam: North-Holland Publishing Company.

INTRILIGATOR, M. D. (1971a). *Mathematical Optimization and Economic Theory*. Englewood Cliffs, N.J.: Prentice Hall.

INTRILIGATOR, M. D. (1971b). "Econometrics and Economic Forecasting," in J. M. English, Ed., *The Economics of Engineering and Social Systems*. New York: John Wiley & Sons, Inc.

ISI (Annual since 1966). *Social Science Citation Index*. Philadelphia: Institute of Scientific Information, Inc.

KLEIN, L. R. (1950). *Economic Fluctuations in the United States, 1921–1941*. Cowles Commission Monograph 11. New York: John Wiley & Sons, Inc.

LEAMER, E. E. (1978). *Specification Searches: Ad Hoc Inference with Nonexperimental Data*. New York: John Wiley & Sons, Inc.

LUCAS, R. E., JR. (1976). "Econometric Policy Evaluation: A Critique." *Journal of Monetary Economics*, 2, Supplement, K. Brunner and A. H. Meltzer, Eds., *The Phillips Curve and Labor Markets*, Vol. 1 of Carnegie-Rochester Conference Series on Public Policy. Amsterdam: North-Holland Publishing Company, pp. 19–46; reprinted in R. E. Lucas, Jr. (1981). *Studies in Business-Cycle Theory*. Cambridge, Mass.: MIT Press, pp. 104–130.

PHELPS, E. S., Ed. (1970). *Microeconomic Foundations of Employment and Inflation Theory*. New York: W.W. Norton & Company, Inc.

PHILLIPS, A. W. (1958). "The Relation between Unemployment and the Rate of Change of Money Wages in the United Kingdom, 1861–1957." *Economica*, 25: 283–299.

PRICE, D. J. DE SOLLA (1961). *Science since Babylon*. New Haven; Conn.: Yale University Press.

PRICE, D. J. DE SOLLA (1963). *Little Science, Big Science*. New York: Columbia University Press.

SIMS, C. A. (1980). "Macroeconomics and Reality." *Econometrica*, 48: 1–48.

SOLARI, L. (1979). "L'économétrie, recherche d'une synthèse entre expérience et théorie" ["Econometrics as the Search for a Synthesis between Empirical Evidence and Theory"], in L. Solari (Ed. F. Carlevaro), *Essais de méthodes et analyses économétriques*. Geneva: Librairie Droz. (This essay was originally published in 1965.)

STONE, R. (1954). *The Measurement of Consumer's Expenditure and Behavior in the United Kingdom, 1920–1938*. Cambridge: Cambridge University Press.

STONE, R. (1965). "The Analysis of Economic Systems." *Scripta Varia*, 28: 1–88.

WALLIS, K. F. (1980). "Econometric Implications of the Rational Expectations Hypothesis." *Econometrica*, 48: 49–73.

2

MODELS, ECONOMIC MODELS, AND ECONOMETRIC MODELS

2.1 WHAT IS A MODEL?

A *model*, by definition, is any representation of an actual phenomenon such as an actual system or process. The actual phenomenon is represented by the model in order to explain it, to predict it, and to control it—purposes corresponding to the three purposes of econometrics discussed in Chapter 1: structural analysis, forecasting, and policy evaluation, respectively. Sometimes the actual system is called the *real-world system* to emphasize the distinction between it and the model system that represents it.

Modeling—the art of model building—is an integral part of most sciences, whether natural or social, because the real-world systems under consideration typically are enormously complex. The system may be an electron moving in an accelerator, prices being set in various markets, or the determination of national income. In these and many other cases, the real-world phenomena are so complicated that they can be treated only by means of a simplified representation—that is, via a model.

Any model represents a compromise between reality and manageability. It must be a "reasonable" representation of the real-world system and in that sense should be "realistic" in incorporating the main elements of the phenomena being represented. On the other hand, it must be manageable in that it yields certain insights or conclusions not obtainable from direct observations of the real-world system. To achieve manageability usually involves various processes of idealization, including the elimination of "extraneous" influences and the simplification of processes. Clearly, this process of idealization usually makes the model less "realistic," yet the process is necessary to ensure that the model system can be reasonably manipulated. Models (of all types) are constantly at the frontier of "unreality," and model users have to be ever vigilant that conclusions drawn from the model will indeed apply to the real-world system.

Striking the proper balance between realism and manageability is the essence of good modeling. A "good" model is both realistic and manageable. It specifies the interrelationships among the parts of a system in a way that is sufficiently detailed and explicit to ensure that the study of the model leads to insights concerning the real-world system. At the same time, however, it specifies them in a way that is sufficiently simplified and manageable to ensure that the model can be readily analyzed and conclusions can be reached concerning the real-world system. One type of "bad" model is one that is highly realistic but so complicated that it becomes unmanageable. In that case there really is no point in building the model in the first place. Another type of bad model goes to the other extreme: it is highly manageable but so idealized that it is unrealistic in not accounting for important components of the real-world system. In that case the process of idealization has been carried too far: influences that have been assumed away are in fact important, and/or real-world processes involve greater complexities than have been postulated in the model. This extreme may be highly dangerous in that the conclusions reached via the model may or may not be relevant to the real-world system; the trouble is that one never knows in advance whether the conclusions are or are not relevant. In this case it is certainly true that "a little bit of knowledge is a dangerous thing."

To the extent that it is impossible to convey precisely how to build a good model, modeling is partly an art and partly a science. Following certain general precepts and knowing previous modeling attempts are helpful, but it takes experience to become a good modeler.[1]

As a general rule the first models of a phenomenon are quite simple, emphasizing manageability at the cost of not treating reality in great detail. The extreme case is the so-called "black box" of Figure 2.1, where no attempt is made to reproduce reality. In this case the model treats only inputs to the system and the system outputs without considering the system itself. A black-box description of a television set, for example, would merely identify the inputs of electricity and control signals by the operator and the outputs of audio and video signals. It would treat only the inputs and outputs without attempting to analyze how the two are related.

The process of modeling usually entails starting with a black box and then elaborating on what lies inside the box. The initial model is a simple black-box model, which treats only inputs and outputs, sometimes called a *descriptive model*. Tracking inputs forward and outputs backward then leads to more elaborate models, eventually resulting in an *analytic model*, a "white-box" model, which explicitly treats all the interconnections between inputs and outputs. A white-box model of a television set, for example, might consist of a com-

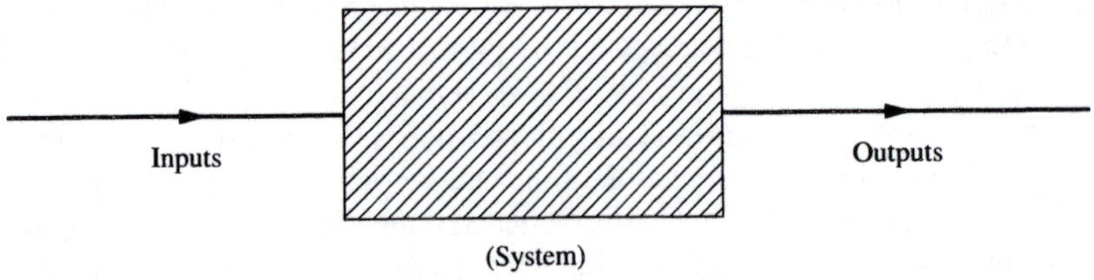

Figure 2.1 Black Box

[1]In Appendix A we describe an econometric research project that involves building a model. All readers, but especially students, are encouraged to undertake this project, a case study in formulating an original econometric model, collecting relevant data, estimating the model, and interpreting results. The discussions in the "applications" chapters of this book—Chapters 7, 8, 12, and 13—should aid the reader both in understanding the process of modeling and in carrying out the research project.

plete circuit diagram. The process of modeling typically entails a continuing attempt to formulate more and more analytic models, which are able to analyze more and more of the various interconnections of the real-world system. An example is the development of models of the macroeconomy, starting with simple models, such as the one presented in Section 2.6 and eventually reaching highly detailed macroeconometric models, some of which are discussed in Chapter 12. In the process, the understanding of the model builder usually increases, but it should be recognized that understanding is itself a subjective concept.

2.2 TYPES OF MODELS: VERBAL/LOGICAL, PHYSICAL, AND GEOMETRIC

Many types of models exist in each of the various fields to which models have been applied. Among the most important types are verbal/logical models, physical models, geometric models, and algebraic models, involving alternative forms of representation of a model.

Perhaps the simplest type of model and the one usually used first in any field of inquiry is the *verbal/logical model*. This approach uses verbal analogies, such as the metaphor and simile, and the resulting model is sometimes called a *paradigm*. Such models often treat the system "as if" it were, in some sense, purposeful. Thus in physics the "principle of least action" states that a particle in motion acts *as if* it were minimizing the energy required for its motion. This is most definitely a model in that a real-world system, the moving particle, is represented in this case by a purposeful entity.

In economics two of the earliest and still two of the best paradigms were developed by the founder of the Classical School, Adam Smith.[2] The first was the pin factory. Smith used the simple operation of manufacturing pins to illustrate the concept of *division of labor*, according to which if each person performs those tasks for which he or she has a comparative advantage, such a division of labor can significantly increase total output. This concept is applicable at the national and international level, but the participants and processes become so numerous and their interrelations so manifold that the principle can be lost. Smith therefore used an analogy or verbal model, discussing the principle with reference to a pin factory, where it could readily be grasped. Obviously, Smith was not particularly interested in pin factories per se. Rather, he found in a pin factory a convenient *model* of the productive working of the entire national and international economies.

The second paradigm employed by Smith was that of the "invisible hand," an important principle in economics and one of the most important contributions of economics to the analysis of social processes. He considered a decentralized free-enterprise economy in which each economic agent, consumer or producer, acts solely out of individual self-interest, seeking selfishly to maximize his or her own welfare. The *price system*, however, ensures that (under suitable conditions) the aggregation of numerous such individual actions attains a coherent equilibrium for the economy as a whole and serves to "promote the public interest." Under the price system each agent is guided in his or her actions by a system of price signals. For example, goods and services are delivered at the appropriate time and place, their delivery being guided by the relevant prices. Smith observed that the system, in this case the total economy, acts *as if* there were an "invisible hand" directing all

[2]Smith (1776).

individual decisions for the "general welfare" of society. Again, a complex process, in this case one of rationalizing all economic actions, was represented by a simple analogy.

A second type of model is the *physical model*. Consider one of the everyday meanings of the word "model," namely a person (usually female, young, and svelte) hired to wear clothes for publicity purposes. Such a person is a "model" in our sense of the term as well because this clothing model represents what the articles of clothing will look like, to a rough approximation, when worn by a typical consumer (the real-world system). Thus, this is a perfectly good example of a physical model (although many a lady of mature years, with a full figure, has discovered that the stunning fashion creation, which looked marvelous when worn by the svelte young model, doesn't do a thing for her, illustrating the previous point that model users have to be careful about drawing conclusions from the model and applying them to the real-world system). In other physical models, the real world is of unmanageable size, so that the model is obtained by appropriate scaling, up or down. Thus an airframe for a new airplane is typically tested by constructing a scaled-down version and testing it in a wind tunnel. This representation is realistic in that the influences omitted (e.g., the interior color scheme) are indeed extraneous. At the same time it is manageable in that it can be constructed and tested easily and inexpensively. Another example is an astronomer's physical model of the solar system. To consider scaling in the opposite direction, physicists sometimes use physical models of the atom, indicating protons and neutrons in the nucleus and electrons in orbit around the nucleus. Molecular biologists similarly use physical models such as those of a protein molecule or the DNA molecule. Such models are scaled-up versions of the real-world system under study and are certainly more manipulable than the actual entities under consideration.

Physical models can also be utilized to study nonphysical phenomena. Thus hydraulic models have been utilized to study macroeconomic variables, such as gross national product, aggregate consumption, aggregate investment, and the money supply, with flows of fluids representing monetary flows in the economy.[3] In general, however, the most useful of these physical models have been those relying upon electric circuits, as in the modern analog computer. The electric network may represent a wide variety of phenomena, including those from physics, engineering, and economics.[4]

Of enormous importance to the development of economic theory has been the third type of model, the *geometric model*, representing relationships geometrically. To appreciate its importance, thumb through almost any introductory or intermediate economic theory text; numerous diagrams of one sort or another will be found. A geometric model uses a diagram to indicate the relationships between variables. The previous chapter included three such diagrams, all of which are geometric models. For example, Figure 1.3 is a geometric model of a linear aggregate consumption function. Later in this chapter, Figure 2.5 is a geometrical representation of the prototype micro model, which can thus be considered (in this sense) a geometric model. Similarly, the determination of national income can be represented as a geometric model, as illustrated in Figure 2.2.

Geometric models are very useful in indicating the principal relationships among the major variables representing the phenomena under investigation. Because of the limited

[3]This approach was advocated in the 1920s and 1930s by Irving Fisher.

[4]For applications of electronic analog models to economics, see Morehouse, Strotz, and Horwitz (1950), Enke (1951), Strotz, McAnulty, and Naines (1953), and Tustin (1953). In recent years, electronic analog models have been less widely used in economics. By contrast, the digital computer, whether of the mainframe or micro (desktop) variety, has been widely used in econometrics.

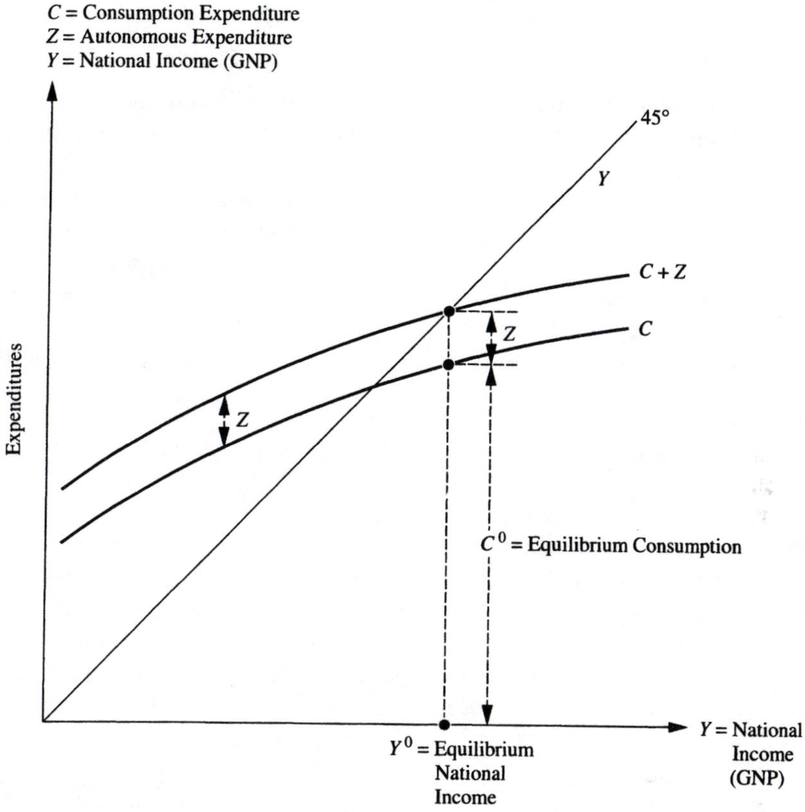

Figure 2.2 Determination of Equilibrium National Income

number of dimensions available, it is necessary to restrict geometric models to relatively few variables. To deal with a larger number of variables, generally an algebraic (rather than a geometric) model is employed, as discussed in the following section.

2.3 ALGEBRAIC MODELS

The *algebraic model*,[5] for purposes of econometrics, is the most important type of model; it represents the real-world system by a system of equations.[6] A macroeconomic model of income determination (shown graphically in Figure 2.2) can be expressed algebraically as

[5]This model and the other types are often studied using a computer. This approach may in fact involve some aspects of *all* the types of models discussed here, including verbal/logical statements, physical analogies (e.g., using hybrid digital/analog computers), graphical treatment, and algebraic expressions. In general, such an approach is utilized when the phenomena become so complex and unmanageable that they cannot be treated (e.g., solved) analytically. Resort is then often made to *simulation* of the behavior of the model system under different conditions or assumptions using a computer. The "system dynamics" models of Forrester (1961, 1969, 1971) exemplify this approach. Such models have been used to study an individual firm (sales, inventories, workforce, etc.), a city (population, buildings, jobs, etc.), a nation, world resource flows, and economic policies (see Naylor, Wertz, and Wonnacott, 1968; Naylor, 1971). For a further discussion of simulation, see Section 16.6.

[6]Sometimes, inequalities are also part of the system.

$$C = C(Y), \tag*{*(2.3.1)}$$

$$Y = C + Z. \tag*{*(2.3.2)}$$

The variables of this model are consumption C, national income Y, and exogenous expenditure Z. (In this simple model, Z includes autonomous investment, government expenditures, and net exports.) Given the consumption function $C(Y)$ and autonomous expenditure Z, the system of equations determines the equilibrium values of consumption C^0 and national income Y^0. Equation (2.3.1) is the consumption function, a behavioral relation indicating how consumers in aggregate respond to income in terms of consumption-saving decisions. Equation (2.3.2) is an equilibrium condition, stating that in equilibrium total income is the sum of consumption expenditure and exogenous expenditure. Equilibrium national income is obtained by inserting (2.3.1) into (2.3.2) and solving for Y^0 as

$$Y^0 \equiv C(Y^0) + Z. \tag{2.3.3}$$

Equilibrium consumption is then obtained from (2.3.1) as

$$C^0 \equiv C(Y^0). \tag{2.3.4}$$

Equations (2.3.3) and (2.3.4) are written as identities because they define Y^0 and C^0, respectively. It should be noted that, so far, the model and the equilibrium obtained are exactly as in Figure 2.2, the geometric and algebraic models constituting different representations of the same model of national income determination.

There are, however, a number of advantages of the algebraic over the geometric representation of a model. One is the ease of manipulation. To illustrate this ease, differentiate both sides of the identity (2.3.3) with respect to Z to obtain

$$\frac{dY^0}{dZ} = \frac{dC}{dY^0}\frac{dY^0}{dZ} + 1. \tag{2.3.5}$$

Collecting terms and noting that dC/dY^0 is the marginal propensity to consume (MPC), defined in (1.5.1), evaluated at the equilibrium level of national income,

$$\frac{dY^0}{dZ} = \frac{1}{1 - \text{MPC}}. \tag*{*(2.3.6)}$$

This result is known as the *multiplier*, indicating the multiple effect of a change in exogenous expenditure such as government expenditure on equilibrium national income. The multiplier depends critically on the value of the MPC. For example, an MPC of 0.8 (i.e., 80 cents out of every additional dollar of income is consumed rather than saved) implies a multiplier of 5; that is, there is a fivefold effect on national income of a change in exogenous expenditure. In this case an increase of $1 billion in government expenditure would lead to an increase of $5 billion in national income. If, however, the MPC were 0.75, the multiplier would be 4, so the added $1 billion of government expenditure would increase national income by $4 billion. Clearly, small changes in the value of MPC can lead to large changes in the multiplier, and hence in forecasts and policy evaluations made on the basis of the model.

Another advantage of algebraic over geometric models is the ease of adding new variables and equations. This advantage will be seen in Section 2.6 in the development of the prototype macro model. Geometry is, by its very nature, confined to only two or three dimensions. Algebra, however, is not so confined, and the algebraic models can therefore be enlarged, disaggregated, and generalized in many ways.

The simple macroeconomic model defined by (2.3.1) and (2.3.2) illustrates the general nature of algebraic models. Such models consist of several *equations*, which may be behavioral, such as the consumption function (2.3.1), an equilibrium condition, such as the national income equilibrium condition (2.3.2), or some other type, but each such equation has a separate meaning and role in the model. All of these fundamental or basic equations of the model may be termed *structural equations*. The model determines values of certain variables, called *endogenous variables*, the jointly dependent variables of the model, which are determined simultaneously by the relations of the model. In this case consumption and national income are the endogenous variables, which are to be explained or predicted. The model also contains other variables, called *exogenous variables*, which are determined outside the system but which influence it by affecting the values of the endogenous variables. They affect the system but are not in turn affected by it. Here exogenous expenditure is such a variable. The model also contains certain *parameters*, which are generally estimated using econometric techniques and relevant data. In this case the parameters are those appearing in the consumption function. Of course, there is a wide choice of functional forms available for an algebraic model, and the choice of a particular one depends on theoretical acceptability, plausibility, ease of estimation, goodness of fit, forecasting ability, and other factors.

2.4 ECONOMETRIC MODELS[7]

Typically an econometric model is a special type of algebraic model: namely, a *stochastic* model that includes one or more random variables. It represents a system by a set of stochastic relations among the variables of the system. An econometric model is either linear or nonlinear. In the linear case the model is linear in the parameters. The linearity assumption is a very important one, both for proving mathematical and statistical theorems concerning such models and for computing values taken by variables in such models. The macro model of Section 2.3, defined in (2.3.1) and (2.3.2), is linear if the consumption function is of the form

$$C(Y) = a + bY. \tag{2.4.1}$$

Here a and b are the relevant parameters, b having the interpretation of the marginal propensity to consume, assumed constant here. The multiplier is then

$$\frac{dY^0}{dZ} = \frac{1}{1-b}. \tag{2.4.2}$$

The reason for assuming linearity (in parameters) is the convenience and manageability of this assumption. In particular, the econometric techniques developed in Parts II and IV are applicable primarily to linear models. While a considerable amount of work has been done on nonlinear models, the linear case is still the more important and common one, for which there exists a wealth of techniques and applications. Generally, it is only where nonlinearity enters in an essential way that it is treated explicitly.

[7]For general discussions of economic and econometric models, see Beach (1957), Suits (1963), Christ (1966), Bergstrom (1967), Ball (1968), Kendall (1968), Brown (1970), Zellner (1979), Eckstein (1983), Intriligator (1983), and Bodkin, Klein, Marwah (1991).

One should not exaggerate the importance of the linearity assumption. First, many economic relationships and relationships in other social sciences are, by their very nature, linear. The national income equilibrium condition (2.3.2), for example, is linear, as are the definitions of expenditure, revenue, cost, and profit. Second, the linearity assumption applies only to parameters, not to variables of the model. Thus the quadratic form of the consumption function

$$C(Y) = a + bY + cY^2, \tag{2.4.3}$$

while nonlinear in the variable Y, is still linear in the parameters, in this case the parameters a, b, c.[8] Variables such as Y^n can be similarly introduced into the equation.

A third reason is that often a model can be transformed into a linear model. The logarithmic transformation can be employed in many cases. For example, the model of constant proportionate growth of Section 1.6,

$$N = N_0 e^{\alpha t} \tag{2.4.4}$$

under a logarithmic transformation becomes

$$\ln N = \ln N_0 + \alpha t, \tag{2.4.5}$$

which is linear in the parameters $\ln N_0$, the intercept, and α, the slope. Similarly, consider the constant elasticity demand function

$$q = q_0 p^{-\varepsilon} I^{\eta}, \tag{2.4.6}$$

where q is the quantity demanded, p is price, and I is income, q_0, ε, and η being parameters, the latter two being the price and income elasticities of demand, respectively. Using a logarithmic transformation yields

$$\ln q = \ln q_0 - \varepsilon \ln p + \eta \ln I, \tag{2.4.7}$$

an equation that is linear in the parameters.[9] A third example is the Cobb–Douglas production function

$$Y = AK^{\alpha} L^{\beta}, \tag{2.4.8}$$

where Y is output, K is capital, L is labor, and A, α, and β are parameters. This production function can be transformed into a linear model by taking logarithms. The result is

$$\log Y = a + \alpha \log K + \beta \log L \qquad (a = \log A), \tag{2.4.9}$$

which is linear in the parameters a, α, and β.[10]

A fourth reason not to exaggerate the linearity assumption is that any smooth function can be reasonably approximated in an appropriate range by a linear function (e.g., via a Taylor's series expansion). Consider, for example, the general production function

$$Y = F(K, L), \tag{2.4.10}$$

[8]Note that is this case MPC = $b + 2cY$ and the multiplier is

$$\frac{dY^0}{dZ} = \frac{1}{1 - b - 2cY^0},$$

where Y^0 is the equilibrium level of national income. Thus in this case the multiplier varies with the equilibrium level of national income.

[9]See the discussion in Chapter 7.

[10]See the discussion of the Cobb–Douglas production function in Chapter 8.

expressing output as a general function of capital and labor, a function that will be treated in some detail in Chapter 8. If the function is continuously differentiable, it can be approximated as a linear function in an appropriate range simply by taking the linear portion of the Taylor's series expansion. Expanding about the base levels of (K_0, L_0) yields

$$Y \cong F(K_0, L_0) + \frac{\partial F}{\partial K}(K_0, L_0)(K - K_0) + \frac{\partial F}{\partial L}(K_0, L_0)(L - L_0), \quad (2.4.11)$$

where the function and its partial derivatives are all evaluated at the base level. Thus in a small range around the point (K_0, L_0),

$$Y \cong a + bK + cL, \quad (2.4.12)$$

where, denoting the partial derivatives by marginal products, written MP_K and MP_L, we obtain

$$a = F(K_0, L_0) - \text{MP}_K(K_0, L_0)K_0 - \text{MP}_L(K_0, L_0)L_0, \quad (2.4.13)$$

$$b = \text{MP}_K(K_0, L_0), \quad (2.4.14)$$

$$c = \text{MP}_L(K_0, L_0). \quad (2.4.15)$$

Another important characteristic of an econometric model is the fact that it is stochastic rather than deterministic. A *stochastic* model includes random variables, whereas a *deterministic* model does not.[11] Typically, the pattern of model building involves construction initially of deterministic models and eventually, where appropriate, construction and utilization of stochastic models. Physics presents an excellent illustration of this pattern. Early models, such as those of Newtonian mechanics, are deterministic, while later models, such as those of quantum mechanics, are stochastic. Indeed, the quantum revolution in physics consisted of the revolutionary observation that one could not identify, for example, the exact location of an elementary particle but one could determine a probability distribution for its location.

To appreciate the nature of stochastic models in economics, consider again the simple macro model (2.3.1) and (2.3.2), where (2.3.1) has been replaced by the linear consumption function (2.4.1). This function specifies that at any given level of national income Y, consumption is determined exactly as the number $a + bY$. Is this reasonable? Clearly not! Many factors other than income affect consumption, such as wealth, prices, and tastes. Furthermore, the relationship may not be quite as simple as that given in (2.4.1), and variables may be measured inaccurately. It is therefore more reasonable to estimate C at a given level of Y, as *on average* $a + bY$. In general, consumption will fall within a certain confidence interval, that is,

$$C = a + bY \pm \Delta, \quad (2.4.16)$$

where C is consumption at the given level of national income Y and Δ indicates the level above or below the average value such that with a high degree of confidence, consumption falls in the defined interval. The value of Δ can be determined by assuming that C is itself a random variable with a particular density function. Because of the central limit theorem the normal distribution is typically assumed, and, in this case, C can be represented as in

[11]In fact, there can be stochastic elements in *all* types of models, including not only the algebraic models, such as those of econometrics, but also verbal, physical, and geometric models.

Figure 2.3.[12] The term "on average" generally refers to the mean or expected value, so $a + bY$ is the mean of C. (Recall that Y is given, so $a + bY$ is just a number.) The Δ can then be chosen, as illustrated, so that 90% of the distribution is included in the confidence interval (2.4.16), where each of the tails of the distribution contains 5% of the distribution.[13] In general, an econometric model uniquely specifies the probability distribution of each endogenous variable, given the values taken by all exogenous variables and given the values of all parameters of the model.

So far one particular value of Y has been considered. Now consider all possible values of Y. At each level of Y, as shown in Figure 2.4, an appropriate (normal) distribution can be constructed, as in Figure 2.3. Connecting the upper and lower levels of the 90% confidence intervals leads to a 90% confidence interval for the entire consumption function. The resulting "band," representing confidence levels for consumption, together with the point values on the function itself, representing mean values, summarize what is known about the *stochastic* (and linear) relationship between consumption and income. The deterministic (i.e., nonstochastic) case can then be interpreted as the one in which the variance of the relevant probability distribution vanishes. In that case $\Delta = 0$. The assumption of zero variance, however, is generally unwarranted, in that not all is known about the relationship. For example, relevant variables have been omitted, and even included variables may be measured subject to error.

Algebraically, the stochastic nature of the relationship is usually represented, for the consumption function, as

$$C = a + bY + \varepsilon, \qquad *(2.4.17)$$

where ε is an additive *stochastic disturbance term* that plays the role of a chance mechanism. In general, each equation of an econometric model, other than definitions, equilibrium conditions, and identities, is assumed to contain an additive stochastic disturbance

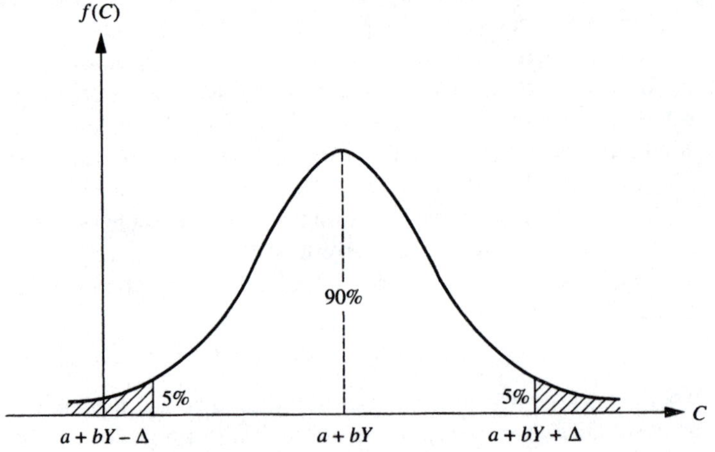

Figure 2.3 Normal Distribution for Consumption C

[12]See Appendix C, Section C.4, for a discussion of the central limit theorem.

[13]It might be recalled that for the normal distribution, if μ is the mean and σ is the standard deviation, $\mu \pm 1.64\sigma$ contains 90% of the distribution.

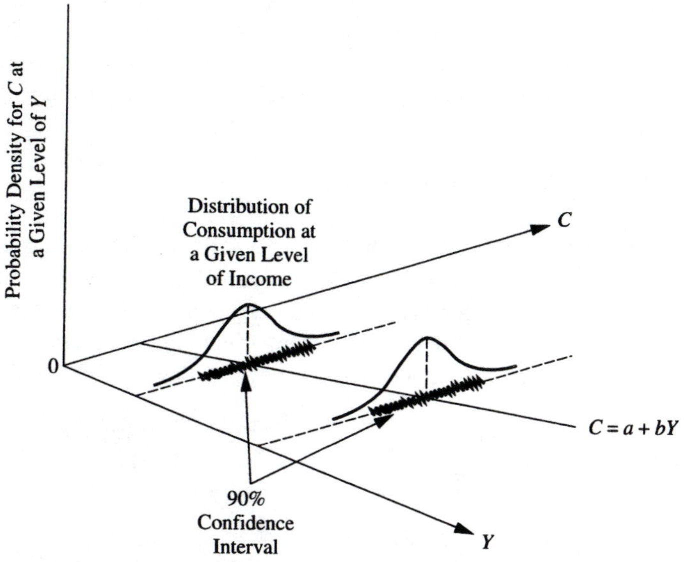

Figure 2.4 Stochastic Relationship between Consumption and Income

term, as in (2.4.17).[14] The stochastic terms are unobservable random variables with certain assumed properties (e.g., means, variances, and covariances). The values taken by these variables of the model are not known with certainty; rather, they can be considered random drawings from a probability distribution. As indicated above, possible sources of such stochastic perturbations could be relevant explanatory variables which have been omitted from the relationships shown in the model, or possibly the effects of measurement errors in the variables. Other sources of such stochastic disturbances could be misspecified functional forms, such as assuming a linear relationship when the true relationship is nonlinear, or errors of aggregation, which might be introduced into a macro equation when not all individuals possess the same underlying micro relationship. Yet another possibility is the fundamentally indeterminate or random nature of human behavior. It might be noted that the sources of these perturbations can be quite important in practice; thus the treatment of measurement error will be, in general, quite different, depending on whether the measurement error is found in the dependent variable or in one or more of the explanatory variables. In any case, the inclusion of such stochastic disturbance terms in the model is basic to the use of tools of statistical inference to estimate parameters of the model.

Econometric models can be either static or dynamic. A *static model* involves no explicit dependence on time, so time is not essential in the model. Simply adding time subscripts to variables does not convert a static model into a dynamic model. A *dynamic model* is one in which time plays an essential role (e.g., if lagged variables or differences of variables over

[14]If the stochastic disturbance term has a variance that is always identically zero, the model reduces to a deterministic one. The other extreme case is where the model is purely stochastic [e.g., (2.4.17), where a and b are identically zero]. There are some examples of such a model in economics; one of the best known is the random walk model for the movement of prices in the stock market, as in Cootner, ed. (1964). The econometric models to be studied, however, are usually neither deterministic nor purely stochastic; they usually have both deterministic elements [e.g., $a + bY$ in (2.4.17)] and nontrivial stochastic elements [e.g., ε in (2.4.17)].

time are part of the model). Thus, if any equation of the model is a difference equation, the model is dynamic. Time also plays an essential role if variables and their time rates of change are explicitly considered, such as in a differential equation. In the next two sections we treat a static model, the prototype micro model, and a dynamic model, the prototype macro model.

2.5 THE PROTOTYPE MICRO MODEL

The first example of an econometric model—a stochastic, algebraic model—is the prototype micro model for an agricultural good. While this model could be represented as a generalization of a graphical model of price determination in a single market, it also illustrates the advantage of algebraic over geometrical models in terms of possible generalizations to more variables. The model consists of the following three equations:

$$q^D = \gamma_1 p + \beta_1 I + \delta_1 + \varepsilon^D, \qquad *(2.5.1)$$

$$q^S = \gamma_2 p + \beta_2 r + \delta_2 + \varepsilon^S, \qquad *(2.5.2)$$

$$q^D = q^S. \qquad *(2.5.3)$$

Here q^D is the quantity demanded of a particular good, q^S is the quantity supplied, p is price, I is income, r is rainfall, ε^D is the stochastic disturbance term for demand, and ε^S is the stochastic disturbance term for supply.[15]

All econometric models contain variables, which are either endogenous or exogenous; stochastic disturbance terms; and parameters in a system of structural equations. The *endogenous variables* are those variables whose values are determined simultaneously by the model and which the model is designed to explain, in this case q^D, q^S, and p. The *exogenous variables* are variables whose values are determined outside the model but which influence the model. From a formal standpoint the exogenous variables are assumed to be statistically independent of all stochastic disturbance terms of the model, while the endogenous variables are not statistically independent of those terms. In this case the exogenous variables are I and r. In general, the exogenous variables are either historically given, policy variables, or are determined by a separate mechanism outside the model.

The *stochastic disturbance terms*, in this case ε^D and ε^S, are random variables that typically are added to all equations of the model other than identities or equilibrium conditions. As suggested above, there are four justifications for including such a term in each nondefinitional equation. First, variables that may influence demand and supply have, in fact, been omitted from the two equations. For example, other prices or variables reflecting the distribution of income, which have been omitted, may, in fact, affect the quantity demanded. Second, the equations may be misspecified in that the particular functional forms chosen, here linear in both parameters and variables, may be incorrect. Third, the variables included may be measured inaccurately. (Again, it is important to distinguish sharply between measurement errors in the dependent and independent variables.) Fourth, there may be basic randomness in behavior on the part of both demanders and suppliers. The stochastic terms can account for any or all of these considerations.[16]

[15]It is possible to interpret q^D, q^S, I, and r as *logarithms* of quantity demanded, quantity supplied, income, and rainfall, respectively. In that case (2.5.1) is similar to the constant elasticity demand function (2.4.7).

[16]More detailed discussions of errors in variables and specification error appear in Chapter 5.

The explicit parameters of the model are the constant coefficients that multiply the variables of the model. In this case the model contains six explicit parameters: γ_1 and γ_2, multiplying p; β_1, multiplying I; β_2, multiplying r; and δ_1 and δ_2, which may be thought of as multiplying 1. The model also contains some implicit parameters, namely those defining the probability distributions for ε^D and ε^S. These explicit and implicit parameters are the *structural parameters*. The equations of the model as given in (2.5.1) to (2.5.3) are the *structural equations*. Each has a separate meaning and identity, and the set of all structural equations, the *structural form*, is the initial stage in model building. In this model, for example, the first equation is a demand equation, the second is a supply equation, and the third is an equilibrium condition.

The demand equation (2.5.1) specifies that the quantity demanded is a linear function of price, income, and an additive stochastic disturbance term. The parameters are γ_1, β_1, and δ_1, where γ_1 is generally negative (downward-sloping demand curve; i.e., the good is not a *Giffen good*) and β_1 is generally positive (added income leads to increased demand; i.e., the good is a *superior good*).[17] Given values for the parameters, income, and the stochastic disturbance term, the resulting relationship between q^D and p can be represented geometrically as a linear demand curve, *DD* in Figure 2.5. As any of these values (parameters, income, stochastic disturbance term) change, this demand curve will shift, as in Figure 2.5. For example, the demand curve will shift outward, from *DD* to *D′D′*, if income increases from I to I'.

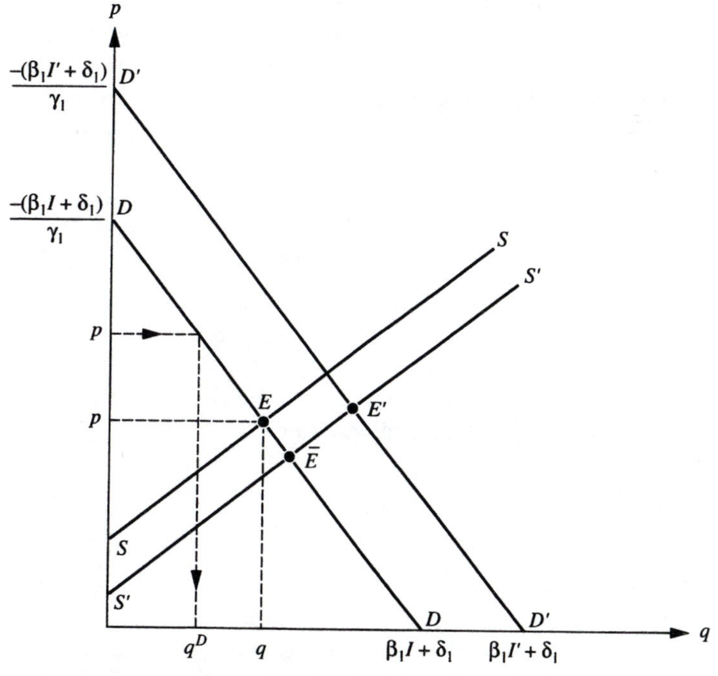

Figure 2.5 Geometric Representation of the Prototype Micro Model

[17]For discussions of Giffen good and superior good, see Chapter 7.

The right-hand side of (2.5.1) includes two random variables. The first is the stochastic disturbance term ε^D. The second is the variable p, which is endogenous and hence influenced by both stochastic disturbance terms [see (2.5.9) below]. Thus the left-hand side, the quantity demanded, is also stochastic. In general, it is assumed that the stochastic disturbance term has a zero expected value:[18]

$$E(\varepsilon^D) = 0. \tag{2.5.4}$$

It therefore follows that the expected quantity demanded is

$$E(q^D) = \gamma_1 E(p) + \beta_1 I + \delta_1. \tag{2.5.5}$$

Figure 2.5 illustrates for a given level of income and a zero value of the stochastic disturbance term the (expected) quantity demanded at any given level of (expected) price.

The supply equation (2.5.2) specifies that the quantity supplied is a linear function of price, rainfall, and a stochastic disturbance term. The parameters are γ_2, β_2, and δ_2, where generally γ_2 is positive (rising supply curve) and β_2 can be either positive (in case of drought) or negative (in case of flood). Thus, in drought conditions added rainfall shifts out supply, while in flood conditions added rainfall shifts in supply. Given these parameters, the levels of r, and the expected value of zero for ε^S, the resulting relationship is a linear supply curve, shown as SS in Figure 2.5. The supply curve will shift outward (e.g., to $S'S'$) for an increase (decrease) in rainfall, given conditions of drought (flood).

Equation (2.5.3) is the equilibrium condition, stating that demand equals supply. This equation, defining equilibrium, does not entail a stochastic disturbance term. The equilibrium values of q and p are shown at the equilibrium point E in Figure 2.5.

In general, equilibrium conditions, such as (2.5.3) and other comparable equations, such as definitions or other identities, can be eliminated. In this case letting q be the equilibrium quantity—that is, the common value of q^D and q^S—the model can be written as the two equations

$$q = \gamma_1 p + \beta_1 I + \delta_1 + \varepsilon^D, \tag*{*(2.5.6)}$$

$$q = \gamma_2 p + \beta_2 r + \delta_2 + \varepsilon^S. \tag*{*(2.5.7)}$$

The prototype micro model then consists of these two structural equations, which determine values of the two endogenous variables q and p in terms of the exogenous variables I and r.

A convenient way of expressing this model and in fact most linear econometric models is to use vector-matrix notation.[19] In this notation the *structural form* is the set of structural equations

$$(q \quad p)\begin{pmatrix} 1 & 1 \\ -\gamma_1 & -\gamma_2 \end{pmatrix} + (I \quad r \quad 1)\begin{pmatrix} -\beta & 0 \\ 0 & -\beta_2 \\ -\delta_1 & -\delta_2 \end{pmatrix} = (\varepsilon^D \quad \varepsilon^S). \tag*{*(2.5.8)}$$

The row vector $(q \quad p)$ is the *vector of endogenous variables*, while $(I \quad r \quad 1)$ is the *vector of exogenous variables* (where 1 accounts for the intercepts), and $(\varepsilon^D \quad \varepsilon^S)$ is the *vec-*

[18] Other assumptions on the stochastic disturbance terms, involving variances and covariances, are introduced in Chapter 4.

[19] See Appendix B for a review of matrices.

tor of stochastic disturbance terms. The two coefficient matrices are *matrices of structural coefficients*, summarizing all parameters of the structural equations—the γ's, β's, and δ's.

Equations (2.5.6) and (2.5.7) can be solved simultaneously simply by equating one to the other. Solving for p and then for q yields

$$p = \frac{\beta_1}{\gamma_2 - \gamma_1} I - \frac{\beta_2}{\gamma_2 - \gamma_1} r + \frac{\delta_1 - \delta_2}{\gamma_2 - \gamma_1} + \frac{\varepsilon^D - \varepsilon^S}{\gamma_2 - \gamma_1}, \qquad *(2.5.9)$$

$$q = \frac{\gamma_2\beta_1}{\gamma_2 - \gamma_1} I - \frac{\gamma_1\beta_2}{\gamma_2 - \gamma_1} r + \frac{\gamma_2\delta_1 - \gamma_1\delta_2}{\gamma_2 - \gamma_1} + \frac{\gamma_2\varepsilon^D - \gamma_1\varepsilon^S}{\gamma_2 - \gamma_1}. \qquad *(2.5.10)$$

Each of these equations, called *reduced-form equations*, expresses one of the endogenous variables as a function of all exogenous variables and stochastic disturbance terms. The set of all reduced-form equations is the *reduced form*, which is used both for analysis and for estimation of the model. In vector-matrix notation it would be written

$$(q \quad p) = (I \quad r \quad 1)\begin{pmatrix} \dfrac{\gamma_2\beta_1}{\gamma_2 - \gamma_1} & \dfrac{\beta_1}{\gamma_2 - \gamma_1} \\ \dfrac{-\gamma_1\beta_2}{\gamma_2 - \gamma_1} & \dfrac{-\beta_2}{\gamma_2 - \gamma_1} \\ \dfrac{\gamma_2\delta_1 - \gamma_1\delta_2}{\gamma_2 - \gamma_1} & \dfrac{\delta_1 - \delta_2}{\gamma_2 - \gamma_1} \end{pmatrix} + \left(\frac{\gamma_2\varepsilon^D - \gamma_1\varepsilon^S}{\gamma_2 - \gamma_1} \quad \frac{\varepsilon^D - \varepsilon^S}{\gamma_2 - \gamma_1}\right), \qquad *(2.5.11)$$

where the coefficient matrix is the *matrix of reduced-form coefficients*. The reduced form (2.5.11) could have been obtained directly from the structural form (2.5.8) by solving for the vector of endogenous variables $(q \quad p)$. To obtain such a solution both sides of equation (2.5.8) would be postmultiplied by the inverse matrix[20]

$$\begin{pmatrix} 1 & 1 \\ -\gamma_1 & -\gamma_2 \end{pmatrix}^{-1} = \frac{1}{\gamma_2 - \gamma_1}\begin{pmatrix} \gamma_2 & 1 \\ -\gamma_1 & -1 \end{pmatrix} \qquad (2.5.12)$$

and the result solved for $(q \quad p)$.

The coefficients of the reduced-form equations summarize the comparative statics results of this model. By *comparative statics* is meant a comparison of two equilibrium values of each of the endogenous variables, where the only change that occurs is in one of the exogenous variables. For example, from (2.5.9) or (2.5.11),

$$\frac{\partial p}{\partial I} = \frac{\beta_1}{\gamma_2 - \gamma_1}. \qquad (2.5.13)$$

Since the denominator is always positive ($\gamma_2 > 0$ being the slope of the supply curve and $\gamma_1 < 0$ being the slope of the demand curve), to the extent that $\beta_1 > 0$ (the good being a superior good) the partial derivative is positive. Thus a *ceteris paribus* increase in income would tend to increase the equilibrium price.[21] Similarly,

[20]For a discussion of the concept of an inverse matrix, see Appendix B. In general, any square matrix with a nonzero determinant has an inverse. Here the determinant, given by $\gamma_1 - \gamma_2$, is nonzero. It is, in fact, negative, since $\gamma_1 < 0$ and $\gamma_2 > 0$.

[21]The expression *ceteris paribus* means other things are held equal; here the "other" things are rainfall and the stochastic disturbance terms.

$$\frac{\partial q}{\partial I} = \frac{\gamma_2 \beta_1}{\gamma_2 - \gamma_1} > 0. \tag{2.5.14}$$

For rainfall,

$$\frac{\partial p}{\partial r} = \frac{-\beta_2}{\gamma_2 - \gamma_1} \lesseqgtr 0, \tag{2.5.15}$$

$$\frac{\partial q}{\partial r} = \frac{-\gamma_1 \beta_2}{\gamma_2 - \gamma_1} \gtreqless 0, \tag{2.5.16}$$

where the top (bottom) sign indicates the direction of change with added rainfall under drought (flood) conditions. For example, in drought added rainfall decreases the price and increases the quantity, as shown geometrically by comparing the equilibrium at E to that at $\overline{E}$.

The comparative statics results, indicating the directions of change of each of the endogenous variables for a change in the exogenous variables, can be summarized as in Table 2.1.[22] Note that two of the signs, corresponding to shifts in the intercepts, are indeterminate. Also note that this table is simply the matrix of reduced-form coefficients in (2.5.11).

In general, economic theory stops and econometrics begins at this point, where the model and the signs of some of the relevant partial derivatives have been determined. The next logical step would be the statistical estimation of numerical values for these partial derivatives, or, what is the same thing, the estimation of the matrix of reduced-form coefficients in (2.5.11). Estimation of these reduced-form coefficients entails the use of data on the endogenous and exogenous variables and the use of econometric techniques. With numerical estimates of these coefficients it would be possible to perform *structural analysis* (e.g., test the hypotheses that price is highly responsive to income but not responsive to rainfall), to use the model for purposes of *forecasting* (e.g., forecast the price of the agricultural good next year), and to use it for purposes of *policy evaluation* (e.g., determine how policies affecting income would affect the price and quantity of the good). The estimation of the reduced-form coefficients is also sometimes the first step in the estimation of the structural-form coefficients.

TABLE 2.1 Comparative Statics of the Prototype Micro Model

Exogenous Variables	Endogenous Variables q	Endogenous Variables p
I	$\frac{\gamma_2\beta_1}{\gamma_2 - \gamma_1} > 0$	$\frac{\beta_1}{\gamma_2 - \gamma_1} > 0$
r	$\frac{-\gamma_1\beta_2}{\gamma_2 - \gamma_1} \gtreqless 0$	$\frac{-\beta_2}{\gamma_2 - \gamma_1} \lesseqgtr 0$
1	$\frac{\gamma_2\delta_1 - \gamma_1\delta_2}{\gamma_2 - \gamma_1}$?	$\frac{\delta_1 - \delta_2}{\gamma_2 - \gamma_1}$?

[22]An entire theory has developed concerning comparative statics, with particular reference to the comparative statics matrix of signs. It is called *qualitative economics* and stems largely from Samuelson (1947).

2.6 THE PROTOTYPE MACRO MODEL

The second example of an econometric model is the *prototype macro model*. This is a generalization of the graphical model of national income determination of Figure 2.2, and, like the prototype micro model, it illustrates the generalization feasible with an algebraic model. It is a prototype for the various macro-econometric models discussed in Chapter 12. Unlike the prototype micro model, which was a *static model* in which time played no essential role, the prototype macro model is a *dynamic model* in which time enters essentially. Specifically, one endogenous variable is specified as dependent on the value taken by another endogenous variable in the preceding year.

The prototype macro model consists of the following three structural equations:

$$C_t = \gamma_1 Y_t + \beta_1 + \varepsilon_t^C, \qquad *(2.6.1)$$

$$I_t = \gamma_2 Y_t + \beta_2 Y_{t-1} + \beta_3 + \varepsilon_t^I, \qquad *(2.6.2)$$

$$Y_t = C_t + I_t + G_t. \qquad *(2.6.3)$$

Here C_t, I_t, and Y_t represent, respectively, consumption, investment, and national income, in year t, and these three variables are the endogenous variables of the model. G_t is government spending in year t, treated as exogenous, and Y_{t-1} is income of the preceding year, a *lagged* endogenous variable. The variables ε_t^C and ε_t^I are stochastic disturbance terms for consumption and investment, respectively. The γ's and β's are five structural parameters to be estimated.

The first equation (2.6.1) is the consumption function, as before. The second equation (2.6.2) determines investment spending on the basis of both current and lagged values of income. The case in which investment is autonomous, as in previous treatments, is the special case in which γ_2, β_2, and ε_t^I are all identically zero, so I_t is the constant β_3. Another important special case is that in which $\beta_2 = -\gamma_2$, where investment follows the accelerator mechanism. In that case levels of investment are based on *changes* in national income, since then

$$I_t = \gamma_2(Y_t - Y_{t-1}) + \beta_3 + \varepsilon_t^I. \qquad (2.6.4)$$

The last equation of the model (2.6.3) is the equilibrium condition giving national income as the sum of consumption, investment, and government expenditure.[23]

Figure 2.6 is a *flow diagram*, also called an *arrow scheme*, which is a common graphical method of illustrating the workings of such a model. It shows the effects of both the exogenous and the lagged endogenous variables on the current endogenous variables; it also shows the interactions among the endogenous variables. The value of current national income influences future investment, as shown by the dashed line, which would connect to income in the following year.

Just as in the prototype micro model, the equilibrium condition can be used to eliminate one equation and one endogenous variable. In this case any one of the three endogenous variables could be eliminated. To eliminate I, equation (2.6.2) can be substituted into (2.6.3) to obtain the two structural equations, (2.6.1) and

[23]Net exports [i.e., exports less imports (the net balance of trade on current account)] are either omitted altogether or included in either investment I_t or government spending G_t (depending on whether or not an endogenous treatment is desired).

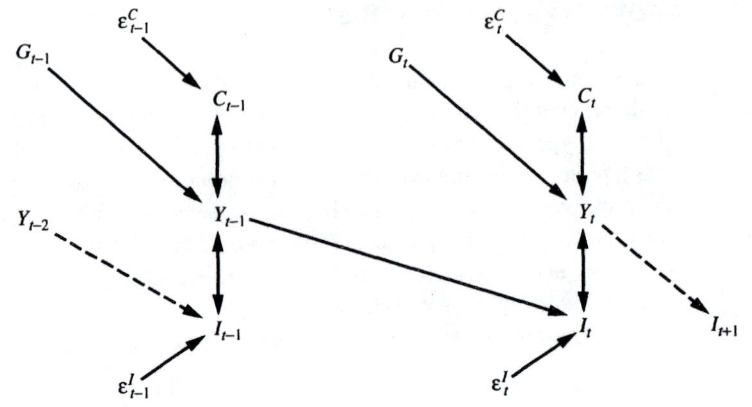

Figure 2.6 Flow Diagram of the Prototype Macro Model

$$Y_t = \left(\frac{1}{1-\gamma_2}\right)C_t + \left(\frac{\beta_2}{1-\gamma_2}\right)Y_{t-1} + \left(\frac{1}{1-\gamma_2}\right)G_t + \frac{\beta_3}{1-\gamma_2} + \frac{\varepsilon_t^I}{1-\gamma_2}. \qquad *(2.6.5)$$

The structural form is thus, in matrix notation,

$$(C_t \quad Y_t)\begin{pmatrix} -1 & \dfrac{1}{1-\gamma_2} \\ \gamma_1 & -1 \end{pmatrix} + (Y_{t-1} \quad G_t \quad 1)\begin{pmatrix} 0 & \dfrac{\beta_2}{1-\gamma_2} \\ 0 & \dfrac{1}{1-\gamma_2} \\ \beta_1 & \dfrac{\beta_3}{1-\gamma_2} \end{pmatrix} = \left(-\varepsilon_t^C \quad \frac{-\varepsilon_t^I}{1-\gamma_2}\right). \qquad *(2.6.6)$$

The reduced-form equations are easily obtained by substitution or by inverting the 2×2 matrix that postmultiplies the vector of endogenous variables, postmultiplying by this inverse in (2.6.6), and solving for $(C_t \quad Y_t)$. The result is

$$Y_t = \frac{\beta_2}{1-\gamma_1-\gamma_2}Y_{t-1} + \frac{1}{1-\gamma_1-\gamma_2}G_t + \frac{\beta_1+\beta_3}{1-\gamma_1-\gamma_2} + \frac{\varepsilon_t^C+\varepsilon_t^I}{1-\gamma_1-\gamma_2}, \qquad *(2.6.7)$$

$$C_t = \frac{\gamma_1\beta_2}{1-\gamma_1-\gamma_2}Y_{t-1} + \frac{\gamma_1}{1-\gamma_1-\gamma_2}G_t + \frac{\gamma_1\beta_3+(1-\gamma_2)\beta_1}{1-\gamma_1-\gamma_2} + \frac{\gamma_1\varepsilon_t^I+(1-\gamma_2)\varepsilon_t^C}{1-\gamma_1-\gamma_2}. \qquad *(2.6.8)$$

These equations determine current income and consumption as functions of lagged income and current government expenditure. In general, the *reduced-form equations* give each current endogenous variable as a function of all lagged endogenous variables, all exogenous variables, and all stochastic disturbance terms. The set of all exogenous and lagged endogenous variables is called the set of *predetermined variables*, since the lagged endogenous variables were determined in a previous period, while the exogenous variables are determined by a system other than the one under consideration. In either case they are assumed to be determined before the current endogenous variables.

Equation (2.6.7) shows the effect of a *ceteris paribus* change in current government expenditure on income as

$$\frac{\partial Y_t}{\partial G_t} = \frac{1}{1 - \gamma_1 - \gamma_2}. \quad *(2.6.9)$$

This result is known as the *impact multiplier*, since it indicates the impact of government spending on income. It is also called the *short-term multiplier*, since it shows the effect of current government spending on current income. In the special case in which investment is predetermined, for which $\gamma_2 = 0$, the impact multiplier is the same as the multiplier in (2.3.6), the reciprocal of unity less the marginal propensity to consume:

$$\left.\frac{\partial Y_t}{\partial G_t}\right|_{\gamma_2 = 0} = \frac{1}{1 - \gamma_1} = \frac{1}{1 - \text{MPC}}. \quad (2.6.10)$$

The reduced-form equation for Y, (2.6.7), is a first-order difference equation, which may be written

$$Y_t = \pi_1 Y_{t-1} + \pi_2 G_t + \pi_3 + u_t, \quad *(2.6.11)$$

where

$$\begin{aligned} \pi_1 &= \beta_2 \pi_2, \\ \pi_2 &= \frac{1}{1 - \gamma_1 - \gamma_2}, \\ \pi_3 &= (\beta_1 + \beta_3)\pi_2, \\ u_t &= (\varepsilon_t^C + \varepsilon_t^I)\pi_2. \end{aligned} \quad (2.6.12)$$

If this difference equation is solved, the result, known as the *final-form equation*, will permit the calculation of all the multipliers, long and short term, for income.

To solve the difference equation by iteration, note that (2.6.11) implies that

$$Y_{t-1} = \pi_1 Y_{t-2} + \pi_2 G_{t-1} + \pi_3 + u_{t-1}. \quad (2.6.13)$$

Substitution of (2.6.13) into (2.6.11) yields

$$Y_t = \pi_1^2 Y_{t-2} + \pi_2(G_t + \pi_1 G_{t-1}) + \pi_3(1 + \pi_1) + (u_t + \pi_1 u_{t-1}). \quad (2.6.14)$$

Similarly, determining Y_{t-2} from (2.6.11) and inserting the result in (2.6.14) yields

$$\begin{aligned} Y_t = \pi_1^3 Y_{t-3} + \pi_2(G_t + \pi_1 G_{t-1} + \pi_1^2 G_{t-2}) + \pi_3(1 + \pi_1 + \pi_1^2) \\ + (u_t + \pi_1 u_{t-1} + \pi_1^2 u_{t-2}). \end{aligned} \quad (2.6.15)$$

Continuing this process of iteration back to the base year, $t = 0$, yields

$$\begin{aligned} Y_t = \pi_1^t Y_0 &+ \pi_2(G_t + \pi_1 G_{t-1} + \pi_1^2 G_{t-2} + \cdots + \pi_1^{t-1} G_1) \\ &+ \pi_3(1 + \pi_1 + \pi_1^2 + \cdots + \pi_1^{t-1}) \\ &+ (u_t + \pi_1 u_{t-1} + \pi_1^2 u_{t-2} + \cdots + \pi_1^{t-1} u_1). \end{aligned} \quad *(2.6.16)$$

This equation is known as the *final-form equation* for income.[24] From it all the multipliers for income, both short and long term, can be calculated. Thus the impact multiplier, giving the effect on current income of a change in current government expenditure, is obtained from (2.6.16) as

$$\frac{\partial Y_t}{\partial G_t} = \pi_2 = \frac{1}{1 - \gamma_1 - \gamma_2}, \tag{2.6.17}$$

as before.

Consider now the effect on current income of a change in government spending in the preceding period. From (2.6.16),

$$\frac{\partial Y_t}{\partial G_{t-1}} = \pi_2 \pi_1. \tag{2.6.18}$$

Adding (2.6.17) and (2.6.18) gives the effect of a change in government spending over both the current and preceding periods. The result is the *two-period cumulative multiplier*

$$\left.\frac{\partial Y_t}{\partial G_t}\right|_{\Delta G_{t-1} = \Delta G_t} = \pi_2(1 + \pi_1) = \frac{1 - \gamma_1 - \gamma_2 + \beta_2}{(1 - \gamma_1 - \gamma_2)^2}. \tag{2.6.19}$$

Similarly, the *three-period cumulative multiplier* is

$$\left.\frac{\partial Y_t}{\partial G_t}\right|_{\Delta G_{t-2} = \Delta G_{t-1} = \Delta G_t} = \pi_2(1 + \pi_1 + \pi_1^2). \tag{2.6.20}$$

In general, the *τ-period cumulative multiplier* is the response to an increase in government expenditure over both the current and previous $\tau - 1$ periods. It is given as

$$\left.\frac{\partial Y_t}{\partial G_t}\right|_{\Delta G_{t-i} = \Delta G_t, i=1,2,\ldots,\tau-1} = \pi_2(1 + \pi_1 + \pi_1^2 + \cdots + \pi_1^{\tau-1}). \tag{2.6.21}$$

Letting τ approach infinity gives the *long-term multiplier*

$$\begin{aligned}\left.\frac{\partial Y_t}{\partial G_t}\right|_{\text{long term}} &= \pi_2(1 + \pi_1 + \pi_1^2 + \cdots) = \frac{\pi_2}{1 - \pi_1} \\ &= \frac{1}{1 - \gamma_1 - \gamma_2 - \beta_2},\end{aligned} \tag{2.6.22}$$

where use has been made both of the result on the sum of a geometric series (assuming that $0 < \pi_1 < 1$) and the definitions in (2.6.12). The long-term multiplier has the interpretation of the change in income arising from a one-unit increase in government spending over not only the current period but also every past period, stretching back toward the infinite past; it is thus the response to a sustained new level in government spending. Alternatively, it can be interpreted as the change in future income arising from a permanent increase in government spending.

If β_2, γ_2, and γ_1 were all positive, the impact multiplier (2.6.9) or (2.6.17) and the long-term multiplier (2.6.22) would yield the lower and upper bounds, respectively, for all government spending multipliers, giving the effect of a unit change in government spending on income a value between

[24]See Sections 2.9 and 14.5. A rigorous proof of this equation would entail the technique of mathematical induction.

$$\frac{1}{1-\gamma_1-\gamma_2} \quad \text{and} \quad \frac{1}{1-\gamma_1-\gamma_2-\beta_2}, \tag{2.6.23}$$

depending on the number of years for which the change was implemented. Thus, to give a quantitative example, if γ_1, the marginal propensity to consume, were 0.7; γ_2, the effect of current income on investment, were 0.05; and β_2, the effect of past income on investment, were also 0.05, the impact multiplier of 4 and long-term multiplier of 5 would give the bounds on all government spending multipliers. In general, the longer the "run," in the sense of the more periods over which government expenditure changes (either in the past or in the future), the larger is the multiplier. (This result, however, will not necessarily generalize to larger, more complicated models.)

With the estimated parameters of the model it is possible to obtain numerical values for the various multipliers (part of *structural analysis*). With these estimates it is also possible to *forecast* (e.g., forecast national income next year) and to conduct *policy evaluation* (e.g., evaluate alternative levels of government expenditure in terms of impacts on national income, consumption, and investment).

2.7 RELATED APPROACHES TO ECONOMETRIC MODELING

In this section and the two that follow, we consider some more general points as well as some alternative approaches to econometric modeling. The prototype macro model of Section 2.6 can be regarded as the basis for more sophisticated macroeconometric models, which are discussed in Chapter 12.[25] Macroeconometric models, which now have a history of greater than half a century, dating from the pioneering efforts of Jan Tinbergen in the 1930s, are among the most important applications of econometrics.

Moreover, the macroeconometric model need not be fitted solely for developed economies such as the United States but can also be adapted successfully for less developed countries (LDCs).[26] At least part of the model of aggregate demand (a simple version of which was sketched in Section 2.6) can be adapted, while production is a universal phenomenon. Thus one might model the production relationships by an input–output system, as discussed below, but at a minimum, the macroeconometric model of an LDC should contain a disaggregation into three productive sectors: agriculture, private nonagriculture, and government production. Careful attention must be paid to differing institutional characteristics of the LDCs. For example, the monetary and financial structures of many LDCs differ strikingly from those of the developed economies. Data, which present many problems even in nearly ideal circumstances (see Chapter 3), may present even greater difficulties in the case of the LDCs. In particular, where aggregative data are either in very short supply or nonexistent, these could be supplemented or replaced by survey (cross-sectional) data. Nevertheless, the past quarter-century has largely confirmed Klein's (1965) cautious optimism about this type of possible macroeconometric model.

[25]A brief synoptic history of macroeconometric modeling, which could be regarded as a brief overview of Chapter 12, appears in Intriligator (1983). Systems of demand equations and production models containing production functions, and competitive first-order conditions for profit maximization, amplifying on the presentations of Chapters 7 and 8, are also discussed in Intriligator (1983). A more detailed history of macroeconometric modeling appears in Bodkin, Klein, Marwah (1991).

[26]See Klein (1965).

It is useful to distinguish the equations of an econometric model into two categories of equations: stochastic equations (i.e., those with stochastic disturbance terms) and identities or equilibrium conditions (i.e., those without disturbance terms). A further distinction can be made by dividing the equations of an econometric model into four categories: behavioral conditions, technical conditions, institutional relationships, and definitional relationships.[27] The *behavioral relations*, which are the essence of econometric (and economic) modeling, are typically based, at least in principle, on rational, optimizing decisions of economic agents, which determine their behavior. (Of course, in a macroeconometric model some aggregation is essential.) The *technical conditions* generally refer to the state of technology, as embodied in production functions, cost functions, and the like, and they generally contain stochastic disturbance terms. The *institutional relationships* summarize relevant laws or institutions; a tax receipts function would be an example. Finally, *definitional relationships* include identities and equilibrium conditions and thus generally do not contain stochastic disturbance terms. Finally, we note that Solari also made a distinction between *forecasting models*, on the one hand, and *decision or policy models*, on the other. Thus, forecasting models frequently make use of whatever autoregressive structure may be found in the economy and hence employ many lagged endogenous variables. By contrast, policy models may or may not include lagged endogenous variables, but such models will include a number of "instruments" or "policy handles" (which may be virtually absent from the forecasting models), among the predetermined variables. By contrast, the discussion in Chapter 1 suggested that, ideally, a "good" econometric model should be useful in both types of applications.

Another approach to modeling economic relationships is that of *microanalytic simulation*, as developed by Orcutt and his colleagues.[28] They argue that valuable information is lost in the process of aggregation which underlies most econometric models and that these models therefore become less precise, as it becomes difficult or impossible to distinguish among competing hypotheses. Instead, they argue that one should ideally represent the behavioral relationships of individual agents, whether consumers, firms, other private organizations, or even individual government units. After such relationships have in principle been described at the microeconomic level of the individual decision unit, the desired amount of aggregation, whether at the regional level, at the national level, by income class, at the industry level, or by whatever aggregation desired, could be carried out within the model itself. This approach, involving a focus on behavior at the individual level and aggregation explicitly within the model context, would, it is asserted, represent a more methodologically suitable approach to modeling economic behavior and would improve the quality of the model building. By contrast, this approach is certainly more costly than conventional approaches, so it is held (by critics) that the putative gains do not justify the costs.[29]

[27]See Solari (1979).

[28]See Orcutt (1962), Orcutt, Watts, and Edwards (1968), and Orcutt, Merz, and Quinke (1986).

[29]In 1962, Orcutt estimated the cost of such a model for the U.S. economy at $50 million; one can only speculate how much more such a model would cost today. An alternative that should be mentioned is a *computable general equilibrium model*. As this is mainly a theoretical effort with parameters supplied from preexisting research, the cost of this approach to problems of economic policy is considerably more modest. Computable general equilibrium models have been used in studying problems of taxation policy, alternative approaches to economic planning in LDCs, and the possible gains to freer trade between the United States and Canada, in anticipation of the 1989 Free Trade Agreement. A good introduction to this approach to economic modeling may be found in Scarf and Shoven (1984) and Piggott and Whalley (1985).

Still another approach to economic modeling is that of *input–output*, developed by Leontief and his colleagues.[30] This approach focuses on the interindustry relationships in the economy, and it determines the requirements for the gross outputs of the various industries of the economy for a given level of final demand for the output of the various industries. The input–output relationships can be interpreted in terms of a particularly simple form of the production function, as discussed in Chapter 8; this form implies that there is a fixed ratio of each of the productive inputs in any single industry to the gross output of that industry. The assumption of fixed input–output coefficients can be extended to the primary factors of labor, capital, land, and other natural resources. The input–output approach has very large demands for data, which increase very rapidly with the number of industries into which the economy is partitioned. The system is therefore generally not estimated statistically, as is also the case for the computable general equilibrium models and unlike the econometric and microanalytic simulation approaches. Instead, the input–output coefficients are typically estimated on the basis of a single observation of the components of the ratio in question. For a number of years now, input–output submodels have been incorporated into some of the large-scale macroeconometric models as a means of representing the technology employed in the economy.[31]

2.8 THE GENERAL LINEAR ECONOMETRIC MODEL: STRUCTURAL FORM AND REDUCED FORM[32]

The *general linear econometric model* is an algebraic, linear (in parameters) stochastic model. Assuming that there are g endogenous (jointly dependent) variables $y_1, y_2, \ldots, y_g$ and k predetermined (exogenous or lagged endogenous) variables $x_1, x_2, \ldots, x_k$, the general linear econometric model can be written

$$\begin{aligned}
y_1\gamma_{11} + y_2\gamma_{21} + \cdots + y_g\gamma_{g1} + x_1\beta_{11} + x_2\beta_{21} + \cdots + x_k\beta_{k1} &= \varepsilon_1 \\
y_1\gamma_{12} + y_2\gamma_{22} + \cdots + y_g\gamma_{g2} + x_1\beta_{12} + x_2\beta_{22} + \cdots + x_k\beta_{k2} &= \varepsilon_2 \\
&\vdots \\
y_1\gamma_{1g} + y_2\gamma_{2g} + \cdots + y_g\gamma_{gg} + x_1\beta_{1g} + x_2\beta_{2g} + \cdots + x_k\beta_{kg} &= \varepsilon_g,
\end{aligned} \qquad *(2.8.1)$$

where $\varepsilon_1, \varepsilon_2, \ldots, \varepsilon_g$ are g stochastic disturbance terms (random variables), the γ's are coefficients of endogenous variables, and the β's are coefficients of predetermined variables.[33] The linear system of equations is *complete* if there are as many independent equations as endogenous variables. The system of equations then jointly determines values of the en-

[30]See Leontief (1941, 1953, 1986). Leontief's philosophical and methodological approach to input–output modeling are clearly expressed in Leontief (1971).

[31]See, for example, the Brookings and Wharton models for the United States, the CANDIDE model for Canada, and the models developed for the Economic Planning Agency of Japan, summarized in Chapter 12. [See, in particular, Committee on Econometric Methods (1965), and Duesenberry et al. (1965), for the original references.]

[32]For a more complete discussion of the general linear econometric model, including a discussion of the stochastic specification of the disturbance terms, see Chapter 9. It might be noted that the general linear econometric model is also referred to as the *simultaneous equations model* and the *structural equations model*. Other disciplines, such as psychology and sociology, use other terms to refer to similar models, including *linear causal scheme*, *path analysis*, and *dependence analysis* (see Goldberger and Duncan, 1973).

[33]In some econometrics texts the roles of the γ's and β's are reversed, so that the γ's are coefficients of predetermined variables and the β's are the coefficients of endogenous variables.

dogenous variables in terms of values of the predetermined variables and values taken by the stochastic disturbance terms.

Each equation in (2.8.1) contains up to $g + k$ parameters, $\gamma_{1h}, \gamma_{2h}, \ldots, \gamma_{gh}$ and $\beta_{1h}, \beta_{2h}, \ldots, \beta_{kh}$, for $h = 1, 2, \ldots, g$. Of course, some of these parameters may be specified as zero; that is, it may be specified that the corresponding variable, endogenous or predetermined, does not have any influence in a particular equation.[34] Intercept terms can be taken into account by specifying one of the predetermined variables, conventionally the last, x_k, to be identically unity, so $\beta_{k1}, \beta_{k2}, \ldots, \beta_{kg}$ are the intercepts.

The econometric models of Sections 2.5 and 2.6 provide examples of this general formulation. In particular, (2.5.6) and (2.5.7) are the structural equations of the prototype micro model, while (2.6.1) and (2.6.5) are the structural equations of the prototype macro model.

As noted in Section 2.7, each equation of the system (2.8.1) has an independent significance, reflecting a behavioral relation (e.g., a demand function or a consumption function), a technological relation (e.g., a production function), or some other specific relation suggested by theory for the system under study. Each equation, because it represents one aspect of the structure of the system, is called a *structural equation*, and the set of all structural equations (2.8.1) is called the *structural form*. Some equations may be deterministic (e.g., definitions, identities, and equilibrium conditions), and for these equations the stochastic disturbance terms are identically zero. In general, however, these equations can be eliminated, reducing both the number of equations and the number of endogenous variables.

The general nature of the econometric model is summarized in Figure 2.7 by a flow diagram. Values taken by the predetermined variables, together with values of stochastic disturbance terms, determine the current values of the endogenous variables. The dashed line indicates that the current values of the endogenous variables become, in the next period, the values of the lagged endogenous variables, which influence future endogenous variables. A specific illustration of such a flow diagram was presented in Figure 2.6 in connection with the prototype macro model.[35]

The structural equations may be written in either of two additional ways, which are equivalent to (2.8.1) but more compact in terms of notation. One uses summation notation, expressing the equations as

$$\sum_{h'=1}^{g} y_{h'}\gamma_{h'h} + \sum_{j=1}^{k} x_j\beta_{jh} = \varepsilon_h, \qquad h = 1, 2, \ldots, g. \qquad *(2.8.2)$$

Here h' is an index of the endogenous variable, h is an index of the equation, and j is an index of the predetermined variable ($h, h' = 1, 2, \ldots, g; j = 1, 2, \ldots, k$). The other uses vector-matrix notation, in which the *structural form* is written[36]

[34] In fact, as discussed in Section 2.10, such zero restrictions play an important role in ensuring that the structural parameters can be estimated.

[35] See Figure 12.1 for another illustration of such a diagram. Note that arrows cannot point leftward in these diagrams, since future variables cannot influence current variables. (Note that expectations variables are current variables.)

[36] Note that vectors and matrices appear in boldface type. It might be noted that some econometrics books use the convention that all vectors are column vectors, in which case (2.8.3) would be written

$$\mathbf{y}'\mathbf{\Gamma} + \mathbf{x}'\mathbf{B} = \boldsymbol{\varepsilon}'.$$

Here, defining $\mathbf{y}$, $\mathbf{x}$, and $\boldsymbol{\varepsilon}$ as row vectors makes it unnecessary to transpose them.

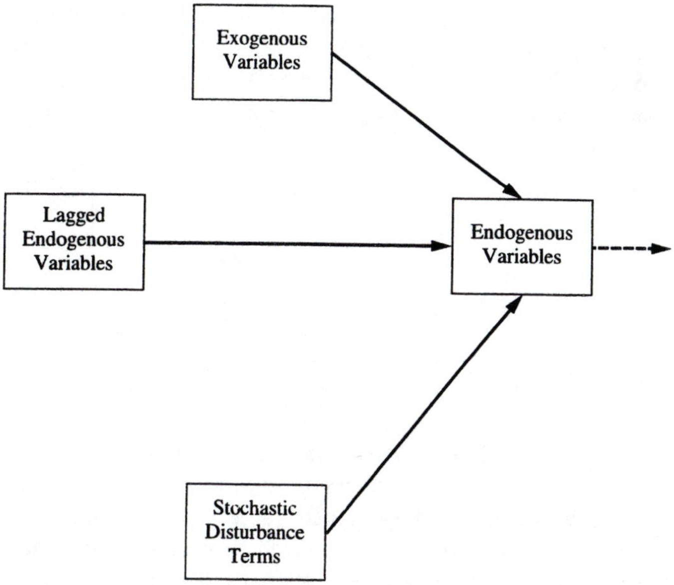

Figure 2.7 Flow Diagram of the General Econometric Model

$$\underset{1\times g}{\mathbf{y}}\ \underset{g\times g}{\boldsymbol{\Gamma}} + \underset{1\times k}{\mathbf{x}}\ \underset{k\times g}{\mathbf{B}} = \underset{1\times g}{\boldsymbol{\varepsilon}}. \qquad *(2.8.3)$$

In this notation **y** and **x** are row vectors of g endogenous and k predetermined variables, respectively:

$$\mathbf{y} = (y_1 \quad y_2 \quad \cdots \quad y_g), \qquad (2.8.4)$$

$$\mathbf{x} = (x_1 \quad x_2 \quad \cdots \quad x_k), \qquad (2.8.5)$$

and $\boldsymbol{\varepsilon}$ is a row vector consisting of g additive stochastic disturbance terms, one for each equation:

$$\boldsymbol{\varepsilon} = (\varepsilon_1 \quad \varepsilon_2 \quad \cdots \quad \varepsilon_g). \qquad (2.8.6)$$

The matrices $\boldsymbol{\Gamma}$ and **B** are the matrices of g^2 and gk structural coefficients, respectively:

$$\underset{g\times g}{\boldsymbol{\Gamma}} = (\gamma_{h'h}) = \begin{pmatrix} \gamma_{11} & \gamma_{12} & \cdots & \gamma_{1g} \\ \gamma_{21} & \gamma_{22} & \cdots & \gamma_{2g} \\ \vdots & \vdots & & \\ \gamma_{g1} & \gamma_{g2} & \cdots & \gamma_{gg} \end{pmatrix}, \qquad (2.8.7)$$

$$\underset{k\times g}{\mathbf{B}} = (\beta_{jh}) = \begin{pmatrix} \beta_{11} & \beta_{12} & \cdots & \beta_{1g} \\ \beta_{21} & \beta_{22} & \cdots & \beta_{2g} \\ \vdots & \vdots & & \\ \beta_{k1} & \beta_{k2} & \cdots & \beta_{kg} \end{pmatrix}, \qquad (2.8.8)$$

representing the complete set of coefficients of endogenous and predetermined variables, respectively. Thus, the hth columns of $\boldsymbol{\Gamma}$ and **B** contain all structural parameters in the hth equation of the system, for $h = 1, 2, \ldots, g$. The structural form in vector-matrix notation

(2.8.3) is the most convenient and the most easily manipulated of the three forms of expressing the structural equations. It will generally be used throughout the remainder of this book. Both of the prototype models have been expressed in this form—in equations (2.5.8) and (2.6.6), respectively. This structural form can be written as follows:

$$(y_1 \quad y_2 \quad \cdots \quad y_g)\begin{pmatrix} \gamma_{11} & \gamma_{12} & \cdots & \gamma_{1g} \\ \gamma_{21} & \gamma_{22} & \cdots & \gamma_{2g} \\ \vdots & \vdots & & \vdots \\ \gamma_{g1} & \gamma_{g2} & \cdots & \gamma_{gg} \end{pmatrix} + (x_1 \quad x_2 \quad \cdots \quad x_k)\begin{pmatrix} \beta_{11} & \beta_{12} & \cdots & \beta_{1g} \\ \beta_{21} & \beta_{22} & \cdots & \beta_{2g} \\ \vdots & \vdots & & \vdots \\ \beta_{k1} & \beta_{k2} & \cdots & \beta_{kg} \end{pmatrix} = (\varepsilon_1 \quad \varepsilon_2 \quad \cdots \quad \varepsilon_g). \tag{2.8.9}$$

There is a trivial indeterminacy in the structural equations in that multiplying all terms in each of these equations by a nonzero constant does not change the equation. This indeterminacy is eliminated by choosing a *normalization rule*, a rule for selecting a particular numerical value for one of the nonzero structural coefficients in each equation. The most common such rule divides all coefficients of equation h by $-\gamma_{hh}$, so that

$$\gamma_{hh} = -1, \qquad h = 1, 2, \ldots, g. \tag{2.8.10}$$

According to this rule all elements along the principal diagonal of $\mathbf{\Gamma}$, the matrix of coefficients of endogenous variables, are chosen to be –1. This normalization corresponds to the usual convention of writing one endogenous variable on the left-hand side of the equation, with a coefficient of 1. The prototype macro model (2.6.6) uses this normalization. Other normalization rules can be used, however. For example, the prototype micro model (2.5.8) uses the normalization $\gamma_{1h} = 1$ for $h = 1, 2$.

The structural form thus consists of g equations, each of which has an independent role and meaning in the model and which, together, determine, for given values of the parameters, the endogenous variables in terms of the predetermined variables and the stochastic disturbance terms. To the extent that every one of the equations has a stochastic disturbance term, it has been assumed that all identities, definitions, and equilibrium conditions have been removed, as was done in each of the prototype models. If the matrix of coefficients of endogenous variables $\mathbf{\Gamma}$ is nonsingular in having a nonzero determinant and hence an inverse, as will be assumed, the equation system can be solved for the endogenous variables as functions of all predetermined variables and stochastic disturbance terms. Postmultiplying (2.8.3) by the inverse of $\mathbf{\Gamma}$ yields

$$\mathbf{y\Gamma\Gamma}^{-1} + \mathbf{xB\Gamma}^{-1} = \boldsymbol{\varepsilon}\mathbf{\Gamma}^{-1}. \tag{2.8.11}$$

Thus, solving for $\mathbf{y}$ yields

$$\mathbf{y} = -\mathbf{xB\Gamma}^{-1} + \boldsymbol{\varepsilon}\mathbf{\Gamma}^{-1}. \tag{2.8.12}$$

Introducing the notation

$$\underset{k\times g}{\mathbf{\Pi}} \equiv -\underset{k\times g}{\mathbf{B}}\;\underset{g\times g}{\mathbf{\Gamma}^{-1}}, \tag*{*(2.8.13)}$$

$$\underset{1\times g}{\mathbf{u}} \equiv \underset{1\times g}{\boldsymbol{\varepsilon}}\;\underset{g\times g}{\mathbf{\Gamma}^{-1}}, \tag*{*(2.8.14)}$$

(2.8.12) can be written

$$\underset{1\times g}{\mathbf{y}} = \underset{1\times k}{\mathbf{x}}\ \underset{k\times g}{\mathbf{\Pi}} + \underset{1\times g}{\mathbf{u}}, \qquad *(2.8.15)$$

which is the the *reduced form*. It relates each endogenous variable to all predetermined variables and stochastic disturbance terms according to the following expression:

$$(y_1 \quad y_2 \quad \cdots \quad y_g) = (x_1 \quad x_2 \quad \cdots \quad x_k)\begin{pmatrix} \pi_{11} & \pi_{12} & \cdots & \pi_{1g} \\ \pi_{21} & \pi_{22} & \cdots & \pi_{2g} \\ \vdots & \vdots & & \vdots \\ \pi_{k1} & \pi_{k2} & \cdots & \pi_{kg} \end{pmatrix} + (u_1 \quad u_2 \quad \cdots \quad u_g). \qquad (2.8.16)$$

In summation notation the reduced form can be expressed as

$$y_h = \sum_{j=1}^{k} x_j \pi_{jh} + u_h, \qquad h = 1, 2, \ldots, g. \qquad *(2.8.17)$$

Written out in full, it states that

$$\begin{aligned} y_1 &= x_1\pi_{11} + x_2\pi_{21} + \cdots + x_k\pi_{k1} + u_1, \\ y_2 &= x_1\pi_{12} + x_2\pi_{22} + \cdots + x_k\pi_{k2} + u_2, \\ &\vdots \\ y_g &= x_1\pi_{1g} + x_2\pi_{2g} + \cdots + x_k\pi_{kg} + u_g. \end{aligned} \qquad *(2.8.18)$$

Whether in matrix notation, summation notation, or written out in full, in the reduced form each of the endogenous variables is expressed as a linear function of the predetermined variables and stochastic disturbance terms. The reduced form thus uniquely determines the probability distributions of the endogenous variables, given the exogenous variables and given the probability distributions of the stochastic disturbance terms.

For the prototype micro model the reduced-form equations are (2.5.9) and (2.5.10) or, in vector-matrix notation (2.5.11), while for the prototype macro model the reduced-form equations are (2.6.7) and (2.6.8) or, in vector-matrix notation,

$$(Y_t \quad C_t) = (Y_{t-1} \quad G_t \quad 1)\begin{pmatrix} \dfrac{\beta_2}{1-\gamma_1-\gamma_2} & \dfrac{\gamma_1\beta_2}{1-\gamma_1-\gamma_2} \\ \dfrac{1}{1-\gamma_1-\gamma_2} & \dfrac{\gamma_1}{1-\gamma_1-\gamma_2} \\ \dfrac{\beta_1+\beta_3}{1-\gamma_1-\gamma_2} & \dfrac{\gamma_1\beta_3+(1-\gamma_2)\beta_1}{1-\gamma_1-\gamma_2} \end{pmatrix} + \left(\frac{\varepsilon_t^I+\varepsilon_t^C}{1-\gamma_1-\gamma_2} \quad \frac{\gamma_1\varepsilon_t^I+(1-\gamma_2)\varepsilon_t^C}{1-\gamma_1-\gamma_2}\right). \qquad *(2.8.19)$$

Thus, in this case, using the notation of (2.8.15),

$$\begin{pmatrix} \pi_{11} & \pi_{12} \\ \pi_{21} & \pi_{22} \\ \pi_{31} & \pi_{32} \end{pmatrix} = \frac{1}{1-\gamma_1-\gamma_2}\begin{pmatrix} \beta_2 & \gamma_1\beta_2 \\ 1 & \gamma_1 \\ \beta_1+\beta_3 & \gamma_1\beta_3+(1-\gamma_2)\beta_1 \end{pmatrix} \qquad (2.8.20)$$

and

$$(u_1 \quad u_2) = \left(\frac{\varepsilon_t^C + \varepsilon_t^I}{1 - \gamma_1 - \gamma_2} \quad \frac{\gamma_1 \varepsilon_t^I + (1 - \gamma_2)\varepsilon_t^C}{1 - \gamma_1 - \gamma_2} \right). \tag{2.8.21}$$

The elements of the matrix of reduced-form coefficients have a useful interpretation as *comparative statics results*, indicating the extent of change in each endogenous variable as any of the predetermined variables change. By differentiating (2.8.17), we obtain

$$\frac{\partial y_h}{\partial x_j} = \pi_{jh}, \qquad j = 1, 2, \ldots, k; \quad h = 1, 2, \ldots, g. \qquad *(2.8.22)$$

Thus the *jh* element of the **Π** matrix of reduced-form coefficients is a measure of the change in the *h*th endogenous variable as the *j*th predetermined variable changes, all other predetermined variables and all stochastic disturbance terms being held constant. The estimation of the elements of the **Π** matrix is therefore an important part of structural analysis.

2.9 THE FINAL FORM

In Section 2.8 we introduced the structural and reduced forms of the econometric model. If the predetermined variables include lagged endogenous variables, it is possible to derive yet another form of the model, the final form.[37] The *final form* expresses the current endogenous variables as functions of base values and all relevant current and lagged exogenous variables and stochastic disturbance terms. It is important for structural analysis, since from it all short- and long-term multipliers can be determined. It thus reveals the short- and long-run comparative statics of the model.

If the system is first-order, involving only one lag, and if the lagged endogenous variables are included first, the vector of predetermined variables can be partitioned as

$$\mathbf{x}_t = (\mathbf{y}_{t-1} \mid \mathbf{z}_t \mid \mathbf{z}_{t-1}), \qquad *(2.9.1)$$

$$\mathbf{x}_t = (y_{1t-1} \cdots y_{gt-1} \mid z_{1t} \cdots z_{kt} \mid z_{1t-1} \cdots z_{kt-1}). \tag{2.9.2}$$

Here $\mathbf{y}_{t-1}$ is the vector of lagged endogenous variables, $\mathbf{z}_t$ is the vector of current exogenous variables, and $\mathbf{z}_{t-1}$ is the vector of lagged exogenous variables. Partitioning the **B** matrix of (2.8.3) to conform to this partition of **x** gives us

$$\mathbf{B} = \begin{pmatrix} \mathbf{B}_1 \\ \hline \mathbf{B}_2 \\ \hline \mathbf{B}_3 \end{pmatrix}. \qquad *(2.9.3)$$

The structural form can be written

[37] See Theil and Boot (1962).

$$\mathbf{y}_t\mathbf{\Gamma} + (\mathbf{y}_{t-1} \mid \mathbf{z}_{t-1})\begin{pmatrix}\mathbf{B}_1 \\ \hdashline \mathbf{B}_2 \\ \hdashline \mathbf{B}_3\end{pmatrix} = \boldsymbol{\varepsilon}_t. \tag{2.9.4}$$

Thus

$$\mathbf{y}_t\mathbf{\Gamma} + \mathbf{y}_{t-1}\mathbf{B}_1 + \mathbf{z}_t\mathbf{B}_2 + \mathbf{z}_{t-1}\mathbf{B}_3 = \boldsymbol{\varepsilon}_t. \qquad *(2.9.5)$$

The reduced form (2.8.15) then becomes

$$\mathbf{y}_t = \mathbf{y}_{t-1}\mathbf{\Pi}_1 + \mathbf{z}_t\mathbf{\Pi}_2 + \mathbf{z}_{t-1}\mathbf{\Pi}_3 + \mathbf{u}_t = (\mathbf{y}_{t-1}\ \mathbf{z}_t\mathbf{z}_{t-1})\begin{pmatrix}\mathbf{\Pi}_1 \\ \mathbf{\Pi}_2 \\ \mathbf{\Pi}_3\end{pmatrix} + \mathbf{u}_t, \qquad *(2.9.6)$$

where $\mathbf{\Pi}_1$, $\mathbf{\Pi}_2$, and $\mathbf{\Pi}_3$ are submatrices of $\mathbf{\Pi}$ satisfying

$$\mathbf{\Pi}_1 = -\mathbf{B}_1\mathbf{\Gamma}^{-1}, \qquad \mathbf{\Pi}_2 = -\mathbf{B}_2\mathbf{\Gamma}^{-1}, \qquad \mathbf{\Pi}_3 = -\mathbf{B}_3\mathbf{\Gamma}^{-1} \qquad *(2.9.7)$$

and $\mathbf{u}_t$ is as in (2.8.14). The final form is obtained by solving the reduced form (2.9.6) iteratively, as in (2.6.11) to (2.6.16) for the prototype macro model, substituting for lagged endogenous variables by using the lagged form of (2.9.6). In the first iteration

$$\begin{aligned}\mathbf{y}_t = \mathbf{y}_{t-2}\mathbf{\Pi}_1 + \mathbf{z}_{t-1}\mathbf{\Pi}_2 + \mathbf{z}_{t-2}\mathbf{\Pi}_3 + \mathbf{u}_{t-1})\mathbf{\Pi}_1 + \mathbf{z}_t\mathbf{\Pi}_2 \\ + \mathbf{z}_{t-1}\mathbf{\Pi}_3 + \mathbf{u}_t,\end{aligned} \tag{2.9.8}$$

$$\begin{aligned}\mathbf{y}_t = \mathbf{y}_{t-2}\mathbf{\Pi}_1^2 + [\mathbf{z}_t\mathbf{\Pi}_2 + \mathbf{z}_{t-1}(\mathbf{\Pi}_2\mathbf{\Pi}_1 + \mathbf{\Pi}_3) + \mathbf{z}_{t-2}\mathbf{\Pi}_3\mathbf{\Pi}_1] \\ + [\mathbf{u}_t + \mathbf{u}_{t-1}\mathbf{\Pi}_1].\end{aligned} \tag{2.9.9}$$

Continuing the iteration back to the base period $t = 0$ yields

$$\begin{aligned}\mathbf{y}_t = \mathbf{y}_0\mathbf{\Pi}_1^t + [\mathbf{z}_t\mathbf{\Pi}_2 + \mathbf{z}_{t-1}(\mathbf{\Pi}_2\mathbf{\Pi}_1 + \mathbf{\Pi}_3) + \mathbf{z}_{t-2}(\mathbf{\Pi}_2\mathbf{\Pi}_1 + \mathbf{\Pi}_3)\mathbf{\Pi}_1 \\ + \mathbf{z}_{t-3}(\mathbf{\Pi}_2\mathbf{\Pi}_1 + \mathbf{\Pi}_3)\mathbf{\Pi}_1^2 + \cdots + \mathbf{z}_0\mathbf{\Pi}_3\mathbf{\Pi}_1^{t-1}] \\ + [\mathbf{u}_t + \mathbf{u}_{t-1}\mathbf{\Pi}_1 + \mathbf{u}_{t-2}\mathbf{\Pi}_1^2 + \cdots + \mathbf{u}_1\mathbf{\Pi}_1^{t-1}].\end{aligned} \qquad *(2.9.10)$$

(Again, a rigorous proof would entail the technique of mathematical induction.) This is the *final form*, in which each of the endogenous variables is expressed as a function of base-period values, current and lagged exogenous variables, and stochastic disturbance terms.

Equation (2.6.16) is an example of such a final-form equation. The successive coefficients of the current and lagged $\mathbf{z}$'s in (2.9.10), given as

$$\mathbf{\Pi}_2, \quad (\mathbf{\Pi}_2\mathbf{\Pi}_1 + \mathbf{\Pi}_3), \quad (\mathbf{\Pi}_2\mathbf{\Pi}_1 + \mathbf{\Pi}_3)\mathbf{\Pi}_1, \ \ldots \qquad *(2.9.11)$$

measure the influence on the current value of the endogenous variables of successively lagged values of the exogenous variables, starting from the current (nonlagged) exogenous variables and given as

$$\frac{\partial \mathbf{y}_t}{\partial \mathbf{z}_{t-j}} = \begin{cases}\mathbf{\Pi}_2, & j = 0, \\ (\mathbf{\Pi}_2\mathbf{\Pi}_1 + \mathbf{\Pi}_3)\,\mathbf{\Pi}_1^{j-1}, & j = 1, \ldots, t-1 \\ \mathbf{\Pi}_3\mathbf{\Pi}_1^{t-1} & j = t.\end{cases} \qquad *(2.9.12)$$

An example, in the case of the prototype macro model, is the set of equations (2.6.17) and (2.6.18), giving the first two elements of the successive coefficients in (2.9.11). The estimation of these short- and long-run multipliers is an important aspect of structural analysis, which also has major implications for forecasting and policy evaluation.

2.10 IDENTIFICATION OF THE GENERAL ECONOMETRIC MODEL; CONCLUDING REMARKS

An important issue in econometric model building is that of *identification.*[38] Several important approaches to the estimation of the structural equations start by estimating the reduced-form equations

$$\mathbf{y} = \mathbf{x}\boldsymbol{\Pi} + \mathbf{u} \qquad *(2.10.1)$$

from observed data on the g endogenous variables $\mathbf{y}$ and on the k predetermined variables $\mathbf{x}$. The resulting estimators are summarized by the $k \times g$ matrix $\hat{\boldsymbol{\Pi}}$.[39] This information is then used to estimate the coefficients of the endogenous and predetermined variables in the structural form

$$\mathbf{y}\boldsymbol{\Gamma} + \mathbf{x}\mathbf{B} = \boldsymbol{\varepsilon}, \qquad *(2.10.2)$$

namely $\boldsymbol{\Gamma}$ and $\mathbf{B}$, respectively. It has been shown in (2.8.13) that

$$\boldsymbol{\Pi} = -\mathbf{B}\boldsymbol{\Gamma}^{-1}, \qquad *(2.10.3)$$

but clearly, information on the estimated elements of $\boldsymbol{\Pi}$ is not enough to "disentangle" the effects of $\mathbf{B}$ and $\boldsymbol{\Gamma}$ in determining $\boldsymbol{\Pi}$. Trying to determine $\mathbf{B}$ and $\boldsymbol{\Gamma}$ from $\boldsymbol{\Pi}$, given (2.10.3), is a bit like trying to determine two numbers the product of which is known to be 12. Clearly, more information is needed to determine $\mathbf{B}$ and $\boldsymbol{\Gamma}$. This is usually referred to as *a priori information*, since it precedes estimation. By contrast, the information contained in (2.10.3) is called *a posteriori information*, since it is based on (and thus follows) estimation of the reduced-form equations, specifically the estimation of $\boldsymbol{\Pi}$.

Basically, the problem of identification is that of providing enough a priori information to enable determination of structural parameters $\mathbf{B}$ and $\boldsymbol{\Gamma}$ from the reduced-form parameters $\boldsymbol{\Pi}$. With insufficient a priori information it is impossible to determine $\mathbf{B}$ and $\boldsymbol{\Gamma}$ from $\boldsymbol{\Pi}$, and this situation is called the *underidentified case* (or the *unidentified case*). In this case it is impossible to distinguish the true structural parameters from "bogus" parameters. With "just enough" information it is possible to determine uniquely (after normalization) the elements of $\mathbf{B}$ and $\boldsymbol{\Gamma}$, the so-called *just identified* (or exactly identified) case, in which only one set of structural parameters is consistent with the a priori information and the reduced-form parameters. With more information there would be more than one way to determine the elements of $\mathbf{B}$ and $\boldsymbol{\Gamma}$ from $\boldsymbol{\Pi}$ and the a priori information. This is the *overidentified case*, which is thought to be the typical case in most econometric models.[40]

[38] See Chapter 9 for a further and a more general discussion of identification.

[39] In general, "hats," as in $\hat{\boldsymbol{\Pi}}$, are used to denote estimators in econometrics. This convention differs from that in elementary statistics, where Greek letters usually designate true parameters and corresponding Roman letters designate their estimators, such as μ and m or σ and s.

[40] However, the dissenting view of Sims (1980), summarized in Section 1.7, may be recalled. Sims argues that macroeconomists in particular may overestimate the number of coefficients that can realistically be set equal to zero, and hence they may overstate the degree of identification.

A priori information can take several forms, but the most common is *zero restrictions*. The information in this case takes the form of zero values of certain elements of the **B** and/or **Γ** matrices, implying that certain variables that appear in certain equations of the model do not appear in other equations. In the prototype micro model (2.5.8), for example, the **B** matrix contains two zeros, reflecting the assumptions that demand does not depend on rainfall and supply does not depend on income, where both variables enter the model. In the prototype macro model (2.6.6), similarly, two zeros appear in the **B** matrix, reflecting the assumptions that consumption does not depend on lagged income or government expenditure.

In general, zero restrictions convey a priori information that can be used to estimate the structural form. For example, in the prototype micro model, from (2.5.11),

$$\begin{pmatrix} \pi_{11} & \pi_{12} \\ \pi_{21} & \pi_{22} \\ \pi_{31} & \pi_{32} \end{pmatrix} = \frac{1}{\gamma_2 - \gamma_1}\begin{pmatrix} \gamma_2\beta_1 & \beta_1 \\ -\gamma_1\beta_2 & -\beta_2 \\ \gamma_2\delta_1 - \gamma_1\delta_2 & \delta_1 - \delta_2 \end{pmatrix}. \tag{2.10.4}$$

In this case the structural parameters—the β's, γ's, and δ's—can be determined *uniquely* from the reduced-form parameters—the π's—as

$$\begin{aligned} \gamma_1 &= \frac{\pi_{21}}{\pi_{22}}, & \gamma_2 &= \frac{\pi_{11}}{\pi_{12}}, \\ \beta_1 &= \pi_{12}\left(\frac{\pi_{11}}{\pi_{12}} - \frac{\pi_{21}}{\pi_{22}}\right), & \beta_2 &= -\pi_{22}\left(\frac{\pi_{11}}{\pi_{12}} - \frac{\pi_{21}}{\pi_{22}}\right), \\ \delta_1 &= \pi_{31} - \pi_{32}\frac{\pi_{21}}{\pi_{22}}, & \delta_2 &= \pi_{31} - \pi_{32}\frac{\pi_{11}}{\pi_{12}}. \end{aligned} \tag{2.10.5}$$

This is the case of *just identification*, in which the structural parameters are given as unique functions of the reduced-form parameters.

By contrast, consider the simple demand–supply model:

$$\begin{aligned} q^D &= \gamma_1 p + \delta_1 + \varepsilon^D, \\ q^S &= \gamma_2 p + \delta_2 + \varepsilon^S, \\ q^D &= q^S. \end{aligned} \tag{2.10.6}$$

This model may be considered the special case of the prototype micro model for which the coefficient of income in the demand equation (β_1) and the coefficient of rainfall in the supply equation (β_2) both vanish. Thus no exogenous influences are present in either equation of the model. The reduced-form equations are

$$(q \quad p) = \begin{pmatrix} \dfrac{\gamma_2\delta_1 - \gamma_1\delta_2}{\gamma_2 - \gamma_1} & \dfrac{\delta_1 - \delta_2}{\gamma_2 - \gamma_1} \end{pmatrix} + \begin{pmatrix} \dfrac{\gamma_2\varepsilon^D - \gamma_1\varepsilon^S}{\gamma_2 - \gamma_1} & \dfrac{\varepsilon^D - \varepsilon^S}{\gamma_2 - \gamma_1} \end{pmatrix}, \tag{2.10.7}$$

so the reduced-form parameters are

$$(\pi'_{11} \quad \pi'_{12}) = \frac{1}{\gamma_2 - \gamma_1}(\gamma_2\delta_1 - \gamma_1\delta_2 \quad \delta_1 - \delta_2). \tag{2.10.8}$$

In this case knowing only π'_{11} and π'_{12} will *not* reveal the structural coefficients γ_1, γ_2, δ_1, and δ_2; many possible values of γ's and δ's are consistent with (2.10.8). This case is therefore one of an *underidentified* (or *unidentified*) model. The underidentification of this model is revealed also geometrically. Consider Figure 2.5 again. Suppose that the initial equilibrium is at E, defined by the pair (q, p). Suppose that because of the presence of the stochastic disturbance terms (rather than because of a shift in income), demand and supply shift to D' and S', implying the new equilibrium E', defined by (q', p'). Information on quantities and prices contained in these two equilibrium points, and, in fact, any number of such points, will not yield information on the slopes and intercepts of the demand or supply curves.

Another variant of the prototype micro model will illustrate an overidentified model. Consider the model

$$\begin{aligned} q^D &= \gamma_1 p + \beta_1 I + \beta_1' A + \delta_1 + \varepsilon^D, \\ q^S &= \gamma_2 p + \beta_2 r + \beta_2' w + \delta_2 + \varepsilon^S, \\ q^D &= q^S, \end{aligned} \tag{2.10.9}$$

where A is advertising and w is the average wage, both of which are treated as exogenous. The reduced form (ignoring the error terms) is

$$(q \quad p) = (I \quad A \quad r \quad w \quad 1)\frac{1}{\gamma_2 - \gamma_1}\begin{pmatrix} \gamma_2\beta_1 & \beta_1 \\ \gamma_2\beta_1' & \beta_1' \\ -\gamma_1\beta_2 & -\beta_2 \\ -\gamma_1\beta_2' & -\beta_2' \\ \gamma_2\delta_1 - \gamma_1\delta_2 & \delta_1 - \delta_2 \end{pmatrix}. \tag{2.10.10}$$

Thus the reduced-form parameters are

$$\begin{pmatrix} \pi_{11}'' & \pi_{12}'' \\ \pi_{21}'' & \pi_{22}'' \\ \pi_{31}'' & \pi_{32}'' \\ \pi_{41}'' & \pi_{42}'' \\ \pi_{51}'' & \pi_{52}'' \end{pmatrix} = \frac{1}{\gamma_2 - \gamma_1}\begin{pmatrix} \gamma_2\beta_1 & \beta_1 \\ \gamma_2\beta_1' & \beta_1' \\ -\gamma_1\beta_2 & -\beta_2 \\ -\gamma_1\beta_2' & -\beta_2' \\ \gamma_2\delta_1 - \gamma_1\delta_2 & \delta_1 - \delta_2 \end{pmatrix}. \tag{2.10.11}$$

In this case some of the structural-form parameters can be determined from these reduced-form parameters in two different ways. For example, two alternative estimators of γ_2 are

$$\frac{\pi_{11}''}{\pi_{12}''} \quad \text{and} \quad \frac{\pi_{21}''}{\pi_{22}''}, \tag{2.10.12}$$

and two alternative estimators of γ_1 are

$$\frac{\pi_{31}''}{\pi_{32}''} \quad \text{and} \quad \frac{\pi_{41}''}{\pi_{42}''}. \tag{2.10.13}$$

This is the case of an *overidentified* model, in which there is more than one way to infer structural parameters from reduced-form parameters.

These three cases—just identification, underidentification, and overidentification—illustrate the three possibilities for identification. In general, the problem of identification is that of combining a priori information contained in the specification of the model with a posteriori information contained in the estimation of the reduced form of the model in order to determine estimates of the structural parameters of the system. Specific conditions of identification are discussed in Chapter 9.

Finally, to conclude on an even more general note, in most of the discussion in this chapter (and, indeed, in most theoretical economics) it is assumed that the particular model under examination is true and the discussion proceeds from that point of view. In fact, one of the most difficult aspects of an applied problem of economics is exactly that of model selection, namely the *specification problem* in econometrics. In the concluding chapter of this book, Chapter 17, we return to this theme in more detail. For the moment, note simply that the variety of approaches to econometric modeling surveyed in this chapter obviously gives rise to a variety of models and that the selection of a particular model (or perhaps a small subset of models) for a particular problem is by no means a trivial task. Indeed, the selection of an appropriate model takes experience, judgment, and maturity.

PROBLEMS

2-A Using the geometric model of income determination shown in Figure 2.2, analyze the effects of:

1. An increase in autonomous expenditures.
2. Introduction of a tax on household income.
3. A thrift campaign on the part of households.

What other changes could be analyzed using this diagram?

2-B Generalize the prototype micro model to allow explicitly for both a tariff on factors used in the production of the good and the distribution of income, both of which are treated as exogenous. For the generalized model:

1. State the structural equations and express them as a matrix equation.
2. Obtain the reduced form.
3. Obtain the matrix of comparative statics results, giving signs of the partial derivatives of each endogenous variable with respect to each exogenous variable.

2-C Consider a disequilibrium version of the prototype micro model, where the equilibrium condition that the quantity demanded equals the quantity supplied is replaced by the tâtonnement condition that the change in price is proportional to the excess of the quantity demanded over the quantity supplied. For this model, obtain:

1. The reduced form and comparative statics results.
2. The final form and long- and short-run multipliers.

2-D In the prototype macro model, develop the structural form, reduced form, and final form if:

1. C is eliminated, so the endogenous variables are Y and I.
2. Y is eliminated, so the endogenous variables are C and I.

2-E In a model of the money market the demand for money (M^D) depends linearly on national income (Y), the interest rate (r), and population (N); the supply of money (M^S) depends linearly on national income and lagged interest rate (r_{-1}); and, in equilibrium, money demand equals money supply. National income and population are treated as exogenous, while the interest rate and stock of money (M) are treated as endogenous. All equations contain constant terms (intercepts) and are nonstochastic.

1. State the structural equations and express them as a matrix equation.
2. Obtain the reduced-form equations in matrix form.
3. What is the final-form equation for r?
4. Obtain the matrix of comparative statics results, giving signs of the partials of each endogenous variable with respect to each exogenous variable.

2-F In a certain political–economic model the proportion of votes cast for the Democratic Party (D) depends linearly on unemployment (U) and union membership (M); unemployment depends linearly on the government deficit ($G - T$) and war (W, a dummy variable, equal to 1 if war, 0 if no war); and the government deficit depends linearly on unemployment and war. D, U, and $G - T$ are treated as endogenous. All equations contain constant terms (intercepts) and are stochastic.

1. Obtain the structural form and the reduced form.
2. What hypotheses could be tested with the estimated matrices of structural and reduced-form coefficients?

2-G In a certain model of inflation and unemployment the rate of inflation (i) depends on the growth of the money supply (m), the interest rate (r), past wage increases (w_{-1}), and the government deficit (d). Unemployment (u) depends on inflation (i), the interest rate (r), current wages (w), and union membership (n). Treat i and u as endogenous.

1. Find the structural form and reduced form of this model.
2. What hypotheses could you test with the estimated model?

2-H Generalize the development of the reduced form and final form to a model including lags of both endogenous and predetermined variables up to and including those of order p. Write out the equations in both matrix and summation notation. What happens when $p \to \infty$?

2-I In the Smithies multiplier-accelerator model savings depends linearly on current income and previous peak income while investment depends linearly on past income, previous peak income, and the difference between lagged full-capacity output and previous peak income.[41] In equilibrium savings equals investment. Assume that income, savings, and investment are endogenous while all other variables are exogenous.

1. What are the structural equations of this model?
2. What is the meaning of the endogenous–exogenous assumptions?
3. What are the reduced-form equations?
4. What is the comparative statics matrix of this model?

2-J In the Kaldor model of the trade cycle, savings depends on current income and lagged capital stock, investment is the change in capital stock, and the change in income is a function of the difference between savings and investment.[42] Assume that all current values of income, savings, investment, and capital stock are the endogenous variables of the model. Assume, in contrast to Kaldor, that all functions are linear.

1. Obtain the structural and reduced-form equations of the model.
2. Obtain the final-form equations for income and capital stock.
3. Obtain short- and long-run multipliers for income.

2-K In the Harrod–Domar model of economic growth, savings at time t, S_t, is a constant proportion s of income at time t, Y_t; capital at time t, K_t, is a constant multiple β of output at time t, Y_t; investment at time t, I_t, is the change in the capital stock ($K_{t+1} - K_t$); and in equilibrium, savings equals investment.[43]

1. What are the structural equations and the reduced-form equations of the model? Which variables are endogenous?
2. Obtain the final-form equation for output, and show that output grows at the rate s/β—that is, at a rate given by the ratio of the savings ratio to the capital/output ratio.

[41] See Smithies (1957).

[42] See Kaldor (1940).

[43] See Domar (1957) and Tinbergen and Bos (1962).

2-L Gravity models are a generalization of the law of gravitational attraction, according to which the gravitational force F_{ij} attracting two point masses i and j is proportional to the product of the masses, $m_i m_j$, and inversely proportional to the square of the distance between them, d_{ij}^2. In the *generalized gravity model*

$$F_{ij} = \gamma m_i^{\alpha_i} m_j^{\alpha_j} d_{ij}^{-\beta_{ij}} e^u,$$

where u is a random variable that is normally distributed with mean zero and variance σ^2. Using logarithms, convert this model to a linear model and indicate the values of coefficients corresponding to the law of gravitational attraction. Also show geometrically the density functions for both u and e^u.

2-M Show that by appropriate transformations of variables (e.g., logarithms, reciprocals) the following nonlinear models relating y to the explanatory variables x_1 and x_2 and the stochastic disturbance term u can be converted to models that are linear in the parameters.

1. $y = Ax_1^{\beta_1} x_2^{\beta_2} e^u$ (constant elasticity)
2. $y = \exp(\beta_0 + \beta_1 x_1 + \beta_2 x_2 + u)$ (exponential)
3. $y = (\beta_0 + \beta_1 x_1 + \beta_2 x_2 + u)^{-1}$ (reciprocal)
4. $y = [1 + \exp(\beta_0 + \beta_1 x_1 + \beta_2 x_2 + u)]^{-1}$ (logistic)

Also show that the following models are nonlinear and cannot be converted into models linear in the parameters. Obtain linear approximations for each.

5. $y = Ax_1^{\beta_1} x_2^{\beta_2} + u$
6. $y = \beta_1 + \beta_2 \exp(\beta_3 x) + u$
7. $y = \beta_1 (x - \beta_2)^2 + u$

Finally, determine whether the following can be converted into models that are linear in the parameters.

8. $y = \beta_0 + \beta_1 \rho^{x_1} + u, \quad 0 < \rho < 1$
9. $y = \exp(\beta_0 + \beta_1 x + \beta_2 x^2) + u$
10. $y = \beta_0 (e^{\beta_1 x_1} + e^{\beta_2 x_2}) + u$

BIBLIOGRAPHY

BALL, R. J. (1968). "Econometric Model Building," in *Mathematical Model Building in Economics and Industry*. London: Charles Griffin & Co., Ltd.

BEACH, E. F. (1957). *Economic Models: An Exposition*. New York: John Wiley & Sons, Inc.

BERGSTROM, A. R. (1967). *Selected Economic Models and Their Analysis*. New York: American Elsevier Publishing Company, Inc.

BODKIN, R. G., L. R. KLEIN, K. MARWAH (1991). *A History of Macroeconometric Model-Building*. Aldershot, Hants, England: Edward Elgar Publishing Ltd.

BROWN, T. M. (1970). *Specification and Uses of Econometric Models*. Toronto: Macmillan Company of Canada Ltd.

CHRIST, C. (1966). *Econometric Models and Methods*. New York: John Wiley & Sons, Inc.

COMMITTEE ON ECONOMETRIC METHODS (1965). *Econometric Models for Medium-Term Economic Plan, 1964–1968*. Tokyo: Economic Planning Agency, Government of Japan.

COOTNER, P. H., Ed. (1964). *The Random Character of Stock Market Prices*, rev. ed. Cambridge, Mass.: MIT Press.

DOMAR, E. D. (1957). *Essays in the Theory of Economic Growth*. New York: Oxford University Press.

DUESENBERRY, J. S., G. FROMM, L. R. KLEIN, and E. KUH, Eds. (1965). *The Brookings Quarterly Econometric Model of the United States*. Chicago: Rand McNally & Company.

ECKSTEIN, O. (1983). *The DRI Model of the U.S. Economy*. New York: McGraw-Hill Book Company.

ENKE, S. (1951). "Equilibrium among Spatially Separated Markets: Solution by Electric Analogue." *Econometrica*, 19: 40–47.

FORRESTER, J. (1961). *Industrial Dynamics*. Cambridge, Mass.: MIT Press; New York: John Wiley & Sons, Inc.

FORRESTER, J. (1969). *Urban Dynamics*. Cambridge, Mass.: MIT Press.

FORRESTER, J. (1971). *World Dynamics*. Cambridge, Mass.: Wright-Allen Press.

GOLDBERGER, A. S., and O. D. DUNCAN, Eds. (1973). *Structural Equation Models in the Social Sciences*. New York: Seminar Press.

INTRILIGATOR, M. D. (1983). "Economic and Econometric Models," in Z. Griliches and M. D. Intriligator, Eds., *Handbook of Econometrics*, Vol. 1. Amsterdam: North-Holland Publishing Company.

KALDOR, N. (1940). "A Model of the Trade Cycle." *Economic Journal*, 50: 78–92.

KENDALL, M. G. (1968). "Introduction to Model Building and Its Problems," in *Mathematical Model Building in Economics and Industry*. London: Charles Griffin & Co. Ltd.

KLEIN, L. R. (1965). "What Kind of Macroeconometric Model for Developing Economies?" *Econometric Annual of the Indian Economic Journal*, 13: 313–324; reprinted in A. Zellner, Ed. (1968). *Readings in Economic Statistics and Econometrics*. Boston: Little, Brown and Company.

LEONTIEF, W. W. (1941). *The Structure of the American Economy, 1919–1929*. New York: Oxford University Press, Inc.

LEONTIEF, W. W., Ed. (1953). *Studies in the Structure of the American Economy*. New York: Oxford University Press, Inc.

LEONTIEF, W. W. (1971). "Theoretical Assumptions and Nonobserved Facts." *American Economic Review*, 61: 1–7.

LEONTIEF, W. W. (1986). *Input–Output Economics*, 2nd ed. New York: Oxford University Press, Inc.

MOREHOUSE, N. F., R. H. STROTZ, and S. J. HORWITZ (1950). "An Electro-Analog Method for Investigating Problems in Economic Dynamics: Inventory Oscillations." *Econometrica*, 18: 313–328.

NAYLOR, T. H. (1971). "Policy Simulation Experiments with Macroeconometric Models: The State of the Art," in M. D. Intriligator, Ed., *Frontiers of Quantitative Economics*. Amsterdam: North-Holland Publishing Company.

NAYLOR, T. H., K. WERTZ, and T. WONNACOTT (1968). "Some Methods for Evaluating the Effects of Economic Policies Using Simulation Experiments." *Review of the International Statistical Institute*, 36: 184–200.

ORCUTT, G. H. (1962). "Microanalytic Models of the United States Economy: Need and Development." *American Economic Review, Papers and Proceedings*, 52: 229–240.

ORCUTT, G. H., J. MERZ, and H. QUINKE, Eds. (1986). *Microanalytic Simulation Models to Support Social and Financial Policy*. New York: North-Holland Publishing Company.

ORCUTT, G. H., H. W. WATTS, and J. B. EDWARDS (1968). "Data Aggregation and Information Loss." *American Economic Review*, 58: 772–787.

PIGGOTT, J., and J. WHALLEY, Eds. (1985). *New Developments in Applied General Equilibrium Analysis*. New York: Cambridge University Press.

SAMUELSON, P. A. (1947). *Foundations of Economic Analysis*. Cambridge: Harvard University Press.

SCARF, H. E., and J. B. SHOVEN, Eds. (1984). *Applied General Equilibrium Analysis*. New York: Cambridge University Press.

SIMS, C. A. (1980). "Macroeconomics and Reality." *Econometrica*, 48: 1–48.

SMITH, A. (1776). *The Wealth of Nations*. Edited by Edwin Cannan (1937). New York: The Modern Library.

SMITHIES, A. (1957). "Economic Fluctuations and Growth." *Econometrica*, 25: 1–52.

SOLARI, L. (1979). "Contenu et portée des modèles économétriques" [Content and Scope of Econometric Models], in L. Solari (Ed. F. Carlevaro), *Essais de méthodes et analyses économétriques*. Geneva: Librairie Droz. (This essay was originally published in *Dialectica*, 1963.)

STROTZ, R. H., J. C. MCANULTY, and J. B. NAINES, JR. (1953). "Goodwin's Nonlinear Theory of the Business Cycle: An Electro-Analog Solution." *Econometrica*, 21: 390–411.

SUITS, D. (1963). *The Theory and Application of Econometric Models*. Athens: Center of Economic Research.

THEIL, H., and J. C. G. BOOT (1962). "The Final Form of Econometric Equation Systems." *Review of the International Statistical Institute*, 30: 136–152; reprinted in A. Zellner, Ed. (1968). *Readings in Economic Statistics and Econometrics*. Boston: Little, Brown and Company.

TINBERGEN, J., and H. C. BOS (1962). *Mathematical Models of Economic Growth*. New York: McGraw-Hill Book Company.

TUSTIN, A. (1953). *The Mechanism of Economic Systems*. Cambridge, Mass.: Harvard University Press.

ZELLNER, A. (1979). "Statistical Analysis of Econometric Models." *Journal of the American Statistical Association*, 74: 628–643, with "Comments" by D. A. Belsley and E. Kuh (643–645). C. F. Christ (645–646), P. M. Robinson (646–648), and T. J. Rothenberg (648–650), and "Rejoinder" of Zellner (650–651).

3

DATA AND REFINED DATA

3.1 WHAT ARE DATA?

An econometric study entails the use of.data to estimate an algebraic linear stochastic model, such as those treated in Chapter 2, via econometric techniques. Pure theory can treat the phenomenon or system under study only up to a certain point. That point is typically the comparative static analysis of the signs of certain partial derivatives, namely the coefficients of the reduced form. To proceed beyond this point, in particular to estimate the values of the coefficients of both the reduced form and the structural form, requires a relevant set of data on all variables of the model. For example, the prototype micro model would require data on price, quantity, income, and rainfall, while the prototype macro model would require data on national income, consumption, investment, and government spending.

Thus it is difficult to overstate the importance of data to the working econometrician. Nevertheless, there is often an uneasy alliance between econometricians and economic data, as econometricians often have ambivalent feelings toward their data. (Often, these data are imperfect and do not provide striking confirmation of the models employed by econometric researchers.) In this connection it must be remembered that most economic data are collected by noneconomists, usually for purposes quite different from economic research. Indeed, at times data may even be reported by nonprofessionals who do not even have any stake in the precision of the information that they are conveying. At times, economists have attempted to remedy these defects by collecting their own data, as discussed briefly in Section 3.4, in the context of social experimentation. This has proved, however, to be a far more difficult task than originally believed and has taught economists a number of lessons, not the least of which was a certain amount of humility in this domain.[1]

[1]For general discussions of data employed in econometric studies, see Morgenstern (1963) and Griliches (1986).

The data relevant to a particular study summarize the facts concerning the phenomena under investigation. These facts may be of different types, and they may be derived from different sources, with the theory underlying the phenomena used to choose among the various alternatives. They may be fundamentally quantitative, fundamentally qualitative, or a mixture of both types. Whatever their type, source, or nature, they are expressed in a quantitative way in carrying out an econometric study. The set of all such quantitatively expressed facts is the *data* of the study.

An econometric model requires, for its estimation, data on all of the variables included in the model. Values taken by endogenous, exogenous, and, where appropriate, lagged endogenous or exogenous variables, are necessary to estimate the parameters of the model. Indeed, the first and often the most serious pitfall in performing an econometric study is simply lack of data. It is relatively easy to construct models of all types, sizes, and so on. They can easily be manipulated in various ways, as discussed in Chapter 2. Finding the data relevant to a particular model is another story, however. In general, the data are either not available or not available in the form wanted. As a result, various proxies are sometimes used for certain variables of the model. An example is a time trend used as a proxy for changing tastes or changing technology, as will be seen in Chapters 7 and 8. Furthermore, choices must be made on such questions as whether to express the data in the form of real or nominal quantities, total or per capita quantities, levels or first differences or percentage differences, stocks or flows, and so on. Examples of these alternatives appear in Chapters 7 and 8. Finally, the data must sometimes be refined or "massaged" in various ways, such as by the elimination of a trend and the use of seasonal adjustment, to make various series comparable and to focus on certain phenomena of interest. This chapter deals with the various types of data (Sections 3.2 to 3.4), problems with the data (Section 3.5), how data are refined to make them more useful (Section 3.6), the particular problem of their accuracy (Section 3.7), and some major sources of data (Section 3.8).

3.2 QUANTITATIVE VERSUS QUALITATIVE DATA; DUMMY VARIABLES

Data can be of different types, and several distinctions can be drawn between the varieties of data available. While data, as a matter of definition, are quantitative, they may, in fact, represent either quantitative or qualitative facts. Quantitative facts, which are already expressed as numbers, lead directly to data in the form of these numbers or some suitable transformation of them. Thus the prototype micro model might, as applied to the wheat market, include data on such quantitative facts as the price of wheat, measured in dollars per bushel; the quantity of wheat, measured in (millions of) bushels per year; income, measured in (billions of) dollars per year; and rainfall, measured in inches of rain per year. Where specific measures exist for a particular set of facts, such as these measures for the facts relevant to the prototype micro model, they typically form the data. Thus the data relevant to the prototype micro model as applied to wheat in the United States, 1961–1981, are presented in Table 3.1. (Note that data on rainfall are omitted here.) Similarly, data relevant to the prototype macro model for the United States, 1961–1985, are presented in Table 3.2.[2]

[2]The generation of these macroeconomic data requires considerable effort and expenditure. They are, in fact, the end products of a set of very complex estimation procedures transforming raw sources of data with differing levels of accuracy and different biases, such as tax returns and profit and loss statements, into carefully constructed estimates of the national aggregates.

TABLE 3.1 Data Relevant to the Prototype Micro Model, as Applied to the Wheat Market of the United States, 1961–1981

	Endogenous Variables		Exogenous Variable
Year	p Price of Wheat ($/bushel)	q Quantity of Wheat (millions of bushels per year)	I Income (billions of dollars of GNP per year)
1961	1.83	1235	520
2	2.04	1094	560
3	1.85	1142	589
4	1.37	1291	629
5	1.35	1316	685
6	1.63	1312	750
7	1.39	1522	790
8	1.24	1576	864
9	1.24	1460	930
1970	1.33	1352	982
1	1.34	1618	1063
2	1.84	1546	1171
3	3.58	1711	1307
4	4.68	1782	1434
5	3.81	2122	1549
6	3.34	2142	1718
7	2.53	2046	1918
8	3.17	1776	2164
9	3.98	2134	2418
1980	4.30	2374	2732
1	4.33	2799	3053

Source U.S. Bureau of the Census, *Statistical Abstract of the United States.* Washington, D.C.: U.S. Government Printing Office, various years.

Qualitative facts, for which no numerical measure exists, can also be expressed in the form of data. Often these qualitative facts refer to either-or situations. Thus something either happened or it did not happen, an attitude or position was adopted or it was not, and so on. These qualitative facts can encompass qualitative variables (e.g., male or female, married or unmarried), qualitative shifts over time or space (e.g., war or peace time, industrialized or developing countries), or even the aggregation of quantitative facts into qualitative facts (e.g., rich or poor, rather than the quantitative level of income). These sort of qualitative facts are typically expressed as numerical data on appropriate *dummy variables*. The dummy variable takes one of two possible values, one value signifying one qualitative possibility and the other value signifying the other possibility. By convention the dummy variable customarily assumes a value of zero or unity, unity usually referring to the occurrence of an event or the presence of a characteristic, and zero referring to the nonoccurrence of the event or the absence of the characteristic.[3]

[3]The dummy variable usually distinguishes only two characteristics, since it would otherwise introduce a scaling effect, with the results of the analysis depending on the particular scale chosen for the dummy variable (see Problem 3-B).

TABLE 3.2 Data Relevant to the Prototype Macro Model, as Applied to the United States, 1961–1985

	Endogenous Variables		Predetermined Variables		
Year	Y (billions of dollars of GNP per year)	C (billions of dollars of consumption spending of per year)	Y (billions of dollars of last year's GNP per year)	G (billions of dollars of government spending per year)	ITC (dummy: 1 in those years in which the investmest tax credit was in force; 0 for other years)
1961	520	335	504	108	0
2	560	355	520	117	1
3	589	374	560	123	1
4	629	399	589	128	1
5	685	433	629	137	1
6	750	466	685	157	0
7	790	492	750	178	0
8	864	536	790	200	0
9	930	580	864	210	0
1970	982	619	930	219	1
1	1063	668	982	234	1
2	1171	733	1063	253	1
3	1307	810	1171	270	1
4	1434	888	1307	304	1
5	1549	976	1434	340	1
6	1718	1084	1549	362	1
7	1918	1204	1718	394	1
8	2164	1346	1918	432	1
9	2418	1507	2164	474	1
1980	2732	1733	2418	530	1
1	3053	1915	2732	588	1
2	3166	2051	3053	642	1
3	3406	2234	3166	675	1
4	3772	2430	3406	736	1
5	4015	2629	3772	821	1

Source U.S. Bureau of the Census, *Statistical Abstract of the United States*. Washington, D.C.: U.S. Government Printing Office, various years; U.S. tax laws.

Consider, for example, the investment tax credit in the United States, which was enacted in 1962, suspended in 1966, reinstated in 1970, and eliminated with the Tax Reform Act of 1986. The presence of the investment tax credit can be represented by a dummy variable ITC, which takes the value 1 in those years in which the investment tax credit was in force (1962–1965 and 1970–1986) and 0 for other years (before 1962, 1966–1969, and 1987 on). This dummy variable might be utilized in a study of investment. Thus the investment function of the prototype macro model of Section 2.6 might be modified to

$$I_t = \gamma_2 Y_t + \beta_2 Y_{t-1} + \beta_3 + \beta_4(\text{ITC})_t + \varepsilon_t^I, \tag{3.2.1}$$

where ITC is the dummy variable and β_4, presumably positive, is a measure of the efficacy of the tax credit. The model might be estimated on the basis of data in Table 3.2. If β_4 is estimated to be large, positive, and statistically significant, it might be concluded that the investment tax credit was important in stimulating additional investment. For the years in which the credit did not exist the investment function is

$$I_t = \gamma_2 Y_t + \beta_2 Y_{t-1} + \beta_3 + \varepsilon_t^I \qquad \text{(where ITC = 0)}, \tag{3.2.2}$$

while for years in which it did exist the function is

$$I_t = \gamma_2 Y_t + \beta_2 Y_{t-1} + (\beta_3 + \beta_4) + \varepsilon_t^I \qquad \text{(where ITC = 1)}. \tag{3.2.3}$$

Thus the investment tax credit variable ITC shifts out the investment function by increasing the intercept from β_3 to $\beta_3 + \beta_4$.

If it were assumed that the investment tax credit affected not only the intercept of the investment function but also possibly each of the slope coefficients as well, the model could be represented by the two equations

$$I_t = \gamma_2 Y_t + \beta_2 Y_{t-1} + \beta_3 + \varepsilon_t^I \qquad \text{(for ITC = 0)}, \tag{3.2.4}$$

$$I_t = \gamma_2' Y_t + \beta_2' Y_{t-1} + \beta_3' + \varepsilon_t^I \qquad \text{(for ITC = 1)}, \tag{3.2.5}$$

where the parameters γ_2, β_2, and β_3 refer to the situation without the investment tax credit and the corresponding parameters γ_2', β_2', and β_3' refer to the situation with the investment tax credit. In terms of the dummy variable this model can be summarized by

$$I_t = (\gamma_2 + \gamma_2''\text{ITC})Y_t + (\beta_2 + \beta_2''\text{ITC})Y_{t-1} + (\beta_3 + \beta_3''\text{ITC}) + \varepsilon_t^I, \tag{3.2.6}$$

where the parameters γ_2, β_2, and β_3 are as in (3.2.4), when ITC = 0. By setting ITC = 1,

$$\gamma_2' = \gamma_2 + \gamma_2'', \qquad \beta_2' = \beta_2 + \beta_2'', \qquad \beta_3' = \beta_3 + \beta_3''. \tag{3.2.7}$$

Estimating (3.2.6) is equivalent to estimating the two equations (3.2.4) and (3.2.5)—that is, estimating two separate investment functions, one for years when ITC = 0 and the other for years when ITC = 1. The simpler specification in (3.2.1), where only the intercept is affected, is the special case for which

$$\gamma_2'' = 0, \qquad \beta_2'' = 0, \qquad \beta_3'' = \beta_4 \tag{3.2.8}$$

(i.e., where the investment tax credit does not shift the slope coefficients, in particular, not affecting the influence of income and past income on investment). Clearly, (3.2.6)—or, equivalently, (3.2.4) and (3.2.5)—is a more general specification of the model than (3.2.1) in that it subsumes the latter as one special case. Nevertheless, specifications such as (3.2.1) are often utilized simply because there are not enough data to estimate (3.2.6) or, equivalently, (3.2.4) and (3.2.5), which require adequate data for each of the two situations.[4] In general, however, if adequate data are available, it is preferable to estimate separate regressions.

3.3 TIME-SERIES VERSUS CROSS-SECTION DATA; POOLING; MICRODATA

Another important distinction to be drawn with reference to the data is that between time-series and cross-section data. Most data utilized in econometric model estimation are of one of these types.

[4]More than one dummy variable can be included in a particular regression equation to serve as explanatory variables, to distinguish among several qualitative characteristics or attributes, such as educational level, occupation, or region. If there are more than two possible qualitative characteristics to be distinguished, several dummy variables can be used. If a regression uses only dummy variables as explanatory variables, it is equivalent to an analysis of variance. The case of a qualitative *dependent* variable is discussed in Section 5.10.

Time-series data measure a particular variable during successive time periods or at different dates. The time period is often a year (i.e., annual data), but it can be a quarter, month, or week (i.e., quarterly, monthly, or weekly data). For other purposes a longer time period is used, such as two years, five years, a decade, or longer. Usually, the observations are successive and equally spaced in time. Examples of time-series data are given in Tables 3.1 and 3.2, presenting annual time-series data for the prototype micro model and the prototype macro model, respectively.

Cross-section data measure a particular variable at a given time for different entities. Just as the "time period" can assume different values in time-series data, the "entity" can assume different identities in cross-section data. The entities might, for example, be different countries, as in Table 3.3, which gives cross-section data relevant to the prototype macro model for selected countries. Another example, for a different entity, could be data for the prototype micro model, on a statewide or countywide basis. Other cross-section data could refer to the situations of firms, industries, families, households, or individuals at a given date. Such data are frequently obtained from surveys of the entities involved (e.g., questionnaires mailed to heads of households to obtain data at the household level).

Sometimes cross-section and time-series data are merged or *pooled*. The result could be interpreted as a cross section of time series or a time series of cross sections. An exam-

TABLE 3.3 Data Relevant to the Prototype Macro Model for Selected Countries, 1972

	Endogenous Variables		Predetermined Variables	
Country	Y Per Capita National Income in Market Prices in 1972	C Per Capita Private Final Consumption Expenditure in 1972	Y_{-1} Per Capita National Income in Market Prices in 1971	G Per Capita Government Final Consumption Expenditure in 1972
North America				
United States	$4984	$3143	$4580	$946
Canada	4235	2420	3755	826
Western Europe				
Belgium	3346	2023	2733	500
France	3403	2017	2831	423
Germany (F.R.)	3769	2036	3182	664
Italy	1984	1272	1735	294
Netherlands	3165	1767	2587	528
Sweden	4669	2509	4025	1077
United Kingdom	2503	1594	2252	469
Asia–Oceania				
Australia	3426	2032	2928	167
Japan	2439	1269	1893	221

Source United Nations, Department of Economic and Social Affairs, *Monthly Bulletin of Statistics*, January 1975, 29: xxvii–xxviii, 191–197.

Note All figures are in per capita terms and are measured in U.S. dollars per year. Per capita consumption and per capita government spending are calculated from the national accounts figures as percentages of gross domestic product, which are then applied to per capita national income.

ple is given in Table 3.4, which is pooled cross-section/time-series data on per capita national income in market prices for selected countries, 1969–1972. (Note that two columns of this table have already been reported in two of the columns of Table 3.3.) Any column of the table is a cross section over countries for a particular year, and any row is a time series for a particular country.

In general, cross-section and time-series data yield different estimates of a model. These data and their resulting estimates are generally not comparable. For example, it is generally found that estimated income elasticities of demand using cross-section data are greater than those obtained using time-series data. Neither estimate is "wrong," and which to use depends on the purpose. For structural analysis, in studying certain long-run elasticities it might be appropriate to use cross-section data, while for purposes of short-run forecasting time-series data might be appropriate.[5] Sometimes, if pooled data are available, certain parameters (e.g., income elasticities) are estimated using the cross-section data, and then other parameters (e.g., price elasticities) are estimated using time-series data.[6] This approach incorporates more information in the model, avoids certain problems with the data, and can be used to construct individual behavioral equations.

Panel data (or *longitudinal data*) are a special type of pooled cross-section/time-series data in which the same individual units of observation are sampled over time. (Some writers reserve the term *panel data* for cross sections in which the number of entities is quite

TABLE 3.4 Per Capita National Income in Market Prices in Selected Countries, 1969–1972

Variable	Per Capita National Income in Market Prices (in U.S. dollars)			
Country	1969	1970	1971	1972
North America				
United States	$4139	$4289	$4580	$4984
Canada	3109	3369	3755	4235
Western Europe				
Belgium	2177	2421	2733	3346
France	2492	2550	2831	3403
Germany (F.R.)	2288	2752	3182	3769
Italy	1437	1591	1735	1984
Netherlands	2013	2232	2587	3165
Sweden	3372	3736	4025	4669
United Kingdom	1829	1990	2252	2503
Asia-Oceania				
Australia	2439	2633	2928	3426
Japan	1400	1649	1893	2439

Source United Nations, Department of Economic and Social Affairs, *Monthly Bulletin of Statistics*, January 1975, 29: xxvii–xxviii. (Also reported in United Nations, *Statistical Yearbook*, annual.)

[5]In general, time-series data usually reflect short-run behavior, while cross-section data reflect long-run behavior, in particular a greater adjustment to long-run equilibrium (see Meyer and Kuh, 1957). See also the discussion in Kuznets (1966) of the inappropriateness of using cross-section data to make inferences about past long-term trends.

[6]See the discussion in Section 5.6.

large relative to the number of time periods available, but the terms *pooled cross section*, *panel data*, and *longitudinal data* are used interchangeably here.) An example is panel data on family expenditure, where certain selected families keep records of their expenditures over several years. Another is the Nielsen ratings of the popularity of television shows. Panel data are generally *microdata* pertaining to individual economic agents, such as families or firms. Microdata are generally preferable to macrodata (which pertain to aggregates of individual agents) since they avoid aggregation problems and allow one to estimate models containing behavioral relations applicable to individual agents.[7] Such data are not always available, however, since they are expensive to obtain and their publication may reveal proprietary or confidential information.

3.4 NONEXPERIMENTAL VERSUS EXPERIMENTAL DATA: SOCIAL EXPERIMENTATION

A third distinction that may be drawn is that between nonexperimental and experimental data. *Nonexperimental data* are obtained typically from observations of a system not subject to experimental control. By contrast, *experimental data* are obtained from a controlled experiment—that is, a situation in which the system or process under investigation is isolated from outside influences and, to whatever extent possible, influences on the system are subject to the control of the experimenter.

It has often been stated that an important aspect of the distinction between the social sciences and the natural sciences is the type of data each utilizes. Typically, data utilized in the natural sciences are experimental, resulting from controlled experiments, while in the social sciences they are nonexperimental, in which the underlying conditions are not subject to control and cannot be replicated. Although generally valid, this distinction does not apply in all cases. The laboratory natural sciences, including chemistry and physics, typically do utilize controlled experiments. A physicist, for example, performing an experiment in high-energy physics will often utilize an accelerator—a controlled environment providing experimental data that can be replicated. Astrophysicists, however, generally cannot perform laboratory experiments but must instead rely upon observations over which they have no control. The same is true, in general, of meteorologists, geologists, and classical (but not molecular) biologists.

Conversely, while social scientists—including sociologists and political scientists as well as economists—generally rely on observational, nonexperimental data, much as astrophysicists do, some social science experiments have generated experimental data. An example is that of experiments with a negative income tax.[8] These experiments enrolled in-

[7]Of course, as noted in Chapter 2, conclusions of a macroeconomic type can be obtained from micro relations only via aggregation. For a discussion of the use of microdata, see Orcutt et al. (1961) and Orcutt (1962), who advocate the *microanalysis* of socioeconomic systems. An example of microdata is the U.S. National Longitudinal Surveys (NLS). These surveys obtained information on a variety of economic, educational, sociological, and other variables and their influence on labor-force behavior and work attitudes for four cohorts of the U.S. civilian population: men, age 45–59; women, age 30–44; young men, age 14–24; and young women, age 14–24, where ages refer to the beginning year of the survey. The surveys were conducted over a 20-year period, from the mid-1960s to the mid-1980s, for national probability samples of approximately 5000 people in each of these four groups. See Parnes (1975).

[8]See Cain and Watts (1973), Kershaw and Fair (1976), and Ferber and Hirsch (1978, 1982). For a study based on Canadian data (from Manitoba), see Hum and Simpson (1991).

dividuals and families in a program to test the effect of direct subsidies to those with incomes below a defined poverty level. The experimenters selected sites where they could achieve some isolation of the subjects from extraneous influences and could use control groups. Other large-scale social experiments have been conducted to test the influence of health insurance for the poor and near poor and to test the influence of housing allowances. The experimental data obtained in these experiments typically relate to groups of individuals or families enrolled in specific programs, such as housing subsidies programs, day care programs, and electricity peak-load pricing schemes. Since they generally include observations over several years, they typically yield pooled cross-section/time-series data.[9]

Most data used in econometric model building, such as standard national accounts data on GDP and its components, are not, however, experimental data. Recently, data-gathering agencies have been supplementing their conventional national accounts data with financial flow data and with national balance sheet data.[10] None of these numbers represents experimental data, but all of them can be very useful in the construction of an econometric model. In particular, with the "decision-sample" approach to data outcomes, where the universe is regarded as the set of all conceivable decisions economic agents might have made, standard probability and econometric theory can be applied to data like these, as explained in Chapter 4.

3.5 PROBLEMS WITH THE DATA

Although experimental data are being collected in some situations, most econometric studies must rely on nonexperimental data. The problems these data present may be referred to, in the terminology of astronomy, as problems of "bad seeing."

The first is the *degrees-of-freedom problem*—that the available data simply do not include enough observations to allow an adequate estimate of the model. In the use of nonexperimental data it is impossible to replicate the conditions that gave rise to them, so additional data points cannot be generated. In some cases the available data may be inadequate for estimating a particular model but adequate for estimating a simpler model.

Second is the *multicollinearity problem*—the tendency of the data to bunch or move together rather than being "spread out." For example, in time-series data the variables tend to exhibit the same trends, cyclical and secular, over time. With experimental data it may be possible to vary the conditions of the experiment to obtain an adequate spread. With nonexperimental data such control does not exist, and the real-world system may involve very small independent variation in the data, in particular a high degree of interdependence among certain variables.

Third is the *serial-correlation problem*—the fact that when using time-series data, underlying changes occur very slowly over time. Thus conditions in time periods that are close

[9]For a description of social experimentation, see Ferber and Hirsch (1978, 1982). This survey reviewed several such studies and concluded that social experimentation is not as promising as it first appeared and hence that it should be undertaken, like surgery, only as a last resort. Moreover, as often arises with research with human subjects, difficult ethical issues often arise.

It is interesting to note that recently there have been some examples of economic data generated directly in a "laboratory." See, for example, Smith (1982) and Smith et al. (1982); both of these articles are oriented toward formulating and testing some propositions of microeconomic theory. Smith (1994) discusses these questions in a broader, philosophical framework.

[10]See Statistics Canada (1985), in which national balance data and national wealth estimates were obtained based on methods developed by Goldsmith (1982) for the United States.

together tend to be similar. To the extent that the stochastic disturbance term represents conditions relevant to the model but not accounted for in it explicitly, such as omitted variables, serial correlation manifests itself in a dependence of the stochastic disturbance term in one period on that in another period.

Fourth is the *structural-change problem*—that there may have been a discontinuous change in the real world so that the data refer to different populations. An example for times-series data is a war period, which often must be excluded as being unrepresentative.

Fifth is the *errors-in-measurement problem*—that data are measured subject to various inaccuracies and biases. In fact, data are sometimes revised because of a later recognition of these inaccuracies and biases. More fundamentally, potential inaccuracies result from a lack of precision in conceptualization. For example, the GNP accounts are revised from time to time on the basis of such changes in conceptualization (e.g., defining what is included in consumption). Such changes in conceptualization necessitate refining the data to make them comparable and consistent over time.

All of these problems are treated in detail in later chapters, particularly in Chapters 4 and 5. Because of these problems the data are usually refined in several ways. A refinement that helps overcome one of the problems, however, may aggravate one of the others. For example, replacing annual time-series data by quarterly data increases the number of data points but tends to aggravate both the multicollinearity and the serial-correlation problems. Eliminating "unrepresentative" data points, such as those referring to unusual periods (e.g., war years) helps overcome the structural-change problem but aggravates both the degrees of freedom and the multicollinearity problems. Replacing variables by their first differences can help overcome the serial-correlation problem, but it can aggravate the errors-in-measurement problem. Clearly, judicious choices must be made in obtaining relevant and usable data from a set of raw data.

3.6 REFINING THE DATA

The data obtained from various sources often must be refined or "massaged" in various ways to make them usable in an econometric study. Refining is performed to obtain a consistent set of data representing comparable series, which can be used to study specific phenomena under investigation. For time-series data refinement can take a variety of forms, including interpolation, extrapolation, splicing, and smoothing.[11]

Interpolation refers to the determination of values that lie between values that are known. In time-series data, for example, data on one or more variables for a particular period may be missing. The method used to obtain values for these missing observations is that of *interpolation*. The simplest case is *linear interpolation*, where a missing point is simply a linear combination of the given data points. Thus if x_t is an observation or an estimate of a variable at time t and x_{t+2} is an observation or estimate of the same variable at time $t + 2$, the linearly interpolated estimate at time $t + 1$, $\hat{x}_{t+1}$, assumed equally spaced between t and $t + 2$, is given as

[11]See Brown (1963), Anderson (1971), Nelson (1973), Granger and Watson (1984), Hendry, Pagan, and Sargan (1984), Granger (1989), and Harvey (1990).

$$\hat{x}_{t+1} = \frac{x_t + x_{t+2}}{2}. \tag{3.6.1}$$

Another method of interpolation, *exponential interpolation*, uses the geometric mean

$$\hat{x}_{t+1} = \sqrt{x_t x_{t+2}}, \tag{3.6.2}$$

which is linear in the logarithms of the variables. This method is equivalent to that of fitting an exponential function between x_t and x_{t+2}, so

$$\hat{x}_{t+1} = x_t e^{\alpha t} \quad \text{where} \quad x_{t+2} = x_{t+1} e^{\alpha t} = x_t e^{2\alpha t}, \tag{3.6.3}$$

where α can be calculated from

$$\alpha = \frac{1}{2t} \ln \frac{x_{t+2}}{x_t}. \tag{3.6.4}$$

The choice of method depends on the characteristics of the time series under study. For example, if the series involves linear (exponential) growth, linear (exponential) interpolation would be appropriate.

Extrapolation is a related problem, involving the prediction of points beyond the given data set. This problem can arise in using time-series data, for example, if data are available on certain variables for more periods than they are available on other variables and if one wants to use a data set longer than the shortest period for which a complete set of data is available. The techniques of extrapolation are similar to those of interpolation. For example, under linear extrapolation, given x_t and x_{t+1} observations on the variable x, the extrapolated value at time $t + 2$, given as $\hat{x}_{t+2}$, satisfies

$$\hat{x}_{t+2} - x_{t+1} = x_{t+1} - x_t \quad \text{so} \quad \hat{x}_{t+2} = 2x_{t+1} - x_t. \tag{3.6.5}$$

Under exponential extrapolation

$$\hat{x}_{t+2} = x_{t+1} e^{\alpha t} \quad \text{where} \quad x_{t+1} = x_t e^{\alpha t}, \tag{3.6.6}$$

so α can be calculated from

$$\alpha = \frac{1}{t} \ln \frac{x_{t+1}}{x_t}. \tag{3.6.7}$$

Further techniques of extrapolation are discussed in Section 4.7 and in Chapter 15, both of which refer to these simple techniques.

Splicing refers to the problem of refining a series to make it consistent when the base changes. Such a problem arises frequently in using time-series data in index form, such as a consumer price index. This index is calculated relative to certain base levels of purchases of goods and services, and these base levels are revised periodically. The series must then be spliced at this point. Usually, there are some points of overlap between the old and new series, so the new series can simply be multiplied by the ratio of the values of the old series to the new at the point of overlap (or by an average, if there are several points of overlap). Equivalently, the old series can be divided by the (average) level of this ratio at the point of overlap. If no points of overlap are reported, it is possible to extrapolate the old series to obtain one or more points of overlap in order to splice the series.[12]

[12]Simple linear regression analysis, discussed in Chapter 4, is sometimes used as a more sophisticated technique for splicing data. The dependent variable is taken to be the series to be extended, while the explanatory variable is the one for which observations exist in the time periods during which the other series is incomplete.

Yet another type of refining is *smoothing*, involving eliminating trend or cycle components. A national income model using time-series data, for example, occasionally requires the elimination of trends and cycles—especially if national income aggregates are being related to certain "real" economic phenomena, such as real wages. Elimination of the trend—for example, the exponential time trend $e^{\alpha t}$, where α is the "average" growth rate of the variable(s) in question—might be accomplished by replacing the original data x_t by the refined data $\hat{x}_t$, defined by

$$\hat{x}_t = x_t e^{-\alpha t} = \frac{x_t}{e^{\alpha t}}, \tag{3.6.8}$$

in which the time trend has been eliminated. Here the trend factor $e^{\alpha t}$ has been used to deflate the original data. Similarly, cycles can be taken out by

$$\hat{x}_t = \frac{x_t}{\cos(\theta t + \varphi)}, \tag{3.6.9}$$

where $\cos(\theta t + \varphi)$ has been used to deflate the original data, θ being a measure of the frequency of the cycle and φ a measure of the phase shift. Such a technique can, for example, be applied to seasonal variables to perform a seasonal adjustment of the data on such variables.[13]

In general, any time series, say x_t, can be decomposed into four basic components: trend, T, representing long-term movements; cycle, C, representing sinusoidal movements; seasonal, S, representing cyclical movements within a period of a year; and irregular, I, representing residual movements. A multiplicative structure of the form

$$x = T \cdot C \cdot S \cdot I \tag{3.6.10}$$

is often assumed. Various methods are then available to isolate these components.[14] The series can be adjusted after they are isolated. If, for example, T and C in (3.6.10) are represented by

$$T = e^{\alpha t}, \tag{3.6.11}$$

$$C = \cos(\theta t + \varphi), \tag{3.6.12}$$

as in (3.6.8) and (3.6.9), the series

$$\hat{x}_t = \frac{x_t e^{-\alpha t}}{\cos(\theta t + \varphi)} \tag{3.6.13}$$

is the time series adjusted for both trend and cycle. Another example is based on taking logs of (3.6.10), where

$$y_t = f(t) + u_t. \tag{3.6.14}$$

Here y_t is log x_t; $f(t)$ represents the (log of the) trend, cycle, and seasonal components; and u_t is the log of I. Equation (3.6.14) decomposes an observed time series y_t into "signal" $f(t)$ and "noise" u_t. If the signal tends to be less erratic than the noise, then the time series can

[13]A more sophisticated approach is that of spectral analysis. See Fishman (1969) and Dhrymes (1970), and for an application of spectral analysis to seasonal adjustment, Nerlove (1964). Yet another approach is that of Box and Jenkins (1970), discussed in Chapter 6. It may also be observed that the elimination of a cyclical component is rarely performed at present, as the current emphasis in applied macroeconomics is on a more general explanation of business cycles.

[14]See the references in footnotes 11 and 13. The methods of spectral analysis are applicable to isolating cyclical and seasonal components.

be "smoothed" by taking moving averages of the y_t, such as the two-period moving average defined by

$$y'_t = \tfrac{1}{2}(y_t + y_{t-1}). \quad (3.6.15)$$

This process of smoothing eliminates unwanted random roughness in the data.[15]

The student or beginning practitioner is warned sternly that each of these several ways of refining the data can entail certain difficulties or problems. This is particularly true of an extrapolation of some data sets, which can at times give quite misleading results due to major structural breaks. In addition, there is also a danger of overrefining the data, which could conceivably introduce spurious relationships among several of the basic series. Thus refining can, on occasion, introduce as many problems as it resolves. Accordingly, such techniques should be used only when clearly necessary. (Unfortunately, it is hard to lay down objective criteria for such "clear necessity"; experience is probably the best guide in this regard.)

3.7 ACCURACY OF ECONOMIC DATA

Several points must be emphasized about the accuracy of economic and other social science data. First, social science data are almost never precise or exact. Just as astronomers have the problem of "bad seeing," economists and other social scientists have very imperfect measures and measuring rods of the variables they study. In fact, social science data are fundamentally less accurate than physical science data, since they are subject to additional inaccuracy in the measurement and reporting of human behavior. Newspaper accounts may refer to a rise of 0.2% in the consumer price index, but the index is so imprecise that such small changes have little meaning. Similarly, national income figures such as GNP or total consumption are often reported to the billion-dollar level of accuracy (or even tenths of billions) as in Table 3.2, implying an accuracy (for large industrialized economies) of better than 1%. Because of a variety of possible sources of error, however, including observation error, roundoff and approximation error, hiding of information, and errors of computation, national income measures probably involve inaccuracies of 15% or more.[16] Both the "statistical discrepancy" that is part of the national accounts and the revisions of the preliminary national income series into final figures are consistent with this extent of inaccuracy, but nevertheless, the preliminary figures (and final figures) are often naively taken as accurate to the last tenth of a billion dollars! In the physical sciences few observations are accurate to more than five significant digits, and probably no observations are even this accurate in the social sciences. Even a relatively simple problem such as counting the population is subject to several sources of inaccuracy. The reported population of the United States of 248,710,000 on April 1, 1990, for example, is probably accurate only to the first two figures.[17] It might better be reported as 249 ± 4 million. In general, two, three, or four figures of accuracy are all that can be expected of social science data. Any more is specious accuracy, and it is improper to treat these data as of greater accuracy, a point that is very frequently ovelooked or misunderstood. A classic (but apocryphal)

[15]See Problem 3-F.

[16]See Morgenstern (1963, 1972) for a detailed account of the sources of error in economic statistics. Morgenstern's basic thesis was that economic data are too fragile or inaccurate for most, if not all, of the uses to which econometricians and economic statisticians wish to put them (see also Leontief, 1971; Griliches, 1986).

[17]The population figure is reported in the U.S. Bureau of the Census, *Statistical Abstract of the United States, 1991* (Washington, D.C.: U.S. Government Printing Office), p. 20.

example is that of a man who, when asked the age of a river, stated that it was 3,000,021 years old because in a book published 21 years earlier its age was given as 3 million years![18]

If counting population is subject to large inaccuracies, measuring economic quantities and prices is subject to even greater ones. All items on any balance sheet or profit and loss statement of any individual or firm are subject to inaccuracy. Many are based on arbitrary accounting conventions, others are measured subject to various biases, and all are subject to reporting and other errors. Data on prices are particularly inaccurate, given various discounts, tie-in sales, quality considerations, and so on, which are typically not taken into account in price statistics.[19] Similarly, Griliches (1986) gives the example that the measured U.S. trade deficit with Canada for 1982 was either $12.8 or $7.9 billion (in U.S. dollars), depending on whether the source was U.S. or Canadian government publications. (It should be noted that this discrepancy undoubtedly remained even after senior officials in the two countries had held consultations in an attempt to minimize the disagreement.)

A second point to be made about social science data is that they vary considerably in their accuracy. Some are relatively precise, others relatively imprecise. In the physical sciences, particularly where experimentation is possible, the differences in accuracy of measurement are indicated numerically by error brackets. Some figures may be known with an accuracy of 3%, others with an accuracy of 0.1%, and yet others with an accuracy of 10%. In the social sciences, however, these error brackets are usually not provided, so one has only indirect evidence or subjective opinion as to the precision of reported data.[20]

A third point is that the errors in accuracy of economic data are generally not symmetric. There are often biases in one direction, so the error brackets are not equal in both directions. An example is total corporate profit as derived from corporate income tax returns. To the extent that corporations bias their profits downward to avoid paying taxes, the total figure may be subject to an error of 20% on the positive side but only 1% on the negative side.

Griliches points out that there are fundamentally four responses to the Morgenstern criticisms (in footnote 16) of the unusability of economic data: (1), the data aren't that bad; (2), the data are bad, but it really doesn't matter for our purposes; (3), the data are bad but we have learned their foibles, so can make appropriate adjustments; and (4) the available data are "the only game in town" and if we wish to "play" (test our theoretical hypotheses), we have to use what is available.[21] Griliches considers that all of these refutations have some merit. To these four a fifth may be added: the data are in general improving as data-gathering agencies learn more about the needs of their users and try to be more responsive to these needs.[22]

[18]Morgenstern (1963) presents this example. He also notes that the mathematician Norbert Wiener, after reading the first edition of *On the Accuracy of Economic Observations*, remarked that "economics is a one or two digit science."

[19]See Stigler and Kindahl (1970). Griliches (1971) provides an example of an attempt to account for quality considerations in the price of automobiles using "hedonic" price indexes, where such indexes relate the price of a good to its qualities, so that the regression coefficients in an estimation of this relationship measure the partial effects of any one quality on the price of the good. This study illustrates both the seriousness of the problem of quality change and the difficulties involved in overcoming it.

[20]For a formal treatment of accuracy of measurement, see Section 5.8.

[21]See Griliches (1986). For a balanced appraisal of the Morgenstern view, one may still consult with profit the late N. D. Ruggles' penetrating book review (1964) of Morgenstern (1963). Ruggles found that Morgenstern's pessimism was overblown, in part because Morgenstern does not distinguish between constant biases and random errors that affect the periodic measure of an economic variable.

[22]See Ruggles (1964).

Although somewhat reassuring, these hopeful notes should not lull the working econometrician into complacency. Rather, the econometrician should always keep the inaccuracies of the data in mind. Thus the alternative of improving the data or obtaining new data should be seriously considered in such a situation. Indeed, in some circumstances one should seriously consider rejecting the data rather than the hypothesis being tested.

3.8 SOURCES OF ECONOMIC DATA

There is a wide variety of sources of economic data. Among the most useful compilations at the national level are the statistical abstracts published by various national governments. These usually summarize the detailed studies and refer to a single year. Cross-section data can often be found within the statistical abstract for one year, while time-series data can be constructed by comparing the abstracts over several years. For example, for the United States, the *Statistical Abstract of the United States*, published annually by the U.S. Bureau of the Census, is an excellent starting point for finding data at the national and statewide levels. A companion volume, *Historical Statistics of the United States*, also published by the U.S. Department of Commerce, provides summary statistics on the United States back to colonial times. For many of the tables in the current *Statistical Abstract of the United States*, comparable statistical time series are reported in *Historical Statistics of the United States*. An excellent overall reference for data and data sources at the national and international levels is the *Statistical Yearbook*, published annually by the United Nations.

Table 3.5 summarizes some useful published sources of data for economic studies.[23] The major sources are various government agencies, which generally provide macrodata on an annual basis. In an effort to protect confidentiality, microdata pertaining to individuals or firms are generally not available or not released. Some special studies have, however, obtained such microdata.[24] As to the time period covered, certain data are now regularly reported on a quarterly, monthly, or weekly basis, but the annual period still predominates. Some private groups have generated data on specialized topics, of which perhaps the most important for the United States are business-cycle and other data compiled by the National Bureau of Economic Research.[25]

PROBLEMS

3-A Show that a dummy variable can take any two arbitrary values, not just 0 and 1. Give an example of such a case.

3-B Show that a dummy variable distinguishing between two characteristics introduces no scaling effect, while one distinguishing between more than two characteristics introduces a scaling effect (i.e., the estimated coefficients are sensitive to the particular choice of values assumed by the dummy variable).

[23]Yet other sources of data are the several large computerized data banks available through Data Resources, Inc., Chase Econometric Associates, the National Bureau of Economic Research, the Bureau of Economic Analysis (BEA) of the U.S. government, and other organizations (see, e.g., Data Resources, Inc. (1976); and Eckstein (1976)).

[24]Examples are the U.S. Census Survey, summarizing microdata from a 1/1000 sample and available on computer tapes, and microdata available from the Personal Survey on Income Distribution (PSID) and the National Longitudinal Survey (NLS), already mentioned.

[25]Other examples of specialized data are those furnished on spreadsheets used on personal computers and machine-readable data designed to serve as input to computer programs.

TABLE 3.5 Sources of Data

Sources: International

United Nations (Annual, since 1948)
Statistical Yearbook. New York: U.N.

United Nations (Monthly)
Monthly Bulletin of Statistics. New York: U.N.

United Nations (Annual)
Demographic Yearbook. New York: U.N.

United Nations (Annual)
Compendium of Social Statistics. New York: U.N.

United Nations (Annual)
Yearbook of National Accounts Statistics. New York: U.N.

United Nations (Annual)
Yearbook of International Trade Statistics. New York: U.N.

United Nations (1966)
The Growth of World Industry, 1953–1965. New York: U.N.

UNESCO (Annual)
Statistical Yearbook. Paris: U.N.

International Labour Office (Annual)
Yearbook of Labour Statistics. Geneva: ILO

World Health Organization (Annual)
World Health Statistics Annual. Geneva: WHO

Food and Agriculture Organization (Annual)
Production Yearbook. Rome: FAO

International Monetary Fund (Monthly)
International Financial Statistics. Washington, D.C.: IMF

Organization for Economic Cooperation and Development (Monthly)
Main Economic Indicators. Paris: OECD

The Institute for Strategic Studies (Annual)
The Military Balance. London: ISS

Wasserman, P., and J. Paskar (1974)
Statistics Sources, 4th ed. Detroit, Mich.: Gale Research Co.

Kendall, M. G., and A. G. Doig (1962–1968)
Bibliography of Statistical Literature. Edinburgh: Oliver & Boyd

Sources: United States

U.S., Bureau of Economic Analysis (1973)
Long Term Economic Growth. Washington, D.C.: U.S. Government Printing Office

U.S., Bureau of Labor Statistics (Monthly)
Monthly Labor Review. Washington, D.C.: U.S. Government Printing Office

U.S., Council of Economic Advisers (Annual)
Economic Report of the President. Washington, D.C: U.S. Government Printing Office

U.S., Board of Governors of the Federal Reserve System (Monthly)
Federal Reserve Bulletin. Washington, D.C.: U.S. Government Printing Office

American Statistics Index (Annual)
Washington, D.C.: Congressional Information Service

Various states (Annual)
Statistical Abstract (or other similar title), e.g., *California Statistical Abstract, New York State Statistical Yearbook*, published by a state agency, a university, or other organization (see Appendix to the *Statistical Abstract of the United States*)

Andriot, J. L. (1973)
Guide to U.S. Government Statistics, 4th ed. McLean, Va.: Documents Index

Harvey, J. M. (1971)
Sources of Statistics, 2nd ed. Hamden, Conn.: Linnet Books

Morton, J. E. (1972)
"A Student's Guide to American Federal Government Statistics." *Journal of Economic Literature*, 10: 371–397

Wasserman, P., and J. Paskar (1974).
Statistics Sources, 4th ed. Detroit, Mich.: Gale Research Co.

National Bureau of Economic Research
Various publications. New York: NBER

U.S., Department of Commerce, Bureau of the Census (Annual, since 1878)
Statistical Abstract of the United States. Washington, D.C.: U.S. Government Printing Office

U.S., Department of Commerce, Bureau of the Census (1976)
Historical Statistics of the United States, Colonial Times to 1970. Washington, D.C.: U.S. Government Printing Office

U.S., Department of Commerce, Bureau of the Census (Monthly)
Business Conditions Digest. Washington, D.C.: U.S. Government Printing Office

U.S., Bureau of Economic Analysis (Monthly)
Survey of Current Business. Washington, D.C.: U.S. Government Printing Office

TABLE 3.5 *(Continued)*

Sources: Canada

Bank of Canada (Monthly)
Bank of Canada Review. Ottawa

Canadian Labour Market and Productivity Centre (1988)
A Guide to Current Analysis of the Canadian Economy. Ottawa

The Conference Board in Canada (1979)
Handbook of Canadian Consumer Markets, 1979. Ottawa

Government of Canada, Statistics Canada (Annual, since 1905)
The Canada Yearbook

Government of Canada, Statistics Canada (Annual and Quarterly)
National Income and Expenditure Accounts. Catalogue nos. 13-201, 13-001, and 13-549E. Ottawa

Government of Canada, Statistics Canada (Quarterly)
Financial Flow Accounts. Catalogue no. 13-002. Ottawa

Government of Canada, Statistics Canada (1985)
National Balance Sheet Accounts, 1961–1984. Catalogue no. 13-124. Ottawa

Harvey, J. M. (1973)
Statistics America. Beckenham, Kent, England: C.B.D. Research, Ltd.

Leacy, F. H., and M. C. Urquhart (1983)
Historical Statistics of Canada, 2nd ed. Ottawa: Supply and Services, Canada

Sources: Europe

Harvey, J. M. (1972)
Statistics Europe. 2nd ed. Beckenham, Kent, England: C.B.D Research Ltd.

Harvey, J. M. (1971)
Sources of Statistics, 2nd ed. Hamden, Conn.: Linnet Books

Kendall, M. G., and A. G. Doig (1962–1968)
Bibliography of Statistical Literature. Edinburgh: Oliver & Boyd; Vol. 1: 1950–1958; Vol. 2, 1940–1949; Vol. 3, Pre-1940, 1962–1968

United Kingdom (Annual, since 1854)
Statistical Abstract, London: HMSO

Sources: Other

Harvey, J. M. (1970)
Statistics Africa. Beckenham, Kent, England: C.B.D. Research Ltd.

Harvey, J. M. (1973)
Statistics America. Beckenham, Kent, England: C.B.D. Research Ltd.

3-C Suppose that the ITC dummy variable in (3.2.1) affects only the slope coefficient γ_2. How should the equation be specified?

3-D Suppose that a study must distinguish between gender (male, female), race (white, nonwhite), and location (urban, suburban, rural).

1. How many different characteristics must be distinguished?
2. What is the minimum number of dummy variables needed to distinguish these characteristics? How could they be defined?

3-E Show how six different characteristics can be distinguished by three, four, five, or six dummy variables.

3-F In discussing smoothing, based on (3.6.14), $y_t = f(t) + u_t$, assume that u_t is a random variable for which

$$E(u_t) = 0,$$
$$E(u_t^2) = \mathrm{Var}(u_t) = \sigma^2,$$
$$E(u_t u_t +_s) = 0 \qquad s \neq 0.$$

Consider the weighted moving average

$$y_t^* = \sum_{s=-m}^{m} c_s y_{t+s},$$

where the coefficients c_s are nonnegative and normalized to sum to unity. Thus

$$y_t^* = \sum_{s=-m}^{m} c_s f(t+s) + u_t^* \quad \text{where} \quad u_t^* = \sum_{s=-m}^{m} c_s u_{t+s}.$$

Find the variance of u_t^* and prove that it is less than σ^2, the variance of u_t. What is $E(u_t^* u_{t+s}^*)$?

3-G Consider Table 3.6, which is analyzed further in Section 4.8.

TABLE 3.6 Number of U.S. Economists, 1950–1988, Selected Years

Year	t	$N(t)$	$y(t) = \ln N(t)$
1950	0	6,936	8.84448
1	1	7,068	8.86333
2	2	7,267	8.89110
3	3	7,335	8.90041
4	4	7,486	8.92079
5	5	7,555	8.92996
6	6	8,450	9.04192
7	7	8,600	9.05952
8	8	9,189	9.12576
9	9	10,159	9.22611
1960	10	10,837	9.29072
1	11	11,054	9.31055
2	12	11,285	9.33123
3	13	11,973	9.39041
4	14	13,025	9.47463
5	15	14,127	9.55584
6	16	15,229	9.63096
7	17	16,675	9.72167
8	18	17,835	9.78892
9	19	19,061	9.85540
1970	20	18,908	9.84734
1	21	18,080	9.80256
2	22	17,286	9.75765
3	23	17,933	9.79440
4	24	18,766	9.83980
5	25	19,582	9.88236
6	26	19,028	9.85366
7	27	17,368	9.76238
8	28	18,901	9.84697
1980	30	19,459	9.87606
4	34	19,886	9.89761
8	38	20,647	9.93532

Note $N(t)$, membership in the American Economic Association; $\ln N(t)$, natural logarithm of $N(t)$.

Source Data for 1950–1959, *The American Economic Review*, Vol. 59, No. 6 (December 1969), *1969 Handbook of the American Economic Association*; data for 1960–1973, *The American Economic Review*, Vol. 64, No. 5 (October 1974), *1974 Directory of Members*; data for 1974–1977, *American Economic Review*, Vol. 68, No. 6 (December 1978), *1978 Survey of Members* (with an estimated correction, based on the final reference, to take account of an omitted category, "Complimentary Memberships"); data for 1978, 1980, and 1984, *American Economic Review*, Vol. 75, No. 6 (December 1985), *1985 Survey of Members*; 1988 datum, *American Economic Review*, Vol. 79, No. 6 (December 1989), *1989 Survey of Members*.

1. Taking only the years to 1973, graphically fit a linear semilogarithmic trend to these data and project the number of U.S. economists in the year 2000.
2. Using the additional information presented in this table, fit a quadratic semilogarithmic trend to *all* the data of the table and correct your projection from part 1. On the basis of this example, what can you infer about the perils of forecasting from a simple trend?

BIBLIOGRAPHY

ANDERSON, T. W. (1971). *The Statistical Analysis of Time Series.* New York: John Wiley & Sons, Inc.

BOX, G. E. P., and G. M. JENKINS (1970). *Time Series Analysis; Forecasting and Control.* San Francisco: Holden-Day & Co.

BROWN, R. G. (1963). *Smoothing, Forecasting and Prediction of Discrete Time Series.* Englewood Cliffs, N.J.: Prentice Hall.

CAIN, G. G., and H. W. WATTS, EDS. (1973). *Income Maintenance and Labor Supply.* New York: Academic Press, Inc.

DATA RESOURCES, INC. (1976). *The Data Resources National Economic Information System.* Amsterdam: North-Holland Publishing Company.

DHRYMES, P. (1970). *Econometrics.* New York: Harper & Row, Publishers, Inc.

ECKSTEIN, O. (1976). "Econometric Models and Business Expectations." *Economic Impact,* 16: 44–51.

FERBER, R., and W. Z. HIRSCH (1978). "Social Experimentation and Economic Policy: A Survey." *Journal of Economic Literature,* 16: 1379–1414.

FERBER, R., and W. Z. HIRSCH (1982). *Social Experimentation and Economic Policy.* Cambridge: Cambridge University Press.

FISHMAN, G. S. (1969). *Spectral Methods in Econometrics.* Cambridge, Mass.: Harvard University Press.

GOLDSMITH, R. W. (1982). *The Balance Sheet of the United States, 1953–1980.* Chicago: The University of Chicago Press.

GRANGER, C. W. J. (1989). *Forecasting in Business and Economics,* 2nd ed. Boston: Academic Press, Inc.

GRANGER, C. W. J., and M. W. WATSON (1984). "Time Series and Spectral Methods in Econometrics," in Z. Griliches and M. D. Intriligator, Eds., *Handbook of Econometrics,* Vol. 2. Amsterdam: North-Holland Publishing Company.

GRILICHES, Z., ED. (1971). *Price Indexes and Quality Change.* Cambridge, Mass.: Harvard University Press.

GRILICHES, Z. (1986). "Economic Data Issues," in Z. Griliches and M. D. Intriligator, Eds., *Handbook of Econometrics,* Vol. 3. Amsterdam: North-Holland Publishing Company.

HARVEY, A. C. (1990). *The Econometric Analysis of Time Series,* 2nd ed. Cambridge, Mass.: MIT Press.

HENDRY, D. F., A. R. PAGAN, and J. D. SARGAN (1984). "Dynamic Specification," in Z. Griliches and M. D. Intriligator, Eds., *Handbook of Econometrics,* Vol. 2. Amsterdam: North-Holland Publishing Company.

HUM, D., and W. SIMPSON (1991). *Income Maintenance, Work Effort, and the Canadian Mincome Experiment.* Ottawa: Supply and Services Canada (prepared for the Economic Council of Canada).

KERSHAW, D., and J. FAIR (1976). *The New Jersey Income-Maintenance Experiment.* New York: Academic Press, Inc.

KUZNETS, S. (1966). *Modern Economic Growth.* New Haven, Conn.: Yale University Press.

LEONTIEF, W. W. (1971). "Theoretical Assumptions and Nonobserved Facts." *American Economic Review*, 61: 1–7.

MEYER, J., and E. KUH (1957). "How Extraneous Are Extraneous Estimates?" *Review of Economics and Statistics*, 39: 380–393.

MORGENSTERN, O. (1963). *On the Accuracy of Economic Observations*, 2nd ed. Princeton, N.J.: Princeton University Press.

MORGENSTERN, O. (1972). "Thirteen Critical Points in Contemporary Economic Theory: An Interpretation." *Journal of Economic Literature*, 10: 1163–1189.

NELSON, C. R. (1973). *Applied Time Series Analysis for Managerial Forecasting.* San Francisco: Holden-Day & Co.

NERLOVE, M. (1964). "Spectral Analysis of Seasonal Adjustment Procedures." *Econometrica*, 32: 241–286.

ORCUTT, G. H. (1962). "Microanalytic Models of the United States Economy: Need and Development." *American Economic Review*, 52: 229–240.

ORCUTT, G. H., M. GREENBERGER, J. KORBEL, and A. M. RIVLIN (1961). *Microanalysis of Socioeconomic Systems: A Simulation Study.* New York: Harper & Row, Publishers, Inc.

PARNES, H. S. (1975). "The National Longitudinal Surveys: New Vistas for Labor Market Research." *American Economic Review*, 65: 244–249.

RUGGLES, N. D. (1964). "Book Review of O. Morgenstern (1963)." *American Economic Review*, 54: 445–447.

SMITH, V. L. (1982). "Microeconomic Systems as an Experimental Science." *American Economic Review*, 72: 923–955.

SMITH, V. L. (1994). "Economics in the Laboratory." *Journal of Economic Perspectives*, 8: 113–131.

SMITH, V. L., A. W. WILLIAMS, W. K. BRATTON, and M. G. VANNONI (1982). "Competitive Market Institutions: Double Auctions vs. Sealed-Bid Auctions." *American Economic Review*, 72: 58–77.

STATISTICS CANADA (GOVERNMENT OF CANADA) (1985). *National Balance Sheet Accounts, 1961–1984*, Catalogue no. 13–214. Ottawa: Department of Supply and Services Canada.

STIGLER, G. J., and J. K. KINDAHL (1970). *The Behavior of Industrial Prices.* National Bureau of Economic Research. New York: Columbia University Press.

4

THE BASIC LINEAR REGRESSION MODEL

4.1 INTRODUCTION

This chapter is devoted to the statistical treatment of the basic linear regression model, in which a single endogenous variable is linearly dependent on a set of exogenous variables and an unobservable random disturbance term. The basic model is introduced in Section 4.2. The method of least squares (LS) is presented in Section 4.3, and the statistical properties of the LS estimators are discussed in Section 4.4. The relation of the least squares estimator to the maximum likelihood estimator (MLE) and the method of moments estimators is discussed in Section 4.5. The generalization of the LS method to models with restricted coefficients is treated in Section 4.6. Hypothesis testing and predictions are discussed in Sections 4.7 and 4.8, respectively. Examples are given in Section 4.9. Finally, issues of model selection and nonnested hypothesis testing and an alternative Bayesian formulation are discussed in Section 4.10 and 4.11, respectively.

4.2 THE LINEAR REGRESSION MODEL

Suppose that a sample of data is given in the form of a vector of n observed values of a single endogenous variable $\mathbf{y}$ and a matrix of n observed values of a $1 \times k$ vector of exogenous variables $\mathbf{x}'$,

$$\underset{n \times 1}{\mathbf{y}} = \begin{pmatrix} y_1 \\ \vdots \\ y_n \end{pmatrix}, \qquad \underset{n \times k}{\mathbf{X}} = \begin{pmatrix} \mathbf{x}_1' \\ \vdots \\ \mathbf{x}_n' \end{pmatrix} = \begin{pmatrix} x_{11} & x_{12} & \cdots & x_{1k} \\ x_{21} & x_{22} & \cdots & x_{2k} \\ \vdots & \vdots & \ddots & \vdots \\ x_{n1} & x_{n2} & \cdots & x_{nk} \end{pmatrix}. \tag{4.2.1}$$

The elements of the $n \times 1$ vector $\mathbf{y}$ are the numbers y_i, where y_i is the value of the variable y at observation i, with i being an index of observations. Here $i = 1,2, \ldots, n$, where n is the sample size.[1] The elements of $\mathbf{X}$ are the numbers x_{ij}, where x_{ij} is the value of the variable x_j at the observation i. The $n \times k$ matrix $\mathbf{X}$ is known as the *design matrix*. Observations on y and $\mathbf{x}$ can be made over time, the case of *time-series data*, or they can be made over individuals, objects, geographic areas, and so on, at a given time, the case of *cross-section data*. Of course, observations of a number of people over time can also be made, representing a *panel* or *pooled times-series and cross-section data*, and involving a double subscript, *it*, to indicate observations of the ith unit at the tth time period.

Suppose that there is a simple linear relation in which the endogenous variable y_i is a linear function of the k exogenous variables $(x_{i1}, \ldots, x_{ik})$ and the unobserved additive stochastic disturbance term u_i,

$$y_i = \beta_1 x_{i1} + \beta_2 x_{i2} + \cdots + \beta_k x_{ik} + u_i, \qquad i = 1, 2, \ldots, n,$$

or in matrix form,

$$\mathbf{y} = \mathbf{X}\boldsymbol{\beta} + \mathbf{u}, \qquad *(4.2.2)$$

where $\boldsymbol{\beta} = (\beta_1, \ldots, \beta_k)'$ is a $k \times 1$ vector of constants, to be called *regression parameters*. The regression model (4.2.2) specifies a "causal" relationship among y, $\mathbf{x}$, and u. The variables $\mathbf{x}$ and the unobserved quantity u are considered to be the "causes" that determine the value of y. Hence y is called the *dependent* or *endogenous* variable. The $\mathbf{x}$ are called the *explanatory* or *exogenous* or *independent* variables, because their values are determined by forces outside the model (4.2.2). To allow for an intercept in this equation, one variable, say the last, is identically unity, so $x_{ik} \equiv 1$, and the last regression parameter β_k is thus the intercept.

The stochastic relation (4.2.2), involving the stochastic disturbance term u_i, is a very convenient way to formulate the relation between y and the k variables $\mathbf{x}$. Had the relation been written in the exact (nonstochastic) form

$$y_i = \beta_1 x_{i1} + \cdots + \beta_k x_{ik}, \qquad i = 1, \ldots, n, \qquad (4.2.3)$$

any sample observations that do not satisfy (4.2.3) would imply a contradiction to this formulation. Therefore, model (4.2.3) has to be discarded because it is too rigid. A more reasonable formulation is to assume that the factors determining y are partly unknown. The errors u_i appear because the model is a simplification of reality. A deterministic specification implies that the k variables in $\mathbf{X}$ are the sole determinants of $\mathbf{y}$, but in fact, there could be innumerable factors that determine the outcome of $\mathbf{y}$, as summarized by u_i. Equation (4.2.2) can also be viewed as one of the reduced-form equations of an econometric model discussed in Chapter 2, where the β's can be interpreted as one column of the $\boldsymbol{\Pi}$ matrix. The disturbance term $\mathbf{u}$ represents the effects of all other factors that affect $\mathbf{y}$ but are not taken explicitly into account. The term $\mathbf{u}$ is considered stochastic (random) because the lack of knowledge about the process generating it gives it the nature of a random variable. It will be called the *error* or *residual* or *stochastic disturbance term*. The u_i's are commonly assumed to have mean zero and variance σ^2.

It follows from (4.2.2) that if $\mathbf{u}$ is random, so is $\mathbf{y}$. There is a distribution of y for every fixed value of $\mathbf{x}$. Each observed value y_i is a realization of the random variable y; that

[1] In general, i will index the observation, whether the data represent a cross section or a time series. In certain contexts in which time-series data are used (e.g., Chapters 6 and 11), however, i will be replaced by the time index t.

is, it can be considered to have been selected according to the probability distribution of y for the corresponding value of $\mathbf{x}$, say $\mathbf{x}_i$. Therefore, another way of describing (4.2.2) is to say that the model specifies the conditional distribution of the endogenous variable y given that $\mathbf{x} = \mathbf{x}_i$.

This conditional distribution formulation suggests that the exogenous variable $\mathbf{x}$ may also be viewed as a random variable. In this formulation, there is a joint density of the observables given by $f(y, \mathbf{x}; \boldsymbol{\theta})$, where $\boldsymbol{\theta}$ is a vector of unknown parameters characterizing the joint distribution, which includes the $\boldsymbol{\beta}$ parameters. Rewriting the joint density as the product of the conditional density and the marginal density,

$$f(y, \mathbf{x}; \boldsymbol{\theta}) = f(y|\mathbf{x}; \boldsymbol{\theta}_1)f(\mathbf{x}; \boldsymbol{\theta}_2), \tag{4.2.4}$$

where $\boldsymbol{\theta}' = (\boldsymbol{\theta}_1', \boldsymbol{\theta}_2')$. Provided that there is no relationship between $\boldsymbol{\theta}_1$ and $\boldsymbol{\theta}_2$, then $\mathbf{x}$ is defined as *weakly exogenous* by Engle, Hendry, and Richard (1983), and regression analysis can be defined as statistical inferences on $\boldsymbol{\theta}_1$. In the case of regression model (4.2.2), $\boldsymbol{\theta}_1$ includes $\boldsymbol{\beta}$ and the parameters characterizing the probability distribution of u.

When $\mathbf{x}$ represents economic quantities, it can often be assumed that their values result from random phenomena, such as an income variable in the consumption function or a price variable in the demand function. However, many cases exist in which certain exogenous variables cannot be considered as random, such as a time trend or seasonal dummies. Because regression analysis involves only the conditional distribution of y for fixed values of $\mathbf{x}$, the methods and properties treated here are equally applicable whether the exogenous variables are fixed or random. As a result, it is possible to avoid the unnecessary complication of specifying the joint distribution of $(y, \mathbf{x}')$ and simply treat $\mathbf{x}$ as exogenous.

The aim of regression analysis is to make inferences about the unknown parameters in (4.2.2), including the regression coefficients $\boldsymbol{\beta}$, from observed $\mathbf{y}$ and $\mathbf{X}$. To make any progress, it is necessary to make some assumptions on how the observed data were generated. The maintained hypotheses for the simple linear regression model are, in addition to the linear model (4.2.2),

A.4.1. $E(\mathbf{u}|\mathbf{X}) = \mathbf{0}$.

A.4.2. $E(\mathbf{u}\mathbf{u}'|\mathbf{X}) = \sigma^2\mathbf{I}_n$, where $\mathbf{I}_n$ is the $n \times n$ identity matrix.

A.4.3. $\text{rank}(\mathbf{X}) = k$.

Assumption A.4.1 specifies that the expected value of the stochastic disturbance term $\mathbf{u}$ is zero whatever the values of the $\mathbf{X}$. In other words, given the model (4.2.2), the expected value of y given the $k \times 1$ vector of exogenous variables $\mathbf{x}$ is $\mathbf{x}'\boldsymbol{\beta}$. An important implication of A.4.1 is that

$$E(\mathbf{X}'\mathbf{u}) = E[E(\mathbf{X}'\mathbf{u}|\mathbf{X})] = E[\mathbf{X}'E(\mathbf{u}|\mathbf{X})|\mathbf{X}] = \mathbf{0}. \tag{4.2.5}$$

In other words, the additive error term $\mathbf{u}$ is not correlated with the explanatory variables $\mathbf{x}$. The elements of $\mathbf{u}$ are called *disturbance terms* because they take values that are sometimes positive and sometimes negative for any values of the exogenous variables.

When the design matrix $\mathbf{X}$ consists of fixed constants for the exogenous variables, the conditional statements of A.4.1 and A.4.2 are equivalent to the following unconditional statements:

A.4.1*. $E\mathbf{u} = \mathbf{0}$.

A.4.2*. $E\mathbf{u}\mathbf{u}' = \sigma^2\mathbf{I}_n$.

For ease of exposition, A.4.1* and A.4.2* will be used in place of A.4.1 and A.4.2 when there is no confusion.

A.4.2* (and A.4.2) are compact ways of writing two assumptions using matrix notation. Since $\mathbf{u}$ is an $n \times 1$ vector, the product $\mathbf{uu}'$ is an $n \times n$ symmetric matrix of cross products, and since the operation of taking expected values is to be applied to each element of this matrix,

$$E(\mathbf{uu}') = E_x E(\mathbf{uu}'|\mathbf{X}) = E_x \left\{ \left[\begin{array}{cccc} E(u_1^2) & E(u_1u_2) & \cdots & E(u_1u_n) \\ E(u_2u_1) & E(u_2^2) & \cdots & E(u_2u_n) \\ \vdots & \vdots & \ddots & \vdots \\ E(u_nu_1) & E(u_nu_2) & \cdots & E(u_n^2) \end{array} \right] \middle| \mathbf{X} \right\} \quad *(4.26)$$

$$= \begin{bmatrix} \sigma^2 & 0 & \cdots & \cdots \\ 0 & \sigma^2 & 0 & \cdots \\ \vdots & \vdots & \ddots & \cdots \\ 0 & \cdots & \cdots & \cdots\sigma^2 \end{bmatrix},$$

where E_x denotes the expectation with respect to X. The terms on the main diagonal show that $E(u_i^2) = \sigma^2$ for all i; that is, the u_i have constant variance $\sigma^2 < \infty$, a property that is referred to as *homoskedasticity*. Each off-diagonal term gives $E(u_iu_j) = 0$ for $i \neq j$; that is, the u_i values are uncorrelated.

The homoskedasticity assumption reinforces the condition already included in A.4.1 that the mean of u_i is zero whatever the values of the $\mathbf{x}$. Here it is assumed that the distribution of each u has a variance and that this variance is unchanged whatever the values of the $\mathbf{x}$. If the distribution of $\mathbf{u}$ is characterized by its first two moments, such as the normal distribution, these assumptions imply that, independent of the values of $\mathbf{x}$, the distribution of $\mathbf{u}$ is unchanged.

The assumption that u_i and u_j are uncorrelated for $i \neq j$ implies that the sources of the effects of unobserved factors are different for different observations. Thus different observations are not affected by certain unobservable common factors.

In the case of simple linear regression where $k = 2$ and $x_{i2} = 1$, the implications of A.4.1 and A.4.2 for model (4.2.2) can be illustrated geometrically. The assumptions that $E(u\,|\,\mathbf{x}) = 0$ and $E(u^2\,|\,\mathbf{x}) = \sigma^2$ imply that the means of the distribution of $\mathbf{y}$ all lie on a straight line and that the spread of $\mathbf{y}$ around their means is independent of $\mathbf{x}$, as shown in Figure 4.1.

Assumption A.4.3 about the rank of $\mathbf{X}$ implies that the number of observations n exceeds k, the number of regression parameters to be estimated, and that no exact linear relations exist between any of the $\mathbf{X}$ variables. If, for example, one explanatory variable were a multiple of another, or one were an exact linear function of several others, the rank of $\mathbf{X}$ would be less than k and thus the rank of $\mathbf{X}$ would be less than k. As will be seen, the rank of $\mathbf{X}$ plays a crucial role in the estimation procedure.

Models satisfying the linear relation (4.2.2) and assumptions A.4.1 to A.4.3 are referred to as the *basic linear regression model*. In any practical application it should be noted that these conditions may be restrictive, and there are many important cases in which one or more of these conditions do not hold. Statistical methods for dealing with these violations of the basic linear regression model form a large part of econometric theory, and they are treated in later chapters. In the present chapter we consider statistical methods only when appropriate to the basic linear regression model.

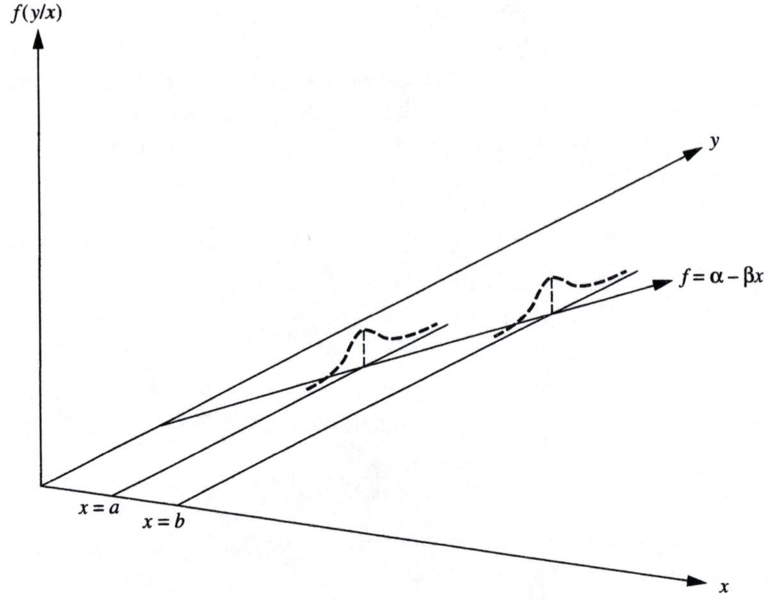

Figure 4.1 The Basic Linear Regression Model with a Single Explanatory Variable

4.3 ESTIMATION USING THE METHOD OF LEAST SQUARES

The $k + 1$ unknown parameters of the basic linear regression model, (4.2.2) with assumptions A.4.1 and A.4.2, are the k coefficients $\boldsymbol{\beta}$ and the variance σ^2. *Regression analysis* is concerned with drawing inferences about these parameters from the observed $\mathbf{y}$ and $\mathbf{X}$. There are, in fact, many methods to estimate $\boldsymbol{\beta}$ and σ^2. For given values of $\boldsymbol{\beta}$, the conditional mean of y_i given the $k \times 1$ vector $\mathbf{x}_i$ under A.4.1 is $E(y_i) = \mathbf{x}_i'\boldsymbol{\beta}$, and the corresponding deviation from the actual value of y_i is $u_i = y_i - E(y_i)$. The *method of least squares* is to choose the values of $\boldsymbol{\beta}$ that minimize the sum of the squares of the deviations between the actual values of y_i and the predicted conditional means $\hat{y}_i$. To put it formally, the *method of least squares* uses as estimates of $\boldsymbol{\beta}$ those values that minimize the sum of the squares of the estimated residuals along the y-axis, S, defined as

$$\begin{aligned} S &= \sum_{i=1}^{n}(y_i - \mathbf{x}_i'\boldsymbol{\beta})^2 \\ &= \sum_{i=1}^{n} u_i^2 = \mathbf{u}'\mathbf{u} \qquad (4.3.1) \\ &= (\mathbf{y} - \mathbf{X}\boldsymbol{\beta})'(\mathbf{y} - \mathbf{X}\boldsymbol{\beta}) = \mathbf{y}'\mathbf{y} - 2\boldsymbol{\beta}'\mathbf{X}'\mathbf{y} + \boldsymbol{\beta}'\mathbf{X}'\mathbf{X}\boldsymbol{\beta}, \end{aligned}$$

where the two cross-product terms are collected as the middle term since they are transposes of each other and they are scalars.

To find those values of $\boldsymbol{\beta}$ that minimize this sum, differentiate S in (4.3.1) with respect to $\boldsymbol{\beta}$:

$$\frac{\partial S}{\partial \boldsymbol{\beta}} = -2\mathbf{X}'\mathbf{y} + 2\mathbf{X}'\mathbf{X}\boldsymbol{\beta}, \tag{4.3.2}$$

which follows from differentiating the linear term in $\boldsymbol{\beta}$ in (4.3.1), $-2\boldsymbol{\beta}'\mathbf{X}'\mathbf{y}$, and the quadratic term in $\boldsymbol{\beta}$ in (4.3.1), $\boldsymbol{\beta}'\mathbf{X}'\mathbf{X}\boldsymbol{\beta}$, noting that the derivative of a quadratic such as $c\beta_1^2$ is $2c\beta_1$. Equating (4.3.2) to zero and putting a "hat" on $\boldsymbol{\beta}$ to indicate the resulting estimated value of $\boldsymbol{\beta}$ yields the *normal equations* of the least squares estimator $\hat{\boldsymbol{\beta}}$,

$$\mathbf{X}'\mathbf{X}\hat{\boldsymbol{\beta}} = \mathbf{X}'\mathbf{y}. \tag{4.3.3}$$

If $\mathbf{X}'\mathbf{X}$ is of full rank, which follows from A.4.3, the *least squares estimator* of $\boldsymbol{\beta}$ can be solved from this system of k linear equations in the unknowns as

$$\hat{\boldsymbol{\beta}} = (\mathbf{X}'\mathbf{X})^{-1}\mathbf{X}'\mathbf{y}, \tag{4.3.4}$$

which expresses the least squares estimator as an explicit function of the data represented by $\mathbf{y}$ and $\mathbf{X}$. This function is linear in $\mathbf{y}$ but nonlinear in $\mathbf{X}$.

It is useful to have an explicit formula for a subset of the least squares estimator $\hat{\boldsymbol{\beta}}$. Suppose that $\hat{\boldsymbol{\beta}}$ is partitioned as $\hat{\boldsymbol{\beta}}' = (\hat{\boldsymbol{\beta}}_1', \hat{\boldsymbol{\beta}}_2')$, where $\hat{\boldsymbol{\beta}}_1$ and $\hat{\boldsymbol{\beta}}_2$ are $k_1 \times 1$ and $k_2 \times 1$ vectors, respectively, with $k_1 + k_2 = k$. Partitioning $\mathbf{X}$ conformably as $\mathbf{X} = (\mathbf{X}_1, \mathbf{X}_2)$, the normal equations (4.3.3) can be written in partitioned form as

$$\mathbf{X}_1'\mathbf{X}_1\hat{\boldsymbol{\beta}}_1 + \mathbf{X}_1'\mathbf{X}_2\hat{\boldsymbol{\beta}}_2 = \mathbf{X}_1'\mathbf{y} \tag{4.3.5}$$

and

$$\mathbf{X}_2'\mathbf{X}_1\hat{\boldsymbol{\beta}}_1 + \mathbf{X}_2'\mathbf{X}_2\hat{\boldsymbol{\beta}}_2 = \mathbf{X}_2'\mathbf{y}. \tag{4.3.6}$$

Solving (4.3.5) for $\hat{\boldsymbol{\beta}}_1$ and inserting it into (4.3.6) yields

$$\hat{\boldsymbol{\beta}}_2 = (\mathbf{X}_2'\mathbf{M}_1\mathbf{X}_2)^{-1}\mathbf{X}_2'\mathbf{M}_1\mathbf{y}, \tag{4.3.7}$$

where $\mathbf{M}_1 = \mathbf{I} - \mathbf{X}_1(\mathbf{X}_1'\mathbf{X}_1)^{-1}\mathbf{X}_1'$. Similarly, (4.3.6) can be solved for $\hat{\boldsymbol{\beta}}_1$ using (4.3.5) to obtain

$$\hat{\boldsymbol{\beta}}_1 = (\mathbf{X}_1'\mathbf{M}_2\mathbf{X}_1)^{-1}\mathbf{X}_1'\mathbf{M}_2\mathbf{y} = (\mathbf{X}_1'\mathbf{X}_1)^{-1}\mathbf{X}_1'\left(\mathbf{y} - \mathbf{X}_2\hat{\boldsymbol{\beta}}_2\right), \tag{4.3.8}$$

where $\mathbf{M}_2 = \mathbf{I} - \mathbf{X}_2(\mathbf{X}_2'\mathbf{X}_2)^{-1}\mathbf{X}_2'$.

Often, the design matrix $\mathbf{X}$ contains a vector of constants. Letting the last (kth) column of $\mathbf{X}$ be $\mathbf{e}$, where $\mathbf{e}$ is an $n \times 1$ vector of ones, from (4.3.6),

$$\hat{\beta}_k = \bar{y} - \bar{x}_1\hat{\beta}_1 - \cdots - \bar{x}_{k-1}\hat{\beta}_{k-1}, \tag{4.3.9}$$

where $\bar{x}_j = 1/n\,\Sigma_{i=1}^n x_{ij}$ is the jth mean of the jth exogenous variable for $j = 1, \ldots, k-1$, and $\bar{y}_j = 1/n\,\Sigma_{i=1}^n y_i$ is the mean of the dependent variable. Thus, by (4.3.9), the least squares line passes through the mean of y and $\mathbf{x}$. Furthermore, the sum of the estimated residuals $\Sigma_{i=1}^n \hat{u}_{ij} = \Sigma_{i=1}^n (y_i - \mathbf{x}_i'\hat{\boldsymbol{\beta}}) = 0$, so, as already noted, some of the least squares residuals are positive and some are negative, their average being zero.

Substituting $\mathbf{X}_2 = \mathbf{e}$ into (4.3.8) yields

$$\hat{\boldsymbol{\beta}}_1 = \begin{pmatrix} \sum_{i=1}^{n}(x_{i1}-\bar{x}_1)^2 & \sum_{i=1}^{n}(x_{i1}-\bar{x}_1)(x_{i2}-\bar{x}_2) & \cdots & \sum_{i=1}^{n}(x_{i1}-\bar{x}_1)(x_{ik-1}-\bar{x}_{k-1}) \\ & \vdots & \vdots & \vdots \\ & \vdots & \vdots & \sum_{i=1}^{n}(x_{ik-1}-\bar{x}_{k-1})^2 \end{pmatrix}^{-1} \cdot \begin{pmatrix} \sum_{i=1}^{n}(x_{i1}-\bar{x}_1)(y_i-\bar{y}) \\ \vdots \\ \sum_{i=1}^{n}(x_{ik-1}-\bar{x}_{k-1})(y_i-\bar{y}) \end{pmatrix}. \tag{4.3.10}$$

Equations (4.3.8) and (4.3.9) also provide an alternative method to obtain the least squares estimator. First, transform each variable into the form of deviations from their respective sample means, $\dot{y}_i = y_i - \bar{y}$, $\dot{x}_{ij} = x_{ij} - \bar{x}_j$, $j = 1, \ldots, k-1$. Second, obtain the least squares estimator $\hat{\beta}_1, \ldots, \hat{\beta}_{k-1}$ by regressing $\dot{y}_i$ on $\dot{x}_{i1}, \ldots, \dot{x}_{i,k-1}$. Third, substitute these estimates into (4.3.9) to obtain $\hat{\beta}_k$.

Given the least squares estimator $\hat{\boldsymbol{\beta}}$, the *predicted value* of $\mathbf{y}$ is defined as

$$\hat{\mathbf{y}} = \begin{pmatrix} \hat{y}_1 \\ \vdots \\ \hat{y}_n \end{pmatrix} = \mathbf{X}\hat{\boldsymbol{\beta}} = \mathbf{X}(\mathbf{X}'\mathbf{X})^{-1}\mathbf{X}'\mathbf{y} = \mathbf{P}\mathbf{y}, \tag{4.3.11}$$

and the *least squares residuals* are defined as

$$\hat{\mathbf{u}} = \mathbf{y} - \mathbf{X}\hat{\boldsymbol{\beta}} = [\mathbf{I} - \mathbf{X}(\mathbf{X}'\mathbf{X})^{-1}\mathbf{X}']\mathbf{y} = \mathbf{M}\mathbf{y} = \mathbf{M}\mathbf{u}, \tag{4.3.12}$$

where $\mathbf{P} = \mathbf{X}(\mathbf{X}'\mathbf{X})^{-1}\mathbf{X}'$ and $\mathbf{M} = \mathbf{I} - \mathbf{P}$. $\mathbf{M}$ and $\mathbf{P}$ are the *fundamental idempotent matrices* of least squares as they satisfy the idempotent condition $\mathbf{M}^2 = \mathbf{M}$, $\mathbf{P}^2 = \mathbf{P}$ and are symmetric, with the properties that $\mathbf{PX} = \mathbf{X}$ and $\mathbf{MX} = \mathbf{0}$. Therefore,

$$(\mathbf{P}\mathbf{y})'[\mathbf{M}\mathbf{y}] = \mathbf{0}. \tag{4.3.13}$$

Since

$$\begin{aligned} \mathbf{y} &= \mathbf{X}\hat{\boldsymbol{\beta}} + \hat{\mathbf{u}} \\ &= \mathbf{P}\mathbf{y} + \mathbf{M}\mathbf{y}, \end{aligned} \tag{4.3.14}$$

and since both $\mathbf{P}$ and $\mathbf{M}$ are projection matrices with $\mathbf{P} + \mathbf{M} = \mathbf{I}$, the least squares estimation can be regarded geometrically as decomposing $\mathbf{y}$ into two orthogonal components, with $\mathbf{P}$ projecting $\mathbf{y}$ onto the space spanned by the column vectors of $\mathbf{X}$ and $\mathbf{M}$ projecting $\mathbf{y}$ onto the space orthogonal to the space spanned by the column vectors of $\mathbf{X}$.[2] Thus $\mathbf{y}$ can be viewed as the sum of two vectors that are orthogonal, forming the sides of a right triangle.

[2]Let ζ be a subspace of V and $\zeta^{\perp}$ the orthogonal complement of ζ. The operator $\mathbf{P}$ that projects on ζ along $\zeta^{\perp}$ is called an *orthogonal projector*. The projector $\mathbf{P}$ is an idempotent matrix (i.e., $\mathbf{P}^2 = \mathbf{P}$). Its complement $\mathbf{I} - \mathbf{P}$ is also a projector that projects on $\zeta^{\perp}$ along ζ. Thus for an $n \times r$ matrix $\mathbf{A}$ of rank r, $\mathbf{P} = \mathbf{A}(\mathbf{A}'\mathbf{A})^{-1}\mathbf{A}'$ and $\mathbf{I} - \mathbf{P}$ are orthogonal projection operators (see Rao, 1973, Sec. 1.c).

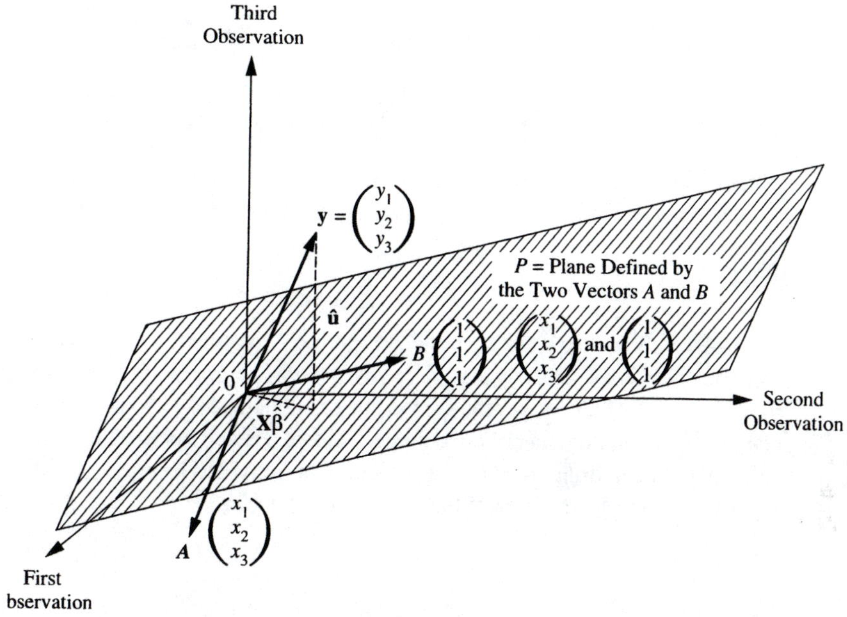

Figure 4.2 Geometrical Interpretation of Least Squares Estimation
Note: The P plane consists of all linear combinations $\mathbf{X}\boldsymbol{\beta}$. $\mathbf{X}\hat{\boldsymbol{\beta}}$ is the perpendicular projection of $\mathbf{y}$ on P, $\hat{\boldsymbol{\beta}}$ is the least squares estimator, $\hat{\mathbf{u}}$ is the least squares residual vector, $\mathbf{y} - \mathbf{X}\hat{\boldsymbol{\beta}}$.

Letting $\mathbf{y}$ and $\mathbf{X}$ represent $k + 1$ vectors in an n-dimensional space, the least squares estimation can be interpreted as the decomposition of the $\mathbf{y}$ vector into two orthogonal components. One is $\mathbf{Py}$, which is $\mathbf{X}\hat{\boldsymbol{\beta}}$, the projection of the vector $\mathbf{y}$ onto the space spanned by the columns of the design matrix $\mathbf{X}$. The other is $\mathbf{My}$, which is $\hat{\mathbf{u}}$ or $(\mathbf{I} - \mathbf{P})\mathbf{y}$, the projection of the $\mathbf{y}$ vector onto the space orthogonal to that spanned by $\mathbf{X}$. This geometrical interpretation of least squares is illustrated in Figure 4.2 for the case in which $n = 3$ and $k = 2$. Note that $\mathbf{X}\hat{\boldsymbol{\beta}}$ lies in the plane defined by the columns of the 3×2 design matrix $\mathbf{X}$, while $\hat{\mathbf{u}}$ is orthogonal to this plane.

Using $\hat{\mathbf{u}}$ from (4.3.12), the residual sum of squares, $\hat{\mathbf{u}}'\hat{\mathbf{u}}$, which is the minimized sum of squares S in (4.3.1), can be written as the following quadratic form in $\mathbf{y}$ and also in $\mathbf{u}$:

$$\hat{\mathbf{u}}'\hat{\mathbf{u}} = \mathbf{y}'\mathbf{M}\mathbf{y} = \mathbf{u}'\mathbf{M}\mathbf{u}. \qquad *(4.3.15)$$

The first equality follows from the idempotent property of the matrix $\mathbf{M}$. The second equality follows from the orthogonality between $\mathbf{M}$ and $\mathbf{X}$ (i.e., the condition $\mathbf{MX} = \mathbf{0}$). Using the geometric interpretation (4.3.14), which decomposes the vector $\mathbf{y}$ into two orthogonal vectors $\mathbf{X}\hat{\boldsymbol{\beta}}$ and $\hat{\mathbf{u}}$, it is possible to measure the proportion of the variance of the dependent variable $\mathbf{y}$ that is explained by the regression $\mathbf{y} = \mathbf{X}\hat{\boldsymbol{\beta}}$. Let $\mathbf{e} = (1, \ldots, 1)'$ be an $n \times 1$ vector of ones, so the mean of $\mathbf{y}$ is $\bar{y} = 1/n\,\mathbf{e}'\mathbf{y}$. Subtracting $\mathbf{e}\bar{y}$ from both sides of (4.3.14) and premultiplying each side of the result by its own transpose, the sum of squares of the deviation of y_i from its mean values, $\dot{y}_i = y_i - \bar{y}$, is obtained as

$$\begin{aligned}\|\dot{\mathbf{y}}\|^2 &= \dot{\mathbf{y}}'\dot{\mathbf{y}} = (\mathbf{y} - \mathbf{e}\bar{y})'(\mathbf{y} - e\bar{y}) = \sum_{i=1}^{n}(y_i - \bar{y})^2 \\ &= (\hat{\mathbf{y}} - \mathbf{e}\bar{y})'(\hat{\mathbf{y}} - \mathbf{e}\bar{y}) + \hat{\mathbf{u}}'\hat{\mathbf{u}} + 2(\hat{\mathbf{y}} - \mathbf{e}\bar{y})'\hat{\mathbf{u}} \\ &= (\hat{\mathbf{y}} - \mathbf{e}\bar{y})'(\hat{\mathbf{y}} - \mathbf{e}\bar{y}) + \hat{\mathbf{u}}'\hat{\mathbf{u}} - 2\bar{y}\mathbf{e}'\hat{\mathbf{u}},\end{aligned} \tag{4.3.16}$$

where the last equality follows from (4.3.13). If, in addition, the design matrix $\mathbf{X}$ contains a constant term, then $\mathbf{e}'\hat{\mathbf{u}} = 0$, which follows from (4.3.9). Equation (4.3.16) then becomes

$$\begin{aligned}\|\dot{\mathbf{y}}\|^2 &= (\hat{\mathbf{y}} - \mathbf{e}\bar{y})'(\hat{\mathbf{y}} - \mathbf{e}\bar{y}) + \hat{\mathbf{u}}'\hat{\mathbf{u}} \\ &= \|\dot{\hat{\mathbf{y}}}\|^2 + \|\hat{\mathbf{u}}\|^2.\end{aligned} \tag{4.3.17}$$

Figure 4.3 shows the right triangle of Figure 4.2, in which $\dot{\mathbf{y}}$ is the hypotenuse and $\dot{\hat{\mathbf{y}}}$ and $\hat{\mathbf{u}}$ are the other sides. Thus (4.3.17) expresses the Pythagorean theorem for this right triangle. The total sum of squares is the sum of the explained sum of squares, which is the first term on the right, and the unexplained sum of squares, $\hat{\mathbf{u}}'\hat{\mathbf{u}}$. This total sum of squares is the sum of squared deviations from the mean and, when divided by the degrees of freedom, $n - 1$, thus is the sample variance of the dependent variable:

$$s_{\dot{y}}^2 = \frac{1}{n-1}\|\dot{y}\|^2.$$

The *coefficient of determination* for a regression, R^2, is the proportion of the total of the dependent variable y that is explained by the regression. From the above, this proportion can be expressed in various equivalent ways:

$$\begin{aligned}R^2 &= \frac{\|\dot{\hat{\mathbf{y}}}\|^2}{\|\dot{\mathbf{y}}\|^2} = \frac{\|\dot{\mathbf{y}}\|^2 - \|\hat{\mathbf{u}}\|^2}{\|\dot{\mathbf{y}}\|^2} = 1 - \frac{\|\hat{\mathbf{u}}\|^2}{\|\dot{\mathbf{y}}\|^2} \\ &= \frac{\dot{\hat{\mathbf{y}}}'\dot{\hat{\mathbf{y}}}}{\dot{\mathbf{y}}'\dot{\mathbf{y}}} = \frac{\sum \dot{\hat{y}}_i^2}{\sum \dot{y}_i^2} = 1 - \frac{\sum \hat{u}_i^2}{\sum \dot{y}_i^2}.\end{aligned} \tag{4.3.18}$$

From the last two expressions for R^2, since a ratio of sums of squares cannot be negative,

$$0 \le R^2 \le 1. \tag{4.3.19}$$

The higher the R^2, the lower is the sum of squared errors $\|\hat{\mathbf{u}}\|^2$ relative to the total sum of squares $\|\dot{\mathbf{y}}\|^2$. In the extreme case when all residuals are zero, $\|\hat{\mathbf{u}}\|^2$ vanishes, $R^2 = 1$, and all of the total sum of squares is explained by the regression. At the other extreme, when all coefficients are zero, $\|\hat{\mathbf{u}}\|^2$ equals $\|\dot{\mathbf{y}}\|^2$, so $R^2 = 0$, and none of the sum of squares is explained by the regression. Thus R^2 is a measure of the explanatory power of the regression—

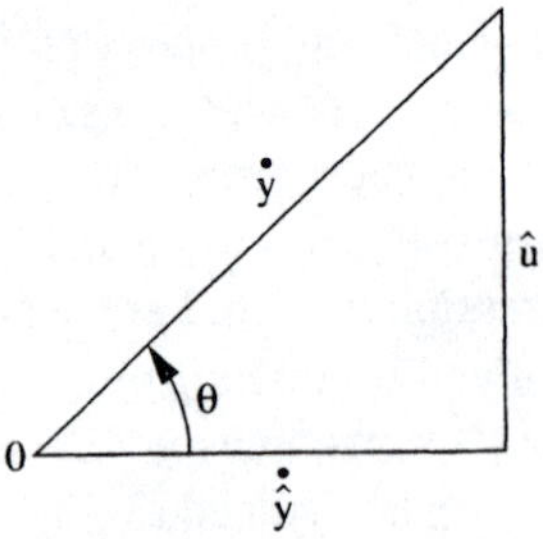

Figure 4.3 Right Triangle of Figure 4.2, Where Variables Are Measured as Deviations from Mean Values

Note Elements of $\dot{\mathbf{y}}$ are $y_i - \bar{y}$. Elements of $\dot{\hat{\mathbf{y}}}$ are $\hat{y}_i - \bar{y} = x_i\hat{\boldsymbol{\beta}} - \bar{y}$.

in particular, a measure of how well the model, as estimated, fits the available data. If, for example, $R^2 = 0.9$, then 90% of the variance of the dependent variable is explained by the regression, with 10% left unexplained. Some further examples of the coefficient of determination in the context of completely worked out examples of simple and multiple linear regressions are given in Section 4.9.

It is also possible to give a trigonometric interpretation for the coefficient of determination, using the right triangle of Figure 4.3. Again measuring variables as deviations from mean values, in Figure 4.3 the angle θ is that between $\dot{\mathbf{y}}$ and $\dot{\hat{\mathbf{y}}}$. Since the cosine of an angle is the ratio of the length of the adjacent side to the length of the hypotenuse,

$$\cos\theta = \frac{\|\dot{\hat{\mathbf{y}}}\|}{\|\dot{\mathbf{y}}\|}, \tag{4.3.20}$$

and since $\|\dot{\hat{\mathbf{y}}}\|^2$ and $\|\dot{\mathbf{y}}\|^2$, being sums of squares, are, from the Pythagorean theorem, the squared lengths, it follows that the coefficient of determination, geometrically, is the square of the cosine of the angle:

$$R^2 = \cos^2\theta = \frac{\|\dot{\hat{\mathbf{y}}}\|^2}{\|\dot{\mathbf{y}}\|^2}. \tag{4.3.21}$$

From this geometrical interpretation it also follows that R^2 is bounded by 0 and 1, as already expressed in (4.3.19).

The *multiple correlation coefficient* R is defined as the nonnegative square root of R^2, or, equivalently,

$$R = \cos\theta \quad \text{where} \quad -\frac{\pi}{2} \le \theta \le \frac{\pi}{2}, \quad \text{so} \quad 0 \le R \le 1. \tag{4.3.22}$$

Thus, when $\mathbf{y}$ lies in the plane P in Figure 4.2, so $\hat{\mathbf{u}}$ is the zero vector, it follows that $\theta = 0$, so $R = 1$ and the coefficient of determination $R^2 = 1$. At the other extreme, when $\mathbf{y}$ is perpendicular to the plane, so $\hat{\boldsymbol{\beta}}$ is the zero vector, it follows that $\theta = \pm\pi/2$ radians, so $R = 0$ and $R^2 = 0$. These extremes correspond, respectively, to a perfect fit (all residuals are zero) and no fit at all (all slope parameters are zero).

4.4 THE GAUSS–MARKOV THEOREM AND PROPERTIES OF THE LEAST SQUARES ESTIMATOR

There are, in fact, many different ways to estimate $\boldsymbol{\beta}$. The least squares method uses the criterion of minimizing the sum of squares of the deviations to obtain (4.3.4). However, one can also obtain estimates of $\boldsymbol{\beta}$ by minimizing the sum of the absolute values of the deviations or by some other criterion. What is so special about the least squares method? It turns out that the attractive features of the least squares estimator are provided by a fundamental theorem in regression analysis called the *Gauss–Markov theorem*.

First, note that the least squares estimator of $\boldsymbol{\beta}$ for the basic linear regression model as given in (4.3.4) is a *linear estimator*, in that it is a linear function of the sample data for the dependent variable y. Equivalently, an estimator is a linear estimator if it can be expressed as a linear function of the true parameters $\boldsymbol{\beta}$ and the disturbance values $\mathbf{u}$.

The least squares estimator of $\boldsymbol{\beta}$ is also unbiased, where an estimator is called *unbiased* if and only if its expected value is equal to its true value. Combining (4.2.2) and (4.3.4) yields

$$\begin{aligned}\hat{\boldsymbol{\beta}} &= (\mathbf{X}'\mathbf{X})^{-1}\mathbf{X}'(\mathbf{X}\boldsymbol{\beta} + \mathbf{u}) \\ &= \boldsymbol{\beta} + (\mathbf{X}'\mathbf{X})^{-1}\mathbf{X}'\mathbf{u}.\end{aligned} \tag{4.4.1}$$

Taking expected values of both sides yields

$$E(\hat{\boldsymbol{\beta}}) = E[E(\hat{\boldsymbol{\beta}}\,|\,\mathbf{X})] = E[\boldsymbol{\beta} + (\mathbf{X}'\mathbf{X})^{-1}\mathbf{X}'E(\mathbf{u}\,|\,\mathbf{X})] = \boldsymbol{\beta} \tag{4.4.2}$$

because, from A.4.1, $E(\mathbf{u}|\mathbf{X}) = \mathbf{0}$. Thus $\hat{\boldsymbol{\beta}}$ is unbiased.

From (4.4.1) it follows that

$$\hat{\boldsymbol{\beta}} - \boldsymbol{\beta} = (\mathbf{X}'\mathbf{X})^{-1}\mathbf{X}'\mathbf{u}. \tag{4.4.3}$$

Therefore, conditional on **X**, the covariance matrix of the least squares estimator is equal to

$$\begin{aligned}\text{Cov}(\hat{\boldsymbol{\beta}}|\mathbf{X}) &= E[(\hat{\boldsymbol{\beta}} - E\hat{\boldsymbol{\beta}})(\hat{\boldsymbol{\beta}} - E\hat{\boldsymbol{\beta}})'|\mathbf{X}] = E[(\hat{\boldsymbol{\beta}} - \boldsymbol{\beta})(\hat{\boldsymbol{\beta}} - \boldsymbol{\beta})'|\mathbf{X}] \\ &= E[(\mathbf{X}'\mathbf{X})^{-1}\mathbf{X}'\mathbf{u}\mathbf{u}'\mathbf{X}(\mathbf{X}'\mathbf{X})^{-1}\,|\mathbf{X}] \\ &= (\mathbf{X}'\mathbf{X})^{-1}\mathbf{X}'E(\mathbf{u}\mathbf{u}'|\mathbf{X})\mathbf{X}(\mathbf{X}'\mathbf{X})^{-1} \\ &= \sigma^2(\mathbf{X}'\mathbf{X})^{-1}.\end{aligned} \tag{4.4.4}$$

The last equality follows from A.4.2: $E(\mathbf{u}\mathbf{u}'|\mathbf{X}) = \sigma^2\mathbf{I}_n$. Hence the variance of $\hat{\beta}_j$ is the jth term in the principal diagonal of $(\mathbf{X}'\mathbf{X})^{-1}$ multiplied by σ^2, the variance of the u_i, while the covariance of any pair of estimates, $\hat{\beta}_j$ and $\hat{\beta}_l$, is the product of σ^2 and the (j, l)th term in $(\mathbf{X}'\mathbf{X})^{-1}$.

An estimator is considered *more efficient* than another if it has a smaller "spread" about the true parameter. In the scalar case, the *mean squared error* of an estimator $\hat{\theta}$ of θ is defined as

$$M(\hat{\theta}) = E(\hat{\theta} - \theta)^2, \tag{4.4.5}$$

an expression similar to that for the variance but where $E(\hat{\theta})$ is replaced by the true parameter θ. The *bias* of an estimator is defined as

$$B(\hat{\theta}) = E(\hat{\theta}) - \theta. \tag{4.4.6}$$

Then

$$\begin{aligned}M(\hat{\theta}) &= E[(\hat{\theta} - E\hat{\theta}) + (E\hat{\theta} - \theta)]^2 \\ &= E(\hat{\theta} - E\hat{\theta})^2 + (E\hat{\theta} - \theta)^2 + 2(E\hat{\theta} - \theta)E(\hat{\theta} - E\hat{\theta}) \\ &= \text{Var}(\hat{\theta}) + [B(\hat{\theta})]^2.\end{aligned} \tag{4.4.7}$$

In particular, if an estimator is unbiased so that the bias vanishes, its mean squared error is the same as its variance. In this scalar case, the estimator $\hat{\theta}^1$ is said to be *at least as efficient* as $\hat{\theta}^2$ if

$$M(\hat{\theta}^1) \le M(\hat{\theta}^2) \quad \text{i.e.,} \quad M(\hat{\theta}^1) - M(\hat{\theta}^2) \le 0. \tag{4.4.8}$$

This concept of efficiency, based on mean squared error, from (4.4.7), takes account of both variance and bias.

In the vector case, the *mean squared error matrix* is defined, analogously to (4.4.5), as

$$M(\hat{\boldsymbol{\theta}}) = E[(\hat{\boldsymbol{\theta}} - \boldsymbol{\theta})(\hat{\boldsymbol{\theta}} - \boldsymbol{\theta})'] = \text{Cov}(\hat{\boldsymbol{\theta}}) + \mathbf{B}(\hat{\boldsymbol{\theta}})\mathbf{B}(\hat{\boldsymbol{\theta}})', \tag{4.4.9}$$

where $\text{Cov}(\hat{\boldsymbol{\theta}})$ is the *covariance matrix* of the estimator, defined as $E[(\hat{\boldsymbol{\theta}} - E(\hat{\boldsymbol{\theta}}))(\hat{\boldsymbol{\theta}} - E(\hat{\boldsymbol{\theta}})')]$, and $\mathbf{B}(\hat{\boldsymbol{\theta}})$ is the *bias* of the estimator, defined as $E(\hat{\boldsymbol{\theta}}) - \boldsymbol{\theta}$. The vector estimator $\hat{\boldsymbol{\theta}}^1$ is then said to be *at least as efficient as* $\hat{\boldsymbol{\theta}}^2$ if, analogously to (4.4.8),

$$M(\hat{\boldsymbol{\theta}}^1) - M(\hat{\boldsymbol{\theta}}^2) \text{ is negative semidefinite,} \tag{4.4.10}$$

meaning that if $\mathbf{a}$ is any nonzero vector of constants, then

$$\mathbf{a}'\left[M(\hat{\boldsymbol{\theta}}^1) - M(\hat{\boldsymbol{\theta}}^2)\right]\mathbf{a} = \mathbf{a}'M(\hat{\boldsymbol{\theta}}^1)\mathbf{a} - \mathbf{a}'M(\hat{\boldsymbol{\theta}}^2)\mathbf{a} \le 0. \tag{4.4.11}$$

Thus the mean squared error of the linear combination $\mathbf{a}'\hat{\boldsymbol{\theta}}^1$ is no larger than the mean-squared error of $\mathbf{a}'\hat{\boldsymbol{\theta}}^2$. If all the elements of $\mathbf{a}$ are zero except for the jth, which is set equal to unity, (4.4.11) implies that, as in (4.4.8),

$$M(\hat{\theta}_j^1) \le M(\hat{\theta}_j^2) \qquad \text{for } j = 1, \ldots, k. \tag{4.4.12}$$

By way of summary, the least squares estimator (4.3.4) has been shown to be linear and unbiased. It will also be shown that among all possible linear unbiased estimators, the least squares estimator is the most efficient in the sense of (4.4.10). This is commonly referred to as the BLUE property of the least squares estimator, where BLUE is an acronym for *best linear unbiased estimator*. These results on the optimality of the least squares estimator are summarized in the following theorem:

Theorem 4.1: Gauss–Markov Theorem. *In the case of the basic regression model (4.2.2) with assumptions A.4.1 to A.4.3, the least squares estimator is the best among the class of linear unbiased estimators.*

To prove this theorem, note that the least squares estimator is linear and unbiased and that the class of linear estimators of $\boldsymbol{\beta}$ can be defined as those estimators of the form $\tilde{\boldsymbol{\beta}} = \mathbf{C}'\mathbf{y}$ for any $n \times k$ constant matrix $\mathbf{C}$. For $\mathbf{C}'\mathbf{y}$ to be unbiased,

$$\begin{aligned} E\boldsymbol{\beta} &= E\mathbf{C}'\mathbf{y} = E\mathbf{C}'(\mathbf{X}\boldsymbol{\beta} + \mathbf{u}) \\ &= \mathbf{C}'\mathbf{X}\boldsymbol{\beta} = \boldsymbol{\beta}, \end{aligned} \tag{4.4.13}$$

it is necessary that $\mathbf{C}$ satisfy

$$\mathbf{C}'\mathbf{X} = \mathbf{I}. \tag{4.4.14}$$

Since $\tilde{\boldsymbol{\beta}} = \hat{\boldsymbol{\beta}} + [\mathbf{C}' - (\mathbf{X}'\mathbf{X})^{-1}\mathbf{X}']\mathbf{y}$, by imposing (4.4.14) it follows that

$$\begin{aligned} \tilde{\boldsymbol{\beta}} &= \hat{\boldsymbol{\beta}} + [\mathbf{C}' - (\mathbf{X}'\mathbf{X})^{-1}\mathbf{X}']\mathbf{y} \\ &= \hat{\boldsymbol{\beta}} + [\mathbf{C}' - (\mathbf{X}'\mathbf{X})^{-1}\mathbf{X}']\mathbf{u}. \end{aligned} \tag{4.4.15}$$

Hence the covariance matrix of a linear unbiased estimator $\tilde{\boldsymbol{\beta}}$ is of the form

$$\text{Cov}(\tilde{\boldsymbol{\beta}}) = \sigma^2(\mathbf{X}'\mathbf{X})^{-1} + \sigma^2[\mathbf{C}' - (\mathbf{X}'\mathbf{X})^{-1}\mathbf{X}'][\mathbf{C}' - (\mathbf{X}'\mathbf{X})^{-1}\mathbf{X}']'. \tag{4.4.16}$$

The theorem then follows by noting that the second term of (4.4.16) is a nonnegative semidefinite matrix.

To obtain an unbiased estimator of σ^2, note that[3]

$$\begin{aligned} E(\hat{\mathbf{u}}'\hat{\mathbf{u}}) &= E_x[E(\hat{\mathbf{u}}'\hat{\mathbf{u}}|\mathbf{X})] \\ &= E_x[E(\mathbf{u}'\mathbf{M}\mathbf{u}|\mathbf{X})] \\ &= \operatorname{tr} E_x[\mathbf{M}E(\mathbf{u}\mathbf{u}'|\mathbf{X})] \\ &= (n-k)\sigma^2. \end{aligned} \quad (4.4.17)$$

Therefore, the unbiased estimator of the variance σ^2, $\hat{s}^2$, is provided by[4]

$$\hat{s}^2 = \frac{1}{n-k}\sum_{i=1}^{n}\hat{u}_i^2. \quad (4.4.18)$$

An intuitive reason for dividing the sum of the squares of the estimated residuals by $n - k$ rather than n is that from the normal equations (4.3.3),

$$\mathbf{X}'(\mathbf{y} - \mathbf{X}\hat{\boldsymbol{\beta}}) = \mathbf{X}'\hat{\mathbf{u}} = \mathbf{0}. \quad (4.4.19)$$

Thus, although there are n estimated residuals, $\hat{u}_i$, they have to satisfy the k equations (4.4.19), which determine the k-dimensional vector $\hat{\boldsymbol{\beta}}$. Therefore, only $(n - k)$ out of n values of the residuals can take arbitrary values, where $(n - k)$ is referred to as the *degrees of freedom.*

Substituting $\hat{s}^2$ for σ^2 in (4.4.4), estimates of the variances and covariances of $\hat{\beta}_j$ and $\hat{\beta}_\ell$ can be obtained. The *standard errors* of the regression coefficients are the positive square roots of the variances of these estimated parameters, so the jth estimated standard error is $\hat{s} \cdot \sqrt{[(\mathbf{X}'\mathbf{X})^{-1}]_{jj}}$.

The least squares estimators, under certain conditions, also satisfy the desirable property of consistency. An estimator $\hat{\boldsymbol{\theta}}$ is a *consistent estimator* of $\boldsymbol{\theta}$ if and only if, letting $|\hat{\boldsymbol{\theta}} - \boldsymbol{\theta}|$ be any scalar measure of the distance between the estimator and the true value, for any $\boldsymbol{\varepsilon} > 0$,

$$\lim_{n\to\infty} P(|\hat{\boldsymbol{\theta}} - \boldsymbol{\theta}| < \varepsilon) = 1. \quad (4.4.20)$$

Here $P(\cdot)$ is the probability that this distance is less than an arbitrarily prescribed distance $\boldsymbol{\varepsilon}$. The estimator is consistent if and only if as the sample size increases without limit, this probability approaches unity.[5] Thus, with a sufficiently large sample, a consistent estimator will have as high a probability as required of being "close" (within an ε distance) to the true population value. Sometimes property (4.4.20) is written in the more compact form, using the notion of a *probability limit*, as

[3]This proof involves tr, the *trace* of a matrix, the sum of its diagonal elements, which satisfies the conditions that the trace of a scalar is the same as the scalar itself and that tr(**ABC**) = tr(**BCA**) for any three matrices **A, B, C** such that the product exists.

[4]Note that (4.4.18) is not a linear estimator because it is a quadratic function of **y**.

[5]Recall that the sequence a_n *converges* to a if and only if

$$\lim_{n\to\infty}|a_n - a| = 0,$$

that is, if and only if given any prespecified distance there is a number N such that for all $n > N$ the absolute difference $|a_n - a|$ is less than the prespecified distance. The concept of consistency is similar to this concept of convergence for a sequence, although it is phrased in terms of the probability statement of (4.4.20) because of the presence of the random variable $\hat{\boldsymbol{\theta}}$.

$$\text{plim } \hat{\boldsymbol{\theta}} = \boldsymbol{\theta}, \tag{4.4.21}$$

stating that the random vector $\hat{\boldsymbol{\theta}}$ converges in probability to the true vector $\boldsymbol{\theta}$. The concept of a probability limit is an extremely useful one. It satisfies the properties

$$\text{plim}\left(\hat{\boldsymbol{\theta}}^1 + \hat{\boldsymbol{\theta}}^2\right) = \text{plim}\,\hat{\boldsymbol{\theta}}^1 + \text{plim}\,\hat{\boldsymbol{\theta}}^2, \tag{4.4.22}$$

$$\text{plim}\left(\hat{\boldsymbol{\theta}}^1\hat{\boldsymbol{\theta}}^2\right) = \text{plim}\,\hat{\boldsymbol{\theta}}^1 \cdot \text{plim}\,\hat{\boldsymbol{\theta}}^2, \tag{4.4.23}$$

$$\text{plim}\left(\hat{\boldsymbol{\theta}}^1\right)^{-1} = \left(\text{plim}\,\hat{\boldsymbol{\theta}}^1\right)^{-1} \quad \text{if } \hat{\boldsymbol{\theta}}^1 \text{ is a square and nonsingular matrix.} \tag{4.4.24}$$

These properties are all special cases of a general *invariance property (Slutsky theorem)*, which states that, if plim $\hat{\boldsymbol{\theta}} = \boldsymbol{\theta}$, then if $f(\hat{\boldsymbol{\theta}})$ is any continuous function of the estimator,

$$\text{plim } f(\hat{\boldsymbol{\theta}}) = f(\boldsymbol{\theta}). \tag{4.4.25}$$

Thus any continuous function of a consistent estimator is itself a consistent estimator of the same function of the original parameters.

If an estimator "collapses" to the true population value $\boldsymbol{\theta}$ in that it is both *asymptotically unbiased*, its mean going to the true population value in the sense that $\lim_{n\to\infty}\mathbf{B}(\hat{\boldsymbol{\theta}}) = \mathbf{0}$, and also *asymptotically certain*, the entire distribution of the estimator falling at $\boldsymbol{\theta}$, so that

$$\lim_{n\to\infty} \mathbf{B}(\hat{\boldsymbol{\theta}}) = \mathbf{0} \quad \text{and} \quad \lim_{n\to\infty} \text{Cov}(\hat{\boldsymbol{\theta}}) = \mathbf{0}, \tag{4.4.26}$$

the estimator is consistent. These conditions are, however, sufficient but not necessary for consistency.[6]

Theorem 4.2: Least Squares Consistency Theorem. *The conditions guaranteeing consistency of the least squares estimator $\hat{\boldsymbol{\beta}}$ are A.4.1 to A.4.3 together with the additional assumption.*

A.4.4. The matrix $(1/n)\mathbf{X}'\mathbf{X}$ *converges to a nonsingular matrix* $\mathbf{Q}$ *as* $n \to \infty$.[7]

The proof is straightforward. First note that from (4.4.2) the least squares estimators are unbiased and hence asymptotically unbiased in that

$$\lim_{n\to\infty} E(\hat{\boldsymbol{\beta}}) = \boldsymbol{\beta}, \tag*{*(4.4.27)}$$

Second, the least squares estimator $\hat{\boldsymbol{\beta}}$ has a covariance matrix,

$$\text{Cov}(\hat{\boldsymbol{\beta}}) = \sigma^2(\mathbf{X}'\mathbf{X})^{-1} = \frac{\sigma^2}{n}\left(\frac{1}{n}\mathbf{X}'\mathbf{X}\right)^{-1}, \tag*{*(4.4.28)}$$

which has been written in such a way that the limit can be taken. Taking the limit as $n \to \infty$ yields

[6]For an example of an estimator that does not satisfy these properties but is nevertheless consistent, see Problem 4-R. However, (4.4.26) is often easier to check than a direct proof of consistency.

[7]In general, when taking limits as $n \to \infty$, it is necessary to include the $1/n$ factors. In the matrix $\mathbf{X}'\mathbf{X}$ each element is the sum of n terms. Thus to make each such element meaningful as $n \to \infty$, it is necessary to divide it by n, as indicated.

$$\lim_{n\to\infty} \text{Cov}(\hat{\beta}) = \lim \frac{\sigma^2}{n}\left(\frac{1}{n}\mathbf{X}'\mathbf{X}\right)^{-1} = \lim \frac{\sigma^2}{n}\mathbf{Q}^{-1} = \mathbf{0}, \tag{4.4.29}$$

where $\mathbf{Q}^{-1}$ is the matrix to which $((1/n)\mathbf{X}'\mathbf{X})^{-1}$ converges. It has therefore been shown that the least squares estimator is both asymptotically unbiased and asymptotically certain. It then follows from (4.4.26) that the least squares estimator is a consistent estimator of $\boldsymbol{\beta}$,

$$\text{plim}\,\hat{\boldsymbol{\beta}} = \boldsymbol{\beta}. \tag{4.4.30}$$

4.5 MAXIMUM LIKELIHOOD AND THE METHOD OF MOMENTS ESTIMATORS

Let $\mathbf{y}' = (y_1, \ldots, y_n)$ be a random sample from a population with a known probability density function characterized by unknown parameters $\boldsymbol{\theta}$. The probability density of observing $\mathbf{y}$ is thus given by $f(\mathbf{y} \mid \boldsymbol{\theta})$. Alternatively, $f(\mathbf{y} \mid \boldsymbol{\theta})$ can be viewed as a function of $\boldsymbol{\theta}$ given $\mathbf{y}$, which is known as the *likelihood function*. The *maximum likelihood estimators* (MLEs) of $\boldsymbol{\theta}$ are those values of $\boldsymbol{\theta}$, say $\hat{\boldsymbol{\theta}}$, that maximize the likelihood function, $f(\mathbf{y} \mid \hat{\boldsymbol{\theta}}) \geq f(\mathbf{y} \mid \tilde{\boldsymbol{\theta}})$, where $\tilde{\boldsymbol{\theta}}$ is any other estimator of $\boldsymbol{\theta}$. The initutive idea of the MLE is that the parameter values which imply a large probability density of the sample actually drawn are preferred to those parameter values which imply that the sample is less probable to be observed.

The MLE has many desirable properties. It can be shown that the MLE is consistent and has the smallest covariance matrix among all asymptotically unbiased estimators (both linear and nonlinear estimators). The covariance matrix of the MLE in the limit is equal to the negative of the inverse of the *information matrix*,

$$-E\left[\frac{\partial^2 \log f(\mathbf{y};\boldsymbol{\theta})}{\partial\boldsymbol{\theta}\partial\boldsymbol{\theta}'}\right]^{-1}, \tag{4.5.1}$$

also known as the *Cramer–Rao lower bound* for an unbiased estimator.

For the regression model (4.2.2), the sample consists of $\mathbf{y}$ and $\mathbf{X}$. To obtain the conditional distribution of $\mathbf{y}$ given $\mathbf{X}$, it is necessary to know the distribution of $\mathbf{u}$. Generally, normality is assumed:

A.4.5. $\mathbf{u}$ is normally distributed with mean $\mathbf{0}$ and covariance matrix $\sigma^2\mathbf{I}_n$, written $\mathbf{u} \sim N(\mathbf{0}, \sigma^2\mathbf{I}_n)$.

Thus $\mathbf{u}$ is assumed to have a probability density of the form

$$(2\pi)^{-n/2}\left(\sigma^2\right)^{-n/2} \exp\left(-\frac{1}{2\sigma^2}\sum_{i=1}^{n} u_i^2\right), \tag{4.5.2}$$

which is the product of the n univariate normal density function for each of the u_i's.

The relationship between the probability distribution of $\mathbf{y}$ and that of $\mathbf{u}$ can be established with the help of the following theorem:[8]

[8]For a proof, see Apostol (1974).

Theorem 4.3: Change of Variable Theorem. If the variable in $\mathbf{u} = (u_1, \ldots, u_n)'$ *have a joint probability density* $g(\mathbf{u})$ *and if* $\mathbf{v} = (v_1, \ldots, v_n)' = \mathbf{h}(\mathbf{u})$ *are functions of* **u** *such that there is a one-to-one correspondence between* **u** *and* **v**, *the probability density of* **v** *is*

$$f(\mathbf{v}) = \text{mod}|\mathbf{J}|\, g(\mathbf{h}^{-1}(\mathbf{v})), \tag{4.5.3}$$

where "mod" means modulus or absolute value and

$$|\mathbf{J}| = \left|\frac{\partial u_i}{\partial v_j}\right|$$

is the Jacobian, that is, the determinant of the matrix of partial derivatives of the components of **u** *with respect to the components of* **v**.

The importance of Theorem 4.3 lies in the fact that, under general conditions, it enables one to determine the probability distribution of the observed variables from the assumed probability distribution of the unobserved random variables. Thus in the context of the basic linear regression model (4.2.2) with assumptions A.4.1 to A.4.3, assumption A.4.5 with regard to the probability distribution of u_i gives the probability distribution of y_i given $\mathbf{x}_i$. Since from (4.2.2) there is a one-to-one correspondence between **y** and **u**, the joint density of **y** can be obtained from the joint density of **u** as

$$f(\mathbf{y}) = g(\mathbf{y} - \mathbf{X}\boldsymbol{\beta})\ \text{mod}|\mathbf{J}|, \tag{4.5.4}$$

where mod | **J** | is the absolute value of the determinant of the Jacobian

$$\begin{vmatrix} \frac{\partial u_1}{\partial y_1} & \frac{\partial u_1}{\partial y_2} & \cdots & \frac{\partial u_1}{\partial y_n} \\ \frac{\partial u_2}{\partial y_1} & \frac{\partial u_2}{\partial y_2} & \cdots & \frac{\partial u_2}{\partial y_n} \\ \vdots & \vdots & \cdots & \vdots \\ \frac{\partial u_n}{\partial y_1} & \frac{\partial u_n}{\partial y_2} & \cdots & \frac{\partial u_n}{\partial y_n} \end{vmatrix} = \begin{vmatrix} 1 & 0 & \cdots & 0 \\ 0 & 1 & \cdots & 0 \\ \vdots & & \ddots & \\ 0 & \cdots & \cdots & 1 \end{vmatrix} = 1.$$

From A.4.5, the fact that the u_i's are normal and uncorrelated means that they are also independent. Consequently, the likelihood function for the observed data y_i given $\mathbf{x}_i$ is

$$\begin{aligned} L = f(y_1, \ldots, y_n) &= \prod_{i=1}^{n} f(y_i) \\ &= \left(2\pi\sigma^2\right)^{-n/2} \exp\left[-\frac{1}{2\sigma^2}\sum_{i=1}^{n}(y_i - \mathbf{x}_i'\boldsymbol{\beta})^2\right]. \end{aligned} \tag{4.5.5}$$

Given the data, the likelihood function (4.5.5) may be regarded as a function of the $k + 1$ parameters $\boldsymbol{\theta}' = (\boldsymbol{\beta}', \sigma^2)$ rather than **y**. When so regarded, it is called the *likelihood function* of $\boldsymbol{\theta}$ for given **y**. Since the values of the parameters that maximize L are the same as those that maximize its logarithmic transformation ($\log L$) and since the logarithmic transformation has the advantage of transforming the function from product form to additive form, the log of the likelihood function is typically maximized instead of maximizing the likelihood function directly to find the MLE. Therefore, the maximum likelihood estimator of the basic linear regression model under normality can be obtained by maximizing

$$\log L = -\frac{n}{2}\log 2\pi - \frac{n}{2}\log\sigma^2 - \frac{1}{2\sigma^2}(\mathbf{y} - \mathbf{X}\boldsymbol{\beta})'(\mathbf{y} - \mathbf{X}\boldsymbol{\beta}), \tag{4.5.6}$$

with respect to the unknown parameters $\boldsymbol{\beta}$ and σ^2.

Differentiating (4.5.6) with respect to $\boldsymbol{\beta}$ and σ^2 yields

$$\frac{\partial \log L}{\partial \boldsymbol{\beta}} = -\frac{1}{\sigma^2}\mathbf{X}'(\mathbf{y} - \mathbf{X}\boldsymbol{\beta}), \tag{4.5.7}$$

$$\frac{\partial \log L}{\partial \sigma^2} = -\frac{n}{2\sigma^2} + \frac{1}{2\sigma^4}(\mathbf{y} - \mathbf{X}\boldsymbol{\beta})'(\mathbf{y} - \mathbf{X}\boldsymbol{\beta}). \tag{4.5.8}$$

Equating (4.5.7) to zero yields the MLE of $\boldsymbol{\beta}$, which turns out to be the same as the least squares estimator (4.3.4). Substituting the MLE of $\boldsymbol{\beta}$ into (4.5.8) and equating the resulting equation to zero yields the MLE of σ^2 as

$$\hat{\sigma}^2 = \frac{1}{n}(\hat{\mathbf{u}}'\hat{\mathbf{u}}) = \frac{1}{n}\mathbf{y}'\mathbf{M}\mathbf{y}. \tag{4.5.9}$$

The estimator $\hat{\sigma}^2$ is a biased estimator. However, it is consistent and asymptotically unbiased as $n \to \infty$. Multiplying by $n/(n-k)$ yields the unbiased estimator $\hat{s}^2$ of (4.4.18), which is used in empirical work. With this adjustment, the maximum likelihood estimates under normality are the same as the least squares estimates.

Another popular method of estimation is the *method of moments* (MM), discussed in Hansen (1982). It relies on the fact that the probability distributions of random variables are typically characterized by their moments. The idea of MM estimators is to approximate population moments by their sample analogs and to solve for the unknown parameters accordingly. Thus for the model (4.2.2) under A.4.1 and A.4.2, it is known that

$$E\mathbf{X}'\mathbf{u} = E_x[\mathbf{X}'E\mathbf{u}|\mathbf{X}] = E\mathbf{X}'(\mathbf{y} - \mathbf{X}\boldsymbol{\beta}) = \mathbf{0}. \tag{4.5.10}$$

Conditioning on $\boldsymbol{\beta} = \hat{\boldsymbol{\beta}}$, the $\mathbf{u}$ can be replaced by the sample estimator $\hat{\mathbf{u}} = \mathbf{y} - \mathbf{X}\hat{\boldsymbol{\beta}}$. Then substituting $\hat{\mathbf{u}}$ for $\mathbf{u}$ and imposing the condition that the covariance between $\hat{\mathbf{u}}$ and $\mathbf{X}$ is zero, $\boldsymbol{\beta}$ can be solved from the following equation:

$$\frac{1}{n}\sum_{i=1}^{n}\mathbf{x}_i\left(y_i - \mathbf{x}_i'\hat{\boldsymbol{\beta}}\right) = \mathbf{0}. \tag{4.5.11}$$

Equation (4.5.11) is identical to the normal equations (4.3.3) for the least squares estimator, so the MM estimator for the basic linear regression model (4.2.2) turns out to be the same as the least squares estimator (and also the same as the maximum likelihood estimator assuming normality).

There are k moment conditions (4.5.10) and k unknowns for the basic linear regression model. Therefore, a unique solution for $\boldsymbol{\beta}$ is obtained by equating the sample moments with the values of the population moments in (4.5.11). In circumstances where there are more moment conditions than the number of unknowns, the method of moments estimator is obtained by minimizing some distance measure of the sample moments with respect to the unknown parameters. Thus suppose that given the parameter vector $\boldsymbol{\theta}$, there are p moment conditions $\mathbf{m}(\boldsymbol{\theta}) = \mathbf{0}$. Then a method of moments estimator of $\boldsymbol{\theta}$ could be the $\hat{\boldsymbol{\theta}}$ that minimizes $\hat{\mathbf{m}}(\boldsymbol{\theta})'\,\hat{\mathbf{m}}(\boldsymbol{\theta})$, where $\hat{\mathbf{m}}(\boldsymbol{\theta})$ denotes the sample moments.

4.6 LINEAR RESTRICTIONS ON THE COEFFICIENTS

Economic theory often suggests that coefficients of a relation should satisfy certain restrictions. For instance, consider a Cobb–Douglas production function relation between output q_i and inputs K_i, L_i, and Z_i, representing capital, labor, and materials, respectively,

$$q_i = AK_i^{\beta_1} L_i^{\beta_2} Z_i^{\beta_3} e^{u_i}, \tag{4.6.1}$$

where i can be an index of time, using time-series data, or of nations or plants, using cross-section data. Taking the logarithmic transformation of (4.6.1) yields the linear regression model (4.2.2) with $k = 4$, $y_i = \log q_i$, $x_{i4} = 1$, $x_{i1} = \log K_i$, $x_{i2} = \log L_i$, $x_{i3} = \log Z_i$, and $\beta_4 = \log A$. If it is known, a priori, that constant returns to scale holds, the coefficients of (4.6.1) or (4.2.2) should satisfy the following linear restriction on the parameters β_1, β_2, and β_3:

$$\beta_1 + \beta_2 + \beta_3 = 1. \tag{4.6.2}$$

Alternatively, consider (4.2.2) as a demand relation with explanatory variables x_{i1}, x_{i2}, and x_{i3} representing the variables nominal price, nominal income, and price deflator. The absence of the money illusion on the part of consumers implies that

$$\beta_1 + \beta_2 + \beta_3 = 0. \tag{4.6.3}$$

Furthermore, if it is also known that there is no autonomous demand, the value of the intercept, β_4, is zero; that is,

$$\beta_4 = 0. \tag{4.6.4}$$

There are essentially two ways to deal with such prior restrictions. One method is to substitute the linear restrictions directly into the regression model (4.2.2) prior to the application of the least squares method. Thus model (4.2.2) subject to (4.6.2) can be transformed into the form

$$y_i^* = \beta_1 x_{i1}^* + \beta_2 x_{i2}^* + \beta_4 + u_i, \tag{4.6.5}$$

where $y_i^* = y_i - x_{i3}$, $x_{i1}^* = x_{i1} - x_{i3}$, and $x_{i2}^* = x_{i2} - x_{i3}$. Similarly, (4.2.2) subject to (4.6.3) and (4.6.4) can be transformed into the form

$$y_i = \beta_1 x_{i1}^* + \beta_2 x_{i2}^* + u_i. \tag{4.6.6}$$

The least squares method can then be applied to the transformed model (4.6.5) or (4.6.6).

The other method is to apply the *constrained least squares method*. Write the general linear restrictions on the parameters in the form

$$\mathbf{R\beta} = \mathbf{r}, \tag{4.6.7}$$

where $\mathbf{R}$ and $\mathbf{r}$ are a $q \times k$ matrix and a $q \times 1$ vector of known constants, respectively; $\boldsymbol{\beta}$ is the $k \times 1$ vector of regression coefficients; and q is the number of linearly independent a priori restrictions. For example, to incorporate restriction (4.6.2) into (4.2.2),

$$\mathbf{R} = [1 \quad 1 \quad 1 \quad 0], \qquad r = 1. \tag{4.6.8}$$

Similarly, to incorporate restrictions (4.6.4) and (4.6.3),

$$\mathbf{R} = \begin{bmatrix} 1 & 0 & 0 & 0 \\ 0 & 1 & 1 & 1 \end{bmatrix}, \qquad \mathbf{r} = \begin{bmatrix} 0 \\ 0 \end{bmatrix}. \tag{4.6.9}$$

To derive the constrained least squares estimator, note that, the constrained estimated coefficient vector, $\hat{\boldsymbol{\beta}}_c$, must be chosen so as to minimize $(\mathbf{y} - \mathbf{X\beta})'(\mathbf{y} - \mathbf{X\beta})$ subject to (4.6.7). Define the Lagrangian function[9]

$$L = (\mathbf{y} - \mathbf{X\beta})'(\mathbf{y} - \mathbf{X\beta}) - \boldsymbol{\lambda}'(\mathbf{R\beta} - \mathbf{r}). \tag{4.6.10}$$

[9] For a discussion of constrained optimization, including the method of Lagrange multipliers, see Intriligator (1971).

where $\boldsymbol{\lambda}$ is a $q \times 1$ vector of Lagrange multipliers. Differentiating (4.6.10) with respect to $\boldsymbol{\beta}$ and $\boldsymbol{\lambda}$, and setting the resulting equations to zero to solve for the constrained estimator, $\hat{\boldsymbol{\beta}}_c$ and $\hat{\boldsymbol{\lambda}}$, yields

$$\frac{\partial L}{\partial \boldsymbol{\beta}} = -2\mathbf{X}'\mathbf{y} + 2(\mathbf{X}'\mathbf{X})\hat{\boldsymbol{\beta}}_c - \mathbf{R}'\hat{\boldsymbol{\lambda}} = \mathbf{0}, \tag{4.6.11}$$

$$\frac{\partial L}{\partial \boldsymbol{\lambda}} = \mathbf{R}\boldsymbol{\beta}_c - \mathbf{r} = \mathbf{0}. \tag{4.6.12}$$

Premultiplying (4.6.11) by $\mathbf{R}(\mathbf{X}'\mathbf{X})^{-1}$ and solving for $\hat{\boldsymbol{\lambda}}$ yields

$$\hat{\boldsymbol{\lambda}} = 2[\mathbf{R}(\mathbf{X}'\mathbf{X})^{-1}\mathbf{R}']^{-1}[\mathbf{R}\hat{\boldsymbol{\beta}}_c - \mathbf{R}\hat{\boldsymbol{\beta}}], \tag{4.6.13}$$

where $\hat{\boldsymbol{\beta}}$ is the unconstrained least squares estimator (4.3.4). Substituting (4.6.13) and (4.6.12) into (4.6.11) yields the *constrained least squares estimator*

$$\hat{\boldsymbol{\beta}}_c = \hat{\boldsymbol{\beta}} + (\mathbf{X}'\mathbf{X})^{-1}\mathbf{R}'\left[\mathbf{R}(\mathbf{X}'\mathbf{X})^{-1}\mathbf{R}'\right]^{-1}(\mathbf{r} - \mathbf{R}\hat{\boldsymbol{\beta}}). \tag{4.6.14}$$

Substituting $\hat{\boldsymbol{\beta}} = \boldsymbol{\beta} + (\mathbf{X}'\mathbf{X})^{-1}\mathbf{X}'\mathbf{u}$ from (4.4.1) into (4.6.14) yields

$$\begin{aligned}\hat{\boldsymbol{\beta}}_c = \boldsymbol{\beta} &+ (\mathbf{X}'\mathbf{X})^{-1}\mathbf{R}'\left[\mathbf{R}(\mathbf{X}'\mathbf{X})^{-1}\mathbf{R}'\right]^{-1}(\mathbf{r} - \mathbf{R}\boldsymbol{\beta}) \\ &+ \left\{\mathbf{I} - (\mathbf{X}'\mathbf{X})^{-1}\mathbf{R}'\left[\mathbf{R}(\mathbf{X}'\mathbf{X})^{-1}\mathbf{R}'\right]^{-1}\mathbf{R}\right\}(\mathbf{X}'\mathbf{X})^{-1}\mathbf{X}'\mathbf{u}.\end{aligned} \tag{4.6.15}$$

It follows that the expectation of the constrained estimator is

$$E(\hat{\boldsymbol{\beta}}_c) = \boldsymbol{\beta} + (\mathbf{X}'\mathbf{X})^{-1}\mathbf{R}'\left[\mathbf{R}(\mathbf{X}'\mathbf{X})^{-1}\mathbf{R}'\right]^{-1}(\mathbf{r} - \mathbf{R}\boldsymbol{\beta}) \tag{4.6.16}$$

and its covariance matrix is

$$\begin{aligned}\mathrm{Cov}(\hat{\boldsymbol{\beta}}_c) &= E\left[\hat{\boldsymbol{\beta}}_c - E(\hat{\boldsymbol{\beta}}_c)\right]\left[\hat{\boldsymbol{\beta}}_c - E(\hat{\boldsymbol{\beta}}_c)\right]' \\ &= \sigma^2\left\{(\mathbf{X}'\mathbf{X})^{-1} - (\mathbf{X}'\mathbf{X})^{-1}\mathbf{R}'\left[\mathbf{R}(\mathbf{X}'\mathbf{X})^{-1}\mathbf{R}'\right]^{-1}\mathbf{R}(\mathbf{X}'\mathbf{X})^{-1}\right\}.\end{aligned} \tag{4.6.17}$$

From (4.6.16) the constrained least squares estimator (4.6.14) is unbiased if the prior restriction (4.6.7) holds for the true $\boldsymbol{\beta}$. The difference between the covariance matrix of the least squares estimator (4.4.4) and that for the constrained least squares estimator (4.6.17) is a nonnegative semidefinite matrix. Therefore, if the prior restriction (4.6.7) is true, (4.6.14) is more efficient than the least squares estimator (4.3.4). If the constraint (4.6.7) is not valid, however, then from (4.6.16), (4.6.14) is a biased estimator. However, it is not necessarily the case that the mean squared error of the constrained estimator is larger than that of the unconstrained estimator. There are cases when imposing invalid restrictions may yield smaller mean squared error than the unconstrained estimator, as discussed in Wallace (1972) and Toro-Vizcarrondo and Wallace (1968).

4.7 STATISTICAL INFERENCE

4.7.1 The Probability Distribution for the Least Squares Estimator

In many applications of the basic linear regression model there are certain hypotheses about individual parameters or linear combinations of parameters that may be tested. To derive significance tests and confidence intervals for both the k coefficient parameters $\boldsymbol{\beta}$ and the variance of the stochastic disturbance term σ^2, the probability distributions of their least squares estimators must be either known or estimated.

From (4.4.1) the difference $(\hat{\boldsymbol{\beta}} - \boldsymbol{\beta})$ is a linear combination of the u_i given as $(\mathbf{X}'\mathbf{X})^{-1}\mathbf{X}'\mathbf{u}$. Therefore, under the normality assumption A.4.5, conditional on $\mathbf{X}$, the least squares estimator, $\hat{\boldsymbol{\beta}}$, is distributed as a multivariate normal distribution with mean $\boldsymbol{\beta}$ and variance–covariance matrix $\sigma^2(\mathbf{X}'\mathbf{X})^{-1}$,

$$\hat{\boldsymbol{\beta}} \sim N\left(\boldsymbol{\beta}, \sigma^2(\mathbf{X}'\mathbf{X})^{-1}\right). \tag{4.7.1}$$

Since σ^2 is typically unknown, it is typically replaced by the unbiased estimator $\hat{s}^2$ in (4.4.18). From (4.3.15) the residual sum of squares $\hat{\mathbf{u}}'\hat{\mathbf{u}}$ is a quadratic form in $\mathbf{u}$, where the weighting matrix $\mathbf{M}$ is symmetric and idempotent. Because the trace of $\mathbf{M}$ is equal to

$$\begin{aligned} \operatorname{tr}\mathbf{M} &= \operatorname{tr}\left(\mathbf{I}_n - \mathbf{X}(\mathbf{X}'\mathbf{X})^{-1}\mathbf{X}'\right) \\ &= \operatorname{tr}\mathbf{I}_n - \operatorname{tr}\mathbf{X}(\mathbf{X}'\mathbf{X})^{-1}\mathbf{X}' \\ &= n - \operatorname{tr}(\mathbf{X}'\mathbf{X})^{-1}(\mathbf{X}'\mathbf{X}) = n - k, \end{aligned} \tag{4.7.2}$$

it follows that the rank of $\mathbf{M}$ is $(n-k)$. Furthermore, $\mathbf{M}$ is symmetric, and it is possible to find an orthogonal matrix $\mathbf{C}$ such that $\mathbf{C}'\mathbf{M}\mathbf{C} = \mathbf{D}_{n-k}$, where $\mathbf{D}_{n-k}$ is a diagonal matrix with $n-k$ units and k zeros on the main diagonal. Transforming the $\mathbf{u}$ vector into a vector $\mathbf{v}$ by $\mathbf{C}'$ yields

$$\mathbf{v} = \mathbf{C}'\mathbf{u}, \quad \mathbf{u} = \mathbf{C}\mathbf{v}, \quad \text{and} \quad E\mathbf{v}\mathbf{v}' = \sigma^2\mathbf{I}_n. \tag{4.7.3}$$

Substituting (4.7.3) into (4.3.15) gives

$$\begin{aligned} \hat{\mathbf{u}}'\hat{\mathbf{u}} &= \mathbf{u}'\mathbf{M}\mathbf{u} \\ &= \mathbf{v}'\mathbf{C}'\mathbf{M}\mathbf{C}\mathbf{v} = \mathbf{v}'\mathbf{D}_{n-k}\mathbf{v} \\ &= v_1^2 + v_2^2 + \cdots + v_{n-k}^2. \end{aligned} \tag{4.7.4}$$

From (4.7.3) it follows that if the u_i are independently and normally distributed with mean zero and constant variance σ^2, so are the v_i. Equation (4.7.4) expresses the residual sum of squares as the sum of squares of $(n-k)$ independent normal variates, v_i. Hence $(n-k)(\hat{s}^2/\sigma^2)$ has a chi-square distribution with $n-k$ degrees of freedom,

$$\frac{(n-k)\hat{s}^2}{\sigma^2} \sim \chi^2(n-k). \tag{4.7.5}$$

Furthermore, (4.7.5) is distributed independently of (4.7.1). To show this, all that is needed is to show that $\hat{\mathbf{u}}$ is distributed independently of $\hat{\boldsymbol{\beta}}$. Since $\hat{\mathbf{u}}$ and $\hat{\boldsymbol{\beta}}$ are each linear functions of normal variates, independence follows from

$$\begin{aligned} E[\hat{\mathbf{u}}(\hat{\boldsymbol{\beta}} - \boldsymbol{\beta})'] &= E\left\{\left[\mathbf{I}_n - \mathbf{X}(\mathbf{X}'\mathbf{X})^{-1}\mathbf{X}'\right]\mathbf{u}\mathbf{u}'\mathbf{X}(\mathbf{X}'\mathbf{X})^{-1}\right\} \\ &= \sigma^2\mathbf{X}(\mathbf{X}'\mathbf{X})^{-1} - \sigma^2\mathbf{X}(\mathbf{X}'\mathbf{X})^{-1} = \mathbf{0}. \end{aligned} \tag{4.7.6}$$

As discussed in Section 4.4, when $n \to \infty$, $\operatorname{Cov}(\hat{\boldsymbol{\beta}}) \to \mathbf{0}$ under assumption A.4.4. That is, $\hat{\boldsymbol{\beta}}$ will have a degenerate distribution as $n \to \infty$. Therefore, in discussing the probability distribution of an estimator, a relevant concept is to multiply a scale factor to $(\hat{\boldsymbol{\beta}} - \boldsymbol{\beta})$ so that the resulting distribution is no longer degenerate. Given assumption A.4.4, the relevant scale factor would be $\sqrt{n}$ because $\operatorname{Var}(\sqrt{n}\hat{\boldsymbol{\beta}}) = \sigma^2(1/n\mathbf{X}'\mathbf{X})^{-1} \neq 0$ as $n \to \infty$. So another way of stating (4.7.1) is that $\sqrt{n}(\hat{\boldsymbol{\beta}} - \boldsymbol{\beta})$ has a multivariate normal distribution with mean $\mathbf{0}$ and covariance matrix $\sigma^2(1/n\mathbf{X}'\mathbf{X})^{-1}$.

When the $\mathbf{u}$ are not normally distributed, the exact distribution of $\hat{\boldsymbol{\beta}}$ (or other estimators) may be difficult to derive. In this circumstance, the way to approximate the probability distribution of $\hat{\boldsymbol{\beta}}$ is to consider the limiting property of $\sqrt{n}(\hat{\boldsymbol{\beta}} - \boldsymbol{\beta})$ as $n \to \infty$. Under certain very general conditions, in particular, if A.4.1 to A.4.4 hold, from the central limit-theorem $\sqrt{n}(\hat{\boldsymbol{\beta}} - \boldsymbol{\beta})$ approaches a normal distribution with mean $\mathbf{0}$ and covariance matrix $\sigma^2\mathbf{Q}^{-1}$ as $n \to \infty$. The approximating distribution (in this case, a normal distribution) is called the *limiting* or *asymptotic distribution*[10] of $\sqrt{n}(\hat{\boldsymbol{\beta}} - \boldsymbol{\beta})$. The scale factor, say $\sqrt{n}$, of a consistent estimator, $\hat{\boldsymbol{\beta}}$, is often referred to as the *speed of convergence*. A least squares estimator under A.4.1 to A.4.4 is called $\sqrt{n}$*-consistent* because it converges to $\boldsymbol{\beta}$ at the speed of $\sqrt{n}$.

4.7.2 Significance of Coefficients and Confidence Intervals

A frequent test performed on the estimated coefficients of the basic linear regression model (4.2.2) is whether they equal a particular value, say zero. Considering the jth coefficient β_j, the null hypothesis to be tested is

$$H_0: \beta_j = 0. \tag{4.7.7}$$

Testing this hypothesis tests whether the corresponding explanatory variable, x_j, exerts no statistically significantly linear influence on the dependent variable.

Under assumption A.4.5, the estimated coefficients are normally distributed, as given in (4.7.1). In particular, $\hat{\beta}_j$ is distributed normally with mean β_j and variance $\sigma^2(\mathbf{X}'\mathbf{X})^{-1}_{jj}$, the jth diagonal element of the covariance matrix. Thus the ratio

$$\frac{\hat{\beta}_j - \beta_j}{\sqrt{\sigma^2(\mathbf{X}'\mathbf{X})^{-1}_{jj}}} \tag{4.7.8}$$

is distributed as the standardized normal with zero mean and unit variance. But from (4.7.5), $\hat{s}^2$ is distributed independently as $[\sigma^2/(n-k)]\,\chi^2\,(n-k)$, so the ratio

$$t = \frac{\left(\hat{\beta}_j - \beta_j\right)/\sqrt{\sigma^2(\mathbf{X}'\mathbf{X})^{-1}_{jj}}}{\sqrt{\hat{s}^2/\sigma^2}} \qquad *(4.7.9)$$

is distributed as the t distribution with $n-k$ degrees of freedom. Defining the jth *standard error* as

$$\hat{s}_j = \sqrt{\hat{s}^2(\mathbf{X}'\mathbf{X})^{-1}_{jj}} = \sqrt{\left(\frac{1}{n-k}\sum \hat{u}_i^2\right)(\mathbf{X}'\mathbf{X})^{-1}_{jj}}, \qquad *(4.7.10)$$

it follows that

[10]A function F from the real line into [0, 1] which is monotone nondecreasing, continuous from the right, and has $F(-\infty) = 0$, $F(\infty) = 1$ is a distribution function. Let $\{F_t\}$, $t = 1, 2, \ldots$, be the sequence of distribution functions of the random variables $\{X_t(\cdot)\}$, $t = 1, 2, \ldots$. This sequence of the random variables $\{X_t(\cdot)\}$ is said to converge in distribution to a random variable $X(\cdot)$ with distribution function F if $\lim_{t\to\infty} F_t(X) = F(X)$ as $t \to \infty$ at all continuity points of F. For further details, see Amemiya (1985) or Theil (1971).

$$t = \frac{\hat{\beta}_j - \beta_j}{\hat{s}_j} \sim t(n-k). \qquad (4.7.11)$$

From the probability statement

$$P\left(-t_{\varepsilon/2} < t < t_{\varepsilon/2}\right) = 1 - \varepsilon, \qquad (4.7.12)$$

it then follows that

$$P\left(\hat{\beta}_j - t_{\varepsilon/2}\hat{s}_j < \beta_j < \hat{\beta}_j + t_{\varepsilon/2}\hat{s}_j\right) = 1 - \varepsilon, \qquad (4.7.13)$$

where $t_{\varepsilon/2}$ is the value of the t distribution for a level of significance $\varepsilon/2$ and with $n-k$ degrees of freedom. Thus the $100(1-\varepsilon)\%$ confidence interval for the jth coefficient is given by

$$\hat{\beta}_j \pm t_{\varepsilon/2}\hat{s}_j. \qquad (4.7.14)$$

For example, the 95% confidence interval is given as the estimated coefficient, $\hat{\beta}_j$, plus or minus the t distribution for a 0.025 level of significance times the relevant standard error. The coefficient $\hat{\beta}_j$ is significantly different from zero, rejecting the null hypothesis in (4.7.7), whenever the confidence interval in (4.7.14) does not include the value of zero. Conversely, the coefficient is insignificant [i.e., not significantly different from zero (H_0 accepted)] whenever the confidence interval includes the value of zero. These two cases are shown in Figure 4.4.

Assuming $\hat{\beta}_j$ is positive, if the confidence interval (4.7.14) includes the origin, then solving at this point for the value of t yields the *t ratio* for the jth coefficient:

$$t_j = \frac{\hat{\beta}_j}{\hat{s}_j}. \qquad (4.7.15)$$

Thus the t ratio is the ratio of the estimated regression coefficient to its standard error. This ratio determines the significance of the coefficient: in general the null hypothesis that β_j is zero is accepted if the absolute value $|t_j|$ is less than the value of t corresponding to a particular level of significance, and it is rejected if $|t_j|$ exceeds this value. A low t ratio implies that the coefficient is *not significant* in that the dependent variable is not linearly dependent on the relevant explanatory variable. If, however, the t ratio exceeds the critical value (at a suitably chosen level of significance), then the coefficient is *significant* (i.e., the dependent variable does depend linearly on the relevant explanatory variable). For large degrees of freedom (e.g., $n-k > 30$) the t distribution is approximately the same as the normal distribution, and in this case a general rule of thumb is that if the t ratio exceeds 2, the coefficient is significant. Conversely, a t ratio less than 2 in this case indicates lack of significance (i.e., a coefficient not statistically different from zero).

The t ratio in (4.7.15) used to test the hypothesis that β_j is zero can easily be successively generalized to consider more and more general hypotheses on the coefficients. As will be seen, the resulting tests will be either t or F tests.

First, consider the hypothesis that the jth coefficient is equal to a prescribed value:

$$H_0: \beta_j = \beta_j^0. \qquad (4.7.16)$$

Assuming that $\hat{\beta}_j$ exceeds β_j^0, it is possible to determine the confidence interval in (4.7.14) so as to include β_j^0:

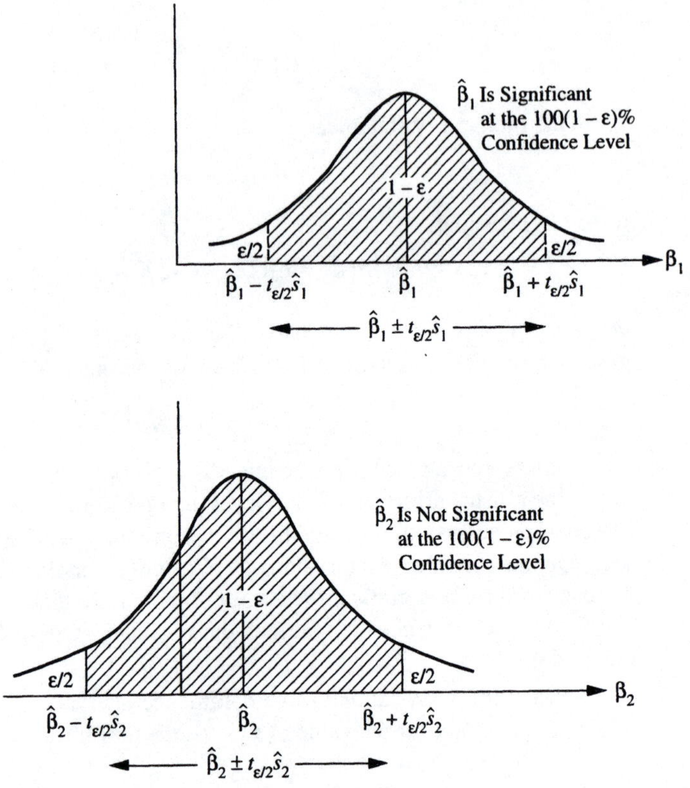

Figure 4.4 Significant and Insignificant Coefficients

$$\hat{\beta}_j - t_{\varepsilon/2}\hat{s}_j = \beta_j^0, \tag{4.7.17}$$

and solving for t, we obtain

$$t = \frac{\hat{\beta}_j - \beta_j^0}{\hat{s}_j}. \tag{4.7.18}$$

In general, if the absolute value of t so defined, $|t|$, exceeds the value of $t_{\varepsilon/2}$ for $n - k$ degrees of freedom, then at the $100(1 - \varepsilon)\%$ level of significance the hypothesis is rejected. If $|t|$ falls below this critical value, the hypothesis is accepted.

4.7.3 General Linear Hypotheses: Wald, Likelihood Ratio, and Lagrange Multiplier Tests

A generalization of the previous tests of the significance of a particular coefficient is to test whether the set of coefficients of a regression model satisfies a set of certain linear restrictions. The null hypothesis for q linear restrictions on the coefficient parameters is

$$H_0: \mathbf{R}\boldsymbol{\beta} = \mathbf{r}, \tag{4.7.19}$$

where, as in (4.6.7), $\mathbf{R}$ and $\mathbf{r}$ are $q \times k$ and $q \times 1$ matrices, respectively, with known elements and $\mathbf{R}$ has rank q. From the normal distribution for $\hat{\boldsymbol{\beta}}$ (4.7.1), it follows that

$$\mathbf{R}\hat{\boldsymbol{\beta}} \sim N\left[\mathbf{R}\boldsymbol{\beta}, \sigma^2\mathbf{R}(\mathbf{X}'\mathbf{X})^{-1}\mathbf{R}'\right]. \tag{4.7.20}$$

Therefore, under the null hypothesis (4.7.19) the test statistic

$$\frac{1}{\sigma^2}(\mathbf{R}\hat{\boldsymbol{\beta}} - \mathbf{r})'\left[\mathbf{R}(\mathbf{X}'\mathbf{X})^{-1}\mathbf{R}'\right]^{-1}(\mathbf{R}\hat{\boldsymbol{\beta}} - \mathbf{r}) \sim \chi^2_{(q)}, \tag{4.7.21}$$

which, as indicated, is distributed as the chi-square with q degrees of freedom. Furthermore, (4.7.21) is distributed independently of (4.7.5). Thus to test (4.7.19) against the alternative hypothesis,

$$H_1 : \mathbf{R}\boldsymbol{\beta} \neq \mathbf{r}, \tag{4.7.22}$$

involves use of the following test statistic

$$\xi_w = \frac{(\mathbf{R}\hat{\boldsymbol{\beta}} - \mathbf{r})'\left[\mathbf{R}(\mathbf{X}'\mathbf{X})^{-1}\mathbf{R}'\right]^{-1}(\mathbf{R}\hat{\boldsymbol{\beta}} - \mathbf{r})}{q\hat{s}^2} \sim F(q, n-k), \tag{4.7.23}$$

which, as indicated, is distributed as the F distribution with q and $(n-k)$ degrees of freedom (in numerator and denominator, respectively). This result reduces to (4.7.9) if $q = 1$, $\mathbf{r} = 0$, and $\mathbf{R}$ is a $1 \times k$ vector with 1 in the jth element and zero elsewhere since $F(1, n-k) = t^2_{(n-k)}$

Note that

$$\begin{aligned}(\mathbf{y} - \mathbf{X}\boldsymbol{\beta})'(\mathbf{y} - \mathbf{X}\boldsymbol{\beta}) &= [(\mathbf{y} - \mathbf{X}\hat{\boldsymbol{\beta}}) + \mathbf{X}(\hat{\boldsymbol{\beta}} - \boldsymbol{\beta})]'[(\mathbf{y} - \mathbf{X}\hat{\boldsymbol{\beta}}) + \mathbf{X}(\hat{\boldsymbol{\beta}} - \boldsymbol{\beta})] \\ &= \hat{\mathbf{u}}'\hat{\mathbf{u}} + (\hat{\boldsymbol{\beta}} - \boldsymbol{\beta})'\mathbf{X}'\mathbf{X}(\hat{\boldsymbol{\beta}} - \boldsymbol{\beta}).\end{aligned} \tag{4.7.24}$$

Substituting $\hat{\boldsymbol{\beta}}_c$ for $\boldsymbol{\beta}$ in (4.7.24) and using the relation (4.6.14), it follows that the numerator of (4.7.23) is equal to the difference of the residual sum of squares between the constrained regression and unconstrained regression of (4.2.2). Thus the F statistic in (4.7.23) can be rewritten as

$$\frac{\hat{\mathbf{u}}_c'\hat{\mathbf{u}}_c - \hat{\mathbf{u}}'\hat{\mathbf{u}}}{q\hat{s}^2} \sim F(q, n-k). \tag{4.7.25}$$

where $\hat{\mathbf{u}}_c'\hat{\mathbf{u}}_c$ is the residual sum of squares in the regression of $\mathbf{y}$ on $\mathbf{X}$ subject to the constraint that $\mathbf{R}\boldsymbol{\beta} = \mathbf{r}$. The numerator of (4.7.25) gives the excess in the sum of squares when the model is estimated subject to the linear restrictions (4.7.19). If this excess is large such that the F test statistic defined in (4.7.25) exceeds a critical value of F given by the probability distribution under the null hypothesis, the hypothesis is rejected.

A special case of (4.7.25) is to test the null hypothesis that all coefficients of the regression other than the intercept (assuming that $x_{ik} \equiv 1$) are zero,

$$H_0 : \beta_1 = \beta_2 = \cdots = \beta_{k-1} = 0. \tag{4.7.26}$$

This hypothesis is equivalent to setting $\mathbf{r}$ equal to a $(k-1) \times 1$ vector of zeros and $\mathbf{R}$ equal to a $(k-1) \times k$ matrix of the form $(\mathbf{I}_{k-1}, \mathbf{0})$. From (4.3.18), the total sum of squares about the mean of $\mathbf{y}$ can be decomposed into the explained sum of squares due to the complete set of explanatory variables and the residual or unexplained sum of squares. Therefore, the test statistic (4.7.23) or (4.7.25) can be written

$$F = \frac{\|\dot{\mathbf{y}}\|^2/(k-1)}{\|\hat{\mathbf{u}}\|^2/(n-k)} = \frac{R^2}{1-R^2} \cdot \frac{n-k}{k-1} \sim F(k-1, n-k). \tag{4.7.27}$$

This F statistic leads directly to the *analysis of variance for the regression*. Table 4.1 summarizes the analysis of variance, where the ratio of the mean squares—in particular, the ratio of explained to unexplained variance—is distributed as the F distribution with $k-1$ and $n-k$ degrees of freedom under (4.7.26). If the ratio defined in (4.7.27) exceeds the critical value of $F(k-1, n-k)$ for a particular level of confidence, the null hypothesis of no dependence on the explanatory variables is rejected. If so, the evidence indicates that not all regression slopes are zero, and the model has some explanatory power. Otherwise, the hypothesis (4.7.26) that all regression slopes are zero is accepted, and the model has no explanatory power if F is too small, in particular, less than the critical value of $F(k-1, n-k)$. An example of the analysis of variance for a regression appears in Section 4.9.

The test statistic (4.7.23) or (4.7.25) is commonly referred to as the *Wald statistic*. It is also possible to derive a test statistic for testing (4.7.19) against (4.7.22) from the likelihood principle. Let $L(\mathbf{y}; \hat{\boldsymbol{\theta}}_c)$ and $L(\mathbf{y}; \hat{\boldsymbol{\theta}})$ be the log-likelihood under the null and alternative hypotheses, respectively, where $\boldsymbol{\theta}' = (\boldsymbol{\beta}', \sigma^2)$ is the vector of all $k+1$ parameters. Under general conditions, the likelihood ratio test statistic,

$$\xi_{\text{LR}} = -2\left(\mathcal{L}\left(\mathbf{y},\hat{\boldsymbol{\theta}}_c\right) - \mathcal{L}\left(\mathbf{y},\hat{\boldsymbol{\theta}}\right)\right), \tag{4.7.28}$$

has a limiting chi-square distribution with q degrees of freedom under the null when $n \to \infty$ (as discussed in Amemiya, 1985, pp. 142–144).

It is interesting to note that in the context of the likelihood ratio test the Lagrangian for the restricted log-likelihood can be written

$$H = L(\mathbf{y};\boldsymbol{\theta}) - \boldsymbol{\lambda}'\mathbf{h}(\boldsymbol{\theta}), \tag{4.7.29}$$

where $\mathbf{h}(\boldsymbol{\theta}) = \mathbf{0}$ is a q-vector-valued differentiable function, representing the q prior restrictions on $\boldsymbol{\theta}$. In the case of (4.7.19), $\mathbf{h}(\boldsymbol{\theta}) = \mathbf{R}\boldsymbol{\beta} - \mathbf{r} = \mathbf{0}$. The $q \times 1$ vector $\boldsymbol{\lambda}$ is that of Lagrange multipliers, measuring the shadow price of each of the constraints. If the shadow price is high, the constraint should be rejected as inconsistent with the data. This leads to the Lagrange multiplier test of Aitcheson and Silvey (1958) and Silvey (1959). The first-order conditions of (4.7.29) are

TABLE 4.1 Analysis of Variance for a Regression

Source	Sum of Squares	Degrees of Freedom	Mean Square
Explained (by regression)	$\lVert\hat{\mathbf{y}}\rVert^2 = R^2\lVert\dot{\mathbf{y}}\rVert^2$	$k-1$	$\lVert\hat{\mathbf{y}}\rVert^2/(k-1)$
Unexplained (residual)	$\lVert\hat{\mathbf{u}}\rVert^2 = (1-R^2)\lVert\dot{\mathbf{y}}\rVert^2$	$n-k$	$\lVert\hat{\mathbf{u}}\rVert^2 = n-k$
Total	$\lVert\dot{\mathbf{y}}\rVert^2 = \Sigma\dot{y}_i^2$	$n-1$	

where

$\lVert\hat{\mathbf{y}}\rVert^2 = \hat{\mathbf{y}}'\hat{\mathbf{y}}$ = sum of squares explained by the regression

$\lVert\hat{\mathbf{u}}\rVert^2 = \hat{\mathbf{u}}'\hat{\mathbf{u}}$ = sum of squares of error terms

$\lVert\dot{\mathbf{y}}\rVert^2 = \dot{\mathbf{y}}'\dot{\mathbf{y}}$ = total sum of squares (of deviations from the mean value)

Note The ratio of the mean squares tests the hypothesis that all slope coefficients vanish.

$$\frac{\partial H}{\partial \boldsymbol{\theta}} = \frac{\partial L(\mathbf{y};\boldsymbol{\theta})}{\partial \boldsymbol{\theta}}\bigg|_{\hat{\boldsymbol{\theta}}_c} - \frac{\partial \mathbf{h}'(\boldsymbol{\theta})}{\partial \boldsymbol{\theta}}\bigg|_{\hat{\boldsymbol{\theta}}_c} \hat{\boldsymbol{\lambda}} = \mathbf{0}, \tag{4.7.30}$$

$$\frac{\partial H}{\partial \boldsymbol{\lambda}} = \mathbf{h}\left(\hat{\boldsymbol{\theta}}_c\right) = \mathbf{0}; \tag{4.7.31}$$

that is,

$$\frac{\partial L(\mathbf{y};\boldsymbol{\theta})}{\partial \boldsymbol{\theta}}\bigg|_{\hat{\boldsymbol{\theta}}_c} = \frac{\partial \mathbf{h}'(\boldsymbol{\theta})}{\partial \boldsymbol{\theta}}\bigg|_{\hat{\boldsymbol{\theta}}_c} \hat{\boldsymbol{\lambda}}. \tag{4.7.32}$$

Thus the test based on the Lagrange multipliers is identical to Rao's (1948) *score test*, which is defined as

$$-\frac{\partial L(\mathbf{y};\boldsymbol{\theta})}{\partial \boldsymbol{\theta}'}\bigg|_{\hat{\boldsymbol{\theta}}_c} \left[E \frac{\partial^2 L(\mathbf{y};\boldsymbol{\theta})}{\partial \boldsymbol{\theta} \partial \boldsymbol{\theta}'}\bigg|_{\hat{\boldsymbol{\theta}}_c} \right]^{-1} \frac{\partial L(\mathbf{y};\boldsymbol{\theta})}{\partial \boldsymbol{\theta}}\bigg|_{\hat{\boldsymbol{\theta}}_c}. \tag{4.7.33}$$

In each case it has a limiting chi-square distribution with q degrees of freedom under the null hypothesis.

In the case of the basic linear regression model (4.2.2) with $\mathbf{u}$ normally distributed, the null hypothesis (4.7.19) implies that

$$\frac{\partial H}{\partial \boldsymbol{\beta}} = \frac{\partial L(\mathbf{y};\boldsymbol{\theta})}{\partial \boldsymbol{\beta}} - \mathbf{R}'\boldsymbol{\lambda} = \frac{1}{\hat{\sigma}_c^2}\mathbf{X}'\left(\mathbf{y} - \mathbf{X}\hat{\boldsymbol{\beta}}_c\right) - \mathbf{R}'\hat{\boldsymbol{\lambda}} = \mathbf{0}, \tag{4.7.34}$$

$$\frac{\partial H}{\partial \sigma^2} = \frac{\partial L(\mathbf{y};\boldsymbol{\theta})}{\partial \sigma^2} = -\frac{n}{2\hat{\sigma}_c^2} + \frac{1}{2\hat{\sigma}_c^4}\left(\mathbf{y} - \mathbf{X}\hat{\boldsymbol{\beta}}_c\right)'\left(\mathbf{y} - \mathbf{X}\hat{\boldsymbol{\beta}}_c\right) = 0, \tag{4.7.35}$$

$$\frac{\partial H}{\partial \boldsymbol{\lambda}} = \mathbf{R}\hat{\boldsymbol{\beta}}_c - \mathbf{r} = \mathbf{0}. \tag{4.7.36}$$

Thus, from (4.7.35), the maximum likelihood estimator of σ^2 is equal to

$$\hat{\sigma}_c^2 = \frac{1}{n}\left(\mathbf{y} - \mathbf{X}\hat{\boldsymbol{\beta}}_c\right)'\left(\mathbf{y} - \mathbf{X}\hat{\boldsymbol{\beta}}_c\right) = \frac{1}{n}\hat{\mathbf{u}}_c'\hat{\mathbf{u}}_c \tag{4.7.37}$$

under the null, and from (4.5.8), the MLE of σ^2 is equal to

$$\hat{\sigma}^2 = \frac{1}{n}(\mathbf{y} - \mathbf{X}\hat{\boldsymbol{\beta}})'(\mathbf{y} - \mathbf{X}\hat{\boldsymbol{\beta}}) = \frac{1}{n}\hat{\mathbf{u}}'\hat{\mathbf{u}} \tag{4.7.38}$$

under the alternative. Substituting (4.7.37) or (4.7.38) into their respective likelihood functions, the exponential terms are equal to exp($-n/2$). Therefore, the likelihood ratio statistic of (4.7.28) becomes

$$\begin{aligned} \xi_{\text{LR}} &= n \log \frac{\hat{\mathbf{u}}_c'\hat{\mathbf{u}}_c}{\hat{\mathbf{u}}'\hat{\mathbf{u}}} = n \log\left(\frac{\hat{\mathbf{u}}_c'\hat{\mathbf{u}}_c - \hat{\mathbf{u}}'\hat{\mathbf{u}}}{\hat{\mathbf{u}}'\hat{\mathbf{u}}} + 1 \right) \\ &= n \log\left(1 + \frac{q}{n-k}\xi_w \right), \end{aligned} \tag{4.7.39}$$

where ξ_w is the Wald statistic in (4.7.23).

Premultiplying (4.7.34) by $\mathbf{R}(\mathbf{X}'\mathbf{X})^{-1}$ and solving for $\boldsymbol{\lambda}$ yields

$$\begin{aligned} \hat{\boldsymbol{\lambda}} &= \frac{1}{\hat{\sigma}_c^2}\left[\mathbf{R}(\mathbf{X}'\mathbf{X})^{-1}\mathbf{R}'\right]^{-1}\mathbf{R}(\mathbf{X}'\mathbf{X})^{-1}\frac{\partial L(\mathbf{y};\boldsymbol{\theta})}{\partial \hat{\boldsymbol{\beta}}_c} \\ &= \frac{1}{\hat{\sigma}_c^2}\left[\mathbf{R}(\mathbf{X}'\mathbf{X})^{-1}\mathbf{R}'\right]^{-1}\mathbf{R}\left(\hat{\boldsymbol{\beta}} - \hat{\boldsymbol{\beta}}_c\right). \end{aligned} \tag{4.7.40}$$

Substituting (4.6.14) into (4.7.40) the values of the Lagrange multipliers are

$$\hat{\boldsymbol{\lambda}} = \frac{1}{\hat{\sigma}_c^2}\left[\mathbf{R}(\mathbf{X}'\mathbf{X})^{-1}\mathbf{R}'\right]^{-1}(\mathbf{R}\hat{\boldsymbol{\beta}} - \mathbf{r}). \tag{4.7.41}$$

If the restrictions are correct, then as $n \to \infty$, $\hat{\sigma}_c^2$ converges to σ^2 in probability, and $\hat{\boldsymbol{\lambda}}$ has a limiting normal distribution

$$\hat{\boldsymbol{\lambda}} \sim N\left(0, \left[\sigma^2\mathbf{R}(\mathbf{X}'\mathbf{X})^{-1}\mathbf{R}'\right]^{-1}\right). \tag{4.7.42}$$

Therefore, the quadratic form, after replacing σ^2 by $\hat{\sigma}_c^2$ in (4.7.37), is the *Lagrange multiplier test*,

$$\xi_{\text{LM}} = \frac{1}{\hat{\sigma}_c^2}(\mathbf{R}\hat{\boldsymbol{\beta}} - \mathbf{r})'[\mathbf{R}(\mathbf{X}'\mathbf{X})\mathbf{R}']^{-1}(\mathbf{R}\hat{\boldsymbol{\beta}} - \mathbf{r}), \tag{4.7.43}$$

which is approximately chi-square distributed with q degrees of freedom and can be written

$$\xi_{\text{LM}} = \left(\frac{nq}{n-k}\xi_w\right)\left(1 + \frac{q}{n-k}\xi_w\right)^{-1}, \tag{4.7.44}$$

where ξ_w is again the Wald statistic of (4.7.23).

Essentially, the Lagrange multiplier approach starts at the null and asks whether movement toward the alternative would be an improvement, while the Wald approach starts at the alternative and considers movement toward the null. The likelihood ratio method compares the two hypotheses on an equal basis as discussed in Engle (1984). Their relations can be illustrated using Figure 4.5, which plots the log-likelihood function against $\boldsymbol{\theta}$ for a particular realization, $\mathbf{y}$. The Wald test is based on the horizontal difference between $\hat{\boldsymbol{\theta}}$ and $\hat{\boldsymbol{\theta}}_c$, the likelihood ratio test is based on the vertical difference, and the Lagrange multiplier test is based on the slope of the likelihood function at $\hat{\boldsymbol{\theta}}_c$. In the limit, as $n \to \infty$, the Wald, likelihood ratio, and Lagrange multiplier test statistics all approach the same chi-square distribution with q degrees of freedom. In finite samples, it can be shown, by comparing (4.7.23) and (4.7.43), that testing for the linear hypothesis of a linear model

$$\xi_w \geq \xi_{\text{LR}} \geq \xi_{\text{LM}}, \tag{4.7.45}$$

as discussed in Berndt and Savin (1975).

4.7.4 Test of Structural Break

In many practical applications, the question arises as to whether a structural shift in some relation has taken place between two time periods. As long as the number of observations in each class exceeds the number of parameters to be estimated, the testing techniques discussed in the preceding subsection can be applied directly. For example, it may be suspected that there are two regression regimes for the n observed sample, with the first n_1 observations following

$$\mathbf{y}_1 = \mathbf{X}_1\boldsymbol{\beta}_1 + \mathbf{u}_1, \tag{4.7.46}$$

where $\mathbf{X}_1$ is the $n_1 \times k$ design matrix for the first n_1 observations and with the last $n - n_1$ observations following

$$\mathbf{y}_2 = \mathbf{X}_2\boldsymbol{\beta}_2 + \mathbf{u}_2, \tag{4.7.47}$$

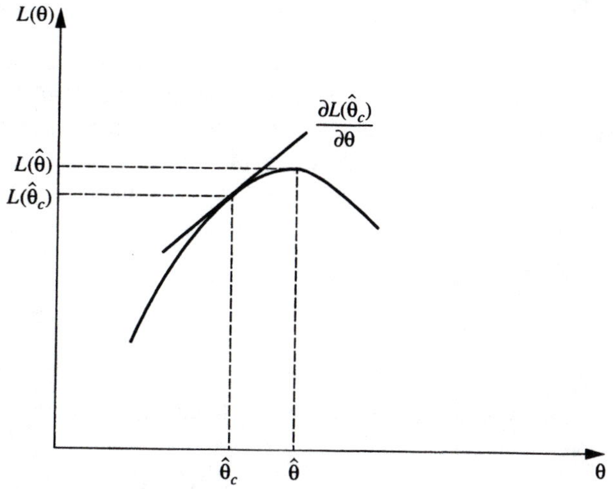

Figure 4.5 Log-Likelihood Value, L, as a Function of the Parameter θ, for a Given Sample

where $\mathbf{X}_2$ is the $(n - n_1) \times k$ design matrix for the last $n - n_1$ observations. The null hypothesis is

$$H_0 : \boldsymbol{\beta}_1 = \boldsymbol{\beta}_2, \qquad *(4.7.48)$$

while the alternative hypothesis is

$$H_1 : \boldsymbol{\beta}_1 \neq \boldsymbol{\beta}_2. \qquad *(4.7.49)$$

Stacking (4.7.46) and (4.7.47) together yields a general model of the form

$$\mathbf{y} = \begin{pmatrix} \mathbf{y}_1 \\ \mathbf{y}_2 \end{pmatrix} = \begin{pmatrix} \mathbf{X}_1 & \mathbf{0} \\ \mathbf{0} & \mathbf{X}_2 \end{pmatrix} \begin{pmatrix} \boldsymbol{\beta}_1 \\ \boldsymbol{\beta}_2 \end{pmatrix} + \begin{pmatrix} \mathbf{u}_1 \\ \mathbf{u}_2 \end{pmatrix}. \qquad (4.7.50)$$

The null hypothesis (4.7.48) is equivalent to imposing the restriction

$$[\mathbf{I}_k \quad -\mathbf{I}_k] \begin{bmatrix} \boldsymbol{\beta}_1 \\ \boldsymbol{\beta}_2 \end{bmatrix} = \mathbf{0}, \qquad (4.7.51)$$

on (4.7.50). Therefore, as in (4.7.23) or (4.7.25), an F-test statistic

$$\frac{\hat{\mathbf{u}}'\hat{\mathbf{u}} - (\hat{\mathbf{u}}_1'\hat{\mathbf{u}}_1 + \hat{\mathbf{u}}_2'\hat{\mathbf{u}}_2)}{\hat{\mathbf{u}}_1'\hat{\mathbf{u}}_1 + \hat{\mathbf{u}}_2'\hat{\mathbf{u}}_2} \frac{n - 2k}{k} \sim F(k, n - 2k), \qquad *(4.7.52)$$

with k and $n - 2k$ degrees of freedom, can be used to test the hypothesis (4.7.48) against the alternative (4.7.49), where $\hat{\mathbf{u}}'\hat{\mathbf{u}}$, $\hat{\mathbf{u}}_1'\hat{\mathbf{u}}_1$, and $\hat{\mathbf{u}}_2'\hat{\mathbf{u}}_2$ are the residual sums of squares of the least squares regression of (4.2.2), (4.7.46), and (4.7.47), respectively.

A special case arises when the number of observations in one class is less than the number of parameters. For example, $(n - n_1)$ may be smaller than k; then $\hat{\mathbf{u}}_2'\hat{\mathbf{u}}_2 = 0$. In this case, Chow (1960) has shown that the appropriate test is given by

$$\frac{\hat{\mathbf{u}}'\hat{\mathbf{u}} + \hat{\mathbf{u}}_1'\hat{\mathbf{u}}_1}{\hat{\mathbf{u}}_1'\hat{\mathbf{u}}_1} \frac{n_1 - k}{n - n_1} \sim F(n - n_1, n_1 - k), \qquad (4.7.53)$$

which is distributed as the distribution F with $(n - n_1)$ and $n_1 - k$ degrees of freedom under the null (4.7.48). This is the *Chow test* for structural break.

4.8 PREDICTION

The Gauss–Markov theorem provides a justification for the use of least squares estimators for purposes of prediction—that is, the estimation of the value of the dependent variable for certain given levels of the explanatory variables. The *least squares predictor* for a future value of y, given as $\hat{y}_f$, is obtained by setting all coefficients equal to their least squares estimators $\hat{\beta}$, all explanatory variables at their given levels $\mathbf{x}_f$, and the stochastic disturbance term equal to its expected value of zero: namely,

$$\hat{y}_f = \mathbf{x}'_f\hat{\boldsymbol{\beta}}. \qquad *(4.8.1)$$

Given $\mathbf{x}_f$,

$$E(\hat{y}_f \mid \mathbf{x}_f) = \mathbf{x}'_f E\hat{\boldsymbol{\beta}} = \mathbf{x}'_f\boldsymbol{\beta} = E(y_f \mid \mathbf{x}_f). \qquad (4.8.2)$$

The mean squared prediction error of $\hat{y}_f$ conditional on $\mathbf{x}_f$, a measure of the inaccuracy of the prediction, is given by

$$\begin{aligned} E[(\hat{y}_f - y_f)|\mathbf{x}_f]^2 &= E[\mathbf{x}'_f(\hat{\boldsymbol{\beta}} - \boldsymbol{\beta}) - \mathbf{u}_f|\mathbf{x}_f]^2 \\ &= \sigma^2 + \mathbf{x}'_f E[(\hat{\boldsymbol{\beta}} - \boldsymbol{\beta})(\hat{\boldsymbol{\beta}} - \boldsymbol{\beta})']\mathbf{x}_f \\ &= \sigma^2[1 + \mathbf{x}'_f(\mathbf{X}'\mathbf{X})^{-1}\mathbf{x}_f], \end{aligned} \qquad (4.8.3)$$

where the last equality follows from the assumption of independence between u_f and $\hat{\boldsymbol{\beta}}$, with u_f being the disturbance term in the period to which the forecast refers. Equation (4.8.3) demonstrates that (4.8.1) is the unique *best linear unbiased predictor* of the dependent variable y, given that $\mathbf{x} = \mathbf{x}_f$. This is because $\hat{\boldsymbol{\beta}}$ is the BLUE of $\boldsymbol{\beta}$. Specifically, among the class of linear and unbiased predictors, the least squares predictor has minimum variance. The variance, as given in (4.8.3), increases with the error variance σ^2 and decreases with the "spread" of the data on the explanatory variables as measured by $(\mathbf{X}'\mathbf{X})$ for which the estimation of $\boldsymbol{\beta}$ is based, and in general, increases with the values taken by the explanatory variables $\mathbf{x}_f$ (in particular, with their deviations from sample means).[11]

The least squares predictor conditional on $\mathbf{x}$ and $\mathbf{x}_f$ has expected value equal to $\mathbf{x}'_f\boldsymbol{\beta} = Ey_f$ and the mean square error of $\hat{y}_f - y_f$ is equal to $\sigma^2(1 + \mathbf{x}'_f(\mathbf{X}'\mathbf{X})^{-1}\mathbf{x}_f)$. Therefore, if the stochastic disturbance term $\mathbf{u}$ is normally distributed, as in assumption A.4.5, the $100(1 - \varepsilon)\%$ confidence interval for y_f is given by

$$\mathbf{x}'_f\hat{\boldsymbol{\beta}} \pm t_{\varepsilon/2}\hat{s}\sqrt{1 + \mathbf{x}'_f(\mathbf{X}'\mathbf{X})^{-1}\mathbf{x}_f}, \qquad *(4.8.4)$$

where $t_{\varepsilon/2}$ is the value of the t distribution for a level of significance of $\varepsilon/2$ and $n - k$ degrees of freedom, and the expression multiplying $t_{\varepsilon/2}$ is the *standard error of prediction* using the estimated standard deviation of the stochastic term $\hat{s}$. For example, a 95% confidence interval would be given by the point prediction $\mathbf{x}'_f\hat{\boldsymbol{\beta}}$ plus or minus the last term in (4.8.4) with a value of t for a 0.025 level of significance. The nature of the confidence is illustrated in Figure 4.6 for the case of simple linear regression.

The confidence interval in (4.8.4) also leads to a test of the hypothesis that a new data point $(y, \mathbf{x}')$ is generated by the same structure. The t value for this data point is given by

[11] See Bodkin (1970).

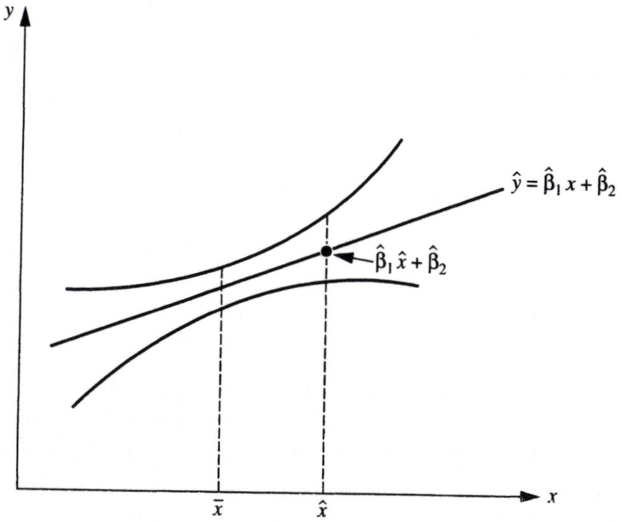

Figure 4.6 The Confidence Interval for Prediction in the Case of Simple Regression

$$t = \frac{\mathbf{x}'\hat{\boldsymbol{\beta}} - y}{\hat{s}\sqrt{1 + \mathbf{x}'(\mathbf{X}'\mathbf{X})^{-1}\mathbf{x}}}. \tag{4.8.5}$$

If the absolute value of t, $|t|$, computed for this observation exceeds the value $t_{(1/2)\varepsilon}$, it would imply that at the $100\varepsilon\%$ level of significance, the new observation is generated by a different structure. If, for example, it exceeds $t_{0.005}$, it would imply that at a 1% level of significance, the observation is generated by a different structure.

4.9 EXAMPLES

A few specific examples may help in understanding the results of this chapter and the next. In this section we give first an example of simple linear regressions and then one of multiple linear regression.

4.9.1 Example of Simple Linear Regression

The example to be pursued borrows from the methodology of Price in studying the history of science, as discussed in Section 1.6. Let $N(t)$ be the number of U.S economists (defined as members of the American Economic Association) at time t; data on $N(t)$ appear in Table 3.6. If a constant exponential growth (subject to a stochastic perturbation) of the number of economists is assumed,[12] it follows that

$$N(t) = N_0 e^{gt} u_t. \tag{4.9.1}$$

[12]In point of fact, a graph on semilogarithmic paper, $N(t)$ plotted against time, indicates that this is an oversimplification. However, as the principal goal of this section is to illustrate the principles with some relatively simple calculations, this assumption will be maintained in this subsection. See, however, Problem 3-G of Chapter 3.

Here N_0 is the number of economists in the base year (when $t = 0$, which we take to be 1950), and g is the annual growth rate of the group of economists (subject to continuous compounding theoretically):

$$g = \frac{1}{n}\frac{dN}{dt}. \tag{4.9.2}$$

Taking logs of equation (4.9.1) yields

$$\ln N(t) = \ln N_0 + gt + \ln u_t \tag{4.9.3}$$

or

$$y = a + gt + v, \tag{4.9.4}$$

where y is $\ln N(t)$, a is $\ln N_0$, and v is $\ln u_t$. The problem of estimating the parameters a and g in regression equation (4.9.4) from data on y and t is one of simple linear regression. For ease of the calculations, the natural logarithms of $N(t)$ are given in Table 3.6 (although a variety of transformations, including that to natural logarithms, is available with many programs on the personal computer and mainframe). Next, we note that for the bivariate case, equation (4.3.10) simplifies to

$$\hat{g} = \frac{\sum_1^n (y_t - \bar{y})(t - \bar{t})}{\sum_1^n (t - \bar{t})^2}, \tag{4.9.5}$$

where $\hat{g}$ is the least squares estimator of the parameter g, y_t is the logarithm of the number of economists in year t, $\bar{y}$ is the mean of y_t over the sample, $\bar{t}$ is the mean of t over the sample, and n is the number of observations in the sample (32 in this case). The intercept can be estimated from a simplification of (4.3.9) as

$$\hat{a} = \bar{y} - \hat{g}\bar{t}. \tag{4.9.6}$$

From a specialization of the results in Section 4.4, the standard error of the slope coefficient, s_g, is given by the formula

$$s_{\hat{g}}^2 = \frac{\hat{s}^2}{\sum_1^n (t - t)^2}, \tag{4.9.7}$$

where $\hat{s}^2$ is the unbiased estimator of the universe variance of the disturbance terms from (4.4.4), which is here given by the sum of squares of the estimated residuals divided by the quantity $n - 2$. [In turn, the easiest way to calculate the sum of squared residuals is simply to take the total sum of squared deviations of the dependent variable and then subtract the explained sum of squared deviations due to the regression, as developed in (4.3.18) or Table 4.1.]

When these results are applied to the entire sample of 32 observations, the calculations show that

$$\begin{aligned} \hat{g} &= \frac{113.2622}{3149.5} = 0.0359618, & \hat{a} &= 9.476557 - 0.0359618(15.875) = 8.90566, \\ \hat{s}^2 &= \frac{0.5840}{32 - 2} = 0.019467, & s_{\hat{g}}^2 &= \frac{0.019467}{3149.5}. \end{aligned} \tag{4.9.8}$$

Thus the estimated regression equation is found, after rounding, to be[13]

$$y = 8.95066 + \underset{(0.002486)}{0.03596t} + v, \qquad r^2 = 0.8746, \quad \hat{s} = 0.1395, \tag{4.9.9}$$

where the t ratio on the slope coefficient (roughly 14.5) indicates that the estimated growth rate (3.6% per annum) is statistically significant by any reasonable standard. At such a rapid growth rate, the number of economists would be expected to double every 20 years or so. Thus, letting $t = 50$ and substituting into equation (4.9.9), we can calculate a projected value for y in the year 2000. This predicted value for y turns out to be 10.70375, which corresponds to a predicted value of $N(50)$ equal roughly to 44,500. In the present (mid-1995) perspective, this prediction seems highly inflated.

These considerations [and also a study of the time diagram of $N(t)$ against time on semi-logarithmic paper] might lead the reader to wonder whether a somewhat more realistic projection could be obtained by calculating a simple regression for the last 12 observations (those for the 12 observations during the subperiod 1970–1988). (Another alternative would be to fit a *quadratic* trend, but this would no longer be an example of a simple linear regression.) By reasoning similar to that used for the entire period, the following results are obtained:

$$\hat{g} = \frac{2.2443}{317} = 0.0070798, \qquad \hat{a} = 9.84134 - 0.0070798(26.5) = 9.96573,$$
$$\hat{s}^2 = \frac{0.01101}{12-2} = 0.001101, \qquad s_{\hat{g}}^2 = \frac{0.001101}{317} = 3.4373 \times 10^{-6}. \tag{4.9.10}$$

Collecting the results together for the subperiod regression for 1970–1988, we obtain

$$y = 9.96573 + \underset{(0.00186)}{0.00708t}, \qquad r^2 = 0.59, \quad s = 0.0332. \tag{4.9.11}$$

It may be noted that the estimated growth rate, while still statistically significant at conventional levels ($t = 3.8$ with 10 degrees of freedom), shows a considerable reduction, at only 0.7% per year. At these modest growth rates, it would take roughly 100 years to double the stock of economists. Finally, a confidence interval for the predicted number of economists may be determined, using the methods of Section 4.8. In the bivariate case, (4.8.4) reduces to

$$a + g(t^*) \pm t_{0.025}s\left[1 + \frac{1}{n} + \frac{(t_f - t)^2}{\sum_1^n (t-t)^2}\right]^{1/2}$$

(where t_f is the value of the independent variable in the forecast year, and is equal to 50 in this case) (4.9.12)

$$= 10.31972 \pm 0.073928(2.84211)^{1/2}$$
$$= (10.19509, 10.44435).$$

[13]We do not bother to calculate the standard error for the constant term, as the statistical significance of this parameter is of secondary interest. We also do not bother to calculate an F statistic for the entire (simple) regression, as this test is formally equivalent to a test of statistical significance on the slope coefficient, $\hat{g}$. Finally, we note that in the case of simple regression, the coefficient of determination is simply the square of a bivariate correlation coefficient and so is denoted as r^2 (rather than R^2).

Thus, if the predictions are based on the final 12 observations of Table 3.6, the point estimate of the number of American economists in 2000 is roughly 30,360, with the 95% confidence lying between 26,800 and 34,400. This seems intuitively more reasonable.

4.9.2 Example of Multiple Linear Regression

Consider now an example of multiple linear regression, specifically the problem of estimating one of the reduced-form equations of the prototype macro model of Section 2.6. In fact, as discussed in considerable detail in Chapter 10, the first step in estimating a simultaneous-equations econometric model such as the prototype macro model is usually that of estimating each of its reduced-form equations. Consider (2.6.7), which may be written[14]

$$Y_t = (Y_{t-1} \quad G_t \quad 1)\begin{pmatrix} \beta_1 \\ \beta_2 \\ \beta_3 \end{pmatrix} + u_t = \beta_1 Y_{t-1} + \beta_2 G_t + \beta_3 + u_t. \qquad (4.9.13)$$

Here Y_t, current national income, is a linear function of lagged income Y_{t-1} and current government spending G_t. The three parameters to be estimated are the two slope parameters β_1 and β_2 and the intercept β_3. Table 3.2 provides 25 data points for the years 1961 and 1985, which can be used in the estimation of the model.

It will be assumed that all the assumptions used to derive the optimality properties of the least squares estimators discussed above are applicable.[15] The least squares estimators are then

$$\hat{\boldsymbol{\beta}} = (\mathbf{X}'\mathbf{X})^{-1}\mathbf{X}'\mathbf{y}, \qquad (4.9.14)$$

where **X** and **y**, from Table 3.2 and the specification of (4.9.13), are given as

$$\mathbf{X} = \begin{pmatrix} 0.504 & 0.108 & 1 \\ 0.520 & 0.117 & 1 \\ 0.560 & 0.123 & 1 \\ 0.589 & 0.128 & 1 \\ 0.629 & 0.137 & 1 \\ \vdots & \vdots & \vdots \\ 2.732 & 0.588 & 1 \\ 3.053 & 0.642 & 1 \\ 3.166 & 0.675 & 1 \\ 3.406 & 0.736 & 1 \\ 3.772 & 0.821 & 1 \end{pmatrix}, \qquad \mathbf{y} = \begin{pmatrix} 0.520 \\ 0.560 \\ 0.589 \\ 0.625 \\ 0.685 \\ \vdots \\ 3.053 \\ 3.166 \\ 3.406 \\ 3.772 \\ 4.015 \end{pmatrix}, \qquad (4.9.15)$$

where, for convenience in the calculations, variables are measured in trillions, rather than billions, of dollars. Here[16]

$$(\mathbf{X}'\mathbf{X}) = \begin{pmatrix} 84.2742 & 18.51026 & 38.674 \\ & 4.07146 & 8.632 \\ & & 25 \end{pmatrix}, \qquad (4.9.16)$$

[14]Note that the β's in (4.9.13) are not the same as the β's used in Section 2.6.

[15]In fact, one of the explanatory variables is a lagged endogenous variable, implying that these assumptions need not hold. Here this fact is not taken explicitly into account. See, however, Section 6.8.4.

[16]Since the matrix is symmetric, only elements on and above the diagonal need be reported. It should also be noted that because of roundoff error in (4.9.17), multiplying $(\mathbf{X}'\mathbf{X})$ by $(\mathbf{X}'\mathbf{X})^{-1}$ yields a matrix close to but not exactly the identity matrix.

yielding the inverse matrix

$$(\mathbf{X}'\mathbf{X})^{-1} = \begin{pmatrix} 13.94075 & -65.89448 & 1.18626 \\ & 312.3828 & -5.92362 \\ & & 0.250217 \end{pmatrix}. \tag{4.9.17}$$

Furthermore,

$$\mathbf{X}'\mathbf{y} = \begin{pmatrix} 91.832084 \\ 20.176344 \\ 42.185 \end{pmatrix}. \tag{4.9.18}$$

Thus the least squares estimators are

$$\hat{\boldsymbol{\beta}} = (\mathbf{X}'\mathbf{X})^{-1}\mathbf{X}'\mathbf{y} = \begin{pmatrix} 0.7407 \\ 1.6285 \\ -0.02518 \end{pmatrix}. \tag{4.9.19}$$

The sum of the squared errors is

$$\sum \hat{u}_i^2 = (\mathbf{y} - \mathbf{X}\hat{\boldsymbol{\beta}})'(\mathbf{y} - \mathbf{X}\hat{\boldsymbol{\beta}}) = 0.32544, \tag{4.9.20}$$

so an unbiased estimate of the variance of the stochastic disturbance term is

$$\hat{s}^2 = \frac{1}{n-k}\sum \hat{u}_i^2 = \frac{1}{22}(0.32544) = 0.0140793. \tag{4.9.21}$$

The estimate of the covariance matrix of the estimated coefficients is thus

$$\widehat{\text{Cov}}\,\hat{\boldsymbol{\beta}} = \hat{s}^2(\mathbf{X}'\mathbf{X})^{-1} = \begin{pmatrix} 0.2062 & -0.9748 & 0.01755 \\ & 4.621 & -0.08763 \\ & & 0.003701 \end{pmatrix}, \tag{4.9.22}$$

and the square roots of the diagonal elements of this matrix are the standard errors of the estimated coefficients.

The value of the coefficient of determination can be obtained as

$$R^2 = 1 - \frac{\sum \hat{u}_i^2}{\sum \dot{y}_i^2} = 0.9968, \tag{4.9.23}$$

where $\sum \dot{y}_i^2$ is the sum of squared deviations of the dependent variable (current national income) from the mean value.

The analysis of variance for the regression is shown in Table 4.2. From this table the F value for the regression is

$$F = \frac{R^2/(k-1)}{(1-R^2)/(n-k)} = \frac{0.9968/2}{0.0032/22} = 3374. \tag{4.9.24}$$

Comparing this value to the $F(2, 22)$ value of 3.44 at a 5% level of significance (or 5.72 at a 1% level), it is clear that the overall regression is highly significant and that the hypothesis that all coefficients are zero is overwhelmingly rejected.

All the results so far can be summarized by the estimated equation and related statistics

$$\begin{gathered} Y_t = 0.741Y_{t-1} + 1.628G_t - 0.0252, \\ (0.454) \qquad (2.15) \qquad (0.0608) \\ R^2 = 0.997, \qquad \hat{s} = 0.122, \qquad F = 3370, \end{gathered} \tag{4.9.25}$$

TABLE 4.2 Analysis of Variance for the Regression for the Reduced-Form Equation for Y in the Prototype Macro Model

Source	Sum of Squares	Degrees of Freedom	Mean Square
Explained (by regression)	99.81498	2	49.907
Unexplained (residual)	0.32544	22	0.014793
Total	100.14042	24	

where numbers have been rounded and standard errors are shown in parentheses.[17] According to (4.9.24), Y_t depends positively on both lagged nominal income and current government expenditure, but the latter variable is clearly statistically insignificant. Even lagged income is of marginal statistical significance (roughly the 6% level with a one-tailed test). Multicollinearity is clearly the villain of the piece, as the overall regression is highly significant, as we have seen.[18] For what it is worth, the point estimates of this relationship would be quite satisfying for a Keynesian; the fitted equation suggests an impact multiplier of 1.6 and a long-term or "equilibrium" multiplier nearly four times as large. However, the relatively high standard errors warn us that other interpretations (based on other theories of the macroeconomy) are indeed possible.

4.10 NONNESTED HYPOTHESIS TESTING AND MODEL SELECTION CRITERIA

4.10.1 Nonnested Hypothesis Testing

So far it has been assumed that the data are generated from the model (4.2.2). However, in economics and other social sciences the data are typically not generated through a controlled experiment. Instead, only certain phenomena are observed, and the goal is to arrange them in a meaningful way. The data are produced by an unknown structure, and the effects of a change in this structure are one of the objects of the study. Yet none of these changes was produced by an investigator as in a laboratory experiment, and often the impact of one factor is confounded with the impacts of other factors.

To reduce complex real-world phenomena into manageable proportions, an economist has to make a theoretical abstraction. The result is a logical model hypothesizing the data-generating process as described in the model (4.2.2). However, a model always represents some but not all of the features of the situation. A given theory may not characterize the perceived world correctly and completely. Given the complexity of economic relationships there is often disagreement about the fundamental relationships among economic vari-

[17]It is appropriate to round at this stage but not earlier. In manual calculations, rounding off in prior calculations can significantly affect later estimates, particularly rounding off before calculating the inverse moment matrix. This is a problem that will not arise with a computer program in double precision.

[18]The presence of multicollinearity is evident in the high values of the terms along the principal diagonal of the inverse moment matrix (see also Section 5.2).

ables. Therefore, instead of (4.2.2), an alternative model (data-generating process) might be considered:

$$\mathbf{y} = \mathbf{Z}\gamma + \mathbf{v}, \tag{4.10.1}$$

where $\mathbf{Z}$ is an $n \times l$ matrix of constants, γ is an $l \times 1$ vector of regression coefficients, and $\mathbf{v}$ is the alternative model stochastic disturbance term, satisfying $E\mathbf{v} = 0$, and $E\mathbf{v}\mathbf{v}' = \sigma_v^2 I_n$.

If $\mathbf{Z}$ is a subset of $\mathbf{X}$, then (4.2.2) can be reduced to (4.10.1) by imposing linear restrictions on its parameters as in (4.6.7) and (4.10.1) is said to be *nested* within (4.2.2). In this case, the F test statistic (4.7.23) can be used to test (4.10.1) against (4.2.2). On the other hand, if $\mathbf{Z}$ is not a subset of $\mathbf{X}$ and $\mathbf{X}$ is not a subset of $\mathbf{Z}$, neither may be obtained from the other by the imposition of appropriate restrictions (or as a limiting form of a suitable approximation), and (4.2.2) and (4.10.1) are said to be *nonnested.* In these situations, the various test statistics discussed in Section 4.7 for nested hypotheses cannot be used. Instead, nonnested hypothesis tests have to be used.

In a nested hypothesis-testing framework the null is treated differently from the alternative and the test statistic is derived under the null. In a nonnested framework, competing models are treated the same. Therefore, each competing model takes turns to be specified as the null with the test statistics derived accordingly. Although there are differences among researchers as to the appropriate ways to test separate families of hypotheses, most of them are based on Cox's (1961, 1962) centered log-likelihood ratio method and Atkinson's (1970) artificial nesting method, as discussed in Pesaran (1982) and MacKinnon (1983).[19]

In the setting that the hypothesis H_1 is (4.2.2) with likelihood $L_1(\boldsymbol{\theta}_1)$ and the hypothesis H_2 is (4.10.1) with likelihood $L_2(\boldsymbol{\theta}_2)$, where $\boldsymbol{\theta}_1$ and $\boldsymbol{\theta}_2$ are parameters of the respective likelihood functions, the Cox's centered likelihood ratio method is to assume tentatively that H_1 is true and form the test statistic

$$T_1 = \log\frac{L_1(\hat{\boldsymbol{\theta}}_1)}{L_2(\hat{\boldsymbol{\theta}}_2)} - E_1\left\{\log\frac{L_1(\hat{\boldsymbol{\theta}}_1)}{L_2(\hat{\boldsymbol{\theta}}_{12})}\right\}, \tag{4.10.2}$$

where $\hat{\boldsymbol{\theta}}_i$ denotes the maximum likelihood estimate of $\boldsymbol{\theta}_i$ under H_i; $E_i(\cdot)$ denotes expectation corresponding to the distribution under H_i; and $\hat{\boldsymbol{\theta}}_{ij}$ denotes the probability limit of $\hat{\boldsymbol{\theta}}_j$ under H_i evaluated at $\boldsymbol{\theta}_i = \hat{\boldsymbol{\theta}}_i$. When the sample size is large, T_1 is approximately normally distributed with mean zero and variance, say v_1^2. Therefore, a test of H_1 against H_2 is to check whether $|T_1|/v_1$ is greater than or less than the critical value given by the standard normal distribution specified by the significance level. However, a crucial distinction between nested and nonnested hypothesis testing is that when one model is nested within another model, there is one null model. This is not so when the models are nonnested. A model is specified as the null only temporarily. Thus it is equally plausible to treat (4.10.1) (H_2) as the null. If H_2 is treated as the null, a centered log likelihood ratio statistic will take the form

$$T_2 = \log\frac{L_2(\hat{\boldsymbol{\theta}}_2)}{L_1(\hat{\boldsymbol{\theta}}_1)} - E_2\left\{\log\frac{L_2(\hat{\boldsymbol{\theta}}_2)}{L_1(\hat{\boldsymbol{\theta}}_{21})}\right\}, \tag{4.10.3}$$

[19]For the link between Cox's methods and the artificial nesting procedures, see Fisher (1983).

Compared with the classical procedure in which the performance of a null model is examined against the general alternative, Cox's procedure is concerned with the ability to detect the departure from a (temporary) null model in the light of specific models that are being seriously entertained. When a test rejects (4.2.2), it does not automatically lead to the acceptance of (4.10.1). To test the validity of (4.10.1), it is necessary to reverse the roles of the two models and compute the relevant test statistic. These tests may indicate rejection of both (4.2.2) and (4.10.1) or rejection of neither (4.2.2) nor (4.10.1). In other words, it may not be possible to obtain a complete ranking of the models being considered.

Often, Cox's procedure is not straightforward to compute. As an alternative, Davidson and MacKinnon (1981) suggest formulating a composite model of the form

$$\mathbf{y} = \mathbf{X}\boldsymbol{\beta}(1-\alpha) + (\mathbf{Z}\hat{\boldsymbol{\gamma}})\alpha + \boldsymbol{\varepsilon}, \tag{4.10.4}$$

to test the null model of (4.2.2) against the alternative model (4.10.1), where $\hat{\boldsymbol{\gamma}}$ is an estimate of $\boldsymbol{\gamma}$. The null model (4.2.2) is "tested" by testing the restriction in (4.10.4) that $\alpha = 0$. In the J test of Davidson and MacKinnon (1981) the coefficient vector $\boldsymbol{\gamma}$ is estimated as

$$\hat{\boldsymbol{\gamma}} = (\mathbf{Z}'\mathbf{Z})^{-1}\mathbf{Z}'\mathbf{y}, \tag{4.10.5}$$

which is the least squares estimate of $\boldsymbol{\gamma}$ under the alternative (4.10.1). If the null (4.2.2) is true, then $\alpha = 0$ and $\boldsymbol{\varepsilon} = \mathbf{u}$. Since $\mathbf{Z}\hat{\boldsymbol{\gamma}}$ is asymptotically independent of $\boldsymbol{\varepsilon}$, it is possible to test whether $\alpha = 0$ in (4.10.4) by using the t statistic for $\hat{\alpha}$, which is asymptotically $N(0, 1)$. Of course, other estimates of the coefficient vector $\boldsymbol{\gamma}$ can also be substituted into (4.10.4). For instance, McAleer and Fisher (1982) propose using, as the estimate of $\boldsymbol{\gamma}$ in (4.10.3),

$$\hat{\boldsymbol{\gamma}} = (\mathbf{Z}'\mathbf{Z})^{-1}\mathbf{Z}'\mathbf{X}(\mathbf{X}'\mathbf{X})^{-1}\mathbf{X}'\mathbf{y}, \tag{4.10.6}$$

which is a consistent estimate of the probability limit of $(\mathbf{Z}'\mathbf{Z})^{-1}\mathbf{Z}'\mathbf{y}$ under the null. They call the resulting test the J_A test. The J_A test gives an exact t distribution under the null. Unfortunately, its power is relatively low under the alternative, as demonstrated by Godfrey and Pesaran (1983).

In the nonnested framework, the relationship between the model (4.2.2) and the alternative (4.10.1) is symmetric. It is equally plausible, however, to treat (4.10.1) as the null and (4.2.2) as the alternative. If, by contrast, (4.10.1) is treated as the null, the role of $\boldsymbol{\beta}$ and $\boldsymbol{\gamma}$ in (4.10.4) should be reversed in the sense of replacing $\boldsymbol{\beta}$ rather than $\boldsymbol{\gamma}$ with the corresponding estimate $\hat{\boldsymbol{\beta}}$. Thus the composite model is now of the form

$$\mathbf{y} = \mathbf{Z}\boldsymbol{\gamma}(1-\alpha) + (\mathbf{X}\hat{\boldsymbol{\beta}})\alpha + \boldsymbol{\varepsilon}^* \tag{4.10.7}$$

and the test is of the restriction that $\alpha = 0$.

The Davidson–MacKinnon J test can be viewed as a special case arising from a comprehensive model

$$\mathbf{y} = \mathbf{X}\boldsymbol{\beta} + \mathbf{Z}\boldsymbol{\gamma} + \boldsymbol{\eta}, \tag{4.10.8}$$

where, for ease of exposition, $\mathbf{X}$ and $\mathbf{Z}$ are supposed to be nonoverlapping. Model (4.10.8) encompasses both (4.2.2) and (4.10.1) as special cases. A test of (4.2.2) against (4.10.1) can be formulated as a conventional test of $\boldsymbol{\gamma} = \mathbf{0}$ in the nested framework. On the other hand, when (4.10.1) is treated as the null, an F test of $\boldsymbol{\beta} = \mathbf{0}$ can be conducted. Compared to (4.10.4), the classical F test examines the performance of a null model against the general alternative, while the J test is concerned with the ability to detect departure from a temporary (null) model in the light of specific models that are being seriously entertained. However, the classical F test has an exact distribution. The Davidson–MacKinnon J-test statistics are derived under the assumption that the sample size is large. When the sample size is small, the results of nonnested tests should be interpreted with caution. In fact, the relationship between the classical nested tests and nonnested tests can be illustrated more clearly in terms of the likelihood ratio statistics, since their limiting distributions are derived under the assumption that n approaches infinity. In this framework, the Davidson–MacKinnon composite model (4.10.4) or (4.10.7) can be viewed as the constrained model of (4.10.8). Under (4.10.8), a likelihood ratio test of $\boldsymbol{\gamma} = \mathbf{0}$ uses the test statistic $n \log (\hat{\mathbf{u}}'\hat{\mathbf{u}}/\hat{\boldsymbol{\eta}}'\hat{\boldsymbol{\eta}})$ as illustrated in (4.7.39). A likelihood ratio test of $\boldsymbol{\alpha} = \mathbf{0}$ for the model (4.10.4) uses the statistic $n \log (\hat{\mathbf{u}}'\hat{\mathbf{u}}/\hat{\boldsymbol{\varepsilon}}'\hat{\boldsymbol{\varepsilon}})$. Since $\hat{\boldsymbol{\varepsilon}}'\hat{\boldsymbol{\varepsilon}} \geq \hat{\boldsymbol{\eta}}'\hat{\boldsymbol{\eta}}$, the nonnested test statistic $n \log (\hat{\mathbf{u}}'\hat{\mathbf{u}}/\hat{\boldsymbol{\varepsilon}}'\hat{\boldsymbol{\varepsilon}})$ cannot be larger than the conventional likelihood ratio test statistic $n \log (\hat{\mathbf{u}}'\hat{\mathbf{u}}/\hat{\boldsymbol{\eta}}'\hat{\boldsymbol{\eta}})$. The former has an asymptotic chi-square distribution with one degree of freedom, while the latter has an asymptotic chi-square distribution with l degrees of freedom. Under the null of $\boldsymbol{\gamma} = \mathbf{0}$, $\hat{\boldsymbol{\varepsilon}}'\hat{\boldsymbol{\varepsilon}}$ would be close to $\hat{\boldsymbol{\eta}}'\hat{\boldsymbol{\eta}}$ and $n \log (\hat{\mathbf{u}}'\hat{\mathbf{u}}/\hat{\boldsymbol{\varepsilon}}'\hat{\boldsymbol{\varepsilon}})$ would be close to $n \log (\hat{\mathbf{u}}'\hat{\mathbf{u}}/\hat{\boldsymbol{\eta}}'\hat{\boldsymbol{\eta}})$. However, with a given significance level, the critical value of a chi-square distribution with one degree of freedom lies to the left of the critical value of the chi-square distribution with l degrees of freedom. Thus the application of a nonnested test is more likely to result in overrejection of the null hypothesis even when the null happens to be true. Monte Carlo experiments carried out by Godfrey and Pesaran (1983) have shown that this is indeed the case if one or more the following circumstances holds: (1) the true model fits poorly; (2) the correlation among the regressors of the two models is weak; and (3) the false model includes more regressors than the correct specification.[20]

4.10.2 Model Selection

Evaluation of the adequacy of a model is often approached either as a model selection problem or as a problem in statistical inference in which the hypothesis of interest is tested against general or specific alternatives. The distinction between these two general approaches basically stems from the way alternatives are treated. In the hypothesis-testing framework, the null hypothesis is treated differently from the alternatives and the test statistics are derived under the assumption that the null is true. In the case of model selection, all the models under consideration are treated the same a priori. The aim is to choose the model that is likely to perform best with respect to a particular loss function when using a particular model instead of the true one. In the case of hypothesis testing, a probabilistic statement is made with regard to model selection. Rejection or acceptance of all the models is not ruled out when the models are nonnested. By contrast, the application of model selection strategy always leads to one model being chosen in preference to other models.

Theil's adjusted R^2. The coefficient of determination, R^2, is used to measure the explanatory power of a regression. When the dependent variable is the same in comparing models with different explanatory variables, R^2 is sometimes used to choose between alternative models. However, the value of R^2 can never decrease as more explanatory

[20]See Mizon and Richard (1986) for a further discussion of artificial nesting and comprehensive or encompassing testing procedures.

variables are added. Because of this, R^2 is frequently adjusted for degrees of freedom to overcome this weakness, as suggested in Theil (1961). The adjusted R^2, denoted by $\bar{R}^2$, is based on the consideration that an unbiased estimator of σ^2 is $\sum \hat{u}_i^2/(n-k)$; hence a degree-of-freedom adjusted measure of the proportion of the variance that is unexplained is defined as

$$1-\bar{R}^2 = \frac{[1/n-k]\sum \hat{u}_i^2}{[1/n-1]\sum \dot{y}_i^2} = \frac{n-1}{n-k}(1-R^2), \tag{4.10.9}$$

where $\dot{y}_i$ denotes the deviation of y_i from its mean, $\bar{y}$, $y_i - \bar{y}$. Here the degrees of freedom associated with the residuals is $n-k$, as in the calculation of $\hat{s}^2$, the unbiased estimator of σ^2, in (4.4.18), while the degrees of freedom associated with the dependent variable is $n-1$, and each sum of squares is deflated in (4.10.9) by the associated degrees of freedom. Thus the *adjusted coefficient of determination* is obtained as

$$\bar{R}^2 = 1-(1-R^2)\frac{n-1}{n-k} = R^2 - \frac{k-1}{n-k}(1-R^2). \qquad *(4.10.10)$$

This is another measure of the goodness of fit or the explanatory power of the regression. In general, $\bar{R}^2 < R^2$ (unless $k = 1$ or $R^2 = 1$, in which case $R^2 = \bar{R}^2$), and it is possible for $\bar{R}^2$ to be negative. While the (unadjusted) coefficient of determination can never decrease as added explanatory variables are taken into account, the adjusted coefficient of determination can decrease if the reduction in $1 - R^2$ is more than offset by the increase in $(n-1)/(n-k)$ in (4.10.9). In using this statistic the strategy is to choose the regression with the highest $\bar{R}^2$. It is essential, however, that the dependent variable should be the same in comparing alternative models.

Prediction criterion. A major reason for econometric estimation is for the purpose of prediction. Therefore, it makes sense in some cases where prediction is a major goal to select a model based on some measure of the efficiency of prediction. Mean squared prediction error is thus often used as a criterion. However, to evaluate the mean squared prediction error, it is necessary to know the true model. But if the true model is known, there is no problem of choosing a model. Amemiya (1980) proposed getting around this dilemma by evaluating the mean squared prediction error of the predictor derived from each model, assuming in turn that each model is the true model. Thus, for model (4.2.2), assuming that

$$E\mathbf{x}_f\mathbf{x}'_f = \frac{1}{n}\mathbf{X}'\mathbf{X}, \tag{4.10.11}$$

it follows that the *unconditional mean squared prediction error* can be derived by taking the expected value of (4.8.3) with respect to $\mathbf{x}_f$, as

$$\begin{aligned} E(\hat{y}-y)^2 &= E\{E[(\hat{y}-y)^2 \mid \mathbf{x}_f]\} \\ &= \sigma^2 + n^{-1}E(\hat{\boldsymbol{\beta}}-\boldsymbol{\beta})'\mathbf{X}'\mathbf{X}(\hat{\boldsymbol{\beta}}-\boldsymbol{\beta}) \\ &= \sigma^2(1+n^{-1}k). \end{aligned} \tag{4.10.12}$$

However, σ^2 is unknown. Amemiya suggested that σ^2 be replaced by its unbiased estimator $\hat{s}^2$ of (4.4.18). The *prediction criterion* then chooses the model with the smallest unconditional mean squared prediction error. Compared to Theil's $\bar{R}^2$, the prediction criterion imposes a higher penalty for increasing the number of regressors.

Alternatively, Mallows (1973) assumed that the true data-generating process of y depends on the most comprehensive model, which in the case of comparing (4.2.2) and (4.10.1), is the union of the design matrix $\mathbf{X}$ and the alternative design matrix $\mathbf{Z}$. Then the unconditional mean squared prediction error for the least squares predictor of (4.2.2) is equal to

$$\text{MC} = \frac{1}{n}\left(2k\sigma^2 + \mathbf{y}'\mathbf{M}\mathbf{y}\right). \tag{4.10.13}$$

Mallows suggested estimating σ^2 by $(n-m)^{-1}\mathbf{y}'[\mathbf{I}-\mathbf{W}(\mathbf{W}'\mathbf{W})^{-1}\mathbf{W}']^{-1}\mathbf{y}$, where $\mathbf{W}$ consists of distinct column vectors of $\mathbf{X}$ and $\mathbf{Z}$ and m is the number of column vectors of $\mathbf{W}$.

Information criterion. The information criterion seeks to measure the closeness of an estimated model to the true data-generating process over the domain of y using the Kullback–Leibler information measure,

$$I = \int [\ln g(y) - \ln f(y|\boldsymbol{\theta})]g(y)\,dy, \tag{4.10.14}$$

where $g(y)$ is the true density of y and $f(y \mid \boldsymbol{\theta})$ is the density of the postulated model. This measure is positive unless $g(y) = f(y \mid \boldsymbol{\theta})$ almost everywhere. Akaike (1973) proposed selecting the model that minimizes (4.10.14), and this approach is called the *Akaike information criterion* (AIC). When this criterion is applied to the regression model (4.2.2), it reduces to

$$\text{AIC} = \log\hat{\sigma}^2 + \frac{2k}{n}, \tag{4.10.15}$$

where $\hat{\sigma}^2$ is the ML (biased) estimator of σ^2, as given in (4.5.9).[21]

4.11 BAYESIAN ANALYSIS OF THE LINEAR REGRESSION MODEL

4.11.1 Bayesian Inference and Bayes' Theorem

As discussed before, the observed values of economic variables are typically viewed as the outcomes of an experiment. Let $f(\mathbf{y}; \boldsymbol{\theta})$ denote the probability law generating the observations $\mathbf{y}$, where $\boldsymbol{\theta}$ is a vector of parameters. In statistical analysis, the investigator has the data $\mathbf{y}$ but does not know $\boldsymbol{\theta}$, using $f(\mathbf{y}; \boldsymbol{\theta})$ indirectly to make inferences about the value of $\boldsymbol{\theta}$ given the n data values. There are generally two methods by which this may be attempted: sampling theory and Bayesian inference. The discussion thus far follows the sampling (or "classical") approach. In this section we briefly discuss the alternative Bayesian approach.

In the classical sampling approach, inferences are made by directing attention to the probability model $f(\mathbf{y}; \boldsymbol{\theta})$. Estimators $\hat{\boldsymbol{\theta}}(\mathbf{y})$ of the parameters $\boldsymbol{\theta}$, which are functions of the data $\mathbf{y}$, are chosen so that their sampling distributions, in repeated experiments, are, in some

[21]See Vuong (1989) for a synthesis of nonnested hypothesis-testing and model selection criteria.

sense, concentrated as closely as possible about the true values of $\boldsymbol{\theta}$. For instance, to provide some idea of how far away the calculated quantities $\hat{\boldsymbol{\theta}}(\mathbf{y})$ might be from the true values, *confidence intervals* are calculated. The $1 - \varepsilon$ confidence interval for a parameter θ_j is computed as

$$\hat{\theta}_{j1}(\mathbf{y}) < \theta_j < \hat{\theta}_{j2}(\mathbf{y}),$$

where $\hat{\theta}_{j1}(\mathbf{y})$ and $\hat{\theta}_{j2}(\mathbf{y})$ are functions of $\mathbf{y}$ that are chosen so that in repeated sampling the computed confidence intervals include the value θ_j a proportion $1 - \varepsilon$ of the time.

In the Bayesian approach, a different line is taken. First, all quantities, including the parameters, are considered random variables. Second, all probability statements are conditional, so that in making a probability statement it is necessary to refer to the conditioning event as well as to the event whose probability is being discussed. Therefore, as part of the model, a *prior* distribution of the parameter $\boldsymbol{\theta}$, $p(\boldsymbol{\theta})$, is introduced. The *prior* is supposed to express a state of knowledge (or ignorance) about $\boldsymbol{\theta}$ before the data are obtained. Given the prior distribution, the probability model $f(\mathbf{y}; \boldsymbol{\theta})$, and the data $\mathbf{y}$, the probability distribution of $\boldsymbol{\theta}$ is revised to $p(\boldsymbol{\theta} \mid \mathbf{y})$, which is called the *posterior distribution* of $\boldsymbol{\theta}$. From this distribution, inferences about the parameters are made.

Bayes' theorem plays a central role in combining prior information with current sample information so as to produce the "revision" of the probability as the posterior probability distribution. According to *Bayes' theorem*, the probability of B given A, written $P(B \mid A)$, is

$$\begin{aligned} P(B|A) &= \frac{P(A|B)P(B)}{P(A)} \\ &\propto P(A|B)P(B), \end{aligned} \tag{4.11.1}$$

where $P(\cdot)$ is a generic symbol for a probability labeled by its argument and the sign "$\propto$" denotes "is proportional to," with the factor of proportionality being a normalizing constant.

Now, given the prior information, $p(\boldsymbol{\theta})$, the probability model, or the likelihood function, $f(\mathbf{y} \mid \boldsymbol{\theta})$, and the data $\mathbf{y}$, Bayes' theorem (4.11.1) implies that the posterior probability density function (pdf) $p(\boldsymbol{\theta} \mid \mathbf{y})$, after observing the data $\mathbf{y}$, is proportional to the prior pdf times the likelihood function.

$$\begin{aligned} \text{posterior pdf} &= p(\boldsymbol{\theta}|\mathbf{y}) \\ &\propto \text{prior pdf} \times \text{likelihood function} \\ &\propto p(\boldsymbol{\theta}) \times f(\mathbf{y}|\boldsymbol{\theta}), \end{aligned} \tag{4.11.2}$$

where $p(\boldsymbol{\theta})$ is $P(B)$ in (4.11.1), $f(y \mid \boldsymbol{\theta})$ is $P(A \mid B)$, and $p(\boldsymbol{\theta} \mid \mathbf{y})$ is $P(B \mid A)$. The likelihood function $f(\mathbf{y} \mid \boldsymbol{\theta})$ plays a very important role in Bayes' formula. It is the function that determines how the data $\mathbf{y}$ modify prior knowledge of $\boldsymbol{\theta}$. It represents the information about $\boldsymbol{\theta}$ coming from the data. The posterior distribution and the likelihood function are both often defined up only to a multiplicative constant, as it is only their relative value which is of importance.

Given the posterior pdf of $\boldsymbol{\theta}$, $p(\boldsymbol{\theta} \mid \mathbf{y})$, the marginal and conditional posterior pdf's that are of interest can be derived. Let $\boldsymbol{\theta}$ be partitioned as $\boldsymbol{\theta}' = (\boldsymbol{\theta}_1', \boldsymbol{\theta}_2')$ and suppose that interest centers on $\boldsymbol{\theta}_1$. For example, $\boldsymbol{\theta}_2$ may be a vector of *nuisance parameters* that are of little interest to the investigator. Integrating $p(\boldsymbol{\theta} \mid \mathbf{y})$ analytically or numerically with respect to $\boldsymbol{\theta}_2$ yields the *marginal posterior pdf* of $\boldsymbol{\theta}_1$,

$$p(\boldsymbol{\theta}_1 | \mathbf{y}) = \int p(\boldsymbol{\theta}_1, \boldsymbol{\theta}_2 | \mathbf{y}) \, d\boldsymbol{\theta}_2. \tag{4.11.3}$$

Furthermore, the joint posterior pdf may be decomposed in the following form:

$$p(\boldsymbol{\theta}_1, \boldsymbol{\theta}_2 | \mathbf{y}) = p(\boldsymbol{\theta}_1 | \boldsymbol{\theta}_2, \mathbf{y}) p(\boldsymbol{\theta}_2 | \mathbf{y}), \tag{4.11.4}$$

and the conditional posterior pdf $p(\boldsymbol{\theta}_1 | \boldsymbol{\theta}_2, \mathbf{y})$ for various assigned values for $\boldsymbol{\theta}_2$ can be used to determine how sensitive inferences about $\boldsymbol{\theta}_1$ are to what is assumed about $\boldsymbol{\theta}_2$. See Box and Tiao (1973), Leamer (1978), and Zellner (1971a) for many examples of such *sensitivity analysis*.

4.11.2 Bayesian Regression Analysis

Conjugate prior. Application of the Bayesian approach requires determination of the likelihood function and the choice of a prior distribution. To apply this approach to the regression model (4.2.2), the nature of the distribution of the stochastic disturbance terms, u_i, must be specified. Assuming that the u_i are independently normally distributed with mean zero and constant variance σ^2, as in assumption A.4.6, the likelihood function for $\mathbf{y}$ is given by (4.5.5), which can be written in terms of proportionality (omitting the normalizing constant) as

$$f(\mathbf{y} | \mathbf{X}, \boldsymbol{\beta}, \sigma^2) \propto \frac{1}{\sigma^n} \exp\left\{ -\frac{1}{2\sigma^2} \left[v\hat{s}^2 + (\boldsymbol{\beta} - \hat{\boldsymbol{\beta}})' \mathbf{X}'\mathbf{X} (\boldsymbol{\beta} - \hat{\boldsymbol{\beta}}) \right] \right\}, \tag{4.11.5}$$

where $\hat{\boldsymbol{\beta}}$ is the least squares estimator of $\boldsymbol{\beta}$, (4.3.4); $\hat{s}^2$ is the unbiased estimator of σ^2, defined in (4.4.18), and v is the number of degrees of freedom, $n - k$. Derivation of this equation makes use of the identity

$$\begin{aligned}
(\mathbf{y} - \mathbf{X}\boldsymbol{\beta})'(\mathbf{y} - \mathbf{X}\boldsymbol{\beta}) &= [(\mathbf{y} - \mathbf{X}\hat{\boldsymbol{\beta}}) - \mathbf{X}(\boldsymbol{\beta} - \hat{\boldsymbol{\beta}})]'[(\mathbf{y} - \mathbf{X}\hat{\boldsymbol{\beta}}) - \mathbf{X}(\boldsymbol{\beta} - \hat{\boldsymbol{\beta}})] \\
&= (\mathbf{y} - \mathbf{X}\hat{\boldsymbol{\beta}})'(\mathbf{y} - \mathbf{X}\hat{\boldsymbol{\beta}}) + (\boldsymbol{\beta} - \hat{\boldsymbol{\beta}})'\mathbf{X}'\mathbf{X}(\boldsymbol{\beta} - \hat{\boldsymbol{\beta}}) \\
&= \hat{\mathbf{u}}'\hat{\mathbf{u}} + (\boldsymbol{\beta} - \hat{\boldsymbol{\beta}})'\mathbf{X}'\mathbf{X}(\boldsymbol{\beta} - \hat{\boldsymbol{\beta}})
\end{aligned} \tag{4.11.6}$$

and the orthogonality of $\mathbf{X}$ and $\hat{\mathbf{u}}$:

$$(\boldsymbol{\beta} - \hat{\boldsymbol{\beta}})'\mathbf{X}'(\mathbf{y} - \mathbf{X}\hat{\boldsymbol{\beta}}) = (\boldsymbol{\beta} - \hat{\boldsymbol{\beta}})'[\mathbf{X}'\mathbf{y} - \mathbf{X}'\mathbf{X}(\mathbf{X}'\mathbf{X})^{-1}\mathbf{X}'\mathbf{y}] = \mathbf{0}. \tag{4.11.7}$$

Notice that the likelihood function (4.11.5) depends on the sample only through $\hat{s}^2$ and $\hat{\boldsymbol{\beta}}$, given a fixed $\mathbf{X}$, of course. Since the data enter Bayes' formula (4.11.2) only through the likelihood, it follows that all other aspects of the data, with the exception of $\hat{s}^2$ and $\hat{\boldsymbol{\beta}}$ are irrelevant in deciding the posterior distribution of $\boldsymbol{\beta}$ and σ^2 and hence in making inferences about $\boldsymbol{\beta}$ and σ^2. Therefore, the statistics $\hat{\boldsymbol{\beta}}$ and $\hat{s}^2$ are *sufficient statistics* in conveying all relevant information.

In principle, the likelihood function can be combined with whatever prior density $p(\boldsymbol{\theta})$ the econometrician may wish to consider. However, for model (4.2.2) with $\boldsymbol{\theta}' = (\boldsymbol{\beta}', \sigma^2)$, if the prior $p(\boldsymbol{\beta}', \sigma^2)$ is chosen quite freely, there is a risk that the calculation of the posterior distribution will be very laborious. Two of the most frequently used families of prior distributions are the *conjugate prior* and the *diffuse prior*.

The *conjugate prior* is a form of the prior distribution that is of the same form as the likelihood function, so that it can be combined easily to form the posterior distribution, as discussed in Raiffa and Schlaifer (1961). For the likelihood function (4.11.5), note that conditional on σ, $\hat{s}^2$ is a multiplicative constant, and the marginal probability distribution function of $\boldsymbol{\beta}$ is multivariate normal of the form

$$p(\boldsymbol{\beta}|\sigma,\hat{\boldsymbol{\beta}}) \propto \frac{1}{\sigma^k}\exp\left[-\frac{1}{2\sigma^2}(\boldsymbol{\beta}-\hat{\boldsymbol{\beta}})'\mathbf{X}'\mathbf{X}(\boldsymbol{\beta}-\hat{\boldsymbol{\beta}})\right]. \tag{4.11.8}$$

Furthermore, given $\hat{\boldsymbol{\beta}}$, the marginal distribution of σ is an *inverted gamma* of the form

$$p(\sigma|\hat{\boldsymbol{\beta}}) \propto \frac{1}{\sigma^\upsilon}\exp\left(-\frac{\upsilon\hat{s}^2}{2\sigma^2}\right). \tag{4.11.9}$$

Therefore, conditional on σ, if the prior distribution of $\boldsymbol{\beta}$ is normal, so is the posterior distribution of $\boldsymbol{\beta}$. Suppose that the prior of $\boldsymbol{\beta}$ given σ is chosen to be of the form

$$p(\boldsymbol{\beta}|\sigma) \sim N(\bar{\boldsymbol{\beta}},\sigma^2\boldsymbol{\Omega}), \tag{4.11.10}$$

where $\bar{\boldsymbol{\beta}}$ is the prior mean vector and $\sigma^2\boldsymbol{\Omega}$ is the prior covariance matrix. Then the posterior density of $\boldsymbol{\beta}$ for the regression model (4.2.2), upon completion of the square (as discussed in Box and Tiao, 1973, App. A7.1), is given by

$$\begin{aligned} p(\boldsymbol{\beta}|\mathbf{y},\mathbf{X}) &\propto \exp\left[-\frac{1}{2\sigma^2}(\boldsymbol{\beta}-\boldsymbol{\mu})'(\mathbf{X}'\mathbf{X}+\boldsymbol{\Omega}^{-1})(\boldsymbol{\beta}-\boldsymbol{\mu})\right] \\ &\times \exp\left[-\frac{1}{2\sigma^2}(\hat{\boldsymbol{\beta}}-\bar{\boldsymbol{\beta}})'\mathbf{X}'\mathbf{X}(\mathbf{X}'\mathbf{X}+\boldsymbol{\Omega}^{-1})^{-1}\boldsymbol{\Omega}^{-1}(\hat{\boldsymbol{\beta}}-\bar{\boldsymbol{\beta}})\right], \end{aligned} \tag{4.11.11}$$

where

$$\boldsymbol{\mu} = (\mathbf{X}'\mathbf{X}+\boldsymbol{\Omega}^{-1})^{-1}(\mathbf{X}'\mathbf{X}\hat{\boldsymbol{\beta}}+\boldsymbol{\Omega}^{-1}\bar{\boldsymbol{\beta}}). \tag{4.11.12}$$

The second term on the right of (4.11.11) is a multiplicative constant that introduces only a proportionality factor. Therefore, the posterior distribution of $\boldsymbol{\beta}$ for a given σ is multivariate normally distributed with mean $\boldsymbol{\mu}$ and covariance matrix $\sigma^2[\mathbf{X}'\mathbf{X}+\boldsymbol{\Omega}^{-1}]^{-1}$. The posterior mean $\boldsymbol{\mu}$ is a weighted average of the prior mean $\bar{\boldsymbol{\beta}}$ and the least squares estimator $\hat{\boldsymbol{\beta}}$, where (4.11.12) shows that the weighting matrices are inversely proportional to their respective covariances.

When σ is unknown, the likelihood function (4.11.5) cannot be factored into the two separate components, (4.11.8) and (4.11.9). In this case a conjugate prior is the one that has the same form as (4.11.5):

$$p(\boldsymbol{\beta},\sigma) \propto \sigma^{-(\tau+1)}\exp\left\{-\frac{1}{2\sigma^2}\left[(\tau-k)s_1^2+(\boldsymbol{\beta}-\bar{\boldsymbol{\beta}})'\Omega^{-1}(\boldsymbol{\beta}-\bar{\boldsymbol{\beta}})\right]\right\}. \tag{4.11.13}$$

This prior has the property that for a given σ, the conditional distribution of $\boldsymbol{\beta}$ is normal, centered at $\bar{\boldsymbol{\beta}}$ with covariance matrix $\sigma^2\boldsymbol{\Omega}$, and a marginal pdf for σ in the inverted gamma form with parameters $\tau-k$ and s_1^2. For a given $\boldsymbol{\beta}$, the dispersion of the conditional distribution of σ decreases as τ increases.

Combining the prior (4.11.13) with the likelihood function (4.11.5) yields a posterior pdf which is of the same form as the prior, as discussed in Zellner (1971a, Chap. 3),

$$p(\boldsymbol{\beta},\sigma|\mathbf{y}) \propto \frac{1}{\sigma^{n+r+1}}\exp\left\{-\frac{1}{2\sigma^2}\left[v^*s^{*2} + (\boldsymbol{\beta}-\boldsymbol{\mu})'(\mathbf{X}'\mathbf{X}+\boldsymbol{\Omega}^{-1})(\boldsymbol{\beta}-\boldsymbol{\mu})\right]\right\}, \tag{4.11.14}$$

where

$$v^* = n + \tau - k \quad \text{and} \quad v^*s^{*2} = (\mathbf{y}-\mathbf{X}\hat{\boldsymbol{\beta}})'(\mathbf{y}-\mathbf{X}\hat{\boldsymbol{\beta}}) + (\tau - k)s_1^2. \tag{4.11.15}$$

Diffuse prior. With appropriate choices as to $\bar{\boldsymbol{\beta}}$, $\sigma^2\boldsymbol{\Omega}$, τ, and s_1^2, in (4.11.15), the *conjugate prior* provides information about the parameters, and hence it is sometimes called an *informative prior*. If little is known a priori relative to what the data have to tell us about $\boldsymbol{\theta}$, the specification of the prior should not suggest that some values of the parameters are more likely than others. In other words, the combination of the prior in this case with the likelihood function should yield a posterior pdf that reflects mainly sample information. Such a prior is referred to as a *diffuse prior* or a *noninformative prior*.

One commonly used noninformative prior for $\boldsymbol{\beta}$ and σ treats $\boldsymbol{\beta}$ and σ as independent, with the marginal distribution of $\boldsymbol{\beta}$ proportional to a constant and the marginal distribution of σ proportional to σ^{-1}, that is,[22]

$$p(\boldsymbol{\beta},\sigma) = p(\boldsymbol{\beta})p(\sigma) \propto \frac{1}{\sigma}, \qquad -\infty < \boldsymbol{\beta} < \infty, \quad 0 < \sigma < \infty. \tag{4.11.16}$$

Combining (4.11.16) with (4.11.5) yields the posterior pdf of $\boldsymbol{\beta}$ and σ as

$$p(\boldsymbol{\beta},\sigma|\mathbf{y},\mathbf{X}) \propto \frac{1}{\sigma^{n+1}}\exp\left\{-\frac{1}{2\sigma^2}\left[v\hat{s}^2 + (\boldsymbol{\beta}-\hat{\boldsymbol{\beta}})'\mathbf{X}'\mathbf{X}(\boldsymbol{\beta}-\hat{\boldsymbol{\beta}})\right]\right\}. \tag{4.11.17}$$

From (4.11.17), it is clear that given σ, $\boldsymbol{\beta}$ has a multivariate normal distribution with mean $\hat{\boldsymbol{\beta}}$ and covariance matrix $\sigma^2(\mathbf{X}'\mathbf{X})^{-1}$. Since σ is usually unknown, (4.11.17) can be integrated with respect to σ to obtain the marginal posterior distribution for $\boldsymbol{\beta}$, as discussed in Zellner (1971a,b), to yield

$$p(\boldsymbol{\beta}|\mathbf{y},x) \propto \left[v\hat{s}^2 + (\boldsymbol{\beta}-\hat{\boldsymbol{\beta}})'\mathbf{X}'\mathbf{X}(\boldsymbol{\beta}-\hat{\boldsymbol{\beta}})\right]^{-(v+k)/2}, \tag{4.11.18}$$

which takes the form of a multivariate Student-*t* distribution. For $v > 1$, the mean of (4.11.18) is $\hat{\boldsymbol{\beta}}$. Further, the marginal pdf for one of the elements of $\boldsymbol{\beta}$, say β_j, is of the univariate Student-*t* form; that is, $(\beta_j - \hat{\beta}_j)/s_{\hat{\beta}j}$ has a univariate t pdf with v degrees of freedom, where $s^2_{\hat{\beta}j}$ equals $\hat{s}^2$ times the jth diagonal element of $(\mathbf{X}'\mathbf{X})^{-1}$.

Furthermore, integrating (4.11.17) with respect to the elements of $\boldsymbol{\beta}$ yields the marginal posterior pdf for σ:

$$p(\sigma|\mathbf{y}) \propto \sigma^{-(v+1)}\exp\left(\frac{-v\hat{s}^2}{2\sigma^2}\right). \tag{4.11.19}$$

From the posterior pdf (4.11.14) and (4.11.17), it follows that as the sample size grows, the posterior distributions assume a normal shape with mean approximately equal to $\hat{\boldsymbol{\beta}}$ (the MLE) and covariance matrix equal to $\sigma^2(\mathbf{X}'\mathbf{X})^{-1}$ (the inverse of the second derivatives of the log-likelihood function).

From (4.11.18) it follows that the location of the posterior distribution is not affected by the use of the prior (4.11.16). Further, while (4.11.16) is an *improper prior* in the sense that its integral is infinite, this does not preclude deriving a *proper* posterior pdf.

[22]See Jeffreys (1961), Box and Tiao (1973), Leamer (1978), and Zellner (1971b, 1977) for further discussions on how to represent "knowing little a priori."

4.11.3 Bayesian Point and Interval Estimation

Given a *loss function,* $L(\boldsymbol{\theta}, \hat{\boldsymbol{\theta}}_n)$, and the posterior distribution for $\boldsymbol{\theta}$, $p(\boldsymbol{\theta} \mid \mathbf{y})$, a *Bayesian point estimate* can be derived by minimizing the expected loss. Explicitly, the solution to the minimization problem

$$\min_{\hat{\boldsymbol{\theta}}_B} \int L\left(\boldsymbol{\theta}, \hat{\boldsymbol{\theta}}_B\right) p(\boldsymbol{\theta} \mid \mathbf{y})\, d\boldsymbol{\theta}, \tag{4.11.20}$$

denoted by $\hat{\boldsymbol{\theta}}_B^*$, is the *Bayesian point estimate*. In particular, if the loss function, $L(\boldsymbol{\theta}, \hat{\boldsymbol{\theta}}_B)$, is quadratic, so

$$L\left(\boldsymbol{\theta}, \hat{\boldsymbol{\theta}}_B\right) = \left(\hat{\boldsymbol{\theta}}_B - \boldsymbol{\theta}\right)^1 \mathbf{Q}\left(\hat{\boldsymbol{\theta}}_B - \boldsymbol{\theta}\right), \tag{4.11.21}$$

where $\mathbf{Q}$ is a given positive-definite symmetric matrix, then

$$\begin{aligned} EL\left(\boldsymbol{\theta}, \hat{\boldsymbol{\theta}}_B\right) &= E\left(\hat{\boldsymbol{\theta}}_B - \boldsymbol{\theta}\right)' \mathbf{Q}\left(\hat{\boldsymbol{\theta}}_B - \boldsymbol{\theta}\right) \\ &= E\left[\hat{\boldsymbol{\theta}}_B - \bar{\boldsymbol{\theta}} - (\boldsymbol{\theta} - \bar{\boldsymbol{\theta}})\right]' \mathbf{Q}\left[\hat{\boldsymbol{\theta}}_B - \bar{\boldsymbol{\theta}} - (\boldsymbol{\theta} - \bar{\boldsymbol{\theta}})\right] \\ &= \left(\hat{\boldsymbol{\theta}}_B - \bar{\boldsymbol{\theta}}\right)' \mathbf{Q}\left(\hat{\boldsymbol{\theta}}_B - \bar{\boldsymbol{\theta}}\right) + E(\boldsymbol{\theta} - \bar{\boldsymbol{\theta}})' \mathbf{Q}(\boldsymbol{\theta} - \bar{\boldsymbol{\theta}}), \end{aligned} \tag{4.11.22}$$

where $\bar{\boldsymbol{\theta}}$ is the posterior mean of $\boldsymbol{\theta}$. From (4.11.22) the value of $\hat{\boldsymbol{\theta}}_B$ that minimizes expected loss is $\hat{\boldsymbol{\theta}}_B^* = \bar{\boldsymbol{\theta}}$, the posterior mean.

To appraise the general sampling properties of Bayes' estimates, let $\tilde{\boldsymbol{\theta}} = \tilde{\boldsymbol{\theta}}(\mathbf{y})$ be an estimator of $\boldsymbol{\theta}$. Relative to a specific loss function $L(\boldsymbol{\theta}, \tilde{\boldsymbol{\theta}})$, the expected loss associated with the estimator $\tilde{\boldsymbol{\theta}}$ for which the expectation is taken with respect to $\mathbf{y}$ is called the *risk* and is given by

$$r(\boldsymbol{\theta}) = \int_{\mathbf{y}} L(\boldsymbol{\theta}, \tilde{\boldsymbol{\theta}}) f(\mathbf{y} \mid \boldsymbol{\theta})\, d\mathbf{y}, \tag{4.11.23}$$

where $f(\mathbf{y} \mid \boldsymbol{\theta})$ is a proper pdf for $\mathbf{y}$, given $\boldsymbol{\theta}$, and the integral in (4.11.23) is assumed to converge. The risk function (4.11.23) depends on the value of the unknown parameter vector $\boldsymbol{\theta}$. Since it is impossible to find a $\tilde{\boldsymbol{\theta}}$ that minimizes $r(\boldsymbol{\theta})$ for all possible values of $\boldsymbol{\theta}$, the best we can do is to seek an estimator that minimizes average risk or *Bayes risk* (BR), defined as

$$\mathrm{BR} = \int_{\boldsymbol{\theta}} r(\boldsymbol{\theta}) p(\boldsymbol{\theta})\, d\boldsymbol{\theta}, \tag{4.11.24}$$

where $p(\boldsymbol{\theta})$ is the pdf or weighting function for $\boldsymbol{\theta}$ in regions of the parameter space. Such an estimator is *admissible* if there is no other estimator that has a smaller risk, $r(\boldsymbol{\theta})$, as given in (4.11.23), over the parameter space of $\boldsymbol{\theta}$.

Upon substituting (4.11.23) into (4.11.24),

$$\mathrm{BR} = \int_{\boldsymbol{\theta}} \int_{\mathbf{y}} L(\boldsymbol{\theta}, \tilde{\boldsymbol{\theta}}) f(\mathbf{y} \mid \boldsymbol{\theta}) p(\boldsymbol{\theta})\, d\mathbf{y}\, d\boldsymbol{\theta}. \tag{4.11.25}$$

Using $f(\mathbf{y} \mid \boldsymbol{\theta}) p(\boldsymbol{\theta}) = p(\boldsymbol{\theta} \mid \mathbf{y}) f(\mathbf{y})$ and interchanging the order of integration, (4.11.25) can be expressed as

$$\mathrm{BR} = \int_{\mathbf{y}} \left[\int_{\boldsymbol{\theta}} L(\boldsymbol{\theta}, \tilde{\boldsymbol{\theta}}) p(\tilde{\boldsymbol{\theta}} \mid \mathbf{y})\, d\boldsymbol{\theta}\right] f(\mathbf{y})\, d\mathbf{y}. \tag{4.11.26}$$

The estimator $\tilde{\boldsymbol{\theta}}$ that minimizes the expression in brackets will minimize expected risk, provided that BR is finite, and this estimator is defined as the *Bayes estimator*. Furthermore, by construction, the Bayes estimator is *admissible* because if there were another estimator that had lower risk $r(\boldsymbol{\theta})$ over the parameter space of $\boldsymbol{\theta}$, it would have lower BR—a contradiction.

In *interval estimation* an interval is sought within which the parameter's value lies with a specified posterior probability, say $1-\varepsilon$. Given the posterior distribution of $\boldsymbol{\beta}$, integration will obtain the marginal posterior pdf for a parameter, say β_j, $p(\beta_j \mid \mathbf{y})$. From $p(\beta_j \mid \mathbf{y})$, it is possible to construct intervals with posterior probability $1-\varepsilon$. Since such intervals are not unique, Zellner (1971a) suggests that of all possible intervals with posterior probability $1-\varepsilon$, the one to be selected should be the shortest such interval. Formally, the length of the interval, say $b-a$, is minimized subject to the condition that $P(a < \beta_j < b \mid \mathbf{y}) = \int_a^b p(\beta_j \mid \mathbf{y})\, d\beta_j = 1-\varepsilon$. For a unimodal symmetric posterior probability density function, the solution is to take $p(\beta_j = a \mid \mathbf{y}) = p(\beta_j = b \mid \mathbf{y})$. This interval has posterior densities associated with it that are greater than those of any other interval with posterior probability $1-\varepsilon$, and it is called a *posterior highest density interval.*

For the regression model (4.2.2) with a diffuse prior (4.11.16), the posterior density for a regression coefficient β_j has been shown to be of the univariate Student-t form. Then, with given probability $1-\varepsilon$, say 0.95, β_j is in the given interval $\hat{\beta}_j \pm c\hat{s}_{\beta_j}$, where c is obtained from t tables with $v = n-k$ degrees of freedom such that $\Pr(-c < t(v) < c) = 1-\varepsilon$ and $\hat{s}_{\beta j}$ is the standard error for the jth regression coefficient. Further, a posterior region for the regression coefficient vector can be computed using the multivariate Student-t property of (4.11.18), namely

$$\frac{(\boldsymbol{\beta}-\hat{\boldsymbol{\beta}})'\mathbf{X}'\mathbf{X}(\boldsymbol{\beta}-\hat{\boldsymbol{\beta}})}{k\hat{s}^2 \sim F(k,v)}, \tag{4.11.27}$$

has a posterior F distribution with k and v degrees of freedom.

4.11.4 Bayesian Prediction and Posterior Odds Ratio

Let y_f represent an as yet unobserved variable with probability density function $f(y_f \mid \boldsymbol{\theta})$. The fact that $\boldsymbol{\theta}$ is unknown makes it difficult to use $f(y_f \mid \boldsymbol{\theta})$ to make probability statements about possible values of y_f. However, $f(y_f \mid \boldsymbol{\theta})$ and $P(\boldsymbol{\theta} \mid \mathbf{y})$ can be combined to derive the *predictive density function* for $\mathbf{y}_f$:

$$P(y_f \mid \mathbf{y}) = \int f(y_f \mid \boldsymbol{\theta}) p(\boldsymbol{\theta} \mid \mathbf{y})\, d\boldsymbol{\theta}. \tag{4.11.28}$$

From (4.11.28) the *predictive density function* can be interpreted as an average of $f(y_f \mid \boldsymbol{\theta})$ with $p(\boldsymbol{\theta} \mid \mathbf{y})$ serving as the weighting function. Moments of y_f can be evaluated using (4.11.28). The *Bayesian point prediction,* $\hat{y}_f$, can also be constructed, once a loss function, $L(y_f, \hat{y}_f)$, is specified. When a quadratic loss function is specified, just like the *Bayesian point estimation,* the mean of the predictive density (4.11.28), $\hat{y}_f$, is an optimal point prediction.

For the regression model (4.2.2), let a future observation y_f be given by

$$y_f = \mathbf{x}'_f\boldsymbol{\beta} + u_f. \tag{4.11.29}$$

Suppose that the posterior density function for $\boldsymbol{\beta}$ given σ is (4.11.17). Then the conditional distribution of y_f, given σ, is normal with mean $\mathbf{x}'_f\hat{\boldsymbol{\beta}}$ and covariance $\sigma^2[1+\mathbf{x}'_f(\mathbf{X}'\mathbf{X})^{-1}\mathbf{x}_f]$. Multiplying this conditional predictive density function of y_f by the posterior for σ (4.11.19) and integrating with respect to σ yields

$$p(y_f \mid \mathbf{y}, \mathbf{X}, \mathbf{x}_f) \propto \left[\frac{\upsilon \hat{s}^2 + (y_f - \hat{y}_f)^2}{[1 + \mathbf{x}'_f(\mathbf{X}'\mathbf{X})^{-1}\mathbf{x}_f]}\right]^{-(\upsilon+1)/2}, \tag{4.11.30}$$

where $\hat{y}_f = \mathbf{x}'_f \hat{\boldsymbol{\beta}}$. Thus

$$\frac{y_f - \hat{y}_f}{\hat{s}\left[1 + \mathbf{x}'_f(\mathbf{X}'\mathbf{X})^{-1}\mathbf{x}_f\right]} \tag{4.11.31}$$

has a Student-t distribution with $\upsilon = n - k$ degrees of freedom.

Bayesian methods are also available for analyzing hypotheses about parameter values and for comparing and choosing between alternative hypotheses or models, be they nested or nonnested. In classical sampling theory, one hypothesis (e.g., the null hypothesis) or one of two models is assumed to be "true" and a test statistic distribution is derived under an assumed true null hypothesis or model. In the Bayesian approach, prior probabilities are assigned to hypotheses or models that reflect the degree of confidence associated with each, and Bayes' theorem is employed to compute posterior probabilities for them that reflect the information in the sample data.

To illustrate the Bayesian approach for analyzing hypotheses or model selection, consider the following hypotheses: H_1: $\boldsymbol{\theta} = \boldsymbol{\theta}^1$ with probability P_1 and H_2: $\boldsymbol{\theta} = \boldsymbol{\theta}^2$ with probability P_2. The prior odds for H_1 versus H_2, denoted by K_{12}, are

$$K_{12} = \frac{P_1}{P_2}. \tag{4.11.32}$$

These prior odds summarize the initial views of the hypotheses about H_1 and H_2. If data $\mathbf{y}$ are observed relating to $\boldsymbol{\theta}$'s possible value, the *posterior odds* of $P(H_1 \mid \mathbf{y})$ to $P(H_2 \mid \mathbf{y})$ can be obtained via Bayes' theorem (4.10.2) as

$$\frac{P(H_1 \mid \mathbf{y})}{P(H_2 \mid \mathbf{y})} = \frac{P_1 \times f(\mathbf{y} \mid \boldsymbol{\theta} = \boldsymbol{\theta}^1)}{P_2 \times f(\mathbf{y} \mid \boldsymbol{\theta} = \boldsymbol{\theta}^2)}. \tag{4.11.33}$$

Given a loss function, it is possible to choose a hypothesis so as to minimize expected loss. That is, in considering two hypotheses, a two-action/two-state loss structure can be formulated, with L_{12} denoting the loss incurred when H_1 is selected and H_2 is appropriate, a *type II error*, and L_{21} denoting the loss incurred when H_2 is selected and H_1 is appropriate, a *type I error*. Then H_1 is chosen if

$$L_{12} P(H_2 \mid \mathbf{y}) < L_{21} P(H_1 \mid \mathbf{y}) \tag{4.11.34}$$

and H_2 is chosen if the inequality is reversed. In the case of a symmetric loss function, where $L_{12} = L_{21}$, the decision rule in (4.11.34) reduces to choosing H_1 if the *posterior odds ratio* (4.11.33) is greater than 1 and to choosing H_2 otherwise.

In short, Bayesian procedures for analyzing different kinds of hypotheses involve a statement of uncertainty about alternative hypotheses in the form of prior probabilities and prior distributions for parameters whose values may not be specified by the hypotheses under consideration. Using these prior probabilities, likelihood functions, and Bayes' theorem, posterior odds and probabilities can be computed, analytically or numerically, to evaluate alternative hypotheses that reflect the information in the data.

There are arguments both for and against the Bayesian approach to estimation, as opposed to the classical approach.[23] On the one hand, the Bayesian approach represents a general learning mode, which should aid the researcher in combining various types of information. It also combines prior and sample information in a formal way, which facilitates sensitivity analysis, testing for the separate influences of prior and sample information. Furthermore, it avoids the necessity of assuming repeated samples and of using arbitrary levels of significance. On the other hand, it is difficult to assess a joint density over even a moderately large number of random variables, and while the forms taken by the prior pdf are quite flexible, the requirement that there be a prior pdf is an inflexible one. After taking these various arguments into account, one might well conclude that the best course to follow is an eclectic one. Rather than siding either with the Bayesians or with those employing classical methods, it may be optimal to use the Bayesian approach if the problem is amenable to this approach (e.g., a small number of parameters, with explicit prior information) and otherwise rely on the classical approach to estimation.

PROBLEMS

4-A The word *regression* stems from an early study relating the height of sons, S, to the height of their fathers, F, where

$$S = \beta_1 F + \beta_2.$$

The study found a *regression* toward the mean, where "regression" means a return to a previous state, in that fathers who are taller (shorter) than average tend to have sons who are also taller (shorter) than average but closer to the average height. What values for the estimates of the parameters yield this result? Prove that these values imply a regression toward the mean, and illustrate geometrically.

4-B Consider the simple linear regression model $y_i = \beta_1 x_i + \beta_2$ estimated using the maximum-likelihood technique under the usual normality assumption.

1. Prove that the estimator of the slope coefficient $\hat{\beta}_1$ is distributed normally as

$$\hat{\beta}_1 \sim N\left(\beta_1, \frac{\sigma^2}{\sum \dot{x}_i^2}\right).$$

2. Show geometrically in a scatter diagram such as Figure 4.1 how the variance decreases as n increases, σ^2 decreases, or $\sum \dot{x}_i^2$ increases.
3. What is the distribution of the estimator of the intercept $\hat{\beta}_2$?
4. What is Cov($\hat{\boldsymbol{\beta}}$), where $\boldsymbol{\beta} = (\beta_1, \beta_2)'$?

4-C Prove that the estimated regression coefficients for a linear regression equation with an intercept term are identical to those obtained for the same linear regression equation without an intercept term, but for which all variables are replaced by deviations from their mean values.

4-D One way of interpreting the least squares estimators is in terms of the solutions to the problem of minimizing the variance of the estimator, given the constraint that the estimator is linear and unbiased. In the case of simple linear regression assume that the slope estimator is linear and unbiased:

$$\hat{\beta}_1 = \sum c_i y_i = \sum c_i(\beta_1 x_i + \beta_2 + u_i),$$
$$E(\hat{\beta}_1) = \beta_1 \sum c_i x_i + \beta_2 \sum c_i = \beta_1,$$

[23]See Zellner (1971a,b, 1983), Rothenberg (1971), and Poirier (1988).

requiring that

$$\sum c_i x_i = 1, \qquad \sum c_i = 0.$$

Subject to these two constraints, minimize the variance

$$\text{Var}(\hat{\beta}_1) = \sigma^2 \sum c_i^2$$

using the Lagrangian

$$L(\hat{\beta}_1, \lambda_1, \lambda_2) = \sigma^2 \sum c_i^2 + \lambda_1(\sum c_i x_i - 1) + \lambda_2(\sum c_i),$$

where λ_1 and λ_2 are Lagrange multipliers. Show that the resulting estimators are the least squares estimators. Carry out a similar proof for β_2.

4-E Yet another way of interpreting the least squares estimators is in terms of the problem of prediction. In the case of simple linear regression, assume that the problem is to predict y at a particular level of x, given as $\hat{x}$. Assume a linear and unbiased predictor

$$\hat{y} = \sum c_i y_i = \sum c_i(\beta_1 x_i + \beta_2 + u_i),$$
$$E(\hat{y}) = \beta_1 \sum c_i x_i + \beta_2 \sum c_i = \beta_1 \hat{x} + \beta_2,$$

requiring that

$$\sum c_i x_i = \hat{x}, \qquad \sum c_i = 1.$$

Subject to these two constraints, minimize the variance of the prediction $\hat{y}$:

$$\text{Var}(\hat{y}) = E[\hat{y} - E(\hat{y})]^2 = \sigma^2 \sum c_i^2,$$

proceeding as in Problem (4-D) to show that the best linear unbiased predictors are given as

$$\hat{y} = \hat{\beta}_1 \hat{x} + \hat{\beta}_2,$$

as in (4.8.1), where $\hat{\beta}_1$ and $\hat{\beta}_2$ are the least squares estimators.

4-F Consider the multiple linear regression with two explanatory variables

$$y_i = x_{i1}\beta_1 + x_{i2}\beta_2 + \beta_3 + u_i.$$

Show that if $\hat{v}_i$ are the least squares residuals in the simple regression of y_i on x_{i2} and $\hat{w}_i$ are the least squares residuals in the simple regression of x_{i1} on x_{i2}, then the least squares estimator for β_1 can be obtained as the estimated slope in the simple regression of $\hat{v}_i$ on $\hat{w}_i$.

4-G Derive the normal equations of least squares for a multiple linear regression using summation notation. Using Cramer's rule, solve for the least squares estimators and show that the results are the same as those using matrix notation.

4-H Prove that in the case of maximum likelihood estimation for multiple linear regression, assuming homoskedasticity and absence of serial correlation, the multivariate normal density function can be written as in (4.5.6). Also prove that $\hat{\boldsymbol{\beta}}$ and $\hat{\sigma}^2$ in (4.3.4) and (4.5.9), respectively, satisfy both first- and second-order conditions for maximization of the likelihood function in (4.5.6).

4-I Consider the fundamental idempotent matrix of least squares $\mathbf{M}$, defined in (4.3.12) as

$$\mathbf{M} = \mathbf{I} - \mathbf{X}(\mathbf{X}'\mathbf{X})^{-1}\mathbf{X}'.$$

Prove that:

1. $\mathbf{M}$ is a symmetric and idempotent matrix.
2. $\mathbf{MX} = \mathbf{0}$, $\hat{\mathbf{u}} = \mathbf{Mu}$, $\hat{\mathbf{u}}'\hat{\mathbf{u}} = \mathbf{u}'\mathbf{Mu}$, $E\hat{\mathbf{u}}\hat{\mathbf{u}} = \sigma^2\mathbf{M}$.
3. $\text{rank}(\mathbf{M}) = \text{tr}(\mathbf{M}) = n - k = \text{d.f.}$
4. $\mathbf{y}'\mathbf{My} \geq 0$, so $\mathbf{M}$ is positive semidefinite.
5. $\mathbf{M} = \mathbf{I} - \mathbf{XX}^{+} = \mathbf{M}^{+}$, where $\mathbf{M}^{+}$ is the generalized inverse of $\mathbf{M}$ (see Appendix B).

4-J An important property of maximum likelihood estimators is that they are invariant with respect to nonsingular transformations. Illustrate this property by proving that the (biased) maximum likelihood estimator of the standard deviation of the stochastic disturbance term, $\hat{\sigma}$, equals the square root of the (biased) maximum likelihood estimator of the variance, $\hat{\sigma}^2$, given in (4.5.9). Show by contrast that the square root of the unbiased estimator $\hat{s}^2$ (4.4.18) is *not* an unbiased estimator of the standard deviation.

4-K Show that $\hat{s}^2$ is a consistent estimator of σ^2, assuming that $\mathbf{u}$ is distributed as in (4.5.2).

4-L An example of an estimator that is consistent even though neither its bias nor its variance tends to zero is the estimator $\hat{\beta}^{(n)}$ of the parameter β defined as[24]

$$\hat{\beta}^{(n)} = \begin{cases} \beta & \text{with probability } 1 - (1/n), \\ n & \text{with probability } 1/n. \end{cases}$$

Show that, as $n \to \infty$:

1. $E(\hat{\beta}^{(n)}) \to \beta + 1 \neq \beta$
2. $\text{Var}(\hat{\beta}^{(n)}) \to \infty$
3. $P(|\hat{\beta}^{(n)} - \beta| < \varepsilon) \to 1$

so that this estimator is consistent even though it is neither asymptotically unbiased nor asymptotically "certain."

4-M Consider the linear form $z = \boldsymbol{\alpha\beta}$, where $\boldsymbol{\alpha}$ is a nonzero row vector of fixed weights and $\boldsymbol{\beta}$ is the column vector of parameters in the basic linear regression model. Letting $\hat{\boldsymbol{\beta}}$ be the least squares estimators, show, using the Gauss–Markov theorem, that

$$\hat{z} = \boldsymbol{\alpha}\,\hat{\boldsymbol{\beta}}$$

is the best linear unbiased estimator of z.[25]

4-N Under the assumptions of the Gauss–Markov theorem of Section 4.4, show that the least squares residual vector

$$\hat{\mathbf{u}} = \mathbf{My} = (\mathbf{I} - \mathbf{X}(\mathbf{X}'\mathbf{X})^{-1}\mathbf{X}')\mathbf{y}$$

is a BLUE estimator of the stochastic disturbance vector $\mathbf{u}$, where

$$E(\hat{\mathbf{u}} - \mathbf{u}) = \mathbf{0}, \qquad \text{Cov}(\hat{\mathbf{u}} - \mathbf{u}) = \sigma^2(\mathbf{I} - \mathbf{M})$$

and where, if $\hat{\hat{\mathbf{u}}}$ is any linear unbiased estimator of $\mathbf{u}$, then

$$\text{Cov}(\hat{\mathbf{u}} - \mathbf{u}) - \text{Cov}(\hat{\hat{\mathbf{u}}} - \mathbf{u}) \quad \text{is negative semidefinite.}$$

4-O Assume that the variables y and x depend on time t, where all three variables have mean zero. Let y_t^* and x_t^* be the detrended variables, namely the calculated residuals from the least squares regressions of y on t and x on t, respectively. Show, for the following regressions,

$$\begin{aligned} y_t &= \beta_1 x_t + \gamma_1 t \\ &= \beta_2 x_t^* \\ &= \beta_3 x_t^* + \gamma_3 t, \\ y_t^* &= \beta_4 x_t^* \\ &= \beta_5 x_t^* + \gamma_5 t, \end{aligned}$$

[24]See Sewell (1969).

[25]This result implies that the minimum variance property of least squares is preserved for any weighted combination of estimators. It also implies that it is impossible to improve on the least squares estimator of one of the parameters in $\boldsymbol{\beta}$ even by sacrificing precision in the estimators of all other elements of $\boldsymbol{\beta}$.

that the least squares estimates of the slope parameter are all equal:

$$\hat{\beta}_1 = \hat{\beta}_2 = \hat{\beta}_3 = \hat{\beta}_4 = \hat{\beta}_5.$$

Generalize to a vector of explanatory variables.

4-P Consider the model

$$y_i = \beta_1 x_{1i} + \beta_2 x_{2i} + u_i,$$
$$E(u_i) = 0,$$
$$E(u_i u_j) = \begin{cases} \sigma^2 & \text{if } i = j \\ 0 & \text{if } i \neq j, \end{cases}$$

where all three variables have mean zero. If β_1 is estimated from the regression of y on x_1, with x_2 omitted, show that the resulting estimate is, in general, biased but has a smaller variance than the estimate obtained with x_2 included. When will the mean squared error $E(\hat{\beta}_1 - \beta_1)^2$ be smaller for the regression with x_2 omitted?

4-Q Consider the case of simple linear regression in which $n - 1$ of the data points are clustered around the point (x_0, y_0) and the last data point (x_n, y_n) is an outlier lying much farther away from (x_0, y_0) than any of the other data points:

1. Show the situation in a diagram, and indicate the least squares regression line in the diagram.
2. Prove that the least squares regression line will be close to the line passing through (x_0, y_0) and (x_n, y_n).
3. Prove that the slope of the least squares regression line $\hat{\beta}_1$ is more sensitive to variations in the outlier point (x_n, y_n) than to variations in any one of the points in the cluster (x_i, y_i), $i = 1, 2, \ldots, n - 1$. Specifically, assuming that the x values are fixed, calculate $\partial\hat{\beta}_1/\partial y_n$ and $\partial\hat{\beta}_1/\partial y_i$, and show that the former is larger (here $\hat{\beta}_1$ is the slope estimate for the simple linear regression). What can you conclude concerning where to spend time and effort in improving the measurement of various data points?

4-R Prove that whenever an additional explanatory variable enters a regression equation, the multiple correlation coefficient R^2 either increases or remains constant. Under what circumstances would R^2 remain constant?

4-S Consider the regression equation

$$\mathbf{y} = \mathbf{X}\boldsymbol{\beta} + \mathbf{u}$$

and assume that $\mathbf{y}$ is replaced by $\mathbf{y}^*$, a linear combination of $\mathbf{y}$ and the columns of the $\mathbf{X}$ matrix defined by

$$\mathbf{y}^* = a_0\mathbf{y} + \sum_{j=1}^{k} a_j \mathbf{x}_j,$$

where $\mathbf{x}_j$ is the jth column of $\mathbf{X}$. Consider the new regression equation

$$\mathbf{y}^* = \mathbf{X}\boldsymbol{\beta}^* + \mathbf{u}^*,$$

where $\mathbf{X}$ is the same as before.

1. Show that the least squares estimators and residuals are changed (i.e., $\hat{\boldsymbol{\beta}} \neq \hat{\boldsymbol{\beta}}^*$, $\hat{\mathbf{u}} \neq \hat{\mathbf{u}}^*$).
2. Show that the coefficient of determination R^2 is generally different [i.e., $R^2 \neq (R^*)^2$].

4-T Verify that the multiple correlation coefficient R can be expressed as the correlation coefficient between $\mathbf{y}$ and $\hat{\mathbf{y}}$:

$$R = \frac{\mathrm{Cov}(\mathbf{y}, \hat{\mathbf{y}})}{\sqrt{\mathrm{Var}(\mathbf{y})\,\mathrm{Var}(\hat{\mathbf{y}})}} = \frac{\sum \dot{y}_i \hat{\dot{y}}_i}{\sqrt{\left(\sum \dot{y}_i^2\right)\left(\sum \hat{\dot{y}}_i^2\right)}},$$

where $\hat{\mathbf{y}} = \mathbf{X}\hat{\boldsymbol{\beta}}$.

4-U Prove, in the case of the simple regression

$$\dot{y} = \beta_1 \dot{x},$$

where variables are measured as deviations from their mean values, that

$$R^2 = \hat{\beta}_1^2 \frac{\sum \dot{x}_i^2}{\sum \dot{y}_i^2} = \hat{\beta}_1^2 \frac{s_x^2}{s_y^2},$$

where s_x^2 and s_y^2 are the sample variances of x and y, respectively, given as

$$s_x^2 = \frac{1}{n-1} \sum \dot{x}_i^2, \qquad s_y^2 = \frac{1}{n-1} \sum \dot{y}_i^2.$$

4-V Consider R^2 for a linear regression model that does not include an intercept term.

1. Show that $\sum \hat{u}_i$ need not vanish, so that (4.3.18) need not hold.
2. If R^2 is defined as $\|\hat{\mathbf{y}}\|^2/\|\Sigma$;, show that R^2 will always be nonnegative but that it can exceed 1.
3. If R^2 is defined as $1 - (\|\hat{\mathbf{u}}\|^2/\|\mathbf{y}\|^2$, show that R^2 will always be less than or equal to 1 but that it can be negative.

4-W Consider tests of significance for estimated parameters of the dummy variable representing the investment tax credit (3.2.1).

1. Show that the t ratio $\hat{\beta}_3/\hat{s}_3$, where $\hat{s}_3$ is the standard error corresponding to β_3, tests the significance of the intercept without the tax credit.
2. Show that the t ratio $\hat{\beta}_4/\hat{s}_4$, where $\hat{s}_4$ is the standard error corresponding to β_4, tests whether there is any significant difference between the intercept with and without the tax credit.

4-X One of the reduced-form equations of the prototype micro model determines price p as a function of income I and rainfall r:

$$p = \beta_1 I + \beta_2 r + \beta_3 + u = (I \quad r \quad 1)\begin{pmatrix} \beta_1 \\ \beta_2 \\ \beta_3 \end{pmatrix} + u,$$

where the notation of (2.5.9) has been simplified. Assume that over the sample the stochastic disturbance term is independently and identically distributed as $N(0, \sigma^2)$. Using the following data for wheat:

Years	Price	Income	Rainfall
1951–1955	2.0	2.0	2.0
1956–1960	1.8	2.2	3.2
1961–1965	1.7	2.6	2.7
1966–1970	1.3	2.9	3.3
1971–1975	1.8	3.2	3.8

do the following *without* the aid of a computer (show all calculations):

1. Obtain the least squares estimators $(\hat{\beta}_1 \quad \hat{\beta}_2 \quad \beta_3)' = \hat{\boldsymbol{\beta}}$ and $\text{Cov}(\hat{\boldsymbol{\beta}})$.
2. Find standard errors and t values for the estimated coefficients. Which, if any, are significant at the 0.90 level?
3. Find the coefficient of determination R^2 and perform an analysis of variance to test for the significance of the entire regression.
4. Forecast the price of wheat in 1976–1980, assuming that income is 3.5 and rainfall is 3.4. Find a 90% confidence interval for the forecasted price.

4-Y Using the geometric approach to least squares of Figure 4.2, prove and illustrate the fact that the coefficient of determination R^2 will not change if the design matrix $\mathbf{X}$ changes as long as the space defined by the columns of $\mathbf{X}$ remains the same. Give several illustrations of the types of changes in $\mathbf{X}$ that will not change the space defined by its columns.

BIBLIOGRAPHY

AITCHESON, J., and S. D. SILVEY (1958). "Maximum Likelihood Estimation of Parameters Subject to Restraints." *Annals of Mathematical Statistics*, 29: 812–822.

AKAIKE, H. (1973). "Information Theory and an Extension of the Maximum Likelihood Principle." *Proceedings of the 2nd International Symposium on Information Theory*, pp. 267–281.

AMEMIYA, T. (1980). "Selection of Regressors." *International Economic Review*, 21: 331–345.

AMEMIYA, T. (1985). *Advanced Econometrics*. Cambridge, Mass.: Harvard University Press.

APOSTOL, T. M. (1974). *Mathematical Analysis*, 2nd ed. Reading, Mass: Addison-Wesley Publishing Company, Inc.

ATKINSON, A. C. (1970). "A Method for Discriminating between Models" (with discussion). *Journal of the Royal Statistical Society*, B32: 323–353.

BERNDT, E. R., and N. E. SAVIN (1975). "Estimation and Hypothesis Testing in Singular Equation Systems with Autoregressive Disturbances." *Econometrica*, 43: 931–957.

BODKIN, R. G. (1970). "A Note on the Standard Error of Prediction in the Multivariate Case." *Metroeconomica*, 22: 149–164.

BOX, G. E. P., and G. C. TIAO (1973). *Bayesian Inference in Statistical Analysis*. Reading, Mass.: Addison-Wesley Publishing Company, Inc.

CHOW, G. (1960). "Tests for Equality between Sets of Coefficients in Two Linear Regressions." *Econometrica*, 28: 591–605.

COX, D. R. (1961). "Tests of Separate Families of Hypotheses," in J. Neyman, Ed., *Proceedings of the 4th Berkeley Symposium on Mathematical Statistics and Probability*, Vol. 1. Berkeley; Calif.: University of California Press, pp. 105–123.

COX, D. R. (1962). "Further Results on Tests of Separate Families of Hypotheses." *Journal of the Royal Statistical Society*, B, 24: 406–424.

DAVIDSON, R., and J. G. MACKINNON (1981). "Several Tests for Model Specification in the Presence of Alternative Hypotheses." *Econometrica*, 49: 781–793.

ENGLE, R. (1984). "Wald, Likelihood Ratio, and Lagrange Multiplier Tests in Econometrics," in Z. Griliches and M. D. Intriligator, Eds., *Handbook of Econometrics*, Vol. 2. Amsterdam, North-Holland Publishing Company.

ENGLE, R., D. F. HENDRY, and J. F. RICHARD (1983). "Exogeneity." *Econometrica*, 51: 277–304.

FISHER, G. R. (1983). "Tests for Two Separate Regressions." *Journal of Econometrics*, 21:117–132.

GODFREY, L., and M. H. PESARAN (1983). "Tests of Non-Nested Regression Models: Small Sample Adjustments and Monte Carlo Evidence." *Journal of Econometrics*, 21: 133–154.

HANSEN, L. P. (1982). "Large Sample Properties of Generalized Method of Moments Estimators." *Econometrica*, 50: 1029–1054.

INTRILIGATOR, M. D. (1971). *Mathematical Optimization and Economic Theory.* Englewood Cliffs, N.J.: Prentice Hall, Inc.

JEFFREYS, H. (1961). *Theory of Probability*, 3rd ed. Oxford: Clarendon Press.

LEAMER, E. (1978). *Specification Searches.* New York: John Wiley & Sons, Inc.

MACKINNON, J. (1983). "Model Specification Tests against Nonnested Alternatives" (with discussions). *Econometric Review*, 2: 85–158.

MALLOWS, C. L. (1973). "Choosing Variables in a Linear Regression: A Graphical Aid." Paper presented at the Central Region Meeting of the Institute of Mathematical Statistics, Manhattan, Kans.

MCALEER, M., and G. R. FISHER (1982). "Testing Separate Regression Models Subject to Specification Error." *Journal of Econometrics*, 19: 125–145.

MIZON, G., and J. F. RICHARD (1986). "The Encompassing Principle and Its Application to Non-Nested Hypotheses." *Econometrica*, 54: 657–678.

PESARAN, M. H. (1986). "Comparison of Local Power of Alternative Tests of Non-Nested Regression Models." *Econometrica*, 50: 1287–1305.

POIRIER, D. J. (1988). "Frequentist and Subjectivist Perspectives on the Problems of Model Building in Economics." *Journal of Economic Perspectives* (with comments by J. Rust, A. Pagan, and J. Geweke), 2: 121–170.

RAIFFA, H., and R. SCHLAIFER (1961). *Applied Statistical Decision Theory*. Cambridge; Mass.: Harvard University Press.

RAO, C. R. (1948). "Tests of Significance in Multivariate Analysis." *Biometrika*, 35: 58–79.

RAO, C. R. (1973). *Linear Statistical Inference and Its Applications*, 2nd ed. New York: John Wiley & Sons, Inc.

ROTHENBERG, T. (1971). "The Bayesian Approach in Econometrics," in M. D. Intriligator, Ed., *Frontiers of Quantitative Economics*. Amsterdam: North-Holland Publishing Company.

SEWELL, W. P. (1969). "Least Squares, Conditional Predictions, and Estimator Properties." *Econometrica*, 37: 39–43.

SILVEY, S. D. (1959). "The Lagrangian Multiplier Test." *Annals of Mathematical Statistics*, 30: 389–407.

THEIL, H. (1961). *Economic Forecasts and Policy*, 2nd ed. Amsterdam: North-Holland Publishing Company.

THEIL, H. (1971). *Principles of Econometrics.* New York: John Wiley & Sons, Inc.

TORO-VIZCARRONDO, C., and T. D. WALLACE (1968). "A Test of the Mean Square Error Criterion for Restrictions in Linear Regression." *Journal of the American Statistical Association*, 63: 558–572.

VUONG, Q. (1989). "Likelihood Ratio Tests for Model Selection and Non-Nested Hypothesis." *Econometrica*, 57: 257–306.

WALLACE, T. D. (1972). "Weaker Criteria and Tests for Linear Restrictions in Regression." *Econometrica*, 40: 689–698.

ZELLNER, A. (1971a). *An Introduction to Bayesian Inference Econometrics*. New York: John Wiley & Sons, Inc.

Zellner, A. (1971b). "The Bayesian Approach in Econometrics," in M. D. Intriligator, Ed. *Frontiers of Quantitative Economics*. Amsterdam: North-Holland Publishing Company.

Zellner, A. (1977). "Jeffrey–Bayes Posterior Odds Ratio and the Akaike Information Criterion for Discriminating between Models," Graduate School of Business, University of Chicago.

Zellner A. (1983). "Statistical Theory and Econometrics," in Z. Griliches and M. D. Intriligator, Eds., *Handbook of Econometrics*, Vol. 1. Amsterdam: North-Holland Publishing Company.

5

EXTENSIONS OF THE SIMPLE LINEAR REGRESSION MODEL

5.1 PROBLEMS: THEIR DIAGNOSIS AND TREATMENT

In econometrics, because of the complexity of phenomena and the impossibility of experimentation, it is customary to hypothesize a data-generating process (e.g., equation (4.2.2) and assumptions A.4.1 to A.4.6) that represents the actual process by which the values of the observed quantities have been determined. Consequently, statistical inference (in the sense of making probability statements about the state of nature) is made conditional on the hypothesized data-generating process. However, in practice, various problems may arise that violate the basic assumptions of the basic linear regression model. The least squares estimators will therefore not necessarily be the best linear unbiased estimators (BLUE). Other problems involve the basic structure of the model. In this chapter we treat some of the more important of these problems.[1] The approach taken will be very much like that of a physician caring for a sick patient. The first step is that of *diagnosis*, subjecting the model, data, or estimates to appropriate tests to see if certain specific problems are, in fact, present. The second step is that of *treatment*, which typically involves reformulating the model, data, or estimation technique to overcome these problems.

Section 5.2 treats the issue of multicollinearity (A.4.3). Section 5.3 treats the generalizations of the Gauss–Markov theorem to the case when the covariance matrix of the error terms is not proportional to an identity matrix (A.4.2) for both the single-equation and multiple-equation models; specific issues of heteroskedasticity and serial correlation are discussed in Sections 5.4 and 5.5, respectively; error components models, which are frequently used for pooling cross-section and time-series data, are discussed in Section 5.6; in Section 5.7 we discuss specification errors; issues of measurement errors and the method of in-

[1]See also Amemiya (1985), Davidson and MacKinnon (1993), Goldfeld and Quandt (1972), Greene (1990), Johnston (1985), Judge et al. (1985), Maddala (1992), Malinvaud (1980), and Theil (1971) for related discussions of these problems.

strumental variables are discussed in Section 5.8; Section 5.9 covers nonlinear regression models; discrete dependent variables and censored or truncated regression models are described in Sections 5.10 and 5.11, respectively; Sections 5.12 and 5.13 treat robust regression and semiparametric or nonparametric estimation; finally, in Section 5.14 we briefly review basic methodologies of empirical modeling.

5.2 MULTICOLLINEARITY

One of the assumptions made in Chapter 4 was the rank condition (A.4.3) that

$$\text{rank}(\mathbf{X}) = k, \tag{5.2.1}$$

so that the columns of the $n \times k$ design matrix $\mathbf{X}$ of data on the explanatory variables are linearly independent. Under this assumption it follows that $\mathbf{X}'\mathbf{X}$ is nonsingular, so it can be inverted to obtain the least squares estimator $\hat{\boldsymbol{\beta}}$ as in (4.3.4). If, however, one column of $\mathbf{X}$ is a linear combination of the other columns of the matrix, the rank condition is violated,

$$\text{rank}(\mathbf{X}) < k, \tag{5.2.2}$$

implying that

$$|\mathbf{X}'\mathbf{X}| = 0. \tag{5.2.3}$$

In other words, $\mathbf{X}'\mathbf{X}$ is a singular matrix that cannot be inverted. This situation is one of *perfect multicollinearity*, in which the normal equations of least squares (4.3.3) cannot be solved for the estimator $\hat{\boldsymbol{\beta}}$. This problem does, in fact, arise on occasion. If one of the explanatory variables is constant over the sample, it is a multiple of the unity variable included to account for the intercept. One column of $\mathbf{X}$ is thus a multiple of another, so $\mathbf{X}'\mathbf{X}$ is singular. Another example is a case in which the data on one of the explanatory variables have been obtained by averaging over several other included explanatory variables. A third example is where *dummy variables*, each representing the presence or absence of a characteristic, are included in the regression, and the dummy variables include all possibilities. For example, suppose that the regression includes dummy variables representing seasonal influences, where d_s is 1 if an observation is taken in season s and 0 otherwise, where $s = 1, 2, 3, 4$. If all four dummy variables d_1, d_2, d_3, and d_4 are included (as well as an intercept term), there is perfect multicollinearity. In such a case, (any) one of the dummy variables or the unity variable must be dropped to avoid this problem of linear dependence.

A situation of perfect multicollinearity is readily identified by the inability to calculate the required inverse matrix. Following this "diagnosis," the "treatment" is clear: remove the offending explanatory variable(s)—namely, those that can be expressed as linear combinations of the other explanatory variables—and estimate the model after such variables have been eliminated. This is equivalent to estimating not the coefficients in $\boldsymbol{\beta}$ but rather, certain linear combinations of these coefficients. For example, if the first two explanatory variables are equal, and thus the first and second columns of $\mathbf{X}$ are the same, there is perfect multicollinearity. In such a case, it is possible to estimate the sum of the coefficients $\beta_1 + \beta_2$ (measuring the combined effect of the first two explanatory variables by deleting either the first or second columns of $\mathbf{X}$), and it is possible to estimate the other coefficients $\beta_3, \beta_4, \ldots, \beta_k$ (assuming that no other linear dependencies are present), but it is impossible to distinguish β_1 from β_2; that is, it is impossible to determine the separate effects of the first two explanatory variables. More generally, with perfect multicollinearity, certain linear combinations of coefficients can be estimated uniquely even if the coefficients themselves cannot be so estimated.[2] More typically, the situation is not one of perfect multicollinearity but rather one of a *multicollinearity problem*, in which case **X'X** is not singular but is "close to" singular in that[3]

$$|\mathbf{X}'\mathbf{X}| \approx 0. \qquad *(5.2.4)$$

In this case the data on the explanatory variables have the property that while none is an *exact* linear combination of the others, the values of one or more of them are *almost* given by such linear combinations of the values of the others. This situation, in which the explanatory variables tend to move together, arises very often in empirical studies, particularly in those using time-series data. Indeed, the problem of multicollinearity is one of the most ubiquitous, significant, and difficult problems in applied econometrics. Economic data, by their very nature, tend to move together, often reflecting common underlying factors such as trends and cycles. For example, in working with macroeconomic time-series data, the national income aggregates all tend to move together, so that including two or more of these variables among the explanatory variables in a regression equation will almost inevitably lead to a multicollinearity problem, as we have seen in Section 4.9.

When **X'X** is close to singular, it is typically possible still to obtain the least squares estimates, and the resulting estimators remain best linear unbiased. However, simply knowing that the least squares estimators have all the desirable properties is cold comfort because, under a high degree of multicollinearity, it becomes very difficult to identify precisely the separate effects of the variables involved in that specific estimates may have very large errors; these errors may be highly correlated, one with another; and the sampling variances of the coefficients may be very large. Investigators may be misled into dropping variables

[2]More formally, with perfect multicollinearity it is possible to estimate certain linear combinations of the coefficients, given by $\mathbf{w}'\boldsymbol{\beta}$, where $\mathbf{w}'$ is a given $1 \times k$ vector of weights. Assuming that the estimator of $\mathbf{w}'\boldsymbol{\beta}$ is a linear estimator, of the form $\mathbf{a}'\mathbf{y}$, where $\mathbf{a}'$ is a $1 \times n$ vector, for it to be unbiased

$$E(\mathbf{a}'\mathbf{y}) = \mathbf{a}'\mathbf{X}\boldsymbol{\beta} = \mathbf{w}'\boldsymbol{\beta},$$

which is satisfied if

$$\mathbf{w}' = \mathbf{a}'\mathbf{X}.$$

This condition requires that each of the weights be a fixed linear combination of the elements of the corresponding column of **X**. If **w** satisfies this condition for some **a**, the best linear unbiased estimator of $\mathbf{w}'\boldsymbol{\beta}$ is given as $\mathbf{w}'\mathbf{z}$, where **z** is any solution of the normal equations

$$(\mathbf{X}'\mathbf{X})\mathbf{z} = \mathbf{X}'\mathbf{y}.$$

Although **z** need not be unique, the estimator $\mathbf{w}'\mathbf{z}$, given that $\mathbf{w}' = \mathbf{a}'\mathbf{X}$, is unique, and $\mathbf{w}'\mathbf{z}$ is the unique BLUE estimator of $\mathbf{w}'\boldsymbol{\beta}$. In the case without perfect multicollinearity, the **z** solving the normal equations above is the unique least squares estimator $\hat{\boldsymbol{\beta}}$ and **a** can be expressed as

$$\mathbf{a}' = \mathbf{w}'(\mathbf{X}'\mathbf{X})^{-1}\mathbf{X}'$$

and the estimator of $\mathbf{w}'\boldsymbol{\beta}$ is

$$\mathbf{w}'\mathbf{z} = \mathbf{w}'\hat{\boldsymbol{\beta}} = \mathbf{w}'(\mathbf{X}'\mathbf{X})^{-1}\mathbf{X}'\mathbf{y} = \mathbf{a}'\mathbf{y}.$$

Thus, in the case without perfect multicollinearity, all vectors of weights **w** yield unique estimators.

[3]If the determinant is not zero but is very close to zero, most computer programs will not calculate the inverse, even though it does exist. Such a situation is not one of perfect multicollinearity, but for practical purposes it can be treated as such.

incorrectly from an analysis because their coefficients are not statistically significantly different from zero or find that coefficient estimates are very sensitive to the addition or deletion of a few observations or the deletion of an apparently insignificant variable.

The sensitivity of the precision (as measured by the reciprocals of the estimated standard errors) of the least squares estimates to the collinear relations among the **X** variables may be demonstrated using the singular-value decomposition of the **X** matrix. Note that an $n \times k$ matrix **X** may be decomposed as

$$\mathbf{X} = \mathbf{UDV}', \tag{5.2.5}$$

where **U** and **V** are $n \times k$ and $k \times k$ matrices with $\mathbf{U}'\mathbf{U} = \mathbf{V}'\mathbf{V} = \mathbf{I}_k$ and **D** is a $k \times k$ diagonal matrix with nonnegative diagonal elements d_l, $l = 1, \ldots, k$, called the *singular values* of **X**. Using (5.2.5), write **X′X** in the form

$$\mathbf{X}'\mathbf{X} = \mathbf{VD}^2\mathbf{V}'. \tag{5.2.6}$$

V is an orthogonal matrix that diagonalizes **X′X**, so the diagonal elements of $\mathbf{D}^2$, the squares of the singular values, are the eigenvalues of **X′X**, while the orthogonal columns of **V** are the eigenvectors of **X′X**. Making use of (5.2.6), the covariance matrix of the least squares estimator $\hat{\boldsymbol{\beta}}$, is

$$\text{Var}\left(\hat{\boldsymbol{\beta}}\right) = \sigma^2(\mathbf{X}'\mathbf{X})^{-1} = \sigma^2\mathbf{VD}^{-2}\mathbf{V}', \tag{5.2.7}$$

where the variance of the jth component of $\hat{\boldsymbol{\beta}}$ is

$$\text{Var}(\hat{\beta}_j) = \sigma^2 \sum_{l=1}^{k} \frac{v_{jl}^2}{d_l^2}, \tag{5.2.8}$$

the d_l's being the singular values and v_{jl} being the (j, l)th component of the **V** matrix. Equation (5.2.8) summarizes what is known about the precision with which the jth coefficient β_j may be estimated. Therefore, other things being equal, near dependencies imply small values of d_l^2, which, in turn, imply a large variance for $\hat{\beta}_j$.

From the preceding discussion, multicollinearity is a data problem, having to do with specific characteristics of the design matrix **X** and not with the statistical aspects of the linear regression model (4.2.2). That is, multicollinearity is a data problem, not a statistical problem. Nevertheless, one aim of a multiple regression is to identify separately the impact of each variable. Therefore, detecting the presence of multicollinear relationships among the data series and assessing the extent to which these relationships have imprecisely estimated coefficients, which we may term *degraded*, from the one where the design matrix **X** has nearly orthogonal columns can be very useful to investigators. Many procedures have been suggested to detect multicollinearity. For instance, if the estimated t ratios indicate that most of the estimated coefficients, which we may term degraded, are not statistically significantly different from zero and, at the same time, R^2 is high and the F test rejects the hypothesis that all coefficients are zero, such a combination of "symptoms" is frequently interpreted as indicating the presence of a multicollinearity problem. In this section we also briefly introduce the *condition index* measure and the *variance decomposition proportions* suggested by Belsley, Kuh, and Welsh (1980) as a means to assess the *degree of multicollinearity*.

Equations (5.2.5) and (5.2.6) imply that for each exact linear dependency among the columns of **X**, there is one zero singular value. Extending this property to near dependencies leads one to suggest that the presence of near dependencies will result in "small" singular values. But how small is "small"? Belsley, Kuh, and Welsh (1980) suggest using the relation between the singular value and the maximum singular value, d_{max}, which they call the *condition index*

$$\eta_j \equiv \frac{d_{max}}{d_j}, \qquad j = 1, \ldots, k, \tag{5.2.9}$$

as a basis for assessing smallness. To avoid the sensitivity of η_j to the unit of measurement, they suggest standardizing the **X** matrix by scaling each column to have unit length before computing the singular values. A singular value that is small relative to its yardstick, d_{max}, has a high condition index. There are as many near dependencies among the columns of a design matrix **X** as there are high condition indexes. However, just what is to be considered a "large" condition index is a matter to be determined empirically. Belsley et al. suggest that weak dependencies are associated with condition indexes around 5 or 10, whereas moderate to strong relations are associated with condition indexes of 30 to 100.

To assess the extent to which multicollinear relationships may have degraded estimated coefficients and to determine specifically which columns of the data matrix are involved in each near dependency (and therefore also those not involved), Belsley et al. (1980) further suggest using a *variance-decomposition* method. Let

$$\varphi_{jl} = \frac{v_{jl}^2}{d_l^2} \quad \text{and} \quad \varphi_j \equiv \sum_{l=1}^{k} \varphi_{jl}, \qquad l = 1, \ldots, k. \tag{5.2.10}$$

They define the (j, l)th *variance-decomposition proportion* as the proportion of the variance of the jth regression coefficient associated with the lth component of its decomposition in (5.2.8):

$$\pi_{lj} = \frac{\varphi_{jl}}{\varphi_j}, \qquad j, l = 1, \ldots, k. \tag{5.2.11}$$

Reflecting the fact that two or more columns of **X** must be involved in any near dependency, the degradation of a regression estimate due to a particular multicollinear relationship can be observed only when a singular value, d_l, is associated with a large proportion of the variance of two or more coefficients. Belsley et al. (1980) propose that the estimates be deemed degraded when more than 50% of the variances of two or more coefficients are associated with a single high condition index. Thus an investigator seeking patterns of high variance decompositions may be aided by the use of a summary table (the **Π** matrix) in the form of Table 5.1.

To illustrate the method of the condition index and variance-decomposition proportions in assessing the impact of multicollinearity, Belsley et al. (1980) use a data matrix,

TABLE 5.1 Variance-Decomposition Proportions

Associated Singular Value	Proportions of:				Condition Index
	$\text{Var}(\hat{\beta}_1)$	$\text{Var}(\hat{\beta}_2)$	$\cdots$	$\text{Var}(\hat{\beta}_k)$	
d_1	π_{11}	π_{12}		π_{1k}	η_1
d_2	π_{21}	π_{22}		π_{2k}	η_2
$\vdots$	$\vdots$	$\vdots$		$\vdots$	η_3
$\vdots$	$\vdots$	$\vdots$		$\vdots$	$\vdots$
d_k	π_{kl}	π_{k2}		π_{kk}	η_k

$$\mathbf{X} = [\mathbf{X}_1 \;\; \mathbf{X}_2] = \begin{bmatrix} -74 & 80 & 18 & -56 & -112 \\ 14 & -69 & 21 & 52 & 104 \\ 66 & -72 & -5 & 764 & 1{,}528 \\ -12 & 66 & -30 & 4{,}096 & 8{,}192 \\ 3 & 8 & -7 & -13{,}276 & -26{,}552 \\ 4 & -12 & 4 & 8{,}421 & 16{,}842 \end{bmatrix}. \quad (5.2.12)$$

This design matrix has the property that its fifth column is exactly twice its fourth, and both of these are in turn orthogonal to the first three columns. Belsley et al. (1980) use these data to compute the variance-decomposition proportions matrix, which is given in Table 5.2.

Table 5.2 exhibits several properties. First, the small singular value d_5 associated with the exact linear dependency between columns 4 and 5 of (5.2.12) accounts for virtually all the variance of $\hat{\beta}_4$ and $\hat{\beta}_5$. Second, the orthogonality of the first three columns of (5.2.12) to the last two involved in the linear dependency isolates their estimated coefficients from these deleterious effects of multicollinearity. Third, the singular value d_3 accounts for 97% or more of Var($\hat{\beta}_1$), Var($\hat{\beta}_2$), and Var($\hat{\beta}_3$), suggesting that a second near dependency is present in (5.2.12) that involves the first three columns. Fourth, to the extent that there are two separate near dependencies in (5.2.12) (one among the first three columns, one between the last two), the $\mathbf{\Pi}$ matrix provides a means for determining which variates are involved in which near dependency.

As the example above illustrates, the joint occurrence of high variance-decomposition proportions for two or more regression coefficient variances associated with a single singular value having a "high" condition index would indicate the presence of degrading multicollinearity. Unfortunately, the problem of multicollinearity is a sample problem in which the sample does not provide "rich" enough information on the explanatory variables to meet the requirements of the model. If controlled experimentation were available, it might be possible to generate a "richer" data set exhibiting greater variability in the behavior of the explanatory variables. The data used to estimate econometric models are typically non-experimental, however, so such a richer data set generally cannot be obtained simply by a choice of experimental design. Nor will additional data of the same type be likely to solve the problem, as they will generally exhibit the same problem of multicollinearity.

The problem of multicollinearity, when viewed as a sample problem, can be considered one of a gap between the information requirements of the model, as specified, and the information provided by the sample data. It is a manifestation of the fact that the data are

TABLE 5.2 Variance-Decomposition Proportions: Modified Bauer Matrix

Associated Singular Value	Proportions of:				
	Var($\hat{\beta}_1$)	Var($\hat{\beta}_2$)	Var($\hat{\beta}_3$)	Var($\hat{\beta}_4$)	Var($\hat{\beta}_5$)
$d_1 = 170.7$	0.002	0.009	0.000	0.000	0.000
$d_2 = 60.5$	0.019	0.015	0.013	0.000	0.000
$d_3 = 7.6$	0.976	0.972	0.983	0.000	0.000
$d_4 = 36{,}368.4$	0.000	0.000	0.000	0.000	0.000
$d_5 = 1.3 \times 10^{-12}$	0.003	0.005	0.003	1.000	1.000

Source Belsley et al. (1980, p. 111).

not rich enough in terms of independent variation of the explanatory variables to estimate adequately the model as specified. Viewing the problem this way—as one of a gap between the data required by the model as specified and the sample of data available—suggests three alternative ways to deal with multicollinearity.

One approach is to augment the sample of data by additional data or other information to facilitate the estimation of the model as specified. As already noted, additional data of the same type generally will not help. What could help are additional data of a different type, specifically data exhibiting significant differences from those that are already available, as illustrated by Silvey (1969). If data representing a different situation are added to the data already available, the combined sample would exhibit less multicollinearity. For example, consider macroeconomic time-series data. Sometimes data referring to "unrepresentative" periods, such as war years, years of major strike activity, or years of "credit crunch," are excluded.[4] Such exclusion of data can exclude periods in which the model may not be applicable, but it can also exclude precisely the variation in the sample that can reduce the problem of multicollinearity. Clearly, some balancing is called for between excluding periods in which the data exhibit variability and excluding periods in which the model may not be applicable. In general, it is best to avoid the extremes of excluding all "unrepresentative" periods—for which the resulting data will exhibit a significant multicollinearity problem and will not yield precise estimators—and, at the other extreme, accepting all periods uncritically—for which the resulting data might reflect fundamentally different underlying mechanisms. The same types of considerations apply to cross-section data (e.g., the issue of whether to include both industrialized and developing economies in a cross section of national economies and that of whether to include the very rich and very poor in a cross section of individuals).

Another method of augmenting the sample is to provide information directly on some of the parameters to be estimated. An example is that of extraneous estimates obtained from a different approach or sample. Thus, in estimating elasticities of demand, use is sometimes made of extraneous estimates of income elasticities obtained from cross-section data when estimating price elasticities from time-series data, given the multicollinearity among data on prices and income.[5] Another example is prior information on parameters—that is, restrictions on parameters imposed before estimation by theory or the results of other studies. In either case, the problem of estimation, rather than that of estimating the k parameters in $\boldsymbol{\beta}$, becomes that of estimating the $k - k_1$ remaining parameters, given values for k_1 of the elements in $\boldsymbol{\beta}$. For example, using least squares, the sum of squares is minimized by the choice of the remaining $k - k_1$ parameters.[6]

A second approach to the treatment of the problem of multicollinearity is to scale down the model to the data available. If other data, extraneous estimates, prior information,

[4]See the discussion of structural break in Section 4.7.4.

[5]See Tobin (1950) and Stone (1954) for examples. See Meyer and Kuh (1957), Maddala (1971a), and Hsiao (1986) for discussions of the use of extraneous estimators.

[6]The problem can be formulated as minimizing the sum of squares subject to the k_1 linear restrictions provided by the given values of the k_1 parameters. The general problem of least squares subject to linear restrictions is formulated and solved in Section 4.6 (see also Problem 4-R). See Theil and Goldberger (1961) and Theil (1963, 1971) for general approaches to mixed estimation, in which estimates reflect both prior information and sample data. For another approach in which prior information (and judgments) are modified on the basis of sample data, see the discussion of Bayesian estimation in Section 4.11.

and so on, are not available, the gap between the data and the model might be reduced by simplifying the model. Essentially, the model, as specified, is asking too much of the data available. By its very nature, multicollinearity means that some of the explanatory variables, as sampled, are not conveying much information over and above that conveyed by other variables. This observation suggests a simple and direct way to scale down the model: to change the specification by dropping some of the explanatory variables (as in the case of perfect multicollinearity) or to average or aggregate certain groups of variables.[7] For example, a model of the credit markets that includes several different interest rates on different types of securities could very well lead to a problem of multicollinearity, which would be reduced by averaging the interest rates into representative long- and short-term rates. The method suggested by Belsley et al. (1980) to detect collinear relations among variables is also useful in suggesting which specific variables to drop. To determine which variables to average, principal component analysis, which identifies linear combinations of explanatory variables that tend to move together, can be used. However, it should be noted that in either case, the estimated coefficients will represent the sum or the average effects of the relevant variables.

The third approach to treating the problem is simply to recognize the problem of multicollinearity and not try to change either the data or model. Other data, extraneous estimates, and so on, may not be available to augment the sample. At the same time, if the model as specified is based on a well-developed underlying theory, there is no justification for changing the specification. Such a change, such as omitting variables, would induce a specification error into the analysis (discussed in Section 5.7), creating biases in all the estimated coefficients. This specification error could lead to more problems, so that the "cure" might be worse than the "disease." The approach of "leaving things alone" is consistent with the view that multicollinearity is basically a property of the sample. The fact that precise statements about the separate influences of each of the explanatory variables cannot be given, in this view, is a very real fact, and there is little or no justification for tampering with the data or specification to attempt to make estimators more precise than they really are.

Which of these three approaches to use—augmenting the data, reducing the model, or "living with" the problem—depends on the specific problem, the purpose, and to some extent, the temperament of the investigator. For example, if the model is based directly on a well-developed theory, it would probably be inappropriate to change the specification, while if the model reflects only ad hoc and casual reasoning as to which variables might be considered relevant, it might be appropriate to change the specification. If other data or extraneous estimates are available, they might be employed. The purpose of the study should also play a role. If the purpose is primarily forecasting, the accuracy of the prediction is not affected by the presence of multicollinearity, provided that the same relationships among explanatory variables exist in the forecast period. If, however, the purpose is structural analysis, specifically that of disentangling the separate influences of explanatory variables, multicollinearity is a very serious problem that must be addressed.

[7]Yet other approaches to changing the specification of the model include transformations of variables and the explicit consideration of relationships among the variables. In the latter case, the original equation is embedded in a system of simultaneous equations.

5.3 GENERALIZED LEAST SQUARES METHOD AND SEEMINGLY UNRELATED REGRESSION MODELS

When the error terms, $\mathbf{u}$, exhibit homoskedasticity and absence of serial correlation, as expressed in A.4.2 or A.4.2*, they are referred to as *spherical disturbances*. When these assumptions do not hold, however, they can be replaced by the more general assumption that

A.5.1. $E(\mathbf{uu}' \mid \mathbf{X}) = \sigma^2\mathbf{\Omega} = \mathbf{V}$,

where trace $(\mathbf{\Omega}) = \text{tr}\,\mathbf{\Omega} = n$. The matrix $\mathbf{\Omega}$ is symmetric positive definite of order n. The condition that tr $\mathbf{\Omega} = n$ serves as a normalizing factor for the unique determination of the value of σ^2.

Model (4.2.2) under assumptions A.4.1, A.4.3, and A.5.1 can still be estimated using the least squares method. The least squares estimator is still linear, is unbiased, and under very general conditions, is also consistent. But it is no longer efficient. Moreover, the covariance matrix of the least squares estimator, $\hat{\boldsymbol{\beta}}$, is no longer the one given by (4.4.4). Rather, the covariance matrix of the least squares estimator under A.5.1 is

$$\begin{aligned} \text{Var}(\hat{\boldsymbol{\beta}} \mid \mathbf{X}) &= E[(\mathbf{X}'\mathbf{X})^{-1}\mathbf{X}'\mathbf{uu}'\mathbf{X}(\mathbf{X}'\mathbf{X})^{-1} \mid \mathbf{X}] \\ &= \sigma^2(\mathbf{X}'\mathbf{X})^{-1}\mathbf{X}'\mathbf{\Omega}\mathbf{X}(\mathbf{X}'\mathbf{X})^{-1} \\ &= (\mathbf{X}'\mathbf{X})^{-1}\mathbf{X}'\mathbf{V}\mathbf{X}(\mathbf{X}'\mathbf{X})^{-1}, \end{aligned} \qquad *(5.3.1)$$

where (5.3.1) becomes (4.4.4) when $\mathbf{\Omega} = \mathbf{I}_k$, in the special case of spherical disturbances.

An efficient estimator of $\boldsymbol{\beta}$ can be derived from the least squares principle if the original model can be transformed into the one that satisfies the conditions of the Gauss–Markov theorem (Theorem 4.1). A result from matrix theory states that any symmetric positive-definite matrix can be expressed in the form $\mathbf{PP}'$, where $\mathbf{P}$ is a nonsingular matrix. Thus let

$$\mathbf{\Omega} = \mathbf{PP}'. \qquad (5.3.2)$$

Then

$$\mathbf{P}^{-1}\,\mathbf{\Omega}\,\mathbf{P}^{-1'} = \mathbf{I} \qquad (5.3.3)$$

and

$$\mathbf{\Omega}^{-1} = \mathbf{P}^{-1'}\mathbf{P}^{-1}. \qquad (5.3.4)$$

Premultiplying the model (4.2.2) by $\mathbf{P}^{-1}$ yields the modified model

$$\mathbf{y}^m = \mathbf{X}^m\boldsymbol{\beta} + \mathbf{u}^m, \qquad (5.3.5)$$

where

$$\mathbf{y}^m = \mathbf{P}^{-1}\mathbf{y}, \quad \mathbf{X}^m = \mathbf{P}^{-1}\mathbf{X}, \quad \text{and} \quad \mathbf{u}^m = \mathbf{P}^{-1}\mathbf{u}, \qquad (5.3.6)$$

so the data in $\mathbf{y}$ and $\mathbf{X}$ are modified by being scaled by $\mathbf{P}^{-1}$. From (5.3.3) and (5.3.4),

$$E(\mathbf{u}^m \mid \mathbf{X}^m) = \mathbf{P}^{-1}E(\mathbf{u} \mid \mathbf{X}) = \mathbf{0} \qquad (5.3.7)$$

and

$$E(\mathbf{u}^m\mathbf{u}^{m\prime} \mid \mathbf{X}^m) = \sigma^2\mathbf{I}. \qquad (5.3.8)$$

Thus the revised model (5.3.5) satisfies all the conditions of the Gauss–Markov theorem. The least squares estimator of (5.3.5) is

$$
\begin{aligned}
\hat{\boldsymbol{\beta}}_{\text{GLS}} &= (\mathbf{X}^{m\prime}\mathbf{X}^m)^{-1}\mathbf{X}^{m\prime}\mathbf{y}^m \\
&= (\mathbf{X}'\mathbf{P}^{-1\prime}\mathbf{P}^{-1}\mathbf{X})^{-1}\mathbf{X}'\mathbf{P}^{-1\prime}\mathbf{P}^{-1}\mathbf{y} \\
&= (\mathbf{X}'\boldsymbol{\Omega}^{-1}\mathbf{X})^{-1}\mathbf{X}'\boldsymbol{\Omega}^{-1}\mathbf{y} \\
&= (\mathbf{X}'\mathbf{V}^{-1}\mathbf{X})^{-1}\mathbf{X}'\mathbf{V}^{-1}\mathbf{y}.
\end{aligned} \qquad *(5.3.9)
$$

It is the BLUE estimator with covariance matrix

$$
\begin{aligned}
\text{Var}(\hat{\boldsymbol{\beta}}_{\text{GLS}}) &= \sigma^2(\mathbf{X}^{m\prime}\mathbf{X}^m)^{-1} \\
&= \sigma^2(\mathbf{X}'\boldsymbol{\Omega}^{-1}\mathbf{X})^{-1} = (\mathbf{X}'\mathbf{V}^{-1}\mathbf{X})^{-1}.
\end{aligned} \qquad *(5.3.10)
$$

The estimator (5.3.9) is called the *generalized least squares (GLS) or Aitken estimator.* Further, if $\mathbf{u}$ is assumed to be normally distributed, so is $\mathbf{u}^m$. The generalized least squares estimator, $\hat{\boldsymbol{\beta}}_{\text{GLS}}$, is also a maximum likelihood estimator. The usual significance tests and confidence intervals for $\boldsymbol{\beta}_k$ can be constructed from the estimator (5.3.9) and its covariance matrix (5.3.10).

An unbiased estimator of σ^2 is given by

$$
\begin{aligned}
\hat{s}^2 &= \frac{1}{n-k}(\mathbf{y}^m - \mathbf{X}^m\hat{\boldsymbol{\beta}}_{\text{GLS}})'(\mathbf{y}^m - \mathbf{X}^m\hat{\boldsymbol{\beta}}_{\text{GLS}}) \\
&= \frac{1}{n-k}(\mathbf{y} - \mathbf{X}\hat{\boldsymbol{\beta}}_{\text{GLS}})'\Omega^{-1}(\mathbf{y} - \mathbf{X}\hat{\boldsymbol{\beta}}_{\text{GLS}}).
\end{aligned} \qquad (5.3.11)
$$

As for predicting the future value y_f given $\mathbf{x}_f$, $\mathbf{y}$ and $\mathbf{X}$, note that

$$
y_f = \mathbf{x}_f'\boldsymbol{\beta} + u_f, \qquad (5.3.12)
$$

where $Eu_f = 0$ and $Eu_f^2 = \sigma_f^2$. If u_f is uncorrelated with $\mathbf{u}$, then $E(u_f \mid \mathbf{u}) = 0$. The best linear unbiased predictor (BLUP) of y_f is simply the prediction regressor, $\mathbf{x}_f$, multiplied by the BLUE of $\boldsymbol{\beta}$. When

$$
E(u_f\mathbf{u}) = \begin{bmatrix} Eu_1u_f \\ Eu_2u_f \\ \vdots \\ Eu_nu_f \end{bmatrix} = \mathbf{w} \neq \mathbf{0}, \qquad *(5.3.13)
$$

it is possible to improve the accuracy of the prediction by also predicting u_f using the interdependence of u_f and the sample residuals $\mathbf{u}$. It was shown by Goldberger (1964) that the BLUP is[8]

$$
\hat{y}_f = \mathbf{x}_f'\hat{\boldsymbol{\beta}}_{\text{GLS}} + \mathbf{w}'\mathbf{V}^{-1}(\mathbf{y} - \mathbf{X}\hat{\boldsymbol{\beta}}_{\text{GLS}}). \qquad *(5.3.14)
$$

This discussion is based on the assumption that $\mathbf{V}$ or $\boldsymbol{\Omega}$ is known. When $\boldsymbol{\Omega}$ is unknown but the n^2 elements of $\boldsymbol{\Omega}$ are functions of a finite number of parameters (or increase at a much

[8]Define a linear predictor $\hat{y}_f = \mathbf{c}'\mathbf{y}$, where $\mathbf{c}$ is a vector of n constants. If $\hat{y}_f$ is to be unbiased, $E\hat{y}_f = Ey_f = \mathbf{x}_f'\boldsymbol{\beta}$, $\mathbf{c}$ must satisfy $\mathbf{c}'\mathbf{X} = \mathbf{x}_f'$ and the prediction error of $\hat{y}_f$ is $\hat{y}_f - y_f = \mathbf{c}'(\mathbf{X}\boldsymbol{\beta} + \mathbf{u}) - (\mathbf{X}_f'\boldsymbol{\beta} + u_f) = \mathbf{c}'\mathbf{u} - u_f$. Then the prediction variance is $\sigma_{\hat{y}_f}^2 = E(\mathbf{c}'\mathbf{u} - u_f)^2 = \mathbf{c}'\mathbf{V}\mathbf{c} + \sigma_f^2 - 2\mathbf{c}'\mathbf{w}$. To minimize $\sigma_{\hat{y}_f}^2$ subject to $\mathbf{c}'\mathbf{X} = \mathbf{x}_f'$, form the Lagrangian $\psi = \mathbf{c}'\mathbf{V}\mathbf{c} - 2\mathbf{c}'\mathbf{w} - 2(\mathbf{c}'\mathbf{X} - \mathbf{x}_f')\boldsymbol{\lambda}$, where $\boldsymbol{\lambda}$ is a $k \times 1$ vector of Lagrangian multipliers. Differentiating ψ with respect to $\mathbf{c}$ and $\boldsymbol{\lambda}$, setting the results equal to zero, and making use of the rule for the inverse of a partitioned matrix yields $\mathbf{c} = \mathbf{V}^{-1}[\mathbf{I} - \mathbf{X}(\mathbf{X}'\mathbf{V}^{-1}\mathbf{X})^{-1}\mathbf{X}'\mathbf{V}^{-1}]\mathbf{w} + \mathbf{V}^{-1}\mathbf{X}(\mathbf{X}'\mathbf{V}^{-1}\mathbf{X})^{-1}\mathbf{x}_f$, which leads to (5.3.14).

slower rate than n), consistent estimation of $\mathbf{\Omega}$ is possible by first applying the least squares method to (4.2.2) to obtain a consistent estimate of $\boldsymbol{\beta}$, then using the least squares residuals (4.3.12) to estimate $\mathbf{\Omega}$. Substituting the estimated $\hat{\mathbf{\Omega}}$ for the true $\mathbf{\Omega}$ into (5.3.9) yields a two-step or feasible GLS (FGLS) estimator. This feasible GLS estimator has the same asymptotic efficiency as the GLS estimator.[9]

The technique of generalized least squares can be applied to systems of equations as well as to individual equations. According to the technique of *seemingly unrelated regressions* (SUR), it is possible to construct a GLS estimator for a system of equations.[10] Consider a system of g equations where

$$\underset{n\times 1}{\mathbf{y}_h} = \underset{n\times k_h}{\mathbf{X}_h}\ \underset{k_h\times 1}{\boldsymbol{\beta}_h} + \underset{n\times 1}{\mathbf{u}_h}, \qquad h = 1, 2, \ldots, g. \tag{5.3.15}$$

Since the $\mathbf{y}_h$ are all column vectors, all g such vectors can be stacked and written as one gn column vector by "stacking" the vectors. Similarly, all $\boldsymbol{\beta}_h$ can be stacked and written as one vector of length

$$k^* = \sum_{h=1}^{g} k_h,$$

and all $\mathbf{u}_h$ can be written as one vector of length gn. The entire system can thus be written in the "star" notation of "stacked" variables as

$$\underset{gn\times 1}{\mathbf{y}^*} = \underset{gn\times k^*}{\mathbf{X}^*}\ \underset{k^*\times 1}{\boldsymbol{\beta}^*} + \underset{gn\times 1}{\mathbf{u}^*}, \tag{*(5.3.16)}$$

which represents the system

$$\begin{pmatrix} \mathbf{y}_1 \\ \mathbf{y}_2 \\ \vdots \\ \mathbf{y}_g \end{pmatrix} = \begin{pmatrix} \mathbf{X}_1 & 0 & \ldots & 0 \\ 0 & \mathbf{X}_2 & \ldots & 0 \\ \vdots & & & \\ 0 & 0 & \ldots & \mathbf{X}_g \end{pmatrix} \begin{pmatrix} \boldsymbol{\beta}_1 \\ \boldsymbol{\beta}_2 \\ \vdots \\ \boldsymbol{\beta}_g \end{pmatrix} + \begin{pmatrix} \mathbf{u}_1 \\ \mathbf{u}_2 \\ \vdots \\ \mathbf{u}_g \end{pmatrix}. \tag{5.3.17}$$

If $\mathbf{\Sigma}^*$ is the covariance matrix for $\mathbf{u}^*$, given as $E(\mathbf{u}^*\mathbf{u}^{*\prime})$, then

$$\hat{\boldsymbol{\beta}}^*_{\text{sur}} = (\mathbf{X}^{*\prime}\Sigma^{*-1}\mathbf{X}^*)^{-1}\mathbf{X}^{*\prime}\Sigma^{*-1}\mathbf{y}^* \tag{*(5.3.18)}$$

is the seemingly unrelated regressions estimator, which is the best linear unbiased estimator.[11] These estimators are the same as the ordinary least squares estimators for each equation if the disturbance terms are uncorrelated between any two different equations or if the

[9]The feasible GLS estimator has the same limiting distribution as GLS estimator if:

1. $\text{plim}(n^{-1}\mathbf{X}'\hat{\mathbf{\Omega}}^{-1}\mathbf{X}) = \text{plim}(n^{-1}\mathbf{X}'\mathbf{\Omega}^{-1}\mathbf{X})$
2. $\text{plim}(n^{-1/2}\mathbf{X}'(\hat{\mathbf{\Omega}}^{-1} - \mathbf{\Omega}^{-1})\mathbf{u}) = \mathbf{0}$. For details, see Theil (1971, Sec. 8.6).

[10]See Zellner (1962, 1963) and Zellner and Huang (1962). For a discussion of tests of hypotheses involving coefficients from different equations, see Theil (1971), and for an extension to simultaneous-equations system, see Section 11.7.

[11]To utilize this method it is necessary to estimate the Σ^* matrix. It is generally assumed that the system satisfies the conditions

$$E(\mathbf{u}_h\mathbf{u}'_{h'}) = \sigma_{hh'}\mathbf{I} \qquad \text{for all } h,\ h'.$$

Thus the first step in employing this method is to estimate the covariance matrix of the residuals using the ordinary least squares estimates of each equation. The second step is then to use this estimated covariance matrix to estimate all equations simultaneously using (5.3.18).

[12]See Problems 5-L and 9-B.

$\mathbf{X}_h$ matrices of explanatory variables are all identical.[12] If, however, the disturbance terms are correlated or the set of explanatory variables is not the same for each equation, this method yields estimators that are asymptotically more efficient than those obtained by applying ordinary least squares to each equation individually. In fact, the gain in efficiency is greater, the greater is the correlation of the residuals and the lesser is the correlation of the explanatory variables in the different equations of the system.

5.4 HETEROSKEDASTICITY

A special case of nonspherical disturbances is what is commonly referred to as *heteroskedasticity*, namely,

$$\text{Var}(u_i) \neq \text{Var}(u_{i'}), \qquad i \neq i', \tag{5.4.1}$$

so in contrast to assumption A.4.2, the elements along the principal diagonal of the covariance matrix $E(\mathbf{uu}')$ are not all equal:

$$\text{Var}(\mathbf{u}) = \sigma^2\mathbf{\Omega} = \begin{pmatrix} \sigma_1^2 & 0 & \cdots & 0 \\ 0 & \sigma_2^2 & & 0 \\ \vdots & & \ddots & \\ 0 & \cdots & \cdots & \sigma_n^2 \end{pmatrix} = \mathbf{V}. \qquad *(5.4.2)$$

Heteroskedasticity can occur in both cross-section and time-series data. For instance, in cross-section studies there is often a problem of heteroskedasticity because there is typically a large variation in the size of the entities for which data are obtained, whether households with widely different income levels, firms with widely different scales of operation, or nations with widely different levels of output. A historically important example is the estimation of the simple savings function,

$$s = \beta_1 x + \beta_2 + u, \tag{5.4.3}$$

where s is family savings; x is family income; β_1 and β_2 are parameters, β_1 being the marginal propensity to save; and u is the stochastic disturbance term. Figure 5.1 shows a hypothetical scatter of cross-section observations representing family savings and income for a group of families. Clearly, the variation in savings behavior is much greater for high-income than for low-income families. Low-income families do not have much to save, so they cannot differ appreciably in their levels of savings. High-income families, by contrast, exhibit wide ranges, from the penny-pinching millionaire who saves virtually all his income to the "nouveau riche" family who save virtually nothing. Clearly, a cross-section sample of data on savings and income behavior that might be used to estimate (5.4.3) does not satisfy the homoskedasticity assumption.[13]

Heteroskedasticity is a special case of assumption A.5.1. Hence, as discussed in Section 5.3, it has two important implications for estimation. The first is that the least squares estimators, while still linear and unbiased, are no longer efficient, no longer providing minimum variance ("best") estimators among the class of linear unbiased estimators. The second implication is that (4.4.4) is a biased estimator of the covariance matrix of the least squares estimator.

If the pattern of heteroskedasticity is known, the covariance matrix of the least squares estimator can be obtained by using (5.3.1). If the pattern of heteroskedasticity is unknown,

[13] See Prais and Houthakker (1955), as discussed in Section 7.4.

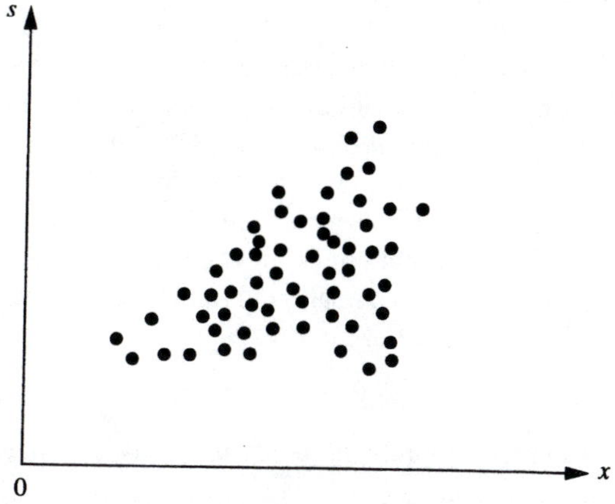

Figure 5.1 Family Savings and Family Income

to correct the bias of the estimated variances so that statistical inferences about $\boldsymbol{\beta}$ can be made based on the least squares estimates of $\boldsymbol{\beta}$, Eicker (1963) and White (1980) have shown that (5.3.1) can be estimated consistently by

$$\begin{aligned}\operatorname{Var}(\hat{\boldsymbol{\beta}}) &= (\mathbf{X}'\mathbf{X})^{-1}\mathbf{X}'\begin{pmatrix} \hat{u}_1^2 & 0 & \cdots & 0 \\ 0 & \hat{u}_2^2 & & \\ \vdots & & \ddots & \\ 0 & & & \hat{u}_n^2 \end{pmatrix}\mathbf{X}(\mathbf{X}'\mathbf{X})^{-1} \qquad (5.4.4) \\ &= \left(\sum_{i=1}^n \mathbf{x}_i\mathbf{x}_i'\right)^{-1}\left(\sum_{i=1}^n \hat{u}_i^2\mathbf{x}_i\mathbf{x}_i'\right)\left(\sum_{i=1}^n \mathbf{x}_i\mathbf{x}_i'\right)^{-1},\end{aligned}$$

where $\hat{u}_i$ are the least squares residuals (4.3.12), provided that $(\mathbf{x}_i', u_i)$ are independently distributed with finite fourth moments.

To obtain the efficient estimate of $\boldsymbol{\beta}$, as discussed in Section 5.3, a GLS estimator should be used. The inverse of the covariance matrix (5.4.2) is of the form

$$\mathbf{V}^{-1} = \begin{pmatrix} \frac{1}{\sigma_1^2} & & & 0 \\ & \frac{1}{\sigma_2^2} & & \\ & & \ddots & \\ 0 & & & \frac{1}{\sigma_n^2} \end{pmatrix}. \qquad (5.4.5)$$

Using the form (5.3.4) for (5.4.5) yields

$$\mathbf{P}^{-1} = \begin{pmatrix} \frac{1}{\sigma_1} & & & 0 \\ & \frac{1}{\sigma_2} & & \\ & & \ddots & \\ 0 & & & \frac{1}{\sigma_n} \end{pmatrix}, \qquad (5.4.6)$$

where the $\mathbf{P}^{-1}$ matrix is a diagonal matrix, the diagonal elements of which are the reciprocals of the corresponding standard deviations of the stochastic disturbance terms. Using (5.3.5), it follows that both dependent and explanatory variables are weighted at each observation by the reciprocal of the standard deviation of the dependent variable (or stochastic disturbance term) at that observation. The larger the σ_i, the smaller the weight of that observation is in the estimation of $\boldsymbol{\beta}$. Therefore, the GLS estimator under heteroskedasticity is sometimes called the *weighted least squares* estimator.

If the σ_i^2 or their pattern is known, the weighted least squares estimator can be applied. For instance, in the estimation of family savings behavior (5.4.3), if the variances are proportional to the square of income

$$\text{Var}(u_i) = \sigma^2 x_i^2, \qquad i = 1, \ldots, n, \tag{5.4.7}$$

the way to correct the problem of heteroskedasticity is to estimate the dependence of the savings *ratio* equation,

$$\frac{s}{x} = \beta_1 + \frac{\beta_2}{x} + u^*, \qquad \text{where} \quad u^* = \frac{u}{x} \tag{5.4.8}$$

rather than (5.4.3).[14]

When σ_i^2 is related to a set of explanatory variables, a gain in asymptotic efficiency would be expected in using the appropriately defined feasible GLS estimator. When heteroskedasticity is unrestricted, namely, when heteroskedasticity is not a known function with a finite number of parameters, each σ_i^2 is an unknown parameter. Clearly, these variances cannot be estimated consistently because there is only one observation per variance. However, it is still possible to estimate $\boldsymbol{\beta}$ consistently and more efficiently than by the least squares method, as discussed in Chamberlain (1982), Cragg (1983), and White (1982). Consider the matrix $\mathbf{Z} = [\mathbf{X}, \mathbf{W}]$, where $\mathbf{W}$ is an $n \times N$ matrix of constants such that the rank of $\mathbf{Z}$ is $k + N$. Premultiply (4.2.2) by $\mathbf{Z}'$, yielding

$$\mathbf{Z}'\mathbf{y} = \mathbf{Z}'\mathbf{X}\boldsymbol{\beta} + \mathbf{Z}'\mathbf{u}. \tag{5.4.9}$$

The transformed error term $\mathbf{Z}'\mathbf{u}$ has mean $E(\mathbf{Z}'\mathbf{u}) = \mathbf{Z}'E\mathbf{u} = \mathbf{0}$, and covariance matrix $\mathbf{Z}'E\mathbf{u}\mathbf{u}'\mathbf{Z} = \mathbf{Z}'\mathbf{V}\mathbf{Z}$. Application of GLS to (5.4.9) yields

$$\hat{\boldsymbol{\beta}}_{\text{PGLS}} = [\mathbf{X}'\mathbf{Z}(\mathbf{Z}'\mathbf{V}\mathbf{Z})^{-1}\mathbf{Z}'\mathbf{X}]^{-1}\mathbf{X}'\mathbf{Z}(\mathbf{Z}'\mathbf{V}\mathbf{Z})^{-1}\mathbf{Z}'\mathbf{y}. \qquad {}^*(5.4.10)$$

A feasible GLS for (5.4.10) would replace $\mathbf{V}$ by

$$\hat{\mathbf{V}} = \begin{pmatrix} \hat{u}_1^2 & 0 & \cdots & 0 \\ 0 & \ddots & & \vdots \\ \vdots & & & \\ 0 & & \cdots & \hat{u}_n^2 \end{pmatrix}, \tag{5.4.11}$$

the $\hat{u}_i$ being the least squares residuals (4.3.12). Amemiya (1983) has suggested choosing $\mathbf{W}$ such that $\mathbf{W}'\mathbf{X} = \mathbf{0}$. Then (5.4.9) becomes

$$\mathbf{X}'\mathbf{y} = \mathbf{X}'\mathbf{X}\boldsymbol{\beta} + \mathbf{X}'\mathbf{u} \tag{5.4.12}$$

and

$$\mathbf{W}'\mathbf{y} = \mathbf{W}'\mathbf{u}. \tag{5.4.13}$$

[14]See Madansky (1964), however, for a warning on the use of ratios.

When GLS (5.4.10) is applied to (5.4.12) and (5.4.13), it becomes

$$\hat{\boldsymbol{\beta}}_{\text{PGLS}} = \hat{\boldsymbol{\beta}} - (\mathbf{X}'\mathbf{X})^{-1}\mathbf{X}'\mathbf{V}\mathbf{W}(\mathbf{W}'\mathbf{V}\mathbf{W})^{-1}\mathbf{W}'\mathbf{y} \tag{5.4.14}$$

and is called the *partially generalized* least squares (PGLS) estimator, where $\hat{\boldsymbol{\beta}}$ is the least squares estimator (4.3.4). The PGLS estimator is more efficient than the least squares estimator because

$$\text{Var}(\hat{\boldsymbol{\beta}}) - \text{Var}(\hat{\boldsymbol{\beta}}_{\text{PGLS}}) = (\mathbf{X}'\mathbf{X})^{-1}\mathbf{X}'\mathbf{V}\mathbf{W}(\mathbf{W}'\mathbf{V}\mathbf{W})^{-1}\mathbf{W}'\mathbf{V}\mathbf{X}(\mathbf{X}'\mathbf{X})^{-1} \tag{5.4.15}$$

is nonnegative definite. It is, however, less efficient than the GLS estimator.

To test for heteroskedasticity, a simple scatter diagram such as Figure 5.1 can help to detect possible problems of heteroskedasticity. An alternative approach is to relate the variances σ_i^2 explicitly to m exogenous variables, $\mathbf{z}_i$, with the last element equal to unity. For instance, Breusch and Pagan (1979) consider that

$$\sigma_i^2 = h(\mathbf{z}_i'\boldsymbol{\alpha}), \tag{5.4.16}$$

where h is a function independent of i and $\boldsymbol{\alpha}' = (\boldsymbol{\alpha}^{*\prime}, \alpha_m)$ is an $1 \times m$ vector of unknown coefficients. Thus specifications such as $\sigma_i^2 = \mathbf{z}_i'\boldsymbol{\alpha}$ and $\sigma_i^2 = \exp(\mathbf{z}_i'\boldsymbol{\alpha})$ are all special cases of (5.4.16). The null hypothesis of homoskedasticity is equivalent to

$$H_0: \quad \boldsymbol{\alpha}^* = \mathbf{0}. \tag{5.4.17}$$

Under the assumption that the u_i are independently normally distributed, Breusch and Pagan (1979) show that the Lagrange multiplier test statistic does not depend on the function h and is given by

$$\eta = \frac{\mathbf{q}'\mathbf{Z}(\mathbf{Z}'\mathbf{Z})^{-1}\mathbf{Z}'\mathbf{q}}{2\hat{\sigma}^4}, \tag{5.4.18}$$

where $\mathbf{q} = \ddot{\mathbf{u}} - \hat{\sigma}^2\mathbf{e}, \mathbf{e}' = (1, \ldots, 1)$, $\ddot{\mathbf{u}} = (\hat{u}_1^2, \ldots, \hat{u}_n^2)'$, $Z = (\mathbf{z}_i')$, and $\hat{\sigma}^2 = \hat{\mathbf{u}}'\hat{\mathbf{u}}/n$. Under H_0, η is asymptotically chi-square distributed with $m - 1$ degrees of freedom.

When heteroskedasticity is not parameterized, White (1980) has proposed to test the hypothesis $\sigma_i^2 = \sigma^2$ for all i by comparing (5.4.4) with $\hat{\sigma}^2(\mathbf{X}'\mathbf{X}')^{-1}$. Equivalently, White considers elements of $\mathbf{X}'\hat{\mathbf{V}}\mathbf{X} - \hat{\sigma}^2\mathbf{X}'\mathbf{X}$. The test statistic proposed by White is to regress $\hat{u}_i^2$ on $x_{ji}x_{li}$ for $1 \leq j, l \leq k$, and $j \leq l$. Under the null hypothesis of homoskedasticity, the nR^2 from this regression is asymptotically distributed as chi-square with $(k^2 + k)/2$ degrees of freedom.

5.5 SERIAL CORRELATION

Another common problem in applied econometrics is serial correlation (or autocorrelation), in which the stochastic disturbance terms are not independent of one another, that is,

$$\text{Cov}(u_i, u_{i'}) \neq 0, \qquad i \neq i' \text{ for some } i, i'. \tag{5.5.1}$$

Thus, in contrast to assumption A.4.2, the elements off the principal diagonal of the covariance matrix $E(\mathbf{uu}')$ are not all zero.[15] The problem of serial correlation is a frequent one when using

[15] The assumption that $E(\mathbf{y}) = \mathbf{0}$ is still being made, so $E(\mathbf{u}\hat{\mathbf{u}}')$ is the $n \times n$ covariance matrix of $\mathbf{u}$.

time-series data due to inertia in the system. It can also occur with cross-section data when the data are ordered in a specific way (e.g., according to one of the explanatory variables).

As in the case of heteroskedasticity, serial correlation results both in least squares estimators that are not efficient and in bias when using (4.4.4) as the estimated covariance matrix of the least squares estimator. Furthermore, as (5.3.14) demonstrates, (4.8.1) is an inefficient predictor. As discussed in Section 5.3, the BLUE in this case is the GLS estimator (5.3.9).

To illustrate the implications of the presence of serial correlation in the disturbance term in a regression model, the disturbances are frequently assumed to take the form of a *Markov process* or *first-order autoregressive process*,

$$u_i = \rho u_{i-1} + v_i, \qquad |\rho| < 1, \tag*{*(5.5.2)}$$

where v_i satisfies the assumption

$$\begin{aligned} &E(v_i \mid \mathbf{X}) = 0, \\ &E(v_i v_{i'} \mid \mathbf{X}) = \begin{cases} \sigma_v^2 & \text{if } i = i', \\ 0 & \text{if } i \neq i'. \end{cases} \end{aligned} \tag*{*(5.5.3)}$$

There are both statistical and economic reasons for wishing to constrain $|\rho| < 1$. Note that by successive substitution

$$\begin{aligned} u_i &= \rho u_{i-1} + v_i \\ &= \rho(\rho u_{i-2} + v_{i-1}) + v_i \\ &= v_i + \rho v_{i-1} + \rho^2 v_{i-2} + \cdots . \end{aligned} \tag{5.5.4}$$

Thus, from (5.5.4), if $|\rho| \geq 1$, it implies that every disturbance that happened early tends to propagate or amplify over time. Therefore, u_i will not have a finite variance even if v_i does. On the other hand, if $|\rho| < 1$, the impact of what happened in the past gradually dies out. In this case, u_i will have a finite variance if v_i does.

Because of the assumption that

$$E(u_i \mid \mathbf{X}) = 0, \tag{5.5.5}$$

it follows that

$$\begin{aligned} E(u_i^2 \mid \mathbf{X}) &= E(v_i^2 \mid \mathbf{X}) + \rho^2 E(v_{i-1}^2 \mid \mathbf{X}) + \rho^4 E(v_{i-2}^2 \mid \mathbf{X}) + \cdots \\ &= (1 + \rho^2 + \rho^4 + \cdots)\sigma_v^2 \\ &= \frac{\sigma_v^2}{1 - \rho^2} . \end{aligned} \tag{5.5.6}$$

Furthermore,

$$\begin{aligned} E(u_i u_{i-1} \mid \mathbf{X}) &= E[(v_i + \rho v_{i-1} + \rho^2 v_{i-2} + \cdots)(v_{i-1} + \rho v_{i-2} + \cdots) \mid \mathbf{X}] \\ &= E\{[v_i + \rho(v_{i-1} + \rho v_{i-2} + \cdots)](v_{i-1} + \rho v_{i-2} + \cdots) \mid \mathbf{X}\} \\ &= \rho E[(v_{i-1} + \rho v_{i-2} + \cdots)^2 \mid \mathbf{X}] \\ &= \frac{\rho \sigma_v^2}{1 - \rho^2}, \end{aligned} \tag{5.5.7}$$

and, in general,

$$E(u_i u_{i-s}) = \frac{\rho^{|s|} \sigma_v^2}{1 - \rho^2}. \tag{5.5.8}$$

Thus

$$E(\mathbf{uu}' \mid \mathbf{X}) = \frac{\sigma_v^2}{1-\rho^2}\begin{bmatrix} 1 & \rho & \cdots & \rho^{n-1} \\ \rho & 1 & & \rho^{n-2} \\ \vdots & & \ddots & \vdots \\ \rho^{n-1} & \rho^{n-2} & \cdots & 1 \end{bmatrix} = \frac{\sigma_v^2}{1-\rho^2}\mathbf{\Omega}. \qquad *(5.5.9)$$

So, if the value of ρ is known, the GLS estimator (5.3.9) can be applied with

$$\mathbf{\Omega}^{-1} = \frac{1}{1-\rho^2}\begin{bmatrix} 1 & -\rho & 0 & \cdots & 0 & 0 & 0 \\ -\rho & 1+\rho^2 & -\rho & & & & \\ 0 & -\rho & 1+\rho^2 & -\rho & & \ddots & \\ \vdots & 0 & \ddots & \ddots & \ddots & \ddots & \ddots \\ & & & & -\rho & 1+\rho^2 & -\rho \\ 0 & 0 & 0 & \cdots & \cdots & -\rho & 1 \end{bmatrix}. \qquad *(5.5.10)$$

Ignoring the scalar constant $(1-\rho^2)^{-1}$ in (5.5.10) and using the form (5.3.4), the data can be adjusted using

$$\mathbf{P}^{-1} = \begin{bmatrix} \sqrt{1-\rho^2} & 0 & \cdots & & 0 \\ -\rho & 1 & & & \\ 0 & -\rho & 1 & & \ddots \\ \vdots & \vdots & \ddots & & \ddots \\ 0 & 0 & \cdots & -\rho & 1 \end{bmatrix}. \qquad (5.5.11)$$

Thus the GLS estimator may be obtained by a simple two-stage procedure: first, transform the original observations into

$$\mathbf{y}^* = \mathbf{P}^{-1}\mathbf{y} = \begin{bmatrix} \sqrt{1-\rho^2}y_1 \\ y_2 - \rho y_1 \\ \vdots \\ y_n - \rho y_{n-1} \end{bmatrix} \qquad \mathbf{X}^* = \mathbf{P}^{-1}\mathbf{X} = \begin{bmatrix} \sqrt{1-\rho^2}\mathbf{x}_1' \\ \mathbf{x}_2' - \rho\mathbf{x}_1' \\ \vdots \\ \mathbf{x}_n' - \rho\mathbf{x}_{n-1}' \end{bmatrix} \qquad (5.5.12)$$

and then apply least squares to the transformed data $\mathbf{y}^*$ and $\mathbf{X}^*$.

Often the GLS estimator is approximated by using the $(n-1)\times n$ matrix

$$\mathbf{P}_1^{-1} = \begin{bmatrix} -\rho & 1 & 0 & 0 & 0 \\ 0 & -\rho & 1 & & \vdots \\ \vdots & \ddots & \ddots & & \vdots \\ 0 & \cdots & 0 & -\rho & 1 \end{bmatrix} \qquad (5.5.13)$$

to transform the data. This is equivalent to applying least squares to the *pseudo-differenced model*

$$\begin{aligned} y_i - \rho y_{i-1} &= (\mathbf{x}_i' - \rho\mathbf{x}_{i-1}')\boldsymbol{\beta} + (u_i - \rho u_{i-1}) \\ &= (\mathbf{x}_i' - \rho\mathbf{x}_{i-1}')\boldsymbol{\beta} + v_i, \qquad i = 2, \ldots, n. \end{aligned} \qquad (5.5.14)$$

The transformed model expresses the variable $y_i - \rho y_{i-1}$ as linear functions of the variables in $\mathbf{x}_i - \rho\mathbf{x}_{i-1}$. If $\rho = 1$, the model is one in first differences, while if $\rho = -1$, it treats a two-period moving average. The model is of the same form as the original model, except that now there are only $(n-1)$ observations and the error terms, v_i, are serially uncorrelated.

When the error terms follow a first-order autoregressive process (5.5.2), efficient prediction can be obtained using (5.3.14) and the covariance pattern (5.5.8). For instance, suppose that there are sample data for periods 1 to n, where the values of the explanatory variables in period $n+1$, $\mathbf{x}_{n+1}$ are given. Then the BLUP for y_{n+1} is

$$\hat{y}_{n+1} = \mathbf{x}'_{n+1}\hat{\boldsymbol{\beta}}_{\text{GLS}} + \rho\hat{u}_n, \tag{5.5.15}$$

where $\hat{\boldsymbol{\beta}}_{\text{GLS}}$ is the GLS estimator and $\hat{u}_n = y_n - \mathbf{x}'_n\hat{\boldsymbol{\beta}}_{\text{GLS}}$.

In general, of course, neither the structure of the serial correlation nor the values of the parameters characterizing the structure of the serial correlation are known, so the GLS estimates cannot be computed directly. A feasible GLS estimator has to be applied. For instance, suppose that the error terms are assumed to follow the first-order autoregressive process (5.5.2). Then it is possible first to apply least squares to (4.2.2) and to obtain the least squares residuals $\hat{\mathbf{u}} = \mathbf{y} - \mathbf{X}\hat{\boldsymbol{\beta}}$. Then regress $\hat{u}_i$ on $\hat{u}_{i-1}$, for $i = 2, \ldots, n$, to obtain a consistent estimate of ρ as

$$\hat{\rho} = \frac{\sum_{i=2}^{n} \hat{u}_i \hat{u}_{i-1}}{\sum_{i=2}^{n} \hat{u}_{i-1}^2}. \tag{5.5.16}$$

Substituting $\hat{\rho}$ for ρ in (5.5.12) to transform the data, least squares can then be applied to the transformed data.

Durbin (1960) has suggested an alternative method to obtain an initial estimate of ρ, where (5.5.14) is rewritten in the form

$$\begin{aligned} y_i &= \rho y_{i-1} + \mathbf{x}'_i\boldsymbol{\beta} - \mathbf{x}'_{i-1}\boldsymbol{\beta}\rho + v_i \\ &= \rho y_{i-1} + \mathbf{x}'_i\mathbf{a}_1 + \mathbf{x}'_{i-1}\mathbf{a}_2 + v_i, \qquad i = 2, \ldots, n, \end{aligned} \tag{5.5.17}$$

where

$$\mathbf{a}_2 = -\mathbf{a}_1\rho. \tag{5.5.18}$$

Ignoring the constraint (5.5.18), the resulting least squares regression of y_i on y_{i-1}, $\mathbf{x}_i$ and $\mathbf{x}_{i-1}$ will still yield consistent estimates of ρ and $\boldsymbol{\beta}$. Therefore, the least squares estimate $\tilde{\rho}$ can be used for ρ to transform the data as in (5.5.12), and then the least squares principle can be applied again to the transformed data to estimate $\boldsymbol{\beta}$.

Since the properties of the least squares estimator depend on the property of the disturbance term, it is common to test the null hypothesis that successive disturbances are uncorrelated against the alternative hypothesis that they are correlated. A convenient start is to examine the correlations between u_i and the immediately preceding u_{i-s}. (Here $s = 1$ and perhaps some slightly higher integers.) Therefore, a test of independence usually starts with a test of first-order serial correlation being zero,

$$H_0 : \rho = 0. \tag{5.5.19}$$

If the u_i are observable, the *von Neumann ratio*[16]

[16]For large n, (5.5.20) is approximately normally distributed with mean $\frac{2n}{n-1}$ and variance $\frac{4n^2(n-2)}{(n+1)(n-3)^3}$.

$$\frac{\delta^2}{s^2} = \frac{\sum_{i=2}^{n}(u_i - u_{i-1})^2/n-1}{\sum_{i=1}^{n}u_i^2/n}$$
$$= \frac{n}{n-1}\frac{\sum_{i=2}^{n}(u_i - u_{i-1})^2}{\sum_{i=1}^{n}u_i^2} = \frac{n}{n-1}d \qquad *(5.5.20)$$

is used to test the null hypothesis (5.5.19). This statistic, apart from the factor $n/n-1$, is the ratio of the sum of squares of successive differences of residuals to the sum of the squared residuals (d). Note that the sum in the numerator of d ranges from 2 to n because of the presence of u_{i-1}, while the sum in the denominator ranges from 1 to n. Carrying out the square in the numerator and recognizing that for n large enough,

$$\sum_{i=2}^{n} u_i^2 \approx \sum_{i=2}^{n} u_{i-1}^2 \approx \sum_{i=1}^{n} u_i^2, \qquad (5.5.21)$$

it follows that d can be approximated as

$$d \approx 2\left(1 - \frac{\sum_{i=2}^{n} u_i u_{i-1}}{\sum_{i=1}^{n} u_i^2}\right). \qquad (5.5.22)$$

This approximation can motivate the use of the *von Neumann ratio* statistic (5.5.20). Suppose that u_i and u_{i-1} are usually of the same sign, the case of positive first-order serial correlation. In that case, $u_i u_{i-1}$ in (5.5.22) would tend to be positive, so d would lie significantly below 2. Conversely, if u_i and u_{i-1} are usually of the opposite sign, the case of negative serial correlation, then $\sum u_i u_{i-1}$ would tend to be negative, so d would be significantly above 2.

Unfortunately, the u_i are usually unobservable. Only the estimated residuals, the $\hat{u}_i$, are available. For the method of last squares, these residuals are

$$\hat{u}_i = y_i - \mathbf{x}_i'\hat{\boldsymbol{\beta}}$$
$$= u_i + \mathbf{x}_i'(\boldsymbol{\beta} - \hat{\boldsymbol{\beta}}), \qquad (5.5.23)$$

where

$$\hat{\boldsymbol{\beta}} - \boldsymbol{\beta} = (\mathbf{X}'\mathbf{X})^{-1}\mathbf{X}'\mathbf{u}. \qquad (5.5.24)$$

In small samples, the sequence of the estimated residuals depends not only on the sequence of errors but also on the values taken by the exogenous variables, $\mathbf{x}$. To test the null hypothesis (5.5.19), Durbin and Watson (1950, 1951) propose using the statistic $\hat{d}$ determined by the estimated residuals,

$$\hat{d} = \frac{\sum_{i=2}^{n}(\hat{u}_i - \hat{u}_{i-1})^2}{\sum_{i=1}^{n}\hat{u}_i^2}, \qquad *(5.5.25)$$

and have given the lower and upper limits of its significance levels. The statistic $\hat{d}$ (5.5.25) is called the *Durbin–Watson statistic*. If $\hat{d} \ll 2$, positive first-order serial correlation is indicated, while if $\hat{d} \gg 2$, negative first-order serial correlation is indicated. If $\hat{d} \approx 2$, the absence of first-order serial correlation, as in (5.5.19), is indicated. Tables of significant values of the Durbin–Watson statistic are based on normally distributed disturbances and fixed explanatory variables. These tables give, for a particular sample size n and a particular num-

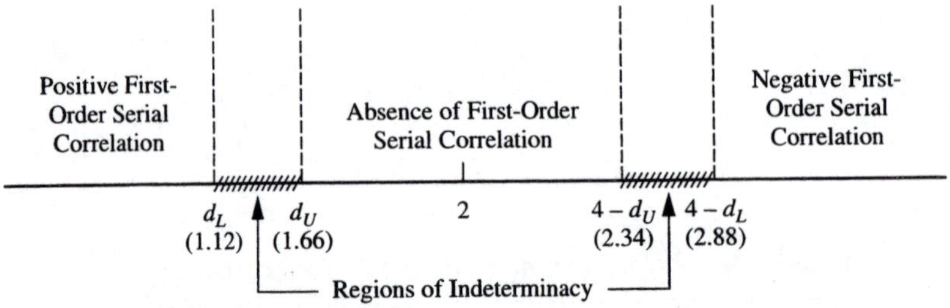

Figure 5.2 Significance Points for the Durbin–Watson Statistic d
Note Numbers refer to the $n=25$, $k=4$ case for a 5% level of significance (see Durbin and Watson (1950).)

ber of coefficients to be estimated k, lower and upper values for $\hat{d}$, called d_L and d_U, representing bounds on the significance level for any set of explanatory variables. For example, if $n=25$ and $k=4$, the values for a 5% level of significance are $d_L=1.12$ and $d_U=1.66$. To understand the meaning and use of these values, construct an axis for $\hat{d}$, as shown in Figure 5.2. The distribution of the statistic is symmetric about 2, so $4-d_U$ and $4-d_L$ are shown as significant points. If the test statistic $\hat{d}$ lies in the middle region close to 2, specifically between d_U and $4-d_L$ (here 1.66 to 2.34), the test indicates the absence of first-order serial correlation.[17] If $\hat{d}$ lies significantly below 2, however, specifically below d_L (here 1.12), it indicates the presence of positive first-order serial correlation. Similarly, if $\hat{d}$ lies above $4-d_L$ (here 2.88), it indicates the presence of negative first-order serial correlation. In the two remaining regions of indeterminacy the test fails, but in those cases, it is customary to reject the hypothesis of absence of first-order serial correlation.[18]

While the Durbin–Watson test is most widely used to test for serial correlation, other tests have also been proposed. For instance, in Section 6.4.4 we discuss the Q test of Box and Pierce (1970) for the null hypothesis of no serial dependence by testing several orders of serial correlations simultaneously equal to zero. If serial independence is rejected using the Durbin–Watson test or other tests, there are two possible treatments, each involving a change in the specification of the original model. One treatment is to identify the pattern of serial correlations in the residuals and apply the GLS approach as outlined above (see also Chapter 6). The other is to call for a respecification of the regression model. If a significant serial correlation of errors exists, it often indicates some flaw in the model. For instance, if important variables are omitted from the specification, the error terms would also represent the effects of these variables, of which no explicit account has been taken in the model. If

[17]If a lagged endogenous variable is included among the explanatory variables, the $\hat{d}$ statistic will be biased toward 2, indicating no serial correlation even though such correlation may be present. Intuitively, this bias stems from the fact that the dependence of the error terms on lagged values is "absorbed" in the included lagged endogenous variable. The test is not conclusive and is not recommended in such a case of an included lagged endogenous variable (see also Section 6.4).

[18]The regions of indeterminacy are large for small numbers of explanatory variables, leading to an inconclusive test in many situations. A test statistic has been constructed by Theil and Nagar (1961) that excludes these regions of indeterminacy. This test statistic requires, however, that each of the explanatory variables move smoothly, in particular, that the first and second differences of each explanatory variable are small in absolute value compared with the range of the variable itself. The test statistic is identical to the Durbin–Watson $\hat{d}$ of (5.5.25), and the critical value d^* is generally near d_U. For example, for $n=25$, $k=4$, and a 5% level of significance, d^* is 1.65 compared to 1.66 for d_U. In this case, using the Theil–Nagar test, there is no first-order serial correlation if $1.65 < d < 2.35$; positive serial correlation if $\hat{d} < 1.65$; and negative serial correlation if $\hat{d} > 2.35$, where 2.35 is obtained as $4-d^*$.

the evolution of these variables, as with many economic quantities, show more regularity than a purely random series, the error terms will exhibit some time dependence.[19] It could also be an indication of a misspecification of the functional relationship among the variables. An example is the case of estimation of a linear relationship when the actual relationship is nonlinear, as shown in Figure 5.3. Note that here $\hat{u}_1$ to $\hat{u}_3$ are negative while $\hat{u}_5$ to $\hat{u}_{13}$ are positive and $\hat{u}_{14}$ to $\hat{u}_{16}$ are negative. Thus $\hat{u}_i\hat{u}_{i-1}$ will be positive for all i other than $i = 4, 5, 13$, and 14. Since the $\hat{u}_i$ and $\hat{u}_{i-1}$ tend to be of the same sign, the $\hat{d}$ will be significantly below 2, indicating positive first-order serial correlation. It could also arise because the conditional variance of u_i, given past u_i, depends on the size of the squared error terms in previous time periods, the *autoregressive conditional heteroskedasticity* (ARCH) model of Engle (1982) and its various extensions. The idea of volatility clustering has been found useful in the analysis of financial markets because residuals of financial models often exhibit the pattern of being small for a number of successive periods of time, then much larger for a while, then smaller again, and so on. There are many different ways to model this basic idea, as discussed in Bollerslev, Chou, and Kroner (1992). A simple example is the ARCH(p) model, in which the error term u_i conditional on $u_{i-1}, \ldots$ is of the form

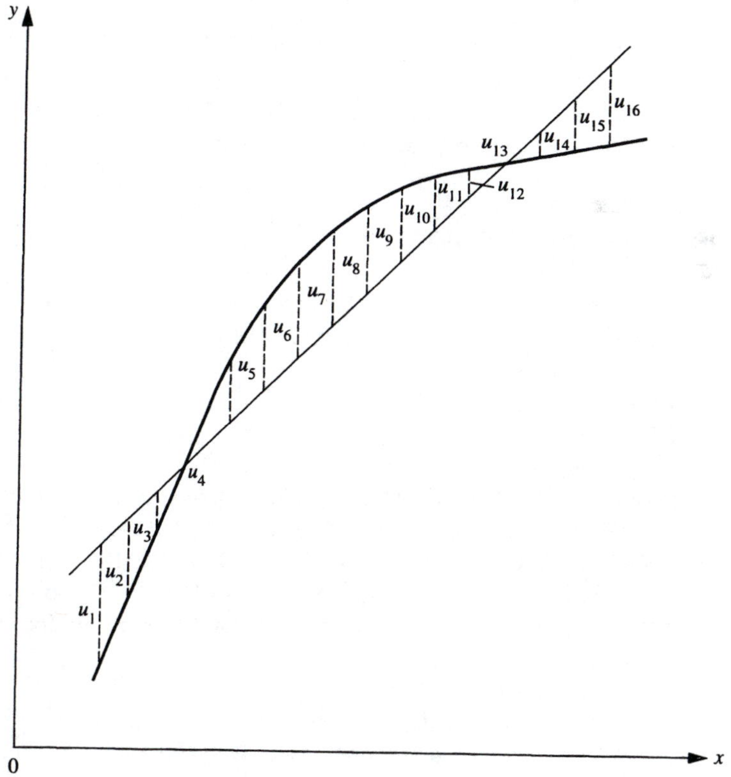

Figure 5.3 Positive First-Order Correlation When a Nonlinear Relationship Is Estimated by a Linear Relationship

[19]For example, see Hendry (1974).

$$(u_i \mid u_{i-1}, \ldots) = \varepsilon_i h_i \quad (5.5.26)$$

$$h_i^2 = E(u_i^2 \mid u_{i-1}, \ldots) = \alpha_0 + \alpha_1 u_{i-1}^2 + \cdots + \alpha_p u_{i-p}^2, \quad (5.5.27)$$

where ε_i is i.i.d. (independent and identically distributed) with mean 0 and variance 1, the α_j are assumed to be positive to ensure $h_i > 0$, and the ARCH process is assumed stable.[20] Note that in this type of model the error term u_i remains uncorrelated over time and the un-conditional variance $E(u_i^2) = \sigma^2 = \alpha_0(1 - \Sigma_{j=1}^{p} \alpha_j)^{-1}$ remains homoskedastic. However, the fact that the conditional variance of u_i depends on $u^2_{i-1}, u^2_{i-2}, \ldots$ could give a misleading impression of the existence of serial correlation, particularly if the sample is small (Milhøj, 1990).

Which of these treatments should be used? It is difficult to give an answer that will cover all contingencies, but, generally, if the DW statistic is significant, it is desirable first to explore the possibility of model misspecification. To test for the omission of relevant explanatory variables, t or F statistics can be used to examine the significance of including additional explanatory variables. To test for the appropriateness of the functional form, Bierens (1990) or Ramsey (1969) have developed statistics which explore the idea that a correctly specified model should have residuals independent of the functions of the explanatory variables, **x** (conditional moment or RESET test; see Section 5.7). To test the ARCH effect, the F statistics for the hypothesis that $\alpha_1 = \alpha_2 = \cdots = \alpha_p = 0$ of the regression model

$$\hat{u}_i^2 = \alpha_0 + \alpha_1 \hat{u}_{i-1}^2 + \cdots + \alpha_p^2 \hat{u}_{i-p} + \text{residual} \quad (5.5.28)$$

can be used, where $\hat{u}_i$ denotes the least squares residual of the model. Only when all these test statistics fail to show misspecification is the GLS estimator (5.5.11), based on consistently estimated serial correlation coefficients, used.

5.6 ERROR COMPONENTS MODELS

A *panel* (or *longitudinal* or *temporal cross-sectional*) *data* set is one that follows the same sample of individuals over time and thus provides multiple observations on each individual in the sample. Examples of these include the University of Michigan's Panel Study of Income Dynamics (PSID) and the National Longitudinal Surveys of Labor Market Experience (NLS). The PSID has been collecting annual economic information from a representative national sample of about 6000 families and 15,000 individuals since 1968. The data set contains over 5000 variables, including employment, income, and human capital variables as well as information on housing, travel to work, and mobility. The NLS has followed samples of several age–gender cohorts: men 45 to 59 in 1966, young men 14 to 24 in 1966, women 30 to 44 in 1967, young women 14 to 24 in 1968, and youth of both sexes 14 to 21 in 1979. The first four cohorts were interviewed periodically for 15 years. The youth cohort interviews were planned to continue annually for 6 years. The original sample size for each of the 1960s cohorts was about 5000 individuals, and the 1979 cohort started with over 12,000 individuals. The list of variables collected is running into the thousands, and as Borus (1981) puts it, "includes everything you always wanted to know about individuals that the Census Bureau was not afraid to ask."

[20]See Sections 6.2 and 6.3 for a discussion of stability conditions.

In addition to the PSID and NLS data sets, there are many panel data sets in several Western countries, including the United States, Canada, France, Germany, and Switzerland.[21] At least two factors have contributed to the proliferation of longitudinal data. One is that such panel data allow economists and other social scientists to analyze, in depth, complex economic and related issues that could not have been treated with equal rigor using time-series or cross-section data alone. Like cross-section data, panel data describe each of a number of individuals. Like time-series data, they describe changes through time. By blending characteristics of both cross-section and time-series data, more reliable research methods can be used in order to investigate phenomena that could not otherwise have been treated.[22]

The second factor is that the cost of developing useful longitudinal data sets is no longer prohibitive. In some cases, computerized matching of existing administrative records can produce inexpensive longitudinal information, such as the Social Security Administration's Continuous Work History Sample (CWHS). In other cases, valuable longitudinal data bases can be generated by computerized matching of existing administrative and survey data, such as the PSID and the U.S. Current Population Survey. Even in cases where the desired longitudinal information can be collected only by initiating new surveys, such as the series of negative income tax experiments in the United States and Canada, recent advances in computerized data management systems have made longitudinal data development cost-effective over the last 20 years, as discussed in Chapter 3 and Ashenfelter and Solon (1982).

Panel data permit construction and testing of realistic behavioral models, which could not be treated using cross-section or time-series data alone. The availability of new data sources also raises new issues, however. New methods are constantly being introduced, and points of view are changing. In this section we review some basic econometric methodologies that have been used to study the individual entities within a pooled data base and to draw generalized inferences about the population.

To utilize the information on both the cross-individual differences and intertemporal dynamics found in a panel data set, it is convenient to classify economic variables into one of three types: individual time invariant, period individual invariant, and individual time-varying variables. The individual time-invariant variables are variables that are the same for a given cross-sectional unit through time but which vary across cross-sectional units. Examples of these are gender and socioeconomic background for individuals, and attributes of individual firm management variables. The period individual-invariant variables are variables that are the same for all cross-sectional units at a given point in time but that vary through time. Examples of these are prices, interest rates, and attitudes such as widespread optimism or pessimism. The individual-time-varying variables are variables that vary across cross-sectional units at a point in time and also exhibit variations through time. Examples of these variables are individuals' wages and firm profits, sales, and capital stock.

Since any econometric model is a simplification of a real-world phenomenon, there are large numbers of factors that affect the outcome but are not explicitly included as explanatory variables. It is natural to assume that the effects of all the omitted variables are also driven by these three types of variables. For ease of exposition, it will be assumed that the effects

[21]For the sources of U.S. (labor market) data sets, see Ashenfelter and Solon (1982) and Borus (1981). For examples of marketing data, see Beckwith (1972); biomedical data, see Sheiner, Rosenberg, and Melmon (1972); for a financial market data base, see Dielman, Nantell, and Wright (1980).

[22]For more details, see Hsiao (1985a, 1986).

of period individual-invariant variables can be amalgamated with the effects of the individual-time-varying variables so that the effects of omitted variables v_{it} can be represented by

$$v_{it} = \alpha_i + u_{it}, \qquad i = 1, \ldots, N; \quad t = 1, \ldots, T. \tag{5.6.1}$$

Here the α_i represent the individual specific effects, while the u_{it} represent the individual-period varying effects. Typically, α_i and u_{it} are assumed to be independent of each other.

Now consider the linear regression model

$$y_{it} = \mathbf{x}'_{it}\boldsymbol{\beta} + v_{it}, \qquad i = 1, \ldots, N; \quad t = 1, \ldots, T, \tag{5.6.2}$$

where v_{it} represents the effects of all the omitted variables with the decomposition typified by (5.6.1). Assume that u_{it} are independent of $\mathbf{x}_{it}$. When the α_i are treated as fixed constants, the model is referred to as a *fixed effects* model. When the α_i are treated as random variables, the model is called a *random effects* model.

If the α_i are treated as fixed constants, the least squares estimation of the model (5.6.2) under the assumption (5.6.1) is called the *least squares dummy variable* (LSDV) *estimators* of $\boldsymbol{\beta}$ and α_i, $i = 1, \ldots, N$, because α_j can be viewed as the coefficients of the dummy variables d_{jt} where $d_{jt} = 1$ for $i = j$ and zero otherwise. The LSDV estimators of $\boldsymbol{\beta}$ and α_i are [see (4.3.7) and (4.3.8)]

$$\hat{\boldsymbol{\beta}}_w = \left[\sum_{i=1}^{N}\sum_{t=1}^{T}(\mathbf{x}_{it} - \bar{\mathbf{x}}_i)(\mathbf{x}_{it} - \bar{\mathbf{x}}_i)'\right]^{-1}\left[\sum_{i=1}^{N}\sum_{t=1}^{T}(\mathbf{x}_{it} - \bar{\mathbf{x}}_i)(y_{it} - \bar{y}_i)\right], \tag*{*(5.6.3)}$$

$$\hat{\alpha}_i = \bar{y}_i - \hat{\boldsymbol{\beta}}'_w\bar{\mathbf{x}}_i, \qquad i = 1, \ldots, N, \tag*{*(5.6.4)}$$

where $\bar{\mathbf{x}}_i = \Sigma_{t=1}^{T}\mathbf{x}_{it}/T$ and $\bar{y}_i = \Sigma_{t=1}^{T}y_{it}/T$ are the mean values of the time series of the ith individual. Note that, of course, $\hat{\boldsymbol{\beta}}'_w\bar{\mathbf{X}}_i$ is equivalent to $\bar{\mathbf{X}}'_i\hat{\boldsymbol{\beta}}_w$.

The LSDV estimator of $\boldsymbol{\beta}$ is also called the *within-group* or *covariance* estimator because it is the least squares estimator of the transformed model

$$y_{it} - \bar{y}_i = \boldsymbol{\beta}'(\mathbf{x}_{it} - \bar{\mathbf{x}}_i) + (u_{it} - \bar{u}_i), \qquad i = 1, \ldots, N; \quad t = 1, \ldots, T, \tag{5.6.5}$$

where $\bar{u}_i = \Sigma_{t=1}^{T}u_{it}/T$ is the time-series mean of u. This transformation of the data obtained by subtracting from each observation the time-series mean for the corresponding cross-sectional unit is called the *covariance transformation*. Such a transformation eliminates the need to include dummy variables to handle the individual effects in the matrix of explanatory variables. Hence it is only necessary to invert a matrix of order $k \times k$, not a matrix of order $(N + k) \times (N + k)$.

The LSDV estimator (5.6.3) is independent of the incidental parameters α_i and is consistent when either N or T or both tend to infinity. By contrast, the estimator $\hat{\alpha}_i$ (5.6.4) is consistent only when T tends to infinity. The LSDV estimator is the best linear unbiased estimator (BLUE) if u_{it} is independently and identically distributed (i.i.d) with mean zero and variance σ_u^2. Furthermore, if u_{it} is normally distributed, it is also the MLE.

If α_i are treated as random, the residuals v_{it} and v_{is} become serially correlated since both contain α_i. Typically, it is assumed that $E\alpha_i = 0$ and $E\alpha_i\alpha_j = \sigma_\alpha^2$ if $i = j$, and $= 0$ if $i \neq j$. Then the covariance matrix of $\mathbf{v}_i$ is of the form

$$E\mathbf{v}_i\mathbf{v}'_i = \sigma_u^2 I_T + \sigma_\alpha^2\mathbf{e}\mathbf{e}' = \mathbf{V}, \qquad E\mathbf{v}_i\mathbf{v}'_j = \mathbf{0}, \tag{5.6.6}$$

where $\mathbf{e}$ is a $T \times 1$ vector of $(1, \ldots, 1)'$ and $\mathbf{I}_T$ is an identity matrix of order T. The inverse of $\mathbf{V}$ then has the form

$$\mathbf{V}^{-1} = \frac{1}{\sigma_u^2}\left(\mathbf{I}_T - \frac{\sigma_\alpha^2}{\sigma_u^2 + T\sigma_\alpha^2}\mathbf{ee}'\right). \tag{5.6.7}$$

When the α_i are random, the covariance transformation can still be applied to eliminate the individual-period-invariant effect, and the LS regression for the transformed model (5.6.5) remains unbiased and consistent, but it is no longer the BLUE. Rather, the BLUE is the generalized least squares (GLS) estimator.

If the α_i are independent of $\mathbf{x}_{it}$ and u_{it} are i.i.d., the GLS estimator of $\boldsymbol{\beta}$ is the weighted average of the between- and within-group estimators, as in Maddala (1971b),

$$\hat{\boldsymbol{\beta}}_{\text{GLS}} = \Delta\hat{\boldsymbol{\beta}}_b + (\mathbf{I}_k - \Delta)\hat{\boldsymbol{\beta}}_w, \qquad *(5.6.8)$$

where $\hat{\boldsymbol{\beta}}_b$ is the between-group estimator

$$\hat{\boldsymbol{\beta}}_b = \left[\sum_{i=1}^{N}(\bar{\mathbf{x}}_i - \bar{\mathbf{x}})(\bar{\mathbf{x}}_i - \bar{\mathbf{x}})'\right]^{-1}\left[\sum_{i=1}^{N}(\bar{\mathbf{x}}_i - \bar{\mathbf{x}})(\bar{y}_i - \bar{y})\right],$$

$$\psi = \frac{\sigma_u^2}{\sigma_u^2 + T\sigma_\alpha^2}, \qquad *(5.6.9)$$

$$\Delta = \psi T\left[\sum_{i=1}^{N}\sum_{t=1}^{T}(\mathbf{x}_{it} - \bar{\mathbf{x}}_i)(\mathbf{x}_{it} - \bar{\mathbf{x}}_i)' + \psi T\sum_{i=1}^{N}(\bar{\mathbf{x}}_i - \bar{\mathbf{x}})(\bar{\mathbf{x}}_i - \bar{\mathbf{x}})'\right]^{-1} \cdot \left[\sum_{i=1}^{N}(\bar{\mathbf{x}}_i - \bar{\mathbf{x}})(\bar{\mathbf{x}}_i - \bar{\mathbf{x}})'\right],$$

and the $\bar{x}$ and $\bar{y}$ are the means

$$\bar{\mathbf{x}} = \frac{\sum_{i=1}^{N}\sum_{t=1}^{T}\mathbf{x}_{it}}{NT} = \frac{\sum_{i=1}^{N}\bar{\mathbf{x}}_i}{N},$$

$$\bar{y} = \frac{\sum_{i=1}^{N}\sum_{t=1}^{T}y_{it}}{NT} = \frac{\sum_{i=1}^{N}\bar{y}_i}{N}.$$

If $\psi \to 1$, then $\hat{\boldsymbol{\beta}}_{\text{GLS}}$ converges to the OLS. If $\psi \to 0$, the GLS estimator of $\boldsymbol{\beta}$ becomes the LSDV (within) estimator. In essence, ψ, as defined in (5.6.9), measures the weight given to the between-group variation. In the LSDV procedure (or *fixed effects model*), this source of variation is completely ignored. The OLS procedure corresponds to $\psi = 1$, where the between- and within-group variations are just added up. Thus the OLS and LSDV estimators may be viewed as corresponding to all-or-nothing ways, respectively, of utilizing the between-group variation. The procedure of treating α_i as random provides a solution intermediate to treating them all as different and treating them all as equal. However, when T tends to infinity, the GLS estimator converges to the LSDV estimator. This is because when T goes to infinity, there is an infinite number of observations for each i. Therefore, each α_i can be considered as a random variable that has been drawn once and forever so that for each i they can be treated like fixed parameters.

Computationally, the GLS estimator is fairly simple to implement. The data are transformed by subtracting a fraction $(1 - \psi^{1/2})$ of individual means $\bar{y}_i$ and $\bar{\mathbf{x}}_i$ from their corresponding y_{it} and $\mathbf{x}_{it}$ values and then $[y_{it} - (1 - \psi^{1/2})\bar{y}_i]$ is regressed on $[\mathbf{x}_{it}\ (1 - \psi^{1/2})\bar{\mathbf{x}}_{it}]$. When σ_α^2 and σ_u^2 are unknown, their consistent estimates may be substituted for them. For instance, the estimators

$$\hat{\sigma}_u^2 = \frac{\sum_{i=1}^{N}\sum_{t=1}^{T}[(y_{it} - \bar{y}_i) - \hat{\boldsymbol{\beta}}'_w(\mathbf{x}_{it} - \bar{\mathbf{x}}_i)]^2}{N(T-1)-k}, \tag{5.6.10}$$

$$\hat{\sigma}_\alpha^2 = \frac{\sum_{i=1}^{N}(\bar{y}_i - \hat{\boldsymbol{\beta}}'_w\bar{\mathbf{x}}_1)^2}{N-k} - \frac{1}{T}\hat{\sigma}_u^2 \tag{5.6.11}$$

are consistent. The feasible GLS estimator using an estimated covariance matrix is asymptotically equivalent to the GLS estimator.

To unify the random effects and fixed effects formulations, it may be assumed from the outset that the effects are random. The fixed effects model can then be viewed as one where investigators make inferences conditional on the effects that are in the sample. The random effects model, by contrast, can then be viewed as one where investigators make unconditional or marginal inference with respect to the population of all effects. There is really no distinction in the "nature of the effects." It is up to the investigator to decide whether to make inferences with respect to the population characteristics or only with respect to the effects that are in the sample.

In general, whether one wishes to consider the conditional likelihood function or the marginal likelihood function depends on the context of the data, the manner in which they were gathered, and the environment from which they came. For instance, consider an example where several technicians care for machines. The effects of the technicians may be assumed to be random. But if the situation is not that each technician comes and goes, randomly sampled from all employees, but that all are available, and if the purpose is to assess differences between these specific technicians, then the fixed effects model would be more appropriate. Conversely, if an experiment involves hundreds of individuals that are considered a random sample from some larger population, the random effects model would be more appropriate. If, however, the situation is one of analyzing just a few individuals, say five or six, where the sole interest lay in just these individuals, then the individual effects would more appropriately be fixed and not random. The situation to which a model applies and the inferences based on it are the deciding factors in determining whether effects should be treated as random or fixed. When individual units in the sample are of interest, the effects are more appropriately considered fixed. When inferences are to be made about the characteristics of a population from which those in the data are considered to be a random sample, the effects should be considered random.[23]

Closely related to the question of fixed effects or random effects inference is the impact of nonorthogonality between the effects α_i and the included explanatory variables, $\mathbf{x}_{it}$, on the appropriateness of either approach. There are arguments which suggest that the individual effects and the explanatory variables are correlated, as in Mundlak (1961, 1978). For example, in a panel of farms observed over several years, suppose that y_{it} is a measure of the output of the ith farm in the tth season, $\mathbf{x}_{it}$ are measured inputs, α_i represents the input reflecting soil quality and other characteristics of the farm's location, which are known to the farmer but unknown to the investigating econometricians, and u_{it} reflects unmeasured inputs which are not under the farmer's control (e.g., rainfall). The factor input decisions $\mathbf{x}_{it}$ are generally made before knowing u_{it} but are conditional on α_i. Treating α_i as an unknown parameter is equivalent to adding a

[23]In this sense, if N becomes large, one would not be interested in the specific effects of each individual but rather in the characteristics of the population. A random effects framework would be more appropriate.

time-invariant variable to the set of explanatory variables $\mathbf{x}_{it}$. Therefore, using a fixed effects model can eliminate the bias arising from the correlation between the unobserved time-invariant effects and the included explanatory variables. On the other hand, random effects inference ignoring the correlation between the effects and the explanatory variables can lead to biased estimation. However, this is a consequence of misspecification rather than of the inappropriateness of random effects inference (e.g., Hsiao, 1986, Chap. 3; 1991).

5.7 SPECIFICATION ERROR

Estimators are based on both the model and the data. Thus errors in the model and errors in the data both give rise to errors in the estimators. In this section we treat specification error, that is, errors in the estimators stemming from errors in formulating the model. In the next section we treat errors in the variables, which are errors in the estimators stemming from errors in measuring the variables.

There are several types of possible errors in specifying the model. Among them are the exclusion of relevant variables, the inclusion of irrelevant variables, an incorrect form of the relationship (e.g., treating a nonlinear model as if it were linear), and an incorrect specification of the stochastic disturbance form (e.g., incorrect variances or covariance or an incorrect form of the distribution).[24] In Section 5.5 the consequence of misspecified functional form was discussed. The discussion here will first be on the consequences of the first two types of misspecification, relating to variable exclusion/inclusion, then on tests of misspecification.[25] Assume that the true model is of the form

$$\mathbf{y} = \mathbf{X}\boldsymbol{\beta} + \mathbf{u}, \tag{5.7.1}$$

where $\mathbf{X}$ has k columns. The model that has been specified, however, is of the form

$$\mathbf{y} = \mathbf{X}_1\boldsymbol{\beta}_1 + \mathbf{u}_1, \tag{5.7.2}$$

where $\mathbf{X}_1$ has k_1 columns. The least squares estimator of $\boldsymbol{\beta}_1$ in (5.7.2) is given as

$$\hat{\hat{\boldsymbol{\beta}}}_1 = (\mathbf{X}_1'\mathbf{X}_1)^{-1}\mathbf{X}_1'\mathbf{y}, \tag{5.7.3}$$

the two hats being a reminder that this is an estimator for the misspecified model. Using the true model, however, and taking expectations, assuming that $\mathbf{X}$ and $\mathbf{X}_1$ are matrices of fixed numbers, yields

$$E(\hat{\hat{\boldsymbol{\beta}}}_1) = (\mathbf{X}_1'\mathbf{X}_1)^{-1}\mathbf{X}_1'\mathbf{X}\boldsymbol{\beta}. \tag{*5.7.4}$$

Each column of the matrix $(\mathbf{X}_1'\mathbf{X}_1)^{-1}\mathbf{X}_1\mathbf{X}$ here multiplying the vector of true parameters $\boldsymbol{\beta}$ is simply the least squares regression of one of the variables in $\mathbf{X}$, the explanatory variables of the true model, on all the variables in $\mathbf{X}_1$, the explanatory variables in the misspecified model.

This formulation can be used to illustrate two important special cases: that of omitted relevant variables and that of included irrelevant variables.[26] In the former case, in which relevant variables have been omitted, the true model (5.7.1) can be written

[24]For a discussion of nonlinear models, see Goldfeld and Quandt (1972).

[25]For a further discussion of specification error, see Theil (1971). For an extension to simultaneous equations, see Fisher (1961).

[26]In general, of course, it is possible both to omit relevant variables and to include irrelevant variables.

$$\mathbf{y} = (\mathbf{X}_1 : \mathbf{X}_2)\begin{pmatrix}\boldsymbol{\beta}_1 \\ \boldsymbol{\beta}_2\end{pmatrix} + \mathbf{u} = \mathbf{X}_1\boldsymbol{\beta}_1 + \mathbf{X}_2\boldsymbol{\beta}_2 + \mathbf{u}. \tag{5.7.5}$$

The misspecification in (5.7.5) thus is the omission of the variables in $\mathbf{X}_2$. In the misspecified model only the variables in $\mathbf{X}_1$ are included, and the error terms $\mathbf{u}_1$ are

$$\mathbf{u}_1 = \mathbf{X}_2\boldsymbol{\beta}_2 + \mathbf{u}. \tag{5.7.6}$$

If $\mathbf{X}_1$ and $\mathbf{X}_2$ are correlated,

$$E(\mathbf{u}_1 \mid \mathbf{X}_1) \neq \mathbf{0}, \tag{5.7.7}$$

so assumption A.4.1 is violated.

When (5.7.7) holds, the least squares estimator of the coefficients of (5.7.2) is biased and inconsistent. Intuitively, the bias and inconsistency in these estimators stem from the influences of the omitted variables $\mathbf{X}_2$ on $\mathbf{y}$, which are represented in part by $\mathbf{u}$, but also in part by $\mathbf{X}_1\boldsymbol{\beta}_1$. The included variables $\mathbf{X}_1$ take account both of the influences of themselves and of the influences of the omitted variables on $\mathbf{y}$.

More formally, the least squares estimators of the coefficients of the included variables are

$$\hat{\hat{\boldsymbol{\beta}}}_1 = (\mathbf{X}_1'\mathbf{X}_1)^{-1}\mathbf{X}_1' y = (\mathbf{X}_1'\mathbf{X}_1)^{-1}\mathbf{X}_1'[\mathbf{X}_1\boldsymbol{\beta}_1 + \mathbf{X}_2\boldsymbol{\beta}_2 + \mathbf{u}] \tag{5.7.8}$$

$$\hat{\hat{\boldsymbol{\beta}}}_1 = \boldsymbol{\beta}_1 + (\mathbf{X}_1'\mathbf{X}_1)^{-1}\mathbf{X}_1'\mathbf{X}_2\boldsymbol{\beta}_2 + (\mathbf{X}_1'\mathbf{X}_1)^{-1}\mathbf{X}_1'\mathbf{u}. \tag{5.7.9}$$

Taking expectations, the bias in estimating $\boldsymbol{\beta}_1$ is

$$B(\hat{\hat{\boldsymbol{\beta}}}_1) = E(\hat{\hat{\boldsymbol{\beta}}}_1) - \boldsymbol{\beta}_1 = (\mathbf{X}_1'\mathbf{X}_1)^{-1}\mathbf{X}_1'\mathbf{X}_2\boldsymbol{\beta}_2. \qquad *(5.7.10)$$

This specification bias is therefore directly proportional to the magnitudes in $\boldsymbol{\beta}_2$, so that the smaller are the coefficients of the omitted variables, the smaller will be the implied bias. This bias is also smaller the smaller is the correlation between included and excluded variables, as measured by $\mathbf{X'}_1\mathbf{X}_2$. The specification error vanishes in the limit as either $\boldsymbol{\beta}_2$ or $\mathbf{X'}_1\mathbf{X}_2$ approaches zero. However, in the case in which a collinear variable has been dropped, where $\mathbf{X'}_1\mathbf{X}_2$ is large, the bias may be substantial. The bias need also not disappear as the sample size increases, so the estimator $\hat{\hat{\boldsymbol{\beta}}}_1$ is an inconsistent one. Furthermore, the estimates of the variances of the estimated coefficients of included variables are also biased in this case of omitted relevant explanatory variables.

The obverse case is that in which irrelevant variables have been included. In that case the true model is as in (5.7.1), while the estimated model is (5.7.2), where

$$\mathbf{X}_1 = (\mathbf{X} \vdots \mathbf{X}_2). \tag{5.7.11}$$

Thus the misspecified model is

$$y = (\mathbf{X} \vdots \mathbf{X}_2)\begin{pmatrix}\boldsymbol{\beta}_0 \\ \cdots \\ \boldsymbol{\beta}_2\end{pmatrix} + \mathbf{u}_1. \tag{5.7.12}$$

Since the misspecified model is still consistent with the Gauss–Markov theorem assumptions (assuming that $\mathbf{X}_2$ is uncorrelated with $\mathbf{u}_1$), the least squares estimator of (5.7.12) may be written in this case as

$$\begin{pmatrix} \hat{\hat{\boldsymbol{\beta}}}_0 \\ \cdots \\ \hat{\hat{\boldsymbol{\beta}}}_2 \end{pmatrix} = [(\mathbf{X} \vdots \mathbf{X}_2)'(\mathbf{X} \vdots \mathbf{X}_2)]^{-1}(\mathbf{X} \vdots \mathbf{X}_2)'\mathbf{y}$$

$$= \left[\begin{pmatrix} \mathbf{X}' \\ \cdots \\ \mathbf{X}_2' \end{pmatrix} (\mathbf{X} \vdots \mathbf{X}_2)\right]^{-1} \begin{pmatrix} \mathbf{X}' \\ \cdots \\ \mathbf{X}_2' \end{pmatrix} \mathbf{y} \tag{5.7.13}$$

$$= \begin{pmatrix} \mathbf{X}'\mathbf{X} & \vdots & \mathbf{X}'\mathbf{X}_2 \\ \cdots & \cdots & \cdots \\ \mathbf{X}_2'\mathbf{X} & \vdots & \mathbf{X}_2'\mathbf{X}_2 \end{pmatrix}^{-1} \begin{pmatrix} \mathbf{X}'\mathbf{y} \\ \cdots \\ \mathbf{X}_2'\mathbf{y} \end{pmatrix}.$$

Here $\hat{\hat{\boldsymbol{\beta}}}_0$ is the estimator from the misspecified model of the true parameters $\boldsymbol{\beta}$, the coefficients of $\mathbf{X}$. Using the true model (5.7.1) for $\mathbf{y}$ and taking expectations, assuming $\mathbf{X}$ and $\mathbf{X}_2$ are matrices of fixed numbers, we obtain

$$E\begin{pmatrix} \hat{\hat{\boldsymbol{\beta}}}_0 \\ \cdots \\ \hat{\hat{\boldsymbol{\beta}}}_2 \end{pmatrix} = \begin{pmatrix} \mathbf{X}'\mathbf{X} \vdots \mathbf{X}'\mathbf{X}_2 \\ \cdots \\ \mathbf{X}_2'\mathbf{X} \vdots \mathbf{X}_2'\mathbf{X}_2 \end{pmatrix}^{-1} \begin{pmatrix} \mathbf{X}'\mathbf{X}\boldsymbol{\beta} \\ \cdots \\ \mathbf{X}_2'\mathbf{X}\boldsymbol{\beta} \end{pmatrix}. \tag{5.7.14}$$

It follows that the expectation of $\hat{\hat{\boldsymbol{\beta}}}_0$ is the true coefficient vector[27]

$$E(\hat{\hat{\boldsymbol{\beta}}}_0) = \boldsymbol{\beta} \quad \text{and} \quad E(\hat{\hat{\boldsymbol{\beta}}}_2) = \mathbf{0} \qquad *(5.7.15)$$

Thus, in this case of included irrelevant variables, $\hat{\hat{\boldsymbol{\beta}}}_0$ is an unbiased estimator. It is also a consistent estimator. In addition, the estimators of the variances of the coefficients of the relevant variables are unbiased. These sample variances of the estimators of coefficients of relevant variables will tend to increase, however, as more irrelevant variables are included.

The asymmetry between the results in these two cases is because in the former case assumption A.4.1 is violated, while in the latter case it is not. Excluding relevant variables yields biased and inconsistent estimators, while including irrelevant variables yields unbiased and consistent estimators; thus in terms of bias and consistency, it is better to include "too many" than to include "too few" explanatory variables. Such practice is *not* generally recommended, however, because of other problems that can arise with included irrelevant variables: multicollinearity, inefficiency, and reduced degrees of freedom. Considerable judgment, in fact, is called for in the specification of the model, balancing between including "too few" and "too many" variables. Theoretical justifications should be available for including each explanatory variable in the model, but it should be recognized that in a general equilibrium setting, where "everything affects everything else," theoretical considerations are not sufficient to justify including explanatory variables. In general, an appealing approach is to include only explanatory variables that, on theoretical grounds, *directly* influence the dependent variable and that are not accounted for by other included variables and to perform formal statistical tests for specification error.

When specific alternatives are considered, conventional t—or F—statistics can be used to test for the significance of the inclusion of specific variables. When the general al-

[27]This result follows from inverting the partitioned matrix in (5.7.14) (see Problem 5-M).

ternative that some unspecified variables have been omitted and/or the functional form is misspecified are considered, Ramsey (1969) has suggested a regression specification error test (RESET) for which the error term under the alternative is assumed to take the polynomial form

$$u_i = \alpha_0 + \alpha_1 \hat{y}_i^2 + \alpha_2 \hat{y}_i^3 + \ldots + \alpha_q \hat{y}_i^{q+1} + v_i, \tag{5.7.16}$$

where $\hat{y}_i = \mathbf{x}_i'\hat{\boldsymbol{\beta}}$ and v_i is the disturbance term assumed to be independently normally distributed. The test procedure is simply to apply the usual F test for the hypothesis that all the α's are zero. However, when the least squares residual $\hat{\mathbf{u}} = \mathbf{Mu}$ is used in place of $\mathbf{u}, \hat{\mathbf{u}}$ has a multivariate normal distribution with mean $\mathbf{0}$ and singular covariance matrix $\sigma^2\mathbf{M}$, where $\mathbf{M}=\mathbf{I}-\mathbf{X}(\mathbf{X}'\mathbf{X})^{-1}\mathbf{X}'$ is of rank $n-k$. Therefore, Ramsey suggests using $\tilde{\mathbf{u}} = \mathbf{A}\hat{\mathbf{u}}$, and $\tilde{\mathbf{y}}^j = \mathbf{A}\hat{\mathbf{y}}^j$ in (5.7.16), where $\mathbf{A}$ is an $(n-k) \times n$ matrix such that $\mathbf{AMA}' = \mathbf{I}$ [e.g., the Theil (1965) BLUS residual]. Then the F test statistic under the null that all α_j's are zero has an F distribution with $q + 1$ and $n - k - (q + 1)$ degrees of freedom.

The Ramsey RESET test is a special case of the conditional moment tests (Newey, 1985). As discussed above and in Section 5.5, if a model is misspecified either because of the omission of relevant variables or because of using an incorrect functional form, the residuals of the model will be correlated with functions of $\mathbf{x}$. Thus if the null hypothesis that $E(y \mid \mathbf{x}) = f(\mathbf{x}; \boldsymbol{\theta})$ is true,[28] it is expected that $E[(y-f(\mathbf{x}; \boldsymbol{\theta}))w_j(\mathbf{x}; \boldsymbol{\theta})]=0$, where $w_j(\mathbf{x}; \boldsymbol{\theta})$ are weighting functions of $\mathbf{x}$. Bierens (1990) suggests using $\boldsymbol{\Phi}(\mathbf{x})$ as a weighting function, where $\boldsymbol{\Phi}(\mathbf{x})$ is any bounded one-to-one transformation of $(x_1, \ldots, x_k)$. For example, $\boldsymbol{\Phi}(\mathbf{x})$ can take the form

$$\boldsymbol{\Phi}(\mathbf{x}_i) = \left(\tan^{-1}\frac{x_{i1} - \bar{x}_1}{s_{x_1}}, \ldots, \tan^{-1}\frac{x_{ik} - \bar{x}_k}{s_{x_k}}\right)', \tag{5.7.17}$$

where $\bar{x}_j$ and s_{x_j} are the sample mean and the sample standard deviation of x_j. Under H_0, the statistic

$$\hat{M}(\boldsymbol{\lambda}) = \frac{1}{n}\sum_{i=1}^{n}[y_i - f(\mathbf{x}_i; \hat{\boldsymbol{\theta}})] \exp[\boldsymbol{\lambda}'\boldsymbol{\Phi}(\mathbf{x}_i)] \tag{5.7.18}$$

will converge to zero in probability, where $\hat{\boldsymbol{\theta}}$ is a consistent estimator and $\boldsymbol{\lambda}$ is a $k \times 1$ nonzero vector of constants. A chi-square with one degree of freedom test of functional form proposed by Bierens (1990) takes the form

$$\hat{W}(\boldsymbol{\lambda}) = \frac{n\hat{M}^2(\boldsymbol{\lambda})}{\hat{s}^2(\boldsymbol{\lambda})}, \tag{5.7.19}$$

where

$$\hat{s}^2(\boldsymbol{\lambda}) = \frac{1}{n}\sum_{i=1}^{n}[y_i - f(\mathbf{x}_i; \hat{\boldsymbol{\theta}})]^2\left\{\exp[\boldsymbol{\lambda}'\boldsymbol{\Phi}(\mathbf{x}_i)] - \hat{\mathbf{b}}(\boldsymbol{\lambda})'\hat{A}^{-1}\frac{\partial}{\partial\boldsymbol{\theta}}f(\mathbf{x}_i; \hat{\boldsymbol{\theta}})\right\}^2, \tag{5.7.20}$$

$$\hat{\mathbf{b}}(\boldsymbol{\lambda}) = \frac{1}{n}\sum_{i=1}^{n}\frac{\partial}{\partial\boldsymbol{\theta}}f(\mathbf{x}_i; \hat{\boldsymbol{\theta}}) \exp[\boldsymbol{\lambda}'\boldsymbol{\Phi}(\mathbf{x}_i)], \tag{5.7.21}$$

$$\hat{\mathbf{A}} = \frac{1}{n}\sum_{i=1}^{n}\left\{\left[\frac{\partial}{\partial\boldsymbol{\theta}}f(\mathbf{x}_i; \hat{\boldsymbol{\theta}})\right]\left[\frac{\partial}{\partial\boldsymbol{\theta}'}f(\mathbf{x}_i; \hat{\boldsymbol{\theta}})\right]\right\} \tag{5.7.22}$$

[28] If $f(\mathbf{x}; \boldsymbol{\theta})$ is linear, then $f(\mathbf{x}; \boldsymbol{\theta}) = \mathbf{x}_i'\boldsymbol{\beta}$.

To test the hypothesis that the errors are normally distributed, it is noted that for a normal distribution, the third central moment, which determines *skewness*, is zero and the fourth central moment, which determines *kurtosis*, is equal to three times the variance. It was shown by Jarque and Bera (1980) that the test statistic

$$\frac{1}{6n}\left(\sum_{i=1}^{n} e_i^3\right)^2 + \frac{1}{24n}\left[\sum_{i=1}^{n}(e_i^4 - 3)\right]^2 \tag{5.7.23}$$

converges to a chi-square distribution with two degrees of freedom under normality, where

$$e_i = \frac{\hat{u}_i - \bar{\hat{u}}}{\hat{\sigma}}, \tag{5.7.24}$$

$\hat{u}_i$ and $\hat{\sigma}$ are the maximum likelihood estimators of the residual and the variance, respectively, and $\bar{\hat{u}}$ is the sample mean of $\hat{u}_i$, which is zero if the model contains an intercept term.

5.8 ERRORS IN VARIABLES AND THE METHOD OF INSTRUMENTAL VARIABLES

Variables, both dependent and independent, are measured subject to error. In particular, the available data may not refer to the variable as specified, as in the use of proxy variables, or there may be systematic biases in the collection or publication of the data. If the measurement errors are systematic, in general, auxiliary equations can be specified to capture these errors.[29] Therefore, this section focuses on only the impact of random measurement errors on the regression model.

Suppose that the true linear regression model is of the usual form

$$\mathbf{y} = \mathbf{X}\boldsymbol{\beta} + \mathbf{u}, \tag{5.8.1}$$

where $\mathbf{y}$ represents the true values of the dependent variable and $\mathbf{X}$ represents the true values of the explanatory variables. Generally, none of these variables is measured without error. Rather, what are observed are $\mathbf{y}_1$ and $\mathbf{X}_1$, where

$$\mathbf{y}_1 = \mathbf{y} + \mathbf{y}_E, \tag{5.8.2}$$

$$\mathbf{X}_1 = \mathbf{X} + \mathbf{X}_E. \tag{5.8.3}$$

Here $\mathbf{y}_E$ is a vector of random errors and $\mathbf{X}_E$ is a matrix of random errors. It is generally assumed that $\mathbf{u}$, $\mathbf{y}_E$, and $\mathbf{X}_E$ are uncorrelated, with zero means and constant covariance matrices.

Errors in measuring $\mathbf{y}$ present no new complications, since the $\mathbf{y}_E$ errors can be merged with the additive stochastic disturbance term $\mathbf{u}$ in (5.8.1). Thus the model is of the form

$$\mathbf{y}_1 = \mathbf{X}_1\boldsymbol{\beta} + (\mathbf{v} - \mathbf{X}_E\boldsymbol{\beta}), \qquad \text{where} \qquad \mathbf{v} = \mathbf{u} + \mathbf{y}_E. \tag{5.8.4}$$

This model cannot be treated as if it were the same as the basic linear regression model, since the measured explanatory variables $\mathbf{X}_1$ are not distributed independently of the stochastic disturbance term $\mathbf{v} - \mathbf{X}_E\boldsymbol{\beta}$. In other words, $E(\mathbf{v} - \mathbf{X}_E\boldsymbol{\beta} \mid \mathbf{X}_1)$ is a function of $\mathbf{X}_1$.[30] Again, assumption A.4.1 is violated. The least squares estimator of (5.8.4) is

[29] For example, see Griliches (1971).

[30] If $\mathbf{X}$ and $\mathbf{X}_E$ are independently normally distributed with mean $\boldsymbol{\mu}$ and $\mathbf{0}$ and variance–covariance matrices $\boldsymbol{\Sigma}_X$ and $\boldsymbol{\Sigma}_E$, respectively, $E(\mathbf{v} - \mathbf{X}_E\boldsymbol{\beta} \mid \mathbf{X}_1) = -\boldsymbol{\Sigma}_E(\boldsymbol{\Sigma}_E + \boldsymbol{\Sigma}_X)^{-1}(\mathbf{X}_1 - \boldsymbol{\mu})\boldsymbol{\beta}$.

$$\hat{\boldsymbol{\beta}} = (\mathbf{X}_1'\mathbf{X}_1)^{-1}\mathbf{X}_1'\mathbf{y}_1 = \boldsymbol{\beta} + (\mathbf{X}_1'\mathbf{X}_1)^{-1}\mathbf{X}_1'(\mathbf{v} - \mathbf{X}_E\boldsymbol{\beta}). \tag{5.8.5}$$

This estimator is, in general, biased, the bias being given as

$$B(\hat{\boldsymbol{\beta}}) = E(\hat{\boldsymbol{\beta}}) - \boldsymbol{\beta} = -E[(\mathbf{X}_1'\mathbf{X}_1)^{-1}\mathbf{X}_1'\mathbf{X}_E\boldsymbol{\beta}]. \tag{5.8.6}$$

Taking the probability limit of (5.8.5) to check consistency,

$$\text{plim}\,\hat{\boldsymbol{\beta}} = \boldsymbol{\beta} - \text{plim}\left(\frac{1}{n}\mathbf{X}_1'\mathbf{X}_1\right)^{-1} \text{plim}\left(\frac{1}{n}\mathbf{X}_1'\mathbf{X}_E\boldsymbol{\beta}\right), \tag{5.8.7}$$

where it has been assumed that the measured explanatory variables are uncorrelated in the probability limit with the stochastic disturbance terms

$$\text{plim}\left(\frac{1}{n}\mathbf{X}_1'\mathbf{v}\right) = \mathbf{0}. \tag{5.8.8}$$

Replacing $\mathbf{X}_1'$ by $\mathbf{X}' + \mathbf{X}_E'$, from (5.8.3), in (5.8.7),

$$\text{plim}\,\hat{\boldsymbol{\beta}} = \boldsymbol{\beta} - \text{plim}\left(\frac{1}{n}\mathbf{X}_1'\mathbf{X}_1\right)^{-1}\left[\text{plim}\left(\frac{1}{n}\mathbf{X}'\mathbf{X}_E\right) + \text{plim}\left(\frac{1}{n}\mathbf{X}_E'\mathbf{X}_E\right)\right]\boldsymbol{\beta}. \tag{5.8.9}$$

Even assuming that the true values of the explanatory variables $\mathbf{X}$ are uncorrelated in the probability limit with the error matrix $\mathbf{X}_E$ (so that the first term in the bracketed expression vanishes), the second term does not vanish. Thus (5.8.9) implies that the least squares estimators are generally inconsistent in the case of errors in explanatory variables, so in this case least squares estimators are both biased and inconsistent.

A specific illustration of this problem in economics is the *permanent income theory of the consumption function*, which is an errors-in-variables model.[31] According to this model measured income, Y_1, has a permanent (true) component, Y, and a transitory component, Y_E:

$$Y_1 = Y + Y_E. \tag{5.8.10}$$

Measured consumption expenditure, C_1, similarly, has a permanent (true) component, C, and a transitory component, C_E:

$$C_1 = C + C_E. \tag{5.8.11}$$

The transitory components represent accidental or chance factors, including cyclical variations. They can, however, be treated as the errors in measuring income and consumption. It is usually assumed that the errors, on average, vanish:

$$E(Y_E) = E(C_E) = 0. \tag{5.8.12}$$

It is also usually assumed that the errors are correlated neither with each other nor with the permanent components:

$$\text{Cov}(Y, Y_E) = \text{Cov}(C, C_E) = \text{Cov}(Y_E, C_E) = 0. \tag{5.8.13}$$

According to the permanent-income hypothesis,

$$C = \beta_1 Y + \beta_2 + u \tag{5.8.14}$$

[31] See Friedman (1957).

—that is, permanent consumption is a linear function of permanent income, where β_1 and β_2 are constant parameters and u is a stochastic disturbance term.[32] Combining (5.8.14) with (5.8.10) and (5.8.11) yields

$$C_1 = \beta_1 Y_1 + \beta_2 + (v - \beta_1 Y_E), \qquad v = u + C_E, \tag{5.8.15}$$

which is a simple linear regression model of the same form as (5.8.4). In this case, (5.8.9) implies that if $\hat{\beta}_1$ is the least squares estimator of the marginal propensity to consume, β_1, then

$$\text{plim}\,\hat{\beta}_1 = \beta_1 - \frac{\sigma_E^2}{\sigma_1^2}\beta_1 = \beta_1 \frac{\sigma_1^2 - \sigma_E^2}{\sigma_1^2}, \tag{5.8.16}$$

where σ_E^2 is the variance of the transitory component of income and σ_1^2 is the variance of the measured income. But from (5.8.10) and (5.8.13)

$$\sigma_1^2 = \sigma^2 + \sigma_E^2, \tag{5.8.17}$$

where σ^2 is the variance of permanent income. Combining with (5.8.16) yields

$$\text{plim}\,\hat{\beta}_1 = \beta_1 \frac{\sigma^2}{\sigma_1^2} = \beta_1 - \beta_1 \frac{\sigma_E^2}{\sigma^2 + \sigma_E^2} < \beta_1. \tag{5.8.18}$$

Thus the estimated marginal propensity to consume, $\hat{\beta}_1$, even in the probability limit, systematically underestimates the true β_1. The greater the variance of transitory income, the greater will be the underestimation. Only when the variance of the transitory (error) component of income vanishes is the least squares estimator of β_1 a consistent estimator. To solve this problem, it is necessary to construct a measure of permanent income Y before estimating the consumption function.

The general problem of errors in variables can be treated in various ways. The major treatment is simply that of correcting for errors, particularly in the explanatory variables, as in the replacement of measured income by permanent income in the estimation of the mar-

[32]Friedman (1957) also specified that $\beta_2 = 0$, so that β_1 is both the marginal and the average propensity to consume out of permanent income. This specification of the structural equation ensures for the normally distributed case that the model is identified—that is, that it is possible to infer the structural parameters [β_1, $E(Y)$, Var(Y), Var(Y_E), Var(C_E)] from the observable parameters [$E(Y_1)$, $E(C_1)$, Var(Y_1), Var(C_1), Cov(C_1, Y_1)]. For (5.8.14) in the normally distributed case these two sets of parameters are related by

$$\begin{aligned}
E(Y_1) &= E(Y + Y_E) = E(Y),\\
E(C_1) &= E(\beta_1 Y + \beta_2 + C_E) = \beta_1 E(Y) + \beta_2,\\
\text{Var}(Y_1) &= \text{Var}(Y + Y_E) = \text{Var}(Y) + \text{Var}(Y_E),\\
\text{Var}(C_1) &= \text{Var}(\beta_1 Y + \beta_2 + C_E) = \beta_1^2\,\text{Var}(Y) + \text{Var}(C_E),\\
\text{Cov}(C_1, Y_1) &= \text{Cov}(\beta_1 Y + \beta_2 + C_E, Y + Y_E) = \beta_1\,\text{Var}(Y).
\end{aligned}$$

In general, then, it is not possible to solve for the six unknowns on the right [β_1, β_2, $E(Y)$, Var(Y), Var(Y_E), Var(C_E)] given the five observables on the left (i.e., the model is not identified). If, however, $\beta_2 = 0$, it is possible to solve for the structural parameters unknowns from the observables [e.g., $\hat{\beta}_1 = E(C_1)/E(Y_1)$], so the model is identified. For a discussion of identification in the context of simultaneous equations estimations, where the observables are the estimates of the reduced form and the unknowns are the structural-form parameters, see Chapter 9. See also Problem 5-N and Aigner et al. (1985), Konijn (1962), and Hsiao (1976, 1977, 1979a).

ginal propensity to consume. A second approach is to determine the sensitivity of the estimated coefficients to various errors in the variables by performing several regressions for alternative assumptions regarding the errors. It would then be possible to determine an interval estimate for each coefficient, reflecting the likely range of errors in the variables. A third approach is to find the bound of the least squares estimates (e.g., Leamer, 1978a). A fourth approach is to use the method of instrumental variables, provided that appropriate instrumental variables are available.[33]

This instrumental variable method can be viewed as a special case of the method of moments. Suppose that there exist n observations of the k variables $\mathbf{Z} = (\mathbf{z}_i')$ with the following properties:

$$\text{plim}\left(\frac{1}{n}\mathbf{Z}'\mathbf{v}\right) = \mathbf{0}, \qquad *(5.8.19)$$

$$\text{plim}\left(\frac{1}{n}\mathbf{Z}'\mathbf{X}_E\right) = \mathbf{0}, \qquad *(5.8.20)$$

and

$$\text{plim}\left(\frac{1}{n}\mathbf{Z}'\mathbf{X}_1\right) = \Sigma_{zx_1} \quad \text{exists and is nonsingular.} \qquad *(5.8.21)$$

Then the variables $\mathbf{z}_i$ are referred to as the *instrumental variables* for $\mathbf{X}_1$.

Premultiplying (5.8.4) by $\mathbf{Z}'$ and dividing both sides of the equality by the sample size yields

$$\frac{1}{n}\mathbf{Z}'\mathbf{y}_1 = \frac{1}{n}\mathbf{Z}'\mathbf{X}_1\boldsymbol{\beta} + \frac{1}{n}\mathbf{Z}'(\mathbf{v} - \mathbf{X}_E\boldsymbol{\beta}). \qquad (5.8.22)$$

The probability limit of the last term on the right-hand side of (5.8.22) is zero. The instrumental variable estimator of $\boldsymbol{\beta}$ is obtained by setting the sample moments of this term equal to their population values and solving for $\boldsymbol{\beta}$,

$$\hat{\boldsymbol{\beta}}_{\text{IV}} = (\mathbf{Z}'\mathbf{X}_1)^{-1}\mathbf{Z}'\mathbf{y}_1. \qquad *(5.8.23)$$

The instrumental variable estimator is consistent. Substituting (5.8.4) into (5.8.23) yields

$$\hat{\boldsymbol{\beta}}_{\text{IV}} = \boldsymbol{\beta} + (\mathbf{Z}'\mathbf{X}_1)^{-1}\mathbf{Z}'(\mathbf{v} - \mathbf{X}_E\boldsymbol{\beta}). \qquad (5.8.24)$$

The probability limit of (5.8.24) is

$$\begin{aligned} \text{plim}\,\hat{\boldsymbol{\beta}}_{\text{IV}} &= \boldsymbol{\beta} + \text{plim}\left(\frac{1}{n}\mathbf{Z}'\mathbf{X}_1\right)^{-1} \text{plim}\left[\frac{1}{n}\mathbf{Z}'(\mathbf{v} - \mathbf{X}_E\boldsymbol{\beta})\right] \\ &= \boldsymbol{\beta} + \Sigma_{zx_1}^{-1} \cdot \mathbf{0} = \boldsymbol{\beta}. \end{aligned} \qquad *(5.8.25)$$

The asymptotic covariance matrix of the instrumental variable estimator is

[33]The Wald (1940) method of fitting straight lines involves grouping the sample, for example, into three groups of approximately equal size and then obtaining an estimate of the relationship by passing a line through the means of the two end groups. This approach can be viewed as regression using grouped data with categorical dummies as instruments, as discussed in Angrist (1991), Bowden and Turkington (1984), Durbin (1954), and Griliches (1986).

$$\text{Asy. Cov}(\hat{\boldsymbol\beta}_{IV}) = \text{plim}[(\mathbf{Z}'\mathbf{X}_1)^{-1}\mathbf{Z}'(\mathbf{v}-\mathbf{X}_E\boldsymbol\beta)(\mathbf{v}-\mathbf{X}_E\boldsymbol\beta)'\mathbf{Z}(\mathbf{X}_1'\mathbf{Z})^{-1}]$$
$$= n^{-1}\,\text{plim}\left(\frac{1}{n}\mathbf{Z}'\mathbf{X}_1\right)^{-1}\text{plim}\left[\frac{1}{n}\mathbf{Z}'(\mathbf{v}-\mathbf{X}_E\boldsymbol\beta)(\mathbf{v}-\mathbf{X}_E\boldsymbol\beta)'\mathbf{Z}\right] \qquad (5.8.26)$$
$$\text{plim}\left(\frac{1}{n}\mathbf{X}_1'\mathbf{Z}\right)^{-1}$$

In practice, (5.8.26) is approximated by

$$s_1^2(\mathbf{Z}'\mathbf{X}_1)^{-1}(\mathbf{Z}'\mathbf{Z})(\mathbf{X}_1'\mathbf{Z})^{-1}, \qquad (5.8.27)$$

where

$$s_1^2 = \frac{1}{n-k}(\mathbf{y}-\mathbf{X}_1\hat{\boldsymbol\beta}_{IV})'(\mathbf{y}-\mathbf{X}_1\hat{\boldsymbol\beta}_{IV}) \qquad (5.8.28)$$

is the unbiased estimator of the variance.

From the discussion above, the criterion for the k variables in $\mathbf{Z}$ to be valid instruments is that they should be uncorrelated with the error terms in the equation and correlated with the explanatory variables in the equation as in conditions (5.8.19) through (5.8.21). Equation (5.8.26) further indicates that the higher the correlation between the instruments and the explanatory variables, the smaller the asymptotic variances of the instrumental variable estimators. In the case that $\mathbf{X}_E = 0$, namely, $\mathbf{X} = \mathbf{X}_1$, the best instruments for $\mathbf{X}$ are $\mathbf{X} = \mathbf{Z}$.

It may be noted that the normal equations of the instrumental variable estimator are

$$\mathbf{Z}'\mathbf{y}_1 = \mathbf{Z}'\mathbf{X}\hat{\boldsymbol\beta}_{IV}, \qquad (5.8.29)$$

which are of the same form as the normal equations of the least squares estimator (4.3.3). Therefore, the least squares estimator can be also viewed as an instrumental variable estimator.

5.9 NONLINEAR LEAST SQUARES ESTIMATOR: GAUSS–NEWTON AND NEWTON–RAPHSON METHODS FOR SOLVING NONLINEAR EQUATIONS

So far it has been assumed that the endogenous or dependent variable depends linearly on the parameters. There are situations in which this is not true. For instance, in the case of the linear regression model with error terms following a first-order autoregressive process (5.5.2), the transformed model (5.5.17) is nonlinear in parameters. Another example is the constant elasticity of substitution (CES) production function, discussed in Chapter 8 (see also Bodkin and Klein, 1967), that relates the output y_i to the labor and capital inputs L_i and K_i of the form

$$y_i = A[\delta K_i^{-\rho} + (1-\delta)L_i^{-\rho}]^{-1/\rho}\, e^{u_i}, \qquad (5.9.1)$$

where A, δ, and ρ are parameters, which is linear neither in parameters nor in variables. In this section we consider the properties of least squares in nonlinear models.

Consider the model

$$y_i = g(\mathbf{x}_i, \boldsymbol\theta) + u_i, \qquad i = 1, \ldots, n, \qquad (5.9.2)$$

where g is a real-valued function, $\boldsymbol\theta$ is a $p \times 1$ vector of unknown parameters, and u_i is independent of $\mathbf{x}_i$ and independently distributed with mean 0 and variance σ_u^2. Model (5.9.2) is nonlinear if $g(\mathbf{x}_i, \boldsymbol{\theta})$ is nonlinear in either $\mathbf{x}$ or $\boldsymbol{\theta}$.[34]

The *nonlinear least squares* (NLLS) estimator of $\boldsymbol{\theta}$ is the value $\hat{\boldsymbol{\theta}}$ that minimizes the sum of squares of the residuals

$$S_n = S_n(\boldsymbol{\theta}) = \sum_{i=1}^{n}[y_i - g(\mathbf{x}_i; \boldsymbol{\theta})]^2. \tag{5.9.3}$$

Under fairly general conditions the NLLS estimator is consistent and asymptotically normally distributed.[35] However, (5.9.3) generally cannot be solved explicitly for $\hat{\boldsymbol{\theta}}$. Instead, it must be solved iteratively, where, starting from an initial estimate, say $\hat{\boldsymbol{\theta}}^{(1)}$, a sequence of estimates $\{\hat{\boldsymbol{\theta}}^{j}\}$ is obtained by iteration, which will ideally converge to the NLLS estimator $\hat{\boldsymbol{\theta}}$. Numerous iterative methods have been proposed. Here, only the Newton–Raphson and Gauss–Newton iterative methods will be considered.[36]

The *Gauss–Newton iterative formula* is given by

$$\hat{\boldsymbol{\theta}}^{(j)} = \hat{\boldsymbol{\theta}}^{(j-1)} - \left[\sum_{i=1}^{n}\frac{\partial g_i}{\partial \boldsymbol{\theta}}\bigg|_{\hat{\boldsymbol{\theta}}^{(j-1)}} \frac{\partial g_i}{\partial \boldsymbol{\theta}'}\bigg|_{\hat{\boldsymbol{\theta}}^{(j-1)}}\right]^{-1} \left\{\sum_{i=1}^{n}\frac{\partial g_i}{\partial \boldsymbol{\theta}}\bigg|_{\hat{\boldsymbol{\theta}}^{(j-1)}} [y_i - g_i(\hat{\boldsymbol{\theta}}^{(j-1)})]\right\}, \tag{5.9.4}$$

where $\hat{\boldsymbol{\theta}}^{(j)}$ denotes the jth iterative solution, $g_i(\hat{\boldsymbol{\theta}}^{(j)})$ is $g(\mathbf{x}_i; \boldsymbol{\theta})$ evaluated at $\hat{\boldsymbol{\theta}}^{(j)}$, and $\frac{\partial g_i}{\partial \boldsymbol{\theta}}\Big|_{\hat{\boldsymbol{\theta}}^{(j)}} = \frac{\partial g(\mathbf{x}_i; \boldsymbol{\theta})}{\partial \boldsymbol{\theta}}\Big|_{\hat{\boldsymbol{\theta}}^{(j)}}$ denotes the vector of partial derivatives of $g(\mathbf{x}_i; \boldsymbol{\theta}) = g_i(\boldsymbol{\theta}) = g_i$ with respect to $\boldsymbol{\theta}$ evaluated at $\boldsymbol{\theta} = \hat{\boldsymbol{\theta}}^{(j)}$. Equation (5.9.4) is derived by taking the linear approximation of $g_i(\boldsymbol{\theta})$ using a Taylor's series expansion around $\hat{\boldsymbol{\theta}}^{(j-1)}$:

$$g_i(\boldsymbol{\theta}) \simeq g_i(\hat{\boldsymbol{\theta}}^{(j-1)}) + \frac{\partial g_i}{\partial \boldsymbol{\theta}'}\bigg|_{\hat{\boldsymbol{\theta}}^{(j-1)}} (\boldsymbol{\theta} - \hat{\boldsymbol{\theta}}^{(j-1)}). \tag{5.9.5}$$

Substituting (5.9.5) into (5.9.3), (5.9.4) is obtained by minimizing $S_n(\boldsymbol{\theta})$ with respect to $\boldsymbol{\theta}$.

The *Newton–Raphson method* is based on a quadratic Taylor's series approximation of the objective function (here, the sum of squares of the residuals)

$$\begin{aligned} S_n(\boldsymbol{\theta}) \simeq\; & S_n(\hat{\boldsymbol{\theta}}^{(j-1)}) + \frac{\partial S_n(\hat{\boldsymbol{\theta}}^{(j-1)})}{\partial \boldsymbol{\theta}'}(\boldsymbol{\theta} - \hat{\boldsymbol{\theta}}^{(j-1)}) \\ & + \frac{1}{2}(\boldsymbol{\theta} - \hat{\boldsymbol{\theta}}^{(j-1)})' \frac{\partial^2 S_n(\hat{\boldsymbol{\theta}}^{(j-1)})}{\partial \boldsymbol{\theta}\partial \boldsymbol{\theta}'}(\boldsymbol{\theta} - \hat{\boldsymbol{\theta}}^{(j-1)}), \end{aligned} \tag{5.9.6}$$

where $S_n(\hat{\boldsymbol{\theta}}^{(j-1)})$ is $S_n(\boldsymbol{\theta})$ evaluated at $\hat{\boldsymbol{\theta}}^{(j-1)}$ and $\frac{\partial S_n(\hat{\boldsymbol{\theta}}^{(j-1)})}{\partial \boldsymbol{\theta}}$ and $\frac{\partial^2 S_n(\hat{\boldsymbol{\theta}}^{(j-1)})}{\partial \boldsymbol{\theta}\partial \boldsymbol{\theta}'}$ are the $p \times 1$ first derivatives and $p \times p$ second derivatives of $\mathbf{S}_n(\boldsymbol{\theta})$ with respect to $\boldsymbol{\theta}$, evaluated at $\hat{\boldsymbol{\theta}}^{(j-1)}$, respectively (the gradient vector and Hessian matrix evaluated at this point). Minimizing (5.9.6) with respect to $\boldsymbol{\theta}$ yields the Newton–Raphson jth round estimator

$$\hat{\boldsymbol{\theta}}^{(j)} = \hat{\boldsymbol{\theta}}^{(j-1)} - \left[\frac{\partial^2 S_n(\hat{\boldsymbol{\theta}}^{(j-1)})}{\partial \boldsymbol{\theta}\partial \boldsymbol{\theta}'}\right]^{-1} \frac{\partial S_n(\hat{\boldsymbol{\theta}}^{(j-1)})}{\partial \boldsymbol{\theta}}. \tag{5.9.7}$$

[34]The model (5.9.2) is a special case of the more general formulation $f(y_i, \mathbf{x}_i; \boldsymbol{\theta}) = u_i$.

[35]For instance, see Amemiya (1985).

[36]See Draper and Smith (1981) and Quandt (1983).

The Gauss–Newton and Newton–Raphson method can be used to solve for general nonlinear estimators, including the NLLS estimator or the MLE. The iteration repeats until $\|\hat{\boldsymbol{\theta}}^{(j)} - \hat{\boldsymbol{\theta}}^{(j-1)}\|$ is less than some preset criterion, where $\|\cdot\|$ some distance measure (e.g., Euclidean distance). When the initial estimator is a consistent estimator, further iterations do not improve the asymptotic efficiency.[37] However, in finite samples, it may pay to iterate until convergence.

The Gauss–Newton and Newton–Raphson methods suffer from the problem of the possibility of an exact or near singularity of the matrices to be inverted in (5.9.4) and (5.9.7) and that of the possibility of either too much or too little change from $\hat{\boldsymbol{\theta}}^{(j-1)}$ to $\hat{\boldsymbol{\theta}}^{(j)}$. To deal with the first problem $\alpha \mathbf{I}_p$ or $-\alpha \mathbf{I}_p$ is added to $\sum_{i=1}^{n} \frac{\partial g_i}{\partial \boldsymbol{\theta}}\Big|_{\hat{\boldsymbol{\theta}}^{(j-1)}} \frac{\partial g_i}{\partial \boldsymbol{\theta}'}\Big|_{\hat{\boldsymbol{\theta}}^{(j-1)}}$ or $\frac{\partial^2 S_n(\hat{\boldsymbol{\theta}}^{(j-1)})}{\partial \boldsymbol{\theta} \partial \boldsymbol{\theta}'}$ as the matrices to be inverted in (5.9.4) or (5.9.7), where α is a positive scalar to be appropriately chosen. To deal with the second problem, an appropriately chosen scalar λ is multiplied to the term that adjusts $\boldsymbol{\theta}^{(j-1)}$ to $\boldsymbol{\theta}^{(j)}$ in (5.9.4) or (5.9.7). For further details, see Amemiya (1985), Goldfeld and Quandt (1972), Quandt (1983), Marquardt (1963), and Hartley (1961).

5.10 DISCRETE RESPONSE MODELS: LINEAR PROBABILITY, PROBIT, AND LOGIT MODELS

So far it has been assumed that the dependent variable y can take any value between $-\infty$ and ∞. There are cases, however, where y can take only a finite number of values. In this section we briefly review some of the most widely used discrete response models.

First consider the case in which the dependent variable y can assume only two values, which for convenience and without loss of generality will be the value of 1 if an event occurs and 0 if it does not. Examples of this include purchases of durables in a given year, participation in the labor force, the decision to enter college, and the decision to move. Suppose that given $\mathbf{x}_i$ the probability is p_i that y_i takes the value 1 and $(1 - p_i)$ that y_i takes the value 0. Then the expected value of y_i given $\mathbf{x}_i$,

$$E(y_i \mid \mathbf{x}_i) = p_i \cdot 1 + (1 - p_i) \cdot 0 = p_i, \tag{5.10.1}$$

is the probability that the event will occur. Therefore, the linear model

$$y_i = \mathbf{x}_i' \boldsymbol{\beta} + u_i \tag{5.10.2}$$

is called the *linear probability model.*

Since y_i can only take the values 0 and 1, when $y_i = 1$, $u_i = 1 - \mathbf{x}_i'\boldsymbol{\beta}$, and when $y_i = 0$, $u_i = -\mathbf{x}_i'\boldsymbol{\beta}$. That is, u_i can take only one of the two values above. To impose the assumption that

$$E(u_i \mid \mathbf{x}_i) = f(u_i = 1 - \mathbf{x}_i'\boldsymbol{\beta}) \cdot (1 - \mathbf{x}_i'\boldsymbol{\beta}) + f(u_i = -\mathbf{x}_i'\boldsymbol{\beta}) \cdot (-\mathbf{x}_i'\boldsymbol{\beta}) = 0 \tag{5.10.3}$$

implies that the probability that $f(u_i = 1 - \mathbf{x}_i'\boldsymbol{\beta}) = \mathbf{x}_i'\boldsymbol{\beta}$ and $f(u_i = -\mathbf{x}_i'\boldsymbol{\beta}) = -\mathbf{x}_i'\boldsymbol{\beta}$. Furthermore, the variance of u_i given $\mathbf{x}_i$,

[37] For details, see Amemiya (1985, Sec. 4.4.2).

$$\begin{aligned}\operatorname{Var}(u_i \mid \mathbf{x}_i) &= (1 - \mathbf{x}_i'\boldsymbol{\beta})^2 \mathbf{x}_i'\boldsymbol{\beta} + (-\mathbf{x}_i'\boldsymbol{\beta})^2 (1 - \mathbf{x}_i'\boldsymbol{\beta}) \\ &= (\mathbf{x}_i'\boldsymbol{\beta})(1 - \mathbf{x}_i'\boldsymbol{\beta}),\end{aligned} \tag{5.10.4}$$

is heteroskedastic.

The linear probability model can be estimated by least squares or weighted least squares, but it has the obvious defect that $E(y_i \mid \mathbf{x}_i) = \boldsymbol{\beta}'\mathbf{x}_i = p_i$ has to lie between 0 and 1, as any probability should. Clearly, without further restrictions, $\boldsymbol{\beta}'\mathbf{x}_i$ is not constrained to lie between 0 and 1. To avoid constraining the value of $\boldsymbol{\beta}'\mathbf{x}_i$, the discrete response model can be considered in terms of a *latent continuous random variable crossing threshold*. Let a continuous random variable y^* be the linear function of $\mathbf{x}$,

$$y_i^* = \mathbf{x}_i'\boldsymbol{\beta} + v_i, \tag{5.10.5}$$

and

$$y_i = \begin{cases} 1 & \text{if } y_i^* > 0, \\ 0 & \text{if } y_i^* \leq 0. \end{cases}$$

If v_i has a standard normal distribution[38]

$$\phi(v_i) = (2\pi)^{1/2} \exp\left(-\frac{v_i^2}{2}\right), \tag{5.10.6}$$

then

$$\begin{aligned}E(y_i \mid \mathbf{x}_i) &= \int_{-\mathbf{x}_i'\boldsymbol{\beta}}^{\infty} \phi(v_i)\, dv_i = 1 - \int_{-\infty}^{-\mathbf{x}_i'\boldsymbol{\beta}} \phi(v_i)\, dv_i \\ &= 1 - \Phi(-\mathbf{x}_i'\boldsymbol{\beta}) \\ &= \Phi(\mathbf{x}_i'\boldsymbol{\beta}) = \int_{-\infty}^{\mathbf{x}_i'\boldsymbol{\beta}} \phi(v_i)\, dv_i.\end{aligned} \tag{5.10.7}$$

This is called the *probit model*, involving the cumulative normal distribution. If, by contrast, v_i has a logistic distribution,

$$f(v_i) = \frac{e^{-v_i}}{(1 + e^{-v_i})^2} \tag{5.10.8}$$

and

$$\begin{aligned}E(y_i \mid \mathbf{x}_i) &= \int_{-\mathbf{x}_i'\boldsymbol{\beta}}^{\infty} \frac{e^{-v_i}}{(1 + e^{-v_i})^2}\, dv_i \\ &= \frac{e^{\mathbf{x}_i'\boldsymbol{\beta}}}{1 + e^{\mathbf{x}_i'\boldsymbol{\beta}}},\end{aligned} \tag{5.10.9}$$

which is called the *logit model*.[39]

The cumulative normal distribution and the logistic distribution are very close to each other, except that the logistic distribution has slightly heavier tails (Cox, 1970). Moreover, the cumulative normal distribution Φ is reasonably well approximated by a linear function for the range of probabilities between 0.3 and 0.7. Amemiya (1981) has suggested an ap-

[38]The reason for assuming that v has a standard normal distribution is that with a dichotomous dependent variable there is no information on the spread of the random variable. In other words, one cannot identify β and σ^2 simultaneously.

[39]The linear probability model of (5.10.2) corresponds to v having a two-point distribution: $(1 - \boldsymbol{\beta}'\mathbf{x}_i)$ and $-\boldsymbol{\beta}'\mathbf{x}_i$, with probabilities $(\boldsymbol{\beta}'\mathbf{x}_i)$ and $(1 - \boldsymbol{\beta}'\mathbf{x}_i)$, respectively, where $0 \leq \boldsymbol{\beta}'\mathbf{x}_i \leq 1$.

proximate conversion rule for the coefficients of these models, where the coefficients for the linear probability, probit, and logit models are denoted as $\hat{\boldsymbol{\beta}}_{\text{LP}}, \hat{\boldsymbol{\beta}}_{\Phi}$, and $\hat{\boldsymbol{\beta}}_{L}$, respectively. Then

$$\begin{aligned} \hat{\boldsymbol{\beta}}_{L} &\simeq 1.6\hat{\boldsymbol{\beta}}_{\Phi}, \\ \hat{\boldsymbol{\beta}}_{\text{LP}} &\simeq 0.4\hat{\boldsymbol{\beta}}_{\Phi} \qquad \text{except for the constant term,} \end{aligned} \tag{5.10.10}$$

and

$$\hat{\beta}_{\text{LP}} \simeq 0.4\hat{\beta}_{\Phi} + 0.5 \qquad \text{for the constant term.}$$

For a random sample of n individuals, the likelihood function for all three models can be written in general form as

$$L = \prod_{i=1}^{n} F(\boldsymbol{\beta}'\mathbf{x}_i)^{y_i}[1 - F(\boldsymbol{\beta}'\mathbf{x}_i)]^{1-y_i}, \tag{5.10.11}$$

where $F(\boldsymbol{\beta}'\mathbf{x}_i) = \boldsymbol{\beta}'\mathbf{x}_i$ for the linear probability model, $F(\boldsymbol{\beta}'\mathbf{x}_i) = \Phi(\boldsymbol{\beta}'\mathbf{x}_i)$ for the probit model, and $F(\boldsymbol{\beta}'\mathbf{x}_i) = e^{\boldsymbol{\beta}'\mathbf{x}_i}(1 + e^{\boldsymbol{\beta}'\mathbf{x}_i})^{-1}$ for the logit model. Differentiating the logarithm of the likelihood function yields the vector of first derivatives and the matrix of second-order derivatives as

$$\frac{\partial \log L}{\partial \boldsymbol{\beta}} = \sum_{i=1}^{n} \frac{y_i - F(\boldsymbol{\beta}'\mathbf{x}_i)}{F(\boldsymbol{\beta}'\mathbf{x}_i)[1 - F(\boldsymbol{\beta}'\mathbf{x}_i)]} F'(\boldsymbol{\beta}'\mathbf{x}_i)\mathbf{x}_i \tag{5.10.12}$$

and

$$\begin{aligned} \frac{\partial^2 \log L}{\partial \boldsymbol{\beta}\, \partial \boldsymbol{\beta}'} = \Bigg\{ &-\sum_{i=1}^{n} \left[\frac{y_i}{F(\boldsymbol{\beta}'\mathbf{x}_i)^2} + \frac{1 - y_i}{[1 - F(\boldsymbol{\beta}'\mathbf{x}_i)]^2} \right] [F'(\boldsymbol{\beta}'\mathbf{x}_i)]^2 \\ &+ \sum_{i=1}^{n} \frac{y_i - F(\boldsymbol{\beta}'\mathbf{x}_i)}{F(\boldsymbol{\beta}'\mathbf{x}_i)[1 - F(\boldsymbol{\beta}'\mathbf{x}_i)]} F''(\boldsymbol{\beta}'\mathbf{x}_i) \Bigg\} \mathbf{x}_i\mathbf{x}_i', \end{aligned} \tag{5.10.13}$$

where $F'(\boldsymbol{\beta}'\mathbf{x}_i)$ and $F''(\boldsymbol{\beta}'\mathbf{x}_i)$ denote the first and second derivatives of $F(\boldsymbol{\beta}'\mathbf{x}_i)$ with respect to $\boldsymbol{\beta}'\mathbf{x}_i$, respectively. The MLE is obtained by setting (5.10.12) equal to zero and solving for $\boldsymbol{\beta}$. However, the resulting equations are highly nonlinear. A Newton–Raphson method of iterative rule

$$\hat{\boldsymbol{\beta}}^{(j)} = \hat{\boldsymbol{\beta}}^{(j-1)} - \left(\frac{\partial^2 \log L}{\partial \boldsymbol{\beta}\, d\boldsymbol{\beta}'}\right)^{-1}_{\boldsymbol{\beta}=\boldsymbol{\beta}^{(j-1)}} \left(\frac{\partial \log L}{\partial \boldsymbol{\beta}}\right)_{\boldsymbol{\beta}=\hat{\boldsymbol{\beta}}^{(j-1)}}, \tag{5.10.14}$$

can be used to find the MLE of $\boldsymbol{\beta}$, where $\hat{\boldsymbol{\beta}}^{(j)}$ denotes the solution at the jth iteration. If $E\left(\frac{\partial^2 \log L}{\partial \boldsymbol{\beta} \partial \boldsymbol{\beta}'}\right)_{\boldsymbol{\beta}=\hat{\boldsymbol{\beta}}^{(j-1)}}$ is substituted for $\left(\frac{\partial^2 \log L}{\partial \boldsymbol{\beta} \partial \boldsymbol{\beta}'}\right)_{\boldsymbol{\beta}=\hat{\boldsymbol{\beta}}^{(j-1)}}$, the iteration formula (5.10.14) is called the *method of scoring*.

In the case in which there are repeated observations of y for a specific value of $\mathbf{x}$, the proportion of $y = 1$ for individuals with the same characteristic, $\mathbf{x}$, is a consistent estimator of $F(\boldsymbol{\beta}'\mathbf{x})$. Transforming $F(\boldsymbol{\beta}'\mathbf{x})$ into a linear function of $\boldsymbol{\beta}$, the weighted least squares method can be applied to estimate $\boldsymbol{\beta}$.[40] The resulting estimator, which is generally referred to as the *minimum chi-square estimator*,[41] has the same asymptotic efficiency as the maximum like-

[40]For the logit model, $\log[p/(1 - p)] = \boldsymbol{\beta}'\mathbf{x}$. For the probit model, $\Phi^{-1}(p) = \boldsymbol{\beta}'\mathbf{x}$.

[41]For a brief survey of the minimum chi-square estimator, see Hsiao (1985b).

lihood estimator (MLE) and computationally may be simpler than the MLE. Moreover, in finite samples, the minimum chi-square estimator may even have a smaller mean squared error than the MLE as discussed in Amemiya (1974, 1976, 1980), Berkson (1955, 1957, 1980), Ferguson (1958), and Neyman (1949). However, despite its statistical attractiveness, the minimum chi-square method is probably less useful than the maximum likelihood method in analyzing survey data, although it is useful in the laboratory setting. Application of this method requires repeated observations for each value of the vector of explanatory variables. In survey data most explanatory variables are continuous. The survey sample size has to be extremely large for the possible configurations of explanatory variables. Furthermore, if the proportion of $y = 1$ is 0 or 1 for a given $\mathbf{x}$, the minimum chi-square method is not defined, but the maximum likelihood method can still be applied.

When the dependent variable y can assume more than two values, things are more complicated. These cases can be classified into ordered and unordered variables. An example of an ordered variable is

$$y = \begin{cases} 0 & \text{if the price of a home bought is} < \$49{,}999, \\ 1 & \text{if the price of a home bought is} = \$50{,}000 - \$99{,}999, \\ 2 & \text{if the price of a home bought is} > \$100{,}000, \end{cases}$$

while an example of an unordered variable is

$$y = \begin{cases} 1 & \text{if mode of transport is car,} \\ 2 & \text{if mode of transport is bus,} \\ 3 & \text{if mode of transport is train.} \end{cases}$$

In general, ordered models are used whenever the values taken by the discrete random variable y correspond to the intervals within which a continuous latent random variable y^* falls. Unordered models are used when more than one latent continuous random variable is needed to characterize the responses of y.

Assume that the dependent variable y_i takes $m_i + 1$ values $0, 1, 2, \ldots, m_i$ for the ith unit. Define $\Sigma_{i=1}^{N}(m_i + 1)$ binary variables as

$$y_{ij} = \begin{cases} 1 & \text{if } y_i = j, \ \ j = 0, 1, \ldots, m_i, \\ 0 & \text{if } y_i = j, \ \ i \neq 0, 1, \ldots, \mathrm{N}, \end{cases} \tag{5.10.15}$$

and write the likelihood function as

$$L = \prod_{i=1}^{N} \prod_{j=0}^{m_i} F_{ij}^{y_{ij}}. \tag{5.10.16}$$

General results concerning the methods of estimation and their asymptotic distributions for the dichotomous case also apply here. However, by contrast to the univariate case, the similarity between probit and logit specifications no longer holds. In general, they will lead to very different inferences.

5.11 CENSORED OR TRUNCATED REGRESSION MODELS

In economics, the ranges of dependent variables are often constrained in some way. For instance, in his pioneering work on household expenditure on durable goods, Tobin (1958) used a regression model that specifically took account of the fact that the expenditure (the dependent variable of his regression model) cannot be negative. Another example is the New Jersey negative income experiment, which excluded all families in the geographic areas of the experiment with incomes above 1.5 times the officially defined poverty level. When the truncation is based on earnings, uses of the data that treat components of earnings (specifically, wages or hours) as dependent variables are constrained and will often create what is commonly referred to as *selection bias*, as discussed in Hausman and Wise (1977), Heckman (1976, 1979), and Hsiao (1974). Tobin called this type of model the model of *limited dependent variables*. It and its various generalizations are known popularly among economists as *Tobit models* because of their similarities to probit models.[42] In statistics they are known as *censored* or *truncated* regression models. The model is called *truncated* if the observations outside a specified range are lost, while it is called *censored* if only some of the explanatory variables can at least be observed.

To see that by constraining the range of the dependent variable the least squares regression will lead to biased estimates, consider a regression model

$$y_i^* = \boldsymbol{\beta}'\mathbf{x}_i + u_i \tag{5.11.1}$$

that satisfies assumptions A.4.1 to A.4.3. Suppose that the y^* are unobserved. Instead, only nonnegative values of y are observed where[43]

$$y_i = \begin{cases} y_i^* & \text{if} \quad y_i^* > 0, \\ 0 & \text{if} \quad y_i^* \leq 0. \end{cases} \tag{5.11.2}$$

This censored regression model in terms of y is then of the form

$$y_i = E(y_i \mid \mathbf{x}_i) + v_i, \tag{5.11.3}$$

where $E(v_i \mid \mathbf{x}_i) = 0$. However, the expected value of y_i given $\mathbf{x}_i$ is

$$\begin{aligned} E(y_i \mid \mathbf{x}_i) &= \text{Prob}(u_i \leq -\mathbf{x}_i\boldsymbol{\beta}) \cdot 0 + \text{Prob}(u_i > -\mathbf{x}_i'\boldsymbol{\beta})E(y_i^* \mid \mathbf{x}_i;\, u_i > -\mathbf{x}_i'\boldsymbol{\beta}) \\ &= \text{Prob}(u_i > -\mathbf{x}_i'\boldsymbol{\beta})\mathbf{x}_i'\boldsymbol{\beta} + \text{Prob}(u_i > -\mathbf{x}_i'\boldsymbol{\beta})E(u_i \mid u_i > -\mathbf{x}_i'\boldsymbol{\beta}) \\ &\neq \mathbf{x}_i'\boldsymbol{\beta} \text{ (in general).} \end{aligned} \tag{5.11.4}$$

If u_i is independently normally distributed with mean 0 and variance σ^2, then

$$\text{Prob}(u_i > -\mathbf{x}_i'\boldsymbol{\beta}) = \Phi(\mathbf{x}_i'\boldsymbol{\alpha}) \tag{5.11.5}$$

and

$$E(u_i \mid u_i > -\mathbf{x}_i'\boldsymbol{\beta}) = \sigma \frac{\phi(\mathbf{x}_i'\boldsymbol{\alpha})}{\Phi(\mathbf{x}_i'\boldsymbol{\alpha})}, \tag{5.11.6}$$

where $\phi(\cdot)$ and $\Phi(\cdot)$ are standard normal density and cumulative (or integrated) normal, respectively, and where $\boldsymbol{\alpha} = (1/\sigma)\boldsymbol{\beta}$. Hence the specification of the linear model

$$y_i = \mathbf{x}_i'\boldsymbol{\beta} + \varepsilon_i \tag{5.11.7}$$

will have stochastic disturbance terms

$$\varepsilon_i = v_i + E(y_i \mid \mathbf{x}_i) - \mathbf{x}_i'\boldsymbol{\beta}, \tag{5.11.8}$$

[42]See Amemiya (1985) for further discussion of various types of Tobit models.

[43]There is no loss of generality in assuming that the truncation point is 0 because if the truncation point is L, the model can always be transformed into (5.11.2) with the new coefficient of the constant term $\beta_k^* = \beta_k - L$.

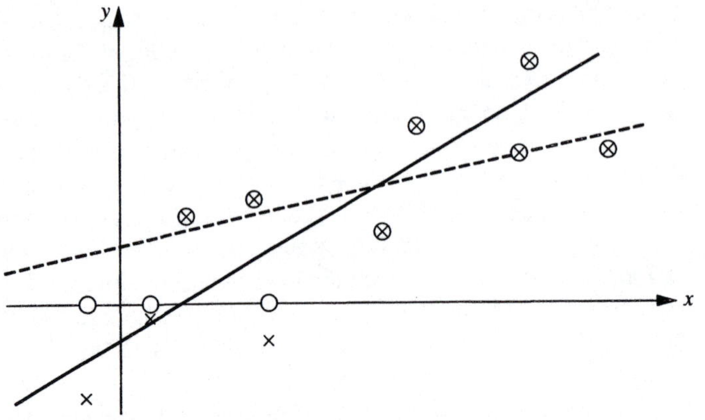

Figure 5.4 Least Squares Bias for Censored Regression Models

with $E(\varepsilon_i \mid \mathbf{x}_i) \neq 0$. As a result, the least squares regression of y on $\mathbf{x}$ yields biased and inconsistent estimates of $\boldsymbol{\beta}$.

The source of the least squares bias for censored or truncated regression models can be illustrated graphically. In Figure 5.4 let the upward-sloping solid line indicate the "average" relation between y^* and x and let the crosses represent the realized y^* around this mean for selected x. All realized y^* below zero would be moved to 0. Therefore, in regressing y on x, instead of using the crossed points, the researcher would use the circled points. This would tend to underestimate the effect of x on y. In other words, limiting the range of dependent variables introduces correlation between right-hand variables and the error term, which leads to a downward biased regression line, as the dashed line in Figure 5.4 indicates.

Although the least squares estimate of $\boldsymbol{\beta}$ is inconsistent, the MLE is consistent.[44] When u_i are independently normally distributed, the likelihood function for the censored model is

$$L = \prod_{i \in \psi} \left[1 - \Phi\left(\frac{\boldsymbol{\beta}'\mathbf{x}_i}{\sigma}\right)\right] \prod_{i \in \bar{\psi}} \frac{1}{\sqrt{2\pi}\,\sigma} \exp\left[-\frac{1}{2\sigma^2}(y_i - \mathbf{x}_i'\boldsymbol{\beta})^2\right], \tag{5.11.9}$$

and the likelihood function for the truncated model is

$$L = \prod_{i \in \bar{\psi}} \Phi\left(\frac{\boldsymbol{\beta}'\mathbf{x}_i}{\sigma}\right)^{-1} \frac{1}{\sqrt{2\pi}\,\sigma} \exp\left[-\frac{1}{2\sigma^2}(y_i - \mathbf{x}_i'\boldsymbol{\beta})^2\right], \tag{5.11.10}$$

where $\psi = \{i \mid y_i = 0\}$ and $\bar{\psi}$ is the complement of ψ. The MLE of $\boldsymbol{\beta}$ has asymptotic covariance matrix $-E\left[\frac{\partial^2 \log L}{\partial \boldsymbol{\beta} \partial \boldsymbol{\beta}'}\right]^{-1}$.

A Newton–Raphson interative method can be used to find the MLE. Alternatively, the nonlinear regression technique can be used to obtain a consistent estimate of $\boldsymbol{\beta}$ because, from (5.11.4) to (5.11.6), (5.11.3) is a nonlinear regression model, as discussed in Hsiao (1973). Another method is to note that given (5.11.1) and (5.11.2), it is possible to introduce the dummy variable w_i, where

[44] See Amemiya (1973, 1985).

$$w_i = \begin{cases} 1 & \text{if } y_i > 0, \\ 0 & \text{if } y_i \le 0. \end{cases} \tag{5.11.11}$$

The likelihood function for w_i is of the standard probit form

$$L^* = \prod_{i \in \overline{\psi}} \Phi(\mathbf{x}_i'\boldsymbol{\alpha}) \prod_{i \in \psi} [1 - \Phi(\mathbf{x}_i'\boldsymbol{\alpha})], \tag{5.11.12}$$

where $\boldsymbol{\alpha} = (1/\sigma)\boldsymbol{\beta}$. Maximizing (5.11.12) yields the consistent estimate of $\boldsymbol{\alpha}$. Heckman (1976) proposes the following two-step estimator:

1. Estimate $\boldsymbol{\alpha}$ by the probit MLE, yielding $\hat{\boldsymbol{\alpha}}$.
2. Substitute $\hat{\boldsymbol{\alpha}}$ for $\boldsymbol{\alpha}$ into the truncated model

$$\begin{aligned} y_i &= E(y_i \mid \mathbf{x}_i) + v_i \\ &= \mathbf{x}_i'\boldsymbol{\beta} + \sigma \frac{\phi(\mathbf{x}_i'\boldsymbol{\alpha})}{\Phi(\mathbf{x}_i'\boldsymbol{\alpha})} + v_i \qquad \text{for } i \text{ such that } y_i > 0, \end{aligned} \tag{5.11.13}$$

where $E(v_i \mid \mathbf{x}_i) = 0$ and $\operatorname{Var}(v_i \mid \mathbf{x}) = \sigma^2 \left[1 - \mathbf{x}_i'\boldsymbol{\alpha} \frac{\phi(\mathbf{x}_i'\boldsymbol{\alpha})}{\Phi(\mathbf{x}_i'\boldsymbol{\alpha})} - \left(\frac{\phi(\mathbf{x}_i'\boldsymbol{\alpha})}{\Phi(\mathbf{x}_i'\boldsymbol{\alpha})} \right)^2 \right]$.

Regress y_i on $\mathbf{x}_i$ and $\dfrac{\phi(\mathbf{x}_i'\hat{\boldsymbol{\alpha}})}{\Phi(\mathbf{x}_i'\hat{\boldsymbol{\alpha}})}$ by least squares, using only the positive observations of y_i.

The Heckman two-step estimator is consistent. But it is not as efficient as the MLE. Furthermore, its asymptotic covariance matrix is somewhat difficult to compute. One way is to approximate it by the formula

$$(\mathbf{Z}'\mathbf{Z})^{-1}\mathbf{Z}'\mathbf{A}\mathbf{Z}(\mathbf{Z}'\mathbf{Z})^{-1}, \tag{5.11.14}$$

where $\mathbf{Z} = [\mathbf{x}_i', \phi(\mathbf{x}_i'\hat{\boldsymbol{\alpha}})[\Phi(\mathbf{x}_i'\hat{\boldsymbol{\alpha}})]^{-1}]$ and $\mathbf{A}$ is the diagonal matrix with the ith diagonal element equal to $\left[y_i - \mathbf{x}_i'\hat{\boldsymbol{\beta}} - \hat{\sigma} \dfrac{\phi(\mathbf{x}_i'\hat{\boldsymbol{\alpha}})}{\Phi(\mathbf{x}_i'\hat{\boldsymbol{\alpha}})} \right]^2$.

5.12 ROBUST METHODS

If the errors are independently and identically distributed (i.i.d.), the least squares estimator is the BLUE. Furthermore, if the errors are normal, the least squares estimator is simply best unbiased.[45] The normality assumption is often justified by a vague appeal to the central limit theorem. However, this represents a tenuous prior belief rationalized by mathematical tractability. There are numerous instances in which "typical" data are longer tailed than the normal distribution. For example, Jeffreys (1961) remarks that errors from careful scientific measurements made under uniform circumstances tend to be better described by the t distribution with low degrees of freedom than by the normal distribution. Even in instances in which economic data may be meaningfully viewed as realizations of an i.i.d.

[45]One can prove this by using the Cramer–Rao inequality, as in Theil (1971).

process (e.g., stock market rates of return), as in Blattberg and Gonedes (1974), or individual productivity measurements, as in Roy (1950), long-tailed distributions like the t distribution and the Pareto distribution[46] seem to fit considerably better than the normal distribution.

If normal error distributions are not the usual state of affairs in econometrics, the question naturally arises as to whether the least squares principle can be justified by appealing to vague continuity or stability principles, such as one for which a minor inaccuracy in the mathematical model should cause only a small error in the final conclusions. Unfortunately, the answer to this question is often a "no." The following classical example from Tukey (1960) illustrates this point clearly. Consider the model

$$y_i = \mu + \mu_i, \qquad i = 1, \ldots, n. \tag{5.12.1}$$

Suppose that there are "good" observations, which are normal with mean μ and standard deviation σ, and "bad" observations, which are also normal with the same mean, but standard deviation 3σ. Each observation is, with probability $1-\varepsilon$, a good one, and with probability ε, a bad one. In other words, the observations are assumed to be independent with the common distribution function

$$F(y) = (1-\varepsilon)\Phi\left(\frac{y-\mu}{\sigma}\right) + \varepsilon\Phi\left(\frac{y-\mu}{3\sigma}\right), \tag{5.12.2}$$

where Φ is the standard normal distribution. The least squares estimator of μ is the sample mean $\bar{y} = (1/n)\sum_{i=1}^{n} y_i$. However, for $\varepsilon = 0.0018$ (i.e., barely 2 bad observations in 1000), there is no superiority of sample mean over sample median as an estimator for μ.[47]

The problem with the least squares principle is that too much weight is given to the outlying observations in minimizing the sum of squares of the residuals. As a result, just one extreme outlying observation may spoil the least squares estimate. Hence, in the case where one is uncertain if the error terms are independently identically distributed, it seems sensible to use estimators that have reasonably good performance in the ideal situation but are rather insensitive to deviations from the model. Unfortunately, a procedure having high absolute efficiency for any arbitrary underlying distribution is currently unavailable. Indeed, there is a plethora of techniques that have been introduced.[48] The discussion here treats only one approach that avoids giving too much weight to extreme observations but still has high efficiency under the normality assumption of the error terms, **u**.

One way to reduce the weight given to large residuals is to formulate the problem as one of *weighted regression*. Huber (1964) has suggested replacing the squares u_i^2 in the

[46]The Pareto distribution is defined as $\Pr[x \geq X] = (k/X)^a$, $k > 0$, $a > 0$; x, $X \geq k$, and it has been used to describe the distribution of income, of firms, and so on.

[47]The sample median is the estimator based on least absolute deviation $\sum_{i=1}^{n} | y_i - \hat{\mu} |$ and the result is based on the measure of asymptotic relative efficiency. The asymptotic relative efficiency (ARE) of d_n relative to s_n is defined as

$$\text{ARE} = \lim_{n\to\infty} \frac{\text{Var}(s_n)/(Es_n)^2}{\text{Var}(d_n)/(Ed_n)^2},$$

where $d_n = (1/n)\sum_{i=1}^{n} |y_i - \hat{\mu}$ and $s_n = [(1/n)\sum_{i=1}^{n}(y_i - \hat{\mu})^2]^{1/2}$

[48]See, for example, Huber (1973, 1981) and Koenker (1982).

sum of squares function $\sum_{i=1}^{n} u_i^2$ to be minimized in least squares by some function $\rho(u_i)$. Let the derivative of $\rho(u_i)$ be denoted by $\psi(u_i)$. Huber suggests the following forms for this derivative $\psi(u_i)$:

$$\psi(u_i; c) = \begin{cases} -c & u_i < -c, \\ u_i & -c < u_i < c, \\ c & u_i > c, \end{cases} \tag{5.12.3}$$

where c may be a certain multiple of a robust measure of dispersion of u_i, such as its interquantile range or its median absolute deviation. Integrating the ψ function above yields the weighting function

$$\rho(u_i; c) = \begin{cases} -cu_i & u_i < -c, \\ \frac{1}{2}u_i^2 & -c < u_i < c, \\ cu_i & u_i > c. \end{cases} \tag{5.12.4}$$

When $c = \infty$, the method employing the weighting function (5.12.4) yields the least squares estimator. At the other extreme, when c is very small, it gives the least absolute derivation estimator. Carroll (1980a, 1980b) and Bickel and Doksum (1984) investigate the consequences of replacing $\rho(u_i) = \frac{1}{2}u_i^2$ with the weighting function (5.12.4). Their asymptotic theory and Monte Carlo calculations confirm the view that Huber's approach will dramatically improve on the MLE based on the normality assumption when the distribution of u_i is long tailed.

5.13 NONPARAMETRIC AND SEMIPARAMETRIC ESTIMATION

5.13.1 Nonparametric Estimation

So far the focus has been on the parametric approach for analyzing economic data, where the probability distribution of the data or the conditional distribution, given exogenous variables, depends on finitely many unknown parameters. This approach usually leads to point estimators that, at least in large samples, are approximately normally distributed about the true parameter point and are as efficient as possible. It also leads to estimators of their large-sample covariance matrices so that hypothesis testing and interval estimation can be conducted. However, the quality and extent of information provided by economic theory need not warrant taking a parametric model very seriously. Thus it would be desirable to obtain good rules of statistical inference that operate in the absence of a finite parameter specification. *Nonparametric methods* are concerned primarily with such statistical inference problems, where there is no explicit assumption as to the form taken by the underlying probability distribution generating the sample observations.

A large body of nonparametric procedures is now available for producing satisfactory estimators of distributional properties such as probability density functions and regression functions, as in Izenman (1991) and Robinson (1986, 1988a). All the numerous methods of nonparametrically estimating the joint or conditional probability density function (pdf) feature a "bandwidth" or "smoothing" number, which measures the size of the "neighborhood" containing the observations S; they also feature some form of weighting of the observations. The most popular nonparametric estimate has been the *kernel* estimate, in which the weighting is provided by a probability density function (pdf), $k(\cdot)$, that is, a bounded symmetric function that integrates to 1, such as

$$k(u) = \begin{cases} \frac{1}{2}, & |u| \le 1 \\ 0, & |u| > 1 \end{cases} \tag{5.13.1}$$

or

$$k(u) = (2\pi)^{½} \exp\left(-\frac{1}{2}u^2\right). \tag{5.13.2}$$

Noting that $k(u)\,du = \frac{1}{h}k\left(\frac{y_i - y_a}{h}\right)dy_i$, where $u = \frac{y_i - y_a}{h}$, a *kernel estimate* of the pdf at the point y_a is obtained by weighting the observations, as deviations from y_a,

$$\hat{f}(y_a) = \frac{1}{nh}\sum_{i=1}^{n} k\left(\frac{y_i - y_a}{h}\right), \tag{5.13.3}$$

where h is a positive number called the *bandwidth* or *smoothing parameter*. The larger the h, the larger the degree of smoothing.

When $k(u)$ satisfies the two properties of a pdf,

$$k(u) \ge 0 \tag{5.13.4}$$

and

$$\int k(u)\,du = 1, \tag{5.13.5}$$

so does the kernel estimate (5.13.3)

$$\hat{f}(y) \ge 0, \tag{5.13.6}$$

$$\int \hat{f}(y)\,dy = 1, \tag{5.13.7}$$

Both the kernel function $k(\cdot)$ and h are chosen by the practitioner. It is possible to use alternative $k(\cdot)$'s satisfying (5.13.4) and (5.13.5) (i.e., pdf's) and still achieve properties (5.13.6) and (5.13.7). The optimal $k(\cdot)$ (in terms of bias, variance, etc.) generally depends on the unknown pdf, f. However, for good properties of a kernel estimate, it is generally believed that the choice of h is far more crucial than that of k. Alternative estimates are often computed from several representative choices of h to obtain the desired degree of smoothing. There is also a need for h to approach zero at a suitable rate, as $n \to \infty$, for good asymptotic statistical properties to result.

A kernel estimate of a multivariate pdf can be constructed similarly. Let the $m \times 1$ vector of random variables $(y_i, \mathbf{x}_i')$ be denoted by $\mathbf{w}_i'$. Let k_m be a function on m-dimensional (real) space, R^m, with

$$\int_{R^m} k_m(\mathbf{w})\,d\mathbf{w} = 1. \tag{5.13.8}$$

Let H_m be a positive-definite matrix. A *kernel estimate of a multivariate pdf* at $\mathbf{w}_a$, $f(\mathbf{w}_a)$, is

$$\hat{f}(\mathbf{w}_a) = \frac{1}{n|H_m|}\sum_{i=1}^{n} k_m\left(H_m^{-1}(\mathbf{w}_i - \mathbf{w}_a)\right). \tag{5.13.9}$$

For instance, it is possible to take

$$k_m(\mathbf{u}) = \prod_{j=1}^{m} k(u_j), \qquad \mathbf{u}' = (u_1, \ldots, u_m), \tag{5.13.10}$$

$$H_m = \operatorname{diag}(h_1, h_2, \ldots, h_m), \tag{5.13.11}$$

where $\int k(u_j)\,du_j = 1$, $\text{diag}(h_1, \ldots, h_m)$ denotes a diagonal matrix with diagonal elements equal to $h_1, \ldots, h_m$, and $h_j > 0$ for $j = 1, \ldots, m$, or let $h_1 = h_2 = \cdots = h_m = h$. Or $k_m(\cdot)$ could be taken to be a manageable function, such as the multinormal pdf with a nondiagonal H_m.

Kernel estimates of a conditional pdf, $f(y_a \mid \mathbf{x}_a)$, or conditional expectations $Eg(\mathbf{w} \mid \mathbf{w}_a)$ can be derived from the kernel estimates of the joint pdf and the marginal pdf. Thus the conditional pdf may be estimated by

$$\hat{f}(y_a|\mathbf{x}_a) = \frac{\hat{f}(\mathbf{w}_a)}{\hat{f}(\mathbf{x}_a)}, \tag{5.13.12}$$

and the conditional expectation by

$$E\hat{g}(\mathbf{w}|\mathbf{w}_a) = \frac{1}{n\,|H_m|} \sum_{i=1}^{n} g(\mathbf{w}_i) k_m\left(H_m^{-1}(\mathbf{w}_i - \mathbf{w}_a)\right) / \hat{f}(\mathbf{w}_a). \tag{5.13.13}$$

The kernel estimates tend to be based on fewer observations in the tails than at the center. Alternatively, it is possible to vary $|H_m|$ with $\mathbf{w}_a$ and use *nearest neighbors*, namely, averaging the N $\mathbf{w}_i$ closest to $\mathbf{w}_a$, where N is much smaller than n, and N/n can be thought of as the bandwidth.

The computation of nonparametric shape estimates is relatively straightforward yet tedious, because typically a separate estimate has to be computed at each observation. Their consistency can be proved and formulas for standard errors derived as in Robinson (1986, 1988). However, in finite samples, there can be many possible shape estimates. For nonparametric procedures to provide useful estimates of the shape of the distribution function, a very large sample size is required and the larger the nonparametric estimate's dimension, the larger n must be. Moreover, compared to the parametric approach, the nonparametric estimates of the parametric model have zero asymptotic efficiency. That is, in a parametric specification, a consistent estimator, whether it is efficient or not, usually converges to the true parameter at the rate of $n^{1/2}$ ($\sqrt{n}$-consistent) [like the least squares estimator for the regression model (4.3.1) with heteroskedastic u_i]. By contrast, nonparametric estimates of a shape function at a fixed point are consistent at a slower than $n^{1/2}$ rate unless the function is constant in a neighborhood of that point. This is because asymptotic bias can only be avoided by giving negligible weight, as $n \to \infty$, to all but a vanishing small proportion of the data, in a shrinking neighborhood of the point.

5.13.2 Semiparametric Estimation

A *semiparametric* model combines a "parametric" component, of known form, with a "nonparametric" or infinite-dimensional one, of unknown form. Examples are:

1. *Linear regression model*

$$y_i = \boldsymbol{\beta}'\mathbf{x}_i + u_i, \qquad i = 1, 2, \ldots, n, \tag{5.13.14}$$

where $E(u_i \mid \mathbf{x}_i) = 0$, as before, but where the serial dependence, heteroskedastic, or distribution properties of u_i have unknown functional form.

2. *Censored regression model*

$$y_i = \begin{cases} y_i^* & \text{if } y_i^* > 0, \\ 0 & \text{if } y_i^* \le 0, \end{cases} \tag{5.13.15}$$

as in (5.11.2), where

$$y_i^* = \boldsymbol{\beta}'\mathbf{x}_i + u_i, \tag{5.13.16}$$

as in (5.11.1) but with u_i's distribution unknown.

3. *Index model*

$$E(y_i|\mathbf{x}_i) = F(\boldsymbol{\beta}'\mathbf{x}_i), \tag{5.13.17}$$

where F is unknown. Both the binary choice and censored regression models discussed in Sections 5.10 and 5.11 are special cases of this general model.

4. *Partly linear model*

$$y_i = \boldsymbol{\beta}'\mathbf{x}_i + \lambda(\mathbf{z}_i) + u_i, \tag{5.13.18}$$

where λ is an unknown function of observables $\mathbf{z}_i$, as discussed in Robinson (1988b). This structure can arise if the precise role of only a subset of a list of candidate regressors is known; from linear models with both observed and latent explanatory variables in which the latter's expectations, conditional on observables $\mathbf{z}_i$, are unknown functions; from certain censored or truncated regression models in which the disturbances have a distribution of unknown form, as in (5.11.7) and (5.11.8); and from similar structures.

In all these cases, the parametric model, reflecting in some fashion what has been learned from economic theory and previous empirical experience, is completed by supplementing the parameters describing features of greatest interest with parameters of secondary importance, commonly referred to as *nuisance parameters*. In previous sections, the nuisance parameters were assumed to be finite. In the semiparametric approach, the finite-dimensional nuisance parameter specification is replaced by a *nonparametric* or *infinite-dimensional* one, of unknown form.

If the nuisance component can be finitely parameterized, it is usually possible to obtain efficient estimators for the parameters of primary interest. For instance, if serial dependence or heteroskadasticity for the linear regression model (5.13.14) is of known form, efficiency can be achieved (see Sections 5.3 to 5.5). Similarly, if u_i is independently normally distributed for the censored regression model, as in (5.13.15) and (5.13.16), or if the distribution function F is known for the index model (say, the probit or logit model), or the function λ is known for the partly linear model (say, linear in $\mathbf{z}$), the MLE is consistent and efficient (see Sections 5.10 and 5.11). But if the nuisance component is misspecified, it typically will incur loss of efficiency and sometimes inconsistency in estimating the parameters of interest. For example, for the censored regression model (5.13.15) and (5.13.16), the MLE under the normality assumption is generally consistent though inefficient under serial dependence, as discussed in Robinson (1982), but inconsistent under heteroskedasticity or nonnormality.

A challenging question for semiparametric econometric models is how well the parametric component can be estimated and how to construct rules of inference with good statistical properties. The techniques of semiparametric estimation are many and various. A common theme appears to be the incorporation of the nonparametric estimates of the nuisance "shape" function, or a regression function such as the conditional variance of u_i given $\mathbf{x}_i$, $\text{Var}(u_i \mid \mathbf{x}_i)$, to estimate the parameter of interest. The property of *adaptation* refers to the existence of an estimate of the parameters in a semiparametric model that is as efficient over a broad class of f as an efficient estimate employing a correct finite parameterization of f. Such an estimate is termed "adaptive" in Manski (1984).

Thus the semiparametric estimation of the linear regression model with heteroskedasticity takes the form

$$\hat{\boldsymbol{\beta}} = \left[E\left(\frac{1}{\sigma^2(\mathbf{x})}\mathbf{x}\mathbf{x}'\right)\right]^{-1} E\left(\frac{1}{\sigma^2(\mathbf{x})}\mathbf{x}y\right), \tag{5.13.19}$$

where

$$\sigma^2(\mathbf{x}) = \text{Var}(y|\mathbf{x}). \tag{5.13.20}$$

The estimation of the partly linear model takes the form

$$\hat{\boldsymbol{\beta}} = \{E[\mathbf{x} - E(\mathbf{x}|\mathbf{z})][\mathbf{x} - E(\mathbf{x}|\mathbf{z})]'\}^{-1} E[\mathbf{x} - E(\mathbf{x}|\mathbf{z})][\mathbf{y} - E(\mathbf{y}|\mathbf{z})]. \tag{5.13.21}$$

The estimation of the index model makes use of the relation

$$\frac{\partial}{\partial \mathbf{x}} E(y|\mathbf{x}) = \boldsymbol{\beta} f(\boldsymbol{\beta}'\mathbf{x}), \tag{5.13.22}$$

where $f(u) = \frac{d}{du}F(u)$. The estimator $\tilde{\boldsymbol{\beta}}$ is then proportional to

$$\int \frac{\partial}{\partial \mathbf{x}} E(y|\mathbf{x})\, r(\mathbf{x})\, d\mathbf{x}, \tag{5.13.23}$$

where $r(\mathbf{x})$ denotes the pdf of $\mathbf{x}$.

In principle, the nonparametric estimators discussed in Section 5.13.1 can be used either directly or indirectly to obtain the unknown shape function based on some initial consistent estimate of $\boldsymbol{\beta}$. For instance, for the heteroskedastic model, the conditional variance, $\text{Var}(u_i \mid \mathbf{x}_i) = \sigma^2(\mathbf{x}_i)$, can be estimated by inserting the kernel estimates of $E(y_i^2 \mid \mathbf{x}_i)$ and $E(y_i \mid \mathbf{x}_i) = \sigma^2(\mathbf{x}_i) = E(y_i^2 \mid \mathbf{x}_i) - E(y_i \mid \mathbf{x}_i))^2$ as in Rose (1978) or replacing u_i by the least squares residuals in the kernel estimate of $\sigma^2(\mathbf{x}_i) = E(u_i^2 \mid \mathbf{x}_i)$, as in Carroll (1982) or Robinson (1988b). The so-obtained nonparametric estimate of the shape function is then inserted into the formula above to give *adaptive estimators* of $\boldsymbol{\beta}$, as in Stone (1977). The success of this practice tends to vary with the smoothness of the shape function. If the shape function, f, is sufficiently smooth, then as n increases, it is possible to shrink the neighborhood of the point being evaluated at a suitable rate to ensure simultaneous improvement in precision and bias, entailing convergence of the estimate of f in a manner that would make the consequent estimate of $\boldsymbol{\beta}$ have the same distribution as the one using a correctly finitely parameterized f. In practice, the computation can be very complex. There is also the issue of having to choose a particular type of shape estimate out of many possibilities. Moreover, even in the case for which the semiparametric estimators can be shown to be asymptotically efficient, their convergence is likely to be slow. Indeed, it must be emphasized that the asymptotic properties of semiparametric estimators may be poor approximations, even in quite large samples. Therefore, econometricians faced with finite samples may as well use various parametric approaches and combine them with statistical testing to detect and eliminate bad approximations as discussed in Mountain and Hsiao (1989).

5.14 APPROACHES TO ANALYZING ECONOMIC DATA

As noted in Chapter 1, econometrics is concerned primarily with analyzing numerical data to provide clear and concise descriptions of the economy, to generate predictions, and to evaluate policy. However, by contrast to most of the natural and biological sciences, data available for economic analysis are rarely generated from controlled experiments. Most are simply observed data. The process that generates these observed data is typically unknown to the investigators. To provide descriptions of the economy and to test economic theories, two approaches have been adopted: the *structural approach* (e.g., Hendry, 1993; Spanos, 1986) and the *data-based approach* (e.g., Engle and Granger, 1987; Granger, 1969; Hsiao, 1979b,c, 1981, 1982a, 1982b; Liu, 1960; Sims, 1980). The structural approach makes use of prior information and hypothesizes a data-generating process (DGP). The analysis of the relevant data proceeds under this hypothetical maintained hypothesis that is supposed to mimic the essential properties of the (unknown) true data-generating process. By contrast, the data-based approach is not to impose any prior restrictions and let the "data speak for themselves." The regression analysis may be viewed as an example of the former approach, while nonparametric approaches and time-series analysis (Chapters 6 and 11) may be viewed as examples of the latter approach.

The structural approach hypothesizes a data-generating process and "modelling is seen as an attempt to characterize data properties in simple parametric relationships that are interpretable in light of economic knowledge, remain reasonably constant over time, and account for the findings of pre-existing models" (Hendry and Ericsson, 1991). The methodology espoused by Hendry and his associates involves a progressive research strategy that formulates and selects an empirical model through sequences of transformations and reductions.[49] Typical transformations include aggregation over space, time, agents, and goods as well as the standard mathematical operations of division, logarithms, and so on. Typical reductions consist of eliminating unwanted variables, referred to as *marginalization*, and conditioning the analysis on other variables, which are not to be explained. As a consequence, *all empirical models are derived entities*. Additionally, given the observed data and a formal model specification, the model's error process must contain everything in the data not explicitly allowed for by the model, and hence it is also derived rather than autonomous. This implies that models can be designed to satisfy preassigned criteria, as when residual serial correlation can be removed by the transformation, like (5.3.6). Thus for model design and model evaluation, Hendry and Richard (1982) propose using the criteria: (1) theoretical consistency (the empirical model reproduces the theory under the conditions assumed by the theory), (2) innovation errors (errors are serially uncorrelated), (3) (weak) exogeneity [the conditioning variables are weakly exogenous in the sense of Engle, Hendry, and Richard (1983) for the parameters of interest], (4) parameter constancy, (5) data admissibility (the model's predictions satisfy all data constraints implied by the theoretical model), and (6) encompassing (the model is able to account for the results obtained by other models). The progressive research strategy starts with a specification of a general model that encompasses contending models as a tentative maintained hypothesis. The standard statistical tests, such as the test of the null hypothesis [e.g., (4.7.16) and (4.7.22)], goodness of fit [(4.3.18) and (4.10.10)], the absence of heteroskedasticity [(5.4.18) or White, 1980] and the residual serial correlation [d statistic (5.5.22) or Box–Pierce Q sta-

[49]See Hendry and Mizon (1990), Hendry and Richard (1982), and Spanos (1986).

tistic (6.4.23) or (6.4.24)], predictive ability and parameter constancy (Chow) test for structural break [(4.7.52) and (4.7.53)] as well as the Hausman (1978) and Wu (1973) test for exogeneity (Section 11.4), Jarque and Bera (1980) test for normality (5.7.23), and Engle (1982) test for autoregressive conditional heteroskedasticity (ARCH) (5.5.28), as summarized in Table 5.3, are used as criteria to narrow down the scope of the model in the light of the data. The aim is to formulate a model that achieves the maximum of explanation with the minimum of factors.

The Hendry approach of starting with a collection of numerical data bearing on the question under study, subjecting them to sophisticated econometric techniques of estimation and tests of significance, and ending with a single hypothesis that can account for results obtained by other models is attractive. However, it is not the only way to formulate an empirical model. Another way is to examine variables one or two at a time and then to build up a general model from a collection of simple hypotheses. It can be argued that the Hendry general-to-specific approach has desirable statistical properties because it is generally incorrect to test hypotheses in one model and infer that the outcome will hold in generalizations of that model unless all the additional influences are uncorrelated with those already included. However, this approach is often hampered by multicollinearity, limited degrees of freedom, and other problems that make the resulting test statistics hard to interpret. Passing various test criteria is a necessary condition for an empirical model to satisfy the criteria put forward by Hendry and Richard, but it is not sufficient. With so many tests being conducted, it is impossible to estimate the probability that an empirical model could have arisen from chance. As Griliches (1986) notes, "We may be asking too much of our data. We want them to test our theories, provide us with estimates of important parameters, and disclose to us the exact time form of the interrelationships between the variables."[50] On the other hand,

TABLE 5.3 Hendry Criteria for Evaluating and Designing Econometric Models

Alternative Hypothesis	Statistic
First-order residual serial correlation	Durbin–Watson (1950) d, (5.5.25)
qth-order residual serial correlation	Box–Pierce (1970) Q, (6.4.24)
q invalid parameter restrictions	F, (4.7.23)
pth-order ARCH	Engle (1982), (5.5.28)
Skewness and excess kurtosis	Jarque and Bera (1980), (5.7.23)
Heteroskedasticity	Breusch and Pagan (1979), (5.4.18); White (1980)
Omission of important explanatory variables or wrong functional form	Ramsey (1969), (5.7.16); Bierens (1990), (5.7.18)
Parameters not constant over subsamples	Chow (1960), (4.7.52), (4.7.53)
Test for exogeneity	Hausman (1978), Wu (1973, Section 11.4)

Source Hendry and Richard (1982).

[50]This comment may also apply to the data-based approach.

examining variables one or two at a time can yield insights that cannot be obtained from a sweeping regression analysis, as in Friedman and Schwartz (1982). Both approaches, and others (e.g., Leamer, 1978b) have their use. None should be relied on exclusively. Furthermore, the adequacy of an empirical specification should be evaluated in light of the results of the sensitivity analysis to see if an inference "holds up" to minor and/or major changes in the model as discussed in Leamer (1978b) and to test hypotheses on bodies of data other than those from which an empirical specification is derived (Friedman, 1957). "The real proof of [the] pudding is whether it produces a satisfactory explanation of data not used in baking it—data for subsequent or earlier years, for other countries, or for other variables" (Friedman and Schwartz, 1991). It makes no sense to proceed with a single approach to the analysis of economic data.

PROBLEMS

5-A Show that if all four seasonal dummy variables d_1, d_2, d_3, and d_4 are included as explanatory variables in a model that also has an intercept term, there will be perfect multicollinearity, specifically a linear dependence in the columns of the **X** matrix.

5-B One approach to multicollinearity takes account of extraneous estimates of some of the parameters. Assume that the $k \times 1$ coefficient vector $\boldsymbol{\beta}$ is partitioned as

$$\begin{pmatrix} \boldsymbol{\beta}_1 \\ \cdots \\ \boldsymbol{\beta}_2 \end{pmatrix},$$

where $\boldsymbol{\beta}_1$ is given by the k_1 extraneous estimates $\bar{\boldsymbol{\beta}}_1$. Find the least squares estimates of the $k - k_1$ remaining parameters $\hat{\boldsymbol{\beta}}_2$ by formulating the problem as one of least squares subject to the linear restrictions that $\boldsymbol{\beta}_1 = \bar{\boldsymbol{\beta}}_1$. Generalize to the case of several linear restrictions on parameters, of the form

$$\mathbf{c} = \mathbf{A}\boldsymbol{\beta} + \mathbf{v}$$

using the formulation

$$\begin{pmatrix} \mathbf{y} \\ \cdots \\ \mathbf{c} \end{pmatrix} = \begin{pmatrix} \mathbf{X} \\ \cdots \\ \mathbf{A} \end{pmatrix}\boldsymbol{\beta} + \begin{pmatrix} \mathbf{u} \\ \cdots \\ \mathbf{v} \end{pmatrix}.$$

5-C Show that the Durbin–Watson statistic of (5.5.25) can be expressed as

$$\hat{d} = \frac{\hat{\mathbf{u}}'\mathbf{A}\hat{\mathbf{u}}}{\hat{\mathbf{u}}'\hat{\mathbf{u}}},$$

where **A** is the symmetric $n \times n$ matrix defined by

$$\mathbf{A} = \begin{pmatrix} 1 & -1 & 0 & \cdots & 0 & 0 & 0 \\ -1 & 2 & -1 & \cdots & 0 & 0 & 0 \\ 0 & -1 & 2 & \cdots & 0 & 0 & 0 \\ \vdots & \vdots & \vdots & & \vdots & \vdots & \vdots \\ 0 & 0 & 0 & & 2 & -1 & 0 \\ 0 & 0 & 0 & & -1 & 2 & -1 \\ 0 & 0 & 0 & & 0 & -1 & 1 \end{pmatrix}.$$

5-D The Markov process (5.5.2) relates $\hat{u}_i$ to $\hat{u}_{i-1}$ in the case of first-order serial correlation.

1. Illustrate positive and negative first-order serial correlation geometrically in terms of the clustering of points in various quadrants of the $\hat{u}_i$, $\hat{u}_{i-1}$ plane.
2. Illustrate the Markov process using this plane.
3. Prove that $\hat{\rho}$ in (5.5.16) is the least squares estimator of the parameter ρ in the Markov process.
4. Prove that $\hat{\rho}$ is a biased but consistent estimator of ρ.

5-E Consider the second-order autoregressive scheme

$$u_i = \rho_1 u_{i-1} + \rho_2 u_{i-2} + v_i.$$

1. Find the transformed model, comparable to (5.5.14).
2. Obtain a test statistic comparable to the Durbin–Watson test statistic to test the hypothesis

$$H_0 : \rho_1 = \rho_2 = 0.$$

3. How could ρ_1 and ρ_2 be estimated?

5-F Consider the model

$$\begin{aligned} y_i &= \beta x_i + u_i \\ u_i &= v_i + \delta v_{i-1}, \qquad |\delta| < 1 \\ E(v_i) &= 0 \\ E(v_i v_{i'}) &= \begin{cases} \sigma_v^2 & \text{if } i = i' \\ 0 & \text{if } i \neq i'. \end{cases} \end{aligned}$$

1. Show that the least squares estimator of β is unbiased.
2. Assuming that δ is known, obtain the GLS estimator of β.

5-G Show that in the *equicorrelated case*, in which the covariance matrix $\mathbf{\Omega}$ in (A.5.1) (p. 133) exhibits homoskedasticity (equal diagonal elements) and equal covariances (equal off-diagonal elements, which are not necessarily all zero), the GLS estimator (5.3.9) reduces to the ordinary least squares estimator.

5-H Prove that if all the assumptions for the Gauss–Markov theorem other than homoskedasticity and absence of serial correlation are met, the least-squares estimators are still linear, unbiased, and consistent but they are no longer most efficient (best).

5-I Prove the GLS version of the Gauss–Markov theorem—that the GLS estimators are BLUE—and the GLS version of the least squares consistency theorem—that the GLS estimators are consistent (proofs can be patterned after those of Section 4.4).

5-J In the case of heteroskedasticity, develop the likelihood function and show that the GLS estimator using (5.4.2) is equivalent to that obtained by maximizing this likelihood function.

5-K Prove that if $\mathbf{\Omega}$ is given as in (5.5.9) with $\sigma^2 = 1$, then

$$\mathbf{\Omega}^{-1} = \frac{1}{1-\rho^2}\begin{pmatrix} 1 & -\rho & 0 & \cdots & 0 & 0 \\ -\rho & 1+\rho^2 & -\rho & \cdots & 0 & 0 \\ 0 & -\rho & 1+\rho^2 & \cdots & 0 & 0 \\ \vdots & \vdots & \vdots & \cdots & \vdots & \vdots \\ 0 & 0 & 0 & \cdots & 1+\rho^2 & -\rho \\ 0 & 0 & 0 & \cdots & -\rho & 1 \end{pmatrix}.$$

Show that the GLS estimator is then the least squares estimator of the transformed model

$$\mathbf{Py} = \mathbf{PX\beta} + \mathbf{Pu},$$

where here

$$\mathbf{P} = \frac{1}{\sqrt{1-\rho^2}} \begin{pmatrix} \sqrt{1-\rho^2} & 0 & 0 & \cdots & 0 & 0 \\ -\rho & 1 & 0 & \cdots & 0 & 0 \\ 0 & -\rho & 1 & \cdots & 0 & 0 \\ \vdots & \vdots & \vdots & & \vdots & \vdots \\ 0 & 0 & 0 & \cdots & 1 & 0 \\ 0 & 0 & 0 & \cdots & -\rho & 1 \end{pmatrix}.$$

Give an interpretation for the transformed model.

5-L For the technique of "seemingly unrelated equations" of Section 5.3:

1. Derive the estimator $\hat{\boldsymbol{\beta}}^*$, assuming that $\Sigma^{-1} = (\sigma^{jj'})$, where

$$\boldsymbol{\Sigma}^{*-1} = \boldsymbol{\Sigma}^{-1} \otimes \mathbf{I} = \begin{pmatrix} \sigma^{11}\mathbf{I} & \sigma^{12}\mathbf{I} & \cdots & \sigma^{1g}\mathbf{I} \\ \vdots & \vdots & & \vdots \\ \sigma^{g1}\mathbf{I} & \sigma^{g2}\mathbf{I} & \cdots & \sigma^{gg}\mathbf{I} \end{pmatrix}.$$

2. Show that if $\sigma^{jj'} = 0$ for $j \neq j'$ or if $\mathbf{X}^1 = \mathbf{X}^2 = \cdots = \mathbf{X}^g$, the estimator reduces to the set of ordinary least squares estimators for each equation considered alone.

5-M For the problem of specification error:

1. Prove (5.7.15) by inverting the partitioned matrix in (5.7.14).
2. Prove that the inclusion of irrelevant variables $\mathbf{X}_2$, as in (5.7.10), yields inefficient estimators for the parameters of the true model (5.7.1).

5-N Consider the identification of the errors-in-variables model, as discussed in footnote 32. Show that the model is identified if $\beta_2 = 0$. Also show that the model is identified if $\mathrm{Var}(Y_E)$ is known, if $\mathrm{Var}(C_E)$ is known, or if the ratio of these variances is known. For each case, obtain the estimator for β_1.

5-O Consider the simple Tobit model for $t = 1, \ldots, n$:

$$y_t = \begin{cases} \mathbf{z}_t'\boldsymbol{\beta} + u_t & \text{if } \mathbf{z}_t'\boldsymbol{\beta} + u_t > 0 \\ 0 & \text{otherwise,} \end{cases}$$

where the u_t's are i.i.d. $N(0, \sigma^2)$.

1. Let $I_t = 1$ if $\mathbf{z}_t'\boldsymbol{\beta} + u_t > 0$ and $I_t = 0$ otherwise. Show that the log-likelihood of the Tobit model is the sum of the log-likelihood of a probit model which depends only on $\boldsymbol{\gamma} = \boldsymbol{\beta}/\sigma$, and of a function L_c which depends on σ and $\boldsymbol{\gamma}$. Suggest a simple consistent estimator of γ.
2. Suppose that γ is known. Maximize L_c with respect to σ. Given a consistent estimator of $\boldsymbol{\gamma}$, suggest a simple (consistent) estimator of σ and $\boldsymbol{\beta}$.

5-P *Binary logit model.* Suppose that utility is

$$U_i = \mathbf{B}'\mathbf{z}_i + \varepsilon_i, \qquad i = 1, 2$$

and stochastic terms ε_i are i.i.d. with the extreme value distribution, whose cdf is

$$F(\varepsilon) = \exp\left[-\exp\left(\frac{-\varepsilon - a}{b}\right)\right]$$

1. Compute the mean and variance of the distribution. [*Hint*:

$$\int_0^\infty e^{-x} \ln x \, dx = -\gamma$$

$$\int_0^\infty e^{-x} (\ln x)^2 \, dx = \frac{\pi^2}{6} + \gamma^2,$$

where

$$\gamma = \text{Euler's constant} = 0.5772157\ldots$$
$$= \lim_{\rho \to \infty} \left(\sum_{n=1}^{\rho} \frac{1}{n} - \ln \rho \right).$$

2. Show that the cdf of $(\varepsilon_2 - \varepsilon_1)$ is logistic, that is,

$$G(x) = \Pr(\varepsilon_2 - \varepsilon_1 \le x) = \frac{1}{1 + e^{-x/b}}.$$

3. Show that the probability of choosing alternative 1 is logit, that is,

$$P_1 = \frac{\exp(\mathbf{B}'\mathbf{z}_1/b)}{\exp(\mathbf{B}'\mathbf{z}_1/b) + \exp(\mathbf{B}'\mathbf{z}_2/b)}.$$

Note that a has no effect on this probability, and that changing b has the same effect as multiplying all components of $\mathbf{B}$ by a constant. Hence we usually normalize $a = 0$, $b = 1$.

4. Show that only the *difference* $\mathbf{z}_1 - \mathbf{z}_2$ affects P_1.

5-Q Let y_i be a random variable that can take only the values zero or 1; let x_i be a variable that can take any value. Consider the model

$$y_i = \alpha + \beta x_i + u_i, \qquad i = 1, \ldots, n. \tag{1}$$

1. Show that u_i must necessarily have a two-point distribution with variance σ_i^2 equal to $(\alpha + \beta x_i)(1 - \alpha - \beta x_i)$.
2. Discuss the issues involved if one uses $\hat{y}_i(1 - \hat{y}_i)$ to estimate σ_i^2, where $\hat{y}_i = \hat{\alpha} + \hat{\beta} x_i$ is the least squares predictor of y_i.
3. What would happen to the coefficients and variance of equation (1) if the binary variable y were presented by a (0, 2) variable rather than by a (0, 1) variable? What does this suggest to you about the interpretation of the estimated least squares parameters?
4. Prove that the model

$$P(y_i = 1 \mid x_i) = F(\alpha + \beta x_i),$$

where F is a cumulative uniform probability function, yields a linear probability model $P(y_i = 1 \mid x_i) = \alpha^* + \beta^* x_i$ with the constraint that $0 \le \alpha^* + \beta^* x_i \le 1$.

5. Suppose that (1) is valid and least squares is used to estimate β. How would you approximate the variance of the least squares estimate of β assuming that x_i is independently, identically distributed? (You do not need to prove your assertion. Some intuitive explanation is sufficient.)

5-R Consider the model

$$\begin{aligned} y_t &= \boldsymbol{\beta}'\mathbf{x}_t + u_t, \\ u_t &= \rho u_{t-1} + \varepsilon_t \end{aligned} \qquad t = 1, \ldots, T,$$

where $\mathbf{x}_t$ is exogenous and ε_t is assumed to be independently, normally distributed with mean zero and variance σ_ε^2.

1. Derive the Lagrangian multiplier test of serial independence. Show that is is asymptotically equivalent to the Durbin–Watson statistic. (*Hint*: Conditional on y_1 being fixed, the likelihood function of $y_2, \ldots, y_T$ is

$$f(y_2, \ldots, y_T \mid y_1) = (2\pi\sigma_\varepsilon^2)^{-(T-1)/2} \exp\left\{-\frac{1}{2\sigma_\varepsilon^2} \sum_{t=2}^{T} [y_t - \rho y_{t-1} - \beta x_t + \rho\beta x_{t-1}]^2\right\}$$

and the information matrix is block diagonal.)

2. Suppose that $\mathbf{x}_t$ contains lagged dependent variable y_{t-1}. Can you still use the Durbin–Watson statistic to test for serial independence? Give an intuitive explanation of your argument. What alternative test would you suggest?

5-S Suppose that in the classical regression model

$$\mathbf{y} = \mathbf{X}\boldsymbol{\beta} + \boldsymbol{\varepsilon} \qquad \boldsymbol{\varepsilon} \sim N(\mathbf{0}, \sigma^2\mathbf{I}_m)$$

we wish to develop a general test for heteroskedasticity.

1. Let $\mathbf{A} = \text{diag}(\sigma_i^2)$, so that in fact $\boldsymbol{\varepsilon} \sim N(\mathbf{O}, \mathbf{A})$. What is the covariance matrix of the OLS estimator $\hat{\boldsymbol{\beta}} = (\mathbf{X}'\mathbf{X})^{-1}\mathbf{X}'\mathbf{y}$?
2. Can **A** be consistently estimated? How?
3. Based on an affirmative answer to part 2, propose a consistent test of the hypothesis of homoskedasticity (White, 1980), developing its sampling properties, and so on.
4. Is there a corresponding GLS estimator in the event that the hypothesis of homoskedasticity is rejected?

5-T Consider the following model for $t = 1, \ldots, T$:

$$y_{1t} = \beta z_t + u_{1t}, \tag{1}$$

$$y_{2t} = u_{2t}, \tag{2}$$

where y_{1t}, y_{2t}, and z_t are scalar random variables. It is assumed that the vectors (z_t, u_{1t}, u_{2t}), $t = 1, 2, \ldots,$ are independently and identically distributed, and satisfy for any t:

$$E(u_{it}) = 0, \qquad E(u_{it}u_{jt}) = \sigma_{ij} < \infty, \tag{3}$$

$$E(z_t^2) \neq 0, \qquad E(u_{it}z_t) = 0 \tag{4}$$

for $i, j = 2$. Throughout you may assume that the model (1)–(2) with the stochastic assumptions (3)–(4) is correctly specified. It may be convenient to denote by $\mathbf{Y}_1$, $\mathbf{Y}_2$ and $\mathbf{Z}$ the $T \times 1$ vectors of observations on y_1, y_2, and z.

1. Suppose that the σ_{ij}'s are known, and treat **Z** as fixed. Show that the best linear unbiased estimator of β is

$$b = (\mathbf{Z}'\mathbf{Z})^{-1}\mathbf{Z}'\mathbf{Y}_1 - \frac{\sigma_{12}}{\sigma_{22}}\mathbf{Z}'\mathbf{Y}_2. \tag{5}$$

   Why is the OLS estimator of β on equation (1) not best linear unbiased? (*Hint*: Think seemingly unrelated or stacked regression model.)

2. From now on, the σ_{ij}'s are unknown. Suppose that you have available consistent estimators s_{ij} of the σ_{ij}'s. How would you use equation (5) to estimate consistently β? Establish the consistency of your proposed estimator. Propose some consistent estimators of the σ_{ij}'s. [You may asume that the vector (u_{1t}, u_{2t}, z_t) has finite fourth moments.]
3. Suppose from now on that the errors u_{it} are normally distributed. Show that (conditional on z_t) the joint density (y_{1t}, y_{2t}) is

$$f(y_{1t}, y_{2t}) = \frac{1}{(2\pi\omega)^{1/2}} \exp\left[-\frac{1}{2\omega}(y_{1t} - \beta z_t - \lambda y_{2t})^2\right] \cdot \frac{1}{(2\pi\sigma_{22})^{1/2}} \exp\left(-\frac{1}{2\sigma_{22}} y_{2t}^2\right), \tag{6}$$

   where

$$\omega \equiv \sigma_{11} - \frac{\sigma_{12}^2}{\sigma_{22}}, \qquad \lambda \equiv \frac{\sigma_{12}}{\sigma_{22}}. \tag{7}$$

4. Using equations (6) and (7) and the invariance property of maximum likelihood (ML) estimation, state how the ML estimators $\hat{\beta}$, $\hat{\sigma}_{11}$, $\hat{\sigma}_{12}$, $\hat{\sigma}_{22}$ can be obtained. Give explicit expressions for $\hat{\beta}$, $\hat{\sigma}_{11}$, $\hat{\sigma}_{12}$, $\hat{\sigma}_{22}$. In particular, show that $\hat{\beta}$ can be obtained from equation (5), where the σ_{ij}'s are estimated by $s_{ij} = \tilde{U}_i'\tilde{U}_j/T$, with $\tilde{U}_i$ being the $T \times 1$ vector of unrestricted OLS residuals obtained by regressing y_{it} on z_t.

5. We want to test H_0: $\beta = 0$ against H_A: $\beta \neq 0$. Show that the constrained ML estimators of σ_{11}, σ_{12}, σ_{22} are given by $\tilde{\sigma}_{ij} = Y_i'Y_j/T$. Give an expression of the statistic used in the likelihood ratio test in terms of $\hat{\omega}$, $\hat{\sigma}_{22}$, $\tilde{\sigma}_{11}$, $\tilde{\sigma}_{12}$, and $\tilde{\sigma}_{22}$, where $\hat{\omega}$ is the unconstrained ML estimator of ω defined in part 3. How would you perform the test?

BIBLIOGRAPHY

AIGNER, D. J., C. HSIAO, A. KAPTEYN, and T. WANSBEEK (1985). "Latent Variable Models in Econometrics," in Z. Griliches and M. D. Intriligator, Eds., *Handbook of Econometrics*, Vol. 2. Amsterdam: North-Holland Publishing Company.

AMEMIYA, T. (1973). "Regression Analysis When the Dependent Variable Is Truncated Normal." *Econometrica*, 41: 997–1016.

AMEMIYA, T. (1974). "Bivariate Probit Analysis: Minimum Chi-Square Methods." *Journal of the American Statistical Association*, 69: 940–944.

AMEMIYA, T. (1976). "The Maximum Likelihood, the Minimum Chi-Square and the Nonlinear Weighted Least Squares Estimator in the General Qualitative Response Model." *Journal of the American Statistical Association*, 71: 347–351.

AMEMIYA, T. (1980). "The n^{-2}-Order Mean Squared Errors of the Maximum Likelihood and the Minimum Logit Chi-Square Estimator." *Annals of Statistics*, 8: 488–505.

AMEMIYA, T. (1981). "Qualitative Response Models: A Survey." *Journal of Economic Literature*, 19: 483–536.

AMEMIYA, T. (1983). "Partially Generalized Least Squares and Two-Stage Least Squares Estimators." *Journal of Econometrics*, 23: 275–283.

AMEMIYA, T. (1985). *Advanced Econometrics*. Cambridge, Mass.: Harvard University Press.

ANGRIST, J. D. (1991). "Grouped-Data Estimation and Testing in Single Labor Supply Models." *Journal of Econometrics*, 47: 243–266.

ASHENFELTER, P., and G. SOLON (1982). "Longitudinal Labor Market Data-Sources, Uses and Limitations," in *What's Happening to American Labor Force and Productivity Measurements*. Kalamazoo, Mich.: W.E. Upjohn Institute for Economic Research.

BECKWITH, N. (1972). "Multivariate Analysis of Sales Response of Competing Brands to Advertising." *Journal of Marketing Research*, 9: 168–176.

BELSLEY, D., E. KUH, and R. E. WELSH (1980). *Regression Diagnostics*. New York: John Wiley & Sons, Inc.

BERKSON, J. (1955). "Maximum Likelihood and Minimum χ^2 Estimates of the Logistic Function." *Journal of the American Statistical Association*, 50: 130–162.

BERKSON, J. (1957). "Tables for Use in Estimating the Normal Distribution Function by Normit Analysis." *Biometrika*, 44: 411–435.

BERKSON, J. (1980). "Minimum Chi-Square, Not Maximum Likelihood." *Annals of Statistics*, 8: 457–487.

BICKEL, P. J., and K. DOKSUM (1984). "An Analysis of Transformations Revisited." *Journal of the American Statistical Association*, 76: 296–312.

BIERENS, H. B. (1990). "A Consistent Conditional Moment Test of Functional Form." *Econometrica*, 58: 1443–1458.

BLATTBERG, R. C., and N. J. GONEDES (1974). "A Comparison of the Stable and Student Distributions as Statistical Models for Stock Prices." *Journal of Business*, 47: 244–279.

BODKIN, R. G., and L. R. KLEIN (1967). "Nonlinear Estimation of Aggregate Production Functions." *Review of Economics and Statistics*, 39: 28–44.

BOLLERSLEV, T., R. Y. CHOU, and K. F. KRONER (1992). "ARCH Modeling in Finance: A Review of the Theory and Empirical Evidence." *Journal of Econometrics*, 52: 5–59.

BORUS, M. E. (1981). "An Inventory of Longitudinal Data Sets of Interest to Economists." Mimeograph, Ohio State University.

BOWDEN, R., and D. TURKINGTON (1984). *Instrumental Variables*. Cambridge: Cambridge University Press.

BOX, G. E. P., and D. A. PIERCE (1970). "Distribution of Residual Autocorrelations in Autoregressive–Integrated Moving Average Time Series Models." *Journal of the American Statistical Association*, 65: 1509–1526.

BREUSCH, T. S., and A. R. PAGAN (1979). "A Simple Test for Heteroscedasticity and Random Coefficient Variation." *Econometrica*, 47: 1287–1294.

CARROLL, R. J. (1980a). "Robust Methods for Factorial Experiments with Outliers." *Applied Statistics*, 29: 246–251.

CARROLL, R. J. (1980b). "A Robust Method for Testing Transformations to Achieve Approximate Normality." *Journal of the Royal Statistical Society*, B 42: 71–78.

CARROLL, R. J. (1982). "Adapting for Heteroscedasticity in Linear Models." *Annals of Statistics*, 10: 1224–1233.

CHAMBERLAIN, G. (1982). "Multivariate Regression Models for Panel Data." *Journal of Econometrics*, 18: 5–46.

CHOW G. (1960). "Tests for Equality between Sets of Coefficient in Two Linear Regressions." *Econometrica*, 28: 591–605.

COX, D. R. (1970). *Analysis of Binary Data*. London: Methuen & Company Ltd.

CRAGG, J. G. (1983). "More Efficient Estimation in the Presence of Heteroscadasticity of Unknown Form." *Econometrica*, 51: 751–763.

DAVIDSON, R., and J. G. MACKINNON (1993). *Estimation and Inferences in Econometrics*. Oxford: Oxford University Press.

DIELMAN, T., T. NANTELL, and R. WRIGHT (1980). "Price Effects of Stock Repurchasing: A Random Coefficient Regression Approach." *Journal of Financial and Quantitative Analysis*, 15: 175–189.

DRAPER, N. R., and H. SMITH (1981). *Applied Regression Analysis*, 2nd ed. New York: John Wiley & Sons, Inc.

DURBIN, J. (1954). "Errors in Variables." *Review of the International Statistical Institute*, 22: 23–32.

DURBIN, J. (1960). "Estimation of Parameters in Time Series Regression Models." *Journal of the Royal Statistical Society*, B 22: 139–153.

DURBIN, J., and G. S. WATSON (1950). "Testing for Serial Correlation in Least Squares Regression I." *Biometrika*, 37: 409–428.

DURBIN, J., and G. S. WATSON (1951). "Testing for Serial Correlation in Least Squares Regression II." *Biometrika*, 38: 159–178.

EICKER, F. (1963). "Asymptotic Normality and Consistency of the Least Squares Estimators for Families of Linear Regression." *Annals of Mathematical Statistics*, 34: 447–456.

ENGLE, R. F. (1982). "Autoregressive Conditional Heteroscedasticity with Estimates of the Variance of United Kingdom Inflation." *Econometrica*, 50: 987–1007.

ENGLE, R. F., and C. W. J. GRANGER (1987). "Cointegration and Error Correction: Representation, Estimation and Testing." *Econometrica*, 55: 251–276.

ENGLE, R. F., D. F. HENDRY, and J. R. RICHARD (1983). "Exogeneity." *Econometrica*, 51: 277–304.

FERGUSON, T. S. (1958). "A Method of Generating Best Asymptotically Normal Estimates with Application to the Estimation of Bacterial Densities." *Annals of Mathematical Statistics*, 29: 1046–1062.

FISHER, F. M. (1961). "On the Cost of Approximate Specification in Simultaneous Equation Estimation." *Econometrica*, 29: 361–366.

FRIEDMAN, M. (1957). *A Theory of the Consumption Function*. Princeton, N.J.: Princeton University Press.

FRIEDMAN, M., and A. J. SCHWARTZ (1982). *Monetary Trends in the United States and the United Kingdom: Their Relation to Income, Prices and Interest Rates, 1867–1975*. Chicago: University of Chicago Press.

FRIEDMAN, M., and A. J. SCHWARTZ (1991). "Alternative Approaches to Analyzing Economic Data." *American Economic Review*, 81: 39–49.

GOLDBERGER, A. S. (1964). *Econometric Theory*. New York: John Wiley & Sons, Inc.

GOLDFELD, S. M., and R. E. QUANDT (1972). *Nonlinear Methods in Econometrics*. Amsterdam: North-Holland Publishing Company.

GRANGER, C. W. J. (1969). "Investigating Causal Relations by Econometric Models and Cross-Spectral Models." *Econometrica*, 37: 424–438.

GREENE, W. H. (1990). *Econometric Analysis*. New York: Macmillan Publishing Company.

GRILICHES, Z., Ed. (1971). *Price Indexes and Quality Change*. Cambridge, Mass.: Harvard University Press.

GRILICHES, Z. (1986). "Economic Data Issues," in Z. Griliches and M. D. Intriligator, Eds., *Handbook of Econometrics*, Vol. 3. Amsterdam: North-Holland Publishing Company.

HARTLEY, H. O. (1961). "The Modified Gauss–Newton Method for the Fitting of Nonlinear Regression Functions by Least Squares." *Technometrics*, 3: 269–280.

HAUSMAN, J. A. (1978). "Specification Tests in *Econometrica*." *Econometrica*, 46: 1251–1271.

HAUSMAN, J. A., and D. A. WISE (1977). "Social Experimentation, Truncated Distributions, and Efficient Estimation." *Econometrica*, 45: 919–938.

HECKMAN, J. J. (1976). "The Common Structure of Statistical Models of Truncation, Sample Selection, and Limited Dependent Variables and a Simple Estimator for Such Models." *Annals of Economic and Social Measurement*, 5: 475–492.

HECKMAN, J. J. (1979). "Sample Selection Bias as a Specification Error." *Econometrica*, 47: 153–161.

HENDRY, D. F. (1974). "Stochastic Specification in an Aggregate Demand Model of the United Kingdom." *Econometrica*, 42: 559–578.

HENDRY, D. F. (1993). *Econometrics: Alchemy or Science*. Oxford: Blackwell Scientific Publications Ltd.

HENDRY, D. F., and N. R. ERICSSON (1991). "An Econometric Analysis of U.K. Money Demand in Monetary Trends in the United States and the United Kingdom by Milton Friedman and Anna J. Schwartz." *American Economic Review*, 81: 8–38.

HENDRY, D. F., and G. E. MIZON (1990). "Procrustean Econometrics: Or Stretching and Squeezing Data," in C. W. J. Granger, Ed., *Modelling Economic Series: Readings in Econometric Methodology*. Oxford: Clarendon Press, pp. 121–136.

HENDRY, D. F., and J.-F. RICHARD (1982). "On the Formulation of Empirical Models in Dynamic Econometrics." *Journal of Econometrics*, 20: 3–33.

HSIAO, C. (1973). "Regression Analysis with Limited Dependent Variable, 1P-186, IBER and CRMS," University of California, Berkeley.

HSIAO, C. (1974). "The Estimation of Labor Supply of Low Income Workers: Some Economic Consideration." Working paper 970–1. Washington, D.C.: The Urban Institute.

HSIAO, C. (1976). "Identification and Estimation of Simultaneous Equation Models with Measurement Error." *International Economic Review*, 17: 319–339.

HSIAO, C. (1977). "Identification for a Linear Dynamic Simultaneous Error-Shock Model." *International Economic Review*, 18: 181–194.

HSIAO, C. (1979a). "Measurement Error in a Dynamic Simultaneous Equation Model with Stationary Disturbances." *Econometrica*, 47: 475–494.

HSIAO, C. (1979b). "Autoregressive Modelling of Canadian Money and Income Data." *Journal of the American Statistical Association*, 74: 553–566.

HSIAO, C. (1979c). "Causality Tests in Econometrics." *Journal of Economic Dynamics and Control*, 1: 321–346.

HSIAO, C. (1981). "Autoregressive Modelling and Money-Income Causality Detection." *Journal of Monetary Economics*, 7: 85–106.

HSIAO, C. (1982a). "Autoregressive Modelling and Causal Ordering of Economic Variables." *Journal of Economic Dynamics and Control*, 4: 243–259.

HSIAO, C. (1982b). "Time Series Modelling and Causal Ordering of Canadian Money, Income, and Interest Rate," in O. D. Anderson, Ed., *Time Series Analysis: Theory and Practice*, Vol. 1. Amsterdam: North Holland Publishing Company, pp. 671–698.

HSIAO, C. (1985a). "Benefits and Limitations of Panel Data." *Econometric Review*, 4: 121–174.

HSIAO, C. (1985b). "Minimum Chi-Square," in S. Kutz and N. Johnson, Eds., *Encyclopedia of Statistical Science*, Vol. 5. New York: John Wiley & Sons, Inc.

HSIAO, C. (1986). *Analysis of Panel Data*. Econometric Society Monographs No. 11. New York: Cambridge University Press.

HSIAO, C. (1991). "Panel Analysis for Metric Data," in G. Arminger, C. C. Clogg, and M. E. Sobel, Eds., *Handbook of Statistical Modelling in the Social and Behavioral Sciences*. London: Plenum Press.

HUBER, P. J. (1964). "Robust Estimation of a Location Parameter." *Annals of Statistics*, 35: 73–101.

HUBER, P. J. (1973). "Robust Regression, Asymptotics, Conjectures and Monte Carlo." *Annals of Statistics*, 1: 799–821.

HUBER, P. J. (1981). *Robust Statistics*. New York: John Wiley & Sons, Inc.

IZENMAN, A. J. (1991). "Recent Developments in Nonparametric Density Estimation." *Journal of the American Statistical Association*, 86: 205–224.

JARQUE, C. M., and A. K. BERA (1980). "Efficient Tests for Normality, Homoscedasticity and Serial Independence of Regression Residuals." *Economics Letters*, 6: 255–259.

JEFFREYS, H. (1961). *Theory of Probability*, 3rd ed. London: Oxford University Press.

JOHNSTON, J. (1985). *Econometric Methods*, 3rd ed. New York: McGraw-Hill Book Company.

JUDGE, G., W. GRIFFITHS, R. HILL, H. LÜTKEPOHL, and T. LEE (1985). *The Theory and Practice of Econometrics*, 2nd ed. New York: John Wiley & Sons, Inc.

KOENKER, R. (1982). "Robust Methods in Econometrics" (with discussion). *Econometric Reviews*, 1: 213–289.

KONIJN, H. S. (1962). "Identification and Estimation in a Simultaneous Equations Model with Errors in the Variables." *Econometrica*, 30: 79–87.

LEAMER, E. E. (1978a). "Least-Squares versus Instrumental Variables Estimation in a Single Errors in Variables Model." *Econometrica*, 46: 961–968.

LEAMER, E. (1978b). *Specification Searches*. New York: John Wiley & Sons, Inc.

LIU, T.C. (1960). "Underidentification, Structural Estimation, and Forecasting." *Econometrica*, 28: 855–865.

MADANSKY, A. (1964). "Spurious Correlation Due to Deflating Variables." *Econometrica*, 32: 652–655.

MADDALA, G. S. (1971a). "The Use of Variance Components Models in Pooling Cross Section and Time Series Data." *Econometrica*, 39: 341–358.

MADDALA, G. S. (1971b). "The Likelihood Approach to Pooling Cross-Section and Time Series Data." *Econometrica*, 39: 939–953.

MADDALA, G. S. (1992). *Introduction to Econometrics*, 2nd ed. New York: Macmillan Publishing Company.

MALINVAUD, E. (1980). *Statistical Methods of Econometrics*, 3rd rev. ed. Amsterdam: North-Holland Publishing Company.

MANSKI, C. F. (1984). "Adaptive Estimation of Nonlinear Regression Models." *Econometric Reviews*, 3: 145–194.

MARQUARDT, D. W. (1963). "An Algorithm for Least Squares Estimation of Non-linear Parameters." *Journal of the Society of Industrial Applied Mathematics*, 11: 431–441.

MEYER, J., and E. KUH (1957). "How Extraneous Are Extraneous Estimates?" *Review of Economics and Statistics*, 39: 380–393.

MILHØJ, A. (1990). "Distribution of Empirical Autocorrelations of a Squared First Order ARCH Process." Unpublished manuscript, Department of Statistics, University of Copenhagen.

MOUNTAIN, D., and C. HSIAO (1989). "A Combined Structural and Flexible Functional Approach for Modeling Energy Substitution." *Journal of the American Statistical Association*, 84: 76–87.

MUNDLAK, Y. (1961). "Empirical Production Function Free of Management Bias." *Journal of Farm Economics*, 43: 44–56.

MUNDLAK, Y. (1978). "On the Pooling of Time Series and Cross Section Data." *Econometrica*, 46: 69–85.

NEWEY, W. K. (1985). "Maximum Likelihood Specification Testing and Conditional Moments Tests." *Econometrica*, 53: 1047–1070.

NEYMAN, J. (1949). "Contributions to the Theory of the χ^2 Test," in J. Neyman, Ed., *Proceedings of the First Berkeley Symposium on Mathematical Statistics and Probabilities*. Berkeley: University of California Press.

PRAIS, S. J., and H. S. HOUTHAKKER (1955). *The Analysis of Family Budgets*. New York: Cambridge University Press.

QUANDT, R. E. (1983). "Computational Problems and Methods," in Z. Griliches and M. D. Intriligator, Eds., *Handbook of Econometrics*, Vol. 1. Amsterdam: North-Holland Publishing Company.

RAMSEY, J. B. (1969). "Tests for Specification Errors in Classical Linear Least-Squares Regression Analysis." *Journal of the Royal Statistical Society*, B 31: 350–371.

ROBINSON, P. M. (1982). "On the Asymptotic Properties of Estimators of Models Containing Limited Dependent Variables." *Econometrica*, 50: 27–41.

ROBINSON, P. M. (1986). "Nonparametric Methods in Specification." *The Economic Journal*, Supplement, 96: 134–141.

ROBINSON, P. M. (1988a). "Semiparametric Econometrics: A Survey." *Journal of Applied Econometrics*, 3: 35–51.

ROBINSON, P. M. (1988b). "Notes on Nonparametric and Semiparametric Estimation." Mimeograph, London School of Economics.

ROSE, R. L. (1978). "Nonparametric Estimation of Weights in Least Squares Regression Analysis." Unpublished Ph.D. dissertation, University of California at Davis.

ROY, A. D. (1950). "The Distribution of Earnings and of Individual Output." *Economic Journal*, 60: 489–505, 831–836.

SHEINER, L., B. ROSENBERG, and K. MELMON (1972). "Modeling of Individual Pharmacokinetics for Computer-Aided Drug Dosage." *Computers and Biomedical Research*, 5: 441–459.

SILVEY, S. D. (1969). "Multicollinearity and Imprecise Estimation." *Journal of the Royal Statistical Society*, B 31: 539–552.

SIMS, C. A. (1980). "Macroeconomics and Reality." *Econometrica*, 48: 1–48.

SPANOS, A. (1986). *Statistical Foundations of Econometric Modelling*. Cambridge: Cambridge University Press.

STONE, C. J. (1975). "Adaptive Maximum Likelihood Estimation of a Location Parameter." *Annals of Statistics*, 3: 267–284.

STONE, C. J. (1977). "Consistent Nonparametric Regressions" (with discussion). *Annals of Statistics*, 5: 595–645.

STONE, J. R. N. (1954). *The Measurement of Consumers' Expenditure and Behavior in the United Kingdom, 1920–1938*. New York: Cambridge University Press.

THEIL, H. (1963). "On the Use of Incomplete Prior Information in Regression Analysis." *Journal of the American Statistical Association*, 58: 401–414.

THEIL, H. (1965). "The Analysis of Disturbances in Regression Analysis." *Journal of the American Statistical Association*, 60: 1067–1079.

THEIL, H. (1971). *Principles of Econometrics*. New York: John Wiley & Sons, Inc.

THEIL, H., and A. S. GOLDBERGER (1961). "On Pure and Mixed Statistical Estimation in Economics." *International Economic Review*, 2: 65–78.

THEIL, H., and A. NAGAR (1961). "Testing the Independence of Regression Disturbances." *Journal of the American Statistical Association*, 56: 793–806.

TOBIN, J. (1950). "A Statistical Demand Function for Food in the U.S.A." *Journal of the Royal Statistical Society*, Series A: 113–141.

TOBIN, J. (1958). "Estimation of Relationships for Limited Dependent Variables." *Econometrica*, 26: 24–36.

TUKEY, J. W. (1960). "A Survey of Sampling from Contaminated Distribution," in I. Olkin et al., Eds., *Contributions to Probability and Statistics: Essays in Honor of Harold Hotelling*. Stanford; Calif.: Stanford University Press.

WALD, A. (1940). "The Fitting of Straight Lines If Both Variables Are Subject to Error." *Annals of Mathematical Statistics*, 11: 284–300.

WHITE, H. (1980). "A Heteroscedasticity-Consistent Covariance Matrix Estimator and a Direct Test for Heteroscedasticity." *Econometrica*, 48: 817–838.

WHITE, H. (1982). "Instrumental Variables Regression with Independent Observations." *Econometrica*, 50: 483–499.

WU, D. M. (1973). "Alternative Tests of Independence between Stochastic Regressors and Disturbances." *Econometrica*, 41: 733–750.

ZELLNER, A. (1962). "An Efficient Method of Estimating Seemingly Unrelated Regressions and Tests for Aggregation Bias." *Journal of the American Statistical Association*, 57: 348–368.

ZELLNER, A. (1963). "Estimators for Seemingly Unrelated Regression Equations: Some Exact Finite Sample Results." *Journal of the American Statistical Association*, 58: 977–992.

ZELLNER, A., and D. S. HUANG (1962). "Further Properties of Efficient Estimators for Seemingly Unrelated Regression Equations." *International Economic Review*, 3: 300–313.

6

INTRODUCTION TO TIME-SERIES ANALYSIS AND DYNAMIC SPECIFICATION

6.1 INTRODUCTION

A time series is a sequence of observations of certain variables that are ordered in time. In principle, the measurement of many quantities, such as temperature, voltage, and seismic waves, can be made *continuously* and is sometimes recorded continuously in the form of a graph. In practice, however, the measurements are often made discretely in time; in other cases, such as the quarterly profit of a firm, the measurements are made at definite intervals of time. In this chapter we treat time series that are recorded *discretely in time*, that is, at regular intervals. Furthermore, we will be concerned primarily with statistical methods for analyzing a *univariate time series*, that is, one type of measurement made repeatedly on the same object or person. The focus will be on an understanding of the mechanism generating the series and the prediction of its future based on knowledge of its past.

The basic approach of time-series analysis is to investigate the past patterns of a variable and use that information to infer something about its future behavior.[1] For samples generated through controlled experiments, the observations in certain cases may be statistically independent. In time series, however, successive observations are typically *dependent*, where the dependence is related to the *positions* in the sequence. The feature of time-series analysis that distinguishes it from most of the statistical techniques discussed so far is the explicit recognition of the importance of the *order* in which the observations are made.

To facilitate the investigation of the time dependence of an actual observed series, y_t, for time period $t = 1, \ldots, n$, it is often convenient to postulate that y_t is a realization of some statistical or probabilistic model of the form

$$y_t = f(t) + u_t, \qquad t = 1, 2, \ldots, n, \qquad *(6.1.1)$$

[1]General references on time-series analysis include Anderson (1971), Box and Jenkins (1970), Granger and Newbold (1986), Hamilton (1994), and Harvey (1990), among others.

in which the observed sequence is made up of a completely determined sequence $\{f(t)\}$, which may be called the *systematic part*, and of a random part, given by a stochastic sequence $\{u_t\}$, which obeys a probability law. The interpretation of (6.1.1) is that if one can repeat the entire situation, obtaining a new set of observations y_t, the $f(t)$ would be the same as before, but the random terms u_t would be different, as new realizations occur according to the probability law governing their generation. In general, while y_t is observable, its two components $f(t)$ and u_t are not observable, as they are theoretical constructs. In fact, the decomposition of y_t into $f(t)$ and u_t illustrates two of the essential stages in model building: first, to determine the class of models that seem appropriate, and second, to estimate the parameter values of the model.

The possible sequences of y together with their laws of generation will be referred to collectively as the *process* $\{y_t\}$. When $u_t = 0$, $\{y_t\}$ is referred to as a *deterministic process*. The future values of y can then be determined from past values of y using the relation $f(\cdot)$. When $u_t \neq 0$, the model generating the time series is not deterministic but is described by a probability law. The process $\{y_t\}$ is generally called a *stochastic process*.

The early development of time-series analysis was based on models in which the effect of time was made in the systematic part but not in the random part. More specifically, it was assumed that $Eu_t = 0$, $\text{Var}(u_t) = \sigma^2$, $Eu_tu_s = 0$ if $t \neq s$, as in the basic linear regression model of Chapter 4. These specifications essentially force any effects of time to be made in the systematic part $f(t)$. If $f(t)$ is a known function of time or some other observable quantities, the regression techniques discussed in earlier chapters can be applied.

The effects of time, however, may be present both in the systematic part $f(t)$ (e.g., as a trend in time) and in the random part u_t. For example, an economic time series may consist of a long-run movement and seasonal variation, which together constitute $f(t)$, and an oscillatory component and other irregularities, which constitute u_t.

It has long been customary to distinguish time-series observations into different types of evolution that may have their effects combined in various ways. Most commonly, the economic times series are assumed to be composed of:

1. A *trend*: a slow movement in some specific direction, which is maintained over a long period of time
2. A *cycle*: a quasi-periodic movement, alternately increasing and decreasing
3. A *seasonal component*: regular weekly, monthly, quarterly, or other such variations arising from changing seasons and the rhythm of human behavior
4. A *random component*: representing influences of all kinds of events on the quantity in question, which may be considered as realizations from a stable probability law

Exactly what such a decomposition means depends not only on the data, but in part, on what is thought of as repetitions of the experiment giving rise to the data. To explain the phenomenon described by a series, or to predict future values of the observed quantity, it is generally worthwhile to consider each movement in isolation. Therefore, in most cases the discussion assumes that the component in question has been observed. Procedures to combine different components will be discussed only after the discussion of estimating the components.

It is useful to study time-series techniques because the data requirements for time-series models are usually less than that for econometric models. Time-series models are easy to construct and usually do not need prior information on the causal structures of the variables. They often can provide good short-run predictions and, in many cases, dominate the predictions generated by econometric models, in particular if the latter are hampered by shortages of degrees of freedom, severe multicollinearity, and so on (e.g., Cooper, 1972; Nelson, 1972). Moreover, time-series techniques can be used in conjunction with econometric methods to achieve a better model specification.

In this chapter we introduce some well-known time-series methods and then illustrate the relationships between time-series models and econometric methods. In Section 6.2 some basic tools are introduced. In Section 6.3 we review the basic property of a *stationary* process. The Box–Jenkins procedure to model stationary time series is discussed in Section 6.4. Nonstationary time series are discussed in Section 6.5. An example is given in Section 6.6. The theory of forecasting is discussed in Section 6.7. In Section 6.8 we discuss the transfer function models that lead to the autoregressive models and distributed lag models widely used in econometrics. Multiple time-series issues involving cointegration, causality detection, and dynamic simultaneous equations models are deferred until Chapter 11.

6.2 SOME BASIC TOOLS

6.2.1 The Lag Operator and Its Algebra

Before more sophisticated models are considered, the lag operator L (or backward operator) is introduced. The lag operator L, which is frequently used for notational convenience, is an operator on a time sequence with the property that shifts the observation made at time t to the observation at time $t-1$. Thus the operator L is said to be the *lag operator* if it defines the transformation

$$Ly_t = y_{t-1},$$

where

1. The kth power of the lag operator, L^k, means that the operator L is successively applied k times, that is,

$$L^k y_t = y_{t-k}.$$

2. The lag operator L satisfies the law of exponents

$$L^{k+s} = L^k L^s = L^s L^k.$$

3. $L^0 = 1$, so that $L^0 y_t = y_t$.
4. The lag operator is a linear operator, satisfying

$$cL = Lc,$$
$$(a+b)L = aL + bL,$$
$$(ab)L = a(bL),$$
$$L(c+v) = Lc + Lv.$$

5. If $T_1 = \sum_{j=0}^{n} c_{1j}L^j$ and $T_2 = \sum_{j=0}^{m} c_{2j}L^j$ are two polynomial operators of degrees n and m in L, where $m < n$, then

$$T_1 + T_2 = \sum_{j=0}^{m}(c_{1j} + c_{2j})L^j + \sum_{j=m+1}^{n} c_{1j}L^j,$$

$$aT_1 = \sum_{j=0}^{n} ac_{1j}L^j,$$

$$T_1 \cdot T_2 = \sum_{j=0}^{m}\sum_{i=0}^{n} c_{1i}c_{2j}L^iL^j = \sum_{r=0}^{m+n} c_r^* L^r,$$

where

$$c_r^* = \sum_{j=0}^{\min(r,m)} c_{1r-j}c_{2j} \text{ for } r = 0, 1, \ldots, m+n \quad \text{and} \quad c_{1n+j} = 0, c_{2m+j} = 0 \text{ for } j > 0.$$

Consider, for example, the *distributed lag model*

$$y_t = \sum_{j=0}^{\infty} w_j x_{t-j} + u_t.$$

Noting that $x_{t-j} = L^j x_t$, this model can be written in terms of the polynomial $W(L)$:

$$y_t = W(L)x_t + u_t, \qquad \text{where} \quad W(L) = \sum_{j=0}^{\infty} w_j L^j.$$

As another example, consider the special case in which $w_j = \alpha\lambda^j$, where $|\lambda| < 1$, known as the *Koyck distributed lag model*. Then

$$W(L) = \alpha \sum_{j=0}^{\infty} \lambda^j L^j$$

$$= \frac{\alpha}{1 - \lambda L},$$

using the geometric series result that[2]

$$(1 - \lambda L)^{-1} = 1 + \lambda L + \lambda^2 L^2 + \cdots.$$

6.2.2 Linear Difference Equations

A *pth-order linear homogeneous difference equation* is an iterative equation of the form

$$x_t = \sum_{j=1}^{p} a_j x_{t-j}, \qquad *(6.2.1)$$

which determines the sequence x_t from p starting values, the *boundary conditions*. The solution of (6.2.1) is of the polynomial form

$$x_t = \sum_{k=1}^{p} A_k G_k^t, \qquad (6.2.2)$$

where G_k^{-1}, $k = 1, \ldots, p$, are the roots of the associated *determinantal equation*

$$a(z) = 1 - a_1 z - a_2 z^2 - \cdots - a_p z^p = 0, \qquad *(6.2.3)$$

assuming no multiple roots and where the constants A_k are determined by the initial values (or boundary conditions). To see this, substituting (6.2.2) into (6.2.1), and rearranging the terms yields

[2] If $S = 1 + \lambda L + \lambda^2 L^2 + \cdots$, then $\lambda LS = \lambda L + \lambda^2 L^2 + \cdots$, so $(1 - \lambda L)S = 1$, implying that $S = (1 - \lambda L)^{-1}$.

$$A_1G_1^t\left[1-a_1G_1^{-1}-\cdots-a_pG_1^{-p}\right]+A_2G_2^t\left[1-a_1G_2^{-1}-\cdots-a_pG_2^{-p}\right]$$
$$+\cdots+A_pG_p^t\left[1-a_1G_p^{-1}-\cdots-a_pG_p^{-p}\right]=0. \tag{6.2.4}$$

So the solution is correct if G_k^{-1}, $k = 1, \ldots, p$, are the roots of the equation $a(z) = 0$, as in (6.2.3), with the constants $A_1, \ldots, A_p$ chosen so that the boundary conditions are satisfied.

If the roots G_k are real, the polynomial expression (6.2.2) must produce real values for the sequence x_t. Any complex value of G_k^{-1} must be matched by its complex conjugate. The pair of complex conjugates, $|G_k|e^{\pm i\theta_k}$ will have a contribution of the form $|G_k|^t \cos(\theta_k t + \phi_k)$. Thus the solution to (6.2.1) will either be a mixture of exponentials through time or a mixture of exponentials and cosine (or sine) waves.

For large t, the form of the solution (6.2.2) will be dominated by $A_i|G^*|^t$, where $|G^*| = \max(|G_k|, k = 1, \ldots, p)$. If $|G^*| < 1$ the solution is said to be *stationary*. If $|G^*| > 1$, the solution is said to be *explosive*. Therefore, a necessary and sufficient condition for the solution to be stationary is that all the roots of the equation $a(z) = 0$ in (6.2.3) are greater than 1 in absolute value (i.e., lie outside the unit circle $|z| = 1$), as the roots are the reciprocals G_k^{-1}. This is called the *stationarity condition*. If (6.2.3) satisfies this *stationarity condition*, x_t is a linear combination of the tth powers of the roots, all of which are less than 1 in absolute value, with (a) the contribution of a positive root being a decreasing exponential function, (b) the contribution of a negative root being an exponential function alternating in sign and decreasing in absolute value, and (c) the contribution of a pair of complex conjugate roots being an oscillating trigonometric function, decreasing in absolute value, whose period of oscillation depends on the argument of the complex roots.

On many occasions a pth-order linear difference equation of order p takes the *nonhomogeneous* form

$$x_t = \sum_{j=1}^{p} a_j x_{t-j} + y_t. \tag{6.2.5}$$

The general solution of (6.2.5) is the sum of the solution to the pth-order linear homogeneous difference equation (6.2.1) (without y_t) and the particular solution

$$x_t^* = a(L)^{-1} y_t, \tag{6.2.6}$$

where $a(L) = 1 - \sum_{j=1}^{P} a_j L_j$.

6.3 STATIONARY PROCESSES

6.3.1 Definitions

A *stationary process* is the one with a distribution that remains the same as time progresses (i.e., it is a process for which the probability structure does not change with time). A stochastic process is said to be *stationary in the strict sense* if

$$P\{y_{t_1} \le b_1, \ldots, y_{t_n} \le b_n\} = P\{y_{t_1+m} \le b_1, \ldots, y_{t_n+m} \le b_n\}, \tag{6.3.1}$$

that is, the probability measure for the sequence $\{y_t\}$ is the same as that for $\{y_{t+m}\}$ for every integer m, so that the probability that y_t falls in a particular interval is the same as it was or as it will ever be.

If the first-order moment exists, stationarity implies that it is a constant mean value:

$$Ey_t = Ey_{t+m} = \mu, \qquad t, m = \ldots, -1, 0, 1, \ldots. \tag{6.3.2}$$

Since (y_{t_1}, y_{t_2}) has the same distribution as (y_{t_1+m}, y_{t_2+m}), the existence of the second-order moments and stationarity imply that

$$\gamma(t_1, t_2) = E(y_{t_1} - \mu)(y_{t_2} - \mu) = \gamma(t_1 + m, t_2 + m) = \gamma(t_2 - t_1) = \gamma_{t_2 - t_1}. \tag{6.3.3}$$

In other words, the covariance between y_{t_1} and y_{t_2} depends only on the difference in time $|t_2 - t_1|$ and is denoted by $\gamma(t_2 - t_1)$or $\gamma_{(t_2-t_1)}$.

If a process satisfies (6.3.2) and (6.3.3), it is called *weakly stationary* or *stationary in the wide sense*.

If the joint distribution of $(y_1, \ldots, y_t)$ is normal, the distribution is characterized by the means Ey_t, the variances, $E(y_t - Ey_t)^2$, and the covariances $E(y_t - Ey_t)(y_s - Ey_s)$. If the joint distributions of $\{y_t\}$ are not normal, these first- and second-order moments, nevertheless, give relevant and important information about the process. For example, the correlation between y_t and y_{t+s} is a measure of linear association between the two random variables.

If the process is stationary, all variances are the same and all covariances depend only on the difference between the two indices involved as in (6.3.3). These moments

$$E[y_t - Ey_t][y_{t+s} - Ey_{t+s}] = \gamma_s, \qquad s = \ldots, -1, 0, 1, \ldots \tag{6.3.4}$$

constitute the *covariance function*. The covariances γ_s will be called *autocovariances*. Because the autocovariances are dependent on the underlying units of measurement of the y process, it is sometimes more convenient to consider the normalized quantities

$$\tau_s = \frac{\gamma_s}{\gamma_0}, \qquad s = \ldots, -1, 0, 1, \ldots, \tag{6.3.5}$$

which will be called the *autocorrelations* of the process. The autocorrelations are expressed as pure numbers, and they are independent of the units of measurement of the underlying process. The sequence τ_s for $s = \ldots, -1, 0, 1, 2, \ldots$ indicates the extent to which one value of the process is correlated with previous values. If the process is stationary, then from the definition (6.3.5),

$$\tau_0 = 1, \qquad \tau_{-s} = \tau_s. \tag{6.3.6}$$

The plot of τ_s against s for $s = 0, 1, 2, \ldots$ is called the *theoretical correlogram*, and the values comprising this diagram are the major quantities used to characterize the (linear) properties of the generating mechanism of the process.

A compact way of summarizing the information held in some sequence is to use a *generating function*. For instance, for the sequence $\lambda_0, \lambda_1, \lambda_2, \ldots, \lambda_j, \ldots$, which may be of infinite length, the generating function is defined as the polynomial function:

$$\lambda(z) = \sum_j \lambda_j z^j. \tag{6.3.7}$$

Each of the λ_j's can be retrieved from $\lambda(z)$ by taking the relevant order partial derivative and evaluating it at $z = 0$. The function $\lambda(z)$ often can be manipulated in simpler ways than the entire sequence. The quantity z does not necessarily have any interpretation and should be considered as simply the carrier of the information in the sequence. As an example, if $\lambda_j = (b^j/j!)\exp(-b)$, then (through the Maclaurin series) $\lambda(z) = \exp[b(z-1)]$ and $\lambda_j = (j!)^{-1}\frac{\partial^j \lambda(z)}{\partial z^j}\Big|_{z=0}$.

For a sequence of autocovariances λ_s, the *autocovariance generating function* is defined as

$$\gamma(z) = \sum_{s=-\infty}^{\infty} \gamma_s z^s, \tag{6.3.8}$$

and the corresponding autocorrelation generating function is

$$\tau(z) = \sum_{-\infty}^{\infty} \tau_s z^s = \frac{\gamma(z)}{\gamma_0}. \tag{6.3.9}$$

Typically, a stationary process can be written as

$$y_t^* = y_t - Ey_t = \sum_{s=0}^{\infty} \psi_s \varepsilon_s, \tag{6.3.10}$$

where $E\varepsilon_s = 0$, $E\varepsilon_s^2 = \sigma_\varepsilon^2$, $E\varepsilon_s\varepsilon_t = 0$, $s \neq t$, and $\sum_{s=0}^{\infty} \psi_s^2 < \infty$ with $\psi_0 = 1$. The convergence of $\sum_{s=0}^{\infty} \psi_s^2$ ensures that the process has a finite variance. This is the so-called *Wold decomposition theorem.*[3] The theorem suggests that the true generating mechanism of a process can be approximated adequately by a linear stochastic process plus some type of deterministic process. However, since an objective of time-series analysis is to develop models that can "explain" the movement of a time series y_t, the representation of the general linear process by (6.3.10) would not be very useful in practice if it contains an infinite number of parameters ψ_s. Therefore, in this section we introduce some simple and important finite parameter models that are representationally useful for analysis and generating prediction.

6.3.2 White Noise Process

A series is *white noise* if it has virtually no discernible structure or pattern to it. If such a series is denoted by y_t, the formal definition is that $\{y_t\}$ be a sequence of independently and identically distributed random variables with

$$Ey_t = \mu, \qquad \text{Var}(y_t) = \sigma^2. \tag{6.3.11}$$

Then

$$\gamma(t-s) = \begin{cases} \sigma^2 & \text{if } t = s, \\ 0 & \text{if } t \neq s, \end{cases} \tag{6.3.12}$$

and the covariance generating function is of the form

$$\gamma(z) = \sigma^2. \tag{6.3.13}$$

This process is stationary in the strict sense. Dropping the requirement that y_t is identically distributed, the resulting distribution is still stationary in the wide sense.

[3] See Wold (1954). An alternative version of Wold's theorem is that any stationary series can be considered to be the sum of the two parts, a self-deterministic component and a moving average of possibly infinite order. However, it is the general view that virtually all series arising in business and economics do not contain a self-deterministic component, except possibly a seasonal component.

6.3.3 Moving Average Process

If $\ldots, \varepsilon_{-1}, \varepsilon_0, \varepsilon_1, \ldots$ is a sequence of independently and identically distributed (i.i.d.) random variables with $E\varepsilon_t = 0$ and $\text{Var}(\varepsilon_t) = \sigma_\varepsilon^2$, and $\theta_0, \theta_1, \ldots, \theta_q$ are $q + 1$ numbers, then

$$\begin{aligned} y_t &= \mu + \theta_0 \varepsilon_t + \theta_1 \varepsilon_{t-1} + \cdots + \theta_q \varepsilon_{t-q} \\ &= \mu + \theta(L)\varepsilon_t \end{aligned} \tag{6.3.14}$$

$$\theta(L) = \theta_0 + \theta_1 L + \cdots + \theta_q L^q \tag{6.3.15}$$

(where θ_0 is often normalized to be equal to 1) is called a *qth-order moving average process*, written MA(q). The MA(q) process has the property that

$$Ey_t = \mu \tag{6.3.16}$$

and

$$\gamma_s = \gamma_{-s} = \begin{cases} \text{Cov}(y_t, y_{t+s}) = \sigma_\varepsilon^2(\theta_0\theta_{|s|} + \theta_1\theta_{|s|+1} + \cdots + \theta_{q-|s|}\theta_q) \\ = \sigma_\varepsilon^2 \sum_{j=0}^{q-|s|} \theta_j \theta_{j+|s|} \qquad |s| \le q, \\ = 0, \qquad |s| > q. \end{cases} \tag{6.3.17}$$

Therefore, $\{y_t\}$ is stationary in the wide sense. Depending on the values of θ_j's, a qth-order moving average series can be smoother than white noise series or it can be less smooth. For instance, in the case of y_t being a MA(1), y_t is smoother than the white noise series if $\theta_1 > 0$ and less smooth if $\theta_1 < 0$.

Noting that

$$\begin{aligned} \theta(L)\theta(L^{-1}) &= \sum_{j,k=0}^{q} \theta_j\theta_k L^{j-k} \\ &= \sum_{s=-q}^{q} L^s \sum_{j=0}^{q-|s|} \theta_j\theta_{j+|s|}, \end{aligned} \tag{6.3.18}$$

by putting $j - k = s$ and taking $\theta_j = 0$ for $j > q$, the autocovariance generating function of the MA process can be written

$$\gamma(z) = \sigma_\varepsilon^2 \theta(z)\theta(z^{-1}). \tag{6.3.19}$$

6.3.4 Autoregressive Process

Let $a(L) = (1 + a_1 L + \cdots + a_p L^p)$ and ε_t be i.i.d. with mean zero; a *pth-order autoregressive process*, written AR(p), is the one generated by

$$a(L)y_t = \varepsilon_t; \tag{6.3.20}$$

that is,

$$y_t + a_1 y_{t-1} + \cdots + a_p y_{t-p} = \varepsilon_t.$$

An AR(p) model is an alternative way to a MA(q) model of producing a series with more structure than white noise. For y_t to be stationary, the solution of the *associated polynomial equation* (or *characteristic equation*)

$$a(z) = \sum_{r=0}^{p} a_r z^r = 0 \tag{6.3.21}$$

must have roots greater than 1 in absolute value, where $a_0 = 1$. This is called the *stability* or *stationarity* condition of an AR process.

Before discussing the general case, consider the first-order AR process

$$y_t = \rho y_{t-1} + \varepsilon_t, \tag{6.3.22}$$

where $\rho = -a_1$. Replacing y_{t-1} in (6.3.22) by the right-hand side of (6.3.22) with t replaced by $t-1$ (i.e., $y_{t-1} = \rho y_{t-2} + \varepsilon_{t-1}$), yields

$$y_t = \varepsilon_t + \rho\varepsilon_{t-1} + \rho^2 y_{t-2}. \tag{6.3.23}$$

Successive substitution yields

$$y_t = \varepsilon_t + \rho\varepsilon_{t-1} + \rho^2\varepsilon_{t-2} + \cdots + \rho^s\varepsilon_{t-s} + \rho^{s+1}y_{t-(s+1)} \tag{6.3.24}$$

or

$$y_t - (\varepsilon_t + \rho\varepsilon_{t-1} + \cdots + \rho^s\varepsilon_{t-s}) = \rho^{s+1}y_{t-(s+1)}. \tag{6.3.25}$$

Thus if $\{y_t\}$ is a stationary process, the difference between y_t and the linear combination of the $s+1$ ε_r's is $\rho^{s+1}y_{t-(s+1)}$ and this becomes small when s increases if $|\rho| < 1$. In particular, if second-order moments exist,

$$E[y_t - (\varepsilon_t + \rho\varepsilon_{t-1} + \cdots + \rho^s\varepsilon_{t-s})]^2 = \rho^{2(s+1)}Ey_{t-(s+1)}^2, \tag{6.3.26}$$

which does not depend on t because of the assumed stationarity. As s increases, (6.3.26) goes to zero. Then writing

$$y_t = \sum_{r=0}^{\infty} \rho^r \varepsilon_{t-r}, \tag{6.3.27}$$

the series on the right *converges in the mean* (or in *the mean square* or in *quadratic mean*) to y_t. Thus the condition for the AR(1) process to be stationary is that $|\rho| < 1$, which is equivalent to the solution of the associated polynomial equation, $1 + a_1 z = 0$, being greater than 1 in absolute value.

Consider now the general case. AR(p) in (6.3.20) can be written

$$y_t = \varepsilon_t - a_1 y_{t-1} - \cdots - a_p y_{t-p}. \tag{6.3.28}$$

Substituting the relation y_{t-1} into (6.3.28), it follows that

$$y_t = \varepsilon_t - a_1\varepsilon_{t-1} - (a_2 - a_1^2)y_{t-2} - \cdots + a_1 a_p y_{t-1-p}, \tag{6.3.29}$$

and using this procedure s times yields

$$y_t = a(L)^{-1}\varepsilon_t, \tag{6.3.30}$$

where

$$a(L)^{-1} = \sum_{r=0}^{\infty} \delta_r L^r. \tag{6.3.31}$$

That is, the δ_r's are the coefficients in the infinite-order MA process

$$\left(\sum_{r=0}^{p} a_r z^r\right)^{-1} = \sum_{r=0}^{\infty} \delta_r z^r, \tag{6.3.32}$$

and they can be determined by formal long division as

$$
\begin{aligned}
&\frac{1}{1+a_1 z+\cdots+a_p z^p}\\
&=1-\frac{a_1 z+\cdots+a_p z^p}{1+a_1 z+\cdots+a_p z^p}\\
&=1-a_1 z-\frac{(a_2-a_1^2)z^2+\cdots+(a_p-a_1 a_{p-1})z^p-a_1 a_p z^{p+1}}{1+a_1 z+\cdots+a_p z^p}\\
&=1+\delta_1 z+\cdots+\delta_s z^s+\frac{\alpha_{s1} z^{s+1}+\cdots+\alpha_{sp} z^{s+p}}{1+a_1 z+\cdots+a_p z^p}\\
&=1+\delta_1 z+\cdots+\delta_s z^s+\alpha_{s1} z^{s+1}\\
&\qquad+\frac{(\alpha_{s2}-\alpha_{s1}\alpha_1)z^{s+2}+\cdots+(\alpha_{sp}-\alpha_{s1}a_{p-1})z^{s+p}-\alpha_{s1}a_p z^{s+p+1}}{1+a_1 z+\cdots+a_p z^p},
\end{aligned}
\tag{6.3.33}
$$

where

$$
\begin{aligned}
\delta_{s+1}&=\alpha_{s1},\\
\alpha_{s+1,j}&=\alpha_{s,j+1}-\alpha_{s1}a_j, \qquad j=1,\ldots,p-1,\\
\alpha_{s+1,p}&=-\alpha_{s1}a_p.
\end{aligned}
\tag{6.3.34}
$$

For y_t to be stationary, it must converge in the mean to

$$y_t=\sum_{j=0}^{\infty}\delta_j \varepsilon_{t-j}, \tag{6.3.35}$$

where $\sum_{j=0}^{\infty}\delta_j^2<\infty$ (because y_t is expected to have a finite variance). If the p roots of the associated polynomial equation (6.3.21), denoted by $z_1,\ldots,z_p$, are greater than 1 in absolute value, then for any z such that $|z|<\min|z_i|$, the series

$$\frac{1}{\sum_{r=0}^{p}a_r z^r}=\frac{1}{\prod_{i=1}^{p}(1-z/z_i)}=\prod_{i=1}^{p}\sum_{v=0}^{\infty}\left(\frac{z}{z_i}\right)^v=\sum_{r=0}^{\infty}\delta_r z^r \tag{6.3.36}$$

converges absolutely. Hence, from (6.3.33),

$$\frac{\alpha_{s1}z+\cdots+\alpha_{sp}z^p}{1+a_1 z+\cdots+a_p z^p} \tag{6.3.37}$$

converges to zero for $|z|<\min|z_i|$ (in particular, for $|z|=1$). This implies that $\alpha_{si}\to 0$ (as $s\to\infty$) for each i. Thus

$$E\left(y_t-\sum_{j=0}^{s}\delta_j\varepsilon_{t-j}\right)^2=E(\alpha_{s1}y_{t-s-1}+\cdots+\alpha_{sp}y_{t-s-p})^2 \tag{6.3.38}$$

converges to zero. Then (6.3.35) follows in the sense of convergence in mean. In other words, if all the roots of the polynomial equation (6.3.21) associated with the stochastic difference equation (6.3.20) are greater than 1 in absolute value, y_t can be written as an infinite linear combination of $\varepsilon_t, \varepsilon_{t-1}, \ldots$. Thus $\{y_t\}$ is stationary in the strict sense. (If the ε_t's are uncorrelated and have common mean and variance, the process is stationary in the wide sense.) Furthermore, because $\varepsilon_t, \varepsilon_{t-1}, \ldots$ are independent of $\varepsilon_{t+1}, \varepsilon_{t+2}, \ldots$, y_t is independent of $\varepsilon_{t+1}, \varepsilon_{t+2}, \ldots$.

When all the roots of (6.3.21) are greater than 1 in absolute value, y_t can be written as (6.3.30). From (6.3.19), the autocovariance generating function for a stationary AR process is equal to

$$\gamma(z) = \frac{\sigma_\varepsilon^2}{a(z)a(z^{-1})}. \tag{6.3.39}$$

More specifically, the autocovariances or autocorrelations of an AR(p) process satisfy the *Yule–Walker equations*

$$\gamma_k + a_1\gamma_{k-1} + \cdots + a_p\gamma_{k-p} = 0, \qquad k > 0. \tag{6.3.40}$$

Equation (6.3.40) is obtained by multiplying (6.3.20) by y_{t-k} and taking expected values of the resultant equation, noting that $E(\varepsilon_t y_{t-k}) = 0$.

As shown in Section 6.2.2, the solution to (6.3.40) is of the form

$$\gamma_k = A_1G_1^k + A_2G_2^k + \cdots + A_pG_p^k, \tag{6.3.41}$$

where G_i^{-1} are the roots of the associated polynomial equation $a(z) = 0$, as in (6.3.21). For stationarity, it is necessary that $|G_i| < 1$. Therefore, as discussed at the end of Section 6.2, the autocovariance or autocorrelation function of a stationary autoregressive process, in general, will consist of a mixture of damped exponentials and damped sine waves.

6.3.5 Autoregressive Moving Average Process

The two previous models are frequently combined to obtain a mixed *autoregressive moving average model of order p and q*, written ARMA(p,q):

$$a(L)y_t = \theta(L)\varepsilon_t, \tag*{*(6.3.42)}$$

$$a(L) = a_0 + a_1L + \cdots + a_pL^p, \tag*{*(6.3.43)}$$

$$\theta(L) = \theta_0 + \theta_1L + \cdots + \theta_qL^q, \tag*{*(6.3.44)}$$

$$a_0 = \theta_0 = 1, \quad E\varepsilon_t^2 = \sigma_\varepsilon^2 \quad \text{and} \quad E\varepsilon_t\varepsilon_s = 0, \quad t \neq s.$$

If the associated polynomial

$$a(z) = \sum_{j=0}^{p} a_jz^j = 0 \tag{6.3.45}$$

has roots greater than 1 in absolute value, (6.3.42) can be divided by $a(L)^{-1}$ to obtain

$$y_t = a(L)^{-1}\theta(L)\varepsilon_t$$
$$= \sum_{j=0}^{\infty} \psi_j\varepsilon_{t-j}. \tag{6.3.46}$$

From the results of Section 6.3.4, it follows that $\sum_{j=0}^{\infty}\psi_j^2 < \infty$ and the process is stationary.

Equation (6.3.32) has shown that a finite-order AR process can be represented as an infinite-order MA process. Similarly, if (6.3.14) or (6.3.42) is divided by the moving average operator $\theta(L)$, the process can be expressed as an infinite-order AR:

$$y_t = \phi_1y_{t-1} + \phi_2y_{t-2} + \cdots + \varepsilon_t. \tag{6.3.47}$$

If the roots of $\theta(z) = 0$ are less than 1 in absolute value, the weights ϕ_j diverge in the expansion (6.3.47). Then, at time t, current y_t depends on $y_{t-1}, y_{t-2}, \ldots, y_{t-j}, \ldots$ with weights that increase as j increases. Typically, this situation is avoided by requiring that the weights ϕ_j form a convergent series. This requires that the roots of $\theta(z) = 0$ be greater than 1 in absolute value, called the *invertibility condition*. However, the invertibility condition is not required for the process to be stationary.

Rewriting the process as MA(∞),

$$y_t = \frac{\theta(L)}{a(L)}\varepsilon_t, \tag{6.3.48}$$

the autocovariance generating function of an ARMA(p,q) process can be written

$$\gamma(z) = \sigma_\varepsilon^2 \frac{\theta(z)\theta(z^{-1})}{a(z)a(z^{-1})}. \tag{6.3.49}$$

The exact pattern of the autocovariance of an ARMA(p,q) process can also be derived by multiplying (6.3.42) by y_{t-k} and taking expectations

$$\gamma_k = -a_1\gamma_{k-1} - \cdots - a_p\gamma_{k-p} + \gamma_{y\varepsilon,k} + \theta_1\gamma_{y\varepsilon,k-1} + \cdots + \theta_q\gamma_{y\varepsilon,k-q} \tag{6.3.50}$$

where $\gamma_{y\varepsilon,k} = E(\varepsilon_t y_{t-k})$. Since y_{t-k} depends only on the ε that have occurred up to time $t-k$, it follows that $\gamma_{y\varepsilon,k} = 0,\ k > 0$ and $\gamma_{y\varepsilon,k} \neq 0,\ k \leq 0$. Therefore,

$$\gamma_k = -a_1\gamma_{k-1} - \cdots - a_p\gamma_{k-p}, \qquad k \geq q+1, \tag{6.3.51}$$

and hence

$$\tau_k = -a_1\tau_{k-1} - \cdots - a_p\tau_{k-p}, \qquad k \geq q+1, \tag{6.3.52}$$

or $a(L)\tau_k = 0$, $k \geq q + 1$. In other words, for the ARMA(p,q) process, there will be q autocorrelations $\tau_q, \tau_{q-1}, \ldots, \tau_1$ whose values depend directly, through (6.3.49), on the q moving average parameters, θ_j's, as well as on the p autoregressive parameters, a_j's. Also, the p values $\tau_q, \tau_{q-1}, \ldots, \tau_{q-p+1}$ provide the necessary starting values for the difference equation $a(L)\tau_k = 0$, where $k \geq q + 1$, which then entirely determines the autocorrelations at higher lags. If $q - p < 0$, the entire autocorrelation function τ_j for $j = 0, 1, 2, \ldots$ will consist of a mixture of damped exponentials and/or damped sine waves whose nature is given by the polynomial $a(L)$ and the starting values. If, however, $q - p \geq 0$, there will be $q - p + 1$ initial values $\tau_0, \tau_1, \ldots, \tau_{q-p}$ that do not follow this general pattern.

6.4 BOX–JENKINS PROCEDURE FOR BUILDING LINEAR (STATIONARY) TIME-SERIES MODELS

6.4.1 Model-Building Philosophy

Consider a sequence of stationary time-series observations $y_1, y_2, \ldots, y_t, \ldots$. The objective is to derive a stochastic model that could have generated the series and to use this model to generate forecasts of future values of the series. The Box–Jenkins (1970) procedure for building a linear time-series model is based on the principle of *parsimony*, that is, employing the *smallest possible* number of parameters for a model that adequately mimics the properties of the sample (e.g., autocorrelations). A parsimonious model has several advantages. First, it improves the accuracy of parameter estimates. As discussed before, the variance of an estimator is usually proportional to the inverse of the degrees of freedom, where the degrees of freedom is defined as the size of the sample observations minus the number of parameters. A more accurately estimated model in general will allow for more reliable inference and yield more accurate forecasts. Second, a parsimonious model can avoid the issue of *model multiplicity* (or *common factor*) when appropriate stationarity and invertibility conditions are imposed. In Section 6.3 it has been shown that a given ARMA model has a unique covariance structure. The converse is not true, however. To see this, consider an ARMA model

$$a(L)y_t = \theta(L)\varepsilon_t, \tag{6.4.1}$$

where

$$a(L) = 1 + a_1 L + \cdots + a_p L^p \tag{6.4.2}$$

and

$$\theta(L) = 1 + \theta_1 L + \cdots + \theta_q L^q, \tag{6.4.3}$$

where it is assumed that $a(z) = 0$ and $\theta(z) = 0$ have no roots in common. The autocovariance generating function of (6.4.1) is then of the form

$$\gamma(z) = \sigma_\varepsilon^2 \psi(z)\psi(z^{-1}), \tag{6.4.4}$$

where

$$\psi(z) = a(z)^{-1}\theta(z). \tag{6.4.5}$$

Multiplying both sides of (6.4.1) by any common factor, say $(1 - \delta_1 L)$, the resulting model will have the same autocovariance structure (6.4.4) as the original model. In other words, if the parsimony principle is not imposed, there can be infinitely many different models yielding the same autocovariance structure. Furthermore, when there are common roots in $a(z) = 0$ and $\theta(z) = 0$, the estimation methods usually fail to converge.

The Box–Jenkins strategy is not based on any optimality criterion. Rather, it is a practical one. The procedure consists of a three-step iterative cycle of (1) model identification, (2) model estimation, and (3) diagnostic checks on model adequacy. The central idea of this strategy is to fit an ARMA model to a given (stationary) time series. At the identification stage, a particular model or a few models are chosen from the class of ARMA models (6.4.1); that is, values are selected for p and q, using statistics that can readily be calculated from the data. However, there is no irrevocable commitment to the model chosen, nor is there a constraint to choose only one model. In fact, a subclass of models may be considered.

At the estimation stage of the model building cycle, the tentatively entertained model is fitted to the data, and its parameters are estimated using efficient statistical techniques. Then diagnostic checks are applied to determine whether or not the chosen model adequately represents the given set of data. If no inadequacy is indicated, the model is ready to use. If any inadequacy is found, the iterative cycle of identification, estimation, and diagnostic checking is repeated until a suitable representation is found.

6.4.2 Identification

The term *identification* as used by Box and Jenkins (1970) is different from its common usage in econometrics (see Chapter 9). Identification here means a rough procedure applied to a set of data to indicate the kind of representational model that is worthy of further investigation. In this stage, graphical methods are particularly useful and judgment must be exercised. The principal tools are the autocorrelation and the partial autocorrelation functions.

The autocorrelation function indicates the degree of comovements between time-series observations. Table 6.1 summarizes the properties of the autocorrelation functions for the AR(p), MA(q), and ARMA(p,q) processes.

TABLE 6.1 Properties of Stationary AR, MA, and ARMA Processes

	AR(p) $a(L)y_t = \varepsilon_t$	MA(q) $y_t = \theta(L)\varepsilon_t$	ARMA(p,q) $a(L)y_t = \theta(L)\varepsilon_t$
Stationarity condition	Roots of $a(z) = 0$ greater than 1 in absolute value	Always stationary	Roots of $a(z) = 0$ greater than 1 in absolute value
Invertibility condition	Stationary AR always invertible	Roots of $\theta(z) = 0$ greater than 1 in absolute value	Roots of $\theta(z) = 0$ greater than 1 in absolute value
Autocorrelation function	Infinite (damped exponentials and/or damped sine waves)	Finite	Infinite (damped exponentials and/or damped sine waves after first $q - p$ lags)
	Tails off	Cuts off (at q)	Tails off
Partial autocorrelation function	Finite	Infinite (dominated by damped exponentials and/or sine waves)	Infinite (dominated by damped exponentials and/or sine waves after first $p - q$ lags)
	Cuts off (at p)	Tails off	Tails off

The partial autocorrelation function is a device which exploits the fact that whereas an AR(p) process has an autocorrelation function which is infinite in extent, it can by its very nature be described in terms of p nonzero functions of the autocorrelations. Denote by a_{kj} the jth coefficient in an autoregressive process of order k, so that a_{kk} is the last coefficient. From (6.3.40), a_{kj} satisfies the set of equations

$$\tau_j = -a_{k1}\tau_{j-1} - \cdots - a_{k(k-1)}\tau_{j-k+1} - a_{kk}\tau_{j-k}, \qquad j = 1, 2, \ldots . \tag{6.4.6}$$

The coefficient a_{kj}, regarded as function of the lag k, is called the *partial autocorrelation function.*

It follows from (6.3.40) that for an autoregressive process of order p, the partial autocorrelations will be nonzero for orders less than or equal to p and zero for order greater than p. For an invertible MA or ARMA process, as the inversion of $\theta(L)$ in (6.3.47) demonstrates, the partial autocorrelation is of infinite order and its pattern is determined by the roots of $\theta(z) = 0$.

The properties of autocorrelation and partial autocorrelation functions are summarized in Table 6.1.

These theoretical characteristics can be employed to help identify an appropriate model. However, the theoretical autocorrelation and partial autocorrelations are unknown, and they must be estimated from the given time-series realizations. A number of estimates of the autocorrelation and partial autocorrelation functions have been suggested by statisticians. One way to estimate the kth lag autocorrelation τ_k is to let

$$r_k = \frac{c_k}{c_0}, \tag{6.4.7}$$

where

$$c_k = \frac{1}{n}\sum_{t=1}^{n-k}(y_t - \bar{y})(y_{t+k} - \bar{y}), \qquad k = 0, 1, 2, \ldots, p \tag{6.4.8}$$

is the estimate of the autocovariance γ_k and $\bar{y}$ is the mean of the time series. The partial autocorrelations may be estimated by fitting successively autoregressive processes of orders

1, 2, 3, . . . , using least squares and using the estimates $\hat{a}_{11}$, $\hat{a}_{22}$, $\hat{a}_{33}$, . . . of the last coefficient fitted at each stage.

Since the estimated values will differ somewhat from their theoretical counterparts, it is important to have some indication of how far an estimated value may differ from the corresponding theoretical value. In particular, it is necessary to establish some means for judging whether the autocorrelations and partial autocorrelations are effectively zero after a specific lag q. For this purpose, for *larger lags*, Box and Jenkins (1970) suggest computing the variance of estimated autocorrelations τ_k from the simplified form of Bartlett's formula, in Bartlett (1946),

$$\mathrm{Var}(r_k) \simeq n^{-1}\{1 + 2(\tau_1^2 + \cdots + \tau_q^2)\} \qquad \text{for } k > q, \tag{6.4.9}$$

with sample estimates r_j replacing theoretical autocorrelations τ_j. Davies and Newbold (1980) show that a slightly better approximation is obtained if n is replaced by $\dfrac{n(n+2)}{n-k}$. For the partial autocorrelations, Box and Jenkins (1970) use the result that under the hypothesis that the process is autoregressive of order p, the variance for partial autocorrelations of order $p + 1$ and higher is

$$\mathrm{Var}(\hat{a}_{kk}) \simeq \frac{1}{n}, \qquad k > p. \tag{6.4.10}$$

Thus, for moderately large samples, plus or minus two standard deviations about zero can be used to provide a guide in assessing whether the theoretical autocorrelations and partial autocorrelations are in fact zero.

The estimated autocorrelations can have rather large variances, and they can be highly autocorrelated with each other. For this reason, detailed adherence to the theoretical autocorrelation function cannot be expected in the estimated function. In particular, moderately large estimated autocorrelations can occur after the theoretical autocorrelation function has damped out, and apparent ripples and trends can occur in the estimated function which have no basis in the theoretical function. In employing the estimated autocorrelation function as a tool for identification, it is usually possible to be fairly sure about broad characteristics, but more subtle indications may or may not represent real effects, and two or more related models may need to be entertained and investigated further at the estimation and diagnostic checking stages of model building.

6.4.3 Estimation

Estimation of time-series models can be carried out by the maximum likelihood method. For an AR(p) process, y_t conditional on $y_{t-1}, \ldots, y_{t-p}$ has the form of a linear regression model,

$$y_t = -a_1 y_{t-1} - \cdots - a_p y_{t-p} + \varepsilon_t. \tag{6.4.11}$$

Then the joint likelihood function of $y_1, \ldots, y_n$ can be written

$$\begin{aligned} f(y_1, \ldots, y_n) &= f(y_{p+1}, \ldots, y_n | y_1, \ldots, y_p) f(y_1, \ldots, y_p) \\ &= \prod_{t=p+1}^{n} f(y_t | y_{t-1}, \ldots, y_{t-p}) f(y_1, \ldots, y_p). \end{aligned} \tag{6.4.12}$$

Since $\varepsilon_{p+1}, \ldots, \varepsilon_n$ are independent of $y_1, \ldots, y_p$, the conditional probability density of $\varepsilon_{p+1}, \ldots, \varepsilon_n$, given $y_1, \ldots, y_p$, is the same as the unconditional probability density. Because the joint distribution of the ε's determines the joint distribution of y's (which are observed), if the ε_t's are normally distributed, the MLE of the a_r's conditional on $y_1, \ldots, y_p$ is identical to the least squares estimator. If n is large, there is little difference between $f(y_1, \ldots, y_n)$ and $f(y_{p+1}, \ldots, y_n \mid y_1, \ldots, y_p)$ and hence between the MLE and LS estimator. If n is finite, the MLE is to find the $\hat{a}_r$'s to maximize (6.4.12), which involves the marginal distribution of $y_1, \ldots, y_p$. Since $f(y_1, \ldots, y_p)$ is nonlinear in a_r's, the MLE will be nonlinear.

For the moving average and the ARMA processes, the likelihood function involves the inverse of the covariance matrix of the y's. Unfortunately, although the covariance matrix has a reasonably simple form, the inverse matrix is not simple. The maximum likelihood equations are complicated to solve and nonlinear techniques must be used.

The complication of the MLE arises because, in general, the determinant and the inverse of the covariance matrix of a time-correlated variable are not simple forms of the parameters. To avoid computing the inverse and the determinant of the covariance matrix of y_t conditioning on $y_{t-1}, \ldots, y_{t-p}$, it is noted by Box and Jenkins that when ε_t is assumed to be independently normally distributed, the exponent of the likelihood function is proportional to $-\sum_{t=1}^{n} \varepsilon_t^2$. Therefore, they suggest approximating the MLE by minimizing the sum of squares $\sum_{t=1}^{n} \varepsilon_t^2$.

For an ARMA(p,q) model,

$$\varepsilon_t = y_t + a_1 y_{t-1} + \cdots + a_p y_{t-p} - \theta_1 \varepsilon_{t-1} - \cdots - \theta_q \varepsilon_{t-q}. \qquad *(6.4.13)$$

Given the a's, θ's $y_t, \ldots, y_{t-p}$, and $\varepsilon_{t-1}, \ldots, \varepsilon_{t-q}$, ε_t can be calculated from (6.4.13). The recursive relation can be initiated given initial estimates of the a's and θ's and substituting the unavailable y's and ε's by their unconditional expectations, $E\varepsilon = 0$, and $Ey = 0$ if the model contains no deterministic part. However, this approximation can be poor if some of the roots of $a(z) = 0$ are close to the boundary of the unit circle. In this case, the initial predicted values $\varepsilon_1, \varepsilon_2, \ldots$ could deviate considerably from their true values, and the introduction of starting values of this sort could introduce a large transient, which would be slow to die out. To reduce the impact of the transient, Box and Jenkins suggest replacing the unconditional expectations by their predicted values.

To obtain predicted values of the unobserved y's and ε's, they note that (6.4.1) may also be written in the form

$$\prod_{i=1}^{p}(1 - G_i L) y_t = \prod_{j=1}^{q}(1 - H_j L)\varepsilon_t, \qquad (6.4.14)$$

where the G_i^{-1} and H_j^{-1} are the roots of $a(z) = 0$ and $\theta(z) = 0$, respectively. Using (6.4.14), the covariance generating function for y is

$$\gamma(L) = \sigma_\varepsilon^2 \prod_{i=1}^{p}(1 - G_i L)^{-1}(1 - G_i L^{-1})^{-1} \prod_{j=1}^{q}(1 - H_j L)(1 - H_j L^{-1}). \qquad (6.4.15)$$

Because of the form of this expression, the covariance generating function $\gamma(L)$ remains unchanged if in (6.4.14) the term $(1 - G_i L)$ is replaced by $(1 - G_i L^{-1})$ and/or $(1 - H_j L)$ by $(1 - H_j L^{-1})$. However, the representation

$$\prod_{i=1}^{p}(1 - G_i L^{-1}) y_t = \prod_{j=1}^{q}(1 - H_j L^{-1})\varepsilon_t \qquad (6.4.16)$$

expresses y_t in terms of future y's and ε's. Thus the backward forms, obtained by reversing time in the ARMA function above,

$$\varepsilon_t = y_t + a_1 y_{t+1} + \cdots + a_p y_{t+p} - \theta_1 \varepsilon_{t+1} - \cdots - \theta_q \varepsilon_{t+q}, \qquad (6.4.17)$$

may be used to calculate the initial y's and ε's that are needed to start off the forward recursion (6.4.13). The back-calculation begins from the end of the series where the unavailable y_{n+r} and ε_{n+r} are replaced by their unconditional expectations. In general, the effect of this approximation is to introduce a transient into the system which, because $a(L)$ and $\theta(L)$ are stationary operators, will, for series of moderate length, almost certainly be negligible by the time the beginning of the series is reached and thus will not affect the calculation of the ε_t's. Once the initial y's and ε's are calculated, they can be substituted into (6.4.13) and this formula can be used recursively to obtain the unconditional sum of squares $\sum_{t=1}^{n}\hat{\varepsilon}_t^2$.

In computing the $\hat{\varepsilon}_t$, the parameters $\boldsymbol{\beta}$ need to be known, where $\boldsymbol{\beta}' = (\mathbf{a}', \boldsymbol{\theta}')$. To obtain the estimated $\boldsymbol{\beta}$ that minimizes $\sum_{t=1}^{n}\hat{\varepsilon}_t^2$, Box and Jenkins use the Gauss–Newton iterative method [see Section 5.9, equations (5.9.4) and (5.9.5)] by first taking a Taylor series expansion of $\hat{\varepsilon}_t$ based on some initial estimates, $\hat{\boldsymbol{\beta}}^{(i-1)}$,

$$\hat{\varepsilon}_t \simeq \hat{\varepsilon}_t^{(i-1)} - \left(\boldsymbol{\beta} - \hat{\boldsymbol{\beta}}^{(i-1)}\right)' \mathbf{x}_t^{(i-1)}, \tag{6.4.18}$$

and then taking the least squares regression of $\hat{\varepsilon}_t^{(i-1)}$ on $\mathbf{x}_t^{(i-1)}$ to obtain the adjustment $(\boldsymbol{\beta} - \hat{\boldsymbol{\beta}}^{(i-1)})$, where

$$\mathbf{x}_t^{(i-1)} = -\frac{\partial \hat{\varepsilon}_t}{\partial \boldsymbol{\beta}}\bigg|_{\boldsymbol{\beta}=\hat{\boldsymbol{\beta}}^{(i-1)}}, \tag{6.4.19}$$

and $\hat{\varepsilon}_t^{(i-1)}$ is constructed from (6.4.13) assuming that $\boldsymbol{\beta} = \hat{\boldsymbol{\beta}}^{(i-1)}$.

Because the $\hat{\varepsilon}$'s are not exactly linear in the parameters $\boldsymbol{\beta}$, a single adjustment will not immediately produce the least squares values. The adjusted values are typically substituted as new initial estimates, and the process is repeated until convergence occurs. Convergence is faster if reasonably good estimates are used initially. One way to obtain such initial estimates is to solve for parameter values from the sample autocorrelation and partial autocorrelation functions obtained from the identification stages using (6.3.17) and/or (6.3.40).

Since, conditional on σ_ε^2, the residual sum of squares $\sum_{t=1}^{n}\varepsilon_t^2 = S_n$ divided by $-2\sigma_\varepsilon^2$ is an approximation to the log-likelihood and since the asymptotic covariance matrix of the MLE is equal to the inverse of the information matrix, the covariance matrix of the nonlinear least squares can be approximated by

$$\mathrm{Var}(\hat{\boldsymbol{\beta}}) \simeq 2\sigma_\varepsilon^2 \left(\frac{\partial^2 S_n}{\partial \boldsymbol{\beta}\, \partial \boldsymbol{\beta}'}\right)^{-1}_{\boldsymbol{\beta}=\hat{\boldsymbol{\beta}}^{(i-1)}}. \tag{6.4.20}$$

6.4.4 Model Diagnostic Checking

When a model is identified and the parameters estimated, the question remains of deciding whether the model is adequate. If there should be evidence of serious inadequacy, the model should be modified in the next iterative cycle. Since it is always possible that characteristics in the data of an unexpected kind can be overlooked, no system of diagnostic checks can ever be comprehensive. However, if thoughtfully devised diagnostic checks applied to a model fitted to a reasonably large body of data fail to show serious discrepancies, it is reasonable to feel more comfortable about using that model. Alternatively, if any inadequacies are revealed, they may suggest alternatives that appear more appropriate.

Box and Jenkins suggest two ways to perform diagnostic checking: the method of overfitting and diagnostic checks applied to residuals. The method of overfitting makes use of the assumption that a particular ARMA model of order (p,q) implicitly imposes the restrictions that in the more general model

$$\begin{aligned}(1 + a_1 L + \cdots + a_p L^p + a_{p+1} L^{p+1} + \cdots + a_{p+r} L^{p+r})y_t \\ = (1 + \theta_1 L + \cdots + \theta_q L^q + \theta_{q+1} L^{q+1} + \cdots + \theta_{q+s} L^{q+s})\varepsilon_t,\end{aligned} \tag{6.4.21}$$

the coefficients a_{p+j}, $j = 1, \ldots, r$, and θ_{q+j}, $j = 1, \ldots, s$, are zero. This is a testable hypothesis. Thus if it is thought desirable to do so, the model identified can be extended by adding extra coefficients. The augmented model can then be estimated and the standard deviations of the estimates of the added coefficients will indicate whether or not the additional coefficients differ significantly from zero, via the usual t-test. However, because of the issue of model multiplicity discussed in Section 6.4.1, as a practical consideration, in fitting extra coefficients one should not add terms simultaneously to both sides of the ARMA model. Instead, it would be more appropriate to add such terms to the autoregressive operator and moving average operator *sequentially*.

Diagnostic checks applied to residuals assume that if a time-series model is correctly specified, the errors (or "innovations") ε_t constitute a white-noise process. If the series $\varepsilon_1, \ldots, \varepsilon_n$ were available, natural checks on model adequacy could be based on the sample autocorrelations of this series. Anderson (1942) has shown that the sample autocorrelations of white noise are asymptotically independently normally distributed with zero means and standard errors $n^{-1/2}$. Hence the statistic $n\sum_{k=1}^{K} \hat{\tau}_k^2$ is asymptotically distributed as chi-square with K degrees of freedom, where the $\hat{\tau}_k$'s are the sample autocorrelations. This statistic could be used to test whether the ε_t's are uncorrelated.

In practice, however, the ε_t's are unknown, so only the residuals from the fitted ARMA(p,q) models, $\hat{\varepsilon}_t$ are available. For a univariate time-series model, the fitted value is the one-step-ahead forecast error. For example, with an AR(1) model where $\hat{a}_1$ is the estimate, the fitted value at time t is $-\hat{a}_1 y_{t-1}$ and the estimated residual $\hat{\varepsilon}_t$ is $\hat{\varepsilon}_t = y_t + \hat{a}_1 y_{t-1}$. When sample autocorrelations are calculated from $\hat{\varepsilon}_t$, as

$$r_k = \frac{[1/(n-k)] \sum_{t=k+1}^{n} \hat{\varepsilon}_t \hat{\varepsilon}_{t-k}}{(1/n) \sum_{t=1}^{n} \hat{\varepsilon}_t^2}, \tag{6.4.22}$$

the statistic

$$Q(K) = n \sum_{k=1}^{K} r_k^2 \tag{6.4.23}$$

is better approximated by a chi-square distribution with $K - p - q$ degrees of freedom, as shown in Box and Pierce (1970). However, for $n < 100$, the approximation can be rather poor. Ljung and Box (1978) suggest using, instead of $Q(K)$,

$$Q^*(K) = n(n+2) \sum_{k=1}^{K} \frac{r_k^2}{n-k}. \tag{6.4.24}$$

If several models are estimated and all pass the diagnostic checks, the model selection criteria, say the Akaike information criterion, as discussed in Section 4.10, could be used to select a specific model representation.

6.4.5 Seasonal Models

Economic time series often exhibit a seasonal pattern. Observations s periods apart may be similar due to institutional or climatic factors, particularly over the course of a year. Thus parts of the series consist of some shape that is continually repeated with little variation in a periodic and fairly regular fashion.

The number s which is required for successive observations to go through a complete cycle is called the *period.* When a series exhibits seasonal behavior with known periodicity s, say, $s = 4$ for quarterly data or $s = 12$ for monthly data, there are not one but two time intervals of importance. Relationships are expected to occur (1) between successive observations and (2) between the observations s periods apart. Therefore, it would be useful to consider the data in the form of a table containing s columns and n/s (assuming that n/s is an integer) rows. For instance, if $\{y_t\}$ is a sequence of quarterly observations, it would be convenient to consider the data in the form of Table 6.2, where there is a relation among observations in the same column and a relation among observations in the same row.

There are a variety of techniques to describe these two types of relations. For instance, the different effects in a series may be assumed additive, that is,

$$y_t = S(t) + y_t^*, \tag{6.4.25}$$

where $S(t)$ denotes the seasonal factor and y_t^* denotes the remainder. If the seasonal factor is periodic in nature, a *periodic function* of period s (4 for quarterly data, 12 for monthly data, etc.),

$$S(t + s) = S(t) \qquad \text{for all } t, \tag{6.4.26}$$

possibly with the normalization

$$\sum_{t=1}^{s} S(t) = 0, \tag{6.4.27}$$

can be used.

A simple specification for a perfectly regular seasonal component $S(t)$ is

$$S(t) = \sum_{j=0}^{s-1} d_j D_{jt} \tag{6.4.28}$$

with the side condition $\sum_{j=0}^{s-1} d_j = 0$, where D_{jt} are dummy variables such that $D_{jt} = 1$ if $(t - j - 1)/s$ is an integer and zero otherwise. For example, if monthly data are used, $s = 12$; $D_{0t} = 1$ every January, is zero in every other month, and so on (assuming that the series begins with the January figure).

TABLE 6.2 Quarterly Time-Series Data y_t

	Quarter			
Year	I	II	III	IV
1	.	.	.	.
2	.	.	.	.
⋮	⋮	⋮	⋮	⋮

Alternatively, because the trigonometric functions possess the property that $\cos(t + 2\pi l) = \cos t$, $\sin(t + 2\pi l) = \sin t$ for $l = 0, \pm 1, \pm 2, \ldots$, they can be used to represent regular seasonal periodic movement. For example, let

$$\begin{aligned} S(t) &= \sum_{j=1}^{\frac{1}{2}s} \left(\alpha_j \cos \frac{2\pi j}{s} t + \beta_j \sin \frac{2\pi j}{s} t \right) \\ &= \sum_{j=1}^{\frac{1}{2}s} d_j \left(\cos \frac{2\pi jt}{s} \cos \theta_j + \sin \frac{2\pi jt}{s} \sin \theta_j \right) \qquad (6.4.29) \\ &= \sum_{j=1}^{\frac{1}{2}s} d_j \cos\left(\frac{2\pi jt}{s} - \theta_j \right), \end{aligned}$$

where $\theta_j = \arctan(\beta_j/\alpha_j)$ and $d_j = (\alpha_j^2 + \beta_j^2)^{1/2}$. The period for the jth trigometric function is s/j while the reciprocal j/s is called the *frequency* because this is the number of periods in the unit interval; that is, the function goes through its pattern this number of times. The effect of the multiplication by $2\pi j/s$ is to expand or contract the time scale. The effect of subtracting θ_j is to translate the cosine curve. The maximum of $\cos[2\pi j/s - \theta_j]$ occurs at $2\pi jt/s = \theta_j + 2\pi l$, $l = 0, \pm 1, \ldots$; that is, at times satisfying $t = (\theta_j + 2\pi l)s/2\pi j$. The angle θ_j is called the *phase*, and at $t = 0$, the trigonometric function is $\cos \theta_j$. The coefficient d_j is called the *amplitude* of the function. Equation (6.4.29) is mathematically equivalent to (6.4.28). The formulation is useful because it allows seasonality to be interpreted as *cyclical*. By construction, the elements, $\cos(2\pi jt/s)$ and $\sin(2\pi jt/s)$, are cyclical processes at the seasonal frequencies $2\pi j/s, j = 1, \ldots, \frac{1}{2}s$, and the coefficients α_j and β_j represent the contribution of each cycle to the seasonal process $S(t)$.

Under the additive assumption (6.4.25) and the assumption $Ey_t^* = 0$, the coefficients d_j or α_j and β_j can be estimated by regression techniques as discussed in Chapters 4 and 5. The additive formulation (6.4.25) also provides a simple procedure to remove seasonality from observed series once the seasonal component has been estimated. The *seasonally adjusted* series of y_t is simply $y_t^* = y_t - \hat{S}(t)$. However, the regression methods would work well only if the seasonal component consists of a regular shape that reoccurs regularly (e.g., every 12 months). If the seasonal component slowly evolves over time, it would be extremely difficult to identify its form from actual time series of a length typically available to economists. Furthermore, the seasonal component may well not be deterministic but rather stochastic in nature. In this situation, an integrated approach that handles the different components of the trend, seasonal, and random components simultaneously in a model may depict a given time series more faithfully.

As mentioned earlier, a unique feature of seasonal time series is that there are relations (1) between successive observations, and (2) between the observations s periods apart. There are two ways to combine these two relations. One is to rely on a single ARMA representation using polynomial terms in both L and L^s. The other is to take the product of two ARMA representations. To describe the relation s periods apart (i.e., the relation in the same column in Table 6.2), the lag operator L^{is}, $i = 0, 1, 2, \ldots$, is particularly useful. Thus an ARMA(p^*,q^*) specification may be used to describe the seasonal relation

$$y_t = \frac{\theta^*(L^s)}{a^*(L^s)} y_t^*, \qquad (6.4.30)$$

where

$$a^*(L^s) = 1 + a_1^* L^s + \cdots + a_{p*}^* L^{p*s}, \tag{6.4.31}$$

$$\theta^*(L^s) = 1 + \theta_1^* L^s + \cdots + \theta_{q*}^* L^{q*s}. \tag{6.4.32}$$

Then the deseasonalized series takes the form

$$y_t^* = \frac{a^*(L^s)}{\theta^*(L^s)} y_t. \tag{6.4.33}$$

To describe the relation of the deseasonalized series, y_t^*, an ARMA(p,q) representation of (6.4.2) and (6.4.3) can be used. Combining (6.4.31), (6.4.32) with (6.4.2), (6.4.3), yields a multiplicative model ARMA$(p,q) \times (p^*,q^*)_s$,

$$a(L)a^*(L^s)y_t = \theta(L)\theta^*(L^s)\varepsilon_t. \tag{6.4.34}$$

The approach to seasonal model building is again composed of an iterative cycle of identification, estimation, and diagnostic checking. For the identification of p,p^*,q,q^*, one again examines the patterns followed by the autocorrelation and partial autocorrelation functions of y_t. For instance, it is noted by Granger and Newbold (1986, pp. 102–103) that

1. If y_t is a multiplicative autoregressive process of order p and p^* (where $q,q^* = 0$), its autocorrelations will die out according to the difference equation

$$a(L)a^*(L^s)\tau_r = 0 \qquad \text{for all } r > 0, \tag{6.4.35}$$

and its partial autocorrelations will obey

$$a_{kk} = 0 \qquad \text{for all } k > p + sp^*. \tag{6.4.36}$$

2. If y_t is a multiplicative MA process of order q,q^* (where $p,p^* = 0$), its autocorrelations will obey

$$\tau_r = 0 \qquad \text{for} \quad \begin{aligned} &q < r < s - q, \\ &s + q < r < 2s - q, \\ &(q^* - 1)s + q < r < q^* s - q, \\ &q^* s + q < r. \end{aligned} \tag{6.4.37}$$

3. If y_t is a multiplicative ARMA of order $(p,q) \times (p^*,q^*)\hat{s}$, its autocorrelations will obey

$$a(L)a^*(L^s)\tau_r = 0 \qquad \text{for all } r > q + sq^*. \tag{6.4.38}$$

For many lower-order members of the class (6.4.34), more comprehensive conditions than the above can be derived. For details, see Box and Jenkins (1970, App. A9.1).

Estimation of the model and diagnostic checking would use essentially the same principles as those described in Sections 6.4.3 and 6.4.4. However, in the case of seasonal models, simulation evidence reported in Ansley and Newbold (1980) indicates a stronger advantage for the maximum likelihood method.

6.5 NONSTATIONARY TIME SERIES

Many time series behave as though they have no fixed mean but exhibit a gradual movement, which may be called a *trend*. Indeed, except in physical data, it is rare to find a series that is truly stationary. In dropping the assumption of stationarity, there is scarcely any restriction on the model. For this reason it is all the more difficult to specify a model, or even to specify some of the statistical properties of the variates, such as first and second moments. This section treats three popular methods of modeling nonstationary time series: (1) a deterministic function of time; (2) an explosive ARMA process; and (3) a unit root or integrated process.

6.5.1 Deterministic Function of Time

When the effects in a time series are assumed additive, a common approach is to assume an "error model," one that specifies the observable y_t as composed of a trend in time $f(t)$ and an (unobservable) error u_t; that is,

$$y_t = T(t) + u_t, \qquad t = 1, 2, \ldots, n. \tag{6.5.1}$$

When there is no theory to specify the broad movement of a time series, it may be possible to approximate it by a polynomial in time,

$$T(t) = \alpha_0 + \alpha_1 t + \cdots + \alpha_m t^m. \tag{6.5.2}$$

The polynomial trend is primarily a descriptive device; it summarizes succinctly the overall characteristics of the series. To do this usefully, the degree of the polynomial, m, should be small relative to n, the number of observations.

A first-degree polynomial function ($m = 1$) represents a uniform movement upward or downward. A second-degree polynomial function can display a decrease followed by an increase, or vice versa, and similarly for higher-degree polynomials. It is advantageous to represent a trend by a polynomial of low degree because the curve is smoother, the presumed "explanation" is simpler, and the function is more economical. However, if the underlying mean value of the observed variable is not even approximately a low-degree polynomial, the investigator may want to use a polynomial of higher degree.

The model of (6.5.1) and (6.5.2) uses the familiar regression framework, and the customary regression techniques discussed in Chapters 4 and 5 can be used. However, the investigator typically does not know in advance the degree of polynomial to fit. The investigator is then confronted with a multiple-decision problem. The disadvantage of too low a degree is a bias in estimating the trend, while the disadvantage of too high a degree is an unnecessarily large variability in the estimation of the trend.

If the investigator knows the maximum possible degree, say m, the problem is one of deciding to which of the following mutually exclusive sets the parameter point $(\alpha_1, \ldots, \alpha_m)$ belongs:

$$\begin{aligned} &H_m\colon \alpha_m \neq 0, \\ &H_{m-1}\colon \alpha_{m-1} \neq 0, \qquad \alpha_m = 0, \\ &\vdots \\ &H_1\colon \alpha_1 \neq 0, \qquad \alpha_2 = \cdots = \alpha_m = 0, \\ &H_0\colon \alpha_1 = \alpha_2 = \cdots = \alpha_m = 0, \end{aligned}$$

where the set H_i implies that the polynomial is of degree i. Thus a sequence of significance tests can be conducted, first testing $\alpha_m = 0$, then $\alpha_{m-1} = 0$, and so on, in turn, until either such a hypothesis is rejected or all such hypotheses are accepted.

With regard to the choice of significance levels for the sequential tests, in general, it is necessary to balance the desirability of not overestimating the degree with that of sensitivity of the procedure to nonzero coefficients. A reasonable approach is to set m fairly large but make the significance level very small for i near m. If the effect of the ith degree is relatively large, there is a chance of learning that fact. If high degrees are not needed, the probability is small that a high degree will be used (see, for example, Anderson, 1971).

Sometimes time series exhibit trends that are best described by functions that are nonlinear in the parameters. For example, population studies often reveal a characteristic trend in the growth of populations which may be reasonably well described by the *logistic growth curve*. The formula for the logistic curve as a function of time is

$$T(t) = \frac{\alpha_1}{1 + \alpha_2 e^{-\alpha_3 t}}, \tag{6.5.3}$$

where α_1, α_2, and α_3 are parameters to be estimated. Such nonlinear trends can be estimated by the method of nonlinear least squares as discussed in Section 5.9.

The fitted polynomial or nonlinear trend can usually be used for *interpolation*, but must be used cautiously for *extrapolation* since there is a question of how good an approximation the polynomial is to the underlying trend outside the range of the given data. While a low-degree polynomial (e.g., third degree) might give a good fit, such a fitted third-degree polynomial is generally not good for prediction, particularly for the long-term future. Outside the range of the observed data, such a polynomial can increase or decrease indefinitely at an increasing rate of increase or decrease. For an example, see Anderson (1971, p. 46).

6.5.2 Explosive ARMA Process

Another way of modeling nonstationary behavior is to assume that although the process is not invariant under time translation, the relation generating it is and can be represented by a stochastic model with a multiplicative structure to capture the different effects in a series. One such model would be to relax the stationarity condition of an ARMA model by assuming that the autoregressive operator $\tilde{a}(L)$ can be factored into the product $a^*(L) \cdot a(L)$, where the roots of $a^*(z) = 0$ lie on or inside the unit circle and the roots of $a(z) = 0$, as in (6.3.45), lie outside the unit circle. If some of the roots of $\tilde{a}(z) = 0$ lie inside the unit circle, after a short induction period, the series "breaks loose" and essentially follows an exponential curve. The generating ε's play almost no further role. In other words, when some of the roots of $\tilde{a}(z) = 0$ lie inside the unit circle, the process becomes *explosive*.

6.5.3 Integrated Process

As described above, an ARMA model with some of the roots of the determinantal equation $\tilde{a}(z) = 0$ lying inside the unit circle represents explosive or evolutionary behavior. However, the types of economic and industrial series typically encountered, while nonstationary, do not exhibit explosive behavior. In fact, they exhibit what Box and Jenkins call *homogeneous nonstationary behavior*, where there is homogeneity in the sense that, apart from local level, or perhaps local level and trend, one part of the series behaves much like any other part. Models that describe such homogeneous nonstationary behavior can be obtained by assuming some suitable difference of the process to be stationary. That is, letting ∇ be the *difference operator*

$$\nabla = 1 - L, \tag{6.5.4}$$

it is assumed that

$$\nabla^d y_t = w_t \tag{6.5.5}$$

is stationary, where $d \geq 1$. Thus

$$\nabla y_t = y_t - y_{t-1} \quad \nabla^2 y_t = \nabla(\nabla y_t) = y_t - 2y_{t-1} + y_{t-2} \quad \text{and} \quad \nabla^d = \sum_{j=0}^{d}(-1)^d \binom{d}{j} y_{t-j}.$$

Inverting (6.5.5) yields

$$y_t = S^d w_t, \tag{6.5.6}$$

where S is the *infinite summation operator* defined by

$$S = \nabla^{-1} = (1-L)^{-1} = 1 + L + L^2 + \cdots. \tag{6.5.7}$$

Thus

$$Sw_t = \sum_{j=0}^{\infty} w_{t-j} \tag{6.5.8}$$

$$\begin{aligned} S^2 w_t &= S\left(\sum_{j=0}^{\infty} w_{t-j}\right) \\ &= Sw_t + Sw_{t-1} + Sw_{t-2} + \cdots \\ &= \sum_{j=0}^{\infty}\sum_{h=0}^{\infty} w_{t-j-h} \end{aligned} \tag{6.5.9}$$

$$S^3 w_t = \sum_{j=0}^{\infty}\sum_{h=0}^{\infty}\sum_{l=0}^{\infty} w_{t-j-h-l}, \tag{6.5.10}$$

and so on. Equation (6.5.6) implies that the process y_t can be obtained by summing (or integrating) the stationary process w_t d times. Therefore, the process (6.5.5) is called an *integrated process*. When the stationary process w_t can be represented by an ARMA(p,q),

$$a(L)w_t = \theta(L)\varepsilon_t, \tag{6.5.11}$$

where $a(L)$ and $\theta(L)$ are defined in the form as (6.3.43) and (6.3.44), respectively, with roots of $a(z) = 0$ and $\theta(z) = 0$ lying outside the unit circle, (6.5.5) can be combined with (6.5.11) to obtain

$$a(L)(1-L)^d y_t = \theta(L)\varepsilon_t. \tag{6.5.12}$$

The process (6.5.12) is called an *autoregressive integrated moving average* process of order (p,d,q), ARIMA(p,d,q). The ARIMA model can also be viewed as a special case of the ARMA model with d of the roots of the generalized autoregressive operator,

$$\begin{aligned} \tilde{a}(L) &= a(L)(1-L)^d \\ &= 1 + \tilde{a}_1 L + \cdots + \tilde{a}_{p+d} L^{p+d}, \end{aligned} \tag{6.5.13}$$

lying on the unit circle.

The ARIMA model or the generalized autoregressive operator (6.5.13) with d unit roots has played a central role in empirical modeling of economic time series because it possesses several appealing features:

1. The case of d roots of $a^*(z) = 0$ lying on the unit circle provides a process that is neatly balanced between an overtly nonstationary one and the stationary situation.

2. An mth polynomial trend, $T(t)$, equation (6.5.2), can be eliminated through successive differencing,[4]

$$\nabla^{m+r}T(t) = (1 - L)^{m+r}T(t) = 0, \qquad r = 1, 2, \ldots, \tag{6.5.14}$$

because each difference reduces the degree of polynomial by 1.

3. In many situations, trends are creations of the authorities. There is no reason to expect a single long-term trend to prevail as one might approximate or extrapolate by curve fitting. For instance, the stock of money in the United States is subject to control by political authorities, either by alteration of the monetary arrangements, or, more recently, by continuous discretionary control. Nothing outside the political sphere prevents a shift from one trend to another or produces a return to an earlier trend after a departure. Differencing allows for a trend to shift drastically from time to time.

4. Differencing requires no decision about the kind of trend to fit or the period to cover. The observations for any one period do not depend on the far distant observations for other periods that affect fitted trends. The series can be extended backward or forward without either recomputing or extrapolating trends.

To transform a series into a stationary one when the nonstationary time series exhibits seasonal behavior with known periodicity, the differencing operator $(1-L)^d(1-L^s)^D$ can be used to link the relationships between successive observations and the relationships s periods apart, where

$$(1-L)^d(1-L^s)^D y_t = w_t, \tag{6.5.15}$$

for $d \geq 0$ and $D \geq 0$.

The seasonal differencing operator $(1 - L^s)$ eliminates any fixed seasonal pattern, where $S(t) = S(t-s)$ in the series. It also removes the trend in the series. Factoring $(1 - L^s)$ into

$$1 - L^s = (1 - L)(1 + L + \cdots + L^{s-1}), \tag{6.5.16}$$

the operation

$$\begin{aligned}(1 - L^s)y_t &= y_t - y_{t-s} \\ &= (1 - L)(1 + L + \cdots + L^{s-1})y_t \\ &= (1 - L)sy_t^*\end{aligned} \tag{6.5.17}$$

can be viewed as removing the trend from the (deseasonalized) series that is the average of y_t over the seasonal interval, s, where $y_t^* = (1/s)(y_t + y_{t-1} + \cdots + y_{t-s+1})$.

If w_t can also be modeled by the form (6.4.28), the result is a multiplicative ARIMA model of order $(p,d,q) \times (P,D,Q)_s$:

$$a(L)a^*(L^s)(1 - L)^d(1 - L^s)^D y_t = \theta(L)\theta^*(L^s)\varepsilon_t. \tag{6.5.18}$$

Experience suggests that $d, D = 0$ or 1 will be appropriate for most observed series, although occasionally $d = 2$ is required.

[4]Differencing a variable having deterministic trend may, however, produce spurious variations as discussed in Chan, Hayya, and Ord (1977), Nelson and Kang (1981), and Durlauf and Phillips (1988).

6.5.4 Tests for the Unit Root Hypothesis

The possible presence of unit roots in time series has important implications for hypothesis testing, estimation, prediction, and control. For stationary time series, the effects of a shock gradually diminish as time progresses, as demonstrated in (6.3.24) or (6.3.27). There is a tendency for the process to revert to the mean. Time series with unit roots imply that the effects of a shock will persist over time, as suggested by (6.5.8), and there is no complete reversion to the mean. Theories designed to explain movements in time series with unit roots differ substantially from theories designed to explain stationary series as discussed in Anderson (1959) and White (1958). This is also the fundamental reason that Box and Jenkins suggest using the difference operation ∇^d to transform a nonstationary time series to a stationary time series. However, before employing the ∇^d operator to transform a time series, some formal statistical procedures to decide on the appropriate values of d would be useful.

An ARIMA(p,d,q) model (6.5.12) can be viewed as an ARMA($p + d$, q) model with an extended autoregressive operator (6.5.13). Clearly, the solution of $a^{\sim}(z) = 0$ has d unit roots. In fact, if one or more roots of the autoregressive operator are on the unit circle, the time-series process $\{y_t\}$ is correspondingly said to possess one or more unit roots, and the process $\{y_t\}$ is nonstationary. Thus unit roots can be 1, –1, or complex with absolute values equal to 1. Here only roots of 1 in $\tilde{a}(L)$ will be discussed, so that $\tilde{a}(L) = (1 - L)^d a(L)$, where d is the number of unit roots and $a(L) = 0$ has roots lying outside the unit circle. Therefore, a test for the order of integration of a series is also referred to as testing for unit roots.[5]

There are essentially two types of statistics to test for the unit root hypothesis. The first type is based on the null hypothesis of unit root versus the alternative hypothesis of stationarity and makes use of the estimated coefficient in the regression of y_t on y_{t-1}. However, when the sequence $\{y_t\}$ is integrated of order one and hence nonstationary, the usual sample moment matrix of y_{t-1} diverges while the matrix of sample moments between the regressors and the errors converges weakly to a random matrix. Thus, for a first-order autoregressive process,

$$y_t = \alpha y_{t-1} + \varepsilon_t, \qquad t = 1, \ldots, n, \tag{6.5.19}$$

where ε_t is independent normal with mean 0 and variance σ_ε^2, the least squares estimator

$$\hat{\alpha} = \frac{\sum_{t=1}^{n} y_t y_{t-1}}{\sum_{t=1}^{n} y_{t-1}^2} \tag{6.5.20}$$

has a nonstandard limiting distribution, where $n(\hat{\alpha} - 1)$ converges in distribution to $\frac{1}{2}[W^2(1) - 1] \Big/ \int_0^1 W^2(r)\,dr$ and $W(r)$ is a Gaussian process [for fixed r, $W(r)$ is $N(0, \sigma_\varepsilon^2 r)$] with independent increments [$W(s)$ is independent of $W(r) - W(s)$ for all $0 < s < r \leq 1$]. To obtain the critical values for the test of the null hypothesis H_0: $\alpha = 1$ against the stationarity alternative H_1: $\alpha < 1$ for various sample sizes, Dickey and Fuller (1979) use the Monte Carlo method to calculate the percentage points of the finite sample as well as the asymptotic distribution of the test statistic $\gamma_\mu = n(\hat{\alpha} - 1)$ as that of Table 8.5.1 of Fuller (1976).[6]

[5]For additional discussion, see Diebold and Nerlove (1989).

[6]The Dickey–Fuller simulation is based on the assumption that $y_0 = 0$. Evans and Savin (1981) have provided analytical results on the exact finite sample distribution of $\hat{\alpha}$ showing in particular its dependence on y_0/σ. Also, see Chan and Wei (1988) for the link between the functional central limit theory and the approach based on the ratio of quadratic forms.

Dickey and Fuller (1979) also use the Monte Carlo method to calculate the percentage points of the conventional Student-t test statistic

$$\gamma_\eta = \frac{\hat{\alpha} - 1}{\left[\hat{s}^2\left(\sum_{t=2}^{n} y_{t-1}^2\right)^{-1}\right]^{1/2}}, \tag{6.5.21}$$

where s^2 is the usual unbiased variance estimator. This test statistic can be easily obtained from the usual t-test statistic in the regression

$$\nabla y_t = (\alpha - 1)y_{t-1} + \varepsilon_t. \tag{6.5.22}$$

To test the null of unit root against the alternatives of nonzero mean stationary process

$$y_t - \mu = \alpha(y_{t-1} - \mu) + \varepsilon_t, \tag{6.5.23}$$

and trend stationary process

$$y_t - a - bt = \alpha[y_{t-1} - a - b(t-1)] + \varepsilon_t, \tag{6.5.24}$$

Dickey (1976), Fuller (1976), and Dickey and Fuller (1979) provide test statistics similar to γ_μ and γ_η and their critical values for various sample sizes from the least squares estimates of the model

$$y_t = c + \alpha y_{t-1} + \varepsilon_t \tag{6.5.25}$$

for (6.5.23) and

$$y_t = c^* + b^* t + \alpha y_{t-1} + \varepsilon_t \tag{6.5.26}$$

for (6.5.24). The null of unit root for (6.5.25) is $c = \mu(1 - \alpha) = 0$ and $\alpha = 1$. The null for (6.5.26) is random walk with drift, $c^* = a(1 - \alpha) + b = b$, $b^* = b(1 - \alpha) = 0$, and $\alpha = 1$.

If the residuals of an AR(1) process are not i.i.d., lagged y can be added as a means to eliminate the serial correlation. Thus, instead of using

$$y_t = \alpha y_{t-1} + u_t, \qquad t = 1, \ldots, n, \tag{6.5.27}$$

an AR(p) process

$$y_t + \sum_{j=1}^{p} \alpha_j y_{t-j} = \varepsilon_t \tag{6.5.28}$$

is considered. Rewriting (6.5.28) as

$$y_t = \rho_1 y_{t-1} + \sum_{j=2}^{p} \rho_j \left(y_{t-j+1} - y_{t-j}\right) + \varepsilon_t, \tag{6.5.29}$$

where $p \geq 2$, $\rho_1 = -\sum_{j=1}^{p}\alpha_j$ and $\rho_i = \sum_{j=1}^{p}\alpha_j$, $i = 2, \ldots, p$. If there is a unit root [which implies $1 + \sum_{j=1}^{p}\alpha_j = 0$], then $\rho_1 = 1$. Dickey (1976) and Fuller (1976) show that under the assumptions that the initial values of the y_j's are considered fixed and ε_t is independently normally distributed with mean 0 and variance σ_ε^2, there exists a scalar c such that in the limiting distribution of the least squares regression of (6.5.29), $nc(\hat{\rho}_1 - 1)$ has the same asymptotic distribution as $n(\hat{\alpha} - 1)$ for the first-order case (6.5.19). However, the constant c can be difficult or impossible to determine in practice. On the other hand, the studentized statistic for the null hypothesis of $\rho_1 = 1$ has the same asymptotic distribution as γ_η. Therefore, Dickey and Fuller suggest that a test of the unit root be conducted by estimating a regression of the form:

$$\nabla y_t = \beta y_{t-1} + \sum_{j=2}^{p} \rho_j \nabla y_{t-j+i} + \varepsilon_t. \tag*{*(6.5.30)}$$

Under the null hypothesis, $\beta = \rho_1 - 1 = 0$, a test could be performed using the ratio of $\hat{\beta}$ to its standard error. This *t-ratio* is termed the *augmented Dickey–Fuller statistic* (ADF); however, ADF does not have the *t* distribution. Dickey and Fuller provide tables of the ADF for various sample sizes using Monte Carlo methods.

The number of lags of ∇y_t in (6.5.30) is usually chosen to ensure that the regression residual is approximately white noise. If *no* lagged ∇y_t are required, the *t*-ratio is termed the Dickey–Fuller (DF) statistic. The critical values for the DF and ADF statistics for a single variable are the same and can be found in Fuller (1976).

When u_t is not i.i.d. but stationary, an alternative to the procedure of adding lagged ∇y_t to (6.5.22) is to stay with the framework of (6.5.22) but take account of the non-i.i.d. nature of u_t. Phillips (1987) proposes the modified statistic

$$n(\hat{\alpha} - 1) - \left[\tfrac{1}{2}\left(s_{nl}^2 - s^2\right)\Big/\left(n^{-2}\sum_{t=2}^{n} y_{t-1}^2\right)\right] \tag{6.5.31}$$

for this case, where

$$s^2 = \frac{1}{n}\sum_{t=1}^{n} \hat{u}_t^2 \tag{6.5.32}$$

$$s_{nl}^2 = \frac{1}{n}\sum \hat{u}_t^2 + 2\sum_{\tau=1}^{l} n^{-1} w_{\tau l} \sum_{t=\tau+1}^{n} \hat{u}_t \hat{u}_{t-\tau}, \tag{6.5.33}$$

$$\hat{u}_t = y_t - \hat{\alpha} y_{t-1}, \tag{6.5.34}$$

$$w_{\tau l} = 1 - \frac{\tau}{l+1}, \tag{6.5.35}$$

and l increases with n at the speed slower than $n^{1/4}$, say $l = n^{1/5}$. The critical values of (6.5.31) are again given in Fuller (1976, Table 8.5.1).

One of the problems with unit root tests is that the tests have low power, in particular, if the root is close to unity. Adding lagged ∇y_t to transform the residuals into white noise is one way to improve the power of these tests. Another way is to add stationary regressors that are correlated with the residuals. For further discussion of this procedure, see Park (1990) and Hansen (1993).

If the time-series process $\{y_t\}$ contains more than one unit root, Dickey and Pantula (1987) propose the following sequential procedure for testing the null of multiple unit roots: First, assume that the true number of unit roots is no greater than m. Then test the null of m unit roots against the alternative of $(m - 1)$ unit roots by regressing $\nabla^m y_t$ on $\nabla^{m-1} y_{t-1}$ (and other relevant variables). If this null is rejected, one then tests the null of $(m - 1)$ unit roots against the alternative of $(m - 2)$ unit roots by regressing $\nabla^{m-1} y_t$ on $\nabla^{m-2} y_t$, and so on.

The second type of test is based on the null hypothesis of stationarity versus the alternative of a unit root. Since stationarity implies that $\beta = 0$ for the following auxiliary linear time trend model

$$y_t = \mu + \beta t + v_t, \qquad t = 1, \ldots, n, \tag{6.5.36}$$

a natural way to test the null of stationarity versus the alternative of a unit root is to rely on the estimated regression coefficient $\hat{\beta}$ of (6.5.36). Bierens and Guo (1993) have shown that the ratios

$$s_n = \frac{\gamma_{1n}}{\zeta_n} \tag{6.5.37}$$

and

$$s_n^* = \frac{\gamma_{1n}}{\zeta_n^*} \tag{6.5.38}$$

converge to the Cauchy (0,1) distribution under the null hypothesis that y_t is stationary, where

$$\gamma_{1n} = 2\left[r_n\hat{\beta} - \tfrac{1}{2}(\sqrt{3})(\sqrt{n}\,\xi_n)\right]$$

$$r_n = \left[\frac{(n+1)^3 - 3(n+1)^2 - 2(n+1)}{12}\right]^{1/2}$$

$$\xi_n = \left(\frac{1}{n}\right)\sum_{t=1}^{n} y_t - \left(\frac{1}{[\frac{1}{2}n]}\right)\sum_{t=1}^{[\frac{1}{2}n]} y_t$$

$$\zeta_n = \left[1 - \exp\left\{-\left[\sqrt{n}(1-\hat{\alpha})\right]^4\right\}\right]\gamma_{2n} + \exp\left\{-\left[\sqrt{n}(1-\hat{\alpha})\right]^4\right\}\frac{\gamma_{2n}}{n}$$

$$\gamma_{2n} = \sqrt{n}\,\xi_n$$

$$\zeta_n^* = \left[1 - \exp\left\{-\left[\sqrt{n}(1-\hat{\alpha})\right]^4\right\}\right]\gamma_{2n} + \exp\left\{-\left[\sqrt{n}(1-\hat{\alpha})\right]^4\right\}\frac{\gamma_{1n}}{n}.$$

Here, $[\frac{1}{2}n] = \frac{1}{2}n$ if n even and $\frac{1}{2}(n=1)$ if n odd, and $\hat{\beta}$ and $\hat{\alpha}$ are the least squares estimate of the slope coefficients in the model (6.5.36) and $y_t = \mu + \alpha y_{t-1} + u_t$, respectively. Under the alternative hypothesis that y_t is nonstationary, plim$(1/n)s_n = 1$ and $(1/n)s_n^*$ converges to a noncentral Cauchy distribution. Monte Carlo studies appear to indicate that (6.5.38) performs better when the process $\{y_t\}$ has a root near 0, while (6.5.37) performs better in the near unit root case. Both tests, however, suffer from severe size distortion in the near unit-root case.

In practice, when n is finite, the graphic method remains the easiest to implement, although it may appear somewhat arbitrary. A stationary time series has finite variance and tends to fluctuate a lot. A nonstationary time series is smoother and has infinite variance. Thus a plot of time-series observations or their differenced series would give a fairly clear idea of whether or not the series is stationary. Furthermore, the autocorrelation of an ARMA(p,q) process has the form

$$\tau_k = A_1 G_1^k + \cdots + A_p G_p^k, \qquad k > q - p. \tag{6.5.39}$$

Inspection of (6.5.39) shows that in the case of a stationary model in which none of the roots lies close to the boundary of the unit circle, the autocorrelation function will quickly "die out" for moderate and large k. On the other hand, if one or more roots are on the unit circle or approach unity, the autocorrelation will not die out quickly. Therefore, irrespective of the value of the estimated autocorrelations, a tendency for the autocorrelation function not to die out quickly is taken as an indication that a root close to unity may exist and that the underlying stochastic process is nonstationary. Thus Box and Jenkins suggest that the degree of differencing d is reached when the autocorrelation function of $w_t = (1-L)^d y_t$ dies out fairly quickly. Once d is determined, the procedure outlined in Section 6.4 can be followed to identify and to estimate an ARMA(p,q) model for the transformed series $w_t = \nabla^d y_t$.

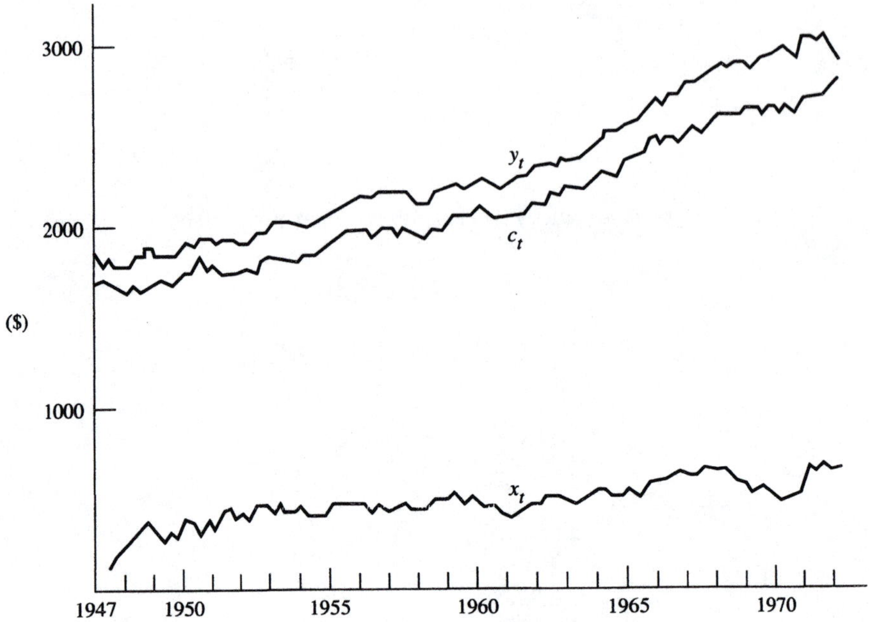

Figure 6.1 Plots of Data

6.6 EXAMPLE

Figure 6.1 presents the plot from Zellner and Palm (1974) of seasonally adjusted quarterly, price-deflated, per capita consumption (c_t), disposable income (y_t), and gross investment (x_t) for the United States for the period 1947.1–1972.2. From this figure it is seen that the variables apparently have trends and thus are nonstationary. Box and Jenkins suggest differencing a nonstationary series until it is stationary. Plots of the first differences are presented in Figure 6.2. It is clear that they are less subject to trend than are the levels of the variables, so d is set equal to 1.

Zellner and Palm (1974) then compute estimates of the autocorrelation and partial autocorrelation functions of the first differenced series. These are presented in Figures 6.3 and 6.4. Also indicated in these figures are $2s$ confidence bands, where s is the standard error for the sample autocorrelations or partial autocorrelations. The standard errors for the r_k are calculated under the assumption that $\tau_k = 0$ for $k \leq 12$. For $k > 12$, they are calculated using (6.4.9) assuming that $\tau_v = r_v$ for $v \leq 12$ and $\tau_v = 0$, $v > 12$. The standard error for the partial autocorrelation is computed using (6.4.10).

For the first difference of the consumption series, all the estimated autocorrelations lie within the $2s$ band except for that of lag 2 in Figure 6.3. Therefore, it is possible to choose either a (0, 1, 2) model as in Zellner and Palm (1976) or a (2, 1, 0) model as in Wallis (1977). For income it appears that none of the autocorrelations or partial autocorrelations is significantly different from zero in Figure 6.4. Therefore, a *random walk* model (0, 1, 0) is selected by Zellner and Palm. However, the autocorrelation and partial autocorrelation at lag 4 are about 0.2, so Wallis prefers to select a seasonal representation $(0, 1, 0) \times (1, 0, 0)_4$, where the subscript 4 denotes the period of seasonality.

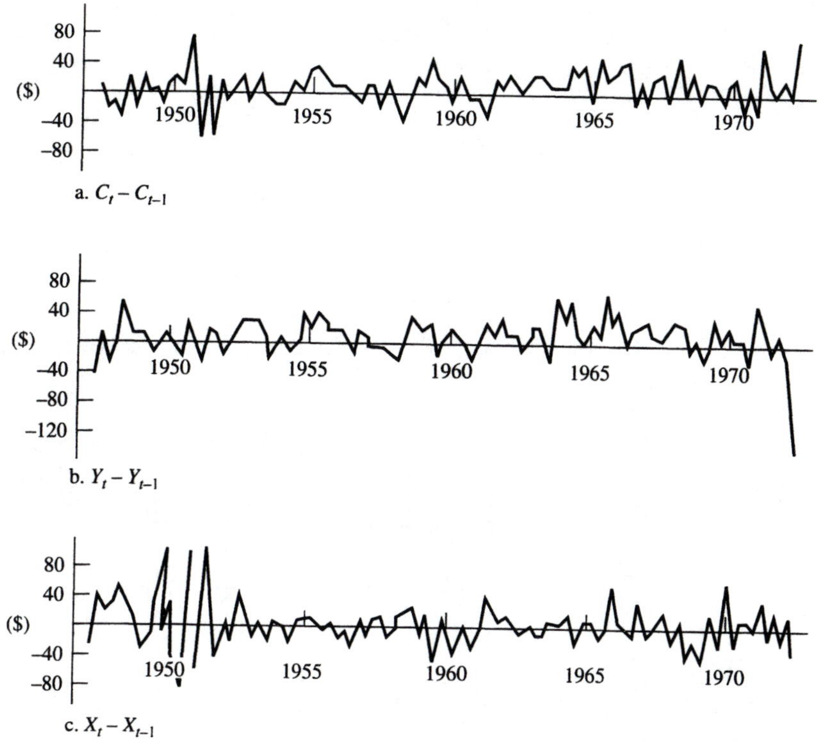

Figure 6.2 Plots of Data for First Differences

For the first difference of the gross investment series, the autocorrelations alternate in sign and show some significant values for lags less than or equal to 5. The partial autocorrelation function has a cutoff at lag 4 in Figure 6.5. Thus Zellner and Palm choose a (4, 1, 0) specification for this series. Noting that the second and third autocorrelations are insignificant but the autocorrelation at lag 5 is significant and opposite in sign to those at lags 1 and 4, Wallis selects a multiplicative seasonal model $(1, 1, 0) \times (1, 0, 0)_4$.

Using the Box and Jenkins nonlinear least squares algorithm, Zellner and Palm (1974) obtain the estimates of their specifications as

$$c_t - c_{t-1} = \underset{}{\varepsilon_t} + \underset{(0.101)}{0.021}\varepsilon_{t-1} + \underset{(0.101)}{0.278}\varepsilon_{t-2} + \underset{(2.96)}{10.73}, \qquad \hat{\sigma}_\varepsilon^2 = 530;$$

$$y_t - y_{t-1} = \varepsilon_t + \underset{(8.336)}{10.03}, \qquad \hat{\sigma}_\varepsilon^2 = 842;$$

$$(1 + \underset{(0.0942)}{0.263}L - \underset{(0.0976)}{0.0456}L^2 + \underset{(0.0970)}{0.0148}L^3 + \underset{(0.0933)}{0.376}L^4)(x_t - x_{t-1})$$

$$= \varepsilon_t + \underset{(3.265)}{7.738}, \qquad \hat{\sigma}_\varepsilon^2 = 939,$$

where standard errors are given in parentheses.

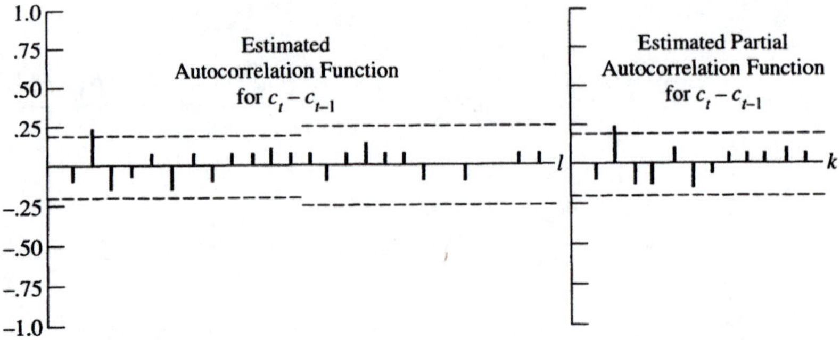

Figure 6.3 Plot of Estimated Autocorrelation and Partial Autocorrelation Function for c_t

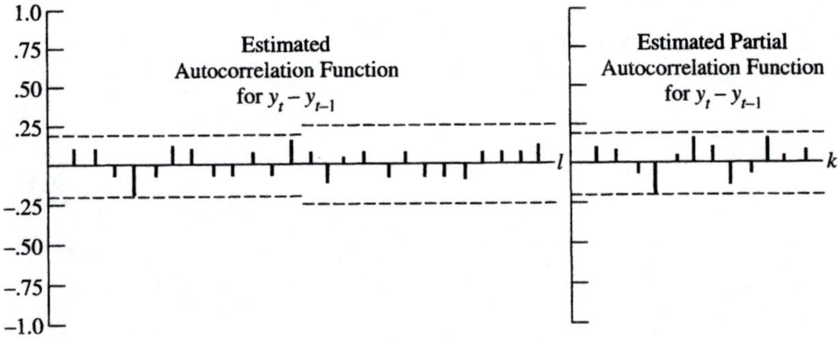

Figure 6.4 Plot of Estimated Autocorrelation and Partial Autocorrelation Function for y_t

Wallis (1977), on the other hand, uses the exact MLE estimator and obtains as estimates for the alternative specifications

$$\underset{}{(1 + \underset{(0.099)}{0.064}L - \underset{(0.100)}{0.258}L^2)(c_t - c_{t-1}) = \underset{(2.69)}{8.56} + \varepsilon_t,}$$

$$\hat{\sigma}_\varepsilon^2 = 516.3, \qquad Q(18) = 14.55;$$

$$(1 + \underset{(0.115)}{0.283}L^4)(y_t - y_{t-1}) = \underset{(3.21)}{13.74} + \varepsilon_t$$

$$\hat{\sigma}_\varepsilon^2 = 794, \qquad Q(19) = 11.73;$$

$$(1 + \underset{(0.098)}{0.249}L)(1 + \underset{(0.095)}{0.334}L^4)(x_t - x_{t-1}) = \underset{(3.15)}{7.92} + \varepsilon_t,$$

$$\hat{\sigma}_\varepsilon^2 = 928, \qquad Q(18) = 12.01,$$

where, again, standard errors are in parentheses and $Q(K)$ is the diagnostic statistic $n\sum_{k=1}^{K} r_k^2$ (6.4.23).

As can be seen from this example, the same sample information can yield different specifications and parameter estimates. The diagnostic checkings applied to the Zellner and

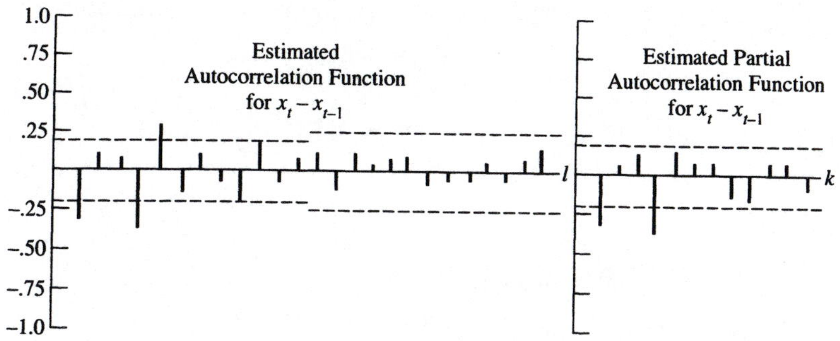

Figure 6.5 Plot of Estimated Autocorrelation and Partial Autocorrelation Function for x_t

Palm specification and to the Wallis specification fail to discover any inadequacy for their specifications. In this sense, either one will serve the purpose. However, if one were to select a specification using the Akaike information criterion of Section 4.10, the Wallis specification has a slight edge.

6.7 MINIMUM MEAN SQUARE ERROR FORECAST

6.7.1 Forecast for Stationary Processes

In considering the building of linear stationary time-series models, it is assumed that the models satisfy the following invertibility condition. Let

$$y_t = \psi(L)\varepsilon_t, \tag{6.7.1}$$

where

$$\psi(L) = 1 + \psi_1 L + \cdots \tag{6.7.2}$$

is a general representation of such models. Let $\hat{y}_{t+v}$ be the linear predictor of y_{t+v}, based on knowledge of the past, $y_t, y_{t-1}, \ldots$ (as indicated, one is forecasting v periods into the future),

$$\begin{aligned} \hat{y}_{t+v} &= \sum_0^\infty \Pi_j y_{t-j} \\ &= \Pi(L) y_t. \end{aligned} \tag{6.7.3}$$

Substituting (6.7.1) into (6.7.3), $\hat{y}_{t+v}$ can be expressed in terms of the past innovations $\varepsilon_t, \varepsilon_{t-1}, \ldots,$

$$\begin{aligned} \hat{y}_{t+v} &= \sum_0^\infty \delta_j \varepsilon_{t-j} \\ &= \delta(L)\varepsilon_t, \end{aligned} \tag{6.7.4}$$

where

$$\delta(L) = \psi(L)\Pi(L). \tag{6.7.5}$$

The mean square prediction error of (6.7.3) or (6.7.4) is given by

$$\begin{aligned}\sigma_v^2 &= E(y_{t+v} - \hat{y}_{t+v})^2 \\ &= E\left[\sum_0^\infty \psi_j \varepsilon_{t+v-j} - \sum_0^\infty \delta_j \varepsilon_{t-j}\right]^2 \\ &= \sigma_\varepsilon^2\left[\sum_{j=0}^{v-1}\psi_j^2 + \sum_0^\infty (\psi_{j+v} - \delta_j)^2\right].\end{aligned} \tag{6.7.6}$$

From (6.7.6), σ_v^2 is minimized when

$$\delta_j = \psi_{j+v}. \tag{6.7.7}$$

In other words, the minimum mean square error predictor of y_t is obtained by taking the MA representation of y_{t+v} of (6.7.1) and setting the unknown future disturbances, ε_{t+1}, $\varepsilon_{t+2}, \ldots, \varepsilon_{t+v}$ equal to their expected values of zero.

Using the bracket notation that for any power series $\gamma(L) = \sum_{-\infty}^{\infty} \gamma_j L^j$,

$$[\gamma(L)]_+ = \sum_{j=0}^{\infty} \gamma_j L^j, \tag{6.7.8}$$

$$[\gamma(L)]_- = \sum_{-\infty}^{-1} \gamma_{-j} L^{-j}, \tag{6.7.9}$$

the minimum mean square error predictor is obtained by setting

$$\delta(L) = \left[\frac{\psi(L)}{L^v}\right]_+. \tag{6.7.10}$$

However, the form (6.7.3) is more convenient because it expresses $\hat{y}_{t+v}$ directly in terms of observed quantities, $y_t, y_{t-1}, \ldots$. From (6.7.5) and (6.7.10),

$$\Pi(L) = \frac{1}{\psi(L)}\left(\sum_{j=0}^{\infty} \psi_{j+v} L^j\right) = \frac{1}{\psi(L)}\left[\frac{\psi(L)}{L^v}\right]_+. \tag{6.7.11}$$

Equation (6.7.11) is the basic formula determining the coefficients of the minimum mean square error predictor. The minimum prediction error variance, from (6.7.10) [or (6.7.6) with (6.7.7)] is

$$\sigma_v^2 = \sigma_\varepsilon^2\left(\sum_{j=0}^{v-1} \psi_j^2\right). \tag{6.7.12}$$

As an example, if y_t is an AR(1) model of the form $y_t - a_1 y_{t-1} = \varepsilon_t$, then $\psi(L) = (1 - a_1 L)^{-1} = \sum_{j=0}^{\infty} a_1^j L^j$ and $\Pi(L) = (1 - a_1 L)\sum_0^\infty a_1^{j+v} L^j = a_1^v$. That is,

$$\hat{y}_{t+v} = a_1^v y_t \quad \text{and} \quad \sigma_v^2 = \sigma_\varepsilon^2 \sum_{j=0}^{v-1} a_1^{2j} = \frac{\sigma_\varepsilon^2(1 - a_1^{2v})}{1 - a_1^2}.$$

As v increases, $\hat{y}_{t+v}$ tends to the unconditional value of y_{t+v}, zero, and σ_v^2 tends to the unconditional variance σ_y^2.

More generally, for an AR(p) process, in general it will be the case that $\hat{y}_{t+v}$ is a function of the last p observed y values alone and is, in fact, recursively determined by the autoregressive relation

$$\sum_{j=1}^{p} a_j y_{t-j+\tau} = \varepsilon_{t+\tau}, \qquad \tau = 1, 2, \ldots, \tag{6.7.13}$$

with the values $\varepsilon_{t+\tau}$ set equal to zero. These recursive relations with the substitution $\varepsilon_{t+1} = \cdots = \varepsilon_{t+\tau} = 0$ give the same relation for $\hat{y}_{t+v}$ as (6.7.3).

As another example, if y_t is an MA(1) process, $y_t = (1 - \psi_1 L)\varepsilon_t$ with $|\psi_1| < 1$, then $\Pi(L) = -(1 - \psi_1 L)^{-1}\psi_1$ if $v = 1$ and $\Pi(L) = 0$ if $v > 1$. That is, if $v = 1$, the predictor will be $\hat{y}_{t+1} = -\sum_0^\infty \psi^{j+1} y_{t-j}$. If $v > 1$, the observed past conveys no information as to y_{t+v}, so that the best predictor is just the unconditional mean value and σ_v^2 equals the unconditional variance $(1 + \psi_1^2)\sigma_\varepsilon^2$.

As a third example, consider the stationary, invertible ARMA(1,1) process $(1 - a_1 L)y_t = (1 - \theta_1 L)\varepsilon_t$. Then

$$\psi(L) = \frac{1 - \theta_1 L}{1 - a_1 L} \quad \text{and}$$

$$\Pi(L) = \frac{1 - a_1 L}{1 - \theta_1 L}\left[\frac{\sum_0^\infty a_1^j L^j - \theta_1 \sum_0^\infty a_1^j L^{j+1}}{L^v}\right]_+ = (a_1 - \theta_1)a_1^{v-1}\sum_0^\infty \theta_1^j L^j.$$

Thus $\hat{y}_{t+v} = (a_1 - \theta_1)a_1^{v-1}\sum_0^\infty \theta_1^j y_{t-j}$.

When $\psi(L)$ is unknown, the estimated values are substituted into (6.7.10) or (6.7.11) and treated as if they were known. Of course, substituting estimated values for the true values will introduce additional error into the predictor. But if the unknown parameters are estimated using an efficient method, this procedure will provide the minimum mean square error predictor for y_{t+v}.

6.7.2 Forecast for Nonstationary Time Series

The prediction formula for the stationary time series can be extended to the ARIMA(p,d,q) process by working with the extended ARMA($p + d$, q) model using the generalized operator $\tilde{a}(L)$ (6.5.13). Letting

$$\begin{aligned}\psi(L) &= \tilde{a}(L)^{-1}\theta(L) \\ &= (1 - L)^{-d} a(L)^{-1}\theta(L),\end{aligned} \tag{6.7.14}$$

the generalized prediction formula follows automatically from (6.7.10) or (6.7.11).

As an example, let y_t be generated by the ARIMA(1, 1, 0) model

$$(1 - 0.8L)(1 - L)y_t = \varepsilon_t, \tag{6.7.15}$$

where ε_t is i.i.d. with mean 0 and variance σ_ε^2. The generalized autoregressive operator is defined as

$$\begin{aligned}\tilde{a}(L) &= (1 - 0.8L)(1 - L) \\ &= (1 - 1.8L + 0.8L^2)\end{aligned} \tag{6.7.16}$$

$$\psi(L) = \tilde{a}(L)^{-1}. \tag{6.7.17}$$

Substituting (6.7.16) into (6.7.10) and (6.7.11), the v period-ahead predictor is

$$\begin{aligned}\hat{y}_{t+v} &= \left[\frac{\psi(L)}{L^v}\right]_+ \hat{\varepsilon}_t \\ &= \left[(1 - L)^{-1}(1 - 0.8)^{-1} - (0.8)^{v+1}(1 - 0.8)^{-1}(1 - 0.8L)^{-1}\right]\hat{\varepsilon}_t\end{aligned} \tag{6.7.18}$$

or

$$\begin{aligned}\hat{y}_{t+v} &= \Pi(L)y_t \\ &= \psi(L)^{-1}\left[\frac{\psi(L)}{L^v}\right]_+ y_t \\ &= \left\{1 + 4(1-L)\left[1-(0.8)^v\right]\right\}y_t.\end{aligned} \tag{6.7.19}$$

Thus (6.7.19) is identical to predicting $\hat{y}_{t+v}$ using the following recursive relation:

$$\begin{aligned}\hat{y}_{t+1} &= 1.8y_t - 0.8y_{t-1} \\ \hat{y}_{t+2} &= 1.8\hat{y}_{t+1} - 0.8y_t \\ \hat{y}_{t+3} &= 1.8\hat{y}_{t+2} - 0.8\hat{y}_{t+1} \\ \hat{y}_{t+v} &= 1.8\hat{y}_{t+v-1} - 0.8\hat{y}_{t+v-2}, \qquad v \geq 3.\end{aligned} \tag{6.7.20}$$

The difference between forecasting a stationary process and a nonstationary process is that the v-period-ahead forecast error variance for a stationary process approaches an upper bound given by the variance of the stationary process itself, while the forecast error variance for a nonstationary process is unbounded as $v \to \infty$.

6.8 TRANSFER FUNCTION MODELS

6.8.1 Introduction

Often, a variable y, which may be called the *output*, is related to another variable x, which may be called the *input*. Because of the inertia in the system, upon a change in x from one level to another, the full impact on y may not necessarily be realized immediately. Instead, changes in x may produce a delayed response with y, eventually coming to *equilibrium* at a new level. Such a change is commonly referred to as a *dynamic* response, and a model that describes this dynamic response is called a *transfer function model.*

The dynamic relationship connecting an output y and an input x can often be expressed in terms of a linear model or *linear filter*,

$$\begin{aligned}y_t &= \alpha_0 x_t + \alpha_1 x_{t-1} + \alpha_2 x_{t-2} + \cdots \\ &= \alpha(L)x_t.\end{aligned} \tag*{*(6.8.1)}$$

The linear filter

$$\alpha(L) = \alpha_0 + \alpha_1 L + \alpha_2 L^2 + \cdots \tag*{*(6.8.2)}$$

is said to be *stable* if (6.8.2) converges for $|L| \leq 1$. The series of weights $\alpha_0, \alpha_1, \ldots$ which appear in the transfer function (6.8.2) is called the *impulse response function.*

The transfer function model (6.8.2) provides another interpretation for the ARIMA model discussed in previous sections. The time-series process $\{y_t\}$ could be viewed as being generated by passing white noise ε_t through a linear filter with a transfer function $\tilde{a}(L)^{-1}\theta(L)$ as in (6.5.12) and (6.5.13). The difference between a transfer function model and an ARIMA model is that in the former case the input variable x is observable, while in the latter case the innovation (or error) ε is not observable.

For brevity, $\alpha(L)$ can frequently be represented with sufficient accuracy by the ratio of two polynomials of low degree in L:

$$\alpha(L) = \frac{\beta(L)}{\delta(L)}. \tag{6.8.3}$$

This approximation allows the dynamic relation between the input and output to be represented parsimoniously by

$$\delta(L)y_t = \beta(L)x_t, \tag{6.8.4}$$

where

$$\delta(L) = 1 + \delta_1 L + \cdots + \delta_r L^r \tag{6.8.5}$$

$$\beta(L) = \beta_0 + \beta_1 L + \cdots + \beta_s L^s. \tag{6.8.6}$$

Often, the relationship between y_t and x_t is affected by disturbances (or noise or omitted variables), whose net effect is to modify the output predicted by the transfer function model by an amount u_t. The combined transfer function–noise model can then be written

$$y_t = \alpha(L)x_t + u_t, \tag{6.8.7}$$

where u_t and x_t are independent. In the econometrics literature model (6.8.7) is referred to as a *distributed lag model*. When $\alpha(L)$ may be approximated by (6.8.3) and u_t may be described by an ARMA(p,q) process

$$u_t = \frac{\theta(L)}{a(L)}\varepsilon_t, \tag{6.8.8}$$

the combined model

$$y_t = \frac{\beta(L)}{\delta(L)}x_t + \frac{\theta(L)}{a(L)}\varepsilon_t \tag{6.8.9}$$

is called a *rational distributed lag model* by econometricians (e.g., Jorgenson 1966). When x_t is a dummy variable indicating the presence or absence of an event, (6.8.9) is called an *intervention model* in time-series literature (e.g., Box and Tiao, 1975).

6.8.2 Box–Jenkins Transfer Function Model Building

In the same way that the autocorrelation function was used to identify stochastic models, the data analysis tool employed for the identification of transfer function models is the *cross-correlation function* between the input (x) and output (y). The *cross-covariance coefficients* between two stationary series x and y at lag s are defined as

$$\gamma_{xy}(s) = E[(x_t - Ex_t)(y_{t+s} - Ey_{t+s})], \qquad s = 0, 1, 2, \ldots. \tag{6.8.10}$$

The *cross-correlation coefficient* at lag s is defined as the dimensionless ratio

$$\rho_{xy}(s) = \frac{\gamma_{xy}(s)}{\gamma_{xx}(0)^{1/2}\gamma_{yy}(0)^{1/2}}. \tag{6.8.11}$$

The sample estimates of (6.8.10) or (6.8.11) can be derived in the same way that sample autocovariance or autocorrelation estimates are derived. However, in contrast to the autocovariance or correlation function of a stationary time series, the cross-covariance coefficients $\gamma_{xy}(s)$ or the correlation coefficients $\rho_{xy}(s)$ are in general not equal to $\gamma_{xy}(-s)$ or $\rho_{xy}(-s)$, respectively.

The cross-covariance or correlation coefficients provide information about the impulse response function $\alpha(L)$. This can be seen by multiplying x_{t-j} to both sides of (6.8.7) for $s \geq 0$,

$$x_{t-j}y_t = \alpha_0 x_t x_{t-j} + \alpha_1 x_{t-1}x_{t-j} + \alpha_2 x_{t-2}x_{t-j} + \cdots + x_{t-j}u_t \tag{6.8.12}$$

and taking expectations in (6.8.12), assuming that $Ex_t = 0$,

$$\gamma_{xy}(j) = \alpha_0\gamma_{xx}(j) + \alpha_1\gamma_{xx}(j-1) + \cdots. \tag{6.8.13}$$

Furthermore, note that

$$\begin{aligned}\delta(L)\alpha(L) &= (1 + \delta_1 L + \cdots + \delta_r L^r)(\alpha_0 + \alpha_1 L + \cdots) \\ &= \beta(L) = \beta_0 + \beta_1 L + \cdots + \beta_s L^s\end{aligned} \tag{6.8.14}$$

or

$$\alpha_j = \begin{cases} -\delta_1\alpha_{j-1} - \delta_2\alpha_{j-2} - \cdots - \delta_r\alpha_{j-r} + \beta_j, & j = 0, 1, \ldots, s, \quad (6.8.15) \\ -\delta_1\alpha_{j-1} - \delta_2\alpha_{j-2} - \cdots - \delta_r\alpha_{j-r}, & j > s, \quad (6.8.16) \end{cases}$$

where $\alpha_{-i} = 0$ for $i > 0$. The weights $\alpha_s, \alpha_{s-1}, \ldots, \alpha_{s-r+1}$ provide r starting values for the difference equation

$$\delta(L)\alpha_j = 0, \qquad j > s. \tag{6.8.17}$$

The solution of this difference equation applies to all values α_j for which $j \geq s - r + 1$. Thus, in general, the impulse response weights α_j consist of (1) $s - r + 1$ values $\alpha_0, \alpha_1, \ldots, \alpha_{s-r}$ following no fixed pattern (no such values occur if $s < r$); and (2) values α_j with $j \geq s - r + 1$ following the pattern dictated by the rth-order difference equation, which has r starting values $\alpha_s, \alpha_{s-1}, \ldots, \alpha_{s-r+1}$.

Therefore, Box and Jenkins suggest the following identification procedure: (1) Derive rough estimates $\hat{\alpha}_j$ of the impulse response weights α_j in (6.8.7); and (2) use the estimates $\hat{\alpha}_j$ so obtained to make guesses of the orders r and s of the operators $\delta(L)$ in (6.8.5) and $\beta(L)$ in (6.8.6) based on the rules established in the last paragraph.

Considerable simplification in deriving the rough estimates $\hat{\alpha}_j$ can be achieved by "prewhitening" the input process. Box and Jenkins note that the usual identification and estimation method will lead to a model for the x_t process

$$a_x(L)\theta_x(L)^{-1}x_t = \eta_t, \tag{6.8.18}$$

which, to a close approximation, transforms the correlated input series x_t to the uncorrelated white noise series η_t. At the same time, an estimate s_η^2 of σ_η^2 can be obtained from the sum of squares of the $\hat{\eta}_t$'s. Applying this same transformation to y_t to obtain

$$y_t^* = a_x(L)\theta_x(L)^{-1}y_t, \tag{6.8.19}$$

the model may be written

$$y_t^* = \alpha(L)\eta_t + u_t^*, \tag{6.8.20}$$

where

$$u_t^* = a_x(L)\theta_x(L)^{-1}u_t. \tag{6.8.21}$$

Multiplying (6.8.20) by η_{t-s} and taking expectations gives

$$\gamma_{\eta y^*}(s) = E(\eta_{t-s}y_t^*) = \alpha_s\sigma_\eta^2. \tag{6.8.22}$$

Thus

$$\alpha_s = \frac{\gamma_{\eta y^*}(s)}{\sigma_\eta^2}, \tag{6.8.23}$$

or, in terms of the cross-correlations,

$$\alpha_s = \frac{\rho_{\eta y^*}(s)\sigma_{y^*}}{\sigma_\eta}, \qquad s = 0, 1, 2, \ldots . \tag{6.8.24}$$

Hence, after prewhitening the input, the cross-correlation function between the prewhitened input and the correspondingly transformed output is directly proportional to the input response function, where the effect of prewhitening is to convert the nonorthogonal set of equations (6.8.13) into the orthogonal set (6.8.22).

In practice, the theoretical cross-correlation function $\rho_{\eta y^*}(s)$ is not known, so estimates $\hat{\rho}_{\eta y^*}(s)$ are substituted into (6.8.24). A crude check of whether the cross correlation between y_t^* and η_{t-s} is effectively zero may be made by comparing the corresponding cross-correlation estimates with their approximate standard errors obtained from the following approximation from Bartlett (1946).

$$\text{Cov}\left[\hat{\rho}_{\eta y^*}(j), \hat{\rho}_{\eta y^*}(j+s)\right] \simeq (n-j)^{-1}\rho_{y^*y^*}(s) \tag{6.8.25}$$

$$\text{Var}\left[\hat{\rho}_{\eta y^*}(j)\right] \simeq (n-j)^{-1}. \tag{6.8.26}$$

The resulting preliminary estimates $\hat{\alpha}_j$ are again, in general, statistically inefficient, but they can provide a rough basis for selecting suitable operators $\delta(L)$ and $\beta(L)$ in the transfer function model. Once a tentative model is identified, Box and Jenkins suggest estimating the unknown parameters using a nonlinear least squares routine with initial estimates of δ and β obtained by substituting the estimates $\hat{\alpha}_j$, r, and s into (6.8.15) and (6.8.16). The efficiently estimated model is then subject to diagnostic checks. These include the autocorrelation check of the residual using the Q statistic of (6.4.23) and the cross-correlation check of the input x and the estimated residual $\hat{\varepsilon}_t$, given $r_{x\varepsilon}(s)$. Statistically significant nonzero autocorrelations of $\hat{\varepsilon}_t$, or cross-correlations between x_t and $\hat{\varepsilon}_{t+s}$ would indicate the inadequacy of the initial model specification, and the iterative cycle of identification, estimation, and diagnostic checking would have to be repeated.

The analysis above is based on the assumption that both y and x are stationary. If y and x are nonstationary, the same procedure can be applied to the difference terms $\nabla^d y_t$ and $\nabla^d x_t$, where d is the order required to achieve stationarity.

6.8.3 The Distributed Lag Model

Economic models, in particular the reduced-form models of Chapter 2, describe how one endogenous variable is determined from the values taken by certain exogenous variables. However, dependent variables often react to a change in one or more of the explanatory variables only after a lapse of time. This delayed reaction suggests the inclusion of lagged explanatory variables into the specification of the model, resulting in a dynamic model. In such a model, rather than an instantaneous response, there is generally a time structure of response in the gradual reaction of the dependent variable to a change in an explanatory variable.

There are several reasons why there might be a lag in the system, especially a lapse of time between a change in an explanatory variable and a change in the dependent variable. One reason is *technical*: production requires time, and durable goods last more than one period. Thus agricultural supply depends on lagged variables, such as lagged prices, since these variables may influence planting, but there is a lag between planting and harvesting. The durability of capital goods implies that current output depends, in part, on past investment decisions. A second reason is *institutional*: it takes time to respond to external events (e.g., to adjust contracts), and certain rules (e.g., the timing of payments) lead to lagged responses. A third reason is *psychological*: behavior is often based on inertia and habit, and expectations about future events are often based on past behavior. For all these reasons lagged variables often enter econometric models as explanatory variables. An example is the prototype macro model of Chapter 2, in which investment depends on both lagged and current income. This dependence on lagged income can be justified in terms of all three reasons: it takes time to produce capital goods (a technical reason), there are lags in response to external conditions (an institutional reason), and expected future output may depend on current and past income (a psychological reason). Another example is the Markov process of (5.5.2), in which the stochastic disturbance term u_t depends on the lagged term u_{t-1}, leading, in (5.5.14), to lagged variables in the transformed model.

It becomes necessary to take explicit account of lagged variables when the lag between the change in an explanatory variable and that in the dependent variable exceeds the period of observation of the variables. For example, lagged variables become increasingly important when annual models are replaced by quarterly or monthly models. They also become important when the model includes expectations variables that depend on past events.

In the simplest case of one dependent (endogenous) variable y and one explanatory (exogenous) variable x, the general relation, taking accout of all possible lags over time t, is given by

$$y_t = f_t(x_t, x_{t-1}, x_{t-2}, \ldots) + u_t, \qquad t = 1, 2, \ldots, \qquad *(6.8.27)$$

where u_t is the customary additive stochastic disturbance term. In this model all present and past values of the exogenous variable can influence the dependent variable. Thus the effects of a change in the explanatory variable can be spread out over time, with the dependent variable gradually adjusting, over time, to a change in the explanatory variable. This "ripple effect" is much like that caused by a stone tossed in a pond. Model (6.8.27) is called the *general distributed lag model.*

In the linear case with time-invariant parameters the general relation becomes the *linear distributed lag model*[7]

$$\begin{aligned} y_t &= c + \beta_0 x_t + \beta_1 x_{t-1} + \beta_2 x_{t-2} + \cdots + u_t \\ &= c + \sum_{j=0}^{\infty} \beta_j x_{t-j} + u_t, \end{aligned} \qquad *(6.8.28)$$

where c and the β's are the parameters to be estimated. The term β_j is the jth *reaction coefficient*, and it is usually assumed that

$$\lim_{j \to \infty} \beta_j = 0, \qquad *(6.8.29)$$

$$\sum_{j=0}^{\infty} \beta_j = \beta < \infty. \qquad *(6.8.30)$$

[7]For surveys of distributed lag models, see Griliches (1967), Sims (1974), and Dhrymes (1981).

The vanishing of the β_j in the limit means that, following a change in the explanatory variable x, the dependent variable y eventually reaches, perhaps in asymptotic fashion, a new equilibrium. If all β_j after β_m vanish, the model reduces to a finite distributed lag, for which the upper limit of the summation sign in (6.8.28) is m. The finiteness of the sum of the coefficients in (6.8.30) means that any finite change in x that persists indefinitely results in a finite change in y.

The relation between y and x in the distributed lag can be represented as in Figure 6.6. Assume that x_t has been constant over a sufficiently long period so that y is constant, as shown. At $\bar{t}$ the variable x increases by a unit amount to a permanently higher level. The immediate effect is to increase y by β_0, as

$$\Delta y_{\bar{t}} = \sum_{j=0}^{\infty} \beta_j \Delta x_{\bar{t}-j} = \beta_0 \Delta x_{\bar{t}} = \beta_0 \qquad \text{since} \quad \Delta x_{\bar{t}} = 1. \tag{6.8.31}$$

The effect in the next period is to increase y by β_1, as

$$\Delta y_{\bar{t}+1} = \beta_0 \Delta x_{\bar{t}+1} + \beta_1 \Delta x_{\bar{t}} = \beta_1 \qquad \text{since} \quad \Delta x_{\bar{t}+1} = 0. \tag{6.8.32}$$

Similarly, in period $\bar{t}+2$ the increase is β_2, and in general, in period $\bar{t}+j$ the increase is β_j. Assuming, as in (6.8.29), that the β_j's eventually diminish to zero, the total effect is given by

$$\Delta y = \sum_{j=0}^{\infty} \beta_j = \beta, \tag{6.8.33}$$

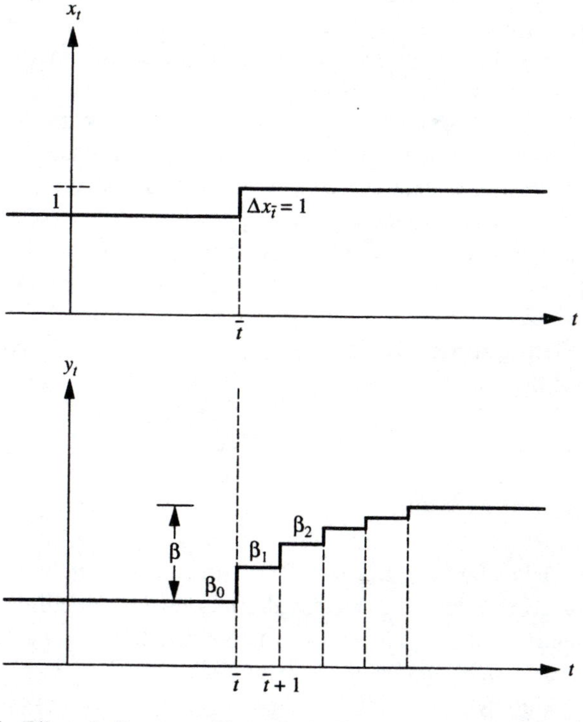

Figure 6.6 Effect of a Permanent Change in the Explanatory Variable for a Distributed Lag Relationship

as shown in the figure. The sum of the coefficients, β, represents the long-term effect of a change in x on y, and the gradual asymptotic approach of y to the long-term increment of β should be noted in the figure. The time shape of the adjustment in y in response to the change in x is the "signature" of the particular distributed lag under consideration. If the weights w_j are defined as

$$w_j = \frac{\beta_j}{\beta}, \tag{6.8.34}$$

the distributed lag model can be written in normalized form as

$$y_t = \alpha + \beta \sum_{j=0}^{\infty} w_j x_{t-j} + u_t. \tag{6.8.35}$$

By definition the weights sum to unity, and if all the β_j are positive, so are all the weights, so that

$$w_j \geq 0, \qquad \sum_{j=0}^{\infty} w_j = 1. \tag{6.8.36}$$

From (6.8.34) the weight w_j may be interpreted as the fraction of the long-term effect β accomplished in period $t - j$.

The linear distributed lag in econometrics is a special case of the transfer function model. The Box–Jenkins procedure to identify a transfer function model, discussed in Section 6.8.2, is a purely statistical one, which will work well if the sample size is large. If, however, the number of time-series observations is small and if the variables are subject to severe multicollinearity, preliminary estimates $\hat{\beta}_j$ tend to jump around and can be very far away from the true value of β_j. In such a case it is hard to implement the Box–Jenkins procedure.

Very often there is some a priori information about the coefficients $\beta_0, \beta_1, \ldots$. For example, the influence of an exogenous variable might be in one direction only so that the β_j are all positive or negative. As another example, the impact of changes in exogenous variable could at first increase with time but must eventually be continuously decreasing once the maximum has been reached. It would be advantageous to take account of this kind of prior knowledge in modeling to overcome the problems of shortages of degrees of freedom and severe multicollinearity stemming from the fact that there are large numbers of parameters and the explanatory variables are all lagged values of the same basic variable.

The geometric or Koyck (1954) lag. The *geometric* or *Koyck lag model* is defined by

$$\begin{aligned} y_t &= \beta \sum_{j=0}^{\infty} \lambda^j x_{t-j} + u_t \\ &= \frac{\beta}{1 - \lambda L} x_t + u_t, \end{aligned} \tag*{*(6.8.37)}$$

as developed by Koyck (1954). This model is an infinite lag model, for which the lag response coefficients decline geometrically, so that the infinite lag response depends on only two parameters, β and λ. An important example of this model is the *partial adjustment (or stock adjustment) model* of Nerlove (1958).

Multiplying (6.8.37) by $(1 - \lambda L)$ yields

$$y_t = \lambda y_{t-1} + \beta x_t + v_t, \tag*{*(6.8.38)}$$

where $v_t = u_t - \lambda u_{t-1}$. If the v_t are i.i.d, the least squares method can be applied. If, however, the u_t are i.i.d., v_t is correlated with y_{t-1}, and least squares will yield inconsistent estimates. Instrumental variable methods using (x_{t-1}, x_t) as instruments for (y_{t-1}, x_t) can be used to obtain consistent estimates of λ and β. Hatanaka (1974) has suggested a three-step estimator, which is asymptotically as efficient as the MLE.

The Almon lag. A very flexible form for the finite-length distributed lag model was suggested by Almon (1965). In the *Almon lag*, starting with an a priori specified lag length of say N, where

$$y_t = \sum_{j=0}^{N} \beta_j x_{t-j} + u_t, \qquad *(6.8.39)$$

the coefficients β_j for $j = 0, 1, \ldots, N$ are approximated by polynomials in the lag j of degree $q < N$.

$$\beta_j = \delta_0 + \delta_1(j) + \delta_2(j)^2 + \cdots + \delta_q(j)^q. \qquad (6.8.40)$$

When considering β_j as a function of j, this lag distribution can have a humped or even more complicated shape. With a second-degree polynomial the β's can, for example, at first rise, then fall, and with a third-degree polynomial the β's can, for example, fall, then rise, and finally fall again. In fact, any complicated shape for the β's can be allowed by choosing a sufficiently high-degree polynomial. Usually, however, only polynomials of relatively low degree are employed.

Letting $\boldsymbol{\beta} = (\beta_0, \beta_1, \ldots, \beta_N)'$, $\boldsymbol{\delta} = (\delta_0, \delta_1, \ldots, \delta_q)'$, and

$$\mathbf{J} = \begin{bmatrix} 1 & 0 & 0 & \cdots & 0 \\ 1 & 1 & 1 & \cdots & 1 \\ 1 & 2 & 2^2 & \cdots & 2^q \\ \vdots & \vdots & \vdots & \ddots & \\ 1 & N & N^2 & & N^q \end{bmatrix}, \qquad (6.8.41)$$

the Almon lag can be represented as

$$\boldsymbol{\beta} = \mathbf{J}\boldsymbol{\delta}. \qquad (6.8.42)$$

Substituting (6.8.42) into (6.8.39), $\boldsymbol{\delta}$ can be estimated by regressing $\mathbf{y}$ on $\mathbf{XJ}$, where $\mathbf{y}$ is an $n \times 1$ vector, the tth element of which is y_t, and $\mathbf{X}$ is an $n \times (N+1)$ matrix, the $(t, j+1)$th element of which is x_{t-j}. Alternatively, (6.8.40) can be written as

$$\nabla^{q+1}\beta_j = 0. \qquad (6.8.43)$$

For instance, for $q = 2$,

$$\begin{aligned} \nabla\beta_j &= \beta_j - \beta_{j-1} \\ &= \left(\delta_0 + \delta_1 j + \delta_2 j^2\right) - \left[\delta_0 + \delta_1(j-1) + \delta_2(j-1)^2\right] \\ &= (\delta_1 - \delta_2) + 2\delta_2 j, \end{aligned} \qquad (6.8.44)$$

$$\nabla^2\beta_j = \nabla\beta_j - \nabla\beta_{j-1} = 2\delta_2, \qquad (6.8.45)$$

$$\begin{aligned} \nabla^3\beta_j &= \nabla^2\beta_j - \nabla^2\beta_{j-1} \\ &= \beta_j - 3\beta_{j-1} + 3\beta_{j-2} - \beta_{j-3} \\ &= 0. \end{aligned} \qquad (6.8.46)$$

Thus, model (6.8.39)–(6.8.40) can also be estimated by the method of constrained regression as discussed in Section 4.6, subject to the constraint (6.8.43).

Some researchers prefer to impose the end constraint $\beta_{N+1} = 0$. This amounts to imposing another restriction

$$\delta_0 + \delta_1(N+1) + \cdots + \delta_q(N+1)^q = 0. \tag{6.8.47}$$

The Shiller lag. Instead of imposing the exact constraint (6.8.43), Shiller (1973) lets β_j follow a stochastic constraint

$$\nabla^{q+1}\beta_j = \eta, \tag{6.8.48}$$

where η is normally distributed with mean zero and variance σ_η^2. Then $\boldsymbol{\beta}$ can be estimated using the Theil and Goldberger (1961) mixed regression technique, which is the generalized least squares method applied to the stacked model:

$$\begin{pmatrix} \mathbf{y} \\ \mathbf{0} \end{pmatrix} = \begin{pmatrix} \mathbf{X} \\ \mathbf{R} \end{pmatrix} \boldsymbol{\beta} + \begin{pmatrix} \mathbf{u} \\ \boldsymbol{\eta} \end{pmatrix}, \tag{6.8.49}$$

where $\mathbf{R}$ is the constraint matrix implied by (6.8.48). For instance, if $q = 2$,

$$\mathbf{R} = \underset{(N+1-3)\times(N+1)}{\begin{bmatrix} -1 & 3 & -3 & 1 & 0 & \cdots & \cdots & 0 \\ 0 & -1 & 3 & -3 & 1 & \cdots & \cdots & 0 \\ \vdots & & \ddots & & & & & \vdots \\ \vdots & & & & \ddots & & & \vdots \\ \vdots & & & & & & & 0 \\ 0 & & & & -1 & 3 & -3 & 1 \end{bmatrix}}. \tag{6.8.50}$$

The spline lag. The Almon lag assumes that all $N + 1$ coefficients are defined by a qth-order polynomial. In many cases a low-order polynomial may not approximate $\beta_0, \beta_1, \ldots, \beta_N$ well. Therefore, several low-order polynomials may be used, each only approximating part of the intervals over the set $\beta_0, \beta_1, \ldots, \beta_N$, with these different polynomials subject to certain smoothness conditions. A *spline function* is a piecewise function in which the pieces are joined together in a suitably smooth fashion. Usually, the pieces are chosen to be polynomials of low degree, and the smoothness requirement is interpreted in terms of continuity of the spline and its derivatives. For instance, consider the case of two qth-degree polynomials for the interval 0 to N, where it is assumed that the first polynomial $f_1(j)$ is used to approximate $\beta_0, \ldots, \beta_k$ and the second polynomial $f_2(j)$ is used to approximate $\beta_k, \beta_{k+1}, \ldots, \beta_N$. The point k where the two polynomials connect is called the *knot*. Usually, in addition to imposing the continuity condition at k,

$$f_1(k) = f_2(k), \tag{6.8.51}$$

smoothness conditions involving the first $(q-1)$ derivatives

$$\begin{gathered} f_1'(k) = f_2'(k) \\ \vdots \\ f_1^{q-1}(k) = f_2^{q-1}(k) \end{gathered} \tag{6.8.52}$$

are also imposed. For instance, for a cubic spline the continuity and smoothness conditions at the knot k are

$$\begin{aligned}\delta_{10} + \delta_{11}k + \delta_{12}k^2 + \delta_{13}k^3 &= \delta_{20} + \delta_{21}k + \delta_{22}k^2 + \delta_{23}k^3,\\ \delta_{11} + 2\delta_{12}k + 3\delta_{13}k^2 &= \delta_{21} + 2\delta_{22}k + 3\delta_{23}k^2,\\ 2\delta_{12} + 6\delta_{13}k &= 2\delta_{22} + 6\delta_{23}k.\end{aligned} \tag{6.8.53}$$

Again, the estimation of $\boldsymbol{\beta}$ can be obtained through a constrained regression method. Of course, in this case, in addition to the a priori chosen N, q, one also has to decide on the knot. For further details, see Poirier (1976).

6.8.4 Autoregressive Models

Another commonly used transfer function form is that of autoregressive (AR) models, in which the explanation of the value taken by a quantity during a certain period is based on the value of the same quantity in preceding periods,

$$y_t = -a_1 y_{t-1} - \cdots - a_p y_{t-p} + \boldsymbol{\beta}'\mathbf{x}_t + u_t. \qquad *(6.8.54)$$

Model (6.8.54) is said to contain *lagged endogenous variables*, which, together with the exogenous variables, determine the current endogenous variables. Alternatively, the expression *predetermined variables* is used to denote both the exogenous variables and the lagged endogenous variables.

If the roots of the associated polynomial equation,

$$a(z) = 1 + a_1 z + \cdots + a_p z^p = 0, \qquad *(6.8.55)$$

as in (6.3.21), are greater than 1 in absolute value, if u_t is i.i.d. with zero mean and finite variance, and if the limit or probability limit of $(1/n)\sum_{t=1}^{n} \mathbf{x}_t\mathbf{x}_t'$ is a finite constant matrix, the least squares estimator of (6.8.54) is consistent and asymptotically normally distributed, with asymptotic covariance matrix given by (4.4.28). However, in finite samples, the least squares estimator is biased, where the order of bias is $1/n$, as discussed in Hurwicz (1950).

If the stochastic disturbances u_t are serially correlated, u_t will be correlated with the lagged endogenous variables so that the least squares estimator will be inconsistent. For instance, consider the simple AR model

$$y_t = -a_1 y_{t-1} + u_t \tag{6.8.56}$$

$$u_t = \rho u_{t-1} + \varepsilon_t, \qquad |\rho| < 1, \tag{6.8.57}$$

where the ε_t are i.i.d. with zero mean and finite variance. The least squares estimator of a_1 is

$$\begin{aligned}\hat{a}_1 &= -\frac{\Sigma y_t y_{t-1}}{\Sigma y_{t-1}^2}\\ &= -\frac{(\rho - a_1)\Sigma y_{t-1}^2 + \rho a_1 \Sigma y_{t-1}y_{t-2} + \Sigma\,\varepsilon_t y_{t-1}}{\Sigma y_{t-1}^2}\\ &= -(\rho - a_1) - \rho a_1 \frac{\Sigma y_{t-1}y_{t-2}}{\Sigma y_{t-1}^2} + \frac{\Sigma\,\varepsilon_t y_{t-1}}{\Sigma y_{t-1}^2},\end{aligned} \tag{6.8.58}$$

where the second equality follows from substituting y_t by the relation

$$y_t = (\rho - a_1)y_{t-1} + \rho a_1 y_{t-2} + \varepsilon_t. \tag{6.8.59}$$

Taking probability limits of (6.8.58) yields

$$\text{plim}\ \hat{a}_1 = -(\rho - a_1) + \rho a_1\ \text{plim}\ \hat{a}_1 + 0, \tag{6.8.60}$$

so

$$\text{plim } \hat{a}_1 = \frac{a_1 - \rho}{1 - \rho a_1}. \tag{6.8.61}$$

The difference between the probability limit of the least squares estimator and the true value is

$$\text{plim } \hat{a}_1 - a_1 = \frac{\rho(a_1^2 - 1)}{1 - \rho a_1}, \tag{6.8.62}$$

and this difference can be large for high values of ρ and low values of a_1. For example, if $\rho = 0.8$ and $a_1 = -0.2$, the difference is -0.66; that is, the probability limit of the least squares estimator is -0.86, while the true value of a_1 is -0.2. This difference underscores the fact that least squares is inappropriate in such cases of lagged dependent variables and serially correlated stochastic disturbance terms as in (6.8.57). The appropriate estimation method in this case is again GLS, where, as discussed in Section 5.3, the GLS method can be viewed as the method of least squares applied to the transformed model, the transformed residuals being serially uncorrelated here. For the example of (6.8.57), the covariance is given in (5.5.9), where σ_v^2 is replaced by σ_ε^2, and the GLS estimator (5.3.9) can be obtained if ρ is known. If ρ is unknown, a two-step procedure can be employed by first obtaining a consistent estimate of ρ using instrumental variable methods.

Because of the potential bias of the least squares estimator for an autoregressive model with serially correlated residuals, it is important to test for serial correlation. Likelihood ratio tests can be conducted. However, they can be computationally tedious. In the case with a single lagged endogenous variable (i.e., when $p = 1$), Durbin (1970) suggests an alternative test that can be used with the least squares residuals. He shows that, under the null hypothesis, the residuals are serially uncorrelated and the *Durbin h-statistic*

$$h = \hat{\rho}\sqrt{\frac{n}{1 - n \operatorname{Var}(\hat{a}_1)}} \tag{6.8.63}$$

is asymptotically normally distributed with mean zero and variance 1, where $\hat{\rho}$ is the estimated first-order serial correlation computed from the least squares residuals, and $\operatorname{Var}(\hat{a}_1)$ is the variance of the least squares estimate of a_1.

PROBLEMS

6-A Consider the time series 1, 2, 3, 4, 5, 6, . . . , 20. Is this series stationary? Calculate the sample autocorrelation function $\hat{\rho}_k$ for $k = 1, 2, \ldots, 5$. Can you explain the shape of this function?

6-B Table 6.3 shows the data of 10 years of monthly rate of return of IBM shares. Calculate the sample autocorrelation function $\hat{\rho}_k$ for $k = 1, 2, \ldots, 12$. Does it exhibit stationarity and/or seasonality? Calculate the sample autocorrelations for the original series and the differenced series $\nabla r_t = r_t - r_{t-1}$. Does the differenced series appear stationary?

6-C Let y_t follow the process

$$y_t = 0.9y_{t-1} - 0.8y_{t-2} + \varepsilon_t,$$

where ε_t has mean 0, variance 1, and is uncorrelated with ε_s, $t \neq s$. Find the autocorrelation of $\{y_t\}$. Plot the autocorrelation function.

6-D Suppose that the autocorrelation function of a time series consisting of 100 quarterly observations has $r_1 = 0.31$, $r_2 = 0.37$, $r_3 = 0.05$, $r_4 = 0.42$, $r_5 = -0.01$, $r_6 = 0.11$, $r_7 = 0.08$, $r_8 = 0.20$, $r_9 = 0.12$,

TABLE 6.3 Monthly Rate of Return of IBM Shares

	1983	1984	1985	1986	1987	1988	1989	1990	1991	1992
Jan.	0.029	0.034	0.066	–0.052	0.119	0.027	–0.065	0.108	–0.026	0.073
Feb.	–0.043	–0.017	–0.062	0.011	–0.014	0.01	–0.026	–0.009	0.003	0.092
Mar.	–0.063	0.052	–0.122	–0.029	–0.034	0.028	0.034	–0.052	0.004	0.076
Apr.	0.13	–0.004	–0.016	–0.06	0.075	0.15	–0.002	–0.004	0.031	0.067
May	–0.018	–0.022	0.025	0.017	–0.029	–0.041	–0.044	0.025	–0.018	0.006
June	–0.004	–0.035	0.061	–0.015	–0.014	0.081	–0.019	–0.038	–0.039	0.016
July	0.092	–0.049	0.111	–0.03	0.082	0.001	0.047	0.062	–0.096	–0.009
Aug.	0.049	0.016	0.017	–0.002	0.087	0.001	0.127	–0.028	0.055	0.053
Sept.	–0.051	–0.032	–0.021	–0.018	0.041	0.062	0.004	–0.022	–0.031	–0.105
Oct.	–0.046	–0.079	0.039	–0.048	0.089	–0.001	0.012	0.048	–0.081	–0.187
Nov.	0.031	0.06	0.035	0.075	0.094	–0.066	–0.023	0.085	0.037	–0.087
Dec.	0.108	–0.013	–0.044	0.044	0.113	0.039	0.011	0.113	–0.056	0.043

$r_{10} = 0.01$, $r_{11} = 0.05$, $r_{12} = -0.07$. Suggest a time-series model that may be appropriate. Explain your result.

6-E Show that the infinite-order MA process $\{y_t\}$ defined by

$$y_t = \varepsilon_t + c(\varepsilon_{t-1} + \varepsilon_{t-2} + \cdots),$$

where c is a constant and ε_t is i.i.d. with mean 0 and variance σ_ε^2, is nonstationary. Also show that the series of first differences defined by

$$w_t = y_t - y_{t-1}$$

is a first-order MA process and is stationary. Find the autocorrelation function of $\{w_t\}$.

6-F Fit an ARMA model for the U.S. quarterly consumer price index from 1970.1 to 1990.4, using the methodology of Box–Jenkins. Compare your predicted 1991–1992 CPI against the actual.

6-G For the model

$$(1 - L)(1 - 0.2L)y_t = (1 - 0.5L)\varepsilon_t, \qquad t = 1, \ldots, T.$$

1. Find forecasts for one and two steps ahead, and show that a recursive expression for forecasts three or more steps ahead is given by
$$\hat{y}_{T+K} = 1.2\hat{y}_{T+K-1} - 0.2\hat{y}_{T+K-2}, \qquad K \geq 3.$$
2. If $y_T = 4$, $y_{T-1} = 3$, $\varepsilon_T = 1$, and $\sigma_\varepsilon^2 = 2$, show $\hat{y}_{T+1}$ and the standard error of the corresponding forecast error.
3. Find the variance of the one-, two-, and three-steps-ahead forecast errors.

6-H Obtain an equation that could be used to estimate a more general distributed lag model of the Koyck type:

1. In which the coefficients decline geometrically only after j_0 periods.
2. In which there are two different explanatory variables x and z for which both lag distributions are characterized by the parameter λ.
3. As in item 2 except that the two lag distributions are characterized by the two parameters λ_1 and λ_2, respectively, where $\lambda_1 \neq \lambda_2$.

6-I In the *adaptive expectations* model of capital stock growth the level of capital is set at a multiple of anticipated output Y_t^*,

$$K_t = \delta Y_t^*,$$

where the change in anticipated output over time is proportional to the gap between actual and past anticipated output:

$$Y_t^* - Y_{t-1}^* = \alpha(Y_t - Y_{t-1}^*) + w_t, \qquad 0 < \alpha \leq 1.$$

Determine for these equations an equation involving only observable magnitudes (anticipated output not being observable), and contrast it to that obtained for the partial adjustment model (6.8.38).

6-J The partial adjustment model of (6.7.38) can be obtained from the adaptive expectations model of Problem 6-I to yield the model

$$K_t^* = \delta Y_t^*,$$

$$K_t - K_{t-1} = \gamma(K_t^* - K_{t-1}) + v_t, \qquad 0 < \gamma \leq 1,$$

$$Y_t^* - Y_{t-1}^* = \alpha(Y_t - Y_{t-1}^*) + w_t, \qquad 0 < \alpha \leq 1.$$

Combine these equations into a single equation that can be estimated. Which of the parameters δ, γ, and α can be estimated from this equation?

6-K A simple model leading to the partial adjustment model of (6.8.38) is one in which total cost is the sum of the cost of not maintaining the desired capital stock and the cost of changing capital stock. In the quadratic case

$$C = \alpha(K_t - K_t^*)^2 + \beta(K_t - K_{t-1})^2,$$

where α and β are given nonnegative constants. Show that the choice of K_t to minimize C yields (6.8.38).

6-L 1. Show that the polynomial distributed lag model

$$y_t = \beta_0 x_t + \beta_1 x_{t-1} + \cdots + \beta_h x_{t-h} + u_t,$$
$$\beta_j = \gamma_0 + \gamma_1 j$$

can be rewritten as a rational distributed lag model.

2. Comment on this result when $h \to \infty$.
3. Devise a test of the hypothesis that the order of the approximating polynomial to β_j is 1 against the alternative hypothesis that the order is 2. That is, for $\beta_j = \gamma_0 + \gamma_1 j + \gamma_2 j^2$, test $H_0: \gamma_2 = 0$ against $H_1: \gamma_2 \neq 0$.

6-M Consider the simple autoregressive model with autocorrelated errors:

$$y_t = \alpha y_{t-1} + u_t, \qquad u_t = \rho u_{t-1} + \varepsilon_t,$$

where the ε_t are independent $N(0, \sigma^2)$ random variables. This can be written as

$$(*) \qquad y_t = (\alpha + \rho) y_{t-1} - \alpha\rho y_{t-2} + \varepsilon_t.$$

1. Assuming (without proof) that $\text{plim}\,(1/T)\Sigma y_t^2$ and $\text{plim}\,(1/T)\Sigma y_t y_{t-1}$ exist, find the probability limit of the least squares estimator $a = \Sigma yy_{-1}/\Sigma y_{-1}^2$. [*Hint*: Multiply (*) by y_{t-1} and sum.]
2. Using (*), write the likelihood function for a sample of size T. Find the asymptotic information matrix for α and ρ (assuming that σ is known). [*Hint*: Let $A = Ey_t^2 = \text{plim}(1/T)\Sigma y_t^2$ and use part 1 to express $E(yy_{-1}) = \text{plim}(1/T)\Sigma yy_{-1}$ in terms of A; write your answer in terms of A without explicitly evaluating it.] Inverting the information matrix, give an expression (in terms of α, ρ, and A) for the asymptotic variance of an efficient estimator of α.
3. Suppose that ρ were known. What is an efficient estimator for α? Using Theil's Theorem 8.5 (Theil, 1971, p. 412), give the asymptotic variance of this estimator. Show that this variance is the same as that obtained by inverting the one-by-one information matrix (assuming ρ and σ^2 known).
4. Compare the variance calculated in part 2 with the variance calculated in part 3. For what values of α and ρ does the knowledge of ρ have the greatest value? Let r_t be a consistent estimator of ρ. If you replaced ρ by r_t in the estimator given in part 3, would you still get the same variance? [*Hint*: Do not try to calculate the asymptotic variance. Simply use the fact that the variance calculated in part 2 is the minimum for all estimates not depending on the true ρ.]

BIBLIOGRAPHY

ALMON, S. (1965). "The Distributed Lag between Capital Appropriations and Expenditure." *Econometrica*, 33: 178–196.

ANDERSON, R. L. (1942). "Distribution of the Serial Correlation Coefficient." *Annals of Mathematical Statistics*, 13: 1–13.

ANDERSON, T. W. (1959). "On Asymptotic Distributions of Estimates of Parameters of Stochastic Difference Equations." *Annals of Mathematical Statistics*, 30: 676–687.

ANDERSON, T. W. (1971). *The Statistical Analysis of Time Series*. New York: John Wiley & Sons, Inc.

ANSLEY, C. F., and P. NEWBOLD (1980). "Finite Sample Properties of Estimators for Autoregressive–Moving Average Models." *Journal of Econometrics*, 13: 159–183.

BARTLETT, M. S. (1946). "On the Theoretical Specification of Sampling Properties of Autocorrelated Time Series." *Journal of the Royal Statistical Society*, 8: 27–41.

BARTLETT, M. S. (1966). *An Introduction to Stochastic Processes*, 2nd ed. Cambridge: Cambridge University Press.

BIERENS, H. J., and S. GUO (1993). "Testing Stationarity and Trend Stationarity against the Unit Root Hypothesis." *Econometric Reviews*, 12: 1–32.

BOX, G. E. P., and G. M. JENKINS (1970). *Time Series Analysis, Forecasting and Control*. San Francisco: Holden-Day, Inc.

BOX, G. E. P., and D. A. PIERCE (1970). "Distribution of Residual Autocorrelation in Autoregressive-Integrated Moving Average Time Series Models." *Journal of the American Statistical Association*, 65: 1509–1526.

BOX, G. E. P., and G. C. TIAO (1975). "Intervention Analysis with Applications to Economic and Environmental Problems." *Journal of the American Statistical Association*, 70: 70–79.

CHAN, K. H., J. C. HAYYA, and T. K. ORD (1977). "A Note on Trend Removal Methods: The Case of Polynomial Trend versus Variate Differencing." *Econometrica*, 45: 737–744.

CHAN, N. H., and C. Z. WEI (1988). "Limiting Distributions of Least Squares Estimates of Unstable Autoregressive Processes." *Annals of Statistics*, 16: 367–401.

COOPER, R. L. (1972). "The Predictive Performance of Quarterly Econometric Models of the United States," in B. G. Hickman, Ed., *Econometric Models of Cyclical Behavior*. New York: Columbia University Press.

DAVIES, N., and P. NEWBOLD (1980). "Sample Moments of the Autocorrelations of Moving Average Processes and a Modification to Bartlett's Asymptotic Variance Formula." *Communication of Statistics*, A9: 1473–1481.

DHRYMES, P. J. (1981). *Distributed Lags*, 2nd ed. Amsterdam: North-Holland Publishing Company.

DICKEY, D. A. (1976). "Estimation and Testing of Nonstationary Times Series." Ph.D. thesis, Iowa State University.

DICKEY, D. A., and W. A. FULLER (1979). "Distribution of the Estimators for Autoregressive Time Series with a Unit Root." *Journal of the American Statistical Association*, 74: 427–431.

DICKEY, D. A., and S. G. PANTULA (1987). "Determining the Order of Differencing in Autoregressive Processes." *Journal of Business and Economic Statistics*, 5: 455–462.

DIEBOLD, F. X., and M. NERLOVE (1989). "Unit Roots in Economic Time Series: A Survey," in T. B. Fomby and G. F. Rhodes, Eds., *Advances in Econometrics: Cointegration, Spurious Regressions, and Unit Roots*. Greenwich, Conn.: JAI Press, Inc.

DURBIN, J. (1970). "Testing for Serial Correlation in Least Squares Regression When Some of the Regressors Are Lagged Dependent." *Econometrica*, 38: 410–421.

DURLAUF, S. N., and P. C. B. PHILLIPS (1988). "Trends versus Random Walks in Time Series Analysis." *Econometrica*, 56: 1333–1354.

EVANS, G. B. A., and N. E. SAVIN (1981). "Testing for Unit Roots I." *Econometrica*, 49: 753–779.

FULLER, W. A. (1976). *Introduction to Statistical Time Series*. New York: John Wiley & Sons, Inc.

GRANGER, C. W. J., and P. NEWBOLD (1986). *Forecasting Economic Time Series*, 2nd ed. San Diego: Academic Press, Inc.

GRILICHES, Z. (1967). "Distributed Lags: A Survey." *Econometrica*, 35: 16–49.

HAMILTON, J. D. (1994). *Time Series Analysis*. Princeton, N.J.: Princeton University Press.

HANSEN, B. (1993). "Rethinking the Univariate Approach to Unit Root Tests: How to Use Covariates to Increase Power." Mimeograph, University of Rochester.

HARVEY, A. C. (1990). *The Econometric Analysis of Time Series*, 2nd ed. Cambridge, Mass: MIT Press.

HATANAKA, M. (1974). "An Efficient Two-Step Estimator for the Dynamic Adjustment Model with Autoregressive Errors." *Journal of Econometrics*, 2: 199–220.

HURWICZ, L. (1950). "Least Squares Bias in Time Series," in *Statistical Inference in Dynamic Economic Models*. New York: John Wiley & Sons, Inc.

JORGENSON, D. (1966). "Rational Distributed Lag Functions." *Econometrica*, 34: 135–149.

KOYCK, L. M. (1954). *Distributed Lags and Investment Analysis*. Amsterdam: North-Holland Publishing Company.

LJUNG, G. M., and G. E. P. BOX (1978). "On a Measure of Lack of Fit in Time Series Models." *Biometrika*, 65: 297–303.

NELSON, C. R. (1972). "The Prediction Performance of the F.R.B.–M.I.T.–PENN Model of the U.S. Economy." *American Economic Review*, 62: 902–917.

NELSON, C. R., and H. KANG (1981). "Spurious Periodicity in Inappropriately Detrended Time Series." *Econometrica*, 49: 741–751.

NERLOVE, M. (1958). *The Dynamics of Supply: Estimation of Farmers' Response to Price*. Baltimore: Johns Hopkins University Press.

PARK, J. (1990). "Testing for Unit Roots and Cointegration by Variable Addition," in T. B. Fomby and G. F. Rhodes, Eds., *Advances in Econometrics*. Greenwich, Conn.: JAI Press, Inc.

PHILLIPS, P. C. B. (1987). "Time Series Regression with a Unit Root." *Econometrica*, 55: 277–301.

POIRIER, D. J. (1976). *The Econometrics of Structural Change*. Amsterdam: North-Holland Publishing Company.

SHILLER, R. J. (1973). "A Distributed Lag Estimator Derived from Smoothness Priors." *Econometrica*, 41: 775–788.

SIMS, C. A. (1974). "Distributed Lags," in M. D. Intriligator and D. A. Kendrick, Eds., *Frontiers of Quantitative Economics*, Vol. 2. Amsterdam: North-Holland Publishing Company.

THEIL, H. (1971). *Principles of Econometrics*. New York: John Wiley & Sons, Inc.

THEIL, H., and A. S. GOLDBERGER (1961). "On Pure and Mixed Statistical Estimation in Economics." *International Economic Review*, 2: 65–78.

WALLIS, K. F. (1977). "Multiple Time Series Analysis and the Final Form of Econometric Models." *Econometrica*, 45: 1481–1497.

WHITE, J. S. (1958). "The Limiting Distribution of the Serial Correlation Coefficient in the Explosive Case." *Annals of Mathematical Statistics*, 29: 1188–1197.

WOLD, H. (1954). *A Study in the Analysis of Stationary Time Series*, 2nd ed. Uppsala: Almquist & Wiksell Förlag.

ZELLER, A., and F. PALM (1974). "Time Series Analysis and Simultaneous Equation Econometric Models." *Journal of Econometrics*, 2: 17–54.

7

APPLICATIONS TO HOUSEHOLDS; DEMAND ANALYSIS

7.1 INTRODUCTION

One of the oldest and most important uses of econometrics is its application to households in the estimation of demand relationships and consumer behavior.[1] Pioneer empirical analyses of demand, starting early in the twentieth century, led, in fact, to later studies of general issues in econometric theory.

Econometric studies of demand have involved all three of the basic objectives of econometrics discussed in Chapter 1. Virtually all involve some aspects of *structural analysis*, particularly the estimation of the impacts of prices and income on demand, as measured by elasticities of demand. Some are oriented toward *forecasting*, in particular forecasting quantities and/or prices of particular commodities in either the short- or long-range future. Others are oriented toward *policy evaluation*, in particular, impacts of policies that may affect markets for consumer goods, such as taxes or (de)regulation. For example, from estimated demand curves it is possible to estimate the effects of excise taxes, such as the effects on the quantities demanded and the tax yield from taxes on gasoline, as in Section 1.4.

Two seminal studies, those by Wold and Jureen, and Stone, illustrate all three uses of empirical studies of demand.[2] Both utilized interwar data from the 1920s and 1930s in order to estimate demand functions for various commodities in Sweden and the United Kingdom, respectively, in the 1950s. Each study estimated elasticities of demand, and some of these results are reported below. Each was also concerned with forecasting the pattern of demand once wartime regulations, in particular rationing, were lifted, and they

[1]Basic references for econometric studies of consumer demand are Powell (1974), Deaton and Muellbauer (1980), Phlips (1983), and Deaton (1986). While "demand" can refer to the demand by firms for factors of production as well as the demand by households for goods, the discussion in this chapter is confined to the latter. For the former, see Chapter 8.

[2]See Wold and Jureen (1953) and Stone (1954a).

both played some role in policy toward eliminating such regulations. In fact, their forecasts were remarkably accurate, considering that the data each utilized were from a much earlier period.

In Section 7.2 we review the basic theory of the household, or consumer, and the demand functions derived from this theory. While the theory presented in this section is usually considered part of microeconomic theory rather than econometrics, it is included here because the specification of the econometric model is (or should be) guided by the underlying theory. In Section 7.3 we contrast the two major types of demand studies—those of single demand functions and those of systems of demand functions. The next two sections present summaries of past econometric studies of single demand equations and systems of demand equations, respectively. The remaining sections treat some important econometric issues in estimating demand relationships, specifically the questions of functional form, identification, aggregation, and dynamic considerations. Included in these sections are examples from the literature of estimated demand functions. It should become clear, as a result of these summaries of past studies, that there is no single ideal model for empirical research on demand. Rather, it is necessary to "tailor make" the model to the particular phenomenon under study. The same type of conclusion will follow from the survey of empirical studies of production and cost in Chapter 8 and the surveys of applications of simultaneous equations in Chapters 12 and 13.

7.2 THE THEORY OF THE HOUSEHOLD

The problem of the household (or consumer), from a formal point of view, is that of choosing levels of consumption of goods (including services) so as to maximize a utility function subject to a given budget constraint.[3] Considering the simplest case of two goods, in which purchases by a single household are measured by x_1 and x_2, respectively, the problem of the household can be stated as

$$\max_{x_1, x_2} U(x_1, x_2) \quad \text{subject to} \quad p_1 x_1 + p_2 x_2 = I. \qquad *(7.2.1)$$

Here $U(x_1, x_2)$ is the utility function, p_1 and p_2 are the prices of the two goods, and I is the level of income of the household. Income and both prices are assumed to be given positive constants. The utility function is an ordinal representation of tastes in that the household prefers a bundle of goods $\mathbf{x} = (x_1, x_2)$ with a higher value of utility to a bundle with a lower value of utility.[4] The budget constraint requires that total expenditures, obtained by totaling expenditures on each of the goods, equal income. The household thus chooses among bundles that satisfy the budget constraint so as to attain the highest available level of utility.

Geometrically, the problem and its solution can be depicted as in Figure 7.1. The *budget line* indicates alternative possible bundles of goods that can be purchased at the given prices and income. The curves are *indifference curves*, each of which indicates those bun-

[3]Basic references for the theory of the household include Intriligator (1971), Barten and Böhm (1982), Phlips (1983), Deaton (1986), Kreps (1990), and Varian (1990).

[4]The theory described here refers to *ordinal utility*, where any monotonically increasing transformation of the utility function is a valid utility function for the household. The utility function can itself be derived from the more basic concept of a preference relation under certain conditions (see Intriligator, 1971).

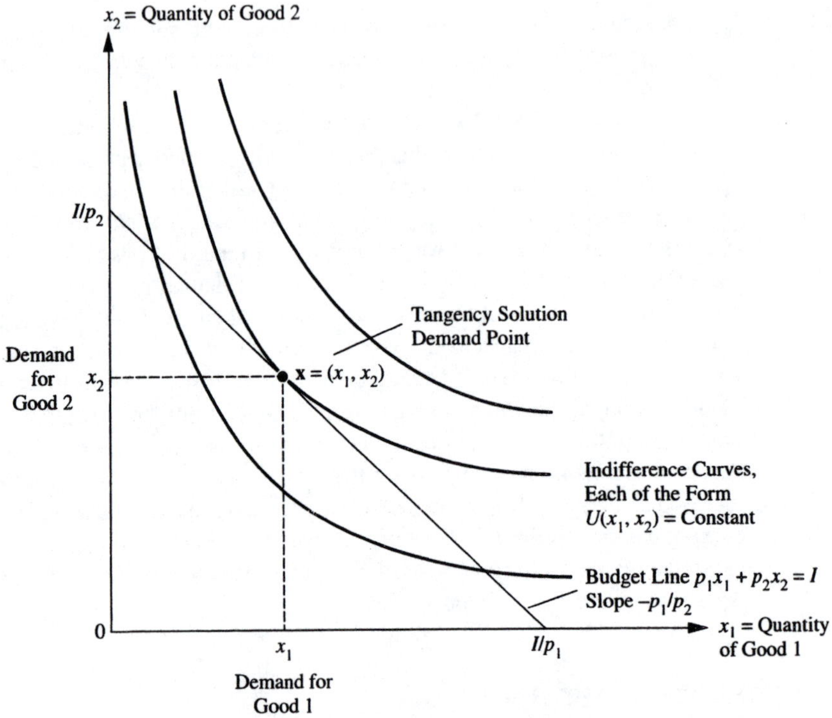

Figure 7.1 Equilibrium of the Consumer

dles that have the same level of utility and therefore among which the consumer is indifferent. They are the level curves of the utility function.

In this "classical" case of smooth and smoothly varying indifference curves the solution is at the *tangency point* **x**. At this point the slope of the budget line, which is the (negative) ratio of prices, equals the slope of the indifference curve, which is called the (negative) *marginal rate of substitution.*[5] The optimal quantities demanded are then x_1 and x_2, as shown.

The *demand functions* give the dependence of the (optimal) quantities demanded on all parameters of problem (7.2.1), namely both prices and income:

$$\left.\begin{aligned} x_1 &= x_1(p_1, p_2, I) \\ x_2 &= x_2(p_1, p_2, I) \end{aligned}\right\} \quad \text{or} \quad x_j = x_j(p_1, p_2, I), \quad j = 1, 2. \qquad *(7.2.2)$$

[5]The slope of the budget line is $-p_1/p_2$. Given a continuous utility function and an indifference curve of the form $U(x_1, x_2)$ = constant, totally differentiating both sides yields

$$\frac{\partial U}{\partial x_1} dx_1 + \frac{\partial U}{\partial x_2} dx_2 = 0.$$

The marginal rate of substitution, the slope, is therefore given as

$$\text{MRS} \equiv -\frac{dx_2}{dx_1} = \frac{\partial U/\partial x_1}{\partial U/\partial x_2}.$$

Thus, at the tangency point,

$$\frac{\partial U/\partial x_1}{\partial U/\partial x_2} = \text{MRS} = \frac{p_1}{p_2}$$

These functions indicate the amount demanded of each of the goods at alternative combinations of prices and income.

Special cases of the demand functions, in which two of the three parameters are held constant, are also widely discussed in the literature on partial equilibrium analysis. Thus, holding p_2 and I constant in the first equation gives the *demand curve* for the first good:

$$x_1 = D_1(p_1) = x_1(p_1, \bar{p}_2, \bar{I}), \qquad *(7.2.3)$$

where the bars indicate that p_2 and I are held constant. This is the same form as (1.4.1), and Figure 1.2, the demand curve for gasoline, illustrates such a demand curve. Similarly, the demand curve for the second good is

$$x_2 = D_2(p_2) = x_2(\bar{p}_1, p_2, \bar{I}). \qquad *(7.2.4)$$

These demand curves indicate the effect of a change in the price of a good on the quantity demanded, holding other price(s) and income constant (i.e., the *ceteris paribus* effect of a change in "own" price). If the other price(s) or income change, the result will be a shift in the demand curve. A second partial equilibrium approach holds p_1 and p_2 constant, to yield the *Engel curves*:[6]

$$\begin{aligned} \bar{p}_1 x_1 &= E_1(I) = \bar{p}_1 x_1(\bar{p}_1, \bar{p}_2, I), \\ \bar{p}_2 x_2 &= E_2(I) = \bar{p}_2 x_2(\bar{p}_1, \bar{p}_2, I). \end{aligned} \qquad *(7.2.5)$$

These Engel curves indicate the effect of a change in income on the expenditure for each good at fixed prices. If the prices change, the result will be a shift in each of the Engel curves.

The demand curves and Engel curves can be derived geometrically from the equilibrium as portrayed in Figure 7.1. Figure 7.2 indicates the derivation of the demand curve (7.2.3). If p_2 and I are held constant, the intercept on the x_2 axis of the budget line is fixed, so varying p_1 is equivalent, geometrically, to a rotation of the budget line about this intercept, as shown in Figure 7.2. For each budget line there is a tangency point at which the consumer is at an equilibrium. Connecting the (x_1, x_2) pairs in the figure gives the *price-consumption path* for p_1, from which the demand curve for good 1 can be obtained, as shown. Note that if the other price p_2 or income I changes, there will be a shift in the demand curve.

The Engel curve can be similarly derived, as shown in Figure 7.3. Holding prices constant implies that the slope of the budget line is constant. Thus changing income is shown geometrically as a parallel shift of the budget line. In the figure it is assumed that $p_1 = 1$, so the horizontal intercepts of the budget lines give the two levels of income. With each budget line there is an associated equilibrium at a tangency with an indifference curve. Connecting the (x_1, x_2) pairs from the figure gives the *income-consumption path*, from which the Engel curve for good 2 can be obtained, as shown. Note that a change in either price will generally lead to a shift in the Engel curve.

Engel's law refers to a property of the Engel curve for food. The law states that the proportion of income consumers spend on food decreases as their income increases. Thus, if x_2 is food, the law states that eventually the ratio p_2x_2/I decreases as I increases.

Elasticities of demand can be defined using the demand function, the demand curve, or the Engel curve. These elasticities are convenient summaries of the responsiveness of the quantity demanded to factors influencing it, in part because they are independent of the units of measurement of the good, prices, income, and so on. Thus comparisons of elasticities

[6]Named for Ernst Engel, the statistician, not to be confused with Karl Marx's collaborator Friedrich Engels.

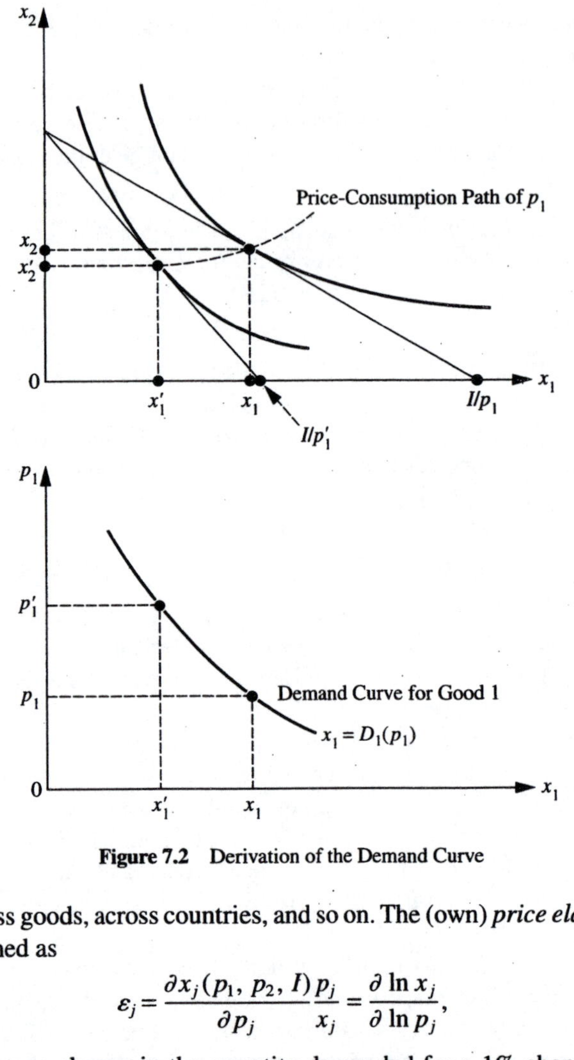

Figure 7.2 Derivation of the Demand Curve

can be made across goods, across countries, and so on. The (own) *price elasticity of demand* for good j is defined as

$$\varepsilon_j = \frac{\partial x_j(p_1, p_2, I)}{\partial p_j}\frac{p_j}{x_j} = \frac{\partial \ln x_j}{\partial \ln p_j}, \qquad *(7.2.6)$$

giving the percentage change in the quantity demanded for a 1% change in the price of this good. Usually, the price elasticity, so defined, is negative.[7] The good is said to be *price elastic* if $|\varepsilon_j| > 1$ and *price inelastic* if $|\varepsilon_j| < 1$. The *income elasticity of demand* for good j is

$$\eta_j = \frac{\partial x_j(p_1, p_2, I)}{\partial I}\frac{I}{x_j} = \frac{\partial \ln x_j}{\partial \ln I}, \qquad *(7.2.7)$$

giving the percentage change in the quantity demand for a 1% change in income. Usually the income elasticity, so defined, is positive. (The elasticity is negative for an inferior good, for which demand falls as income rises.) The good is said to be *income elastic* if $\eta_j > 1$ and *income inelastic* if $\eta_j < 1$. In terms of elasticities, Engel's law states that food is income in-

[7] Frequently, the magnitude of the price elasticity of demand is reported as a positive number, referring to its absolute value and not to its sign.

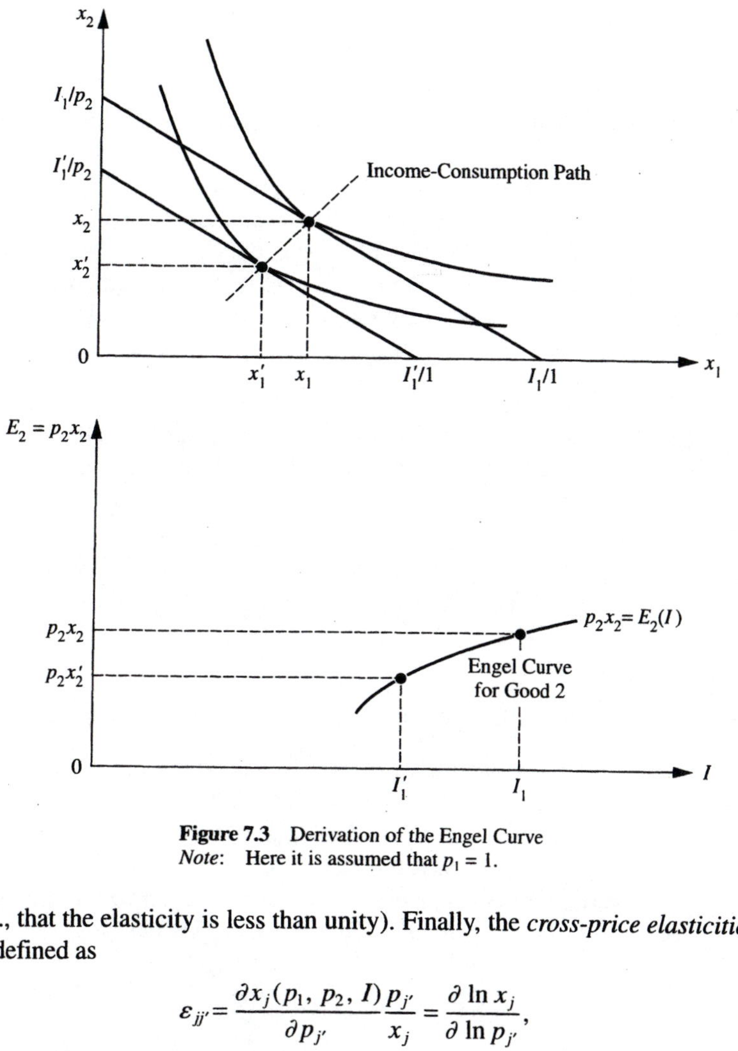

Figure 7.3 Derivation of the Engel Curve
Note: Here it is assumed that $p_1 = 1$.

elastic (i.e., that the elasticity is less than unity). Finally, the *cross-price elasticities* of demand are defined as

$$\varepsilon_{jj'} = \frac{\partial x_j(p_1, p_2, I)}{\partial p_{j'}} \frac{p_{j'}}{x_j} = \frac{\partial \ln x_j}{\partial \ln p_{j'}}, \qquad *(7.2.8)$$

indicating the effect of a change in the price of one good on the demand for the other good. From these definitions $\varepsilon_{jj} = \varepsilon_j$ (the own price elasticity) and, in general, $\varepsilon_{jj'} \neq \varepsilon_{j'j}$ for $j \neq j'$. While the elasticities are sometimes treated as approximately constant over a limited range of variations of the variables influencing demand, in general all elasticities depend on all prices and income, so that in this case of two goods all six elasticities, ε_1, ε_2, η_1, η_2, ε_{12}, and ε_{21}, vary with p_1, p_2, and I.

Economic theory suggests that the demand functions (7.2.2) must satisfy certain restrictions. First, they must satisfy the *budget constraint*:

$$p_1x_1(p_1, p_2, I) + p_2x_2(p_1, p_2, I) = I \qquad *(7.2.9)$$

since they solve problem (7.2.1), which contains this constraint. Dividing both sides of this constraint by income, I, the constraint can be expressed as

$$s_1 + s_2 = 1, \qquad *(7.2.10)$$

where s_1 and s_2 are the *budget shares*, defined as the proportions of income spent on each of the goods:

$$s_j = \frac{p_j x_j}{I}, \quad j = 1, 2. \qquad *(7.2.11)$$

It is convenient to express some of the restrictions on the demand functions in terms of these budget shares.

Second, a scaling of both prices and income, from (p_1, p_2, I) to $(\alpha p_1, \alpha p_2, \alpha I)$ does not change the basic problem (7.2.1) since the budget constraint is unchanged and prices and income do not enter the utility function. Hence such scaling should not change the solution as embodied in the demand functions. Thus an equiproportionate change in all prices and income should have no effect on the quantity demanded of either good:[8]

$$x_1(\alpha p_1, \alpha p_2, \alpha I) = x_1(p_1, p_2, I),$$
$$x_2(\alpha p_1, \alpha p_2, \alpha I) = x_2(p_1, p_2, I). \qquad *(7.2.12)$$

These homogeneity conditions state that the demand functions are homogeneous of degree zero in all explanatory variables. It then follows from Euler's theorem on homogeneous functions that[9]

$$\frac{\partial x_1}{\partial p_1} p_1 + \frac{\partial x_1}{\partial p_2} p_2 + \frac{\partial x_1}{\partial I} I = 0,$$
$$\frac{\partial x_2}{\partial p_1} p_1 + \frac{\partial x_2}{\partial p_2} p_2 + \frac{\partial x_2}{\partial I} I = 0. \qquad *(7.2.13)$$

These are the *homogeneity conditions*, which should also be satisfied by the demand functions. These conditions can be expressed in elasticity form as

$$\varepsilon_1 + \varepsilon_{12} + \eta_1 = 0,$$
$$\varepsilon_{21} + \varepsilon_2 + \eta_2 = 0, \qquad *(7.2.14)$$

which state that the sum of all elasticities for any good must vanish.

A third set of conditions are the *Slutsky conditions*, which are based on the comparative static effects of changing prices and income and determining the resulting changes in demand.[10] They include, first, the *negativity conditions*:

$$\frac{\partial x_1}{\partial p_1} + \frac{\partial x_1}{\partial I} x_1 \leq 0,$$
$$\frac{\partial x_2}{\partial p_2} + \frac{\partial x_2}{\partial I} x_2 \leq 0 \qquad *(7.2.15)$$

[8]These conditions are sometimes referred to as "absence of money illusion," where, for example, halving or doubling all prices and income has no effect on quantities demanded.

[9]Euler's theorem on homogeneous functions states that if $f(x_1, x_2, \ldots, x_n)$ is homogeneous of degree h, as defined by

$$f(\alpha x_1, \alpha x_2, \ldots, \alpha x_n) = \alpha^h f(x_1, x_2, \ldots, x_n), \quad \text{all } (x_1, x_2, \ldots, x_n),$$

then

$$\sum_{j=1}^{n} \frac{\partial f}{\partial x_j} x_j = hf(x_1, x_2, \ldots, x_n).$$

[10]These conditions refer to the negative semidefiniteness and symmetry of the matrix of substitution effects in the Slutsky equation (see Intriligator, 1971). The j, k *substitution effect* $(\partial x_j / \partial p_k)_{\text{comp}}$ is defined as the compensated change in the quantity demanded of good j as the price of good k changes, where the compensation in

and second, the *symmetry condition*:

$$\frac{\partial x_1}{\partial p_2} + \frac{\partial x_1}{\partial I} x_2 = \frac{\partial x_2}{\partial p_1} + \frac{\partial x_2}{\partial I} x_1. \qquad *(7.2.16)$$

Using the budget shares defined in (7.2.11), these conditions can also be expressed in elasticity form as

$$\begin{aligned} \varepsilon_1 + s_1\eta_1 &\leq 0, \\ \varepsilon_2 + s_2\eta_2 &\leq 0, \end{aligned} \qquad *(7.2.17)$$

and

$$\frac{1}{s_2}\varepsilon_{12} + \eta_1 = \frac{1}{s_1}\varepsilon_{21} + \eta_2. \qquad *(7.2.18)$$

A fourth set of conditions are the *aggregation conditions* obtained by differentiating the budget constraint (7.2.9). First is the *Engel aggregation condition*:

$$p_1\frac{\partial x_1}{\partial I} + p_2\frac{\partial x_2}{\partial I} = 1 \qquad *(7.2.19)$$

obtained by differentiating with respect to income. It states that the sum of the marginal expenditures is unity, so that an increase in income is spent on some good(s). It is therefore also called the *"adding up" condition.* In terms of income elasticities this condition stipulates that

$$s_1\eta_1 + s_2\eta_2 = 1. \qquad *(7.2.20)$$

The second of the aggregation conditions are the *Cournot aggregation conditions*, which state that

$$\begin{aligned} p_1\frac{\partial x_1}{\partial p_1} + p_2\frac{\partial x_2}{\partial p_1} + x_1 &= 0, \\ p_1\frac{\partial x_1}{\partial p_2} + p_2\frac{\partial x_2}{\partial p_2} + x_2 &= 0. \end{aligned} \qquad *(7.2.21)$$

They can be obtained by differentiating the budget constraint (7.2.9) with respect to each of the prices. In terms of elasticities again:

$$\begin{aligned} \varepsilon_1 + \frac{s_2}{s_1}\varepsilon_{21} + 1 &= 0, \\ \frac{s_1}{s_2}\varepsilon_{12} + \varepsilon_2 + 1 &= 0, \end{aligned} \qquad *(7.2.22)$$

where s_1 and s_2 are again the budget shares.

---

income keeps the household at the same level of utility. Here the substitution effect, which enters the Slutsky equation

$$\frac{\partial x_j}{\partial p_k} = \left(\frac{\partial x_j}{\partial p_k}\right)_{\text{comp}} - \left(\frac{\partial x_j}{\partial I}\right)x_k, \quad \text{all } j, k,$$

has been replaced by $(\partial x_j/\partial p_k) + (\partial x_j/\partial I)x_k$ in order to emphasize those changes that are, at least in principle, observable. Conditions (7.2.15) could have been written, equivalently, as

$$\left(\frac{\partial x_j}{\partial p_k}\right)_{\text{comp}} \leq 0 \quad \text{for } j = k.$$

See also footnote 13 and Problem 7-H.

These nine conditions, including the budget constraint, two homogeneity conditions, three Slutsky conditions, and three aggregation conditions, represent the principal content of the classical theory of the consumer of two goods.[11] These conditions are, however, not independent (e.g., the Slutsky symmetry condition can be derived from the other conditions). It should also be noted that the elasticities ε_j, $\varepsilon_{jj'}$, η_j, and the budget shares s_j, in general, vary as the parameters p_1, p_2, and I change. They are *not*, in general, parameters to be estimated, although some specialized functional forms used to estimate demand functions treat certain of these parameters as constant, as noted below.

A good is said to be *normal* if it has a downward sloping demand curve or, equivalently, a negative own price elasticity. Otherwise, it is a *Giffen good* with an upward-sloping demand curve (which is not inconsistent with the basic theory but is rare). A good is said to be *superior* if it has an upward-sloping Engel curve or, equivalently, a positive income elasticity. Otherwise, it is an *inferior good* with a downward-sloping Engel curve. From the Slutsky conditions (7.2.15),

$$\frac{\partial x_1}{\partial p_1} \leqslant -\frac{\partial x_1}{\partial I} x_1, \qquad *(7.2.23)$$

so a Giffen good (for which $\partial x_1/\partial p_1 > 0$) cannot be a superior good (for which $\partial x_1/\partial I > 0$). All goods can thus be classified as belonging to one of the three types indicated in Table 7.1. Some goods are superior and hence normal, so that if income rises, more is demanded, and if price rises, less is demanded. Examples are fresh milk and butter. Other goods are normal but inferior, so that if price rises, less is demanded, but if income rises, *less* is demanded. An example is condensed milk.[12] The last type is the Giffen good, for which if income rises, less is demanded, and if price rises, more is demanded. Examples might be certain staple foods among the very poor, such as bread, corn, potatoes, or rice.

TABLE 7.1 The Three Types of Goods

	Effect of Change in Income	
Effect of Change in Own Price	Superior $\frac{\partial x_1}{\partial I} > 0$	Inferior $\frac{\partial x_1}{\partial I} < 0$
Normal $\frac{\partial x_1}{\partial p_1} < 0$	Normal superior good Examples: milk, butter	Normal inferior good Example: condensed milk
Giffen $\frac{\partial x_1}{\partial p_1} > 0$	[No entries here]	Giffen good Example: staple foods among the very poor

[11]For the generalization to n goods, see Problem 7-F. For a discussion of the modern approach to the theory of the household using duality, see below and Problem 7-H.

[12]For empirical evidence on fresh milk, butter, and condensed milk, see Table 7.5.

The modern approach to the theory of the household is based on the concept of duality.[13] Inserting the demand functions (7.2.2) into the utility function (7.2.1) defines the *indirect utility function*

$$U^* = U[x_1(p_1, p_2, I), x_2(p_1, p_2, I)] = U^*(p_1, p_2, I), \qquad *(7.2.24)$$

where $U^*(p_1, p_2, I)$ is the maximum utility that is attainable at prices p_1 and p_2 and income (expenditure) I. Maximization of the direct utility function $U(x_1, x_2)$ with respect to the quantities for given prices and income, subject to the budget constraint, leads to the same level for utility as maximization of the indirect utility function $U^*(p_1, p_2, I)$ with respect to the prices and income for given quantities. The demand functions of (7.2.2) are sometimes called *Marshallian (or uncompensated) demand functions* (to distinguish them from "Hicksian" demand functions discussed below). According to *Roy's identity*, these Marshallian demand functions, expressing the quantities demanded as functions of prices and income, can be obtained as the ratios of the partial derivatives of the indirect utility function with respect to prices to that with respect to income:

$$x_j = -\frac{\partial U^*/\partial p_j}{\partial U^*/\partial I} = x_j(p_1, p_2, I), \qquad j = 1, 2. \qquad *(7.2.25)$$

Dual to the indirect utility function is the *expenditure (or cost) function*, defined as the minimum expenditure needed to attain the utility level U:

$$\begin{aligned} E^* &= E^*(p_1, p_2, U) \\ &= \min_{x_1, x_2} [p_1x_1 + p_2x_2] \quad \text{subject to} \quad U(x_1, x_2) \geq U. \end{aligned} \qquad *(7.2.26)$$

The solutions to this problem of expenditure minimization are the *Hicksian (or compensated) demand functions*, $x_j(p_1, p_2, U)$ for $j = 1, 2$, as opposed to the Marshallian demand functions shown in (7.2.25). These yield the same quantities for the demands for each good, but they indicate how these demands change with prices for a fixed level of utility U. According to *Shephard's lemma*, the Hicksian demand functions are the partial derivatives of the expenditure function $E^*(p_1, p_2, U)$ with respect to prices:

$$x_j = \frac{\partial E^*}{\partial p_j} = x_j(p_1, p_2, U), \qquad j = 1, 2. \qquad *(7.2.27)$$

The indirect utility function and expenditure function are dual to one another in that

$$\begin{aligned} U^*[p_1, p_2, E^*(p_1, p_2, U^*)] &= U^* \quad \text{and} \\ E^*[p_1, p_2, U^*(p_1, p_2, E^*)] &= E^*. \end{aligned} \qquad *(7.2.28)$$

The direct and indirect utility function, the budget constraint, the expenditure function, and the Marshallian demand functions and Hicksian demand functions and their properties form the principal content of the theory of the household.

[13]See McFadden (1978), Deaton and Muellbauer (1980), Diewert (1982), Phlips (1983), Deaton (1986), Kreps (1990), and Varian (1990). The Slutsky equation of footnote 10 can be obtained using the duality approach (see also Problem 7-H), where $\partial x_j/\partial p_k$ refers to the partial derivatives of the Marshallian demand functions of (7.2.25), while the compensated partial derivatives, compensated to keep the household at the same level of utility, are those of the Hicksian demand functions of (7.2.27).

7.3 SINGLE DEMAND EQUATIONS VERSUS SYSTEMS OF DEMAND EQUATIONS

The application of econometrics to the theory of the household requires, in addition to data, a specific formal econometric model. The demand functions of the last section, equations (7.2.2), can be generalized for a consumer of n goods as

$$x_j = x_j(p_1, p_2, \ldots, p_j, \ldots, p_n, I), \qquad j = 1, 2, \ldots, n. \qquad *(7.3.1)$$

These n equations indicate the quantity demanded of each of the goods as a function of all prices and income.

Econometric studies of demand include both single demand equation studies and studies of systems of demand equations. A single demand equation study would select one equation from (7.3.1) and estimate its parameters. For example, taking the first equation, and adding a stochastic term, u_1, to account for omitted variables, misspecification of the equation, and errors in measuring variables, a single demand equation study would estimate

$$x_1 = x_1(p_1, p_2, \ldots, p_n, I, u_1), \qquad *(7.3.2)$$

where the reason(s) for including the stochastic disturbance term would determine both the specification of the inclusion of u_1 and the method of estimation. A specialization of this equation is represented by partial equilibrium analysis and would involve the estimation of a demand curve or an Engel curve for the first good:

$$x_1 = D_1(p_1, u_1) = x_1(p_1, \bar{p}_2, \ldots, p_n, \bar{I}, u_1), \qquad (7.3.3)$$

$$\bar{p}_1 x_1 = E_1(I, u_1) = \bar{p}_1 x_1(\bar{p}_1, \bar{p}_2, \ldots, \bar{p}_n, I, u_1). \qquad (7.3.4)$$

An example is the estimation of the price elasticity of demand for gasoline, as in Section 1.4. Of the nine conditions on demand functions introduced in Section 7.2, only two are applicable to the case of a single demand equation, the homogeneity condition and the negativity condition, which in this case require that

$$\sum_{k=1}^{n} \frac{\partial x_1}{\partial p_k} p_k + \frac{\partial x_1}{\partial I} I = 0, \qquad (7.3.5)$$

$$\frac{\partial x_1}{\partial p_1} + \frac{\partial x_1}{\partial I} x_1 \leqslant 0. \qquad (7.3.6)$$

(The other conditions apply to two or more demand equations.)

An econometric study of the *system* of demand equations would estimate the complete system for a single household or group of households. A stochastic term is introduced in each equation, and the budget constraint is added, so the complete system consists of the $n + 1$ equations

$$x_j = x_j\left(p_1, p_2, \ldots, p_n, I, u_j\right), \qquad j = 1, 2, \ldots, n,$$
$$\sum_{j=1}^{n} p_j x_j = I. \qquad *(7.3.7)$$

In the next two sections we consider single demand equations and systems of demand equations, respectively. They include discussions of both functional forms and specific studies.

7.4 SINGLE DEMAND EQUATIONS

To estimate either the single demand equation (7.3.2) or the system of demand equations (7.3.7), it is necessary to specify a particular functional form for the general relationship indicated. A variety of functional forms have, in fact, been utilized in both cases. This section treats single demand equations; the next treats systems of demand equations.

Perhaps the simplest functional form for a single demand equation is the linear one. Such a *linear demand equation*, that for good 1, can be written, assuming an additive stochastic disturbance term, as[14]

$$x_1 = a_1 + b_1 p_1 + b_2 p_2 + \cdots + b_n p_n + c_1 I + u_1, \qquad *(7.4.1)$$

where, typically, the prices $p_1, p_2, \ldots, p_n$ and income I are treated as (exogenous) explanatory variables. This equation, or special cases of it, have been estimated in several early studies, although they lack any basis in utility theory.

One early study, by Schultz, estimated linear demand curves for agricultural products, treating per capita consumption as a linear function of the price of the product relative to a general price index and an annual time trend. For example, the estimated equation for sugar in the United States over the period 1896–1914 was[15]

$$\underset{}{x_t = 92.9 - \underset{(1.01)}{3.34 p_t} + \underset{(0.15)}{0.92 t}.} \qquad (7.4.2)$$

The implied price elasticity of demand, evaluated at the mean value for price and quantity, was estimated as

$$\varepsilon = \frac{\partial x}{\partial p}\frac{\bar{p}}{\bar{x}} = -3.34\frac{\bar{p}}{\bar{x}} = -0.26, \qquad (7.4.3)$$

where $\bar{p}$ and $\bar{x}$ are the mean values. Some price elasticities of demand estimated by Schultz for the United States, 1915–1929 (excluding 1917 to 1921) are reported in Table 7.2. In general he found that the demands for agricultural commodities were price inelastic, all reported elasticities in the table being, in absolute value, less than unity.

Early studies also estimated linear Engel curves, Allen and Bowley, for example, estimated the following linear Engel curve from cross-section data on 112 British city families in 1926:[16]

$$E_1 = 0.47I + 62.66. \qquad (7.4.4)$$

Here E_1 is measured as expenditure on food, rent, and clothing and I as total expenditure. The elasticity of these expenditures with respect to total expenditure, measured at the mean values, was 0.8.

[14]One interpretation of this equation is that it is based on taking a Taylor's series approximation for (7.3.2) and dropping all nonlinear terms. Thus

$$x_1 \approx x_1(\bar{p}_1, \bar{p}_2, \ldots, \bar{p}_n, \bar{I}) + \frac{\partial x_1}{\partial p_1}(p_1 - \bar{p}_1) + \frac{\partial x_1}{\partial p_2}(p_2 - \bar{p}_2)$$
$$+ \cdots + \frac{\partial x_1}{\partial p_n}(p_n - \bar{p}_n) + \frac{\partial x_1}{\partial I}(I - \bar{I}).$$

[15]See Schultz (1938). The Schultz estimates have been rounded. Numbers in parentheses are standard errors. Note that Schultz does not use income as an explanatory variable. The time trend might be a proxy for the effects of increasing income, among other phenomena.

[16]See Allen and Bowley (1935).

TABLE 7.2 Estimated Price Elasticities of Demand for the United States, 1915–1929 (Excluding 1917–1921)

Commodity	Price Elasticity of Demand
Wheat	-0.08 ± 0.04
Sugar	-0.28 ± 0.09
Potatoes	-0.31 ± 0.30
Barley	-0.42 ± 0.20
Corn	-0.48 ± 0.15
Oats	-0.54 ± 0.42
Hay	-0.62 ± 0.28

Source Schultz (1938).

Note The error brackets are given by the standard errors.

A second specification of a functional form is the *semilogarithmic demand function*:

$$x_1 = a_1 + b_1 \ln p_1 + b_2 \ln p_2 + \cdots + b_n \ln p_n + c_1 \ln I + u_1. \tag{7.4.5}$$

The Engel curve for this function was utilized by Prais and Houthakker in their study of budgets of British middle-class families in 1938.[17] Some of the income elasticities they estimated are given in Table 7.3. The demand for margarine was found to be essentially independent of income, while that for coffee was highly dependent on income. The income elasticity of tea was significantly lower than that for coffee, suggesting that coffee was more of a luxury good than tea for middle-class British families in 1938. Condensed milk was apparently an inferior good, with a negative income elasticity, a result consistent with other studies.

A third functional form and, in fact, the one that has been the most commonly used is the *log-linear* or *constant elasticity form*. It specifies the demand function as

$$x_1 = A_1 p_1^{b_1} p_2^{b_2} \cdots p_n^{b_n} I^c e^{u_1}. \qquad *(7.4.6)$$

Taking logarithms leads to the log-linear representation

$$\begin{aligned} \ln x_1 &= a_1 + b_1 \ln p_1 + b_2 \ln p_2 + \cdots \\ &\quad + b_n \ln p_n + c \ln I + u_1 \quad (a_1 = \ln A_1). \end{aligned} \qquad *(7.4.7)$$

In particular, it should be evident that the demand curve will be a line when plotted on double-log graph paper, the slope of the line being b_1, where b_1 is the elasticity of demand with respect to price:

$$b_1 = \varepsilon_1 = \frac{\partial \ln x_1}{\partial \ln p_1} = \frac{\partial x_1}{\partial p_1}\frac{p_1}{x_1}. \qquad *(7.4.8)$$

All of the coefficients are in fact elasticities, where

$$b_j = \varepsilon_{1j} = \frac{\partial \ln x_1}{\partial \ln p_j} = \frac{\partial x_1}{\partial p_j}\frac{p_j}{x_1}, \quad j = 1, 2, \ldots, n, \qquad *(7.4.9)$$

$$c = \eta_1 = \frac{\partial \ln x_1}{\partial \ln I} = \frac{\partial x_1}{\partial I}\frac{I}{x_1}, \qquad *(7.4.10)$$

and a defining characteristic of this specification of the demand function is that all $n + 1$ price and income elasticities are constant. While commonly used, this specification again lacks any basis in utility theory.

[17]See Prais and Houthakker (1955).

TABLE 7.3 Estimated Income Elasticities of Demand for British Middle-Class Families, 1938

Commodity	Income Elasticity of Demand
Margarine	0.02 ± 0.06
Butter	0.35 ± 0.04
Rice	0.41 ± 0.08
Tea	0.68 ± 0.08
Coffee	1.42 ± 0.20
Condensed milk	-0.08 ± 0.18

Source Prais and Houthakker (1955).

Note The error brackets are given by the standard errors.

An example of the log-linear specification is the Houthakker study of Engel curves.[18] He estimated the following Engel curve for food, using 1950 data for U.S. urban households (numbers in parentheses being standard errors)

$$\ln E_1 = a + \underset{(0.002)}{0.69} \ln I + \underset{(0.002)}{0.22} \ln N, \tag{7.4.11}$$

where E_1 is household expenditure on food, I is total household expenditures, and N is the number of persons in the household. The implied income elasticity was estimated to be 0.69, which is less than 1, as expected from Engel's law. The income elasticity was estimated to be less than 1 for both food and housing (0.89) but greater than 1 for clothing (1.28) and for other items of expenditure (1.25). The elasticity of demand with respect to the number of persons in the household was estimated to be 0.22, indicating, since it is less than 1, that there are economies of scale in terms of family size.[19]

A second example of the log-linear specification is the later Houthakker study of demand elasticities.[20] He considered the model for commodity j:

$$\ln x_j = a_j + \varepsilon_j \ln p_j + \eta_j \ln I + \delta_j t + u_j, \tag{7.4.12}$$

where x_j is per capita expenditure in constant prices, p_j is relative price, I is total per capita expenditure in constant prices, and t is time. The estimated coefficients ε_j and η_j provide direct estimates of price and income elasticities, respectively, and the estimated δ_j provides an estimate of the trend in demand, since

$$\delta_j = \frac{\partial \ln x_j}{\partial t} = \frac{1}{x_j}\frac{\partial x_j}{\partial t}. \tag{7.4.13}$$

[18]See Houthakker (1957). Results have been rounded. Data used in this study were group means of observations of individual households in U.S. cities, obtained from the Survey of Consumer Expenditure conducted by the Bureau of Labor Statistics.

[19]Note that if the Engel curve were for *per capita* expenditure and such expenditure were independent of family size, then

$$\frac{E_1}{N} = AI^c,$$

so that

$$\ln E_1 = a + c \ln I + \ln N,$$

where the elasticity of total household demand with respect to family size is unity. In (7.4.11) the elasticity is less than unity, implying economies of scale.

[20]Houthakker (1965).

TABLE 7.4 Estimated Price and Income Elasticities of Demand for Various Countries, 1948–1959

Country	Food		Clothing		Rent		Durables	
	Price	Income	Price	Income	Price	Income	Price	Income
United States	−0.34	0.32	0.42	0.78	0.08	1.67	1.09	2.03
Canada	−0.29	0.69	−0.38	−0.09	−0.09	1.27	0.96	3.44
Belgium	−0.69	0.92	0.32	0.06	0.05	0.33	0.44	2.23
France	−0.16	0.68	0.53	1.47	−0.17	0.87	−0.15	2.53
Italy	−0.26	0.78	−0.19	0.59	−0.10	0.70	0.41	2.72
Netherlands	0.59	0.57	0.47	1.81	0.36	0.32	−2.19	1.99
Sweden	0.06	0.38	−1.81	−0.94	−0.33	1.57	0.52	2.87
United Kingdom	0.12	0.73	−0.09	1.04	−0.19	0.66	−1.46	3.01
Combined (weighted average)	0.08	0.71	−0.10	0.71	−0.29	1.29	−0.12	2.36

Source Houthakker (1965).

Note Here "income" refers to total expenditure. Results have been rounded.

Some of Houthakker's results are reported in Table 7.4. Note that for all countries food is income inelastic, as implied by Engel's law. Also note that the income elasticity for food in the United States fell from the earlier estimate of 0.69 in 1950 to 0.32 here. This fall in the elasticity as average incomes rise is expected and is typically found. The table similarly indicates a lower income elasticity for food for higher-income countries. It also shows that durables tend to be income elastic and nondurables tend to be income inelastic (the exceptions: rent is income elastic in the United States, Canada, and Sweden, while clothing is income elastic in France and the Netherlands, the United Kingdom being a borderline case). The estimated price elasticities are not as consistent as those for income (e.g., many have the wrong sign).

A third example of the log-linear specification is the study by Stone of demand functions in the United Kingdom.[21] His specification was similar to (7.4.12), of the form

$$\ln x_j = a_j + \varepsilon_j \ln p_j + \sum_{j'} \varepsilon_{jj'} \ln p_{j'} + \eta_j \ln I + \delta_j t + u_j, \tag{7.4.14}$$

where ε_j and η_j are elasticities as in (7.4.12), δ_j is a time trend as in (7.4.12), and $\varepsilon_{jj'}$ is the cross-price elasticity of demand, as in (7.2.8). The sum in (7.4.14) is taken not over all commodities, but rather over those believed, on the basis of a priori reasoning or other studies, to be related to the good as complement or substitute goods. The x_j variable is per capita consumption, and I is per capita real income, relative to a general price index. The income elasticities were estimated from a cross-section sample of household budgets in the United Kingdom, 1937–1939, and these estimates were used in estimating the remaining coefficients in (7.4.14) on the basis of time-series data for the United Kingdom over the period 1920–1938. First differences were utilized to reduce first-order serial correlation of the stochastic disturbance term u_t. Table 7.5 presents some of Stone's results for food items.

For fresh milk Stone found that demand was price inelastic and exhibited a positive income elasticity, both elasticities being approximately 0.5. Thus a 10% increase in price would reduce demand for fresh milk by 5%, and a 10% increase in income would increase

[21] Stone (1954a). A similar specification was used in Wold and Jureen (1953).

TABLE 7.5 Estimated Demand Elasticities for the United Kingdom, 1920–1938

Commodity	Own Price Elasticity ε_j	Cross-Price Elasticities $\varepsilon_{jj'}$		Income Elasticity η_j	Trend Coefficient δ_j	R^2 / d
Fresh milk	−0.49 (0.13)	0.73 (0.15)	Beef and veal	0.50 (0.18)	0.004 (0.004)	0.81 2.01
		−0.23 (0.07)	Cream			
Condensed milk	−1.23 (0.32)	2.25 (0.53)	Fresh milk	−0.53 (0.18)	−0.047 (0.016)	0.82 1.85
		0.80 (0.23)	Margarine			
		1.06 (0.35)	Tea			
		0.43 (0.19)	Cheese			
Butter	−0.41 (0.13)	−0.21 (0.11)	Flour	0.37 (0.08)	0.040 (0.009)	0.61 1.84
		0.56 (0.26)	Cakes and biscuits			
		0.63 (0.30)	Carcass meat			
Margarine	0.01 (0.17)	1.01 (0.17)	Butter	−0.16 (0.11)	0.016 (0.010)	0.77 1.76
		1.02 (0.26)	Chocolate and confectionary			
		−0.46 (0.31)	Cakes and biscuits			
Tea	−0.26 (0.07)	0.14 (0.08)	Coffee	0.04 (0.04)	0.003 (0.003)	0.56 2.15
		0.08 (0.05)	Beer			

Source Stone (1954a), reported by Phlips (1983).

Note Income elasticities are based on budget surveys of 1937–1939. Other elasticities are based on time-series data over the entire period.

demand by 5%.[22] The cross-price elasticities indicate that beef is a substitute for milk (e.g., both provide protein for the diet) and that cream is a complement for milk.[23] Increasing the price of beef, which lowers the amount of beef demanded, increases the amount of milk demanded. Increasing the price of cream, however, lowers the amount of cream demanded but also reduces the amount of milk demanded. The trend coefficient shows a slight increase in per capita consumption after allowing for price and income effects.

[22]The income elasticity estimate of 0.50 for fresh milk is consistent with the range of 0.35 to 0.53 for the income elasticity of dairy produce given by Prais and Houthakker (1955) in their study of family budgets based on U.K. data of 1937 to 1939.

[23]A better measure of substitutes and complements, which is usually considered the theoretically correct measure, is the *compensated* cross-price elasticities, compensated for changes in real income. The uncompensated cross-price elasticities, as reported in Table 7.5, include income as well as substitution effects. Since real rather than money income is used, however, the price elasticities are closer to compensated than to uncompensated elasticities.

The results for the other goods can be contrasted to those for fresh milk. For example, the demand for condensed milk is elastic; it is an inferior good, as also found by Prais and Houthakker; it exhibits a secular decline over time, and fresh milk, margarine, tea, and cheese are all substitutes. Butter is more like fresh milk in terms of own price and income elasticities, has a more significant positive trend, and is a complement with flour (e.g., they often go into recipes together) and a substitute for cakes and biscuits and carcass meat. The demand for margarine is highly inelastic, with a somewhat negative income elasticity. Butter and chocolate and confectionary are substitutes, while cakes and biscuits are complements. The demand for tea is price and income inelastic, and coffee and beer are substitutes. In general, demands for most commodities are both price inelastic and income inelastic; of 32 reported income elasticities 23 were in the range 0 to 1, while of 36 reported own price elasticities 26 were in the range 0 to –1.

7.5 SYSTEMS OF DEMAND EQUATIONS[24]

Systems of demand functions involve the n demand equations

$$x_j = x_j(p_1, p_2, \ldots, p_n, I, u_j), \qquad j = 1, 2, \ldots, n, \qquad {}^*(7.5.1)$$

which, together with the budget equation, which the n demand equations are assumed to satisfy, form a complete system, as in (7.3.7). In such systems the variables $x_1, x_2, \ldots, x_n$, the quantities consumed of each of the goods, are typically treated as endogenous variables, while the variables $p_1, p_2, \ldots, p_n$, the prices of each of the goods, and I, the income, are typically treated as exogenous variables. The estimation of the complete system is important in identifying the interdependence among the goods, specifically the effects of changes in prices of certain goods on the demand for other goods.

Various functional forms have been employed in estimating the system (7.5.1).[25] One such functional form is the *linear system*:

$$x_j = a_j + \sum_k b_{jk} p_k + c_j I + u_j, \qquad j = 1, 2, \ldots, n, \qquad {}^*(7.5.2)$$

and another is the *log-linear* or *constant elasticity* system, for which

$$\ln x_j = a'_j + \sum_k b'_{jk} \ln p_k + c'_j \ln I + u'_j, \qquad j = 1, 2, \ldots, n. \qquad {}^*(7.5.3)$$

Each of these is a straightforward generalization of the corresponding single-equation demand function and, as before, each lacks any basis in utility theory.

One of the most widely used functional forms is one that does have a basis in utility theory, the *linear expenditure system*, which can be written[26]

$$p_j x_j = p_j x_j^0 + \beta_j\left(I - \sum_{k=1}^{n} p_k x_k^0\right), \qquad j = 1, 2, \ldots, n, \qquad {}^*(7.5.4)$$

[24]See Powell (1974), Barten (1977), Deaton and Muellbauer (1980), Deaton (1986), and Theil and Clements (1987).

[25]See the references cited in footnote 24; see also Problem 7-N for a general additive utility function that implies several possible functional forms for the system of demand functions, depending on the parameters. Note that the restrictions on demand functions imply restrictions on the parameters in (7.5.2) and (7.5.3) (see Problem 7-J).

[26]See Stone (1954b, 1972), Barten (1977), Deaton and Muellbauer (1980), Phlips (1983), and Deaton (1986).

where $x_j - x_j^0 > 0$, $0 < \beta_j < 1$, $\sum \beta_j = 1$. This system can be interpreted as stating that expenditure on good j, given as $p_j x_j$, can be decomposed into two components. The first is the expenditure on a certain "base amount" x_j^0 of good j, which is the minimum expenditure to which the consumer is committed. The second is a fraction β_j of the *supernumerary income*, defined as the income above the "subsistence income" $\sum p_k x_k^0$ needed to purchase base amounts of all goods. These two components correspond, respectively, to committed and discretionary expenditure on good j. Dividing through (7.5.4) by the price p_j gives the corresponding system of demand equations:

$$x_j = x_j^0 + \frac{\beta_j}{p_j}\left(I - \sum p_k x_k^0\right), \qquad *(7.5.5)$$

which is hyperbolic in own price and linear in income. The demand curve can be written, again using bars to denote variables held constant, as in (7.2.3), as

$$x_j = x_j^0(1 - \beta_j) + \beta_j\left(\bar{I} - \sum_{k \neq j} \bar{p}_k x_k^0\right)p_j^{-1}, \qquad (7.5.6)$$

which, aside from the translation of the axis by the term $x_j^0(1 - \beta_j)$, represents a hyperbola in the (x_j, p_j) plane of Figure 7.2. The Engel curve is of the form

$$E_j = \bar{p}_j x_j = \left(\bar{p}_j x_j^0 - \beta_j \sum \bar{p}_k x_k^0\right) + \beta_j I \qquad (7.5.7)$$

and is thus a linear relationship in the (I, E_j) plane of Figure 7.3.

The linear expenditure system is widely used for three reasons. First, it has a straightforward and reasonable interpretation as given after (7.5.4). Second, it is one of the few systems that automatically satisfy all nine theoretical restrictions in Section 7.2 on systems of demand equations. Third, it can be derived from a specific utility function.[27] The system is estimated from data on quantities x_j and prices p_j of the n goods and data on income I (or total expenditure). The parameters that are estimated are the *n base quantities* $x_1^0, x_2^0, \ldots, x_n^0$ and the *n marginal budget shares* $\beta_1, \beta_2, \ldots, \beta_n$. The linear expenditure system has been used in several empirical studies of demand, and it and the constant elasticity system are two of the most widely used specifications employed in estimating systems of demand equations.[28]

The estimation of the linear expenditure system presents certain complications because, while it is linear in the variables, it is nonlinear in the parameters, involving the product of β_j and each x_k^0 in (7.5.4) and (7.5.5). There are, in fact, several approaches to the estimation of this system. One approach determines the base quantities x_k^0 on the basis of extraneous information or prior judgments. The system (7.5.4) then implies that expenditure on each good in excess of base expenditure $(p_j x_j - p_j x_j^0)$ is a linear function of supernumerary income, so each of the marginal budget shares β_j can be estimated using the usual single-equation simple linear regression methods. A second approach reverses this

[27]The specific utility function from which the linear expenditure system can be derived is the Stone–Geary utility function (also called the Klein–Rubin utility function) given in Problem 7-L, of which a particular case appears in Problem 7-I and a generalization appears in Problem 7-N.

[28]For the constant-elasticity system (7.5.3), see Sato (1972). There are, in general, three ways of specifying systems of demand functions. One is based on a specified utility function, as in the linear expenditure system and in Problem 7-I. Another is based on a specified indirect utility function, as discussed in Problem 7-H. The third is to specify directly a form for the demand functions, such as the constant elasticity system (see Barten, 1977).

procedure by first determining the marginal budget shares β_j on the basis of extraneous information or prior judgments [or Engel curve studies, which estimate the β_j from the relationship between expenditure and income, as in (7.5.7)]. It then estimates the base quantities x_k^0 by estimating the system in which the expenditure less the marginal budget share times income $(p_j x_j - \beta_j I)$ is a linear function of all prices. The total sum of squared errors—over all goods as well as all observations—is then minimized by choice of the x_k^0. A third approach is an iterative one, using the estimates of the β_j conditional on the x_k^0 (as in the first approach) and the estimates of the x_k^0 conditional on the β_j (as in the second approach) iteratively so as to minimize the total sum of squares. The process would continue, choosing β_j based on the last estimated x_k^0 and then choosing x_k^0 based on the last estimated β_j, until convergence of the sum of squares is obtained. A fourth approach selects β_j and x_j^0 simultaneously by setting up a grid of possible values for the $2n - 1$ parameters (the -1 based on the fact that the β_j sum to unity) and obtaining that point on the grid where the total sum of squares over all goods and all observations is minimized.

Estimates of the linear expenditure system for the United States, Canada, and the United Kingdom from the Goldberger and Gamaletsos study are presented in Table 7.6.[29] This table reports estimated base quantities, measured in units of the domestic currency, of expenditures per capita, and estimated marginal budget shares, which sum to unity. For the United States, for example, since the units of measurement are thousands of dollars, base quantities are \$330 worth of food per capita, \$140 worth of clothing, and so on. According to the marginal budget shares, 8.1% of income over supernumerary income goes to food, 5.5% to clothing, and so on. For all three countries the base quantities for clothing, rent, and durables were similar and significantly lower than the base quantity for food, as might be expected. Leaving aside the heterogeneous "other" category, the marginal budget shares indicate that in the United States and Canada incremental income (above supernumerary income) tends to go for rent, while in the United Kingdom such income tends to go for durables.

TABLE 7.6 Estimates of the Linear Expenditure System for the United States, Canada, and the United Kingdom, 1950–1961

	United States		Canada		United Kingdom	
Commodity Group	x_j^0	β_j	x_j^0	β_j	x_j^0	β_j
Food	0.33	0.081	0.19	0.177	0.21	0.172
Clothing	0.14	0.055	0.09	0.029	0.08	0.130
Rent	0.14	0.190	0.06	0.279	0.06	0.052
Durables	0.15	0.096	0.07	0.133	0.06	0.269
Other	0.52	0.578	0.32	0.382	0.30	0.377

Source Goldberger and Gamaletsos (1970).

Note x_j^0 = base quantity; β_j = marginal budget share. For all countries units of measurement are thousands of U.S. dollars, where use has been made of the 1961 exchange rates of 98.73 U.S. cents per Canadian dollar and 280.27 U.S. cents per U.K. pound sterling.

[29]See Goldberger and Gamaletsos (1970). They obtained estimates of the linear expenditure system for 13 OECD countries. They also estimated a constant-elasticity system, using the same data, and obtained estimates of elasticities that were, in general, similar to those obtained for the linear expenditure system. For other estimates of the linear expenditure system, see Lluch and Powell (1975).

Two other systems of demand equations are the "almost ideal demand system" and the Rotterdam system.[30] In the *almost ideal demand system (AIDS)*, the shares s_j as defined in (7.2.11) are functions of the logs of real income and of the logs of all the prices in a semi-logarithmic form, where

$$s_j = \alpha_j + \beta_j \ln(I/P) + \sum \gamma_{jk} \ln p_k, \qquad j = 1, \ldots, n, \qquad *(7.5.8)$$

and where in the last term the summation is over all k, from 1 to n. Real income, the term in parentheses, is defined as nominal income I divided by the price level P, where

$$\ln P = \alpha_0 + \sum \alpha_j \ln p_j + \tfrac{1}{2} \sum \sum \gamma_{jk} \ln p_j \ln p_k \qquad *(7.5.9)$$

and where the first summation is over all j while the second is over all j and k. If prices are constant and units are chosen so that the prices are unity, each share is simply a linear function of the log of nominal income, called *Working's model.*

The *Rotterdam system* uses a differential approach, treating changes in demand rather than levels of demand. It can be written in terms of continuous changes, as

$$s_j d(\ln x_j) = a_j + b_j\left[d(\ln I) - \sum s_k d(\ln p_k)\right] + \sum c_{jk} d(\ln p_k), \qquad *(7.5.10)$$

where both summations are over all k. Since, for any variable z, the differential $d(\ln z)$ is the proportionate change dz/z, the left-hand side is the share-weighted proportionate change in the demand for good j or, equivalently, the quantity component of the change in the budget share of good j. In the Rotterdam system this quantity change is given as a linear function of the proportionate change in real income and of the proportionate changes in all prices. The term in brackets, the proportionate change in real income, is the proportionate change in income less the share-weighted proportionate changes in prices, the latter being known as the *Divisia price index.* Since the term in brackets is the proportionate change in income less the proportionate changes in prices, it can be interpreted as a quantity index. It is the share-weighted proportionate changes in quantities, $\sum s_k d(\ln x_k)$, known as the *Divisia quantity index* (or *Divisia volume index*). The left-hand variable in (7.5.10) can thus be interpreted as the contribution of good j to the Divisia quantity index. A finite-change version of the Rotterdam system is used in empirical estimation.

The Rotterdam system of demand equations provides a local first-order approximation to any set of demand functions in which quantities depend on prices and income. It is expressed in terms of *changes* in quantities being explained by *changes* in real income and *changes* in prices. It is an example of a "flexible functional form," which guarantees that it is an arbitrarily close local approximation to any general set of demand functions and which allows at least one free parameter for measurement of each effect of interest, such as the effect of total expenditure and the effects of the n prices. Thus in (7.5.10) the b_j's measure the effects of a change in real income, while the c_{jk} measure the effects of changes in prices.

The concept of a flexible functional form is a very useful one that can be used to obtain a quadratic approximation of preferences as well as demand. For example, the *indirect translog* is a second-order Taylor's series approximation of the indirect utility function, given by the quadratic expression in the logs of the elements of the vector **r** of normalized prices p/I:

[30]For the AIDS system, see Deaton and Muellbauer (1980) and Deaton (1986); for the Rotterdam system, see Theil (1975–76), Barten (1977), and Deaton (1986); for the translog system, see Jorgenson, Lau, and Stoker (1982) and Deaton (1986).

$$U^*(r) = \alpha_0 + \sum \alpha_j \ln r_j + \tfrac{1}{2}\sum\sum \beta_{jk} \ln r_j \ln r_k, \qquad *(7.5.11)$$

where the first summation is over all goods j, while the second is over all pairs of goods j and k. Many other flexible functional forms have been used to approximate demand functions, utility functions, indirect utility functions, or expenditure functions. Other examples of flexible functional forms are presented in Chapter 8, including the translog cost function.

There are several difficulties in actually estimating systems of demand equations, such as the linear expenditure system. One such difficulty is the multicollinearity among the prices, which all tend to move together. This difficulty is partly offset by the constraints imposed on the system by theory, as summarized in Section 7.2. Three additional difficulties, which apply both to individual demand equations and systems of demand equations, are identification, aggregation, and dynamic factors, the subjects of the next three sections of this chapter.

7.6 IDENTIFICATION

An important question in estimating demand relationships is that of *identification*: has the demand equation been identified and, in particular, can it be distinguished from the supply equation?[31] Consider, for example, the simple demand supply system for a single good:

$$q^D = a - bp + u^D, \qquad (7.6.1)$$

$$q^S = c + dp + u^S, \qquad (7.6.2)$$

$$q^D = q^S, \qquad (7.6.3)$$

treated in Section 2.10. This system consists of linear demand and supply curves and an equilibrium condition equating demand to supply. The system is, in general, *not* identified, and Figure 7.4 illustrates the difficulties caused by underidentification of each of the two behavioral equations of (7.6.1)–(7.6.3). Suppose that D and S are the demand and supply curves, respectively, in one year. They define an equilibrium at E, consisting of q and p as quantity and price, respectively. In the next year both stochastic terms have values different from their previous values (e.g., because of changes in variables not explicitly included in the model). Such variables may include income and climate, as in the prototype micro model of Section 2.5. The result is that the demand curve shifts to D', and the supply curve shifts to S'. The new equilibrium is at E'. Similar shifts occur in the next year, leading to the quantity–price pair at E''.

Now suppose one were performing an econometric study and attempting to determine the parameters a, b, c, and d in the simple demand–supply system. Clearly, one does not, in fact, know or observe the demand curves or the supply curves of Figure 7.4—they are to be determined. The data are simply the quantity–price pairs given by E, E', and E''. Fitting a curve to these points would not permit estimation of either the demand or the supply curve. Nor is the problem alleviated by more data; estimating the relationship determined by any number of data points would not provide enough information upon which to estimate the values of the four parameters in (7.6.1)–(7.6.3).

One of two approaches is generally utilized to overcome this problem of lack of identification. The first is to obtain identification by zero restrictions. This approach adds rele-

[31] See Section 2.10 and Chapter 9.

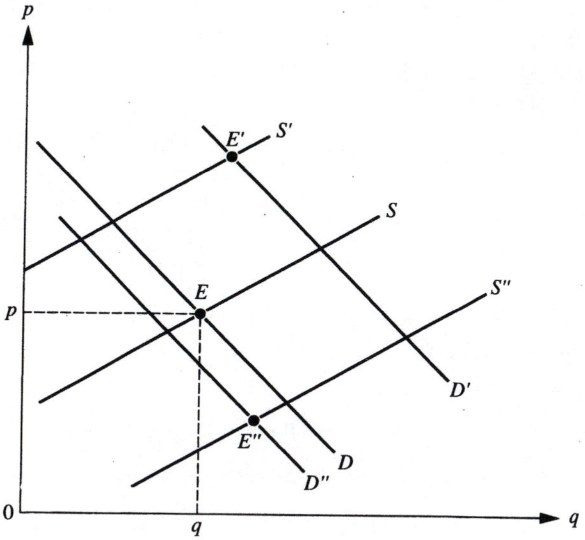

Figure 7.4 Problem of Lack of Identification

vant variables to certain equations but not to others in order to differentiate the demand equation from the supply equation and thus to estimate each. One example is the prototype micro model of Section 2.5, which may be written

$$q = \gamma_1 p + \beta_1 I + \delta_1 + \varepsilon^D, \tag{7.6.4}$$

$$q = \gamma_2 p + \beta_3 r + \delta_2 + \varepsilon^S. \tag{7.6.5}$$

This model is exactly identified, as discussed in Section 2.10, since it includes income as an exogenous variable in the demand equation that does not appear in the supply equation and it includes rainfall as an exogenous variable in the supply equation that does not appear in the demand equation. This model can be estimated from observed data on quantity, price, income, and rainfall. In terms of Figure 7.4 the identification problem is overcome because at least one of the factors causing each of the curves to shift has been explicitly included in the model. To the extent that the shifts in demand are based upon changes in income and shifts in supply are based upon changes in rainfall, the magnitude of the shifts can be taken into account from knowledge of these two exogenous variables.

A model similar to the prototype micro model was used by Fox to estimate demand for and supply of farm products.[32] His structural equations for the market for pork were:

$$\ln p = \alpha_1 \ln q + \alpha_2 \ln I + u^D, \tag{7.6.6}$$

$$\ln q = \alpha_3 \ln p + \alpha_4 \ln z + u^S. \tag{7.6.7}$$

The first equation is a constant elasticity demand function, solved for log p rather than log q. It is the same as (7.6.4), except variables are measured in terms of logarithmic deviations from their means (so the constant term falls out) and it is solved for log p. The second equation is a supply equation giving the quantity as a log-linear function of price and

[32]See Fox (1953).

production (z), assumed exogenous. Fox estimated the reduced-form equations using U.S. data 1922–1941 on per capita consumption (q) and production (z) of pork, on per capita income (I), and on retail price of pork (p). He obtained the following estimated reduced-form equations:

$$\ln p = \underset{(0.10)}{0.97} \ln I - \underset{(0.11)}{0.96} \ln z, \qquad R^2 = 0.92, \tag{7.6.8}$$

$$\ln q = -\underset{(0.06)}{0.66} \ln I + \underset{(0.07)}{0.84} \ln z, \qquad R^2 = 0.91. \tag{7.6.9}$$

The structural estimates were then obtained from the relationships between the structural and reduced-form coefficients.[33] In this case the estimated structural-form equations were

$$\ln p = -1.14 \ln q + 0.90 \ln I, \tag{7.6.10}$$

$$\ln q = -0.062 \ln p + 0.77 \ln z, \tag{7.6.11}$$

with supply largely independent of price in (7.6.11). The implied estimates of the price and income elasticities of demand for pork are obtained by taking the reciprocals of the estimated coefficients in (7.6.10), given as

$$\varepsilon = \frac{-1}{1.14} = -0.88, \qquad \eta = \frac{1}{0.90} = 1.11. \tag{7.6.12}$$

Another approach to identification utilizes relative variances. Suppose that the variance of the stochastic term for the demand equation in (7.6.1), σ_D^2, is considerably smaller than the corresponding variance for the supply equation, σ_S^2, in (7.6.2):

$$\sigma_D^2 << \sigma_S^2. \tag{7.6.13}$$

Then the simple demand–supply system can be depicted as in Figure 7.5. In this case estimating a line through the observed quantity–price combinations yields an approximation to the demand curve. This is the case in which the demand curve is identified via relative variances. An example is the work of Schultz, discussed in Section 7.4, who estimated demand curves for agricultural commodities. For an agricultural commodity the variance of demand is likely to be rather low, since these commodities enter into basic foodstuffs. At the same time, the variance of supply is likely to be rather large because of the influence of weather conditions on harvests. Thus it can be argued that Schultz was, in fact, estimating demand curves, rather than supply curves or some combination of demand and supply curves, because of the relative variances.

[33]The reduced-form equations can be written

$$\ln p = \frac{\alpha_2}{1 - \alpha_1\alpha_3} \ln I + \frac{\alpha_1\alpha_4}{1 - \alpha_1\alpha_3} \ln z,$$

$$\ln q = \frac{\alpha_2\alpha_3}{1 - \alpha_1\alpha_3} \ln I + \frac{\alpha_4}{1 - \alpha_1\alpha_3} \ln z,$$

by solving the structural equations simultaneously and omitting the disturbances. Thus the ratio of the two coefficients of $\ln I$ yields $\hat{\alpha}_3$, while the ratio of the two coefficients of $\ln z$ yields $\hat{\alpha}_1$. The coefficient of $\ln I$ in the first equation times $(1 - \hat{\alpha}_1\hat{\alpha}_3)$ yields $\hat{\alpha}_2$, while the coefficient of $\ln z$ in the second equation times $(1 - \hat{\alpha}_1\hat{\alpha}_3)$ yields $\hat{\alpha}_4$.

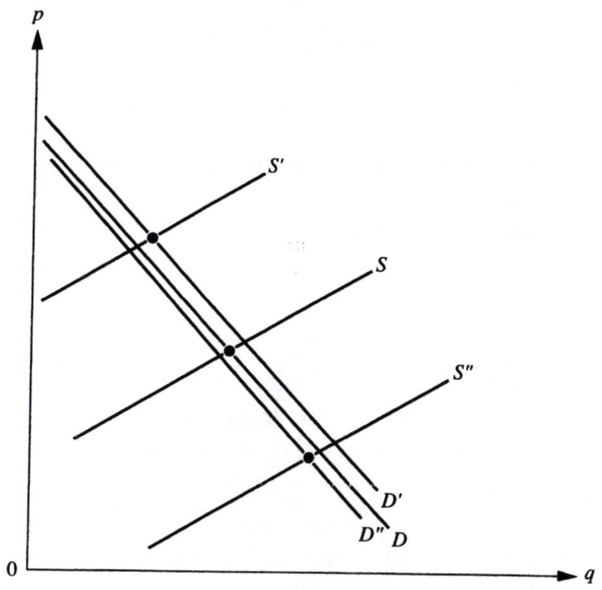

Figure 7.5 Identification Achieved via Relative Variances, where $\sigma_D^2 << \sigma_S^2$

7.7 AGGREGATION

Another issue in empirical work on household demand is that of aggregation.[34] The basic theory of demand, as developed in Section 7.2, refers to a single consuming unit, such as an individual or family. Empirical work, however, usually involves market phenomena, such as the total quantity purchased in a country. The problem of aggregation is that of reconciling the two. Usually, certain conditions must be met to overcome the problem of aggregation.

A simple example of the aggregation problem and conditions of aggregation is that of the linear demand equation (7.4.1). Considering only own price and income as explanatory variables, the equation is written for individual household h, designated by a superscript, as

$$x_1^h = a^h + b^h p_1 + c^h I^h + u_1^h, \qquad h = 1, 2, \ldots, H, \tag{7.7.1}$$

where there are H households. Under what conditions can these H demand equations be aggregated into a similar demand equation for the market as a whole? Summing over the H households,

$$\sum x_1^h = \sum a^h + \sum b^h p_1 + \sum c^h I^h + \sum u_1^h, \tag{7.7.2}$$

where all sums are over h, from 1 to H. The left-hand side is the aggregate quantity demanded of good 1.

$$x_1 = \sum x_1^h. \tag{7.7.3}$$

On the right-hand side the individual intercepts aggregate to a market intercept:

$$a = \sum a^h. \tag{7.7.4}$$

[34]Basic references on aggregation are Theil (1954), Green (1964), and Deaton and Muellbauer (1980).

The price p_1 is assumed common to all, so

$$bp_1 = p_1 \sum b^h \quad \text{where} \quad b = \sum b^h. \tag{7.7.5}$$

The aggregate stochastic term is the sum of the individual terms:

$$u_1 = \sum u_1^h. \tag{7.7.6}$$

The term that creates an aggregation problem, however, is that involving income, since both c^h and I^h, in general, vary from one household to another. If, however, it is assumed that the c^h are the same for all households,

$$c^h = c, \quad \text{all } h, \tag{7.7.7}$$

then

$$cI = \sum c^h I^h \quad \text{where} \quad I = \sum I^h, \tag{7.7.8}$$

where I is aggregate income of all households. Under the assumption (7.7.7), that of parallel linear Engel curves, distribution of income will not affect aggregate demand, and the individual demand equations can be aggregated into the market demand curve:

$$x_1 = a + bp_1 + cI + u_1. \tag{7.7.9}$$

Here the assumption that the response of demand to income is the same for all households is the aggregation condition for this problem. The condition can be stated as the condition that the Engel curves are all linear, with identical slopes across households. Under this condition the market behavior of an aggregate of different households is the same as if it were the market behavior of a single representative household.

In general, aggregation conditions must be imposed in order to develop aggregate demand equations from individual household demand equations. Such conditions usually require that if an explanatory variable changes among different micro units (e.g., income), but the coefficients are the same for each such unit [as in (7.7.7)], then the macro relationship is of the same form, where the explanatory variable is the sum of the micro variables [as in (7.7.8)]. They also require that if an explanatory variable is the same for all the micro units (e.g., price), then the macro relationship is of the same linear form but the coefficient in the macro relationship is the sum of the coefficients for the micro relationships [as in (7.7.5)]. In practice, however, such aggregation conditions are usually ignored, with the totality of various individual households treated as if it were a single "representative" household. There is usually an aggregation over commodities as well as households; empirical studies almost always refer to a group of individuals consuming not specific commodities but groups of commodities, as indicated in the above tables. In fact, most empirical studies treat fewer than 10 commodities, which clearly entails aggregation of individual commodities into broad commodity groups.

An important practical implication of the problem of aggregation involves the type of data utilized and the nature of the hypotheses being tested. To the extent that the data utilized in an econometric study are aggregate data, constructed either by the investigator or by others, such data have typically been constructed on the basis of certain assumptions, which take the role of maintained hypotheses. These assumptions are illustrated by the above conditions of aggregation. It would then be inappropriate to test for these conditions, which would, in effect, amount to testing a maintained hypothesis. Nevertheless, such studies are often conducted. The investigator must be aware of the assumptions that are built into the data and avoid testing for them. A specific example is presented in the next chapter [see (8.3.25) to (8.3.31)].

7.8 DYNAMIC DEMAND ANALYSIS

So far the specifications of demand relationships have been largely static, referring to situations in which time plays no essential role. There are several ways of extending these relationships to situations in which time enters essentially—that is, to *dynamic demand functions*.

Perhaps the most straightforward of the dynamic specifications is that of a *time trend* in the demand function. An example is the log-linear (constant elasticity) model (7.4.12), where δ_j is the time trend, as given in (7.4.13), with dimension (1/time). This demand function shifts out over time at the rate $100\delta_j$ percent per time period. Another example is the linear expenditure system (7.5.4), in which the base quantitites and marginal budget shares change over time.[35]

A second approach to dynamic demand analysis involves *lagged variables*. An example is the *cobweb model*, according to which the quantity demanded depends on current price, while the quantity supplied depends on lagged price—that is, the price of a previous time period. Such a model may be a valid representation of situations in which there is a significant time lag in the production process. In such a situation, decisions to initiate production depend on the then current price, so the amount supplied, at the end of the production process, depends on the lagged price. Such an approach has been utilized in the market for certain agricultural commodities and for construction, such as house building and shipbuilding. In the simplest linear case without stochastic disturbances the model is of the form

$$q_t^D = a - bp_t, \qquad *(7.8.1)$$

$$q_t^S = c + dp_{t-1}, \qquad *(7.8.2)$$

where q_t^D and q_t^S are the quantities demanded and supplied, respectively, at time t, and p_t and p_{t-1} are current and lagged prices, respectively. At an equilibrium $p_t = p_{t-1} = \bar{p}$, and demand equals supply, so

$$q^D = a - b\bar{p} = c + d\bar{p} = qS, \qquad (7.8.3)$$

$$\bar{p} = \frac{a-c}{b+d}. \qquad (7.8.4)$$

Setting demand equal to supply in each period leads to

$$a - bp_t = c + dp_{t-1}, \qquad (7.8.5)$$

implying the first-order linear difference equation

$$p_t + \frac{d}{b}p_{t-1} = \frac{a-c}{b}. \qquad *(7.8.6)$$

Solving this equation yields[36]

$$p_t = (p_0 - \bar{p})\left(-\frac{d}{b}\right)^t + \bar{p}. \qquad *(7.8.7)$$

Thus p_t approaches $\bar{p}$ in the limit (as $t \to \infty$) provided that $d < b$—that is, provided that the slope of the supply curve is less than the (absolute value of the) slope of the demand curve. Such a case is illustrated in Figure 7.6, where, because of the convention of setting q on the

[35]See Stone (1966).

[36]See Allen (1959). Since (7.8.6) is a linear difference equation, its solution is the sum of a homogeneous solution (of the form km^t) and a particular solution (here the constant $\bar{p}$).

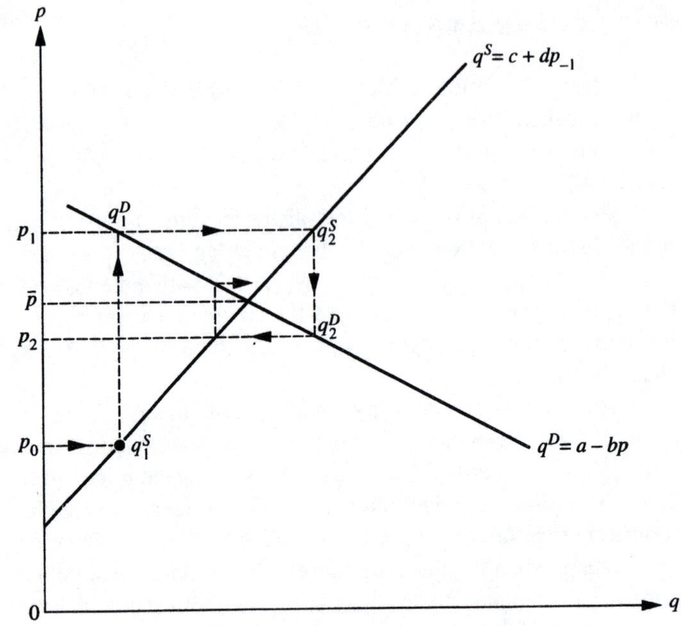

Figure 7.6 Cobweb Model
Note: Here it is assumed that $d > b$.

horizontal axis, the slope is relative to the *horizontal*, rather than the vertical, axis. Given any historical price p_0, the supply curve gives the supply available in the next period q_1^S, which must equal q_1^D on the demand curve. The resulting price p_1 determines q_2^S, and so on, leading, in this case, to the equilibrium price $\bar{p}$. If, however, $d = b$, the solution cycles about $\bar{p}$, while if $d > b$, the solution explodes, moving farther and farther away from $\bar{p}$.

A third approach to dynamic demand analysis is the specification of a *distributed lag* relationship. Such a relationship is often utilized in studying the demand for consumer durables, such as houses, automobiles, and household appliances, which are goods that last more than one year. The analysis of consumer durables is frequently based upon a *partial adjustment model*.[37] Letting x_t be the stock of the durable and x_t^* be the desired stock at time t, the stock adjustment model is

$$x_t - x_{t-1} = \gamma(x_t^* - x_{t-1}) + v_t, \qquad 0 < \gamma < 1. \tag{7.8.8}$$

According to the model, the change in the stock of the durable good is proportional to the gap between the current desired and the past actual stock level. Here γ is the adjustment coefficient, indicating the speed of adjustment, and v_t is the stochastic disturbance term. Assuming that the desired stock is a linear function of price p and income I,

$$x_t^* = a + bp_t + cI_t, \tag{7.8.9}$$

leads to

$$x_t = (1 - \gamma)x_{t-1} + a\gamma + b\gamma p_t + c\gamma I_t + v_t. \tag{7.8.10}$$

[37]See Section 6.8, Harberger (1960), and Stone and Rowe (1960). See also Nerlove (1958), as discussed in Problem 7-T.

This equation is equivalent to a distributed lag model of the Koyck type, where

$$x_t = \frac{\alpha\gamma}{1-\gamma} + b \sum_{j=0}^{\infty} \gamma(1-\gamma)^j p_{t-j} + c \sum_{j=0}^{\infty} \gamma(1-\gamma)^j I_{t-j} + u_t, \qquad (7.8.11)$$

indicating the dependence of the current stock of the durable on current and all past levels of prices and income. The coefficients b and c are long-run coefficients, showing the impact of price and income, respectively. The coefficients $b\gamma$ and $c\gamma$ are the corresponding short-run coefficients.[38]

The stock adjustment model was used by Chow to study the demand for new automobiles in the United States.[39] Using data covering the years 1921–1953, he found that

$$\underset{}{x_t = 0.078} - \underset{(0.047)}{0.231S_{t-1}} - \underset{(0.0026)}{0.0201p_t} + \underset{(0.0011)}{0.0117I_t}, \quad R^2 = 0.858, \qquad (7.8.12)$$

where x_t is the annual purchases of new automobiles per capita, S_{t-1} the stock of automobiles per capita at the end of the previous year, p_t the price of automobiles relative to the consumer price index, and I_t the disposable income in constant prices per capita. The per capita stock changes according to

$$S_t - S_{t-1} = x_t - dS_{t-1}, \qquad (7.8.13)$$

where d is the depreciation rate. Assuming that d is 0.25 yields an estimate of the adjustment coefficient, γ, of 0.48.[40] The coefficients of p_t and I_t in (7.8.12) imply that the long-run price and income elasticities of demand for new automobiles, computed at mean values, are –0.63 and 3.0, respectively.

A related but fourth approach to dynamic demand analysis is a specification based on *changes* rather than levels of the quantity demanded. An example is the Suits estimation of a demand equation for new automobiles in the United States.[41] Using data from 1929–1956 (excluding 1942–1948 as unrepresentative years of war and its aftermath), he estimated the demand function as

$$\begin{aligned} \Delta A = 0.115 + \underset{(0.011)}{0.106\Delta I} - \underset{(0.086)}{0.507\Delta S} - \underset{(0.088)}{0.234\Delta(p/m)} \\ - \underset{(0.261)}{0.827PS}, \qquad R^2 = 0.85. \end{aligned} \qquad (7.8.14)$$

Here A is annual retail sales of new passenger automobiles, and ΔA, the change in these sales, is the dependent variable. The explanatory variables are the change in real disposable income, ΔI; the change in the stock of passenger automobiles, ΔS; the change in average retail price deflated by the average duration of automobile loans, $\Delta(p/m)$; and a dummy vari-

[38]Using a related model, which is log-linear rather than linear, Stone and Rowe (1958) estimated the speed of adjustment as very small for durable household goods (0.09), small for clothing (0.27), and larger than unity for certain habit-forming goods (e.g., 1.31 for beer, 1.47 for other alcoholic beverages, and 1.20 for tobacco).

[39]See Chow (1957).

[40]The adjustment coefficient is the difference between d and the coefficient of S_{t-1} in (7.8.12). See Problem 7-V. Phlips (1983) notes that (7.8.13) should, in fact, be adjusted to allow for the depreciation of goods purchased at the beginning of year t. One simple approach is to depreciate the average stock over the year, replacing S_{t-1} on the right-hand side in (7.8.13) by $(S_t + S_{t-1})/2$.

[41]See Suits (1958).

able to take account of years of severe production shortages (*PS*). All regression coefficients are statistically significant at the 1% level. The implied stock elasticities of demand, evaluated at the mean values, were estimated to be 4.2 with respect to real disposable income, –3.7 with respect to the stock of automobiles, and –0.6 with respect to the deflated average retail price. The elasticities with respect to income and price were similar to those obtained by Chow, reported above, indicating a price-inelastic but income-elastic demand for new automobiles.

The demand for automobiles and other such durables can be based, in part, on the existing stock, as in the Chow and Suits studies. The Houthakker–Taylor approach to dynamic demand analysis, which is the fifth approach, extends this concept to nondurables as well.[42] It is based on the idea that consumption involves some aspect of *habit formation* or *inertia*, as individual consumers become accustomed to certain amounts of a good. This habit formation can be accounted for by an observable stock of goods in the case of certain habit-forming durables, such as stocks of books or compact disks, which have the property that the larger the stock, other things being equal, the greater will be the demand for the good. Houthakker and Taylor extended this line of reasoning to all goods, nondurable as well as durable. In the case of nondurables, however, the stock is unobservable and is essentially a psychological construct. The model stipulates that the demand for a good, x, is a linear function of price, income, and the unobservable stock of the good:

$$x = a + bp + cI + eS + u. \qquad *(7.8.15)$$

This demand equation is the same as the linear demand function (7.4.1), except that other prices have been omitted for simplicity (they can, in fact, be easily added) and the dependence on the stock of the good is included. The stock grows according to

$$\Delta S = x - dS, \qquad *(7.8.16)$$

as in (7.8.13). Thus the quantities purchased at any time add to the stock, but the stock is depleted by depreciation at the rate d. This equation is the same as the one that states that the rate of change of capital stock is the (gross) rate of investment less depreciation. For durable goods the stock is observable, but for nondurable goods the analog, S, is not, so empirical estimation requires the elimination of this variable from the equation. This is accomplished by taking first differences in (7.8.15) and inserting (7.8.16) to obtain

$$\Delta x = b\Delta p + c\Delta I + e(x - dS) + \Delta u. \qquad (7.8.17)$$

Now, replacing S by solving (7.8.15) for S yields

$$\begin{aligned}\Delta x = {} & ad + (e - d)x + b\,\Delta p + bdp \\ & + c\,\Delta I + cdI + (\Delta u + du).\end{aligned} \qquad *(7.8.18)$$

According to this equation, the rate of change of demand is a linear function of the level of demand and the levels and rates of change of both price and income.

For a long-term equilibrium, x and S both remain constant over time. Denoting these long-term equilibrium levels by $\bar{x}$ and $\bar{S}$, it follows from (7.8.15) and (7.8.16) that

$$\bar{x} = a + b\bar{p} + c\bar{I} + e\bar{S} + u = d\bar{S}, \qquad *(7.8.19)$$

where $\bar{p}$ and $\bar{I}$ represent price and income levels in the long-term equilibrium. When p and I are equal to their long-term equilibrium values, it follows from (7.8.15) that for deviations

[42]See Houthakker and Taylor (1970). See also Stone and Rowe (1957), Pollak (1970), and Phlips (1983) for related dynamic models.

of the stock from its long-term level

$$x - \bar{x} = e(S - \bar{S}). \qquad *(7.8.20)$$

Thus the deviation of the current purchases of a good from its long-term level is proportional to the deviation of the current stock of the good from its long-term level. If the parameter e is negative, *current* purchases are above the long-term level if the stock is below its long-term level; this is the situation of *stock adjustment* (e.g., for durables). If, however, e is positive, both deviations have the same sign; this is the situation of *habit formation.* In the latter case the more of the good that is consumed, the more will be purchased.

Equation (7.8.18) can be written:[43]

$$x_t = A_0 + A_1 x_{t-1} + A_2\,\Delta I_t + A_3 I_{t-1} + A_4\,\Delta p_t + A_5 p_{t-1} + v_t. \qquad *(7.8.21)$$

Here use is made of the definition of the first difference:

$$\Delta x_t \equiv x_t - x_{t-1}. \qquad (7.8.22)$$

Thus this specification is also that of a Koyck distributed lag model in which the current variable, demand for a good, depends on its lagged value and current values of explanatory variables.

Houthakker and Taylor estimated their model for 83 commodities using constant dollar per capita expenditure in the United States over the period 1929–1964 (excluding the war years 1942–1945). Some of their results are reported in Table 7.7.[44] In their estimations, however, I is total consumption expenditure per capita, rather than income.[45] According to these results, stock adjustment (negative e) was found for automobiles, as might be expected, and also for purchased meals and clothing (although for the latter two the estimate of e is not as significant). The other goods listed exhibited habit formation (positive e), particularly electricity, alcoholic beverages, and gasoline and oil. The rates of depreciation of the stock, d, were smallest for clothing and automobiles, which are durable goods, and largest for jewelry and medical care (values of 2 were assumed for alcoholic beverages and electricity). The greatest short-run own price elasticity was for purchased meals and the least was for electricity, as might be expected. As to income elasticities, automobiles exhibited by far the greatest responsiveness to income, again indicating the demand for automobiles to be income-elastic, while electricity exhibited the smallest responsiveness to income among the goods included in the table.

[43]The linear demand equation

$$x_t = a + bp_t + cI_t + eS_t + u_t,$$

as in (7.8.15), for which the stochastic disturbance terms follows a Markov process

$$u_t = \rho u_{t-1} + v_t,$$

as in (5.5.2), would imply (7.8.21) provided that $e = 0$. Thus (7.8.21) can be considered a generalization of the static model with first-order serial correlation of stochastic disturbance terms (see Problem 7-W).

[44]Houthakker and Taylor (1970) also report results based on 1947–1964 data and results for other countries.

[45]Empirical studies sometimes use total expenditure rather than total income because data on income are either not available or subject to various errors and biases. Reported elasticities with respect to total expenditure, as in Table 7.7 and some earlier tables, should, however, be approximately the same as the corresponding elasticities with respect to income, since the elasticity of total expenditure with respect to income is close to unity.

TABLE 7.7 **Habit-Formation Demand Functions for the United States, 1929–1964 (excluding 1942–1945)**

Commodity	Estimates of $x = a + bp + cI + eS$: $\Delta S = x - dS$				Short-Run Elasticity	
	b	c	e	d	Own Price	Income (Expenditure)
Alcoholic beverages	—	0.011 (0.004)	1.067 (0.231)	2	—	0.29
Purchased meals	−1.40 (0.35)	0.068 (0.017)	−0.026 (0.012)	0	−2.27	1.61
Jewelry	−0.026 (0.013)	0.0057 (0.0019)	0.36 (0.73)	0.92 (0.83)	−0.41	1.00
Clothing	—	0.092 (0.016)	−0.15 (0.08)	0.12 (0.08)	—	1.14
Electricity	0.027 (0.014)	0.0018 (0.0008)	1.92 (0.09)	2	−0.13	0.13
Medical care	−0.0088 (0.0026)	0.0020 (0.0008)	0.37 (0.51)	0.56 (0.56)	−0.31	0.69
Automobiles	—	−0.26 (0.04)	−0.64 (0.16)	0.16 (0.04)	—	5.46
Gasoline and oil	—	0.017 (0.003)	0.17 (0.06)	0.28 (0.07)	—	0.55

Source Houthakker and Taylor (1970).

PROBLEMS

7-A Figure 7.2 shows the derivation of a demand curve for a normal good, and Figure 7.3 shows the derivation of an Engel curve for a superior good.

1. Show in a diagram comparable to Figure 7.2 the derivation of a demand curve for a Giffen good.
2. Show in a diagram comparable to Figure 7.3 the derivation of an Engel curve for an inferior good.
3. From the geometrical derivation show that a Giffen good must be an inferior good.

7-B The many specifications of the demand curve in various studies have included the following equations:

1. $x_1 = a - bp_1$ (linear)
2. $\ln x_1 = a - b \ln p_1$ (logarithmic or double logarithmic)
3. $x_1 = a - b \ln p_1$ (semilogarithmic)
4. $\ln x_1 = a - bp_1$ (inverse semilogarithmic)
5. $x_1 = a + b/p_1$ (linear in reciprocal)
6. $\ln x_1 = a + b/p_1$ (inverse semilogarithmic in reciprocal)

For each, determine the price elasticity of demand. Which permit a *threshold level* of price above which the consumer does not purchase the good (represented by zero, negative, or undefined values of x_1)? Which permit a *saturation level*, for which the demand curve approaches an asymptote? How would the results be modified if income I were substituted for price p_1 in each equation, the sign of b changed, and the set of equations were considered alternative specifications of the Engel curve?

7-C Engel's law states that the proportion of income spent on food decreases as income increases, or, equivalently, that the demand for food is income-inelastic. Prove that these two properties are equivalent.

7-D The Törnquist–Engel curves are given by

$$x = \frac{\alpha I}{I+\beta}, \qquad x = \alpha\frac{I-\gamma}{I+\beta}, \qquad x = \alpha I\frac{I-\gamma}{I+\beta},$$

where the parameters α, β, and γ depend on prices.[46] For each, find the income elasticity and asymptote and indicate the general shape it exhibits. Why are they referred to as Engel curves for "necessities," "relative luxuries," and "luxuries," respectively?

7-E Consider the nine conditions on demand functions in the case of two goods, as summarized by equations (7.2.10), (7.2.14), (7.2.17), (7.2.18), (7.2.20), and (7.2.22). Show that they are not independent by deriving the Slutsky symmetry condition in (7.2.18) from the other conditions.

7-F For the complete system of n demand equations (7.3.7) write out, using summation notation, all the theoretical restrictions that were developed for the case of two goods in Section 7.2, specifically:

1. One budget constraint
2. n homogeneity conditions
3. $n + \frac{n(n-1)}{2}$ Slutsky conditions
4. $n + 1$ aggregation conditions

7-G Prove that for an *additive utility function*, where overall utility is the sum of utilities for each of the goods,[47]

$$\varepsilon_{jj'} = \delta_{jj'}\phi\eta_j + \eta_j s_{j'}(1 - \phi\eta_{j'}), \qquad j, j' = 1, 2, \ldots, n,$$

where $\varepsilon_{jj'}$ is the cross-price elasticity (7.2.8), η_j the income elasticity (7.2.7), $s_{j'}$ the budget share (7.2.11), $\delta_{jj'}$, the Kronecker delta ($\delta_{jj'} = 1$ if $j = j'$, 0 if $j \neq j'$), and ϕ, the *income flexibility*, is defined as:

$$\frac{1}{\phi} = \frac{\partial \ln U^*}{\partial \ln I} = \frac{I}{U^*}\frac{\partial U^*}{\partial I} = \frac{I}{U^*}\frac{\partial^2 y^*}{\partial I^2},$$

where U^* is maximized utility and y^* is the Lagrange multiplier for problem (7.2.1). Thus the reciprocal of the income flexibility is the income elasticity of the marginal utility of income. From this result it may be noted that if s_j is small, the own price elasticity is proportional to the income elasticity:

$$\varepsilon_j = \varepsilon_{jj} \approx \phi\eta_j.$$

7-H Using the modern approach to the theory of the household, based on the concept of duality[48]:

1. Prove Shephard's lemma (7.2.27):

$$x_j = \frac{\partial E^*}{\partial p_j} = x_j(p_1, p_2, U), \qquad j = 1, 2.$$

2. Prove Roy's identity (7.2.25):

$$x_j = -\frac{\partial U^*/\partial p_j}{\partial U^*/\partial I} = x_j(p_1, p_2, I), \qquad j = 1, 2.$$

3. From these results, prove the Slutsky equation (see footnote 10).

[46]See Wold and Jureen (1953).

[47]See Frisch (1959).

[48]See footnote 13 and the references cited there.

4. Prove that the shares s_j of (7.2.11) satisfy

$$s_j = \frac{\partial \ln E_*}{\partial \ln p_j}.$$

7-I Given a logarithmic utility function:

$$U = \beta_1 \ln x_1 + \beta_2 \ln x_2, \qquad \beta_1, \beta_2 > 0, \quad \beta_1 + \beta_2 = 1,$$

show that the demand functions are of the form

$$x_j = \frac{\beta_j I}{p_j}, \qquad j = 1, 2$$

so that the expenditure on each good is a constant proportion of income. How are the demand functions modified if the normalization rule $\beta_1 + \beta_2 = 1$ is not assumed? (*Note*: Problem 7-M is a generalization of this problem.)

7-J Consider the linear and log-linear systems of demand equations as given in (7.5.2) and (7.5.3). What restrictions are imposed on the b's and c's by the theory of the consumer? How many coefficients remain to be estimated?

7-K Verify that the linear expenditure system of demand equations (7.5.4) satisfies all theoretical restrictions, in particular the homogeneity, Slutsky, and aggregation conditions on systems of demand equations.

7-L Show that the linear expenditure system of demand equations (7.5.4) solves the problem of maximizing utility subject to a budget constraint, where the utility function is of the Stone–Geary type:

$$U = \sum_{j=1}^{n} \beta_j \ln(x_j - x_j^0), \quad \text{where} \quad x_j > x_j^0, \qquad \text{all } j,$$

$$0 < \beta_j < 1, \quad \sum \beta_j = 1.$$

(*Note*: Problem 7-I refers to the special case in which $n = 2$ and $x_j^0 = 0$, all j, while Problem 7-O generalizes this problem.)

7-M For the linear expenditure system of demand equations (7.5.4):

1. Obtain price and income elasticities of demand, and show that there can be neither inferior goods nor price-elastic goods (assuming that $x_j > 0$).
2. Show that the budget shares s_j defined in (7.2.11) can be represented as the linear combination

$$s_j = (1 - r)\beta_j + r s_j^*,$$

where r is the *subsistence ratio*, the ratio of subsistence income to total income,

$$r = \frac{\sum p_k x_k^0}{I}, \qquad 0 \leqslant r \leqslant 1,$$

and s_j^* is the *subsistence budget share*, the proportion of subsistence income devoted to the purchase of the base quantity of the good:

$$s_j^* = \frac{p_j x_j^0}{\sum_k p_k x_k^0}.$$

3. Express the own and cross-price elasticities, ε_j and $\varepsilon_{jj'}$, as specific functions of the income elasticities η_j, the subsistence ratio r, and the budget shares s_j.

7-N Consider the general additive utility function

$$U = \sum_{j=1}^{n} \frac{\beta_j}{\alpha_j} \left(\frac{x_j - x_j^0}{\beta_j} \right)^{\alpha_j}$$

where the constant parameters satisfy $\alpha_j < 1, \beta_j > 0$, and $x_j^0 < x_j$.

1. What form does the utility function take in the limit as $\alpha_j \to 0$?
2. Find the demand functions implied by this utility function.
3. Show that if $x_j^0 = 0$ and all α_j are equal, the utility function assumes the same form as the CES production function (of Section 8.3) and that if, in addition, $\alpha_j = 0$, the form is the same as the Cobb–Douglas production function (also of Section 8.3). What are the implied demand functions in each of these cases? What are the demand functions if $x_j^0 = 0$ but α_j are not all equal (but $\alpha_j < 1$)?
4. Assume that $x_j^0 > 0$ (but $x_j^0 < x_j$). Show that if $\alpha_j = 0$, the demand functions are those of the linear expenditure system (7.5.5). What form do they take if the α_j are all equal (but not zero)?

7-O Show in a diagram analogous to Figure 7.5 that if $\sigma_S^2 << \sigma_D^2$, the supply curve would be identified. In which markets would this assumption about relative variances likely be met?

7-P Consider the estimation of elasticities as

$$\hat{\delta} = \frac{\sum p_i q_i}{\sum p_i^2},$$

where p_i and q_i here are the logarithms of price and quantity, measured as deviations from the means of the logarithms. According to the model:

$$q_i^D = \beta p_i + u_i \qquad \text{where} \quad u_i \sim N(0, \sigma_u^2),$$

$$q_i^S = \gamma p_i + v_i \qquad \text{where} \quad v_i \sim N(0, \sigma_v^2),$$

$$E(u_i u_{i'}) = E(v_i v_{i'}) = 0 \qquad \text{for } i \neq i',\ E(u_i v_{i'}) = 0, \quad \text{all } i, i',$$

show that

$$E(\hat{\delta}) = \frac{\gamma\sigma_u^2 + \beta\sigma_v^2}{\sigma_u^2 + \sigma_v^2}$$

and indicate those circumstances in which $\hat{\delta}$ is an acceptable estimate of the price elasticity of demand.

7-Q Consider the aggregation condition given in Section 7.7, stating that the Engel curves are all linear, with identical slopes across all consumers. Show that this condition is both necessary and sufficient for any redistribution of income among the consumers not to have any behavioral repercussions on aggregate demand. Illustrate geometrically.

7-R Consider the problem of aggregation for log-linear demand curves. What are the conditions of aggregation in this case?

7-S Consider the homogeneity restriction for aggregate demand functions, assuming all individual demand functions exhibit homogeneity. Show that aggregate demand does not change when aggregate income and all prices change by the same proportion only if it is also assumed that all individual incomes change by the same proportion.

7-T In the Nerlove model of adaptive expectations, sellers adapt their expectations of price according to past mistakes, in that the change in expected price is proportional to the deviation between actual and expected prices in the last period.[49] Thus

$$p_t^* - p_{t-1}^* = h(p_{t-1} - p_{t-1}^*), \qquad 0 < h \leq 1,$$

[49]See Nerlove (1958); see also Section 6.8.

where p_t^* is the expected price in period t, p_t the actual price in period t, and h the expectation adjustment coefficient. Demand depends linearly on actual price

$$q_t^D = a - bp_t$$

and supply depends linearly on expected price

$$q_t^S = c + dp_t^*,$$

where market clearing occurs in each period:

$$q_t^D = q_t^S.$$

1. Show that the behavior of expected prices can be obtained from a Koyck distributed lag relating expected prices to actual prices.
2. Show that the model reduces to the cobweb model of (7.8.1)–(7.8.7) for $h = 1$.
3. For any h within the given bounds obtain the implied difference equation and solve it for the behavior of price over time, starting from p_0.
4. Prove that price converges to an equilibrium price $\bar{p}$ only if

$$1 - \frac{2}{h} < -\frac{d}{b}.$$

   Compare this condition to that for convergence of the cobweb model. In particular, show that adaptive expectations can stabilize an otherwise unstable cobweb model.
5. Generalize the model to allow for stochastic disturbance terms and discuss the estimation of parameters of the model.

7-U Schultz (1938) estimated the following cobweb model for sugar:

$$p(t) = 2.34 - 1.34q^D(t) \qquad \text{(demand)},$$
$$q^S(t) = 0.5 + 0.6p(t-1) \qquad \text{(supply)},$$

where $p(t)$ is price at time t, $q^D(t)$ is demand at time t, and $q^S(t)$ is supply at time t.

1. What is the equilibrium price?
2. Find the time trend for the price.
3. Does the system converge to the equilibrium price?

7-V Prove that, for the Chow stock adjustment model in (7.8.12) and (7.8.13), the adjustment coefficient γ is the difference between d and the coefficient of S_{t-1} in (7.8.12).

7-W For the Houthakker–Taylor model of (7.8.15)–(7.8.22):

1. Solve for a, b, c, d, and e of (7.8.18) in terms of A_0 to A_5 of (7.8.21).
2. Show that the case $d = 2$ leads to:

$$x_t = A_0 + A_1 x_{t-1} + A_2 I_t + A_4 p_t + v_t,$$

   as in the Koyck distributed lag. Treat the case $d = -2$ similarly.
3. Show that the static model with first-order serial correlation of stochastic disturbance terms, as given in footnote 43, implies (7.8.21) provided that $e = 0$.

7-X For the almost ideal demand system (AIDS) system of demand equations, combine (7.5.8) and (7.5.9) into a single set of equations, show that α_0 is unidentified, and determine how many parameters are in each equation of the system. How many data points are needed to estimate the complete set of n equations? What do the theoretical restrictions on demand equations of Section 7.2 imply as restrictions on the α_j, β_j, and γ_{jk} parameters? Obtain the income elasticities of the related Working's model.

7-Y For the Rotterdam system of demand equations (7.5.10) in the case of two goods, what do the theoretical restrictions on demand equations of Section 7.2 imply as restrictions on the a_j, b_j, and c_{jk} parameters?

BIBLIOGRAPHY

ALLEN, R. G. D. (1959). *Mathematical Economics*, 2nd ed. London: Macmillan and Co. Ltd.

ALLEN, R. G. D., and A. L. BOWLEY (1935). *Family Expenditure*. London: P.S. King.

BARTEN, A. P. (1977). "The Systems of Consumer Demand Functions Approach: A Review." *Econometrica*, 45: 23–51. Also in M. D. Intriligator, Ed., *Frontiers of Quantitative Economics*, Vol. 3. Amsterdam: North-Holland Publishing Company.

BARTEN, A. P., and V. BÖHM (1982). "Consumer Theory," in K. J. Arrow and M. D. Intriligator, Eds., *Handbook of Mathematical Economics*, Vol. 2. Amsterdam: North-Holland Publishing Company.

CHOW, G. C. (1957). *Demand for Automobiles in the United States*. Amsterdam: North-Holland Publishing Company.

DEATON, A. S. (1986). "Demand Analysis," in Z. Griliches and M. D. Intriligator, Eds., *Handbook of Econometrics*, Vol. 2. Amsterdam: North-Holland Publishing Company.

DEATON, A. S., and J. MUELLBAUER (1980). *Economics and Consumer Behavior*. Cambridge: Cambridge University Press.

DIEWERT, W. E. (1982). "Duality Approaches to Microeconomic Theory," in K. J. Arrow and M. D. Intriligator, Eds., *Handbook of Mathematical Economics*, Vol. 2. Amsterdam: North-Holland Publishing Company.

FOX, K. A. (1953). *The Analysis of Demand for Farm Products*. Technical Bulletin 1081. Washington, D.C.: U.S. Department of Agriculture.

FOX, K. A. (1958). *Econometric Analysis for Public Policy*. Ames, Iowa: Iowa State College Press.

FRISCH, R. (1959). "A Complete Scheme for Computing All Direct and Cross Demand Elasticities in a Model with Many Sectors." *Econometrica*, 27: 117–196.

GOLDBERGER, A., and T. GAMALETSOS (1970). "A Cross-Country Comparison of Consumer Expenditure Patterns." *European Economic Review*, 1: 357–400.

GREEN, H. A. J. (1964). *Aggregation in Economic Analysis: An Introductory Survey*. Princeton, N.J.: Princeton University Press.

HARBERGER, A., Ed. (1960). *The Demand for Durable Goods*. Chicago: University of Chicago Press.

HOUTHAKKER, H. S. (1957). "An International Comparison of Household Expenditure Patterns Commemorating the Centenary of Engel's Laws." *Econometrica*, 25: 532–551.

HOUTHAKKER, H. S. (1965). "New Evidence on Demand Elasticities." *Econometrica*, 33: 277–288.

HOUTHAKKER, H. S., and L. D. TAYLOR (1970). *Consumer Demand in the United States, 1929–1970*, 2nd enlarged ed. Cambridge, Mass.: Harvard University Press.

INTRILIGATOR, M. D. (1971). *Mathematical Optimization and Economic Theory*. Englewood Cliffs, N.J.: Prentice Hall.

JORGENSON, D. W., L. J. LAU, and T. STOKER (1982). "The Transcendental Logarithmic Model of Aggregate Consumer Behavior." *Advances in Econometrics*, Vol. 1. Greenwich, Conn.: JAI Press, Inc.

KREPS, D. M. (1990). *A Course in Microeconomic Theory*. Princeton, N.J.: Princeton University Press.

LLUCH, C., and A. A. POWELL (1975). "International Comparisons of Expenditure Patterns." *European Economic Review*, 5: 275–303.

MCFADDEN, D. (1978). "Costs, Revenue, and Profit Functions," in M. Fuss and D. McFadden, Eds., *Production Economics: A Dual Approach to Theory and Applications*. Amsterdam: North-Holland Publishing Company.

NERLOVE, M. (1958). "Adaptive Expectations and Cobweb Phenomena." *Quarterly Journal of Economics*, 72: 227–240.

PHLIPS, L. (1983). *Applied Consumption Analysis*, revised and enlarged ed. Amsterdam: North-Holland Publishing Company.

POLLAK, R. A. (1970). "Habit Formation and Dynamic Demand Functions." *Journal of Political Economy*, 78: 745–763.

POWELL, A. A. (1974). *Empirical Analytics of Demand Systems*. Lexington, Mass.: Lexington Books.

PRAIS, S. J., and H. S. HOUTHAKKER (1955). *The Analysis of Family Budgets*. New York: Cambridge University Press.

SATO, K. (1972). "Additive Utility Functions with Double-Log Consumer Demand Functions." *Journal of Political Economy*, 80: 102–124.

SCHULTZ, H. (1938). *The Theory and Measurement of Demand*. Chicago: University of Chicago Press.

STONE, R. (1954a). *The Measurement of Consumers' Expenditure and Behavior in the United Kingdom, 1920–1938*. New York: Cambridge University Press.

STONE, R. (1954b). "Linear Expenditure Systems and Demand Analysis; An Application to the Pattern of British Demand." *Economic Journal*, 64: 511–527.

STONE, R. (1966). "The Changing Pattern of Consumption," in R. Stone, Ed., *Mathematics in the Social Sciences and Other Essays*. London: Chapman & Hall Ltd.

STONE, R. (1972). *A Computable Model of Economic Growth: A Programme for Growth*, Vol. 1. Cambridge: Chapman & Hall Ltd.

STONE, R., and D. A. ROWE (1957). "The Market Demand for Durable Goods." *Econometrica*, 25: 423–443.

STONE, R., and D. A. ROWE (1958). "Dynamic Demand Functions: Some Econometric Results." *Economic Journal*, 68: 256–270.

STONE, R., and D. A. ROWE (1960), "The Durability of Consumers' Durable Goods." *Econometrica*, 28: 407–416.

SUITS, D. B. (1958). "The Demand for New Automobiles in the United States, 1929–1956." *The Review of Economics and Statistics*, 40: 273–280.

THEIL, H. (1954). *Linear Aggregation of Economic Relations*. Amsterdam: North-Holland Publishing Company.

THEIL, H. (1975–76). *Theory and Measurement of Consumer Demand*, Vols. 1 and 2. Amsterdam: North-Holland Publishing Company.

THEIL, H., and K. W. CLEMENTS (1987). *Applied Demand Analysis*. Cambridge, Mass.: Ballinger Publishing Co.

VARIAN, H. (1990). *Microeconomic Analysis,* 2nd ed. New York: W.W. Norton & Company, Inc.

WOLD, H., and L. JUREEN (1953). *Demand Analysis*. New York: John Wiley & Sons, Inc.

8

APPLICATIONS TO FIRMS; PRODUCTION FUNCTIONS AND COST FUNCTIONS

8.1 INTRODUCTION

The second important area of application of single-equation estimation is to the firm, the firm and the household constituting the two basic units of microeconomics. The firm is the basic production unit, producing goods (and services) using certain inputs called *factors of production*, such as labor and capital.

The applications of econometrics to the firm include the estimation of production functions, cost curves, factor demand equations, and technical change. Each of these subjects will be treated in this chapter, following a summary of salient aspects of the theory of the firm.

8.2 THE THEORY OF THE FIRM

The problem of the firm, from a formal point of view, is that of maximizing profits subject to a given technology.[1] Profits equal revenue minus cost; revenue is the level of output times the price of output; and cost is the sum, over all inputs, of the level of each input times the wage of each input. In the neoclassical formulation the technology is summarized by a *production function*, a technical relationship based on physical or engineering considerations indicating the (maximum) output attainable for alternative combinations of all conceivable

[1]See Intriligator (1971), Nadiri (1982), Samuelson (1983), Varian (1984), Malinvaud (1985), and Kreps (1990). The basic assumption of profit maximization has been repeatedly challenged. For example, Baumol (1967) suggests sales (or growth of sales) maximization, Williamson (1964) suggests managerial utility maximization, and Simon (1959) suggests replacing profit maximizing by profit satisficing. Nevertheless, profit maximization is still the most widely used basic assumption for the firm, and these alternative goals frequently imply profit maximization—at least in the long run.

inputs of factors of production. In the case of a firm producing a single output from two inputs, the production function can be represented as:

$$y = f(x_1, x_2) \qquad *(8.2.1)$$

where y is the (maximum possible) level of output, x_1 and x_2 are the levels of the two inputs, and $f(\cdot,\cdot)$ is a function that is generally assumed to be continuously differentiable, so that the partial derivatives are continuous. The production function indicates the level of output y associated with any combination of inputs (x_1, x_2).

The problem of the firm in this case of one output and two inputs can be stated as that of choosing the output and inputs so as to

$$\max_{y,x_1,x_2} \Pi = py - w_1x_1 - w_2x_2 \quad \text{subject to} \quad y = f(x_1, x_2). \qquad *(8.2.2)$$

Here Π is profits, given as revenue (py) less cost $(w_1x_1 + w_2x_2)$, p is the price of output, and w_1 and w_2 are the wages (the prices) of the inputs. When the production function constraint is substituted into the definition of profits, the problem can be stated as the unconstrained problem

$$\max_{x_1,x_2} \Pi = pf(x_1, x_2) - w_1x_1 - w_2x_2. \qquad *(8.2.3)$$

In the case of perfect competition, in which all three prices p, w_1, and w_2 are given parameters determined on the relevant product and factor markets, the necessary (first-order) conditions for a maximum are:[2]

$$\frac{\partial \Pi}{\partial x_1} = p\frac{\partial f}{\partial x_1} - w_1 = 0, \qquad (8.2.4)$$

$$\frac{\partial \Pi}{\partial x_2} = p\frac{\partial f}{\partial x_2} - w_2 = 0. \qquad (8.2.5)$$

These conditions require that

$$\frac{\partial f}{\partial x_j} \equiv \text{MP}_j = \frac{w_j}{p}, \qquad j = 1, 2, \qquad *(8.2.6)$$

where the partial derivatives are the *marginal products* MP_j, defined as the increase in output per unit increase in one input, the other input being held constant. These conditions state that the marginal product of each input must equal *its real wage*, namely the wage (input price) divided by the price of output. The two marginal-product conditions in (8.2.6) plus the production function in (8.2.1) form a system of three simultaneous equations that determine profit-maximizing output y and inputs x_1 and x_2.[3]

The two conditions in (8.2.6) imply that the ratio of the marginal products must equal the ratio of the wages:

$$\text{MRTS}_{jk} \equiv \frac{\text{MP}_j}{\text{MP}_k} = \frac{w_j}{w_k}, \qquad j, k = 1, 2, \qquad *(8.2.7)$$

where MRTS_{jk} is the *marginal rate of technical substitution* between inputs j and k, defined as the ratio of the marginal products of these inputs. In the case of two inputs, (8.2.7) gives one condition—that MRTS_{12} equal w_1/w_2.

[2]For a discussion of second-order conditions, see Intriligator (1971).

[3]This system can, in fact, be divided into two subsystems—the two equations in (8.2.6), determining x_1 and x_2, and the equation in (8.2.1), determining y.

The equilibrium of the firm can be shown geometrically as in Figure 8.1. The lines are *isocosts*, defined as the locus of input combinations (x_1, x_2) for which cost C, the total payment to both inputs, is constant:

$$C = w_1x_1 + w_2x_2 \equiv \text{constant}. \tag{8.2.8}$$

Totally differentiating this identity yields

$$w_1\,dx_1 + w_2\,dx_2 \equiv 0, \tag{8.2.9}$$

so the slope of the isocosts is the ratio of the wages:

$$\frac{dx_2}{dx_1} = -\frac{w_1}{w_2}. \tag{8.2.10}$$

For each (positive) level of the constant in (8.2.8) an isocost is defined, and each isocost has a slope equal to the negative of the ratio of the wages of the inputs. A family of these isocosts is illustrated in the figure.

The curves in the figure are *isoquants*, each of which is the locus of input combinations for which output is fixed, that is, level curves of the production function defined by:

$$y = f(x_1, x_2) \equiv \text{constant}. \tag*{*(8.2.11)}$$

Each curve corresponds to a particular constant in this equation. Totally differentiating (8.2.11) gives

$$\frac{\partial f}{\partial x_1}dx_1 + \frac{\partial f}{\partial x_2}dx_2 = 0, \tag{8.2.12}$$

so the slope of any isoquant at any point is given by

$$\frac{dx_2}{dx_1} = -\frac{\partial f/\partial x_1}{\partial f/\partial x_2} = -\frac{\text{MP}_1}{\text{MP}_2} = -\text{MRTS}_{12}. \tag{8.2.13}$$

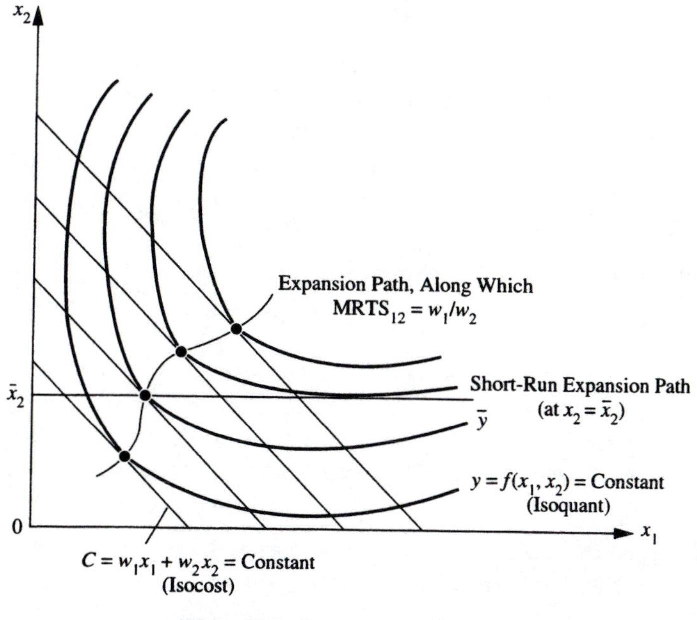

Figure 8.1 Expansion Paths for the Firm

Thus the slope of the isoquant is the negative of the marginal rate of technical substitution, which generally varies as the inputs change, as shown by the change in the slope of any one of the isoquants as one input is substituted for another.

The equilibrium of the firm in the long run, when both inputs can be freely varied, is at the tangency of an isocost to an isoquant. Only at such a point is output maximized for a given cost or, equivalently, is cost minimized for a given output. The former follows by moving along any one isocost: if at any one point it crosses an isoquant it is possible to increase output with no additional cost—by moving toward the tangency point. Similarly, moving along any one isoquant, if at any one point it crosses an isocost, it is possible to decrease cost while holding output constant—by moving toward the tangency point. The locus of tangency points is the set of possible equilibrium points for the firm; it is called the *expansion path* and is characterized by the equality of slopes of isocost and isoquant. From the above results on these slopes, the geometric tangency is in fact equivalent to the algebraic condition (8.2.7), stating that, for profit maximization, the marginal rate of technical substitution must equal the ratio of wages.

The possible equilibrium points along the expansion path of Figure 8.1 indicate at each such point an output, y, from the isoquant, and a level of cost, C, from the isocost. The set of all possible pairs of output and cost along the expansion path defines the *cost curve*:

$$C = C(y), \qquad *(8.2.14)$$

in this case the long-run total cost curve, since it represents total cost:

$$C = w_1x_1 + w_2x_2 \qquad (8.2.15)$$

in the long-run situation in which all factor inputs can be varied freely. A *short-run cost curve* is defined using an alternative expansion path that reflects whatever factors are fixed in any particular short run. An example would be the expansion path defined by the horizontal line at $\bar{x}_2$, where the second input is fixed at this level and the first input is free to vary. The short-run cost curve defined by the output and cost along such an alternative expansion path $C_S(y)$ must satisfy

$$C_S(y) \geqslant C(y) \qquad \text{at each } y \qquad (8.2.16)$$

since at all points other than those for which the two expansion paths cross the short-run situation involves producing a particular level of output y at higher cost.

Average cost curves in the long run and short run are defined by:

$$\text{AC}(y) = \frac{C(y)}{y}, \qquad \text{AC}_S(y) = \frac{C_S(y)}{y} \qquad *(8.2.17)$$

and marginal cost curves in these cases are defined by:

$$\text{MC}(y) = \frac{dC(y)}{dy}, \qquad \text{MC}_S(y) = \frac{dC_S(y)}{dy}. \qquad *(8.2.18)$$

The various cost curves introduced here are illustrated geometrically in Figure 8.2. The upper diagram shows (total) cost curves in the long run and short run, and the lower diagram shows corresponding average and marginal cost curves in the long run and short run. Because all inputs can be freely varied in the long run, the cost at zero output is zero:

$$C(0) = 0. \qquad (8.2.19)$$

In a short run, however, certain factors are fixed, and so there will be some cost at zero output—the fixed cost defined by

$$C_S(0) = \text{FC} > 0. \qquad (8.2.20)$$

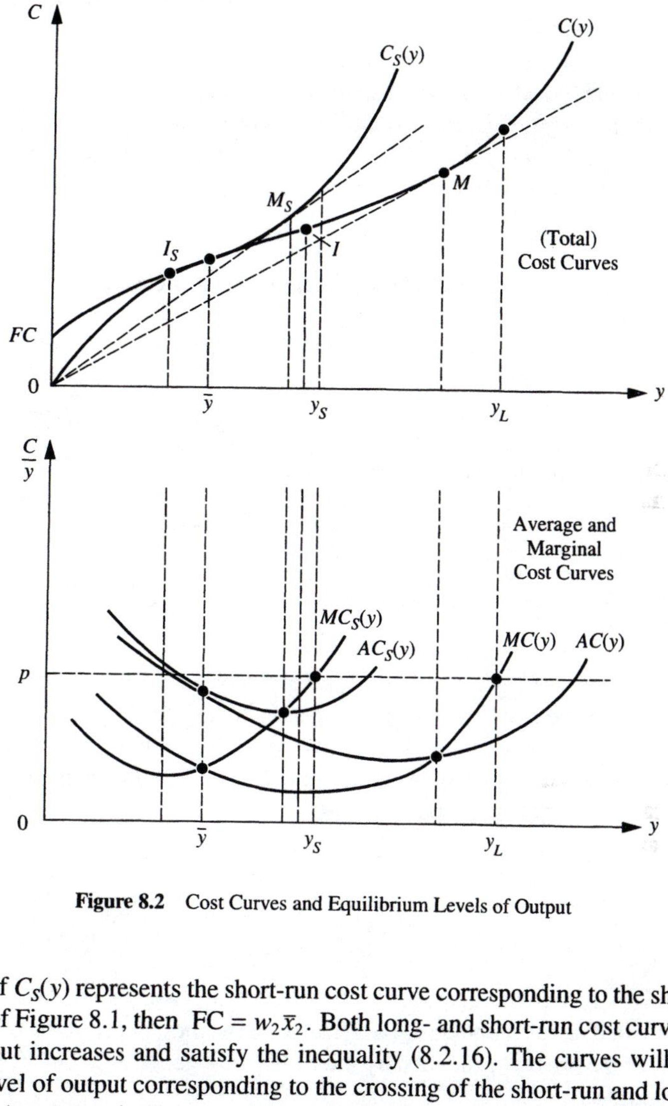

Figure 8.2 Cost Curves and Equilibrium Levels of Output

For example, if $C_S(y)$ represents the short-run cost curve corresponding to the short-run expansion path of Figure 8.1, then $FC = w_2\bar{x}_2$. Both long- and short-run cost curves must increase as output increases and satisfy the inequality (8.2.16). The curves will touch one another at a level of output corresponding to the crossing of the short-run and long-run expansion paths (e.g., at $\bar{y}$ in Figure 8.1, shown also in Figure 8.2). The shape of the cost curves reflects underlying assumptions concerning the technology—that initially cost increases at a decreasing rate, corresponding to increased specialization and division of labor, while at higher levels of output cost increases at an increasing rate, corresponding to managerial diseconomies in large enterprise.

The lower diagrams show average and marginal cost curves, plotted on a separate diagram since the dimension of both, cost divided by output, differs from that of total cost. Geometrically, average cost is the slope of a ray connecting the origin and a point on the total cost curve, while marginal cost is the slope of the total cost curve itself. Thus average cost is at a minimum where the ray is tangent to the curve—at M and M_S—so at this point marginal cost and average cost are equal. The marginal cost curves reach minimum levels corresponding to inflection points of the total cost curves at I and I_S. At the point $\bar{y}$, at which the total cost curves touch, both average cost curves and both marginal cost curves give identical values.

The equilibrium of the competitive firm is also shown in Figure 8.2.[4] A given price of the product, p, is shown in the lower diagram as the horizontal line; it is in the lower diagram since p has the dimension of cost *per unit*. The equilibrium is found at that output for which the price line intersects the marginal cost and marginal cost is increasing—at y_S in the short run and y_L in the long run. Algebraically, since

$$\Pi = py - C(y), \qquad *(8.2.21)$$

maximizing profit by choice of output calls for choosing y so that:

$$\frac{d\Pi}{dy}(y) = p - \frac{dC}{dy}(y) = p - \text{MC}(y) = 0. \qquad (8.2.22)$$

Thus a first-order condition of profit maximization is:

$$p = \text{MC}(y). \qquad *(8.2.23)$$

The second-order condition is:

$$\frac{d^2\Pi}{dy^2} = -\frac{d^2C}{dy^2} = -\frac{d\,\text{MC}(y)}{dy} \leqslant 0, \qquad (8.2.24)$$

so

$$\frac{d\,\text{MC}(y)}{dy} \geqslant 0. \qquad (8.2.25)$$

Equations (8.2.23) and (8.2.25) give, algebraically, the conditions that price equals marginal cost where marginal cost is increasing, as at y_S and y_L in Figure 8.2.

Given the optimal (profit-maximizing) output, the choice of inputs is given at that point where the corresponding isoquant intersects the relevant expansion path of Figure 8.1. The corresponding optimal inputs are x_1 and x_2, where output is given as

$$y = f(x_1, x_2). \qquad (8.2.26)$$

The optimal inputs, in general, depend on both wages and output price:

$$x_j = x_j(w_1, w_2, p), \qquad j = 1, 2. \qquad (8.2.27)$$

This system of equations is called the system of *factor demand functions*. They are also called *derived demand functions* because they are derived from the underlying demand for the product produced by the firm. More generally, for a firm using n inputs to produce output,

$$x_j = x_j(w_1, w_2, \ldots, w_n, p), \qquad j = 1, 2, \ldots, n, \qquad *(8.2.28)$$

where w_j is the price of input j. If output price and all wages other than that of the input itself are held constant, the resulting curve

$$x_j = D_j(w_j) = x_j(\overline{w}_1, \overline{w}_2, \ldots, w_j, \ldots, \overline{w}_n, \overline{p}) \qquad (8.2.29)$$

is the jth *factor demand curve*.

The optimal level of output is also a function of input wages and output price. In the two-input case,

[4]For the case of the firm in imperfect competition, see Problem 8-E.

$$y = y(w_1, w_2, p) = f[x_1(w_1, w_2, p), x_2(w_1, w_2, p)] \tag{8.2.30}$$

is the *output supply function*, and in the n-input case it is:

$$y = y(w_1, w_2, \ldots, w_n, p). \qquad *(8.2.31)$$

If all wages are held constant, the resulting curve,

$$y = S(p) = y(\overline{w}_1, \overline{w}_2, \ldots, \overline{w}_n, p), \tag{8.2.32}$$

is the *output supply curve*. Both the factor demand functions and the output supply function are determined on the basis of the technology, as represented by the production function.

Comparative statics, as applied to the firm, is concerned with the effect of changes in input wages and output prices on the factor demand functions in (8.2.28) and on the output supply function in (8.2.31). The first-order conditions for profit maximization can be written as the identities:

$$p\frac{\partial f}{\partial x_j}[x_1(w_1, \ldots, w_n, p), \ldots, x_n(w_1, \ldots, w_n, p)] \equiv w_j, \qquad j = 1, 2, \ldots, n, \tag{8.2.33}$$

which, together with the identities:

$$y \equiv f[x_1(w_1, \ldots, w_n, p), \ldots, x_n(w_1, \ldots, w_n, p)], \tag{8.2.34}$$

$$\Pi \equiv pf[x_1(w_1, \ldots, w_n, p), \ldots, x_n(w_1, \ldots, w_n, p)] - \sum_{j=1}^{n} w_j x_j(w_1, \ldots, w_n, p) \tag{8.2.35}$$

define the equilibrium inputs, output, and profits. Differentiating these conditions with respect to wages and price gives the comparative statics results.[5] One important set of results are the *symmetry conditions:*

$$\frac{\partial x_j}{\partial w_k} = \frac{\partial x_k}{\partial w_j}, \qquad \text{all } j, k, \tag{8.2.36}$$

which state, for profit-maximizing inputs, that the change in the jth factor demand for a change in the kth wage is equal to the change in the kth factor demand for a change in the jth wage (i.e., the cross effects of wages on the inputs are symmetric). For $j \neq k$, inputs j and k are *substitutes* if $\partial x_j/\partial w_k$ is positive and they are *complements* if this partial derivative is negative.

Another set of comparative statics results are the *sign conditions* on profit-maximizing inputs and output,

$$\frac{\partial x_j}{\partial w_j} < 0, \qquad *(8.2.37)$$

$$\frac{\partial x_j}{\partial p} > 0 \qquad \text{for some } j, \qquad *(8.2.38)$$

$$\frac{\partial y}{\partial p} > 0, \qquad *(8.2.39)$$

$$\frac{\partial y}{\partial w_j} < 0 \qquad \text{for some } j. \qquad *(8.2.40)$$

[5]For proofs using profit and cost functions, see below. For more classical proofs, see Intriligator (1971, Chap. 8).

These conditions are analogous to the negativity of own substitution effects in the theory of the consumer. Condition (8.2.37) is that of a negatively sloped demand curve for factors, so that there can be no "Giffen factor" comparable to the Giffen good of the theory of the household. Condition (8.2.39) is that of a rising supply curve for output. The positive slope of the supply curve is also shown geometrically in Figure 8.2—raising p will clearly increase both y_S and y_L, as the optimum point moves up the marginal cost curve. In fact, the marginal cost curve in the long run above average cost is the long-run supply curve, while the marginal cost curve in the short run above average variable cost is the short-run supply curve, average variable cost being $[C_S(y) - C_S(0)]/y$. Furthermore,[6]

$$\frac{\partial x_j}{\partial p} = -\frac{\partial y}{\partial w_j}, \qquad \text{all } j. \tag*{*(8.2.41)}$$

Inputs for which

$$\frac{\partial x_j}{\partial p} = -\frac{\partial y}{\partial w_j} < 0 \tag*{*(8.2.42)}$$

are called *inferior inputs*, for which demand decreases as output price (and hence output) increases or, equivalently, for which output increases when the wage of the factor increases. By (8.2.38) and (8.2.40), not all inputs can be inferior.[7]

Another set of comparative static conditions follows from the homogeneity of the factor demand equations and the output supply function. Scaling price and wages by a positive scale factor, from $(w_1, w_2, \ldots, w_n, p)$ to $(\alpha w_1, \alpha w_2, \ldots, \alpha w_n, \alpha p)$, where $\alpha > 0$, scales profits by α, from Π to $\alpha\Pi$. But maximizing $\alpha\Pi$ is equivalent to maximizing Π if $\alpha > 0$. Thus the solutions for profit-maximizing factor demands and output supply are invariant to such a change (i.e., they are homogeneous to degree zero in all wages and price):

$$x_j(\alpha w_1, \alpha w_2, \ldots, \alpha w_n, \alpha p) = x_j(w_1, w_2, \ldots, w_n, p), \qquad \text{all } j, \text{ all } \alpha > 0, \tag{8.2.43}$$

$$y(\alpha w_1, \alpha w_2, \ldots, \alpha w_n, \alpha p) = y(w_1, w_2, \ldots, w_n, p), \qquad \text{all } \alpha > 0. \tag{8.2.44}$$

Euler's theorem on homogeneous functions then implies that:

$$\sum_{k=1}^{n} w_k \frac{\partial x_j}{\partial w_k} + p\frac{\partial x_j}{\partial p} = 0, \qquad \text{all } j, \tag*{*(8.2.45)}$$

$$\sum_{k=1}^{n} w_k \frac{\partial y}{\partial w_k} + p\frac{\partial y}{\partial p} = 0, \tag*{*(8.2.46)}$$

which are the *homogeneity conditions*. They can be expressed in elasticity form as

$$\sum_{k=1}^{n} \frac{w_k}{x_j}\frac{\partial x_j}{\partial w_k} + \frac{p}{x_j}\frac{\partial x_j}{\partial p} = 0, \qquad j = 1, 2, \ldots, n, \tag*{*(8.2.47)}$$

$$\sum_{k=1}^{n} \frac{w_k}{y}\frac{\partial y}{\partial w_k} + \frac{p}{y}\frac{\partial y}{\partial p} = 0, \tag*{*(8.2.48)}$$

stating that the sum of all elasticities vanishes both for each factor demand equation and for the output supply function.

[6]This relation follows from the homogeneity of the input demand functions discussed below (see Problem 8-B).

[7]Note that inferior inputs do not involve a negative marginal product; even though output increases as the level of input decreases, other inputs are also changing.

The modern approach to the theory of the firm is based on the concept of duality, using the profit function and cost function.[8] Profit is defined as:

$$\Pi \equiv py - \sum w_j x_j \tag{8.2.49}$$

so, assuming competitive markets, where the output price and factor wages are given, inserting the output supply function (8.2.31) and the factor demand functions (8.2.28) into this identity yields

$$\begin{aligned}\Pi(w_1, w_2, \ldots, w_n, p) &= py(w_1, w_2, \ldots, w_n, p)\\ &\quad - \sum w_j x_j(w_1, w_2, \ldots, w_n, p).\end{aligned} \qquad *(8.2.50)$$

This function, stating the dependence of profits on all wages and price, is called the *profit function*. This function, which is defined for the long-run situation in which all inputs and outputs are freely variable, is continuous, homogeneous of degree one, convex, decreasing in each wage, and increasing in output price. Furthermore, if the profit function is continuously differentiable at a certain set of input wages and output price, then, according to *Hotelling's lemma*, the profit-maximizing levels of inputs and output can be expressed as the following partial derivatives of the profit function:

$$x_j = -\frac{\partial \Pi}{\partial w_j}, \qquad j = 1, 2, \ldots, n, \qquad *(8.2.51)$$

$$y = \frac{\partial \Pi}{\partial p}. \qquad *(8.2.52)$$

From these conditions the comparative statics results readily follow. The symmetry conditions (8.2.36) follow from the equality of the mixed second-order partial derivatives:

$$\frac{\partial x_j}{\partial w_k} = -\frac{\partial^2 \Pi}{\partial w_j\, \partial w_k} = -\frac{\partial^2 \Pi}{\partial w_k\, \partial w_j} = \frac{\partial x_k}{\partial w_j}, \qquad \text{all } j, k. \qquad *(8.2.53)$$

The rising supply curve (8.2.39) follows from

$$\frac{\partial y}{\partial p} = \frac{\partial^2 \Pi}{\partial p^2} > 0, \qquad *(8.2.54)$$

where the inequality follows from the convexity of the profit function in p. Intuitively, the marginal effect of an increase in price on profits is itself increasing as price rises. Similarly, the falling factor demand curve (8.2.37) follows from the convexity in w_j:

$$\frac{\partial x_j}{\partial w_j} = -\frac{\partial^2 \Pi}{\partial w_j^2} < 0, \qquad \text{all } j. \qquad *(8.2.55)$$

Intuitively, the marginal effect of an increase in any wage on profits is itself increasing as that wage rises. Condition (8.2.41) follows from

$$\frac{\partial x_j}{\partial p} = -\frac{\partial^2 \Pi}{\partial p \partial w_j} = -\frac{\partial^2 \Pi}{\partial w_j\, \partial p} = -\frac{\partial y}{\partial w_j}, \qquad \text{all } j. \qquad *(8.2.56)$$

The *cost function* is the special case of the profit function corresponding to fixed output.[9] It is given in the long-run case in which all inputs are free to vary as $C(w_1, w_2, \ldots, w_n, y)$,

[8]See Shephard (1970), Fuss and McFadden (1978), Diewert (1982), Samuelson (1983), Varian (1984), and Kreps (1990); see also Problem 8-C.

[9]See the references in footnote 8. See also Problems 8-D, 8-Y, and 8-Z. Another formulation of duality, assuming constant returns to scale, is in terms of the *price function*, giving the price of output as a function of the prices of all inputs (see Christensen, Jorgenson, and Lau, 1973; Jorgenson, 1986).

defined as the minimum level of cost for any set of input wages $w_1, w_2, \ldots, w_n$, at a given level of output y, so that:

$$C(w_1, w_2, \ldots, w_n, y) \text{ solves } \min_{x_1, x_2, \ldots, x_n} C \equiv \sum_{j=1}^{n} w_j x_j \quad *(8.2.57)$$

$$\text{such that } y = f(x_1, x_2, \ldots, x_n).$$

Such a cost function is dual to the production function. If it is assumed that the cost function is continuously differentiable in w for fixed y, the optimal factor inputs satisfy *Shephard's lemma*:

$$x_j = \frac{\partial C}{\partial w_j}, \quad *(8.2.58)$$

where the cost function is nondecreasing in wages for each fixed y. Since the cost function is concave in wages for each fixed y,

$$\frac{\partial x_j}{\partial w_j} = \frac{\partial^2 C}{\partial w_j^2} < 0, \qquad \text{all } j \quad *(8.2.59)$$

as in (8.2.37). The cost curve of (8.2.14) then corresponds to the cost function with given input wages

$$C(y) = C(\overline{w}_1, \overline{w}_2, \ldots, \overline{w}_n, y). \quad *(8.2.60)$$

Of these various functions, the ones most frequently estimated using econometric techniques are the production function (8.2.1), the cost curve (8.2.14), factor demand functions (8.2.28), the profit function (8.2.50), and the cost function (8.2.57).

8.3 ESTIMATION OF PRODUCTION FUNCTIONS

A basic problem in applied econometrics is that of estimating the production function, representing the technological relationship between output (value added) and factor inputs.[10] In most empirical applications the production function gives output y as a function of only two homogeneous inputs—labor L and capital K:

$$y = f(L, K). \quad *(8.3.1)$$

Data for the estimation include cross-section or time-series data on some or all three variables and related variables, such as prices and wages. Output is typically measured as value added per year, deflated for price changes in time-series studies. It can also, however, be measured as physical units of output per year or gross value of output per year. The inputs should, in theory, be measured in terms of *services* of the input per unit of time, but such data are generally not available, so they are instead typically measured by the amount of the input utilized or available in the production process. Labor input is typically measured as labor hours employed per year, but it is also sometimes measured as number of employees. Capital input is typically measured by the net capital stock (net of depreciation), but it is also sometimes measured by the gross capital stock and by certain direct measures (e.g., number of tractors in use for agriculture). Among the other inputs that could be included in the production func-

[10] For surveys of production functions and their estimation, see Walters (1963, 1968), Frisch (1965), Hildebrand and Liu (1965), Nerlove (1967), Solow (1967), Brown (1967), Ferguson (1969), Johansen (1972), and Sato (1975).

tion are raw materials, fuel, and land. Furthermore, labor and capital can be disaggregated, for example, into skilled and unskilled labor, and for capital, plant and equipment.

Of these variables, the one that creates the most problems is the capital input. While data on output and labor are generally available, data on capital are either not available or of questionable validity. Enormously complex problems of measurement arise with respect to capital as an input to the production process. First, capital generally represents an aggregation of very diverse components, including various types of machines, plant, inventories, and so on. Even machines of the same type may cause aggregation problems if they are of different vintages, with different technical characteristics, particularly different levels of productivity or efficiency. Second, some capital is rented but most is owned. For the capital stock that is owned, however, it is necessary to impute rental values to take account of capital services. Such an imputation depends, in part, on depreciation of capital. Depreciation figures are generally unrealistic, however, since they entail both tax avoidance by the firm and the creation by the tax authorities of incentives to invest via accelerated depreciation. Third, there is the problem of capacity utilization. Only capital that is actually utilized should be treated as an input, so measured capital should be adjusted for capacity utilization. Accurate data on capacity utilization are, however, difficult or impossible to obtain.[11] Other problems could be cited as well, but all these suggest that, if at all possible, the use of an explicit measure of the capital stock should be avoided, since it is virtually impossible to find data adequately representing capital stock.

To estimate the production function requires the further development of its properties, leading to the specification of an explicit functional form. In particular, it is generally assumed that the production function satisfies the properties:

$$f(0, K) = f(L, 0) = 0, \tag{8.3.2}$$

$$\frac{\partial f}{\partial L} \geqslant 0, \qquad \frac{\partial f}{\partial K} \geqslant 0, \tag{8.3.3}$$

$$\frac{\partial^2 f}{\partial L^2} \leqslant 0, \qquad \frac{\partial^2 f}{\partial K^2} \leqslant 0, \qquad \frac{\partial^2 f}{\partial L^2}\frac{\partial^2 f}{\partial K^2} - \left(\frac{\partial^2 f}{\partial L \partial K}\right)^2 \geqslant 0. \tag{8.3.4}$$

Here (8.3.2) indicates that both factor inputs are indispensable in the production of output, (8.3.3) states that both marginal products are nonnegative, and (8.3.4) states that the Hessian matrix of second-order partial derivatives of the production function is negative semidefinite, ensuring the proper curvature of the isoquants.

The production function (8.3.1) can, in certain cases, exhibit certain *returns-to-scale* phenomena at particular points. Thus at the point (L, K) the production function exhibits local

$$\begin{Bmatrix} \text{constant} \\ \text{increasing} \\ \text{decreasing} \end{Bmatrix} \text{ returns to scale} \quad \text{if} \quad f(\lambda L, \lambda K) \begin{Bmatrix} = \\ > \\ < \end{Bmatrix} \lambda f(L, K), \text{ all } \lambda > 1. \tag{8.3.5}$$

[11] An early approach to capacity utilization was to assume that the percentage of capital utilized was the same as the percentage of labor utilized and thus to reduce the total capital available by the (labor) unemployment rate, as in Solow (1957). More recently, there are various methods used to adjust capital for the degree of utilization which are independent of the unemployment rate. For example, the Wharton capacity utilization rate method assumes 100% utilization at local peaks of the industry output series, with capacity assumed to grow linearly from peak to peak. Capacity utilization is then obtained as the percentage of output relative to the value obtained on the linearly interpolated capacity series.

The constant-returns-to-scale case, that in which the production function exhibits (global) constant returns to scale for all positive λ, is that in which it is positive homogeneous of degree one (sometimes called "linearly homogeneous"), satisfying

$$f(\lambda L, \lambda K) = \lambda f(L, K), \quad \text{all } \lambda > 0. \quad \text{all } (L, K). \qquad *(8.3.6)$$

In this case, at any levels of the inputs, scaling both inputs by the same multiplicative factor scales output by the same multiplicative factor. Then Euler's theorem on homogeneous functions implies that

$$\frac{\partial f}{\partial L} L + \frac{\partial f}{\partial K} K = f(L, K). \qquad (8.3.7)$$

This condition implies, from (8.2.6), assuming perfect competition, that

$$wL + rK = pf(L, K). \qquad *(8.3.8)$$

Here the left-hand side is total income, the sum of labor income and capital income, w and r being the wages rates of labor and capital, respectively. The right-hand side is the value of output, given as output price times the level of output. Condition (8.3.8) thus states that, assuming profit maximization and perfect competition, a constant-returns-to-scale production function implies that total income equals total output. This result is sometimes called the "adding-up theorem." More generally, the production function is positive homogeneous of degree h if

$$f(\lambda L, \lambda K) = \lambda^h f(L, K), \quad \text{all } \lambda > 0. \quad \text{all } (L, K), \qquad (8.3.9)$$

the case $h = 1$ being that of constant returns to scale. If the production function is homogeneous of degree h and $h > 1$, then it exhibits (global) increasing returns to scale, while if $h < 1$, it exhibits (global) decreasing returns to scale.[12]

The production function is said to be *homothetic* if it can be expressed as

$$y = F[g(L, K)], \qquad (8.3.10)$$

where F is a monotonic increasing function of a single variable and g is a function that is homogeneous of degree one in L and K. The case of homogeneity of degree one of the production function, as represented by (8.3.6), is thus a special case of homotheticity. Homotheticity ensures that all isoquants, as in Figure 8.1, are "radial blowups" of a given isoquant, since the isoquants passing through a given ray from the origin all have the same slope.

Another important property of production functions, in addition to that of returns to scale, is that of the *substitutability of inputs* for one another. A local measure of such substitutability is the *elasticity of substitution* σ, defined as the ratio of the proportionate change in the ratio of factor inputs (called "factor proportions") to the proportionate change in the ratio of marginal products (the marginal rate of technical substitution at given levels of inputs):[13]

$$\sigma = \frac{d \ln(K/L)}{d \ln(\mathrm{MP}_L/\mathrm{MP}_K)} = \frac{d \ln(K/L)}{d \ln(\mathrm{MRTS}_{LK})}. \qquad *(8.3.11)$$

[12] Of course, production functions need not be homogeneous of any degree. A local measure of returns to scale is given by the *elasticity of production* at the point (L, K):

$$\varepsilon(L, K) = \frac{L}{y}\frac{dy}{dL} = \frac{K}{y}\frac{dy}{dK} \quad \text{where} \quad \frac{dL}{L} = \frac{dK}{K}$$

and thus is defined for a proportional change in each of two inputs (see Problem 8-G).

[13] See Arrow et al. (1961) and Nadiri (1982).

In this definition the numerator involves the ratio of capital to labor, while the denominator involves the ratio of the marginal product of labor to that of capital, ensuring that σ is non-negative.

Assuming perfect competition and profit maximization, the ratio of the marginal products is the ratio of the factor prices, as in (8.2.7). Thus σ can, under these assumptions, be written:

$$\sigma = \frac{d \ln(K/L)}{d \ln(w/r)} = \frac{d(K/L)(K/L)}{d(w/r)(w/r)} = \frac{(w/r)\, d(K/L)}{(K/L)\, d(w/r)}. \qquad *(8.3.12)$$

The elasticity of substitution is thus a measure of how rapidly factor proportions change for a change in relative factor prices. It is therefore a measure of the curvature of the isoquants. Figure 8.3 illustrates σ by showing isoquants for each of two production functions. In this case isoquant 1 exhibits greater elasticity of substitution than isoquant 2, since the same change in relative factor prices elicits for 1 a greater change in factor proportions, shown geometrically as the change in the slope of the ray from the origin to the tangency between isocost and isoquant.

One of the most widely used production functions for empirical estimation is the *Cobb–Douglas production function*, of the form:[14]

$$y = AL^{\alpha}K^{\beta}, \qquad *(8.3.13)$$

where A, α, and β are fixed positive parameters. This specification is identical to that of the last chapter for constant elasticity demand functions. In this case the exponents are the elasticities of output with respect to each input:

$$\alpha = \frac{L}{y}\frac{\partial y}{\partial L}, \quad \beta = \frac{K}{y}\frac{\partial y}{\partial K}, \quad 0 < \alpha < 1, \ 0 < \beta < 1, \ \alpha + \beta \leq 1. \qquad (8.3.14)$$

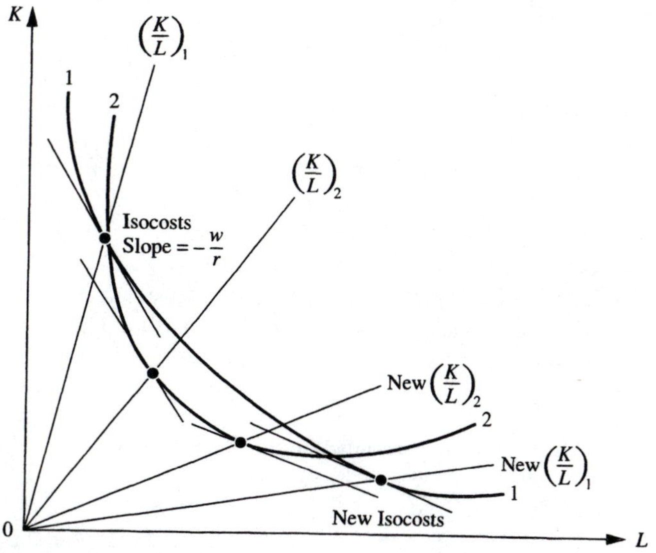

Figure 8.3 Elasticity of Substitution of Isoquant 1 > Isoquant 2

[14]See Douglas (1948), Heady and Dillon (1961), Walters (1963), Nerlove (1965), and Samuelson (1979).

The constancy of these elasticities is a characteristic of the Cobb–Douglas production function, and the inequalities in (8.3.14) ensure that conditions (8.3.2)–(8.3.4) are satisfied. The sum of the elasticities is the degree of homogeneity of the function, since

$$f(\lambda L, \lambda K) = A(\lambda L)^{\alpha}(\lambda K)^{\beta} = \lambda^{\alpha+\beta} AL^{\alpha}K^{\beta} = \lambda^{\alpha+\beta} f(L, K). \qquad (8.3.15)$$

The Cobb–Douglas function is linear in the logarithms of the variables. Considering cross-section studies, the Cobb–Douglas function for the ith firm, after taking logarithms and adding a stochastic disturbance term u_i to account for variations in the technical or productive capabilities of the ith firm, is:[15]

$$\ln y_i = a + \alpha \ln L_i + \beta \ln K_i - u_i \quad (a = \ln A). \qquad *(8.3.16)$$

It is assumed here that the parameters α and β (and also the prices) are the same for all firms, differences among firms being summarized by the u_i. One way of estimating the parameters a, α, and β is to estimate this equation directly, given data on output y_i, labor input L_i, and capital input K_i. Since such data are often not available, especially data on capital, the function has generally been estimated indirectly. Even if these data were available, however, a direct estimation of (8.3.16) would be a somewhat questionable procedure, since the explanatory variables $\ln L_i$ and $\ln K_i$ are endogenous variables, jointly determined with $\ln y_i$, and are not independent of the stochastic disturbance term, leading to a problem of simultaneous-equations estimation, specifically an endogenous explanatory variable. They also tend not to be independent of one another, leading to a possible problem of multicollinearity. Furthermore, the variance of the stochastic disturbance term need not be constant, leading to a problem of heteroskedasticity.

The classical approach to estimating the Cobb–Douglas production function is to assume perfect competition and profit maximization, so conditions (8.2.6) are applicable. These conditions require that marginal productivity equal the real wage:

$$\frac{\partial y_i}{\partial L_i} = \alpha \frac{y_i}{L_i} = \frac{w}{p}, \qquad \frac{\partial y_i}{\partial K_i} = \beta \frac{y_i}{K_i} = \frac{r}{p}. \qquad (8.3.17)$$

These conditions can be written:

$$\alpha = \frac{wL_i}{py_i}, \qquad \beta = \frac{rK_i}{py_i}. \qquad *(8.3.18)$$

Here the common denominator is py_i, the value of output. The numerator wL_i is payments to labor, and the other numerator, rK_i, is payments to capital. Thus these conditions require that labor's share of total income be the parameter α, while the share of capital be the parameter β. Since the total value of output equals total income (the sum of labor income and capital income),

[15]An additive stochastic disturbance term here means that in the original formulation the stochastic disturbance is multiplicative, (8.3.13) taking the form:

$$y_i = AL_i^{\alpha} K_i^{\beta} e^{u_i}.$$

The multiplicative nature of this stochastic disturbance term is justified mainly by convenience. Bodkin and Klein (1967) suggest that there is little difference between multiplicative and additive stochastic disturbance terms in terms of the resulting estimated parameters, their standard errors, and so on, so the convenience of using a multiplicative stochastic disturbance term in the original formulation can be justified on pragmatic grounds.

$$py_i = wL_i + rK_i, \tag{8.3.19}$$

conditions (8.3.18) and (8.3.19) require that:

$$\alpha + \beta = 1. \tag{8.3.20}$$

This condition is precisely the condition that the Cobb–Douglas function exhibit constant returns to scale.

Assuming constant returns to scale, equation (8.3.16) implies that

$$\ln y_i = a + \alpha \ln L_i + (1 - \alpha)\ln K_i + u_i, \tag{8.3.21}$$

which, further, implies that

$$\ln\left(\frac{y_i}{L_i}\right) = a + (1 - \alpha)\ln\left(\frac{K_i}{L_i}\right) + u_i. \tag*{*(8.3.22)}$$

This equation is the production function in *intensive form*, relating output per worker to the capital-labor ratio. Estimating this equation yields an estimate of $1 - \alpha$, the elasticity of output with respect to capital, where α is the elasticity with respect to labor. Using this equation rather than (8.3.16) also reduces the problems of multicollinearity and heteroskedasticity, the use of ratios to reduce the problem of heteroskedasticity having been discussed in Section 5.4.

An alternative method of estimation, assuming constant returns to scale, perfect competition, and profit maximization, is based on the share of labor income in output. From (8.3.17) and constant returns to scale,

$$\alpha = \frac{wL_i}{py_i} = s_L, \qquad \beta = 1 - \alpha, \tag*{*(8.3.23)}$$

where s_L is the share of labor in national income. Thus the shares yield direct estimates of both α and β under these assumptions.[16] This method requires no data on capital inputs, either in total [as in (8.3.16)] or relative to labor [as in (8.3.22)], but it does depend on the assumption of constant returns to scale and hence cannot be used to test hypotheses about returns to scale.

Assuming constant returns to scale, perfect competition, and profit maximization, the marginal productivity equation (8.3.17) implies a log-linear relation between output per worker and the real wage:

$$\ln \frac{y_i}{L_i} = \ln \frac{w}{p} - \ln \alpha. \tag{8.3.24}$$

Adding a stochastic disturbance term to this relation, to account for errors made by firms in choosing inputs so as to maximize profits, leads to a regression equation. The estimated intercept then provides an estimate of the (negative of the logarithm of the) elasticity α.

There are, then, at least four different methods of estimating the parameters of the production function, involving alternative assumptions and econometric problems.[17] The first is that of estimating the *production function itself* in log-linear form, (8.3.16). This method requires no further assumptions (e.g., as to returns to scale), but it typically leads to economet-

[16]With cross-section or time-series data the shares can be estimated as the *geometric* means of shares calculated for each production unit or at each time period (see Problem 8-K).

[17]See Walters (1963) and Nerlove (1965). A fifth method is discussed in footnote 18.

ric problems of simultaneity (endogenous explanatory variable), multicollinearity, and heteroskedasticity. The second method is that of estimating the *intensive production function* in log-linear form, (8.3.22). This method reduces the problems of multicollinearity and heteroskedasticity, but it does require the assumption of constant returns to scale and hence cannot be used to test for increasing or decreasing returns to scale. It also has an endogenous explanatory variable. The third and fourth methods, those of *factor shares*, (8.3.23), and of the *marginal productivity relation*, (8.3.24), respectively, eliminate the simultaneity, multicollinearity, and heteroskedasticity problems, but require the assumptions of constant returns to scale, perfect competition, and profit maximization. None of these methods dominates the others. Each is appropriate in particular situations, depending upon what can be assumed and what is to be investigated.[18] The resulting parameter estimates will generally be different, and there is little evidence to suggest which estimates come closest to true values.

Table 8.1 presents some estimates of the Cobb–Douglas production function for the macroeconomy of a nation or state using time-series data and the technique of least squares, as applied to (8.3.16). The discussion of Section 8.2 referred, however, to a single firm. Estimates of production relationships for macroeconomies, such as those of Table 8.1, are based on the further assumption that the macroeconomic entity acts as if it were representative of the underlying microeconomic entities.[19] The index i then ranges over time.

The four alternative estimates for the United States and the two alternative estimates for New Zealand in Table 8.1 are based on alternative ways of measuring inputs and out-

[18]A fifth method is to estimate the simultaneous system consisting of the production function and the first-order conditions for profit maximization:

$$y_i = AL_i^{\alpha} K_i^{\beta} e^{u_i},$$

$$\frac{\partial y_i}{\partial L_i} = \frac{\alpha y_i}{L_i} = \frac{w}{p} e^{v_i},$$

$$\frac{\partial y_i}{\partial K_i} = \beta \frac{y_i}{K_i} = \frac{r}{p} e^{w_i}.$$

Here u_i is a technical disturbance term, affecting the efficiency of the production process, and v_i and w_i are economic disturbance terms, affecting the attainment of the two profit-maximization conditions. Taking logarithms gives the linear system:

$$\ln y_i = a + \alpha \ln L_i + \beta \ln K_i + u_i,$$

$$\ln y_i = -\ln \alpha + \ln L_i + \ln \frac{w}{p} + v_i,$$

$$\ln y_i = -\ln \beta + \ln K_i + \ln \frac{r}{p} + w_i,$$

which is the structural form for a system in which $\ln y_i$, $\ln L_i$, and $\ln K_i$ are the endogenous variables and $\ln w/p$ and $\ln r/p$ are the exogenous variables (assuming perfect competition). See Marschak and Andrews (1944), Nerlove (1965), Hildebrand and Liu (1965), Zellner, Kmenta, and Drèze (1966), Griliches and Ringstad (1971), and Problem 8-I. The first method of estimation entails estimating only the first equation of this system. Estimating the complete system is generally superior to estimating only the first equation from both economic and econometric standpoints. From an economic standpoint, estimating the complete system expresses the assumption that the data reflect both the behavior of the decision maker (the firm) and the technology, while the first equation reflects only the technology. From an econometric standpoint, the estimator of only the first equation involves simultaneous-equations bias, so the estimators will be biased and inconsistent, as discussed in Chapter 10.

[19]Formally, under certain aggregation conditions, it may be possible to aggregate microeconomic production functions into macroeconomic production functions. The aggregation conditions here are comparable to those for a household, as discussed in Section 7.7. Several new issues arise here, however, with regard to aggregation.

TABLE 8.1 Estimates of the Cobb–Douglas Production Function

Country, Time Period	Labor Elasticity α	Capital Elasticity β	Returns to Scale $\alpha+\beta$	Average Labor Share s_L
United States I 1899–1922	0.81 (0.15)	0.23 (0.06)	1.04	0.61
United States II 1899–1922	0.78 (0.14)	0.15 (0.08)	0.93	0.61
United States III 1899–1922	0.73 (0.12)	0.25 (0.05)	0.98	0.61
United States IV 1899–1922	0.63 (0.15)	0.30 (0.05)	0.93	0.61
New Zealand I 1915–1916 and 1918–1935	0.42 (0.11)	0.49 (0.03)	0.91	0.52
New Zealand II 1923–1940	0.54 (0.02)			0.54
New South Wales, Australia 1901–1927	0.78 (0.12)	0.20 (0.08)	0.98	
Victoria, Australia 1902–1929	0.84 (0.34)	0.23 (0.17)	1.07	

Source Douglas (1948).

Note Numbers in parentheses are standard errors.

put. Douglas concluded, based on the results reported in this table and other results (some based on cross-section rather than time-series data), that production exhibits approximately constant returns to scale. He also concluded that the factors of production receive approximately the share they would receive under competitive conditions, given as the elasticity of output with respect to the factor. Later authors have questioned these conclusions, however. One criticism was based on the multicollinearity in the data used. Another was based on the condition that the total value of output equal total income (8.3.19), which creates a bias of the estimated production function toward these results.[20]

One is that of *reswitching*, where different ratios of inputs are used at different ratios of input prices. For example, reswitching occurs if one method of production is better than another available method at a low interest rate, worse at a higher interest rate, and then becomes better again at even a higher interest rate. Others are *efficiency* and *technical change*, which are both affected by and affect aggregation of micro production functions into macro production functions. Also, some exogeneity assumptions change (e.g., factor prices). On the general problems of aggregation, see Walters (1963), Green (1964), and Problem 8-K. For a study of efficiency and aggregation, see Houthakker (1955–56), who derived a macro Cobb–Douglas production function on the basis of micro fixed-coefficients (input–output) production functions [introduced in (8.3.33)], assuming a specific probability distribution (the Pareto distribution) of firms over possible values of the input coefficients. Generalizations and related approaches appear in Johansen (1972) and Sato (1975).

[20]See Cramer (1969). The bias toward constant returns to scale is an example of the practical problem stemming from the aggregation problem, as discussed in Section 7.7. Aggregate output is calculated from the total value of payments to factors of production, so using this value for output to test for returns to scale is questionable. Similarly, if aggregate capital data are constructed by subtracting the value of labor input from the value of output and deflating, then a test of returns to scale is also questionable.

To show this bias, using index numbers in (8.3.16), it follows that (ignoring the stochastic disturbance term):

$$\ln \frac{y_i}{\bar{y}_i} = \alpha \ln \frac{L_i}{\bar{L}_i} + \beta \ln \frac{K_i}{\bar{K}_i}, \tag{8.3.25}$$

where $\bar{y}_i$, $\bar{K}_i$, and $\bar{L}_i$ are base-year quantities of output, capital, and labor, respectively, for the ith firm.[21] But if y_i, K_i, and L_i do not vary appreciably from the base quantities, the ratios are close to unity, so

$$\ln \frac{y_i}{\bar{y}_i} \approx \frac{y_i}{\bar{y}_i} - 1, \qquad \ln \frac{L_i}{\bar{L}_i} \approx \frac{L_i}{\bar{L}_i} - 1, \qquad \ln \frac{K_i}{\bar{K}_i} \approx \frac{K_i}{\bar{K}_i} - 1. \tag{8.3.26}$$

Thus (8.3.25) implies that:

$$\frac{y_i}{\bar{y}_i} \approx \alpha \frac{L_i}{\bar{L}_i} + \beta \frac{K_i}{\bar{K}_i} + (1 - \alpha - \beta), \tag{8.3.27}$$

so that

$$py_i = \left(\alpha p \frac{\bar{y}_i}{\bar{L}_i}\right) L_i + \left(\beta p \frac{\bar{y}_i}{\bar{K}_i}\right) K_i + (1 - \alpha - \beta) p\bar{y}_i. \tag{8.3.28}$$

Comparing this equation to (8.3.19), however, it follows that:

$$\alpha p \frac{\bar{y}_i}{\bar{L}_i} \approx w, \quad \beta p \frac{\bar{y}_i}{\bar{K}_i} \approx r, \qquad (1 - \alpha - \beta)p \approx 0. \tag{8.3.29}$$

These results imply that

$$\alpha + \beta \approx 1, \tag{8.3.30}$$

which means returns to scale are approximately constant, and

$$\frac{w\bar{L}_i}{p\bar{y}_i} \approx \alpha, \quad \frac{r\bar{K}_i}{p\bar{y}_i} \approx \beta, \tag{8.3.31}$$

which means that factor shares are approximately the elasticities, α and β, the shares received under competitive conditions. Thus, assuming only small variations in output and inputs, the form of the production function and the equality of the values of output and income imply that the production function exhibits approximately constant returns to scale and that factor shares are approximately the elasticities.

A second example of the Cobb–Douglas production function is the estimation by Kimbell and Lorant of a production function for physicians' services.[22] The data were obtained from an American Medical Association survey of physician activities in 1970. Altogether there were 844 observations on physicians in both solo and group practices. The estimated function is:

[21]The intercept drops out of the equation, since, if

$$y_i = AL_i^\alpha K_i^\beta, \qquad \bar{y}_i = A\bar{L}_i^\alpha \bar{K}_i^\beta$$

then, taking ratios,

$$\frac{y_i}{\bar{y}_i} = \left(\frac{L_i}{\bar{L}_i}\right)^\alpha \left(\frac{K_i}{\bar{K}_i}\right)^\beta.$$

Taking logarithms of this equation yields (8.3.25).

[22]See Kimbell and Lorant (1974).

$$\begin{aligned}\ln(py) = 2.826 &+ \underset{(0.052)}{0.255}\ln h + \underset{(0.037)}{0.708}\ln d + \underset{(0.030)}{0.302}\ln a \\ &+ \underset{(0.042)}{0.074}\ln r, \qquad R^2 = 0.906.\end{aligned} \tag{8.3.32}$$

Here py is gross revenue from medical practice, a measure of output for the heterogeneous services provided by physicians; h is the average number of hours worked by (full-time) physicians in the practice; d is the number of (full-time equivalent) physicians in the practice; a is the number of (full-time equivalent) allied health personnel (e.g., nurses) employed by the practice; and r is the number of rooms used in the practice, a measure of capital input. According to these results, the elasticity of gross revenue with respect to physicians' hours is 0.255, so a 10% increase in hours would increase gross revenue by about 2.6%. The elasticity for aides implies that increasing the number of aides by one-third would increase gross revenue by about 10%. The sum of the elasticities is 1.084, which is significantly greater than unity at the 0.01 confidence level, indicating increasing returns to scale for physicians' services.

Another form of the production function is the *input–output production function*:[23]

$$y = \min\left(\frac{L}{a}, \frac{K}{b}\right), \qquad a, b > 0. \tag*{*(8.3.33)}$$

Here the isoquants are right-angled (L-shaped), as shown in Figure 8.4, and the production function permits no substitution between the inputs. The condition of profit maximization, given positive factor wages, is:

$$\frac{L}{a} = \frac{K}{b}, \tag{8.3.34}$$

that is, operation at the vertex of the isoquants. Then,

$$a = \frac{L}{y}, \quad b = \frac{K}{y}, \tag{8.3.35}$$

so the parameters a and b are, respectively, the input of labor per unit of output and the input of capital per unit of output—the fixed proportions of inputs to output. The equations in (8.3.35) are typically used to estimate the parameters a and b, which are called *technical coefficients*. The estimation is typically based on a single observation, so regression techniques are not used. The estimated production function is used in input–output studies concerned with the interrelationships among productive sectors that arise from the fact that the inputs of any one sector consist of portions of the outputs of other sectors.[24]

One of the most widely used production functions in empirical work is the *constant elasticity of substitution* (CES) production function, of the form:[25]

[23] See Leontief (1951, 1966) and Chenery and Clark (1959).

[24] Let x_{ij} be the input of commodity i, as produced by sector i, that is used in the production of commodity j by sector j. If x_j is the output of sector j, the technical coefficients comparable to (8.3.35) are given as:

$$a_{ij} = \frac{x_{ij}}{x_j}, \qquad i, j = 1, 2, \ldots$$

See Intriligator (1971).

[25] See Arrow et al. (1961), Brown and de Cani (1963), Minhas (1963), Griliches (1967), Nerlove (1967), Nadiri (1970), and Berndt (1976, 1991). Note that β here plays an entirely different role from the β in the Cobb–Douglas production function.

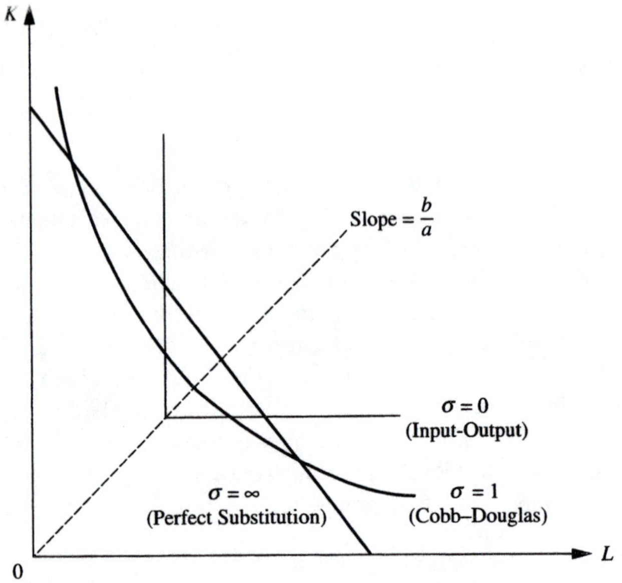

Figure 8.4 Isoquants of the CES Production Function Corresponding to Different Values of the Elasticity of Substitution, σ

$$y = A\left[\delta L^{-\beta} + (1-\delta)K^{-\beta}\right]^{-1/\beta}. \qquad *(8.3.36)$$

The parameters defining this production function are:

A: scale parameter, $A > 0$
δ: distribution parameter, $0 < \delta < 1$
β: substitution parameter, $\beta \geqslant -1$

The name of the function is based on the concept of the elasticity of substitution, σ, defined in (8.3.11). In general, the elasticity of substitution σ varies with K and L. Assuming σ is constant, however, and solving the resulting differential equation yields, in the constant-returns-to-scale case, precisely the CES function, where

$$\sigma = \frac{1}{1+\beta}, \qquad *(8.3.37)$$

justifying the interpretation of β as the substitution parameter. As defined in (8.3.11), σ must be nonnegative, so

$$\beta \geqslant -1. \qquad (8.3.38)$$

At the extreme value of $\beta = -1$ the CES function reduces to the linear function:

$$y = A\left[\delta L + (1-\delta)K\right] \quad \text{if} \quad \beta = -1, \text{ i.e., } \sigma = \infty. \qquad *(8.3.39)$$

The isoquants for this case are linear, the slope of each being $-\delta/(1-\delta)$. In this case of perfect substitution $\sigma = \infty$, meaning that certain slight changes in w/r would lead to discontinuous changes in K/L (e.g., from one boundary point to another). At the other extreme value for β, namely in the limit as β approaches ∞, from (8.3.37), σ approaches zero and, in this case, in the limit of the CES as $\beta \to \infty$, it approaches the input–output production function, as in (8.3.33),

$$y = \min\left(\frac{L}{a}, \frac{K}{b}\right) \quad \text{if} \quad \beta \to \infty, \text{ i.e., } \sigma \to 0. \tag{8.3.40}$$

In the limit as β approaches zero, σ approaches unity; this is the case of the Cobb–Douglas production function, where, taking the limit as $\beta \to 0$, the CES approaches (8.3.13):

$$y = A_0 L^{\delta} K^{1-\delta} \quad \text{if} \quad \beta \to 0, \text{ i.e., } \sigma \to 1. \tag{8.3.41}$$

Thus the CES is a family of production functions that includes, as special cases, the Cobb–Douglas, input–output, and linear production functions. The isoquants of these various cases are shown in Figure 8.4, and estimation of σ gives information on the curvature of the isoquants. The isoquants of the CES production function intersect the axes if $\sigma > 1$, and they are asymptotic to horizontal and vertical lines if $\sigma < 1$. When σ approaches 1 in the limit, the isoquants become those of the Cobb–Douglas production function, which are asymptotic to the axes.[26]

The CES can be estimated by using the conditions of profit maximization (8.2.6). The marginal product of labor can be written:

$$\frac{\partial y}{\partial L} = A'\left(\frac{y}{L}\right)^{1+\beta}, \tag{8.3.42}$$

where A' is a constant, so setting the marginal product equal to the real wage yields:

$$A'\left(\frac{y}{L}\right)^{1+\beta} = \frac{w}{p}. \tag{8.3.43}$$

Solving for output per labor hour (labor productivity) y/L yields:

$$\frac{y}{L} = A''\left(\frac{w}{p}\right)^{1/1+\beta}, \tag{8.3.44}$$

where A'' is another constant, so, taking logs and using (8.3.37) gives

$$\ln\frac{y}{L} = a + \frac{1}{1+\beta}\ln\frac{w}{p} = a + \sigma\ln\frac{w}{p}, \quad a = \ln A''. \tag{8.3.45}$$

This equation relates output per worker to the real wage, where a and σ are constants, σ being the coefficient of $\ln(w/p)$. The special case of the Cobb–Douglas for which $\sigma = 1$ was presented earlier in (8.3.24). Equation (8.3.45), with an additive stochastic disturbance term on the right-hand side, can be estimated using least squares regression. Alternatively, the equation can be solved for the real wage and the resulting equation,

$$\ln\frac{w}{p} = a' + (1+\beta)\ln\frac{y}{L}, \tag{8.3.46}$$

in which the dependent and explanatory (exogenous) variables have switched roles, can be estimated to obtain $1/(1+\beta)$ as an estimate of σ. An estimation based on (8.3.45) could, for example, utilize cross-section data on output, y, labor, L, and the real wage, w/p, assuming the real wage is exogenous and all entities in the cross section use the

[26]See Problem 8-N. As noted there, the case $\sigma > 1$ is excluded if both factors are essential in that output is zero if either factor input is zero—conditions (8.3.2). The case $\sigma < 1$ is consistent with factors being essential in this sense.

same underlying production function. This was the approach used by Arrow et al., who estimated σ in (8.3.45) using cross-section data for specific industries from 19 different countries over the period 1950–1956. They found that their estimates of σ tended to cluster below unity, with 10 out of 24 industries having an estimated σ statistically different from (and below) unity. Their approach was extended by Fuchs, who, using the same data, distinguished developed from less developed countries in the sample of 19 countries. He showed, using analysis of covariance, that the developed and less developed countries exhibit different intercept a in (8.3.45), but the same σ, and he reestimated σ, using a dummy variable to reflect the different intercept in the developed countries.[27] His estimates tend to cluster around unity, ranging from a low of 0.658 for clay products to a high of 1.324 for grain and mill products and only one of the estimates is statistically significantly different from unity. Thus the Fuchs study provides justification for continued use of the Cobb–Douglas function. Various other studies also find that the estimated elasticity of substitution does not differ significantly from unity, justifying use of the Cobb–Douglas production function.[28]

The CES production function can be extended to the case of nonconstant-returns-to-scale, but homogeneous case, for which the function can be written:

$$y = A\left[\delta L^{-\beta} + (1-\delta)K^{-\beta}\right]^{-h/\beta}, \qquad *(8.3.47)$$

where h is the degree of homogeneity of the function. This case reduces to (8.3.36) if $h = 1$, the constant-returns-to-scale case. The general function was estimated by Dhrymes using cross-section data on U.S. states.[29] From his results for h, most industries operate at or above constant returns to scale ($h = 1$), with textile mill products exhibiting the lowest degree of homogeneity. From his results for σ, most consumer goods (e.g., textile mill products, furniture) are produced with an elasticity of substitution of approximately unity (i.e., close to the Cobb–Douglas production function). Most producer goods (e.g., machinery, chemicals), however, are produced with an elasticity of substitution significantly below unity, approaching in some cases the input–output production function. However, other studies have arrived at radically different results for certain industries. The study by Ferguson,

[27]See Fuchs (1963).

[28]See Griliches (1967), Zarembka (1970), and Griliches and Ringstad (1971). Griliches (1967) found only one industry (paper) out of 17 in which use of the Cobb–Douglas production function was not justified. It might be noted, however, that Nerlove (1967), in surveying over 40 papers, found conflicting estimates of the elasticity of substitution, with values ranging from 0.068 to 1.16. He concluded that the estimates are sensitive to the period under consideration and the concepts employed. In a later survey, Mayor (1969) found that studies using cross-section data obtain estimates of the elasticity of substitution close to unity while those using time series obtain estimates considerably less than unity, clustering around one-half. Johansen (1972) attributes this difference between cross-section and time-series studies to the "putty-clay" nature of technology, according to which substitution possibilities are reduced once investment has occurred and capital is in place. Johansen suggests that the firm decides factor proportions before investment in new plant and equipment occurs and that, after this investment has occurred, subsequent decisions involve only the scale of operation. Cross-section estimates may reveal *ex-ante* substitution possibilities, before capital is in place, and so exhibit relatively high elasticities of substitution. Time-series estimates, by contrast, tend to reveal *ex-post* substitution possibilities, after capital is in place, and so exhibit relatively low elasticities of substitution. For further discussion of the putty-clay model, which distinguishes ex-ante and ex-post substitution possibilities, such as substitution possibilities ex-ante but fixed coefficients ex-post, see Johansen (1959, 1972) and Bliss (1968).

[29]See Dhrymes (1965), Kmenta (1967), and Zarembka (1970). See also Brown and de Cani (1963), where the derivation and estimation of the CES production function allowed for $h \neq 1$.

for example, of U.S. manufacturing industries, using time-series data from the U.S. Census for 18 industries, 1949–1961, found an estimate of σ for nonelectrical machinery of 1.041 (0.04), in contrast to the Dhrymes value of 0.050, and for chemicals of 1.248 (0.072), in contrast to the Dhrymes value of 0.506. Some of the other industries yielded somewhat comparable estimates, however—for example, for textile mill products [1.104 (0.44) vs. 0.936], lumber and wood [0.905 (0.067) vs. 1.109], furniture and fixtures [1.123 (0.045) vs. 1.001], and food [0.241 (0.20) vs. 0.469].[30]

It has already been noted that the Cobb–Douglas production function is a special case of the CES production function, corresponding to an elasticity of substitution of unity. Conversely, the CES production function can be viewed as a generalization of the Cobb–Douglas production function to the case of a nonunitary, but constant, elasticity of substitution. For example, expanding ln y in a Taylor's series approximation of the CES around $\beta = 0$ yields:[31]

$$\ln y \approx a + h\delta \ln L + h(1-\delta)\ln K - \frac{\beta h\delta(1-\delta)}{2}(\ln L - \ln K)^2. \qquad (8.3.48)$$

The first several terms on the right are those of the Cobb–Douglas production function, and the last term accounts for $\sigma \neq 1$. This approximation is better the closer the elasticity of substitution is to unity, and it reduces to the Cobb–Douglas case if $\beta = 0$.

While the CES production function represents one generalization of the Cobb–Douglas production function, the Cobb–Douglas has also been generalized in several other ways. One such way is the *transcendental production function*, of the form:[32]

$$y = AL^{\alpha}K^{\beta}e^{\alpha' L + \beta' K}, \qquad A > 0, \quad \alpha', \beta' \leqslant 0. \qquad (8.3.49)$$

This case reduces to the Cobb–Douglas if α' and β' vanish. Taking logarithms yields:

$$\ln y = a + \alpha \ln L + \beta \ln K + \alpha' L + \beta' K, \qquad (8.3.50)$$

so ln y is a linear function of the inputs L and K, as well as the logarithms of the inputs ln L and ln K. For this function it is possible for marginal products to rise before eventually falling. This function also permits variable elasticity of production and variable elasticity of substitution over the range of inputs.

A second approach to generalizing the Cobb–Douglas production function is the *Zellner–Revankar production function*, of the form:[33]

$$ye^{cy} = AL^{\alpha}K^{\beta}, \qquad c \geqslant 0. \qquad (8.3.51)$$

This case reduces to the Cobb–Douglas form if $c = 0$. Taking logarithms gives:

$$\ln y + cy = a + \alpha \ln L + \beta \ln K. \qquad (8.3.52)$$

[30]See Ferguson (1965) and Nerlove (1967).

[31]See Kmenta (1967) and Griliches and Ringstad (1971). This approximation can be used to estimate the parameters of the CES production function. Using this approach, Kmenta estimated σ as 0.672 and h as 1.179. Neither of these estimates, however, was significantly different from unity, so a Cobb–Douglas production function with constant returns to scale is not ruled out by his findings. It should be noted, however, that the estimated σ is not invariant to a change in units of measurement.

[32]See Halter, Carter, and Hocking (1957). Note that α' and β' are not invariant to a change in units of measurement. For a discussion of other functional forms not necessarily related to the Cobb–Douglas production function, see Heady and Dillon (1961).

[33]See Zellner and Revankar (1969).

This case is essentially the obverse of the transcendental case. In the transcendental case inputs and logarithms of inputs enter on the right-hand side, while in this case output and the logarithm of output enter on the left-hand side.

A third approach to generalizing the Cobb–Douglas production function is the *Nerlove–Ringstad production function*, of the form:[34]

$$y^{1+c\ln y} = AL^{\alpha}K^{\beta}, \quad c \geqslant 0. \tag{8.3.53}$$

This case reduces to the Cobb-Douglas form if $c = 0$. Taking logarithms yields:

$$(1 + c\ln y)\ln y = a + \alpha\ln L + \beta\ln K, \tag{8.3.54}$$

so $\ln y$ and $(\ln y)^2$ appear on the left-hand side.

A fourth approach to generalizing the Cobb–Douglas production function is the *translog production function*, of the form:[35]

$$\ln y = a + \alpha\ln L + \beta\ln K + \gamma\ln L\ln K + \delta(\ln L)^2 + \varepsilon(\ln K)^2. \tag{8.3.55}$$

This function, which is quadratic in the logarithms of the variables, reduces to the Cobb–Douglas case if the parameters γ, δ, and ε all vanish; otherwise, it exhibits nonunitary elasticity of substitution. In general, this function is quite flexible in approximating arbitrary production technologies in terms of substitution possibilities. It provides a local approximation to any production frontier.[36]

The last several production functions have been extensions of the Cobb–Douglas production function. The CES production function has also been generalized in different ways. One such generalization is the two-level production function.[37] For this function factors are combined according to the CES at one level to form "higher-level" factors, which are combined again according to the CES to produce output. An example is the production function:

$$\begin{aligned} y = A\Big\{&\left[\delta_1 x_1^{-\beta_1} + (1-\delta_1)x_2^{-\beta_1}\right]^{-\beta/\beta_1} \\ &+ \left[\delta_2 x_3^{-\beta_2} + (1-\delta_2)x_4^{-\beta_2}\right]^{-\beta/\beta_2}\Big\}^{-1/\beta}. \end{aligned} \tag{8.3.56}$$

Here x_1 and x_2 are combined into a "higher-level" factor, where the elasticity of substitution is $(1 + \beta_1)^{-1}$, while x_3 and x_4 are combined with an elasticity of substitution of $(1 + \beta_2)^{-1}$. The higher-level inputs are then combined with an elasticity of substitution of $(1 + \beta)^{-1}$. Another generalization of the CES is the *VES production function* (i.e., the variable-elasticity-of-substitution production function).[38] For this function the elasticity of substitution

[34]See Nerlove (1963) and Ringstad (1967).

[35]*Translog* is short for *transcendental logarithmic*. See Christensen, Jorgenson, and Lau (1973) and Griliches and Ringstad (1971). More generally, for n inputs, the translog function is

$$\ln y = \alpha_0 + \sum_{i=1}^{n} \alpha_i \ln x_i + \sum_{i=1}^{n}\sum_{j=1}^{n} \gamma_{ij} \ln x_i \ln x_j,$$

where x_i is the ith input and $\gamma_{ij} = \gamma_{ji}$. Note that this function is also not invariant to a change of units. This function is applied below to the cost function in equation (8.4.13). See Jorgenson (1986) and Lau (1986).

[36]It can also be applied to other frontiers (e.g., to demand functions or to price frontiers).

[37]See Sato (1967).

[38]See Sato and Hoffman (1968); see also Lu and Fletcher (1968), Revankar (1971), and Lovell (1973). It can also be applied to other frontiers, including demand functions and price frontiers (see Jorgenson, 1986; Lau, 1986).

varies with the factor proportions (the ratio of the inputs). Such a relationship can be estimated by regressing the log of output per worker on both the real wage [as in (8.3.45)] and the capital/labor ratio.[39]

8.4 ESTIMATION OF COST CURVES AND COST FUNCTIONS

Cost curves, based on economic theory, were developed in Section 8.2, equations (8.2.14)–(8.2.20), and illustrated in Figure 8.2. A variety of cost curves, including total, average, and marginal cost curves, have been estimated empirically for particular industries.[40]

A simple example of a total cost curve that satisfies the curvature postulated in Figure 8.2 is the *cubic cost curve*:

$$C = a_0 + a_1 y + a_2 y^2 + a_3 y^3, \qquad *(8.4.1)$$

where a_0, a_1, a_2, and a_3 are given parameters. The average cost associated with the cubic cost curve is

$$\text{AC} = \frac{a_0}{y} + a_1 + a_2 y + a_3 y^2 \qquad (8.4.2)$$

and marginal cost is given as

$$\text{MC} = a_1 + 2a_2 y + 3a_3 y^2. \qquad (8.4.3)$$

For U-shaped average and marginal cost curves, as illustrated in Figure 8.2, the parameters must satisfy the restrictions:

$$a_0 \geqslant 0,\ \ a_1 > 0,\ \ a_2 < 0,\ \ a_3 > 0, \qquad (8.4.4)$$

where a_0 is the fixed cost, the cost at zero output.

Empirical studies of cost curves typically estimate a long-run cost curve using cross-sectional data on firms in the industry, specifically data on total costs, output, and other relevant variables. Assuming that the same technology applies to all firms, that observed outputs are close to planned outputs, and that firms are seeking to minimize costs at each planned output level, it follows that the cost curve estimated from a scatter diagram of cost-output points represents an estimate of the long-run cost curve. The specific curve estimated is usually an average cost curve; and taking ratios as called for in such a curve reduces problems of heteroskedasticity.[41] In the long-run case, a_0 in the cubic cost curve (8.4.1), which is fixed cost, vanishes, so the average cost curve in this case is

$$\text{AC} = a_1 + a_2 y + a_3 y^2. \qquad (8.4.5)$$

This quadratic long-run average cost curve has been estimated for many industries.

For a wide variety of industries, including manufacturing, mining, distribution, transportation, and trade, it has been found that the long-run average cost curves are L-shaped rather than U-shaped.[42] Thus, as illustrated in Figure 8.5, average cost at first falls sharply

[39]See Hildebrand and Liu (1965). In most industries the coefficient of the capital/labor ratio is significant.

[40]For surveys of cost curves, see Johnston (1960) and Walters (1963, 1968). For cost functions, see Shephard (1970).

[41]Note that if u is an additive stochastic disturbance term for the total cost curve and $\text{Var}(u) = Ky^2$, where K is a positive constant, then $\text{Var}(u/y) = K$; with this assumption the additive stochastic disturbance term in the average cost curve exhibits constant variance for all levels of output y.

[42]See Johnston (1960), Walters (1963), Wiles (1963), and Gold (1966).

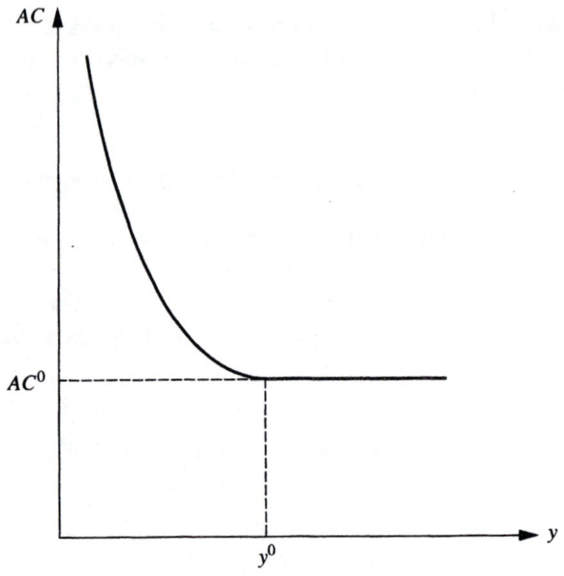

Figure 8.5 Estimated Average Cost Curve

(based, in part, on spreading fixed costs over more output) but then reaches or asymptotically approaches a certain minimum level AC^0 at a critical level of output, y^0, and remains flat at this level.[43] The critical level of output y^0 is the minimal efficient scale; it is the point at which there is a "knee" in the average cost curve.

Various explanations have been suggested for the L-shaped nature of the long-run average cost curve. Some are based on econometric reasoning, involving certain biases present in the estimation or in the measurement of costs or output.[44] Others are based on economic reasoning. For example, a profit-maximizing firm would, assuming the cost curve applies to a particular plant, build new plants (until the minimum average cost level is attained) rather than move up the rising portion of the average cost curve for its existing plants. Thus the rising portion of the curve would never be observed.

Estimated cost curves have been used to study the question of economies of scale. A local measure of economies of scale is given by the *elasticity of cost*, γ, the elasticity of the cost curve with respect to output, given as

$$\gamma = \gamma(y) = \frac{y}{C(y)} \frac{\partial C(y)}{\partial y}, \tag{8.4.6}$$

[43]In the case of a linear cost curve, of the form:

$$C = a + by,$$

average cost is

$$\frac{C}{y} = \frac{a}{y} + b,$$

which asymptotically approaches b, marginal cost, here assumed constant.

[44]There are, indeed, manifold problems in measuring cost. One is the fact that certain costs are unobservable, including the costs of capital, self-employed labor, stocks of factors, and certain other inputs.

where factor prices are assumed given.[45] There are

$$\text{local}\left\{\begin{matrix}\text{economies of}\\ \text{constant returns to}\\ \text{diseconomies of}\end{matrix}\right\}\text{scale at } y \quad \text{if} \quad \gamma(y)\left\{\begin{matrix}<\\=\\>\end{matrix}\right\}1. \tag{8.4.7}$$

Local economies of scale hold if and only if the average cost curve is decreasing, while increasing average cost is equivalent to local diseconomies of scale. Thus in Figure 8.5 there are local economies to scale up to y^0, and neither economies nor diseconomies of scale (i.e., constant returns to scale) beyond this point. The point y^0 is thus the *minimal efficient scale* (MES), that is, the smallest output level at which average cost reaches its minimum value, or, equivalently, the smallest output for which the elasticity of cost is unity.

In the special case of a production function that is positive homogeneous of degree h, as in (8.3.9), it follows that:

$$\gamma = \frac{1}{h}, \tag{8.4.8}$$

so in this case, if $h > 1$ there are economies of scale everywhere and if $h < 1$ there are diseconomies of scale everywhere. For example, in the Cobb–Douglas case γ is given as the reciprocal of the sum of the elasticities:

$$\gamma = \frac{1}{\alpha + \beta}, \tag{8.4.9}$$

so if this sum exceeds unity it means that there are economies of scale everywhere.

An alternative to the estimation of the production function is the estimation of the cost function $C(w_1, w_2, \ldots, w_n, y)$, defined in (8.2.57) as the minimum level of cost obtained by choice of inputs for any set of input wages $w_1, w_2, \ldots, w_n$ at a given level of output y.[46] The cost function is *dual* to the production function in that it provides an alternative yet equivalent description of the relevant technology. From it all the parameters of the related production function can be obtained. In the estimation of the production function it is typically assumed that output is endogenous and input quantities are exogenous, whereas in the estimation of the cost function it is typically assumed that cost and input quantities are endogenous while input prices and output are exogenous. Frequently, the latter are more reasonable assumptions to make, particularly at the relatively more disaggregated level of a firm. In such relatively more micro cases, the production function can be estimated indirectly by first estimating the cost function and then, from its estimation, recovering all the parameters of the related production function. Most of the standard production functions treated earlier have related cost functions that can be formulated explicitly. For example, for the Cobb–Douglas production function of (8.3.13), or in its log-linear form (8.3.16), the related *Cobb–Douglas cost function* is of the constant elasticity form, where

$$C(w, r, y) = A'(w^{\alpha} r^{\beta} y)^{1/(\alpha+\beta)} \qquad *(8.4.10)$$

Here the elasticity of the cost function with respect to output is $1/(\alpha + \beta)$, the reciprocal of the degree of homogeneity of the production function, as in (8.4.9). Considering firm i, tak-

[45] The intimate connections between cost curves and production functions is indicated by the fact that the elasticity of production, defined in footnote 12, is the reciprocal of the elasticity of cost (see Problem 8-G).

[46] See Nerlove (1963), Fuss and McFadden (1978), Jorgenson (1986), and Berndt (1991); see also Problems 8-Y and 8-Z.

ing logarithms, and adding the stochastic disturbance term u_i, the elasticities α and β can be estimated from the linear model:

$$\ln C_i = a' + \frac{\alpha}{\alpha+\beta}\ln w + \frac{\beta}{\alpha+\beta}\ln r + \frac{1}{\alpha+\beta}\ln y_i + u_i, \tag{8.4.11}$$

where u_i, C_i, and y_i vary with the firm, but α, β, w, and r are assumed to be the same for all firms (and hence are not subscripted). This approach provides yet another way of estimating the Cobb–Douglas production function. The parameters of the original production function can be recovered from the estimation of this cost function, where the estimated coefficient of $\ln y$ is an estimator of the reciprocal of the sum of the elasticities $\alpha + \beta$. Given this estimate, the labor elasticity α can be obtained by multiplying the estimated coefficient of $\ln w$ by the estimate of the sum of the elasticities, while the capital elasticity β can be obtained by multiplying the estimated coefficient of $\ln r$ by the estimate of the sum of the elasticities. Similarly, the CES production function of (8.3.36) can be estimated from its associated cost function.

Another frequently used cost function is the *generalized Leontief cost function*:

$$C = \left(\sum_{i=1}^{n}\sum_{j=1}^{n} b_{ij} w_i^{1/2} w_j^{1/2}\right). \tag{8.4.12}$$

where constant returns to scale are assumed and $b_{ij} = b_{ji}$. This is the cost function related to the input–output production function (8.3.33).

A flexible form for the cost function is the *translog cost function*, which represents any arbitrary cost function in terms of a second-order Taylor's series approximation in logarithms, of the form:

$$\begin{aligned}\ln C = \alpha_0 &+ \sum \alpha_i \ln w_i + \sum\sum \gamma_{ij} \ln w_i \ln w_j \\ &+ \beta_0 \ln y + \beta_1 (\ln y)^2 + \sum \delta_i \ln w_i \ln y,\end{aligned} \tag{8.4.13}$$

where the first sum is over all i, the second sum is over all i and j, and the γ's form a symmetric matrix so $\gamma_{ij} = \gamma_{ji}$. This is the cost function related to the translog production function (8.3.55).[47] This function can be estimated directly or indirectly. For the latter, differentiate $\ln C$ with respect to $\ln w_i$ to obtain the elasticity of cost with respect to the wage of any factor and then use Shephard's lemma to obtain an equation in the share that input i represents of total cost. This equation can be estimated subject to the restriction that the shares sum to unity and to the symmetry condition on the γ_{ij} to obtain the parameters of the translog cost function. Additional restrictions can account for constant returns to scale or other conditions imposed by the technology.

8.5 ESTIMATION OF FACTOR DEMAND EQUATIONS

Another aspect of the theory of the firm is the system of factor demand equations, (8.2.28), of the form:[48]

$$x_j = x_j(w_1, w_2, \ldots, w_n, p), \qquad j = 1, 2, \ldots, n. \tag*{*(8.5.1)}$$

[47]See Diewert (1982) and Problem 8-Z.

[48]For a survey of factor demand equations, see Nadiri (1970).

This system can be estimated using alternative approaches that correspond to the estimation of consumer demand equations of the last chapter.

The partial equilibrium approach is to estimate a single equation of this system, specifically the factor demand curve for factor j, of the form:

$$x_j = D_j(w_j) = x_j(\overline{w}_1, \ldots, \overline{w}_{j-1}, w_j, \overline{w}_{j+1}, \ldots, \overline{w}_n, \overline{p}). \tag*{*(8.5.2)}$$

Various specifications have been utilized in estimating such a factor demand curve, including the linear- and the log-linear function. The latter is of the form:

$$x_j = A w_j^{\varepsilon_j} e^{u_j} \tag{8.5.3}$$

where u_j is the stochastic disturbance term. Taking logs gives

$$\ln x_j = a + \varepsilon_j \ln w_j + u_j, \tag*{*(8.5.4)}$$

where ε_j is the elasticity of demand for factor j.

The general equilibrium approach is to estimate the complete system, and various specifications have been used for systems of factor demand equations. One of the most common is the constant elasticity form:

$$x_j = A w_1^{\varepsilon_{1j}} w_2^{\varepsilon_{2j}} \cdots w_n^{\varepsilon_{nj}} p^{\gamma_j} e^{u_j}, \qquad j = 1, 2, \ldots, n \tag{8.5.5}$$

which, in log form, is the linear system:

$$\begin{aligned} \ln x_j &= a + \varepsilon_{1j} \ln w_1 + \varepsilon_{2j} \ln w_2 + \cdots \\ &\quad + \varepsilon_{nj} \ln w_n + \gamma_j \ln p + u_j, \qquad j = 1, 2, \ldots, n. \end{aligned} \tag*{*(8.5.6)}$$

This system reduces to (8.5.3) and (8.5.4) if all wages other than that of the factor itself and output price are held constant. The ε_{jj} in (8.5.6) is then the same as ε_j in (8.5.4).

A system of factor demand equations can be derived from the first-order conditions of profit maximization, assuming that a production function is given and all prices are given. Consider, for example, the case of the Cobb–Douglas production function:

$$y = A L^{\alpha} K^{\beta}. \tag*{*(8.5.7)}$$

The first-order conditions of profit maximization require that:

$$\frac{\partial y}{\partial L} = \alpha A L^{\alpha-1} K^{\beta} = \frac{\alpha y}{L} = \frac{w}{p}, \tag{8.5.8}$$

$$\frac{\partial y}{\partial K} = \beta A L^{\alpha} K^{\beta-1} = \frac{\beta y}{K} = \frac{r}{p}, \tag{8.5.9}$$

where w is the given wage of labor, r the given rental on capital, and p the given output price. Combining these gives

$$\frac{K}{L} = \frac{\beta}{\alpha} \frac{w}{r}, \tag{8.5.10}$$

so the capital/labor ratio is constant. Solving this equation for K and inserting the result in (8.5.7) yields the demand for labor. Solving for L and taking logs, the demand-for-labor equation is:

$$\ln L = a' - \frac{\beta}{\alpha+\beta} \ln \frac{w}{r} + \frac{1}{\alpha+\beta} \ln y. \tag*{*(8.5.11)}$$

This factor demand function and the comparable one for ln K [where the coefficient of ln (r/w) is $-\alpha/(\alpha+\beta)$] are of the log-linear constant elasticity type, as in (8.5.6).[49] Labor de-

[49] A similar approach can be used to estimate factor demand functions using other production functions, such as the CES (see Problem 8-V).

mand functions of this type have been combined, by Waud, with an assumed log-linear specification of a demand function for the output of the firm to explain the behavior of production worker labor-hours at the two-digit level in U.S. manufacturing industry, 1954–1964.[50] Some of his findings are summarized in Table 8.2, including estimated elasticities of labor hours with respect to wage, the cost of capital, and GNP (treated here as an exogenous shift variable in the demand function for output). In some industries, notably apparel, labor-hours are relatively insensitive to the wage or cost of capital, while in others, such as machinery, they are highly sensitive to both. In general, employment in manufacturing durables goods exhibits greater sensitivity to GNP than such employment in nondurables manufacturing. (The Durbin–Watson figures for the last two industries are quite low, however, and an alternative specification might be used in these cases.)

A related approach, the labor-requirements approach to factor demand, starts from the production function and solves it for the labor required as a function of capital and output. Thus, solving the Cobb–Douglas production function for L:

$$L = A^{-1/\alpha}K^{-\beta/\alpha}y^{1/\alpha}, \tag{8.5.12}$$

so, in log form,

$$\ln L = a_0 - \frac{\beta}{\alpha}\ln K + \frac{1}{\alpha}\ln y. \tag{8.5.13}$$

TABLE 8.2 Production Worker Labor-Hour Behavior in U.S. Manufacturing Industry, 1954–1964

	Elasticity with Respect to:			
Industry	Wage	Cost of Capital	GNP	R^2/d
Food	–0.506 (0.145)	0.157 (0.066)	–0.036 (0.101)	0.920 2.137
Apparel	–0.287 (0.442)	0.136 (0.154)	0.796 (0.173)	0.726 1.596
Paper	–0.613 (0.345)	0.364 (0.095)	0.583 (0.152)	0.846 2.109
Chemicals	–0.654 (0.270)	0.339 (0.115)	0.690 (0.136)	0.674 1.789
Rubber and plastics	–1.334 (0.748)	0.675 (0.228)	1.400 (0.211)	0.861 1.737
Stone, clay, and glass	–1.967 (0.776)	0.445 (0.182)	1.466 (0.334)	0.574 1.505
Fabricated metals	–2.366 (0.708)	0.317 (0.124)	1.683 (0.244)	0.771 1.938
Machinery, except electrical	–2.103 (0.922)	0.995 (0.206)	2.340 (0.462)	0.791 1.399
Electrical machinery	–2.142 (0.838)	0.943 (0.217)	1.256 (0.259)	0.771 0.910

Source Waud (1968).

Note Coefficients of dummy variables, representing cyclical factors, which were included in these regressions, are not reported here.

[50]See Waud (1968).

One problem with this approach is that data on capital are generally not available. Nevertheless it has been utilized, and such labor-requirement functions have been estimated.[51]

The labor-requirements approach is sometimes combined with a labor-adjustment model allowing gradual adjustment of labor input to its equilibrium level. Equation (8.5.12) is modified by interpreting the labor input as a required or desired amount of labor input at time t, designated by L_t^* and defined by

$$L_t^* = A^{-1/\alpha} K_t^{-\beta/\alpha} y_t^{1/\alpha}, \tag{8.5.14}$$

where capital input and output are treated as given in the short run. The labor-adjustment equation is then typically assumed to be of the log-linear form:[52]

$$\frac{L_t}{L_{t-1}} = \left(\frac{L_t^*}{L_{t-1}}\right)^{\lambda}, \qquad 0 \leq \lambda < 1, \tag{8.5.15}$$

where λ is the adjustment coefficient. Combining the last two equations and taking logarithms yields:

$$\ln L_t = (1-\lambda)\ln L_{t-1} - \frac{\lambda}{\alpha}\ln A - \frac{\beta\lambda}{\alpha}\ln K_t + \frac{\lambda}{\alpha}\ln y_t. \qquad *(8.5.16)$$

This equation, or variants of it, have been estimated by several authors.[53]

A variant of this approach replaces the labor-requirements function by the relation of desired labor input to the wage, which is typically assumed to be of the constant elasticity form:

$$L_t^* = Aw^{\beta}. \tag{8.5.17}$$

For example, from (8.3.17) for the Cobb–Douglas production function β is -1. Combining with (8.5.15) yields, in this case,

$$\ln L_t = a_0 + a_1 \ln L_{t-1} + a_2 \ln w, \qquad a_1 = 1-\lambda,\ a_2 = \lambda\beta, \qquad *(8.5.18)$$

where a_2 is the elasticity of labor demand with respect to the real wage and the elasticity of desired labor with respect to the wage, the β in (8.5.17), is estimated as $a_2/(1-a_1)$.

Recent estimates of input demand functions are based on the cost functions of Section 8.4. Shephard's lemma (8.2.58) states that each of the (optimal) factor inputs is the partial derivative of the cost function with respect to the corresponding wage. Thus input demand functions can be derived from the generalized Leontief cost function of (8.4.12) or the translog cost function of (8.4.13). For example, for the generalized Leontief cost function, differentiating the cost function with respect to w_j yields:

$$x_j = \left[b_{jj} + \frac{1}{2}\sum_{i \neq j} b_{ij}\left(\frac{w_i}{w_j}\right)^{1/2}\right] y \qquad *(8.5.19)$$

showing the dependence of input demand on relative wages and on output. This is clearly a generalization of the Leontief production function result, which follows if $b_{ij} = 0$ for $i \neq j$, when the equation reduces to fixed input–output coefficients, as given by the b_{jj} [e.g., the parameters a and b in (8.3.35)].[54]

[51]See Wilson and Eckstein (1964) and Kuh (1965).

[52]This labor-adjustment model is a variant of the stock adjustment model of Section 6.8. See Fair (1969).

[53]For a survey, see Fair (1969). See also Nadiri and Rosen (1973) for a simultaneous equations model of employment, investment, and inventories.

[54]For an example of the use of cost functions to estimate input demand functions, see Berndt and Wood (1975, 1979) and Berndt (1991).

8.6 TECHNICAL CHANGE

Technical change can be analyzed and estimated using production functions.[55] One such type of technical change is a shift in the production function over time reflecting greater efficiency in combining inputs. It is called *disembodied technical change*, and it can be represented by the production function:

$$y = f(L, K, t), \quad \text{i.e.,} \quad y(t) = f(L(t), K(t), t), \qquad *(8.6.1)$$

where t is time.[56] The change in output over time is given as:

$$\frac{dy}{dt} = \frac{\partial f}{\partial L}\frac{dL}{dt} + \frac{\partial f}{\partial K}\frac{dK}{dt} + \frac{\partial f}{\partial t}. \qquad *(8.6.2)$$

The first two terms on the right indicate the change in output due to increased inputs of labor and capital, respectively (i.e., a movement along the production function). The last term on the right indicates the change in output due to disembodied technical change (i.e., a shift in the production function). This type of technical change is called "disembodied" because it is not embodied in the factor inputs; rather, it involves a reorganization of the inputs. It can occur with or without increases in the inputs. Dividing both sides of (8.6.2) by output y, to convert to proportionate rates of change, yields:

$$\frac{1}{y}\frac{dy}{dt} = \left(\frac{L}{y}\frac{\partial y}{\partial L}\right)\frac{1}{L}\frac{dL}{dt} + \left(\frac{K}{y}\frac{\partial y}{\partial K}\right)\frac{1}{K}\frac{dK}{dt} + \frac{1}{y}\frac{\partial y}{\partial t}, \qquad *(8.6.3)$$

where all terms have been expressed as proportionate rates of change. The first two terms on the right are the proportionate rates of change of the two inputs, each weighted by the elasticity of output with respect to the input. The third term is the proportionate rate of disembodied technical change.

Technical change is *neutral* (or *Hicks neutral*) if it does not change the marginal rate of substitution between the inputs. Geometrically, for a given ratio of factor prices, neutral technical change shifts the isoquants of the production function uniformly toward the origin, leaving unchanged the slope of the isoquant along any ray from the origin. Thus factor proportions remain unchanged as long as the ratio of factor prices remains unchanged. Assume, for example, that the elasticities of output with respect to labor and capital are constant and given by α and β, respectively, as in the Cobb–Douglas case. Assume further that the proportionate rate of disembodied technical change is constant at the rate m. Then (8.6.3) implies that:

$$\frac{1}{y}\frac{dy}{dt} = \alpha\frac{1}{L}\frac{dL}{dt} + \beta\frac{1}{K}\frac{dK}{dt} + m, \qquad *(8.6.4)$$

where m is the rate of neutral disembodied technical change. The assumption of constant elasticities is, as already noted, that of the Cobb–Douglas production function, and (8.6.4) could, in fact, be derived from such a production function with the scale parameter A increasing exponentially over time:

$$y = \left(A_0 e^{mt}\right) L^{\alpha} K^{\beta}. \qquad *(8.6.5)$$

Thus taking logarithms gives

$$\ln y = a_0 + \alpha \ln L + \beta \ln K + mt, \quad a_0 = \ln A_0 \qquad *(8.6.6)$$

[55]See Brown (1966), Nadiri (1970), Kennedy and Thirwall (1972), Baily (1981, 1982), Jorgenson, Gollop, and Fraumeni (1987), Jorgenson (1988), Baily and Schultze (1990), and Boskin and Lau (1991).

[56]See Solow (1957).

and differentiating yields:

$$\frac{d\ln y}{dt} = \frac{1}{y}\frac{dy}{dt} = \alpha\frac{1}{L}\frac{dL}{dT} + \beta\frac{1}{K}\frac{dK}{dt} + m, \qquad *(8.6.7)$$

as in (8.6.4). The exponential time trend term in (8.6.5) thus accounts for neutral disembodied technical change. The rate of disembodied change, m, can be obtained from (8.6.4) as:

$$m = \frac{1}{y}\frac{dy}{dt} - \alpha\left(\frac{1}{L}\frac{dL}{dT}\right) + \beta\left(\frac{1}{K}\frac{dK}{dt}\right), \qquad *(8.6.8)$$

that is, as the proportionate change in output less the sum of the proportionate changes in all inputs, each such proportionate change being weighted by the elasticity of output with respect to that input. Solow used this formulation, with values of 0.65 for α and 0.35 for β, values based on relative shares, and with observed proportionate changes in y, L, and K, in order to infer the rate of disembodied technical change for U.S. nonfarm output, 1909–1949. He estimated m to be 0.015, representing a trend increase for productivity of 1.5% per year over this period.[57] He also found that the rate was about 1% per year during the 1909–1929 period and about 2% per year during the 1929–1949 period, indicating an acceleration in the rate of disembodied technical change. Over the entire period he found that technical change accounted for about 90% of the increase in output per labor-hour, with the increase in capital per labor hour accounting for only 10%.

A related study by Aukrust for Norway, 1900–1955, excluding 1940 to 1945, obtained, as an estimate of (8.6.6):[58]

$$\ln y = 2.62 + \underset{(0.10)}{0.76} \ln L + \underset{(0.19)}{0.20} \ln K + \underset{(0.003)}{0.018}t. \qquad *(8.6.9)$$

Thus he estimated elasticities with respect to labor and capital of 0.76 and 0.20, respectively, and a rate of disembodied technical change (m) of 1.8% per year. Thus, with no increase in labor or capital, output would grow at the rate of 1.8% per year. Since output (real national product) grew at an average rate of 3.4% during 1948–1955, during this period over half of the growth rate is accounted for via disembodied technical change.

Another related study, by Brown, estimated the model:

$$\Delta \ln y = \alpha \Delta \ln L + \beta \Delta \ln K + m, \qquad *(8.6.10)$$

obtained by taking first differences of (8.6.6).[59] He estimated this model over various historical periods, treating U.S. private domestic nonfarm output in 1929 prices as a function of labor-hours employed and net capital stock in 1929 prices adjusted for capital utilization. His results are presented in Table 8.3. The estimates of elasticities and returns to scale are different from those obtained by Douglas, as reported in Table 8.1 for all periods other than 1947–1960. In general, the Brown results involve labor elasticities that are lower and capital elasticities that are higher than those estimated by Douglas. Technical change was highest in 1921–1939 and lowest in 1890–1906.

[57]See Solow (1957). The study by Arrow et al. (1961) calculated the rate of technical change over the same period using a CES production function to be slightly higher—about 1.8% per year. Other studies yield similar estimates; for example, Morishima and Saito (1964), using a Cobb–Douglas production function, found the rate to be about 1.5% per year over the period 1902–1952, while David and van de Klundert (1965), using a CES production function, found the rate to be 1.85% per year over the period 1899–1960.

[58]See Aukrust (1959).

[59]See Brown (1966).

TABLE 8.3 Estimates of Technical Change in the United States

Period	Elasticity with Respect to: Labor α	Capital β	Technical Change m	Returns to Scale $\alpha+\beta$	$\bar{R}^2$ / d
1890–1960	0.325 (0.088)	0.552 (0.048)	0.0061 (0.0014)	0.877	0.887 1.49
1890–1906	0.690 (0.230)	0.416 (0.092)	0.0018 (0.0034)	1.106	0.867 1.98
1921–1939	0.383 (0.162)	0.505 (0.100)	0.0077 (0.0025)	0.888	0.928 1.81
1940–1960	0.453 (0.175)	0.489 (0.131)	0.0069 (0.0026)	0.942	0.775 1.27
1947–1960	0.659 (0.194)	0.379 (0.112)	0.0062 (0.0021)	1.038	0.891 1.90

Source Brown (1966). Results have been rounded.

The discussion thus far has referred to *disembodied* technical change—that is, technical change that is not embodied in the factor inputs. By contrast, *embodied* technical change involves an augmentation in the effectiveness of factor inputs due to various possible improvements in their quality or efficiency over time. It can be represented by a *vintage model*, in which later vintages of inputs are more effective than earlier vintages.[60] A production function incorporating both embodied and disembodied technical change was estimated by Intriligator for aggregate U.S. manufacturing output, 1929–1958.[61] Various time series for labor input were considered, involving alternative adjustments in the effectiveness of the labor force, including adjustments for the changes in working hours, education, and the age–gender composition of the labor force. For capital input, alternative rates of embodied technical change, corresponding to improvements in the technical efficiency of capital, were considered. The best estimate was:

$$y = 0.869e^{0.0167t}L^{0.862}K^{0.138}, \quad R^2 = 0.993, d = 2.159, \qquad *(8.6.11)$$
$$(0.0026) \quad (0.044)$$

where L refers to labor input of unchanging quality and K refers to capital input for embodied technical change of 4% annually. Thus, according to these estimates, disembodied technical change is 1.67% annually, no technical change is embodied in labor, and technical change embodied in capital amounts to 4% annually.[62]

A study of capital and productivity by Boskin and Lau used the translog production function to estimate how much of the observed output growth in the United States, Japan, Germany, France, and the United Kingdom can be attributed to capital formation and tech-

[60]See Solow (1960, 1962) and Phelps (1962).

[61]See Intriligator (1965).

[62]Some authors have sought to explain changes in output and technology by explicitly accounting for as many influences as possible, including nonconstant returns to scale, changes in education, improvement in capital, etc. (see Jorgenson and Griliches, 1967). Later studies of productivity and technical change have taken account explicitly of additional inputs, explaining output not only in terms of labor and capital but also in terms of energy, material inputs, and purchased services, using "KLEMS" data on inputs of capital, labor, energy, material inputs, and purchased services, respectively (see Jorgenson, Gollop, and Fraumeni, 1987; Jorgenson, 1988; Baily and Schultze, 1990).

nical change, as opposed to labor growth.[63] They found that over 70% of the output change in the United States can be attributed to capital formation and technical change, while over 95% of growth in the other four nations can be so attributed to capital formation and technical change. Furthermore, they found that technical change is capital-augmenting and that capital growth is capital-saving, rather than labor-saving, and thereby not, by itself, leading to (labor) unemployment. They also found that overall economy-wide production exhibits sharply decreasing local returns to scale and that the elasticity of substitution between labor and capital lies strictly between zero and 1.

PROBLEMS

8-A Consider the following cost curves $C(y)$, where y is output. For each, determine what conditions economic theory imposes on the coefficients, assuming fixed cost is nonnegative; average and marginal costs are both positive; and average and marginal costs initially decrease but eventually increase. For each, also determine the output level at which average cost is a minimum.

1. $C = a_1y + a_2y^2 + a_3y^3$ (cubic cost curve)
2. $C = a_0 + a_1y + a_2y^{1/2}$
3. $C = a_1 y^{a_2} e^{a_3 y}$
4. $C = a_1 y^{a_2} e^{a_3(\log y)^2}$
5. $C = a_1 y^{1/a_2}(a_2 + a_3 y)^{-1/a_2}$

8-B Prove the comparative statics relation (8.2.41), using the production function, the homogeneity of the input demand functions, and the first-order conditions for profit maximization.

8-C For the profit function $\Pi(w_1, w_2, \ldots, w_n, p)$ defined in (8.2.50):

1. Prove that the profit function is positive homogeneous of degree one in all variables:
$$\Pi(\alpha w_1, \alpha w_2, \ldots, \alpha w_n, \alpha p) = \alpha\Pi(w_1, w_2, \ldots, w_n, p), \quad \text{all } \alpha > 0.$$
2. Prove that the demands for inputs x_j satisfy Hotelling's lemma:
$$x_j = -\frac{\partial \Pi}{\partial w_j} \quad \text{where} \quad \frac{\partial x_j}{\partial w_j} = -\frac{\partial^2 \Pi}{\partial w_j^2} < 0.$$
3. Prove that the supply of output y satisfies
$$y = \frac{\partial \Pi}{\partial p} \quad \text{where} \quad \frac{\partial y}{\partial p} = \frac{\partial^2 \Pi}{\partial p^2} > 0.$$
4. Prove that the $n \times n$ matrix consisting of the partial derivatives $\partial x_j/\partial w_k$ is symmetric and negative semidefinite. What are the economic implications of this result?

8-D For the cost function $C(w_1, w_2, \ldots, w_n, y)$ defined in (8.2.57):

1. Find the first-order conditions characterizing this function and illustrate them geometrically.
2. Prove that the cost function is positive homogeneous of degree one in all factor prices for fixed y:
$$C(\alpha w_1, \alpha w_2, \ldots, \alpha w_n, y) = \alpha\, C(w_1, w_2, \ldots, w_n, y), \quad \text{all } \alpha > 0.$$
3. Prove that the demands for inputs x_j satisfy Shephard's lemma,
$$x_j = \frac{\partial C}{\partial w_j} \quad \text{where} \quad \frac{\partial x_j}{\partial w_j} = \frac{\partial^2 C}{\partial w_j^2} < 0, \quad \text{all } j.$$

[63] See Boskin and Lau (1991).

8-E Consider the case of the firm in *imperfect competition*, where either output price or input prices are not given parametrically, but rather vary with the output or input levels chosen by the firm.

1. For a *monopolist* the output price falls with the level of output, since the firm faces the entire market demand curve for the product. Obtain the first-order conditions characterizing profit maximization in such a case. Illustrate geometrically.
2. For a *monopsonist* the input prices rise with the levels of input, since the firm faces the entire market supply curve for the input. Obtain the first-order conditions characterizing profit maximization in such a case. Illustrate geometrically.

8-F The production function $y = f(x_1, x_2)$ exhibits constant returns to scale if it is positive homogeneous of degree one, so

$$f(\alpha x_1, \alpha x_2) = \alpha f(x_1, x_2), \quad \text{all } \alpha > 0,$$

as in (8.3.6). Prove that if the production function exhibits constant returns to scale:

1. Marginal products and average products depend only on factor proportions $x_1/x_2 = k$.
2. The elasticity of substitution defined in (8.3.11) depends only on factor proportions, and it can be expressed in the following ways:

$$\sigma = \frac{(\partial f/\partial x_1)(\partial f/\partial x_2)}{y(\partial^2 f/\partial x_1 \partial x_2)} = \frac{d\ln(y/x_1)}{d\ln(\partial f/\partial x_1)} = \frac{d\ln(y/x_2)}{d\ln(\partial f/\partial x_2)} = \frac{-g'(g - kg')}{kgg''},$$

where $k = x_1/x_2$ and $g(k) = g(x_1/x_2) = f(x_1/x_2, 1)$.

3. Real wages w_1/p and w_2/p depend only on factor proportions and there exists a *factor price frontier* $w_1/p = \varphi(w_2/p)$, where $\varphi' < 0$, $\varphi'' > 0$ and where the elasticity of w_1/p with respect to w_2/p is the relative share (i.e., the ratio of real payments to the two factors).[64]

8-G The *elasticity of production*, a local measure of returns to scale, is defined for the production function $y = f(L, K)$ as:[65]

$$\varepsilon = \varepsilon(L, K) = \frac{L}{y}\frac{dy}{dL} = \frac{K}{y}\frac{dy}{dK} \quad \text{where} \quad \frac{dL}{L} = \frac{dK}{K}.$$

It is therefore the elasticity of output with respect to an equiproportionate increase in all inputs.

1. Prove that if the production function is homogeneous of degree h, then $\varepsilon = h$.
2. Prove that the elasticity of production at any point is the sum of the elasticities of output with respect to all inputs at this point:

$$\varepsilon = \frac{L}{y}\frac{\partial y}{\partial L} + \frac{K}{y}\frac{\partial y}{\partial K}.$$

3. Prove that the elasticity of cost, γ, defined in (8.4.6) is the reciprocal of the elasticity of production:

$$\gamma = \frac{1}{\varepsilon}.$$

8-H For the Cobb–Douglas production function (8.3.13), show that a change of units from (y, L, K) to $(c_0 y, c_1 L, c_2 K)$ changes the constant A but does not change the exponents (elasticities) α and β. How does A change? Consider a similar change in units for other production functions, specifically the CES, transcendental, Zellner–Revankar, Nerlove–Ringstad, and translog production functions. Which parameters are invariant to a change in units?

[64]See Samuelson (1962). The factor price frontier can be defined as the locus of real wages such that the cost function is constant, for given output.

[65]See footnote 12 and Intriligator (1971). It is called the *passus coefficient* in Frisch (1965) and the *scale elasticity* in Johansen (1972).

8-I Consider the four alternative methods of estimating the Cobb–Douglas production function as discussed following (8.3.24). Assuming data y_i, L_i, K_i, and $(w/p)_i$ are available for $i = 1, 2, \ldots, n$, where n is the number of firms in a cross-section sample, determine for each method the estimator of α, the elasticity of output with respect to labor input. Give economic interpretations for these estimators, and compare them to one another.

8-J Consider the structural form defined in footnote 18 for the estimation of the Cobb–Douglas production function. Write the system as a matrix equation, and obtain the reduced form of this system. What restrictions must be placed on α and β? Show that the system is not identified (see Chapter 9). What method(s) might be employed in estimating the elasticities α and β?

8-K A simple example of the aggregation problem, as discussed in footnote 19, is that of an industry consisting of F firms producing the same output from the same inputs of labor and capital, using Cobb–Douglas production functions with different parameters. Show that for this industry there exists an aggregate Cobb–Douglas production function for which the parameters are weighted averages of those of the firms, provided aggregates of all variables are geometric means.

8-L For the Kimbell–Lorant production function for physicians' services in (8.3.32), find the implied demand curve for allied health personnel as a function of the real wage of such personnel, w/p.

8-M The dependence of output on one factor input, assuming all others are held constant, is called a *product curve* (or *returns curve*). In the two-factor case, holding capital constant at K and varying labor leads to the total product. average product, and marginal product curves:

$$\text{TP}(L) = f(L, \overline{K}),$$

$$\text{AP}(L) = \frac{1}{L} f(L, \overline{K}),$$

$$\text{MP}(L) = \frac{\partial f}{\partial L}(L, \overline{K}).$$

Obtain these curves algebraically and geometrically for the:

1. Cobb–Douglas production function.
2. Input–output production function.

8-N The isoquants of the CES production function (8.3.36) intersect the axes if $\sigma > 1$ and are asymptotic to horizontal and vertical lines if $\sigma < 1$.

1. In the case $\sigma > 1$, find the values at which the isoquants intersect the axes.
2. In the case $\sigma < 1$, find the values of the inputs defining the horizontal and vertical lines that the isoquants approach asymptotically. Show that the assumption that factor inputs are indispensable (8.3.2) excludes the case $\sigma > 1$.

8-O For the CES production function (8.3.36), show that the relative share of labor is given as:

$$s_L = \frac{\delta}{1-\delta}\left(\frac{L}{K}\right)^{-\beta}.$$

8-P Assuming output and both inputs are endogenous variables and output and input prices are exogenous, develop a simultaneous system of equations for the CES production function comparable to that developed for the Cobb–Douglas production function in footnote 18 and Problem 8-J. What is the reduced form?

8-Q For the transcendental production function (8.3.49), show that the elasticity of substitution is:

$$\sigma = 1 + \frac{1}{(\beta/\alpha' K) + (\beta'/\alpha' - r/w)}.$$

8-R Prove by differentiating the average cost function that local economies of scale, defined in (8.4.7), hold if and only if the average cost curve is decreasing.

8-S Consider a chemical engineering process for which liquids are processed in a spherical tank. Assume that the output of the process is proportional to the volume of the tank, while the cost of the process is proportional to the surface of the tank. Letting C be cost and y be output, show, on the basis of geometrical considerations, that:

$$C \sim y^{2/3},$$

so that the elasticity of the cost curve with respect to output is:

$$\gamma = \tfrac{2}{3},$$

implying, by (8.4.7), economies of scale at each y.[66] Why, then, would such tanks be large, but not enormous?

8-T Consider the cost function for the Cobb–Douglas production function, as given in (8.4.10).

1. Derive this function from the conditions for profit maximization, solving explicitly for the constant term A'.
2. Show that the implied cost curve is linear in the case of constant returns to scale.
3. By setting marginal cost equal to price, obtain the output supply function and show that it is proportional to $p^{(\alpha+\beta)/(1-\alpha-\beta)}$. What is the shape of this supply function in the constant-returns-to-scale case?

8-U A production function implies a cost function.

1. Show for the extended CES production function (8.3.47) that the cost function is given as:

$$C(w, r, y) = A'y^{1/h}\left[\delta^{1/(1+\beta)}w^{\beta/(1+\beta)} + (1-\delta)^{1/(1+\beta)}r^{\beta/(1+\beta)}\right]^{(1+\beta)/\beta}.$$

2. Show for the Zellner–Revankar production function (8.3.51) that the cost function is given as:

$$C(w, r, y) = A'\left(w^{\alpha}r^{\beta}ye^{cy}\right)^{1/(\alpha+\beta)}.$$

[Note that this reduces to the Cobb–Douglas cost function (8.4.10) if $c = 0$.]

8-V Consider the demand-for-labor equation (8.5.11).

1. Solve for a'.
2. Prove that a comparable demand-for-labor equation for the CES production function (8.3.47) is given as:

$$\ln L = a'' - \frac{1}{1+\beta}\ln w + \frac{1}{\beta}\ln\left[\delta^{1/(1+\beta)}w^{\beta/(1+\beta)} + (1-\delta)^{1/(1+\beta)}r^{\beta/(1+\beta)}\right] + \frac{1}{h}\ln y$$

and solve for a''.

8-W An *engineering production function* is estimated on the basis of physical and engineering principles. An example of such a production function is that for transmission from a boiler, as determined by Smith:[67]

$$y = x_1 - \frac{a}{b + cx_2}.$$

[66]See Moore (1959); see also Haldi and Whitcomb (1967) and Silberston (1972). Note that an elasticity of 2/3 implies that doubling output increases costs by only two-thirds, known as the "two-thirds" (or, sometimes, "six-tenths") rule of thumb in the chemical engineering literature (see Scherer, 1980).

[67]See Smith (1961); see also Chenery (1949, 1953).

Here y is the heat output, x_1 the heat input, and x_2 the thickness of the insulation material, where x_1 and x_2 are treated as the two inputs to the production process.

1. Determine the marginal rate of substitution between heat input and insulation material, and draw several isoquants.
2. Given w_1 and w_2 as the cost of heat input and thickness of insulation material, respectively, determine the demand functions for each of the inputs.

8-X Another example of an engineering production function is that for transmission of crude oil in a pipeline, as determined by Cookenboo:[68]

$$y^a = bx_1 + x_2^c.$$

Here y is the output of crude oil, x_1 the horsepower of the transmission pump, and x_2^c the inside diameter of the pipe. As in Problem 8-W, determine the marginal rate of substitution, draw several isoquants, and determine the demand functions for the two inputs.

8-Y Using Shephard's lemma (8.2.58), obtain the demand for inputs for the generalized Leontief cost function in (8.4.12), and, from this result, show that this cost function implies a generalization of input–output demand equations for the inputs, as in the input–output production function (8.3.33).

8-Z For the translog cost function (8.4.13), differentiate ln C with respect to ln w_j to obtain the elasticity of cost with respect to the wage of any factor and then use Shephard's lemma to obtain an equation in the share that input i represents of total cost.

BIBLIOGRAPHY

ARROW, K. J., H. B. CHENERY, B. S. MINHAS, and R. M. SOLOW (1961). "Capital-Labor Substitution and Economic Efficiency." *Review of Economics and Statistics*, 43: 225–235.

AUKRUST, O. (1959). "Investment and Economic Growth." *Productivity Measurement Review*, 16: 35–53.

BAILY, M. N. (1981). "Productivity and the Services of Capital and Labor." *Brookings Papers on Economic Activity*, 1: 1–50.

BAILY, M. N. (1982). "The Productivity Growth Slowdown by Industry." *Brookings Papers on Economic Activity*, 2: 423–454.

BAILY, M. N., and C. L. SCHULTZE (1990). "The Productivity of Capital in a Period of Slower Growth." *Brookings Papers on Economic Activity*, 10: 369–420.

BAUMOL, W. J. (1967). *Business Behavior, Value and Growth*, rev. ed. New York: Harcourt Brace Jovanovich, Inc.

BERNDT, E. R. (1976). "Reconciling Alternative Estimates of the Elasticity of Substitution." *Review of Economics and Statistics*, 58: 59–68.

BERNDT, E. R. (1991). *The Practice of Econometrics: Classic and Contemporary*. Reading, Mass.: Addison-Wesley Publishing Company, Inc.

BERNDT, E. R., and D. O. WOOD (1975). "Technology, Prices and the Derived Demand for Energy." *Review of Economics and Statistics*, 57: 259–268.

BERNDT, E. R., and D. O. WOOD (1979). "Engineering and Econometric Interpretations of Energy–Capital Complementarity." *American Economic Review*, 69: 342–354.

BLISS, C. (1968). "On Putty-Clay." *Review of Economic Studies*, 35: 105–132.

BODKIN, R. G., and L. R. KLEIN (1967). "Nonlinear Estimation of Aggregate Production Functions." *Review of Economics and Statistics*, 39: 28–44.

[68] See Cookenboo (1955).

BOSKIN, M., and L. J. LAU (1991). "Capital and Productivity: A New View." Paper presented at the IUI seminar "Capital: Its Value, Its Rate of Return, and Its Productivity," Stockholm, March.

BROWN, M. (1966). *On the Theory and Measurement of Technological Change*. New York: Cambridge University Press.

BROWN, M., Ed. (1967), *The Theory and Empirical Analysis of Production*. National Bureau of Economic Research. New York: Columbia University Press.

BROWN, M., and J. S. DE CANI (1963). "Technological Change and the Distribution of Income." *International Economic Review*, 4: 289–309.

CHENERY, H. B. (1949). "Engineering Production Functions." *Quarterly Journal of Economics*, 63: 507–531.

CHENERY, H. B. (1953). "Process and Production Functions from Engineering Data," in W. W. Leontief et al., Eds., *Studies in the Structure of the American Economy*. New York: Oxford University Press.

CHENERY, H. B., and P. G. CLARK (1959). *Industry Economics*. New York: John Wiley & Sons, Inc.

CHRISTENSEN, L. R., D. W. JORGENSON, and L. J. LAU (1973). "Transcendental Logarithmic Production Frontiers." *Review of Economics and Statistics*, 55: 28–45.

COOKENBOO, L. J. (1955). *Crude Oil Pipe Lines and Competition in the Oil Industry*. Cambridge, Mass.: Harvard University Press.

CRAMER, J. S. (1969). *Empirical Econometrics*. Amsterdam: North-Holland Publishing Company.

DAVID, P. A., and T. VAN DE KLUNDERT (1965). "Biased Efficiency Growth and Capital–Labor Substitution in the U.S., 1899–1960." *American Economic Review*, 55: 357–394.

DHRYMES, P. J. (1965). "Some Extensions and Tests for the CES Class of Production Functions." *Review of Economics and Statistics*, 47: 357–366.

DIEWERT, W. E. (1982). "Duality Approaches to Microeconomic Theory," in K. J. Arrow and M. D. Intriligator, Eds., *Handbook of Mathematical Economics*, Vol 2. Amsterdam: North-Holland Publishing Company.

DOUGLAS, P. H. (1948). "Are There Laws of Production?" *American Economic Review*, 38: 1–41.

FAIR, R. C. (1969). *The Short-Run Demand for Workers and Hours*. Amsterdam: North-Holland Publishing Company.

FERGUSON, C. E. (1965). "Time Series Production Functions and Technological Progress in American Manufacturing Industry." *Journal of Political Economy*, 73: 135–147.

FERGUSON, C. E. (1969). *The Neoclassical Theory of Production and Distribution*. New York: Cambridge University Press.

FRISCH, R. (1965). *Theory of Production*. Dordrecht, The Netherlands: D. Reidel Publishing Co.; Chicago: Rand McNally & Company.

FUCHS, V. R. (1963). "Capital–Labor Substitution: A Note." *Review of Economics and Statistics*, 45: 436–438.

FUSS, M., and D. MCFADDEN, Eds. (1978). *Production Economics: A Dual Approach to Theory and Applications*. Amsterdam: North-Holland Publishing Company.

GOLD, B. (1966). "New Perspectives on Cost Theory and Empirical Findings." *Journal of Industrial Economics*, 14: 161–194.

GREEN, H. A. J. (1964). *Aggregation in Economic Analysis*. Princeton; N.J.: Princeton University Press.

GRILICHES, Z. (1967). "Production Functions in Manufacturing: Some Preliminary Results," in Brown. Ed. (1967).

GRILICHES, Z., and V. RINGSTAD (1971). *Economies of Scale and the Form of the Production Function*. Amsterdam: North-Holland Publishing Company.

HALDI, J., and D. WHITCOMB (1967). "Economies of Scale in Industrial Plants." *Journal of Political Economy*, 75: 373–385.

HALTER, A. N., H. O. CARTER, and J. G. HOCKING (1957). "A Note on Transcendental Production Functions." *Journal of Farm Economics*, 39: 966–974.

HEADY, E. O., and J. L. DILLON (1961). *Agricultural Production Functions*. Ames, Iowa: Iowa State University Press.

HILDEBRAND, G. H., and T. C. LIU (1965). *Manufacturing Production Functions in the United States*. Ithaca, N.Y.: Cornell University Press.

HOUTHAKKER, H. (1955–56). "The Pareto Distribution and the Cobb–Douglas Production Function in Activity Analysis," *Review of Economic Studies*, 23: 27–31.

INTRILIGATOR, M. D. (1965). "Embodied Technical Change and Productivity in the United States, 1929–1958." *Review of Economics and Statistics*, 47: 65–70.

INTRILIGATOR, M. D. (1971). *Mathematical Optimization and Economic Theory*. Englewood Cliffs, N.J.: Prentice Hall.

JOHANSEN, L. (1959). "Substitution vs. Fixed Production Coefficients in the Theory of Economic Growth: A Synthesis." *Econometrica*, 27: 157–176.

JOHANSEN, L. (1972). *Production Functions*. Amsterdam: North-Holland Publishing Company.

JOHNSTON, J. (1960). *Statistical Cost Analysis*. New York: McGraw-Hill Book Company.

JORGENSON, D. W. (1986). "Econometric Methods for Modeling Producer Behavior," in Z. Griliches and M. D. Intriligator, Eds., *Handbook of Econometrics*, Vol. 3. Amsterdam: North-Holland Publishing Company.

JORGENSON, D. W. (1988). "Productivity and Postwar U.S. Economic Growth." *Journal of Economic Perspectives*, 2: 23–41.

JORGENSON, D. W., F. M. GOLLOP, and B. M. FRAUMENI (1987). *Productivity and U.S. Economic Growth*. Amsterdam: North-Holland Publishing Company.

JORGENSON, D. W., and Z. GRILICHES (1967). "Explanation of Productivity Change." *Review of Economic Studies*, 34: 249–283.

KENNEDY, C., and A. P. THIRWALL (1972). "Technical Progress: A Survey." *Economic Journal*, 82: 11–72.

KIMBELL, L. J., and J. LORANT (1974). "Physician Productivity and Returns to Scale," Chapter 20 in University of Southern California, Human Resources Research Center, *An Original Comparative Economic Analysis of Group Practice and Solo Fee-for-Service Practice: Final Report*. Publication PB 241 546. Springfield, Va.: National Technical Information Service, U.S. Department of Commerce.

KMENTA, J. (1967). "On Estimation of the CES Production Function." *International Economic Review*, 8: 180–189.

KREPS, D. M. (1990). *A Course in Microeconomic Theory*. Princeton; N. J.: Princeton University Press.

KUH, E. (1965). "Income Distributions and Employment over the Business Cycle," in J. Duesenberry et al., Eds., *The Brookings Quarterly Econometric Model of the United States*. Amsterdam: North-Holland Publishing Company.

LAU, L. J. (1986). "Functional Forms in Economic Model Building," in Z. Griliches and M. D. Intriligator, Eds., *Handbook of Econometrics*, Vol. 3. Amsterdam: North-Holland Publishing Company.

LEONTIEF, W. W. (1951). *The Structure of the American Economy, 1919–1939*, 2nd ed. New York: Oxford University Press.

LEONTIEF, W. W. (1966). *Input–Output Economics*. New York: Oxford University Press.

LOVELL, C. A. K. (1973). "Estimation and Prediction with CES and VES Production Functions." *International Economic Review*, 14: 676–692.

LU, Y., and L. B. FLETCHER (1968). "A Generalization of the CES Production Function." *Review of Economics and Statistics*, 50: 449–452.

MALINVAUD, E. (1985). *Lectures on Microeconomic Theory*, 2nd rev. ed. (first English ed., 1972). Amsterdam: North-Holland Publishing Company.

MARSCHAK, J., and W. H. ANDREWS (1944). "Random Simultaneous Equations and the Theory of Production." *Econometrica*, 12: 143–205.

MAYOR, T. H. (1969). "Some Theoretical Difficulties in the Estimation of the Elasticity of Substitution from Cross-Section Data." *Western Economic Journal*, 7: 153–163.

MINHAS, B. S. (1963). *An International Comparison of Factor Costs and Factor Use*. Amsterdam: North-Holland Publishing Company.

MOORE, F. T. (1959). "Economics of Scale: Some Statistical Evidence." *Quarterly Journal of Economics*, 73: 232–245.

MORISHIMA, M., and SAITO, M. (1964). "A Dynamic Analysis of the American Economy, 1902–1952." *International Economic Review*, 5: 125–164.

NADIRI, M. I. (1970). "Some Approches to the Theory and Measurement of Total Factor Productivity." *Journal of Economic Literature*, 8: 1137–1177.

NADIRI, M. I. (1982). "Producer's Theory," in K. J. Arrow and M. D. Intriligator, Eds., *Handbook of Mathematical Economics*, Vol. 2. Amsterdam: North-Holland Publishing Company.

NADIRI, M. I., and S. ROSEN (1973). *A Disequilibrium Model of Demand for Factors of Production*. National Bureau of Economic Research. New York: Columbia University Press.

NERLOVE, M. (1963). "Returns to Scale in Electricity Supply," in C. F. Christ et al., Eds., *Measurement in Econometrics: Studies in Mathematical Economics and Econometrics in Memory of Yehuda Grunfeld*. Stanford, Calif.: Stanford University Press; reprinted in Nerlove (1965).

NERLOVE, M. (1965). *Estimation and Identification of Cobb–Douglas Production Functions*. Amsterdam: North-Holland Publishing Company.

NERLOVE, M. (1967). "Recent Empirical Studies of the CES and Related Production Functions," in Brown, Ed. (1967).

PHELPS, E. S. (1962). "The New View of Investment: A Neoclassical Analysis." *Quarterly Journal of Economics*, 76: 548–567.

REVANKAR, N. S. (1971). "A Class of Variable Elasticity of Substitution Production Functions." *Econometrica*, 39: 61–71.

RINGSTAD, V. (1967). "Econometric Analysis Based on a Production Function with Neutrally Variable Scale Elasticity." *Swedish Journal of Economics*, 69: 115–133.

SAMUELSON, P. A. (1962). "Parable and Realism in Capital Theory: The Surrogate Production Function." *Review of Economic Studies*, 29: 193–206.

SAMUELSON, P. A. (1979). "Paul Douglas' Measurement of Production Functions and Marginal Productivities." *Journal of Political Economy*, 87: 923–939.

SAMUELSON, P. A. (1983). *Foundations of Economic Analysis*, 2nd ed. (first ed., 1947). Cambridge, Mass.: Harvard University Press.

SATO, K. (1967). "A Two Level Constant-Elasticity-of-Substitution Production Function." *Review of Economic Studies*, 34: 201–218.

SATO, K. (1975). *Production Functions and Aggregation*. Amsterdam: North-Holland Publishing Company.

SATO, R., and R. F. HOFFMAN (1968). "Production Functions with Variable Elasticity of Factor Substitution: Some Analysis and Testing." *Review of Economics and Statistics*, 50: 453–460.

SCHERER, F. M. (1980). *Industrial Market Structure and Economic Performance*, 2nd ed. Chicago: Rand McNally & Company.

SHEPHARD, R. (1970). *Theory of Cost and Production Functions*. Princeton, N.J.: Princeton University Press.

SILBERSTON, A. (1972). "Economies of Scale in Theory and Practice." *Economic Journal*, 82: 369–391.

SIMON, H. (1959). "Theories of Decision-Making in Economics and Behavioral Science." *American Economic Review*, 59: 253–283.

SMITH, V. L. (1961). *Investment and Production*. Cambridge, Mass.: Harvard University Press.

SOLOW, R. M. (1957). "Technical Change and the Aggregate Production Function." *Review of Economics and Statistics*, 39: 312–320.

SOLOW, R. M. (1960). "Investment and Technical Progress," in K. J. Arrow, S. Karlin, and F. Suppes, Eds., *Mathematical Methods in the Social Sciences, 1959*. Stanford, Calif.: Stanford University Press.

SOLOW, R. M. (1962). "Technical Progress, Capital Formation, and Economic Growth." *American Economic Review, Papers and Proceedings*, 52: 76–86.

SOLOW, R. M. (1967). "Some Recent Developments in the Theory of Production," in Brown, Ed. (1967).

VARIAN, H. (1984). *Microeconomic Analysis*, 2nd ed. New York: W.W. Norton & Company, Inc.

WALTERS, A. A. (1963). "Production and Cost Functions: An Econometric Survey." *Econometrica*, 31: 1–66.

WALTERS, A. A. (1968). "Econometric Studies of Production and Cost Functions." *Encyclopedia of the Social Sciences*.

WAUD, R. N. (1968). "Man-Hour Behavior in U.S. Manufacturing: A Neoclassical Interpretation." *Journal of Political Economy*, 76: 407–427.

WILES, P. (1963). *Price, Cost, and Output*, rev. ed. New York: Praeger Publishers.

WILLIAMSON, O. E. (1964). *The Economics of Discretionary Behavior: Managerial Objectives in a Theory of the Firm*. Englewood Cliffs, N.J.: Prentice Hall.

WILSON, T. A., and O. ECKSTEIN (1964). "Short Run Productivity Behavior in U.S. Manufacturing." *Review of Economics and Statistics*, 46: 41–56.

ZAREMBKA, P. (1970). "On the Empirical Relevance of the CES Production Function." *Review of Economics and Statistics*, 52: 47–53.

ZELLNER, A., J. KMENTA, and J. DRÈZE (1966). "Specification and Estimation of Cobb–Douglas Production Function Models." *Econometrica*, 34: 727–729.

ZELLNER, A., and N. REVANKAR (1969). "Generalized Production Functions." *Review of Economic Studies*, 36: 241–250.

9

THE SIMULTANEOUS-EQUATIONS SYSTEM AND ITS IDENTIFICATION

9.1 THE SIMULTANEOUS-EQUATIONS SYSTEM

The discussion of the last five chapters has concentrated on single equations, their estimation, and their applications. This chapter returns to the simultaneous-equations model introduced in Chapter 2 in Sections 2.8 to 2.10. It is presented in its general form in this section, and the next two sections are concerned with its identification. Section 9.5 treats recursive models. In the last section we discuss the identification of nonlinear simultaneous equations models. In particular, this chapter develops the specification of the stochastic disturbance terms of equation (2.8.3) and the relevance of this specification for identification. The next chapter then takes up the estimation of the simultaneous-equations model. In Chapter 11 we consider the generalization to the dynamic model and its relation to dynamic systems, and Chapters 12 and 13 consider applications of this model.

A simultaneous-equations model determines the values of one set of variables, the *endogenous variables*, in terms of another set of variables, the *predetermined variables*. The linear simultaneous-equations model can be written in the *structural form* as the g simultaneous equations

$$\underset{1\times g}{\mathbf{y}_i}\ \underset{g\times g}{\boldsymbol{\Gamma}} + \underset{1\times k}{\mathbf{x}_i}\ \underset{k\times g}{\mathbf{B}} = \underset{1\times g}{\boldsymbol{\varepsilon}_i}, \quad i = 1, 2, \ldots, n. \qquad *(9.1.1)$$

Here $\mathbf{y}_i$ is the vector of g endogenous variables at the ith observation, $\mathbf{x}_i$ is a vector of k predetermined (exogenous or lagged endogenous) variables at the ith observation, and $\boldsymbol{\varepsilon}_i$ is a vector of g stochastic disturbance terms at the ith observation. The index i ranges over the sample of observations, from 1 to n, where n is the sample size (the number of observations). The coefficient matrices to be estimated are $\boldsymbol{\Gamma}$ and $\mathbf{B}$, representing, respectively, coefficients of endogenous and predetermined variables.[1] The $\mathbf{\Gamma}$ matrix is square and is assumed nonsingular, while $\mathbf{B}$ is generally not square. The structural form contains g equations that jointly determine, for each observation, the values of the g endogenous variables, given the k predetermined variables, the g stochastic disturbance terms, and the $g^2 + gk$ coefficients of the system.

As noted in Section 2.8, there is a trivial indeterminacy in each of the structural equations in that multiplying all terms by any nonzero constant does not change the meaning of the equation. This indeterminacy is eliminated by normalization, which usually involves choosing a specific nonzero numerical value for any one of the nonzero parameters in each equation. A frequently used normalization, as in (2.8.10), sets all diagonal elements of $\mathbf{\Gamma}$ equal to -1:

$$\gamma_{hh} = -1, \qquad h = 1, 2, \ldots, g \tag{9.1.2}$$

assuming $\gamma_{hh} \neq 0$. This normalization is equivalent to multiplying equation h by the constant $-1/\gamma_{hh}$. With this normalization equation h can be written, in the summation notation of (2.8.2), as

$$y_{ih} = \sum_{\substack{h'=1 \\ h' \neq h}}^{g} y_{ih'}\gamma_{h'h} + \sum_{j=1}^{k} x_{ij}\beta_{jh} - \varepsilon_{ih}, \qquad h = 1, 2, \ldots, g. \qquad *(9.1.3)$$

In this form the y_{ih} plays a role comparable to the dependent variable of single-equation estimation, while the $y_{ih'}$ (for $h' \neq h$, where $\gamma_{h'h} \neq 0$) and the x_{ij} (for j, where $\beta_{jh} \neq 0$) play a role comparable to the explanatory variables of single-equation estimation. The $y_{ih'}$ are explanatory endogenous variables, and the presence of such variables distinguishes simultaneous-equations estimation from single-equation estimation.

Returning to the structural form (9.1.1), it is typically assumed that the stochastic disturbance term row vectors $\boldsymbol{\varepsilon}_i$ satisfy certain assumptions. First, they are assumed to have a zero mean:

$$E(\boldsymbol{\varepsilon}_i) = \underset{1\times g}{\mathbf{0}}, \qquad \text{all } i. \qquad *(9.1.4)$$

This assumption is a vector generalization of the comparable assumption, in (A.4.1) for the single-equation case, of the form $E(u_i) = 0$. Second, the covariance matrix of the $\boldsymbol{\varepsilon}_i$ is assumed the same at each observation:

$$\text{Cov}(\boldsymbol{\varepsilon}_i) = E(\boldsymbol{\varepsilon}_i'\boldsymbol{\varepsilon}_i) = \underset{g\times g}{\Sigma} = \begin{pmatrix} \sigma_{11} & \sigma_{12} & \cdots & \sigma_{1g} \\ \sigma_{21} & \sigma_{22} & \cdots & \sigma_{2g} \\ \vdots & & & \\ \sigma_{g1} & \sigma_{g2} & \cdots & \sigma_{gg} \end{pmatrix}, \qquad \text{all } i, \qquad *(9.1.5)$$

[1]As noted in Chapter 2 some studies reverse the role of the $\mathbf{\Gamma}$ and $\mathbf{B}$ matrices. They also frequently premultiply column vectors of variables (rather than, as here, postmultiply row vectors of variables), writing the system (9.1.1) as

$$\mathbf{B}\mathbf{y}_i + \mathbf{\Gamma}\mathbf{x}_i = \mathbf{u}_i,$$

where $\mathbf{u}_i$ is the stochastic disturbance term column vector. The notation employed in this chapter in general uses row vectors, but column vectors are employed occasionally. The student should develop a mind-set flexible enough to deal with both.

where $\boldsymbol{\Sigma}$ is a symmetric positive-definite matrix of variances and covariances. This assumption is a vector generalization of the assumption of homoskedasticity in A.4.2, of the form $\text{Var}(u_i) = \sigma^2$. In fact, it reduces to this assumption if $g = 1$. Third, the $\boldsymbol{\varepsilon}_i$ are assumed to be uncorrelated over the sample,

$$E(\boldsymbol{\varepsilon}_i' \boldsymbol{\varepsilon}_j) = \underset{g\times g}{\mathbf{0}}, \qquad \text{all } i, j, \quad i \neq j, \qquad *(9.1.6)$$

so that each stochastic disturbance term is uncorrelated with any stochastic disturbance term (including itself) at any other point in the sample. This assumption is a vector generalization of the assumption of absence of serial correlation in A.4.2, of the form $\text{Cov}(u_i u_j) = 0$. These assumptions are satisfied, for example, if the stochastic disturbance terms $\boldsymbol{\varepsilon}_i$ are independently and identically distributed over the sample, with a zero mean vector and a constant covariance matrix $\boldsymbol{\Sigma}$. Under these assumptions, while the stochastic disturbance terms are, by (9.1.6), uncorrelated *over the sample*, from (9.1.5) the stochastic disturbance terms *between equations* can be correlated. This latter phenomenon of correlation between stochastic disturbance terms in different equations is, in fact, the essence of the simultaneous-equation system and the principal reason why it must be estimated as a system, rather than as a set of separate single equations.

In the single-equation case specific assumptions were sometimes made as to the distribution of the stochastic disturbance terms, particularly in the derivation of maximum likelihood estimators. The situation is similar here in dealing with simultaneous-equations systems. When additional assumptions are made as to the form of the distribution of the $\boldsymbol{\varepsilon}_i$, it is generally assumed that they are distributed independently, identically, and *normally* at each observation, so

$$\boldsymbol{\varepsilon}_i \sim \mathbf{N}(\mathbf{0}, \boldsymbol{\Sigma}). \qquad *(9.1.7)$$

Since it is assumed that $\boldsymbol{\Gamma}$ is a nonsingular matrix, it is possible to solve for the vector of endogenous variables $\mathbf{y}_i$ by postmultiplying (9.1.1) by $\boldsymbol{\Gamma}^{-1}$. The result is:

$$\mathbf{y}_i = -\mathbf{x}_i \mathbf{B} \boldsymbol{\Gamma}^{-1} + \boldsymbol{\varepsilon}_i \boldsymbol{\Gamma}^{-1} \qquad (9.1.8)$$

or

$$\underset{1\times g}{\mathbf{y}_i} = \underset{1\times k}{\mathbf{x}_i} \; \underset{k\times g}{\boldsymbol{\Pi}} + \underset{1\times g}{\mathbf{u}_i}, \qquad (9.1.9)$$

where

$$\underset{k\times g}{\boldsymbol{\Pi}} = -\underset{k\times g}{\mathbf{B}} \; \underset{g\times g}{\boldsymbol{\Gamma}^{-1}} \qquad (\text{or } \boldsymbol{\Pi}\boldsymbol{\Gamma} = -\mathbf{B}), \qquad *(9.1.10)$$

$$\underset{1\times g}{\mathbf{u}_i} = \underset{1\times g}{\boldsymbol{\varepsilon}_i} \; \underset{g\times g}{\boldsymbol{\Gamma}^{-1}} \qquad (\text{or } \mathbf{u}_i \boldsymbol{\Gamma} = \boldsymbol{\varepsilon}_i). \qquad *(9.1.11)$$

Equation (9.1.9) is the *reduced form*, which expresses each of the endogenous variables $\mathbf{y}_i$ as a linear function of all predetermined variables $\mathbf{x}_i$ and the stochastic disturbance terms $\mathbf{u}_i$. The coefficient matrix $\boldsymbol{\Pi}$, defined in (9.1.10), is known as the matrix of *reduced-form coefficients*, and $\mathbf{u}_i$, defined in (9.1.11), is known as the vector of *reduced-form stochastic disturbance terms*. The stochastic assumptions made on $\boldsymbol{\varepsilon}_i$ imply corresponding conditions on $\mathbf{u}_i$, since from (9.1.11) the reduced-form stochastic disturbance terms are linear functions of the structural equation disturbance terms. From (9.1.4) and (9.1.11) it follows that

$$E(\mathbf{u}_i) = \mathbf{0}, \qquad \text{all } i, \qquad *(9.1.12)$$

so that "on average" the reduced-form model is "correct" in that

$$E(\mathbf{y}_i) = \mathbf{x}_i\mathbf{\Pi}. \tag{9.1.13}$$

Furthermore, using (9.1.5) and (9.1.11) gives

$$\text{Cov}(\mathbf{u}_i) = E(\mathbf{u}_i'\mathbf{u}_i) = \mathbf{\Gamma}^{-1\prime}E(\boldsymbol{\varepsilon}_i'\,\boldsymbol{\varepsilon}_i)\,\mathbf{\Gamma}^{-1} = \mathbf{\Gamma}^{-1\prime}\mathbf{\Sigma}\mathbf{\Gamma}^{-1} = \mathbf{\Omega}, \qquad \text{all } i. \tag{9.1.14}$$

Here $\mathbf{\Omega}$ is the covariance matrix of $\mathbf{u}_i$. Since $\mathbf{\Sigma}$ is a symmetric and positive-definite matrix, $\mathbf{\Omega}$ is also. From the last equality in (9.1.14) it follows by premultiplying by $\mathbf{\Gamma}'$ and post-multiplying by $\mathbf{\Gamma}$ that

$$\mathbf{\Sigma} = \mathbf{\Gamma}'\mathbf{\Omega}\mathbf{\Gamma}, \tag{9.1.15}$$

showing the relation between the covariance matrix of the structural form $\mathbf{\Sigma}$ and that of the reduced form $\mathbf{\Omega}$. From (9.1.6) and (9.1.11)

$$E(\mathbf{u}_i'\mathbf{u}_j) = \mathbf{0}, \qquad \text{all } i, j, \quad i \neq j, \tag{9.1.16}$$

so the $\mathbf{u}_i$, just as the $\boldsymbol{\varepsilon}_i$, are uncorrelated over the sample. Equations (9.1.12), (9.1.14), and (9.1.16) summarize the stochastic specification of the reduced-form equations. If it is further assumed that the structural equation stochastic disturbance terms are distributed normally, as in (9.1.7), it follows from (9.1.11) that

$$\mathbf{u}_i \sim \mathrm{N}(\mathbf{0}, \mathbf{\Omega}), \qquad *(9.1.17)$$

or, equivalently, from (9.1.9),

$$\mathbf{y}_i \sim \mathrm{N}(\mathbf{x}_i\mathbf{\Pi}, \mathbf{\Omega}). \qquad *(9.1.18)$$

The observations on the endogenous and predetermined variables for both the structural-form and the reduced-form equations can be summarized by the *data matrices*:

$$\underset{n\times g}{\mathbf{Y}} = \begin{pmatrix} \mathbf{y}_1 \\ \mathbf{y}_2 \\ \vdots \\ \mathbf{y}_n \end{pmatrix}, \qquad \underset{n\times k}{\mathbf{X}} = \begin{pmatrix} \mathbf{x}_1 \\ \mathbf{x}_2 \\ \vdots \\ \mathbf{x}_n \end{pmatrix}, \tag{9.1.19}$$

which generalize the data matrices introduced in (4.2.1) for a single equation. (These data matrices reduce to those of a single equation in (4.2.1) for the case $g = 1$, in which case the problems and methods of this part of the book, including this chapter and the next, reduce to those of estimating a single equation, as in Part II, particularly Chapter 4.) The data matrices can be written compactly as the *combined data matrix*:

$$\underset{n\times(g+k)}{(\mathbf{Y} \mid \mathbf{X})} = \begin{pmatrix} y_{11} & \cdots & y_{1g} & x_{11} & \cdots & x_{1k} \\ \vdots & & & \vdots & & \\ y_{n1} & \cdots & y_{ng} & x_{n1} & \cdots & x_{nk} \end{pmatrix}, \qquad *(9.1.20)$$

where each row gives data on all endogenous and predetermined variables at a particular observation point, and each column gives all data at every observation point on one variable of the system.

Each of the reduced-form equations (9.1.9) can be estimated as a single equation, as in Chapter 4. The coefficients of equation h, summarized by the hth column of the $\mathbf{\Pi}$ matrix,

$$\underset{k\times 1}{\mathbf{\Pi}_h} = \begin{pmatrix} \Pi_{1h} \\ \Pi_{2h} \\ \vdots \\ \Pi_{kh} \end{pmatrix}, \qquad h = 1, 2, \ldots, g, \tag{9.1.21}$$

can be estimated, using the least squares estimator (4.3.4) and the data in (9.1.19), as

$$\underset{k\times 1}{\hat{\Pi}_h} = \underset{k\times k}{(\mathbf{X}'\mathbf{X})^{-1}} \underset{k\times n}{\mathbf{X}'} \underset{n\times 1}{\begin{pmatrix} y_{1h} \\ y_{2h} \\ \vdots \\ y_{nh} \end{pmatrix}}, \tag{9.1.22}$$

where it is assumed that rank($\mathbf{X}$) = k, so $\mathbf{X}'\mathbf{X}$ is nonsingular. Lining up these g columns gives the entire matrix of reduced-form coefficients:

$$\hat{\Pi} = (\hat{\Pi}_1, \hat{\Pi}_2, \cdots, \hat{\Pi}_g) = (\mathbf{X}'\mathbf{X})^{-1}\mathbf{X}' \begin{pmatrix} y_{11} & y_{12} & \cdots & y_{1g} \\ y_{21} & y_{22} & & y_{2g} \\ \vdots & \vdots & & \vdots \\ y_{n1} & y_{n2} & \cdots & y_{ng} \end{pmatrix}. \tag{9.1.23}$$

Thus the set of all least squares estimators of the entire reduced-form system can be represented as[2]

$$\underset{k\times g}{\hat{\Pi}} = \underset{k\times k}{(\mathbf{X}'\mathbf{X})^{-1}} \underset{k\times n}{\mathbf{X}'} \underset{n\times g}{\mathbf{Y}}. \tag{*9.1.24}$$

Each column of this matrix, which summarizes all the estimated parameters in one of the reduced-form equations, can be written as the $(\mathbf{X}'\mathbf{X})^{-1}\mathbf{X}'$ matrix of weights times the column of the $\mathbf{Y}$ matrix corresponding to the dependent variable in that particular reduced-form equation. The estimators in (9.1.24) are the unique best linear unbiased and consistent estimators of the reduced form, since they represent least-squares estimators of each of the reduced-form equations and each of these equations satisfies the assumptions of both the Gauss–Markov theorem and the least-squares consistency theorem of Section 4.4.

The covariance matrix of the stochastic disturbance terms for the reduced-form equations $\mathbf{\Omega}$ can be estimated using the matrix generalization of the single-equation estimator in (4.4.4) as

$$\begin{aligned} \hat{\mathbf{\Omega}} &= \frac{1}{n-k}\hat{\mathbf{u}}'\hat{\mathbf{u}} = \frac{1}{n-k}(\mathbf{Y} - \mathbf{X}\hat{\Pi})'(\mathbf{Y} - \mathbf{X}\hat{\Pi}) \\ &= \frac{1}{n-k}\mathbf{Y}'[\mathbf{I} - \mathbf{X}(\mathbf{X}'\mathbf{X})^{-1}\mathbf{X}']\mathbf{Y}. \end{aligned} \tag{*9.1.25}$$

Here $\hat{\mathbf{u}}$ is the matrix of least squares residuals and $\mathbf{I} - \mathbf{X}(\mathbf{X}'\mathbf{X})^{-1}\mathbf{X}'$ is the fundamental idempotent matrix of least squares, as introduced in Section 4.3. This estimator is an unbiased and consistent estimator of $\mathbf{\Omega}$.[3]

[2]One might wonder whether it might be possible to use an estimate of the covariance matrix $\mathbf{\Omega}$ to improve the efficiency of the estimator of the reduced-form coefficients by applying generalized least squares for the system of equations, namely the technique of "seemingly unrelated equations," as discussed in Section 5.3. If, however, the explanatory variables are the same for all equations, as here, where $\mathbf{X}$ summarizes the data for the explanatory variables in each equation, then the technique of seemingly unrelated equations does not improve upon the technique of ordinary least squares applied to each equation separately, as summarized in (9.1.24) (see also Problems 5-L and 9-B). As noted in Problem 9-B, by stacking the stochastic disturbance terms as $\mathbf{u}^*$ in (5.3.16), assumptions (9.1.14) and (9.1.16) can be rewritten:

$$\underset{gn\times gn}{\mathrm{Cov}(\mathbf{u}^*)} = \underset{g\times g}{\mathbf{\Omega}} \otimes \underset{n\times n}{\mathbf{I}}.$$

In the single-equation case, where $g = 1$, this covariance matrix reduces to $\sigma^2\mathbf{I}$, as in A.4.2. (Do not confuse the $g \times g$ matrix $\mathbf{\Omega}$ here with the $n \times n$ matrix $\mathbf{\Omega}$ used in GLS in Section 5.3.)

[3]For an approach to the derivation of (9.1.25) [and also (9.1.24)], see Problem 9-B.

Under certain conditions, to be discussed in the next sections of this chapter, the least-squares estimators of the reduced-form parameters $\hat{\mathbf{\Pi}}$ and $\hat{\mathbf{\Omega}}$, given in (9.1.24) and (9.1.25), which summarize all the relevant information that can be obtained from the sample, can be used to estimate the structural-form parameters $\mathbf{\Gamma}$, $\mathbf{B}$, and $\mathbf{\Sigma}$. The specific techniques of estimation of the structural-form parameters are presented in Chapter 10.

One might wonder why the reduced-form equations were introduced at all. Why not estimate each of the structural form equations directly, using ordinary least squares?[4] This issue is treated in some detail in Chapter 10, but a brief answer is that such direct estimates are generally not only biased but also inconsistent, since the structural-form equations generally include explanatory endogenous variables, as shown in (9.1.3). By contrast, the estimators of structural-form parameters that are obtained from the reduced form using the techniques to be discussed in the next chapter are generally consistent estimators.

9.2 THE PROBLEM OF IDENTIFICATION[5]

The problem of identification is that of obtaining estimates of the parameters of the structural form (9.1.1), namely the coefficient matrices $\mathbf{\Gamma}$ and $\mathbf{B}$ and the covariance matrix $\mathbf{\Sigma}$ of (9.1.5), given estimates of the parameters of the reduced form (9.1.9), namely the coefficient matrix $\mathbf{\Pi}$ and the covariance matrix $\mathbf{\Omega}$ of (9.1.14). This problem can be studied prior to estimation; indeed, it was introduced in Section 2.10 before any discussion of estimation.

Since the reduced-form parameters summarize all relevant information available from the sample data, a structural equation is *identified* if and only if all parameters pertaining to it can be estimated given all the reduced-form parameters. Otherwise, it is *not identified*, in which case there is no way of calculating structural parameters from the reduced-form parameters. A system of structural equations, summarized by the structural form (9.1.1), is *identified* if and only if every equation of the system is identified; if any equation is not identified, then the system is *not identified.*

A structural equation that is identified is *just identified* (or *exactly identified*) if and only if there is a unique way of calculating its parameters from the reduced-form parameters. It is *overidentified* if there is more than one way to calculate its parameters from the reduced-form parameters, leading to restrictions on the reduced-form parameters.

To get a "feel" for the problem of identification one might simply count the numbers of "givens" and "unknowns." The givens are the reduced-form parameters, namely the gk elements of $\mathbf{\Pi}$ and the $g(g + 1)/2$ independent elements of $\mathbf{\Omega}$.[6] The total number of givens G is thus:

[4]The "ordinary" in "ordinary least squares" distinguishes this approach from other techniques of simultaneous-equations estimation, to be introduced in the next chapter, which also utilize the basic idea of least squares.

[5]See Section 2.10, Fisher (1966), and Schmidt (1976). It might be worthwhile to reread Section 2.10, which discusses the general nature of identification and presents some simple examples. For a more general discussion of the problem of identification, treated as that of drawing inferences from observed samples to an underlying theoretical structure, see Rothenberg (1971) and Bowden (1973). Another example of the identification problem is the errors-in-variables model (see Section 5.8, especially footnote 32).

[6]Since $\mathbf{\Omega}$ is a $g \times g$ symmetric matrix, it contains $g[(g + 1)/2]$ independent elements. For example,

$$\mathbf{\Omega} = \begin{pmatrix} \omega_{11} & \omega_{12} \\ \omega_{12} & \omega_{22} \end{pmatrix}$$

contains three independent elements.

$$G = gk + \frac{g(g+1)}{2}. \tag{9.2.1}$$

The unknowns are the structural-form parameters, namely the g^2 elements of $\mathbf{\Gamma}$, the gk elements of $\mathbf{B}$, and the $g(g + 1)/2$ independent elements of $\mathbf{\Sigma}$. Each of the equations can be normalized, however, such as in (9.1.2), accounting for g parameters. The total number of unknowns U is therefore:

$$U = g^2 + gk + \frac{g(g+1)}{2} - g. \tag{9.2.2}$$

There is thus an excess of unknowns over givens, amounting to:

$$U - G = g^2 - g = g(g-1). \tag{9.2.3}$$

This excess implies that without additional information it is impossible to estimate structural parameters from reduced-form parameters.[7]

To demonstrate more formally that the reduced-form parameters in general are not sufficient in and of themselves to estimate the structural parameters, consider a "bogus" system of false structural parameters. Assuming $\mathbf{\Gamma}$, $\mathbf{B}$, and $\mathbf{\Sigma}$ are matrices summarizing the *true* parameters of the structural form defined by (9.1.1) and (9.1.5), consider the "*bogus*" parameters obtained by postmultiplying the system by any $g \times g$ nonsingular matrix $\mathbf{R}$:

$$\mathbf{y}_i\mathbf{\Gamma R} + \mathbf{x}_i\mathbf{BR} = \boldsymbol{\varepsilon}_i\mathbf{R}. \tag{9.2.4}$$

This bogus system is normalized in the same way that the old one was—by choosing a specific numerical value for one of the nonzero parameters in each equation, as in (9.1.2). The stochastic assumptions on the bogus system, from (9.1.4) and (9.1.5), are

$$E(\boldsymbol{\varepsilon}_i\mathbf{R}) = \mathbf{0}, \qquad \text{all } i, \text{ and} \tag{9.2.5}$$

$$\text{Cov}(\boldsymbol{\varepsilon}_i\mathbf{R}) = E(\mathbf{R}'\boldsymbol{\varepsilon}_i\boldsymbol{\varepsilon}_i\mathbf{R}) = \mathbf{R}'\mathbf{\Sigma R}, \qquad \text{all } i. \tag{9.2.6}$$

The matrices summarizing the parameters of this bogus system are thus

$$\overline{\mathbf{\Gamma}} = \mathbf{\Gamma R}, \qquad \overline{\mathbf{B}} = \mathbf{BR}, \qquad \overline{\mathbf{\Sigma}} = \mathbf{R}'\mathbf{\Sigma R}. \tag{9.2.7}$$

The corresponding reduced-form parameters are given by $\overline{\mathbf{\Pi}}$ and $\overline{\mathbf{\Omega}}$, where, from (9.1.10) and (9.1.14):[8]

$$\overline{\mathbf{\Pi}} = -\overline{\mathbf{B}}\overline{\mathbf{\Gamma}}^{-1} = -\mathbf{BRR}^{-1}\mathbf{\Gamma}^{-1} = -\mathbf{B\Gamma}^{-1} = \mathbf{\Pi}, \tag{9.2.8}$$

$$\begin{aligned}\overline{\mathbf{\Omega}} &= \overline{\mathbf{\Gamma}}^{-1\prime}\overline{\mathbf{\Sigma}}\overline{\mathbf{\Gamma}}^{-1} = \mathbf{\Gamma}^{-1\prime}\mathbf{R}^{-1\prime}\mathbf{R}'\mathbf{\Sigma RR}^{-1}\mathbf{\Gamma}^{-1} \\ &= \mathbf{\Gamma}^{-1\prime}\mathbf{\Sigma\Gamma}^{-1} = \mathbf{\Omega}.\end{aligned} \tag{9.2.9}$$

The reduced-form parameters based on the bogus estimates are thus *identical* to those based on the true estimates. The true and bogus estimates are thus *observationally equivalent*, since they yield the same reduced form.[9] Multiplication by the $\mathbf{R}$ matrix combines elements of the various equations of the structural form in a way that is permissible in the sense that it leaves unchanged the reduced form for the system. It therefore follows that if the only

[7]Note that if $g = 1$ the problem disappears, since the single equation is already the reduced form.

[8]Use is made here of the result on matrices that, for two nonsingular matrices $\mathbf{C}$ and $\mathbf{D}$,

$$(\mathbf{CD})^{-1} = \mathbf{D}^{-1}\mathbf{C}^{-1}.$$

[9]More precisely, they are observationally equivalent in implying the same likelihood function for the observed values of the endogenous variables, given the values of the predetermined variables.

available information about the structural form is that of the reduced-form parameters $\mathbf{\Pi}$ and $\mathbf{\Omega}$, called *a posteriori information* and based on estimation of the reduced-form equations, then the system is not identified. In that case many different structural-form parameters, as given in (9.2.7) for alternative $\mathbf{R}$, are consistent with the information available, and it is impossible to distinguish the true parameters $\mathbf{\Gamma}$, $\mathbf{B}$, $\mathbf{\Sigma}$ from the bogus parameters $\bar{\mathbf{\Gamma}}$, $\bar{\mathbf{B}}$, $\bar{\mathbf{\Sigma}}$ in (9.2.7). Additional information about the structural form, obtained from relevant theory or the results of other studies, must be provided in order to restrict the possible values taken in the $\mathbf{R}$ matrix in (9.2.7) Since these restrictions are imposed prior to the estimation of the reduced form, they are called a priori restrictions, which convey *a priori information.*[10] By contrast the information in (9.1.10) and (9.1.14) is *a posteriori information.*

Having assumed that each equation has been normalized by choosing a specific numerical value for one of the nonzero parameters for this equation, such as in (9.1.2), this normalized system is identified if the only $\mathbf{R}$ matrix consistent with the a priori restrictions is the identity matrix:

$$\mathbf{R} = \mathbf{I} = \begin{pmatrix} 1 & & & 0 \\ & 1 & & \\ & & \ddots & \\ 0 & & & 1 \end{pmatrix}. \tag{9.2.10}$$

It is then possible to distinguish each structural equation from any other equation, there being enough information so that only one set of structural coefficients could produce the estimated reduced-form parameters. Without the a priori information, but with normalization, the number of free elements in $\mathbf{R}$ is $g^2 - g$, corresponding to the excess of the number of unknowns over the number of givens in (9.2.3). Identification is achieved by adding enough a priori information to eliminate the free elements from $\mathbf{R}$.

Identification is achieved by imposing a priori restrictions on the structural-form matrices $\mathbf{\Gamma}$, $\mathbf{B}$, $\mathbf{\Sigma}$. One approach to identification is to impose restrictions on the coefficient matrices $\mathbf{\Gamma}$ and $\mathbf{B}$. The most common way of doing so is by imposing zero restrictions, equating some elements of these matrices a priori to zero. This approach, treated in Section 9.3, is based on relevant theory or on other studies, which may suggest that certain variables do not appear in certain equations. More generally, the coefficients might be related to one another via various linear restrictions. An example of such a restriction is

$$\gamma_{11} = -\beta_{11}. \tag{9.2.11}$$

Such a restriction might occur in the prototype macro model equation for investment: under the accelerator hypothesis, the coefficient of lagged income would be the negative of that for current income, as in equation (2.6.4). Such restrictions (and zero restrictions) are treated in Section 9.4 as special cases of general linear restrictions on the coefficients.

The second approach to identification is through the imposition of restrictions on the covariance matrix $\mathbf{\Sigma}$. One way is with zero restrictions, where certain variances or covariances are assumed zero. A second way is with the relative sizes of variances or covariances.

[10]In general, a priori information includes all knowledge of the system prior to parameter estimation. It therefore includes information as to which variables are included, which of the variables are endogenous and which exogenous, the form of the model, and possibly specific information as to values of variables or covariances.

An example is an inequality restriction such as

$$\sigma_1^2 = \sigma_{11} << \sigma_{22} = \sigma_2^2, \tag{9.2.12}$$

which might occur in the prototype micro model if the variance of demand were much less than that of supply, as discussed in Section 7.6.

A third approach is some mixture of the above, where certain restrictions, equalities or inequalities, are imposed on $\mathbf{\Gamma}$, $\mathbf{B}$, and $\mathbf{\Sigma}$. An example treated in Section 9.5 is that of a recursive system, in which certain zero restrictions are imposed on both $\mathbf{\Gamma}$ and $\mathbf{\Sigma}$.[11]

9.3 IDENTIFICATION BY ZERO RESTRICTIONS IN THE NONSTOCHASTIC CASE

In the nonstochastic case, in which $\mathbf{\Sigma}$ and $\mathbf{\Omega}$ do not appear as part of the problem, the structural form is

$$\mathbf{y\Gamma} + \mathbf{xB} = \mathbf{0}, \tag{9.3.1}$$

and the reduced form is

$$\mathbf{y} = \mathbf{x\Pi}, \tag{9.3.2}$$

where the i subscript has been omitted. The relationships among the reduced-form parameters and structural-form parameters are summarized by

$$\mathbf{\Pi} = -\mathbf{B\Gamma}^{-1}. \tag*{*(9.3.3)}$$

The problem of identification is that of using a priori information contained in the specification to determine estimates of $\mathbf{\Gamma}$ and $\mathbf{B}$ from estimates of the reduced-form parameters, where the latter, $\mathbf{\Pi}$, represents the available a posteriori information. In the case of zero restrictions, the a priori information takes the form of zeros in the $\mathbf{\Gamma}$ and $\mathbf{B}$ coefficient matrices, representing, respectively, endogenous and predetermined variables omitted from certain equations.

Consider now, without loss of generality (since equations can be renumbered), the estimation of the first structural equation, which may be written:

$$(y_1 \quad y_2 \quad \cdots \quad y_g)\begin{pmatrix} \gamma_{11} \\ \gamma_{21} \\ \vdots \\ \gamma_{g_1 1} \\ 0 \\ 0 \\ \vdots \\ 0 \end{pmatrix} + (x_1 \quad x_2 \quad \cdots \quad x_k)\begin{pmatrix} \beta_{11} \\ \beta_{21} \\ \vdots \\ \beta_{k_1 1} \\ 0 \\ 0 \\ \vdots \\ 0 \end{pmatrix} = 0. \tag{9.3.4}$$

Here only the first columns of the $\mathbf{\Gamma}$ and $\mathbf{B}$ matrices are indicated, corresponding to the first equation to be estimated. It is assumed that there may be zeros in both columns, and the order of the variables has been changed (that is, variables have been renumbered) so that any zeros come at the end of each of the two column vectors of parameters. In particular, of the g endogenous variables, it is assumed that only g_1 enter the first equation. The re-

[11]See Fisher (1966), Rothenberg (1971), and Hsiao (1983) for discussions of a more general treatment of the case in which restrictions are imposed on both coefficients and covariances.

maining $g - g_1$ endogenous variables which are omitted from the equation are placed last in the row vector $(y_1 \quad y_2 \quad \cdots \quad y_g)$, so the first column of the $\mathbf{\Gamma}$ matrix ends in $g - g_1$ zeros, as shown in (9.3.4). Similarly, of the k predetermined variables it is assumed that only the first k_1 enter the first equation. The remaining predetermined variables are placed last in the vector $(x_1 \quad x_2 \quad \cdots \quad x_k)$, so the first column of the $\mathbf{B}$ matrix ends in $k - k_1$ zeros, as shown. The first equation (9.3.4) can thus be written

$$\left(\gamma_{11}y_1 + \gamma_{21}y_2 + \cdots + \gamma_{g_1 1}y_{g_1}\right) + \left(\beta_{11}x_1 + \beta_{21}x_2 + \cdots + \beta_{k_1 1}x_{k_1}\right) = 0. \qquad (9.3.5)$$

Now consider the matrix equation (9.3.3), which can be written, by postmultiplying by the $\mathbf{\Gamma}$ matrix, as

$$\mathbf{\Pi\Gamma} = -\mathbf{B}. \qquad (9.3.6)$$

Considering only the first columns of $\mathbf{\Gamma}$ and $\mathbf{B}$, corresponding to the first equation of the structural form, and noting the zero values as above, the $\mathbf{\Pi}$ matrix can be partitioned so that this first equation can be represented as

$$\begin{array}{c} k_1 \\ k - k_1 \end{array} \left(\begin{array}{c|c} \mathbf{\Pi}_1 & \mathbf{\Pi}_3 \\ \hline \mathbf{\Pi}_2 & \mathbf{\Pi}_4 \end{array}\right) \begin{pmatrix} \gamma_{11} \\ \vdots \\ \gamma_{g_1 1} \\ \hline 0 \\ \vdots \\ 0 \end{pmatrix} = - \begin{pmatrix} \beta_{11} \\ \vdots \\ \beta_{k_1 1} \\ \hline 0 \\ \vdots \\ 0 \end{pmatrix}, \qquad (9.3.7)$$
$$\qquad\qquad g_1 \qquad g - g_1$$

where $\mathbf{\Pi}_1, \ldots, \mathbf{\Pi}_4$ are submatrices of $\mathbf{\Pi}$ corresponding to the variables included in and excluded from the first equation. The submatrix $\mathbf{\Pi}_2$, for example, is a $(k - k_1) \times g_1$ matrix. Performing the matrix multiplications leads to the two sets of equations:

$$\underset{k_1 \times g_1}{\mathbf{\Pi}_1} \begin{pmatrix} \gamma_{11} \\ \vdots \\ \gamma_{g_1 1} \end{pmatrix} = - \begin{pmatrix} \beta_{11} \\ \vdots \\ \beta_{k_1 1} \end{pmatrix} \qquad (k_1 \text{ equations}) \qquad *(9.3.8)$$

$$\mathbf{\Pi}_2 \begin{pmatrix} \gamma_{11} \\ \vdots \\ \gamma_{g_1 1} \end{pmatrix} = 0 \qquad (k - k_1 \text{ equations}). \qquad *(9.3.9)$$

The problem of identification in this case is that of solving these equations simultaneously for the γ's and β's, given estimates of $\mathbf{\Pi}$. If, however, (9.3.9) can be solved for the γ's, then these estimates can be inserted in (9.3.8) to obtain the β's.[12] The problem thus reduces to that of solving (9.3.9) for the γ's, or, more precisely, for γ's that are unique after normalization. Multiplying both sides of (9.3.9) by a constant, say λ, does not change the equality, but will multiply the γ's by λ. Since λ can be any nonzero number, the γ's are normalized by setting one of them equal to a fixed number, usually 1 or –1, as in (9.1.2).

The system in (9.3.9) is a homogeneous system of $k - k_1$ linear equations in g_1 unknowns. This system has a nontrivial solution that is unique after normalization if and only if the coefficient matrix satisfies the rank condition

$$\text{rank}\,(\mathbf{\Pi}_2) = g_1 - 1, \qquad *(9.3.10)$$

[12]See (9.3.19) to (9.3.24) for details.

that is, the lower left submatrix in (9.3.7) has rank equal to the number of included endogenous variables, less one.[13] This condition is known as the *rank condition of identification.* It is necessary and sufficient for identification of the first equation, and, if it holds, there exist solutions for $\gamma_{11}, \ldots, \gamma_{g_1 1}$ that are unique after normalization. Since $\mathbf{\Pi}_2$ is a $(k - k_1) \times g_1$ matrix, for the rank condition to be satisfied it is necessary that[14]

$$k - k_1 \geqslant g_1 - 1, \qquad *(9.3.11)$$

that is, the number of *excluded* predetermined variables must be at least the number of *included* endogenous variables, less one. This condition, known as the *order condition of identification*, is necessary but not sufficient for identification. Since the order condition is easy to check—it just involves counting zeros in the relevant columns of the $\mathbf{\Gamma}$ and $\mathbf{B}$ matrices—it is usually checked first. If the order condition is not met, then the equation is *underidentified.* If the equation is identified and the order condition is met exactly, then the equation is *just identified*, while if it is met as a strict inequality, the equation is *overidentified.* Thus the equation must fall in one of the following four categories:

$$\left.\begin{array}{l}\text{overidentified}\\ \text{just identified}\\ \text{underidentified}\\ \text{unidentified}\end{array}\right\} \text{ if } \begin{cases}\text{rank}(\mathbf{\Pi}_2) = g_1 - 1 \text{ and } k - k_1 > g_1 - 1\\ \text{rank}(\mathbf{\Pi}_2) = g_1 - 1 \text{ and } k - k_1 = g_1 - 1\\ \qquad\qquad\qquad\qquad k - k_1 < g_1 - 1\\ \text{rank}(\mathbf{\Pi}_2) < g_1 - 1 \text{ and } k - k_1 \geqslant g_1 - 1.\end{cases} \qquad (9.3.12)$$

An underidentified equation cannot be identified, since then the $\mathbf{\Pi}_2$ matrix has too few rows to satisfy the rank condition. If $k - k_1 \geqslant g_1 - 1$, satisfying the order condition, the equation might nevertheless not be identified, since the order condition is necessary but not sufficient. The basic condition is the rank condition, which is both necessary and sufficient for identification.

The rank condition can be stated in a form that is more convenient to use than (9.3.10). Let $\mathbf{A}$ be the matrix of all structural coefficients defined as:

$$\underset{(g+k)\times g}{\mathbf{A}} = \begin{pmatrix}\mathbf{\Gamma}\\ \hline \mathbf{B}\end{pmatrix} = \left(\begin{array}{c|c}\gamma_{11} & \\ \vdots & \mathbf{\Gamma}_0\\ \gamma_{g_1 1} & \\ \hline \mathbf{0} & \mathbf{\Gamma}_1\\ \hline \beta_{11} & \\ \vdots & \mathbf{B}_0\\ \beta_{k_1 1} & \\ \hline \mathbf{0} & \mathbf{B}_1\end{array}\right)\begin{array}{l}g_1\\ \\ g - g_1\\ \\ k_1\\ \\ k - k_1\end{array} \qquad (9.3.13)$$

$$\qquad\qquad 1 \qquad g - 1$$

[13]Note that (9.3.9) is a system of $k - k_1$ linear homogeneous equations in g_1 unknowns, namely $\gamma_{11}, \ldots, \gamma_{g_1 1}$. If the matrix of coefficients $\mathbf{\Pi}_2$ has rank g_1, the only solution would be the trivial solution where $\gamma_{11} = \gamma_{21} = \cdots = \gamma_{g_1 1} = 0$. If the rank were less than $g_1 - 1$, then there would be an infinite number of nontrivial solutions after normalization. It is only when the rank is $g_1 - 1$ that there exist solutions that are unique after normalization. For further discussion, see Section B.6 of Appendix B.

[14]Recall that if $\mathbf{A}$ is an $m \times n$ matrix, then rank $(\mathbf{A}) \leqslant \min(m, n)$, since rank($\mathbf{A}$) is the size of the largest nonvanishing determinant in $\mathbf{A}$. For further discussion, see Section B.4 of Appendix B.

where $\boldsymbol{\Gamma}_0$, $\boldsymbol{\Gamma}_1$, $\mathbf{B}_0$, and $\mathbf{B}_1$ are submatrices forming the last $g - 1$ columns of $\boldsymbol{\Gamma}$ and $\mathbf{B}$. The condition (9.3.10) is equivalent to the condition that:

$$\text{rank}\begin{pmatrix} \boldsymbol{\Gamma}_1 \\ --- \\ \mathbf{B}_1 \end{pmatrix} = g - 1, \qquad *(9.3.14)$$

that is, that the matrix of coefficients in the *other* equations that multiply variables *excluded* from the first equation have rank $g - 1$.[15]

This condition is a convenient one to use since it does not require the computation of the inverse matrix $\boldsymbol{\Gamma}^{-1}$ that is used to calculate $\boldsymbol{\Pi}$. To check this condition, all that is required is to write down the **A** matrix of all coefficients in the structural form, cross out rows in which there are nonzero entries in the first column, strike out the first column itself, and check the rank of the resulting matrix. The necessary and sufficient *rank condition of identification* is that the rank of the remaining matrix be one less than the number of endogenous variables in the *system*. The corresponding *order condition of identification* is:

$$(g - g_1) + (k - k_1) \geqslant g - 1, \qquad *(9.3.15)$$

[15]To prove the equivalence of the two rank conditions (9.3.10) and (9.3.14), note that from (9.3.3) and the definition of **A** in (9.3.13) that:

$$\mathbf{A}\boldsymbol{\Gamma}^{-1} = \begin{pmatrix} \mathbf{I} & | & \mathbf{0} \\ --- & | & --- \\ \mathbf{0} & | & \mathbf{I} \\ --- & | & --- \\ -\boldsymbol{\Pi}_1 & | & -\boldsymbol{\Pi}_3 \\ --- & | & --- \\ -\boldsymbol{\Pi}_2 & | & -\boldsymbol{\Pi}_4 \end{pmatrix},$$

where the **I**'s are identity matrices. Define $\overline{\mathbf{A}}$ as the $[(g - g_1) + (k - k_1)] \times g$ matrix:

$$\overline{\mathbf{A}} = \begin{pmatrix} \mathbf{0} & | & \boldsymbol{\Gamma}_1 \\ -- & | & -- \\ \mathbf{0} & | & \mathbf{B}_1 \end{pmatrix},$$

so that

$$\overline{\mathbf{A}}\boldsymbol{\Gamma}^{-1} = \begin{pmatrix} \mathbf{0} & | & \mathbf{I} \\ --- & | & --- \\ -\boldsymbol{\Pi}_2 & | & -\boldsymbol{\Pi}_4 \end{pmatrix},$$

and defining $\overline{\boldsymbol{\Pi}}$ as the square nonsingular matrix of order $(g - g_1) + (k - k_1)$:

$$\overline{\boldsymbol{\Pi}} = \begin{pmatrix} \mathbf{I} & | & \mathbf{0} \\ --- & | & --- \\ -\boldsymbol{\Pi}_4 & | & -\mathbf{I} \end{pmatrix},$$

it follows that:

$$\overline{\boldsymbol{\Pi}}\,\overline{\mathbf{A}}\boldsymbol{\Gamma}^{-1} = \begin{pmatrix} \mathbf{0} & | & \mathbf{I} \\ -- & | & -- \\ \boldsymbol{\Pi}_2 & | & \mathbf{0} \end{pmatrix}.$$

But the rank of **A** is unchanged by premultiplying and postmultiplying by nonsingular matrices. Thus

since the matrix in (9.3.14) has $(g - g_1) + (k - k_1)$ rows. This condition requires for identification that the total number of variables excluded from the equation must be at least as great as the total number of endogenous variables of the system less one.[16] Clearly, some variables must be excluded; excluding no variables leads to an unidentified equation (assuming $g > 1$). If the equation is identified, then the structural coefficients of the equation can be obtained as functions of the reduced-form coefficients, and if each of the equations of the structural form is identified, then the system is identified.

A simple example of the theory of identification is the prototype micro model (2.5.8). In this case,

$$\mathbf{A} = \begin{pmatrix} 1 & 1 \\ -\gamma_1 & -\gamma_2 \\ \hline -\beta_1 & 0 \\ 0 & -\beta_2 \\ -\delta_1 & -\delta_2 \end{pmatrix}, \tag{9.3.16}$$

where the two columns summarize the two equations of the model. Checking the order condition (9.3.11), both equations are just identified, since in each $k - k_1 = 1 = g_1 - 1$. Equivalently, for each equation $(k - k_1) + (g - g_1) = 1 = g - 1$. According to the rank condition (9.3.14), the first equation, that for demand, is identified if and only if, striking rows in which there are nonzero elements in the first column and then striking the first column itself,

$$\text{rank}\begin{pmatrix} \mathbf{\Gamma}_1 \\ \hline \mathbf{B}_1 \end{pmatrix} = \text{rank}\begin{pmatrix} \not{1} & \not{1} \\ \not{\gamma_1} & \not{-\gamma_2} \\ \not{\beta_1} & \not{0} \\ 0 & -\beta_2 \\ \not{\delta_1} & \not{-\delta_2} \end{pmatrix} = \text{rank}\,(-\beta_2) = 1, \tag{9.3.17}$$

that is, $\beta_2 \neq 0$. If $\beta_2 \neq 0$, there is a variable in the system of equations that does *not* enter the demand equation, namely rainfall. Similarly, the second equation is identified if and only if $\beta_1 \neq 0$, implying that there is a variable in the system, I, that is excluded from the supply equation. For this model, then, since each equation is just identified, there exist unique estimates of the structural parameters in terms of the estimated reduced-form parameters.

$$\text{rank}\,(\bar{\mathbf{A}}) = \text{rank}\,(\bar{\mathbf{\Pi}}\,\bar{\mathbf{A}}\,\mathbf{\Gamma}^{-1}) = (g - g_1) + \text{rank}\,(\mathbf{\Pi}_2).$$

Furthermore, from the definition of $\bar{\mathbf{A}}$,

$$\text{rank}\begin{pmatrix} \mathbf{\Gamma}_1 \\ \hline \mathbf{B}_1 \end{pmatrix} = \text{rank}\,(\bar{\mathbf{A}}) = (g - g_1) + \text{rank}\,(\mathbf{\Pi}_2).$$

Thus

$$\text{rank}\begin{pmatrix} \mathbf{\Gamma}_1 \\ \hline \mathbf{B}_1 \end{pmatrix} = g - 1 \quad \text{if and only if} \quad \text{rank}\,(\mathbf{\Pi}_2) = g_1 - 1,$$

proving the equivalence of the two conditions.

[16]Condition (9.3.15) can be obtained from (9.3.11) by adding $g - g_1$ to both sides of the inequality.

These estimates are given in (2.10.5), and, in general, if a model is just identified, each structural coefficient can be obtained from the reduced-form coefficients by algebraic manipulations such as those in (2.10.5).

In the just-identified case, such as that of the prototype micro model, by normalizing on the first element of the (first) column of the $\mathbf{\Gamma}$ matrix by setting $\gamma_{11} = -1$, as in (9.1.2), the first equation can be written:

$$y_1 = \left(\gamma_{21}y_2 + \gamma_{31}y_3 + \cdots + \gamma_{g_1 1}y_{g_1}\right) + \left(\beta_{11}x_1 + \beta_{21}x_2 + \cdots + \beta_{k_1 1}x_{k_1}\right). \tag{9.3.18}$$

Here the parentheses show the dependence of the first endogenous variable on the remaining $g_1 - 1$ included explanatory endogenous variables and the k_1 included predetermined variables. With this normalization equations (9.3.8) and (9.3.9) can be written:

$$\left(\underset{k_1\times 1}{\mathbf{\Pi}_1^0} \;\vdots\; \underset{k_1\times(g_1-1)}{\mathbf{\Pi}_1^{00}}\right)\begin{pmatrix} -1 \\ --- \\ \boldsymbol{\gamma}_1 \end{pmatrix} = -\boldsymbol{\beta}_1, \tag{*(9.3.19)}$$

$$\left(\underset{(k-k_1)\times 1}{\mathbf{\Pi}_2^0} \;\vdots\; \underset{(k-k_1)\times(g_1-1)}{\mathbf{\Pi}_2^{00}}\right)\begin{pmatrix} -1 \\ --- \\ \boldsymbol{\gamma}_1 \end{pmatrix} = \mathbf{0}, \tag{*(9.3.20)}$$

where $\boldsymbol{\gamma}_1 = (\gamma_{21} \quad \gamma_{31} \quad \cdots \quad \gamma_{g_1 1})'$ is the column vector of the remaining $g_1 - 1$ coefficients of endogenous variables and $\boldsymbol{\beta}_1 = (\beta_1 \quad \beta_{21} \quad \cdots \quad \beta_{k_1 1})'$ is the column vector of the k_1 coefficients of predetermined variables. Here $\mathbf{\Pi}_1^0$ and $\mathbf{\Pi}_2^0$ are simply the first column vectors of $\mathbf{\Pi}_1$ and $\mathbf{\Pi}_2$, respectively, while $\mathbf{\Pi}_1^{00}$ and $\mathbf{\Pi}_2^{00}$ are the matrices of remaining columns of $\mathbf{\Pi}_1$ and $\mathbf{\Pi}_2$, respectively. Carrying out the multiplications yields:

$$-\mathbf{\Pi}_1^0 + \mathbf{\Pi}_1^{00}\gamma_1 = -\boldsymbol{\beta}_1, \tag{9.3.21}$$

$$-\mathbf{\Pi}_2^0 + \mathbf{\Pi}_2^{00}\gamma_1 = \mathbf{0}. \tag{9.3.22}$$

Solving for $\boldsymbol{\gamma}_1$ from (9.3.22) and noting that $\mathbf{\Pi}_2^{00}$ is a square matrix, since it was assumed that this is the just-identified case, where $k - k_1 = g_1 - 1$—yields the estimator for $\boldsymbol{\gamma}_1$:

$$\hat{\boldsymbol{\gamma}}_1 = \left(\hat{\mathbf{\Pi}}_2^{00}\right)^{-1}\hat{\mathbf{\Pi}}_2^0, \tag{*(9.3.23)}$$

where $\mathbf{\Pi}_2^{00}$ and $\mathbf{\Pi}_2^0$ have been replaced by their estimated values. From (9.3.21) it then follows that the estimator for $\boldsymbol{\beta}_1$ is:

$$\hat{\boldsymbol{\beta}}_1 = \hat{\mathbf{\Pi}}_1^0 - \hat{\mathbf{\Pi}}_1^{00}\left(\hat{\mathbf{\Pi}}_2^{00}\right)^{-1}\hat{\mathbf{\Pi}}_2^0, \tag{*(9.3.24)}$$

where $\hat{\mathbf{\Pi}}_1^0, \hat{\mathbf{\Pi}}_1^{00}, \hat{\mathbf{\Pi}}_2^0, \hat{\mathbf{\Pi}}_2^{00}$ are all submatrices of $\hat{\mathbf{\Pi}}$ in (9.1.24). These results, called the *indirect least squares estimators*, indicate the general relationships among the estimated structural coefficients $\hat{\boldsymbol{\gamma}}_1$ and $\hat{\boldsymbol{\beta}}_1$ and the estimated reduced-form coefficients $\hat{\mathbf{\Pi}}$. The prototype micro model illustrates this case, where (2.10.5) indicates the form taken by these relationships.

To summarize, the necessary and sufficient condition for identification of a single equation in this nonstochastic case is the rank condition (9.3.10) or, equivalently, (9.3.14). The order condition (9.3.11) or, equivalently, (9.3.15) is necessary but not sufficient for identification. If an equation is just identified (i.e., identified and meeting the order condition exactly), it is possible to solve uniquely for its structural coefficients as functions of the reduced-form coefficients, yielding indirect least squares estimators, as in (9.3.23) and (9.3.24).

9.4 IDENTIFICATION BY GENERAL LINEAR RESTRICTIONS[17]

General linear restrictions on the coefficient matrices $\mathbf{\Gamma}$ and $\mathbf{B}$ include, as special cases, zero restrictions, as developed in Section 9.3, and equality restrictions, such as (9.2.11). It will be assumed, however, that the covariance matrix $\mathbf{\Sigma}$ is unrestricted. A somewhat more compact notation will facilitate the development of identification by general linear restrictions. This notation uses the $\mathbf{A}$ matrix of all coefficients of the structural form, as in (9.3.13):

$$\underset{(g+k)\times g}{\mathbf{A}} = \begin{pmatrix} \mathbf{\Gamma} \\ --- \\ \mathbf{B} \end{pmatrix} = (\mathbf{a}_1 \; \mathbf{a}_2 \; \cdots \; \mathbf{a}_g) = \begin{pmatrix} \gamma_{11} & \gamma_{12} & \cdots & \gamma_{1g} \\ \vdots & \vdots & & \vdots \\ \gamma_{g1} & \gamma_{g2} & \cdots & \gamma_{gg} \\ \hline \beta_{11} & \beta_{12} & \cdots & \beta_{1g} \\ \vdots & \vdots & & \vdots \\ \beta_{k1} & \beta_{k2} & \cdots & \beta_{kg} \end{pmatrix}. \tag{9.4.1}$$

Here $\mathbf{a}_h$ is the hth column vector of $\mathbf{A}$, summarizing all the coefficients in equation h, for $h = 1, 2, \ldots, g$, where

$$\mathbf{a}_h = (\gamma_{1h} \; \gamma_{2h} \; \cdots \; \gamma_{gh} \mid \beta_{1h} \; \cdots \; \beta_{kh})'.$$

In this notation the structural form can be written:

$$(\mathbf{y}_i \mid \mathbf{x}_i)\mathbf{A} = (\mathbf{y}_i \mid \mathbf{x}_i)\begin{pmatrix} \mathbf{\Gamma} \\ --- \\ \mathbf{B} \end{pmatrix} = \varepsilon_i, \qquad i = 1, 2, \ldots, n, \tag{9.4.2}$$

and the hth equation of the structural form can be written:

$$(\mathbf{y}_i \mid \mathbf{x}_i)\mathbf{a}_h = \boldsymbol{\varepsilon}_{hi}, \qquad h = 1, 2, \ldots, g. \tag{9.4.3}$$

This notation has already been used in (9.1.20), where data on the $g + k$ variables in (9.4.2) are summarized by an $n \times (g + k)$ matrix.

The a priori information on the hth equation of the system can be summarized as:

$$\underset{r_h\times(g+k)}{\mathbf{\Phi}_h} \; \underset{(g+k)\times 1}{\mathbf{a}_h} = \underset{r_h\times 1}{\mathbf{0}}, \tag*{*(9.4.4)}$$

that is,

$$\begin{pmatrix} \varphi_{h11} & \varphi_{h12} & \cdots & \varphi_{h1,g+k} \\ \varphi_{h21} & \varphi_{h22} & \cdots & \varphi_{h2,g+k} \\ \vdots & & & \\ \varphi_{hr_h1} & \varphi_{hr_h2} & \cdots & \varphi_{hr_h,g+k} \end{pmatrix} \begin{pmatrix} \gamma_{1h} \\ \vdots \\ \gamma_{gh} \\ --- \\ \beta_{1h} \\ \vdots \\ \beta_{kh} \end{pmatrix} = \begin{pmatrix} 0 \\ \vdots \\ 0 \end{pmatrix},$$

where $\mathbf{\Phi}_h$ is a given matrix. Each row of $\mathbf{\Phi}_h$ implies one linear restriction on $\mathbf{a}_h$, and the $\mathbf{r}_h$ rows of this matrix summarize all such a priori restrictions on the hth structural equation.

[17]See Fisher (1966) and Hsiao (1983).

If, for example, one row of $\mathbf{\Phi}_h$ were $(0 \quad 1 \quad 0 \quad \cdots \quad 0)$, it would impose the restriction that $\gamma_{2h} = 0$, and, in general, rows of $\mathbf{\Phi}_h$ that are unit vectors impose zero restrictions on the equation, requiring that certain variables be excluded from this equation. If, however, $g = 2$ and one row of $\mathbf{\Phi}_1$ were $(1 \quad 0 \quad 1 \quad 0 \quad \cdots \quad 0)$, it would impose the restriction that $\gamma_{11} = -\beta_{11}$, as in (9.2.11). Any linear equality restriction can be expressed in this way, and equation (9.4.4) imposes r_h such restrictions on the hth equation. [An example will be presented following equation (9.4.17).]

The a posteriori information on the system, of the form:

$$\mathbf{\Pi} = -\mathbf{B}\mathbf{\Gamma}^{-1} \tag{9.4.5}$$

can be written

$$\mathbf{\Pi}\mathbf{\Gamma} + \mathbf{B} = \mathbf{0}. \tag{9.4.6}$$

Thus, defining $\mathbf{W}$ as the partitioned coefficient matrix and identity matrix

$$\underset{k\times(g+k)}{\mathbf{W}} = (\underset{k\times g}{\mathbf{\Pi}} \mid \underset{k\times k}{\mathbf{I}}) \quad \text{where} \quad \text{rank}(\mathbf{W}) = k, \tag{9.4.7}$$

all a posteriori information can be summarized by the equation

$$\mathbf{W}\mathbf{A} = \mathbf{0}. \tag{9.4.8}$$

This equation states that

$$\mathbf{W}\mathbf{A} = (\mathbf{\Pi} \mid \mathbf{I})\begin{pmatrix} \mathbf{\Gamma} \\ --- \\ \mathbf{B} \end{pmatrix} = \mathbf{\Pi}\mathbf{\Gamma} + \mathbf{B} = \mathbf{0}. \tag{9.4.9}$$

In particular, for the hth equation the a posteriori information is summarized by the k restrictions in $g + k$ unknowns:

$$\underset{k\times(g+k)}{\mathbf{W}} \; \underset{(g+k)\times 1}{\mathbf{a}_h} = \mathbf{0} \tag*{*(9.4.10)}$$

This equation summarizes all k restrictions on the coefficients of the hth equation obtained from the a posteriori information of the reduced form.

The a priori restrictions (9.4.4) and the a posteriori restrictions (9.4.10) for each equation can be combined in the single system of homogeneous equations:

$$\underset{(r_h+k)\times(g+k)}{\begin{pmatrix} \mathbf{\Phi}_h \\ --- \\ \mathbf{W} \end{pmatrix}} \quad \underset{(g+k)\times 1}{\mathbf{a}_h} \quad = \quad \underset{(r_h+k)\times 1}{\mathbf{0}}, \qquad h = 1, 2, \ldots, g, \tag*{*(9.4.11)}$$

which summarizes all $r_h + k$ restrictions on the hth equation. The equation is *identified* if this system of $r_h + k$ homogeneous equations in $g + k$ unknowns has a nontrivial solution. A nontrivial solution that is unique after normalization exists, however, if and only if the matrix in (9.4.11) satisfies the *rank condition*:[18]

[18]To verify this condition, note that following the reasoning of footnote 13, (9.4.11) is a system of $r_h + k$ linear homogeneous equations in $g + k$ unknowns, namely the elements of $\mathbf{a}_h$. If the matrix of coefficients had rank $g + k$, the only solution would be the trivial solution $\mathbf{a}_h = \mathbf{0}$. If the rank were less than $g + k - 1$, there would be an infinite number of nontrivial solutions after normalization. It is only when the rank is $g + k - 1$ that there exist solutions for the elements of $\mathbf{a}_h$ that are unique after normalization.

$$\text{rank}\begin{pmatrix} \mathbf{\Phi}_h \\ --- \\ \mathbf{W} \end{pmatrix} = g + k - 1. \qquad *(9.4.12)$$

A condition that is equivalent to (9.4.12) is the *general rank condition of identification*:[19]

$$\underset{r_h \times g}{\text{rank}\,(\mathbf{\Phi}_h \mathbf{A})} = g - 1. \qquad *(9.4.13)$$

This is a necessary and sufficient condition for the identification of the hth equation that is preferred to (9.4.12) because it does not involve $\mathbf{W}$, making unnecessary the inversion of $\mathbf{\Gamma}$ to determine the $\mathbf{\Pi}$ in $\mathbf{W}$. From (9.4.13) and the fact that multiplying a matrix by another cannot increase its rank, it follows that a necessary condition of identification is

$$\text{rank}\,(\mathbf{\Phi}_h) \geqslant g - 1, \qquad *(9.4.14)$$

which is the *general order condition of identification*. It is called an "order" condition even though it involves the rank of a matrix, and it is necessary, but not sufficient for identification. Since it depends only on $\mathbf{\Phi}_h$, it is easy to check. This order condition generalizes the condition (9.3.15), and it is used to define overidentified, just-identified, and underidentified equations. Thus, following the categories in (9.3.12), equation h is:

[19]Fisher (1966) has shown the equivalence of the two rank conditions using the concept of *column kernel*, defined as the set of column vectors transformed into the zero vector by the matrix. Thus the column kernel of the matrix $\mathbf{M}$ is the set of all column vectors $\mathbf{z}$ satisfying $\mathbf{Mz} = \mathbf{0}$. In the problem at hand, letting $\mathbf{\Psi}_h$ be:

$$\begin{pmatrix} \mathbf{\Phi}_h \\ --- \\ \mathbf{W} \end{pmatrix},$$

suppose that rank$(\mathbf{\Psi}_h) = g + k - 1$, but rank$(\mathbf{\Phi}_h\mathbf{A}) \neq g - 1$. The hth column of $\mathbf{\Phi}_h\mathbf{A}$ contains only zeros because of the a priori restrictions, (9.4.4), so rank$(\mathbf{\Phi}_h\mathbf{A}) < g - 1$. Thus there exist at least two independent column vectors in the column kernel of $\mathbf{\Phi}_h\mathbf{A}$. If these vectors are $\mathbf{v}$ and $\mathbf{w}$, then, by definition of the column kernel,

$$(\mathbf{\Phi}_h\mathbf{A})\mathbf{v} = \mathbf{0}, \qquad (\mathbf{\Phi}_h\mathbf{A})\mathbf{w} = \mathbf{0}.$$

Define

$$\tilde{\mathbf{v}} = \mathbf{Av}, \qquad \tilde{\mathbf{w}} = \mathbf{Aw}$$

where, since $\mathbf{v}$ and $\mathbf{w}$ are independent, so are $\tilde{\mathbf{v}}$ and $\tilde{\mathbf{w}}$ [assuming that rank$(\mathbf{A}) = g$]. But

$$\mathbf{\Phi}_h\tilde{\mathbf{v}} = \mathbf{\Phi}_h\mathbf{Av} = \mathbf{0}, \qquad \mathbf{\Phi}_h\tilde{\mathbf{w}} = \mathbf{\Phi}_h\mathbf{Aw} = \mathbf{0},$$

and since, from (9.4.8), $\mathbf{WA} = \mathbf{0}$,

$$\mathbf{W}\tilde{\mathbf{v}} = \mathbf{WAv} = \mathbf{0}, \qquad \mathbf{W}\tilde{\mathbf{w}} = \mathbf{WAw} = \mathbf{0}.$$

Thus

$$\mathbf{\Psi}_h\tilde{\mathbf{v}} = \mathbf{0}, \qquad \mathbf{\Psi}_h\tilde{\mathbf{w}} = \mathbf{0},$$

so there are at least two independent column vectors in the column kernel of $\mathbf{\Psi}_h$, implying that rank$(\mathbf{\Psi}_h) < g + k - 1$, a contradiction. Conversely, suppose that rank$(\mathbf{\Phi}_h\mathbf{A}) = g - 1$ but rank$(\mathbf{\Psi}_h) \neq g + k - 1$. Since, from (9.4.4) and (9.4.10), $\mathbf{\Psi}_h\mathbf{a}_h = \mathbf{0}$, it follows that rank$(\mathbf{\Psi}_h) < g + k - 1$, so there are at least two independent column vectors in the column kernel of $\mathbf{\Psi}_h$. Call them $\tilde{\mathbf{v}}$ and $\tilde{\mathbf{w}}$. From the definition of $\mathbf{\Psi}_h$ these vectors are in the column kernel of $\mathbf{w}$. But the columns of $\mathbf{A}$ form a basis for this column kernel, so there exist two independent vectors $\mathbf{v}$ and $\mathbf{w}$ such that

$$\tilde{\mathbf{v}} = \mathbf{Av}, \qquad \mathbf{w} = \mathbf{Aw}.$$

But

$$\mathbf{\Phi}_h\mathbf{Av} = \mathbf{\Phi}_h\tilde{\mathbf{v}} = \mathbf{0}, \qquad \mathbf{\Phi}_h\mathbf{Aw} = \mathbf{\Phi}_h\tilde{\mathbf{w}} = \mathbf{0},$$

where $\tilde{\mathbf{v}}$ and $\tilde{\mathbf{w}}$ are in the column kernel of $\mathbf{\Phi}_h$, since they are in the column kernel of $\mathbf{\Psi}_h$. Thus $\mathbf{v}$ and $\mathbf{w}$ are two independent vectors of the column kernel of $\mathbf{\Phi}_h\mathbf{A}$, implying that rank$(\mathbf{\Phi}_h\mathbf{A}) < g - 1$, a contradiction. Thus the equivalence of the two rank conditions is proved.

$$\begin{Bmatrix}\text{overidentified}\\ \text{just identified}\\ \text{underidentified}\\ \text{unidentified}\end{Bmatrix} \quad \text{if} \quad \begin{cases}\text{rank}(\boldsymbol{\Phi}_h\mathbf{A}) = g-1 \text{ and } \text{rank}(\boldsymbol{\Phi}_h) > g-1\\ \text{rank}(\boldsymbol{\Phi}_h\mathbf{A}) = g-1 \text{ and } \text{rank}(\boldsymbol{\Phi}_h) = g-1\\ \qquad\qquad\qquad\qquad\qquad\quad \text{rank}(\boldsymbol{\Phi}_h) < g-1\\ \text{rank}(\boldsymbol{\Phi}_h\mathbf{A}) < g-1 \text{ and } \text{rank}(\boldsymbol{\Phi}_h) \geqslant g-1.\end{cases} \tag{9.4.15}$$

A necessary condition for identification, which is necessary for the general order condition to be met, is:

$$r_h \geqslant g-1, \qquad *(9.4.16)$$

requiring that the number of linear restrictions imposed on each equation be at least the number of endogenous variables of the system, less one.[20] For example, in a system of two equations with two endogenous variables at least one linear restriction must be imposed on each equation for the system to be identified, as was illustrated in Section 2.10. If this condition is violated the equation is *underidentified* and therefore not identified. If there are no a priori restrictions, so $r_h = 0$, the equation can be identified only if $g = 1$, in which case the reduced form and the structural form are equivalent. This is the single-equation case treated earlier.

The rank and order conditions derived in Section 9.3 are special cases of (9.4.13) and (9.4.14), corresponding to the case in which the restrictions on coefficients are all zero restrictions. For example, (9.3.15), which states, as an order condition, that the total number of variables excluded from the equation (i.e., the total number of zero restrictions) must be no less than $g - 1$, is the special case of (9.4.14), in which all rows of $\boldsymbol{\Phi}_h$ are unit vectors, so

$$\text{rank}(\boldsymbol{\Phi}_h) = r_h = (g - g_h) + (k - k_h) \geqslant g - 1 \tag{9.4.17}$$

and $h = 1$, referring to the first equation.

An example should help clarify the nature of the general conditions of identification. Suppose that $g = 3$ and $k = 4$, so, in the normalized case,

$$\mathbf{A} = \begin{pmatrix} -1 & \gamma_{12} & \gamma_{13}\\ \gamma_{21} & -1 & \gamma_{23}\\ \gamma_{31} & \gamma & -1\\ \hline \beta_{11} & \beta_{12} & \beta_{13}\\ \beta_{21} & \beta_{22} & \beta_{23}\\ \beta_{31} & \beta_{32} & \beta_{33}\\ \beta_{41} & \beta_{42} & \beta_{43}\end{pmatrix}. \tag{9.4.18}$$

Assume that the a priori restrictions are given by

$$\gamma_{21} = \beta_{11} = \beta_{32} = \gamma_{23} = \beta_{23} = 0, \qquad \beta_{13} = \beta_{33}. \tag{9.4.19}$$

Considering now the first equation, involving coefficients summarized by the first $\mathbf{A}$ column vector $\mathbf{a}_1$, all a priori restrictions for this equation can be written in the form:

$$\boldsymbol{\Phi}_1\mathbf{a}_1 = \mathbf{0}, \tag{9.4.20}$$

[20]The reason for subtracting one here and earlier is that because of the homogeneity of the equation, subtracting less than one means structural estimators are not defined, while subtracting more than one means that the estimators are not unique after normalization (see footnotes 13 and 18).

where

$$\mathbf{\Phi}_1 = \begin{pmatrix} 0 & 1 & 0 & 0 & 0 & 0 & 0 \\ 0 & 0 & 0 & 1 & 0 & 0 & 0 \end{pmatrix}. \tag{9.4.21}$$

Since

$$\mathbf{\Phi}_1\mathbf{A} = \begin{pmatrix} \gamma_{21} & -1 & \gamma_{23} \\ \beta_{11} & \beta_{12} & \beta_{13} \end{pmatrix}, \tag{9.4.22}$$

it is clear, by inspection, that, barring special coincidences,

$$\operatorname{rank}(\mathbf{\Phi}_1) = 2 = g - 1, \qquad \operatorname{rank}(\mathbf{\Phi}_1\mathbf{A}) = 2. \tag{9.4.23}$$

Thus this equation is just identified. For the second equation,

$$\mathbf{\Phi}_2 = (0 \quad 0 \quad 0 \quad 0 \quad 0 \quad 1 \quad 0), \qquad \operatorname{rank}(\mathbf{\Phi}_2) = 1 < g - 1, \qquad r_2 = 1 < g - 1, \tag{9.4.24}$$

so this equation is underidentified and hence not identified.[21] For the third equation,

$$\mathbf{\Phi}_3 = \begin{pmatrix} 0 & 1 & 0 & 0 & 0 & 0 & 0 \\ 0 & 0 & 0 & 0 & 1 & 0 & 0 \\ 0 & 0 & 0 & 1 & 0 & -1 & 0 \end{pmatrix}, \qquad \operatorname{rank}(\mathbf{\Phi}_3) = 3, \qquad \operatorname{rank}(\mathbf{\Phi}_3\mathbf{A}) = 2, \tag{9.4.25}$$

so this equation is overidentified. Thus, in this example, the first equation can be estimated directly from the reduced form, which yields unique estimators of the structural coefficients of this equation; the second equation cannot be estimated from the reduced form; and the third equation can be estimated in more than one way from the reduced form. Because one equation is not identified, the system is not identified.

In any econometric project involving simultaneous equations the identification of the system is of crucial importance. If an equation is just identified, then it can be estimated from the least squares estimates of the reduced form, using the technique of indirect least squares. If an equation is overidentified, then there are several techniques that can be used in its estimation, as discussed in the next chapter. If, however, any equation is underidentified, then it cannot be estimated, and it is not possible to infer structural coefficients for this equation from reduced-form estimates. In such a case the system might be respecified to avoid underidentified equations. In general, ordinary least squares applied to just-identified or overidentified equations leads to biased and inconsistent estimators, while ordinary least squares applied to underidentified equations yields bogus estimators. The next section, however, summarizes one type of simultaneous-equations system for which ordinary least squares does provide estimators with desirable properties—the recursive system.

9.5 RECURSIVE SYSTEMS

An important type of simultaneous-equations system is the *recursive system*, in which the endogenous variables and the structural equations can be arranged in such an order that $\mathbf{\Gamma}$, the matrix of coefficients of endogenous variables, is a triangular matrix and $\mathbf{\Sigma}$, the matrix of variances and covariances of stochastic disturbance terms, is a diagonal matrix.[22] Thus in this case,

[21]Note that either test would be adequate to show that this equation is underidentified. It fails on both tests, each of which is necessary.

[22]See Wold (1954, 1960, 1964). In Wold's terminology a model that is not recursive is *interdependent*. He argues against such models both philosophically on the basis of a unilateral flow of causation and econometrically on the basis of the difficulties of estimation of interdependent models.

$$\mathbf{\Gamma} = \begin{pmatrix} \gamma_{11} & \gamma_{12} & \gamma_{13} & \cdots & \gamma_{1_g} \\ 0 & \gamma_{22} & \gamma_{23} & \cdots & \gamma_{2_g} \\ 0 & 0 & \gamma_{33} & \cdots & \gamma_{3_g} \\ \vdots & & & \ddots & \\ 0 & 0 & 0 & & \gamma_{gg} \end{pmatrix}, \qquad *(9.5.1)$$

$$\mathbf{\Sigma} = \begin{pmatrix} \sigma_1^2 & 0 & \cdots & 0 \\ 0 & \sigma_2^2 & & \\ \vdots & & \ddots & \\ 0 & & & \sigma_g^2 \end{pmatrix}. \qquad *(9.5.2)$$

The first set of conditions, on the coefficient matrix, requires that the structural equations can be expressed such that no equation includes those endogenous variables included in higher-numbered equations. The second set of conditions, on the covariance matrix, requires that all covariances between the stochastic disturbance terms in any two different equations vanish. It should be noted that the first set of conditions, on the coefficients, is not, by itself, adequate. The conditions on the covariances are also essential for the system to be recursive.

Under the assumptions (9.5.1) and (9.5.2) on a recursive system, the system of equations can then be written, using the usual normalization of diagonal elements, as

$$\begin{aligned} y_1 &= \sum_{j=1}^{k} \beta_{j1} x_j - \varepsilon_1, \\ y_2 &= \gamma_{12} y_1 + \sum_{j=1}^{k} \beta_{j2} x_j - \varepsilon_2, \\ y_3 &= \gamma_{13} y_1 + \gamma_{23} y_2 + \sum_{j=1}^{k} \beta_{j3} x_j - \varepsilon_3, \\ &\vdots \\ y_g &= \sum_{h=1}^{g-1} \gamma_{hg} y_h + \sum_{j=1}^{k} \beta_{jg} x_j - \varepsilon_g. \end{aligned} \qquad (9.5.3)$$

Thus each endogenous variable can be explained in terms of the predetermined variables, stochastic disturbance term, and *lower*-numbered endogenous variables. The assumption that the covariance matrix of the $\boldsymbol{\varepsilon}$'s, the $\mathbf{\Sigma}$ matrix, is diagonal ensures that contemporaneous stochastic disturbance terms are uncorrelated. Each equation therefore stands alone, and its stochastic disturbance term does not "contaminate" the other equations of the system. Every endogenous variable is predetermined with respect to higher-numbered equations in that the direction of flow of impulses is only from lower-numbered to higher-numbered equations. This unidirectional flow is illustrated in Figure 9.1 in an arrow diagram. All the predetermined variables and ε_1 determine y_1. Then y_1, all the predetermined variables, and ε_2 determine y_2. Then y_1, y_2, all the predetermined variables, and ε_3 determine y_3.

Recursive models are always exactly identified. That is, with the zero restrictions in $\mathbf{\Gamma}$ and $\mathbf{\Sigma}$ given in (9.5.1) and (9.5.2) it is always possible to infer the nonzero structural coefficients from the reduced-form coefficents. The normalized system contains $g[(g + 1)/2] - g$ coefficients to be estimated in $\mathbf{\Gamma}$, gk in $\mathbf{B}$, and g in $\mathbf{\Sigma}$, and the reduced form contains the usual number of $gk + g[(g + 1)/2]$ parameters, as in (9.2.1). The number of givens and unknowns is therefore the same:

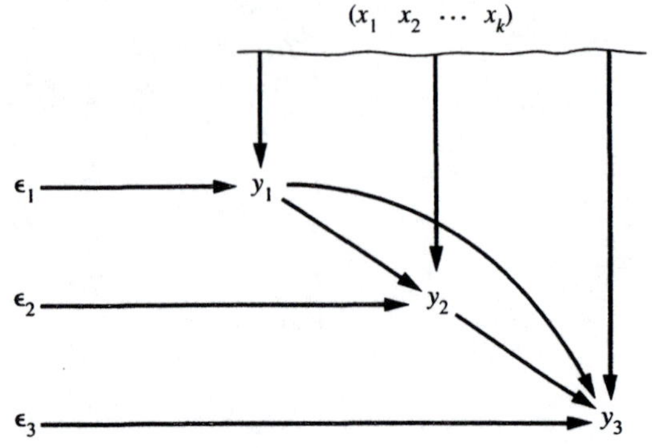

Figure 9.1 Unilateral Flow for a Recursive Model

$$G = U = \frac{g(g+1)}{2} + gk. \tag{9.5.4}$$

For example, if $g = 2$ and $k = 3$, the number of unknowns and givens is 9. In this case, from (9.1.15),

$$\begin{pmatrix} \sigma_1^2 & 0 \\ 0 & \sigma_2^2 \end{pmatrix} = \begin{pmatrix} -1 & 0 \\ \gamma_{12} & -1 \end{pmatrix} \begin{pmatrix} \omega_1^2 & \omega_{12} \\ \omega_{12} & \omega_2^2 \end{pmatrix} \begin{pmatrix} -1 & \gamma_{12} \\ 0 & -1 \end{pmatrix}, \tag{9.5.5}$$

where the ω's are elements of the $\boldsymbol{\Omega}$ matrix, assumed known or estimated. From (9.5.5) it follows that:

$$\begin{aligned} \sigma_1^2 &= \omega_1^2, \\ \gamma_{12} &= \frac{\omega_{12}}{\omega_1^2}, \\ \sigma_2^2 &= \omega_2^2 - \frac{\omega_{12}^2}{\omega_1^2}, \end{aligned} \tag{9.5.6}$$

where ω_1^2 and ω_2^2 are variances of the reduced-form stochastic disturbance terms. But from (9.1.10),

$$\begin{pmatrix} \pi_{11} & \pi_{12} \\ \pi_{21} & \pi_{22} \\ \pi_{31} & \pi_{32} \end{pmatrix} \begin{pmatrix} -1 & \gamma_{12} \\ 0 & -1 \end{pmatrix} = -\begin{pmatrix} \beta_{11} & \beta_{12} \\ \beta_{21} & \beta_{22} \\ \beta_{31} & \beta_{32} \end{pmatrix}, \tag{9.5.7}$$

so, solving for the remaining unknowns, the β's,

$$\begin{aligned} \beta_{11} &= \pi_{11}, & \beta_{12} &= \pi_{12} - \gamma_{12}\pi_{11} \\ \beta_{21} &= \pi_{21}, & \beta_{22} &= \pi_{22} - \gamma_{12}\pi_{21} \\ \beta_{31} &= \pi_{31}, & \beta_{32} &= \pi_{32} - \gamma_{12}\pi_{31}, \end{aligned} \tag{9.5.8}$$

where γ_{12} is given in (9.5.6). These results summarize the indirect least squares estimators for the structural parameters, given the reduced-form coefficients. The coefficients of the first equation are the reduced-form coefficients (since this equation contains only one endogenous variable), while the coefficients of the second equation are obtained using the recursive nature of the system from the coefficients obtained for the first equation and the reduced-form coefficients for the second equation. The first equation is of the form:

$$y_1 = \beta_{11}x_1 + \beta_{21}x_2 + \beta_{31}x_3 - \varepsilon_1, \tag{9.5.9}$$

and the β's are the reduced-form coefficients

$$\beta_{11} = \pi_{11}, \quad \beta_{21} = \pi_{21}, \quad \beta_{31} = \pi_{31}. \tag{9.5.10}$$

The second equation is of the form

$$y_2 = \gamma_{12}y_1 + \beta_{12}x_1 + \beta_{22}x_2 + \beta_{32}x_3 - \varepsilon_2, \tag{9.5.11}$$

so, replacing y_1 from (9.5.9) and (9.5.10) gives

$$y_2 = \gamma_{12}(\pi_{11}x_1 + \pi_{21}x_2 + \pi_{31}x_3) + \beta_{12}x_1 + \beta_{22}x_2 + \beta_{32}x_3 - \varepsilon_2 - \gamma_{12}\,\varepsilon_1, \tag{9.5.12}$$

$$y_2 = (\gamma_{12}\pi_{11} + \beta_{12})x_1 + (\gamma_{12}\pi_{21} + \beta_{22})x_2 + (\gamma_{12}\pi_{31} + \beta_{32})x_3 - \varepsilon_2 - \gamma_{12}\,\varepsilon_1. \tag{9.5.13}$$

Equating the terms in parentheses to the coefficients of the second reduced-form equation yields

$$\beta_{12} = \pi_{12} - \gamma_{12}\pi_{11}, \qquad \beta_{22} = \pi_{22} - \gamma_{12}\pi_{21}, \qquad \beta_{32} = \pi_{32} - \gamma_{12}\pi_{31}, \tag{9.5.14}$$

as in (9.5.8). The nine results in (9.5.6) and (9.5.8) give the normalized structural coefficients as explicit functions of the reduced-form coefficients, illustrating the identification and indirect least squares estimators that are always guaranteed for recursive systems.

9.6 IDENTIFICATION OF NONLINEAR MODELS

9.6.1 The Model

It often happens that behavioral relationships are best described by nonlinear equations. For instance, the CES production function is nonlinear in parameters, the Phillips curve is nonlinear with respect to the unemployment rate, and so on. In general, consider a system of g equations in which the errors appear additively:

$$f_h(\mathbf{y}_i, \mathbf{x}_i; \mathbf{a}) = \varepsilon_{ih}, \qquad h = 1, \ldots, g, \quad i = 1, \ldots, n, \tag{9.6.1}$$

where $\mathbf{y}_i$ and $\mathbf{x}_i$ are vectors of the g endogenous variables and k exogenous variables, respectively, at observation i; f_h is a known function, and $\mathbf{a}$ is an $m \times 1$ vector of parameters. The $g \times 1$ error term $\boldsymbol{\varepsilon}_i = (\varepsilon_{i1}, \ldots, \varepsilon_{ig})'$ is assumed to satisfy (9.1.4) and (9.1.5). The model is nonlinear if $f_h(\mathbf{y}_i, \mathbf{x}_i; \mathbf{a})$ is nonlinear either in the variables $\mathbf{y}$ or in the parameters $\mathbf{a}$.

9.6.2 Models Nonlinear in Parameters

This section treats models that are linear in variables but nonlinear in parameters. The identification of simultaneous equations models that are nonlinear in parameters is much more complicated than that of linear simultaneous equations models. For linear models, if the model is identified, it means that the equations relating the prior and observational restrictions give a unique solution to the structural parameters $\mathbf{a}$. Hence if the linear model is identifiable, it is *globally* identified. For nonlinear models, however, where some of the equations defining the prior and observational restrictions are not linear in the elements of $\mathbf{a}$, it is possible that these equations would admit more than one solution. One of these solutions may correspond to the true structure, so without additional information to distinguish among the solutions there is only *local* identifiability.

For simplicity, assume that the characteristics of the probability density for $\mathbf{y}$ can be summarized by the l population moments ω_j, $j = 1, \ldots, l$, which are continuously differentiable functions of the m-dimensional structural parameters $\omega_j = \psi_j(\mathbf{a})$, $j = 1, \ldots, l$. In addition, it is assumed that $\mathbf{a}$ satisfies a set of continuously differentiable constraint equations $\varphi_\tau(\mathbf{a}) = 0$, $\tau = 1, \ldots, R$. Then $\mathbf{a}$ is globally identifiable if and only if the equations

$$\begin{aligned} \omega_j &= \omega_j(\mathbf{a}), \qquad & j &= 1, \ldots, l, \\ \mathbf{0} &= \varphi_\tau(\mathbf{a}), \qquad & \tau &= 1, \ldots, R, \end{aligned} \tag{9.6.2}$$

have a unique solution for $\mathbf{a}$; it is locally identifiable if all the solutions of (9.6.2) are isolated from each other. A basic condition for (9.6.2) to give a locally unique solution for $\mathbf{a}$ is the following.

A necessary and sufficient condition that $\mathbf{a}^0$ be a locally isolated solution is that the $(l + R) \times m$ Jacobian matrix formed by taking partial derivatives of (9.6.2) with respect to $\mathbf{a}$,

$$J(\mathbf{a}) = \begin{bmatrix} \dfrac{\partial \psi_1(\mathbf{a})}{\partial a_1} & \cdots & \dfrac{\partial \psi_1(\mathbf{a})}{\partial a_m} \\ \dfrac{\partial \psi_2(\mathbf{a})}{\partial a_1} & \cdots & \dfrac{\partial \psi_2(\mathbf{a})}{\partial a_m} \\ \vdots & & \vdots \\ \dfrac{\partial \psi_\ell(\mathbf{a})}{\partial a_1} & \cdots & \dfrac{\partial \psi_\ell(\mathbf{a})}{\partial a_m} \\ \dfrac{\partial \varphi_1(\mathbf{a})}{\partial a_1} & \cdots & \dfrac{\partial \varphi_1(\mathbf{a})}{\partial a_m} \\ \vdots & \ddots & \vdots \\ \dfrac{\partial \varphi_R(\mathbf{a})}{\partial a_1} & \cdots & \dfrac{\partial \varphi_R(\mathbf{a})}{\partial a_m} \end{bmatrix} \tag{9.6.3}$$

have rank m at $\mathbf{a}^0$ and for all $\mathbf{a}$ in some sufficiently small neighborhood of $\mathbf{a}^0$.

For proof of this theorem, see Fisher (1966). For other elaborations, see Hsiao (1983).

9.6.3 Systems Nonlinear in the Variables

Now consider the identifiability of the coefficients of a simultaneous equations system that is linear in parameters but nonlinear in the variables. Such a model can be written as:

$$\mathbf{A}\mathbf{q}(\mathbf{y}_i, \mathbf{x}_i) = \boldsymbol{\varepsilon}_i, \tag{9.6.4}$$

where $\mathbf{q}$ is an $N \times 1$ vector of known functions of $\mathbf{y}$ and $\mathbf{x}$, and $\mathbf{A}$ is the $g \times N$ matrix of unknown coefficients. Assume that (9.6.4) implicitly defines a *unique relevant inverse relationship*:[23]

$$\mathbf{y}_i = \mathbf{s}(\boldsymbol{\varepsilon}_i, \mathbf{x}_i; \mathbf{A}), \tag{9.6.5}$$

where $\mathbf{s}$ is a $g \times 1$ vector of continuous functions. In addition, assume that the coefficient matrix is known to satisfy the linear restrictions:

[23]This is a strong assumption. The inverse relationship often is not unique, as discussed in Goldfeld and Quandt (1972).

$$\boldsymbol{\alpha}_h'\boldsymbol{\Phi}_h = \mathbf{0}, \qquad h = 1, \ldots, g, \tag{9.6.6}$$

where the $1 \times N$ vector $\boldsymbol{\alpha}_h'$ denotes the hth row of $\mathbf{A}$ (the coefficients of the hth equation) and $\boldsymbol{\Phi}_h$ is an $N \times R_h$ known matrix with each of the R_h columns corresponding to a homogeneous linear restriction.

Brown (1983) derives the identification of such a model assuming that (1) $\boldsymbol{\varepsilon}_i$ and $\mathbf{x}$ are independent, and (2) $E(\boldsymbol{\varepsilon}_i \mid \mathbf{x}_i) = \mathbf{0}$. Condition (1) implies that

$$\frac{\partial \boldsymbol{\varepsilon}_i}{\partial \mathbf{x}'} = \mathbf{A}\tilde{\mathbf{Q}}' = \mathbf{0}, \tag{9.6.7}$$

where $\tilde{\mathbf{Q}}'$ is a g-row matrix which forms a basis for the space generated by

$$\tilde{\mathbf{Q}}(\boldsymbol{\varepsilon}_i, \mathbf{x})' = \frac{\partial \mathbf{q}(\mathbf{s}(\boldsymbol{\varepsilon}_i, \mathbf{x}; \mathbf{A}), \mathbf{x})}{\partial \mathbf{x}'}. \tag{9.6.8}$$

Condition (2) implies that

$$\begin{aligned} \mathbf{A}E\mathbf{q}(\mathbf{y}_i, \mathbf{x}_i) &= \mathbf{A}E\{\mathbf{q}[\mathbf{s}(\boldsymbol{\varepsilon}_i, \mathbf{x}_i; \mathbf{A}), \mathbf{x}_i \mid \mathbf{x}_i]\} \\ &= \mathbf{A}\overline{\mathbf{q}}(\mathbf{x}) = \mathbf{0}. \end{aligned} \tag{9.6.9}$$

Combining (9.6.7) and (9.6.9) with (9.6.6), the coefficient vector of the hth equation has to satisfy:

$$\boldsymbol{\alpha}_h'\left(\overline{\mathbf{q}} : \tilde{\mathbf{Q}}' : \boldsymbol{\Phi}_h\right) = \mathbf{0}. \tag{9.6.10}$$

Therefore, a necessary and sufficient condition for the hth equation to be identified (where $\boldsymbol{\alpha}_h$ is unique up to a scalar multiple) is that the hth equation satisfies the *generalized rank condition*:

$$\text{rank}\left(\tilde{\mathbf{q}} : \tilde{\mathbf{Q}}' : \boldsymbol{\Phi}_h\right) = g - 1. \tag*{*(9.6.11)}$$

This generalized rank condition is weaker than the rank condition for the linear simultaneous equation [rank($\boldsymbol{\Phi}_h\mathbf{A}$) $= g - 1$]. Therefore, if the coefficient vector of the hth equation of a nonlinear system satisfies the usual rank condition (9.4.13), the hth equation is identifiable under this assumption. However, even if rank($\boldsymbol{\Phi}_h\mathbf{A}$) $< g - 1$, that does not necessarily mean that the hth equation is unidentifiable. It may still be identifiable provided that it satisfies the generalized rank condition (9.6.11). Thus nonlinearity in variables actually helps identification. Of course, one should note that this is achieved only when the model (9.6.4) admits a unique inverse relation (9.6.5).

PROBLEMS

9-A Prove that the least squares estimator $\hat{\boldsymbol{\Pi}}$ given in (9.1.24) is both an unbiased and a consistent estimator of $\boldsymbol{\Pi}$ and that the estimator $\hat{\boldsymbol{\Omega}}$ given in (9.1.25) is both an unbiased and a consistent estimator of $\boldsymbol{\Omega}$.

9-B The star notation of Sections 5.3 and 10.7 can be used to derive the estimator of the reduced-form system. In this notation the reduced form is:

$$\underset{gn\times 1}{\mathbf{y}^*} = \underset{gn\times gk}{\mathbf{X}^*}\ \underset{gk\times 1}{\boldsymbol{\Pi}^*} + \underset{gn\times 1}{\mathbf{u}^*},$$

where $\mathbf{y}^*$ and $\mathbf{u}^*$ are as in (5.3.16), $\mathbf{X}^*$ is as in (10.7.14) in the next chapter, and $\mathbf{\Pi}^*$ is obtained by stacking the columns of the $\mathbf{\Pi}$ matrix. The stochastic assumptions in (9.1.12), (9.1.14) and (9.1.16) can be written:

$$E(\mathbf{u}^*) = \mathbf{0},$$

$$\text{Cov}(\mathbf{u}^*) = \mathbf{\Omega} \otimes \mathbf{I}.$$

1. Show that the GLS estimators of the column vectors constituting $\mathbf{\Pi}^*$ are given by the columns of $\hat{\mathbf{\Pi}}$ in (9.1.24).
2. Show that if $\hat{\mathbf{\Pi}}^*$ is the GLS estimator of $\mathbf{\Pi}^*$, then

$$\text{Cov}(\hat{\mathbf{\Pi}}^*) = \mathbf{\Omega} \otimes (\mathbf{X}'\mathbf{X})^{-1}.$$

3. Assuming normality,

$$\mathbf{u}^* \sim \mathbf{N}(\mathbf{0}, \mathbf{\Omega} \otimes \mathbf{I}),$$

show that the maximum likelihood estimator of $\mathbf{\Pi}^*$ is the GLS estimator $\hat{\mathbf{\Pi}}^*$ and that the maximum likelihood estimator of $\mathbf{\Omega}$ is the same as (9.1.25) except for the usual division by n rather than $n - k$. Also show that $\hat{\mathbf{\Pi}}^*$ is distributed normally, where

$$\hat{\mathbf{\Pi}}^* \sim \mathbf{N}[\mathbf{\Pi}^*, \mathbf{\Omega} \otimes (\mathbf{X}'\mathbf{X})^{-1}].$$

9-C Give examples of a priori restrictions relating coefficients to one another, such as (9.2.11), for several specific demand functions and production functions.

9-D A macroeconomic model is of the form:

$$C = \alpha_1 + \alpha_2 Y + \alpha_3 W + u_1,$$
$$I = \beta_1 + \beta_2 Y + \beta_3 Y_{-1} + \beta_4 r + u_2,$$
$$Y = C + I + G,$$

where C, I, and Y are endogenous; Y_{-1}, W, r, and G are predetermined; and u_1 and u_2 are stochastic, where W is wealth and r is the interest rate.

1. Determine the reduced-form equations.
2. Determine the identification of the model both without and with the hypothesis that investment satisfies the acceleration hypothesis $\beta_3 = -\beta_2$.

9-E A structural model of a firm using a Cobb–Douglas production function takes the form:

$$\ln y = a_1 + \alpha_1 \ln L + \beta_1 \ln K, \quad (1)$$

$$\ln w = a_2 + \alpha_2 \ln L + \beta_2 \ln K, \quad (2)$$

$$\ln r = a_3 + \alpha_3 \ln L + \beta_3 \ln K, \quad (3)$$

where equation (1) is the log-linear production function and equations (2) and (3) jointly determine the inputs of labor and capital given the factor prices.[24] Assuming that the endogenous variables are $\ln y$, $\ln L$, and $\ln K$ and that the exogenous variables are $\ln w$ and $\ln r$, obtain the reduced form, show that each equation is just identified, and indicate how the structural parameters can be estimated from the reduced-form parameters. How do the results change if stochastic disturbance terms are added to the right-hand sides of all three equations?

9-F The Suits model of the watermelon market treats the demand for and supply of watermelons using the two equations:[25]

[24]See the related system in footnote 18 of Chapter 8.

[25]See Suits (1955). The model has been somewhat simplified.

$$P = a_0 + a_1 \frac{X}{N} + a_2 \frac{Y}{N} + a_3 F,$$

$$X = b_0 + b_1 \frac{P}{W} + b_2 P_{-1} + b_3 C_{-1} + b_4 T_{-1}.$$

Here the first equation is a demand equation, relating price, P, to per capita quantity (demanded), X/N; per capita income, Y/N; and freight costs, F. The second equation is a crop supply schedule, relating the harvest, X, to price relative to the farm wage rate, P/W; lagged price, P_{-1}; lagged price of cotton, C_{-1}, and lagged price of other vegetables, T_{-1}. The endogenous variables are P and X.

1. Show the cobweb behavior of price and quantity in a diagram.
2. Obtain the reduced form and the final form.
3. Determine the identification of the model.

9-G Given the structural equations:

$$(y_1 \quad y_2 \quad y_3)\begin{pmatrix} -1 & \gamma_{12} & 0 \\ 0 & -1 & \gamma_{23} \\ \gamma_{31} & \gamma_{32} & -1 \end{pmatrix}$$

$$+ (x_1 \quad x_2 \quad x_3 \quad x_4)\begin{pmatrix} \beta_{11} & 0 & \beta_{13} \\ \beta_{21} & \beta_{22} & 0 \\ \beta_{31} & 0 & 0 \\ \beta_{41} & \beta_{42} & \beta_{43} \end{pmatrix} = (\varepsilon_1 \quad \varepsilon_2 \quad \varepsilon_3).$$

1. Determine the identification of the model, analyzing, for each equation, the order and rank conditions.
2. For all exactly identified equations, show specifically how the structural parameters can be estimated from the reduced-form parameters.
3. For all overidentified equations, show several ways in which structural parameters can be estimated from the reduced-form parameters.

9-H Answer the same questions as in Problem 9-G for the following $\mathbf{\Gamma}$, $\mathbf{B}$ matrices:

1. $$\mathbf{\Gamma} = \begin{pmatrix} -1 & \gamma_{12} & 0 \\ \gamma_{21} & -1 & 0 \\ \gamma_{31} & 0 & -1 \end{pmatrix}, \quad \mathbf{B} = \begin{pmatrix} \beta_{11} & \beta_{12} & \beta_{13} \\ 0 & \beta_{22} & 0 \\ 0 & 0 & \beta_{33} \\ 0 & \beta_{42} & \beta_{43} \\ \beta_{51} & 0 & 0 \\ \beta_{61} & \beta_{62} & \beta_{63} \end{pmatrix}$$

2. $$\mathbf{\Gamma} = \begin{pmatrix} -1 & \gamma_{12} & \gamma_{13} & \gamma_{14} \\ \gamma_{21} & -1 & \gamma_{23} & \gamma_{24} \\ 0 & 0 & -1 & \gamma_{34} \\ 0 & 0 & \gamma_{43} & -1 \end{pmatrix}, \quad \mathbf{B} = \begin{pmatrix} 0 & 0 & 0 & \beta_{14} \\ \beta_{21} & 0 & 0 & \beta_{24} \\ 0 & \beta_{32} & \beta_{33} & 0 \\ 0 & \beta_{42} & \beta_{43} & 0 \\ \beta_{51} & \beta_{52} & \beta_{53} & \beta_{54} \end{pmatrix}.$$

9-I In a certain model of the steel industry the endogenous variables are shipments (S), price (p), and imports (M), while the predetermined variables are lagged price (p_{-1}), time (t), inventory (I), and unity (1). The equations of the model are:

$$S = f_1(p, M, t),$$

$$p = f_2(S, p_{-1}, I),$$

$$M = f_3(p, t),$$

where all equations are linear and contain intercepts. Show that the model is not identified and re-specify it to yield a related model that is identified.

9-J In the following macroeconomic model the endogenous variables are

$$\Delta Y = \text{change in national income,}$$
$$\Delta S = \text{change in private spending,}$$
$$\Delta W = \text{change in the wage rate,}$$
$$U = \text{unemployment rate,}$$

and the predetermined variables are

$$\Delta G = \text{change in government spending,}$$
$$\Delta M = \text{change in money supply,}$$
$$\Delta W_{-1} = \text{lagged change in the wage rate.}$$

The model states that:

$$\Delta Y = \Delta S + \Delta G,$$
$$\Delta S = \alpha_1 \, \Delta Y + \alpha_2 \, \Delta M + \varepsilon_1,$$
$$\Delta W = \beta_1 \, \Delta Y + \beta_2 U + \beta_3 \, \Delta W_{-1} + \varepsilon_2,$$
$$U = \gamma_1 \, \Delta Y + \gamma_2 \, \Delta W + \varepsilon_3.$$

1. Obtain the reduced form (first eliminate the nonstochastic equation).
2. Analyze the identification of the model.
3. Discuss the implications of the estimated model for monetary and fiscal policies that would promote low unemployment without large wage increases.

9-K Show that for identification by general linear restrictions in the overidentified case as defined in (9.4.15) the number of "excess" restrictions, given by:

$$\text{rank}(\mathbf{\Phi}_h) - (g - 1) = \text{rank}(\mathbf{\Phi}_h) - \text{rank}(\mathbf{\Phi}_h \mathbf{A})$$

represents the number of restrictions imposed on the hth column of the $\mathbf{\Pi}$ matrix.

9-L Suppose that $\mathbf{\Sigma}$ can be expressed as

$$\mathbf{\Sigma} = \sigma^2 \mathbf{I},$$

where σ^2 is the only unknown parameter in the covariance matrix. Prove that the system is identified if $g = 1$ and if $g = 2$ but not if $g > 2$.

9-M Consider the demand–supply model:

$$q = \gamma_1 p + \delta_1 + \varepsilon^D,$$
$$q = \gamma_2 p + \delta_2 + \varepsilon^S,$$

where $\text{Cov}(\boldsymbol{\varepsilon}^D, \boldsymbol{\varepsilon}^S) = 0$ and $\text{Var}(\boldsymbol{\varepsilon}^S) = K\,\text{Var}(\boldsymbol{\varepsilon}^D)$. Assume that K is known, so the covariance matrix

$$\mathbf{\Sigma} = \begin{pmatrix} \sigma^2 & 0 \\ 0 & K\sigma^2 \end{pmatrix}$$

contains only one unknown parameter, σ^2, the variance of demand. Prove that the system is identified.

9-N A recursive model is one in which $\mathbf{\Gamma}$ is triangular and $\mathbf{\Sigma}$ is diagonal.

1. Prove that a recursive model is always identified by showing that the only admissible transformation matrix $\mathbf{R}$ as in (9.2.7) is the identity matrix.
2. Show by using the $\mathbf{R}$ matrix that the triangular nature of $\mathbf{\Gamma}$ and the diagonal nature of $\mathbf{\Sigma}$ are each, by themselves, not sufficient to identify the system.

9-O Show that the following models are recursive. For each depict the unilateral direction of flow in an arrow diagram.

1. The cobweb model of Section 7.8.
2. The Walrasian tâtonnement model of Problem 2-C.

9-P A generalization of the recursive system is the *block recursive* system, in which the system is recursive in certain subsets of variables. In this case $\mathbf{\Gamma}$ is block triangular and $\mathbf{\Sigma}$ is block diagonal:

$$\mathbf{\Gamma} = \begin{pmatrix} \mathbf{\Gamma}_{11} & \mathbf{\Gamma}_{12} & \cdots & \\ \mathbf{0} & \mathbf{\Gamma}_{22} & & \\ & & \ddots & \\ \mathbf{0} & & & \mathbf{\Gamma}_{qq} \end{pmatrix}, \qquad \mathbf{\Sigma} = \begin{pmatrix} \mathbf{\Sigma}_{11} & \mathbf{0} & & \mathbf{0} \\ \mathbf{0} & \mathbf{\Sigma}_{22} & & \mathbf{0} \\ & & \ddots & \\ \mathbf{0} & \mathbf{0} & & \mathbf{\Sigma}_{qq} \end{pmatrix}.$$

Here $\mathbf{\Gamma}_{11}$ and $\mathbf{\Sigma}_{11}$ are square matrices of the same order, $\mathbf{\Gamma}_{22}$ and $\mathbf{\Sigma}_{22}$ are square matrices of the same order (but not necessarily the same order as $\mathbf{\Gamma}_{11}$), and so on. Each equation is then identified with respect to other equations in its own block. Determine the identification of such a model.[26]

9-Q A general definition of identification states that a model is *identified* if and only if its parameters can be obtained from knowledge of the likelihood function. Using the likelihood function for the simultaneous-equations model, as given in (10.8.9), prove that:

1. The reduced-form model is identified.
2. In the absence of a priori information the structural form is not identified. [In particular show that the bogus parameters in (9.2.7) yield the same likelihood function as the true parameters.]

9-R Consider the identification of the first equation of the simultaneous-equations system. Assume that specific numerical values are given for g_1' of the $g_1 - 1$ explanatory endogenous variables and for k_1' of the k_1 included exogenous variables. Given this additional information, obtain the rank and order conditions of identification.

9-S Consider the model:

$$\sum_{j=0}^{p} \mathbf{y}_{t-j}\mathbf{\Gamma}_j + \sum_{j=0}^{q} \mathbf{x}_{t-j}\mathbf{B}_j = \mathbf{u}_t,$$

$$\sum_{j=0}^{r} \mathbf{u}_{t-j}\mathbf{C}_j = \boldsymbol{\varepsilon}_t,$$

$$E(\boldsymbol{\varepsilon}_t) = \mathbf{0},$$

$$E(\boldsymbol{\varepsilon}_{t-\tau}'\boldsymbol{\varepsilon}_t) = \begin{Bmatrix} \mathbf{0} & \tau \neq 0 \\ \mathbf{\Sigma} & \tau = 0 \end{Bmatrix}, \quad \text{all } t.$$

Obtain the reduced form and final form of this system.

BIBLIOGRAPHY

ANDO, A., F. M. FISHER, AND H. A. SIMON (1963). *Essays on the Structure of Social Science Models.* Cambridge, Mass.: MIT Press.

BOWDEN, R. (1973). "The Theory of Parametric Identification." *Econometrica,* 41: 1069–1074.

BROWN, B. W. (1983). "The Identification Problem in Systems Nonlinear in the Variables." *Econometrica,* 51: 175–196.

[26]See Ando, Fisher, and Simon (1963) and Fisher (1965).

Fisher, F. M. (1965). "Dynamic Structure and Estimation in Economy-Wide Econometric Models," in J. S. Duesenberry, G. Fromm, L. R. Klein, and E. Kuh, Eds., *The Brookings Quarterly Econometric Model of the United States*. Chicago: Rand McNally & Company; Amsterdam: North-Holland Publishing Company.

Fisher, F. M. (1966). *The Identification Problem in Econometrics*. New York: McGraw-Hill Book Company.

Goldfeld, S. M., and R. E. Quandt (1972). *Nonlinear Methods in Econometrics*. Amsterdam: North-Holland Publishing Company.

Hsiao, C. (1983). "Identification," in Z. Griliches and M. Intriligator, Eds., *Handbook of Econometrics*, Vol. 1. Amsterdam: North-Holland Publishing Company.

Rothenberg, T. (1971). "Identification in Parametric Models." *Econometrica*, 38: 577–591.

Schmidt, P. (1976). *Econometrics*. New York: Marcel Dekker, Inc.

Suits, D. B. (1955). "An Econometric Model of the Watermelon Market." *Journal of Farm Economics*, 37: 237–251.

Wold, H. (1954). "Causality and Econometrics." *Econometrica*, 22: 162–177.

Wold, H. (1960). "A Generalization of Causal Chain Models." *Econometrica*, 28: 443–463.

Wold, H. (1964). *Econometric Model Building: Essays on the Causal Chain Approach*. Amsterdam: North-Holland Publishing Company.

10

ESTIMATION OF SIMULTANEOUS-EQUATIONS SYSTEMS[1]

10.1 INTRODUCTION

The simultaneous-equations system to be estimated is:

$$\underset{1\times g}{\mathbf{y}_i}\ \underset{g\times g}{\mathbf{\Gamma}} + \underset{1\times k}{\mathbf{x}_i}\ \underset{k\times g}{\mathbf{B}} = \underset{1\times g}{\boldsymbol{\varepsilon}_i}, \qquad i = 1, 2, \ldots, n, \tag{10.1.1}$$

as in (9.1.1). Here $\mathbf{y}_i$ and $\mathbf{x}_i$ are, respectively, vectors of g endogenous and k predetermined variables and $\boldsymbol{\varepsilon}_i$ is the vector of g stochastic disturbance terms, one for each of the g equations of the system. The subscript i refers to the observation number, indexing the n observations.

Several stochastic assumptions are made on $\boldsymbol{\varepsilon}_i$, as in (9.1.4)–(9.1.6). First is the *disturbance assumption* that the stochastic disturbance terms have a zero mean in each period:

$$E(\boldsymbol{\varepsilon}_i) = \mathbf{0}, \qquad \text{all } i. \tag{10.1.2}$$

Second is the *homoskedasticity assumption* that these stochastic disturbances have a constant (and finite) covariance matrix:

$$\text{Cov}(\boldsymbol{\varepsilon}_i) = E(\boldsymbol{\varepsilon}_i'\boldsymbol{\varepsilon}_i) = \underset{g\times g}{\mathbf{\Sigma}}, \qquad \text{all } i, \tag{10.1.3}$$

where $\mathbf{\Sigma}$ is a symmetric positive-definite matrix of variances and covariances. Third is the *absence-of-serial-correlation assumption* that the stochastic disturbance terms are uncorrelated over the sample, implying that

$$E(\boldsymbol{\varepsilon}_i'\boldsymbol{\varepsilon}_{i'}) = \mathbf{0}, \qquad \text{all } i, i', \quad i \neq i'. \tag{10.1.4}$$

[1]General references on the estimation of simultaneous-equations systems include Christ (1966), Dhrymes (1970), Malinvaud (1970), Theil (1971), Madansky (1976), Schmidt (1976), and Hausman (1983). For discussions of Bayesian estimation of simultaneous-equations systems see Zellner (1971), Morales (1971), Harkema (1971), and Drèze and Richard (1983).

The n observations on each of the g endogenous variables can be summarized by the data matrix:

$$\underset{n\times g}{\mathbf{Y}} = \begin{pmatrix} \mathbf{y}_1 \\ \mathbf{y}_2 \\ \vdots \\ \mathbf{y}_n \end{pmatrix} = \begin{pmatrix} y_{11} & y_{12} & \cdots & y_{1g} \\ y_{21} & y_{22} & \cdots & y_{2g} \\ \vdots & & & \\ y_{n1} & y_{n2} & \cdots & y_{ng} \end{pmatrix}, \tag{10.1.5}$$

where $\mathbf{y}_i$ is the vector of data on all g endogenous variables at observation i. Similarly the n observations on each of the k predetermined variables can be summarized by the data matrix:

$$\underset{n\times k}{\mathbf{X}} = \begin{pmatrix} \mathbf{x}_1 \\ \mathbf{x}_2 \\ \vdots \\ \mathbf{x}_n \end{pmatrix} = \begin{pmatrix} x_{11} & x_{12} & \cdots & x_{1k} \\ x_{21} & x_{22} & \cdots & x_{2k} \\ \vdots & & & \\ x_{n1} & x_{n2} & \cdots & x_{nk} \end{pmatrix}, \tag{10.1.6}$$

where $\mathbf{x}_i$ is the vector of data on all k predetermined variables at observation i.

Using these data matrices, which were introduced in (9.1.19), the simultaneous equations system can be written:

$$\underset{n\times g}{\mathbf{Y}}\ \underset{g\times g}{\mathbf{\Gamma}} + \underset{n\times k}{\mathbf{X}}\ \underset{k\times g}{\mathbf{B}} = \underset{n\times g}{\mathbf{E}}, \tag*{*(10.1.7)}$$

where $\mathbf{E}$ is here the $n \times g$ matrix, each row of which is the $\boldsymbol{\varepsilon}_i$ vector of stochastic disturbance terms in (10.1.1). This system is the generalization of the single-equation model to g endogenous variables. It reduces to the single-equation model if $g = 1$, in which case the matrix $\mathbf{Y}$ collapses to the column vector $\mathbf{y}$; the matrix $\mathbf{\Gamma}$ collapses to a single element, which may be chosen as -1 to normalize the equation; the matrix $\mathbf{B}$ collapses to the column vector $\boldsymbol{\beta}$; and the matrix $\mathbf{E}$ collapses to the column vector $-\mathbf{u}$, so

$$\mathbf{y}(-1) + \mathbf{X}\boldsymbol{\beta} = -\mathbf{u}, \tag{10.1.8}$$

or

$$\mathbf{y} = \mathbf{X}\boldsymbol{\beta} + \mathbf{u}, \tag{10.1.9}$$

as in Chapters 4 and 5.

The problem of simultaneous equation estimation is that of using the matrices $\mathbf{Y}$ and $\mathbf{X}$ to estimate the parameters of the system (10.1.7), namely the coefficient matrices $\mathbf{\Gamma}$ and $\mathbf{B}$ and the matrix $\mathbf{\Sigma}$ of covariances of $\boldsymbol{\varepsilon}_i$ in (10.1.3). Some of these coefficients may be specified a priori, as discussed in Chapter 9 with reference to the identification of the system. In fact, the case that will be emphasized here is the normalized system in which some of the coefficients are specified to be zero—the case of zero restrictions as discussed in Section 9.3.

As noted in Chapter 9, each of the equations can be normalized, and a convenient normalization is the one introduced in (9.1.2), which sets each of the n elements along the principal diagonal of the $\mathbf{\Gamma}$ matrix equal to -1:

$$\gamma_{hh} = -1, \qquad h = 1, 2, \ldots, g. \tag{10.1.10}$$

Solving equation h for y_{ih} then yields:

$$y_{ih} = \sum_{\substack{h'=1 \\ h'\neq h}}^{g} y_{ih'}\gamma_{h'h} + \sum_{j=1}^{k} x_{ij}\beta_{jh} - \varepsilon_{ih}, \qquad h = 1, 2, \ldots, g. \tag{10.1.11}$$

as in (9.1.3). Here h is an index of the equation, h' is an index of the endogenous variables, and j is an index of the exogenous variables, as in (2.8.2).[2] In this formulation, also, the simultaneous-equations system collapses to the single-equation model if $g = 1$, in which case the first summation on the right vanishes and the h subscripts can be dropped.

Consider, without loss of generality, the first equation of the system ($h = 1$), and assume that the a priori restrictions on the coefficients are all zero restrictions. The variables can be renumbered, if necessary, so that only the first g_1 endogenous variables ($g_1 < g$) and only the first k_1 exogenous variables ($k_1 < k$) are included in the equation, the other $(g - g_1) + (k - k_1)$ variables having zero coefficients. The first equation can then be written

$$y_{i1} = \sum_{h'=2}^{g_1} y_{ih'}\gamma_{h'1} + \sum_{j=1}^{k_1} x_{ij}\beta_{j1} - \varepsilon_{i1}. \tag{10.1.12}$$

Introducing the vectors,

$$\mathbf{Y}_{i1} = \begin{pmatrix} y_{i2} & y_{i3} & \cdots & y_{ig_1} \end{pmatrix}, \qquad \mathbf{X}_{i1} = \begin{pmatrix} x_{i1} & x_{i2} & \cdots & x_{ik_1} \end{pmatrix}, \tag{10.1.13}$$

for the included explanatory variables and introducing

$$\boldsymbol{\gamma}_1 = \begin{pmatrix} \gamma_{21} & \gamma_{31} & \cdots & \gamma_{g_1 1} \end{pmatrix}', \qquad \boldsymbol{\beta}_1 = \begin{pmatrix} \beta_{11} & \beta_{21} & \cdots & \beta_{k_1 1} \end{pmatrix}' \tag{10.1.14}$$

for the nonzero coefficients, (10.1.12) can be written:

$$y_{i1} = \underset{1\times(g_1-1)}{\mathbf{Y}_{i1}} \underset{(g_1-1)\times 1}{\boldsymbol{\gamma}_1} + \underset{1\times k_1}{\mathbf{X}_{i1}} \underset{k_1\times 1}{\boldsymbol{\beta}_1} - \varepsilon_{i1}. \tag{10.1.15}$$

Here the subscript 1 indicates "included in the first equation." Thus $\mathbf{Y}_{i1}$ is the vector of $g_1 - 1$ explanatory endogenous variables included in the first equation; $\mathbf{X}_{i1}$ is the vector of k_1 exogenous variables included in the first equation; ε_{i1} is the stochastic disturbance term included in the first equation; and $\boldsymbol{\gamma}_1$ and $\boldsymbol{\beta}_1$ are, respectively, the $g_1 - 1$ coefficients of explanatory endogenous and k_1 coefficients of exogenous variables included in the first equation.

The data on all variables of the system, summarized by the **Y** and **X** matrices in (10.1.5) and (10.1.6), can be divided into data on the variables indicated in (10.1.15). Thus the matrix of data on the endogenous variables **Y** can be partitioned into:

$$\underset{n\times g}{\mathbf{Y}} = (\underset{n\times 1}{\mathbf{y}_1} \;\vdots\; \underset{n\times(g_1-1)}{\mathbf{Y}_1} \;\vdots\; \underset{n\times(g-g_1)}{\mathbf{Y}_2}), \tag*{*(10.1.16)}$$

where $\mathbf{y}_1$ is the column vector of data on the dependent endogenous variable (the one on which this equation has been normalized), $\mathbf{Y}_1$ is the matrix of data on the $g_1 - 1$ explanatory endogenous variables in $\mathbf{Y}_{i1}$, and $\mathbf{Y}_2$ is the matrix of data on the $g - g_1$ excluded endogenous variables. Similarly, the matrix of data on the exogenous variables **X** can be partitioned into:

$$\underset{n\times k}{\mathbf{X}} = (\underset{n\times k_1}{\mathbf{X}_1} \;\vdots\; \underset{n\times(k-k_1)}{\mathbf{X}_2}), \tag*{*(10.1.17)}$$

where $\mathbf{X}_1$ is the matrix of data on the k_1 included exogenous variables in $\mathbf{X}_{i1}$ and $\mathbf{X}_2$ is the matrix of data on the $k - k_1$ excluded exogenous variables.

[2]The discussion here and below refers to "exogenous" rather than "predetermined" variables. Lagged endogenous variables as explanatory variables were treated in the single-equation context in Section 6.8, and they are treated in the simultaneous-equations context in Section 10.6.

In terms of the data matrices, equation (10.1.15) can be represented as:

$$\underset{n\times 1}{\mathbf{y}_1} = \underset{n\times(g_1-1)}{\mathbf{Y}_1}\ \underset{(g_1-1)\times 1}{\boldsymbol{\gamma}_1} + \underset{n\times k_1}{\mathbf{X}_1}\ \underset{k_1\times 1}{\boldsymbol{\beta}_1} + \underset{n\times 1}{\boldsymbol{\varepsilon}_1}, \qquad *(10.1.18)$$

where $\boldsymbol{\varepsilon}_1$ is the negative of the vector of n stochastic disturbance terms for the first equation. The subscript ones serve as a reminder that this is the first equation of the system. This equation can be obtained from the system (10.1.7) and the partitioning of the variables in (10.1.16) and (10.1.17) as

$$(\mathbf{y}_1 \,\vdots\, \mathbf{Y}_1 \,\vdots\, \mathbf{Y}_2)\begin{pmatrix} -1 & \cdots \\ \hline \boldsymbol{\gamma}_1 & \cdots \\ \hline \mathbf{0} & \cdots \end{pmatrix} + (\mathbf{X}_1 \,\vdots\, \mathbf{X}_2)\begin{pmatrix} \boldsymbol{\beta}_1 & \cdots \\ \hline \mathbf{0} & \cdots \end{pmatrix} = (-\boldsymbol{\varepsilon}_1 \,\vdots\, \cdots), \qquad (10.1.19)$$

that is, as

$$-\mathbf{y}_1 + \mathbf{Y}_1\boldsymbol{\gamma}_1 + \mathbf{X}_1\boldsymbol{\beta}_1 = -\boldsymbol{\varepsilon}_1. \qquad (10.1.20)$$

Since only the first equation is being considered, only the first columns of $\boldsymbol{\Gamma}$, $\mathbf{B}$, and $\mathbf{E}$ are shown in (10.1.19). The first column of $\boldsymbol{\Gamma}$ is as shown because of the normalization ($\gamma_{11} = -1$), the definition of $\boldsymbol{\gamma}_1$ in (10.1.14), and the zero restrictions. Similarly the first column of $\mathbf{B}$ is as shown because of the definition of $\boldsymbol{\beta}_1$ in (10.1.14) and the zero restrictions. The first column of the $\mathbf{E}$ matrix is written here $-\boldsymbol{\varepsilon}_1$, where the change in sign allows the stochastic disturbance terms to be added, as shown in (10.1.18).[3]

Equation (10.1.18) is the basic equation to be used in developing several of the estimators of the simultaneous-equations system. It represents the first equation of the system, with the subscript 1 serving as a convenient reminder that it is the first equation. More generally, the hth equation can be represented as:

$$\mathbf{y}_h = \mathbf{Y}_h\boldsymbol{\gamma}_h + \mathbf{X}_h\boldsymbol{\beta}_h + \boldsymbol{\varepsilon}_h, \qquad h = 1, 2, \ldots, g, \qquad *(10.1.21)$$

where $\mathbf{y}_h$ is the column vector of data on the dependent endogenous variable, $\mathbf{Y}_h$ is the matrix of data on the $g_h - 1$ explanatory endogenous variables, $\mathbf{X}_h$ is the matrix of data on the included exogenous variables, and $\boldsymbol{\varepsilon}_h$ is the negative of the hth column of $\mathbf{E}$ in (10.1.7).

An example of the form specified in (10.1.18) or (10.1.21) is the consumption function from the prototype macro model of Section 2.6, of the form

$$C = \gamma_1 Y + \beta_1 + \varepsilon^C, \qquad (10.1.22)$$

as in (2.6.1), where γ_1 is the marginal propensity to consume and β_1 is the intercept. This equation is already of the form (10.1.18), where C, consumption, is the normalized endogenous variable; Y, income, is the single explanatory endogenous variable in this equation; and 1 is the single exogenous variable included in this equation. The complete system, of which this is one equation, is the system of two equations given by

$$(C \quad Y)\begin{pmatrix} -1 & \gamma_3 \\ \gamma_1 & -1 \end{pmatrix} + (Y_{-1} \quad G \quad 1)\begin{pmatrix} 0 & \beta_4 \\ 0 & \beta_5 \\ \beta_1 & \beta_6 \end{pmatrix} = (-\varepsilon^C \quad -\varepsilon^Y), \qquad (10.1.23)$$

[3]Here $\boldsymbol{\varepsilon}_1$ is the $n \times 1$ negative of the first column of $\mathbf{E}$, not to be confused with the row vector $\boldsymbol{\varepsilon}_i$ in (10.1.1) for $i = 1$.

as in (2.6.6), where Y_{-1} is lagged income and G is government expenditure.[4] Using the results of Chapter 9, the first equation, that for consumption, as given by (10.1.22), is identified if

$$\text{rank}\begin{pmatrix} \beta_4 \\ \beta_5 \end{pmatrix} = 1, \tag{10.1.24}$$

which is satisfied if either β_4 or β_5 does not vanish. This equation excludes a total of two variables, so

$$(g - g_1) + (k - k_1) = 2 > 1 = g - 1, \tag{10.1.25}$$

implying that the equation is overidentified.

A variant of this model is one in which the lagged variable Y_{-1} does not appear, so in this variant the structural form is:

$$(C \quad Y)\begin{pmatrix} -1 & \gamma_3' \\ \gamma_1' & -1 \end{pmatrix} + (G \quad 1)\begin{pmatrix} 0 & \beta_5' \\ \beta_1' & \beta_6' \end{pmatrix} = \left(-\varepsilon^{C'} \quad -\varepsilon^{Y'}\right). \tag{10.1.26}$$

The first equation is the variant consumption function:

$$C = \gamma_1' Y + \beta_1' + \varepsilon^{C'}, \tag{10.1.27}$$

which is similar in form to (10.1.22) and where γ'_1 and β'_1 are again the marginal propensity to consume and intercept, respectively. In this case, however, the first equation excludes a total of one variable, so (assuming that $\beta'_5 \neq 0$) this equation is just identified. Note that the form of the consumption function is the same for both models, but, because of a change in the other equation of the model, the original consumption function is overidentified while the variant consumption function is just identified.

The methods of estimation to be introduced will be illustrated using both the overidentified original consumption function (10.1.22) and the just-identified variant consumption function (10.1.27). In both cases the parameters to be estimated are the marginal propensity to consume (γ_1 or γ'_1) and the intercept (β_1 or β'_1). In both cases the stochastic disturbance term (ε^C or $\varepsilon^{C'}$) will be assumed to satisfy the conditions (10.1.2) to (10.1.4). The data for the estimation of the original consumption function in the prototype macro model (10.1.23) would be summarized by the data matrices:

$$\left(\begin{array}{c|c|} C_1 & Y_1 \\ C_2 & Y_2 \\ \vdots & \vdots \\ C_n & Y_n \end{array}\right), \quad \left(\begin{array}{c|cc} 1 & Y_0 & G_1 \\ 1 & Y_1 & G_2 \\ \vdots & \vdots & \vdots \\ 1 & Y_{n-1} & G_n \end{array}\right), \tag{10.1.28}$$

as in (10.1.16) and (10.1.17). In this case, as shown by the partitions, there are no excluded endogenous variables, and lagged Y and G are the excluded predetermined variables.

10.2 NAIVE, LIMITED-INFORMATION, AND FULL-INFORMATION APPROACHES

There are three alternative approaches to estimating the simultaneous-equations system in (10.1.1) or (10.1.7) using the data in (10.1.5) and (10.1.6). They are the naive approach, the limited-information approach, and the full-information approach. These approaches differ, as their names indicate, in the amount of information utilized in the estimation process.

[4]Here γ_3 and $\beta_4, \beta_5, \beta_6$ simplify the notation of (2.6.6).

The *naive approach* expresses each equation of the system in the form of (10.1.18) and estimates it as a single equation using the technique of least squares. The approach is identical to that discussed earlier under single-equation estimation, where the explanatory endogenous variables $\mathbf{Y}_1$ and included exogenous variables $\mathbf{X}_1$ constitute the set of $g_1 - 1 + k_1$ explanatory variables. In fact, this approach is called "naive" for precisely this reason: it ignores information as to which of the explanatory variables in the equation under consideration are endogenous and which are exogenous. In this approach they are all lumped together as explanatory variables. Moreover, no use is made of information on variables that are included in the system but are excluded from the equation being estimated. They are ignored altogether, and all explanatory variables are used to estimate the parameters. For example, in the prototype macro model consumption function (10.1.22) the naive approach would estimate the parameters γ_1 and β_1 as the slope and intercept of a simple linear regression of C on Y. In this case and in general, the resulting estimators are biased and inconsistent because of the inclusion of endogenous variables among the set of explanatory variables. This approach, called *ordinary least squares* (OLS), is developed in Section 10.3.

The *limited-information approach* estimates one equation at a time, estimating (10.1.18) as does OLS, but unlike OLS it distinguishes between explanatory endogenous variables $\mathbf{Y}_1$ and included exogenous variables $\mathbf{X}_1$. It also uses information as to which variables, both endogenous and exogenous, are included in the other equations of the system but excluded from the equation being estimated, given as $\mathbf{Y}_2$ and $\mathbf{X}_2$. Thus it utilizes all identifying restrictions pertaining to the equation. The information required is limited, however, to the variables included in or excluded from the equation being estimated. This approach does not require information as to the specification of the other equations of the system—in particular, the identifying restrictions on these other equations. The limited-information approach leads to estimators of (10.1.18) for coefficients $\boldsymbol{\gamma}_1$ of the $g_1 - 1$ explanatory endogenous variables and coefficients $\boldsymbol{\beta}_1$ of the k_1 included exogenous variables. Comparing this equation to the system conveys information as to the $g - g_1$ excluded endogenous variables and the $k - k_1$ excluded exogenous variables. In the consumption function of the prototype macro model (10.1.22) the coefficients are estimated given the information that Y is an explanatory endogenous variable and that Y_{-1} and G are excluded predetermined variables. While the variant consumption function (10.1.27) would result in the same naive OLS estimators as the original consumption function, the limited-information estimators would generally differ, since the excluded predetermined variables are Y_{-1} and G for the original consumption function but only G for the variant consumption function. The limited-information approach includes several specific estimators, of which *indirect least squares (ILS)* is presented in Section 10.4 and *two-stage least squares (2SLS)* and *k-class estimators*, including *limited-information maximum likelihood (LIML)*, are presented in Section 10.5. These estimators can be expressed as *instrumental variable estimators (IV)*, for particular choices of instrumental variables, as discussed in Section 10.6.

The *full-information approach* estimates the entire system of simultaneous equations in (10.1.1) [or (10.1.7) or (10.1.21) for all h] simultaneously in "one fell swoop," using all information available on each of the equations of the system. It estimates all structural parameters of the system, namely $\boldsymbol{\Gamma}$, $\mathbf{B}$, and $\boldsymbol{\Sigma}$, given the model and all identifying restrictions on each equation of the system. For the prototype macro model it would lead to estimators of (10.1.23), including the γ_1 and γ_3 elements of $\boldsymbol{\Gamma}$; the β_1, β_4, β_5, and β_6 elements of $\mathbf{B}$; and the three independent elements of $\boldsymbol{\Sigma}$, σ_{11}, σ_{22}, and σ_{12}. The variant model would result in different estimators because it entails a different specification for one of the equations of the model. The full-information approach includes two specific estimators, of which *three-stage least squares (3SLS)* is presented in Section 10.7 and *full-information maximum likelihood (FIML)* is presented in Section 10.8.

There are, therefore, several different estimators available for simultaneous-equations systems. All, however, are extensions of the two basic techniques of single-equation estimation: least squares and maximum likelihood. As indicated by their names, ordinary least squares, two-stage least squares, and three-stage least squares are extensions of the least-squares technique to simultaneous-equations estimation. Similarly, limited-information maximum likelihood and full-information maximum likelihood are extensions of the maximum-likelihood technique to simultaneous-equations estimation. The choice of a particular technique, in particular the small-sample properties of estimators, is discussed in Section 10.9.

10.3 ORDINARY LEAST SQUARES AND LEAST SQUARES BIAS

The naive approach to estimating the parameters of a system of simultaneous equations is that of *ordinary least squares (OLS)*. This approach applies least squares to each equation of the model separately, ignoring the distinction between explanatory endogenous and included exogenous variables. It also ignores all information available concerning variables not included in the equation being estimated. It will be shown that this approach leads to biased and inconsistent estimators.

The equation to be estimated, the first equation of the system, (10.1.18), can be written:

$$\mathbf{y}_1 = \mathbf{Y}_1\boldsymbol{\gamma}_1 + \mathbf{X}_1\boldsymbol{\beta}_1 + \boldsymbol{\varepsilon}_1 = (\mathbf{Y}_1 \,\vdots\, \mathbf{X}_1)\begin{pmatrix} \boldsymbol{\gamma}_1 \\ --- \\ \boldsymbol{\beta}_1 \end{pmatrix} + \boldsymbol{\varepsilon}_1 = \mathbf{Z}_1\boldsymbol{\delta}_1 + \boldsymbol{\varepsilon}_1. \tag{10.3.1}$$

Here $\mathbf{Z}_1$ lumps together data on all $(g_1 - 1 + k_1)$ included explanatory variables whether endogenous or exogenous:

$$\underset{n\times(g_1-1+k_1)}{\mathbf{Z}_1} = (\underset{n\times(g_1-1)}{\mathbf{Y}_1} \,\vdots\, \underset{n\times k_1}{\mathbf{X}_1}), \tag{10.3.2}$$

and $\boldsymbol{\delta}_1$ is a vector summarizing all coefficients to be estimated in the equation:

$$\underset{(g_1-1+k_1)\times 1}{\boldsymbol{\delta}_1} = \begin{pmatrix} \boldsymbol{\gamma}_1 \\ --- \\ \boldsymbol{\beta}_1 \end{pmatrix}\begin{matrix} g_1-1 \\ \\ k_1 \end{matrix}. \tag{10.3.3}$$

The ordinary least squares estimators of the coefficients are obtained in the same way they were for the single-equation model in Chapter 4. Applying (4.3.4) to (10.3.1) yields the estimator:

$$\hat{\boldsymbol{\delta}}_{1\text{OLS}} = (\mathbf{Z}_1'\mathbf{Z}_1)^{-1}\mathbf{Z}_1'\mathbf{y}_1, \tag{10.3.4}$$

where the inverse exists if $\mathbf{Z}_1$ has rank $g_1 - 1 + k_1$. In terms of the original notation the *OLS estimators* can be written:

$$\begin{pmatrix} \hat{\boldsymbol{\gamma}}_1 \\ --- \\ \hat{\boldsymbol{\beta}}_1 \end{pmatrix}_{\text{OLS}} = \begin{pmatrix} \mathbf{Y}_1'\mathbf{Y}_1 & | & \mathbf{Y}_1'\mathbf{X}_1 \\ ----- & | & ----- \\ \mathbf{X}_1'\mathbf{Y}_1 & | & \mathbf{X}_1'\mathbf{X}_1 \end{pmatrix}^{-1}\begin{pmatrix} \mathbf{Y}_1' \\ --- \\ \mathbf{X}_1' \end{pmatrix}\mathbf{y}_1. \tag*{*(10.3.5)}$$

While the OLS estimators are readily calculated and are utilized extensively, they do have certain limitations. For single-equation models the Gauss–Markov theorem in Section 4.4 established that least squares estimators are unbiased, and it was also shown in Section 4.4 that they are consistent estimators. The proofs of both unbiasedness and consistency in the single-equation case relied, however, on the assumption that the explanatory variables were uncorrelated with the stochastic disturbance terms. This assumption is not valid here, however. In (10.3.1) the $\mathbf{Y}_1$ are *endogenous* variables, which are *not* statistically independent of the stochastic disturbance terms, even in the probability limit. The result is that in a system of simultaneous equations the OLS estimators are *biased* and also generally *inconsistent* estimators.[5] The biased and inconsistent nature of OLS estimators can be easily demonstrated by substituting $\mathbf{Z}_1\boldsymbol{\delta}_1 + \boldsymbol{\varepsilon}_1$ for $\mathbf{y}_1$ in (10.3.4), leading to:

$$\hat{\boldsymbol{\delta}}_1 = (\mathbf{Z}_1'\mathbf{Z}_1)^{-1}\mathbf{Z}_1'(\mathbf{Z}_1\boldsymbol{\delta}_1 + \boldsymbol{\varepsilon}_1) = \boldsymbol{\delta}_1 + (\mathbf{Z}_1'\mathbf{Z}_1)^{-1}\mathbf{Z}_1'\boldsymbol{\varepsilon}_1. \tag{10.3.6}$$

Taking expectations,

$$E(\hat{\boldsymbol{\delta}}_1) = \boldsymbol{\delta}_1 + E\left[(\mathbf{Z}_1'\mathbf{Z}_1)^{-1}\mathbf{Z}_1'\boldsymbol{\varepsilon}_1\right]. \tag{10.3.7}$$

In the single-equation case the term corresponding to $E[(\mathbf{Z}'_1\mathbf{Z}_1)^{-1}\mathbf{Z}'_1\boldsymbol{\varepsilon}_1]$ vanishes because the explanatory variables are nonstochastic fixed numbers (or, stochastic but statistically independent of any of the stochastic disturbance terms). Here, however, $\mathbf{Z}_1$ includes endogenous variables, $\mathbf{Y}_1$, which are stochastic and not independent of the stochastic disturbance term. Thus $E[(\mathbf{Z}'_1\mathbf{Z}_1)^{-1}\mathbf{Z}_1'\boldsymbol{\varepsilon}_1]$ does not vanish, implying that the OLS estimators are biased:

$$E(\hat{\boldsymbol{\delta}}_1) \neq \boldsymbol{\delta}_1. \tag*{*(10.3.8)}$$

This bias does not vanish even in the limit as $n \to \infty$, so the OLS estimators are also asymptotically biased. Nor does it vanish in the probability limit, so the OLS estimators are inconsistent:

$$\text{plim}(\hat{\boldsymbol{\delta}}_1) = \boldsymbol{\delta}_1 + \text{plim}\left(\frac{1}{n}\mathbf{Z}_1'\mathbf{Z}_1\right)^{-1}\left(\frac{1}{n}\mathbf{Z}_1'\boldsymbol{\varepsilon}_1\right) \neq \boldsymbol{\delta}_1. \tag{10.3.9}$$

In terms of the original coefficients and data, the OLS estimators are:

$$\begin{pmatrix} \hat{\boldsymbol{\gamma}}_1 \\ \text{---} \\ \hat{\boldsymbol{\beta}}_1 \end{pmatrix}_{\text{OLS}} = \begin{pmatrix} \boldsymbol{\gamma}_1 \\ \text{---} \\ \boldsymbol{\beta}_1 \end{pmatrix} + \left(\begin{array}{c|c} \mathbf{Y}_1'\mathbf{Y}_1 & \mathbf{Y}_1'\mathbf{X}_1 \\ \hline \mathbf{X}_1'\mathbf{Y}_1 & \mathbf{X}_1'\mathbf{X}_1 \end{array}\right)^{-1} \begin{pmatrix} \mathbf{Y}_1' \\ \text{---} \\ \mathbf{X}_1' \end{pmatrix} \boldsymbol{\varepsilon}_1. \tag{10.3.10}$$

In general, the expectation of the second term on the right does not vanish, even in the probability limit, since the explanatory endogenous variables are not independent of the stochastic disturbance term. The bias is given by

$$\begin{aligned} B\begin{pmatrix} \hat{\boldsymbol{\gamma}}_1 \\ \text{---} \\ \hat{\boldsymbol{\beta}}_1 \end{pmatrix}_{\text{OLS}} &= E\left[\begin{pmatrix} \hat{\boldsymbol{\gamma}}_1 \\ \text{---} \\ \hat{\boldsymbol{\beta}}_1 \end{pmatrix} - \begin{pmatrix} \boldsymbol{\gamma}_1 \\ \text{---} \\ \boldsymbol{\beta}_1 \end{pmatrix}\right] \\ &= E\left[\left(\begin{array}{c|c} \mathbf{Y}_1'\mathbf{Y}_1 & \mathbf{Y}_1'\mathbf{X}_1 \\ \hline \mathbf{X}_1'\mathbf{Y}_1 & \mathbf{X}_1'\mathbf{X}_1 \end{array}\right)^{-1} \begin{pmatrix} \mathbf{Y}_1' \\ \text{---} \\ \mathbf{X}_1' \end{pmatrix} \boldsymbol{\varepsilon}_1\right] \end{aligned} \tag{10.3.11}$$

and this bias does not vanish, even asymptotically.

[5]See Haavelmo (1943, 1947). A simultaneous system in which least squares is appropriate, however, is a recursive system as discussed in Sections 9.5 and 10.8.

The consumption function of the prototype macro model (10.1.22) can be used to illustrate the OLS estimators. Using (10.3.5) yields

$$\begin{pmatrix} \hat{\gamma}_1 \\ \hat{\beta}_1 \end{pmatrix}_{\text{OLS}} = \begin{pmatrix} \Sigma Y_i^2 & \Sigma Y_i \\ \Sigma Y_i & n \end{pmatrix}^{-1} \begin{pmatrix} \Sigma C_i Y_i \\ \Sigma C_i \end{pmatrix}, \tag{10.3.12}$$

leading to the OLS estimator of the slope, the marginal propensity to consume, as:

$$\hat{\gamma}_{1\text{OLS}} = \frac{\Sigma \dot{C}_i \dot{Y}_i}{\Sigma \dot{Y}_i^2}, \tag{10.3.13}$$

in this case of simple linear regression. Here γ_1' and $\dot{Y}_i$ are the ith deviations of consumption and income from their mean values, as defined by:

$$\dot{C}_i = C_i - \overline{C}, \qquad \overline{C} = \frac{1}{n}\Sigma C_i, \tag{10.3.14}$$

$$\dot{Y}_i = Y_i - \overline{Y}, \qquad \overline{Y} = \frac{1}{n}\Sigma Y_i. \tag{10.3.15}$$

In terms of these deviations the structural equations can be written:

$$\dot{C}_i = \gamma_1 \dot{Y}_i + \varepsilon_i^C, \tag{10.3.16}$$

$$\dot{Y}_i = \gamma_3 \dot{C}_i + \beta_4 \dot{Y}_{i-1} + \beta_5 \dot{G}_i + \varepsilon_i^Y. \tag{10.3.17}$$

Using (10.3.16), the OLS estimator of γ_1 can be written

$$\hat{\gamma}_{1\text{OLS}} = \gamma_1 + \frac{\Sigma \varepsilon_i^C \dot{Y}_i}{\Sigma \dot{Y}_i^2}, \tag{10.3.18}$$

which is of the same form as the general expression (10.3.10). Taking expectations, as in (10.3.11), the bias in the estimation of the marginal propensity to consume is:

$$B(\hat{\gamma}_{1\text{OLS}}) = E\left(\frac{\Sigma \varepsilon_i^C \dot{Y}_i}{\Sigma \dot{Y}_i^2}\right) > 0. \tag{10.3.19}$$

The bias is positive, as can readily be seen from the structural equations. Suppose that there were a positive ε_i^C at observation i. The result from (10.3.16) would be a larger γ_1' at this observation than would be expected. But a larger γ_1' would, from (10.3.17), assuming that $\gamma_3 > 0$, lead to a larger Y_i than would be expected. Thus a positive ε_i^C implies a larger $\dot{Y}_i$ than would be expected. Similarly, a negative ε_i^C implies a smaller $\dot{Y}_i$ than would be expected. The expectation of the ratio in (10.3.19) is therefore positive, so the OLS estimator of γ_1 is biased upward:

$$E(\hat{\gamma}_{1\text{OLS}}) > \gamma_1, \tag{10.3.20}$$

overstating the marginal propensity to consume. At the same time OLS understates β_1, the intercept, as illustrated in Figure 10.1, where the OLS estimate of the slope is biased upward, but the OLS estimate of the intercept is biased downward compared to the true consumption function. The inclusion of an explanatory endogenous variable leads to this bias.

The OLS overstatement of the marginal propensity to consume is not corrected by taking a larger sample, so the OLS estimator is inconsistent as well as biased. From (10.3.18), in general,

$$\text{plim } \hat{\gamma}_{1\text{OLS}} = \gamma_1 + \frac{\text{plim}(1/n)\Sigma \varepsilon_i^C \dot{Y}_i^2}{\text{plim}(1/n)\Sigma \dot{Y}_i^2} > \gamma_1, \tag{10.3.21}$$

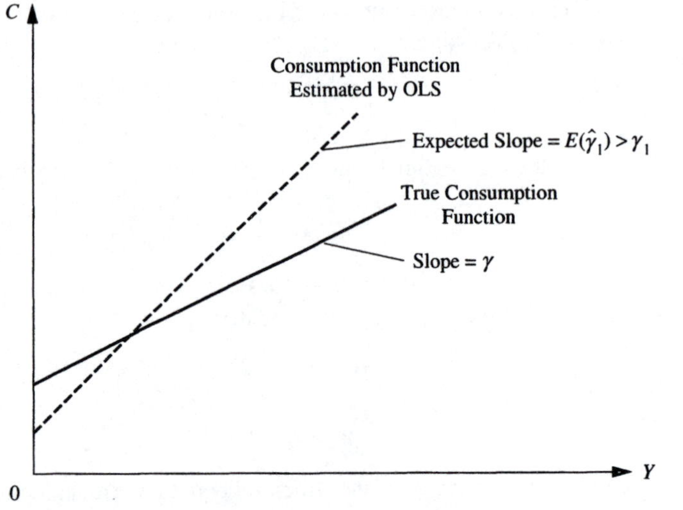

Figure 10.1 Least Squares Bias in Estimating the Consumption Function by OLS

so that the OLS estimator generally overstates the true marginal propensity to consume even in the limit, as the sample size grows without bound.[6]

While OLS yields estimators that are biased and inconsistent, it should not be totally rejected as an estimation technique for simultaneous-equations systems. As will be seen in Section 10.9, the OLS estimators tend to exhibit both efficiency and insensitivity to specification error. Furthermore, as little is known concerning the finite-sample properties of any estimator, OLS may be as good as any other method of estimation, even the consistent estimators to be presented later in this chapter. In fact, as will be seen in Chapters 12 and 13, OLS is indeed used in estimating several specific simultaneous-equations systems.

10.4 INDIRECT LEAST SQUARES

Indirect least squares (ILS) is a limited-information technique that can be used to obtain consistent estimators of a just-identified equation, as discussed in Section 9.3. In the just-identified case the structural parameters are uniquely determined from the reduced-form parameters, so the estimated reduced-form parameters can be used to infer estimated structural parameters indirectly, leading to the name "indirect least squares."

This approach involves two steps. The first is the estimation of the reduced-form parameters $\hat{\mathbf{\Pi}}$ using least squares. The second, which is possible if and only if the equation is just identified, is the estimation of structural-form parameters $\mathbf{\Gamma}$ and $\mathbf{B}$ using the relationships between these parameters and the reduced-form parameters and the identifying restrictions. If the equation is overidentified, the ILS method will not work and either OLS or other approaches, discussed in the next sections, must be employed. It will be seen, however, that these other approaches, which apply both to just-identified and overidentified equations, typically are equivalent to ILS in the just-identified case.

The ILS method starts by estimating the reduced form, which is:

[6]See Problem 10-C for certain special conditions under which the OLS estimator of γ'_1 in the variant model is consistent.

$$\underset{n\times g}{\mathbf{Y}} = \underset{n\times k}{\mathbf{X}}\ \underset{k\times g}{\mathbf{\Pi}} + \underset{n\times g}{\mathbf{U}}, \tag{10.4.1}$$

where

$$\mathbf{\Pi} = -\mathbf{B}\mathbf{\Gamma}^{-1}, \tag{10.4.2}$$

$$\mathbf{U} = \mathbf{E}\mathbf{\Gamma}^{-1}, \tag{10.4.3}$$

as in (9.1.10) and (9.1.11). The least squares estimator of the matrix of reduced-form coefficients $\mathbf{\Pi}$ is given by:

$$\underset{k\times g}{\hat{\mathbf{\Pi}}} = \underset{k\times k}{(\mathbf{X}'\mathbf{X})^{-1}}\ \underset{k\times n}{\mathbf{X}'}\ \underset{n\times g}{\mathbf{Y}}, \tag{10.4.4}$$

as in (9.1.24), where $\mathbf{X}$ and $\mathbf{Y}$ are the data matrices of (10.1.5) and (10.1.6). This estimator is equivalent to estimating each equation of the reduced form separately via least squares, since each column of $\hat{\mathbf{\Pi}}$ is the common matrix of weights $(\mathbf{X}'\mathbf{X})^{-1}\mathbf{X}'$ times the column of the $\mathbf{Y}$ matrix corresponding to the dependent variable in that particular reduced-form equation.

Now consider one just identified equation. The $\mathbf{Y}$ matrix can be partitioned as in (10.1.16), corresponding to the one dependent endogenous variable $\mathbf{y}_1$, the $g_1 - 1$ explanatory endogenous variables $\mathbf{Y}_1$, and the $g - g_1$ excluded endogenous variables $\mathbf{Y}_2$. The $\mathbf{X}$ matrix can be similarly partitioned as in (10.1.17), corresponding to the k_1 included exogenous variables $\mathbf{X}_1$ and the $k - k_1$ excluded variables $\mathbf{X}_2$. The reduced form (10.4.1) can then be written:

$$\left(\underset{n\times 1}{\mathbf{y}_1} \,\vdots\, \underset{n\times(g_1-1)}{\mathbf{Y}_1} \,\vdots\, \underset{n\times(g-g_1)}{\mathbf{Y}_2}\right) = \left(\underset{n\times k_1}{\mathbf{X}_1} \,\vdots\, \underset{n\times(k-k_1)}{\mathbf{X}_2}\right) \begin{pmatrix} \mathbf{\Pi}_1^0 & \mathbf{\Pi}_1^{00} & \mathbf{\Pi}_3 \\ \mathbf{\Pi}_2^0 & \mathbf{\Pi}_2^{00} & \mathbf{\Pi}_4 \end{pmatrix}_{\substack{\\ 1 \quad g_1-1 \quad g-g_1}} + \left(\underset{n\times 1}{\mathbf{u}_0} \,\vdots\, \underset{n\times(g_1-1)}{\mathbf{u}_1} \,\vdots\, \underset{n\times(g-g_1)}{\mathbf{u}_2}\right), \tag*{*(10.4.5)}$$

where the stochastic disturbance terms have been partitioned in the same way as $\mathbf{Y}$, corresponding to the dependent, explanatory, and excluded endogenous variables. The matrix of reduced-form coefficients $\mathbf{\Pi}$ has been partitioned here into six submatrices in order to carry out the matrix multiplication, as in (9.3.7), (9.3.19), and (9.3.20). Its columns have been divided to correspond to the one dependent endogenous variable, the $g_1 - 1$ explanatory endogenous variables, and the $g - g_1$ excluded endogenous variables. Its rows have been divided to correspond to the k_1 included exogenous variables and $k - k_1$ excluded exogenous variables. Thus, for example, the submatrix $\mathbf{\Pi}_2^{00}$ is a $(k - k_1) \times (g_1 - 1)$ matrix. If the equation to be estimated is just identified, then $k - k_1 = g_1 - 1$, so $\mathbf{\Pi}_2^{00}$ is a square matrix.

The relations between the structural-form and reduced-form parameters, (10.4.2), may be written:

$$\mathbf{\Pi}\mathbf{\Gamma} = -\mathbf{B}. \tag{10.4.6}$$

For the first equation, involving only the first columns of $\mathbf{\Gamma}$ and $\mathbf{B}$, using the normalization and zero restrictions, and using the partitioned $\mathbf{\Pi}$ matrix in (10.4.5),

$$\begin{pmatrix} \mathbf{\Pi}_1^0 & \mathbf{\Pi}_1^{00} & \mathbf{\Pi}_3 \\ \mathbf{\Pi}_2^0 & \mathbf{\Pi}_2^{00} & \mathbf{\Pi}_4 \end{pmatrix} \begin{pmatrix} -1 \\ \boldsymbol{\gamma}_1 \\ \mathbf{0} \end{pmatrix} = -\begin{pmatrix} \boldsymbol{\beta}_1 \\ \mathbf{0} \end{pmatrix}. \tag{10.4.7}$$

Writing out the resulting two sets of equations, where elements of $\mathbf{\Pi}$ are replaced by the estimators $\hat{\mathbf{\Pi}}$ in (10.4.2) and the structural coefficients of the first equation are replaced by their estimators $\hat{\boldsymbol{\gamma}}_1$ and $\hat{\boldsymbol{\beta}}_1$,

$$-\hat{\mathbf{\Pi}}_1^0 + \hat{\mathbf{\Pi}}_1^{00}\hat{\boldsymbol{\gamma}}_1 = -\hat{\boldsymbol{\beta}}_1 \qquad (k_1 \text{ equations}), \tag{10.4.8}$$

$$-\hat{\mathbf{\Pi}}_2^0 + \hat{\mathbf{\Pi}}_2^{00}\hat{\boldsymbol{\gamma}}_1 = \mathbf{0} \qquad (k - k_1 \text{ equations}). \tag{10.4.9}$$

As already noted, if the equation to be estimated is just identified, then $\mathbf{\Pi}_2^{00}$ is a square matrix. Assuming it is nonsingular, (10.4.9) can be solved for $\hat{\boldsymbol{\gamma}}_1$, as in (9.3.23), as:

$$\hat{\boldsymbol{\gamma}}_1 = \left(\hat{\mathbf{\Pi}}_2^{00}\right)^{-1}\hat{\mathbf{\Pi}}_2^0. \tag{10.4.10}$$

From this result and (10.4.8), it follows that $\hat{\boldsymbol{\beta}}_1$ can be obtained, as in (9.3.24), as:

$$\hat{\boldsymbol{\beta}}_1 = \hat{\mathbf{\Pi}}_1^0 - \hat{\mathbf{\Pi}}_1^{00}\left(\hat{\mathbf{\Pi}}_2^{00}\right)^{-1}\hat{\mathbf{\Pi}}_2^0. \tag{10.4.11}$$

These are the *indirect least squares (ILS) estimators*, which may be written:

$$\begin{pmatrix} \hat{\boldsymbol{\gamma}}_1 \\ --- \\ \hat{\boldsymbol{\beta}}_1 \end{pmatrix}_{\text{ILS}} = \begin{pmatrix} \left(\hat{\mathbf{\Pi}}_2^{00}\right)^{-1}\hat{\mathbf{\Pi}}_2^0 \\ ------------ \\ \hat{\mathbf{\Pi}}_1^0 - \hat{\mathbf{\Pi}}_1^{00}\left(\hat{\mathbf{\Pi}}_2^{00}\right)^{-1}\hat{\mathbf{\Pi}}_2^0 \end{pmatrix}. \tag*{*(10.4.12)}$$

These estimators use the least squares estimators of reduced-form coefficients, (10.4.4), plus the identifying restrictions to obtain estimators of the structural parameters for one just-identified equation of the simultaneous-equations system. They are the first of several limited-information estimators to be considered.

The ILS estimators are generally biased estimators, as are the OLS estimators, but unlike the OLS estimators, ILS estimators are consistent, where:

$$\text{plim}\begin{pmatrix} \hat{\boldsymbol{\gamma}}_1 \\ --- \\ \hat{\boldsymbol{\beta}}_1 \end{pmatrix}_{\text{ILS}} = \begin{pmatrix} \boldsymbol{\gamma}_1 \\ --- \\ \boldsymbol{\beta}_1 \end{pmatrix}. \tag*{*(10.4.13)}$$

The consistency of the ILS estimators follows from the fact that, as indicated in Section 4.4, continuous functions of consistent estimators are also consistent estimators. The ILS estimators are obtained, however, as continuous functions of the reduced-form estimators $\hat{\mathbf{\Pi}}$, as summarized in (10.4.12), and the reduced-form estimators themselves are consistent from the least squares consistency theorem of Section 4.4.[7]

The ILS estimator can be illustrated using the variant consumption function (10.1.27), which is a just-identified equation. The structural form, from (10.1.26), is:

$$C = \gamma_1' Y + \beta_1' + \varepsilon^{C'}, \tag{10.4.14}$$

[7]While continuous functions of consistent estimators are consistent, continuous functions of unbiased estimators need not be unbiased, and continuous functions of efficient estimators need not be efficient. Thus, even though the reduced-form estimators $\hat{\mathbf{\Pi}}$ are unbiased and efficient by the Gauss–Markov theorem of Section 4.4, the ILS estimators are, in general, neither unbiased nor efficient. It should also be noted that since $\hat{\gamma}_{1_{\text{ILS}}}$, the ILS estimator of γ_1, is consistent, the continuous transformation $(1 - \hat{\gamma}_{1_{\text{ILS}}})$, the estimator of the multiplier, is also a consistent estimator (but not necessarily an unbiased or efficient estimator). It might further be noted that another property that holds over continuous transformations is that of maximum likelihood. Thus if the reduced-form estimators $\hat{\mathbf{\Pi}}$ are maximum likelihood estimators, which they are if the structural- and reduced-form stochastic disturbance terms are normally distributed, then the ILS estimators in (10.4.12) are also maximum likelihood estimators.

$$Y = \gamma_3' C + \beta_5' G + \beta_6' + \varepsilon^{Y'}. \tag{10.4.15}$$

The reduced form is obtained readily by inserting Y from (10.4.15) in (10.4.14) and solving for C and then Y to yield:

$$C = \Pi_1' + \Pi_2' G + u^{C'}, \tag{10.4.16}$$

$$Y = \Pi_3' + \Pi_4' G + u^{Y'}, \tag{10.4.17}$$

where

$$\Pi_1' = \frac{\beta_1' + \gamma_1' \beta_6'}{1 - \gamma_1' \gamma_3'}, \qquad \Pi_2' = \frac{\gamma_1' \beta_5'}{1 - \gamma_1' \gamma_3'}, \qquad u^{C'} = \frac{\varepsilon^{C'} + \gamma_1 \varepsilon^{Y'}}{1 - \gamma_1' \gamma_3'}, \tag{10.4.18}$$

$$\Pi_3' = \frac{\beta_6' + \gamma_3' \beta_1'}{1 - \gamma_1' \gamma_3'}, \qquad \Pi_4' = \frac{\beta_5'}{1 - \gamma_1' \gamma_3'}, \qquad u^{Y'} = \frac{\gamma_3' \varepsilon^{C'} + \varepsilon^{Y'}}{1 - \gamma_1' \gamma_3'}. \tag{10.4.19}$$

But the reduced form can be written, following (10.4.5), as

$$(C \mid Y \mid \quad) = (1 \mid G) \begin{pmatrix} \Pi_1' & \mid & \Pi_3' & \mid & \\ \hline \Pi_2' & \mid & \Pi_4' & \mid & \end{pmatrix} + (u^{C'} \mid u^{Y'} \mid \quad), \tag{10.4.20}$$

where the order of the exogenous variables has been adjusted so the exogenous variable excluded from the consumption function, G, appears last. Following (10.4.7) for the relations between the reduced-form and structural-form coefficients:

$$\begin{pmatrix} \Pi_1' & \mid & \Pi_3' & \mid & \\ \hline \Pi_2' & \mid & \Pi_4' & \mid & \end{pmatrix} \begin{pmatrix} -1 \\ \hline \gamma_1' \end{pmatrix} = - \begin{pmatrix} \beta_1' \\ \hline 0 \end{pmatrix}. \tag{10.4.21}$$

Thus

$$-\Pi_1' + \Pi_3' \gamma_1' = -\beta_1', \tag{10.4.22}$$

$$-\Pi_2' + \Pi_4' \gamma_1' = 0, \tag{10.4.23}$$

where here $\mathbf{\Pi}_1^0$ reduces to Π_1'; $\mathbf{\Pi}_2^0$ reduces to Π_2'; $\mathbf{\Pi}_1^{00}$ reduces to Π_3'; and $\mathbf{\Pi}_2^{00}$ reduces to Π_4'. From (10.4.12), the ILS estimators are:

$$\begin{pmatrix} \hat{\gamma}_1' \\ \hline \hat{\beta}_1' \end{pmatrix}_{\text{ILS}} = \begin{pmatrix} \hat{\Pi}_4'^{-1} \hat{\Pi}_2' \\ \hline \hat{\Pi}_1' - \hat{\Pi}_3' \hat{\Pi}_4'^{-1} \hat{\Pi}_2' \end{pmatrix}, \tag{10.4.24}$$

so that

$$\hat{\gamma}_{1_{\text{ILS}}}' = \frac{\hat{\Pi}_2'}{\hat{\Pi}_4'}, \tag{10.4.25}$$

$$\hat{\beta}_{1_{\text{ILS}}}' = \hat{\Pi}_1' - \frac{\hat{\Pi}_2' \hat{\Pi}_3'}{\hat{\Pi}_4'}. \tag{10.4.26}$$

In this simple example these estimators can also be readily obtained directly from (10.4.18) and (10.4.19) by solving for γ'_1 and β_1'.

Using the least squares estimators of the two simple linear regression equations that constitute the reduced form (10.4.16) and (10.4.17), the ILS estimator of the marginal propensity to consume is:

$$\hat{\gamma}'_{1_{\text{ILS}}} = \frac{\hat{\Pi}'_2}{\hat{\Pi}'_4} = \frac{\Sigma \dot{C}_i \dot{G}_i \,/\, \Sigma \dot{G}_i^2}{\Sigma \dot{Y}_i \dot{G}_i \,/\, \Sigma \dot{G}_i^2} = \frac{\Sigma \dot{C}_i \dot{G}_i}{\Sigma \dot{Y}_i \dot{G}_i}, \tag{10.4.27}$$

where $\dot{C}_i$, $\dot{Y}_i$, and $\dot{G}_i$ represent deviations from mean values. This result can be contrasted with the OLS estimator, which is the same for the variant consumption function as for the original consumption function. From (10.3.13),

$$\hat{\gamma}'_{1_{\text{OLS}}} = \frac{\Sigma \dot{C}_i \dot{Y}_i}{\Sigma \dot{Y}_i^2}. \tag{10.4.28}$$

The OLS estimator is biased and inconsistent, while the ILS estimator is biased but consistent. The consistency of the ILS estimator can be readily seen, since, using (10.4.16) and (10.4.17) in (10.4.27),

$$\hat{\gamma}'_{1_{\text{ILS}}} = \frac{\Sigma \dot{C}_i \dot{G}_i}{\Sigma \dot{Y}_i \dot{G}_i} = \frac{\Pi'_2 + \left(\frac{1}{n} \Sigma u_i^{C'} \dot{G}_i\right) \Big/ \left(\frac{1}{n} \Sigma \dot{G}_i^2\right)}{\Pi'_4 + \left(\frac{1}{n} \Sigma u_i^{Y'} \dot{G}_i\right) \Big/ \left(\frac{1}{n} \Sigma \dot{G}_i^2\right)}. \tag{10.4.29}$$

In any finite sample the expectation of $\hat{\gamma}'_{1_{\text{ILS}}}$ need not be $(\Pi'_2/\Pi'_4) = \gamma'_1$, since the expectation of a ratio is not, in general, the ratio of the expectations. Thus

$$E(\hat{\gamma}'_{1_{\text{ILS}}}) = \gamma'_1. \tag{10.4.30}$$

Taking the probability limit, however, the probability limit of a ratio is the ratio of the probability limits, so, since both $\text{plim}(1/n)\,\Sigma u_i^{C'} \dot{G}_i$ and $\text{plim}(1/n)\,\Sigma u_i^{Y'} \dot{G}_i$ vanish,

$$\text{plim}(\hat{\gamma}'_{1_{\text{ILS}}}) \neq \gamma'_1, \tag{10.4.31}$$

demonstrating the consistency of this indirect least squares estimator.[8]

The indirect least squares approach provides consistent estimators, but it is defined only for just-identified equations. This estimator is not defined in the overidentified case such as the original consumption function of the prototype macro model. The methods to be introduced in the next two sections are limited-information approaches for which estimators are defined in both the overidentified and the just-identified cases. As already noted, however, these estimators are generally equivalent to the indirect least squares estimator in the just-identified case.

10.5 TWO-STAGE LEAST SQUARES AND *k*-CLASS ESTIMATORS[9]

In Sections 10.3 and 10.4 we introduced OLS estimators, which are generally biased and inconsistent, and ILS estimators, which are biased but consistent and defined only for just-identified equations. This section presents a limited-information technique that can be used to estimate either an overidentified or an identified equation from a system of simultaneous equations—the technique of two-stage least squares (2SLS) and its generalization to *k*-class estimators.

[8]A comparable approach for $\hat{\gamma}'_{1_{\text{OLS}}}$ shows that it is inconsistent as well as biased (see Problem 10-E).

[9]For the initial development of two-stage least squares, see Theil (1961) and Basmann (1957, 1959, 1960). Basmann has referred to the technique as a "generalized classical linear" (GCL) estimator. See the next two sections for related presentations of two-stage least squares. For an extension to nonlinear estimation, see Kelejian (1971), Amemiya (1974), and Section 10.10.

Several formulations of the 2SLS estimator will be presented in this section and the next two sections. The first formulation will provide both a motivation for the estimator and a rationale for its name.

Consider the (first) equation to be estimated, as presented in (10.1.18), of the form:

$$\mathbf{y}_1 = \mathbf{Y}_1\boldsymbol{\gamma}_1 + \mathbf{X}_1\boldsymbol{\beta}_1 + \boldsymbol{\varepsilon}_1. \tag{10.5.1}$$

The "problem" in applying least squares directly to estimate this equation is the presence of explanatory endogenous variables, $\mathbf{Y}_1$, which are correlated with the stochastic disturbance terms, $\boldsymbol{\varepsilon}_1$, even in the probability limit. If these variables could be replaced by related variables that are uncorrelated, in the probability limit, with the stochastic disturbance terms, the resulting estimator would be consistent. The method of two-stage least squares accomplishes this by using the estimated reduced form to replace explanatory endogenous variables by their estimated values. Thus, $\mathbf{Y}_1$ is replaced in (10.5.1) by $\hat{\mathbf{Y}}_1$, the estimated values of each of the explanatory endogenous variables at each observation using the reduced form. The least squares estimator of the resulting equation, which is the same as the OLS estimator in (10.3.5) other than $\mathbf{Y}_1$ being replaced by $\hat{\mathbf{Y}}_1$, is the *two-stage least squares (2SLS) estimator*, of the form:

$$\begin{pmatrix} \hat{\boldsymbol{\gamma}}_1 \\ \hline \hat{\boldsymbol{\beta}}_1 \end{pmatrix}_{2SLS} = \left(\begin{array}{c|c} \hat{\mathbf{Y}}_1'\hat{\mathbf{Y}}_1 & \hat{\mathbf{Y}}_1'\mathbf{X}_1 \\ \hline \mathbf{X}_1'\hat{\mathbf{Y}}_1 & \mathbf{X}_1'\mathbf{X}_1 \end{array}\right)^{-1} \begin{pmatrix} \hat{\mathbf{Y}}_1' \\ \hline \mathbf{X}_1' \end{pmatrix} \mathbf{y}_1. \tag{*10.5.2}$$

This first formulation of the 2SLS estimator indicates that it yields estimators of all coefficients of one equation of the system, given data on the dependent endogenous variable $\mathbf{y}_1$, data on the included exogenous variables $\mathbf{X}_1$, and estimated values of the explanatory endogenous variables $\mathbf{Y}_1$. These estimated values are determined, themselves, from the estimated reduced-form coefficients and the data on all exogenous variables of the system. Thus the estimator depends on all exogenous variables, not just those included in the equation to be estimated.

The rationale for the name *two-stage least squares* is indicated by (10.5.2). Least squares regression is, indeed, done in two stages. The first stage uses least squares to estimate the reduced form in order to calculate the $\hat{\mathbf{Y}}_1$ in (10.5.2). The second stage uses least squares once again to estimate the structural-form equation, as seen in (10.5.2), which is a least squares estimator for which $\mathbf{Y}_1$ in (10.5.1) has been replaced by $\hat{\mathbf{Y}}_1$. Thus 2SLS involves two stages, each of which entails the least squares estimation of g equations—those of the reduced form in the first stage and those of the structural form in the second stage.[10]

The formulation of the 2SLS estimator in (10.5.2) uses $\hat{\mathbf{Y}}_1$, and it will be important to specify more formally the computation of these estimates of the explanatory endogenous variables. The reduced form is:

$$\mathbf{Y} = \mathbf{X}\boldsymbol{\Pi} + \mathbf{u} \tag{10.5.3}$$

and the least squares estimators of the reduced-form coefficients $\hat{\boldsymbol{\Pi}}$ are given as:

$$\hat{\boldsymbol{\Pi}} = (\mathbf{X}'\mathbf{X})^{-1}\mathbf{X}'\mathbf{Y}, \tag{10.5.4}$$

[10]The ILS estimator also involves two steps, but only the first step, the estimation of the reduced form in (10.4.4), involves least squares. The second step involves algebraic manipulations of the reduced-form estimators to obtain structural-form estimators, as in (10.4.12).

as in (10.4.4). In this first of the two stages, all exogenous variables are treated as the explanatory variables in each of the g least squares regressions, one for each endogenous variable. The $\hat{\mathbf{\Pi}}$ estimator consists of g columns, each representing the estimators of the coefficients in one such regression. The estimates of the endogenous variables $\hat{\mathbf{Y}}$ are obtained from the estimated $\hat{\mathbf{\Pi}}$ and data on all exogenous variables of the model $\mathbf{X}$ as:

$$\hat{\mathbf{Y}} = \mathbf{X}\hat{\mathbf{\Pi}} = \mathbf{X}(\mathbf{X}'\mathbf{X})^{-1}\mathbf{X}'\mathbf{Y}. \qquad (10.5.5)$$

Furthermore,

$$\mathbf{Y} = \mathbf{X}\hat{\mathbf{\Pi}} + \hat{\mathbf{u}} = \hat{\mathbf{Y}} + \hat{\mathbf{u}}, \qquad (10.5.6)$$

where $\hat{\mathbf{u}}$ is the matrix of reduced-form residuals. Following the usual partitioning based on those variables included in or excluded from the equation to be estimated, as in (10.4.5), equation (10.5.6) can be written

$$(\mathbf{y}_1 \mid \mathbf{Y}_1 \mid \mathbf{Y}_2) = (\mathbf{X}_1 \mid \mathbf{X}_2)\begin{pmatrix} \hat{\mathbf{\Pi}}_1^{0} & \hat{\mathbf{\Pi}}_1^{00} & \hat{\mathbf{\Pi}}_3 \\ \hline \hat{\mathbf{\Pi}}_2^{0} & \hat{\mathbf{\Pi}}_2^{00} & \hat{\mathbf{\Pi}}_4 \end{pmatrix} + (\hat{\mathbf{u}}_0 \mid \hat{\mathbf{u}}_1 \mid \hat{\mathbf{u}}_2). \qquad (10.5.7)$$

Solving for the variables of interest, the explanatory endogenous variables in the equation to be estimated,

$$\mathbf{Y}_1 = \mathbf{X}_1\hat{\mathbf{\Pi}}_1^{00} + \mathbf{X}_2\hat{\mathbf{\Pi}}_2^{00} + \hat{\mathbf{u}}_1 = \hat{\mathbf{Y}}_1 + \hat{\mathbf{u}}_1. \qquad (10.5.8)$$

Thus $\hat{\mathbf{Y}}_1$, the matrix of estimated values of the explanatory endogenous variables in (10.5.2), is given as the linear combination of the exogenous variables:

$$\hat{\mathbf{Y}}_1 = \mathbf{X}_1\hat{\mathbf{\Pi}}_1^{00} + \mathbf{X}_2\hat{\mathbf{\Pi}}_2^{00}. \qquad (10.5.9)$$

Furthermore, from (10.5.5) and (10.5.7),

$$\begin{aligned} \hat{\mathbf{Y}} = (\hat{\mathbf{y}}_1 \mid \hat{\mathbf{Y}}_1 \mid \hat{\mathbf{Y}}_2) &= \mathbf{X}\hat{\mathbf{\Pi}} = \mathbf{X}(\mathbf{X}'\mathbf{X})^{-1}\mathbf{X}'\mathbf{Y} \\ &= \mathbf{X}(\mathbf{X}'\mathbf{X})^{-1}\mathbf{X}'(\mathbf{y}_1 \mid \mathbf{Y}_1 \mid \mathbf{Y}_2), \end{aligned} \qquad (10.5.10)$$

so that $\hat{\mathbf{Y}}_1$ can be expressed as the linear function of the actual $\mathbf{Y}_1$, namely:

$$\hat{\mathbf{Y}}_1 = \mathbf{X}(\mathbf{X}'\mathbf{X})^{-1}\mathbf{X}'\mathbf{Y}_1. \qquad (10.5.11)$$

The $\hat{\mathbf{Y}}_1$ can be also expressed as the actual $\mathbf{Y}_1$ less the relevant reduced-form residuals:

$$\hat{\mathbf{Y}}_1 = \mathbf{Y}_1 - \hat{\mathbf{u}}_1, \qquad (10.5.12)$$

where $\hat{\mathbf{u}}_1$ can be expressed in terms of the fundamental idempotent matrix of least squares (4.3.12) as:

$$\hat{\mathbf{u}}_1 = (\mathbf{I} - \mathbf{X}(\mathbf{X}'\mathbf{X})^{-1}\mathbf{X}')\mathbf{Y}_1 = \mathbf{M}\mathbf{Y}_1. \qquad (10.5.13)$$

The $\hat{\mathbf{Y}}_1$ in (10.5.2) has thus been expressed in three equivalent ways in (10.5.9), (10.5.11), and (10.5.12).

The last formulation of $\hat{\mathbf{Y}}_1$, in (10.5.12), indicates that it can be obtained from the data on explanatory endogenous variables $\mathbf{Y}_1$ by subtracting the relevant estimated reduced-form residuals $\hat{\mathbf{u}}_1$ in order to "purge" the variables of their statistical dependence on the stochastic term. The 2SLS estimator can then be interpreted in terms of the original equation. Combining (10.5.1) and (10.5.12) yields:

$$\mathbf{y}_1 = (\hat{\mathbf{Y}}_1 + \hat{\mathbf{u}}_1)\boldsymbol{\gamma}_1 + \mathbf{X}_1\boldsymbol{\beta}_1 + \boldsymbol{\varepsilon}_1. \qquad (10.5.14)$$

Thus,

$$\mathbf{y}_1 = \hat{\mathbf{Y}}_1\boldsymbol{\gamma}_1 + \mathbf{X}_1\boldsymbol{\beta}_1 + \mathbf{v}_1, \tag{10.5.15}$$

where

$$\mathbf{v}_1 = \hat{\mathbf{u}}_1\boldsymbol{\gamma}_1 + \boldsymbol{\varepsilon}_1. \tag{10.5.16}$$

The 2SLS estimator is the least squares estimator of (10.5.15), which is of exactly the same form as (10.5.1), but in which explanatory endogenous variables are replaced by values estimated from the reduced form.

Combining (10.5.2) and (10.5.12) yields the second formulation of the 2SLS estimator:

$$\begin{pmatrix} \hat{\boldsymbol{\gamma}}_1 \\ \hline \hat{\boldsymbol{\beta}}_1 \end{pmatrix}_{2SLS} = \left(\begin{array}{c|c} \mathbf{Y}_1'\mathbf{Y}_1 - \hat{\mathbf{u}}_1'\hat{\mathbf{u}}_1 & \mathbf{Y}_1'\mathbf{X}_1 \\ \hline \mathbf{X}_1'\mathbf{Y}_1 & \mathbf{X}_1'\mathbf{X}_1 \end{array}\right)^{-1} \begin{pmatrix} \mathbf{Y}_1' - \hat{\mathbf{u}}_1' \\ \hline \mathbf{X}_1' \end{pmatrix}\mathbf{y}_1. \quad *(10.5.17)$$

To obtain this estimator, $\hat{\mathbf{Y}}_1$ in (10.5.2) is replaced by $\mathbf{Y}_1 - \hat{\mathbf{u}}_1$ from (10.5.12). The upper left submatrix in the partitioned matrix to be inverted is then:

$$\hat{\mathbf{Y}}_1'\hat{\mathbf{Y}}_1 = (\mathbf{Y}_1' - \hat{\mathbf{u}}_1')(\mathbf{Y}_1 - \hat{\mathbf{u}}_1) = \hat{\mathbf{Y}}_1'\mathbf{Y}_1 = \mathbf{Y}_1'\mathbf{Y}_1 - \hat{\mathbf{u}}_1'\hat{\mathbf{u}}_1, \tag{10.5.18}$$

where the last two equalities follow from

$$\hat{\mathbf{u}}_1'\mathbf{Y}_1 = \mathbf{Y}_1'\hat{\mathbf{u}}_1 = \hat{\mathbf{u}}_1'\hat{\mathbf{u}}_1 = \mathbf{Y}_1'\mathbf{M}\mathbf{Y}_1, \tag{10.5.19}$$

using the fact that the $\mathbf{M}$ matrix in (10.5.13) is both symmetric and idempotent. The upper right submatrix in the partitioned matrix to be inverted is:

$$\hat{\mathbf{Y}}_1'\mathbf{X}_1 = (\mathbf{Y}_1' - \hat{\mathbf{u}}_1')\mathbf{X}_1 = \mathbf{Y}_1'\mathbf{X}_1, \tag{10.5.20}$$

where the last equality follows from the fact that $\mathbf{MX}$ must vanish.[11] Comparing the 2SLS estimator in (10.5.17) to the OLS estimator in (10.3.5), the only difference is the correction of the explanatory endogenous variables $\mathbf{Y}_1$ using the reduced-form least squares residuals $\hat{\mathbf{u}}_1$. Thus, in this formulation the $\mathbf{Y}_1$ are "purged" of their endogenous nature by netting out the $\hat{\mathbf{u}}_1$ residuals.

It has been stated previously that the 2SLS estimator is defined only for an equation that is just identified or overidentified. This fact can be inferred from the two formulations of the 2SLS estimator in (10.5.2) and (10.5.17). The matrix to be inverted is of the order $g_1 - 1 + k_1$, and for the equation to be just identified or overidentified it is necessary that it fulfill the order condition $k - k_1 \geqslant g_1 - 1$ or, equivalently,

$$g_1 - 1 + k_1 \leqslant k. \tag{10.5.21}$$

But the matrix to be inverted in (10.5.2) and (10.5.17) consists of combinations of the elements of the $\mathbf{X}$ matrix, where $\hat{\mathbf{Y}}_1 = \mathbf{Y}_1 - \hat{\mathbf{u}}_1$ represents, from (10.5.9), linear combinations of $\mathbf{X}$. The matrix to be inverted thus cannot have rank larger than that of the original $\mathbf{X}$ matrix, namely k. Thus, if condition (10.5.21) is not met, in which case the equation is underidentified, the matrix cannot be inverted, so the 2SLS estimator is not defined. It is generally assumed that the matrix does, in fact, have full rank and hence can be inverted if the equation is just identified or overidentified.

[11]Recall that, from Section 4.4,

$$\mathbf{MX} = [\mathbf{I} - \mathbf{X}(\mathbf{X}'\mathbf{X})^{-1}\mathbf{X}']\mathbf{X} = \mathbf{X} - \mathbf{X} = \mathbf{0}.$$

It has also been stated previously that the 2SLS estimator reduces to ILS in the just-identified case. To show this it suffices to express the equation to be estimated in terms of the reduced-form coefficients. Thus combining (10.5.15) and (10.5.9) gives:

$$\mathbf{y}_1 = \left(\mathbf{X}_1\hat{\mathbf{\Pi}}_1^{00} + \mathbf{X}_2\hat{\mathbf{\Pi}}_2^{00}\right)\boldsymbol{\gamma}_1 + \mathbf{X}_1\boldsymbol{\beta}_1 + \mathbf{v}_1. \tag{10.5.22}$$

Collecting terms yields:

$$\mathbf{y}_1 = \mathbf{X}_1\left(\hat{\mathbf{\Pi}}_1^{00}\boldsymbol{\gamma}_1 + \boldsymbol{\beta}_1\right) + \mathbf{X}_2\hat{\mathbf{\Pi}}_2^{00}\boldsymbol{\gamma}_1 + \mathbf{v}_1. \tag{10.5.23}$$

The 2SLS estimator is the least squares estimator of this equation, which can be written:

$$\begin{aligned}\mathbf{y}_1 &= (\mathbf{X}_1 \,\vdots\, \mathbf{X}_2)\begin{pmatrix}\hat{\mathbf{\Pi}}_1^{00}\boldsymbol{\gamma}_1 + \boldsymbol{\beta}_1 \\ \text{--------} \\ \hat{\mathbf{\Pi}}_2^{00}\boldsymbol{\gamma}_1\end{pmatrix} + \mathbf{v}_1 \\ &= \mathbf{X}\begin{pmatrix}\hat{\mathbf{\Pi}}_1^{00}\boldsymbol{\gamma}_1 + \boldsymbol{\beta}_1 \\ \text{--------} \\ \hat{\mathbf{\Pi}}_2^{00}\boldsymbol{\gamma}_1\end{pmatrix} + \mathbf{v}_1.\end{aligned} \tag{10.5.24}$$

The least squares estimation of this equation yields:

$$\begin{pmatrix}\hat{\mathbf{\Pi}}_1^{00}\hat{\boldsymbol{\gamma}}_1 + \hat{\boldsymbol{\beta}}_1 \\ \text{--------} \\ \hat{\mathbf{\Pi}}_2^{00}\hat{\boldsymbol{\gamma}}_1\end{pmatrix} = (\mathbf{X}'\mathbf{X})^{-1}\mathbf{X}'\mathbf{y}_1 = \begin{pmatrix}\hat{\mathbf{\Pi}}_1^{0} \\ \text{---} \\ \hat{\mathbf{\Pi}}_2^{0}\end{pmatrix}, \tag{10.5.25}$$

that is, it is simply the first column of the estimated matrix of reduced-form coefficients. This equality always holds for 2SLS estimators of $\boldsymbol{\gamma}_1$ and $\boldsymbol{\beta}_1$. If, however, the equation is just identified, then $\hat{\mathbf{\Pi}}_2^{00}$ will be square, and, assuming it is nonsingular, solving for $\hat{\boldsymbol{\gamma}}_1$ and $\hat{\boldsymbol{\beta}}_1$ yields:

$$\hat{\boldsymbol{\gamma}}_1 = \left(\hat{\mathbf{\Pi}}_2^{00}\right)^{-1}\hat{\mathbf{\Pi}}_2^{0}, \tag{10.5.26}$$

$$\hat{\boldsymbol{\beta}}_1 = \hat{\mathbf{\Pi}}_1^{0} - \hat{\mathbf{\Pi}}_1^{00}\left(\hat{\mathbf{\Pi}}_2^{00}\right)^{-1}\hat{\mathbf{\Pi}}_2^{0}. \tag{10.5.27}$$

These are precisely the ILS estimators in (10.4.10) and (10.4.11).[12]

Finally, it was stated previously that the 2SLS estimators are consistent estimators. In general 2SLS estimators are biased, as are OLS estimators, but, unlike the OLS estimators, they are consistent. The problem in OLS was the inclusion of $\mathbf{Y}_1$ as explanatory variables, which led to an inconsistent estimator. In 2SLS, however, the $\mathbf{Y}_1$ have been replaced by $\hat{\mathbf{Y}}_1$, which consists of linear combinations of exogenous variables. Since the full set of explanatory variables are either exogenous ($\mathbf{X}_1$) or linear combinations of exogenous variables $\hat{\mathbf{Y}}_1$, the explanatory variables are uncorrelated in the probability limit with the stochastic disturbance terms, ensuring consistency. To show this more formally, consider (10.5.15), which may be written:

$$\mathbf{y}_1 = \left(\hat{\mathbf{Y}}_1 \,\vdots\, \mathbf{X}_1\right)\begin{pmatrix}\boldsymbol{\gamma}_1 \\ \text{---} \\ \boldsymbol{\beta}_1\end{pmatrix} + \mathbf{v}_1 = \hat{\mathbf{Z}}_1\boldsymbol{\delta}_1 + \mathbf{v}_1. \tag{10.5.28}$$

[12]While the estimates in the case of a just-identified equation are the same for both ILS and 2SLS, the 2SLS method also yields information on asymptotic standard errors, which is not available using ILS. See the next section for a discussion of these asymptotic standard errors. See, in particular, the estimator of the variance σ_1^2 in (10.6.35) and the asymptotic covariance matrix in (10.6.37).

In this notation the 2SLS estimator is:

$$\begin{pmatrix} \hat{\boldsymbol{\gamma}}_1 \\ --- \\ \hat{\boldsymbol{\beta}}_1 \end{pmatrix}_{2SLS} = \hat{\boldsymbol{\delta}}_{1_{2SLS}} = \left(\hat{\mathbf{Z}}_1'\hat{\mathbf{Z}}_1\right)^{-1}\hat{\mathbf{Z}}_1'\mathbf{y}_1, \qquad *(10.5.29)$$

where $\hat{\mathbf{Z}}_1$ summarizes the data on estimated explanatory endogenous variables and included exogenous variables:

$$\underset{n\times(g_1-1+k_1)}{\hat{\mathbf{Z}}_1} = (\underset{n\times(g_1-1)}{\hat{\mathbf{Y}}_1} \,\vdots\, \underset{n\times k_1}{\mathbf{X}_1}), \qquad (10.5.30)$$

as in (10.3.2), but where $\mathbf{Y}_1$ is replaced by $\hat{\mathbf{Y}}_1$. From (10.5.28) and (10.5.29),

$$\hat{\boldsymbol{\delta}}_{1_{2SLS}} = \boldsymbol{\delta}_1 + \left(\hat{\mathbf{Z}}_1'\hat{\mathbf{Z}}_1\right)^{-1}\hat{\mathbf{Z}}_1'\mathbf{v}_1. \qquad (10.5.31)$$

Taking expectations gives:

$$E\left(\hat{\boldsymbol{\delta}}_{1_{2SLS}}\right) = \boldsymbol{\delta}_1 + E\left[\left(\hat{\mathbf{Z}}_1'\hat{\mathbf{Z}}_1\right)^{-1}\hat{\mathbf{Z}}_1'\mathbf{v}_1\right], \qquad (10.5.32)$$

where the second term in general does not vanish, given the definition of $\hat{\mathbf{Z}}_1$ in (10.5.30) and the definition of $\mathbf{v}_1$ in (10.5.16). Thus the 2SLS estimator is generally biased:

$$E\left(\hat{\boldsymbol{\delta}}_{1_{2SLS}}\right) \neq \boldsymbol{\delta}_1. \qquad (10.5.33)$$

Returning to the proof of consistency, (10.5.31) can be written:

$$\hat{\boldsymbol{\delta}}_{1_{2SLS}} = \boldsymbol{\delta}_1 + \left(\frac{1}{n}\hat{\mathbf{Z}}_1'\hat{\mathbf{Z}}_1\right)^{-1}\left(\frac{1}{n}\hat{\mathbf{Z}}_1'\mathbf{v}_1\right), \qquad (10.5.34)$$

where the $1/n$ factors, as usual, ensure the meaningfulness of the elements of the matrices shown, each element of which is the sum of n terms. Assuming for the set of explanatory variables

$$\text{plim}\left(\frac{1}{n}\hat{\mathbf{Z}}_1'\hat{\mathbf{Z}}_1\right) = \mathbf{Q}_1, \qquad (10.5.35)$$

where $\mathbf{Q}_1$ is a nonsingular matrix, it follows that

$$\text{plim}\,\hat{\boldsymbol{\delta}}_{1_{2SLS}} = \boldsymbol{\delta}_1 + \mathbf{Q}_1^{-1}\,\text{plim}\left(\frac{1}{\text{n}}\hat{\mathbf{Z}}_1'\mathbf{v}_1\right). \qquad (10.5.36)$$

Thus the 2SLS estimator is consistent if

$$\text{plim}\left(\frac{1}{n}\hat{\mathbf{Z}}_1'\mathbf{v}_1\right) = \begin{pmatrix} \text{plim}\,\frac{1}{n}\hat{\mathbf{Y}}_1'\boldsymbol{\varepsilon}_1 \\ \text{plim}\,\frac{1}{n}\mathbf{X}_1'\boldsymbol{\varepsilon}_1 \end{pmatrix} = \mathbf{0}, \qquad (10.5.37)$$

where $\boldsymbol{\varepsilon}_1$ has replaced $\mathbf{v}_1$, since $(1/n)\hat{\mathbf{Z}}_1'\hat{\mathbf{u}}_1 = \mathbf{0}$, by the properties of least squares, applied to the first-stage regressions. The bottom expression vanishes since the $\mathbf{X}_1$ are exogenous and hence are uncorrelated with the stochastic disturbance terms in the probability limit. The top expression is, from (10.5.9),

$$\text{plim}\,\frac{1}{n}\hat{\mathbf{Y}}_1'\boldsymbol{\varepsilon}_1 = \text{plim}\,\frac{1}{n}\left(\hat{\boldsymbol{\Pi}}_1^{00\prime}\mathbf{X}_1' + \hat{\boldsymbol{\Pi}}_2^{00\prime}\mathbf{X}_2'\right)\boldsymbol{\varepsilon}_1 = \mathbf{0}, \qquad (10.5.38)$$

since both $\mathbf{X}_1$ and $\mathbf{X}_2$ are uncorrelated with $\boldsymbol{\varepsilon}_1$ in the probability limit. Thus 2SLS provides a consistent estimator:

$$\text{plim}\,\hat{\boldsymbol{\delta}}_{1_{2SLS}} = \boldsymbol{\delta}_1. \qquad *(10.5.39)$$

Another way of proving consistency of the 2SLS estimator is based on the k-class estimator to be introduced later in this section and the instrumental variables interpretation of this estimator to be presented in Section 10.6.

The 2SLS estimator, given by (10.5.2), (10.5.17), and (10.5.29), is thus a consistent estimator, which is defined for overidentified and just-identified equations and which reduces to the ILS estimator in the just-identified case. As already noted, the technique is called "two-stage least squares," since it uses two distinct least squares sets of regressions. The first set of regressions, the *first stage*, is the estimation of the coefficients of the reduced form, as given in (10.5.4). These estimators summarize a set of g least squares regressions, one for each of the reduced-form equations. In each such regression, one of the endogenous variables is treated as the dependent variable, and all exogenous variables of the complete model are treated as the explanatory variables.[13] The second set of regressions, the *second stage*, also constitutes g least squares regressions, each of which represents the estimation of the parameters of one of the structural equations. Each such equation is expressed in a form similar to that used in (10.5.15) for the first such equation, where $\hat{\mathbf{Y}}_1 = \mathbf{Y}_1 - \hat{\mathbf{u}}_1$ represents the estimated values of the explanatory endogenous variables, as obtained from the results of the first stage. The result of this second-stage estimation is a set of estimated coefficients for each of the structural equations, the 2SLS estimators.

As noted for (10.5.17), the difference between the OLS estimator and the 2SLS estimator is the fact that in 2SLS the reduced-form residuals $\hat{\mathbf{u}}_1$, as defined in (10.5.13), are netted out from $\mathbf{Y}_1$ to determine $\hat{\mathbf{Y}}_1$. These residuals are zero if the reduced form is estimated exactly, so in this special case $\mathbf{Y}_1 = \hat{\mathbf{Y}}_1$ and the OLS and 2SLS estimates are identical. In this case the coefficient of determination R^2 for each of the relevant reduced-form equations (those for $\mathbf{Y}_1$) is unity. At the opposite extreme, if the values of R^2 for the relevant reduced-form equations are close to zero, then the data on the explanatory endogenous variables are replaced by what are essentially disturbance terms, so the 2SLS estimators are largely meaningless. Thus the method of two-stage least squares works poorly if the R^2 values in the first stage are "too small," i.e., close to zero, while it is only negligibly different from OLS if the R^2 values in the first stage are "too large," i.e., close to unity. It is only in the case of "intermediate" values of R^2 in the first stage that the 2SLS estimators make sense.[14]

[13]In general, the estimation in the first stage is that of the *unrestricted* reduced form not taking explicit account of overidentifying restrictions, which restrict the reduced-form coefficients. In a large econometric model, however, it may be the case that the total number of exogenous variables in the system exceeds the total number of data points available, so that there are insufficient degrees of freedom to estimate the unrestricted first-stage reduced-form equations. In such a case there are several ways to redefine the first-stage equations to obtain a set of equations that can be estimated. One is to select only those exogenous variables that are most closely related to the endogenous variable in the equation, excluding from each equation those exogenous variables believed to be unimportant on the basis of a priori considerations. An example is the partitioning of the model into certain submodels, each involving a particular set of variables, where the only exogenous variables entering the reduced-form equation for any particular endogenous variable are those of the submodel in which the variable appears, as in the Brookings model (see Fisher, 1965a, and Section 12.7). An alternative approach is to replace the set of all exogenous variables by the leading principal components of such variables, as discussed in Kloek and Mennes (1960), Amemiya (1966b), Dhrymes (1970), Malinvaud (1970), and Mitchell (1971). A third approach uses certain instrumental variables; see the references cited in footnotes 21 and 22 (see also Klein, 1973).

[14]It is possible to define a coefficient of determination for the second stage of 2SLS as

$$R^2_{2SLS} = 1 - \frac{\hat{\boldsymbol{\varepsilon}}_1'\hat{\boldsymbol{\varepsilon}}_1}{\dot{\mathbf{y}}_1'\dot{\mathbf{y}}_1},$$

(cont.)

The 2SLS estimator can be illustrated using the consumption function of the prototype macro model (10.1.22). In this overidentified equation there is one explanatory endogenous variable Y. The 2SLS estimators are obtained as the least squares estimators of

$$C = \gamma_1 \hat{Y} + \beta_1 + v^C, \tag{10.5.40}$$

where $\hat{Y}$ is the estimated value of Y. This estimated value is obtained by estimating the reduced-form equation for Y:

$$Y = \Pi_3 + \Pi_4 G + \Pi_5 Y_{-1} + u^Y, \tag{10.5.41}$$

yielding $\hat{\Pi}_3$, $\hat{\Pi}_4$, and $\hat{\Pi}_5$ and determining $\hat{Y}_i$ as:

$$\hat{Y}_i = \hat{\Pi}_3 + \hat{\Pi}_4 G_i + \hat{\Pi}_5 Y_{i-1} \tag{10.5.42}$$

The 2SLS estimators of (10.5.40) are then:

$$\hat{\gamma}_{1\,2SLS} = \frac{\sum \dot{C}_i \dot{\hat{Y}}_i}{\sum \dot{\hat{Y}}_i^2}, \tag{10.5.43}$$

$$\hat{\beta}_{1\,2SLS} = \overline{C} - \hat{\gamma}_1 \overline{\hat{Y}}, \tag{10.5.44}$$

where $\overline{C}$ and $\overline{\hat{Y}}$ are mean values and $\dot{C}$ and $\dot{\hat{Y}}$ are deviations from these mean values.

For the variant consumption function the reduced form for Y is:

$$Y = \Pi_3' + \Pi_4' G + u^{Y'}, \tag{10.5.45}$$

as in (10.4.17), and the least squares estimators of this equation are:

$$\hat{\Pi}_4' = \frac{\sum \dot{Y}_i \dot{G}_i}{\sum \dot{G}_i^2}, \tag{10.5.46}$$

$$\hat{\Pi}_3' = \overline{Y} - \hat{\Pi}_4' \overline{G}, \tag{10.5.47}$$

where $\overline{Y}$ and $\overline{G}$ are mean values and $\dot{Y}_i$ and $\dot{G}_i$ are deviations from mean values. The 2SLS estimators are then given as in (10.5.43) and (10.5.44), where:

$$\hat{Y}_i = \hat{\Pi}_3' + \hat{\Pi}_4' G_i. \tag{10.5.48}$$

Thus $\dot{\hat{Y}}_i = \hat{\Pi}_4' \dot{G}_i$, implying that:

$$\sum \dot{C}_i \dot{\hat{Y}}_i = \hat{\Pi}_4' \sum \dot{C}_i \dot{G}_i, \tag{10.5.49}$$

$$\sum \dot{\hat{Y}}_i^2 = \hat{\Pi}_4'^2 \sum \dot{G}_i^2. \tag{10.5.50}$$

Then, from (10.5.43) and (10.5.46),

$$\hat{\gamma}'_{1\,2SLS} = \frac{1}{\hat{\Pi}_4'} \frac{\sum \dot{C}_i \dot{G}_i}{\sum \dot{G}_i^2} = \frac{\sum \dot{C}_i \dot{G}_i}{\sum \dot{Y}_i \dot{G}_i}, \tag{10.5.51}$$

which is the same estimator as the ILS estimator in (10.4.27), as would be expected in this case of a just-identified equation.

---

where $\dot{\mathbf{y}}_1$ represents deviations from mean values, $\hat{\boldsymbol{\varepsilon}}_1$ represents the residuals in the estimation of (10.5.15), given as

$$\hat{\boldsymbol{\varepsilon}}_1 = \mathbf{y}_1 - (\hat{\mathbf{Y}}_1 + \hat{\mathbf{u}}_1)\hat{\gamma}_1 - \mathbf{X}_1\hat{\boldsymbol{\beta}}_1 = \mathbf{y}_1 - \hat{\mathbf{y}}_1,$$

and $\hat{\gamma}_1$ and $\hat{\boldsymbol{\beta}}_1$ are the 2SLS estimators. The R^2_{2SLS} so defined cannot exceed unity, but it can be negative. It therefore does not have the usual interpretation of R^2 as the proportion of variance explained by the regression (see Problem 10-H).

A general class of limited-information estimators can be introduced as an extension of the two-stage least squares estimator in (10.5.17). Letting k be a scalar parameter, which may be either a fixed number or a number determined by the sample, the *k-class estimator* of the structural parameters in the equation to be estimated is:[15]

$$\begin{pmatrix} \hat{\boldsymbol{\gamma}}_1 \\ --- \\ \hat{\boldsymbol{\beta}}_1 \end{pmatrix}_k = \left(\begin{array}{c|c} \mathbf{Y}_1'\mathbf{Y}_1 - k\hat{\mathbf{u}}_1'\hat{\mathbf{u}}_1 & \mathbf{Y}_1'\mathbf{X}_1 \\ \hline \mathbf{X}_1'\mathbf{Y}_1 & \mathbf{X}_1'\mathbf{X}_1 \end{array}\right)^{-1} \begin{pmatrix} \mathbf{Y}_1' - k\hat{\mathbf{u}}_1' \\ ------- \\ \mathbf{X}_1' \end{pmatrix} \mathbf{y}_1, \qquad *(10.5.52)$$

where $\hat{\mathbf{u}}_1$ is the reduced-form residuals for $\mathbf{Y}_1$. This definition of an entire class of estimators may be motivated by an inspection of (10.5.17) and a comparison of this formulation of the 2SLS estimator with the OLS estimator in (10.3.5). The only differences between these estimators is the subtraction of $\hat{\mathbf{u}}_1'\hat{\mathbf{u}}_1$ in the upper left submatrix of the matrix to be inverted in (10.5.17) and the subtraction of $\hat{\mathbf{u}}_1$ in the upper submatrix of the second matrix on the right in (10.5.17). But the scalar k in the k-class estimator multiplies both of these terms. Thus if $k = 0$, the k-class estimator is the OLS estimator, while if $k = 1$, the k-class estimator is the 2SLS estimator. The k-class interpolates between these by allowing k to be any scalar, and it extends the estimators to other possible k values that may not lie between 0 and 1.

A general result on k-class estimators states that if k satisfies

$$\text{plim}(k - 1) = 0, \qquad *(10.5.53)$$

then the k-class estimator is consistent:[16]

$$\text{plim}\begin{pmatrix} \hat{\boldsymbol{\gamma}}_1 \\ --- \\ \hat{\boldsymbol{\beta}}_1 \end{pmatrix}_k = \begin{pmatrix} \boldsymbol{\gamma}_1 \\ --- \\ \boldsymbol{\beta}_1 \end{pmatrix}. \qquad *(10.5.54)$$

The consistency result for 2SLS, in (10.5.39), is the special case for which $k = 1$.[17]

[15]See Theil (1961, 1971). Do not confuse the k here with the total number of exogenous variables in the system of structural equations.

[16]See Problem 10-J for an approach to proving this result using the method of instrumental variables, to be introduced in Section 10.6.

[17]Another estimator of the k-class that is consistent since it satisfies (10.5.53) is the *limited-information maximum likelihood (LIML) estimator*. This estimator is obtained by maximizing the likelihood function for an individual equation subject only to the a priori restrictions imposed on the equation, without requiring information as to the specification of other equations of the system (other than information on variables in the entire system but not in the particular equation being estimated). In this case $k = \hat{l}$, the smallest root of the polynomial equation:

$$|\mathbf{R}_1 - l\mathbf{R}| = 0,$$

where $\mathbf{R}_1$ and $\mathbf{R}$ are defined as:

$$\mathbf{R}_1 = \begin{pmatrix} \mathbf{y}_1' \\ --- \\ \mathbf{Y}_1' \end{pmatrix} \mathbf{M}_1(\mathbf{y}_1 \,\vdots\, \mathbf{Y}_1),$$

$$\mathbf{R} = \begin{pmatrix} \mathbf{y}_1' \\ --- \\ \mathbf{Y}_1' \end{pmatrix} \mathbf{M}(\mathbf{y}_1 \,\vdots\, \mathbf{Y}_1),$$

and where $\mathbf{M}_1$ and $\mathbf{M}$ are the idempotent matrices:

$$\mathbf{M}_1 = \mathbf{I} - \mathbf{X}_1(\mathbf{X}_1'\mathbf{X}_1)^{-1}\mathbf{X}_1',$$

$$\mathbf{M} = \mathbf{I} - \mathbf{X}(\mathbf{X}'\mathbf{X})^{-1}\mathbf{X}'.$$

(footnote continued on page 369)

10.6 INSTRUMENTAL VARIABLES

The method of instrumental variables (IV) is a general approach to estimating a single equation in a system of equations, and all of the estimators introduced so far can be interpreted as IV estimators for particular choices of instrumental variables.[18] Consider once again the first structural equation, which can be expressed:

$$\mathbf{y}_1 = \mathbf{Z}_1\boldsymbol{\delta}_1 + \boldsymbol{\varepsilon}_1 = (\mathbf{Y}_1 \mid \mathbf{X}_1)\begin{pmatrix} \boldsymbol{\gamma}_1 \\ --- \\ \boldsymbol{\beta}_1 \end{pmatrix} + \boldsymbol{\varepsilon}_1, \tag{10.6.1}$$

as in (10.3.1), where $\mathbf{Z}_1$ lumps together data on all included explanatory variables, whether endogenous or exogenous, and $\boldsymbol{\delta}_1$ summarizes all coefficients to be estimated:

$$\mathbf{Z}_1 = (\mathbf{Y}_1 \mid \mathbf{X}_1), \qquad \boldsymbol{\delta}_1 = \begin{pmatrix} \boldsymbol{\gamma}_1 \\ --- \\ \boldsymbol{\beta}_1 \end{pmatrix}. \tag{10.6.2}$$

A heuristic explanation of the OLS estimator, following the approach outlined in Section 4.5 [in (4.5.10) and (4.5.11)], is based on premultiplying (10.6.1) by $\mathbf{Z}_1'$ to make the matrix multiplying $\boldsymbol{\delta}_1$ square, yielding:

$$\mathbf{Z}_1'\mathbf{y}_1 = \mathbf{Z}_1'\mathbf{Z}_1\boldsymbol{\delta}_1 + \mathbf{Z}_1'\boldsymbol{\varepsilon}_1. \tag{10.6.3}$$

Dropping the term $\mathbf{Z}_1'\boldsymbol{\varepsilon}_1$ and solving the resulting "normal equations" yields the OLS estimator

$$\hat{\boldsymbol{\delta}}_{1\text{OLS}} = (\mathbf{Z}_1'\mathbf{Z}_1)^{-1}\mathbf{Z}_1'\mathbf{y}_1, \tag{10.6.4}$$

as in (10.3.4). In the single-equation context of Chapter 4, dropping the term corresponding to $\mathbf{Z}'_1\boldsymbol{\varepsilon}_1$ was justified because the explanatory variables were exogenous and hence uncorrelated with the stochastic disturbance term. In the simultaneous-equations context, however, dropping this term cannot be so justified, since the explanatory endogenous variables in $\mathbf{Z}_1$ are not statistically independent of $\boldsymbol{\varepsilon}_1$. They are correlated with the $\boldsymbol{\varepsilon}$'s, even in the probability limit.

Suppose, however, that there exists a set of $g_1 - 1 + k_1$ variables (the same number as in $\mathbf{Z}_1$) that are uncorrelated with $\boldsymbol{\varepsilon}_1$ but, at the same time, correlated with $\mathbf{Z}_1$. Such variables

---

This technique, which is also called *least variance ratio (LVR)* and *limited-information single equation (LISE)*, is a limited-information technique that yields consistent estimators, since plim$(\hat{l} - 1) = 0$. The LIML technique can be used to estimate any just-identified or overidentified equation, and, as in the case of 2SLS, it reduces to ILS in the just-identified case. One advantage of the LIML technique over 2SLS and other members of the k-class is its invariance to the choice of normalization—that is, the choice of which included endogenous variable is to be the dependent variable. It is the only member of the k-class with this property.

Assuming normally distributed stochastic terms, the LIML estimator is asymptotically normally distributed, and it has the same limiting distribution as 2SLS. It has the asymptotically efficient property of minimum variance in the class of all estimators with the same a priori information (see also footnote 20).

While LIML is of historical importance, having been used to estimate several major econometric models in the 1950s, it has not been used in recent work and thus is not stressed here. Other reasons for not stressing it here are the findings in studies of exact finite-sample distributions of estimators that LIML has no finite moments and the findings in Monte Carlo studies that the LIML as an estimator exhibits erratic and highly unstable behavior. For references to these studies, see footnote 36. For a further discussion of LIML, see Theil (1971).

[18]See Sargan (1958), Brundy and Jorgenson (1971, 1973, 1974), and Madansky (1976). See also Section 10.7 [e.g., equation (10.7.28)] for the application of instrumental variables to the entire system of equations.

are *instrumental variables*, and data on them are summarized by the $n \times (g_1 - 1 + k_1)$ matrix $\mathbf{W}_1$, where the subscript again refers to the first equation. Then premultiplying (10.6.1) by $\mathbf{W}_1'$ yields:

$$\mathbf{W}_1'\mathbf{y}_1 = \mathbf{W}_1'\mathbf{Z}_1\boldsymbol{\delta}_1 + \mathbf{W}_1'\boldsymbol{\varepsilon}_1. \tag{10.6.5}$$

Dropping $\mathbf{W}_1'\boldsymbol{\varepsilon}_1$, since the variables in $\mathbf{W}_1$ were assumed uncorrelated with $\boldsymbol{\varepsilon}_1$, and solving for $\boldsymbol{\delta}_1$ yields:

$$\hat{\boldsymbol{\delta}}_{1\text{IV}} = \hat{\boldsymbol{\delta}}_1(\mathbf{W}_1) = (\mathbf{W}_1'\mathbf{Z}_1)^{-1}\mathbf{W}_1'\mathbf{y}_1. \qquad *(10.6.6)$$

This is the *instrumental-variables (IV) estimator*, which, as indicated by the functional relationship $\hat{\boldsymbol{\delta}}_1(\mathbf{W}_1)$, depends on the choice of instruments and the data on these instruments.

The IV estimator is extremely useful, since it represents a whole class of estimators, each defined by $\mathbf{W}_1$, the matrix of data on the instrumental variables. As already noted, all of the estimators introduced so far are members of this class and can be interpreted as IV estimators for particular choices of $\mathbf{W}_1$. For example, the OLS estimator is

$$\hat{\boldsymbol{\delta}}_{1\text{OLS}} = \hat{\boldsymbol{\delta}}_1(\mathbf{Z}_1) = (\mathbf{Z}_1'\mathbf{Z}_1)^{-1}\mathbf{Z}_1'\mathbf{y}_1, \tag{10.6.7}$$

where $\mathbf{Z}_1$ itself is used for data on the instrumental variables (although this choice of instrumental variables is not one that satisfies the assumption of independence of the stochastic disturbance term). The example given in (10.3.13) of the OLS estimator of the marginal propensity to consume for the prototype macro model consumption function is of this form. This estimator may be written:

$$\hat{\gamma}_{1\text{OLS}} = (\textstyle\sum \dot{Y}_1^2)^{-1}\sum \dot{Y}_i\dot{C}_i \tag{10.6.8}$$

to emphasize that it is of same form as (10.6.7), where Y_i is the explanatory variable (comparable to $\mathbf{Z}_1$) and C_i is the dependent variable (comparable to $\mathbf{y}_1$). Other examples of estimators developed in previous sections will be similarly shown to be of the same form as the IV interpretation of the estimator.

In the case of a just-identified equation, the number of instrumental variables $g_1 - 1 + k_1$ is equal to the number of exogenous variables in the system k. In this case all exogenous variables can be used as the instrumental variables, so $\mathbf{W}_1$ is simply $\mathbf{X}$, and the indirect least squares estimator can be written:

$$\hat{\boldsymbol{\delta}}_{1\text{ILS}} = \hat{\boldsymbol{\delta}}_1(\mathbf{X}) = (\mathbf{X}'\mathbf{Z}_1)^{-1}\mathbf{X}'\mathbf{y}_1. \tag{10.6.9}$$

The example given in (10.4.29) of the ILS estimator of the marginal propensity to consume for the variant consumption function is of this form. This estimator may be written:

$$\hat{\gamma}_{1\text{ILS}}' = (\textstyle\sum \dot{G}_i\dot{Y}_i)^{-1}\sum \dot{G}_i\dot{C}_i, \tag{10.6.10}$$

to emphasize that it is of the same form as (10.6.9), where G_i is the exogenous variable (comparable to $\mathbf{X}$), Y_i is again the explanatory endogenous variable (comparable to $\mathbf{Z}_1$), and C_i is again the dependent variable (comparable to $\mathbf{y}_1$).

The OLS and ILS estimators have thus been expressed as IV estimators. The 2SLS estimator can also be so expressed as an IV estimator. To understand the IV formulation of 2SLS, note first that the only variables that must be treated via appropriate instrumental variables are the explanatory endogenous variables $\mathbf{Y}_1$ since the included exogenous variables $\mathbf{X}_1$ can be used as their own instrumental variables. In the 2SLS approach the explanatory endogenous variables are replaced by their estimated values $\hat{\mathbf{Y}}_1$, which can serve as instrumental variables. The choice of instrumental variables for 2SLS is thus given by $(\hat{\mathbf{Y}}_1 \mid \mathbf{X}_1)$, consisting of the estimated values of the $g_1 - 1$ explanatory endogenous variables and the actual values of the k_1 included exogenous variables. This choice of instrumental variables, from (10.5.30), can be written:

$$\mathbf{W}_{1_{2SLS}} = (\hat{\mathbf{Y}}_1 \mid \mathbf{X}_1) = \hat{\mathbf{Z}}_1. \tag{10.6.11}$$

Thus the 2SLS estimator can be written as the IV estimator:

$$\hat{\boldsymbol{\delta}}_{1_{2SLS}} = \hat{\boldsymbol{\delta}}_1(\hat{\mathbf{Z}}_1) = (\hat{\mathbf{Z}}_1'\mathbf{Z}_1)^{-1}\hat{\mathbf{Z}}_1'\mathbf{y}_1. \tag{10.6.12}$$

By (10.5.18) and (10.5.19), however,

$$\hat{\mathbf{Z}}_1'\mathbf{Z}_1 = \hat{\mathbf{Z}}_1'\hat{\mathbf{Z}}_1, \tag{10.6.13}$$

leading to the 2SLS estimator as presented in (10.5.29):

$$\hat{\boldsymbol{\delta}}_{1_{2SLS}} = (\hat{\mathbf{Z}}_1'\hat{\mathbf{Z}}_1)^{-1}\hat{\mathbf{Z}}_1'\mathbf{y}_1. \tag{10.6.14}$$

The example given in (10.5.43) of the 2SLS estimator of the marginal propensity to consume for the prototype macro model consumption function is of this form. This estimator may be written:

$$\hat{\gamma}_{1_{2SLS}} = (\sum \dot{\hat{Y}}_i^2)^{-1} \sum \dot{\hat{Y}}_i \dot{C}_i, \tag{10.6.15}$$

to emphasize that it is of the same form as (10.6.14), where $\hat{Y}_i$ is the estimated explanatory endogenous variable (comparable to $\hat{\mathbf{Z}}_1$) and C_i is again the dependent variable (comparable to $\mathbf{y}_1$).

It will prove useful to develop yet another formulation of the 2SLS estimator using the IV approach. To derive this formulation, note that:

$$\hat{\mathbf{Y}}_1 = \mathbf{X}(\mathbf{X}'\mathbf{X})^{-1}\mathbf{X}'\mathbf{Y}_1, \tag{10.6.16}$$

as shown in (10.5.11), and that:

$$\mathbf{X}_1 = \mathbf{X}(\mathbf{X}'\mathbf{X})^{-1}\mathbf{X}'\mathbf{X}_1, \tag{10.6.17}$$

which follows from

$$(\mathbf{X}_1 \mid \mathbf{X}_2) = \mathbf{X} = \mathbf{X}(\mathbf{X}'\mathbf{X})^{-1}\mathbf{X}'\mathbf{X} = \mathbf{X}(\mathbf{X}'\mathbf{X})^{-1}\mathbf{X}'(\mathbf{X}_1 \mid \mathbf{X}_2) \tag{10.6.18}$$

by dropping $\mathbf{X}_2$ from the first and last expressions. The equalities in (10.6.16) and (10.6.17) can be combined as:

$$\mathbf{W}_{1_{2SLS}} = \hat{\mathbf{Z}}_1 = (\hat{\mathbf{Y}}_1 \mid \mathbf{X}_1) = \mathbf{X}(\mathbf{X}'\mathbf{X})^{-1}\mathbf{X}'(\mathbf{Y}_1 \mid \mathbf{X}_1) = \mathbf{X}(\mathbf{X}'\mathbf{X})^{-1}\mathbf{X}'\mathbf{Z}_1, \tag{10.6.19}$$

which is the matrix of estimated values obtained from a regression of all explanatory variables $\mathbf{Z}_1$ on all exogenous variables $\mathbf{X}$. This is the instrumental-variables data matrix used in 2SLS. Thus the 2SLS estimator can be written:

$$\hat{\boldsymbol{\delta}}_{1_{2SLS}} = \hat{\boldsymbol{\delta}}_1(\mathbf{X}(\mathbf{X}'\mathbf{X})^{-1}\mathbf{X}'\mathbf{Z}_1) = [\mathbf{Z}_1'\mathbf{X}(\mathbf{X}'\mathbf{X})^{-1}\mathbf{X}'\mathbf{Z}_1]^{-1}\mathbf{Z}_1'\mathbf{X}(\mathbf{X}'\mathbf{X})^{-1}\mathbf{X}'\mathbf{y}_1, \tag{10.6.20}$$

where $\mathbf{X}$ consists of data on all exogenous variables and $\mathbf{Z}_1$ consists of data on all explanatory variables, both endogenous and exogenous, in the equation. Thus this formulation of the 2SLS estimator involves only actual data matrices.

The 2SLS estimator in (10.6.20) can also be interpreted as the estimator obtained if all exogenous variables are used as instrumental variables, as in the ILS estimator of (10.6.9), but the GLS estimator of (5.3.9) is employed. Thus premultiplying (10.6.1) by $\mathbf{X}'$ yields:

$$\mathbf{X}'\mathbf{y}_1 = \mathbf{X}'\mathbf{Z}_1\boldsymbol{\delta}_1 + \mathbf{X}'\boldsymbol{\varepsilon}_1, \tag{10.6.21}$$

where

$$\text{Cov}(\mathbf{X}'\boldsymbol{\varepsilon}_1) = E(\mathbf{X}'\boldsymbol{\varepsilon}_1\boldsymbol{\varepsilon}_1'\mathbf{X}) = \sigma_1^2(\mathbf{X}'\mathbf{X}). \tag{10.6.22}$$

Using the inverse of this covariance matrix for the GLS estimator,

$$\hat{\boldsymbol{\delta}}_{1\,2SLS} = \left[\mathbf{Z}_1'\mathbf{X}(\mathbf{X}'\mathbf{X})^{-1}\mathbf{X}'\mathbf{Z}_1\right]^{-1}\mathbf{Z}_1'\mathbf{X}(\mathbf{X}'\mathbf{X})^{-1}\mathbf{X}'\mathbf{y}_1, \tag{10.6.23}$$

which is precisely the 2SLS estimator in (10.6.20). Thus the 2SLS estimator has the additional interpretation as the GLS estimator of the equation after having used all exogenous variables as instrumental variables. This interpretation will be important in Section 10.7, since the three-stage least squares estimator uses a similar approach—applying GLS after having used all exogenous variables as instrumental variables—but where the system as a whole, rather than only one equation of the system, is estimated.

To complete this summary of IV interpretations of various estimators, consider the k-class estimator of (10.5.52). This estimator is an IV estimator for which the data on the instruments are given by:

$$\mathbf{W}_1 = (\mathbf{Y}_1 - k\hat{\mathbf{u}}_1 \,\vdots\, \mathbf{X}_1). \tag{10.6.24}$$

Here the instrumental variables for the explanatory endogenous variables are their measured values less k times the reduced-form residuals for these variables, as in (10.5.52), while the included exogenous variables serve as their own instrumental variables. Thus the k-class estimator is:

$$\hat{\boldsymbol{\delta}}_{1_k} = \hat{\boldsymbol{\delta}}_1(\mathbf{Y}_1 - k\hat{\mathbf{u}}_1 \,\vdots\, \mathbf{X}_1) = \left[\begin{pmatrix} \mathbf{Y}_1' - k\hat{\mathbf{u}}_1' \\ \hline \mathbf{X}_1' \end{pmatrix}(\mathbf{Y}_1 \,\vdots\, \mathbf{X}_1)\right]^{-1} \cdot \begin{pmatrix} \mathbf{Y}_1' - k\hat{\mathbf{u}}_1' \\ \hline \mathbf{X}_1' \end{pmatrix}\mathbf{y}_1. \tag{10.6.25}$$

As noted in Section 10.5, this estimator reduces to OLS if $k = 0$, in which case $\mathbf{W}_1 = \mathbf{Z}_1$, as in (10.6.7). It reduces to 2SLS if $k = 1$, in which case $\mathbf{W}_1 = \hat{\mathbf{Z}}_1 = (\hat{\mathbf{Y}}_1 \,\vdots\, \mathbf{X}_1)$, as in (10.6.11).

The instrumental-variable estimator is a consistent estimator under certain conditions. The general IV estimator of (10.6.6) can be combined with the first equation (10.6.1) to yield:

$$\begin{aligned}\hat{\boldsymbol{\delta}}_{1\,IV} &= (\mathbf{W}_1'\mathbf{Z}_1)^{-1}\mathbf{W}_1'\mathbf{y}_1 = (\mathbf{W}_1'\mathbf{Z}_1)^{-1}\mathbf{W}_1'(\mathbf{Z}_1\boldsymbol{\delta}_1 + \boldsymbol{\varepsilon}_1) \\ &= \boldsymbol{\delta}_1 + (\mathbf{W}_1'\mathbf{Z}_1)^{-1}\mathbf{W}_1'\boldsymbol{\varepsilon}_1,\end{aligned} \tag{10.6.26}$$

so that

$$\text{plim}\,\hat{\boldsymbol{\delta}}_{1\,IV} = \boldsymbol{\delta}_1 + \text{plim}\left(\frac{1}{n}\mathbf{W}_1'\mathbf{Z}_1\right)^{-1}\text{plim}\left(\frac{1}{n}\mathbf{W}_1'\boldsymbol{\varepsilon}_1\right). \tag{10.6.27}$$

Assume that the instrumental variables are asymptotically uncorrelated with the stochastic disturbance terms, so

$$\text{plim}\left(\frac{1}{n}\mathbf{W}_1'\boldsymbol{\varepsilon}_1\right) = \mathbf{0} \tag{10.6.28}$$

and that they are asymptotically correlated with the $\mathbf{Z}_1$'s, so

$$\text{plim}\left(\frac{1}{n}\mathbf{W}_1'\mathbf{Z}_1\right) = \mathbf{Q}_1, \tag{10.6.29}$$

where $\mathbf{Q}_1$ exists and is nonsingular. Under these two assumptions on $\mathbf{W}_1$, from (10.6.27) it follows that $\hat{\boldsymbol{\delta}}_{1IV}$ is a consistent estimator:

$$\text{plim}\, \hat{\boldsymbol{\delta}}_{1_{IV}} = \boldsymbol{\delta}_1. \qquad *(10.6.30)$$

Thus if a set of instruments were available that satisfied these two assumptions, it would yield a consistent estimator. Of the specific estimators introduced thus far, the OLS estimator is not consistent, because it fails to satisfy (10.6.28), while the 2SLS estimator is consistent, since both conditions are satisfied. The k-class estimator is consistent if condition (10.5.53) is met.

Furthermore, by a version of central limit theorem it can be shown that $1/\sqrt{n}\,\mathbf{W}_1'\boldsymbol{\varepsilon}_1$ has a limiting normal distribution of the form:

$$\frac{1}{\sqrt{n}}\mathbf{W}_1'\boldsymbol{\varepsilon}_1 \xrightarrow{d} N\left[\mathbf{0},\, \sigma_1^2\left(\frac{1}{n}\mathbf{W}'\mathbf{W}\right)\right], \qquad (10.6.31)$$

since

$$E(\boldsymbol{\varepsilon}_1\boldsymbol{\varepsilon}_1) = \sigma_{11}I = \sigma_1^2 I. \qquad (10.6.32)$$

From (10.6.27), the asymptotic convariance matrix of $\hat{\boldsymbol{\delta}}_{1,IV}$ is obtained by combining (10.6.29) and (10.6.31) as:

$$\text{Asy. Cov}\left(\hat{\boldsymbol{\delta}}_{1_{IV}}\right) = \frac{1}{n}\sigma_1^2\, \text{plim}\left[\left(\frac{1}{n}\mathbf{W}_1'\mathbf{Z}_1\right)^{-1}\left(\frac{1}{n}\mathbf{W}_1'\mathbf{W}_1\right)\left(\frac{1}{n}\mathbf{Z}_1'\mathbf{W}_1\right)^{-1}\right]. \qquad *(10.6.33)$$

The variance of the first equation, σ_1^2, can be estimated as:

$$\hat{\sigma}_1^2 = \frac{1}{n}\hat{\boldsymbol{\varepsilon}}_1'\hat{\boldsymbol{\varepsilon}}_1 = \frac{1}{n}\left(\mathbf{y}_1 - \mathbf{Z}_1\hat{\boldsymbol{\delta}}_1\right)'\left(\mathbf{y}_1 - \mathbf{Z}_1\hat{\boldsymbol{\delta}}_1\right), \qquad *(10.6.34)$$

where $\hat{\boldsymbol{\delta}}_1$ is the IV estimator and $\hat{\boldsymbol{\varepsilon}}_1$ is the vector of residuals in the estimation of the first equation when using this estimator.[19] Using these results, the asymptotic covariance matrix for the 2SLS estimator is given as

$$\text{Asy. Cov}\left(\hat{\boldsymbol{\delta}}_{1_{2SLS}}\right) = \frac{1}{n}\sigma_1^2\, \text{plim}\left(\frac{1}{n}\hat{\mathbf{Z}}_1'\hat{\mathbf{Z}}_1\right)^{-1}$$

$$= \frac{1}{n}\sigma_1^2\, \text{plim}\left[\frac{1}{n}\begin{pmatrix} \hat{\mathbf{Y}}_1'\mathbf{Y}_1 & \mathbf{Y}_1'\mathbf{X}_1 \\ \mathbf{X}_1'\mathbf{Y}_1 & \mathbf{X}_1'\mathbf{X}_1 \end{pmatrix}\right]^{-1}, \qquad (10.6.35)$$

or using (10.6.19), as[20]

[19]Note that no correction is made for degrees of freedom (which would change the denominator to $n - g_1 + 1 - k_1$), since this estimator is primarily relevant only asymptotically, as $n \to \infty$.

[20]The 2SLS estimator is asymptotically efficient within the class of all estimators that use the same a priori restrictions for a single equation, but, as discussed in the next section, it is not asymptotically efficient relative to the full-information technique of three-stage least squares [see (10.7.27) and footnote 30]. The asymptotic efficiency of 2SLS is based upon the fact that, assuming the stochastic disturbance terms at each observation are independently and identically (but not necessarily normally) distributed, the 2SLS estimators are asymptotically normally distributed [i.e., the estimator $\sqrt{n}(\hat{\boldsymbol{\delta}}_{1_{2SLS}} - \boldsymbol{\delta}_1)$ is asymptotically normal] with mean given by the true vector of parameters and an asymptotic covariance matrix given by (10.6.36) (see Malinvaud, 1970; Theil, 1971). The asymptotic covariance matrix of (10.6.36) is also that of the k-class estimator if

$$\text{plim}\, \sqrt{n}(k - 1) = 0.$$

For example, it is the asymptotic covariance matrix for the LIML estimator discussed in footnote 17.

$$\text{Asy. Cov}(\hat{\boldsymbol{\delta}}_{1_{2SLS}}) = \frac{1}{n}\sigma_1^2 \text{ plim}\left[\left(\frac{1}{n}\mathbf{Z}_1'\mathbf{X}\right)\left(\frac{1}{n}\mathbf{X}'\mathbf{X}\right)^{-1}\left(\frac{1}{n}\mathbf{X}'\mathbf{Z}_1\right)\right]^{-1}. \quad (10.6.36)$$

The variance σ_1^2 can be consistently estimated as $\hat{\sigma}_1^2$ in (10.6.34), using the 2SLS estimator for $\hat{\boldsymbol{\delta}}_1$. The resulting consistent estimator of the asymptotic covariance matrix can be used to construct asymptotic tests of hypotheses and interval estimates for structural parameters, as in Chapter 4. For example, asymptotic standard errors, given as the square roots of the diagonal elements of the asymptotic covariance matrix, can be used to construct asymptotic t-tests of statistical significance. While these tests apply only asymptotically, finite-sample approximations are frequently used in applications of the 2SLS approach for given n, $\mathbf{Z}_1$, and $\mathbf{X}$ in (10.6.36) and with σ_1^2 estimated by $\hat{\sigma}_1^2$ in (10.6.34) using the 2SLS estimator for $\hat{\boldsymbol{\delta}}_1$. This practice is supported by the results of Monte Carlo studies, as discussed in Section 10.9.

The major problem in using the instrumental-variables technique is simply that of obtaining a suitable set of instrumental variables that are both sufficiently uncorrelated with the stochastic disturbance terms and sufficiently correlated with the relevant explanatory variables. Furthermore, when there is choice of such instrumental variables, the estimates are usually very sensitive to the particular instrumental variables chosen, leading to a genuine problem of choice of such variables.[21]

It might be noted that while the estimators defined thus far can be applied to simultaneous-equations models with lagged endogenous variables, they generally fail to satisfy any desired properties in such a case. They will certainly fail to satisfy these properties if the stochastic disturbance terms exhibit serial correlation. In that case past disturbances, which influence the lagged endogenous variables, also influence current disturbances, so the lagged endogenous variables will be correlated with current endogenous variables, leading to biased and inconsistent estimators.

Several techniques have been proposed for such a case, one of which is the technique of *iterative instrumental variables* (IIV).[22] This technique starts with the predicted values from the least squares estimates of the restricted reduced form, that is, the reduced form taking account of all overidentifying restrictions, which impose restrictions on reduced-form parameters. These predicted values are then used as instruments for the estimation of the structural form, and the process iterates, such that at each stage of the estimation instrumental variables calculated from the restricted reduced form of the previous stage are used to estimate the structural parameters. This process continues until convergence is achieved—that is, until parameter estimates cease to vary significantly upon iteration.

10.7 THREE-STAGE LEAST SQUARES

The estimators introduced thus far have all been estimators of a single equation from a system of simultaneous equations. By contrast the technique of three-stage least squares (3SLS) and that of full-information maximum likelihood (FIML), to be presented in the next section,

[21]For discussions of the choice of instrumental variables, see Fisher (1965b), Mitchell and Fisher (1970), Mitchell (1971), and Brundy and Jorgenson (1971, 1973, 1974).

[22]See Lyttkens (1970), Dutta and Lyttkens (1974), and Brundy and Jorgenson (1971, 1973, 1974). For other approaches to estimating a system with lagged endogenous variables and serial correlation, see Sargan (1961), Amemiya (1966a), Fair (1970, 1972), Dhrymes and Erlat (1974), Dhyrmes, Berner, and Cummins (1974), and Hatanaka (1976).

are full-information estimation techniques, which estimate all parameters of the structural equations simultaneously.[23] As its name implies, 3SLS can be considered an extension of 2SLS. In fact, the first two of the three stages of 3SLS are those of 2SLS, the first stage being the estimation of all reduced-form coefficients using the least squares estimator, while the second stage is the estimation of all structural coefficients by applying 2SLS to each of the structural equations. The third stage is then the generalized least squares estimation of all of the structural coefficients of the system, using a covariance matrix for the stochastic disturbance terms of the structural equations that is estimated from the second-stage residuals. Using the information contained in this covariance matrix has the effect of improving efficiency. In fact, in terms of properties of estimators, the 3SLS technique is an improvement over 2SLS, since, while both are consistent, 3SLS is asymptotically more efficient than 2SLS. Thus the basic rationale for 3SLS, as opposed to 2SLS, is its use of information on the correlation of the stochastic disturbance terms of the structural equations in order to improve asymptotic efficiency.

The 3SLS technique can be viewed as an extension of the GLS approach of Section 5.3 to the estimation of a system of simultaneous equations. It can also, however, be viewed as an extension of the method of "seemingly unrelated equations," also presented in Section 5.3, to a system of equations in which explanatory endogenous variables are present in some or all of the equations.[24] If there are no explanatory endogenous variables in the system (e.g., if $\mathbf{\Gamma}$ is diagonal), then 3SLS reduces to "seemingly unrelated equations," while if $g = 1$ it reduces to GLS.

In order to develop the 3SLS estimator it is convenient to use the star notation, as in Section 5.3. The hth equation of the system, which contains g_h endogenous and k_h exogenous variables, can be written as in (10.1.21):

$$\begin{aligned} \underset{n\times 1}{\mathbf{y}_h} &= (\underset{n\times(g_h-1)}{\mathbf{Y}_h} \mid \underset{n\times k_h}{\mathbf{X}_h}) \begin{pmatrix} \boldsymbol{\gamma}_h \\ --- \\ \boldsymbol{\beta}_h \end{pmatrix} + \underset{n\times 1}{\boldsymbol{\varepsilon}_h} \\ &= \underset{n\times(g_h-1+k_h)}{\mathbf{Z}_h} \underset{(g_h-1+k_h)\times 1}{\boldsymbol{\delta}_h} + \boldsymbol{\varepsilon}_h, \qquad h = 1, 2, \ldots, g, \end{aligned} \tag{10.7.1}$$

where $\boldsymbol{\delta}_h$ summarizes all the coefficients to be estimated in the equation. It will be assumed that all identities have been eliminated and that all equations are either just identified or overidentified. The star notation basically involves "stacking" the vectors, so that a series of column vectors is written as one "stacked" column vector. The g vectors of dependent

[23]The 3SLS estimator was developed by Zellner and Theil (1962). See also Sargan (1964), Theil (1971), and Madansky (1976).

[24]The following table indicates the relations between 3SLS, 2SLS, and "seemingly unrelated equations."

	No Explanatory Endogenous Variables	Explanatory Endogenous Variables
Estimate a single equation from a system of equations	Estimation of a reduced-form equation using least squares (Section 4.3)	2SLS and k-class estimators (Section 10.5)
Estimate all equations of a system simultaneously	"Seemingly unrelated equations" (Section 5.3)	3SLS (Section 10.7)

endogenous variables and stochastic disturbance terms are stacked to form the column vectors of gn elements:

$$\underset{gn\times 1}{\mathbf{y}^*} = \begin{pmatrix} \mathbf{y}_1 \\ \hline \mathbf{y}_2 \\ \hline \vdots \\ \hline \mathbf{y}_g \end{pmatrix}, \qquad \underset{gn\times 1}{\boldsymbol{\varepsilon}^*} = \begin{pmatrix} \boldsymbol{\varepsilon}_1 \\ \hline \boldsymbol{\varepsilon}_2 \\ \hline \vdots \\ \hline \boldsymbol{\varepsilon}_g \end{pmatrix}, \tag{10.7.2}$$

the star serving as a reminder that these are the stacked vectors. Similarly, the g vectors of coefficients are stacked to form the column vector of k^* coefficients:

$$\underset{k^*\times 1}{\boldsymbol{\delta}^*} = \begin{pmatrix} \boldsymbol{\delta}_1 \\ \hline \boldsymbol{\delta}_2 \\ \hline \vdots \\ \hline \boldsymbol{\delta}_g \end{pmatrix}, \tag{10.7.3}$$

where k^* is the total number of coefficients to be estimated, given as:

$$k^* = \sum_{h=1}^{g} (g_h - 1 + k_h). \tag{10.7.4}$$

The vector $\boldsymbol{\delta}^*$ thus contains all coefficients to be estimated. The matrices of explanatory variables are summarized in the star notation by the single matrix:

$$\mathbf{Z}^* = \left(\begin{array}{c|c|c|c} \mathbf{Z}_1 & \mathbf{0} & \cdots & \mathbf{0} \\ \hline \mathbf{0} & \mathbf{Z}_2 & \cdots & \mathbf{0} \\ \hline \vdots & \vdots & & \vdots \\ \hline \mathbf{0} & \mathbf{0} & \cdots & \mathbf{Z}_g \end{array}\right) = \left(\begin{array}{c|c|c|c} \mathbf{Y}_1 \;\vdots\; \mathbf{X}_1 & \mathbf{0} & \cdots & \mathbf{0} \\ \hline \mathbf{0} & \mathbf{Y}_2 \;\vdots\; \mathbf{X}_2 & \cdots & \mathbf{0} \\ \hline \vdots & \vdots & & \vdots \\ \hline \mathbf{0} & \mathbf{0} & \cdots & \mathbf{Y}_g \;\vdots\; \mathbf{X}_g \end{array}\right), \tag{10.7.5}$$

in which each matrix along the "principal diagonal" of matrices contains all data on explanatory variables in one equation. In this star notation all g equations of the system can be written:

$$\underset{gn\times 1}{\mathbf{y}^*} = \underset{gn\times k^*}{\mathbf{Z}^*} \; \underset{k^*\times 1}{\boldsymbol{\delta}^*} + \underset{gn\times 1}{\boldsymbol{\varepsilon}^*}, \tag{10.7.6}$$

and the problem of estimation is that of estimating $\boldsymbol{\delta}^*$ given the data summarized by $\mathbf{y}^*$ and $\mathbf{Z}^*$.

In the single-equation case the assumptions on the stochastic disturbance terms in (4.2.2) were conveniently represented by A.4.1 and A.4.2. The same is true here, and the star notation facilitates the statement of the assumptions on the stochastic disturbance terms for the simultaneous-equations system. Thus the disturbance assumption (10.1.2) can be written:

$$E(\boldsymbol{\varepsilon}^*) = \mathbf{0}, \tag{10.7.7}$$

which can be considered the generalization of (A.4.1) to the case of simultaneous-equations systems. The homoskedasticity assumption (10.1.3) and the absence of serial correlation assumption (10.1.4) can be written:

$$\text{Cov}(\boldsymbol{\varepsilon}^*) = E(\boldsymbol{\varepsilon}^*\boldsymbol{\varepsilon}^{*\prime}) = \begin{pmatrix} \sigma_{11}\mathbf{I} & \sigma_{12}\mathbf{I} & \cdots & \sigma_{1g}\mathbf{I} \\ \sigma_{21}\mathbf{I} & \sigma_{22}\mathbf{I} & \cdots & \sigma_{2g}\mathbf{I} \\ \vdots & & & \\ \sigma_{g1}\mathbf{I} & \sigma_{g2}\mathbf{I} & \cdots & \sigma_{gg}\mathbf{I} \end{pmatrix} = \boldsymbol{\Sigma} \otimes \mathbf{I}, \tag{10.7.8}$$

where $\boldsymbol{\Sigma} \otimes \mathbf{I}$ is the Kronecker product of these matrices.[25] This is the generalization of (4.2.2) to the case of simultaneous equations. In this expression the covariance matrix has been partitioned into blocks, where each block is an element of the $\boldsymbol{\Sigma}$ matrix times the $n \times n$ identity matrix. In the case of a single equation ($g = 1$), the Kronecker product reduces to $\sigma^2\mathbf{I}$, which is the covariance matrix in this case, as in (4.2.2). Each block is a diagonal matrix, reflecting the independence among noncontemporaneous disturbances. The contemporaneous disturbances can, however, be correlated, as reflected in the elements of $\boldsymbol{\Sigma}$. For example, the matrix $\sigma_{11}\mathbf{I}$ represents the covariance matrix for the first equation. The equal diagonal elements of this block represent the constant variance of the stochastic disturbance terms of the first equation at each observation, while the zero off-diagonal elements of this block represent the assumption of absence of correlation between the disturbance terms of the first equation at different observations. The matrix $\sigma_{12}\mathbf{I}$, referring to the first and second equations, is also a diagonal matrix, where the equal diagonal elements represent the assumption of constant covariance at corresponding observations for the first and second equations, and where the zero off-diagonal elements indicate the assumption that the stochastic disturbance terms of the first and second equations are uncorrelated at different observations.

The star notation can be used to state some of the estimators previously introduced. For example, the OLS estimator is readily expressed in this notation as:

$$\hat{\boldsymbol{\delta}}^*_{\text{OLS}} = (\mathbf{Z}^{*\prime}\mathbf{Z}^*)^{-1}\mathbf{Z}^{*\prime}\mathbf{y}^*. \tag{10.7.9}$$

This estimator summarizes the OLS estimator of each equation, of the form:

$$\hat{\boldsymbol{\delta}}_{h\text{OLS}} = (\mathbf{Z}_h'\mathbf{Z}_h)^{-1}\mathbf{Z}_h'y_h, \qquad h = 1, 2, \ldots, g, \tag{10.7.10}$$

in the star notation.

The 2SLS estimator can be expressed using the star notation as:

$$\hat{\boldsymbol{\delta}}^*_{\text{2SLS}} = \left(\hat{\mathbf{Z}}^{*\prime}\hat{\mathbf{Z}}^*\right)^{-1}\hat{\mathbf{Z}}^{*\prime}\mathbf{y}^*, \tag{10.7.11}$$

that is, as the same estimator as OLS except for the replacement of explanatory variables by their estimated values. Here $\hat{\mathbf{Z}}^*$ is:

[25]For a definition of the Kronecker product of two matrices and a summary of its properties, see Appendix B, equation (B.3.21), and Theil (1971).

$$\hat{\mathbf{Z}}^* = \left(\begin{array}{c|c|c|c} \hat{\mathbf{Y}}_1 \; \vdots \; \mathbf{X}_1 & \mathbf{0} & \cdots & \mathbf{0} \\ \hline \mathbf{0} & \hat{\mathbf{Y}}_2 \; \vdots \; \mathbf{X}_2 & \cdots & \mathbf{0} \\ \hline \vdots & \vdots & & \vdots \\ \hline \mathbf{0} & \mathbf{0} & \cdots & \hat{\mathbf{Y}}_g \; \vdots \; \mathbf{X}_g \end{array}\right) \tag{10.7.12}$$

$$= \left(\begin{array}{c|c|c|c} \hat{\mathbf{Z}}_1 & \mathbf{0} & \cdots & \mathbf{0} \\ \hline \mathbf{0} & \hat{\mathbf{Z}}_2 & \cdots & \mathbf{0} \\ \hline \vdots & \vdots & & \vdots \\ \hline \mathbf{0} & \mathbf{0} & \cdots & \hat{\mathbf{Z}}_g \end{array}\right),$$

representing the estimated values of all explanatory endogenous variables and the actual values of all exogenous variables in each of the equations of the model. Using (10.6.19), however,

$$\hat{\mathbf{Z}}^* = \mathbf{X}^*(\mathbf{X}^{*\prime}\mathbf{X}^*)^{-1}\mathbf{X}^{*\prime}\mathbf{Z}^*, \tag{10.7.13}$$

where $\mathbf{X}^*$ is defined as:

$$\underset{gn\times gk}{\mathbf{X}^*} = \begin{pmatrix} \mathbf{X} & \mathbf{0} & \cdots & \mathbf{0} \\ \mathbf{0} & \mathbf{X} & \cdots & \mathbf{0} \\ \vdots & \vdots & & \vdots \\ \mathbf{0} & \mathbf{0} & \cdots & \mathbf{X} \end{pmatrix} = \underset{g\times g}{\mathbf{I}} \otimes \underset{n\times k}{\mathbf{X}}. \tag{10.7.14}$$

Thus the 2SLS estimator can be expressed as:

$$\hat{\boldsymbol{\delta}}^*_{2SLS} = \left[\mathbf{Z}^{*\prime}\mathbf{X}^*(\mathbf{X}^{*\prime}\mathbf{X}^*)^{-1}\mathbf{X}^{*\prime}\mathbf{Z}^*\right]^{-1}\mathbf{Z}^{*\prime}\mathbf{X}^*(\mathbf{X}^{*\prime}\mathbf{X}^*)^{-1}\mathbf{X}^{*\prime}\mathbf{y}^*. \tag{10.7.15}$$

This estimator is of exactly the same form as (10.6.23) except for the use of starred variables. The 2SLS estimator can also be written, using the properties of the Kronecker product, as:[26]

$$\hat{\boldsymbol{\delta}}^*_{2SLS} = \left\{\mathbf{Z}^{*\prime}\left[\mathbf{I}\otimes\mathbf{X}(\mathbf{X}'\mathbf{X})^{-1}\mathbf{X}'\right]\mathbf{Z}^*\right\}^{-1}\mathbf{Z}^{*\prime}\left[\mathbf{I}\otimes\mathbf{X}(\mathbf{X}'\mathbf{X})^{-1}\mathbf{X}'\right]\mathbf{y}^*. \tag{10.7.16}$$

The problem with the 2SLS estimator of the system, as given in (10.7.11), (10.7.15), and (10.7.16), is the same as that encountered in OLS for one equation of the system, namely the correlation between explanatory variables, specifically the explanatory endogenous variables in $\mathbf{Z}^*$ [shown explicitly as $\mathbf{Y}_1, \mathbf{Y}_2, \ldots, \mathbf{Y}_g$ in (10.7.5)], and the stochastic disturbance term $\boldsymbol{\varepsilon}^*$. The OLS estimator in (10.7.9) takes no account of the distinction between explanatory endogenous and included exogenous variables and is biased and inconsistent. The 2SLS estimator in (10.7.15) and (10.7.15) takes account of this distinction in each equation, but it does not take account of the possible correlation between explanatory endogenous variables of one equation and the stochastic disturbance terms in all other equations. This correlation between stochastic disturbance terms in different equations, leading to the cor-

[26]Note that for the product of Kronecker products

$$(\mathbf{A}_1 \otimes \mathbf{B}_1)(\mathbf{A}_2 \otimes \mathbf{B}_2)(\mathbf{A}_3 \otimes \mathbf{B}_3) = (\mathbf{A}_1\mathbf{A}_2\mathbf{A}_3) \otimes (\mathbf{B}_1\mathbf{B}_2\mathbf{B}_3).$$

relation of dependent endogenous variables with stochastic disturbances in other equations, is represented by the blocks of the covariance matrix (10.7.8) that lie off the principal diagonal of matrices. For example, the block $\sigma_{12}\mathbf{I}$, as noted previously, refers to the correlation between the first and second equations, which results in a correlation of the first endogenous variable $\mathbf{y}_1$ with the contemporaneous stochastic disturbance term of the second equation $\boldsymbol{\varepsilon}_2$. If these off-diagonal blocks of the covariance matrix all vanish—that is, if $\boldsymbol{\Sigma}$ in (10.1.3) is diagonal—then there is no way to improve upon the 2SLS estimator. If, however, these off-diagonal blocks do not vanish, then it is possible to improve upon the asymptotic efficiency of 2SLS by taking explicit account of this inter-equation correlation. This improvement in asymptotic efficiency is incorporated in the 3SLS estimator.

The 3SLS estimator is a GLS estimator of the entire system in (10.7.6) that takes explicit account of the covariance matrix in (10.7.8). GLS was used earlier in this chapter in (10.6.21)–(10.6.23), where it was shown that 2SLS is equivalent to using all exogenous variables as instrumental variables and estimating the resulting equation using GLS. The 3SLS estimator follows exactly the same approach for the entire system of equations. Using all exogenous variables as instruments implies that the equation to be estimated is obtained from (10.7.6) by premultiplying by $\mathbf{X}^{*\prime}$, the matrix defined by:

$$\mathbf{X}^{*\prime} = \begin{pmatrix} \mathbf{X}' & \mathbf{0} & \cdots & \mathbf{0} \\ \mathbf{0} & \mathbf{X}' & \cdots & \mathbf{0} \\ \vdots & \vdots & & \vdots \\ \mathbf{0} & \mathbf{0} & \cdots & \mathbf{X}' \end{pmatrix}, \tag{10.7.17}$$

yielding:

$$\mathbf{X}^{*\prime}\mathbf{y}^* = \mathbf{X}^{*\prime}\mathbf{Z}^*\boldsymbol{\delta}^* + \mathbf{X}^{*\prime}\boldsymbol{\varepsilon}^*. \tag{10.7.18}$$

This is the system obtained by premultiplying each equation by $\mathbf{X}'$, using all exogenous variables as instrumental variables in each equation of the system. It is the systems analog of (10.6.21). The GLS estimator of this equation is the 3SLS estimator:

$$\begin{aligned}\hat{\boldsymbol{\delta}}^*_{3SLS} &= \left\{\mathbf{Z}^{*\prime}\mathbf{X}^*\left[\mathrm{Cov}(\mathbf{X}^{*\prime}\boldsymbol{\varepsilon}^*)\right]^{-1}\mathbf{X}^{*\prime}\mathbf{Z}^*\right\}^{-1} \\ &\cdot \mathbf{Z}^{*\prime}\mathbf{X}^*\left[\mathrm{Cov}(\mathbf{X}^{*\prime}\boldsymbol{\varepsilon}^*)\right]^{-1}\mathbf{X}^{*\prime}\mathbf{y}^*.\end{aligned} \tag{10.7.19}$$

The covariance matrix, however, from (10.7.8), is:

$$\mathrm{Cov}(\mathbf{X}^{*\prime}\boldsymbol{\varepsilon}^*) = \mathbf{X}^{*\prime}\mathrm{Cov}(\boldsymbol{\varepsilon}^*)\mathbf{X}^* = \mathbf{X}^{*\prime}(\boldsymbol{\Sigma} \otimes \mathbf{I})\mathbf{X}^*, \tag{10.7.20}$$

which is the systems analog of (10.6.22). Thus the 3SLS estimator can be written:

$$\begin{aligned}\hat{\boldsymbol{\delta}}^*_{3SLS} &= \left\{\mathbf{Z}^{*\prime}\mathbf{X}^*\left[\mathbf{X}^{*\prime}(\boldsymbol{\Sigma} \otimes \mathbf{I})\mathbf{X}^*\right]^{-1}\mathbf{X}^{*\prime}\mathbf{Z}^*\right\}^{-1} \\ &\cdot \mathbf{Z}^{*\prime}\mathbf{X}^*\left[\mathbf{X}^{*\prime}(\boldsymbol{\Sigma} \otimes \mathbf{I})\mathbf{X}^*\right]^{-1}\mathbf{X}^{*\prime}\mathbf{y}^*,\end{aligned} \tag*{*(10.7.21)}$$

which is the systems analog of (10.6.23). This estimator is of the same form as the 2SLS estimator in (10.7.15), except for the insertion of $\boldsymbol{\Sigma} \otimes \mathbf{I}$ between $\mathbf{X}^{*\prime}$ and $\mathbf{X}^*$ in two places. Thus the 3SLS estimator can be interpreted as taking all the 2SLS results, summarized in (10.7.15), and "correcting" them for the covariance matrix $\boldsymbol{\Sigma}$. In this interpretation the 3SLS estimator is precisely the technique of "seemingly unrelated equations," as discussed in Section 5.3, applied to the set of all second-stage equations of 2SLS. The resulting estimator is both consistent and asymptotically more efficient than the 2SLS estimators, since it takes explicit account of the covariances in $\boldsymbol{\Sigma}$. If all equations were just identified or the covariance matrix $\mathbf{\Sigma}$ were diagonal, the 3SLS estimator would reduce to the 2SLS estimator.[27]

All components of the 3SLS estimator other than the covariance matrix are obtained directly from the data. Thus $\mathbf{Z}^*$ is defined by (10.7.5), $\mathbf{X}^*$ by (10.7.14), and $\mathbf{y}^*$ by (10.7.2). If $\mathbf{\Sigma}$ is given, it is used as given. Typically, however, $\mathbf{\Sigma}$ is not given, and it must be estimated. This is the rationale for referring to a "three-stage" estimator. The result of the first two stages, the 2SLS estimates, yield the information, in the residuals, needed to estimate the covariance matrix. In particular, $\mathbf{\Sigma}$ is estimated as:

$$\hat{\mathbf{\Sigma}} = (\hat{\sigma}_{hh'}) \quad \text{where} \quad \hat{\sigma}_{hh'} = \frac{1}{n}\hat{\boldsymbol{\varepsilon}}_h\hat{\boldsymbol{\varepsilon}}_{h'}$$

$$= \frac{1}{n}\left(\mathbf{y}_h - \mathbf{Z}_h\hat{\boldsymbol{\delta}}_h\right)'\left(\mathbf{y}_{h'} - \mathbf{Z}_{h'}\hat{\boldsymbol{\delta}}_{h'}\right), \qquad (10.7.22)$$

$$h, h' = 1, 2, \ldots, g,$$

and is assumed nonsingular.[28] Here $\hat{\boldsymbol{\delta}}_h$ and $\hat{\boldsymbol{\delta}}_{h'}$ are the 2SLS estimates that are the relevant column-vector components of (10.7.15). The first two stages are performed in the 3SLS technique only to provide estimates of $\mathbf{\Sigma}$; no other use is made of the 2SLS estimates of coefficients $\hat{\boldsymbol{\delta}}_h = \hat{\boldsymbol{\delta}}_{h2SLS}$.

Another way of stating the 3SLS estimator is based on using (10.7.14) so as to express the covariance matrix in (10.7.20) as:

$$\text{Cov}(\mathbf{X}^{*\prime}\boldsymbol{\varepsilon}^*) = \mathbf{X}^{*\prime}(\mathbf{\Sigma} \otimes \mathbf{I})\mathbf{X}^* = (\mathbf{I} \otimes \mathbf{X}')(\mathbf{\Sigma} \otimes \mathbf{I})(\mathbf{I} \otimes \mathbf{X}), \qquad (10.7.23)$$

so that[29]

$$\text{Cov}(\mathbf{X}^{*\prime}\boldsymbol{\varepsilon}^*) = \mathbf{\Sigma} \otimes (\mathbf{X}'\mathbf{X})\,. \qquad (10.7.24)$$

Combining (10.7.21) and (10.7.24), the 3SLS estimator can be written, replacing $\mathbf{\Sigma}$ by $\hat{\mathbf{\Sigma}}$, as:

$$\hat{\boldsymbol{\delta}}^*_{3SLS} = \left\{\mathbf{Z}^{*\prime}\left[\hat{\mathbf{\Sigma}}^{-1} \otimes \mathbf{X}(\mathbf{X}'\mathbf{X})^{-1}\mathbf{X}'\right]\mathbf{Z}^*\right\}^{-1}\mathbf{Z}^{*\prime}\left[\hat{\mathbf{\Sigma}}^{-1} \otimes \mathbf{X}(\mathbf{X}'\mathbf{X})^{-1}\mathbf{X}'\right]\mathbf{y}^*. \qquad *(10.7.25)$$

This statement of the 3SLS estimator, if compared to the 2SLS estimator of (10.7.16), indicates that the 3SLS differs from the 2SLS estimator only in taking explicit account of the estimate of the covariance matrix $\hat{\mathbf{\Sigma}}$.

The 3SLS estimator is thus given by (10.7.25) or, equivalently (10.7.21) with $\mathbf{\Sigma}$ replaced by $\hat{\mathbf{\Sigma}}$ and where $\hat{\mathbf{\Sigma}}$ is estimated from (10.7.22). It is the estimator obtained by using all exogenous variables as instrumental variables and then applying GLS to the whole system, where the 2SLS estimates are used to obtain an estimate of the relevant covariance matrix. The three stages of 3SLS are thus: *first*, estimation of the reduced form, as in (10.5.4); *second*, estimation of each structural equation via 2SLS as in (10.7.15); *third*, GLS estimation of the system after having used all exogenous variables as instrumental variables, as in (10.7.21), where the covariance matrix is estimated from the residuals of the 2SLS estimates, as in (10.7.22). This estimator is both consistent, in that:

$$\text{plim } \hat{\boldsymbol{\delta}}^*_{3SLS} = \boldsymbol{\delta}^*, \qquad *(10.7.26)$$

and asymptotically more efficient than 2SLS, in that:

[27]See Problem 10-L.

[28]Note that $\hat{\sigma}_1^2$ in (10.6.35) is identical to $\hat{\sigma}_{11}$ in (10.7.22) [see also (10.8.13) in Section 10.8].

[29]See footnote 26.

$$\text{Asy. Cov}(\hat{\boldsymbol{\delta}}^*_{3SLS}) - \text{Asy. Cov}(\hat{\boldsymbol{\delta}}^*_{2SLS}) \text{ is negative semidefinite.} \qquad *(10.7.27)$$

In Section 10.6 it was shown that several single-equation estimators could be interpreted as instrumental-variables estimators for particular choices of instrumental variables. The same interpretation can be given the various systems estimators presented here. Given the system in star notation (10.7.6), the instrumental-variables (IV) estimator of $\boldsymbol{\delta}^*$, by analogy to (10.6.6), is:

$$\hat{\boldsymbol{\delta}}^*_{IV} = \hat{\boldsymbol{\delta}}^*(\mathbf{W}^*) = (\mathbf{W}^{*\prime}\mathbf{Z}^*)^{-1}\mathbf{W}^{*\prime}\mathbf{y}^*, \qquad (10.7.28)$$

where $\hat{\boldsymbol{\delta}}^*$ $(\mathbf{W}^*)$ shows the functional dependence of the estimator on $\mathbf{W}^*$, matrix of data on instrumental variables. Thus the OLS estimator in (10.7.9) corresponds to the IV estimator for which $\mathbf{W}^*$ is simply the set of all explanatory variables $\mathbf{Z}^*$:

$$\hat{\boldsymbol{\delta}}^*_{OLS} = \hat{\boldsymbol{\delta}}^*(\mathbf{Z}^*) = (\mathbf{Z}^{*\prime}\mathbf{Z}^*)^{-1}\mathbf{Z}^{*\prime}\mathbf{y}^*, \qquad (10.7.29)$$

which is the systems analog of (10.6.7). The 2SLS estimator in (10.7.11), (10.7.15), and (10.7.16) is the IV estimator for which:

$$\mathbf{W}^*_{2SLS} = \hat{\mathbf{Z}}^* = \mathbf{X}^*(\mathbf{X}^{*\prime}\mathbf{X}^*)^{-1}\mathbf{X}^{*\prime}\mathbf{Z}^* = \left[\mathbf{I} \otimes \mathbf{X}(\mathbf{X}'\mathbf{X})^{-1}\mathbf{X}'\right]\mathbf{Z}^*, \qquad (10.7.30)$$

where, for example, in (10.7.16):

$$\hat{\boldsymbol{\delta}}^*_{2SLS} = \hat{\boldsymbol{\delta}}^*\left(\left[\mathbf{I} \otimes \mathbf{X}(\mathbf{X}'\mathbf{X})^{-1}\mathbf{X}'\right]\mathbf{Z}^*\right). \qquad (10.7.31)$$

Finally the 3SLS estimator in (10.7.25) is the IV estimator for which:

$$\mathbf{W}^*_{3SLS} = \left[\sum{}^{-1} \otimes \mathbf{X}(\mathbf{X}'\mathbf{X})^{-1}\mathbf{X}'\right]\mathbf{Z}^*, \qquad (10.7.32)$$

so that

$$\hat{\boldsymbol{\delta}}^*_{3SLS} = \hat{\boldsymbol{\delta}}^*\left(\left[\sum{}^{-1} \otimes \mathbf{X}(\mathbf{X}'\mathbf{X})^{-1}\mathbf{X}'\right]\mathbf{Z}^*\right). \qquad (10.7.33)$$

For the general IV estimator, using (10.7.6) and (10.7.28),

$$\begin{aligned}\hat{\boldsymbol{\delta}}^*_{IV} &= (\mathbf{W}^{*\prime}\mathbf{Z}^*)^{-1}\mathbf{W}^{*\prime}(\mathbf{Z}^*\boldsymbol{\delta}^* + \boldsymbol{\varepsilon}^*) \\ &= \boldsymbol{\delta}^* + (\mathbf{W}^{*\prime}\mathbf{Z}^*)^{-1}\mathbf{W}^{*\prime}\boldsymbol{\varepsilon}^*,\end{aligned} \qquad (10.7.34)$$

so that

$$\text{plim } \hat{\boldsymbol{\delta}}^*_{IV} = \boldsymbol{\delta}^* + \text{plim}\left(\frac{1}{n}\mathbf{W}^{*\prime}\mathbf{Z}^*\right)^{-1} \text{plim}\left(\frac{1}{n}\mathbf{W}^{*\prime}\,\boldsymbol{\varepsilon}^*\right), \qquad (10.7.35)$$

which is the systems analog of (10.6.27). Assuming that the instrumental variables are asymptotically uncorrelated with the stochastic disturbance terms,

$$\text{plim}\left(\frac{1}{n}\mathbf{W}^{*\prime}\boldsymbol{\varepsilon}^*\right) = \mathbf{0}, \qquad (10.7.36)$$

and that they are asymptotically correlated with the $\mathbf{Z}^*$'s,

$$\text{plim}\left(\frac{1}{n}\mathbf{W}^{*\prime}\mathbf{Z}^*\right) = \mathbf{Q}^*, \qquad (10.7.37)$$

where $\mathbf{Q}^*$ exists and is nonsingular, the IV estimator is consistent:

$$\text{plim } \hat{\boldsymbol{\delta}}^*_{IV} = \boldsymbol{\delta}^*. \qquad (10.7.38)$$

The two conditions for consistency are systems analogs for (10.6.28) and (10.6.29), and they are satisfied for 2SLS and 3SLS, which are both consistent estimators, but not for OLS, which is generally not consistent.

The asymptotic covariance matrix for the IV estimator, as given in (10.7.34), is given as:

$$\text{Asy. Cov}(\hat{\boldsymbol{\delta}}^*_{\text{IV}}) = \frac{1}{n}\,\text{plim}\left[\left(\frac{1}{n}\mathbf{W}^{*\prime}\mathbf{Z}^*\right)^{-1}\left(\frac{1}{n}\mathbf{W}^{*\prime}\boldsymbol{\varepsilon}^*\,\boldsymbol{\varepsilon}^{*\prime}\mathbf{W}^*\right)\left(\frac{1}{n}\mathbf{Z}^{*\prime}\mathbf{W}^*\right)^{-1}\right], \tag{10.7.39}$$

which is the systems analog of (10.6.33). From (10.7.8), however,

$$\text{Asy. Cov}(\hat{\boldsymbol{\delta}}^*_{\text{IV}}) = \frac{1}{n}\,\text{plim}\left\{\left(\frac{1}{n}\mathbf{W}^{*\prime}\mathbf{Z}^*\right)^{-1}\left[\frac{1}{n}\mathbf{W}^{*\prime}(\boldsymbol{\Sigma}\otimes\mathbf{I})\mathbf{W}^*\right]\left(\frac{1}{n}\mathbf{Z}^{*\prime}\mathbf{W}^*\right)^{-1}\right\}, \tag{10.7.40}$$

which is analogous to (10.6.33). This result yields as the asymptotic covariance matrix for 2SLS, using (10.7.31):

$$\begin{aligned}\text{Asy. Cov}(\hat{\boldsymbol{\delta}}^*_{\text{2SLS}}) = \frac{1}{n}\,\text{plim}\Bigg(&\left\{\frac{1}{n}\mathbf{Z}^{*\prime}[\mathbf{I}\otimes\mathbf{X}(\mathbf{X}'\mathbf{X})^{-1}\mathbf{X}']\mathbf{Z}^*\right\}^{-1}\\ &\cdot\left\{\frac{1}{n}\mathbf{Z}^{*\prime}[\boldsymbol{\Sigma}\otimes\mathbf{X}(\mathbf{X}'\mathbf{X})^{-1}\mathbf{X}']\mathbf{Z}^*\right\}\\ &\cdot\left\{\frac{1}{n}\mathbf{Z}^{*\prime}[\mathbf{I}\otimes\mathbf{X}(\mathbf{X}'\mathbf{X})^{-1}\mathbf{X}']\mathbf{Z}^*\right\}^{-1}\Bigg),\end{aligned} \tag{10.7.41}$$

which generalizes (10.6.36) to the entire system. The covariance matrix $\boldsymbol{\Sigma}$ can be consistently estimated as $\hat{\boldsymbol{\Sigma}}$ in (10.7.22), where $\hat{\boldsymbol{\delta}}_h$ and $\hat{\boldsymbol{\delta}}_{h'}$ are the 2SLS estimators. The result in (10.7.40) also yields as the asymptotic covariance matrix for 3SLS, using (10.7.33),[30]

$$\text{Asy. Cov}(\hat{\boldsymbol{\delta}}^*_{\text{3SLS}}) = \frac{1}{n}\,\text{plim}\left(\left\{\frac{1}{n}\mathbf{Z}^{*\prime}\left[\boldsymbol{\Sigma}^{-1}\otimes\mathbf{X}(\mathbf{X}'\mathbf{X})^{-1}\mathbf{X}'\right]\mathbf{Z}^*\right\}^{-1}\right). \tag*{*(10.7.42)}$$

The covariance matrix $\boldsymbol{\Sigma}$ can again be consistently estimated as $\hat{\boldsymbol{\Sigma}}$ in (10.7.22), but where $\hat{\boldsymbol{\delta}}_h$ and $\hat{\boldsymbol{\delta}}_{h'}$ are now the 3SLS estimators. These are the two asymptotic covariance matrices used in (10.7.27), which states that 3SLS is asymptotically more efficient than 2SLS. They can also be used for constructing (asymptotic) tests of significance and confidence intervals, as discussed following (10.6.36).

10.8 FULL-INFORMATION MAXIMUM LIKELIHOOD

The other major full-information technique is that of full-information maximum likelihood (FIML).[31] In this approach the likelihood function for the entire system is maximized by choice of all system parameters, subject to all a priori identifying restrictions. The result-

[30]As in footnote 20, assuming the stochastic disturbance terms at each observation are independently and identically (but not necessarily normally) distributed, the 3SLS estimator is asymptotically normally distributed [that is, the estimator $\sqrt{n}(\hat{\boldsymbol{\delta}}^*_{\text{3SLS}} - \boldsymbol{\delta}^*)$ is asymptotically normal] with mean given by the zero vector and with an asymptotic covariance matrix given by (10.7.42). If there are no restrictions on $\boldsymbol{\Sigma}$, the asymptotic distribution of the 3SLS estimator is identical to that of full-information maximum likelihood. In particular, the asymptotic distribution is normal and the asymptotic covariance matrix (10.7.42) is asymptotically efficient in that it attains the asymptotic Cramer–Rao bound of the full-information maximum likelihood estimator. See footnote 32 of Section 4.5, and Rao (1965). For further discussions of asymptotic efficiency, see Malinvaud (1970), Theil (1971), and Rothenberg (1974).

[31] See Sargan (1964), Fisk (1967), Theil (1971), and Madansky (1976). For an instrumental-variable interpretation, see Hausman (1975). For extensions to nonlinear econometric systems, see Eisenpress and Greenstadt (1966), Chow (1973), and Jorgenson and Laffont (1974).

ing estimators are consistent and asymptotically efficient.[32] They also have the same asymptotic properties as 3SLS, including the same asymptotic covariance matrix. A major advantage of FIML over 3SLS, however, is that with this technique it is possible to use in the estimation process a wide range of a priori information, pertaining not only to each equation individually but also to several equations simultaneously, such as constraints involving coefficients of different structural equations and certain restrictions on the error structure. The major disadvantage of FIML, however, is that it is difficult and expensive to compute, involving the estimation of rather awkward simultaneous nonlinear equations, which usually must be computed via iteration.

It is convenient to use the star notation of Section 10.7 in developing the FIML estimator. In this notation all g equations of the simultaneous system, after normalization, can be written:

$$\underset{gn\times 1}{\mathbf{y}^*} = \underset{gn\times k^*}{\mathbf{Z}^*}\ \underset{k^*\times 1}{\boldsymbol{\delta}^*} + \underset{gn\times 1}{\boldsymbol{\varepsilon}^*}, \tag{10.8.1}$$

as in (10.7.6). The vector of all stochastic disturbances in all equations $\boldsymbol{\varepsilon}^*$ is assumed to satisfy the properties:

$$E(\boldsymbol{\varepsilon}^*) = \mathbf{0}, \tag{10.8.2}$$

$$\text{Cov}(\boldsymbol{\varepsilon}^*) = \boldsymbol{\Sigma} \otimes \mathbf{I}, \tag{10.8.3}$$

as in (10.7.7) and (10.7.8). The FIML technique is one of maximum likelihood, however, and maximum likelihood always requires a specific assumption as to the form of the distribution of the stochastic disturbances. If it is again assumed that the stochastic disturbances are distributed normally,

$$\boldsymbol{\varepsilon}^* \sim \mathbf{N}(\mathbf{0}, \boldsymbol{\Sigma} \otimes \mathbf{I}), \tag{10.8.4}$$

the logarithm of the likelihood function is given by:

$$\begin{aligned}\ln\ L(\boldsymbol{\varepsilon}^*) = &-\frac{gn}{2}\ln\ 2\pi - \tfrac{1}{2}\ln|\boldsymbol{\Sigma}\otimes\mathbf{I}| \\ &-\tfrac{1}{2}(\mathbf{y}^* - \mathbf{Z}^*\boldsymbol{\delta}^*)'(\boldsymbol{\Sigma}^{-1}\otimes\mathbf{I})(\mathbf{y}^* - \mathbf{Z}^*\boldsymbol{\delta}^*).\end{aligned} \tag{10.8.5}$$

This is the likelihood function of the $\boldsymbol{\varepsilon}^*$ disturbance vector, but what is needed is the likelihood function of the endogenous variables $\mathbf{y}^*$, since the objective is to choose values of parameters so as to maximize the likelihood of observing the values given by $\mathbf{y}^*$. But, letting $L(\mathbf{y}^*)$ be the likelihood function for $\mathbf{y}^*$,

$$\ln\ L(\mathbf{y}^*) = \ln\ L(\boldsymbol{\varepsilon}^*) + \ln\left|\frac{\partial\boldsymbol{\varepsilon}^*}{\partial\mathbf{y}^*}\right|, \tag{10.8.6}$$

since the transformation of variables from $\boldsymbol{\varepsilon}^*$ to $\mathbf{y}^*$ multiplies the likelihood function by the determinant of the relevant Jacobian matrix.[33] It is convenient to simplify this expression

[32]The FIML estimator $\hat{\boldsymbol{\delta}}^*_{\text{FIML}}$ is asymptotically normally distributed, and it is asymptotically efficient in that it attains the asymptotic Cramer–Rao bound. In particular, given any estimator $\hat{\boldsymbol{\delta}}^*$ that asymptotically normally distributed Asy. Cov$(\hat{\boldsymbol{\delta}}^*_{\text{FIML}})$ – Asy. Cov$(\hat{\boldsymbol{\delta}}^*)$ is negative semidefinite, where the asymptotic covariance matrix of the FIML estimator is identical to that for 3SLS, as given in (10.7.42) (see Rothenberg and Leenders, 1964; Madansky, 1964, 1976; Sargan, 1964, Rothenberg, 1974).

[33]The likelihood function for the endogenous variables $\mathbf{y}^*$ can be obtained from the likelihood function for the stochastic disturbance terms $\boldsymbol{\varepsilon}^*$ as:

for the likelihood function in order to obtain a form such that the first-order conditions of maximization characterize the estimators of the system parameters, as given by $\boldsymbol{\delta}^*$ and $\boldsymbol{\Sigma}$. One such simplification applies to the determinant of the Jacobian matrix in (10.8.6). From (10.7.2), it follows that:

$$\left|\frac{\partial \boldsymbol{\varepsilon}^*}{\partial \mathbf{y}^*}\right| = \left\|\begin{pmatrix} \boldsymbol{\Gamma} & \mathbf{0} & \cdots & \mathbf{0} \\ & \boldsymbol{\Gamma} & \cdots & \mathbf{0} \\ & & \ddots & \vdots \\ & & \cdots & \boldsymbol{\Gamma} \end{pmatrix}\right\| = |\boldsymbol{\Gamma}|^n, \tag{10.8.7}$$

since, while elements below the principal diagonal of $\boldsymbol{\Gamma}$ matrices may be nonzero, reflecting lagged endogenous variables, all elements above the principal diagonal must be zero, reflecting the fact that future variables do not influence present ones. These zeros ensure that the determinant of the Jacobian is the nth power of the (positive value of the) determinant of $\boldsymbol{\Gamma}$. Another simplification is the replacement of $-\frac{1}{2}\ln|\boldsymbol{\Sigma}\otimes\mathbf{I}|$ in (10.8.5) by $-(n/2)\,|\boldsymbol{\Sigma}|$, since

$$-\tfrac{1}{2}\ln|\boldsymbol{\Sigma}\otimes\mathbf{I}| = -\tfrac{1}{2}\ln|\boldsymbol{\Sigma}|^n = -\frac{n}{2}\ln|\boldsymbol{\Sigma}. \tag{10.8.8}$$

The relevant likelihood function is then:

$$\ln L(\mathbf{y}^*) = -\frac{gn}{2}\ln 2\pi - \frac{n}{2}\ln|\boldsymbol{\Sigma}| + n\ \ln|\boldsymbol{\Gamma}| \\ -\tfrac{1}{2}(\mathbf{y}^* - \mathbf{Z}^*\boldsymbol{\delta}^*)'(\boldsymbol{\Sigma}^{-1}\otimes\mathbf{I})(\mathbf{y}^* - \mathbf{Z}^*\boldsymbol{\delta}^*). \tag{10.8.9}$$

This likelihood function is maximized by choice of the parameters. It is convenient to consider first the choice of elements of the covariance matrix $\boldsymbol{\Sigma}$, where it is assumed that there are no a priori restrictions on $\boldsymbol{\Sigma}$. The last term in (10.8.9) can be written:

$$-\tfrac{1}{2}(\mathbf{y}^* - \mathbf{Z}^*\boldsymbol{\delta}^*)'(\boldsymbol{\Sigma}^{-1}\otimes\mathbf{I})(\mathbf{y}^* - \mathbf{Z}^*\boldsymbol{\delta}^*) \\ = -\tfrac{1}{2}\sum_{h=1}^{g}\sum_{h'=1}^{g}\sigma^{hh'}(\mathbf{y}_h - \mathbf{Z}_h\boldsymbol{\delta}_h)'(\mathbf{y}_{h'} - \mathbf{Z}_{h'}\boldsymbol{\delta}_{h'}), \tag{10.8.10}$$

where superscripted elements $\sigma^{hh'}$ are those of the inverse of the covariance matrix and subscripted elements $\sigma_{hh'}$ continue to be those of the matrix itself:

$$\boldsymbol{\Sigma} = (\sigma_{hh'}), \qquad \boldsymbol{\Sigma}^{-1} = (\sigma^{hh'}). \tag{10.8.11}$$

Using (10.8.10), the first-order conditions for a maximum by choice of elements of the (inverse of the) covariance matrix are[34]

$$\frac{\partial \ln L(\mathbf{y}^*)}{\partial \sigma^{hh'}} = \frac{n}{2}\sigma_{hh'} - \tfrac{1}{2}(\mathbf{y}_h - \mathbf{Z}_h\boldsymbol{\delta}_h)'(\mathbf{y}_{h'} - \mathbf{Z}_{h'}\boldsymbol{\delta}_{h'}) = 0. \tag{10.8.12}$$

$$L(\mathbf{y}^*) = L(\boldsymbol{\varepsilon}^*)\left|\frac{\partial \boldsymbol{\varepsilon}^*}{\partial \mathbf{y}^*}\right|,$$

where the last term is the determinant of the Jacobian matrix of all first-order partial derivatives of elements of $\boldsymbol{\varepsilon}^*$ with respect to elements of $\mathbf{y}^*$. This result on "change of variables" follows from the calculus of several variables, and it is discussed in standard texts on analysis, such as Rudin (1964), Apostol (1974), and Hoffman (1975) (see also Section 4.5).

[34]For the first term on the right, see Problem 10-O.

These conditions lead to the FIML estimator of the elements of the covariance matrix:

$$\hat{\boldsymbol{\Sigma}} = (\hat{\sigma}_{hh'}), \quad \text{where} \quad \hat{\sigma}_{hh'} = \frac{1}{n}\left(\mathbf{y}_h - \mathbf{Z}_h\hat{\boldsymbol{\delta}}_h\right)'\left(\mathbf{y}_{h'} - \mathbf{Z}_{h'}\hat{\boldsymbol{\delta}}_{h'}\right), \quad h, h' = 1, 2, \ldots, g. \tag{10.8.13}$$

These estimators were used previously in the 3SLS estimator in (10.7.22). Using them, the estimate of $\boldsymbol{\Sigma} \otimes \mathbf{I}$ is:

$$\hat{\boldsymbol{\Sigma}} \otimes \mathbf{I} = \frac{1}{n}\left(\mathbf{y}^* - \mathbf{Z}^*\hat{\boldsymbol{\delta}}^*\right)\left(\mathbf{y}^* - \mathbf{Z}^*\hat{\boldsymbol{\delta}}^*\right)'. \tag{10.8.14}$$

Inserting this result in (10.8.9), the matrices in the last term cancel, yielding:

$$\ln L(\mathbf{y}^*) = -\frac{gn}{2}\ln 2\pi - \frac{n}{2}\ln|\hat{\boldsymbol{\Sigma}}| + n\ln|\boldsymbol{\Gamma}| - \frac{ng}{2}. \tag{10.8.15}$$

The FIML estimators of the coefficients are then obtained by maximizing this likelihood function by choice of $\boldsymbol{\delta}^*$ subject to all a priori restrictions. In the unrestricted case, the first-order conditions are:

$$\frac{\partial \ln L(\mathbf{y}^*)}{\partial \boldsymbol{\delta}^*} = -\frac{n}{2}\frac{\partial \ln|\hat{\boldsymbol{\Sigma}}|}{\partial \boldsymbol{\delta}^*} + n\frac{\partial \ln|\boldsymbol{\Gamma}|}{\partial \boldsymbol{\delta}^*} = \mathbf{0}, \tag{10.8.16}$$

where $\hat{\boldsymbol{\Sigma}}$ depends on $\hat{\boldsymbol{\delta}}^*$, as given in (10.8.13). This is the system of nonlinear equations that must be solved for the FIML estimators $\hat{\boldsymbol{\delta}}^*_{\text{FIML}}$. Since $|\boldsymbol{\Gamma}|$ is a function of the coefficient of endogenous variables in all equations, the system of nonlinear equations in unknown coefficients is particularly awkward to solve. For example, for the coefficient $\gamma_{hh'}$,

$$\frac{\partial \ln|\boldsymbol{\Gamma}|}{\partial \gamma_{hh'}} = \gamma^{h'h}, \tag{10.8.17}$$

where $\gamma^{h'h}$ is the (h', h) element of $\boldsymbol{\Gamma}^{-1}$, involving all elements of $\boldsymbol{\Gamma}$ in a nonlinear fashion. Similarly, the partial derivatives of $\ln|\hat{\boldsymbol{\Sigma}}|$ are nonlinear in the parameters. Thus the system is very difficult to solve.[35]

The difficulties of solving for FIML estimators vanish in the recursive case, where $\boldsymbol{\Gamma}$ is triangular and $\boldsymbol{\Sigma}$ is diagonal. Since $\boldsymbol{\Gamma}$ is triangular, the system can be normalized so that $|\boldsymbol{\Gamma}|$ is simply unity. Thus, in this case $\boldsymbol{\delta}^*$ is estimated from:

$$\frac{\partial \ln|\hat{\boldsymbol{\Sigma}}|}{\partial \boldsymbol{\delta}^*} = \mathbf{0}, \tag{10.8.18}$$

since $\ln|\boldsymbol{\Gamma}|$ vanishes in (10.8.16). But here, since $\boldsymbol{\Sigma}$ is diagonal,

$$\begin{aligned} \ln|\hat{\boldsymbol{\Sigma}}| &= \sum_{h=1}^{g}\ln\hat{\sigma}_{hh} = \sum_{h=1}^{g}\ln\frac{1}{n}\left(\mathbf{y}_h - \mathbf{Z}_h\hat{\boldsymbol{\delta}}_h\right)'\left(\mathbf{y}_h - \mathbf{Z}_h\hat{\boldsymbol{\delta}}_h\right) \\ &= \sum_{h=1}^{g}\ln\frac{1}{n}\left(\mathbf{y}_h'\mathbf{y}_h - 2\hat{\boldsymbol{\delta}}_h'\mathbf{Z}_h'\mathbf{y}_h + \hat{\boldsymbol{\delta}}_h'\mathbf{Z}_h'\mathbf{Z}_h\hat{\boldsymbol{\delta}}_h\right), \end{aligned} \tag{10.8.19}$$

[35] Rothenberg and Leenders (1964) have proposed a linearized version of the system with the same asymptotic properties as FIML that is much simpler to compute. It might be noted that for computation of the FIML estimator it is necessary that n, the number of data points, exceed the sum of the number of exogenous variables k and the number of endogenous variables g (see Klein, 1971; Sargan, 1975).

so, differentiating with respect to $\hat{\boldsymbol{\delta}}_h$,

$$\frac{\partial \ln|\hat{\boldsymbol{\Sigma}}|}{\partial \hat{\boldsymbol{\delta}}'_h} = \frac{1}{\hat{\sigma}_{hh}} \frac{1}{n}\left(-2\mathbf{Z}'_h\mathbf{y}_h + 2\mathbf{Z}'_h\mathbf{Z}_h\hat{\boldsymbol{\delta}}_h\right) = \mathbf{0}, \tag{10.8.20}$$

leading to the estimators:

$$\hat{\boldsymbol{\delta}}_h = (\mathbf{Z}'_h\mathbf{Z}_h)^{-1}\mathbf{Z}'_h\mathbf{y}_h, \qquad h = 1, 2, \ldots, g. \tag{10.8.21}$$

These are, of course, the OLS estimators of each of the equations of the system (10.7.1), as presented in (10.3.4). Thus in the case of a recursive system, the OLS estimators are also the FIML estimators and hence are consistent and asymptotically efficient. They are also unbiased if the model does not include lagged endogenous variables. OLS "works" in this case because, assuming that $\boldsymbol{\Gamma}$ is triangular and $\boldsymbol{\Sigma}$ is diagonal, the variables in each equation are not correlated with the stochastic disturbance term in that equation.

10.9 MONTE CARLO STUDIES OF SMALL-SAMPLE PROPERTIES OF ESTIMATORS

While all of the estimators presented so far, other than OLS, have the property of consistency, and some are asymptotically efficient, these properties are asymptotic ones, referring to large samples. Applied econometric studies, however, typically utilize small samples, as will be seen in the next two chapters, and the large-sample properties of consistency and asymptotic efficiency provide no direct information about the small-sample properties of the various estimators. There is thus a real problem of choosing among these estimators.

One way of studying the small-sample properties of estimators is to utilize the Monte Carlo approach.[36] This approach virtually turns the problem on its head: instead of estimating unknown parameters using a specific technique, known parameters, which are chosen beforehand, are estimated using different techniques. The resulting comparisons between estimated and true parameters are used to make inferences about the different techniques. This approach thus simulates the process of estimating parameters using a controlled setting, in which the true parameter values are known. The Monte Carlo approach has been applied not only to the choice of alternative estimators but also to the influence of sample size, multicollinearity, and other factors on the various possible estimators. It provides a type of "laboratory" in which "controlled experiments" on econometric estimators can be studied. As with most laboratory results, however, there can arise the issue of their applicability to "real-world" phenomena. In particular, an important issue in the Monte Carlo approach to simultaneous-equations estimation is whether the results for certain specific models can, in fact, be applied to models in general. Such an application should be made only after extensive testing and systematic treatment of various possible changes in the formulation of the model.

The Monte Carlo approach starts by postulating a specific simultaneous-equations model and assigns numerical values to all parameters, including not only the coefficient ma-

[36]For surveys of various Monte Carlo studies, see Cragg (1967) and Smith (1973). Another approach is to determine the exact finite-sample distribution of the estimators, as discussed by Basmann (1961, 1963, 1974). Yet a third approach is to study approximations of the estimators for finite samples, as in Nagar (1959, 1962), Kadane (1971), Sargan and Mikhail (1971), Anderson and Sawa (1973), Phillips (1983), and Rothenberg (1984).

trices $\mathbf{\Gamma}$ and $\mathbf{B}$ but also the covariance matrix $\mathbf{\Sigma}$. Numerical values are also specified for the values of all exogenous variables $\mathbf{X}$. From the reduced-form equations, the implied values of reduced-form coefficients $\mathbf{\Pi} = -\mathbf{B}\mathbf{\Gamma}^{-1}$ and the assumed values of exogenous variables $\mathbf{X}$, together with a sample of reduced-form disturbances $\mathbf{u}$, generate a sample of data on the endogenous variables $\mathbf{Y}$ via:

$$\mathbf{Y} = \mathbf{X}\mathbf{\Pi} + \mathbf{U}. \tag{10.9.1}$$

Both $\mathbf{X}$ and $\mathbf{\Pi}$ are known; all that is needed to generate $\mathbf{Y}$ is $\mathbf{U}$. But $\mathbf{u}$ is a random variable that, under the usual normality assumptions, is distributed normally as:

$$\mathbf{u} \sim \mathrm{N}(\mathbf{0}, \mathbf{\Omega}), \tag{10.9.2}$$

where $\mathbf{\Omega}$ is known, since

$$\mathbf{\Omega} = \mathbf{\Gamma}^{-1\prime}\mathbf{\Sigma}\mathbf{\Gamma}^{-1} \tag{10.9.3}$$

and both $\mathbf{\Gamma}$ and $\mathbf{\Sigma}$ are known. Random numbers are used to generate a particular sample of values for the reduced-form disturbances $\mathbf{u}$ that are consistent with the known distribution in (10.9.2). The sample size is in the range typically used in an actual econometric study, e.g., 15–50 observations. From this sample for $\mathbf{u}$, equation (10.9.1) yields a sample of values for all endogenous variables $\mathbf{Y}$. Thus the result is a sample of data $\mathbf{Y}$ and $\mathbf{X}$, as in (10.1.5) and (10.1.6), and this sample of data is used to estimate values of structural-form parameters using various alternative estimators. The process of selecting $\mathbf{u}$ and generating a sample for $\mathbf{Y}$ is then replicated (e.g., 50 to 200) times, leading to a series of samples of data, each of a given size, and a series of alternative estimates, each referring to a particular estimation technique. The resulting estimates can then be compared to the known true values of the parameters.[37]

Various criteria are used in the comparison of estimates to the true values of parameters. Letting θ be the known true value of a parameter and $\hat{\theta}_j$ be the estimated value at the jth replication, the mean estimate of this parameter is:

$$\bar{\hat{\theta}} = \frac{1}{N}\sum_{j=1}^{N} \hat{\theta}_j, \tag{10.9.4}$$

where N is the total number of replications. The *bias* is then estimated numerically as:

$$B = \bar{\hat{\theta}} - \theta, \tag{10.9.5}$$

where $\bar{\hat{\theta}}$ is taken as a sample measure of $E(\hat{\theta})$. The bias is one important criterion used in evaluating the small-sample properties of estimators. Another criterion is the *variance*, defined as:

$$V = \frac{1}{N}\sum_{j=1}^{N}\left(\hat{\theta}_j - \bar{\hat{\theta}}\right)^2, \tag{10.9.6}$$

[37]The use of tables of random numbers and replication are the hallmarks of the Monte Carlo technique of simulation by random sampling. To give one example of many that illustrate the application of the Monte Carlo technique and one that is completely different from that presented in this section, consider the problem of approximating the area enclosed by a complicated two-dimensional figure. A Monte Carlo approach to this problem would be to enclose the object in a square and to choose units so that the sides of the square are both of length one, so the square has unit area. A table of uniformly distributed random numbers would then be used to select a random point in the square (as a pair of fractional numbers), and this process of random selection would be replicated many times. The limiting fraction of times the randomly chosen points fall in the figure rather than outside it would then approximate its area (in the units of the square). For a discussion of the Monte Carlo technique, see Hammersley and Handscomb (1964), Hendry (1984), and Naylor, Ed. (1969).

measuring the dispersion of the estimates about their mean value. A third criterion is the *mean squared error*, defined as:

$$M = \frac{1}{N}\sum_{j=1}^{N}\left(\hat{\theta}_j - \theta\right)^2, \tag{10.9.7}$$

measuring the dispersion of the estimates about the true value.[38] These criteria are related by:

$$M = V + B^2, \tag{10.9.8}$$

so that only two of these three criteria are independent. For example, a particular biased estimate may show a smaller mean squared error than a rival unbiased estimate if it more than compensates for the bias by a smaller variance. In addition to these criteria, Monte Carlo studies have used others, such as the median and mode (in addition to the mean) as measures of central tendency; the range, interquartile range, and mean sum of absolute deviations (in addition to the variance and mean squared error) as measures of dispersion; and various higher-order sample moments as measures of skewness and other characteristics of the shape of the distribution of the estimators.

The Monte Carlo studies of small-sample properties of estimators have treated OLS, 2SLS, *k*-class estimators, IV, 3SLS, FIML, and other estimators. The results of these studies are not definitive, since differences between estimators are often not large and the results often vary more significantly with the choice of model and the choice of values for the exogenous variables and elements of the covariance matrix than with the choice of a particular estimator. In terms of actual econometric studies, the data frequently exhibit such inaccuracy and/or the specification of the model is so uncertain that any reasonable rounding off of results would tend to eliminate the differences among the rival estimators. Indeed, in certain applications it is expected that the estimates vary considerably more both over the likely range of data points (e.g., adding or deleting certain data points) and over the likely range of specifications (e.g., adding or deleting an explanatory variable, endogenous or exogenous, in an equation of the model) than over the range of possible estimation techniques.[39] Nevertheless, some guidelines can be drawn from the Monte Carlo studies concerning the choice of estimator.

Starting with the naive and inconsistent technique of OLS, the Monte Carlo studies generally indicate that the OLS estimates have the largest bias among the estimators considered. On the other hand, OLS generally retains the Gauss–Markov property of minimum variance, albeit about a biased mean. The large bias, however, usually more than offsets the small variance, so OLS estimates usually exhibit the largest mean squared error of any technique. Despite these problems the technique still has the advantage of simplicity and low variance and might still be utilized, particularly in preliminary work. OLS is also appropriate if the model is recursive or approximately recursive. More generally, it may be conjectured that OLS is appropriate if the matrix of coefficients of endogenous variables $\mathbf{\Gamma}$ is sparse, containing many zeros. Such sparseness frequently arises as the size of the model increases, since the total number of endogenous variables usu-

[38] Sometimes the square root of the mean squared error, the root mean square error, RMS, is used instead of M. Thus

$$\text{RMS} = \sqrt{M} = \sqrt{V + B^2}.$$

[39] For a specific application plus a discussion of this point, see Denton and Kuiper (1965).

ally increases faster than the number of such variables appearing in a typical equation of the model.[40]

Of the various possible limited-information estimators (e.g., those of the *k* class), the 2SLS estimator generally performs best in terms of both bias and mean squared error. It is also usually more stable than the others; in particular, it is not greatly affected by specification errors. Furthermore, it is also generally easily and inexpensively computed.[41] On the other hand, the 2SLS estimator is significantly affected by multicollinearity. Nevertheless, the 2SLS estimator is generally the best available limited-information estimator.

The full-information techniques, specifically 3SLS and FIML, generally provide the most desirable estimators in terms of both bias and mean squared error when the model is correctly specified and the variables are correctly measured. FIML is, however, extremely sensitive to both specification error and measurement error. A slight misspecification or measurement error can change the results so as to make the FIML estimator less desirable than the limited-information estimators. Such a sensitivity to specification error and measurement error may be expected in this approach, where, because of its computation via a system of nonlinear equations, an error in one equation or in one variable will propagate throughout the whole system in the process of estimation. By contrast, the limited-information approach, which estimates only one equation at a time, confines a misspecification in one equation to that particular equation and confines an error in measurement in one variable to those equations containing that particular variable. In addition to this sensitivity to error, the full-information estimators, particularly FIML, are, as already noted, computationally more complicated than other estimators and hence more costly to use. Furthermore, both FIML and 3SLS require a much larger sample size than the limited-information estimators.

The results of the Monte Carlo studies thus suggest that the 2SLS estimator, while not ideal, is a good compromise choice among the group of various estimators. Thus 2SLS avoids the bias (and inconsistency) of OLS while, at the same time, it avoids the sensitivity to specification error and measurement error (and the cost) of 3SLS and FIML. Of course, other estimators may be more appropriate under certain circumstances. If, for example, the model is nearly recursive, then the 2SLS approach may not be necessary and OLS may be appropriate. OLS may also be appropriate if the first-stage R^2 values are either "too small" or "too large," as discussed in Section 10.5. At the other extreme, if correlations between stochastic disturbance terms in different equations are important and specification errors and sample size are not a problem, then it may be appropriate to improve upon the 2SLS estimates by using the 3SLS approach. Barring such special circumstances, 2SLS is both reasonable and appropriate as an estimation technique. It is, therefore, not at all surprising that 2SLS has emerged as the most widely used technique for estimating simultaneous-equations systems, such as those discussed in Chapters 12 and 13.

[40]For a discussion of the conjecture that OLS may be appropriate when $\mathbf{\Gamma}$ is sparse, see Smith (1973). Both Mosbaek and Wold (1970) and Smith (1973) found that OLS tends to improve relative to the limited-information estimators as the size of the model increases. See also Klein (1960) for a discussion of the use of OLS and Carter (1973) for the use of ordinary least squares in a a preliminary search for a suitable specification.

[41]Studies of the exact finite-sample distribution of estimators, while limited to very small simultaneous systems of two or three endogenous variables, suggest that for 2SLS the number of finite moments is, at most, equal to the number of independent overidentifying restrictions for the equation, higher-order moments generally failing to exist. For example, no finite moments exist if the equation is just identified. Comparisons of estimators involving such moments (e.g., a comparison of the bias for estimators with no finite first moments) are meaningless (see Smith, 1973; Basmann, 1974).

10.10 NONLINEAR SIMULTANEOUS EQUATIONS MODELS

Consider a system of g nonlinear simultaneous equations that accommodates nonlinearity in both parameters and variables:

$$f_h(\mathbf{y}_i, \mathbf{x}_i, \mathbf{a}_h) = \varepsilon_{ih}, \qquad h = 1, \ldots, g; \quad i = 1, \ldots, n, \tag{10.10.1}$$

where $\mathbf{y}_i$ is a $g \times 1$ vector of endogenous variables, $\mathbf{x}_i$ is a $k \times 1$ vector of exogenous variables, $\mathbf{a}_h$ is an $m_h \times 1$ vector of unknown parameters, and f_h is a known function. Not all the elements of $\mathbf{y}_i$ and $\mathbf{x}_i$ may actually appear in the arguments of each f_h. The g-dimensional vector $\boldsymbol{\varepsilon}_i = (\boldsymbol{\varepsilon}_{i1}, \ldots, \boldsymbol{\varepsilon}_{ig})'$ is assumed to satisfy (10.1.2)–(10.1.4). For simplicity, it is assumed that there is a unique relationship between $\boldsymbol{\varepsilon}_i$ and $\mathbf{y}_i$, as in (9.6.5).

The nonlinear least squares estimator of (10.10.1) is inconsistent for the same reason that the least squares estimator is inconsistent for a linear simultaneous equations system (10.1.1). Consistent estimators for (10.10.1), however, can be derived in a way analogous to the derivation of consistent estimators for (10.1.1). First consider the single-equation estimator. Without loss of generality, consider the first equation in the nonlinear system (10.10.1).

Let $\mathbf{f}_1$ be an $n \times 1$ vector, the ith element of which is $f_1(\mathbf{y}_i, \mathbf{x}_i, \mathbf{a}_1)$, which is abbreviated as $f_{i1}(\mathbf{a}_1)$, or simply f_{i1}. Let $\mathbf{W}$ be the $n \times m$ matrix of instruments with $m \geq m_1$. The nonlinear two-stage least squares (NL2S) estimator of $\mathbf{a}_1$ in the model (10.10.1) is the value that minimizes:

$$\mathbf{f}_1'\mathbf{W}(\mathbf{W}'\mathbf{W})^{-1}\mathbf{W}'\mathbf{f}_1. \tag*{*(10.10.2)}$$

Amemiya (1975, 1985) has shown that the NL2S estimator $\hat{\mathbf{a}}_1$ is consistent and asymptotically normally distributed with covariance matrix:

$$\sigma_1^2\left[\left(\frac{\partial \mathbf{f}_1'}{\partial \mathbf{a}_1}\mathbf{W}\right)(\mathbf{W}'\mathbf{W})^{-1}\left(\mathbf{W}'\frac{\partial \mathbf{f}_1}{\partial \mathbf{a}_1'}\right)\right]^{-1}. \tag{10.10.3}$$

Analogously, Jorgenson and Laffont (1974) define the class of nonlinear three-stage least squares (NL3S) estimator of the complete system as the values of $\hat{\mathbf{a}}$ that minimize:

$$\mathbf{f}'\left[\hat{\boldsymbol{\Sigma}}^{-1} \otimes \mathbf{W}(\mathbf{W}'\mathbf{W})^{-1}\mathbf{W}'\right]\mathbf{f}, \tag{10.10.4}$$

where $\mathbf{a}' = (\mathbf{a}_1', \ldots, \mathbf{a}_g')$, $\mathbf{f}' = (\mathbf{f}_1', \mathbf{f}_2', \ldots, \mathbf{f}_g')$ is a $1 \times gn$ vector; $\mathbf{W}$ is an $n \times m$ matrix of instrumental variables with rank $\mathbf{W} = m$, where $m \geq \max(m_1, \ldots, m_g)$; and $\otimes$ is the Kronecker product. $\hat{\boldsymbol{\Sigma}}$ is a consistent estimator of $\boldsymbol{\Sigma}$, such as the average of the scatter matrix of the residuals:

$$\hat{\boldsymbol{\Sigma}} = \frac{1}{n}\sum_{i=1}^{n}\begin{pmatrix}\hat{f}_{i1}\\ \vdots \\ \hat{f}_{ig}\end{pmatrix}\begin{pmatrix}\hat{f}_{i1} & \cdots & \hat{f}_{ig}\end{pmatrix}. \tag{10.10.5}$$

Amemiya (1977) defines the class of the NL3S estimators as the value of $\hat{\mathbf{a}}$ that minimizes:

$$\mathbf{f}'\hat{\boldsymbol{\Lambda}}^{-1}\mathbf{S}\left(\mathbf{S}'\hat{\boldsymbol{\Lambda}}^{-1}\mathbf{S}\right)^{-1}\mathbf{S}'\hat{\boldsymbol{\Lambda}}^{-1}\mathbf{f}, \tag{10.10.6}$$

where $\mathbf{S}$ is a matrix of constants with ng rows and with the rank of $\mathbf{S}$ at least $\Sigma_{i=1}^{g} m_i$, and $\hat{\boldsymbol{\Lambda}}$ is a consistent estimate of $\boldsymbol{\Lambda} = \boldsymbol{\Sigma} \otimes I$. Expression (10.10.6) reduces to the Jorgenson–Laffont formulation (10.10.4) if $\mathbf{S} = \text{diag}(\mathbf{W}, \mathbf{W}, \ldots, \mathbf{W})$ and it reduces to NL2S if $\boldsymbol{\Sigma}$ is diagonal and $\mathbf{S}$ is block diagonal, say $\mathbf{S} = \text{diag}\{\mathbf{W}, \ldots, \mathbf{W}\}$, an $ng \times nm$ matrix.

This NL3S estimator is consistent. Its asymptotic covariance matrix is equal to:

$$\left[G'\Lambda^{-1}\mathbf{S}(\mathbf{S}'\Lambda^{-1}\mathbf{S})^{-1}\mathbf{S}'\Lambda^{-1}G\right]^{-1}, \tag{10.10.7}$$

where $G = \text{diag}\{\mathbf{G}_1, \ldots, \mathbf{G}_g\}$ is an $ng \times (\Sigma_{i=1}^{g} m_i)$ block diagonal matrix with $\mathbf{G}_h = \partial\mathbf{f}_h/\partial\mathbf{a}_h'$, an $n \times m_h$ matrix.

The asymptotic efficiency of instrumental variables estimators depends on the form of the instruments. Amemiya (1977) has shown that the optimal instruments are the expected value of G:

$$\mathbf{S} = EG. \tag{10.10.8}$$

Substituting (10.10.8) into (10.10.7) implies that the lower bound of the covariance matrix of the instrumental variables estimators is:[42]

$$\left[EG'\Lambda^{-1}EG\right]^{-1}. \tag{10.10.9}$$

However, using the optimal instruments presents difficulties since they involve conditional expectations of nonlinear functions of endogenous variables. Their calculation often requires specification of the conditional distribution of the endogenous variables as well as integration. If the conditional expectation is a sufficiently smooth function of unknown parameters, Newey (1990) suggests using nonparametric regression to estimate the conditional expectations that appear in the optimal instruments. Two types of nonparametric regression estimators will be considered, *nearest neighbor* and *series approximation.*

The *nearest neighbor estimates* of conditional expectation $\tau(\mathbf{x}_j) = E[\delta_j = \delta(\mathbf{x}_j) \mid \mathbf{x} = \mathbf{x}_j]$ are calculated from observations δ_i and $\mathbf{x}_i$ $(i = 1, \ldots, n)$ using weighted averages of δ_i, where all observations but those with $\mathbf{x}_i$ among the l closest values to $\mathbf{x}_j$ receive zero weight. "Closeness" for values of $\mathbf{x}$ is defined here using a scaled version of the Euclidean norm $\|\cdot\|$, the distance between $\mathbf{x}_j$ and $\mathbf{x}$ being defined by $\{\Sigma_{k=1}^{K}(x_k - x_{kj})^2/\hat{\sigma}_k^2\}^{1/2}$, where $\hat{\sigma}_k$ is some estimate of the scale of the kth component of $\mathbf{x}$, x_k. Thus

$$\hat{\tau}(\mathbf{x}_j) = \sum_{i=1}^{n} \omega_j(\mathbf{x})\delta(\mathbf{x}_i), \tag{10.10.10}$$

where $\omega_j(\mathbf{x}) = \omega(s, l)$ are the weights for averaging the values of $\delta(\mathbf{x}_i)$ for $\mathbf{x}_i$ among the l closest values to $\mathbf{x}_j$ with:

$$\omega(s, l) \geq 0, \quad \omega(w, l) = 0, \quad s > l; \qquad \sum_{s=1}^{l} \omega(s, l) = 1. \tag{10.10.11}$$

Examples of weights include the uniform weights $\omega(s, l) = 1/l$ and the triangular weights $\omega(s, l) = 2(l - s + 1)/l(l + 1)$, $s \leq l$. The motivation for triangular weights is that $\hat{\tau}(\mathbf{x})$ will be a smoother function of $\mathbf{x}$ than that for uniform weights.[43]

[42]It is sufficient to show that $(1/n)\,EG'\Lambda^{-1}EG - (1/n)\,G'\Lambda^{-1}\mathbf{S}(\mathbf{S}'\Lambda^{-1}\mathbf{S})^{-1}\mathbf{S}'\Lambda^{-1}G$ approaches a positive-semi-definite matrix. Because Λ^{-1} is nonsingular, it is possible to find a nonsingular $\mathbf{C}$ such that $\Lambda^{-1} = \mathbf{CC}'$. Let $\tilde{\mathbf{G}} = \mathbf{C}^{-1}EG$, $\tilde{\mathbf{S}} = \mathbf{C}^{-1}\mathbf{S}$, and note that $\lim(1/n)\,G'\Lambda^{-1}\mathbf{S} = (1/n)\,(EG)'\Lambda^{-1}\mathbf{S}$, and so the difference approaches:

$$\frac{1}{n}\tilde{\mathbf{G}}'[\mathbf{I} - \tilde{\mathbf{S}}(\tilde{\mathbf{S}}'\tilde{\mathbf{S}})^{-1}\tilde{\mathbf{S}}']\tilde{\mathbf{G}},$$

which is positive semidefinite.

[43]For further details on nearest neighbor nonparametric regression, see McFadden (1985) or Stone (1977) (see also Section 5.13).

The *series estimates* of a conditional expectation make use of the first l terms of a sequence of functions $(p_1(\mathbf{x}), p_2(\mathbf{x}), \ldots)$,

$$\mathbf{p}^l(\mathbf{x}) = (p_1(\mathbf{x}), \ldots, p_l(\mathbf{x}))', \tag{10.10.12}$$

calculating the conditional expectation as the predicted value obtained from the regression of $\boldsymbol{\delta}(\mathbf{x})$ on $\mathbf{p}^l(\mathbf{x})$,

$$\hat{\tau}(\mathbf{x}_j) = \mathbf{p}^l(\mathbf{x}_j)'\left[\sum_{i=1}^{n}\mathbf{p}^l(\mathbf{x}_i)\mathbf{p}^l(\mathbf{x}_i)'\right]^+\left[\sum_{i=1}^{n}\mathbf{p}^l(\mathbf{x}_i)\boldsymbol{\delta}(\mathbf{x}_i)\right]. \tag{10.10.13}$$

The presence of the generalized inverse (see Section B.5 of Appendix B) allows for perfect multicollinearity among the columns of $[\mathbf{p}^l(\mathbf{x})']$. One generalized inverse corresponds to the deletion of redundant columns of $[\mathbf{p}^l(\mathbf{x})']$ and the regression of $\boldsymbol{\delta} = (\delta_1, \ldots, \delta_n)$ on the remaining columns as is done by some regression software. One example of $\hat{\mathbf{p}}^l(\mathbf{x})$ involves a power series. Letting $\boldsymbol{\lambda} = (\lambda_1, \ldots, \lambda_k)'$ denote a k-dimensional vector of nonnegative integers and $\mathbf{x}_i^{\boldsymbol{\lambda}} = x_{i1}^{\lambda_1}x_{i2}^{\lambda_2}, \ldots, x_{ik}^{\lambda_k}$ denote a product of powers of the components of $\mathbf{x}$, a basis sequence would take the form:

$$p_s(\mathbf{x}) \equiv \mathbf{x}^{\boldsymbol{\lambda}(s)}, \qquad s = 1, 2, \ldots, \tag{10.10.14}$$

with distinct $\boldsymbol{\lambda}(s)$. Trigonometric series are another example, as discussed in Gallant (1981).

It is conceivable that small sample performance of nearest point or series estimates can be improved by estimating part of this conditional expectation by a preliminary regression, a procedure referred to as "trend removal" by Stone (1977). The idea is that it may be possible to reduce bias for a given number of nearest neighbors or sequence of functions by removing an important part of the conditional expectation, which would then allow one to average over a large number of neighbors or sequences of functions to reduce variance. To describe trend removal, let $t(\mathbf{x}; \boldsymbol{\alpha})$ be a known function of $\mathbf{x}$ and parameters $\boldsymbol{\alpha}$, $\hat{\boldsymbol{\alpha}}$ be the estimates from nonlinear least squares regression of $\boldsymbol{\delta}(\mathbf{x}_i)$ on $t(\mathbf{x}_i; \boldsymbol{\alpha})$ and $\boldsymbol{\delta}^*(\mathbf{x}_i) = t(\mathbf{x}_i; \hat{\boldsymbol{\alpha}})$ the corresponding predicted values. The estimate of $\tau(\mathbf{x}_j)$ can be formed as the sum of $t(\mathbf{x}_j; \hat{\boldsymbol{\alpha}})$ and the weighted average of the residual $\boldsymbol{\delta}(\mathbf{x}_i) - t(\mathbf{x}_i; \hat{\boldsymbol{\alpha}})$. Thus, for nearest point estimates, it yields:

$$\hat{\tau}(\mathbf{x}_j) = t(\mathbf{x}_j; \hat{\boldsymbol{\alpha}}) + \sum_{i=1}^{n}\omega_i(\mathbf{x})[\boldsymbol{\delta}(\mathbf{x}_i) - \boldsymbol{\delta}^*(\mathbf{x}_i)], \tag{10.10.15}$$

while for series estimates, it becomes:

$$\hat{\tau}(\mathbf{x}_i) = t(\mathbf{x}_i; \hat{\boldsymbol{\alpha}}) + \mathbf{p}^l(\mathbf{x}_i)'\left[\sum_{i=1}^{n}\mathbf{p}^l(\mathbf{x}_i)\mathbf{p}^l(\mathbf{x}_i)'\right]^+\left[\sum_{i=1}^{n}\mathbf{p}^l(\mathbf{x}_i)(\boldsymbol{\delta}(\mathbf{x}_i) - \boldsymbol{\delta}^*(\mathbf{x}_i))\right]. \tag{10.10.16}$$

Consistency of the resulting estimator of $\tau(\mathbf{x})$ follows by letting l grow with the sample size at an appropriate rate. Provided the estimates converge sufficiently fast, by analogy with the parametric case, estimation of the optimal instruments would not affect the limiting distribution of the instrumental variable estimator. Consequently, the instrumental variable estimator using these instruments will be asymptotically efficient.

In the linear case, the 2SLS and 3SLS estimators are asymptotically equivalent to the limited and full information maximum likelihood estimates, respectively. In the nonlinear case, Amemiya (1977) shows that if the stochastic disturbance of terms $\boldsymbol{\varepsilon}_i$ are normally distributed, the nonlinear limited and full information maximum likelihood estimators are consistent and, in general, have smaller asymptotic covariance matrices than the best NL2S and

NL3S estimators, respectively. If the $\boldsymbol{\varepsilon}_i$ are not normally distributed, in contrast to the linear case, the nonlinear limited and full information maximum likelihood estimators (based on the assumption of normality) for the nonlinear simultaneous equations model are, in general, not consistent, whereas NL2S and NL3S remain consistent.

To test a hypothesis of the form $\mathbf{h}(\mathbf{a}_1) = \mathbf{0}$ for model (10.10.1), where $\mathbf{h}$ is a q vector of nonlinear functions, it is possible to use a generalized Wald test statistic:

$$\frac{1}{s_1^2}\mathbf{h}(\hat{\mathbf{a}}_1)'\left[\hat{\mathbf{H}}\left(\hat{\mathbf{G}}_1'\mathbf{W}(\mathbf{W}'\mathbf{W})^{-1}\mathbf{W}'\hat{\mathbf{G}}_1\right)^{-1}\hat{\mathbf{H}}'\right]^{-1}\mathbf{h}(\hat{\mathbf{a}}_1). \qquad *(10.10.17)$$

Under the null hypothesis, (10.10.17) is asymptotically distributed as chi-square with q degrees of freedom, where $\hat{\mathbf{H}} = [\partial\mathbf{h}/\partial\mathbf{a}_1']_{\mathbf{a}_1=\hat{\mathbf{a}}_1}$, $\mathbf{G}_1 = [\partial\mathbf{f}_1/\partial\mathbf{a}_1']_{\mathbf{a}_1=\hat{\mathbf{a}}_1}$, and $s_1^2 = (1/n)\sum_{i=1}^n \hat{f}_{i1}^2$.

To generate a predicted value of $\mathbf{y}$, assume that there exists an inverse relation, as in (10.9.1), where:

$$\mathbf{y}_i = \mathbf{g}(\mathbf{x}_i, \boldsymbol{\varepsilon}_i; \mathbf{a}). \qquad (10.10.18)$$

The predictor $\hat{\mathbf{y}}_v$ based on the estimator $\hat{\mathbf{a}}$ and the assumption that $E\boldsymbol{\varepsilon}_v = \mathbf{0}$, given as:

$$\hat{\mathbf{y}}_v = \mathbf{g}(\mathbf{x}_v, \mathbf{0}; \hat{\mathbf{a}}), \qquad (10.10.19)$$

in general, is biased because $E\mathbf{g}(\mathbf{x}_v, \boldsymbol{\varepsilon}_v; \mathbf{a}) \neq g(\mathbf{x}_v, E\boldsymbol{\varepsilon}_v; \mathbf{a})$. One way to generate an unbiased predictor is to use a Monte Carlo predictor:

$$\frac{1}{T}\sum_{j=1}^{T} \mathbf{g}(\mathbf{x}_v, \mathbf{v}_j; \hat{\mathbf{a}}), \qquad (10.10.20)$$

where $\{\mathbf{v}_j\}$ are i.i.d. with the same distribution as $\boldsymbol{\varepsilon}_v$. Another way is to use a residual-based predictor:

$$\frac{1}{n}\sum_{i=1}^{n} \mathbf{g}(\mathbf{x}_v, \hat{\boldsymbol{\varepsilon}}_i; \hat{\mathbf{a}}), \qquad *(10.10.21)$$

where $\hat{\boldsymbol{\varepsilon}}_i = \mathbf{f}(\mathbf{y}_i, \mathbf{x}_i; \hat{\mathbf{a}})$. According to Brown and Mariano (1984) and Mariano and Brown (1983), clearly (10.10.19) is the worst predictor. As for the choice between the Monte Carlo predictor (10.10.20) and the residual-based predictor (10.10.21), the former is favored if T is large and the assumed distribution of $\boldsymbol{\varepsilon}_v$ is true, although the latter is simpler to compute and more robust in the sense that the distribution of $\boldsymbol{\varepsilon}_v$ need not be specified.

PROBLEMS

10-A Show that if the simultaneous-equations system includes a definitional equation, then the covariance matrix $\boldsymbol{\Sigma}$ in (10.1.13) is positive semidefinite rather than positive definite. Will excluding all definitional equations ensure that $\boldsymbol{\Sigma}$ is positive definite?

10-B Express conditions (10.1.2) to (10.1.4) on the stochastic disturbance term for the prototype macro model in (10.1.23).

10-C Consider (10.3.21) for the variant model (10.1.26) in which Y_{i-1} does not appear, so $\beta_4 = 0$. By using the reduced-form equation for Y_i show that the OLS estimator is consistent if any of the following conditions hold:

$$\gamma_1'\gamma_3' = 1,$$
$$\text{Var}(G) = \infty,$$
$$\text{Var}(\varepsilon^{C'}) = 0 \quad \text{and} \quad \text{Cov}(\varepsilon^{Y'}, \varepsilon^{C'}) = 0.$$

10-D Show that the OLS estimators of each equation of a recursive model, in which $\mathbf{\Gamma}$ is triangular and $\mathbf{\Sigma}$ is diagonal, are consistent.

10-E Using (10.4.16) and (10.4.17) as in (10.4.29), show that the OLS estimator of the marginal propensity to consume for the variant model (10.4.28) is both biased and inconsistent.

10-F Consider the prototype micro model of Section 2.5, which takes the form:

$$(q \;\; p)\begin{pmatrix} -1 & -1 \\ \gamma_1 & \gamma_2 \end{pmatrix} + (I \;\; r \;\; 1)\begin{pmatrix} \beta_1 & 0 \\ 0 & \beta_2 \\ \delta_1 & \delta_2 \end{pmatrix} = (\varepsilon^D \;\; \varepsilon^S),$$

where the stochastic disturbance terms are distributed normally:

$$(\varepsilon^D \;\; \varepsilon^S) \sim N\left[(0 \;\; 0), \begin{pmatrix} \sigma_D^2 & \sigma_{SD} \\ \sigma_{SD} & \sigma_S^2 \end{pmatrix}\right].$$

1. Obtain the OLS estimators of both equations and show that they are inconsistent by demonstrating that the explanatory endogenous variable is correlated with the stochastic disturbances in both equations. Find explicit expressions for $E(p_i \varepsilon_i^D)$ and $E(p_i \varepsilon_i^S)$.
2. Obtain the ILS estimators of both equations and determine their distribution.
3. Show that if $\beta_2 = 0$, consistent estimation of the demand equation is impossible.

10-G For the 2SLS approach to estimation:

1. Show that the elements of $\mathbf{v}_1$, as defined in (10.5.16), have zero mean, exhibit constant variance, and are uncorrelated.
2. Show that the 2SLS estimators do not exist if $n < k$.
3. Show that the 2SLS estimators satisfy the orthogonality conditions:

$$\mathbf{X}_1'\hat{\boldsymbol{\varepsilon}}_1 = \mathbf{X}_1'(\mathbf{y}_1 - \mathbf{Y}_1\hat{\boldsymbol{\gamma}}_1 - \mathbf{X}_1\hat{\boldsymbol{\beta}}_1) = \mathbf{0},$$

where $\hat{\boldsymbol{\varepsilon}}_1$ is the vector of 2SLS residuals. How many conditions does this represent?

4. Show that the sum of the 2SLS residuals vanishes.

10-H Prove that the R^2_{2SLS} for the second stage of 2SLS, as defined in footnote 14, cannot exceed unity but can be negative. Under what conditions will it be negative?

10-I Prove that the ILS estimator expressed as an instrumental-variable estimator in (10.6.9) is the same as the ILS estimator in (10.4.12).

10-J Using the interpretation of the k-class estimator as an instrumental-variable estimator in (10.6.25) and the conditions for an instrumental-variable estimator to be consistent in (10.6.28) and (10.6.29), prove that the k-class estimator is consistent if

$$\text{plim}(k - 1) = 0,$$

as in (10.5.53). Also prove that the k-class estimator has the same asymptotic covariance matrix as 2SLS, given in (10.6.35), if

$$\text{plim}\,\sqrt{n}(k - 1) = 0,$$

as in footnote 20.

10-K Prove that the estimator $\hat{\sigma}_1^2$ in (10.6.34) is a consistent estimator of σ_1^2 if $\hat{\boldsymbol{\delta}}_1$ is the 2SLS estimator. Also prove that $\hat{\hat{\sigma}}_1^2$ obtained as in (10.6.34) but where $\mathbf{Z}_1$ is replaced by $\hat{\mathbf{Z}}_1$ (and $\hat{\boldsymbol{\delta}}_1$ is the 2SLS estimator) is not a consistent estimator of σ_1^2.

10-L Prove that the 3SLS estimator in (10.7.21) and the 2SLS estimator in (10.7.16) are identical if either:

1. All equations are just identified, or

2. The error term of any one equation is contemporaneously uncorrelated with the error term of any other equation (i.e., $\mathbf{\Sigma}$ is diagonal).

10-M Prove that the 3SLS estimator can be written:

$$\hat{\boldsymbol{\delta}}^*_{3SLS} = \left[\hat{\mathbf{Z}}^{*\prime}(\mathbf{\Sigma}^{-1} \otimes \mathbf{I})\hat{\mathbf{Z}}^*\right]^{-1}\hat{\mathbf{Z}}^{*\prime}(\mathbf{\Sigma}^{-1} \otimes \mathbf{I})\mathbf{y}^*$$

and from this expression show that the 3SLS estimator is defined only if each equation of the system is either overidentified or just identified.

10-N Prove that the 3SLS estimator is asymptotically more efficient than 2SLS, (10.7.27), using the asymptotic covariance matrices in (10.7.41) and (10.7.42).

10-O Prove that if $\mathbf{\Sigma}$ is the symmetric matrix $(\sigma_{hh'})$ and its inverse is $(\sigma^{hh'})$, then

$$\frac{\partial \ln|\mathbf{\Sigma}^{-1}|}{\partial \sigma^{hh'}} = \sigma_{hh'},$$

as was used in (10.8.12) and (10.8.17).

10-P Prove that ILS estimators are equivalent to FIML estimators if the model is just identified.

10-Q Consider the following simultaneous-equations system:

$$(y_1 \;\; y_2)\begin{pmatrix} -1 & \gamma_2 \\ \gamma_1 & -1 \end{pmatrix} + (x_1 \;\; x_2 \;\; x_3)\begin{pmatrix} \beta_1 & 0 \\ 0 & \beta_2 \\ 0 & \beta_3 \end{pmatrix} = (\varepsilon_1 \;\; \varepsilon_2),$$

where there are no intercepts, since all variables are measured as deviations from mean values. In this system the first equation is overidentified and the second equation is just identified. Given data y_{i1}, y_{i2}, x_{i1}, x_{i2}, x_{i3} for $i = 1, 2, \ldots, n$, construct, using summation notation:

1. The OLS estimator of the first equation.
2. The ILS estimator of the second equation.
3. The 2SLS and k-class estimators of the first equation.
4. The IV estimator of the first equation.
5. The 3SLS estimator of both equations.

10-R An equation widely used in applied econometrics is the constant elasticity equation

$$y = Ax_1^{\alpha_1}x_2^{\alpha_2}\cdots x_k^{\alpha_k}e^u,$$

where y is the dependent variable, the x's are explanatory variables, A and the α's are parameters, and u is a stochastic disturbance term.

1. Why is the equation called a "constant elasticity" equation? Interpret the elasticities in the case of demand equations and in the case of a production function.
2. Assume that $k = 2$ and the x's are exogenous. Given a sample of n data points on y, x_1, and x_2, show specifically how you would estimate the parameters of the model.
3. Again assume that $k = 2$ and x_1 is exogenous, but now suppose that x_2 is endogenous. How would you now estimate the parameters of the model, given a sample of n data points? [Make whatever assumptions you feel appropriate as to the specification of additional equation(s) of the model.]

10-S In a model of the money market, the demand for money depends on the interest rate and population, while the interest rate depends on the quantity of money, the discount rate, and excess reserves. Assume that the money market is in equilibrium, the demand for money equaling the quantity of money, and that the quantity of money (M) and the interest rate (r) are endogenous, while population (N), the discount rate (d), and excess reserves (R) are exogenous. Each equation of the model (other than the equilibrium condition) is linear and stochastic but contains no intercept, variables being measured in terms of deviations from their mean values.

1. Express the structural equations and reduced-form equations as matrix equations, and determine the identification of each of the structural equations, analyzing both order and rank conditions.
2. For each relevant equation obtain the following estimators:

$$\begin{aligned}\text{OLS} &= \text{ordinary least squares,}\\ \text{ILS} &= \text{indirect least squares,}\\ \text{2LS} &= \text{two-stage least squares}\end{aligned}$$

in terms of data on each of the variables of the model: M_t, r_t, N_t, d_t, R_t for $t = 1, 2, \ldots, T$. Which estimators are identical? Which one(s) would you use?

10-T A subject of some debate in the economics literature is whether growth in the money supply is a cause or an effect of inflation. Outline a simultaneous-equations model econometric project that could shed some light on this issue and discuss how such a model might be estimated.

BIBLIOGRAPHY

AMEMIYA, T. (1966a). "Specification Analysis in the Estimation of Parameters of a Simultaneous Equation Model with Autoregressive Residuals." *Econometrica*, 34: 283–306.

AMEMIYA, T. (1966b). "On the Use of Principal Components of Independent Variables in Two-Stage Least Squares Estimation." *International Economic Review*, 7: 283–303.

AMEMIYA, T. (1974). "The Nonlinear Two-Stage Least Squares Estimator." *Journal of Econometrics*, 2: 105–110.

AMEMIYA, T. (1975). "The Nonlinear Limited Information Maximum Likelihood Estimator and the Modified Nonlinear Two-Stage Least Squares Estimator." *Journal of Econometrics*, 3: 375–386.

AMEMIYA, T. (1977). "The Maximum Likelihood and Nonlinear Three-Stage Least Squares Estimator in the General Nonlinear Simultaneous Equation Model." *Econometrica*, 45: 955–968.

AMEMIYA, T. (1985). *Advanced Econometrics*. Cambridge, Mass.: Harvard University Press.

ANDERSON, T. W., and T. SAWA (1973). "Distribution of Estimates of Coefficients of a Single Equation in a Simultaneous System and Their Asymptotic Expansions." *Econometrica*, 41: 683–714.

APOSTOL, T. M. (1974). *Mathematical Analysis*, 2nd ed. Reading, Mass.: Addison-Wesley Publishing Company, Inc.

BASMANN, R. L. (1957). "A Generalized Classical Method of Linear Estimation of Coefficients in a Structural Equation." *Econometrica*, 25: 77–83.

BASMANN, R. L. (1959). "The Computation of Generalized Classical Estimates of Coefficients in a Structural Equation." *Econometrica*, 27: 72–81.

BASMANN, R. L. (1960). "On the Asymptotic Distribution of Generalized Linear Estimators." *Econometrica*, 28: 97–108.

BASMANN, R. L. (1961). "A Note on the Exact Finite Sample Frequency Functions of Generalized Classical Linear Estimators in Two Leading Overidentified Cases." *Journal of the American Statistical Association*, 56: 619–636.

BASMANN, R. L. (1963). "A Note on the Exact Finite Sample Frequency Functions of Generalized Classical Linear Estimators in a Leading Three Equation Case." *Journal of the American Statistical Association*, 58: 161–171.

BASMANN, R. L. (1974). "Exact Finite Sample Distributions for Some Econometric Estimators and Test Statistics: A Survey and Appraisal," in M. D. Intriligator and D. A. Kendrick, Eds., *Frontiers of Quantitative Economics*, Vol. 2. Amsterdam: North-Holland Publishing Company.

BROWN, B. W., and R. S. MARIANO (1984). "Residual-Based Procedures for Prediction and Estimation in a Nonlinear Simultaneous System." *Econometrica*, 52: 321–344.

BRUNDY, J. M., and D. W. JORGENSON (1971). "Efficient Estimation of Simultaneous Equations by Instrumental Variables." *Review of Economics and Statistics*, 53: 207–224.

BRUNDY, J. M., and D. W. JORGENSON (1973). "Consistent and Efficient Estimation of Systems of Simultaneous Equations," in P. Zarembka, Ed., *Frontiers in Econometrics*. New York: Academic Press, Inc.

BRUNDY, J. M., and D. W. JORGENSON (1974). "The Relative Efficiency of Instrumental Variables Estimators of Systems of Simultaneous Equations." *Annals of Economic and Social Measurement*, 3: 679–700.

CARTER, R. A. L. (1973). "Least Squares as an Exploratory Estimator." *Canadian Journal of Economics*, 6: 108–114.

CHOW, G. (1973). "On the Computation of Full Information Maximum Likelihood Estimates for Nonlinear Equation Systems." *Review of Economics and Statistics*, 55: 104–109.

CHRIST, C. F. (1966). *Econometric Models and Methods*. New York: John Wiley & Sons, Inc.

CRAGG, J. (1967). "On the Relative Small-Sample Properties of Several Structural-Equation Estimators." *Econometrica*, 35: 89–110.

DENTON, F. T., and J. KUIPER (1965). "The Effect of Measurement Errors on Parameter Estimates and Forecasts: A Case Study Based on Canadian Preliminary National Accounts." *Review of Economics and Statistics*, 47: 198–206.

DHRYMES, P. J. (1970). *Econometrics: Statistical Foundations and Applications*. New York: Harper & Row, Publishers, Inc.

DHRYMES, P. J., R. BERNER, and D. CUMMINS (1974). "A Comparison of Some Limited Information Estimators for Dynamic Simultaneous Equations Models with Autocorrelated Errors." *Econometrica*, 42: 311–332.

DHRYMES, P. J., and H. ERLAT (1974). "Asymptotic Properties of Full Information Estimation in Dynamic Autoregressive Simultaneous Equation Models." *Journal of Econometrics*, 2: 247–260.

DRÈZE, J. H., and J.-F. RICHARD (1983). "Bayesian Analysis of Simultaneous Equations Systems," in Z. Griliches and M. D. Intriligator, Eds., *Handbook of Econometrics*, Vol. 1. Amsterdam: North-Holland Publishing Company.

DUTTA, M., and E. LYTTKENS (1974). "Iterative Instrumental Variables Method and Estimation of a Large Simultaneous System." *Journal of the American Statistical Association*, 69: 977–986.

EISENPRESS, H., and J. GREENSTADT (1966). "The Estimation of Nonlinear Econometric Systems." *Econometrica*, 34: 851–861.

FAIR, R. C. (1970). "The Estimation of Simultaneous Equation Models with Lagged Endogenous Variables and First Order Serially Correlated Errors." *Econometrica*, 38: 507–516.

FAIR, R. C. (1972). "Efficient Estimation of Simultaneous Equations with Autoregressive Errors by Instrumental Variables." *Review of Economics and Statistics*, 54: 444–449.

FISHER, F. M. (1965a). "Dynamic Structure and Estimation in Economy-Wide Econometric Models," in J. S. Duesenberry, G. Fromm, L. R. Klein, and E. Kuh, Eds., *The Brookings Quarterly Econometric Model of the United States*. Chicago: Rand McNally & Company; Amsterdam: North-Holland Publishing Company.

FISHER, F. M. (1965b). "The Choice of Instrumental Variables in the Estimation of Economy-Wide Econometric Models." *International Economic Review*, 6: 245–274.

FISK, P. R. (1967). *Stochastically Dependent Equations*. London: Charles Griffen & Co. Ltd.

GALLANT, R. A. (1981). "On the Bias in Flexible Functional Forms and an Essentially Unbiased Form: The Fourier Functional Form." *Journal of Econometrics*, 15: 211–245.

HAAVELMO, T. (1943). "The Statistical Implications of a System of Simultaneous Equations." *Econometrica*, 11: 1–12.

HAAVELMO, T. (1947). "Methods of Measuring the Marginal Propensity to Consume." *Journal of the American Statistical Association*, 42: 105–122.

HAMMERSLEY, J. M., and D. C. HANDSCOMB (1964). *Monte Carlo Methods*. New York: John Wiley & Sons, Inc.

HARKEMA, R. (1971). *Simultaneous Equations: A Bayesian Approach*. Rotterdam: Universitaire Pers.

HATANAKA, M. (1976). "Several Efficient Two-Step Estimators for the Dynamic Simultaneous Equation Model with Autoregressive Disturbances." *Journal of Econometrics*, 4: 189–204.

HAUSMAN, J. A. (1975). "An Instrumental Variable Approach to Full Information Estimators for Linear and Certain Nonlinear Econometric Models." *Econometrica*, 43: 727–738.

HAUSMAN, J. A. (1983). "Specification and Estimation of Simultaneous Equation Models," in Z. Griliches and M. D. Intriligator, Eds., *Handbook of Econometrics*, Vol. 1. Amsterdam: North-Holland Publishing Company.

HENDRY, D. F. (1984). "Monte Carlo Experimentation in Econometrics," in Z. Griliches and M. D. Intriligator, Eds., *Handbook of Econometrics*, Vol. 2. Amsterdam: North-Holland Publishing Company.

HOFFMAN, K. (1975). *Analysis in Euclidean Space*. Englewood Cliffs, N.J.: Prentice Hall.

JORGENSON, D. W., and J. J. LAFFONT (1974). "Efficient Estimation of Nonlinear Simultaneous Equations with Additive Disturbances." *Annals of Economic and Social Measurement*, 3: 615–640.

KADANE, J. B. (1971). "Comparison of *k*-Class Estimators When the Disturbances Are Small." *Econometrica*, 39: 723–737.

KELEJIAN, H. H. (1971). "Two Stage Least Squares and Econometric System Linear in Parameters but Nonlinear in the Endogenous Variables." *Journal of the American Statistical Association*, 66: 373–374.

KLEIN, L. R. (1960). "Single Equation vs. Equation System Methods of Estimation in Econometrics." *Econometrica*, 28: 866–871.

KLEIN, L. R. (1971). "Forecasting and Policy Evaluation Using Large-Scale Econometric Models: The State of the Art," in M. D. Intriligator, Ed., *Frontiers of Quantitative Economics*. Amsterdam: North-Holland Publishing Company.

KLEIN, L. R. (1973). "The Treatment of Undersized Samples in Econometrics," in A. A. Powell and R. A. Williams, Eds., *Econometric Studies of Macro and Monetary Relations*. Amsterdam: North-Holland Publishing Company.

KLOEK, T., and L. B. M. MENNES (1960). "Simultaneous Equation Estimation Based on Principal Components of Predetermined Variables." *Econometrica*, 28: 45–61.

LYTTKENS, E. (1970). "Symmetric and Asymmetric Estimation Methods," in Mosbaek and Wold (1970).

MADANSKY, A. (1964). "On the Efficiency of Three-Stage Least Squares Estimation." *Econometrica*, 32: 51–56.

MADANSKY, A. (1976). *Foundation of Econometrics*. Amsterdam: North-Holland Publishing Company.

MALINVAUD, E. (1970). *Statistical Methods of Econometrics*, 2nd rev. ed. Amsterdam: North-Holland Publishing Company.

MARIANO, R. S., and B. W. BROWN (1983). "Prediction-Based Tests for Misspecification in Nonlinear Simultaneous Systems," in S. Karlin, T. Amemiya, and L. A. Goodman, Eds., *Studies in Econometrics, Time Series and Multivariate Statistics*. New York: Academic Press, Inc., pp. 131–151.

MCFADDEN, D. (1985). "Specification of Econometric Models." Presidential address, 1985 meeting of the Econometric Society.

MITCHELL B. (1971). "Estimation of Large Econometric Models by Principal Component and Instrumental Variable Methods." *Review of Economics and Statistics*, 53: 140–146.

MITCHELL, B., and F. M. FISHER (1970). "The Choice of Instrumental Variables in the Estimation of Economy-Wide Econometric Models: Some Further Thoughts." *International Economic Review*, 11: 226–234.

MORALES, J. A. (1971). *Bayesian Full Information Structural Analysis*. Berlin: Springer-Verlag.

MOSBAEK, E. J., and H. O. WOLD, Eds. (1970). *Interdependent Systems: Structure and Estimation*. Amsterdam: North-Holland Publishing Company.

NAGAR, A. L. (1959). "The Bias and Moment Matrix of the General *k*-Class Estimators of the Parameters in Simultaneous Equations." *Econometrica*, 27: 575–595.

NAGAR, A. L. (1962). "Double *k*-Class Estimators of Parameters in Simultaneous Equations and Their Small Sample Properties." *International Economic Review*, 3: 168–188.

NAYLOR, T. H., Ed. (1969). *The Design of Computer Simulation Experiments*. Durham, N.C.: Duke University Press.

NEWEY, W. K. (1990). "Efficient Instrumental Variables Estimation of Nonlinear Models." *Econometrica*, 58: 809–837.

PHILLIPS, P. C. B. (1983). "Exact Small Sample Theory in the Simultaneous Equations Models," in Z. Griliches and M. D. Intriligator, Eds., *Handbook of Econometrics*, Vol. 1. Amsterdam: North-Holland Publishing Company.

RAO, C. R. (1965). *Linear Statistical Inference and Its Applications*. New York: John Wiley & Sons, Inc.

ROTHENBERG, T. J. (1974). *Efficient Estimation with A Priori Information*. New Haven, Conn.: Yale University Press.

ROTHENBERG, T. J. (1984). "Approximating the Distributions of Econometric Estimators and Test Statistics," in Z. Griliches and M. D. Intriligator, Eds., *Handbook of Econometrics*, Vol. 2. Amsterdam: North-Holland Publishing Company.

ROTHENBERG, T. J., and C. T. LEENDERS (1964). "Efficient Estimation of Simultaneous Equation Systems." *Econometrica*, 32: 57–76.

RUDIN, W. (1964). *Principles of Mathematical Analysis*. New York: McGraw-Hill Book Company.

SARGAN, J. D. (1958). "The Estimation of Economic Relationships Using Instrumental Variables." *Econometrica*, 26: 393–415.

SARGAN, J. D. (1961). "The Maximum Likelihood Estimation of Economic Relationships with Autoregressive Residuals." *Econometrica*, 29: 414–426.

SARGAN, J. D. (1964). "Three-Stage Least Squares and Full Information Maximum Likelihood Estimates." *Econometrica*, 32: 77–81.

SARGAN, J. D. (1975). "Asymptotic Theory and Large Models." *International Economic Review*, 16: 75–91.

SARGAN, J. D., and W. M. MIKHAIL (1971). "A General Approximation to the Distribution of Instrumental Variable Estimates." *Econometrica*, 39: 131–169.

SCHMIDT, P. (1976). *Econometrics*. New York: Marcel Dekker, Inc.

SMITH, V. K. (1973). *Monte Carlo Methods*. Lexington, Mass.: Lexington Books.

STONE, C. J. (1977). "Consistent Nonparametric Regression" (with discussion). *Annals of Statistics*, 5: 595–645.

THEIL, H. (1961). *Economic Forecasts and Policy*, 2nd ed. Amsterdam: North-Holland Publishing Company.

THEIL, H. (1971). *Principles of Econometrics*. New York: John Wiley & Sons, Inc.

ZELLNER, A. (1971). *An Introduction to Bayesian Inference in Econometrics*. New York: John Wiley & Sons, Inc.

ZELLNER, A., and H. THEIL (1962). "Three Stage Least Squares: Simultaneous Estimation of Simultaneous Equations." *Econometrica*, 30: 54–78.

11

DYNAMIC SYSTEMS

11.1 INTRODUCTION

Chapters 9 and 10 have covered the identification and estimation of a static system, while this chapter treats some of the issues involved in modeling a dynamic system. It begins in Section 11.2 with a discussion of identification and estimation of a dynamic simultaneous-equations model. We then discuss time-series procedures for modeling a vector of variables. In Section 11.3 we discuss the Tiao and Box approach of modeling unrestricted multiple time-series models. Restricted time-series approaches are then discussed in Sections 11.4 and 11.5, with Section 11.4 on Granger causality and Section 11.5 on cointegration. The relationships between dynamic simultaneous equations models and time-series models are discussed in Section 11.6.

11.2 DYNAMIC SIMULTANEOUS-EQUATIONS MODELS

Consider models of the form:

$$\begin{aligned}\boldsymbol{\Gamma}_0\mathbf{y}_t + \boldsymbol{\Gamma}_1\mathbf{y}_{t-1} + \cdots + \boldsymbol{\Gamma}_p\mathbf{y}_{t-p} + \mathbf{B}_0\mathbf{x}_t + \mathbf{B}_1\mathbf{x}_{t-1} & \\ + \cdots + \mathbf{B}_q\mathbf{x}_{t-q} = \mathbf{u}_t, \qquad t = 1, 2, \ldots, T, & \qquad *(11.2.1)\end{aligned}$$

where $\boldsymbol{\Gamma}_j$ and $\mathbf{B}_j$ are $g \times g$ and $g \times k$ matrices of constants; $\mathbf{y}_t$, $\mathbf{x}_t$, and $\mathbf{u}_t$ are $g \times 1$, $k \times 1$, and $g \times 1$ vectors of observed jointly dependent variables, exogenous variables, and unobserved disturbance terms, respectively. Using the scalar lag operator L to mean the lag operation on each element of $\mathbf{y}_t$ and $\mathbf{x}_t$, (11.2.1) can be written compactly as

$$\boldsymbol{\Gamma}(L)\mathbf{y}_t + \mathbf{B}(L)\mathbf{x}_t = \mathbf{u}_t. \qquad *(11.2.2)$$

The $\boldsymbol{\Gamma}(L)$ and $\mathbf{B}(L)$ are $g \times g$ and $g \times k$ matrix polynomials in order p and q, respectively, in the lag operator L:

$$\boldsymbol{\Gamma}(L) = \boldsymbol{\Gamma}_0 + \boldsymbol{\Gamma}_1 L + \cdots + \boldsymbol{\Gamma}_p L^p, \tag{11.2.3}$$

$$\mathbf{B}(L) = \mathbf{B}_0 + \mathbf{B}_1 L + \cdots + \mathbf{B}_q L^q, \tag{11.2.4}$$

where the $\boldsymbol{\Gamma}_r$'s and $\mathbf{B}_r$'s are $g \times g$ and $g \times k$ matrices, respectively. That is, each element of the matrix polynomial is a polynomial of the corresponding element such that

$$[\boldsymbol{\Gamma}(L)]_{hl} = \gamma_{hl,0} + \gamma_{hl,1} L + \cdots + \gamma_{hl,p} L^p. \tag{11.2.5}$$

It is assumed that the system is stable [i.e., the roots of the polynomial equation $|\boldsymbol{\Gamma}(z)| = 0$ lie outside the unit circle]. If $\mathbf{u}_t$ is i.i.d., the order and rank conditions discussed in Chapter 9 are necessary and sufficient for identification.

If $\mathbf{u}_t$ is serially correlated, the rank condition (9.4.13) is not sufficient to identify (11.2.1). For example, consider the model:

$$y_{1t} + \gamma_{11,1} y_{1,t-1} + \gamma_{12,1} y_{2,t-1} = u_{1t}, \tag{11.2.6}$$

$$\gamma_{21,0} y_{1t} + y_{2t} = u_{2t}. \tag{11.2.7}$$

If the stochastic disturbance terms u_{1t} and u_{2t} are serially uncorrelated, this model satisfies the usual rank condition (9.4.13) and so is identified. However, if u_{1t} and u_{2t} are serially correlated, (11.2.6) and (11.2.7) can be premultiplied by the transformation matrix

$$\mathbf{F}(L) = \mathbf{I} + \begin{bmatrix} 0 & c \\ 0 & 0 \end{bmatrix} L, \tag{11.2.8}$$

which premultiplies (11.2.7) by cL and adds the resulting equation to (11.2.6) to obtain a new system that consists of (11.2.7) and

$$y_{1t} + \gamma^*_{11,1} y_{1,t-1} + \gamma^*_{12,1} y_{2,t-1} = u^*_{1t}, \tag{11.2.9}$$

where $\gamma^*_{11,1} = \gamma_{11,1} + c\gamma_{21,0}$, $\gamma^*_{12,1} = \gamma_{12,1} + c$, and $u^*_{1t} = u_{1t} + cu_{2,t-1}$. Equations (11.2.7) and (11.2.9) satisfy the same prior restrictions as (11.2.6) and (11.2.7). Therefore, the model consisting of (11.2.6) and (11.2.7) is not identified if the $\mathbf{u}_t$ are serially correlated.

This example demonstrates that when both lagged variables and serially correlated stochastic disturbance terms are allowed, there exists the possibility of premultiplication of the system by a nonsingular $g \times g$ polynomial matrix $\mathbf{F}(L)$ while retaining observational equivalence. This additional complexity does not arise for models containing lagged variables alone, since if $\mathbf{u}_t$ is serially uncorrelated, the transformation matrix $\mathbf{F}(L)$ can be at most a nonsingular constant matrix; otherwise, serial correlation will be introduced.

One set of sufficient conditions to identify a dynamic simultaneous-equations model with stationary disturbances consists of:

1. $\boldsymbol{\Gamma}(L)$ and $\mathbf{B}(L)$ have no common polynomial factors.
2. Rank $[\boldsymbol{\Gamma}_p \mathbf{B}_q] = g$.
3. At least $(g-1)$ zeros must be prescribed in each row of

$$\mathbf{A} = [\boldsymbol{\Gamma}_0 \quad \boldsymbol{\Gamma}_1 \quad \cdots \quad \boldsymbol{\Gamma}_p \quad \mathbf{B}_0 \quad \mathbf{B}_1 \quad \cdots \quad \mathbf{B}_q], \tag{11.2.10}$$

and the rank of each submatrix of $\mathbf{A}$ obtained by taking the columns of $\mathbf{A}$ with prescribed zeros in a certain row has to be $g-1$.

Condition 1 eliminates redundancy in the specification. The following is an example of an equation with a redundancy. Let

$$\begin{bmatrix} (1+\rho L)(1+\gamma_{11,1}L) & 0 \\ 0 & (1+\gamma_{22,1}L) \end{bmatrix} \begin{bmatrix} y_{1t} \\ y_{2t} \end{bmatrix} + \begin{bmatrix} (1+\rho L)b_{11} \\ 0 \end{bmatrix} x_t = \begin{bmatrix} u_{1t} \\ u_{2t} \end{bmatrix}. \tag{11.2.11}$$

The first equation has a common factor $(1+\rho L)$.[1] When common factors are allowed, there may be infinitely many structures that are observationally equivalent. Furthermore, redundant specification also poses serious estimation problems, as discussed in Box and Jenkins (1970) and Hannan, Dunsmiur, and Deistler (1980).

Condition 2 constrains the transformation $\mathbf{F}(L)$ to be a constant matrix $\mathbf{F}$. To see this, premultiplying (11.2.1) by $\mathbf{F}(L) = \mathbf{F}_0 + \mathbf{F}_1 L$ yields:

$$\begin{aligned} [\boldsymbol{\Gamma}^*(L) \quad \mathbf{B}^*(L)] &= \mathbf{F}(L)[\boldsymbol{\Gamma}(L) \quad \mathbf{B}(L)] \\ &= [\mathbf{F}_0\boldsymbol{\Gamma}_0 + (\mathbf{F}_0\boldsymbol{\Gamma}_1 + \mathbf{F}_1\boldsymbol{\Gamma}_0)L + \cdots + (\mathbf{F}_0\boldsymbol{\Gamma}_p + \mathbf{F}_1\boldsymbol{\Gamma}_{p-1})L^p \\ &\qquad + \mathbf{F}_1\boldsymbol{\Gamma}_p L^{p+1},\ \mathbf{F}_0\mathbf{B}_0 + \cdots + (\mathbf{F}_0\mathbf{B}_q + \mathbf{F}_1\mathbf{B}_{q-1})L^q \\ &\qquad + \mathbf{F}_1\mathbf{B}_q L^{q+1}]. \end{aligned} \tag{11.2.12}$$

As long as there exists a nonzero $\mathbf{F}_1$ such that:

$$\mathbf{F}_1[\boldsymbol{\Gamma}_p \quad \mathbf{B}_q] = [\mathbf{0} \ \vdots \ \mathbf{0}], \tag{11.2.13}$$

the order conditions for p and q will still be preserved. On the other hand, if $[\boldsymbol{\Gamma}_p \quad \mathbf{B}_p]$ has rank g, multiplication of $\mathbf{F}(L)$ will increase the length of the lag, and thus two structures will not be equivalent unless $\mathbf{F}_j = \mathbf{0}$ for $j \geq 1$. Condition 2 is imposed to eliminate the possibility that $\mathbf{F}_j$, $j \geq 1$ may not be equal to zero.

Condition 3 restricts the transformation matrix $\mathbf{F}(L) = \mathbf{F}_0$ to be a diagonal matrix. Furthermore, a normalization condition, such as letting one element in each row of $\boldsymbol{\Gamma}_0$ be unity, will further constrain $\mathbf{F}_0$ to be an identity matrix. Hence a dynamic structure (11.2.1) satisfying conditions 1, 2, and 3 will be identified. For further elaborations of the identification conditions for a dynamic system, see Hannan (1971), Hatanaka (1975), and Hsiao (1983).

The estimation of (11.2.1) depends critically on the nature of the error process $\mathbf{u}_t$. If $\mathbf{u}_t$ is independently distributed over time, the estimation methods discussed in Chapter 10 can be applied in a straightforward way, except now the set of predetermined variables consists of $(\mathbf{y}_{t-1}, \ldots, \mathbf{y}_{t-p}, \quad \mathbf{x}_t, \ldots, \mathbf{x}_{t-q})$. If $\mathbf{u}_t$ follows an autoregressive process, it is possible to first apply a generalized version of the Cochrane–Orcutt transformation to remove serial correlation and then use the methods of Chapter 10 to estimate the transformed model. If $\mathbf{u}_t$ follows a moving average (MA) or autoregressive moving average (ARMA) process, there is no simple transformation to eliminate the serial correlation, and estimation becomes quite complicated.

Suppose that $\mathbf{u}_t$ follows an sth-order MA process:

$$\mathbf{u}_t = \sum_{j=0}^{s} \boldsymbol{\Theta}_j \boldsymbol{\varepsilon}_{t-j}, \tag{11.2.14}$$

where $\boldsymbol{\Theta}_0 = \mathbf{I}_g$, and $\boldsymbol{\varepsilon}_t$ is a g-dimensional i.i.d. random vector with mean zero and covariance matrix $\boldsymbol{\Omega}$. Because the combination of (11.2.1) and (11.2.14) typically involves a large number of parameters and on many occasions the number of parameters could be

[1] By eliminating redundancy, the transformation matrix $\mathbf{F}(L)$ is restricted to be a *unimodular matrix* $\mathbf{F}(L)$, with the property that its determinant is a constant. Any dynamic system transformed by a unimodular matrix will have the same autocovariance structure. For further details, see MacDuffee (1956) or Hsiao (1983).

larger than the number of observations, an often used formulation (e.g., in Klein, 1973) is to assume that no disturbances from any other equation enters into, say, the hth equation. In that case, $\mathbf{\Theta}_j$ is assumed diagonal, $j = 1, \ldots, s$, so

$$u_{ht} = \sum_{j=0}^{s} \theta_{hj} \varepsilon_{h,t-j}, \qquad h = 1, \ldots, g. \tag{11.2.15}$$

Under the assumption of (11.2.15), efficient estimation of the $\mathbf{B}_r$'s, $\mathbf{\Gamma}_r$'s, and $\mathbf{\Theta}_r$'s can be obtained by an application of the seemingly unrelated estimator that minimizes:

$$S = \sum_{t=1}^{T} \boldsymbol{\varepsilon}_t' \mathbf{\Omega}^{-1} \boldsymbol{\varepsilon}_t. \tag{11.2.16}$$

The Box–Jenkins method of constructing a single equation ε_t, as discussed in Section 6.4, can be extended directly to construct a vector $\boldsymbol{\varepsilon}_t$. The solution of (11.2.16) is then obtained by applying a Gauss–Newton or Newton–Raphson iterative scheme using some consistent estimator of $\mathbf{\Omega}$, which can be obtained by applying the single-equation estimator to each equation in turn, as discussed in Nicholls, Pagan, and Terrell (1975).

When the $\mathbf{\Theta}_j$'s are unrestricted, a frequency-domain approach can be utilized to derive an asymptotically efficient estimator, as discussed in Hannan and Terrell (1973). For additional discussion on dynamic specification, see Hendry, Pagan, and Sargan (1984).

11.3 MODELING UNRESTRICTED MULTIPLE TIME SERIES: THE APPROACH OF TIAO AND BOX

Given that many economic variables are interrelated, it is natural to consider the generalization of the modeling of univariate time series discussed in Chapter 6 to multiple time series. There is considerable interest in modeling multiple time series because it helps in understanding the dynamic relationships among a group of variables and may lead to better forecasts when such relationships are utilized.

Let $\mathbf{y}_t$ be an n-dimensional vector time series, $t = 1, \ldots, T$. For simplicity, assume that $\mathbf{y}_t$ is stationary and purely "nondeterministic."[2] The multivariate generalization of Wold's decomposition theorem states that $\mathbf{y}_t$ can be represented by a weighted average:

$$\mathbf{y}_t = \mathbf{\Psi}(L)\boldsymbol{\varepsilon}_t, \tag*{*(11.3.1)}$$

where $\boldsymbol{\varepsilon}_t$ is i.i.d. with mean zero and covariance matrix $\mathbf{\Omega}$, $\mathbf{\Psi}(L)$ is an $n \times n$ matrix of polynomials in the back-shift operator L:

$$\mathbf{\Psi}(L) = \mathbf{\Psi}_0 + \mathbf{\Psi}_1 L + \cdots, \tag{11.3.2}$$

the $\mathbf{\Psi}_j$'s being $n \times n$ matrices. The (g, h)th element of $\mathbf{\Psi}(L)$ is:

$$\Psi_{gh}(L) = \sum_{j=0}^{\infty} \Psi_{gh,j} L^j. \tag{11.3.3}$$

Thus a typical equation in (11.3.1) is:

$$y_{gt} = \sum_{j=0}^{\infty} \psi_{g1,j} \varepsilon_{1,t-j} + \sum_{j=0}^{\infty} \psi_{g2,j} \varepsilon_{2,t-j} + \cdots + \sum_{j=0}^{\infty} \psi_{gn,j} \varepsilon_{n,t-j}. \tag*{*(11.3.4)}$$

[2] If the observed vector time series is nonstationary and is not cointegrated (see Section 11.5), it is possible to apply the difference operator ∇^d to each series separately to transform them into a stationary vector time series (Section 6.5.3). If the observed series has constant mean, take $\mathbf{y}_t$ as the deviation from the mean.

Operations can be performed on the matrix lag operators $\mathbf{\Psi}(L)$ in the same fashion as they can be performed on scalar lag operators, except that matrix operations are substituted for the corresponding scalar operation. Therefore, if $\mathbf{\Psi}(L)$ is invertible, there is also an autoregressive representation for the $\mathbf{y}_t$ series:

$$\mathbf{\Phi}(L)\mathbf{y}_t = \boldsymbol{\varepsilon}_t, \tag{11.3.5}$$

where $\mathbf{\Theta}(L)$ is an $n \times n$ matrix whose elements are polynomials in the lag operator L. If $\mathbf{\Psi}(L)$ can in some way be approximated by the product of two matrices, $\mathbf{A}(L)^{-1}\mathbf{\Theta}(L)$, each involving only finite-order polynomials in L, the result is a mixed autoregressive moving average (ARMA) model:

$$\mathbf{A}(L)\mathbf{y}_t = \mathbf{\Theta}(L)\boldsymbol{\varepsilon}_t, \qquad *(11.3.6)$$

where $\mathbf{A}(L)$ and $\mathbf{\Theta}(L)$ are the polynomials in the lag operator:

$$\mathbf{A}(L) = \mathbf{A}_0 - \mathbf{A}_1 L - \cdots - \mathbf{A}_p L^p, \tag{11.3.7}$$

$$\mathbf{\Theta}(L) = \mathbf{\Theta}_0 - \mathbf{\Theta}_1 L - \cdots - \mathbf{\Theta}_q L^q, \tag{11.3.8}$$

the $\mathbf{A}_r$'s and $\mathbf{\Theta}_r$'s being $n \times n$ matrices. The roots of the determinantal equations $|\mathbf{A}(L)| = 0$ and $|\mathbf{\Theta}(L)| = 0$ are all assumed to be outside the unit circle to ensure stationarity and invertibility.

Just like the dynamic simultaneous-equations models, such multivariate ARMA models may be unidentified. For instance, multiplying (11.3.5) through by a nonsingular matrix $\mathbf{C}$ or transforming $\mathbf{\Theta}(L)$ to $\mathbf{\Theta}^*(L) = \mathbf{\Theta}(L)\mathbf{C}$ and $\boldsymbol{\varepsilon}_t$ to $\boldsymbol{\varepsilon}_t^* = \mathbf{C}^{-1}\boldsymbol{\varepsilon}_1$ would yield structures that are different. However, they all possess identical second-order moments. Conditions given in Section 11.2 are sufficient for identifying the multivariate ARMA(p, q) process in (11.3.6) and are discussed in Hannan (1971) and Hsiao (1983). Here, without loss of generality, let $\mathbf{A}_0 = \mathbf{I}$ and $\mathbf{\Theta}_0 = \mathbf{I}$.

It is often argued that there does not exist enough prior information to identify a dynamic simultaneous-equation model. Liu (1960) and Sims (1980) have argued that identification of a structure is often achieved not because there is sufficient prior information but only because of the desire that the model be identified. Therefore, as a preliminary analysis they favor building a multiple time-series model as a reduced form representation of a given phenomenon to avoid potential bias in prediction and policy analysis due to the imposition of often incredible and spurious prior restrictions. However, the multivariate ARMA model in (11.3.6) contains a dauntingly large number of parameters $\{n^2(p + q) + \frac{1}{2}n(n + 1)\}$, complicating methods for model building and estimation.

Tiao and Box (1981) have proposed an iterative approach consisting of (1) tentative specification [or "identification" in Box–Jenkins (1970) terminology], (2) estimation, and (3) diagnostic checking. In the tentative specification stage, they suggest employing statistics that can be readily calculated from the data to choose a subclass of models worthy of further examination. The basic tools used are sample cross-covariance or sample cross-correlation matrices and sample partial autocorrelation matrices.

The lag s cross-covariance matrix of a stationary vector time series $\{\mathbf{y}_t\}$ with mean zero is defined as:

$$\mathbf{R}(s) = E\mathbf{y}_t\mathbf{y}'_{t+s}. \tag{11.3.9}$$

Postmultiplying (11.3.6) by $\mathbf{y}'_{t+s}$ and taking expectations, we obtain:

$$\mathbf{R}(s) = \begin{cases} \sum_{j=s-r}^{s-1} \mathbf{A}_{s-j}\mathbf{R}(j) - \sum_{j=0}^{r-s} \mathbf{\Theta}_{j+s}\mathbf{\Omega}\mathbf{\Psi}'_j, & s = 0, \ldots, r, \\ \sum_{j=1}^{r} \mathbf{A}_j \mathbf{R}(s-j), & s > r, \end{cases} \qquad *(11.3.10)$$

where the $\mathbf{\Psi}_j$'s are obtained from the relationship:

$$\mathbf{\Psi}(L) = \mathbf{A}(L)^{-1}\mathbf{\Theta}(L) = \mathbf{I} + \mathbf{\Psi}_1 L + \cdots, \qquad (11.3.11)$$

$\mathbf{\Theta}_0 = -\mathbf{I}$, $r = \max(p, q)$, and it is understood that if $p < q$, $\mathbf{A}_{p+1} = \cdots = \mathbf{A}_r = \mathbf{0}$, and if $q < p$, $\mathbf{\Theta}_{q+1} = \cdots = \mathbf{\Theta}_r = \mathbf{0}$.

When $p = 0$, that is, in the case of the vector moving average, MA(q), the cross-covariance matrix is:

$$\mathbf{R}(s) = \begin{cases} \sum_{j=0}^{q-s} \mathbf{\Theta}_j\, \mathbf{\Omega}\mathbf{\Theta}'_{j+s}, & s = 0, \ldots, q, \\ \mathbf{0}, & s > q, \end{cases} \qquad (11.3.12)$$

where all auto- and cross-covariances are zero when $s > q$. On the other hand, when $q = 0$, in the case of a vector autoregressive model AR(p), the cross-covariance matrix $\mathbf{R}(s)$ in (11.3.10) indicates that the auto- and cross-covariances in general will gradually decay to zero as $|s|$ increases.

The second moment equations (11.3.10) imply that the autocovariance matrices $\mathbf{R}(s)$'s and the autoregressive coefficients are related. Analogous to the partial autocorrelation function for the univariate case, Tiao–Box defined a *partial autoregression matrix* function $\mathbf{P}(j)$ as:[3]

$$\mathbf{P}'(j) = \begin{cases} \mathbf{R}^{-1}(0)\mathbf{R}(1), & j = 1, \\ \left[\mathbf{R}(0) - \mathbf{b}'(j)C^{-1}(j)\mathbf{b}(j)\right]^{-1} \cdot \\ \left[\mathbf{R}(j) - \mathbf{b}'(j)C^{-1}(j)\mathbf{d}(j)\right], & j > 1, \end{cases}$$

where

$$\mathbf{C}(j) = \begin{bmatrix} \mathbf{R}(0) & \mathbf{R}(-1) & \cdots & \mathbf{R}(-p+2) \\ \mathbf{R}(1) & \mathbf{R}(0) & \cdots & \vdots \\ \vdots & \ddots & \ddots & \vdots \\ \vdots & \ddots & \ddots & \mathbf{R}(-1) \\ \mathbf{R}(p-2) & & \mathbf{R}(1) & \mathbf{R}(0) \end{bmatrix}, \qquad (11.3.13)$$

$$\mathbf{b}(j) = \begin{bmatrix} \mathbf{R}(-j+1) \\ \vdots \\ \mathbf{R}(-1) \end{bmatrix}, \qquad \mathbf{d}(j) = \begin{bmatrix} \mathbf{R}(1) \\ \vdots \\ \mathbf{R}(j-1) \end{bmatrix}.$$

It follows from (11.3.5) that if the model is AR(p), $\mathbf{P}(j)$ has the property that:

$$\mathbf{P}(j) = \begin{cases} \mathbf{A}_j, & j \le p, \\ \mathbf{0}, & j > p. \end{cases} \qquad (11.3.14)$$

For general multivariate ARMA models, both the population cross-correlation matrices and the partial autoregression matrices decay only gradually toward $\mathbf{0}$.

[3]It should be noted that the cross-covariance $\mathbf{R}(s)$, in general, is not equal to $\mathbf{R}(-s)$.

Estimates of cross-correlations are calculated using the sample cross-correlations:

$$\hat{\rho}_{gh}(s) = \frac{\sum (y_{gt} - \bar{y}_g)(y_{h,t+s} - \bar{y}_h)}{\left[\sum (y_{gt} - \bar{y}_g)^2 \sum (y_{ht} - \bar{y}_h)^2\right]^{1/2}}, \tag{11.3.15}$$

where $\bar{y}_g$ is the sample mean of the gth component series of $\mathbf{y}_t$. Estimates of the $\mathbf{P}(j)$ and their standard errors can be obtained by fitting autoregressive models of successively higher order $j = 1, 2, \ldots$ by standard multivariate least squares. In principle, it is possible to plot the sample cross-correlations and partial autoregression matrices as in the case of the univariate case (see Chapter 6). However, graphs of this kind become increasingly cumbersome as the number of series is increased. Tiao–Box, therefore, suggest the following simple device. For the pattern of cross-correlation function, instead of the numerical values, a plus sign indicates a value greater than $2T^{-1/2}$, a minus sign indicates a value less than $-2T^{-1/2}$, and a dot indicates a value between $-2T^{-1/2}$ and $2T^{-1/2}$. The motivation is that if the series were white noise, for large T the $\hat{\rho}_{gh}(j)$'s would be normally distributed with mean 0 and variance T^{-1}. The symbols can then be arranged in a form similar to that shown in Table 11.1.

The pattern of partial correlations can similarly be summarized by listing indicator symbols, assigning a plus (minus) sign when a coefficient in $\mathbf{P}(j)$ is greater (less) than 2(–2) times its estimated standard errors, and a dot for values in between. In general, a low-order moving average model has the pattern of indicator symbols for the cross-correlation matrices in the form of having plus signs in the first few of them and dots for the rest. The persistence of large correlations suggests the possibility of autoregressive behavior. The order of an AR(p) process can be tentatively identified by examining the pattern of the partial autoregressive matrices, $\mathbf{P}(j)$, which will be zero for $j > p$. Furthermore, the likelihood ratio statistics can be employed to help determine the order of an autoregressive model. The null hypothesis $\mathbf{A}_l = \mathbf{0}$ against the alternative $\mathbf{A}_l \neq \mathbf{0}$ can be formulated when an AR(l) model is fitted. Let

$$\mathbf{S}(l) = \sum_{t=l+1}^{T} (\mathbf{y}_t - \hat{\mathbf{A}}_1\mathbf{y}_{t-1} - \cdots - \hat{\mathbf{A}}_l\mathbf{y}_{t-l})(\mathbf{y}_t - \hat{\mathbf{A}}_1\mathbf{y}_{t-1} - \cdots - \hat{\mathbf{A}}_l\mathbf{y}_{t-l})' \tag{11.3.16}$$

be the matrix of residual sum of squares and cross-products after fitting an AR(l). Under the null hypothesis, the log-likelihood ratio statistic:

$$-\left(T - l - 1 - \frac{1}{2} - l \cdot n\right) \log \frac{|\mathbf{S}(l)|}{|\mathbf{S}(l-1)|} = M(l) \qquad *(11.3.17)$$

is asymptotically distributed as chi-square with n^2 degrees of freedom.

It should be noted that this procedure to select tentatively the order of an ARMA model for estimation is not based on any formal significance test. Rather, it is a crude signal-to-

TABLE 11.1 Sample Pattern of Cross-Correlation for Each Element in the Matrix over All Lags (n = 3)

	y_1	y_2	y_3
y_1	+++++... ...	......	--------- -------
y_2	....+++	++++++++ +++...	+++++++ ++......
y_3	-----... ...+++	++++++++ +++	++++++++ +++++...

noise ratio guide to help arrive at an initial model. Considerable simplification is almost invariably possible after an initial model has been fitted.

Once the order of the model in (11.3.6) has tentatively been selected, efficient estimates of the associated parameter matrices $\mathbf{A}_1,\ldots,\mathbf{A}_p,\mathbf{\Theta}_1,\ldots,\mathbf{\Theta}_q$ and $\mathbf{\Omega}$ are determined by maximizing the likelihood function. To guide against model misspecification and to search for directions of improvement, diagnostic checks including (1) plots of standardized residual series against time and/or other variables and (2) chi-square tests based on the sample cross-correlations of the residuals have been proposed by, among others, Hoskin (1980) and Li and McLeod (1980).[4]

In addition to the Tiao-Box procedure, Granger and Newbold (1986), Tiao and Tsay (1983), and others have proposed methods for relating multiple time-series models to actual data. However, in general, the procedures are complex and difficult to apply for $g > 2$. Much further work is needed, especially in the identification of mixed autoregressive moving average models and in developing faster estimation algorithms and better tools for diagnostic checking.

As an example, Tiao–Box apply the foregoing approach to quarterly data from 1952 IV to 1967 IV of the *Financial Times* ordinary share index (y_{1t}), U.K. car production (y_{2t}), and the *Financial Times* commodity price index (y_{3t}). Patterns of sample cross-correlations and partial autoregressions are reported in Tables 11.2 and 11.3. Examination of Table 11.2 shows high and persistent auto- and cross-correlations. Examination of Table 11.3 shows that for $j > 2$ most of the elements of $\mathbf{P}(j)$ are small compared with their estimated standard errors and the corresponding likelihood ratio statistics fail to show significance after $j > 2$. Table 11.4 shows that the pattern of the cross-correlations of the residuals after AR(2) is consonant with estimated white noise. However, they also note that there is one large residual correlation at lag 1 after the AR(1) fit, suggesting also the possibility of an ARMA(1, 1) model.

Both an AR(1) and ARMA(1, 1) model were fitted using the exact maximum likelihood method, and the results for the ARMA(1, 1) model:

$$(\mathbf{I} - \mathbf{A}_1 L)\mathbf{y}_t = \boldsymbol{\mu} + (\mathbf{I} - \mathbf{\Theta}_1 L)\boldsymbol{\varepsilon}_t \tag{11.3.18}$$

are given in Table 11.5, because this model produced a marginally better representation and diagnostic checks applied to it suggest that it provides an adequate representation of the data.

Table 11.5 shows the initial unrestricted fit and also the fits for two simpler models by setting to zero coefficients whose estimates are small compared to their standard errors. The final model implies that the system may be approximated by:

TABLE 11.2 Sample Pattern of Cross-Correlation

	y_1: Stocks	y_2: Cars	y_3: Commodities
y_1: Stocks	++++++++....	– –	– –
y_2: Cars	....+++	+++++++++++++ +++....	+++++++++++++ ++.....
y_3: Commodities	– – – – – – –...... ...+++++	+++++++++++++ ++++++..	+++++++++++++ +++++...

[4]See also Section 6.8.

TABLE 11.3 Partial Autoregression and Related Statistics

Lag	Indicator Symbols for Partials	$M(l)$ Statistic $\simeq \chi_9^2$	Diagonal Elements of $\Omega \times 10$
1	+ . .	301.3	0.44
	. + .		0.89
	. . +		1.62
2	− . .	18.6	0.40
	. . .		0.84
	− + −		1.23
3	. . .	9.6	0.37
	. . .		0.81
	. . .		1.21
4	. . .	3.6	0.36
	. . .		0.79
	. . .		1.19
5	. + .	11.9	0.32
	. + .		0.70
	. . .		1.11

TABLE 11.4 Pattern of Cross-Correlation Matrices of Residuals

	Lag							
Model	1	2	3	4	5	6	7	8
AR(1)	. . +	. . .	. . .	. . .	. . .	. . .	. . .	. . .
	. . .	. . .	. . .	. . .	. . .	. . .	. . .	. . .
	. . .	. . .	. . .	. . .	. . .	. . .	. . +	. . .
AR(2)	. . .	. . .	. . .	. . .	. . .	. . .	. . .	. . .
	. . .	. . .	. . .	− . .	. . .	. . .	. . .	. . .
	. . .	. . .	. . .	. . .	. . .	. . .	. . +	. . .

$$(1 - 0.98L)y_{1t} = \varepsilon_{1t}, \tag{11.3.19}$$

$$(1 - 0.93L)y_{2t} = 0.2 + \varepsilon_{2t}, \tag{11.3.20}$$

$$(1 - 0.83L)y_{3t} = 2.8 + 0.40\varepsilon_{1,t-1} + (1 + 0.41L)\varepsilon_{3t}. \tag{11.3.21}$$

All three series behave approximately as random walks with slightly correlated errors. Substituting (11.3.19) into (11.3.21) yields:

$$(1 - 0.83L)y_{3t} = 2.8 + 0.40(1 - 0.98L)y_{1,t-1} + (1 + 0.41L)\varepsilon_{3t}. \tag{11.3.22}$$

From the point of view of forecasting, (11.3.22) is of some interest since it implies that the ordinary share index $y_{1,t-1}$ is a leading indicator at lag 1 for the commodity price index y_{3t}. Its effect is small, however, as can be seen, for example, by the improvement achieved over the corresponding best-fitting univariate model, which was:

$$(1 - 0.78L)y_{3t} = 3.63 + (1 + 0.53L)\varepsilon_{3t}, \qquad \hat{\sigma}_3^2 = 0.151. \tag{11.3.23}$$

The residual variance from the univariate model, $\hat{\sigma}_3^2$, is not much larger than the value 0.134 for the variance of ε_{3t} obtained from the final vector model (11.3.22).

TABLE 11.5 Estimation Results for the Model (11.3.18)

Model	$\hat{\mathbf{c}}$	$\hat{\mathbf{A}}_1$	$\hat{\boldsymbol{\Theta}}$	$\hat{\boldsymbol{\Omega}}$
Full	$\begin{bmatrix} 1.11 \\ (0.64) \\ 1.74 \\ (0.82) \\ 4.08 \\ (1.47) \end{bmatrix}$	$\begin{bmatrix} 0.81 & 0.15 & -0.06 \\ (0.08) & (0.07) & (0.04) \\ -0.07 & 0.98 & -0.09 \\ (0.10) & (0.10) & (0.05) \\ -0.32 & 0.30 & 0.76 \\ (0.18) & (0.17) & (0.08) \end{bmatrix}$	$\begin{bmatrix} -0.29 & 0.23 & 0.06 \\ (0.15) & (0.11) & (0.07) \\ -0.45 & 0.20 & -0.15 \\ (0.22) & (0.17) & (0.11) \\ -0.79 & 0.57 & -0.44 \\ (0.28) & (0.21) & (0.13) \end{bmatrix}$	$\begin{bmatrix} 0.037 & & \\ 0.022 & 0.078 & \\ 0.013 & 0.022 & 0.129 \end{bmatrix}$
Restricted (intermediate)	$\begin{bmatrix} 0.13 \\ (0.09) \\ 0.59 \\ (0.05) \\ 2.48 \\ (1.10) \end{bmatrix}$	$\begin{bmatrix} 0.90 & 0.08 & \\ (0.06) & (0.06) & \cdot \\ & 0.92 & -0.02 \\ \cdot & (0.04) & (0.04) \\ & & 0.85 \\ \cdot & \cdot & (0.07) \end{bmatrix}$	$\begin{bmatrix} \cdot & \cdot & \cdot \\ \cdot & \cdot & \cdot \\ -0.40 & & -0.41 \\ (0.23) & \cdot & (0.12) \end{bmatrix}$	$\begin{bmatrix} 0.042 & & \\ 0.022 & 0.079 & \\ 0.017 & 0.021 & 0.131 \end{bmatrix}$
Restricted (final)	$\begin{bmatrix} 0.12 \\ (0.08) \\ 0.24 \\ (0.10) \\ 2.76 \\ (1.07) \end{bmatrix}$	$\begin{bmatrix} 0.98 & & \\ (0.03) & & \cdot \\ & 0.93 & \\ \cdot & (0.04) & \cdot \\ & & 0.83 \\ \cdot & \cdot & (0.06) \end{bmatrix}$	$\begin{bmatrix} \cdot & \cdot & \cdot \\ \cdot & \cdot & \cdot \\ -0.40 & & -0.41 \\ (0.23) & \cdot & (0.12) \end{bmatrix}$	$\begin{bmatrix} 0.045 & & \\ 0.024 & 0.085 & \\ 0.019 & 0.023 & 0.134 \end{bmatrix}$

Note Standard errors in parentheses.

11.4 GRANGER CAUSALITY

In the case of time-series modeling when no restrictions are imposed, in general, the Box–Jenkins approach works well for univariate time series. Unfortunately, its generalization to multiple time series does not appear as satisfactory in finite samples. This is mainly because when several variables are considered simultaneously, the complicated cross-correlation patterns could arise from many possible models. Each of these choices involves a large number of unknown parameters that requires the implementation of complicated estimation routines. However, there exist statistical procedures that exploit the interrelationships among multiple time series to narrow down possible choices of models. Two of them treated here are Granger causality and cointegration.

A major goal of economic research is to determine the causal relationships among economic variables. In nonexperimental research, such inferences tend to rely on considerations external to the data, as in the case of the classification of endogenous and exogenous variables in regression analysis. However, if one were to assume that (1) the future cannot cause the past (i.e., causality can only occur with the past causing the present or the future) and (2) a cause contains unique information about an effect that is not available elsewhere, time-series techniques can be employed to infer causal relations among variables. Further, because causality implies restrictions on the parameters in a system, it can be used to simplify the specification of a multivariate time-series model.

Granger (1969) has provided a definition of causality called *Granger causality* as follows: Let $F(A \mid B)$ denote the conditional distribution function of A given B. Let Ω_t denote the information set at time t, including past values of x_t and y_t, denoted by $\bar{X}_t = \{\ldots, x_{t-2}, x_{t-1}\}$ and $\bar{Y}_t = \{\ldots, y_{t-2}, y_{t-1}\}$, respectively. Then if

$$F(y_{t+j} \mid \Omega_t) = F(y_{t+j} \mid \Omega_t - \bar{X}_t) \qquad \text{for all } j \geq 0, \tag{11.4.1}$$

where $\Omega_t - \bar{X}_t$ denotes the information set Ω_t other than $\bar{X}_t$, it is said that *x does not cause y relative to the information set* Ω. If (11.4.1) does not hold, then x does *cause* y.

To make this definition operational, Granger let $\Omega_t = \{\mathbf{w}_{t-j}, j = 1, 2, \ldots\}$, where $\mathbf{w}_t$ is a stationary n-dimensional vector of random variables, including y_t and x_t, and $\sigma^2(A \mid B)$ denotes the minimum mean squared prediction error of A given B. If $\sigma^2(y_t \mid \Omega_t) < \sigma^2(y_t \mid \Omega_t - \bar{X}_t)$ (i.e., the prediction of y using past x is more accurate than such prediction without using past x, in the mean squared error sense), then by definition x (Granger) causes y, denoted by $x \Rightarrow y$. If $\sigma^2(y_t \mid \Omega_t) < \sigma^2(y_t \mid \Omega_t - \bar{X}_t)$ and $\sigma^2(x_t \mid \Omega_t) < \sigma^2(x_t \mid \Omega_t - \bar{Y}_t)$, then, by definition, feedback occurs, denoted by $x \Leftrightarrow y$.

These definitions have strong implications for the parameterization of a multivariate time-series model. For instance, consider a stationary bivariate system (y_t, x_t). By the Wold decomposition theorem it has a MA representation of the form:

$$\begin{pmatrix} y_t \\ x_t \end{pmatrix} = \bar{\mathbf{\Psi}}(L)\boldsymbol{\varepsilon}_t = \begin{bmatrix} \psi_{11}(L) & \psi_{12}(L) \\ \psi_{21}(L) & \psi_{22}(L) \end{bmatrix} \begin{bmatrix} \varepsilon_{1t} \\ \varepsilon_{2t} \end{bmatrix}. \tag{11.4.2}$$

If the MA operator is invertible, it will also have an AR representation of the form:

$$\begin{pmatrix} \phi_{11}(L) & \phi_{12}(L) \\ \phi_{21}(L) & \phi_{22}(L) \end{pmatrix} \begin{pmatrix} y_t \\ x_t \end{pmatrix} = \begin{pmatrix} \varepsilon_{1t} \\ \varepsilon_{2t} \end{pmatrix}. \tag{11.4.3}$$

Given these definitions, it follows that if y does not cause x, the following statements are equivalent:[5]

1. $\psi_{21}(L) = 0$.
2. $\phi_{21}(L) = 0$.
3. The least squares estimate of y_t, given the observations $x_t, x_{t-1}, x_{t-2}, \ldots$, is identical to the estimate of y_t given $\{x_t\}$, for $t = \ldots, t-1, t, t+1, \ldots$.
4. If $y \not\Rightarrow > x$ and $x \Rightarrow y$, there exists a unique representation of y with respect to x of the distributed lag form:

$$y_t = \sum_{j=0}^{\infty} \beta_j x_{t-j} + \sum_{j=0}^{\infty} \psi_j \boldsymbol{\varepsilon}_{t-j}, \tag{11.4.4}$$

where $Ex_t\boldsymbol{\varepsilon}_s = 0$.

A number of tests, based on these various equivalent statements, have been proposed, including:

1. *Sims (1972) test*. From statement 3, an F test can be conducted by regressing y on past and future values of x. If y does not cause x, then future values of x in the regression should have coefficients that are, as a group, insignificantly different from zero.

[5]For proof, see Caines and Chan (1975).

2. *Pierce and Haugh (1971) test.* First use separate linear operators in lag operator L on x and y to ensure that each is (very nearly) prewhitened. Then use cross-correlation analysis to determine whether the residuals of the two prewhitened series are cross-correlated. If causality runs from x to y only, all the cross-correlation between the residuals of x and the lagged residuals of y should be insignificantly different from 0. Haugh (1976) shows that, under the null hypothesis that the two series are uncorrelated, the estimated residual cross-correlations, $\hat{r}_k$, are asymptotically normally distributed with mean zero and variance $1/T$. Thus $T\ \Sigma_{k=1}^{Q}\ \hat{r}_k^2$ is chi-square distributed with Q degrees of freedom.
3. *Wu (1973) and Hausman (1978) test.* From statement 4, one way to test for the absence of causality is to test the independence between the stochastic regressor x and disturbances ε. Wu (1973) and Hausman (1978) have suggested various methods for testing exogeneity specification.[6] The fundamental idea of the *Hausman specification test* is as follows: If there are two estimators $\hat{\boldsymbol{\beta}}^{(1)}$ and $\hat{\boldsymbol{\beta}}^{(2)}$ that converge to the true value $\boldsymbol{\beta}$ under the null but converge to different values under the alternative, the null hypothesis can be tested by testing whether the probability limit of the difference of the two estimators, $\hat{\mathbf{q}} = \hat{\boldsymbol{\beta}}^{(1)}$ and $\hat{\boldsymbol{\beta}}^{(2)}$, is zero. Suppose, based on a sample of T observations, that $\hat{\boldsymbol{\beta}}^{(1)}$ attains the asymptotic Cramer–Rao lower bound and both $\sqrt{T}(\hat{\boldsymbol{\beta}}_1 - \boldsymbol{\beta})$ and $\sqrt{T}(\hat{\boldsymbol{\beta}}_2 - \boldsymbol{\beta})$ are asymptotically normally distributed with mean zero and covariance matrix $\mathbf{V}_1$ and $\mathbf{V}_2$, respectively; then Var $(\sqrt{T}\hat{\mathbf{q}}) = \mathbf{V}_2 - \mathbf{V}_1$ and $T\hat{\mathbf{q}}'(\mathbf{V}_2 - \mathbf{V}_1)^{-1}\hat{\mathbf{q}}$ is asymptotically chi-square distributed with k degrees of freedom, where k is the dimension of the vector $\boldsymbol{\beta}$.
4. *Direct test.* From statements 1 and 2, it is possible to test for no causality from y to x by fitting either an AR or an MA model and testing whether $\phi_{21}(L) = 0$ or $\psi_{21}(L) = 0$.

Other things being equal, Hsiao (1979b) has shown that a direct test has more power than other tests. However, all these tests are very sensitive to the choice of the lag order of the preliminary unconstrained model, as discussed in Hsiao (1979a,b, 1981). To avoid having the test results contingent upon an arbitrary preliminary unconstrained model, Hsiao (1979a, 1982) suggests the following system identification procedure:

1. Determine the order of the one-dimensional autoregressive process, say y, using the Akaike information criterion (AIC) of Section 4.10.2.
2. Take y as the only output of the system and assume that x is the manipulated variable which controls the outcome of y. Use the AIC to determine the lag order of x, say p_2, assuming the order of the lag operator of y to be the one specified in step 1, say p_1.
3. To check whether the lagged y might pick up the effects of lagged x when y is treated as a univariate AR process, let the order of the lagged operator $\phi_{12}(L)$ be fixed at p_2 and let the lag operator $\phi_{11}(L)$ vary from 0 to p_1. Compute the corresponding AICs. Choose the order of $\phi_{11}(L)$ that gives the smallest AIC [conditional on the order of $\phi_{12}(L)$ being p_2], say p_1^*. The p_1^* may or may not be equal to p_1.

[6]However, since causality does not necessarily imply exogeneity (e.g., feedback may occur), this test actually imposes much stronger conditions than those required for testing for causality.

4. Compare the smallest AICs of steps 1 and 3. If the former is less than the latter, a one-dimensional autoregressive representation for y is used. If the converse is true, we say that $x \Rightarrow y$, and the optimal model for predicting y is the one including p_1^* lagged y and p_2 lagged x.
5. Repeat steps 1 to 4 for the x process, treating y as the manipulated variable.
6. Put together all single-equation specifications to identify the system. Because the sequential procedure may bias the joint nature of the process and the single-equation approach is equivalent to ignoring the effects of possible correlations within the components of the error terms, diagnostic checks are recommended to examine the adequacy of the model specification. This can be carried out by treating the specification of the system as the maintained hypothesis and performing likelihood ratio tests by deliberately overfitting or underfitting the model.

11.5 COINTEGRATION

11.5.1 Introduction and Definition

Most macroeconomic time series behave in a nonstationary manner. The approaches discussed above all begin by transforming nonstationary time series into stationary time series, either by differencing or detrending. While the nonstationarity of the data was previously considered a nuisance and therefore largely ignored, the recent development of cointegration analysis has pointed to its great potential as a statistical means of distinguishing between long-run relations and short-run dynamic adjustment.

The basic idea of cointegration is that although each of the two or more variables may be nonstationary, a linear combination of them may have the trend terms mutually cancel out so that it becomes stationary. For instance, consider two variables, y_{1t} and y_{2t}, each having extremely important long-run components. However, if the two series are related, then they tend to move closely together. Their long-run relation can be captured by combining them in such a way that the underlying long-run components mutually cancel out. Hence the linear combination of them will be stationary. To put this formally, let $\mathbf{y}_t$ denote a vector of n variables, where each element is integrated of order d, denoted by $\mathbf{y}_t \sim I(d)$. Then $(1-L)^d\mathbf{y}_t$ is stationary. It is generally true that a linear combination of them, say $w_t = \boldsymbol{\gamma}'\mathbf{y}_t$, is also $I(d)$. However, if there exists a vector $\boldsymbol{\gamma}$ such that $w_t = \boldsymbol{\gamma}'\mathbf{y}_t \sim I(d-b)$, $b > 0$, then $\mathbf{y}_t$ is called *cointegrated* and will be denoted by $CI(d, b)$. The vector $\boldsymbol{\gamma}$ is called the *cointegrating vector* (Granger, 1984).

If the vector $\mathbf{y}_t$ contains more than two variables, there could be more than one linear combination of them that is stationary. For instance, suppose that each of the three variables y_{1t}, y_{2t}, y_{3t} is $I(1)$, and there exist vectors $\gamma_{11}y_{1t} + \gamma_{12}y_{2t} \sim I(0)$ and $\gamma_{22}y_{2t} + \gamma_{23}y_{3t} \sim I(0)$; then a linear combination of them is also $I(0)$. In other words, this would imply that there exists a vector $\boldsymbol{\gamma}'_3 = (\gamma_{31}, \gamma_{32}, \gamma_{33})$ such that $\gamma_{31}y_{1t} + \gamma_{32}y_{2t} + \gamma_{33}y_{3t} \sim I(0)$. Moreover, the vector $\boldsymbol{\gamma}_3$ is not unique. In general, if $\mathbf{y}_t$ is $n \times 1$ and $\boldsymbol{\Gamma}$ is an $r \times n$ matrix such that $\boldsymbol{\Gamma}\mathbf{y}_t = \mathbf{u}_t$ is stationary, then $\boldsymbol{\Gamma}^*\mathbf{y}_t = \mathbf{u}_t^*$ is also stationary for $\boldsymbol{\Gamma}^* = \mathbf{C}\boldsymbol{\Gamma}$, $\mathbf{u}_t^* = \mathbf{C}\mathbf{u}_t$ where $\mathbf{C}$ is any arbitrary $r \times r$ constant matrix. Therefore, normalization rules have to be imposed. One normalization rule is to consider only linearly independent cointegrating vectors. For instance, suppose that there are r linearly independent cointegrating vectors such that $\mathbf{\Gamma y}_t = \mathbf{u}_t$, where $\mathbf{\Gamma} = (\mathbf{\Gamma}_1, \mathbf{\Gamma}_2)$ is an $r \times n$ matrix with rank r and $\mathbf{u}_t$ is an $r \times 1$ vector of stationary random variables; if $\mathbf{\Gamma}_1$ is nonsingular, one can use a normalized cointegrating matrix $\mathbf{\Gamma}^* = (\mathbf{I}_r, \mathbf{\Gamma}_2^*)$, where $\mathbf{\Gamma}_2^* = \mathbf{\Gamma}_1^{-1}\mathbf{\Gamma}_2$. The maximum number of linearly independent cointegrating vectors in a system of n nonstationary variables is $n-1$ because if $r = n$, then $\mathbf{y}_t = \mathbf{\Gamma}^{-1}\mathbf{u}_t$, which is stationary and contradicts the basic assumption.

11.5.2 Representation of Cointegrating Processes

When vector time series are cointegrated, this implies that the variables share some common components, and hence a reduction to a more parsimonious and more informative economic and statistical structure is possible. As an example, consider the simple case in which $d = b = 1$, which happens to be the case of greatest practical importance. Because each component of the vector $\mathbf{y}_t$ series is $I(1)$, $(1-L)\mathbf{y}_t$ is stationary and will have a multivariate Wold decomposition representation of the form:

$$(1-L)\mathbf{y}_t = \nabla\mathbf{y}_t = \mathbf{\Psi}(L)\boldsymbol{\varepsilon}_t = [\mathbf{\Psi}_0 + \mathbf{\Psi}_1 L + \cdots]\boldsymbol{\varepsilon}_t, \qquad *(11.5.1)$$

where $\nabla = (1-L)$ and $\boldsymbol{\varepsilon}_t$ is an $n \times 1$ vector of white noise process. Suppose there exists a vector of weights $\boldsymbol{\gamma}$ such that:

$$\mathbf{z}_t = \boldsymbol{\gamma}'\mathbf{y}_t \sim I(0). \qquad (11.5.2)$$

Then

$$\boldsymbol{\gamma}'\mathbf{\Psi}(1) = \boldsymbol{\gamma}'\left[\sum_{j=0}^{\infty}\mathbf{\Psi}_j\right] = 0. \qquad *(11.5.3)$$

To see this, rewrite:

$$\mathbf{\Psi}(L) = \mathbf{\Psi}(1) + (1-L)\mathbf{\Psi}^*(L), \qquad (11.5.4)$$

which can always be done by equating coefficients for powers of L so that

$$\mathbf{\Psi}_j^* = -\sum_{i=j+1}^{\infty}\mathbf{\Psi}_i.$$

Then (11.5.1) becomes:

$$\nabla\mathbf{y}_t = \mathbf{\Psi}(1)\boldsymbol{\varepsilon}_t + \nabla\mathbf{\Psi}^*(L)\boldsymbol{\varepsilon}_t. \qquad *(11.5.5)$$

Multiplying through (11.5.5) by $\boldsymbol{\gamma}'$ yields:

$$\nabla\boldsymbol{\gamma}'\mathbf{y}_t = \nabla\mathbf{z}_t = \boldsymbol{\gamma}'\mathbf{\Psi}(1)\boldsymbol{\varepsilon}_t + \nabla\boldsymbol{\gamma}'\mathbf{\Psi}^*(L)\boldsymbol{\varepsilon}_t. \qquad (11.5.6)$$

If $\boldsymbol{\gamma}'\mathbf{\Psi}(1) = 0$, then

$$\mathbf{z}_t = \boldsymbol{\gamma}'\mathbf{\Psi}^*(L)\boldsymbol{\varepsilon}_t, \qquad (11.5.7)$$

which will generally be $I(0)$. If $\boldsymbol{\gamma}'\mathbf{\Psi}(1) \neq 0$,

$$\mathbf{z}_t = (1-L)^{-1}\boldsymbol{\gamma}'\mathbf{\Psi}(1)\boldsymbol{\varepsilon}_t + \boldsymbol{\gamma}'\mathbf{\Psi}^*(L)\boldsymbol{\varepsilon}_t, \qquad (11.5.8)$$

which will be $I(1)$. Therefore, the condition for cointegration is that the matrix $\mathbf{\Psi}(1)$ have reduced rank. Any vector lying in the null space of $\mathbf{\Psi}(1)$is a cointegrating vector, and the cointegrating rank is the rank of this null space.

The restriction (11.5.3) also provides a convenient interpretation of the cointegrating process y_t in terms of *common trends*. Conditional on the initial value of $\mathbf{y}_0$ and $\boldsymbol{\varepsilon}_0 = \boldsymbol{\varepsilon}_{-1} = \cdots = \mathbf{0}$, from (11.5.5), it is possible to solve for $\mathbf{y}_t$ through continuous substitution as:

$$\begin{aligned} \mathbf{y}_t &= \mathbf{y}_0 + \left(1 + L + L^2 + \cdots + L^{t-1}\right)\left[\bar{\boldsymbol{\Psi}}(1) + (1-L)\bar{\boldsymbol{\Psi}}^*(L)\right]\boldsymbol{\varepsilon}_t \\ &= \mathbf{y}_0 + \bar{\boldsymbol{\Psi}}(1)\left(1 + L + \cdots + L^{t-1}\right)\boldsymbol{\varepsilon}_t + \bar{\boldsymbol{\Psi}}^*(L)\boldsymbol{\varepsilon}_t. \end{aligned} \tag{11.5.9}$$

Since $\bar{\boldsymbol{\Psi}}(1)$ has rank $n - r$, write it as the product of an $n \times (n - r)$ matrix $\mathbf{Q}^*$ and $(n - r) \times n$ matrix $\mathbf{J}^*$, both of rank $(n - r)$,

$$\bar{\boldsymbol{\Psi}}(1) = \mathbf{Q}^*\mathbf{J}^*. \tag{11.5.10}$$

Then express $\mathbf{y}_t$ in terms of the lower-dimensional random walk $\boldsymbol{\tau}_t$:

$$\mathbf{y}_t = \mathbf{y}_0 + \mathbf{Q}^*\boldsymbol{\tau}_t + \bar{\boldsymbol{\Psi}}^*(L)\boldsymbol{\varepsilon}_t, \tag{11.5.11}$$

where $\boldsymbol{\tau}_t$ is an $(n - r)$-dimensional random walk process defined by

$$\begin{aligned} \boldsymbol{\tau}_t &= \boldsymbol{\tau}_{t-1} + \mathbf{J}^*\boldsymbol{\varepsilon}_t \\ &= (1 + L + \cdots + L^{t-1})\mathbf{J}^*\boldsymbol{\varepsilon}_t. \end{aligned} \tag{11.5.12}$$

with initial condition $\boldsymbol{\tau}_0 = 0$. Because the dimension of $\boldsymbol{\tau}_t$ is smaller than $\mathbf{y}_t$, $\boldsymbol{\tau}_t$ can be referred to as the *common trends* in the system (Stock and Watson, 1988). From an economic point of view, $\mathbf{y}_t$ being cointegrated means that there may be latent variables which are responsible for the growth of many separate random variables. In King et al. (1991), these are identified as accumulations of productivity shocks, monetary policy shocks, and other macroeconomic innovations.

It is also possible to represent the common trends in terms of observables. Following Phillips (1991), the $r \times n$ cointegrating matrix $\boldsymbol{\Gamma}$ can be partitioned in the form:

$$\boldsymbol{\Gamma} = (\boldsymbol{\Gamma}_1, \boldsymbol{\Gamma}_2), \tag{11.5.13}$$

where $\boldsymbol{\Gamma}_1$ is $r \times r$ and nonsingular. Premultiplying $\boldsymbol{\Gamma}$ by $\boldsymbol{\Gamma}_1^{-1}$ yields a renormalized cointegrating matrix $\boldsymbol{\Gamma}^* = (\mathbf{I}_r, -\mathbf{B})$, where $\mathbf{B} = -\boldsymbol{\Gamma}_1^{-1}\boldsymbol{\Gamma}_2$. Letting $\mathbf{y}'_t = (\mathbf{y}'_{1t}, \mathbf{y}'_{2t})$ be the conformable partition, the system can be rewritten in the form:

$$\mathbf{y}_{1t} = \mathbf{B}\mathbf{y}_{2t} + \mathbf{u}_{1t}, \tag{11.5.14}$$

$$\nabla\mathbf{y}_{2t} = \mathbf{u}_{2t}, \tag{11.5.15}$$

where the process $\mathbf{u}'_{1t} = (\mathbf{u}'_{1t}, \mathbf{u}'_{2t})$ is assumed to be an invertible stationary process and $\mathbf{y}_{2t} = \nabla^{-1}\mathbf{u}_{2t}$ can be viewed as the common trends.

The fact that variables are cointegrated also implies and is implied by the existence of some adjustment process that prevents the errors in the long-run relationship from becoming larger and larger. This is the *error-correction model*. The error-correction model is a popular macroeconometric specification which integrates the long-run equilibrium analysis and short-run dynamic adjustment by including in the short-term dynamic model a measure of how much out of equilibrium or target the variables are in the last period, as in Pagan and Wickens (1989). It relates changes in $\mathbf{y}_t$, $\nabla\mathbf{y}_t$, to last period's error, $\mathbf{y}^*_{t-1} - \mathbf{y}_{t-1}$, where $\mathbf{y}^*_t$ denotes the target or equilibrium value. To see the relationship between cointegrated variables and an error-correction representation, rewrite (11.5.14) and (11.5.15) in the form:

$$\begin{bmatrix} \mathbf{I}_r & \mathbf{0} \\ \mathbf{0} & \nabla \mathbf{I}_{n-r} \end{bmatrix} \begin{bmatrix} \mathbf{I}_r & -\mathbf{B} \\ \mathbf{0} & \mathbf{I}_{n-r} \end{bmatrix} \begin{bmatrix} \mathbf{y}_{1t} \\ \mathbf{y}_{2t} \end{bmatrix} = \begin{bmatrix} \mathbf{u}_{1t} \\ \mathbf{u}_{2t} \end{bmatrix}, \tag{11.5.16}$$

where

$$\begin{aligned} \mathbf{u}_t &= \begin{bmatrix} \mathbf{u}_{1t} \\ \mathbf{u}_{2t} \end{bmatrix} = [\mathbf{C}_1(L) \quad \mathbf{C}_2(L)] \begin{bmatrix} \boldsymbol{\varepsilon}_{1t} \\ \boldsymbol{\varepsilon}_{2t} \end{bmatrix} \\ &= \mathbf{C}(L)\boldsymbol{\varepsilon}_t, \end{aligned} \tag{11.5.17}$$

and $\boldsymbol{\varepsilon}_t = (\boldsymbol{\varepsilon}'_{1t}, \boldsymbol{\varepsilon}'_{2t})'$ is an $n \times 1$ vector of white noise process. Assuming that $\mathbf{C}(L)$ is invertible, denoting $\mathbf{C}(L)^{-1}$ by $\mathbf{C}^*(L) = [\mathbf{C}_1^*(L), \mathbf{C}_2^*(L)]$, and premultiplying (11.5.16) by $\mathbf{C}(L)^{-1}$ yields:

$$[\mathbf{C}_1^*(L) \quad \mathbf{C}_2^*(L)] \begin{bmatrix} \mathbf{I}_r & \mathbf{0} \\ \mathbf{0} & \nabla \mathbf{I}_{n-r} \end{bmatrix} \begin{bmatrix} \mathbf{I}_r & -\mathbf{B} \\ \mathbf{0} & \mathbf{I}_{n-r} \end{bmatrix} \begin{bmatrix} \mathbf{y}_{1t} \\ \mathbf{y}_{2t} \end{bmatrix} = \begin{bmatrix} \boldsymbol{\varepsilon}_{1t} \\ \boldsymbol{\varepsilon}_{2t} \end{bmatrix}. \tag{11.5.18}$$

Let

$$\mathbf{A}(L) = [\mathbf{C}_1^*(L) \quad \mathbf{C}_2^*(L)] \begin{bmatrix} \mathbf{I}_r & \mathbf{0} \\ \mathbf{0} & \nabla \mathbf{I}_{n-r} \end{bmatrix} \begin{bmatrix} \mathbf{I}_r & -\mathbf{B} \\ \mathbf{0} & \mathbf{I}_{n-r} \end{bmatrix}, \tag{11.5.19}$$

and write

$$\mathbf{A}(L) = \mathbf{A}(1)L + (1 - L)\mathbf{A}^*(L), \tag{11.5.20}$$

which can always be done by equating coefficients for powers of L. Then $|\mathbf{A}^*(L)| = 0$ has roots lying outside the unit circle and

$$\mathbf{A}(1) = \mathbf{C}_1^*(1)[\mathbf{I}_r, -\mathbf{B}]. \tag{11.5.21}$$

Substituting (11.5.20) and (11.5.21) into (11.5.19) yields:[7]

$$\mathbf{A}^*(L)\nabla \mathbf{y}_t = \boldsymbol{\Pi}\mathbf{y}_{t-1} + \boldsymbol{\varepsilon}_t, \tag*{*(11.5.22)}$$

where

$$\boldsymbol{\Pi} = -\mathbf{C}_1^*(1)[\mathbf{I}_r, -\mathbf{B}]. \tag*{*(11.5.23)}$$

Equation (11.5.22) is called the *Granger representation theorem*, as discussed in Engle and Granger (1987). The left-hand side of (11.5.22) is a vector autoregression in the changes in $\mathbf{y}_t$, which are therefore $I(0)$. The right-hand side of (11.5.22) must be $I(0)$, too. This implies that $[\mathbf{I}_r - \mathbf{B}]\mathbf{y}_t$ must be stationary. Furthermore, because $\mathbf{C}(L)$ has full rank for all values of L within or on the unit circle, $\mathbf{C}_1^*(1)$ is of full column rank, here equal to r. Therefore, $[\mathbf{I}_r - \mathbf{B}]$ must be equal to the matrix of cointegrating vectors $\boldsymbol{\Gamma}^*$.

Viewing $\boldsymbol{\Gamma}^*\mathbf{y}_t = \mathbf{z}_t$ as errors reflecting the deviation from the equilibrium,[8] (11.5.22) may be viewed as an *error-correction model* as in Sargan (1964), Hendry and von Ungern–Sternberg (1981), and others, in which the error $\mathbf{z}_{t-1}$ is partially corrected in the next period by setting $\mathbf{y}_t$ according to (11.5.22). The implication of the Granger representation theorem (11.5.22) is that if there is no cointegration, the error correction term does

[7]Note that by rearranging (11.5.20) in an alternative equivalent form $\mathbf{A}(L) = \mathbf{A}(1)L^s + (1 - L)\tilde{\mathbf{A}}(L)$, any set of lags of the $\mathbf{y}$ can be written in the form (11.5.22), thus allowing any type of gradual adjustment toward a new equilibrium.

[8]Note that the equilibrium concept used here is different from the concept used by theorists. Here, it means an observed relationship among variables.

not enter the model. Similarly, if it is assumed that the data follow a vector autoregression in the differences, it is implicitly assumed that there is no cointegration.

11.5.3 Determination of Cointegration Rank

The formulations (11.5.10), (11.5.14), and (11.5.15) assume that the cointegration rank or the variables belonging to the common trends, $\mathbf{y}_{2t}$, are known. In practice, this is rarely the case. Nevertheless, whether the variables are cointegrated has important implications with regard to empirical modeling of time-series processes. Therefore, a series of testing strategies has been proposed. A popular approach is through *residual-based tests*. The basic idea behind these tests is that if the variables are cointegrated $CI(1, 1)$, the residuals calculated from regressions among the variables should be stationary. Tests are designed on the null hypothesis of no cointegration by testing the null that there is a unit root in the residuals against the alternative that the root is less than unity. If the null of a unit root is rejected, the null of no cointegration is also rejected.

The approach begins with the fact that, if $\mathbf{y}_t \sim CI(1, 1)$, any cointegrating variable may be used as the dependent variable in the regression. The reason is that the error process in the regression is $I(0)$ while the variables are $I(1)$ (or higher). That is, the means of the variables are time dependent and will go to infinity. In effect, the growth in the means of the variables swamps the (stationary) error process so that there is no need to require the regressors to be uncorrelated with the (stationary) error term. Arbitrarily selecting a normalization, regress one variable on the other, say y_{1t} on $y_{2t}, \ldots, y_{nt}$:

$$y_{1t} = \hat{\gamma}_2 y_{2t} + \cdots + \hat{\gamma}_n y_{nt} + \hat{u}_t. \tag{11.5.24}$$

If $\hat{\gamma}' = (1, -\hat{\gamma}_2, \ldots, -\hat{\gamma}_n) \neq \gamma'$, the residual $\hat{u}_t$ will be nonstationary and hence will have a very large variance in any finite sample. If $\hat{\gamma} \simeq \gamma$, the estimated variance of $\hat{u}_t$ will be much smaller. The least squares method selects $\hat{\gamma}$ to minimize the variance of $\hat{u}_t$, and it will be extremely good in picking out the cointegrating vector γ if there is cointegration. In fact, Stock (1987) has shown that if $\mathbf{y} \sim CI(1, 1)$, the least squares estimate $\hat{\gamma}$ converges to γ at the speed of T^{-1} rather than the speed of $T^{-1/2}$ for the usual case of stationary regressors (see Chapters 4 and 5).

In other words, if there is cointegration, the residuals $\hat{u}_t$ of (11.5.24) will be stationary. If not, the regression is spurious, as discussed in Granger and Newbold (1974) and Phillips (1986), and the residuals should still have a unit root. Therefore, tests for no cointegration can be formulated using the regression coefficients of $\hat{u}_t$ on $\hat{u}_{t-1}$ of (6.5.17) and/or (6.5.18). However, because the least squares method selects $\hat{\gamma}$ to minimize the variance of the residual series $\hat{u}_t$, even if the variables are not cointegrated, the least squares residuals will look stationary more often than an integrated series $I(1)$. Thus the Dickey–Fuller–Phillips test statistics in (6.5.17) and (6.5.18) may reject the null hypothesis of nonstationarity more often than the significance levels suggested in Tables 8.5.1 of Fuller (1976). To correct for this downward bias, Engle and Granger (1987) and Phillips and Quliaris (1990) have provided the empirical distribution of these tests using Monte Carlo methods.

The residual-based tests are simple to implement and hence are convenient tools to detect the presence of cointegration relations. However, they cannot be used to test for the rank of the cointegration matrix. Other approaches have to be used. For instance, Stock and

Watson (1988) have suggested a *common stochastic trends test*, which exploits the property of the reduced rank of the moving average representation of the cointegrated variables. Johansen (1988, 1991a,b) has suggested a *likelihood ratio test* in a vector autoregressive framework. These tests have the advantage that they may be employed to test for the presence of r linearly independent cointegrating vectors against $r-1$ cointegrating vectors for $r \geq 1$.

Johansen begins by expressing $\mathbf{y}_t$ as an unrestricted vector autoregressive model:

$$\mathbf{y}_t = \sum_{j=1}^{p} \mathbf{A}_j \mathbf{y}_{t-j} + \boldsymbol{\mu} + \boldsymbol{\varepsilon}_t, \tag{11.5.25}$$

where each $\mathbf{A}_j$ is $n \times n$, $\boldsymbol{\mu}$ is an $n \times 1$ vector of constant, and the roots of $| \mathbf{I} - \sum_{j=1}^{p} \mathbf{A}_j z^j | = 0$ are either 1 or outside the unit circle. Reparametrizing the system (11.5.25) in error correction form yields:

$$\nabla \mathbf{y}_t = \boldsymbol{\Pi} \mathbf{y}_{t-1} + \sum_{j=1}^{p-1} \mathbf{A}_j^* \nabla \mathbf{y}_{t-j} + \boldsymbol{\mu} + \boldsymbol{\varepsilon}_t, \tag{11.5.26}$$

where

$$\mathbf{A}_j^* = -\sum_{l=j+1}^{p} \mathbf{A}_l, \qquad j = 1, \ldots, p-1, \tag{11.5.27}$$

and

$$\boldsymbol{\Pi} = \sum_{j=1}^{p} \mathbf{A}_j - \mathbf{I}. \tag{11.5.28}$$

Comparing (11.5.26) with (11.5.23), it follows that the hypothesis of cointegration is defined as:

$$H_r\!: \boldsymbol{\Pi} = \mathbf{Q}\mathbf{J}', \tag{11.5.29}$$

where $\mathbf{Q}$ and $\mathbf{J}$ are $n \times r$ matrices. The hypothesis H_r specifies that the rank of $\boldsymbol{\Pi}$ is less than or equal to r. Furthermore, the hypotheses $H_0, \ldots, H_n$ are nested, with $H_0 \subset H_1 \subset \cdots \subset H_{n-1}$. Using the results in Brownian motion theory, Johansen derived the asymptotic distribution of the likelihood ratio statistics of (11.5.51) and (11.5.52), to be shown in Section 11.5.4. These distribution are tabulated by simulation, as discussed in Johansen and Juselius (1988) and Johansen (1991a).

11.5.4 Estimation and Prediction

There is a vast literature on how best to estimate a cointegrated system.[9] In general, the alternative approaches may be classified in terms of whether unit root restrictions are imposed or not. In the case that unit root restrictions are not imposed, the system can be estimated using a vector autoregression or a vector autoregressive-moving average model. Chan and Wei (1988), Park and Phillips (1989), and Sims, Stock, and Watson (1990) provide detailed studies of the asymptotics in this case. Since, as discussed in Phillips (1991), when unit roots are implicitly estimated in an unrestricted regression, this has nontrivial effects on the asymptotic theory of inference, this section is concerned only with the estimation of cointegrated systems when the unit root restrictions are imposed.

[9]See Phillips and Loretan (1991) for a general discussion.

In the case that the unit root restrictions are imposed, the cointegrating vector can be estimated using the Granger representation theorem (11.5.22).[10] However, this is not easy to implement because there is the cross-equation restriction that the same parameters occur in the level parts of all the equations. One way to simplify the computation is to use the two-step procedure suggested by Engle and Granger (1987). In the first step the least squares method is used to regress one level variable, say y_{1t}, on other level variables, say, $y_{2t}, \ldots, y_{nt}$. In the second step, $\mathbf{A}^*(L)$ and $\mathbf{C}_1^*(1)$ are estimated using the residuals from the first step regression in lieu of $(\mathbf{I}_r - \mathbf{B})\mathbf{y}_{t-1}$ in the error correction representation (11.5.22) as the explanatory variables. The two-step procedure transforms models that are nonlinear in parameters into two separate stages with separate parameters entering into separate stages linearly. The two-step method for estimating $\mathbf{A}^*(L)$ and $\mathbf{C}_1^*$ is asymptotically fully efficient because the estimate of the cointegrating vector $\mathbf{B}$ converges sufficiently rapidly to its true value (at the speed of $1/T$) that it can be taken as the true coefficient for estimation of the remaining coefficients in $\mathbf{A}^*(L)$ and $\mathbf{C}_1^*(1)$ (Stock, 1987). Furthermore, conditional on $(\mathbf{I}_r - \mathbf{B})$ all the variables in (11.5.22) are stationary, so tests for hypotheses on the coefficients in an error correction system can be conducted using conventional χ^2 tests (Johansen and Juselius, 1988; Phillips, 1991).

Although the least squares estimate of $\mathbf{B}$ converges to $\mathbf{B}$ at the speed of $1/T$, it was also shown by Phillips (1991) that the unit roots in $\mathbf{y}_{2t}$ and the endogeneity of the regressor $\mathbf{y}_{2t}$ induce asymptotic bias, asymmetry, and nuisance parameters into the limit distribution. In other words, even though the consistency of the estimates is unaffected, these effects do make the least squares estimator of $\mathbf{B}$ a poor candidate in finite samples. To remove the dependencies of the limit distribution on the serial correlation in the error and endogeneity of the regressor, Park (1992) and Phillips and Hansen (1990), generalizing an idea of Phillips (1991), have suggested a two-step procedure. The first step is to use the least squares regression of $\mathbf{y}_{1t}$ on $\mathbf{y}_{2t}$ to obtain an initial estimate of $\mathbf{B}$ and to derive the estimated residuals $\hat{\mathbf{u}}_t' = (\hat{\mathbf{u}}_{1t}, \hat{\mathbf{u}}_{2t})$ using (11.5.14) and (11.5.15); then use $\hat{\mathbf{u}}_t'$ to estimate the long-run covariance matrix, $\mathbf{\Omega}$, where:

$$\begin{aligned}\mathbf{\Omega} &= E(\mathbf{u}_t\mathbf{u}_t') + \sum_{k=1}^{\infty} E(\mathbf{u}_t\mathbf{u}_{t+k}') + \sum_{k=1}^{\infty} E(\mathbf{u}_{t+k}\mathbf{u}_t') \\ &= \begin{pmatrix} \Omega_{11} & \Omega_{12} \\ \Omega_{21} & \Omega_{22} \end{pmatrix}.\end{aligned} \tag{11.5.30}$$

The correction for endogeneity of $\mathbf{y}_{2t}$ is achieved by constructing:

$$\mathbf{y}_{1t}^* = \mathbf{y}_{1t} - \hat{\Omega}_{12}\hat{\Omega}_{22}^{-1}\nabla\mathbf{y}_{2t}. \tag{11.5.31}$$

However, (11.5.31) does not eliminate the dependence of $\mathbf{u}_{1t}$ in (11.5.14) on the error process that drives the regressor $\mathbf{y}_{2t}$ as shown by (11.5.15). Thus a second-step fully modified estimator that employs both exogeneity and serial correlation corrections is defined as:

$$\mathbf{B}^+ = \left[\sum \mathbf{y}_{1t}^*\mathbf{y}_{2t}' - T\hat{\boldsymbol{\delta}}^+\right]\left[\sum \mathbf{y}_{2t}\mathbf{y}_{2t}'\right]^{-1}, \tag{11.5.32}$$

where

$$\hat{\boldsymbol{\delta}}^+ = \left[\mathbf{I} - \hat{\mathbf{\Omega}}_{12}\hat{\mathbf{\Omega}}_{22}^{-1}\right]\hat{\mathbf{\Delta}}, \tag{11.5.33}$$

and $\hat{\mathbf{\Delta}}$ is a consistent estimate of:

[10] The error correction formulation (11.5.22) eliminates unit roots by construction.

$$\mathbf{\Delta} = \sum_{k=0}^{\infty} E(\mathbf{u}_{t+k}\mathbf{u}'_t). \tag{11.5.34}$$

The two-step estimator $\mathbf{B}^+$ has the same asymptotic behavior as the full-system maximum likelihood estimator.

The long-run covariance matrix $\mathbf{\Omega}$ or $\mathbf{\Delta}$ can be obtained using either a spectral estimator or the approach suggested by Andrews (1991) and Andrews and Monahan (1990). In the Andrews procedure, suppose that $\mathbf{v}_t$ is an $m \times 1$ vector whose long-run covariance matrix is given by $\mathbf{\Omega}$.

1. Prewhiten $\mathbf{v}_t$ by a finite vector autoregression:

$$\mathbf{v}_t = \sum_{j=1}^{b} \hat{\mathbf{H}}_j \mathbf{v}_{t-j} + \hat{\boldsymbol{\eta}}_t, \qquad t = b+1, \ldots, T, \tag{11.5.35}$$

where $\hat{\mathbf{H}}_j$ are $m \times m$ parameter estimates and $\hat{\boldsymbol{\eta}}_t$ are the corresponding residuals.

2. Use an automatic bandwidth for a kernel estimator of the heteroskedastic–autocorrelation covariance matrix:

$$\hat{\mathbf{\Omega}}^*(a_T) = \sum_{j=-T+1}^{T-1} k\left(\frac{j}{a_T}\right)\mathbf{G}(j), \tag{11.5.36}$$

$$\mathbf{G}(j) = \begin{cases} T^{-1} \sum_{t=j+1}^{T} \hat{\boldsymbol{\eta}}_t \hat{\boldsymbol{\eta}}'_{t-j} & \text{for } j \geq 0, \\ T^{-1} \sum_{t=-j+1}^{T} \hat{\boldsymbol{\eta}}_{t-j} \hat{\boldsymbol{\eta}}'_t & \text{for } j < 0, \end{cases} \tag{11.5.37}$$

where a_T is the data-dependent (automatic) bandwidth and $k(\cdot)$ is the real-valued quadratic spectral kernel:

$$k(x) = \frac{25}{12\pi^2 x^2}\left\{\frac{\sin(6\pi x/5) - \cos(6\pi x/5)}{6\pi x/5}\right\}. \tag{11.5.38}$$

3. Recolor to obtain the estimate of the long-run covariance matrix:

$$\hat{\mathbf{\Omega}} = \hat{\mathbf{D}}\hat{\mathbf{\Omega}}^*(a_T)\hat{\mathbf{D}}' \quad \text{and} \quad \hat{\mathbf{D}} = \left[\mathbf{I}_p - \sum_{j=1}^{b} \hat{\mathbf{H}}_j\right]^{-1}. \tag{11.5.39}$$

Johansen (1988, 1991a,b), on the other hand, has suggested a maximum likelihood estimator in the time domain. The method begins by expressing the data generation process in a vector autoregressive model, written in the error correction form (11.5.22), where $\mathbf{\Pi}$ is subject to the constraint (11.5.23). Since $\mathbf{C}_1^*(1)\mathbf{\Lambda}^{-1}\mathbf{\Lambda}[\mathbf{I}_r - \mathbf{B}] = \mathbf{\Pi}$ is unchanged with any $r \times r$ nonsingular matrix $\mathbf{\Lambda}$, for simplicity, $\mathbf{\Pi}$ is written as in (11.5.29), where $\mathbf{Q}$ and $\mathbf{J}$ are $n \times r$ matrices of rank r. Note that only the space spanned by the columns of $\mathbf{J}$ and $\mathbf{Q}$ can be estimated.

If $\boldsymbol{\varepsilon}$ are independently normally distributed with zero mean and covariance matrix $\mathbf{\Omega}$, and $\mathbf{QJ}'$ were known, the model becomes:

$$\mathbf{z}_{0t} = \mathbf{A}\mathbf{z}_{1t} + \mathbf{QJ}'\mathbf{z}_{2t} + \boldsymbol{\varepsilon}_t, \tag{11.5.40}$$

where $\mathbf{z}_{0t} = \nabla\mathbf{y}_t$, $\mathbf{z}_{2t} = \mathbf{y}_{t-1}$, and $\mathbf{z}_{1t} = (\nabla\mathbf{y}'_{t-1}, \nabla\mathbf{y}'_{t-2}, \ldots, \nabla\mathbf{y}'_{t-p+1}, 1)'$ and $\mathbf{A} = (\mathbf{A}_1^*, \ldots, \mathbf{A}_{p-1}^*, \boldsymbol{\mu})$. Given $\mathbf{Q}$ and $\mathbf{J}$, the maximum likelihood estimates of $\mathbf{A}$ could be obtained by the least squares method:

$$\hat{\mathbf{A}} = (\mathbf{M}_{01} - \mathbf{QJ}'\mathbf{M}_{21})\mathbf{M}_{11}^{-1}, \tag{11.5.41}$$

where $\mathbf{M}_{ij} = T^{-1}\sum_{t=1}^{T} \mathbf{z}_{it}\mathbf{z}'_{jt}$, $i, j = 0, 1, 2$. Concentrating the likelihood function with respect to **A** yields:

$$L(\mathbf{Q}, \mathbf{J}, \mathbf{\Omega}) = |\, \mathbf{\Omega} \,|^{-T/2} \exp\left\{-\frac{1}{2}\sum_{t=1}^{T}(\mathbf{R}_{0t} - \mathbf{QJ}'\mathbf{R}_{2t})'\mathbf{\Omega}^{-1}(\mathbf{R}_{0t} - \mathbf{QJ}'\mathbf{R}_{2t})\right\}, \tag{11.5.42}$$

where

$$\mathbf{R}_{it} = \mathbf{z}_{it} - \mathbf{M}_{i1}\mathbf{M}_{11}^{-1}\mathbf{z}_{1t}, \qquad i = 0, 1, 2. \tag{11.5.43}$$

For fixed **J**, this function is easily maximized to give:

$$\hat{\mathbf{Q}}(\mathbf{J}) = \mathbf{S}_{02}\mathbf{J}(\mathbf{J}'\mathbf{S}_{22}\mathbf{J})^{-1}, \tag{11.5.44}$$

where

$$\hat{\mathbf{\Omega}}(\mathbf{J}) = \mathbf{S}_{00} - \mathbf{S}_{02}\mathbf{J}(\mathbf{J}'\mathbf{S}_{22}\mathbf{J})^{-1}\mathbf{J}'\mathbf{S}_{20}, \text{ and} \tag{11.5.45}$$

$$\mathbf{S}_{ij} = \mathbf{M}_{ij} - \mathbf{M}_{i1}\mathbf{M}_{11}^{-1}\mathbf{M}_{1j}. \tag{11.5.46}$$

Substituting (11.5.44) and (11.5.45) into (11.5.42) yields:

$$\begin{aligned} L(\mathbf{J}) &= |\hat{\mathbf{\Omega}}(\mathbf{J})|^{-T/2} \\ &= \left|\mathbf{S}_{00} - \mathbf{S}_{02}\mathbf{J}(\mathbf{J}'\mathbf{S}_{22}\mathbf{J})^{-1}\mathbf{J}'\mathbf{S}_{20}\right|^{-T/2}. \end{aligned} \tag{11.5.47}$$

It was shown by Anderson (1951) that maximizing (11.5.47) subject to the normalization condition:

$$\mathbf{J}'\mathbf{S}_{22}\mathbf{J} = \mathbf{I}_r \tag{11.5.48}$$

yields $\hat{\mathbf{J}} = (\hat{\mathbf{j}}_1, \ldots, \hat{\mathbf{j}}_r)$ as the first r eigenvectors of equations:

$$|\, \lambda\mathbf{S}_{22} - \mathbf{S}_{20}\mathbf{S}_{00}^{-1}\mathbf{S}_{02} \,| = 0, \tag{11.5.49}$$

that are ordered by $\hat{\lambda}_1 > \hat{\lambda}_2 > \cdots > \hat{\lambda}_n > 0$. The maximized likelihood function is then equal to:

$$\hat{L} = |\, \mathbf{S}_{00} \,|^{-T/2}\left[\Pi_{i=1}^{r}\left(1 - \hat{\lambda}_i\right)\right]^{-T/2}. \tag{11.5.50}$$

In other words, the maximum likelihood estimates of **A**, **Π**, and **Ω** are obtained by first solving (11.5.49) for eigenvalues $\hat{\lambda}_1 > \cdots > \hat{\lambda}_r > 0$ and eigenvectors $\hat{\mathbf{j}}_1, \ldots, \hat{\mathbf{j}}_r$. Then let $\hat{\mathbf{J}} = (\hat{\mathbf{j}}_1, \ldots, \hat{\mathbf{j}}_r)$. and substitute it into (11.5.44) and (11.5.45) to obtain $\hat{\mathbf{Q}}$ and $\hat{\mathbf{\Omega}}$. Substituting $\hat{\mathbf{Q}}$ and $\hat{\mathbf{J}}$ into (11.5.41) yields the maximum likelihood estimates of **A**.

The Johansen procedure can also be used to test the rank of the cointegration spaces. The likelihood ratio test statistics of the hypotheses H_r versus H_{r+1} (i.e., r versus $r+1$ cointegrating vectors) or H_n (i.e., at most r cointegrating vectors), as suggested by Johansen (1991a), are given by:

$$H_r \text{ versus } H_{r+1}\text{:} -T\log\left(1 - \hat{\lambda}_{r+1}\right), \text{ and} \tag*{*(11.5.51)}$$

$$H_r \text{ versus } H_n\text{:} -T\sum_{i=r+1}^{n}\log\left(1 - \hat{\lambda}_i\right), \tag*{*(11.5.52)}$$

respectively. Unfortunately, the limiting distribution of (11.5.51) or (11.5.52) is nonstandard. Critical values of the test statistic will have to be derived through Monte Carlo studies (Johansen, 1991a).

The implication of $CI(1, 1)$ for forecasting is apparent from the fact that each component of $\mathbf{y}_t$ is an integrated series but $\mathbf{\Gamma y}_t$ is stationary. As discussed in Section 6.7, the standard error of a v-period-ahead forecast of an integrated series increases with v. On the other hand, the v-period-ahead forecast error of a cointegrating linear combination approaches a finite limit as v increases. The vector of v-step-ahead forecasts will, for large v, obey the linear restrictions $\mathbf{\Gamma}\hat{\mathbf{y}}_{t+v} = \mathbf{0}$. In other words, the forecasts of levels of cointegrated variables will "hang together," whereas forecasts produced in some other way, such as by a group of individual univariate Box–Jenkins models, may well not do so. For further details, see Engle and Yoo (1989).

11.6 RELATIONSHIPS BETWEEN TIME-SERIES MODELS AND STRUCTURAL ECONOMETRIC MODELS

In this section we demonstrate the relationships between various time-series models and structural econometric models. For further details, see Hsiao (1992). Let $\mathbf{w}_t$ be an $n \times 1$ vector of random variables, $t = 1, \ldots, T$. Under fairly general conditions, there exists an autoregressive representation:

$$\mathbf{\Phi}(L)\mathbf{w}_t = \boldsymbol{\varepsilon}_t, \tag{11.6.1}$$

where $\boldsymbol{\varepsilon}_t$ is an $n \times 1$ vector of independently, identically distributed random variables with mean zero and covariance matrix $\mathbf{I}_n$. The $n \times n$ autoregressive operator $\mathbf{\Phi}(L)$ can be further factored into the form:[11]

$$\mathbf{\Phi}(L) = \mathbf{U}(L)\mathbf{M}(L)\mathbf{V}(L), \tag{11.6.2}$$

where $\mathbf{M}(L)$ is an $n \times n$ diagonal matrix, and either $\mathbf{U}(L)$ and $\mathbf{V}(L)$ are $n \times n$ matrices that are nonsingular constant matrices or the roots of $| U(L) | = 0$ and $| V(L) | = 0$ lie outside the unit circle.

If $\mathbf{w}_t$ is stationary, $\mathbf{M}(L)$ equals an $n \times n$ identity matrix. If $\mathbf{w}_t$ is integrated of order 1, $\mathbf{M}(L) = \nabla\mathbf{I}_n = (1 - L)\mathbf{I}_n$, and

$$\begin{aligned}\mathbf{\Phi}(L) &= \mathbf{U}(L)\mathbf{M}(L)\mathbf{V}(L)\\ &= (1 - L)\mathbf{U}(L)\mathbf{V}(L),\end{aligned} \tag{11.6.3}$$

with $\mathbf{\Phi}(1) = \mathbf{0}$ and $\mathbf{\Phi}^*(L) = \mathbf{U}(L)\mathbf{V}(L)$. The roots of $| \mathbf{\Phi}^*(L) | = 0$ lie outside the unit circle. Multiplying $\mathbf{U}(L)^{-1}$ on both sides of (11.6.1) yields the multivariate autoregressive–moving average representation:

$$\mathbf{V}(L)\nabla^d\mathbf{w}_t = \mathbf{\Theta}(L)\boldsymbol{\varepsilon}_t, \qquad d \geq 0, \tag{11.6.4}$$

where

$$\mathbf{\Theta}(L) = \mathbf{U}(L)^{-1}, \tag{11.6.5}$$

[11] Any rectangular polynomial matrix can be transformed into a *canonical diagonal matrix* by elementary row and column operations as demonstrated in Gantmacher (1959, vol. I, pp. 139–141). Yoo (1986) then factors the diagonal matrix of rational polynomials into a component with roots on or within the unit circle and a component whose roots lie outside the unit circle. The latter has an inverse and is combined with the row and column transformation matrices (which are unimodular) to achieve the form (11.6.2).

and the roots of the determinantal equations $|\mathbf{V}(z)| = 0$ and $|\boldsymbol{\Theta}(z)| = 0$ lie outside the unit circle.

Solving (11.6.5) for $\nabla^d \mathbf{w}_t$ yields:

$$\nabla^d \mathbf{w}_t = \mathbf{V}(L)^{-1}\boldsymbol{\Theta}(L)\boldsymbol{\varepsilon}_t, \tag{11.6.6}$$

$$\nabla^d \mathbf{w}_t = |\mathbf{V}(L)|^{-1}\mathbf{V}^*(L)\boldsymbol{\Theta}(L)\boldsymbol{\varepsilon}_t, \tag{11.6.7}$$

where $\mathbf{V}^*(L)$ is the adjoint matrix associated with $\mathbf{V}(L)$ and $|\mathbf{V}(L)|$ is the determinant, which is a scalar, finite polynomial in L. Equation (11.6.6) or (11.6.7) expresses $\nabla^d \mathbf{w}_t$ as an infinite MA process that can be equivalently expressed as a system of finite-order ARIMA equations:

$$|\mathbf{V}(L)|\nabla^d \mathbf{w}_t = \mathbf{V}^*(L)\boldsymbol{\Theta}(L)\boldsymbol{\varepsilon}_t. \tag{11.6.8}$$

The hth equation of (11.6.8) is given by:

$$|\mathbf{V}(L)|\nabla^d w_{ht} = \boldsymbol{\delta}_h'(L)\boldsymbol{\varepsilon}_t, \tag{11.6.9}$$

where $\boldsymbol{\delta}_h'(L)$ is the hth row of $\mathbf{V}^*(L)\boldsymbol{\Theta}(L)$.

As pointed out by Zellner and Palm (1974):

1. Each equation in (11.6.8) is an ARIMA form. Thus the univariate ARIMA processes are compatible with some, perhaps unknown, joint process for a set of random variables.
2. The order and parameters of the autoregressive part of each equation $|\mathbf{V}(L)|\nabla^d \mathbf{w}_{ht}$, $h = 1, \ldots, g$, will usually be the same except for the case where there exist common roots between $|\mathbf{V}(L)|$ and $\boldsymbol{\delta}_h'(L)$.
3. The equations of (11.6.9) are in the form of a restricted seemingly unrelated autoregressive model with correlated moving average processes.

For ease of exposition, consider the case $d = 1$; that is, $\mathbf{w}_t$ is $I(1)$. Partition $\nabla \mathbf{w}_t'$ into $(\nabla \mathbf{y}_t', \nabla \mathbf{x}_t')$ and partition $\mathbf{V}(L)$, $\boldsymbol{\Theta}(L)$ and $\boldsymbol{\varepsilon}_t$ correspondingly, so (11.6.4) can be written:

$$\begin{bmatrix} \mathbf{V}_{11}(L) & \mathbf{V}_{12}(L) \\ \mathbf{V}_{21}(L) & \mathbf{V}_{22}(L) \end{bmatrix} \begin{bmatrix} \nabla \mathbf{y}_t \\ \nabla \mathbf{x}_t \end{bmatrix} = \begin{pmatrix} \boldsymbol{\Theta}_{11}(L) & \boldsymbol{\Theta}_{12}(L) \\ \boldsymbol{\Theta}_{21}(L) & \boldsymbol{\Theta}_{22}(L) \end{pmatrix} \begin{pmatrix} \boldsymbol{\varepsilon}_{1t} \\ \boldsymbol{\varepsilon}_{2t} \end{pmatrix}. \tag*{*(11.6.10)}$$

If

$$\mathbf{V}_{21}(L) \equiv \mathbf{0} \quad \text{and} \quad \boldsymbol{\Theta}_{21} = \mathbf{0}, \tag{11.6.11}$$

$\mathbf{y}_t$ does not Granger cause $\mathbf{x}_t$. If either or both

$$\mathbf{V}_{12}(L) \neq \mathbf{0} \quad \text{or/and} \quad \boldsymbol{\Theta}_{12}(L) \neq \mathbf{0}, \tag{11.6.12}$$

$\mathbf{x}_t$ Granger causes $\mathbf{y}_t$. If, in addition to (11.6.11),

$$\boldsymbol{\Theta}_{12}(L) \equiv \mathbf{0} \tag{11.6.13}$$

also holds, the elements of $\boldsymbol{\varepsilon}_{1t}$ do not affect the elements of $\nabla \mathbf{x}_t$, and the elements of $\boldsymbol{\varepsilon}_{2t}$ affect the elements of $\mathbf{y}_t$ only through the elements of $\mathbf{x}_t$. Then $\mathbf{x}_t$ can be viewed as exogenous variables in the conventional sense and (11.6.10) is in the form of a dynamic simultaneous-equation model with endogenous vector $\nabla \mathbf{y}_t$ generated by:

$$\mathbf{V}_{11}(L)\nabla \mathbf{y}_t + \mathbf{V}_{12}(L)\nabla \mathbf{x}_t = \boldsymbol{\Theta}_{11}(L)\boldsymbol{\varepsilon}_{1t}, \tag*{*(11.6.14)}$$

or

$$\sum_{r=0}^{p} \mathbf{V}_{11,r} L^r \nabla \mathbf{y}_t + \sum_{r=0}^{p} \mathbf{V}_{12,r} L^r \nabla \mathbf{x}_t = \sum_{r=0}^{q} \mathbf{\Theta}_{11,r} L^r \boldsymbol{\varepsilon}_{1t}, \qquad *(11.6.15)$$

where p and q denote the maximum order in the matrix polynomials $\mathbf{V}(L)$ and $\mathbf{\Theta}(L)$, respectively. The $\mathbf{V}_{11}(L)$ and $\mathbf{V}_{12}(L)$ in (11.6.14) would correspond to $\mathbf{\Gamma}(L)$ and $\mathbf{B}(L)$ in (11.2.1), respectively. The vector $\nabla \mathbf{x}_t$ in (11.6.14) is treated as exogenous variables and is assumed to be generated by the ARIMA process:

$$\mathbf{V}_{22}(L) \nabla \mathbf{x}_t = \mathbf{\Theta}_{22}(L) \boldsymbol{\varepsilon}_{2t}. \qquad (11.6.16)$$

Under the assumption that $\mathbf{V}_{11,0}$ is of full rank, the reduced form of $\nabla \mathbf{y}_t$ can be derived as functions of the lagged endogenous and current and lagged exogenous variables in difference form:

$$\nabla \mathbf{y}_t = -\mathbf{V}_{11,0}^{-1} \sum_{r=1}^{p} \mathbf{V}_{11,r} L^r \nabla \mathbf{y}_t - \mathbf{V}_{11,0}^{-1} \sum_{r=0}^{p} \mathbf{V}_{12,r} L^r \nabla \mathbf{x}_t + \mathbf{V}_{11,0}^{-1} \sum_{r=0}^{q} \mathbf{\Theta}_{11,r} \boldsymbol{\varepsilon}_{1t}. \qquad (11.6.17)$$

The "final form" of Theil and Boot (1962) (or "transfer function" of Box–Jenkins) is obtained by multiplying (11.6.14) by $\mathbf{V}_{11}(L)^{-1}$:

$$\nabla \mathbf{y}_t = -\mathbf{V}_{11}(L)^{-1} \mathbf{V}_{12}(L) \nabla \mathbf{x}_t + \mathbf{V}_{11}(L)^{-1} \mathbf{\Theta}_{11}(L) \boldsymbol{\varepsilon}_{1t}. \qquad *(11.6.18)$$

Here each endogenous variable is expressed as an infinite distributed lag function of exogenous variables. Noting that $\mathbf{V}_{11}(L)^{-1} = |\, \mathbf{V}_{11}(L) \,|^{-1} \mathbf{V}_{11}^*(L)$, where $\mathbf{V}_{11}^*(L)$ is the adjoint matrix of $\mathbf{V}_{11}(L)$, the Box–Jenkins (1970) transfer function is derived as:

$$|\, \mathbf{V}_{11}(L) \,| \nabla \mathbf{y}_t = -\mathbf{V}_{11}^*(L) \mathbf{V}_{12}(L) \nabla \mathbf{x}_t + \mathbf{V}_{11}^*(L) \mathbf{\Theta}_{11}(L) \boldsymbol{\varepsilon}_t, \qquad (11.6.19)$$

where each equation relates a given endogenous variable to its own past values and to the exogenous variables, but to no other endogenous variables, whether current or past. As in (11.6.6), the endogenous variables in $\mathbf{y}_t$ have autoregressive parts with identical order and parameters unless there is a cancellation of common factors.

If $\mathbf{w}_t$ are cointegrated with the rank of cointegrating matrix $\mathbf{\Gamma}$ equal to r (namely, $\mathbf{\Gamma w}_t = \mathbf{u}_t$ is stationary), then as shown in (11.5.18),

$$\mathbf{M}(L) = \begin{pmatrix} \mathbf{I}_r & \mathbf{0} \\ \mathbf{0} & \nabla \mathbf{I}_{n-r} \end{pmatrix}. \qquad (11.6.20)$$

Partition $\mathbf{U}(L)$ and $\mathbf{V}(L)$ correspondingly; (11.6.1) and (11.6.2) now take the form

$$\begin{bmatrix} \mathbf{U}_{11}(L) & \mathbf{U}_{12}(L) \\ \mathbf{U}_{21}(L) & \mathbf{U}_{22}(L) \end{bmatrix} \begin{bmatrix} \mathbf{I}_r & \mathbf{0} \\ \mathbf{0} & \nabla \mathbf{I}_{n-r} \end{bmatrix} \begin{bmatrix} \mathbf{V}_{11}(L) & \mathbf{V}_{12}(L) \\ \mathbf{V}_{21}(L) & \mathbf{V}_{22}(L) \end{bmatrix} \begin{bmatrix} \mathbf{w}_{1t} \\ \mathbf{w}_{2t} \end{bmatrix} = \begin{bmatrix} \boldsymbol{\varepsilon}_{1t} \\ \boldsymbol{\varepsilon}_{2t} \end{bmatrix}. \qquad (11.6.21)$$

Multiplying the last $n - r$ rows of (11.6.21) by $\mathbf{U}_{12}(L)\mathbf{U}_{22}(L)^{-1}$ and subtracting the resulting equations from the first r rows yields:

$$\begin{aligned} &\left[\mathbf{U}_{11}(L) - \mathbf{U}_{12}(L)\mathbf{U}_{22}(L)^{-1}\mathbf{U}_{21}(L)\right]\left[\mathbf{V}_{11}(L)\mathbf{w}_{1t} + \mathbf{V}_{12}(L)\nabla \mathbf{w}_{2t}\right] \\ &\qquad = \boldsymbol{\varepsilon}_{1t} - \mathbf{U}_{12}(L)\mathbf{U}_{22}^{-1}(L)\boldsymbol{\varepsilon}_{2t}. \end{aligned} \qquad (11.6.22)$$

Multiplying the first r rows of (11.6.21) by $\mathbf{U}_{21}(L)\mathbf{U}_{11}(L)^{-1}$ and subtracting the resulting equations from the last $n - r$ rows yields:

$$\begin{aligned} &\left[\mathbf{U}_{22}(L) - \mathbf{U}_{21}(L)\mathbf{U}_{11}(L)^{-1}\mathbf{U}_{12}(L)\right]\left[\mathbf{V}_{21}(L)\mathbf{w}_{1t} + \mathbf{V}_{22}(L)\mathbf{w}_{2t}\right] \\ &\qquad = \boldsymbol{\varepsilon}_{2t} - \mathbf{U}_{21}(L)\mathbf{U}_{11}(L)^{-1}\boldsymbol{\varepsilon}_{1t}. \end{aligned} \qquad (11.6.23)$$

Solving (11.6.22) for $\mathbf{w}_{1t}$ yields:

$$\mathbf{w}_{1t} = \mathbf{V}_{11}(L)^{-1}\{-\mathbf{V}_{12}(L)\mathbf{w}_{2t} + [\mathbf{U}_{11}(L) - \mathbf{U}_{12}(L)\mathbf{U}_{22}(L)^{-1}\mathbf{U}_{21}(L)]^{-1} \cdot [\boldsymbol{\varepsilon}_{1t} - \mathbf{U}_{12}(L)\mathbf{U}_{22}(L)^{-1}\boldsymbol{\varepsilon}_{2t}]\}. \tag{11.6.24}$$

Substituting (11.6.24) into (11.6.23) yields:

$$\begin{aligned}\nabla\mathbf{w}_{2t} &= [\mathbf{V}_{22}(L) - \mathbf{V}_{21}(L)\mathbf{V}_{11}(L)^{-1}\mathbf{V}_{12}(L)]^{-1} \\ &\quad \{[\mathbf{U}_{22}(L) - \mathbf{U}_{21}(L)\mathbf{U}_{11}(L)^{-1}\mathbf{U}_{12}(L)]^{-1} \\ &\quad \cdot [\boldsymbol{\varepsilon}_{2t} - \mathbf{U}_{21}(L)\mathbf{U}_{11}(L)^{-1}\boldsymbol{\varepsilon}_{1t}] - \mathbf{V}_{21}(L)\mathbf{V}_{11}(L)^{-1} \\ &\quad [\mathbf{U}_{11}(L) - \mathbf{U}_{12}(L)\mathbf{U}_{22}(L)^{-1}\mathbf{U}_{21}(L)]^{-1} \\ &\quad \cdot [\boldsymbol{\varepsilon}_{1t} - \mathbf{U}_{12}(L)\mathbf{U}_{22}(L)^{-1}\boldsymbol{\varepsilon}_{2t}]\} \\ &= \mathbf{u}_{2t},\end{aligned} \tag{11.6.25}$$

which is of the form (11.5.15) with $\mathbf{w}_{2t} = \mathbf{y}_{2t}$.

Rewrite

$$-\mathbf{V}_{11}(L)^{-1}\mathbf{V}_{12}(L) = \mathbf{B} + (1 - L)\mathbf{B}^*(L), \tag{11.6.26}$$

where

$$\mathbf{B} = -\mathbf{V}_{11}(1)^{-1}\mathbf{V}_{12}(1); \tag{11.6.27}$$

then

$$\mathbf{w}_{1t} = \mathbf{B}\mathbf{w}_{2t} + \mathbf{B}^*(L)\nabla\mathbf{w}_{2t} + \mathbf{V}_{11}(L)^{-1}[\mathbf{U}_{11}(L) - \mathbf{U}_{12}(L)\mathbf{U}_{22}(L)^{-1}\mathbf{U}_{21}(L)]^{-1} \cdot [\boldsymbol{\varepsilon}_{1t} - \mathbf{U}_{12}(L)\mathbf{U}_{22}(L)^{-1}\boldsymbol{\varepsilon}_{2t}]. \tag{11.6.28}$$

Then substituting (11.6.25) for $\nabla\mathbf{w}_{2t}$, (11.6.28) is of the form (11.5.14) with $\mathbf{w}_{1t} = \mathbf{y}_{1t}$, $\mathbf{w}_{2t} = \mathbf{y}_{2t}$, and

$$\mathbf{u}_{1t} = \mathbf{V}_{11}(L)^{-1}[\mathbf{U}_{11}(L) - \mathbf{U}_{12}(L)\mathbf{U}_{22}(L)^{-1}\mathbf{U}_{21}(L)]^{-1} \cdot [\boldsymbol{\varepsilon}_{1t} - \mathbf{U}_{12}(L)\mathbf{U}_{22}(L)^{-1}\boldsymbol{\varepsilon}_{2t}] + \mathbf{B}^*(L)\nabla\mathbf{u}_{2t}. \tag{11.6.29}$$

When

$$\mathbf{U}_{21}(L) \equiv 0 \quad \text{and} \quad \mathbf{V}_{21}(L) \equiv 0, \tag{11.6.30}$$

$\mathbf{w}_{1t}$ does not Granger cause $\mathbf{w}_{2t}$, and then

$$\nabla\mathbf{w}_{2t} \equiv \mathbf{V}_{22}(L)^{-1}\mathbf{U}_{22}(L)^{-1}\boldsymbol{\varepsilon}_{2t}. \tag*{*(11.6.31)}$$

For $\mathbf{w}_{2t}$ to be exogenous, in addition to (11.6.31),

$$\mathbf{U}_{12}(L) \equiv 0 \tag{11.6.32}$$

has to hold.[12] When both (11.6.31) and (11.6.32) hold, the system of (11.6.24) and (11.6.25) becomes:

$$\mathbf{V}_{11}(L)\mathbf{w}_{1t} + \mathbf{V}_{12}(L)\mathbf{w}_{2t} = \mathbf{U}_{11}(L)^{-1}\boldsymbol{\varepsilon}_{1t} \tag*{*(11.6.33)}$$

and (11.6.31). Let $\mathbf{w}_{1t} = \mathbf{y}_t, \mathbf{w}_{2t} = \mathbf{x}_t, \boldsymbol{\Gamma}(L) = \mathbf{V}_{11}(L)$, and $\mathbf{V}_{12}(L) = \mathbf{B}(L)$; then (11.6.33) is identical to the form of a dynamic simultaneous-equations model discussed in Section 9.2, with the process generating exogenous variables given by (11.6.31). If there exists prior in-

[12]This is the same condition as $\boldsymbol{\Theta}_{12}(L) \equiv \mathbf{0}$ in (11.6.13).

formation satisfying the conditions given in Sections 9.3 and 9.4, $\mathbf{V}_{11}(L)$ and $\mathbf{V}_{12}(L)$ can be identified and the long-run relationship between $\mathbf{y}$ and $\mathbf{x}$ is given by $\mathbf{V}_{11}(L)^{-1}\mathbf{V}_{12}(1)$, which is equal to $\mathbf{B}$ in (11.5.14).

To summarize, suppose that:

$$\mathbf{U}(L)\mathbf{M}(L)\mathbf{V}(L)\mathbf{w}_t = \boldsymbol{\varepsilon}_t. \tag{11.6.34}$$

If $\mathbf{w}_t$ is stationary, $\mathbf{M}(L) = \mathbf{I}_n$. If $\mathbf{w}_t \sim I(1)$, $\mathbf{M}(L) = \nabla\mathbf{I}_n$ and if $\mathbf{w}_t \sim CI(1, 1)$, $\mathbf{M}(L) = \begin{bmatrix} \mathbf{I}_r & \mathbf{0} \\ \mathbf{0} & \nabla\,\mathbf{I}_{n-r} \end{bmatrix}$, if there exist r linearly independently cointegrating vectors. If $\mathbf{U}_{21}(L) \equiv \mathbf{0}$ and $\mathbf{V}_{21}(L) \equiv \mathbf{0}$, there is no causality from $\mathbf{w}_{1t}$ to $\mathbf{w}_{2t}$. The variables $\mathbf{w}_{2t}$ can be viewed as exogenous variables if $\mathbf{U}_{21}(L) \equiv 0, \mathbf{V}_{21}(L) \equiv 0,$ and $\mathbf{U}_{12}(L) \equiv 0.$ If each element of $\mathbf{w}_t$ is not cointegrated, the dynamic simultaneous equations model has to be in first-differenced form (11.6.10). If $\mathbf{w}_t \sim CI(1, 1)$, the dynamic simultaneous equations form can be expressed using level variables as in (11.6.33). If prior information on $\mathbf{V}_{11}(L)$ and $\mathbf{V}_{12}(L)$ exists and satisfies the conditions given in Sections 9.3 and 9.4, the dynamic simultaneous equations model can be identified and the long-run relation between $\mathbf{y}$ and $\mathbf{x}$ is given by:

$$\mathbf{V}_{11}(L)\mathbf{y}_t + \mathbf{V}_{12}(L)\mathbf{x}_t = \mathbf{u}_{1t}. \tag*{*(11.6.35)}$$

PROBLEMS

11-A Find the cross-correlations and partial autocorrelations of the system

$$\begin{bmatrix} y_{1t} \\ y_{2t} \end{bmatrix} = \begin{bmatrix} 0.5 & -0.2 \\ -0.3 & 0.4 \end{bmatrix}\begin{bmatrix} y_{1,t-1} \\ y_{2,t-1} \end{bmatrix} + \begin{bmatrix} \varepsilon_{1t} \\ \varepsilon_{2t} \end{bmatrix},$$

where $(\varepsilon_{1t}, \varepsilon_{2t})$ is assumed to be independently identically distributed.

11-B Use the U.S. quarterly data of GNP, M2, investment, and six-month commercial paper rate to construct a univariate and multivariate time-series models. Compare the prediction performance of the univariate time-series model with the multiple time-series model.

11-C 1. Let $\mathbf{A}(L)\mathbf{X}(t) = \mathbf{e}(t)$, where $\mathbf{e}(t)$ is $I(0), \mathbf{X}(t) = [Y(t), W(t)]'$, and $\mathbf{A}(L)$ is a 2×2 matrix given by:

$$\begin{bmatrix} 1-(1-u)L & -uL \\ uL & 1-(1+u)L \end{bmatrix}.$$

State under what condition $Y(t)$ is cointegrated with $W(t)$ and under what condition it is not. What is the cointegration vector for the former?

2. Comment on the following statement. "Suppose that Japan's stock price, $W(t)$, is cointegrated with the U.S. stock price, $Y(t)$. Since Japan's market is closed 10 hours ahead of the U.S. market, we can use $W(t)$ to predict $Y(t)$ optimally (i.e., a money-making machine in the U.S. market).

11-D Consider the bivariate ARMA(1,1) model:

$$\begin{bmatrix} 1+a_{11}L & a_{12}L \\ a_{21}L & 1+a_{22}L \end{bmatrix}\begin{bmatrix} y_t \\ x_t \end{bmatrix} = \begin{bmatrix} \theta_{11,0}+\theta_{11,1}L & \theta_{12,0} \\ \theta_{21,0} & \theta_{22,0}+\theta_{22,1}L \end{bmatrix}\begin{bmatrix} \varepsilon_{1t} \\ \varepsilon_{2t} \end{bmatrix},$$

where $(\boldsymbol{\varepsilon}_{1t}, \boldsymbol{\varepsilon}_{2t})$ are independently identically distributed with mean zero and covariance matrix $\boldsymbol{\Omega}$.

1. Transform the system into an equivalent ARMA(1,1) model with the covariance matrix of an innovation term equal to an identity matrix.

2. Transform y_t as a function of x_t and noise.
3. Transform y_t and x_t into univariate ARMA processes.
4. What are the conditions for y_t to cause x_t and x_t not to cause y_t?

11-E Consider the bivariate cointegrated system:

$$\begin{bmatrix} y_{1t} \\ y_{2t} \end{bmatrix} = \begin{bmatrix} 0 & a_{12} \\ 0 & 1 \end{bmatrix} \begin{bmatrix} y_{1t-1} \\ y_{2t-1} \end{bmatrix} + \begin{bmatrix} u_{1t} \\ u_{2t} \end{bmatrix},$$

where $\mathbf{u}_t = (u_{1t}, u_{2t})'$ is i.i.d. $(0, \Sigma = (\sigma_{ij}))$. Data generated from this system are estimated using a levels vector autoregression with one lag, that is, a VAR(1). Denote the estimates of the coefficients in the first equation obtained in this way by $\hat{a}_{11}$ and $\hat{a}_{12}$.

1. Find the asymptotic distribution of $(\hat{a}_{11}, \hat{a}_{12})$.
2. Show how this asymptotic distribution is related to that of the OLS estimate of a_{12} in the model:

$$y_{1t} = a_{12} y_{2,t-1} + u_{1t}.$$

3. Use this result to explain the presence of simultaneous equations bias in the limit distribution (Phillips, 1992).

11-F Consider the vector autoregression:

$$\begin{bmatrix} y_{1t} \\ y_{2t} \end{bmatrix} = \begin{bmatrix} a_{11} & a_{12} \\ a_{21} & a_{22} \end{bmatrix} \begin{bmatrix} y_{1,\,t-1} \\ y_{2,\,t-1} \end{bmatrix} + \begin{bmatrix} \varepsilon_{1t} \\ \varepsilon_{2t} \end{bmatrix},$$

in which it is known that $a_{11} = 1$, $a_{22} = 0$, and where $\varepsilon_t = (\varepsilon_{1t}, \varepsilon_{2t})'$ is i.i.d. $N(\mathbf{0}, \Sigma)$ with $\Sigma = (\sigma_{ij})$. An investigator wishes to test the causality hypothesis:

$$H_0 \colon a_{12} = 0,$$

and does so by running the single-equation least squares regression:

$$y_{1t} = \hat{a}_{11} y_{1,\,t-1} + \hat{a}_{12} y_{2,\,t-1} + \hat{\varepsilon}_{1t},$$

and by employing a conventional regression t-test. Find the limit distribution of $t(\hat{a}_{12})$, the test statistic used by this investigator. Explain your result (Phillips and Toda, 1990).

BIBLIOGRAPHY

ANDERSON, T. W. (1951). "Estimating Linear Restrictions on Regression Coefficients for Multivariate Normal Distributions." *Annals of Mathematical Statistics*, 22: 327–351 [correction, *Annals of Mathematical Statistics*, 8 (1980): 1400].

ANDREWS, D. K. (1991). "Heteroskedasticity and Autocorrelation Consistent Covariance Matrix Estimation." *Econometrica*, 59: 817–858.

ANDREWS, D. K., and J. C. MONAHAN (1990). "An Improved Heteroskedasticity and Autocorrelation Consistent Covariance Estimator." Cowles Foundation working paper 945, Yale University, New Haven, Conn.

BOX, G. E. P., and G. M. JENKINS (1970). *Time Series Analysis, Forecasting and Control*. San Francisco: Holden-Day, Inc.

CAINES, P. E., and C. W. CHAN (1975). "Feedback between Stationary Stochastic Processes." *IEEE Transactions on Automatic Control*, AC-20: 498–508.

CHAN, N. H., and C. Z. WEI (1988). "Limiting Distribution of Least Squares Estimates of Unstable Autoregressive Processes." *Annals of Statistics*, 27: 168–175.

ENGLE, R. F., and C. W. J. GRANGER (1987). "Cointegration and Error Correction: Representation, Estimation and Testing." *Econometrica*, 55: 251–276.

ENGLE, R. F., and B. SAM YOO (1989). "Cointegrated Economic Time Series: A Survey with New Results." Discussion paper 87-26R. Department of Economics, University of California, San Diego.

FULLER, W. A. (1976). *Introduction to Statistical Time Series*. New York: John Wiley & Sons, Inc.

GANTMACHER, F. R. (1959). *Matrix Theory*, Vol. 1. New York: Chelsea Publishing Company, Inc.

GRANGER, C. W. J. (1969). "Investigating Causal Relations by Econometric Models and Cross-Spectral Models." *Econometrica*, 37: 424–438.

GRANGER, C. W. J. (1984). "Co-Integrated Variables and Error Correction Models." Working paper. Department of Economics, University of California, San Diego.

GRANGER, C. W. J., and P. NEWBOLD (1974). "Spurious Regression in Econometrics." *Journal of Econometrics*, 2: 111–120.

GRANGER, C. W. J., and P. NEWBOLD (1986). *Forecasting Economic Time Series*, 2nd ed. San Diego: Academic Press, Inc.

HANNAN, E. J. (1971). "The Identification Problem of Multiple Equation Systems with Moving Average Errors." *Econometrica*, 41: 229–320.

HANNAN, E. J., and R. D. TERRELL (1973). "Multiple Equation Systems with Stationary Errors." *Econometrica*, 41: 299–320.

HANNAN, E. J., W. DUNSMIUR, and M. DEISTLER (1980). "Estimation of Vector ARMAX Models." *Journal of Multivariate Analysis*, 10: 275–295.

HATANAKA, M. (1975). "On the Global Identification of the Dynamic Simultaneous Equations Model with Stationary Disturbances." *International Economic Review*, 16: 545–554.

HAUGH, L. D. (1976). "Checking the Independence of Two Covariance-Stationary Time Series: A Univariate Residual Cross Correlation Approach." *Journal of the American Statistical Association*, 71: 378–385.

HAUSMAN, J. A. (1978). "Specification Tests in Econometrics." *Econometrica*, 46, 1251–1271.

HENDRY, D. F., A. R. PAGAN, and J. D. SARGAN (1984). "Dynamic Specification," in Z. Griliches and M. D. Intriligator, Eds., *Handbook of Econometrics*, Vol. 2. Amsterdam: North-Holland Publishing Company.

HENDRY, D. F., and T. VON UNGERN-STERNBERG (1981). "Liquidity and Inflation Effects on Consumer's Expenditure," in A. S. Deaton, Ed., *Essays in the Theory and Measurement of Consumer's Behavior*. Cambridge: Cambridge University Press.

HOSKIN, J. R. M. (1980). "The Multivariate Portmanteau Statistic." *Journal of the American Statistical Association*, 74: 652–660.

HSIAO, C. (1979a). "Autoregressive Modelling of Canadian Money and Data Income." *Journal of the American Statistical Association*, 74: 553–566.

HSIAO, C. (1979b). "Causality Tests in Econometrics." *Journal of Economic Dynamics and Control*, 1: 321–346.

HSIAO, C. (1981). "Autoregressive Modelling and Money-Income Causality Detection." *Journal of Monetary Economics*, 7: 85–106.

HSIAO, C. (1982). "Autoregressive Modelling and Causal Ordering of Economic Variables." *Journal of Economic Dynamics and Control*, 4: 243–259.

HSIAO, C. (1983). "Identification," in Z. Griliches and M. D. Intriligator, Eds., *Handbook of Econometrics*, Vol. I. Amsterdam: North-Holland Publishing Company.

HSIAO, C. (1992). "A Note on Multiple Time Series Models, Causality, Co-integration and Dynamic Simultaneous Equations Models." Mimeograph, University of Southern California.

JOHANSEN, S. (1988). "Statistical Analysis of Cointegration Vectors." *Journal of Economic Dynamics and Control*, 12: 231–254.

JOHANSEN, S. (1991a). "Estimation and Hypothesis Testing of Cointegration Vectors in Gaussian Vector Autoregressive Models." *Econometrica*, 59: 1551–1580.

JOHANSEN, S. (1991b). "Estimating Systems of Trending Variables." Preprint 6. Institute of Mathematical Statistics, University of Copenhagen.

JOHANSEN, S., and K. JUSELIUS (1988). "Hypothesis Testing for Cointegration Vectors with an Application to the Demand of Money in Denmark and Finland." Preprint. Institute of Mathematical Statistics, University of Copenhagen.

KING, R., C. I. PLOSSER, J. H. STOCK, AND M. W. WATSON (1991). "Stochastic Trends and Economic Fluctuations." *American Economic Review*, 81: 819–840.

KLEIN, L. (1973). "The Treatment of Undersized Samples in Econometrics," in A. A. Powell and R. A. Williams, Eds., *Econometric Studies of Macro and Monetary Relations*. Amsterdam: North-Holland Publishing Company.

LI, W. K., and A. I. MCLEOD (1980). "Distribution of the Residual Autocorrelations in Multivariate ARMA Time Series Models." TR-80-03. University of Western Ontario.

LIU, T. C. (1960). "Underidentification, Structural Estimation, and Forecasting." *Econometrica*, 28: 855–865.

MACDUFFEE, C. C. (1956). *The Theory of Matrices*. New York: Chelsea Publishing Company, Inc.

NICHOLLS, D. F., A. R. PAGAN, and R. D. TERRELL (1975). "The Estimation and Use of Models with Moving Average Disturbance Terms: A Survey." *International Economic Review*, 16: 113–134.

PAGAN, A. R., and M. R. WICKENS (1989). "A Survey of Some Recent Econometric Methods." *Economic Journal*, 99: 962–1025.

PARK, J. Y. (1992). "Canonical Cointegrating Regressions." *Econometrica*, 60: 119–143.

PARK, J. Y., and P. C. B. PHILLIPS (1989). "Statistical Inference in Regressions with Integrated Processes: Part 2." *Econometric Theory*, 5: 95–131.

PHILLIPS, P. C. B. (1986). "Understanding Spurious Regressions in Econometrics." *Journal of Econometrics*, 33: 311–340.

PHILLIPS, P. C. B. (1991). "Optimal Inference in Cointegrating Systems." *Econometrica*, 59: 283–306.

PHILLIPS, P. C. B. (1992). "Simultaneous Equations Bias in Level VAR Estimation." *Econometric Theory*, 9: 307.

PHILLIPS, P. C. B., and B. E. HANSEN (1990). "Statistical Inference in Instrumental Variables Regression with I(1) Processes." *Review of Economic Studies*, 57: 99–125.

PHILLIPS, P. C. B., and M. LORETAN (1991). "Estimating Long-Run Economic Equilibria." *Review of Economic Studies*, 58: 407–436.

PHILLIPS, P. C. B., and S. QULIARIS (1990). "Asymptotic Properties of Residual Based Tests for Cointegration." *Econometrica*, 58: 165–193.

PHILLIPS, P. C. B., and H. TODA (1990). "Testing Causality in an Autoregression with Cointegrated Regressions." *Econometric Theory*, 7: 409.

PIERCE, D. A., and L. D. HAUGH (1971). "Causality in Temporal Systems: Characterizations and a Survey." *Journal of Econometrics*, 5: 265–294.

SARGAN, J. D. (1964). "Wages and Prices in the United Kingdom: A Study in Econometric Methodology," in P. E. Hart and J. K. Whittaker, Eds., *Econometric Analysis for National Economic Planning*. London: Butterworth & Company (Publishers) Ltd.

SIMS, C. A. (1972). "Money, Income and Causality." *American Economic Review*, 62: 540–552.

SIMS, C. A. (1980). "Macroeconomics and Reality." *Econometrica*, 48: 1–48.

SIMS, C. A., J. H. STOCK, and M. W. WATSON (1990). "Inference in Linear Time Series Models with Some Unit Roots." *Econometrica*, 58: 113–144.

STOCK, J. H. (1987). "Asymptotic Properties of Least Squares Estimators of Cointegrating Vectors." *Econometrica*, 55: 1035–1056.

STOCK, J. H., and M. W. WATSON (1988). "Testing for Common Trends." *Journal of the American Statistical Association*, 83: 1097–1107.

THEIL, H., and J. C. D. BOOT (1962). "The Final Form of Econometric Equation System." *Review of the International Statistical Institute*, 30: 136–152.

TIAO, G. C., and G. E. P. BOX (1981). "Modeling Multiple Time Series with Applications." *Journal of the American Statistical Association*, 76: 802–816.

TIAO, G. C., and R. S. TSAY (1983). "Multiple Time Series Modeling and Extended Sample Cross-Correlations." *Journal of Business Economics and Statistics*, 1: 43–56.

WU, D. M. (1973). "Alternative Tests of Independence between Stochastic Regressors and Disturbances." *Econometrica*, 41: 733–750.

YOO, B. SAM (1986). "Multi-Cointegrated Time Series and Generalized Error-Correction Models." Working paper, Economics Department, University of California, San Diego.

ZELLER, A., and F. PALM (1974). "Time Series Analysis and Simultaneous Equation Econometric Models." *Journal of Econometrics*, 2: 17–54.

12

APPLICATIONS TO MACROECONOMETRIC MODELS

12.1 THE NATURE OF MACROECONOMETRIC MODELS

The earliest and still one of the most important applications of econometric techniques is to macroeconometric models.[1] Such models often utilize a Keynesian framework for the determination of national income [usually measured as gross domestic product (GDP)] and its components, consumption and investment, as well as other macroeconomic variables such as those listed in Table 12.1.[2] Such models are utilized for all three purposes of econometrics: structural analysis (e.g., determination of multipliers), forecasting (e.g., forecasting GDP over the next eight quarters), and policy evaluation (e.g., analyzing the impact of government expenditure and taxation programs), as will be seen in Chapters 14 to 16.

The nature of macroeconometric models can be perhaps easiest understood in terms of the prototype macro model of Chapter 2, of the form

$$C = \gamma_1 Y + \beta_1 + \varepsilon^C, \tag{12.1.1}$$

$$I = \gamma_2 Y + \beta_2 Y_{-1} + \beta_3 + \varepsilon^I, \tag{12.1.2}$$

$$Y = C + I + G. \tag{12.1.3}$$

The first equation is a consumption function, according to which consumption (C) is determined as a linear function of current national income (Y). The second equation is an in-

[1]For surveys of macroeconometric models, see Bodkin, Klein, Marwah (1991) and Uebe and Fischer (1992).

[2]Most of these variables are aggregates of corresponding micro variables, such as household consumption and individual firm investment. For a discussion of the problem of aggregating micro relationships into macro ones, see Section 7.7. The mainstream Keynesian approach to macroeconometric modeling has been subject, in recent years, to considerably more competition from other theoretical paradigms (in particular, those of the New Keynesians, monetarists, and New Classicals) than was the case when the first edition of this book was written. On this point, see Adams and Klein (1991), Helliwell (1993), and Taylor (1993).

TABLE 12.1 Macroeconomic Variables

GDP and its components
Gross domestic product (GDP)
Consumption
Nondurable goods
Durable goods
Services
Investment
Fixed plant and equipment investment
Inventory accumulation
Residential construction
Government
Federal
State and local
Net foreign investment
Exports
Imports
Income
Disposable income
Corporate profits
Income of unincorporated enterprises
Prices, wages, interest rates
Implicit price deflator for GDP
Consumer price index (CPI)
Nonfarm wage rate
Short-term interest rate
Long-term interest rate
Rates of foreign exchange
Employment, unemployment
Employment
Unemployment
Labor force
Unemployment rate
Participation rate
Production
Index of production
Production in various sectors
Assets
Capital stock
Financial assets
Balance on current account (in balance of payments)

Note See Table 16.1 for macroeconomic policy variables.

vestment function, according to which investment is determined as a linear function of current and lagged national income.[3] Both equations are stochastic, where the stochastic disturbance terms, the ε's, are included to represent omitted variables influencing consumption and investment, misspecification of these two behavioral relationships, and errors in mea-

[3]Net foreign investment, exports less imports, is omitted here. The consumption function and investment function have generated considerable interest in their own right. For surveys of econometric studies of the consumption function, see Malinvaud (1970), Bodkin (1977), and Deaton and Muellbauer (1980). For surveys of studies of the investment function, see Jorgenson (1974) and Clark (1979).

suring the included variables. By contrast, the last equation is an equilibrium condition, defining national income as the sum of consumption, investment, and government expenditure (G), and is therefore nonstochastic. These three equations determine values of the three current endogenous variables—C, I, and Y—given values of the one lagged endogenous variable Y_{-1} and the one exogenous variable G.

This model is a prototype of macroeconometric models because all such models generally contain the same basic elements as this one: a consumption function or a group of such functions, an investment function or a group of such functions, and a national income equilibrium condition or a group of such conditions. They generally involve a greater degree of disaggregation than is indicated in the prototype model, however. The prototype macro model disaggregates national income into only three components, two of which are determined endogenously in the model. The macroeconometric models to be discussed below typically further disaggregate these two components. Thus consumption may be disaggregated into consumption of goods and consumption of services, while consumption of goods may be itself further disaggregated into durables (e.g., automobiles) and nondurables (e.g., food). Similarly, investment may be disaggregated into business fixed plant investment, inventory accumulation, and residential construction. Income may itself be disaggregated into various components such as labor income and capital income, while output may be disaggregated by production sector. The macroeconometric models also involve more equations and variables by including certain factors not treated explicitly in the prototype model, which focuses exclusively on national income variables. Among these are prices, wages, interest rates, employment, and unemployment, as indicated in Table 12.1.[4]

In the following sections of this chapter we summarize five different macroeconometric models of the U.S. economy: the Klein interwar and the Klein–Goldberger models, which are small teaching models, composed of six to 25 equations, and the series of Wharton models, the MPS model, and the DRI model, which are all "large" models of over 100 equations. Section 12.7 looks at some other interesting macroeconometric models from the 1970s up to the present. Section 12.8 gives an international dimension to the review, as the LINK system and the CANDIDE model of the Canadian economy are summarized. In the concluding section we look at some trends in macroeconometric model construction.

12.2 THE KLEIN INTERWAR MODEL

The Klein interwar model was developed by Lawrence R. Klein to analyze the economy of the United States during the period between World Wars I and II, 1921–1941.[5] It is a particularly interesting model, both because it is both complicated enough to be challenging and simple enough to be treated fully, being only slightly larger than the prototype macroeconometric model, and also because it has been used to study policy pursued during the Depression years. The variables of the model are summarized in Table 12.2. The

[4]See also Problem 12-A for how some of these variables can enter a macroeconometric model.

[5]See Klein (1950). This model is also called *Klein Model I* in Goldberger (1964), Christ (1966), and Theil (1971). A larger model in Klein (1950), called *Klein Model III*, includes 15 equations, of which 12 are stochastic.

TABLE 12.2 Variables of the Klein Interwar Model

6 Endogenous Variables	4 Exogenous Variables
Y = output (private net national product at market prices)	G = government nonwage expenditure
C = consumption	W_G = public wages
I = investment (net)	T = business taxes
W_p = private wages	t = time
Π = profits	
K = capital stock (at year end)	

Note All variables other than K and t are flows, measured in billions of dollars of 1934 purchasing power per year. K, a stock, is measured in billions of 1934 dollars. Time, t, is measured as annual deviations (positive or negative) from 1931.

six endogenous variables are simultaneously determined by the model. Of the four exogenous variables, one is clearly determined outside the system—time, t. The remaining three are government variables, controlled by government economic policy, and therefore treated as exogenous. The model, as estimated by the full-information maximum likelihood method using annual data on the U.S. economy, 1921–1941, is presented in Table 12.3. The first three equations are the estimated behavioral equations for consumption, investment, and private wages; the last three equations are identities, for income, profits, and net investment.

The interactions of the variables of the model are shown in a flow diagram in Figure 12.1, which follows the approach of Figure 2.7 and can be considered a generalization of Figure 2.6, which represented the prototype macro model in a similar way. Note that in this type of diagram no arrows can point to either lagged endogenous variables or exogenous variables.

This model is clearly only slightly larger than the prototype macro model. Like the prototype model, it includes a single consumption function. In the Klein interwar model, however, consumption in (1) depends not on total income but rather on the components of income: wage income and profit income. Total wage income, the sum of private and government wages, has an associated marginal propensity to consume of 0.8; that is, every dollar of additional wage income increases consumption by 80 cents. By contrast, the marginal propensity to consume out of profit income, either current or lagged, is considerably smaller—0.02 for current profits and 0.23 for lagged profits. The low marginal propensity to consume out of current profit income makes it plausible to include lagged

TABLE 12.3 Estimated Klein Interwar Model

(1) $C = 16.79 + 0.800(W_p + W_G) + 0.020\Pi + 0.235\Pi_{-1}$

(2) $I = 17.78 + 0.231\Pi + 0.546\Pi_{-1} - 0.146K_{-1}$

(3) $W_p = 1.60 + 0.420Y + 0.164Y_{-1} + 0.135t$

(4) $Y = C + I + G$

(5) $\Pi = Y - W_P - T$

(6) $K = K_{-1} + I$

Source Theil and Boot (1962).

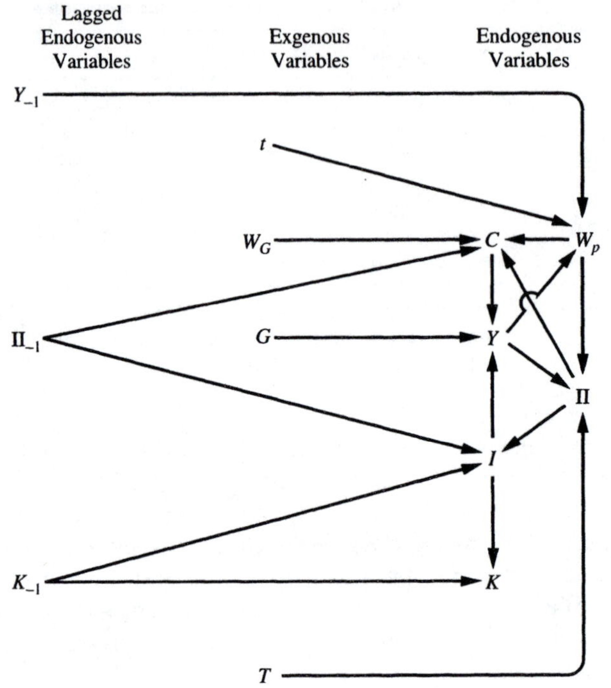

Figure 12.1 Flow Diagram of the Klein Interwar Model

profit income, while the high marginal propensity to consume out of wage income makes it plausible to exclude lagged wage income as a determinant of current consumption expenditure.

The investment function of the model (2) is also only a slight elaboration of that of the prototype model. It takes account, as in the consumption function, of the various types of income, but relies upon current and lagged *profit* income rather than current and lagged total income, since profits are more important for investment than wages. The last term is the depreciation term, suggesting that 15% of capital depreciates each year and must be replaced.

The third equation of the model (3), that for private wages, has no counterpart in the prototype model, because the latter does not treat the separate wage and profit components of income. According to the Klein interwar model, private wages depend on current and lagged income and on a time trend, which is a proxy for increased union strength during the period. This equation may be considered a private demand-for-labor equation, since it determines the wage bill paid by private industry.

The remaining equations of the Klein interwar model are three identities, thereby completing the model, which involves six equations and six endogenous variables. Equation (4) is the national income identity, as in the prototype model. Equation (5) defines total profits of the private sector as the difference between revenue—here, for the national economy—total output, and cost, represented here by private wages and taxes. Finally equation (6) defines net investment as the change in capital stock.

The reduced form of the model is presented in Table 12.4, where endogenous variables have been ordered in such a way that those with included lagged values appear first.[6] Since lagged C, W_P, and I do not appear in the model the coefficients of the lagged variables are zero, giving the last three rows of zeros in the coefficient matrix $\hat{\mathbf{\Pi}}_1$ for the lagged endogenous variables. From $\hat{\mathbf{\Pi}}_2$ a billion-dollar increase in government expenditure in the current period increases income by \$1.930 billion, private wages by \$0.811 billion, consumption by \$0.671 billion, and investment by \$0.259 billion, the circled figures. The balanced-budget income multiplier for government spending (where the change in G is offset by the change in T) is 1.930 – 0.484 = 1.446. The implied long-run multipliers for maintained changes in values of three of the exogenous variables are given in Table 12.5. Thus the long-run balanced-budget income multiplier is 2.323 – 0.569 = 1.754, of which 1.446 occurs in the first year.

In addition to this type of structural analysis, the Klein interwar model has been used both for forecasting and for policy evaluation. It was not very successful in predicting postwar phenomena, however, as compared to various naive models, which tended to work as

TABLE 12.4 Reduced Form of the Klein Interwar Model

$$\mathbf{y} = \mathbf{y}_{-1}\mathbf{\Pi} + \mathbf{z}\mathbf{\Pi}_2,$$

where

$$\mathbf{y} = (\Pi \quad Y \quad K \quad C \quad W_p \quad I)$$
$$\mathbf{y}_{-1} = (\Pi \quad Y \quad K \quad C \quad W_p \quad I)_{-1}$$
$$\mathbf{z} = (W_G \quad T \quad G \quad t)$$

$$\hat{\Pi}_1 = \begin{pmatrix} 0.863 & 1.489 & 0.746 & 0.743 & 0.626 & 0.746 \\ -0.063 & 0.174 & -0.015 & 0.189 & 0.237 & -0.015 \\ -0.164 & -0.283 & 0.816 & -0.098 & -0.119 & -0.184 \\ 0 & 0 & 0 & 0 & 0 & 0 \\ 0 & 0 & 0 & 0 & 0 & 0 \\ 0 & 0 & 0 & 0 & 0 & 0 \end{pmatrix}$$

$$\hat{\Pi}_2 = \begin{pmatrix} 0.895 & 1.544 & 0.207 & 1.337 & 0.649 & 0.207 \\ -1.281 & \textcircled{-0.484} & -0.296 & -0.188 & -0.204 & -0.296 \\ 1.119 & \textcircled{1.930} & 0.259 & \textcircled{0.671} & \textcircled{0.811} & \textcircled{0.259} \\ -0.052 & 0.143 & -0.012 & 0.155 & 0.195 & -0.012 \end{pmatrix}$$

Source Theil and Boot (1962).

TABLE 12.5 Long-Run Multipliers for the Klein Interwar Model

	Π	Y	K	C	W_P	I
W_G	0.773	1.859	4.099	1.859	1.087	0
T	−1.237	(−0.569)	−6.564	−0.569	−0.333	0
G	0.965	(2.323)	5.123	1.323	1.358	0

Source Theil and Boot (1962).

[6]See Theil and Boot (1962).

well or better.[7] This lack of predictive ability may, however, be attributed to the change in the structure of the U.S. economy resulting from World War II. The model has also been used for policy evaluation, specifically the evaluation of policy choices during the Great Depression.[8] This model is therefore useful as an exploratory model for all three purposes of econometrics—structural analysis, forecasting, and policy evaluation. A deficiency of the model, however, which prevents its use for anything more than exploratory work, is its use of highly aggregated variables and its failure to consider factors other than those of national income determination, such as production, price formation, demographic growth, and financial factors. These deficiencies have been remedied in later models.

12.3 THE KLEIN–GOLDBERGER MODEL

Although it is now considered principally a teaching model of relatively small size, at the time the Klein–Goldberger model was viewed as a "medium-sized" econometric model that could be employed for forecasting purposes. Fitted to the U.S. economy for the period 1929–1952 (excluding the war years 1942–1945), the fixed taxes version of this model consists of 20 equations, of which 15 are behavioral or stochastic and 5 are identities.[9] In addition to the 20 endogenous variables, the fixed taxes version of the model has 14 exogenous variables[10]; Table 12.6 summarizes these variables. It should also be noted that the model has been extremely important in influencing the construction of most of the later models of the U.S. economy, at least indirectly.

From the table it is clear that the Klein–Goldberger model involves a greater degree of disaggregation than the very "small" models treated in the two previous sections. Thus five categories of income, five of population and labor force, four of direct tax, three prices,

TABLE 12.6 Variables of the Klein–Goldberger Model (Fixed Taxes Version)

20 Endogenous Variables	14 Exogenous Variables
5 Income	Government expenditure
Consumption	4 Direct taxes
Gross private investment	Indirect tax
Depreciation	5 Population and labor force
Imports	Hours worked
Corporate saving	Excess reserves
Corporate surplus	Import prices
Private employees	
Capital stock	
2 Liquid assets	
3 Prices	
2 Interest rates	

[7]Christ (1951).

[8]See van den Bogaard and Theil (1959) and Chapter 16.

[9]See Klein and Goldberger (1955). Theil (1971, pp. 468–483) contains an excellent summary of the model, together with a critique of some critical points. Bodkin et al. (1991) discuss this model at some length, also.

[10]For forecasting purposes, tax *receipts* were generally explained by tax *functions*, leaving tax *rates* as the exogenous parameters.

two liquid assets, and two interest rates are included in the model. The model includes lags of up to five years, cumulated investment, and time trends. It makes use of the Koyck distributed lag, and it contains several nonlinear equations.

The Klein–Goldberger model was estimated using 20 annual observations from the periods 1929–1941 and 1946–1952; the war years were excluded because it was believed they did not conform to the economic structure described by the model. All variables representing stocks and flows of goods were measured in billions of dollars of 1939 purchasing power. The method of estimation was limited-information maximum likelihood. It might be noted that when the model was reestimated using the same data but using the technique of ordinary least squares, the resulting estimates were not very different.[11]

The Klein–Goldberger model treats both real and monetary phenomena, with most but not all behavioral equations specified in real terms. Most commentators feel that it has been more successful in representing real (rather than monetary) phenomena, particularly the components of GNP other than investment. A major problem with investment is that the model lumps together inventory investment with fixed business investment, precluding a detailed study of inventory cycles.[12] [Indeed, this is one of the reasons why this model is considered today to be a teaching (rather than a working) model.] The model tends, in fact, to be dominated by consumer demand elements, reflecting its Keynesian origins. Thus production is treated in a cursory way, with the role of the production function being one of obtaining the demand for employment by its inversion. It can also be argued that the entire monetary and wage–price sectors of the model, dealing with wages, price levels, and interest rates, are generally inadequate.[13] Later models have sought to remedy these deficiencies.[14]

One study, by Adelman and Adelman, compared the long-term behavior of the Klein–Goldberger model to actual trends and cycles in the U.S. economy.[15] It simulated the performance of the model over time, from 1952 to 2052, with and without additive random shocks, given as artificially generated random numbers in the behavioral and technological equations. Without the random shocks a linearized version of the model exhibited, over the long run, simple linear growth trends for each of its variables, assuming that the exogenous variables follow linear trends. With the addition of the exogenous normally distributed additive random shocks (with variances equal to the residual variances exhibited over the sample), the resulting simulated series exhibited business cycles similar in length, amplitude, and timing to those actually observed for the U.S. economy. In fact, the simulated cycles conformed remarkably well to the usual pattern of lead–lag relationships over the cycle, as

[11] Fox (1958). Where there was a substantial discrepancy, such as when the same coefficient had a different sign, the OLS estimators tended, on the basis of economic considerations, to be superior to the LIML estimators. It might also be noted that it was impossible to estimate the reduced form of the model, since the number of predetermined variables (including the lagged endogenous variables) exceeded the number of observations. Klein and Goldberger therefore restricted the predetermined variables to those that on the basis of a priori considerations seemed most important to "capture the spirit of simultaneity."

[12] This defect was remedied in the next generation of the Klein models, the postwar quarterly model (see Klein, 1961), which was used by Klein and Popkin (1961) to study precisely the issue of whether the short-term postwar business cycle in the United States could reasonably be termed an inventory cycle.

[13] See Goldberger (1959) and Theil (1971).

[14] For an update of more than a decade later of the Klein–Goldberger model, estimated with four types of parameter estimation, see also Klein (1969a).

[15] See Adelman and Adelman (1959); see also Hickman (1972).

formulated and estimated by the National Bureau of Economic Research, and to other measures, such as the mean duration of the cycle and the mean lengths of the expansion and contraction phases. This result supports the validity of the model with the additive random shocks as a representation of the U.S. economy. It is also consistent with the view that cycles represent a response of the economy to exogenous random shocks.

12.4 THE WHARTON MODEL

The Wharton model of the U.S. economy is really a series of models that have evolved gradually, with each new generation closely related to the preceding version. Over time, new developments in macroeconomic theory have been incorporated, and changes in the model have also reflected the lessons of experience. In addition, the size of the Wharton model has been growing larger: the original Wharton model (constructed in the mid-1960s) contained 76 equations, the Mark III version of the mid-1970s contained 201 equations, and the most recent version surveyed (Mark 9, fitted in 1988) contains approximately 620 equations. Thus the scale of this model, which has evolved over the past quarter century, has gone from "medium size" to "large."

Although the Wharton model is a lineal descendant of the Klein–Goldberger model, it differs from previous models in three important respects. First, it is estimated using quarterly rather than annual data, the original estimates of the model being based on 68 observations from the first quarter of 1948 to the fourth quarter of 1964, generally written as 1948.1–1964.4. Second, unlike most of the previous models discussed, it is explicitly designed for developing short-term forecasts of the economy, particularly national income, its components, employment, and aggregate prices.[16] Third, it involves increasingly a greater degree of disaggregation, a better treatment of accounting identities, and a better integration of the monetary sector than the earlier models.

The original Wharton model consisted of 76 equations, of which 47 were behavioral and 29 identities; in addition, there were 42 exogenous variables.[17] Table 12.7 summarizes these variables. From this table it is clear that even this version of the model is considerably more disaggregated than previous ones. For example, while all previous models involved only single aggregate measures of consumption and investment expenditures, the original Wharton model involved five different categories of consumption expenditure and five different categories of investment outlays. It disaggregated the economy into manufacturing and nonmanufacturing sectors, with the latter including regulated industry, trade, and finance. Production relationships in the model were of the Cobb–Douglas type. The treatment of supply conditions, the inclusion of the effects on prices of unit labor costs, and the endogenous determination of capacity utilization are among the main distinguishing features of the Wharton model. The original Wharton model also included a small monetary sector. The exogenous variables of the variables of the original Wharton model are listed in Table 12.7; among these are the policy levers of the model, which included two types of government expenditures, Social Security contributions, the Fed's discount rate, and net free reserves of the banking system.

[16]In the early days, the forecast horizon was generally two years (eight quarters). During the decade of the 1980s, this horizon was extended to *five* years (20 quarters).

[17]See Evans and Klein (1967, 1968) and Evans (1969).

TABLE 12.7 Variables of the Original Wharton Model

76 Endogenous Variables	42 Exogenous Variables
5 Output	2 Output
2 Sales	Income
4 Income	Consumption anticipations
5 Consumption	Farm fixed investment
5 Fixed investment	Farm inventories
4 Depreciation	2 Investment anticipations
Exports	Depreciation
3 Imports	2 Government purchases
2 Corporate profits	Interest payments
Dividends	2 Social Security contributions
2 Retained earnings	Housing starts
Cash flow	Population
Inventory valuation adjustment	5 Labor force
Rent and interest payments	2 Wage bill
3 Taxes	7 Prices
Transfer payments	Discount rate
4 Labor force	Net free reserves
2 Hours worked	Time
2 Wage bill	6 Dummy variables
2 Unemployment rate	Productivity trend
6 Capital stocks	Index of world trade
3 Inventories	Statistical discrepancy
Unfilled orders	
Index of capacity utilization	
10 Prices	
2 Wage rates	
2 Interest rates	

The Wharton model and most of the macroeconometric models of the U.S. economy for the past two decades are quarterly rather than annual models, involving variables and data defined over a three-month period. Estimation of such a model, rather than an annual model, gives a finer and more complete description of both interrelationships among variables and the types of lag structures present in the system. For example, certain short-term business-cycle phenomena that could not be captured in an annual model can be identified using a quarterly model. Quarterly models seem particularly useful for analyzing and forecasting short-term macroeconomic phenomena.

The original Wharton model contained lags of up to nine quarters (later versions contained even longer lags), and it employed the Almon distributed lag in the investment function to account for the lags between investment decisions and capital goods expenditures. The model used first differences for some variables but absolute levels for others. It also contained time trends and six dummy variables relating to periods of war, strikes, shortages, and credit tightness. It contained nonlinear relationships, such as the Phillips curve, which explained the money wage adjustment in terms of an aggregate rate of unemployment, among other explanatory variables.

The original Wharton model was estimated using the technique of two-stage least squares. (By contrast, the Mark 9 version of 1988 is estimated by ordinary least squares.) As already noted, it was built primarily for projecting the U.S. economy ahead eight quarters on a continuing basis, given certain assumptions about the exogenous variables, particularly the policy levers. Over the years, the forecasts, combined with judgments of experts, in the form of "add factors," as discussed in Chapter 15, represent some of the best forecasts available for gross domestic product and its components, regardless of the size of model.

There were three members of the family of Wharton models in the mid-1970s. The Wharton Mark III model[18] contained 201 endogenous and 104 exogenous variables in 67 stochastic equations and 134 identities. This version of the Wharton model involved a more detailed specification of the financial sector, of the nonmanufacturing sector (which was subdivided into the regulated, commercial, government, mining, and agriculture subsectors), and of prices, nominal wages, and labor demand. This model employed 25 policy instruments (as opposed to 7), with a considerably more detailed treatment of both monetary and fiscal policy variables, particularly tax rates. A second, related model of that period was the Wharton Annual and Industry Forecasting model.[19] This model, fitted on an annual basis, yielded more disaggregated forecasts of both quantities and prices than did the original Wharton model, and the horizon of the forecasts (roughly 10 years) was also considerably longer. The Annual and Industry Forecasting model also incorporated an input–output submodel (which was used both on the side of industry output determination and one for the determination of detailed price levels), and it was divided into eight model sectors: final demand, input–output (industry output determination), labor requirements, sector wages, sector prices, final demand prices, income payments, and monetary (financial) relationships. A final related model was the Wharton III Anticipations model.[20] In this model, anticipations variables were added to several of the structural equations: in particular, consumer anticipations, measured on an eight-point index, influence purchases of automobiles and other consumer durables; housing starts (considered a type of anticipations variable) influence residential construction; and investment anticipations affect plant and equipment investment by the manufacturing, regulated, and mining industries. Similar anticipations variables have been incorporated from time to time, but not continuously, in later generations of the Wharton Model.

The latest version of the Wharton Model available at the time of writing, Mark 9, contains roughly 620 endogenous variables, of which approximately 280 are stochastic, and 130 exogenous variables. The model was fitted (by ordinary least squares) to a postwar quarterly sample ending in 1987.4. In addition to its forecasting uses, Mark 9 is also intended for use in developing a number of alternative policy simulations. Among the exogenous variables of the model are roughly 30 monetary and fiscal policy levers, as well as the exchange value of the U.S. dollar.

As for the structure of the model, Mark 9 is a further development of the earlier Wharton models, with important supply side and financial influences. Although short-run movements in output are primarily determined by changes in aggregate demand, considerable attention is paid to the production and pricing sides. On the side of industry output de-

[18]See McCarthy (1972) and Duggal, Klein, and McCarthy (1974).

[19]See Preston (1972, 1975). The Wharton Annual and Industry Model has continued to the present time and has followed the trends toward further elaboration and disaggregation.

[20]See Adams and Duggal (1974).

termination, an input–output submodel is employed to determine measures of output produced by each of eight one-digit industries. These industry output variables determine labor and capital requirements by industry. On the side of prices, input–output information is employed in a "stages of processing" prices submodel, in which producer prices are determined by unit labor costs and other input costs. Mark 9 also contains a detailed trade sector in which eight categories (six of goods and two of services) are modeled individually, for both exports and imports. Each is related to the appropriate income or demand variables as well as to relative prices. As well, the links between the real and the financial sectors of the Wharton model have been strengthened over the years. In addition to their obvious impact on interest incomes, interest rates affect a user cost of capital (employed in the investment demand equations), the relative prices of consumer durables, and the consumer sentiment index (a variable retained from the Wharton III Anticipations model), which in turn influences consumption and investment expenditures. On the other hand, the evolution of the Wharton Model, at least with regard to its size, has not been monotonic. Thus the versions of the early 1980s contained a large, detailed flow-of-funds submodel, but this sector was dropped in the second half of the decade, as its marginal benefit was deemed to be outweighed by its marginal cost (see also the discussion in Section 12.9). Mark 9 also contains fully specified sectors for housing, energy, and automobiles. Finally, important exogenous variables, in addition to the policy levers previously mentioned, include demographic variables, oil prices (an important input into the energy sector), inflation and real growth in the rest of the world, and seasonal patterns.[21]

12.5 THE MPS MODEL

The MPS model is the public version of an econometric model of the U.S. economy developed by the Federal Reserve Board, MIT, and the University of Pennsylvania.[22] The official version, called the FMP model (for *F*ederal Reserve, *M*IT, and *P*ennsylvania), was used for forecasting and policy evaluation by the Federal Reserve System. The public version is called the MPS model (for *M*IT, *P*ennsylvania, and the *S*ocial Science Research Council). It was previously called the FRB-MIT model.

The MPS model is a large-scale quarterly econometric model involving over 100 equations. Its main focus, as might be expected of an econometric model due, in part, to the Federal Reserve Board, is in estimating the impacts of alternative monetary policies.[23] The model includes six major blocks of equations, as summarized in Table 12.8.

The final demand sector treats consumption, investment in plant and equipment, housing, state and local government expenditure (treated as endogenous variables), inventory investment, and imports. The investment portion of this sector involves highly nonlinear functional forms.

[21]The sources of the discussion in these two final paragraphs of this section are Adams and Klein (1991), particularly the appendix to this article, and also some unpublished manuscripts of the WEFA (Wharton Econometric Forecasting Associates) Group.

[22]See Rasche and Shapiro (1968), de Leeuw and Gramlich (1968, 1969), Ando and Modigliani (1969), Ando, Modigliani, and Rasche (1972), and Ando (1974).

[23]See Section 13.2 for a discussion of some equations of the model relating to money demand and supply.

TABLE 12.8 Equations of the MPS Model

	Stochastic Equations	Nonstochastic Equations	Total Equations
Final demand	24	20	44
Distribution of income	5	21	26
Tax and transfer	12	9	21
Labor market	3	10	13
Prices	10	22	32
Financial sector	21	14	35
Total	75	96	171

Note: This listing refers to Version 4.1 of the Federal Reserve–MIT–Penn Model, dated April 15, 1969.

The financial sector of this model was the most detailed of any econometric model to date, including attempts to treat aspects of the operation of commercial banks, commercial loan markets, savings and loan associations, and mutual savings banks. There is an equation for the ratio of dividends paid to share (stock market) prices, which thus makes the stock market an endogenous phenomenon of the system.

Among the fiscal policy variables explicitly considered in this model are components of Federal government purchases of goods and services, transfer payments, and rates and other parameters of the Federal tax system. On the monetary side the model treats the money supply, the monetary base, the basic short-term interest rate, the discount rate, and reserve ratios.

The specification of the model makes extensive use of distributed lags, nonlinear equations, intercept shifts, and corrections for first-order autocorrelation. The model also allows for alternative specification of various equations.

The model, as estimated from quarterly postwar data, has been used to analyze the workings of certain sectors of the economy, particularly the financial, investment, and housing sectors. It has also been used for short-run forecasting, given projected values of all exogenous variables, values of lagged endogenous variables, the parameter estimates, and certain constant adjustment factors, as explained in Chapter 15.[24]

[24]Helliwell et al. (1973) used the MPS model in conjunction with the RDX2 macroeconometric model of the Canadian economy to study linkages between the United States and Canada. They found important links in terms of capital flows and labor migration, in addition to the obvious trade linkages. In its early days, when the Federal Reserve Board was an actively involved user of the model, its most important use was the evaluation of alternative monetary and fiscal policies. Ando and Modigliani continued along these lines, making their model an important tool for evaluating monetarism as a short-hand view of the U.S. macroeconomy. (Of course, this assumes that the model is sufficiently accurate for this purpose.) Their general conclusion was that monetarism is something of an oversimplification; see, for example, Modigliani's presidential address (1977) to the American Economic Association.

In the past decade, the research staff of the Federal Reserve Board has again become interested in macroeconometric model building and has constructed a new, somewhat larger version of a quarterly macroeconometric model, inspired in part by the experience with the MPS model. This larger version, which has 128 behavioral equations (Adams and Klein, 1991), also places emphasis on the financial flows of the economy, with some attention to long-run equilibrium properties.

12.6 THE DRI MODEL

The DRI model, developed by Data Resources, Inc., is one of the largest models of the U.S. economy.[25] It is a highly disaggregated model that was influenced by the Brookings model (briefly discussed in the following section), the Wharton model, and other earlier models, including the Duesenberry, Eckstein, and Fromm model (1960). The current version of the DRI model draws its inspiration from a number of theoretical sources: mainstream Keynesian, neoclassical, and monetarist currents of thinking; as well, it attempts to incorporate the long-run properties of certain well-received models of economic growth.

The 1989 DRI model includes 974 endogenous variables and 286 exogenous variables. Of the endogenous variables, however, an important proportion are not central to the mechanism of the model but rather, are based on a breakdown by industry. Table 12.9 presents a profile of 10 major sectors of the model, indicating the degree of structural detail in each sector. Clearly, this model, in at least several sectors, involves a considerable degree of detail. In particular, the first six sectors (private domestic spending, production and income, government, international transactions, financial, and the prices sectors) all involve a considerable degree of disaggregation. An important part of this disaggregation is an input–output model of 60 SIC (standard industrial classification) industries, with interindustry relations summarized by relevant input–output coefficients that are automatically corrected for systematic trend and cyclical factors.

The DRI model includes several other unique features. One such feature is a flow-of-funds submodel for the household and corporate sectors of the economy that is fully simultaneous with the income-expenditure flows.[26] A second feature is a detailed stage-of-processing model of the inflation process, with which it is possible to trace the impacts of changes in the prices of basic and raw materials, such as world oil or food, through later stages of production to the retail level. A third feature is the inclusion of demographic and supply considerations affecting potential output and determining the composition, by age, gender, and race, of employment and unemployment. A fourth feature is a wholly endogenous and behavioral state and local government sector, which responds to macroeconomic conditions, demographic factors, and financial constraints impinging on that sector's budget. Finally, since 1984 the rate of foreign exchange has been made an endogenous variable; the inflation-adjusted world value of the U.S. dollar is sensitive to the spread between U.S. and foreign bond yields (in real terms) and also to the deficit on current account of the balance of payments.

[25]See Eckstein, Green, and Sinai (1974), Data Resources, Inc. (1976), and Eckstein (1983). The current version of the DRI model is summarized in Adams and Klein (1991) and discussed further in Brinner and Hirsch (1991); however, the principal source of this section is unpublished manuscripts by (and correspondence with) personnel of Data Resources, Inc./McGraw-Hill. This organization maintains a large integrated computerized data bank, which it provides to subscribers in industry and government on the basis of either time-sharing or direct access via a mainframe or personal computer. The DRI model could be regarded as a major by-product of this data bank, as many more series are maintained on the data bank than are used in the estimation of the model; in any case, the model represents a service furnished subscribers. Other commercial ventures that also provide subscribers access to large data banks and various models based on such data include Chase Econometrics Associates, Inc., and Wharton Econometric Forecasting Associates, Inc., which provide (or used to provide) respectively the Chase model and the various Wharton models (discussed in Section 12.4). (These two enterprises have recently merged.)

[26]It appears that this detailed financial submodel yields considerable sensitivity to financial factors for the DRI model, at least in comparison with a model that is more centrally in the Keynesian tradition, such as the BEA model. On this point, see Brinner and Hirsch (1991).

TABLE 12.9 Sectors of the DRI Model

Sector	Basic Behavioral[a]		Identities and Other Nonstochastic Relationships		Exogenous		Total	
I. Private domestic spending	38		129		21		188	
A. Consumption		16		31		0		47
B. Business spending		17		84		19		120
C. Housing		5		14		2		21
II. Production and income	115		107		113		335	
A. Wages		3		3		2		8
B. Capital income		3		16		96[b]		115
C. Industry detail								
1. Production		57		67		10		134
2. Capacity operating rates		5		5		2		12
3. Employment		39		6		1		46
D. Rental, entrepreneurial, etc.		8		10		2		20
III. Government	17		50		44		111	
A. Federal taxes and spending		6		27		36		69
B. State and local government		11		8		6		25
C. Aggregates		0		15		2		17
IV. International transactions (goods and services, prices and quantities)	36		51		12		99	
A. Imports		17		24		3		44
B. Exports		15		25		3		43
C. Exchange rates, foreign interest rates		1		2		3		6
D. Stock markets, foreign		3		0		3		6
V. Financial	92		100		38		230	
A. Monetary and financial aggregates		17		33		18		68
B. Interest rates		22		9		0		31
C. Flow of funds (household, nonfinancial, and mortgage)		50		56		20		126
D. Stock market (domestic)		3		2		0		5
VI. Prices, wages, productivity	48		78		15		141	
A. Wholesale prices		17		39		12		68
B. Deflators and CPI		28		33		1		62
C. Wages and productivity		3		6		2		11
VII. Supply	6		36		26		68	
A. Capital stocks		0[c]		21		10		31
B. Labor supply and employment		2		0		2		4
C. Energy		2		3		13		18
D. Productivity		1		9		1		11
E. Aggregate supply		1		3		0		4
VIII. Expectations	1		4		0		5	
A. Consumer		1		0		0		1
B. Financial		0		4		0		4
IX. Population	0		0		10		10	
X. Aggregates and miscellaneous	1		14		13		28	
Totals	354		569		292		1215	

Principal source Private correspondence with Cynthia Stephens and David Kelly of DRI/McGraw-Hill.

[a]Or stochastic equations.

[b]Includes 94 economic depreciation rates for calculating the book value of the capital stock.

[c]Note that investment spending is included in business spending.

An example of one equation from the DRI model is that for consumer purchases of automobiles, one of 16 categories of consumer spending in the consumption sector of the model. This equation illustrates how day-to-day use and annual rethinking have added significant elements to the basic theoretical structure provided by textbook modeling. The equation, as estimated by ordinary least squares using data from the first quarter of 1969 through the fourth quarter of 1988 (with calculated t ratios below the estimated coefficients) is:

$$\log(\text{CDMV\&P82/HOUSETREND}_{-1}) = \underset{(4.91)}{-6.26}$$

$$+ \underset{(3.82)}{1.635}\left(\sum_{t=0}^{-17} \hat{\alpha}_t \log(\text{YD82} - \text{CSOFI/PC})/\text{HOUSETREND}_{-1}\right)_t$$

$$- \underset{(5.37)}{0.029}\,(\text{RINT}_{-1} - \text{PCEXP79}_{-1}) + \underset{(7.34)}{0.191}\left(\sum_{t=0}^{-2} \text{JATTC}_t\right)$$

$$- \underset{(3.14)}{0.0343}\left(\sum_{t=-1}^{4} \text{CHLPMILE8}_t\right) - \underset{(1.80)}{0.420}\log(\text{WPI141101/PC}) \tag{12.6.1}$$

$$+ \underset{(1.06)}{0.155}\log(((\text{HHNETWORTH} - \text{HHEQUITY})_{-1}/\text{PC})/\text{HOUSETREND}_{-1})$$

$$+ \underset{(1.36)}{0.0434}\log((\text{HHEQUITY}_{-1}/\text{PC})/\text{HOUSESTREND}_{-1}) + \underset{(4.24)}{0.0837}\,\text{DMYINC}$$

$$+ \underset{(1.74)}{0.039}\,\text{GCARDUMMY} - \underset{(5.35)}{1.203 * 10^{-5}}\,\text{DMYSTR371}$$

$$\bar{R}^2 = 0.957, \qquad d = 2.26.$$

The endogenous variable CDMV&P82 is consumer spending on motor vehicles and parts in 1982 dollars (including net used cars, tires, and parts), while HOUSETREND is the normalized value (using a seven-year centered moving average) of the number of households of the U.S. economy. Hence the formulation is in terms of expenditures, income, and wealth *per household* (rather than being in absolute terms or on a per capita basis). The disposable income variable in this version (YD82, disposable income in 1982 dollars) has only a small correction for the real value of "free" (imputed) financial services (CSOFI/PC), which are presumably not relevant to the automobile expenditure decision. To be noted is the fairly high income elasticity in the long term; even the instantaneous effect (not shown here) of increases in real adjusted disposable income is virtually a unit-elastic response in automobile expenditures. [The $\hat{\alpha}_t$ coefficients are estimated weights for the fitted polynomial (Almon) distributed lag.] The variable RINT is a constructed interest rate variable relevant to automobile purchases, which also attempts to take account of the tax deductibility of some of these payments, while PCEXP79 is the expected rate of change (in percentages) of the implicit deflator of consumption expenditures in the national accounts. This term thus measures the relevant real rate of interest, and it may be noted that its effect, with a one-quarter lag, is significantly negative. The variable JATTC is the Michigan Survey Index of Consumer Sentiment, representing consumer confidence; CHLPMILE8 represents an eight-quarter change in the estimated real cost of the gasoline requirements for a unit operation of a representative car; notice that during this period its effect was both negative, as expected (as gasoline and cars are clearly complements), and significant. Another real price variable is WPI141101/PC, the wholesale price index of new passenger cars divided by the implicit deflator of total consumption; note that this equation suggests that the demand for automobiles is price inelastic. This wholesale price deflator was used in preference to the personal consumption deflator for motor vehicles and parts from the national accounts, as the wholesale price deflator explicitly takes account of interest rate incentives.

Two wealth terms follow next; real per household holdings of corporate equities or shares (HHEQUITY) seem to exert a smaller numerical influence than the remaining portion of household net worth, net of depreciation (HHNETWORTH), although neither is statistically significant by conventional tests and the elasticities, although positive as expected, are numerically small.

The final three variables, which are dummy variables or nearly, are intended to measure the effects of special circumstances. The variable DMYSTR371 can be termed a "cluster" variable, as it represents the effects of automobile strikes during the sample period by the number of labor-hours lost to strike activity. In particular, this variable will "cluster" at zero for "normal" periods, but may reach high values during quarters of large strike activity. GCARDUMMY represents the introduction of the compact car in the late 1970s, and DMYINC represents the effects of varying incentive programs attempting to encourage the purchase of motor vehicles. It may be noted that the effects of the strike variable were negative and (although small) highly significant, presumably reflecting a reduced availability (and temporary nonprice rationing) of automobiles; the definition of this variable explains why this is possible. The effect of GCARDUMMY is in the expected direction, although only marginally significant; and the incentives programs of the car manufacturers had a large and significant effect, even though the possibility exists that these effects were only temporary. The fit is quite good, and the equation is apparently free of autocorrelated disturbances. A bridge equation relates consumer spending on new automobiles to total automobile expenditures; other relations translate new car purchases into unit domestic retail sales and unit domestic retail sales of foreign cars, as well as into outlays for tires and parts.

The DRI model is reestimated each year to take advantage of data revisions and new research findings. The model has been used for all three purposes of econometrics. It has been used for structural analysis to evaluate various multipliers and elasticities. Its detailed structure (as illustrated above) describes many economic processes, including cyclical factors, energy aspects, and financial conditions, and it is sufficiently disaggregated that both macro effects of micro changes and micro effects of macro changes can be analyzed in detail. The model has been used for short-run forecasting, providing quarterly forecasts of up to 12 quarters of both the main macroeconomic variables and their detailed components. Dynamic simulations using the model have covered up to a 15-year period. The model has also been employed for policy evaluation, to estimate the impacts of various monetary and fiscal policies on unemployment, price stability, and economic growth.[27] Its highly detailed structure and its inclusion of a number of detailed policy levers make it very useful for analyzing the implications of various policy packages.

12.7 SURVEY OF SOME MACROECONOMETRIC MODELS OF THE U.S. ECONOMY

In earlier sections of this chapter we have treated, in various degrees of detail, five macroeconometric models (or groups of models) of the U.S. economy. There have been many other macroeconometric models of the United States and of other countries.[28] In this section a brief review of 15 other macroeconometric models of the U.S. economy is presented. Many of these have evolved over time, but in the cursory presentation their condition at one point in time (usually, that point at which the greatest amount of documentation is available) is the principal focus of the discussion.

The first macroeconometric model of the United States was the Tinbergen study of U.S. business cycles over the 1919–1932 period. The *Tinbergen model* was quite influential in at least three respects. First, it influenced future research by developing a quantitative approach to the subject of business-cycle analysis. In this connection, Tinbergen showed how stock market speculation could in certain instances be quite destabilizing, in what was otherwise a stable macroeconomy. Second, it fostered further development and use of macroeconometric modeling. Third, it contributed indirectly to later work on problems of estimation of a system of simultaneous equations.[29]

The *Valavanis model*[30] was an unusual model as the units of observation are overlapping decade averages and it treated long-term economic growth over an extended period—from 1869 through 1953. The size of the model and the types of variables used are similar to those of Klein–Goldberger. However, in this one, because of the focus on long-term growth, such variables as those of population and labor force, the employment rate, and the birth rate were treated as *endogenous*, to be explained by the model. The exogenous variables of the model include time, the money supply, the death rate, net immigration, the value of land, standard hours, and the proportion of the labor force that is unionized. In a more complete model, one can easily envisage the latter four variables (and possibly the money supply) as endogenous.

The *Duesenberry–Eckstein–Fromm (or DEF) model*[31] was a quarterly model of the U.S. economy under recession conditions, emphasizing built-in stabilizers such as tax and transfer payments. One of the major conclusions of this study was that the built-in stabilizers could mitigate but could not eliminate exogenous impulses making for cyclical down-

[27] In this connection, see Eckstein (1976, 1978).

[28] See Christ (1975), Fromm and Klein (1976), Bodkin, Klein, Marwah (1991), Adams and Klein (1991), and Uebe and Fischer (1992) for surveys. Related econometric models have been used to study regional economies, interregional and international trade, and economic development; some of this is discussed in the following section.

[29] See Tinbergen (1939, 1959). Criticism of Tinbergen's study by Haavelmo and others led to the postwar development of simultaneous-equations estimation techniques.

[30] See Valavanis (1955).

[31] See Duesenberry, Eckstein, and Fromm (1960).

turns, a conclusion that looked less obvious at the time of study than it does at present. This model was influenced by the Klein–Goldberger model but could not be considered a direct descendant. It, in turn, influenced the development of both the Brookings model and the DRI model, being a model of quarterly movements in GNP.

The *Suits model*[32] was based on an expanded version of the Klein–Goldberger model, where variables of the model were replaced by first differences and where an automobile sector was broken out. As well, Suits placed a heavy emphasis on the use of the model as a tool for forecasting. In addition, Suits estimated the relationships of his model by ordinary least squares, as the sophistication of two-stage least squares (or some other consistent method) was deemed not to repay the additional effort. This model influenced the later Michigan quarterly model, the MQEM model.

The *Liu model*[33] was an exploratory model of effective demand for the immediate postwar U.S. economy, beginning with the first quarter of 1947. By comparison to the Klein–Goldberger model, it entails somewhat greater disaggregation (e.g., four consumption variables plus consumer durables and three investment variables). It also has a monetary sector, which involves five liquid assets, five interest rates, and as exogenous variables, the discount rate and excess reserves relative to required reserves. It influenced the development of the later Liu–Hwa model.

The *Morishima–Saito model* was a small-scale model (seven behavioral equations and two identities) that today we should consider principally as a "classroom" or pedagogical model. Representing the U.S. economy over the period 1902–1952 (excluding the war years 1941–1945), it was intended to be a model of long-term growth. The behavioral relationships were fitted to annual data by the method of two-stage least squares, and they are all log-linear. The model was used for both structural analysis and for policy evaluation, particularly for the study of the relative effectiveness of monetary and fiscal policy. The structure of this model may be described briefly. In addition to a time trend and a dummy variable for postwar shifts after World War II, the other exogenous variables are the size of the population 15 years of age and older (as a simplification, the labor force was taken to be 57% of this magnitude), the stock of money (supposed, in this simplified representation, to be under the control of the monetary authorities), the trade balance (net exports) in real terms, and gross investment spending, also in real terms. Public spending is apportioned between current and capital uses. (In a growth model, it could be argued that taking at least private gross investment to be exogenous is something of an oversimplification.) The two identities are the equality of net national product to the sum of consumption plus gross investment plus net exports less capital consumption allowances (also in real terms), and one for the year-end value in current dollars of the capital stock (equal to last year's stock of capital plus gross investment less capital consumption allowances). The seven behavioral equations are a consumption function, a liquidity preference function (associated, in the first instance, with the determination of the corporate bond rate, which, however, appears to go nowhere in the model), a production function, a labor-share equation, a (nominal) wage rate equation, an equation for determining hours worked per person per year, and a depreciation (capital consumption allowance) equation. As this is a growth model, the heart of this model could be considered to be the production function, which is of the

[32]See Suits (1962, 1967).

[33]See Liu (1963).

Cobb–Douglas form with constant returns to scale (imposed, not estimated) and neutral technological progress of roughly 1.5% per annum. (In addition, there is a shift dummy that suggests a discrete improvement in efficiency of roughly 13% for all 7 years immediately following World War II.) The labor and capital coefficients in the production function are not estimated but are imposed from the results of the labor-share equation, which suggests that the elasticities of output with respect to labor and with respect to capital were roughly 0.82 and 0.18, respectively. The assumption of constant returns to scale might be questioned, particularly in the context of a growth model, as well as the view that all technological progress is of a neutral disembodied kind, rather than being (for instance) related to qualitative changes in the labor and capital inputs.[34]

The *Brookings model* was, at the time of its construction in the early 1960s, the largest and most ambitious macroeconometric model of the U.S. economy.[35] It was a highly disaggregated quarterly model, involving, in the "standard" version, 176 endogenous and 89 exogenous variables.[36] A major goal in building a model of that size was that of advancing the state of the art in model building, both via disaggregation and via the inclusion of sectors not included in previous models. The resulting model, in representing the detailed structure of the economy, was used both for structural analysis of cycles and growth and for policy evaluation.

The Brookings model was estimated using seasonally adjusted quarterly data from 1949 to 1960, amounting to approximately 60 observations. The reader may well wonder how a model of this size, involving so many explanatory variables, could have been estimated (with simultaneous-equations methods) from a sample of this size. Statistical estimation in this case appears to violate the fundamental degrees-of-freedom assumption. However, the division of the model into seven "blocks" of equations, to take account of the approximately block recursive nature of the model, enabled the model builders to overcome these problems and obtain consistent estimators of the model's parameters.[37]

As already noted, the focus of the Brookings model, which was not maintained after 1972, was policy evaluation, in the context of both short-term business cycles and long-run growth. One such study, for example, analyzed the impact of the dramatic 1964 income tax

[34]See Morishima and Saito (1972). The implications of the estimated Morishima–Saito model for multiplier analysis may be examined briefly. In particular, the calculated multipliers tend to support the Keynesian notion that fiscal policy is relatively more effective in reducing unemployment than monetary policy when the rate of unemployment is initially high.

[35]See Duesenberry et al. (1965, 1969), Fromm (1971), and Fromm and Klein (1975). More than 30 economists at various universities and research organizations collaborated in the development of the model, with individual specialists working on particular sectors. A more detailed review of the model, with a consideration of the critique by Basmann (1972), appears in Bodkin, Klein, Marwah (1991).

[36]Other versions have had more than 200 endogenous variables and allow for further expansion to over 400 endogenous variables, depending on the disaggregation of the producing sectors. It should be emphasized that while today the Brookings model would be considered a medium-sized model, at the time it was considered to be gigantic.

[37]See the discussion in Klein (1969a). Recall that the nature of a recursive model from Section 9.5 is one in which the coefficient matrix is triangular and the covariance matrix is diagonal. Here these properties are assumed for *blocks* of variables in both matrices, as indicated in Problem 9-P. The block recursive structure was a particularly convenient one to use, as it enabled individual specialists who participated in developing the model to concentrate on their own specific areas of expertise. The seven blocks of the model were Fixed Business Investment and Exports; Other Final Demand; Sectoral Outputs; Employment and Hours; Labor Supply and Unemployment; Wages, Prices, and Profits; and Interest, Money, and Other Income Shares.

cut with the Brookings model as the instrument of analysis.[38] Perhaps the most important contribution of the Brookings model project was, however, its role in integrating various sectors of the economy, methodologies, and data into a single unified approach and its influence in these respects on later models, approaches to estimation, and data banks. Moreover, it certainly showed the feasibility of larger sizes of macroeconometric models.

The *BEA model*, which was originally called the *OBE model*, is a quarterly model originally based on an early version of the Wharton model and developed by the Bureau of Economic Analysis (formerly, the Office of Business Economics; hence the name change) of the U.S. Department of Commerce.[39] In size and general structure, the original BEA model was similar to the original Wharton model, but both grew larger during the decades of the 1970s and 1980s. However, the BEA model emphasizes the government sector of the economy, while the Wharton model emphasizes the private sector. The original BEA model included three major sectors: the output market, for components of GNP; the labor market, for hours, wage rate, labor force, and labor income; and prices, for price deflators for GNP components and the wage rate. The short-run employment function included in the model converged to a standard Cobb–Douglas production function at potential (full-capacity) output. Another interesting feature of the model was that there were structural equations for *all* income components with the statistical discrepancy treated residually, subject to a constraint on the absolute size of this magnitude. This contrasts with the usual treatment where one income category (usually, property income or corporate profits) is treated residually.[40] The policy variables of the model include various tax rates and monetary policy variables. This model has been used for short-term forecasting and policy evaluation in the Department of Commerce and other government agencies, such as the Council of Economic Advisers.

The *St. Louis model*,[41] which was developed at the Federal Reserve Bank of St. Louis, ran counter to the trend of developing ever larger simultaneous macroeconometric models. It utilized a small linearized model of five semi-reduced-form equations, supplemented by four identities, to study alternative monetary and fiscal policies. It also ran counter to most of the other macroeconometric models summarized in this chapter by taking a strictly monetarist perspective (in contrast to a mainstream Keynesian view or an eclectic one), so it placed a heavy emphasis on monetary aggregates, in assessing monetary and fiscal impacts on total aggregate spending, real national product, unemployment, price levels, and interest rates. Its three exogenous variables were the change in the money stock (M_1), the change in high-employment federal expenditures, and potential full-employment output. According to the original estimated parameters, the money supply, however, was the principal driving force of this model. This conclusion, which was quite controversial,[42] is illustrated in Section 14.9, where the dynamic multiplier properties of the St. Louis model, while broadly displaying the same inverted-U form as the mainstream macroeconometric models, have quite

[38]See Fromm and Taubman (1968) and Klein (1969b).

[39]See Hirsch, Grimm, and Narasimham (1974) for the BEA model, and for its predecessor, Liebenberg, Hirsch, and Popkin (1966), Liebenberg, Green, and Hirsch (1971), and Green, Liebenberg, and Hirsch (1972). A current version, which has 195 behavioral equations, is summarized in Adams and Klein (1991).

[40]In the BEA model, if the statistical discrepancy is "too large," so that some of the income components must be adjusted, all of them are so treated.

[41]See Andersen and Jordan (1968), and Andersen and Carlson (1970, 1974).

[42]For a summary of these critiques, see Bodkin, Klein, Marwah (1991, Chap. 5, Sec. 7).

different qualitative patterns. In particular, the multiplier effects of increased government expenditures are exhausted quite quickly, after only several periods.

The *Michigan quarterly econometric model or MQEM*[43] was influenced by the Suits model (discussed earlier in this section), which had been used earlier at Michigan. It was, however, the direct descendant of a small quarterly model developed in the late 1960s at the Council of Economic Advisers for use in forecasting. MQEM was a medium-sized nonlinear model designed primarily, like its antecedent, for short-term prediction. It consisted of six main blocks or sectors—wages and prices, productivity and employment, expenditures, income flows, interest rates, and the composition of output; these six blocks formed an integrated and interdependent system. The model was also used for policy analysis; thus Hymans employed this model (and also the MPS and BEA models) to study the long-term or steady-state behavior of the Phillips curve (trade-off curve) of the American economy in the late 1960s.[44] As one might expect, the Michigan model contains considerable disaggregation with regard to automobile demand. Also, the late 1980s version of the model has a mechanism for explaining the trade-weighted exchange value of the U.S. dollar.

The *Fair model* of the 1970s was a short-run quarterly forecasting model that was originally constructed as a point of principle to be small in comparison to other quarterly models, consisting of 14 stochastic equations and five identities.[45] It was composed of three sectors: the monthly housing starts sector, the nominal GNP sector, and the price–unemployment–labor force sector. The model explicitly allowed for disequilibrium in the housing sector and treated unemployment as a residual, the difference between total labor force (obtained from participation rate equations) and labor requirements (which followed a short-run production function). This model also provided direct estimates of potential GNP. Included as exogenous variables were expectations with regard to both consumer buying and plant and equipment investment. The estimation technique accounted for both first-order serial correlation (which is Fair's preferred assumption) and any simultaneity present. A unique aspect of Fair's technique of *ex ante* forecasting with this model was that no use was made of subjective add factors adjusting the constant terms, following a running reestimation of the parameters just before the time of the forecast.[46] Fair's model for the 1980s is considerably larger, at 30 behavioral equations and 98 identities. This later model, which is available for use on the personal computer, has been used by Fair himself in recent years to investigate the hypothesis that economic expectations are "rational" (or at least "model consistent"), especially with regard to the financial sector of the economy.[47]

The *Hickman–Coen model*[48] is an annual model of long-term growth. It is used for medium- and long-range prediction purposes, specifically for predictions of the annual time paths of major macroeconomic variables, such as actual and potential GNP, labor force, unemployment, wages, and prices, over a horizon of a decade or so. These predictions are made under alternative assumptions concerning government policies and demographic and techno-

[43]See Hymans and Shapiro (1970, 1974), Adams and Klein (1991), and Fair and Alexander (1991).

[44]See Hymans (1972).

[45]See Fair (1971, 1974). A 1980s version of the Fair model may be found in Fair (1984). See also Adams and Klein (1991) and Fair and Alexander (1991).

[46]In this connection, see Chapter 15, especially Sections 15.3 and 15.6.

[47]See Fair (1979, 1993).

[48]See Hickman, Coen, and Hurd (1975), Hickman and Coen (1976), Coen and Hickman (1984), and Green et al. (1991).

logical trends. The model thus emphasizes long-run growth factors rather than short-run cyclical phenomena. Among its distinguishing features are interrelated firm demand functions for labor and capital as agents of production; consideration of alternative concepts of full-employment, potential, and capacity real GNP; an integrated cost, pricing, and production framework; a variant of a search theory approach to unemployment; a long-run model of housing in which disequilibrium factors act in the short run; and a high proportion of logarithmic stochastic functions (e.g., Cobb–Douglas production functions) and partial adjustment hypotheses. A reworked version of the model for the 1980s includes a separate energy sector as well as energy constraints on total production. Policy simulations with the 1970s version of the model imply that a sustained exogenous increase in federal expenditures (or a reduction in tax receipts) could permanently reduce unemployment, with most of the reduction accomplished in the first five years.[49] Expansionary monetary policy (an increase in unborrowed reserves), by contrast, will decrease unemployment temporarily, but after two or three years the unemployment rate returns approximately to its original level. (This is hardly surprising, given the weak links of the monetary sector with the real variables, in the Hickman–Coen model.)

The *Liu–Hwa model*,[50] a successor of the Liu model described above, was a monthly model of national income determination that was intended for forecasting and policy analysis. It disaggregated the production sector into private nonfarm and general government components and also made use of the CES production function. It included 12 policy instruments, the values of which (in combination with lagged endogenous and exogenous variables) generated *monthly* forecasts of GNP and its components. Indeed, it was the first major monthly econometric model, which gave it an important advantage in attempting to capture the lag structure of the economy. Indeed, Liu and Hwa place considerable emphasis on this aspect of their model. The Liu–Hwa model, although experimental and a tentative effort in a new direction of research, was quite stimulating and showed considerable promise. For a long time this work languished, following the untimely death in 1975 of one of its principal researchers. Recently, the Liu–Hwa work has been taken up again by the Federal Reserve Board, with the particular focus of employing monthly data to sharpen short-term forecasts.[51]

The *Taylor model* of the U.S. economy[52] is interesting for several reasons. First, it is squarely in the "New Keynesian" framework, in which wages and prices are sticky in the short run; wages in particular evolve through staggered contracts. Nevertheless, expectations are expected to be "rational" if the agents have time to learn a changed regime. Second, Taylor embeds his U.S. model in a multicountry modeling context; the other countries modeled explicitly are the G-7 countries of Canada, France, Germany, Italy, Japan, and the United Kingdom. The U.S. model used in the simulations by Adams and Klein had 20 behavioral equations and was fitted to varying periods between 1971 and 1986. Because of the centrality of the rational expectations assumption, the Taylor model reacts quite differently to economic shocks from the typical mainstream macroeconometric model. In the

[49]By contrast, in the 1980s version of the model, the dynamic multipliers resemble much more those of the other American models, so the multiplier impact of a sustained increase in government expenditure rises for a time, then peaks, and then declines.

[50]See Liu (1969) and Liu and Hwa (1974).

[51]See Klein (1991) and Howrey (1991).

[52]See Taylor (1986, 1993) and also Adams and Klein (1991), particularly for the multiplier results mentioned below.

government expenditure multiplier simulations by Adams and Klein, the Taylor model showed more of a response initially than the "average" model, but the effects of stimulation dissipated much more rapidly. Taylor himself has recently used the model to show the effects of a "credible" five-year plan in which the United States cuts its budget deficit from 3% of GDP to zero.

The final model reviewed in this section is Allen Sinai's *Boston Company Economic Advisors (BCEA) model.*[53] With 261 behavioral equations, 270 identities, and 209 exogenous variables, the BCEA model certainly qualifies as a large-scale model. Although there is considerable attention to supply-side detail and to the financial sector, it seems fair to describe the model as being "eclectic," rather than belonging to any particular theoretical camp. The model explains the valuation of stock market equities, based on such fundamentals as interest rates, expected earnings, and expected after-tax returns on these equities. Like the MQEM, the model explains the foreign exchange value of the U.S. dollar (in this case against a trade-weighted average of 15 OECD currencies). The formation of expectations in financial and real markets is a distinguishing feature of the BCEA, with expectations being formed (in particular cases) by either permanent, extrapolative, or model-consistent ("rational," in one interpretation) mechanisms. In the model, expectations have a "quick" effect on asset prices and returns, which gives financial factors some additional force as compared to standard specifications. Nevertheless, Sinai asserts that his model has "standard" government expenditure multiplier properties, but that monetary policy is quite potent in the model. Sinai himself has recently used the model as a framework for disentangling real and monetary factors in recent business cycles or fluctuations. In particular, Sinai is quite proud of the fact that his model was almost unique in both predicting the 1990–1991 recession (in advance), as well as the anemic recovery of the U.S. economy from that recession.[54]

12.8 SOME INTERNATIONAL EXPERIENCE; THE CANDIDE MODEL OF THE CANADIAN ECONOMY

Macroeconometric models have been built for many countries besides the United States; Uebe and Fischer in their tabulations of macroeconometric models list 133 countries (counting subdivisions such as North and South Korea and West and East Germany as two countries) for which at least one such model has been constructed.[55] Moreover, al-

[53]See Sinai (1992) and Adams and Klein (1991).

[54]Two other models employed by Adams and Klein (1991) in their simulation studies of major U.S. macroeconometric models at that time are the model of the Indiana University Center for Econometric Research (IND) and the Washington University Macro Model (WUMM) of Lawrence Meyer & Associates. Both are medium-sized and both pay attention to supposed long-run equilibrium properties, particularly WUMM. In apparent consequence, both have medium-term government expenditure multipliers that diminish sooner and more rapidly than the "representative" model's multipliers [for the case with the money supply (M_1 concept) held constant].

[55]Uebe and Fischer (1992) give simply a tabular presentation for approximately 3500 models (including regional submodels of particular countries); this tabulation gives the number of equations in total (divided into stochastic and definitional equations), the number of exogenous variables, the presence or absence of an endogenous monetary sector, the presence or absence of an input–output submodel, the frequency of the observations, and the type of model surveyed. [More than macroeconometric models are tabulated, for example input–output models, linear programming models, and vector autoregressive (VAR) models.] More detail in an international survey appears in Bodkin, Klein, Marwah (1991), especially Chapters 6 through 12, where the history of macroeconometric model building in the Netherlands, the United Kingdom, France, Canada, Japan, India, and the Latin American countries is surveyed in separate chapters.

though it seems fair to say that there has been more macroeconometric modeling applied to the U.S. economy than to any other single country, it is interesting to note that the first such model was built by Jan Tinbergen for the Dutch economy in the mid-1930s. It was only in the late 1930s, when he was working for the League of Nations, that Tinbergen built the first macroeconometric model of the U.S. economy, which we have surveyed in Section 12.7.

With the number of macroeconometric models currently in the thousands (see footnote 55), an attempt to be comprehensive has had to be abandoned. Instead, one general development of recent years, namely the presentation of a number of *linked* systems of macroeconometric models, is discussed. As well, a Canadian macroeconometric model is summarized, to illustrate macroeconometric model building outside the United States.

One of the earliest systems of linked macroeconometric models is called Project LINK.[56] This project was started in 1968 by a small group of 11 econometricians under the leadership of Lawrence R. Klein and Bert G. Hickman, who worked with seven macroeconometric models of individual countries or, where such models were lacking, with models of aggregated regions (such as a model for the socialist countries as a whole or a model for the less developed countries). However, the philosophy of Project LINK has been to encourage the participation of individual model builders from the particular countries concerned, taking on the view that an indigenous model builder will have a better feeling for his/her own economy than could someone constructing a model of the entire world economy, in one particular location. (Of course, costs of coordination and even problems of inconsistency are greater with the LINK approach.) From this particular beginning, the project has been growing steadily, so that by 1987 there were more than 100 participants and 79 macroeconometric models represented in the project. Trade linkages have, as one might expect, been at the center of simulations of the world economy as depicted in the LINK project, and algorithms have been developed to make the exports of one country consistent with the imports of its trading partners. In addition, import prices have been made consistent with the export prices of the trading partners. Exchange rates against the U.S. dollar are also determined in a subsystem for Belgium, Canada, France, Germany, Italy, Japan, and the United Kingdom, and direct interest rate linkages appear in many of the models for OECD countries. Of course, some coordination of the entire system of all the equations of all the models is required, and this is done at a center termed "LINK Central." The overall system was composed of some 20,000 equations in 1987; accordingly, the solution of such a large system can make use of the computer power of a *supercomputer*. Thus projections of the world economy, typically with a five-year horizon, with emphasis on world trade, are usually prepared twice a year, following semiannual meetings of the participants. In addition, a number of special studies have been carried out with Project LINK; for example, Klein reconsidered the issue of protectionism in the context of this macro model of the world as a whole and showed that protec-

[56]See Waelbroeck (1976), Hickman (1991), and Klein (1983, Chap. 7, "Project LINK"). There have been a number of linked systems of macroeconometric models, and Hickman (1991) discusses explicitly 12 of these, at least briefly. Almost all of them have a different philosophy from Project LINK, with a tight control at the center of the project. However, in this chapter only Project LINK is summarized. (Note, however, that the Taylor multicountry model, alluded to briefly in Section 12.7, is an illustration of an alternative linked system. Another alternative system is described in Bryant et al., 1988.)

tionism entailed definite costs for the world economy as a whole, even if some individual countries at times might be gainers.[57]

Finally, as an example of a model of an economy other than that of the United States, consider the government of Canada's *CANDIDE model* of the Canadian economy.[58] There have been five versions of the CANDIDE model (1.0, 1.1, 1.2, 2.0, and 3.0), but the discussion will concentrate on the second version, as the published documentation is most complete for this version. The acronym stands for "*Can*adian *d*isaggregated *i*nter-*de*partmental *e*conometric," and the individual terms are fairly descriptive. While "Canadian" and "econometric" are fairly obvious, a word of explanation on the other two might be in order. The term *inter-departmental* refers to the fact that the model was originally a cooperative effort of several departments and agencies of the government of Canada, with a leading role for the Economic Council of Canada; rather than having a number of individual government departments construct macroeconometric models, it was decided to build an all-purpose model, in an attempt to economize scarce professional resources. The term *disaggregated* refers to a considerable industrial disaggregation of the model, which was thought desirable to obtain detailed policy handles on complicated issues such as the Canada–USA Automobile Agreement and the issue of increased stability in the construction industry and its possible macroeconomic impacts. This large degree of disaggregation was facilitated by the presence of two input–output submodels as constituent pieces of the entire system; one of these submodels was on the side of industrial output determination (generating outputs of 76 input–output industries, which may be reduced to real domestic product originating in 63 detailed industries or 13 major sectors). The other input–output submodel was on the side of industrial price formation. Of course, such a disaggregation implied a large-scale model; indeed, at roughly 2000 equations (approximately 600 behavioral equations, 400 input–output identities, and 1000 ordinary identities) and approximately 450 exogenous variables, CANDIDE was probably, for its day, the largest macroeconometric model in the world for a single country. (The issue of an optimum scale for a macroeconometric model is discussed in Section 12.9.) Model 1.1 was an annual model, fitted to Canadian data for the period 1955–1971, and it was definitely in the mainstream Keynesian tradition of the model-building profession at that time.

The scope of the model may be indicated by eight "supersectors": final demand by ultimate use, real domestic product by industry, labor supply and requirements, wages and prices, private and government revenues, national income accounting relationships, financial flows, and antecedent relationships. The latter included a rather detailed demographic submodel, because CANDIDE was used for medium-term projections, and of course demographic phenomena influence the development of the Canadian economy, although there were no channels of feedback from the economy to demographic phenomena.[59] Finally, it

[57]See Klein (1985) and Johnson and Klein (1974). The LINK system enables one to draw macroeconomic conclusions for the world as a whole about protectionism, while the laws of comparative advantage could be interpreted to refer strictly to individual countries or even to individual industries.

[58]See McCracken (1973) and Bodkin and Tanny (1975).

[59]In fact, this was not strictly true. Net immigration did depend on the state of the Canadian economy, although with a lag; thus buoyant conditions in Canada would tend to attract larger numbers of immigrants (after taking emigration into account). However, it is true that total population and its components were *predetermined* from the point of view of current economic activity. As the model was used for medium-term projections into the future, it was very useful to have a population calculator embedded in the basic model. For historical simulations, the users tended to ignore the demographic submodel, taking population components as measured by Statistics Canada (the main data-gathering agency of the country).

has already been noted that the perspective of the model was medium term, interpreted as projections some five to 10 years into the future (well beyond the length of the typical business cycle, but it was hoped, not so far into the future that major technological developments or other structural changes would have taken place). Indeed, the major use of the model that was originally envisaged at the Economic Council of Canada was to make projections of what "good" macroeconomic policy might accomplish, in a vague effort to make both public and private economic decision making more "rational," in some sense.[60] Be that as it may, an important input into future projections of an economy (such as the Canadian) according to a macroeconometric model (e.g., CANDIDE) is of course the projected *future* values of exogenous variables. In the case of CANDIDE (like virtually all Canadian econometric models), the exogenous variables included developments in the U.S. economy (in some detail). But where could one find projections of the U.S. economy in such detail? One possibility was (and remains) a compatible medium-term macroeconometric model of the U.S. economy, of course, provided that projections of this model into the medium-term future were readily available. In fact, during a considerable part of the time when the CANDIDE model was actively maintained and used, the project maintained a subscription to the WEFA corporation, principally to obtain the medium-term projections of the Wharton Industry and Annual Forecasting Model, summarized briefly in Section 12.4. Such a procedure is indeed reasonable if one assumes that the American economy greatly influences the Canadian economy but that the feedback influence of the Canadian economy on the U.S. economy is minimal. Given that the size of the U.S. economy is some 10 to 15 times larger (depending on what one assumes about equilibrium exchange rates), this seems a reasonable assumption to make.[61]

12.9 TRENDS IN MACROECONOMETRIC MODEL CONSTRUCTION

It should be apparent in considering their evolution over time, as summarized in the discussion above, that macroeconomic models have tended to increase in size, as measured, for example, by the number of stochastic equations. They have also tended to increase in scope and complexity. This change can be easily understood in terms of a rational choice of scale, reflecting size, scope, and complexity. A rational choice would seek the point at which the marginal benefit of added scale (measured in terms, for example, of more accurate or more complete forecasts) equals the marginal cost of added scale (measured in terms, for example, of the added cost of data collection and information processing), as illustrated in Figure 12.2. The successive models surveyed above were developed, however, during decades in which the marginal cost of added scale fell precipitously as a result of the advent of computers to perform the necessary calculations, library programs for econometric routines, and readily available or even computerized data banks.[62] This change over time is

[60]In this regard, see the *Ninth Annual Review* of the Economic Council of Canada (1972).

[61]Still, one would not wish to make this assumption in analyzing developments in a Vermont border town that is heavily dependent on Canadian tourism. Here, as elsewhere, the intended purpose of a model is not trivial.

[62]In terms of the basic ingredients of an econometric model, as given in Figure 1.1, the econometric techniques and data have become much more readily available and reasonably standardized. As a result, the remaining basic ingredient—the economic model—has become a major focus of attention in recent years.

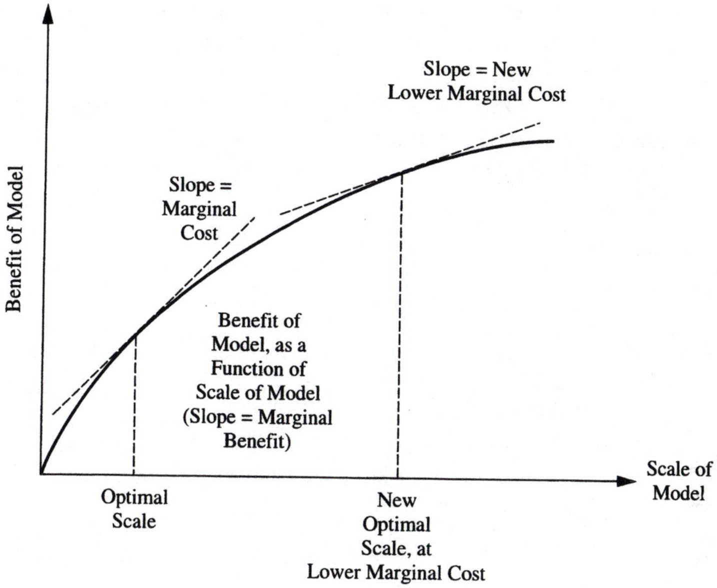

Figure 12.2 Increase of Model's Optimal Scale with a Fall in the Marginal Cost

depicted in Figure 12.2: the fall in the marginal cost of scale has led to an overall increase in scale.[63]

Another trend in macroeconometric model construction has been the attempt to combine several distinct models into a larger integrated model. One aspect of this trend is the inclusion of input–output models into macroeconometric models.[64] Another is the attempt to link together several national macroeconometric models into a global model that can treat international trade as well as national economic phenomena; see Section 12.8. A third aspect is the attempt to relate microeconomic behavior, of individual agents, to macroeconomic phenomena.

A third trend in macroeconometric model construction has been the tendency to rely more and more upon nonlinear rather than linear models. While many phenomena represented in such models are linear or can be approximated by linear relationships, some are inherently nonlinear. Thus, for example, all value terms represent the product of price and quantity; production relationships are typically nonlinear; and ratios, such as those of prices to an average price level, are frequently included in such models. Modern econometric mod-

[63]In the decade of the 1980s, the arrival of very cheap computing costs for small-scale projects in the form of the personal computer (PC) has in part induced a movement back to small and medium-sized macroeconometric models. In technical terms it appears that there are now two typical points of local optimization for a possible macroeconometric project, one small in size using the PC and the other large in scale employing the mainframe computer and/or workstation. The individual researcher (or project manager) must decide the *optimum optimorum.* Chapter 17 considers further aspects of the project management of an econometric model.

[64]Examples include the Brookings model, the Wharton Annual and Industry model, the DRI model, and the CANDIDE model. See Fisher, Klein, and Shinkai (1965), Fromm and Klein (1969), and Kresge (1969) for the Brookings model; Preston (1975) for the Wharton Annual and Industry model; Eckstein (1983) and Eckstein, Green, and Sinai (1974) for the DRI model; and McCracken (1973) and Bodkin and Tanny (1975) for the CANDIDE model.

els usually include such nonlinearities. They must therefore be solved by nonlinear techniques. For example, obtaining the reduced form from the structural form involves solving a system of nonlinear equations.[65]

The uses of the models discussed in this chapter for purposes of structural analysis, forecasting, and policy evaluation will be the topics of Chapters 14, 15, and 16. Chapter 13 will treat some applications of simultaneous-equations models in fields other than the macroeconomy.

PROBLEMS

12-A Consider the following nine-equation macroeconomic model:

$$C_t = \alpha_{11}Y_t + \alpha_{21} + \varepsilon_{1t} \text{ (consumption function)}$$
$$I_t = \alpha_{12}Y_t + \alpha_{22}Y_{t-1} + \alpha_{32}r_t + \alpha_{42}K_{t-1} + \alpha_{52} + \varepsilon_{2t} \text{ (investment function)}$$
$$M_t = \alpha_{13}Y_t + \alpha_{23}r_t + \alpha_{33} + \varepsilon_{3t} \text{ (money supply, demand)}$$
$$L_t = \alpha_{14}w_t + \alpha_{24}Y_t + \alpha_{34}K_t + \alpha_{44} + \varepsilon_{4t} \text{ (employment function)}$$
$$p_t - p_{t-1} = \alpha_{15}(w_t - w_{t-1}) + \alpha_{25}(M_t - M_{t-1}) + \alpha_{35} + \varepsilon_{5t} \text{ (price change function)}$$
$$w_t - w_{t-1} = \alpha_{16}(p_t - p_{t-1}) + \alpha_{26}U_t + \alpha_{36}U_{t-1} + \alpha_{46} + \varepsilon_{6t} \text{ (wage adjustment function)}$$
$$Y_t = C_t + I_t + G_t \text{ (national income identity)}$$
$$U_t = N_t - L_t \text{ (unemployment identity)}$$
$$K_t - K_{t-1} = I_t - \alpha_{42}K_{t-1} \text{ (capital stock identity)}$$

where the nine endogenous variables are:

Y = national income
C = consumption
I = investment
K = capital stock
L = employment
U = unemployment
w = wage rate
p = price level
r = interest rate

and the three exogenous variables are:

G = government expenditure
M = money supply
N = labor force.

1. Show the interrelationships of the model in a flow diagram (arrow diagram) covering the periods $t-1$, t, and $t+1$ (stochastic disturbance terms can be omitted).

[65]The Gauss–Seidel technique is typically used to solve such a nonlinear system for the reduced-form equations. This technique starts from an initial trial solution (e.g., past values of the endogenous variables) and iterates toward the solutions for the endogenous variables by correcting discrepancies at each stage. The process continues until the change in solution values from one iteration to the next is less than a preassigned degree of accuracy (e.g., a percentage change of less than 0.001 in absolute value) (see Fromm and Klein, 1969; Klein and Evans, 1969; Klein, 1983; and Amemiya, 1983, 1985).

2. Formulate the structural form as a matrix equation. Indicate by partitioning the coefficient matrix the clustering of variables.

12-B Consider the following macroeconomic model:

$$C_t = a + bY_t + cC_{t-1},$$
$$Y_t = C_t + I_t,$$
$$I_t = I_0\lambda^t,$$

where the consumption function includes a term representing habit formation and where investment grows exogenously, λ being the (positive) growth factor.

1. Solve for the time path for C_t.
2. Show that, for equilibrium values, the long-run marginal propensity to consume is given by

$$\text{MPC}_L = \frac{b}{1 - c/\lambda} = \frac{\lambda b}{\lambda - c}.$$

3. Show that the equation for consumption is equivalent to the Koyck distributed lag formulation:

$$C_t = \frac{a}{1-c} + b\sum_{j=0}^{\infty} c^j Y_{t-j}.$$

4. Evans estimated the following consumption function for the United States, 1929–1962 (excluding 1942–1946), using annual data in constant dollars:[66]

$$\underset{}{C_t} = \underset{(0.041)}{0.280Y_t} + \underset{(0.052)}{0.676C_{t-1}}.$$

Estimate the short- and long-run marginal propensity to consume (assume $\lambda = 1.02$, corresponding to 2% growth per year), and give 95% confidence intervals for both.

12-C Consider the following model for investment:

$$I_t = K_t - K_{t-1} + D_t, \qquad (1)$$
$$D_t = \delta K_{t-1}, \qquad (2)$$
$$K_t - K_{t-1} = (1-\delta)(K_t^* - K_{t-1}), \qquad (3)$$
$$K_t^* = \alpha Y_t + \beta\left(\frac{w}{r}\right)_t, \qquad (4)$$

where equation (1) identifies gross investment as the change in the capital stock (net investment) plus depreciation; equation (2) stipulates that depreciation is proportional to the existing capital stock; equation (3) is the stock adjustment hypothesis; and equation (4) relates desired capital to output and the wage-rental ratio.

Assuming Y and w/r can be treated as exogenous, show that it is impossible to determine unique parameter estimates for α, β, δ, and λ, but that it is possible to determine the ratio α/β uniquely. If δ were available from extraneous information, show specifically how α, β, and λ could be estimated.

12-D For the Klein interwar model of Table 12.3:

1. Find the dimensions (units of measurement) of each estimated coefficient.
2. Using the order condition, investigate the identification of each equation.

12-E Construct, in general terms, a flow diagram such as that in Figure 12.1 for the original Wharton model.

12-F Construct, in general terms, a flow diagram such as that in Figure 12.1 for the DRI model.

[66]See Evans (1969, Sec. 3.3).

12-G Consider Figure 12.2 and sketch in a curve of total costs of a model construction project, including computing costs. Let this curve be strictly increasing, but the curve should increase slowly in a range of "small" to "medium" models, then increase rapidly in a middle range, and finally increase slowly again in the range of "large" models. (This might be rationalized by the use of PCs in the first range, while the transition to mainframe computers and workstations induces rapidly increasing costs of computation, over the middle range of model scale.) Show graphically that there are indeed two points of local optimum, for the scale of an econometric project. How should the project manager choose between these two points? (Explain very briefly.)

BIBLIOGRAPHY

ADAMS, F. G., and V. G. DUGGAL (1974). "Anticipations Variables in an Econometric Model: The Anticipations Version of Wharton Mark IV." *International Economic Review*, 15: 267–84.

ADAMS, F. G., and L. R. KLEIN (1991). "Performance of Quarterly Econometric Models of the United States: A New Round of Model Comparisons," in L. R. Klein, Ed., *Comparative Performances of U.S. Econometric Models*. New York: Oxford University Press.

ADELMAN, I., and F. ADELMAN (1959). "The Dynamic Properties of the Klein–Goldberger Model." *Econometrica*, 27: 596–625; reprinted in A. Zellner, Ed. (1968). *Readings in Economic Statistics and Econometrics*. Boston: Little, Brown and Company.

AMEMIYA, T. (1983). "Non-linear Regression Models," in Z. Griliches and M. D. Intriligator, Eds., *Handbook of Econometrics*, Vol. 1. Amsterdam: North-Holland Publishing Company.

AMEMIYA, T. (1985). *Advanced Econometrics*. Cambridge, Mass.: Harvard University Press.

ANDERSEN, L. C., and K. M. CARLSON (1970). "A Monetarist Model for Economic Stabilization." *Federal Reserve Bank of St. Louis Review*, 52: 7–25.

ANDERSEN, L. C., and K. CARLSON (1974). "St. Louis Model Revisited." *International Economic Review*, 15: 305–327.

ANDERSEN L. C., and J. L. JORDAN (1968). "Monetary and Fiscal Actions: A Test of Their Relative Importance in Economic Stabilization." *Federal Reserve Bank of St. Louis Review*, 50: 11–23.

ANDO, A. (1974). "Some Aspects of Stabilization Policies, the Monetarist Controversy, and the MPS Model." *International Economic Review*, 15: 541–571.

ANDO, A., and F. MODIGLIANI (1969). "Econometric Analysis of Stabilization Policies." *American Economic Review*, 59: 296–314.

ANDO, A., F. MODIGLIANI, and R. RASCHE (1972). "Equations and Definitions of Variables for the FRB–MIT–Penn Econometric Model, November, 1969," in Hickman, Ed. (1972).

BASMANN, R. L. (1972). "The Brookings Quarterly Econometric Model: Science or Number Mysticism?" in K. Brunner, Ed., *Problems and Issues in Current Econometric Practice*. Columbus, Ohio: College of Administrative Science, Ohio State University.

BODKIN, R. G. (1977). "Keynesian Econometric Concepts: Consumption Functions, Investment Functions, and 'The' Multiplier," in S. Weintraub, Ed., *Modern Economic Thought*. Philadelphia: University of Pennsylvania Press.

BODKIN, R. G., L. R. KLEIN, K. MARWAH (1991). *A History of Macroeconometric Model-Building*. Aldershot, Hants, England: Edward Elgar Publishing Ltd.

BODKIN, R. G., and S. TANNY (1975). *CANDIDE Model 1.1*. CANDIDE Project Paper 18. Ottawa: Information Canada.

BRINNER, R. E., and A. A. HIRSCH (1991). "A Comparative Analysis of the DRI and BEA Models," in L. R. Klein, Ed., *Comparative Performance of U.S. Econometric Models*. New York: Oxford University Press.

BRYANT, R., D. HENDERSON, G. HOLTHAM, P. HOOPER, and S. SYMANSKY, Eds. (1988). *Empirical Macroeconomics for Interdependent Economies*. Washington, D.C.: The Brookings Institution.

CHRIST, C. F. (1951). "A Test of an Econometric Model of the United States, 1921–1947," *Conference on Business Cycles,* New York National Bureau of Economic Research, Inc.

CHRIST, C. F. (1966). *Econometric Models and Methods*. New York: John Wiley & Sons, Inc.

CHRIST, C. F. (1975). "Judging the Performance of Econometric Models of the U.S. Economy." *International Economic Review*, 16: 54–74.

CLARK, P. K. (1979). "Investment in the 1970s: Theory, Performance, and Prediction." *Brookings Papers on Economic Activity*, 1: 73–113.

COEN, R. M., and B. G. HICKMAN (1984). "Tax Policy, Federal Deficits, and U.S. Growth in the 1980s." *National Tax Journal*, 37: 89–104.

DATA RESOURCES, INC. (1976). *The Data Resources National Economic Information System.* Amsterdam: North-Holland Publishing Company.

DEATON, A. S., and J. N. MUELLBAUER (1980). *Economics and Consumer Behaviour.* New York: Cambridge University Press.

DE LEEUW, F., and E. M. GRAMLICH (1968). "The Federal Reserve-M.I.T. Econometric Model." *The Federal Reserve Bulletin*, 54: 11–40.

DE LEEUW, F., and E. M. GRAMLICH (1969). "The Channels of Monetary Policy." *Federal Reserve Bulletin*, 55: 472–491.

DUESENBERRY, J. S., O. ECKSTEIN, and G. FROMM (1960). "Simulation of the United States Economy in Recession." *Econometrica*, 28: 749–809.

DUESENBERRY, J. S., G. FROMM, L. R. KLEIN, and E. KUH, Eds. (1965). *The Brookings Quarterly Econometric Model of the United States*. Chicago: Rand McNally & Company; Amsterdam: North-Holland Publishing Company.

DUESENBERRY, J. S., G. FROMM, L. R. KLEIN, and E. KUH, Eds. (1969). *The Brookings Model: Some Further Results*. Chicago: Rand McNally & Company.

DUGGAL, V. G., L. R. KLEIN, and M. D. MCCARTHY (1974). "The Wharton Model Mark III: A Modern IS-LM Construct." *International Economic Review*, 15: 572–594.

ECKSTEIN, O., Ed. (1976). *Parameters and Policies in the U.S. Economy*. Amsterdam: North-Holland Publishing Company.

ECKSTEIN, O. (1978). *The Great Recession: With a Postscript on Stagflation*. Amsterdam: North-Holland Publishing Company.

ECKSTEIN, O. (1983). *The DRI Model of the U.S. Economy*. New York: McGraw-Hill Book Company.

ECKSTEIN, O., E. W. GREEN, and A. SINAI (1974). "The Data Resources Model: Uses, Structure, and Analysis of the U.S. Economy." *International Economic Review*, 15: 595–615.

ECONOMIC COUNCIL OF CANADA (1972). *The Years to 1980*. Ninth Annual Review of the Economic Council of Canada. Ottawa: Information Canada.

EVANS, M. K. (1969). *Macroeconomic Activity: Theory, Forecasting and Control; An Econometric Approach*. New York: Harper & Row, Publishers, Inc.

EVANS, M. K., and L. R. KLEIN (1967). *The Wharton Econometric Forecasting Model*. Philadelphia: Economics Research Unit, Wharton School, University of Pennsylvania.

EVANS, M. K., and L. R. KLEIN (1968). *The Wharton Econometric Forecasting Model*, 2nd enlarged ed. Philadelphia: Economics Research Unit, Wharton School, University of Pennsylvania.

FAIR, R. C. (1971). *A Short-Run Forecasting Model of the United States Economy*. Lexington, Mass.: Heath Lexington Books.

FAIR, R. C. (1974). "An Evaluation of a Short-Run Forecasting Model." *International Economic Review*, 15: 285–303.

FAIR, R. C. (1979). "An Analysis of a Macro-Econometric Model with Rational Expectations in the Bond and Stock Markets." *American Economic Review*, 69: 539–552.

FAIR, R. C. (1984). *Specification, Estimation and Analysis of Macroeconometric Models*. Cambridge, Mass.: Harvard University Press.

FAIR, R. C. (1993). "Testing Macroeconometric Models." *American Economic Review, Papers and Proceedings*, 83: 287–293.

FAIR, R. C., and L. S. ALEXANDER (1991). "A Comparison of the Michigan and Fair Models," in L. R. Klein, Ed., *Comparative Performance of U.S. Econometric Models*. New York: Oxford University Press.

FISHER, F. M., L. R. KLEIN, and Y. SHINKAI (1965). "Price and Output Aggregation in the Brookings Econometric Model," in Duesenberry et al., Eds. (1965).

FOX, K. A. (1958). *Econometric Analysis for Public Policy*. Ames: Iowa State University Press.

FROMM, G., Ed. (1971). *Tax Incentives and Capital Spending*. Amsterdam: North-Holland Publishing Company.

FROMM, G., and L. R. KLEIN (1969). "Solutions of the Complete System," in Duesenberry et al., Eds. (1969).

FROMM, G., and L. R. KLEIN, Eds. (1975). *The Brookings Model: Perspective and Recent Developments*. Amsterdam: North-Holland Publishing Company.

FROMM, G., and L. R. KLEIN (1976). "The NBER/NSF Model Comparison Seminar: An Analysis of Results." *Annals of Economic and Social Measurement*, 5: 1–28.

FROMM, G., and P. TAUBMAN (1968). *Policy Simulations with an Economic Model*. Amsterdam: North-Holland Publishing Company.

GOLDBERGER, A. S. (1959). *Impact Multipliers and Dynamic Properties of the Klein-Goldberger Model*. Amsterdam: North-Holland Publishing Company.

GOLDBERGER, A. S. (1964). *Econometric Theory*. New York: John Wiley & Sons, Inc.

GREEN, G. R., in association with M. LIEBENBERG and A. A. HIRSCH (1972). "Short- and Long-Term Simulations with the OBE Econometric Model," in Hickman, Ed. (1972).

GREEN, R. J., B. G. HICKMAN, E. P. HOWREY, S. H. HYMANS, and M. R. DONIHUE (1991). "The IS-LM Cores of Three Econometric Models," in L. R. Klein, Ed., *Comparative Performance of U.S. Econometric Models*. New York: Oxford University Press.

HELLIWELL, J. F. (1993). "Macroeconometrics in a Global Economy." *American Economic Review, Papers and Proceedings*, 83: 287–293.

HELLIWELL, J. F., F. W. GORBET, G. R. SPARKS, and I. A. STEWART (1973). "Comprehensive Linkage of Large Models: Canada and the United States," in R. J. Ball, Ed., *The International Linkage of National Economic Models*. Amsterdam: North-Holland Publishing Company.

HICKMAN, B. G., Ed. (1972). *Econometric Models of Cyclical Behavior*. National Bureau of Economic Research. New York: Columbia University Press.

HICKMAN, B. G. (1991). "Project LINK and Multicountry Modelling," in Bodkin, Klein, Marwah (1991).

HICKMAN, B. G., and R. M. COEN (1976). *An Annual Growth Model of the U.S. Economy*. Amsterdam: North-Holland Publishing Company.

HICKMAN, B. G., R. M. COEN, and M. D. HURD (1975). "The Hickman–Coen Annual Growth Model: Structural Characteristics and Policy Responses." *International Economic Review*, 16: 20–37.

HIRSCH, A. A., B. T. GRIMM, and G. L. V. NARASIMHAM (1974). "Some Multiplier and Error Characteristics of the BEA Quarterly Model." *International Economic Review*, 16: 616–631.

HOWREY, E. P. (1991). "New Methods for Using Monthly Data to Improve Forecast Accuracy," in L. R. Klein, Ed., *Comparative Performance of U.S. Econometric Models*. New York: Oxford University Press.

HYMANS, S. H. (1972). "Prices and Price Behavior in Three U.S. Econometric Models," in O. Eckstein, Ed., *The Econometrics of Price Determination Conference*. Washington, D.C.: Board of Governors of U.S. Federal Reserve System.

HYMANS, S. H., and H. T. SHAPIRO (1970). *The DHL III Quarterly Econometric Model of the U.S. Economy*. Research Seminar in Quantitative Economics, University of Michigan.

HYMANS, S. H., and H. T. SHAPIRO (1974). "The Structure and Properties of the Michigan Quarterly Econometric Model of the U.S. Economy." *International Economic Review*, 15: 632–653.

JOHNSON, K., and L. R. KLEIN (1974). "LINK Model Simulations of International Trade: An Evaluation of the Effects of Currency Realignment." *Journal of Finance*, 29: 617–630.

JORGENSON, D. W. (1974). "Investment and Production: A Review," in M. D. Intriligator and D. A. Kendrick, Eds., *Frontiers of Quantitative Economics*, Vol. 2. Amsterdam: North-Holland Publishing Company.

KLEIN, L. R. (1950). *Economic Fluctuations in the United States, 1921–1941*. Cowles Commission Monograph 11. New York: John Wiley & Sons, Inc.

KLEIN, L. R. (1961). "A Postwar Quarterly Model: Description and Applications," in *Models of Income Determination*, Vol. 28 of *Studies in Income and Wealth*. Princeton, N.J.: Princeton University Press (for the N.B.E.R.).

KLEIN, L. R. (1969a). "Estimation of Interdependent Systems in Macroeconomics." *Econometrica*, 37: 171–192.

KLEIN, L. R. (1969b). "Econometric Analysis of the Tax Cut of 1964," in Duesenberry et al., Eds. (1969).

KLEIN, L. R. (1983). *Lectures in Econometrics*. Amsterdam: North-Holland Publishing Company.

KLEIN, L. R. (1985). "Empirical Aspects of Protectionism." *Journal of Policy Modeling*, 7: 35–47.

KLEIN, L. R. (1991). "Past, Present, and Possible Future of Macroeconometric Models and Their Uses," in L. R. Klein, Ed., *Comparative Performance of U.S. Econometric Models*. New York: Oxford University Press.

KLEIN, L. R., and M. K. EVANS (1969). *Econometric Gaming*. New York: Macmillan Publishing Company.

KLEIN, L. R., and A. S. GOLDBERGER (1955). *An Econometric Model of the United States, 1929–1952*. Amsterdam: North-Holland Publishing Company.

KLEIN, L. R., and J. POPKIN (1961). "An Econometric Analysis of the Postwar Relationship between Inventory Fluctuations and Changes in Aggregate Economic Activity," in *Inventory Fluctuations and Economic Stabilization*. Washington, D.C.: U.S. Government Printing Office.

KRESGE, D. T. (1969). "Price and Output Conversion: A Modified Approach," in Duesenberry et al., Eds. (1969).

LIEBENBERG, M., G. GREEN, and A. HIRSCH (1971). *The Office of Business Economics 1970 Quarterly Econometric Model*. Washington, D.C.: U.S. Department of Commerce, Econometrics Branch.

LIEBENBERG, M., A. A. HIRSCH, and J. POPKIN (1966). "A Quarterly Econometric Model of the United States: A Progress Report." *Survey of Current Business*, 46: 13–39.

LIU, T. C. (1963). "An Exploratory Quarterly Econometric Model of Effective Demand in the Post-War U.S. Economy." *Econometrica*, 31: 301–348.

LIU, T. C. (1969). "A Monthly Recursive Econometric Model of United States: A Test of Feasibility." *Review of Economics and Statistics*, 51: 1–13.

LIU, T. C., and E. C. HWA (1974). "Structure and Applications of a Monthly Econometric Model of the U.S. Economy." *International Economic Review*, 15: 328–365.

MALINVAUD, E. (1970). *Statistical Methods of Econometrics*, 2nd rev. ed. Amsterdam: North-Holland Publishing Company.

McCarthy, M. D. (1972). *The Wharton Quarterly Econometric Forecasting Model, Mark III.* Philadelphia: Economics Research Unit, University of Pennsylvania.

McCracken, M. C. (1973). *An Overview of CANDIDE Model 1.0.* CANDIDE Project Paper 1. Ottawa: Information Canada.

Modigliani, F. (1977). "The Monetarist Controversy or, Should We Forsake Stabilization Policies?" *American Economic Review*, 67: 1–19.

Morishima, M., and M. Saito (1972). "A Dynamic Analysis of the American Economy, 1902–1952," in M. Morishima et al., Eds., *The Working of Econometric Models*. New York: Cambridge University Press.

Preston, R. S. (1972). *The Wharton Annual and Industry Forecasting Model*. Philadelphia: Economics Research Unit, Wharton School, University of Pennsylvania.

Preston, R. S. (1975). "The Wharton Long Term Model: Input–Output within the Context of a Macro Forecasting Model." *International Economic Review*, 16: 3–19.

Rasche, R. H., and H. Shapiro (1968). "The FRB–MIT Econometric Model: Its Special Features and Implications for Stabilization Policies." *American Economic Review*, 58: 123–149.

Sinai, A. (1992). "Financial and Real Business Cycles." *Eastern Economic Journal*, 18: 1–54.

Suits, D. B. (1962). "Forecasting and Analysis with an Econometric Model." *American Economic Review*, 52: 104–132.

Suits, D. B. (1967). "Applied Econometric Forecasting and Policy Analysis," in H. O. Wold, G. H. Orcutt, E. A. Robinson, D. B. Suits, and P. de Wolff, Eds., *Forecasting on a Scientific Basis*. Lisbon: Gulbenkian Foundation.

Taylor, J. B. (1986). "Econometric Approaches to Stabilization Policy in Stochastic Models of Macroeconomic Fluctuations," in Z. Griliches and M. D. Intriligator, Eds., *Handbook of Econometrics*, Vol. 3. Amsterdam: North-Holland Publishing Company.

Taylor, J. B. (1993). "The Use of the New Macroeconometrics for Policy Formulation." *American Economic Review, Papers and Proceedings*, 83: 300–305.

Theil, H. (1971). *Principles of Econometrics*. New York: John Wiley & Sons, Inc.

Theil, H., and J. C. G. Boot (1962). "The Final Form of Econometric Equation Systems." *Review of the International Statistical Institute*, 30: 136–152; reprinted in A. Zellner, Ed. (1968). *Readings in Economic Statistics and Econometrics*. Boston: Little, Brown and Company.

Tinbergen, J. (1939). *Statistical Testing of Business Cycle Theories*. Vol. 1: *A Method and Its Application to Investment Activity*. Vol. 2: *Business Cycles in the United States of America, 1919–1932*. Geneva: League of Nations.

Tinbergen, J. (1959). *Selected Papers*. Amsterdam: North-Holland Publishing Company.

Uebe, G., and J. Fischer (1992). *Macro-Econometric Models: An International Bibliography*, 2nd ed. Aldershot, Hants, England: Gower Publishing Co. Ltd.

Valavanis, S. (1955). "An Econometric Model of Growth, U.S.A., 1869–1953." *American Economic Review, Papers and Proceedings*, 45: 208–221.

van den Bogaard, P. J. M., and H. Theil (1959). "Macrodynamic Policy-Making: An Application of Strategy and Certainty Equivalence Concepts to the Economy of the United States, 1933–36." *Metroeconomica*, 11: 149–167; reprinted in A. Zellner, Ed. (1968). *Readings in Economic Statistics and Econometrics*. Boston: Little, Brown and Company.

Waelbroeck, J. L., Ed. (1976). *The Models of Project LINK*. Amsterdam: North-Holland Publishing Company.

13

OTHER APPLICATIONS OF SIMULTANEOUS-EQUATIONS ESTIMATION

13.1 INTRODUCTION

While macroeconometric models, as discussed in Chapter 12, and models of demand and production, as discussed in Chapters 7 and 8, are the oldest and most widely known applications of simultaneous-equations estimation, they are by no means the only such application. In fact, virtually every field of economics (and other social sciences) makes use on a regular basis of econometric techniques, including single-equation estimation; simultaneous-equations estimation; and other econometric techniques, such as time-series methods. In this chapter we survey a few of the many other applications of simultaneous-equations techniques, including applications to monetary economics, industrial organization, labor economics, health economics, alcoholism, and economic history.[1]

Most fields in economics, such as those treated here, have developed in a pattern established by many other scientific disciplines. The first works are typically discourses on various institutional or historical aspects of the field. They lead, as a second phase, to verbal paradigms, such as analogies and case studies. The third phase often involves the use of geometrical models, such as demand and supply curves. The fourth phase is algebraic models, some of which are estimated using single-equation techniques. In the fifth phase, other techniques are used, including simultaneous-equations methods and time-series analyses. In this chapter we report on some of the aspects of the fourth and fifth phases in several fields. Space limitations preclude anything other than a cursory treatment of each of these fields. It is hoped that the reader will become interested in doing further reading, using the references given for each section and the references in Appendix A.

[1]For a bibliography of applications of econometrics to various areas of economics and other social sciences, see the bibliography of Appendix A.

13.2 SIMULTANEOUS-EQUATIONS MODEL OF MONEY DEMAND AND SUPPLY

The field of monetary economics is concerned with the demand for and supply of money and credit; how these factors determine interest rates and other credit conditions; and how they affect and are affected by production, employment, and prices in the economy. The demand for money has been studied by many investigators, both theoretically and empirically, typically assuming, in a single-equation context, that the supply of money is set exogenously by the monetary authorities.[2] If supply is treated as endogenous, the demand for and supply of money form a system of simultaneous equations, treated later in this section.

From a theoretical standpoint, the demand for money is based on various motives for holding money rather than other assets. One is the *transactions motive*, according to which money is held because it is needed to conduct transactions—that is, to buy goods and services. The amount of money held for this motive then depends positively on national income, measured, for example, as gross national product Y. A second is the *precautionary motive*, according to which money is held because there may be an unexpected need for it in the future. The unexpected needs, by their very nature, are difficult to quantify, but the cost of holding money rather than other assets can be measured by the rate of return on such other assets. An asset that is similar in some respects to money but that bears an explicit rate of return is a bond, which yields a return measured by its rate of interest. The interest rate, r, should therefore influence the demand for money negatively in that, as the interest rate rises, it becomes more "expensive" to hold money, in terms of opportunities forgone, so less money is held for precautionary reasons. A third is the *speculative (or portfolio) motive*, according to which money is held because of a fear of capital loss in holding bonds, given the expectation that interest rates will rise in the future, so capital values will fall. The expected future interest rate, r_e, should therefore influence the demand for money positively in that, as the expected future interest rate rises, it is expected that bond prices will fall, so investors will hold money in their optimal portfolios rather than bonds. Combining the factors suggested by all three motives, the demand for money equation can be written:

$$M = M(Y, r, r_e), \qquad *(13.2.1)$$

where M is money balances demanded (perhaps deflated to real per capita terms by dividing by the price level and the population), Y the national income (again perhaps deflated to real terms and put on a per capita basis), r the interest rate (perhaps the real interest rate, net of the inflation rate, either short or long term), and r_e the expected interest rate (again perhaps real and either short or long term).

If it is possible to separate the transactions demand from the other two demands, if the transactions demand is proportional to income, and if the expected interest rate can be omitted (e.g., because it depends on the current income and interest rate), the demand equation would take the form:

$$M = kY + L(r), \qquad *(13.2.2)$$

[2]See Goldfeld (1973, 1976), Judd and Scadding (1982), Laidler (1985), Fair (1987), and Goldfeld and Sichel (1990).

where k is the *Cambridge k*, giving the ratio of money used for transactions to the national income and $L(r)$ is the liquidity preference function, indicating the dependence of precautionary and speculative money balances on the interest rate. The two terms on the right-hand side of (13.2.2) are, respectively, the *transactions demand* and *asset demand* for money. The sums of money held to satisfy these demands are called, respectively, *active balances* and *passive balances*.

Another way of expressing the demand for money in (13.2.1) is:

$$MV = Y = PT, \tag{13.2.3}$$

where V is the *velocity of money*, the rate at which money turns over per year, P is the price level, and T is the volume of transactions or, equivalently, real income (Y/P). This equation expresses the *quantity theory of money*, according to which velocity is a (stable) function of the interest rate, the expected interest rate, income, and possibly other variables, such as the expected rate of inflation, the expected return on equities, and real balances.

Both (13.2.2) and (13.2.3) and other variants of (13.2.1) have been estimated by many investigators. As one example, Klein estimated the following long-run demand function for the United States over the period 1880–1970:[3]

$$\ln\frac{M}{pN} = \underset{(0.177)}{-13.96} + \underset{(0.025)}{1.328}\ln\frac{Y_p}{pN} - \underset{(0.018)}{0.315}(r_s - r_m), \qquad R^2 = 0.988, \quad d = 1.12, \tag{13.2.4}$$

where numbers in parentheses will always refer to standard errors (rather than t statistics). In this estimated demand function M is currency outside banks plus demand deposits plus time deposits at commercial banks, N is the total population, p is the price level, Y_p is permanent income (national income with transitory components removed or, equivalently, the expected permanent return on total wealth), r_s is the short-term (four- to six-month) commercial paper rate, and r_m is the (implicit) rate of interest on demand deposits. The *net interest rate*, defined by the difference $r_s - r_m$, measures the cost of holding money rather than short-term interest-bearing notes. The specification with respect to this net interest rate is semilogarithmic, in part, because this variable can be negative. According to these results, the per capita real demand for money is sensitive to both real per capita permanent income and the cost of holding money. The implied income elasticity of the demand for money is 1.328. Other studies have found roughly similar values for this elasticity over various periods up to 1970, with values typically in the range 1.2 to 1.4.

As another example of a demand for money equation, Goldfeld and Sichel estimated the following partial adjustment model for the United States over various periods:[4]

$$\ln m_t = b_0 + b_1 \ln y_t + b_2 \ln r_t + b_3 \ln m_{t-1} + b_4 \pi_t + u_t. \tag{13.2.5}$$

Here m_t is real money balances (measured as currency plus checkable deposits), y_t the transactions variable (measured as real GNP), r_t represents interest rates (measured as the commercial paper rate and the commercial bank passbook rate), m_{t-1} is the lagged real money balances (lagged one quarter), and π_t is the rate of inflation (measured as $\ln(P_t/P_{t-1})$, where P is the implicit GNP price deflator). Their estimation of this model with quarterly data over the relatively tranquil period 1952.3 (i.e., the third quarter of 1952) to 1974.1 yielded stable

[3]See Klein (1974).

[4]See Goldfeld and Sichel (1990). If $b_4 = 0$, this is a nominal partial adjustment model, while if $b_4 = -b_2$, it is a real partial adjustment model.

and sensible results, with significant income and interest effects and plausible long-run elasticities. They found, however, that the behavior of this "conventional" specification sharply deteriorates after 1974, suggesting that the money demand equation underwent some type of structural change. In particular, the coefficient of the lagged dependent variable becomes essentially unity, implying a misspecified partial adjustment mechanism. Furthermore, the stability that was present earlier disappears after 1974, possibly as a result of the substantial degree of financial deregulation after 1980. There is also a substantial amount of "missing money" in the mid-1970s, representing the difference between the forecast and actual real money balances, possibly due to financial innovation. These results suggest that it may be necessary to rethink this conventional specification, and various extensions have been proposed, including generalized distributed lag models, expectations models, and buffer stock models.

A simultaneous-equations model of money demand and supply can be developed by relaxing the assumption that money supply is exogenous and, instead, treating it as endogenous. Then to the basic demand equation in (13.2.1) is added a supply equation, so the system becomes:

$$M^D = M^D(Y, r, r_e, \ldots), \qquad *(13.2.6)$$

$$M^S = M^S(Y, r, r_e, \ldots). \qquad *(13.2.7)$$

Here M^D is money demand and M^S is money supply, where it is assumed that the monetary authorities are responsive to the same factors that influence demand. Adding a third equation equating demand and supply would give an equilibrium condition, while adding a different equation relating, for example, changes in prices or in interest rates to the difference between money demand and supply would be the corresponding disequilibrium version of this model.

The ellipses (. . .) in the demand and supply equations above represent other variables that could enter either equation. In fact, without either the exclusion of other variables or the exclusion of some of the variables shown in one of the equations, neither equation of the model would be identified, assuming that the model is one of equilibrium and assuming identification via zero restrictions. As presented above, there is no way, empirically, to differentiate the demand equation from the supply equation. Thus one of the first issues in estimating a simultaneous-equations model of money demand and supply is that of identification. Has a demand equation, in fact, been identified? A supply equation?

Several studies have treated simultaneous demand for and supply of money equations. One, by Teigen, treated the model:[5]

$$M^D = M^D(Y, r_s Y, M_{-1}), \qquad (13.2.8)$$

$$M^S = M^* f(r_s - r_d), \qquad (13.2.9)$$

$$M^D = M^S = M. \qquad (13.2.10)$$

[5]See Teigen (1964). Other models treating the supply as well as demand for money appear in Brunner and Meltzer (1964), Modigliani, Rasche, and Cooper (1970), and Gibson (1972). For general discussions of the supply of money, see Brunner and Meltzer (1990) and Papademos and Modigliani (1990). Some of the macroeconometric models of Chapter 12 also include simultaneous monetary submodels. See, for example, Cooper (1974) for the FMP model.

The demand function specifies the demand for money as a function of income, the product of the short-term rate of interest and income, and lagged money stock.[6] The inclusion of lagged money stock allows for a lagged response or partial adjustment to equilibrium. The supply function determines the supply of money as the product of the maximum potential money stock based on reserves supplied by the Federal Reserve System, M^*, and a function $f(\cdot)$ of the difference between r_s, the short-term interest rate, and r_d, the discount rate. The maximum potential money stock is related to reserves by the identity:

$$M^* \equiv \frac{1}{\rho(1-c-h)}R, \tag{13.2.11}$$

where R represents reserves, ρ is the (weighted average) reserve ratio, c the currency ratio, and h the demand deposit ratio. Finally, the last equation is the equilibrium condition, equating the demand for and the supply of money.

The endogenous variables of this model are M, the money stock (measured as M_1), and r_s, the short-term rate of interest (the rate on four- to six-month prime commercial paper). The exogenous variables are Y, national income (in money terms), and r_d, the discount rate.[7]

Teigen estimated this model using quarterly data with 49 observations over the period 1946.4–1959.4 using two-stage least squares. His results for demand and supply, respectively, were:[8]

$$\begin{gathered} M = \underset{(0.0126)}{0.0618}Y - \underset{(0.0007)}{0.0025}r_sY + \underset{(0.0728)}{0.6860}M_{-1} + \underset{(4.9783)}{23.0600} + \cdots, \\ R^2 = 0.992, \quad d = 1.885, \end{gathered} \tag{13.2.12}$$

$$\begin{gathered} M = M^*\left(\underset{(0.0159)}{0.0751}(r_s - r_d) + \underset{(0.0068)}{0.8522} + \cdots\right), \\ R^2 = 0.726, \quad d = 1.536. \end{gathered} \tag{13.2.13}$$

All signs agree with prior expectations, all coefficients are at least three times their standard errors, and the Durbin–Watson statistics indicate no significant serial correlation. The implied short-run elasticity of demand (evaluated at mean values) with respect to the interest rate is –0.0168 and with respect to income is 0.1613. The corresponding long-run elasticities are –0.0538 and 0.5130, respectively. The estimated elasticity of *supply* with respect to the interest rate is 0.1950.

Teigen also found that all of the elasticities appear to have declined significantly in the postwar period, as compared to the prewar years, even though interest rates were very low in the 1930s.[9] This finding casts doubt upon the liquidity-trap hypothesis of high

[6]Several seasonal and structural shift dummy variables are included.

[7]In fact, Teigen considered a somewhat larger model in which national income, Y, is endogenous, and an additional equation determines Y on the basis of its lagged value, exogenous expenditure, and net worth. Since this equation contains no monetary variables, however, the larger system can be divided into a real system, namely the equation for national income, and a monetary system, the equations for money demand and supply, reported here.

[8]The omitted variables are the seasonal and structural shift dummy variables. The equation for Y is also omitted here.

[9]His estimates of the demand elasticities for the prewar years were –0.091 with respect to the interest rate and 0.443 with respect to income.

elasticity of demand at low interest rates. Teigen, however, saw it as reflecting a change in the role of money, with the asset demand for money declining in the postwar years as a result of the advent of newer forms of liquid asset holding.

13.3 SIMULTANEOUS-EQUATIONS MODEL OF INDUSTRIAL-ORGANIZATION RELATIONSHIPS

The field of industrial organization is concerned with the causes and consequences of the structure of industry, including business behavior, its implications, and public policy toward industry. A basic paradigm of this field is the structure–conduct–performance hypothesis (SCP).[10] According to this hypothesis, the structure of an industry, that is, its organizational characteristics, particularly its degree of concentration and conditions of entry, influences the conduct of firms in the industry in their decisions regarding prices, sales, employment, advertising, research and development, and so on. The conduct of the firms, in turn, influences performance, particularly the profits earned in the industry. Econometric studies of industrial organization have tended to focus on various aspects of this hypothesis.[11] Many studies have considered the effect of the concentration ratio, the percentage of output represented by the leading four (or three or eight) firms in the industry, a measure of the structure of an industry, on conduct, such as advertising, and on performance, such as profit. An example was the regression of Weiss for 399 U.S. industries in 1973:[12]

$$\underset{}{\pi} = \underset{(0.010)}{0.193} + \underset{(0.0002)}{0.0011}CR - \underset{(0.0001)}{0.0003}GD + \underset{(0.0002)}{0.0009}(K/O), \qquad R^2 = 0.20, \tag{13.3.1}$$

numbers in parentheses again being standard errors. Here π is the price–cost margin (value of shipments less cost of materials and payroll, all divided by the value of shipments), CR is the four-firm concentration ratio, *GD* is a geographical dispersion index, and *K/O* is the fixed capital/shipments ratio. The regression coefficients for both the concentration ratio and the fixed capital/shipments ratio are statistically significant, the *t*-ratio for *CR* being over 5. The coefficient for *CR* indicates that an increase of 10 percentage points in the four-firm concentration ratio increases the price–cost margin by over 1 percentage point. From this regression, other regressions he estimated, and the results of the many other studies he considered, Weiss concluded that concentration does lead to higher profit margins, particularly for "normal years" not subject to accelerating inflation.

Various other aspects of industrial conduct and performance have also been related to concentration and other variables. Variables such as prices, wages, advertising, research and development expenditures, and productivity have all been related to concentration and other variables. Each of these studies can be considered a single equation from a larger and simultaneous-equations model of industrial organization relationships, which builds on the SCP hypothesis and can test the role played by concentration. Such a simultane-

[10]See Bain (1956, 1968), Scherer (1980), and Schmalensee (1988, 1989).

[11]See Weiss (1971), Comanor and Wilson (1979), Hay and Morris (1979), Scherer (1980), and Waterson (1984).

[12]See Weiss (1974). As he notes, the concentration–profit relationship is one of the most thoroughly tested of all hypotheses in economics. See also Schmalensee (1989) for a discussion of this relationship.

ous-equations model of industrial organization relationships is summarized in Tables 13.1 and 13.2.[13]

Table 13.1 summarizes the six endogenous and six exogenous variables of the model. Industry structure is represented by two variables: concentration, measured by the four-firm

TABLE 13.1 Variables of the Simultaneous-Equations Model of Industrial Organization

Endogenous variables

Structure module

(1) CR = concentration ratio

(2) ΔN = relative change in number of firms

Conduct module

(3) K/L = capital-labor ratio

(4) A/S = advertising-sales ratio

Performance module

(5) Δp = relative change in price

(6) Π = profit rate on net worth

Exogenous variables

Underlying-considerations module

ε_p = price elasticity of demand (negative)

ε_I = income elasticity of demand

MES = minimum efficient size (weighted average of the total asset size class)

Factors external to a particular industry

w = real wage

g = growth in the value of shipments

Δc = relative change in direct costs

TABLE 13.2 Simultaneous-Equations Model of Industrial Organization

Structure

(1) $CR = f_1(K/L, A/S, \Pi; \varepsilon_p, g)$

+ + + + −

(2) $\Delta N = f_2(CR, A/S, \Pi; MES)$

− − + −

Conduct

(3) $K/L = f_3(CR; w)$

+ +

(4) $A/S = f_4(CR, \Pi; \varepsilon_p)$

+ + −

Performance

(5) $\Delta p = f_5(CR, K/L; \Delta c)$

+ − +

(6) $\Pi = f_6(CR, A/S; MES, g, \varepsilon_I)$

+ + + + +

Note Explanatory variables appearing before the semicolon are specified to be endogenous; those appearing after it are specified to be exogenous. Expected signs appear below each explanatory variable.

[13]See Intriligator, Weston, and De Angelo (1975). For other simultaneous-equations models of industrial organization, see Grabowski and Mueller (1970), Comanor and Wilson (1974), Martin (1979, 1983), Caves, Porter, and Spence (1980), Geroski (1982), and Connolly and Hirschey (1984). Schmalensee (1989) notes that the instrumental variables necessary for consistent estimation are rarely available in empirical work in industrial organization using cross-section data. Such studies can, however, if properly designed to use prior information from both theory and prior empirical work, describe relations among the long-run equilibrium values of endogenous variables.

concentration ratio based on the value of shipments (*CR*), and entry, measured by the relative change in the number of firms (ΔN, defined as N/N_{-1}). Conduct, involving the decisions of the firm, is represented by two variables: capital intensity, measured by the capital/labor ratio (*K/L*), and advertising, measured by the advertising-sales ratio (*A/S*). Performance, involving the social performance of the industry, is also represented by two variables: price change, measured by the relative change in price (Δp, defined as p/p_{-1}) and profit, measured by the net profit rate on net worth (Π).

The exogenous variables fall into two categories. First are those factors that may be treated as "underlying considerations," specifically, price and income elasticities of demand (ε_p and ε_I) and the minimum efficient size (*MES*). Second are factors that are endogenous to the overall economy but are treated as exogenous for any particular industry, namely the real wage (w), the growth in the value of shipments (g), and the relative change in direct costs (Δc). The real wage is assumed to be set by aggregate labor markets, which cut across all industries. As to the growth in shipments and the change in direct costs, they reflect considerations that are, from an input–output standpoint, respectively, "downstream" and "upstream" from any particular industry. If the data permitted, an expanded model would treat some of these exogenous variables as endogenous.

The six equations of the model and the expected signs of coefficients of all variables of the model are specified in Table 13.2. It is by no means claimed that the model is either definitive or exhaustive. Rather it is an attempt to represent the SCP paradigm. The variables included and relationships indicated were chosen on the basis of three considerations—their roles in the SCP paradigm, their use in previous studies, and the availability of relevant and usable data.

Data used in the estimation of the model were obtained for 381 four-digit SIC (Standard Industrial Classification) manufacturing industries for the 1963–1966 period. A linear version of the model was then estimated using both ordinary least-squares (OLS) and two-stage least squares (2SLS) techniques. The results of this estimation are given in Table 13.3, which gives both OLS and 2SLS regression coefficients and standard errors.

Several findings emerge from estimation of this model, particularly the 2SLS coefficient and (asymptotic) standard errors. One set of findings concerns the several two-way relationships of the model, in which one variable both influences and is influenced by another. The first is that between the capital-labor ratio and the concentration ratio: *K/L* exerts a statistically significant positive influence on *CR*, and *CR* exerts a statistically significant positive effect on *K/L*. As to *CR* and the advertising/sales ratio, while *CR* exerts a positive influence of borderline statistical significance on *A/S*, the *A/S* variable exerts no statistically significant influence on *CR*. The relationship between *CR* and the profit rate Π has been a major implication of the SCP paradigm. The estimated model, however, indicates that *CR* exerts only an insignificant influence on the profit rate, while the reverse feedback, that of Π on *CR*, shows a positive influence that is statistically significant. The fourth and last of the two-way relationships is that between *A/S* and Π. According to the estimates in Table 13.3, *A/S* exerts a statistically significant positive influence on Π, while Π exerts a positive influence of borderline statistical significance on *A/S*.

A second set of findings concerns the one-way relationships of the estimated model, specifically the lack of a statistically significant influence of *CR* on either ΔN or Δp. A third set of findings relates to the role of concentration. This construct has played a central role in the SCP literature, but the results suggest that while concentration does have some place

TABLE 13.3 Industrial Organization Simultaneous Model, Estimated for 381 Four-Digit Manufacturing Industries

(1)	(2SLS)	CR	=	−0.298	+	$1.26K/L$	−	$2.59A/S$	+	9.75Π	−	$0.037g$	−	$1.03\varepsilon_p$	
				(0.23)		(0.41)		(3.39)		(4.62)		(0.032)		(0.95)	
(1′)	(OLS)	CR	=	0.132	+	$0.745K/L$	+	$1.42A/S$	+	2.24Π	+	$0.004g$	−	$0.074\varepsilon_p$	$R^2 = 0.117$
				(0.06)		(0.144)		(0.75)		(0.89)		(0.017)		(0.74)	$F = 9.97$
(2)	(2SLS)	ΔN	=	0.007	+	$0.002CR$	+	0.054Π	−	$0.067A/S$	−	$0.000002\ MES$			
				(0.0015)		(0.0027)		(0.029)		(0.027)		(0.0000005)			
(2′)	(OLS)	ΔN	=	0.009	+	$0.005CR$	+	0.014Π	−	$0.016A/S$	−	$0.000001MES$			$R^2 = 0.065$
				(0.0005)		(0.00051)		(0.008)		(0.007)		(0.0000002)			$F = 6.56$
(3)	(2SLS)	K/L	=	−0.106	+	$0.176CR$	+	$0.046w$							
				(0.016)		(0.076)		(0.011)							
(3′)	(OLS)	K/L	=	−0.093	+	$0.037CR$	+	$0.062w$							$R^2 = 0.283$
				(0.014)		(0.016)		(0.006)							$F = 74.72$
(4)	(2SLS)	A/S	=	−0.013	+	$0.020CR$	+	0.283Π	−	$0.127\varepsilon_p$					
				(0.010)		(0.014)		(0.196)		(0.053)					
(4′)	(OLS)	A/S	=	−0.025	+	$0.010CR$	+	0.504Π	−	$0.121\varepsilon_p$					$R^2 = 0.237$
				(0.004)		(0.003)		(0.054)		(0.051)					$F = 39.00$
(5)	(2SLS)	Δp	=	0.848	−	$0.036CR$	+	$0.157K/L$	+	$2.56\Delta C$					
				(0.042)		(0.101)		(0.184)		(0.27)					
(5′)	(OLS)	Δp	=	0.861	−	$0.034CR$	+	$0.065K/L$	+	$2.46\Delta C$					$R^2 = 0.272$
				(0.020)		(0.015)		(0.044)		(0.22)					$F = 46.90$
(6)	(2SLS)	Π	=	0.043	+	$0.025CR$	+	$0.450A/S$	+	$0.000002MES$	+	$0.003g$	+	$0.200\varepsilon_I$	
				(0.004)		(0.014)		(0.171)		(0.000002)		(0.001)		(0.099)	
(6′)	(OLS)	Π	=	0.052	+	$0.002CR$	+	$0.393A/S$	+	$0.000006MES$	+	$0.003g$	+	$0.203\varepsilon_I$	$R^2 = 0.311$
				(0.002)		(0.0027)		(0.038)		(0.000002)		(0.001)		(0.084)	$F = 33.87$

in industrial-organization relationships, it perhaps does not occupy the central place it has assumed as a result of an inadequately tested acceptance of the SCP paradigm. While concentration does have a statistically significant effect on capital intensity, it has no significant influence on entry. Nor does it have a significant influence on the two conduct variables of decisions of the firm with regard to capital intensity and advertising or on the two performance variables of the change in price and the profit rate. Even the central doctrine of the SCP paradigm that concentration leads to higher profitability is not supported by the evidence. Furthermore, concentration cannot itself be explained on the basis of considerations such as advertising. These findings concerning the influence and role of the concentration ratio in the system pose serious questions about its central role in the literature on industrial organization.

A fourth set of findings relates to the role of advertising. The evidence points to a mixed answer to the question of whether advertising is a barrier to entry. Advertising does appear to reduce entry, but at the same time, it appears to have no statistically significant effect on concentration. Thus advertising may create a barrier to the entry of new firms without changing the degree of concentration in the industry.

A fifth set of findings relates to the two techniques of estimation, OLS and 2SLS. Comparing the estimates obtained using OLS with those obtained using 2SLS indicates the effect of the estimation technique. Three important shifts take place in moving from OLS to 2SLS estimates. The influence of advertising on concentration is positive and significant using OLS but negative and no longer significant using 2SLS. In the advertising equation, the influence of concentration and profits on advertising intensity is significant using OLS but not using 2SLS. A third switch occurs in the profit equation, where *MES* is no longer significant using 2SLS. Thus the method of estimation does have an important effect on the estimated model, and certain of the results of previous studies using OLS are called into question.

Several conclusions emerge from this study. First, it is possible to specify and estimate a simultaneous-equations model of industrial organization. Second, the OLS and 2SLS techniques provide different estimates, casting some doubt upon previous single-equation studies. Third, the SCP paradigm may be improperly giving too much weight to concentration as an explanatory variable for industry conduct and performance.

13.4 SIMULTANEOUS-EQUATIONS MODEL IN LABOR ECONOMICS

The field of labor economics makes use of econometric techniques in its study of the demand for and supply of labor, wages and hours, labor force participation, unionization, unemployment, human capital, training evaluation, characteristics of workers, job search, job turnover, occupational choice, migration, and other labor-market phenomena.[14] An example of the use of simultaneous-equations models and techniques to treat the joint determination of labor-market variables is the Ashenfelter-Heckman model of family labor supply.[15]

[14]For surveys of econometric applications in labor economics, see Heckman and MaCurdy (1986) and Ashenfelter and Layard (1986).

[15]See Ashenfelter and Heckman (1974). For other studies, see Heckman and MaCurdy (1986) and Ashenfelter and Layard (1986).

The endogenous variables of the model are ΔR_h, the change in the labor supply of the husband; ΔR_w, the change in the labor supply of the wife; and ΔF, the change in total income. The exogenous variables are ΔW_h, the change in the wage rate of the husband, and ΔW_w, the change in the wage rate of the wife. One equation of the model is the identity:

$$\Delta F_k \equiv \Delta(R_{hk} W_{hk}) + \Delta(R_{wk} W_{wk}) + \Delta Y_k, \tag{13.4.1}$$

where ΔY_k is the change in nonlabor income and k is an index of the observation of a particular family. The other two equations of the model take the form:

$$\Delta R_{ik} = S_{ih}\ \Delta W_{hk} + S_{iw}\ \Delta W_{wk} + \beta_i\ \Delta F_k + \varepsilon_{ik}, \qquad i = h, w, \tag{13.4.2}$$

where i indicates husband or wife; S_{ih}, S_{iw}, and β_i are the parameters to be estimated; and ε_{ik} is the stochastic disturbance term.[16] The disturbances ε_{hk} and ε_{wk} are expected to be correlated in that the labor-supply decisions of the husband and the wife in any particular family are likely to be interrelated. Furthermore, ΔF_k is expected to be correlated with both of these stochastic disturbances. The system is therefore estimated via three-stage least squares. Estimates of the two behavioral equations of the system for husbands and wives aged 25 to 54 for 100 metropolitan areas in 1960 are given by:

$$\begin{aligned}\Delta R_h &= \underset{(0.043)}{0.106}\ \Delta W_h + \underset{(0.067)}{0.127}\ \Delta W_w - \underset{(0.067)}{0.102}\ \Delta F,\end{aligned} \tag{13.4.3}$$

$$\begin{aligned}\Delta R_w &= \underset{(0.067)}{0.127}\ \Delta W_h + \underset{(0.273)}{1.233}\ \Delta W_w - \underset{(0.177)}{0.886}\ \Delta F.\end{aligned} \tag{13.4.4}$$

For these estimates the constraint that $S_{wh} = S_{hw}$ in (13.4.2), as implied by basic theory, has been imposed.[17] The estimated substitution effect for husbands, $\hat{S}_{hh} = 0.106$, is statistically different from zero, but it implies the very small value of 0.06 for the substitution elasticity (evaluated at the means). Thus the labor supply of husbands is not very responsive to the husband's wage. For wives, however, the substitution effect, $\hat{S}_{ww} = 1.233$, is much larger than that for husbands, and it implies the relatively large substitution elasticity (again evaluated at the means) of 1.154. Thus the labor supply of wives is highly responsive to wives' wages. The estimated cross effect is positive, indicating that husbands' labor supply responds positively to wives' wages (and wives' labor supply responds positively to husbands' wages). The negative β coefficients, $\hat{\beta}_h = -0.102$ and $\hat{\beta}_w = -0.886$, imply that leisure is a normal good, but $\hat{\beta}_h$ is not statistically significant.

13.5 SIMULTANEOUS-EQUATIONS MODEL OF THE HEALTH SYSTEM

The field of health economics is, broadly, the study of the allocation of resources to the delivery of health services. It considers microeconomic issues, such as the demand for health services by groups of individuals, cost curves for hospital or physician providers of

[16]Equation (13.4.2) is a discrete difference version of the Slutsky decomposition relating the effects of changes in wages and nonlabor income. See Ashenfelter and Heckman (1974) and Section 7.2, especially equation (7.2.14).

[17]This constraint is the symmetry condition of consumer theory, as in (7.2.14). Here this theory has been extended to labor-supply decisions.

health services, and the supply of and demand for nurses and other categories of health personnel. It also considers macroeconomic issues, such as the functioning of the entire health care system in determining quantities of services provided, overall health costs, and related matters. This field includes quantitative econometric studies of various relationships in the health care system, including the formulation, estimation, and utilization of both single-equation models of particular sectors and simultaneous-equations models of the entire system.[18] Such studies are valuable in analyzing, forecasting, and evaluating policy for this important and complex system, including the design of alternative health reform proposals.

The demand for health services is among the most frequent and important of the quantitative studies in health economics. Such studies determine the effects on demand for inpatient and outpatient health services of variables included in the demand studies discussed in Chapter 7, such as price and income, but they also estimate the effects of variables specific to or particularly relevant to the demand for health, such as health insurance, health condition, age, gender, and so on. An example of such a study is that of Newhouse and Phelps, using cross-section data on 2367 U.S. families interviewed in 1963.[19] Their analysis is limited to those individuals with positive observed quantities of the health service considered and their estimated demand curves for hospital length of stay and physician visits are summarized in Table 13.4.

According to these results, disability days are the most significant explanatory variable for length of stay, while the health status variables are the most significant explanatory variables for visits to physicians' offices.[20] The dummy variables for age are also important determinants of length of stay. For example, according to Table 13.4, everything else being equal, a person over 65 stays in the hospital about 12 more days per year than a person not in this age group. These age variables play no significant role in influencing visits to physicians' offices, however. The variable for race plays an important role in determining visits to physicians, with nonwhite persons having almost two fewer visits per year than whites. This variable, however, plays no significant role for hospital length of stay. The price variables allow for the existence of health insurance in that they are the *net* price to the individual consumer, after taking account of the coinsurance rate (the percentage of the hospital or physician bill paid by the consumer).

The elasticities implied by the Newhouse and Phelps demand functions are reported in Table 13.5. The estimated demand functions are clearly both price and income inelastic, with all reported elasticities very small. In fact, none of the estimated price and income elasticities exceeds 0.1 in absolute value. While wage-income elasticities are positive, nonwage

[18]See Grossman (1972, 1982), Perlman (1974), Rossett (1976), van der Gaag and Perlman (1981), Fuchs (1982), van der Gaag, Neenan, and Tsukahara (1982), Williams (1987), Wagstaff (1989), and Duru and Paelinck (1991).

[19]See Newhouse and Phelps (1974). They also present some simultaneous-equations estimates, taking account of the endogeneity of health insurance and price. See also Newhouse and Phelps (1976) and Newhouse (1981).

[20]Those explanatory variables for which the t ratio of the estimated coefficient to its standard error is less than unity in both equations are not reported here. They include nonwage income if greater than $3000, education 9–11 years, education 12 years, age 25–34, and gender.

On health status, respondents were asked whether they would characterize their health as excellent, good, fair, or poor, and responses were entered as dummy variables.

TABLE 13.4 Estimated Demand Equations for Hospital Length of Stay and Physician Office Visits

	Dependent Variable			
Explanatory Variables	Hospital Length of Stay (Days)		Physician Office Visits (Number)	
Price of hospital bed × hospital coinsurance rate	–0.062	(0.036)	–0.034	(0.012)
Price of office visit × physician coinsurance rate	–0.241	(0.193)	–0.054	(0.027)
Wage income/week	0.008	(0.011)	0.004	(0.002)
Nonwage income	–0.001	(0.001)	–0.76E-04	(2.71E-04)
*Education 13–15 years	–3.088	(2.998)	0.396	(0.629)
*Education 16+ years	1.029	(3.027)	–0.765	(0.638)
*Age 35–54	7.051	(5.262)	–0.815	(0.916)
*Age 55–64	10.296	(5.477)	–0.403	(0.983)
*Age 65+	12.142	(5.469)	–0.818	(0.974)
Family size	–0.451	(0.438)	–0.070	(0.119)
*White	0.743	(2.322)	1.616	(0.466)
Disability days	0.029	(0.008)	0.008	(0.004)
*Health status good	–0.256	(2.133)	1.671	(0.419)
*Health status fair	0.575	(2.396)	3.683	(0.539)
*Health status poor	–1.667	(2.646)	6.824	(0.801)
Physicians per 100,000	–0.022	(0.015)	0.006	(0.039)
Beds per 1000	0.250	(0.294)	–0.105	(0.086)
Constant	3.132	(5.910)	3.804	(1.160)
R^2	0.345		0.181	
Number of observations	122		842	

Source Newhouse and Phelps (1974).

Note Standard errors are shown in parentheses. Those explanatory variables for which the t ratio is less than unity for both equations have been omitted (see footnote 20). The notation –0.76E-04 means –0.000076.

*Signifies dummy variable, taking value 1 if characteristic is present, 0 if it is not.

income is found to have no effect on demand for physician office visits. These results indicate that additional physicians per capita would increase visits and decrease length of stay, while additional hospital beds per capita would have precisely the opposite effect.

An example of a simultaneous-equations model of the health care system is the 47-equation macroeconometric model of Yett, Drabek, Intriligator, and Kimbell.[21] The endogenous variables can perhaps best be described in terms of the institutions and personnel explicitly included.

The inpatient institutions treated in the model are:

1. Voluntary and proprietary short-term hospitals
2. State and local governmental hospitals

[21]See Yett et al. (1972, 1974); see also Yett et al. (1975, 1977) for a microeconometric model of the health care system, based on the behavior of individual consumers and providers of health services.

TABLE 13.5 Estimated Demand Elasticities

Explanatory Variables	Dependent Variable: Hospital Length of Stay	Dependent Variable: Physician Office Visits
Price of hospital bed × hospital coinsurance rate	–0.10	–0.10
Price of office visit × physician coinsurance rate	–0.10	–0.06
Wage income/week	0.08	0.08
Nonwage income	–0.07	–0.01
Disability days	0.19	0.02
Physicians per 100,000	–0.28	0.13
Beds per 1000	0.13	–0.09

Source Newhouse and Phelps (1974).

3. Federal and nonfederal short-term general hospitals
4. Skilled nursing homes

The endogenous variables for each are patient days provided and number of beds. In addition the model includes, as endogenous variables, the daily service charges for 1 and 4 and the occupancy rate for 1, 2, and 4.

The outpatient institutions treated in the model are

5. Outpatient clinics of short-term voluntary and proprietary hospitals
6. Outpatient clinics of short-term state and local governmental hospitals
7. Outpatient clinics of federal and nonfederal short-term general hospitals
8. Offices of medical specialists in private practice
9. Offices of surgical specialists in private practice

The endogenous variable for each is patient visits. The model also includes, as endogenous variables, the price per visit for 5, 8, and 9.

The types of personnel treated in the model are:

10. Medical specialist physicians in private practice
11. Surgical specialist physicians in private practice
12. Other specialists in private practice
13. Physicians employed by hospitals
14. Hospital interns and residents
15. Registered nurses
16. Practical nurses
17. Allied health professionals
18. Nonmedical labor

The endogenous variable for each is the number active or employed. In addition, the model includes, as endogenous variables, the annual wage for 15, 16, and 17.

The exogenous and standardizing variables of the model include demographic variables (total population, proportion of the population age 65 and over), economic variables (per capita income, consumer price index), insurance variables (private health insurance, Medicare and Medicaid expenditures), and health labor variables (stocks of registered nurses and practical nurses).

The basic mechanism of the model is that of demand and supply, as applied to inpatient institutions to yield patient days and daily service charges, to outpatient institutions to determine patient visits and prices per visit, and to health labor categories to determine numbers employed and wage rates. The model is not an equilibrium one, however. It allows both for inequality of demand and supply and for lags in the process of adjustment to equilibrium.

The model was estimated using primarily 1970 cross-sectional data on states. The estimated model has been used for various purposes, including forecasts of health services and health personnel and simulation of certain changes in a state health care system. Among the changes simulated using the model are a redistribution of physicians to "shortage" areas and a reduction in the rate of construction of new hospital beds. The model has been able to reveal both primary and secondary consequences of such changes—for example, the magnitude of increase of outpatient visits resulting from reduced bed construction. Through this type of simulation, the estimated model and other estimated models of the health care system can reveal the consequences of various policy changes. They can therefore provide an important vehicle for health care planners to use in evaluating policy alternatives.

13.6 SIMULTANEOUS-EQUATIONS MODEL OF ALCOHOLISM

Alcoholism and alcohol-related deaths are significant social problems in many nations, accounting for a significant fraction of morbidity and mortality and contributing to workdays lost, traffic accidents, and family and societal disruption. Most econometric studies of alcoholism concentrate on the consumption of alcoholic beverages, as in a demand study.[22] A simultaneous-equations model can, however, go beyond the demand for alcohol to account, in addition, for the causes of alcoholism, its effects, and its possible control.[23]

The simultaneous-equations model includes two sets of equations that are estimated using statewide U.S. data for 35 states in 1975. The first set consists of equations for consumption of alcoholic beverages, including the consumption of beer, CB, and of spirits, CS.[24] The second consists of an equation for alcoholism, ASM, and an equation for alcohol-related mortality, ARM. The four equations of this model are, in log-linear (constant elasticity) form:

[22]See Ornstein (1980) for estimated price and income elasticities of demand for beer, wine, and distilled spirits.

[23]See Schweitzer, Intriligator, and Salehi (1983).

[24]In principle, there should be a third equation to account for the consumption of wine, but this was omitted due to lack of data.

$$\begin{aligned}\ln \mathrm{CB} = {} & (a_1 \ln \mathrm{ASM}) + (a_2 \ln \mathrm{I} + a_3 \ln \mathrm{TR} \\ & + a_4 \ln \mathrm{UR} + a_5 \ln \mathrm{TM} + a_6 \ln \mathrm{RG}) \\ & + (a_7 \ln \mathrm{PRB} + a_8 \ln \mathrm{PRS} + a_9 \ln \mathrm{OL} \\ & + a_{10}\, \mathrm{BAN} + a_{11} \ln \mathrm{MDA} + a_{12} \ln \mathrm{UN}) + a_0 + u_1,\end{aligned} \tag{13.6.1}$$

$$\begin{aligned}\ln \mathrm{CS} = {} & (b_1 \ln \mathrm{ASM}) + (b_2 \ln \mathrm{I} + b_3 \ln \mathrm{TR} + b_4 \ln \mathrm{UR} \\ & + b_5 \ln \mathrm{TM} + b_6 \ln \mathrm{RG}) + (b_7 \ln \mathrm{PRS} + b_8 \ln \mathrm{PRB} \\ & + b_9 \ln \mathrm{OL} + b_{10}\, \mathrm{BAN} + b_{11} \ln \mathrm{MDA} \\ & + b_{12} \ln \mathrm{UN}) + b_0 + u_2,\end{aligned} \tag{13.6.2}$$

$$\begin{aligned}\ln \mathrm{ASM} = {} & (c_1 \ln \mathrm{CB} + c_2 \ln \mathrm{CS}) + (c_3 \ln \mathrm{CW} + c_4 \ln \mathrm{UR}) \\ & + (c_5 \ln \mathrm{OL} + c_6 \ln \mathrm{EX} + c_7 \ln \mathrm{UN}) + c_0 + u_3,\end{aligned} \tag{13.6.3}$$

$$\begin{aligned}\ln \mathrm{ARM} = {} & (d_1 \ln \mathrm{CB} + d_2 \ln \mathrm{CS}) + (d_3 \ln \mathrm{CW} + d_4 \ln \mathrm{UR}) \\ & + (d_5 \ln \mathrm{OL} + d_6 \ln \mathrm{EX} + d_7 \ln \mathrm{UN}) + d_0 + u_4.\end{aligned} \tag{13.6.4}$$

In each of these equations the right-hand side of explanatory variables has four sets of variables. The first is a set of explanatory endogenous variables, such as alcoholism influencing consumption in the first two equations and the consumption of beer and of spirits influencing alcoholism and alcohol-related mortality in the last two equations. The second is a set of standardizing exogenous variables, including income, I; tourism, TR; urbanization, UR; temperature, TM; and religion, RG, in the first two equations and CW, consumption of wine, and urbanization in the last two equations. The third is a set of exogenous policy variables, including the price of spirits, PRS; the price of beer, PRB; the number of outlets, OL; a dummy variable for a ban on advertising, BAN; the minimum drinking age, MDA; the unemployment rate, UN; and alcoholism rehabilitation expenses, EX. The unemployment rate is treated in this model as an exogenous policy variable, where industrial policy, educational policy, or other policies taken at a statewide level could influence employment and unemployment. The fourth is the intercept and stochastic disturbance term for each equation. The first two equations are demand equations for beer and spirits, respectively, where, for example, a_2 and b_2 are income elasticities, a_7 and b_7 are (own) price elasticities, and a_8 and b_8 are cross-price elasticities. These equations differ from the more usual demand equations in including alcoholism as an explanatory variable and treating the unemployment rate as an exogenous policy variable which can influence the endogenous variables of the model. The third and fourth equations explain alcoholism and alcohol-related mortality, respectively, in terms of alcohol consumption, standardizing variables, and control variables.

The reduced form of this model explains each of the endogenous variables as a function of all exogenous (standardizing and policy) variables. It thus accounts for all direct and indirect effects of each of the exogenous variables on each of the endogenous variables and it therefore yields the appropriate set of elasticities to be used to study policy initiatives. For example, the number of outlets, OL, has both a direct and an indirect effect on consumption of beer since it enters directly in equation (13.6.1), but it also affects alcoholism in

(13.6.3) and thus influences the ASM variable in (13.6.1). As another example, the minimum drinking age (MDA) has no direct effect on alcoholism, but it has two indirect effects through its effects on both consumption variables.

Both the reduced form and the structural form of this model were estimated using least squares estimation using the data on the 35 states in 1975. The results indicate that the endogenous variables are reasonably well explained by the explanatory variables in both the reduced form and the structural form. There were relatively high adjusted R^2 values for cross-section studies, amounting to over 0.6 for the consumption equations and over 0.5 for the alcoholism equation in the structural form. The equation for alcohol-related mortality did not have as high an adjusted R^2 value, amounting to 0.38 in the structural form and 0.4 in the reduced form. Most of the coefficients were not significant, possibly indicating the presence of multicollinearity, in which groups of explanatory variables tend to move together.

Because of the log-linear specification, all of the coefficients can be interpreted as elasticities other than those for the advertising ban, which was entered directly (rather than in log form) as a dummy variable, and the intercept. In the reduced-form estimation of the equation for beer consumption, the most significant elasticities were those for tourism, with an elasticity of 0.103, significant at the 1% level, and the minimum drinking age, with an elasticity of –0.736, significant at the 5% level. The latter result implies that a 11.1% increase in the minimum drinking age, from 18 to 20, would reduce beer consumption by 8.17% or, on average, from 29.26 to 26.87 gallons per capita. In the reduced-form estimation of the equation for consumption of spirits, tourism continued to be significant at the 1% level, with an elasticity of 0.289, while the minimum drinking age was not significant. Overall, the explanatory variables that appear to be most important in the consumption of beer and spirits, in terms of the size and significance of the estimated elasticities, are tourism, minimum drinking age, income, outlets, advertising, and the price of beer.

In the reduced-form estimation of the equations for alcoholism and for alcohol-related mortality, the unemployment rate was highly significant, with an elasticity of 0.57, significant at the 1% level, in influencing alcoholism and with an elasticity of 0.41, significant at the 5% level, in influencing alcohol-related mortality. Prices of beer and spirits have opposite effects on alcoholism and on alcohol-related mortality, with the price of beer increasing alcoholism and decreasing mortality but the price of spirits *decreasing* alcoholism and *increasing* mortality. Interestingly, average statewide consumption has no significant effect on either alcoholism or alcohol-related mortality, which are apparently determined by the distribution of alcohol consumption, particularly its upper tail involving heavy drinkers, rather than merely its mean value.

The estimated reduced form was used to simulate several policy initiatives that could influence the level of alcoholic beverage consumption, alcoholism, and alcohol-related mortality. These simulations analyzed the potential impact of changes in the policy variables of the model, specifically the minimum drinking age, unemployment, advertising, and increased taxes on alcoholic beverages (which would increase their price). The simulation of the effects of increasing the minimum drinking age used the estimated reduced form to determine the effects of raising all states in the sample that had a minimum drinking age of less than 21 up to one of 21. According to the results of this simulation, such a policy change would lower beer consumption by 8.39%, would lower spirits consumption by 7.28%, would reduce alcoholism by an insignificant 0.37%, and would reduce alcohol-related mortality by 3.23%. Thus there are significant reductions in the consumption of alcoholic beverages but not in alcoholism, due to an increase in the minimum drinking age.

The simulation of the effects of reducing the unemployment rate used the estimated reduced form to determine the effects of lowering the unemployment rate for all states in the sample that were above the average of 8.07% to this level by suitable economic policies. According to the results of this simulation, such a policy change would lead to small reductions in alcohol consumption (3.25% for beer and 2.73% for spirits) but to *substantial* reductions in alcoholism, amounting to 10.87%, and in alcohol-related mortality, by 6.64%. While it takes a number of years of hard drinking to become an alcoholic, differences in unemployment rates across the states frequently persist over long periods, leading to greater alcoholism problems in states with above-average unemployment. At the individual level, those people who are at high risk of developing alcohol-related health problems may well become alcoholics when confronted with the stress of unemployment. These results suggest that reducing unemployment would have substantial value in combating alcoholism over and above its general economic value to society.

As to advertising, the simulation of a ban on advertising for alcoholic beverages indicates that it leads not to a general reduction in consumption of alcohol, but rather, to a shift from beer consumption to spirits consumption, a result that is consistent with the high ratio of beer advertising relative to that of other beverages. While the ban on advertising would reduce alcoholism, it would slightly increase alcohol-related mortality, which appears to be more closely related to spirits consumption and which would increase as a result of the ban. Combining the ban on advertising with an increase in the minimum drinking age would, however, decrease both alcoholism (substantially) and alcohol-related mortality (slightly).

Finally, as to increased taxes on alcoholic beverages, the simulation of a 10% increase in the price of spirits would decrease consumption of spirits by 1.31%, while the consumption of beer would rise by 1.58%, beer being a substitute for spirits and both being highly price inelastic. While these changes are relatively small, there are more substantial effects on alcoholism and on alcohol-related mortality, which would drop by 4.78% and by 9.24%, respectively, suggesting the value of such a policy initiative, despite its relatively small effect on consumption.

This study of alcoholism reached two general conclusions. First, it is important to study alcoholism and alcohol-related mortality *directly* as variables of an econometric model, as opposed to making inferences from the demand for alcoholic beverages alone. The relations between consumption and the effects in terms of alcoholism and alcohol-related mortality are sufficiently complex to warrant the use of a simultaneous-equations approach to aid in understanding the ways in which consumption of alcoholic beverages, alcoholism, and alcohol-related mortality are related to one another. Second, the estimated model is useful in analyzing policy variables to show their relative importance. Several of these policy variables were identified as significant determinants of consumption, alcoholism, and alcohol-related mortality, including the minimum drinking age, unemployment, advertising, and increased taxes on alcoholic beverages. Of particular importance, however, was the role of unemployment as a determinant of alcoholism and alcohol-related mortality, implying that unemployment produces significant social losses stemming from the consumption of alcohol, in addition to its more commonly measured direct economic losses.

13.7 ECONOMIC HISTORY; CLIOMETRICS

The "new" economic history, sometimes called *cliometrics* ("clio" referring to the muse of history), uses econometric techniques to study historical issues.[25] While in a certain sense all of econometrics is a particular, stylized way of studying history, the distinctive feature of cliometrics is that it considers issues treated by economic historians and studies them using the tools of econometrics. This section contains two examples of such studies of U.S. economic history, pertaining to railroad rate fixing before 1900 and cotton price fluctuations in the 1830s.[26]

The first study is the MacAvoy analysis of the success of railroad rate-fixing agreements before 1900.[27] Loyalty to cartel agreements is tested by estimating the relationship:

$$R_T = \alpha + \beta R_0, \tag{13.7.1}$$

where R_T is the rate reported by the Chicago Board of Trade and R_0 is the official cartel rate. Complete loyalty would require that the rate changes only when the official rate changes, so that the estimated coefficients would take the values $\hat{\alpha} = 0$, $\hat{\beta} = 1$, and $R^2 = 1$. If there is cheating on the cartel agreement, however, then $\hat{\beta} < 1$ and $R^2 < 1$, since actual rates change less than official rates, and a portion of the variance in R_T is based on cheating rather than on following changes in R_0.[28] Estimates of equation (13.7.1) using weekly data for successive summer and winter seasons over the period 1871–1874 indicate that $\hat{\beta}$ was not significantly different from 1 and R^2 was high, indicating success of the cartel agreement over this period. During the winter season of 1874–1875, however, both $\hat{\beta}$ and R^2 fell to zero, indicating failure of the cartel agreement, perhaps because one major railroad had at that time just completed a direct line to Chicago.

The second econometric study of history is the Temin analysis of cotton price fluctuations in the United States during the period 1820–1859.[29] The model consists of three interrelated equations, but, because of its special structure each of the equations can be estimated directly using ordinary least squares.[30] The first equation relates the supply of cotton Q to the U.S. price of the previous year P_{-1}^A (because the cotton was planted then) and time t (a proxy for the labor force available). The estimated equation, specified in log-linear form, is

$$\begin{aligned} \log Q = 5.37 - &\underset{(0.09)}{0.05}\log P_{-1}^A + \underset{(0.002)}{0.06}t, \\ R^2 = 0.96&, \quad d = 1.8. \end{aligned} \tag{13.7.2}$$

[25]See Fogel (1966, 1989), Conrad (1968), Fogel and Engerman, Eds. (1971), Wright (1971), Aydelotte, Bogue, and Fogel, Eds. (1972), Sutch (1977), van der Wee and Klep (1977), Ransom, Sutch, and Walton, Eds. (1982), and Goldin and Rockoff, Eds. (1992).

[26]These studies are discussed at length in Wright (1971).

[27]See MacAvoy (1965) and the discussion in Wright (1971).

[28]This argument, in fact, depends on R_0 being exogenously set. If R_0 is based on R_T or if changes in R_T lead to changes in R_0, then the estimates $\hat{\beta} = 1$ and $R^2 = 1$ would not signify success of the cartel.

[29]See Temin (1967) and the discussion in Wright (1971).

[30]The model is a recursive one, as discussed in Section 9.5, assuming that the covariance matrix of the stochastic disturbance terms is diagonal, so that there is no correlation between the disturbances in any two of the three equations.

The insignificance of the estimated elasticity of supply suggests that the size of the cotton crop was not responsive to price (or perhaps that the equation is misspecified). The estimated coefficient of t indicates a 6% outward shift per year in cotton supply.

The estimated demand equation is:

$$\log P^B = -1.28 - \underset{(0.18)}{0.71} \log Q - \underset{(0.23)}{0.94} \log B + \underset{(0.01)}{0.03}t + \log R, \tag{13.7.3}$$

$$R^2 = 0.70, \quad d = 1.6,$$

where P^B is the price of cotton in Britain (the primary market for U.S. cotton); B is the deflated price of bread in London, a proxy for cyclical changes in income; and R is an index of British prices (the coefficient of R is set equal unity, since the equation is meant to explain the *relative* price of cotton). According to (13.7.3) the demand for cotton was price elastic during this period, its estimated elasticity being $-(1/0.71) = -1.4$.

The third equation, which completes the system, estimates the relationship of the U.S. price to the British price as:

$$\log P^A = 0.36 + \underset{(0.09)}{1.02} \log P^B, \qquad R^2 = 0.78, \quad d = 2.1. \tag{13.7.4}$$

Thus the U.S. price followed the British price closely, a 10% increase in the British price raising the U.S. price by 10.2%.

Temin concluded from these and other regressions that the size of the U.S. cotton crop was not sensitive to price, but rather was determined by the growth of the labor force and random factors, such as the weather. In particular he concluded that both the price rise in 1835 and the price fall in 1838 were due to the harvest and conditions in Britain.

Other cliometric studies have treated such issues as the role of railroads in U.S. economic development, the growth of specific industries, and the economics of slavery in the U.S. South.[31]

PROBLEMS

13-A Consider the demand for (nominal) money. Construct a statistical test that would determine whether this demand function is homogeneous of degree one with respect to the price level.

13-B In the Goldfeld and Sichel partial adjustment model (13.2.5), obtain the long-run elasticities. Also obtain the equivalent Koyck distributed lag model.

13-C Consider a stock adjustment model for money, of the form:

$$M_t - M_{t-1} = \gamma(M_t^* - M_{t-1}), \qquad 0 < \gamma < 1,$$

where the desired stock of money is a given function of income and the interest rate:

$$M_t^* = F(Y_t, r_t).$$

1. What is the equivalent Koyck distributed lag formulation of this model?
2. Show that if $M_t^* = kY_t$, where k is a constant, the stock of money is proportional to an exponentially weighted average of all past levels of income ("permanent income"). What happens if k depends on r_t?

[31]See Fogel (1964, 1989) Fogel and Engerman (1969, 1974, 1991), and the references cited in footnote 25.

3. Consider the related log-linear stock adjustment model:

$$\frac{M_t}{M_{t-1}} = \left(\frac{M_t^*}{M_{t-1}}\right)^{\delta}, \quad where \quad M_t^* = Ar_t^{\alpha}Y_t.$$

Show that $\ln M_t$ is an exponentially weighted geometric average of current and past income levels and interest rates. Show that if $\alpha = 0$, then the velocity of circulation is an exponentially weighted average of current and past rates of change of income.

13-D According to *Gresham's law*, money that is overvalued ("bad" money) tends to drive undervalued ("good") money out of circulation. In an exponential model of this process:

$$N(t) = N_0 e^{-\lambda t},$$

where $N(t)$ is the number of good coins in circulation, starting from N_0 in the base year, and λ is the rate at which the undervalued money is driven out of circulation.

1. One way of estimating λ is to calculate the number in circulation at a given date and compare it to the number minted. One study found that in 1969, four years after clad copper dimes first appeared, out of 929 randomly collected dimes 26 were silver and 903 were clad copper. Altogether there were 51.37×10^8 silver dimes and 67.57×10^8 clad copper dimes minted at this point. On the basis of the sample it is estimated that the number of silver dimes in circulation was:

$$\frac{26}{903} \times 67.57 \times 10^8 = 1.945 \times 10^8.$$

What is the estimate of λ, the rate of disappearance of the silver dimes?

2. How would you estimate λ on the basis of n observations, given the relative numbers of each type of coin at each observation and given the total number minted of each type?

13-E Show that a linear version of the Teigen model (13.2.8), (13.2.9), and (13.2.10) is an identified model.

13-F Using the order condition of identification, discuss the identification of the simultaneous-equations model of industrial organization presented in Tables 13.1 and 13.2.

13-G Several measures of concentration have been used in studies of industrial organization. One is the *concentration ratio*, defined as the percentage of output accounted for by the k largest firms in the industry (usually $k = 4$ or 8). Another is the *Herfindahl index*, defined as:

$$H = \sum_{i=1}^{n} s_i^2,$$

where s_i is the share of the ith firm in industry output (that is, x_i/x, where x_i is the output of firm i and x is total industry output) and n is the total number of firms. A third is *entropy*, defined as:

$$E = -\sum_{i=1}^{n} s_i \log s_i,$$

where the log usually refers to base 2 logarithms.

1. Show that:

$$\frac{1}{n} \leqslant H \leqslant 1,$$

and give interpretations for $H = 1/n$ and $H = 1$. Show that $1/H$ is a "numbers equivalent," giving the number of equal-sized firms in an industry with the same value of H.

2. Show that:

$$0 \leqslant E \leqslant \log n,$$

and give interpretations for $E = 0$ and $E = \log n$. Show that F, where $\log F = E$, is a "numbers equivalent," giving the number of equal-sized firms in an industry with the same value of E.

BIBLIOGRAPHY

Money

BRUNNER, K., and A. H. MELTZER (1964). "Some Further Investigations of Demand and Supply Functions for Money." *Journal of Finance*, 19: 240–283.

BRUNNER, K., and A. H. MELTZER (1990). "Money Supply," in B. M. Friedman and F. H. Hahn, Eds., *Handbook of Monetary Economics*, Vol. 1. Amsterdam: North-Holland Publishing Company.

COOPER, J. P. (1974). *Development of the Monetary Sector, Prediction, and Policy Analysis in the FRB-MIT-Penn Model*. Lexington, Mass.: Lexington Books.

FAIR, R. C. (1987). "International Evidence on the Demand for Money." *Review of Economics and Statistics*, 69: 473–480.

GIBSON, W. E. (1972). "Demand and Supply Functions for Money in the United States: Theory and Measurement." *Econometrica*, 40: 361–370.

GOLDFELD, S. M. (1973). "The Demand for Money Revisited." *Brookings Papers on Economic Activity*, 3: 577–638.

GOLDFELD, S. M. (1976). "The Case of the Missing Money." *Brookings Papers on Economic Activity*, 6: 683–730.

GOLDFELD, S. M., and D. E. SICHEL (1990). "The Demand for Money," in B. M. Friedman and F. H. Hahn, Eds., *Handbook of Monetary Economics*, Vol. 1. Amsterdam: North-Holland Publishing Company.

JUDD, J. P., and J. L. SCADDING (1982). "The Search for a Stable Money Demand Function: A Survey of the Post-1973 Literature." *Journal of Economic Literature*, 20: 993–1023.

KLEIN, B. (1974). "Competitive Interest Payments on Bank Deposits and the Long-Run Demand for Money." *American Economic Review*, 64: 931–949.

LAIDLER, D. E. W. (1985). *The Demand for Money: Theories, Evidence, and Problems*, 3rd ed. New York: Harper & Row, Publishers, Inc.

MODIGLIANI, F., R. H. RASCHE, and J. P. COOPER (1970). "Central Bank Policy, the Money Supply, and the Short-Term Rate of Interest." *Journal of Money, Credit, and Banking*, 2: 166–218.

PAPADEMOS, L., and F. MODIGLIANI (1990). "The Supply of Money and the Control of Nominal Income," in B. M. Friedman and F. H. Hahn, Eds., *Handbook of Monetary Economics*, Vol. 1. Amsterdam: North-Holland Publishing Company.

TEIGEN, R. (1964). "Demand and Supply Functions for Money in the United States: Some Structural Estimates." *Econometrica*, 32: 476–509.

Industrial Organization

BAIN, J. S. (1956). *Barriers to New Competition*. Cambridge, Mass.: Harvard University Press.

BAIN, J. S. (1968). *Industrial Organization*, 2nd ed. New York: John Wiley & Sons, Inc.

CAVES, R. E., M. E. PORTER, and A. M. SPENCE (1980). *Competition in the Open Economy: A Model Applied to Canada*. Cambridge, Mass.: Harvard University Press.

COMANOR, W. S., and T. A. WILSON (1974). *Advertising and Market Power*. Cambridge, Mass.: Harvard University Press.

COMANOR, W. S., and T. A. WILSON (1979). "The Effect of Advertising on Competition: A Survey." *Journal of Economic Literature*, 17: 435–476.

CONNOLLY, R. A., and M. HIRSCHEY (1984). "R&D, Market Structure and Profits: A Value-Based Approach." *Review of Economics and Statistics*, 66: 678–681.

GEROSKI, P. A. (1982). "Simultaneous Equations Models of the Structure–Performance Paradigm." *European Economic Review*, 19: 145–158.

GRABOWSKI, H., and D. C. MUELLER (1970). "Industrial Organization: The Role and Contributions of Econometrics." *American Economic Review, Papers and Proceedings*, 60: 100–104.

HAY, D. A., and D. J. MORRIS (1979). *Industrial Economics: Theory and Evidence*. Oxford: Oxford University Press.

INTRILIGATOR, M. D., J. F. WESTON, and H. DE ANGELO (1975). "An Econometric Test of the Structure–Conduct–Performance Paradigm in Industrial Organization." Paper presented at the Econometric Society 3rd World Congress, Toronto.

MARTIN, S. (1979). "Advertising, Concentration, and Profitability: The Simultaneity Problem." *Bell Journal of Economics*, 10: 639–647.

MARTIN, S. (1983). *Market, Firm, and Economic Performance: An Empirical Analysis*. New York: New York University Press.

SCHERER, F. M. (1980). *Industrial Market Structure and Economic Performance*, 2nd ed. Chicago: Rand McNally & Company.

SCHMALENSEE, R. (1988). "Industrial Economics: An Overview." *Economic Journal*, 98: 643–681.

SCHMALENSEE, R. (1989). "Inter-industry Studies of Structure and Performance," in R. Schmalensee and R. D. Willig, Eds., *Handbook of Industrial Organization*, Vol. 2. Amsterdam: North-Holland Publishing Company.

WATERSON, M. (1984). *Economic Theory of Industry*. Cambridge: Cambridge University Press.

WEISS, L. W. (1971). "Quantitative Studies of Industrial Organization," in M. D. Intriligator, Ed., *Frontiers of Quantitative Economics*. Amsterdam: North-Holland Publishing Company.

WEISS, L. W. (1974). "The Concentration–Profits Relationship and Antitrust," in H. J. Goldschmid, H. M. Mann, and J. F. Weston, Eds., *Industrial Concentration: The New Learning*. Boston: Little, Brown and Company.

Labor Economics

ASHENFELTER, O., and J. HECKMAN (1974). "The Estimation of Income and Substitution Effects in a Model of Family Labor Supply." *Econometrica*, 42: 73–86.

ASHENFELTER, O., and R. LAYARD, Eds. (1986). *Handbook of Labor Economics*, Vols. 1 and 2. Amsterdam: North-Holland Publishing Company.

HECKMAN, J., and T. MACURDY (1981). "New Methods for Estimating Labor Supply Functions: A Survey," in R. Ehrenberg, Ed., *Research in Labor Economics*, Vol. 4. London: JAI Press Ltd.

HECKMAN, J., and T. MACURDY (1986). "Labor Econometrics," in Z. Griliches and M. D. Intriligator, Eds., *Handbook of Econometrics*, Vol. 3. Amsterdam: North-Holland Publishing Company.

Health Economics

DURU, G., and J. H. P. PAELINCK, Eds. (1991). *Econometrics of Health Care*. Dordrecht, The Netherlands: Wolters Kluwer NV.

FUCHS, V. R., Ed. (1982). *Economic Aspects of Health*. Chicago: University of Chicago Press.

GROSSMAN, M. (1972). *The Demand for Health: A Theoretical and Empirical Investigation*. New York: Columbia University Press.

GROSSMAN, M. (1982). "The Demand for Health after a Decade." *Journal of Health Economics*, 1: 1–13.

NEWHOUSE, J. P. (1981). "The Demand for Medical Care Services: A Retrospect and Prospect," in van der Gaag and Perlman (1981).

NEWHOUSE, J. P., and C. E. PHELPS (1974). "Price and Income Elasticities for Medical Care Services," in Perlman (1974).

NEWHOUSE, J. P., and C. E. PHELPS (1976). "New Estimates of Price and Income Elasticities," in Rossett (1976).

PERLMAN, M., Ed. (1974). *The Economics of Health and Medical Care*. International Economic Association. London: Macmillan Publishers Ltd.

ROSSETT, R. N., Ed. (1976). *The Role of Health Insurance in the Health Services Sector*. New York: National Bureau of Economic Research.

VAN DER GAAG, J., W. B. NEENAN, and T. TSUKAHARA, JR., Eds. (1982). *Economics of Health Care*. New York: Praeger Publishers.

VAN DER GAAG, J., and M. PERLMAN, Eds. (1981). *Health, Economics, and Health Economics*. Amsterdam: North-Holland Publishing Company.

WAGSTAFF, A. (1989). "Econometric Studies in Health Economics: A Survey of the British Literature." *Journal of Health Economics*, 8: 1–51.

WILLIAMS, A., Ed. (1987). *Health and Economics*. Oxford: Macmillan Publishers Ltd.

YETT, D. E., L. J. DRABEK, M. D. INTRILIGATOR, and L. J. KIMBELL (1972). "Health Manpower Planning: An Econometric Approach." *Health Services Research*, 7: 134–147.

YETT, D. E., L. J. DRABEK, M. D. INTRILIGATOR, and L. J. KIMBELL (1974). "Econometric Forecasts of Health Services and Health Manpower," in Perlman (1974).

YETT, D. E., L. J. DRABEK, M. D. INTRILIGATOR, and L. J. KIMBELL (1975). "A Microeconometric Model of the Health Care System in the United States." *Annals of Economic and Social Measurement*, 4: 407–433.

YETT, D. E., L. J. DRABEK, M. D. INTRILIGATOR, and L. J. KIMBELL (1977). *A Forecasting and Policy Simulation Model of the Health Care Sector: The HRRC Prototype Microeconometric Model*. Lexington, Mass.: Lexington Books.

Alcoholism

ORNSTEIN, S. (1980). "Control of Alcohol Consumption through Price Increases." *Journal of Studies on Alcohol*, 41: 807–818.

SCHWEITZER, S. O., M. D. INTRILIGATOR, and H. SALEHI (1983). "Alcoholism: An Econometric Model of Its Causes, Its Effects, and Its Control," in M. Grant, M. Plant, and A. Williams, Eds., *Economics and Alcohol*. London: Croom Helm Ltd.; New York: Gardner Press, Inc.

Economic History

AYDELOTTE, W. O., A. G. BOGUE, and R. W. FOGEL, Eds. (1972). *The Dimensions of Quantitative Research in History*. Princeton, N.J.: Princeton University Press.

CONRAD, A. H. (1968). "Econometrics and Southern History." *Explorations in Entrepreneurial History*, Second Series, 6: 34–53.

FOGEL, R. W. (1964). *Railroads and American Economic Growth*. Baltimore: Johns Hopkins University Press.

FOGEL, R. W. (1966). "The New Economic History: Its Findings and Methods." *Economic History Review*, 19: 642–656.

FOGEL, R. W. (1989). *Without Consent or Contract: The Rise and Fall of American Slavery*. New York: W.W. Norton & Company, Inc.

FOGEL, R. W., and S. L. ENGERMAN (1969). "A Model for the Explanation of Industrial Expansion during the Nineteenth Century, with an Application to the American Iron Industry." *Journal of Political Economy*, 77: 306–328.

FOGEL, R. W., and S. L. ENGERMAN, Eds. (1971). *The Reinterpretation of American Economic History*. New York: Harper & Row, Publishers, Inc.

FOGEL, R. W., and S. L. ENGERMAN (1974). *Time on the Cross*. Boston: Little, Brown and Company.

FOGEL, R. W., and S. L. ENGERMAN, Eds. (1991). *Without Consent or Contract. Technical Papers: The Rise and Fall of American Slavery*. New York: W.W. Norton & Company, Inc.

GOLDIN, C., and H. ROCKOFF, Eds. (1992). *Strategic Factors in Nineteenth Century American Economic History*. Chicago: University of Chicago Press.

MACAVOY, P. (1965). *The Economic Effects of Regulation: Trunk Line Railroad Cartels and the Interstate Commerce Commission before 1900*. Cambridge, Mass.: MIT Press.

RANSOM, R. L., R. SUTCH, and G. M. WALTON, Eds. (1982). *Explorations in the New Economic History*. New York: Academic Press, Inc.

SUTCH, R. (1977). "United States Economic History," in M. D. Intriligator, Ed., *Frontiers of Quantitative Economics*, Vol. 3. Amsterdam: North-Holland Publishing Company.

TEMIN, P. (1967). "The Cause of Cotton Price Fluctuation in the 1830s." *Review of Economics and Statistics*, 49: 463–470.

VAN DER WEE, H., and P. M. M. KLEP (1977). "Quantitative Economic History in Europe since the Second World War: Survey, Evaluation, and Prospects," in M. D. Intriligator, Ed., *Frontiers of Quantitative Economics*, Vol. 3. Amsterdam: North-Holland Publishing Company.

WRIGHT, G. (1971). "Econometric Studies of History," in M. D. Intriligator, Ed., *Frontiers of Quantitative Economics*. Amsterdam: North-Holland Publishing Company.

14

STRUCTURAL ANALYSIS

14.1 THE USES OF ECONOMETRIC MODELS

This chapter begins the final part of this book, consisting of three chapters on the uses of econometric models and a final chapter concerning certain managerial aspects of these models (particularly their evaluation). The models, data, and estimation techniques of econometrics, as well as several applications, have been developed in previous parts of the book. At this point it is therefore appropriate to assess the significance and impact of these developments. To perform such an assessment it is necessary to return to the ideas developed in Chapter 1 on the nature of the econometric approach, particularly the purposes of econometrics as displayed in Figure 1.1. The three purposes identified there—structural analysis, forecasting, and policy evaluation—will be treated in the next three chapters. They correspond, respectively, to the descriptive, predictive, and prescriptive uses of econometrics.

In developing not only structural analysis but also forecasting and policy evaluation, it is convenient to use a particular format for the econometric model. This format, similar to that developed in Section 2.9, expresses the structural form as:

$$\underset{1\times g}{\mathbf{y}_t}\,\underset{g\times g}{\mathbf{\Gamma}} + \underset{1\times g}{\mathbf{y}_{t-1}}\,\underset{g\times g}{\mathbf{B}_1} + \underset{1\times k}{\mathbf{z}_t}\,\underset{k\times g}{\mathbf{B}_2} = \underset{1\times g}{\boldsymbol{\varepsilon}_t}. \qquad *(14.1.1)$$

Here $\mathbf{y}_t$ is a vector of g current endogenous variables of the model, $\mathbf{y}_{t-1}$ is a vector of the same g endogenous variables in the preceding period, $\mathbf{z}_t$ is a vector of k exogenous variables, and $\boldsymbol{\varepsilon}_t$ is a vector of g stochastic disturbance terms. Taken together, $\mathbf{y}_{t-1}$ and $\mathbf{z}_t$ are the predetermined variables of the system, which can be written:

$$\underset{1\times g}{\mathbf{y}_t}\,\underset{g\times g}{\mathbf{\Gamma}} + \underset{1\times(g+k)}{(\mathbf{y}_{t-1} \,\vdots\, \mathbf{z}_t)}\,\underset{(g+k)\times g}{\begin{pmatrix}\mathbf{B}_1 \\ \hline \mathbf{B}_2\end{pmatrix}} = \underset{1\times g}{\boldsymbol{\varepsilon}_t}. \qquad (14.1.2)$$

The partitioned matrix of coefficients of predetermined variables is the **B** matrix used previously; here the matrix is partitioned to take explicit account of lagged endogenous and exogenous variables.[1]

If $\mathbf{\Gamma}$ is nonsingular, the reduced form can be written:

$$\mathbf{y}_t = \mathbf{y}_{t-1}\mathbf{\Pi}_1 + \mathbf{z}_t\mathbf{\Pi}_2 + \mathbf{u}_t, \qquad *(14.1.3)$$

where the coefficient matrices and reduced-form stochastic disturbance terms are given as

$$\mathbf{\Pi}_1 = -\mathbf{B}_1\mathbf{\Gamma}^{-1}, \qquad \mathbf{\Pi}_2 = -\mathbf{B}_2\mathbf{\Gamma}^{-1}, \qquad \mathbf{u}_t = \boldsymbol{\varepsilon}_t\mathbf{\Gamma}^{-1}. \qquad *(14.1.4)$$

The final form can be obtained by iteration, using the reduced form, as:

$$\mathbf{y}_t = \mathbf{y}_0\mathbf{\Pi}_1^t + \sum_{j=0}^{t-1}\mathbf{z}_{t-j}\mathbf{\Pi}_2\mathbf{\Pi}_1^j + \sum_{j=0}^{t-1}\mathbf{u}_{t-j}\mathbf{\Pi}_1^j. \qquad *(14.1.5)$$

Here each of the g endogenous variables is expressed as a linear function of base values of all endogenous variables ($\mathbf{y}_0$), current and lagged values of all exogenous variables ($\mathbf{z}_t$, $\mathbf{z}_{t-1}$, . . . , $\mathbf{z}_1$), and current and lagged values of all reduced-form stochastic disturbance terms ($\mathbf{u}_t$, $\mathbf{u}_{t-1}$, . . . , $\mathbf{u}_1$).

14.2 THE NATURE OF STRUCTURAL ANALYSIS

One of the major purposes of performing an econometric study is that of using the estimated econometric model for structural analysis. By *structural analysis* is meant an investigation of the underlying interrelationships of the system under consideration in order to understand and to explain relevant phenomena. Structural analysis involves the quantitative estimation of the interrelationships among the variables of the system.

The basic step in structural analysis is the estimation of the coefficients of the system, in particular $\mathbf{\Gamma}$, $\mathbf{B}_1$, and $\mathbf{B}_2$ in the structural form (14.1.1); $\mathbf{\Pi}_1$ and $\mathbf{\Pi}_2$ in the reduced form (14.1.3); and $\mathbf{\Pi}_1^t, \mathbf{\Pi}_2, \mathbf{\Pi}_2\mathbf{\Pi}_1, \mathbf{\Pi}_2\mathbf{\Pi}_1^2, \ldots$, in the final form (14.1.5).

In addition to the estimation of the coefficient matrices themselves, structural analysis is concerned with the interpretation of certain coefficients or combinations of coefficients. Three important ways of interpreting the coefficients are the comparative statics results, the elasticities, and the multipliers. These will be the subjects of the next sections of this chapter.

Another aspect of structural analysis is the testing of rival theories. An example is the CES production function of Section 8.3. The estimation of this function, in particular the estimate of σ, the elasticity of substitution, can be considered a test of rival theories, in particular the Cobb–Douglas and input–output production functions. If $\sigma = 1$, the CES reduces to the Cobb–Douglas case, while if $\sigma = 0$, it reduces to the input–output case. An econometric measurement of σ, together with its estimated standard error, would allow a statistical test of the hypothesis that $\sigma = 1$ or that $\sigma = 0$. Thus if σ is not significantly different from 0, the input-output production function may be accepted as a simpler but adequate theory,

[1]Note that the **B** matrix in (14.1.2) is of order $(g + k) \times g$ rather than $k \times g$ as earlier because of the explicit inclusion of lagged endogenous variables. Also note that lagged exogenous variables are not accounted for explicitly here, whereas they are in equation (2.9.4). These variables can be taken into account by including them within $\mathbf{z}_t$.

while if σ is not significantly different from 1, the Cobb–Douglas form of the function may be so accepted.

14.3 COMPARATIVE STATICS

The comparative statics technique is one of the most useful techniques of economic analysis.[2] It involves the comparison of two equilibrium points of a system of equations describing the phenomenon under consideration. The two equilibrium points typically involve equilibrium before and after displacement by a change in one of the parameters of the system of equations.

Consider the following system of g independent and consistent (i.e., mutually compatible) equations in g variables $y_1, y_2, \ldots, y_g$ involving m parameters $\alpha_1, \alpha_2, \ldots, \alpha_m$:

$$\begin{aligned} f^1(y_1, y_2, \ldots, y_g; \alpha_1, \alpha_2, \ldots, \alpha_m) &= 0, \\ f^2(y_1, y_2, \ldots, y_g; \alpha_1, \alpha_2, \ldots, \alpha_m) &= 0, \\ &\vdots \\ f^g(y_1, y_2, \ldots, y_g; \alpha_1, \alpha_2, \ldots, \alpha_m) &= 0. \end{aligned} \qquad *(14.3.1)$$

If the g functions of $f^1, f^2, \ldots, f^g$ are sufficiently smooth and independent, this system can be solved to obtain a set of equilibrium values for the variables, each of which can be treated as a differentiable function of the parameters of the system:[3]

$$\begin{aligned} y_1^0 &= y_1^0(\alpha_1, \alpha_2, \ldots, \alpha_m), \\ y_2^0 &= y_2^0(\alpha_1, \alpha_2, \ldots, \alpha_m), \\ &\vdots \\ y_g^0 &= y_g^0(\alpha_1, \alpha_2, \ldots, \alpha_m). \end{aligned} \qquad *(14.3.2)$$

Inserting these equilibrium values in the original set of equations yields the identities:

$$\begin{aligned} f^1(y_1^0, y_2^0, \ldots, y_g^0; \alpha_1, \alpha_2, \ldots, \alpha_m) &\equiv 0, \\ f^2(y_1^0, y_2^0, \ldots, y_g^0; \alpha_1, \alpha_2, \ldots, \alpha_m) &\equiv 0, \\ &\vdots \\ f^g(y_1^0, y_2^0, \ldots, y_g^0; \alpha_1, \alpha_2, \ldots, \alpha_m) &\equiv 0. \end{aligned} \qquad (14.3.3)$$

Now consider the effect of a change in one of the parameters, say α_l, on the equilibrium values of the variables. Differentiating each of the identities in (14.3.3) with respect to α_l yields:

$$\sum_{j=1}^{g} \frac{\partial f^i}{\partial y_j^0} \frac{\partial y_j^0}{\partial \alpha_l} + \frac{\partial f^i}{\partial \alpha_l} = 0, \qquad i = 1, 2, \ldots, g. \qquad (14.3.4)$$

Solving for the effect of a change in every α_l on y_j^0 yields, in matrix notation,

$$\underset{g\times m}{\frac{\partial \mathbf{y}^0}{\partial \boldsymbol{\alpha}}} = -\underset{g\times g}{\left(\frac{\partial \mathbf{f}}{\partial \mathbf{y}}\right)^{-1}} \underset{g\times m}{\left(\frac{\partial \mathbf{f}}{\partial \boldsymbol{\alpha}}\right)}, \qquad *(14.3.5)$$

[2]For a general discussion of the theory of comparative statics, see Kalman and Intriligator (1973).

[3]The smoothness and independence assumptions are the conditions on the Jacobian matrix required for the application of the implicit function theorem. See the references listed in Chapter 10, footnote 33.

where

$$\frac{\partial \mathbf{y}^0}{\partial \boldsymbol{\alpha}} = \begin{pmatrix} \frac{\partial y_1^0}{\partial \alpha_1} & \cdots & \frac{\partial y_1^0}{\partial \alpha_m} \\ \vdots & & \\ \frac{\partial y_g^0}{\partial \alpha_1} & \cdots & \frac{\partial y_g^0}{\partial \alpha_m} \end{pmatrix}, \qquad \frac{\partial \mathbf{f}}{\partial \mathbf{y}} = \begin{pmatrix} \frac{\partial f^1}{\partial y_1} & \cdots & \frac{\partial f^1}{\partial y_g} \\ \vdots & & \\ \frac{\partial f^g}{\partial y_1} & \cdots & \frac{\partial f^g}{\partial y_g} \end{pmatrix},$$

$$\frac{\partial \mathbf{f}}{\partial \boldsymbol{\alpha}} = \begin{pmatrix} \frac{\partial f^1}{\partial \alpha_1} & \cdots & \frac{\partial f^1}{\partial \alpha_m} \\ \vdots & & \\ \frac{\partial f^g}{\partial \alpha_1} & \cdots & \frac{\partial f^g}{\partial \alpha_m} \end{pmatrix}. \tag{14.3.6}$$

Equation (14.3.5) expresses the change in the equilibrium levels of each endogenous variable as each of the parameters of the model varies.[4] The effect of a change in any one parameter, α_l, on the equilibrium value of any of the variables, y_j^0, is then given as:

$$dy_j^0 = \frac{\partial y_j^0}{\partial \alpha_l} d\alpha_l, \qquad j = 1, 2, \ldots, g; \quad l = 1, 2, \ldots, m, \tag{14.3.7}$$

where $\partial y_j^0 / \partial \alpha_l$ is the jl element of the matrix $\partial \mathbf{y}^0 / \partial \boldsymbol{\alpha}$ in (14.3.5).

The econometric model is a special case of this system of equations, and so the comparative statics developments are applicable to it. The structural form (14.1.1) is a special case of (14.3.1) for which the f^i functions are linear and the g endogenous variables $y_1, y_2, \ldots, y_g$ are determined on the basis of a certain set of parameters. The parameters include not only the coefficients of the system, embodied in the $\boldsymbol{\Gamma}$, $\mathbf{B}_1$, and $\mathbf{B}_2$ matrices, but also the exogenous and lagged endogenous variables $\mathbf{z}$ and $\mathbf{y}_{-1}$ and the parameters determining the stochastic disturbance terms (e.g., the elements of the covariance matrix). The equilibrium values of the endogenous variables in general all change as any one of these parameters varies.

The comparative statics results can be illustrated most easily in the case of a single-equation model with one exogenous variable where the stochastic disturbance term is set equal to its expected value of zero, in which case the structural form (14.1.1) is:

$$y\gamma + y_{-1}\beta_1 + z\beta_2 = 0. \tag{14.3.8}$$

The reduced form is then:

$$y = -y_{-1}\frac{\beta_1}{\gamma} - z\frac{\beta_2}{\gamma}. \tag{14.3.9}$$

The effect of a change in the coefficient of the endogenous variable γ is then:

$$\frac{\partial y}{\partial \gamma} = \gamma_{-1}\frac{\beta_1}{\gamma^2} + z\frac{\beta_2}{\gamma^2} = -\frac{y}{\gamma}, \tag{14.3.10}$$

a result that could have been obtained either by differentiating (14.3.9) or alternatively from (14.3.5), since here

[4]Note that it has been assumed that the square matrix is nonsingular. This assumption can be justified as constituting a critical part of the sufficient conditions, allowing one to apply the implicit function theorem cited in footnote 3.

$$f(y;\, \gamma,\, \beta_1,\, \beta_2,\, y_{-1},\, z) = y\gamma + y_{-1}\beta_1 + z\beta_2 = 0, \tag{14.3.11}$$

so

$$\frac{\partial y}{\partial \gamma} = -\left(\frac{\partial f}{\partial y}\right)^{-1} \frac{\partial f}{\partial \gamma} = -(\gamma)^{-1} y = -\frac{y}{\gamma}. \tag{14.3.12}$$

Thus the change in the equilibrium value of y stemming from a change in γ is proportional to y, the factor of proportionality being $-1/\gamma$. Once the model is estimated and a value of γ is obtained, (14.3.10) can be used to test the sensitivity of the equilibrium value of the endogenous variable to a change in its parameter. The other comparative statics results, obtained either from (14.3.5) or from differentiating (14.3.9), are:

$$\frac{\partial y}{\partial \beta_1} = -\frac{y_{-1}}{\gamma}, \qquad \frac{\partial y}{\partial \beta_2} = -\frac{z}{\gamma},$$
$$\frac{\partial y}{\partial y_{-1}} = -\frac{\beta_1}{\gamma}, \qquad \frac{\partial y}{\partial z} = -\frac{\beta_2}{\gamma}. \tag{14.3.13}$$

Consider now once again the prototype macro model of Section 2.6. The reduced-form equation for national income can be written:

$$Y = \frac{\beta_2}{1-\gamma_1-\gamma_2} Y_{-1} + \frac{1}{1-\gamma_1-\gamma_2} G + \frac{\beta_1+\beta_3}{1-\gamma_1-\gamma_2}, \tag{14.3.14}$$

as in (2.6.7), where the stochastic disturbance terms have been dropped for simplicity. One of the comparative statics results,

$$\frac{\partial Y}{\partial G} = \frac{1}{1-\gamma_1-\gamma_2}, \tag{14.3.15}$$

has been discussed earlier as the *multiplier*, indicating the changes in the equilibrium level of national income as government expenditure changes. Another result is:

$$\frac{\partial Y}{\partial Y_{-1}} = \frac{\beta_2}{1-\gamma_1-\gamma_2}, \tag{14.3.16}$$

indicating how the equilibrium level of national income changes as national income of the previous year changes.

There are, however, also the comparative statics results obtained by changing the parameters of the model. Changing the intercept of the consumption function, β_1, or the intercept of the investment function, β_3, has the same effect on equilibrium national income, given as:

$$\frac{\partial Y}{\partial \beta_1} = \frac{\partial Y}{\partial \beta_3} = \frac{1}{1-\gamma_1-\gamma_2}, \tag{14.3.17}$$

which, of course, is the same as the multiplier. Thus the multiplier can be more generally interpreted as the effect on national income of any change in one of its autonomous components, whether consumption (β_1), investment (β_3), or government expenditure (G).

The effect of a change in the marginal propensity to consume, γ_1, is given as:

$$\frac{\partial Y}{\partial \gamma_1} = \frac{Y}{1-\gamma_1-\gamma_2} \tag{14.3.18}$$

and the same value is obtained for the change in equilibrium national income as the marginal propensity to invest out of current income γ_2 changes. Finally, the effect of a change in β_2, the coefficient of lagged income in the investment equation, is given as:

$$\frac{\partial Y}{\partial \beta_2} = \frac{Y_{-1}}{1 - \gamma_1 - \gamma_2}. \qquad (14.3.19)$$

These results summarize the comparative statics for equilibrium national income in the prototype macro model. Similar results can be obtained for other models, including the macroeconometric models of Chapter 12. The estimated coefficients of the model, together with relevant (current) values of the variables, could then be used to obtain numerical estimates of all comparative statics results. Such results summarize the interaction between elements of the model, specifically the effect of changes in coefficients of the system and in exogenous and lagged endogenous variables on equilibrium values of all endogenous variables. They provide insight into the quantitative importance of influences contained in the model. As will be seen in Chapters 15 and 16, they are also useful for purposes of forecasting and policy evaluation.

Another structural use of econometric models is an attempt to achieve some insight into simpler systems which have a more straightforward theoretical interpretation. Thus, some years ago, Duggal, Klein, and McCarthy suggested that the intricate Wharton model of the time (Mark III) could be interpreted as an empirical IS-LM construct (admittedly one that was complicated).[5] This point of view is developed further in an article by Green et al. in a more recent volume of simulations on leading U.S. macroeconometric models; here these authors take the Indiana model, the Michigan model (MQEM), and the Hickman–Coen model and perform certain simulations designed to elicit the slopes of the ordinary IS and LM theoretical curves.[6] In general, it is found that the IS curve has a relatively steep slope and the LM curve a relatively flat slope, at least for the three models examined, but there was another conclusion of interest as well: for the three more complicated, dynamic models examined in this paper, the slope of either the IS or LM curve will depend on the number of periods that the system has to adjust to a shift in one of the exogenous variables.

14.4 ELASTICITIES

It is often convenient to express the comparative statics results of structural analysis in the form of elasticities. Assume, as in (14.3.2), that:

$$y_j^0 = y_j^0(\alpha_1, \alpha_2, \ldots, \alpha_m), \qquad j = 1, 2, \ldots, g, \qquad *(14.4.1)$$

expresses the equilibrium value of the jth endogenous variable as a function of the m parameters of the model. Then the elasticity of y_j^0 with respect to α_l is given as:

$$\varepsilon_{jl} = \frac{\alpha_l}{y_j^0} \frac{\partial y_j^0}{\partial \alpha_l}, \qquad j = 1, 2, \ldots, g; \quad l = 1, 2, \ldots, m. \qquad *(14.4.2)$$

An advantage of this representation is that it provides a dimensionless measure of the sensitivity of y_j to changes in α_l. The value of elasticity thus does not depend on the units in which y_j and α_l are measured.

[5]See Duggal, Klein, and McCarthy (1974).

[6]See Green et al. (1991).

Since the elasticity can be written:

$$\varepsilon_{jl} = \frac{\partial \log y_j^0}{\partial \log \alpha_l} = \frac{\alpha_l}{y_j^0}\frac{\partial y_j^0}{\partial \alpha_l}, \tag*{*(14.4.3)}$$

it can be interpreted as the *proportionate* change in the variable y_j^0 given a unit *proportionate* change in the parameter α_l, all other parameters held fixed.

The comparative statics results of the last section can be expressed in elasticity form. Thus, for the single-equation model (14.3.8), the effect of a change in γ, as in (14.3.12), can be written in elasticity form as:

$$\varepsilon_{y\gamma} = \frac{\gamma}{y}\frac{\partial y}{\partial \gamma} = -1. \tag{14.4.4}$$

For example, a 10% increase in γ, holding all other parameters constant, would decrease the equilibrium y by 10%. The results in (14.3.13) can be written, in elasticity form, as:

$$\begin{aligned} \varepsilon_{y\beta_1} &= -\frac{\beta_1}{\gamma}\left(\frac{1}{y/y_{-1}}\right), & \varepsilon_{y\beta_2} &= -\frac{\beta_2}{\gamma}\left(\frac{1}{y/z}\right), \\ \varepsilon_{yy_{-1}} &= -\frac{\beta_1}{\gamma}\left(\frac{1}{y/y_{-1}}\right), & \varepsilon_{yz} &= -\frac{\beta_2}{\gamma}\left(\frac{1}{y/z}\right). \end{aligned} \tag{14.4.5}$$

Thus the elasticity with respect to β_1 is the same as the elasticity with respect to y_{-1}, both being proportional to the reciprocal of the proportionate change in y (given as y/y_{-1}). Similarly, $\varepsilon_{y\beta 2}$ and ε_{yz} are the same, both proportional to the reciprocal of the ratio y/z.

For the prototype macro model, as in (14.3.14):

$$\varepsilon_{YG} = \frac{1}{1-\gamma_1-\gamma_2}\left(\frac{G}{Y}\right), \qquad \varepsilon_{YY_{-1}} = \frac{\beta_2}{1-\gamma_1-\gamma_2}\left(\frac{Y}{Y_{-1}}\right)^{-1}, \tag{14.4.6}$$

so the elasticity with respect to government expenditure is proportional to the fraction of national income spent by the government, while the elasticity with respect to previous national income is inversely proportional to the growth in national income. For changes in the marginal propensity to consume:

$$\varepsilon_{Y\gamma_1} = \frac{\gamma_1}{1-\gamma_1-\gamma_2}, \tag{14.4.7}$$

so this elasticity is independent of Y—at any level of national income a 1% increase in the marginal propensity to consume raises equilibrium national income by a percentage increase equal to the product of the marginal propensity to consume and the multiplier.

A model that is linear in the logarithms of the variables entails constant elasticities, as indicated in (14.4.3). Earlier chapters have considered such models. An example is the constant elasticity demand function of Section 7.4, of the form:

$$x_1 = Ap_1^{b_1}p_2^{b_2}\cdots p_n^{b_n}I^c. \tag{14.4.8}$$

Taking logarithms yields:

$$\begin{aligned} \log x_1 = a + b_1 \log p_1 + b_2 \log p_2 + \cdots \\ + b_n \log p_n + c \log I \qquad (a = \log A), \end{aligned} \tag{14.4.9}$$

so

$$\varepsilon_{x_1p_j} = \frac{\partial \log x_1}{\partial \log p_j} = b_j, \quad j = 1, 2, \ldots, n; \qquad \varepsilon_{x_1I} = \frac{\partial \log x_1}{\partial \log I} = c. \tag{14.4.10}$$

Another example is the Cobb–Douglas production function of Section 8.3, of the form:

$$y = AL^{\alpha}K^{\beta}. \tag{14.4.11}$$

Again, taking logarithms gives

$$\log y = a + \alpha \log L + \beta \log K \qquad (a = \log A), \tag{14.4.12}$$

so

$$\varepsilon_{yL} = \frac{\partial \log y}{\partial \log L} = \alpha, \qquad \varepsilon_{yK} = \frac{\partial \log y}{\partial \log K} = \beta. \tag{14.4.13}$$

For such log-linear models, the exponents of the original multiplicative specification are the elasticities, assumed constant. Estimation of the parameters immediately yields the constant elasticities.

Some specific numerical estimates of such elasticities have been presented in earlier chapters, including Chapters 1, 7, and 8. Some additional estimates of income elasticities of demand for different categories of consumer goods in the United Kingdom 1920–1938 and the Netherlands 1921–1939 and 1948–1958 as estimated by Stone and Barten, respectively, are summarized in Table 14.1. According to this table, for the United Kingdom, margarine was close to if not an inferior good, while meals away from home was a good with a very high income elasticity: a 10% increase in income would have reduced margarine consumption by 1.6% and would have increased meals away from home by about 24%. The elasticities were reasonably similar in both countries and were, in fact, identical for fish—in both countries a 10% increase in income would have increased consumption of fish by 8.8%, although there was a much wider confidence interval for this estimate in the Netherlands than in the United Kingdom, for which the standard error is considerably smaller. The income elasticity for all food was 0.53 in the United Kingdom and 0.67 for the

TABLE 14.1 Income Elasticities of Demand

Category of Consumer Goods	United Kingdom, 1920–1938 Income Elasticity	United Kingdom, 1920–1938 Standard Error	Netherlands, 1921–1939, 1948–1958 Income Elasticity	Netherlands, 1921–1939, 1948–1958 Standard Error
Margarine	–0.16	0.11	—	—
Bread	–0.05	0.04	0.12	0.06
Milk/dairy products	0.50	0.18	0.57	0.13
All food	0.53	0.04	0.67	0.16
Fish	0.88	0.07	0.88	0.41
Vegetables	0.93	0.14	0.84	0.17
Textiles and clothing	—	—	1.84	0.12
Meals away from home	2.39	0.18	—	—

Sources Stone (1954) for the United Kingdom, Barten (1964) for the Netherlands.

Netherlands. This particular elasticity is of considerable interest, since it indicates the responsiveness of a major item of expenditure to income. *Engel's law*, which states that as income increases the proportion of income spent on food decreases, implies that this elasticity should be less than unity, as obtained. It has also been estimated for other countries and periods, e.g., as 0.677 for France, 0.782 for Italy, 0.574 for the Netherlands, 0.381 for Sweden, 0.728 for the United Kingdom, 0.689 for Canada, and 0.319 for the United States for the period 1948–1959.[7]

While the constant elasticity log-linear models are convenient in yielding direct estimates of elasticities, it is frequently important to calculate elasticities for other models, specifically linear models. In a linear model the estimated coefficients are slopes, and the related elasticities vary with the point at which they are evaluated. Usually they are evaluated and reported at mean values for the variables. For example, for the single-equation model (14.3.8), the elasticity of y with respect to z is defined as:

$$\varepsilon_{yz} = \frac{z}{y}\frac{\partial y}{\partial z}. \qquad (14.4.14)$$

Using (14.3.9), this elasticity can be obtained from estimates of β_2 and γ, by evaluating it at mean values of the variables:

$$\hat{\varepsilon}_{yz} = -\frac{\overline{z}}{\overline{y}}\frac{\hat{\beta}_2}{\hat{\gamma}}, \qquad (14.4.15)$$

where $\overline{z}$ and $\overline{y}$ are mean values of the variables and $\hat{\beta}_2$ and $\hat{\gamma}$ are estimates of the parameters of the equation.

14.5 MULTIPLIERS: IMPACT, INTERIM, AND LONG-RUN (THE LINEAR CASE)

The most common way of developing the structural analysis of an econometric model is in terms of multipliers.[8] The multipliers can be recognized as special cases of the comparative statics results corresponding to changes in each of the exogenous variables of the model. Thus the (single) multiplier of the prototype macro model is given as:

$$\frac{\partial Y}{\partial G} = \frac{1}{1 - \gamma_1 - \gamma_2}, \qquad (14.5.1)$$

indicating the effect of a change in government expenditure on equilibrium national income. In fact, this is usually referred to as an *impact multipler*, since it indicates the impact of a change in a current value of an exogenous variable on the current value of an endogenous variable. For the general reduced form (14.1.3) the $k'g'$ *impact multiplier* is given as

$$\frac{\partial y_{t,g'}}{\partial z_{t,k'}} = (\boldsymbol{\Pi}_2)_{k'g'}, \qquad g' = 1, 2, \ldots, g; \quad k' = 1, 2, \ldots, k, \qquad (14.5.2)$$

[7]See Houthakker (1965).

[8]Many commentators on macroeconometric models have suggested that a study of multipliers (e.g., for their plausibility) should be part of the process of model evaluation. This point of view would appear to be implicit in the discussions of Fair (1993) and Helliwell (1993).

that is, as the $k'g'$ element of the $\mathbf{\Pi}_2$ matrix. Since

$$\mathbf{\Pi}_2 = -\mathbf{B}_2\mathbf{\Gamma}^{-1}, \tag{14.5.3}$$

once either the reduced form or the structural form is estimated, all the impact multipliers can be determined. Of course, if g is even moderately large, the problem of numerically inverting $\mathbf{\Gamma}$ in (14.5.3) can be very laborious, suggesting the value of using the estimated reduced form directly. As long as $\mathbf{\Gamma}^{-1}$ is easy to compute, however, there are advantages in terms of efficiency in estimating the structural form, due to use of prior information.

The interim and long-term multipliers of a model are obtained from the final form of the econometric model. For the prototype macro model of Section 2.6, for which the final form for Y is (omitting stochastic disturbance terms):

$$Y_t = Y_0\Pi_1^t + \sum_{j=0}^{t-1} G_{t-j}\Pi_1^j\Pi_2 + \sum_{j=0}^{t-1}\Pi_1^j\Pi_3, \tag{14.5.4}$$

as in (2.6.16), the two-period cumulative multiplier is:

$$\left.\frac{\partial Y_t}{\partial G_t}\right|_{\Delta G_{t-1}=\Delta G_t} = \Pi_2(1+\Pi_1), \tag{14.5.5}$$

as in (2.6.19), and the three-period cumulative multiplier is:

$$\left.\frac{\partial Y_t}{\partial G_t}\right|_{\Delta G_{t-2}=\Delta G_{t-1}=\Delta G} = \Pi_2(1+\Pi_1+\Pi_1^2), \tag{14.5.6}$$

as in (2.6.20). These are both *cumulative interim multipliers*, obtained by treating equal changes in the exogenous variables over two or more periods. More generally, the τ-period cumulative multiplier is:

$$\left.\frac{\partial Y_t}{\partial G_t}\right|_{\tau} = \Pi_2(1+\Pi_1+\Pi_1^2+\cdots+\Pi_1^{\tau-1}), \tag{14.5.7}$$

as in (2.6.21). Taking the limit, as $\tau \to \infty$, yields the long-term multiplier:

$$\left.\frac{\partial Y_t}{\partial G_t}\right|_{L} = \Pi_2(1+\Pi_1+\Pi_1^2+\cdots) = \frac{\Pi_2}{1-\Pi_1}, \tag{14.5.8}$$

as in (2.6.22), assuming that $0 \le \Pi_1 < 1$.

More generally, for the final form of the general linear econometric model, as given in (14.1.5), the $k'g'$ *τ-period cumulative multiplier* is given as:

$$\left.\frac{\partial y_{t,g'}}{\partial z_{t,k'}}\right|_{\tau} = \sum_{j=0}^{\tau-1}\left(\mathbf{\Pi}_2\mathbf{\Pi}_1^j\right)_{k'g'} = \left[\mathbf{\Pi}_2\left(\mathbf{I}+\mathbf{\Pi}_1+\cdots+\mathbf{\Pi}_1^{\tau-1}\right)\right]_{k'g'}. \qquad *(14.5.9)$$

Setting $\tau = 1$ yields the *impact multipliers* as in (14.5.2). Finite values of τ larger than 1 yield the *cumulative interim multipliers*, indicating the change in each endogenous variable as each exogenous variable experiences a sustained increase over a period of τ periods.[9] Taking the limit as $\tau \to \infty$ yields the *long-term multipliers*,

[9]These multipliers can be estimated directly, from estimates of $\mathbf{\Pi}_1$ and $\mathbf{\Pi}_2$, or indirectly, via simulating the response of the endogenous variables to changes in the exogenous variables. The simulation approach is particularly useful for nonlinear models, as discussed in Section 14.6.

$$\left.\frac{\partial y_{t,g'}}{\partial z_{t,k'}}\right| = \left[\mathbf{\Pi}_2(\mathbf{I} - \mathbf{\Pi}_1)^{-1}\right]^{k'g'}, \qquad *(14.5.10)$$

assuming that the power series in (14.5.9) converges.[10] This long-term multiplier (if it exists) measures the effect on the endogenous variable g' when the exogenous variable k' experiences a sustained change in every period.

14.6 MULTIPLIERS: IMPACT, INTERIM, AND LONG-RUN (THE NONLINEAR CASE)

Most current working econometric models contain some essential nonlinearities, so it may be difficult to obtain explicit representations of the reduced-form equations and thus of the final-form equations. Nevertheless, the basic concepts of impact, interim, and long-term multipliers can be carried over to the nonlinear econometric model.[11]

The impact multipliers were obtained, in principle, in Section 14.3, provided that one of the parameters, say α_l, is interpreted as an exogenous variable. In this case the typical impact multiplier becomes $\partial y_j^0 / \partial \alpha_l$ and is obtained, as in equation (14.3.7), from a solution of equation (14.3.4). Another approach, however, is that of simulation.

In the simulation approach to obtaining cumulative interim multipliers for a nonlinear econometric model, the first step is to reformulate the equations constituting the model. As in the case of the linear model, it is assumed that there are only one-period lags in the model, although this assumption could be generalized. The g equations of the general (linear or nonlinear) econometric model may be written:

$$\begin{aligned} &f^i(y_{t1}, y_{t2}, \ldots, y_{tg}; y_{t-1,1}, y_{t-1,2}, \ldots, y_{t-1,g}; \\ &\quad z_{t1}, z_{t2}, \ldots, z_{tk}; \varepsilon_{ti}) = 0, \qquad i = 1, 2, \ldots, g, \quad t = 1, 2, \ldots, T. \end{aligned} \qquad *(14.6.1)$$

Given initial values of all g endogenous variables and the time paths of all k of the exogenous variables and of all g of the stochastic disturbance terms ε_{ti} (usually assumed to be zero), it is possible, in principle, to solve for the time paths of all the endogenous variables. If an *initial solution* for the time path of a typical endogenous variable $\mathbf{y}_{g'}$ is obtained as:

$$y_{1g'}, y_{2g'}, \ldots, y_{\tau g'}, \ldots, y_{Tg'}, \qquad g' = 1, 2, \ldots, g, \qquad (14.6.2)$$

let one of the exogenous variables, say $\mathbf{z}_{k'}$, be changed in value from $z_{tk'}$ to $z_{tk'} + \Delta z_{k'}$ for all t periods from 1 to T. (Note that the increment $\Delta z_{k'}$ is independent of the time period t.) The principles of Section 14.3 can then be used to generate a new set of solution values for each

[10] The power series in (14.5.9), called a *Neumann expansion*, converges if and only if $lim_{\tau \to \infty} \mathbf{\Pi}_1^{\tau} = 0$ or, equivalently, if and only if all characteristic roots of $\mathbf{\Pi}_1$ have modulus less than unity. Note that (14.5.10) could have been obtained directly from (14.1.3) by noting that in the long run $\mathbf{y}_t = \mathbf{y}_{t-1}$, so

$$\mathbf{y}_t = \mathbf{y}_t\mathbf{\Pi}_1 + \mathbf{z}_t\mathbf{\Pi}_2 + \mathbf{u}_t.$$

Solving for $\mathbf{y}_t$ yields:

$$\mathbf{y}_t = \mathbf{z}_t\mathbf{\Pi}_2(\mathbf{I} - \mathbf{\Pi}_1)^{-1} + \mathbf{u}_t(\mathbf{I} - \mathbf{\Pi}_1)^{-1},$$

which implies (14.5.10), provided that $\mathbf{I} - \mathbf{\Pi}_1$ is nonsingular.

[11] See Klein (1983), especially pp. 57–69 and 134–144.

endogenous variable for all periods. Denote the new solution path for $\mathbf{y}_{g'}$ as $\mathbf{y}^*_{g'}$, which may be termed the *shocked solution* and written explicitly as:

$$y^*_{1g'}, y^*_{2g'}, \ldots, y^*_{\tau g'}, \ldots, y^*_{Tg'}, \qquad g' = 1, 2, \ldots, g. \tag{14.6.3}$$

Then the cumulative interim multiplier, that is, the multiplier after τ periods of sustained increase in the time path of $\mathbf{z}_{k'}$, is given by:

$$\left.\frac{\partial y_{t,g'}}{\partial z_{t,k'}}\right|_{\tau} = \frac{y^*_{\tau g'} - y_{\tau g'}}{\Delta z_{k'}}, \ \tau = 1, 2, \ldots, T \quad g' = 1, 2, \ldots, g. \qquad *(14.6.4)$$

Thus the interim multipliers are obtained by taking the differences in the values of the endogenous variables between the shocked and the initial solution values, after normalizing these differences by the variation in the relevant exogenous variable. These are cumulative interim multipliers, which automatically include the buildup of inertial effects from preceding rounds. As one particular case, if the number of periods of the displacement (τ) is only one, (14.6.4) becomes the impact multiplier of system (14.6.1).[12]

The long-term multipliers again present the greatest difficulty in the nonlinear case, as they may or may not exist. If they exist, they may be obtained in one of two approaches. First, it is possible to examine the asymptotic behavior of the cumulative interim multiplier, as given in (14.6.4), as τ (and hence T), the length of time for the change in the relevant exogenous variable, becomes indefinitely longer. If this sequence has a limit, such a limit may be termed the *long-term multiplier*. Equivalently, let $y_{tg'} = y_{t-1,g'} = \bar{y}_{g'}$, for all endogenous variables 1, 2, . . . , g, be a set of constant (through time) values for the endogenous variables that constitute the solution of equations (14.6.1); it is assumed temporarily that such a solution exists. (Such a solution would be based on constant values of the exogenous variables z_{tk} that are also independent of time, say $\bar{z}_{k'}$; as well, the disturbance terms ε_{ti} would be based on given values, $\bar{\varepsilon}_i$, typically equal to zero.) In these circumstances, (14.6.1) reduces to:

$$f^i(\bar{y}_1, \bar{y}_2, \ldots, \bar{y}_g; \bar{y}_1, \bar{y}_2, \ldots, \bar{y}_g; \bar{z}_1, \bar{z}_2, \ldots, \bar{z}_k; \bar{\varepsilon}_i) = 0, \qquad i = 1, 2, \ldots, g. \tag{14.6.5}$$

If this long-term equilibrium system has a solution, explicit or implicit, for the endogenous variables, given as:

$$\bar{y}^*_i = \bar{y}^*_i(\bar{z}_1, \bar{z}_2, \ldots, \bar{z}_k; \bar{\varepsilon}_i), \qquad i = 1, 2, \ldots, g, \tag{14.6.6}$$

then the long-term multipliers are simply the appropriate partial derivatives of these functions (still assuming that these functions do indeed exist). Such partial derivatives may then be obtained by the same techniques as those presented in Section 14.3.

To illustrate these points, a schematic diagram, Figure 14.1, is presented showing the central tendency of interim government expenditure multipliers from the studies reviewed in Sections 14.9 through 14.11. (The key endogenous variable impacted is some variant of real national product.) Note that the impact multipliers generally start moderately low (around 1.0 or 1.25) and then build, after 10 to 16 quarters, to a maximum (shown as 2.5 in Figure 14.1). After the passage of this amount of time, a constant stimulus ap-

[12]In practice, this approach for calculating the cumulative interim multipliers can also be used in the linear case, as noted in footnote 9. The simulation approach is particularly useful when the scale of the linear model is large, so that matrix inversion entails considerable computation.

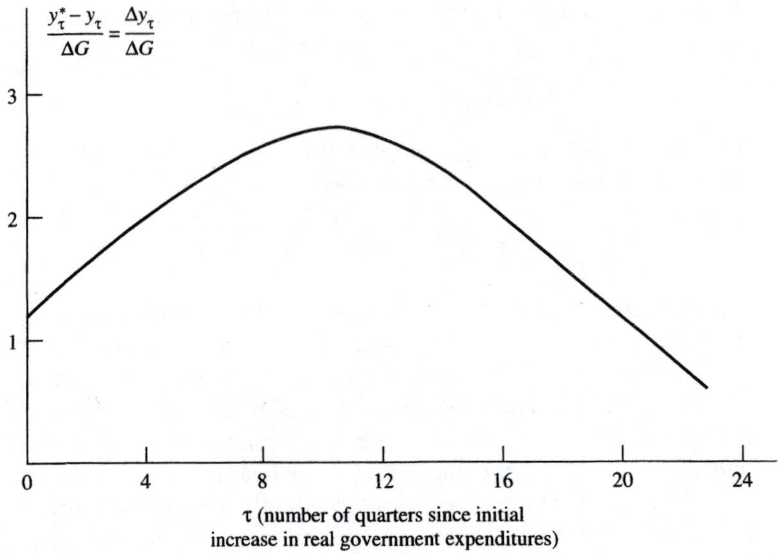

Figure 14.1 Interim Government Expenditure Multipliers (with National Income as the Endogenous Variable under Study), Hypothetical U.S. Macroeconometric Model

pears to lose efficacy, which some writers[13] term "crowding out." After a number of years, the stimulative impact may disappear completely. This "inverted U" pattern for the dynamic multipliers is fairly general and appears to characterize most multiplier studies of large, modern macroeconometric models. In particular, the *lack* of existence of the conceptual long-term multipliers (as described above), namely their nonconvergence, would appear to be a fairly general result.

14.7 EXAMPLE OF MULTIPLIER ANALYSIS: THE SUITS STUDY

Five specific examples of multiplier analysis are discussed in this and in the next four sections in order to indicate the nature of this approach to structural analysis. The first two are the Suits and Goldberger analyses, which are related to a particular macroeconometric model of the U.S. economy, as presented in Sections 12.7 and 12.3, respectively. The next two studies concern comparative multiplier analyses for the U.S. and Canadian economies. Finally, the government expenditures multiplier for the early 1980s version of the DRI model of the U.S. economy (summarized in Section 12.6) rounds out the presentation.

[13]For example, Eckstein (1983).

The Suits analysis of the U.S. economy was based on a 33-equation model of the real economy using first differences of most variables.[14] Some multipliers for government actions are indicated in Table 14.2. The first line indicates that an additional $1 billion in government purchases from firms in 1960 would have increased GNP by $1.304 billion and would have increased total employment by 89,000. The second line indicates the effects of an additional $1 billion in federal wages used to hire 0.2 million new workers. Clearly, such an increase in federal spending would have had a greater effect on GNP than federal purchases from firms and a much greater effect on total employment, which increased by 0.263 million, the added 0.063 million new workers being employed in the private sector. (It might be noted, however, that the more effective of these two policies for causing increases in employment in the private sector is federal purchase from firms.) The last line indicates the effects of a federal personal income tax shift—increasing the personal income tax by $1 billion would have lowered GNP by $1.119 billion and employment by 76,000 workers. This last multiplier can perhaps best be understood in terms of its reciprocal. To increase employment by one million workers would have required a reduction in the federal personal income tax of (1/0.076) or $13.2 billion.

Any particular combination of policies could be analyzed using the multipliers of Table 14.2 and other related multipliers. For example, an increase in federal purchases from firms of $2 billion, coupled with additional federal wages of $0.5 billion and an upward shift in the personal tax schedule of $1.3 billion, would have produced a total change in gross national product (Y) of

$$\Delta Y = (2 \times 1.304) + (0.5 \times 1.692) + [1.3 \times (-1.119)] \cong 2, \qquad (14.7.1)$$

that is, of about $2 billion. Such a change would have produced a total change in employment (N) of

$$\Delta N = (2 \times 0.089) + (0.5 \times 0.263) + [1.3 \times (-0.076)] = 0.211, \qquad (14.7.2)$$

that is, of approximately 211,000 workers.

TABLE 14.2 Multipliers for the Suits Model

	Endogenous Variable Affected	
Exogenous Change	National Income (GNP)	Employment
Federal purchases from firms	1.304	0.089
Federal wages (each $1 billion in federal wages is used to hire 0.2 million new workers)	1.692	0.263
Federal personal income tax shift	−1.119	−0.076

Source Suits (1962).

Note Dollar figures in 1954 dollars; employment figures in millions.

[14]Suits (1962). The Suits model was estimated in 1954 dollars using data from 1947–1960.

14.8 SECOND EXAMPLE OF MULTIPLIER ANALYSIS: THE GOLDBERGER STUDY

A second example of multiplier analysis is the Goldberger study of impact and long-run multipliers for the Klein–Goldberger model.[15] Goldberger calculated the reduced form of the model and interpreted the coefficients as impact multipliers, giving the change in each of the endogenous variables as any of the predetermined variables of the model changed, as summarized above in equation (14.5.2). Some of his impact multipliers are summarized in Table 14.3. The first item in the table is the change in GNP given a change in government expenditure on goods and services. The value of this multiplier—1.39—is similar to that found by Suits in Table 14.2. The multiplier giving the effect of government wages on GNP—1.78—is also similar to that of Suits. It was obtained by adding the multiplier for the government wage bill, 0.39, to the multiplier for government expenditures, 1.39, since the wage-bill multiplier is based on holding government expenditures constant.

Two tax multipliers are shown in Table 14.3: those for wage taxes and for corporate taxes. The wage-tax multiplier is lower in absolute value for the Klein-Goldberger model than for the Suits model, but it is much larger than the corporate-tax multiplier. The two tax multipliers may be combined with the expenditure multipliers to determine the alternative possible effects of government policy within a fixed budget surplus or deficit. Thus, according to this model, increasing both government expenditure and wage taxes by $1 billion would have increased GNP by $0.63 billion. Increasing government wage expenditure and corporate taxes by $1 billion, however, would have increased GNP by $1.24 billion.

Table 14.3 also shows multiplier effects on employment. Government expenditures in this model have a multiplier effect of 0.61 on employment, so an additional $1 billion in government expenditure would have created 610,000 new jobs. The multiplier is larger here than in the Suits model, in part because the period covered extends back further (to 1929) and hence involves smaller average wage payments.

Government wages have a smaller multiplier effect on employment than government expenditures, and the value is equal to the multiplier for wage taxes. Thus lowering wage taxes by $1 billion would have had the same effect on employment as increasing government wages by $1 billion. The employment multiplier for corporate taxes is extremely small (i.e., the level of employment is not sensitive to the level of corporate taxes).

TABLE 14.3 Impact Multipliers for the Klein–Goldberger Model

	Endogenous Variable Affected	
Exogenous Change	National Income (GNP)	Employment
Government expenditures	1.39	0.61
Government wages	1.78	0.34
Wage taxes	–0.76	–0.34
Corporate taxes	–0.15	–0.07

Source Goldberger (1959).
Note Figures have been rounded. The row for government wages was obtained by adding the government wage bill and government expenditure multipliers.

[15]See Goldberger (1959). For a discussion of the Klein–Goldberger model, see Section 12.3 and Klein and Goldberger (1955).

Goldberger also calculated cumulative interim multipliers for the Klein–Goldberger model, and some of his estimates are presented in Table 14.4. A sustained unit increase in government expenditure has the initial multiplier of 1.39, as in Table 14.3, but increases rapidly over the next several years to reach almost 5.0. It then declines somewhat, having overshot the long-term value. Similar multiplier buildups over time in the first several years are indicated for employment.

Somewhat comparable patterns emerge for the cumulative interim multipliers in response to a sustained unit increase in wage taxes, the initial values differing from those of Table 14.3 because of the assumption here that tax rates are given. It might be noted that this model is highly aggregated, so that the effects on particular labor sectors or industries cannot be determined.

14.9 THIRD EXAMPLE OF MULTIPLIER ANALYSIS: STUDY OF COMPARATIVE MULTIPLIERS OF U.S. MACROECONOMETRIC MODELS FROM A MODELS COMPARISONS PROJECT

As part of a more comprehensive effort to evaluate major U.S. macroeconometric models at the time that he was writing, Carl F. Christ tabulated interim (cumulative) multipliers of eight U.S. macroeconometric models of the early 1970s.[16] The analysis studies the models' estimation of the dynamic effects of a sustained $1 billion dollar increase in real government expenditures, without any accommodation in monetary policy. The endogenous variable of interest was, of course, gross national product in constant dollars.

TABLE 14.4 Interim Multipliers for the Klein-Goldberger Model

	Response to a Sustained Unit Increase in Government Expenditure in Year 0		Response to a Sustained Unit Increase in Wage Taxes in Year 0	
Year	National Income	Employment	National Income	Employment
0	1.39	0.61	–0.68	–0.30
1	2.81	1.21	–1.20	–0.53
2	3.88	1.63	–1.44	–0.62
3	4.57	1.84	–1.53	–0.65
4	4.89	1.90	–1.54	–0.64
5	4.92	1.84	–1.53	–0.62
6	4.75	1.69	–1.51	–0.61

Source Goldberger (1959).
Note Figures have been rounded.

[16]See Christ (1975), especially his Figure 4. These models were three versions of the Wharton model, the MPS model, the St. Louis model, the BEA model, the Brookings model, the DRI model, the Michigan quarterly econometric model, and the Hickman–Coen model. (All of these models have been described in Chapter 12.) Christ did not make most of these calculations himself; rather, he relied on calculations done for the NBER/NSF Models Comparison Seminar, as reported in a preliminary version of Fromm and Klein (1976). Christ terms these interim multipliers *dynamic multipliers*.

There is a general agreement among the interim multipliers studied by Christ, with one or two exceptions. In the typical model, the impact multiplier (immediate effect) begins at a low value (not far from 1.0) and then the interim multiplier gradually builds, reaching a peak of 2.25 to 2.75, generally after 8 to 16 quarters. (For the version of the DRI model analyzed by Christ, the peak value, roughly 2.25, occurred only after 28 quarters.) Then the dynamic multipliers fall away, under pressures from increased monetary stringency (sometimes termed *crowding out*), price level increases, and related pressures. Consequently, after 40 quarters, the interim multipliers are all very small or negative, with the three exceptions of the DRI model, the Brookings model, and the Hickman–Coen model. (For the Brookings model and the DRI model, the interim multiplier after 40 quarters remains roughly equal to unity; the special case of the Hickman–Coen model is discussed further in the next paragraph.) Thus it seems fair to conclude that the general shape of the interim expenditures multipliers is that of an inverted "U," as shown in Figure 14.1.

The two exceptions are also of interest. The interim multiplier of the St. Louis model begins at zero, builds rapidly to a peak of 1.0 after several quarters, and then declines rapidly to zero (in fact, to a small negative constant) after another several quarters. However, given that this model was constructed to reflect monetarist theorizing, which is a quite different approach to macroeconomic theory than that employed by most model builders, one need not be surprised that the derived government expenditures multipliers should be weak and of temporary importance. As for the Hickman–Coen model, Christ's graph shows that the interim multipliers build continuously after the first eight quarters, so that after 10 years (40 quarters) the interim multiplier is at its maximum on the graph with a value of roughly 2.9.[17]

Also, with the exception of the St. Louis model, *none* of the remaining seven models appears to possess a long-run or equilibrium expenditures multiplier. In other words, in the case of the remaining seven macroeconometric models, none of the time paths of the model's interim multipliers appeared to converge to a steady-state value. Accordingly, with more "realistic" macroeconometric models, the existence of long-run multipliers may remain only a theoretical possibility.

Fifteen years later, the models comparison project again did a study with comparative multiplier simulations.[18] This time, the comparative multipliers of 10 or 11 leading models of the U.S. economy were surveyed.[19] In general, the pattern of inverted U-shaped interim multipliers on national product continued to hold true, for controlled changes in govern-

[17]In fact, the interim multiplier cycles in the first two years, so that the interim multiplier after one year is larger than both the impact multiplier and the multiplier after two years. More important, this version of the Hickman–Coen model does show an interim multiplier which eventually peaks and then turns down, but as this occurs after 10 years or 40 quarters, this is not apparent in Christ's graphical analysis. Later versions of the Hickman–Coen model did indeed show the familiar inverted-U pattern for the interim expenditures multipliers, which in these cases did then peak before 40 quarters had elapsed.

[18]See Klein (1991a,b) and Adams and Klein (1991).

[19]The 10 original models were the Wharton model, the DRI model, the BEA model, the Fair model, the St. Louis model, the current Federal Reserve Board model (a direct descendant of the MPS model), the Michigan model (MQEM), the Washington University Macro Model (of Lawrence Meyer & Associates), the U.S. model of John Taylor's system of multicountry models, and the Indiana model. Allen Sinai's BCEA model joined the simulation exercises in the middle of these experiments. All of these models have been described (or at least presented) in Chapter 12. It should also be mentioned that a number of dynamic shocks (changes in the exogenous variables) were studied, along with the effects on several key endogenous variables of model, such as the price level, unemployment rate, current account deficit of the balance of payments, and so on. However, in this summary, only the effects on national product of shocks to government expenditures are discussed.

ment expenditure. However, there was considerable divergence in the results for individual models, which led Adams and Klein to present results for the "average" multiplier path in their text and to relegate results for individual models to their appendix. This same divergence also puzzled two of the commentators of the model volume.[20] Finally, again there was no evidence of convergence of the interim government expenditure multipliers to constant long-term values, again with the possible exception of the St. Louis model.

14.10 FOURTH EXAMPLE OF MULTIPLIER ANALYSIS: COMPARATIVE INTERIM MULTIPLIERS WITH CANADIAN MACROECONOMETRIC MODELS

The next example of multiplier analysis is also a comparative study. In the late 1970s, a group of Canadian econometricians studied the comparative properties of their respective macroeconometric models.[21] Although many properties other than comparative real expenditure multipliers were studied, it is this phenomenon that is the focus here. There was a hypothetical experiment in which a weighted mixture of government expenditures was increased by $400 million in 1961, with the increase sustained in real terms over the following 10 years or 40 quarters and with no accommodation in monetary policy (the supply of money was kept unchanged from its historical path). The four models under study were QFM (Quarterly Forecasting Model, University of Toronto), CANDIDE (Government of Canada, particularly the Economic Council of Canada, an annual model), TRACE (University of Toronto, an annual model), and RDX2 (Bank of Canada, a quarterly model). The CANDIDE model was described in Section 12.8. In broad terms, the four Canadian macroeconometric models display the familiar inverted-U pattern of Figure 14.1, with small impact multipliers and interim multipliers rising to a peak and then falling off.[22] In particular, here also there is no evidence of convergence to constant values that would constitute long-run expenditure multipliers.

If the results of these studies are examined in slightly more detail, the impact multipliers are comparable to those of the American macroeconometric models reviewed in the preceding section (between 0.95 and 1.9), which is mildly surprising in view of the much greater openness of the Canadian economy. The dynamic pattern of the interim multipliers was such that the extra stimulation of real national product from increased government spending appeared after 10 years to have largely died away, so that the typical value of the 10-year interim multiplier was roughly equal to 0.5. In the case of the QFM model, the 10-year real expenditure multiplier appeared to have been negative, so

[20]Shiller (1991), in particular, expresses surprise that the models should yield so different results with regard to the expenditures multipliers, given that seven of the 10 have been constructed in the mainstream tradition of neo-Keynesian modeling with some neoclassical features blended in. He cautiously asserts that some of these models may be better than others, but he declines to draw direct conclusions. Visco (1991) attempts to reconcile differences by an intensive study of the structure of particular sectors of the model, an exercise that the present authors find less than convincing.

[21]The details of this experiment may be found in de Bever et al. (1979) and Helliwell, Maxwell, and Waslander (1979).

[22]See in particular Figure 1 of Helliwell, Maxwell, and Waslander (1979). In particular, it should be noted immediately that the TRACE model is the exception that "proves" (tests) this generalization.

that effects of extra real spending apparently disappeared completely if this model is to be believed. In three of four cases, the interim multipliers rose to a maximum between 1.5 and 2.9, after two to four years; the one exception here was the TRACE model, where the interim multiplier declined more or less regularly from the high impact value of 1.9.[23] This lower value (in general) of the interim multiplier at the peak of its inverted U, in comparison to the American studies, is consistent with the greater openness of the Canadian economy. Finally, the QFM model builds to a much higher maximum value (2.9) of the interim multiplier time path than either CANDIDE or RDX2, and furthermore, this peak comes somewhat later (four years instead of two or three) than in the case of the other two; in fact, this study of the structure of interim multipliers of the four Canadian macroeconometric models in question proved useful in calling into question the specifications of the QFM model.[24]

14.11 FINAL EXAMPLE OF MULTIPLIER ANALYSIS: THE DRI MODEL OF THE EARLY 1980s

The final example examined in this chapter comes from the DRI model of the early 1980s.[25] Here, Eckstein employs the concept of interim multipliers to examine some interactions of fiscal policy with monetary policy.

For the interim multipliers presented above, it was assumed that monetary policy was not accommodating, or in other words the stock of money was not adjusted from what it otherwise would have been. Eckstein relaxed this assumption by calculating four sets of interim multipliers for the DRI model of the U.S. economy, under four alternative assumptions. Thus he considered (1) an unchanged nominal money supply (the assumption on which the results above have been based), (2) an unchanged level of net unborrowed reserves (total legally acceptable reserves less borrowings from the Federal Reserve), (3) a constant interest rate for federal funds, in real terms (i.e., after correction for anticipated inflation), and (4) a constant rate of interest for federal funds, in nominal (ordinary) terms. In all four cases, federal government purchases of nondefense goods and services were increased by $10 billion in real terms, and the stimulus was maintained for five years (20 quarters) into the hypothetical future beginning around 1981. The effect on real national product was then observed.

[23]It may be recalled that the TRACE model is an annual model, so that dynamic patterns may not be fully captured when important adjustments take place more rapidly than annually.

[24]The QFM model was subsequently rebuilt under the name of the FOCUS (for *FO*re*C*asting and *U*ser *S*imulation) model. It may be observed that while a model that differs from the mainstream is not necessarily unsuitable or even "incorrect," such a sharp divergence from received opinion or the majority view may often be a sign that some rethinking might be fruitful.

Mention might be made of a similar British models comparison project, which has been carried out for some years now at the University of Warwick under the leadership of K. F. Wallis, in collaboration with a number of associates (see Wallis et al., 1987).

[25]See Eckstein (1983), especially Figure 2.1 on p. 37 and the surrounding discussion. Mention may be made of the later study of Brinner and Hirsch (1991), in the context of the U.S. models comparative simulations project. Broadly speaking, Brinner's simulations with a later version of the DRI model (which are compared in this article to similar simulations with the BEA model) are quite consistent with those presented in this section. [These simulations also indicate that while the fiscal responses of the two models are quite similar (with regard to real national product), the DRI model shows considerably more sensitivity to monetary shocks, such as those associated with monetary policy.]

The results are quite interesting and show the critical importance of monetary policy accommodation (or lack thereof) on the traditional impact and interim multipliers, for national product from expenditure increases. Under the assumption of an unchanged money supply [assumption (1) of the preceding paragraph], the interim multipliers do *not* display the familiar inverted-U pattern. Instead, the impact multiplier begins with a value of roughly 0.75 and then the interim multiplier declines monotonically (with the trivial exception of some meaningless perturbations), so that the interim multiplier is slightly negative (roughly –0.1) after 20 quarters.

By contrast, the time pattern of the impact and interim multipliers is much different in the three remaining cases, which represent some degree of monetary accommodation to fiscal stimulation. In all three cases, the impact multiplier begins at a modest value [between 1.05 for constant nonborrowed reserves (assumption 2) to 1.2 for the remaining two] and then the interim multipliers rise to peak after five or six quarters, thus displaying the familiar inverted-U pattern.[26] The interim multipliers then decline quite rapidly in all three cases, so that after 20 quarters very little of the original stimulation remains; the interim multipliers associated with 20 quarters of stimulation vary from 0.4 to 0.6.[27] Thus it seems clear that the reactions (if any) of the monetary authorities can affect the size and time pattern of interim expenditure multipliers.[28]

Finally, note the absence of the convergence of *any* of the time paths of the interim expenditure multipliers, regardless of which of the four monetary assumptions are considered, to a constant or steady-state value. Here again, there would appear to be *no* evidence of the existence of long-run multipliers.

These five studies of multipliers are illustrative of structural analysis, indicating the responsiveness of endogenous variables of the model to exogenous variables. Of central importance for purposes of both forecasting and policy analysis in the macroeconomic mod-

[26]The peak is highest for the interim multipliers associated with a constant nominal rate of federal funds (assumption 4) at a value slightly in excess of 2.0. By contrast, the peak of the pattern of interim multipliers is lowest (among the three) for assumption 2, a constant level of unborrowed reserves; the associated maximum is a value of the interim multiplier roughly equal to 1.6. As expected, the intermediate assumption, a constant federal funds rate in real terms (assumption 3), yields an intermediate result, namely a maximal value for the interim multipliers approximately equal to 1.8.

[27]Note, however, that this is considerably more important than in the case of the interim multipliers under the assumption of a strictly unchanged nominal supply of money, where it has been seen that the relevant interim multiplier fell to a slightly negative value of –0.1, after 20 quarters of stimulation.

[28]As well, the traditional government expenditures multiplier (with national product as the endogenous variable of interest) can vary in an open economy depending on the assumptions made about the foreign exchange markets. (This was developed in some of the individual studies underlying the symposium on Canadian macroeconometric models reviewed in Section 14.10.) Howrey and Hymans (1995) have examined this issue in the context of an early 1990s version of the Michigan Quarterly Econometric Model in which the international linkages are highly developed, at least in comparison to earlier versions. They then conduct fiscal policy experiments under three different assumptions: (1) key international variables (rate of foreign exchange, import prices in a representative foreign currency, and U.S. exports in real terms) unchanged, (2) exchange rate adjusts so that the ratio of U.S. to foreign interest rates (nominal) remains unchanged, and (3), level of foreign interest rates (nominal) remains unchanged. Three time paths of the traditional government expenditures multipliers (impact and interim) are calculated for 56 quarters. After five or six quarters, the interim multipliers are quite sensitive to the assumptions made about international linkages, and in general the greater the international linkages, the smaller the interim multipliers. (Indeed, after 44 quarters or so, the interim multipliers become negative on the final two assumptions.) Finally, there is apparently no convergence to no long-run multipliers in this case, also.

els is the responsiveness of such key endogenous variables as national income and employment to important government policy variables, such as government expenditure and taxes. The next two chapters consider (among other subjects) the use of these multipliers for purposes of forecasting and policy evaluation.

PROBLEMS

14-A Develop the comparative statics results for the prototype micro model.

14-B Construct confidence intervals for the income elasticities presented in Table 14.1, and determine for which categories of consumer goods the elasticities in the United Kingdom and the Netherlands show no statistically significant difference.

14-C Consider the Klein interwar model as presented in equations (12.2.1)–(12.2.6).

1. Find numerical values of all relevant multipliers, short-run and long-run.
2. Obtain numerical comparative statics results (see Theil, 1971, especially pp. 463–468).

14-D Prove that Engel's law implies that the income elasticity of demand for food must be less than unity.

14-E Consider the following macroeconometric model:

$$C = a + b(Y - T),$$
$$I = c + dY_{-1},$$
$$T = e + fY,$$
$$Y = C + I + G,$$

which is based on that presented by Suits (1962). Here C, I, T, and Y are the four endogenous variables: consumption, investment, tax revenue, and national income, respectively; and Y_{-1} and G are predetermined: last-period income and government expenditure, respectively.

1. Find equilibrium values of the endogenous variables if the last-period income is $\bar{Y}_{-1}$ and current government expenditure is $\bar{G}$.
2. Using a table, trace out the implications over three periods of time for changes in each of the endogenous variables, given a unit increase in government expenditures in the base period.
3. Similarly trace out the implications over time of a unit increase in both government expenditure and taxes in the base period (assume the marginal tax yield of f is constant, but that tax revenue increases by 1 by a shift in e, the intercept of the tax-yield equation).

14-F Using the multipliers of Table 14.2, consider the following policies for the United States:

1. An increase in federal purchases from firms of $10 billion combined with a federal personal income tax shift of $10 billion.
2. An increase in federal wages of $10 billion combined with a federal personal income tax shift of $10 billion.

Contrast the effect of these policies on GNP and total employment. Note that they both have the same (zero) impact on the federal deficit. What can be concluded about the use of the federal deficit as a measure of the impact of the federal government on the economy?

14-G Assume the U.S. federal government wants to increase employment by two million workers in order to reach "full employment." Using Table 14.2, show geometrically the alternative combinations of changes in federal purchases from firms and federal personal income tax shift that will reach full employment. Similarly show the combinations of changes in federal wages and income tax shift that will reach full employment. Determine the implications of several alternative combinations on each diagram for the federal deficit. Can full employment be attained with no additional federal deficit? If so, how?

14-H With nonlinear models, the values of the impact multipliers need no longer be constant; instead, the numerical values of these multipliers may well vary depending on the initial starting position. Moreover, the total impact on the endogenous variables may not be independent of the size of the stimulus from the exogenous variable under consideration.

1. Using the reasoning of Section 14.6, construct a heuristic (intuitive) argument why this should be so.
2. Modify the prototype macro model of Chapter 2 so that the marginal propensity to consume is no longer constant but declines with increasing income. In particular, one could modify (2.6.1) so that consumption now depends *negatively* on the square of national income and the equation becomes:

$$C_t = \gamma_1 Y_t + \delta_1 Y_t^2 + \beta_1 + \varepsilon_t^c,$$

where the parameter δ_1 is both negative and small. Solve for the reduced form as before (one reasonably easy method is to use the quadratic formula), calculate the impact multiplier for government expenditures on national income, and so illustrate the two general propositions stated above with the prototype macro model, as modified.

14-I Write the investment function of Problem 14-E as:

$$I = c + dY_{-1} - hG^2,$$

where the parameter h is positive but small. [One rationalization of this effect is the possible discouraging effect of high government expenditures on business decision makers' expectations, leading them to invest less when government spending is exceptionally high. Another interpretation might be that high government expenditures could put pressure on the complex of interest rates, resulting also in less investment (the so-called phenomenon of "crowding out").] As in Problem 14-H, show both that the size of the impact multiplier of government expenditures on national income is not independent of the initial starting point but rather depends (negatively) on the initial level of government expenditures and also that the total effect on national income (per unit stimulus) is somewhat smaller for a *large* increase in government expenditures (as compared to a small stimulus).

BIBLIOGRAPHY

ADAMS, F. G., and L. R. KLEIN (1991). "Performance of Quarterly Econometric Models of the United States: A New Round of Model Comparisons," in Klein, Ed. (1991a).

BARTEN, A. P. (1964). "Consumer Demand Functions under Conditions of Almost Additive Preferences." *Econometrica*, 32: 1–38.

BRINNER, R. E., and A. A. HIRSCH (1991). "A Comparative Analysis of the DRI and BEA Models," in Klein, Ed. (1991a).

CHRIST, C. F. (1975). "Judging the Performance of Econometric Models of the U.S. Economy." *International Economic Review*, 16: 54–74.

DE BEVER, L., D. K. FOOT, J. F. HELLIWELL, G. V. JUMP, T. MAXWELL, J. A. SAWYER, and H. E. L. WASLANDER (1979). "Dynamic Properties of Four Canadian Macroeconomic Models: A Collaborative Research Project." *Canadian Journal of Economics*, 12: 133–139.

DUGGAL, V. G., L. R. KLEIN, and M. D. MCCARTHY (1974). "The Wharton Model Mark III: A Modern IS-LM Construct." *International Economic Review*, 15: 572–594.

ECKSTEIN, O. (1983). *The DRI Model of the U.S. Economy*. New York: McGraw-Hill Book Company.

FAIR, R. C. (1993). "Testing Macroeconometric Models." *American Economic Review, Papers and Proceedings*, 83: 287–293.

FROMM, G., and L. R. KLEIN (1976). "The NBER/NSF Model Comparison Seminar: An Analysis of Results." *Annals of Economic and Social Measurement*, 5: 1–28.

GOLDBERGER, A. S. (1959). *Impact Multipliers and Dynamic Properties of the Klein–Goldberger Model*. Amsterdam: North-Holland Publishing Company.

GREEN, R. J., B. G. HICKMAN, E. P. HOWREY, S. H. HYMANS, and M. R. DONIHUE (1991). "The IS-LM Cores of Three Econometric Models," in Klein, Ed. (1991a).

HELLIWELL, J. F. (1993). "Macroeconometrics in a Global Economy." *American Economic Review, Papers and Proceedings*, 83: 294–299.

HELLIWELL, J. F., T. MAXWELL, and H. E. L. WASLANDER (1979). "Comparing the Dynamics of Canadian Macromodels." *Canadian Journal of Economics*, 12: 181–194.

HOUTHAKKER, H. S. (1965). "New Evidence on Demand Elasticities." *Econometrica*, 33: 277–288.

HOWREY, E. P., and S. H. HYMANS (1995). "An Open Economy Analysis of the Dynamic Properties of the Michigan Quarterly Econometric Model of the U.S. Economy," in M. Dutta, R. J. Ball, R. G. Bodkin, A. S. Goldberger, S. Ichimura, R. F. Kosobud, J. M. Letiche, R. S. Mariano, J. Popkin, and P. Taubman, Eds., *Economics, Econometrics and the LINK: Essays in Honor of Lawrence R. Klein*. Amsterdam: Elsevier Science B.V.

KALMAN, P. J., and M. D. INTRILIGATOR (1973). "Generalized Comparative Statics, with Application to Consumer and Producer Theory." *International Economic Review*, 14: 473–486.

KLEIN, L. R. (1983). *Lectures in Econometrics*. Amsterdam: North-Holland Publishing Company.

KLEIN, L. R., Ed. (1991a). *Comparative Performance of U.S. Econometric Models*. New York: Oxford University Press.

KLEIN, L. R. (1991b). "Past, Present, and Possible Future of Macroeconometric Models and Their Uses," in Klein (1991a).

KLEIN, L. R., and A. S. GOLDBERGER (1955). *An Econometric Model of the United States Economy*, 1929–1952. Amsterdam: North-Holland Publishing Company.

SHILLER, R. J. (1991). "Model Comparisons and Appraisals," in Klein (1991a).

STONE, R. (1954). *The Measurement of Consumers' Expenditure and Behavior in the United Kingdom, 1920–1938*. New York: Cambridge University Press.

SUITS, D. B. (1962). "Forecasting and Analysis with an Econometric Model." *American Economic Review*, 52: 104–132; reprinted in A. Zellner, Ed. (1968). *Readings in Economic Statistics and Econometrics*. Boston: Little, Brown and Company.

THEIL, H. (1971). *Principles of Econometrics*. New York: John Wiley & Sons, Inc.

VISCO, I. (1991). "A New Round of U.S. Model Comparisons: A Limited Appraisal," in Klein (1991a).

WALLIS, K. F., P. G. FISHER, J. A. LONGBOTTOM, D. S. TURNER, and J. D. WHITLEY (1987). *Models of the UK Economy: A Fourth Review by the ESRC Macroeconomic Modelling Bureau*. Oxford: Oxford University Press.

15

FORECASTING

15.1 THE NATURE OF FORECASTING[1]

One of the major objectives of econometrics is *forecasting*, by which is meant the prediction of values of certain variables outside the available sample of data—typically, a prediction for the future, but, more generally, a prediction for other times and places. It will generally be assumed that the forecast is quantitative, explicit, and unambiguous, and therefore verifiable in that there are conceivable outcomes that would validate or refute it. Examples include, in addition to forecasts of economic phenomena, forecasts of demographic, political, meteorological, astronomical, and many other phenomena. More specific examples include forecasts of national income and its components, population, election outcomes, the weather, and eclipses.

Forecasting is closely related to policy evaluation. In fact, most methods of policy evaluation rely upon a specific type of forecast—one that is conditional upon adoption of a policy (or, more generally, alternate policies). This subject will be discussed at length in the next chapter.

Assuming the vector of variables $\mathbf{y}$ is to be forecast, the problem of forecasting is typically that of predicting values for $\mathbf{y}$ at the future time $T + h$, given the T observations, $\mathbf{y}_1$, $\mathbf{y}_2, \ldots, \mathbf{y}_T$, and, possibly, observations of certain other variables.[2] The time T is often taken

[1]See Theil (1961, 1966), Mincer (1969), Stekler (1970), Klein (1971a, 1983), and McNees (1988b). For general discussions of various approaches to business forecasting, see Chambers, Mullich, and Smith (1971), Granger (1989), and Holden, Peel, and Thompson (1990).

[2]Forecasting can, however, also apply to the period *before* the sample—predicting the value of $\mathbf{y}$ at time $-h$. An example is the prediction of the first electrical engineer in the United States by Price, in Section 1.6. It can also apply to cross-section analyses (e.g., predictions for one family or one nation on the basis of data of other families or other nations).

to be the present, and the positive time interval h is called the *forecast horizon*. A *point forecast* would be:

$$\hat{\mathbf{y}}_{T+h}, \qquad *(15.1.1)$$

representing a prediction of the values of $\mathbf{y}$ at time $T + h$. To the extent that the true values of the variables at this time, $\mathbf{y}_{T+h}$, are determined according to a probability distribution, the point forecast (15.1.1) is generally taken to be the expected value of the distribution as estimated at time T from the data $\mathbf{y}_1, \mathbf{y}_2, \ldots, \mathbf{y}_T$. This expected value can be bracketed by the *forecast interval*—for example, the 90% confidence interval:

$$\left[\bar{\hat{\mathbf{y}}}_{T+h}, \bar{\bar{\hat{\mathbf{y}}}}_{T+h}\right]_{0.90}, \qquad *(15.1.2)$$

defined by

$$P\left(\bar{\hat{\mathbf{y}}}_{T+h} \leq \mathbf{y}_{T+h} \leq \bar{\bar{\hat{\mathbf{y}}}}_{T+h}\right) = 0.90. \qquad *(15.1.3)$$

This forecast interval is illustrated in Figure 15.1 for the scalar case of predicting a single variable $\mathbf{y}$. Because of the greater uncertainty in the more distant future, the forecast interval "fans out" over time.[3] The rate at which the interval fans out determines what

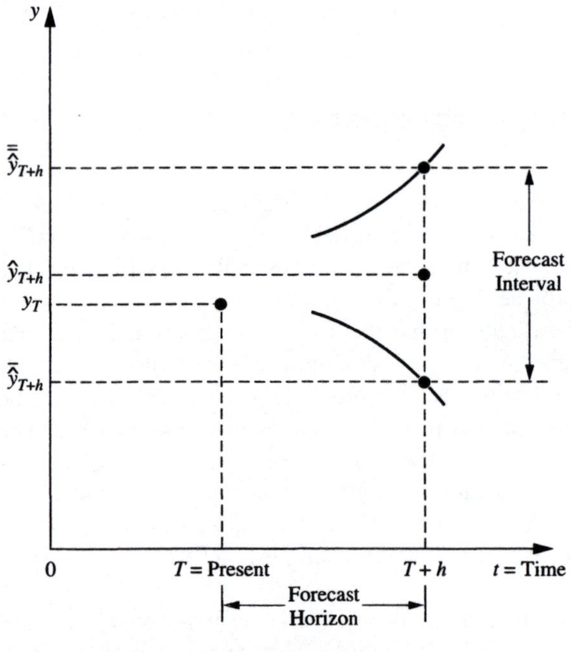

Figure 15.1 Point Forecast and Interval Forecast

[3]From (4.8.5) a $100(1-\varepsilon)\%$ confidence interval for the predicted $\hat{y}$ is:

$$\hat{y} \pm t_{\varepsilon/2}\hat{s}\sqrt{1 + \frac{1}{n} + \frac{(\hat{x}-\bar{x})^2}{\Sigma \dot{x}_j^2}},$$

where $\hat{x}$ is the predicted value of the explanatory variable, $\bar{x}$ is the mean value of this variable over the sample, and $\dot{x}_j$ is the deviation from the mean value. Thus, as $\hat{x} - \bar{x}$ becomes larger—that is, as the value of the explanatory variable moves away from the mean value observed in the sample—the confidence interval widens, as shown in Figure 15.1 (see also Problem 15-A).

constitutes a "short-term" as opposed to a "long-term" forecast. Thus a short-term economic forecast might involve a forecast horizon of one quarter or one year, whereas a short-term weather forecast might involve a forecast horizon of one day. Similarly, a long-term forecast in economics might be of the order of five years, whereas one in meteorology might be one week. The time scale for economic forecasts is much longer than that for weather forecasts, since the confidence interval for weather forecasts fans out much more rapidly. The time scale is then measured in appropriate units (e.g., quarters of a year for economic forecasts and days for weather forecasts). Given these units, the shortest short-term forecast is $\hat{\mathbf{y}}_{T+1}$, while $\hat{\mathbf{y}}_{T+h}$ for sufficiently large h would represent a long-term forecast.

Another type of forecast based on the probability distribution of $\mathbf{y}_{T+h}$ is the *probability forecast*, which reports the probability of a certain statement regarding the future value of the variable. An example is

$$P(\mathbf{y}_{T+h} \geqslant \mathbf{y}^0) = \alpha, \tag{15.1.4}$$

where $\mathbf{y}^0$ is specified and α is the probability forecast. An example is a weather forecast giving the probability of rain. Such forecasts have not been utilized in economics as extensively as point forecasts and interval forecasts, but they may well be more extensively used in the future as the methodology for their construction and evaluation is developed.

It used to be thought that forecasting was the critical test of a particular econometric model.[4] However, in recent years it has become recognized that forecasting contains at least as much art as science, so it is difficult to base critical criteria for the acceptance or rejection of a particular econometric model on its forecasting performance alone. Moreover, this point is reinforced when it is recognized that there is no precise agreement on how to *measure* forecasting performance if the evaluator's objectives are more than single valued.[5]

15.2 ALTERNATIVE APPROACHES TO FORECASTING

There are several different approaches to forecasting. This section introduces approaches other than the econometric approach, and the next section presents the econometric approach. It will be shown, however, that the econometric approach includes as special cases several of the approaches to be presented here.

The oldest approach to forecasting is that of *expert opinion*, based on the informed judgment of experts acquainted with the phenomena in question. An important special case is that of *anticipation surveys*, such as surveys of capital investment anticipations or consumption anticipations, where decision makers themselves are asked to forecast their own future actions. In general, the factors relevant to the forecast, such as anticipations surveys

[4]This point of view may be found in Klein (1971a) and, in principle, in Friedman (1953).

[5]A similar point of view has been expressed by McNees (1988b). The question of the evaluation of an econometric model is considered in more detail in Chapter 17. Also, Taylor (1993) has argued that the rise of what he calls "the new macroeconometrics" has shifted the emphasis in applied work from forecasting to policy evaluation (which is discussed in Chapter 16).

(namely, the plans of other decision makers), budgets and sales, and credit conditions, are not considered in the context of an explicit framework in this approach. Rather, these factors are weighted and evaluated subjectively by the expert.

A modern variant of the method of expert opinion, the *Delphi method*, pools the judgments of a panel of experts in order to obtain forecasts.[6] Each of the experts is consulted and then their forecasts are presented, in summary statistical form, to all. This presentation of responses is usually done anonymously and without face-to-face contact (e.g., via mail questionnaire) to avoid problems of small-group interaction, which might create certain biases in the outcome. The experts are then asked to revise their forecasts on the basis of the summary of all the forecasts and perhaps additional information. This process is repeated until the group of experts reaches a consensus.

A more formal approach is *persistence forecasting*, based on the assumption that the system has a certain momentum, with the future replicating the past. The simplest type is the *status quo* forecast, which predicts that the present value of the variable will continue through time into the future. Assuming a single variable to be forecast, the *status quo* forecast is the point forecast:

$$\hat{y}_{T+1} = y_T, \qquad *(15.2.1)$$

also called the "Naive I" forecast. An example is the forecast that tomorrow's weather will be identical to today's, a forecast that tends to be valid a very high fraction of the time.

Another simple type of persistence forecast predicts the same change from one period to the next:

$$\hat{y}_{T+1} - y_T = y_T - y_{T-1} \quad \text{or} \quad \hat{y}_{T+1} = 2y_T - y_{T-1}, \qquad (15.2.2)$$

also called the "Naive II" forecast, while yet another predicts the same proportionate change:

$$\frac{\hat{y}_{T+1} - y_T}{y_T} = \frac{y_T - y_{T-1}}{y_{T-1}} \quad \text{or} \quad \hat{y}_{T+1} = y_T + \frac{y_T}{y_{T-1}}(y_T - y_{T-1}). \qquad (15.2.3)$$

A general form for most persistence forecasts is the *autoregressive model*, yielding the forecast of the distributed lag form:

$$\hat{y}_{T+1} = \sum_{j=0}^{\infty} a_j y_{T-j}. \qquad *(15.2.4)$$

[6]See Helmer (1966), North and Pyke (1969), Dalkey et al. (1972), Parente and Anderson-Parente (1987), and Granger (1989). The Delphi method has also been applied to areas other than forecasting, including the quantification of both social goals and subjective uncertainty. A specific example of the pooling of expert opinion (but without the revision of forecasts that is part of the Delphi methodology) was the consensus quarterly forecasts of GNP and its components sponsored by the American Statistical Association and the National Bureau of Economic Research (NBER) over the period from the fourth quarter of 1968 through the first quarter of 1990. These ASA–NBER consensus forecasts, which were published regularly by the NBER in *Explorations in Economic Research*, were the arithmetic means of the forecasts produced by the participants, most of whom employed an informal GNP model rather than a formal econometric model. (In the first part of this period, there were roughly 40 regular forecasters; after 1980, the number was slightly less than half of this, as the number of pieces of information requested increased.) The survey has been sufficiently useful and interesting, so that, at the beginning of the 1990s, the Federal Reserve Bank of Philadelphia had taken over the tabulation and distribution of these surveys (see Zarnowitz, 1969; Su and Su, 1975; Zarnowitz and Braun, 1993).

Here the forecasted value is obtained as a weighted linear combination of all past values of the variable. The coefficients a_j may be specified a priori, as in (15.2.1) and (15.2.2), or they may be estimated statistically.[7]

A related approach to forecasting is *trend extrapolation*, based on simple functions of time.[8] An example is the linear trend:

$$y_t = a + bt, \qquad *(15.2.5)$$

for which the forecasted value at $T + 1$ is:

$$\hat{y}_{T+1} = a + b(T + 1), \qquad (15.2.6)$$

where a and b are either postulated or estimated statistically. In fact, this model is a special case of the persistence forecast (15.2.2) based on a constant absolute change from one period to the next, where:

$$\hat{y}_{T+1} - y_T = y_T - y_{T-1} = b. \qquad (15.2.7)$$

Similarly, the exponential trend:

$$y_t = Ae^{\alpha t}, \qquad (15.2.8)$$

yielding the forecast:

$$\hat{y}_{T+1} = Ae^{\alpha(T+1)}, \qquad (15.2.9)$$

is a special case of (15.2.3), where the prediction is based on a constant relative change, given by:

$$\frac{\hat{y}_{T+1} - y_T}{y_T} = \frac{y_T - y_{T-1}}{y_{T-1}} = e^{\alpha} - 1. \qquad (15.2.10)$$

Taking logarithms of (15.2.8) yields:

$$\ln y_t = \ln A + \alpha t, \qquad *(15.2.11)$$

so the forecast at time $T + h$ can be written:

$$\ln \hat{y}_{T+h} = \ln A + \alpha(T + h), \qquad (15.2.12)$$

where α is the proportionate rate of change in y. This is the model used for forecasting the growth of science in Sections 1.6 and 4.9. For example, the model, as used to forecast backward in time, predicted that $y = 1$ when

$$\ln \hat{y}_{T+h} = \ln A + \alpha(T + h) = 0, \qquad *(15.2.13)$$

[7]Mincer and Zarnowitz (1969) and Klein (1971b) argue that this purely autoregressive model should be used as a standard of reference in evaluating forecasts. Note that in (15.2.1) $a_0 = 1$ and $a_j = 0$, for all $j > 0$, while in (15.2.2) $a_0 = 2$, $a_1 = -1$, and $a_j = 0$ for all $j > 1$. Statistical estimation of the more general integrated autoregressive–moving average (ARIMA) model in the variable y_t and with disturbance term ε_t:

$$\phi_p(L)\Delta^d y_t = \theta_q(L)\varepsilon_t$$

is discussed at some length in Chapter 6, where its forecasting uses are also described. The classic reference to this approach is Box and Jenkins (1970), and in some circles this approach is considered synonymous with the time-series approach to forecasting socioeconomic series. A generalization of the autoregressive model to include a vector of *several* variables is called the *vector autoregressive model* (or VAR model); this approach, of which Litterman (1986) is a leading advocate for macroeconomic forecasting, is described in Chapter 11 and in Section 15.6.

[8]See also Section 3.6. It might be noted that in several areas it has been found that trend extrapolation provides more accurate forecasts than anticipations surveys (see Ferber, 1958; Okun 1962).

that is, when the horizon h was equal to h^*, where:

$$T + h^* = -\frac{\ln A}{\alpha}, \tag{15.2.14}$$

obtained from estimates of A and α.

Yet another approach to forecasting is the method of *leading indicators*. To use this approach a forecast for y is based on a related variable x, the leading indicator, where y at time t depends on x at the previous time $t - \theta$. Thus,

$$y_t = f(x_{t-\theta}). \tag{15.2.15}$$

The predicted value of y at time $T + h$ is thus:

$$\hat{y}_{T+h} = f(x_{T+h-\theta}). \tag{15.2.16}$$

In fact, this method is almost exclusively applied not to *levels* of variables but rather to their *rates of change*. In particular, the model:

$$\Delta y_{T+h} = g(\Delta x_{T+h-\theta}) \qquad *(15.2.17)$$

is used to predict turning points, where, for example, a downturn in one variable signals the eventual downturn of another variable. The leading indicators are selected on the basis of their record in predicting (leading) past turning points. Examples of leading indicators for the general level of economic activity include hours worked per week, new incorporations, business failures, wholesale prices that have been judged cyclically sensitive, stock market prices, new orders, and construction contracts, all of which generally lead overall economic activity by approximately six months. Thus a downturn in several of these indicators signals a downturn in overall business conditions in six months time.[9] Another example is the money supply, where a change in the rate of growth of the money supply generally leads to a change in the rate of growth of national income in nine to 12 months.[10]

15.3 THE ECONOMETRIC APPROACH TO FORECASTING; SHORT-TERM FORECASTS

For linear models, the econometric approach to forecasting is based on the reduced-form equations introduced in Section 14.1:

$$\mathbf{y}_t = \mathbf{y}_{t-1}\mathbf{\Pi}_1 + \mathbf{z}_t\mathbf{\Pi}_2 + \mathbf{u}_t. \qquad *(15.3.1)$$

Here $\mathbf{y}_t$ is a vector of g endogenous variables to be forecast; $\mathbf{z}_t$ is a vector of k exogenous variables; $\mathbf{y}_{t-1}$, the lagged endogenous variables, and $\mathbf{z}_t$ together are the predetermined vari-

[9]See Moore (1961), Moore and Shiskin (1967), Hymans (1973), and Klein and Moore (1983). In practice the leading indicators predict virtually all the true turns, but they also predict false turns. The principal way of treating this problem of false turns is to pool the leading indicators. See Shiskin (1967) for an index of leading series. Another way of pooling is via a *diffusion index*, representing the percentage of the group of indicators that is rising. Since the diffusion index is like a first difference, when it turns up it signals a future rise in general business conditions (see Alexander 1958; Alexander and Stekler, 1959). Yet another approach is by a *composite index*, which takes into account the size as well as the direction of changes in the component series (see Moore, 1969, 1983). A critical (but not destructive) evaluation of this approach to economic forecasting may be found in Auerbach (1982). Stock and Watson (1993) have attempted to give new life to the leading indicator approach by employing it in conjunction with a multivariate time-series model, of the sort studied in Chapter 11.

[10]See Friedman and Schwartz (1963). Note that the change in growth of national income can involve a change in the price level and/or real income.

ables; and $\mathbf{u}_t$ is a vector of g stochastic disturbance terms. The coefficient matrices are estimated as $\hat{\mathbf{\Pi}}_1$ and $\hat{\mathbf{\Pi}}_2$, numerical matrices with g^2 and kg elements, respectively. These estimated reduced-form coefficient matrices can be obtained directly from an estimate of the reduced form, or indirectly from the estimated structural form, as in (14.5.3). The time period involved in the lag in (15.3.1) should depend on the system under consideration and, as indicated at the end of Section 15.1, should depend on how rapidly the forecast interval "fans out."

The model in (15.3.1), ideally, is based upon some underlying theory as embodied in the structural-form equations. Sometimes the data are used to help specify the model, in particular to select the exogenous variables (e.g., via an analysis of correlations of variables). The most likely result of this approach, however, will be either spurious correlation (e.g., the correlation of the birth rate with the stork population) or the regression of a variable on itself (e.g., the regression of investment on savings). Such an approach might lead to good fits, including high R^2 values, but generally does not lead to good forecasts.

Given the econometric model, summarized by the estimated reduced-form equations, a *short-term forecast* of values taken by all endogenous variables in the next period is given as:[11]

$$\hat{\mathbf{y}}_{T+1} = \mathbf{y}_T\hat{\mathbf{\Pi}}_1 + \hat{\mathbf{z}}_{T+1}\hat{\mathbf{\Pi}}_2 + \hat{\mathbf{u}}_{T+1}. \qquad *(15.3.2)$$

This prediction of the next-period values of the endogenous variables consists of two systematic components and one judgmental component.

The first systematic component in (15.3.2), $\mathbf{y}_T\hat{\mathbf{\Pi}}_1$, indicates the dependence on current values of the endogenous variables, which are weighted by the estimated coefficients in $\hat{\mathbf{\Pi}}_1$. This term summarizes the systematic dependence of each of the endogenous variables on previous values of all endogenous variables due to factors such as serial correlation, constant growth processes, or distributed lag phenomena. In many instances a very good forecast can be obtained on the basis only of lagged values, as in the case of persistence forecasting.

The second systematic component in (15.3.2) is $\hat{\mathbf{z}}_{T+1}\hat{\mathbf{\Pi}}_2$, based upon a prediction of the future values of the exogenous variables, $\hat{\mathbf{z}}_{T+1}$, and the estimated coefficients, $\hat{\mathbf{\Pi}}_2$. This term reflects the dependence of the endogenous variables on exogenous variables of the model. Since the $\mathbf{z}_T$ are exogenous variables, they are themselves determined on the basis of factors not explicitly treated in the econometric model, so it is reasonable that these variables must be forecast on the basis of factors other than those of the model itself. One important case is that in which the $\mathbf{z}_{T+1}$ are themselves forecasts from another econometric model. For example, several major corporations forecast their sales, employment, etc. on the basis of an econometric model specific to their company or industry. (This is sometimes known as a *satellite* or *peripheral* model.) Such a model typically treats major macroeconomic variables, such as personal income or investment expenditure, as exogenous. To predict corporate sales, therefore, it is necessary to use forecasts of the major macroeconomic variables, which are obtained as forecasts of the endogenous variables of a macroeconometric model (e.g., one of those discussed in Chapter 12). The macroeconometric model itself contains certain exogenous variables, some of which are predicted on the basis of anticipations surveys of consumer behavior and capital spending decisions. In addition to

[11]See Theil (1966) and Klein (1971b, 1983).

the output of another econometric model and anticipations surveys, the future values of the exogenous variables $\hat{\mathbf{z}}_{T+1}$ are sometimes obtained on the basis of expert opinion or extrapolations of past trends in these variables.[12]

The third component in (15.3.2) is the judgmental component $\hat{\mathbf{u}}_{T+1}$, called *add factors*, which can be interpreted as estimates of the future values of the disturbance terms or, alternatively, as adjustments of the intercepts in each of the reduced-form equations. These add factors round out the econometric forecast–the first component in (15.3.2) summarizes the effects of past endogenous variables; the second component summarizes the effects of all other included exogenous variables; and the third component, the add factors, summarizes the effects of all other factors, including variables omitted from the model. The add factors are based on judgments of factors not explicitly included in the model. For example, in a macroeconometric model there may be no explicit account taken of strike activity, but if major union contracts are expiring and a strike appears likely in the forecast period, the forecasts of production should be appropriately revised downward. Many other factors may not have been included in the model because their occurrence is rare or because data are difficult to obtain, but this does not mean that they must be overlooked in formulating a forecast. Indeed, it would be inappropriate to ignore relevant considerations simply because they were omitted from the model. In this sense forecasting with an econometric model is not simply a mechanical exercise but rather a blending of objective and subjective considerations. The subjective considerations, embodied in the add factors, generally improve significantly on the accuracy of the forecasts made with an econometric model.[13]

While the add factors reflect judgmental considerations, choices of values for $\hat{\mathbf{u}}_{T+1}$ can be guided not only by relevant factors that have been omitted from the model but also by past residuals in estimating the model and past errors in forecasts. These residuals and errors are clues not only to omitted variables but also to errors in measurement of coefficients and systematic biases in forecasting exogenous variables. For example, if the recent features of the system are different from those over the entire sample and it is expected that these features will continue into the forecast period, or if the past residuals or forecast errors exhibit positive serial correlation (or a cyclical pattern), then it might be appropriate to use the recent residuals or forecast errors to construct add factors. One such approach would use add factors in such a way that the computed values of the endogenous variables at the most recent observation, as adjusted by the add factors, are the same as the observed value. Another would use add factors such that an average of the last several forecast errors vanishes.[14]

The econometric forecast in (15.3.2) is called an *ex-ante forecast* because it is a true forecast, made before the event occurs. By contrast, an *ex-post forecast*, made after the event, would replace the predicted values of the exogenous variables $\hat{\mathbf{z}}_{T+1}$ by their actual values $\mathbf{z}_{T+1}$ and would replace the add factors $\hat{\mathbf{u}}_{T+1}$ by the zero expected values of the stochastic disturbance terms. Thus the ex-post forecast is:

$$\hat{\hat{\mathbf{y}}}_{T+1} = \mathbf{y}_T\hat{\mathbf{\Pi}}_1 + \mathbf{z}_{T+1}\hat{\mathbf{\Pi}}_2. \tag{15.3.3}$$

[12]For example, the $\mathbf{z}_{T+1}$ might be obtained from an autoregressive model for the $\mathbf{z}$'s comparable to that for the y's in (15.2.4) (see Problem 15-E).

[13]In his discussion of forecast preparation, Klein (1983) gives an extended discussion of the role of add factors.

[14]See Klein (1971b) and Haitovsky, Treyz, and Su (1974).

The relation between the ex-ante forecast $\hat{\mathbf{y}}_{T+1}$ and the ex-post forecast $\hat{\hat{\mathbf{y}}}_{T+1}$ is:

$$\hat{\hat{\mathbf{y}}}_{T+1} = \hat{\mathbf{y}}_{T+1} + (\mathbf{z}_{T+1} - \hat{\mathbf{z}}_{T+1})\hat{\mathbf{\Pi}}_2 - \hat{\mathbf{u}}_{T+1}, \tag{15.3.4}$$

so $\hat{\hat{\mathbf{y}}}_{T+1}$ can be obtained from $\hat{\mathbf{y}}_{T+1}$ after observing $\mathbf{z}_{T+1}$ by correcting both for the errors in predicting the exogenous variables $\mathbf{z}_{T+1} - \hat{\mathbf{z}}_{T+1}$ and for the add factors $\hat{\mathbf{u}}_{T+1}$. The ex-post forecast is useful in focusing on the explicitly estimated parts of the forecast, specifically the estimated coefficient matrices $\hat{\mathbf{\Pi}}_1$ and $\hat{\mathbf{\Pi}}_2$, and eliminating the influence of the other elements of the ex-ante forecast, namely $\hat{\mathbf{z}}_{T+1}$ and $\hat{\mathbf{u}}_{T+1}$, which are generally not explicitly estimated. For example, it is possible to replicate ex-post forecasts, but not ex-ante forecasts.[15]

Another variant on the econometric forecast in (15.3.2) is the *stochastic forecast*. The forecast in (15.3.2) is a *deterministic forecast* in that it is based upon specific values for the current endogenous and future exogenous variables, for the coefficients, and for the future stochastic disturbance terms. All of these (with the possible exception of the current endogenous variables—which may be measured subject to error) are subject to uncertainty. In a stochastic forecast this uncertainty is indicated via the forecast interval (15.1.2) or the probability forecast (15.1.4). One approach to developing such forecasts is to use available estimates of the parameters of the distribution of the coefficients and the stochastic disturbance terms, particularly estimated variances and covariances, together with judgments or statistical inferences as to the distribution of the variables, to determine a probability distribution for $\hat{\mathbf{y}}_{T+1}$. This probability distribution can be described using the forecast interval or the probability forecast. Another approach is the Bayesian one, in which judgments on prior probabilities, together with the likelihood function, would imply posterior (forecast) probabilities.[16]

Yet a third approach is the Monte Carlo technique of stochastic simulation in which a set of alternative forecasts is prepared based on repeated random drawings using the distributions of the parameter estimates and stochastic disturbance terms. This set of forecasts can be described in terms of either the forecast interval (e.g., 90% of the forecasts fall within a certain range) or the probability forecast (e.g., the percent of the forecasts that exceed a certain level.)[17]

Returning to the ex-ante deterministic forecast of (15.3.2), the various approaches to forecasting introduced in the last section can all be interpreted in terms of this econometric forecast. The expert-opinion forecast is the special case in which there is no systematic part, so the forecast can be represented as the purely judgmental one:

$$\hat{\mathbf{y}}_{T+1} = \hat{\mathbf{u}}_{T+1}, \tag{15.3.5}$$

[15]For these reasons, some writers, including Christ (1975), consider that ex-post forecasts are a much better test of an econometric model than ex-ante forecasts.

[16]See Problem 15-C. For a discussion of the Bayesian approach to estimation, see Section 4.11. For a discussion of analytical computations of forecast intervals, see Goldberger, Nagar, and Odeh (1961).

[17]See Klein (1971b), Evans, Klein, and Saito (1972), and Fromm, Klein, and Schink (1972). In the simplest case this approach takes the two systematic components of (15.3.2) and adds to it values for $\mathbf{u}_{T+1}$ obtained from repeated random drawings from a distribution with the stochastic characteristics of $\mathbf{u}$, e.g., $N(\mathbf{0}, \mathbf{\Sigma})$, where $\mathbf{\Sigma}$ is either estimated or assumed. The result is a sample of values for $\hat{\mathbf{y}}_{T+1}$ that can be used to construct forecast intervals or probability forecasts. Fair (1980) uses a more sophisticated version of this technique to decompose the prediction error from an econometric model into components for coefficient error, exogenous variable error, specification error, and inherent randomness.

where $\hat{\mathbf{\Pi}}_1 = \mathbf{0}$ and $\hat{\mathbf{\Pi}}_2 = \mathbf{0}$. In persistence forecasting the first systematic component $\mathbf{y}_T\hat{\mathbf{\Pi}}_1$ is emphasized, since it reflects dependence on past values of the same variables. For example, the *status quo* forecast:

$$\hat{\mathbf{y}}_{T+1} = \mathbf{y}_t \tag{15.3.6}$$

corresponds to the case $\hat{\mathbf{\Pi}}_1 = \mathbf{I}$, $\hat{\mathbf{\Pi}}_2 = \mathbf{0}$, $\hat{\mathbf{u}}_{T+1} = \mathbf{0}$.[18] Other persistence forecasts, such as the autoregressive model of (15.2.4), can be represented using (15.3.2) simply by adding terms for $\mathbf{y}_{T-2}$, $\mathbf{y}_{T-3}$, and so on. Trend extrapolation can be explained in terms of (15.3.2) either by lagged endogenous variables or by including time as an exogenous variable. Leading indicators can be represented in the econometric approach using lagged exogenous variables.[19] Anticipation variables can be directly included in the model, and their inclusion usually leads to improved forecasts.

There are, in fact, several advantages of econometric forecasts, as in (15.3.2), over alternative approaches to forecasting. First, the econometric approach provides a useful structure in which to consider various possible factors, such as past values of the variables to be forecast, values of related variables, and other factors. Second, it is broad enough to allow for treatment of many different considerations, including a synthesis of various systematic and judgmental factors. Third, it leads to forecasts of related variables that are consistent with one another, since they all must satisfy the requirements of the model, particularly its identities. Fourth, it leads to forecasts that are explicitly conditional on predicted values of future exogenous variables $\hat{\mathbf{z}}_{T+1}$, add factors $\hat{\mathbf{u}}_{T+1}$, coefficient matrices $\hat{\mathbf{\Pi}}_1$ and $\hat{\mathbf{\Pi}}_2$, and current values of endogenous variables $\mathbf{y}_T$. It is therefore possible to analyze the relative importance of each of these elements of the forecast individually and to test the sensitivity of the forecast to changes in each, particularly in the light of new data. Fifth, it is possible to replicate a related forecast—the ex-post forecast of (15.3.3). Sixth, and perhaps most important, it has a good record for accuracy, compared to other approaches, such as those of Section 15.2, each of which can be interpreted as emphasizing one aspect of the econometric forecast but excluding its other aspects. Indeed, the best forecasts generally combine an econometric model that includes leading indicators, anticipations data, and time-series analysis with judgmental factors, represented by add factors, as discussed in Sections 15.5 to 15.8.[20]

[18]In this case the reduced form can be written

$$\mathbf{y}_t - \mathbf{y}_{t-1} = \mathbf{u}_t,$$

so the first differences of the endogenous variables are random variables. This model and the implied status quo forecasts work quite well for certain complex systems in which change is influenced by a multitude of random causal factors. An example is the motion of molecules in a gas, called *Brownian motion*, in which each molecule moves randomly. At the macroscopic level, weather conditions also generally change according to this model, so one of the best weather forecasts is the status quo forecast that tomorrow's weather will be the same as today's. An example closer to economics is the behavior of prices in the stock market. Studies of these prices, as discussed in Cootner (1964), Granger and Morgenstern (1970), Fama (1971), and Malkiel (1973), indicate that they change over time, from a statistical standpoint, in a way very much like the molecules in a gas—according to Brownian motion. Thus the best predictors of tomorrow's prices are today's prices.

[19]Note that lagged exogenous variables can appear in $\mathbf{z}_t$ (see Problem 15-F).

[20]When considering nonlinear models, it is necessary to modify the approach of this section since an explicit expression for the reduced-form equations may not even exist. Nevertheless, one-period forecasts can generally be obtained by solving the system of model equations, allowing for add factors if one wishes, and using an approach that follows closely the multiplier analysis of nonlinear econometric models of Chapter 14. See Bianchi and Calzolari (1980), where the prediction errors of such one-period forecasts for a version of the Klein–Goldberger model have been decomposed into coefficient estimation error and intrinsic randomness (see also Problem 15-N).

15.4 LONG-TERM FORECASTS

Long-term forecasts are those for which the forecasting horizon, h in (15.1.1), exceeds some prespecified level, h_0. Thus the long-term point forecast is:

$$\hat{\mathbf{y}}_{T+h}, \qquad h > h_0, \qquad *(15.4.1)$$

consisting of predicted values of all endogenous variables h periods ahead. The level h_0 depends primarily on the nature of the variables being forecast, specifically the rate at which the forecast interval (15.1.2) "fans out" over time. It also depends on the purpose of the forecast. Thus, for example, in forecasting national income aggregates, for certain purposes long-term forecasts might be of the order of eight years, while for other purposes they might be of the order of eight quarters. Customarily, however, in this context long-term forecasts refer to horizons in excess of five years.

Long-term forecasts can be obtained by developing a succession of short-term forecasts—that is, by iterating the forecasts obtained from the reduced form, as in (15.3.2). This technique is valid for either a linear or a nonlinear econometric model. Equivalently, in the linear case, they can be obtained from the final-form equations of Section 14.1. Using this approach, the long-term forecasts can be written:

$$\hat{\mathbf{y}}_{T+h} = \mathbf{y}_T\hat{\mathbf{\Pi}}_1^h + \sum_{j=0}^{h-1} \hat{\mathbf{z}}_{T+h-j}\hat{\mathbf{\Pi}}_2\hat{\mathbf{\Pi}}_1^j + \sum_{j=0}^{h-1} \hat{\mathbf{u}}_{T+h-j}\hat{\mathbf{\Pi}}_1^j. \qquad *(15.4.2)$$

In this formulation the long-term forecasts are explicitly conditional on the current values of the endogenous variables $\mathbf{y}_T$; forecasts of future values of the exogenous variables up to and including time $T + h$, $\hat{\mathbf{z}}_{T+1}, \hat{\mathbf{z}}_{T+2}, \ldots, \hat{\mathbf{z}}_{T+h}$; add factors for all these future periods, $\hat{\mathbf{u}}_{T+1}, \hat{\mathbf{u}}_{T+2}, \ldots, \hat{\mathbf{u}}_{T+h}$; and the estimated coefficient matrices $\hat{\mathbf{\Pi}}_1$ and $\hat{\mathbf{\Pi}}_2$. It is therefore possible to analyze the effects of changes in these considerations on the long-term forecasts. The corresponding ex-post long-term forecast is:

$$\hat{\mathbf{y}}_{T+h} = \mathbf{y}_T\hat{\mathbf{\Pi}}_1^h + \sum_{j=0}^{h-1} \mathbf{z}_{T+h-j}\hat{\mathbf{\Pi}}_2\hat{\mathbf{\Pi}}_1^j \qquad (15.4.3)$$

and stochastic forecasts can be constructed as in the short-term forecast case.

15.5 FORECAST ACCURACY

Given a forecast, whether short-term or long-term, interest centers both on its impact for action and on its accuracy. The former will be the subject of the next chapter, on policy evaluation. As developed in some detail there, forecasts can have significant impacts on the system. The present section covers forecast accuracy.

Various errors must be taken into account in any study of the accuracy of econometric forecasts.[21] First, there is the inaccuracy in the model, which is a simplification of reality and hence omits certain influences and simplifies others. Second, there is the inaccuracy of the data used in the estimation of the model, as discussed in Section 3.7. Third, there is the inaccuracy or bias present in the method of estimation, to which must be added possible errors of computation (e.g., round-off error). Fourth, there are errors in the forecasts of the exogenous variables and in the add factors. Finally, there are possible inaccuracies in

[21]See Morgenstern (1963) and Griliches (1986).

the "actual" data to which the forecast is compared. Of course, some may be offsetting, leading to spurious accuracy in the forecast.[22]

There are several possible measures of the accuracy of a forecast. For simplicity only short-run ex-ante deterministic forecasts are treated here, but similar approaches can be used for studying the accuracy of long-term forecasts.

The absolute error $\hat{\mathbf{e}}_{T+1}$ of the short-term forecast in (15.3.2) is given by combining this equation with (15.3.1):

$$\hat{\mathbf{e}}_{T+1} = \mathbf{y}_{T+1} - \hat{\mathbf{y}}_{T+1} = \left(\mathbf{y}_T\mathbf{\Pi}_1 + \mathbf{z}_{T+1}\mathbf{\Pi}_2 + \mathbf{u}_{T+1}\right) - \left(\mathbf{y}_T\hat{\mathbf{\Pi}}_1 + \hat{\mathbf{z}}_{T+1}\hat{\mathbf{\Pi}}_2 + \hat{\mathbf{u}}_{T+1}\right). \qquad *(15.5.1)$$

Combining terms, $\hat{\mathbf{e}}_{T+1}$ can be expressed as:

$$\hat{\mathbf{e}}_{T+1} = \mathbf{y}_T\left(\mathbf{\Pi}_1 - \hat{\mathbf{\Pi}}_1\right) + \mathbf{z}_{T+1}\left(\mathbf{\Pi}_2 - \hat{\mathbf{\Pi}}_2\right) + (\mathbf{z}_{T+1} - \hat{\mathbf{z}}_{T+1})\hat{\mathbf{\Pi}}_2 + (\mathbf{u}_{T+1} - \hat{\mathbf{u}}_{T+1}). \qquad *(15.5.2)$$

The equation has been arranged in this fashion because each term in the decomposition of the error has a meaning. The first consists of the errors due to incorrect estimation of the coefficient matrix $\mathbf{\Pi}_1$, these errors being weighted by $\mathbf{y}_T$. The second consists of the errors in estimating the coefficient matrix $\mathbf{\Pi}_2$, these being weighted by the *true* values of the future exogenous variables $\mathbf{z}_{T+1}$. The third consists of the errors in forecasting these future exogenous variables, weighted by the *estimated* coefficient matrix $\hat{\mathbf{\Pi}}_2$. The fourth consists of the errors in the disturbance terms, where $\hat{\mathbf{u}}_{T+1}$ are the add factors. All four terms, but particularly the last, can be based, in part, on a change in economic structure over time, which can be a major source of forecast error. Of course, some of these errors can and generally will be offsetting.

The error $\hat{\mathbf{e}}_{T+1}$ is a random variable, since $\hat{\mathbf{\Pi}}_1$, $\hat{\mathbf{\Pi}}_2$, and $\mathbf{u}_{T+1}$ are all random variables. At the time of the forecast, $\mathbf{y}_T$ is presumed to be a known quantity (and hence not random). Taking expectations, if the coefficient matrices $\hat{\mathbf{\Pi}}_1$ and $\hat{\mathbf{\Pi}}_2$ are unbiased estimators, then, assuming that $\mathbf{z}_{T+1}$ and $\hat{\mathbf{u}}_{T+1}$ are deterministic,

$$E(\hat{\mathbf{e}}_{T+1}) = (\mathbf{z}_{T+1} - \hat{\mathbf{z}}_{T+1})\mathbf{\Pi}_2 - \hat{\mathbf{u}}_{T+1}, \qquad (15.5.3)$$

since $\mathbf{u}$ is assumed to have a zero mean. Thus the expected error consists of the error in predicting the exogenous variables, weighted by the *true* coefficient matrix $\mathbf{\Pi}_2$, minus the add factors. The forecast $\hat{\mathbf{y}}_{T+1}$ is an *unbiased forecast* if the absolute error defined in (15.5.1) has a zero expectation:

$$E(\hat{\mathbf{e}}_{T+1}) = \mathbf{0}. \qquad (15.5.4)$$

In this case the mean values of actual and forecast values coincide:

$$E(\mathbf{y}_{T+1}) = E(\hat{\mathbf{y}}_{T+1}). \qquad (15.5.5)$$

From (15.5.3), the forecast is unbiased if

$$\hat{\mathbf{u}}_{T+1} = (\mathbf{z}_{T+1} - \hat{\mathbf{z}}_{T+1})\Pi_2, \qquad (15.5.6)$$

which implies that unless the exogenous variables are forecast without error (or $\mathbf{\Pi}_2 = \mathbf{0}$), *not* including add factors or, equivalently, setting them equal to zero will result in biased forecasts.

[22]Thus Stekler's review (1966) of Suits's forecasts with an early version of the Michigan model (see Suits, 1962) suggested that Suits's skill as a forecaster was so great that he was able to compensate for weakness in the fitted model (in particular, a tendency for his consumption equations to overpredict) by a judicious selection of the exogenous variables.

A convenient way of showing geometrically the accuracy of forecasts in the case of a forecast of a single variable is given in Figure 15 .2.[23] The actual percentage change, shown on the horizontal axis, is:

$$A_T = \frac{y_{T+1} - y_T}{y_t} \times 100, \qquad (15.5.7)$$

and the forecasted percentage change, shown on the vertical axis, is:

$$F_T = \frac{\hat{y}_{T+1} - y_T}{y_T} \times 100. \qquad (15.5.8)$$

In this figure the 45-degree line is the *line of perfect forecasts*, for which the actual and forecasted percentage changes are equal. The first quadrant contains points for which an increase was forecasted and for which the increase actually occurred, and the third quadrant contains points for which a decrease was forecasted and for which the decrease actually occurred. The second and fourth quadrants contain the *turning-point errors* (i.e., incorrect forecasts of the direction of change): in the second quadrant an increase was forecasted but the variable actually decreased in value, and in the fourth quadrant a decrease was forecaster but the variable actually increased in value.

A series of forecasted percentage and actual changes (A_T, F_T) for different variables or different periods can be depicted as a scatter of points as in Figure 15.2. It is generally found, however, for many different variables and for many different periods, that most of these points fall in the shaded cone between the line of perfect forecasts and the actual percentage increase axis, the cone of *underestimation of change*. For example, out of 210 forecasts, using a macroeconometric model for the Netherlands over the period 1953–1962,

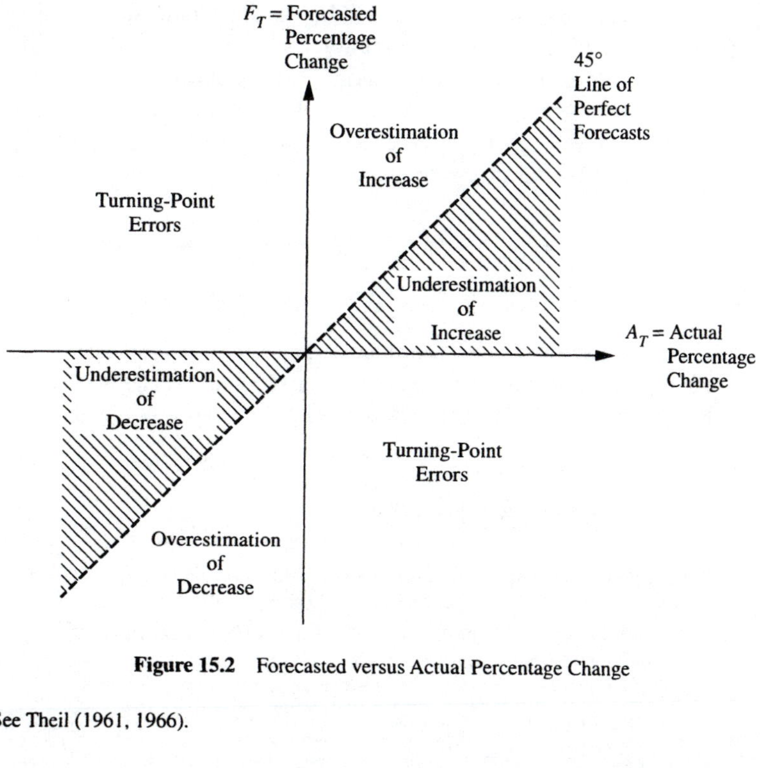

Figure 15.2 Forecasted versus Actual Percentage Change

[23]See Theil (1961, 1966).

59% involved an underestimation of change, 26% involved an overestimation of change, and 15% involved turning-point errors.[24] Such a systematic *underestimation* of change is a general finding for most forecasts.[25] Thus a forecast of 3% increase might, for certain variables, involve, on average, an actual increase of 5%. Typically, in terms of the definitions of A_T and F_T above,

$$|A_T| > |F_T|. \tag{15.5.9}$$

In the case of positive y_T, where y_{T+1} and $\hat{y}_{T+1}$ both exceed y_T, (15.5.9) implies that y_{T+1} exceeds $\hat{y}_{T+1}$—that is, actual levels exceed forecasted levels. Then (15.5.2) implies that:

$$\mathbf{y}_T(\mathbf{\Pi}_1 - \hat{\mathbf{\Pi}}_1) + \mathbf{z}_{T+1}(\mathbf{\Pi}_2 - \hat{\mathbf{\Pi}}_2) + (\mathbf{z}_{T+1} - \hat{\mathbf{z}}_{T+1})\hat{\mathbf{\Pi}}_2 + (\mathbf{u}_{T+1} - \hat{\mathbf{u}}_{T+1}) > 0. \tag{15.5.10}$$

Taking expectations, this inequality implies, on average, that:

$$\hat{\mathbf{u}}_{T+1} < (\hat{\mathbf{z}}_{T+1} - \hat{\mathbf{z}}_{T+1})\mathbf{\Pi}_2, \tag{15.5.11}$$

in contrast to (15.5.6), where equality holds for unbiased forecasts. In the simplest case of a single exogenous variable, where $\Pi_2 > 0$, inequality (15.5.11) is based on both the underestimation of the future value of the exogenous variable ($\hat{z}_{T+1} < z_{T+1}$) and the underestimation of the add factor (e.g., its absence).

One possible explanation of the systematic underestimation of change is that all forecasting methods are based on some explicit or implicit model, and all models involve, in their simplification of reality, an assumption that certain relevant variables either do not change or are accounted for in the stochastic disturbance term. To the extent that these variables actually do change and to the extent that they affect the forecasted variable, the result of this simplification is the observed systematic underestimation of change. The result is a *conservative bias* in forecasting, shading both upward and downward forecasts below their true magnitudes.[26] This bias is reinforced by hedging in forecasts (e.g., adjusting add factors toward zero) so as to avoid taking extreme positions.

An algebraic measure of the overall accuracy of several forecasts is the *inequality coefficient*.[27] If F_{Ti} and A_{Ti} are forecast and actual percent changes, respectively, for period (or variable) i, ranging from 1 to m, the inequality coefficient for this set of forecasts is:

$$U_T = \frac{\sqrt{(1/m)\sum_{i=1}^{m} (A_{Ti} - F_{Ti})^2}}{\sqrt{(1/m)\sum_{i=1}^{m} A_{Ti}^2}}. \tag{*(15.5.12)}$$

Here the numerator is the root-mean-square error in the forecast, while the denominator is the root-mean-square error assuming zero forecasted change. The case of perfect forecasts is that in which $U = 0$. If $F_{Ti} = 0$, so the forecasted percent change were zero, meaning a sta-

[24]See Theil (1966).

[25]In estimating regression equation:

$$F_T = bA_T + v_T, \quad \text{where} \quad E(v_T) = 0, \quad E(A_T v_T) = 0,$$

it is generally found that $0 < b < 1$, so turning-point errors are avoided, but forecasts generally underestimate change (see Theil, 1961, 1966; and Mincer and Zarnowitz, 1969).

[26]Of course, shading downward movement means *overstating* the value of the variable (see Figure 15.2). In fact, however, the underestimation of change applies primarily to upswings. There is a general tendency to miss turning points and/or slightly overestimate downswings.

[27]See Theil (1961, 1966); see also Mincer (1969) and Evans, Haitovsky, and Treyz (1972).

tus quo forecast for all variables in question, then $U = 1$. The case of $U = 1$ is therefore equivalent to a status quo forecast. Of course, U can exceed unity, in which case the forecasts are, in an overall sense, worse than *status quo* forecasts. More generally, if

$$F_{Ti} = kA_{Ti}, \tag{15.5.13}$$

where k is a constant greater than zero (i.e., turning-point errors are avoided) but less than unity (i.e., there is a systematic underestimation of change), then

$$U_T = 1 - k. \tag{15.5.14}$$

For example, if forecasted percentage changes are all 75% of the actual percentage changes, then $U_T = 0.25$.

The inequality coefficient can be decomposed into several terms, reflecting the different causes of inaccuracy. To perform such a decomposition it is convenient to consider the square of (15.5.12). The square of the numerator can be written:

$$\frac{1}{m}\sum_{i=1}^{m}\left[(A_{Ti} - \bar{A}) - (F_{Ti} - \bar{F}) + (\bar{A} - \bar{F})\right]^2, \tag{15.5.15}$$

where $\bar{A}$ and $\bar{F}$ are the mean actual and forecasted percentage changes, respectively. Squaring the terms in brackets leads to the expression:

$$U_T^2 = \frac{1}{(1/m)\sum A_{Ti}^2}\left[(\bar{A} - \bar{F})^2 + (s_A - s_F)^2 + 2(1 - r)s_A s_F\right], \qquad *(15.5.16)$$

where s_A and s_F are the standard deviations of A and F, respectively, and r is the correlation coefficient between A and F. In this expression the square of the inequality coefficient is decomposed into three terms. The first is the squared difference in the means, a measure of the bias—that is, the unequal central tendencies of the actual and forecasted percentage changes. The second is the squared difference between standard deviations, a measure of their unequal variation. The third involves the correlation coefficient and is a measure of their imperfect covariation. This last term represents a nonsystematic random error that cannot be avoided. The first two terms, however, represent systematic errors that should ideally be avoided.

15.6 FORECASTING EXPERIENCE WITH MACROECONOMETRIC MODELS: SPECIFIC STUDIES

Econometric models have been used for forecasting macroeconomic variables such as those listed in Table 12.1, starting with the early macroeconometric models. This experience has yielded knowledge as to what variables econometric models generally forecast accurately, what types of models have the best forecasting abilities, and what are the best approaches to forecasting.

The prototype macro model first introduced in Section 2.6 and later referred to in connection with the macroeconometric models of Chapter 12 can be used to illustrate the nature of forecasting with such models. The reduced-form equation of the prototype model for national income is:

$$Y_t = \Pi_1 Y_{t-1} + \Pi_2 G_t + \Pi_3 + u_t, \tag{15.6.1}$$

as in (2.6.7). A short-term forecast of national income (e.g., national income next year) is then:

$$\hat{Y}_{T+1} = \hat{\Pi}_1 Y_T + \hat{\Pi}_2 \hat{G}_{T+1} + \hat{\Pi}_3 + \hat{u}_{T+1}, \tag{15.6.2}$$

which is of the same form as (15.3.2). This ex-ante deterministic point forecast is conditional upon the current value of national income Y_T; predicted future government expenditure $\hat{G}_{T+1}$; the estimated coefficients $\hat{\Pi}_1$, $\hat{\Pi}_2$, and $\hat{\Pi}_3$; and the predicted future disturbance term $\hat{u}_{T+1}$. The comparable long-term forecast is obtained from the final-form equation for national income, yielding the forecast for Y at time $T + h$ of:

$$\begin{aligned}\hat{Y}_{T+h} = {} & \hat{\Pi}_1^h Y_T + \hat{\Pi}_2\left(\hat{G}_{T+h} + \hat{\Pi}_1 G_{T+h-1} + \hat{\Pi}_1^2 \hat{G}_{T+h-2} + \cdots + \hat{\Pi}_1^{h-1} \hat{G}_{T+1}\right) \\ & + \hat{\Pi}_3\left(1 + \hat{\Pi}_1 + \hat{\Pi}_1^2 + \cdots + \hat{\Pi}_1^{h-1}\right) \\ & + \left(\hat{u}_{T+h} + \hat{\Pi}_1 \hat{u}_{T+h-1} + \hat{\Pi}_1^2 \hat{u}_{T+h-2} + \cdots + \hat{\Pi}_1^{h-1} \hat{u}_{T+1}\right),\end{aligned} \tag{15.6.3}$$

which is of the same form as (15.4.2). This forecast is conditional upon the current value of national income, all predicted future values for government expenditures up to the time horizon, the estimated coefficients, and all predicted future disturbance terms up to the time horizon.

The forecasts in (15.6.2) and (15.6.3), which are the short-term and long-term forecasts of national income from the prototype macro model, are themselves prototypes of the forecasts obtained using macroeconometric models. Such forecasts typically determine the forecasted value as a sum of systematic and judgmental factors. The first set of systematic factors includes the lagged endogenous variables of the model, particularly lagged values of the variable being forecast, here represented by Y_T, the current value of national income in both (15.6.2) and (15.6.3). The second set of systematic factors includes the exogenous variables of the model, which must themselves be forecast or obtained from some source other than the model itself. They are represented by $\hat{G}_{T+1}$ in (15.6.2) and by $\hat{G}_{T+1}, \hat{G}_{T+2}, \ldots, \hat{G}_{T+h}$ in (15.6.3). In general, the exogenous variables can include both policy variables, such as government expenditure here, and nonpolicy exogenous variables, such as variables representing population and the foreign sector. More generally, both sets of systematic factors—lagged endogenous variables and policy and nonpolicy exogenous variables—can contain many variables, specifically all the lagged endogenous and exogenous variables of the model.

The last elements of the forecast are the judgmental factors, namely the add factors, represented by $\hat{u}_{T+1}$ in (15.6.2) and $\hat{u}_{T+1}, \hat{u}_{T+2}, \ldots, \hat{u}_{T+h}$ in (15.6.3). They can be interpreted either as adjustments of the intercepts or as future values of the stochastic disturbance term. For the interpretation as an adjustment of the intercepts, note in (15.6.2) that $\hat{u}_{T+1}$ is added to $\hat{\Pi}_3$. (The fact that it is "added to" the intercept led to the terminology "add factor.") More generally, an econometric forecast typically includes forecasts of all endogenous variables of the model, so there would be add factors for each of these variables. These add factors reflect the judgment of the forecaster concerning factors not specifically included in the model. The forecast also depends on the estimated coefficients of the model, represented in (15.6.2) and (15.6.3) by $\hat{\Pi}_1$, $\hat{\Pi}_2$, and $\hat{\Pi}_3$. More generally, all estimated reduced-form coefficients are used in generating forecasts of all endogenous variables of the model.

The fact that the forecast is explicitly conditional means that it is possible to investigate the sensitivity of the forecast to alternative assumptions. For the short-term forecast in (15.6.2), it is possible to vary the forecasted level of government expenditure $\hat{G}_{T+1}$ to determine alternative forecasts for $\hat{Y}_{T+1}$, each conditional on a particular level of $\hat{G}_{T+1}$. It is also possible to consider alternative add factors $\hat{u}_{T+1}$—for example, one add factor if there will be a major strike and another if there will be no strike. For the long-term forecast (15.6.3) it is possible in principle to vary not only the levels of government expenditure but also the timing of these expenditures. If, for example, the model were a quarterly model, it would be possible to determine the impacts of shifting government expenditure within the fiscal year, such as increasing it in the two quarters before an election and decreasing it in the quarter following the election.[28]

Carl Christ has studied econometric model forecasts for many years.[29] Early econometric models (in particular, Klein's interwar model, discussed in Section 12.2, and the Klein–Goldberger model, discussed in Section 12.3) did not forecast well, in comparison to two "naive models," which were used for comparison purposes. These two naive models were forecasts of an unchanged level and of a constant rate of change, respectively. In addition, the Klein–Goldberger model did not forecast turning points well, even during the sample period. One problem may have been the blunt, aggregated nature of the investment function, which included both inventory investment and fixed capital formation. By contrast, Christ's 1975 study indicated that "working" econometric models could easily outperform the naive models, for both *ex-ante* and *ex-post* forecasts.[30]

McNees has been studying the accuracy of forecasts based on macroeconometric models for some time, also. Due to considerations of space, only his 1988 study[31] is discussed here, but the earlier studies are also interesting, especially as they trace out an evolution in his thinking.[32] Ten organizations or forecasters were surveyed: the consensus forecasts of the ASA–NBER (Victor Zarnowitz; discussed in footnote 6), the BMARK forecasts of Charles Nelson (which are based on the ARIMA technique surveyed in Chapter 6), the BEA model (surveyed in Chapter 12) forecasts, the DRI model (also discussed in Chapter 12) forecasts, the forecasts of Chase Econometrics, those of Georgia State University's Economic Forecasting Project, forecasts of KEDI (Kent Economic and Development Institute), forecasts from the Michigan model (surveyed in Chapter 12 also), the forecasts of the UCLA Anderson Graduate School of Management model (Larry J. Kimbell), and those of WEFA (Wharton Econometric Forecasting Associates). Thus eight of the 10 forecasters surveyed are econometric model forecasters (with judgment playing a role, of course, as indicated in preceding sections). The preponderance of econometric model forecasters in his sample reflects the universe, in McNees's view. Five major conclusions came out of the McNees study. The most important conclusion was that no one forecaster dominates for *all* variables; all forecasters appear to have their respective strengths and weaknesses. As this comment is particularly pertinent if differing horizons are taken into account, a choice of a forecaster for a

[28]In practice, the fluctuations of quarterly variations in key economic variables, such as economic growth rates, are considered to be highly difficult to predict, and hence such forecasts would be of doubtful validity (see Ashley, 1988; McNees, 1988a).

[29]See Christ (1951, 1956, 1975).

[30]A similar contemporaneous finding appeared in both Zarnowitz (1967) and Moore (1969), who found that most model forecasts of GNP and its components were more accurate than simple trend extrapolation, particularly for short-run forecasts.

[31]See McNees (1988a).

[32]See in particular McNees (1975, 1979). While the main conclusions of the earlier studies are not greatly modified by the 1988 study, a greater definitiveness in the major conclusions of the exercise may be noted.

particular client would appear to largely a matter of taste, particularly depending on the important criterion variable or variables for that model user. Second, forecasts of individual quarterly changes (as indicated in footnote 28) are not obviously more accurate than the ARIMA comparative predictions; better results may be obtained by focusing on *cumulative* changes. Third, forecasting errors are usually small and tolerable, but a few egregious errors, such as occurred with the forecasts of real GNP growth in 1982 (see the next paragraph), have tended to give forecasters a bad reputation with both professional economists and the informed public alike. Fourth, forecasting accuracy for the past three decades (1960s through 1980s) has improved over time, slightly in absolute terms but definitely in relative terms, if the comparison is made relative to either intrinsic variability or to "naive models" (of the sort mentioned previously). Finally, McNees notes that, in general, the macroeconometric forecasting models are slightly more accurate than Charles Nelson's "benchmark" ARIMA forecasts; he suggests that forecasts of real and nominal GNP are 20% more accurate, on average; while for the implicit GNP deflator, the improvement is on the order of 10%. Still, how much effort is required to shave off a few percentage points of forecasting error! For forecast users who do not require a great deal of emphasis on accuracy, Nelson's estimates are, in McNees's view, an easy, inexpensive alternative to macroeconometric forecasts.[33]

Litterman has developed a forecasting technique called the *Bayesian vector autoregressive (BVAR) method*.[34] The vector autoregressive (VAR) method, discussed briefly in Chapter 11, expresses a row vector of jointly determined variables $\mathbf{y}(t)$ (with n elements) as a function of the lagged values of all elements of this vector:

$$\mathbf{y}(t) = \mathbf{d}(t) + \sum_{j=1}^{m} \mathbf{y}(t-j)\mathbf{B}_j + \boldsymbol{\varepsilon}(t), \qquad t = 1, 2, \ldots, T. \tag{15.6.4}$$

Here the $\mathbf{B}_j$ matrices represent coefficients for lagged jointly dependent variables $\mathbf{y}(t-j)$ and are square of order n. The maximum lag is denoted by the symbol m. The $\mathbf{d}(t)$ vector represents the deterministic component of the jointly dependent variables (in practice, Litterman uses merely constant terms), while the $\boldsymbol{\varepsilon}(t)$ vector represents the stochastic term; both are row vectors with n elements. In scalar form, the ith equation has the following appearance:

$$\begin{aligned} y_i(t) = {} & d_i(t) + \beta_{1i}^1 y_1(t-1) + \cdots + \beta_{1i}^m y_1(t-m) \\ & + \cdots + \beta_{ii}^1 y_i(t-1) + \cdots + \beta_{ii}^m y_i(t-m) \\ & + \cdots + \beta_{ni}^1 y_n(t-1) + \cdots + \beta_{ni}^m y_n(t-m) + \boldsymbol{\varepsilon}_i(t), \\ & i = 1, 2, \ldots, n; \quad t = 1, 2, \ldots, T. \end{aligned} \tag{15.6.5}$$

[33]The BMARK forecasts are discussed most fully in Nelson (1984). Nelson (1972) showed the potential for ARIMA forecasts to be useful, even in the context of a large and respected macroeconometric model. Nelson studied the predictive accuracy of the FRB–MIT–Penn or MPS model, summarized in Section 12.5, in one-quarter-ahead predictions, both within the sample period and outside of it. The standard of comparison was the set of predictions of ARIMA models of the relevant time series. Nelson concluded that the MPS model beat the naive ARIMA models, 12 times out of 14 for the within-sample predictions and 9 times out of 14 for the predictions outside the sample period. Nevertheless, this superiority was not overwhelming: in particular, if one constructed a "composite" predictor for the postsample developments, with both model and ARIMA predictions as inputs in a regression equation, in most of the cases both "explanatory variables" would have had statistically significant weights. In other words, the ARIMA predictions contained important, alternative evidence for explaining postsample developments.

[34]See Litterman (1986).

So far, this schema is simply a vector autoregressive mechanism; free fits of the coefficient matrices have not yielded impressive forecasting performances.[35] However, Litterman renders this schema "Bayesian" in imposing some a priori structure on the coefficients of equations (15.6.5); thus the coefficients β_{ii}^{1} are generally taken to be unity, while the fitting process gives a dominant weight to the lags of the own variable (the $\boldsymbol{\beta}_{ii}^{j}$ coefficients).[36] These modifications seem to improve the forecasts dramatically, to the point where the BVAR forecasts of macroeconomic variables are at least comparable to those of the macroeconometric models, at least for real variables such as unemployment rates and real GNP growth. In fact, Litterman hints that, on some criteria, his projections are *better* than those of the more formal models, especially when cost is taken into account.[37] On the other hand, McNees points out[38] that the Litterman BVAR forecasts certainly have their area of weakness, namely in the area of inflation (price indices). He also argues that the comparatively good showing of the BVAR approach for real variables for the first half of the 1980s may well reflect a unique incident, namely the dismal underestimate of the severity of the 1982 recession, which was extremely sharp if not prolonged. Most model forecasters had in front of them a very optimistic forecast of a popular, newly elected administration that intended to tighten monetary policy "painlessly"; they also knew that their clients were in no mood for negativism from their forecasting services, especially in view of the fact that some of them had overestimated the length of the brief (and shallow) 1980 recession. It is possible that several of them tailored their forecasts to what they believed the clients wanted to hear. By contrast, Litterman's honest equations blithely forecasted recession, whether popular president was claiming economic miracles or not! Whether this was a unique incident that does not reflect on the accuracy of the forecasting process in general or whether this is more damning than an honest miss will have to be left to the reader.

Wallis has completed a survey of the history of macroeconometric forecasting in the United Kingdom, from the mid-1960s to the end of the 1980s.[39] Four of his major conclusions were as follows. First, no one model forecasts dominated all the others, in terms of the set of criterion variables examined; Wallis considered the history of forecasts from four groups: the London Business School model, the Liverpool model, that of the National Institute of Economic Research, and the model of City University (of London) Business School. The similarity with the conclusions of McNees may be noted. On the other hand, Wallis found that the models' forecasts were better than those of time-series methods, including some generated by the VAR technique (not the version employed by Litterman). Second, some periods are more difficult to forecast than others, for example the period 1975–1976, which was right after the first oil shock.[40] Third, Wallis claims that the accu-

[35]On this point, see Wallis (1989) and Fair and Shiller (1990).

[36]Details may be found in Litterman (1986).

[37]Ashley (1988) would appear to confirm Litterman's own assessment, at least for the period of the first half of the 1980s. Using a standard of the intrinsic variability of the forecasted variable in question (perhaps adjusted for autocorrelation relationships), Ashley finds that Litterman's forecasts easily dominate most of the macroeconometric model forecasts for the period in question. However, Kimbell's projections (from the Anderson Graduate School of Management of UCLA) are even better than the BVAR forecasts; Ashley hints that this may have been a lucky coincidence!

[38]See McNees (1986a,b) for a detailed discussion of the Litterman forecasting technique from the viewpoint of someone sympathetic to the macroeconometric model forecasting approach.

[39]See Wallis (1989).

[40]McNees would appear to agree with this conclusion, as noted above.

racy of the models' forecasting performance has been increasing over time, both absolutely (slightly) and certainly relatively to the intrinsic variability of the economy (or with regard to naive model alternatives). Finally, Wallis asserts that forecasting the rate of foreign exchange is arguably the most difficult single problem that U.K. forecasters must confront.

Finally, mention may be made of Mervin Daub's detailed study of the forecasting "industry" in Canada.[41] Daub takes an industrial organization approach to the activity of economic forecasting; as the number of enterprises engaged in this activity (at least for resale of their services to general clients) is small, he considers the industry to be one of differentiated oligopoly. Thus, as one might expect from some forms of oligopoly theory, the enterprises offering this service do not in general compete on the basis of the straight price of their services. More generally, they compete in nonprice dimensions, such as special services (e.g., special simulation runs, construction of satellite models) offered to the clients. Of course, if one service could achieve greater forecasting accuracy in general, it could achieve a knockout and obtain a dominant market share of the industry. However, technology being general and impossible to keep secret, this does not happen, according to Daub.[42] Daub does find that the macroeconometric model approach to economic forecasting has become the dominant one in recent years.

15.7 FORECASTING EXPERIENCE WITH MACROECONOMETRIC MODELS: GENERAL LESSONS

More recent experience with forecasting using an econometric model has indicated the importance and value of add factors. These add factors, reflecting expert judgment on factors not included in the model, generally improve significantly on model performance. Forecasts with such subjective adjustments have generally been more accurate than those obtained from the purely mechanical application of the econometric model, including ex-post forecasts.[43] Combining an econometric model with expert opinion in this way utilizes the best

[41]See Daub (1987).

[42]However, Bodkin et al. (1979) found just the opposite in their survey of three forecasters [Informetrica Limited's projections of the CANDIDE model, those of a University of Toronto group on the basis of their Quarterly Forecasting Model (QFM), and those of the Conference Board of Canada on the basis of AERIC, their model of the time], along with naive models of the sort summarized in Section 15.2. The study dealt with ex-ante forecasts during the first half of the 1970s. Although all the models beat the naive forecasts (with the exception of QFM and CANDIDE for the two price-level variables surveyed), the AERIC projections emerged as a clear winner in the "horse race" or forecasting contest, on the basis of several criteria, for admittedly only three phenomena of interest (inflation, growth rates of real output, and unemployment).

[43]See Evans, Haitovsky, and Treyz (1972), Haitovsky and Treyz (1972), McNees (1973, 1975, 1990), Haitovsky, Treyz, and Su (1974), Fromm and Klein (1973, 1976), Suits (1962), and Christ (1975), who found that forecasts incorporating add factors were generally better than those without such factors. See also Stekler (1966, 1970). Econometric forecasts with add factors are also generally superior—at least for the short-term—to purely judgmental forecasts that do not use an econometric model at all, although Christ (1975) comments that ex-ante econometric forecasts are, on average, no better than the heavily judgmental ASA–NBER consensus forecasts described in footnote 6. It is possible, however, that the judgmental forecasts are indirectly influenced by the predictions of the econometric models (see also Moore, 1969; Zarnowitz, 1972, 1979; Zarnowitz and Braun, 1993). For the view that the forecasts from one model, the Fair model, do not require add factors due to frequent reestimation, see Fair (1974, 1984). In this connection, McNees (1990) has pointed up the possibility of "overadjusting" the constant terms, namely the introduction of add factors that are too "aggressive" (in terms of forecasting accuracy).

features of each. It combines the explicit objective discipline of the formal econometric model and regression estimators with the implicit subjective expertise of individual experts intimately aware of the real-world system. The econometric model provides a useful starting place for formulating the forecast, it identifies those factors for which judgmental decisions must be made, and it provides a framework that ensures that the forecast is internally consistent. The add factors take account of special circumstances and knowledge not embodied in the formal model, which can substantially improve forecasting performance.[44] They can also take account of revisions and updating of the data, which represent the main links between information on the real-world system and information contained in the model.

Experience with macroeconometric models has also indicated that such models are generally capable of generating accurate forecasts of certain variables but much less accurate forecasts of others. In general, as might be expected, smooth slow-moving variables are more accurately predicted than those that exhibit high variance and large fluctuations from period to period.[45] For example, the forecasting performance for variables such as consumption expenditure and wage income has been very good because these variables tend to exhibit stable patterns of growth with only small variations over time. By contrast, forecasts of variables such as inventory investment, profit income, and short-term interest rates, all of which exhibit large variations over time, have generally been only fair or even poor. Furthermore, the forecast error tends to increase the longer the forecast horizon. Short-term forecasting is comparatively easy, especially if the model includes lagged variables. Real and nominal gross national product, for example, can be forecast up to three quarters ahead with a relative root-mean-square error of less than 1% and up to six quarters with an error of less than 2%.[46] Medium-term and especially long-term forecasts, however, have much larger errors, with the forecasts deteriorating significantly as the horizon increases.[47]

On the types of models that have the best forecasting abilities, one major issue has been the proper extent of disaggregation and size of the model. Small models of

[44]Clearly, the importance in practice of these add factors implies that the associated forecasts become more subjective in the sense that different forecasters would produce different forecasts using the same econometric model. Thus the forecasts are less capable of being replicated and are thus less "scientific." Nevertheless, it can be argued that the forecasting value of an econometric model is most reasonably judged on the basis of its ex-ante forecasts, for which the selection of the add factors is an important part of the art of forecasting (see, e.g., McNees, 1986a,b).

[45]See Christ (1975) and Fromm and Klein (1976).

[46]See Christ (1975). The relative root-mean-square error of forecasts up to τ periods ahead is defined as

$$\text{Rel. RMSE} = \sqrt{\frac{1}{\tau}\sum_{i=1}^{\tau}\left(\frac{\hat{y}_{T+i} - y_{T+i}}{y_{T+i}}\right)^2} \times 100$$

where $\hat{y}_{T+i}$ is the forecast value of the variable y at time $T + i$ and y_{T+i} is the actual value at time $T + i$.

[47]Christ (1975) notes that the root-mean-square error for nine econometric models of the U.S. economy typically doubles or triples in going from forecasts of one quarter ahead to forecasts of five quarters ahead. He concludes: "These econometric models are at best only approximations to the economy as it existed when they were built and estimated; they do not state fundamental immutable laws of human behavior" (p. 64). More recently, Ashley (1988) has confirmed a similar tendency in his review of the forecasts of major U.S. macroeconomic forecasters. However, both Litterman (1986) and McNees (1988a) have found some qualified exceptions to this generalization.

less than 20 endogenous variables, such as the Klein interwar model and the St. Louis model; medium-sized models of between 20 and 250 such variables, such as the Klein–Goldberger and Wharton models; and large models of more than 250 endogenous variables, such as the Wharton Mark III, Chase Econometrics, and DRI models, have all been used for purposes of forecasting major macroeconomic phenomena. While there have been some exceptions, there has been a tendency to build and to use larger models as the data bases have increased and the costs of data retrieval and computation have fallen.

There are several reasons for using larger models, specifically the medium-sized and large models, for purposes of forecasting.[48] First, a fundamental problem with small, highly aggregated models is that they simply do not provide forecasts for variables of interest. For example, it is usually important to disaggregate investment into components and to treat explicitly increases in inventories, which are generally more volatile than the other components and which, to some extent, play the role of a leading indicator. As an illustration of this point, Suits (1967), in a sequel to his pioneering study (1962) of macroeconomic forecasting employing a macroeconometric model, noted that he was driven to increased disaggregation, in particular to the disaggregation of the demand for consumer durables into the components of automobiles and other consumer durables, in order to improve forecasting accuracy. Second, the medium- and large-scale models include many important variables and relationships that must be taken into account when dealing with a complex system such as the determination of national income and related phenomena. It is important, for example, to be specific about exogenous variables that influence the system in order both to allow explicitly for their influence and to test the sensitivity of the forecast to alternative assumptions regarding such variables.[49] In a small model these variables are taken into account only through the stochastic disturbance terms and add factors, but this may put too heavy a burden on such factors. The larger models can take cognizance of these variables explicitly and reserve the add factors for unusual or nonquantitative factors. Third, the medium-sized and large models provide a better framework in which to use expert judgment, in the form of add factors, than the small models. The larger models pinpoint the issues and can make effective use of detailed expert judgment. For example, experts can give informed judgments not only on overall government expenditure but also on its various components. It is therefore not surprising that during the past 15 years or so, greater use has been made of medium-sized and large econometric models, combined with expert judgment in the form of add factors, for the purpose of forecasting macroeconomic (and other) phenomena.

Finally, a generalization that appears to hold up in large number of cases is the systematic tendency to underestimate changes, as noted in Section 15.5. The instance of severe underestimates of negative output changes and unemployment rates in the 1982 recession, pointed up by McNees in his 1986 papers, is another illustration of this tendency.

[48]See Klein (1971b, 1983) and Fromm and Schink (1973). The latter presents evidence that larger models tend to provide more accurate predictions than smaller models.

[49]While the measure of the size of the model suggested earlier involved only the number of endogenous variables, in general, models with many endogenous variables also have many exogenous variables.

15.8 COMBINING FORECASTS AND FORECASTING METHODS

In recent years, there has emerged a tendency for users of economic forecasts (particularly macroeconometric forecasts) to combine these predictions.[50] In this approach, a final forecast is obtained by weighting each of several forecasts from differing sources:

$$F^* = \alpha_1 F_1 + \alpha_2 F_2 + \cdots + \alpha_m F_m, \tag{15.8.1}$$

where F^* is the user's final forecast, F_i, $i = 1, 2, \ldots, m$, are the individual forecasts being combined (m in total), and the α_i's are the weights attached to individual forecasts. (Generally, it is required that the sum of the weights, $\sum_1^m \alpha_i$, be equal to unity.) Granger and his associated authors have shown that if we have a good knowledge of the variances and covariances among the individual forecasts (and also if the forecasts are unbiased), it is possible to select the weights on the basis of this knowledge in order to minimize the variance of the forecast error (equivalent to its mean squared error, in this context). In general, intuitive results are obtained: past forecasts that have displayed small mean squared forecast errors (i.e., are highly accurate) obtain large weights. In some cases, the reduction in the variance of the forecast error of F^* over those of the its components can be substantial.

If not all of the individual forecasts are unbiased, it may be more convenient to produce the final, weighted forecast by a multiple regression.[51] Thus if there are data on (past) forecasts and their realizations, one can run the regression:

$$y_t = \beta_0 + \beta_1 F_{1t} + \cdots + \beta_m F_{mt} + \varepsilon_t, \qquad t = 1, 2, \ldots, T. \tag{15.8.2}$$

Here the t subscript indicates the time date of the observation; as usual, there is a sample of T observations on the past forecasts and their realizations (the y_t's). As usual, the random variable ε_t is a stochastic disturbance. With the estimation of the parameters of this regression, the final (combined) forecast becomes:

$$F^*_{T+1} = \hat{\beta}_0 + \hat{\beta}_1 F_{1,T+1} + \cdots + \hat{\beta}_m F_{m,T+1}. \tag{15.8.3}$$

The constant term may be set equal to zero and the sum of the weights in (15.8.3) may be forced to equal unity; but neither is necessary. Indeed, with biased forecasts, a free fit of the coefficients (permitting a nonzero constant term) may be desirable.[52]

If one doubts the stability of the structure of the relative accuracy of individual forecasts but still wishes to combine such forecasts, a simple unweighted (or equally weighted) average of individual forecasts has been suggested. The simple average of macroeconomic forecasts of the U.S. economy has been used, with good results, in the *Blue Chip Economic Indicators* survey.[53] Indeed, the ASA–NBER mean or consensus forecasts, discussed in footnote 6, were such an unweighted average of individual forecasts; in general, these forecasts were more accurate than those of the typical individual forecaster. Thus in a concrete prob-

[50]The seminal study in this area is Bates and Granger (1969). Excellent descriptions of the technique may be found in Granger and Newbold (1986), Granger (1989), and Holden, Peel, and Thompson (1991) (see also Problem 15-G).

[51]This technique was employed by Nelson (1972) when he wished to obtain combined forecasts from his separate MPS model and ARIMA estimates.

[52]Granger and Ramanathan (1984) demonstrate that the regression method is equivalent to the variance–covariance approach, under the hypothesis of unbiased forecasts.

[53]See McNees (1992). Although this method appears to "work," McNees is very skeptical that such an approach will produce a fundamental increase in forecasting accuracy.

lem, a user of forecasts who has more than one forecast of a particular variable (or set of variables) must decide whether to combine forecasts, and, if so, what weights to use in the combination.[54]

The combination of individual forecasts, with its result of generally improving their accuracy, suggests the possibility of combining *approaches* to economic forecasting. In the field of macroeconomic forecasting, Pindyck and Rubinfeld have suggested that one might wish to combined traditional macroeconometric modeling with the ARIMA approach to the stochastic disturbances of the structural equations.[55] Pindyck and Rubinfeld examine U.S. three-month Treasury bill rates, with a view to providing satisfactory predictions of this financial variable. They find that a regression model in which the disturbances are then taken to follow an ARIMA process gives excellent predictions, which are much better than either those of a straight regression model or a simple ARIMA analysis alone. Interestingly, while formerly one had to fit the parameters of the regression equation, calculate the sample residuals, and then apply the ARIMA analysis, at present all parameters of the system (both those of behavioral equation and those of the ARIMA process) can be estimated simultaneously. It would appear that this leads to an important improvement in forecasting accuracy, so this approach appears to have great promise.

Finally, another approach in combining techniques is the attempt to merge forecasts from a *monthly* macroeconometric model with those from a *quarterly* econometric model.[56] The problem is, broadly speaking, the following: monthly data (said to be "high-frequency" data) are available rapidly but are generally less complete than the quarterly (or annual) aggregates. Accordingly, quarterly models can be much more comprehensive and accurate but their very short-run predictions are less timely. Thus one seeks to merge the two sets of predictions, to capitalize on the strengths of each. As one might imagine, such a merger or combination of separate forecasts from a monthly and a quarterly model of the same phenomena is far from simple, and Corrado and Greene and also Howrey discuss some of these technical problems in detail. In general, Corrado and Greene approach the problem as one of modifying the add factors in the quarterly forecasts to take account of the additional information that the monthly model provides, while Howrey appears to approach the matter as one of obtaining optimal combinations of separate forecasts of the same phenomena. In any case, both sets of authors show that dramatic gains in forecasting accuracy can be obtained by this technique, at least for some variables of interest, for the very short-term forecasts, namely those for economic aggregates one quarter ahead, including those of the incomplete current

[54]This problem is tackled elegantly, largely in a Bayesian context, by Palm and Zellner (1992). Palm and Zellner indicate that it is generally preferable to combine, although the special case of *all* forecasters omitting a theoretical model that the user believes could be important in some circumstances (or with some subjective probability) *could* lead one *not* to combine for a final forecast but to stick with one of the individual forecasts. As for the issue of a simple average versus some selected weights that in principle give more emphasis to forecasts which have been more reliable in the recent past, this is strongly a matter of belief in the future relevance of such evidence, in this view. In particular, if the forecasts to be combined differ in their time dates, one might wish to use greater weights for more recent forecasts, say through an exponential decay scheme.

[55]See Pindyck and Rubinfeld (1991), particularly the final chapter.

[56]See Corrado and Greene (1988), who discuss such a merger of monthly and quarterly versions of the Federal Reserve Board's variant of the MPS model, and Howrey (1991), who studies the possibility of adding an auxiliary monthly model to the Michigan Quarterly Econometric Model (MQEM) of the U.S. economy. From Chapter 12, the reader may recall the pioneering efforts with the Liu–Hwa (1974) monthly macroeconometric model, which showed great promise, particularly for improving forecasting accuracy.

quarter. Still, it must be conceded that the results of Corrado and Greene suggest that gains in forecasting accuracy are rapidly dissipated as the horizon of the forecast lengthens. Nevertheless, both Howrey and Corrado and Green consider that the technique is promising enough that it warrants intensive future study.

PROBLEMS

15-A Consider the problem of forecasting a single endogenous variable where the only exogenous variable is time, representing a time trend. The reduced form is:

$$y_t = a + bt + u_t, \qquad u_t \sim N(0,\sigma^2), \qquad t = -T, -T+1, \ldots, -1, 0, 1, 2, \ldots, T-1, T,$$

and the long-term forecast is:

$$\hat{y}_{T+h} = \hat{a} + \hat{b}(T+h).$$

1. Show that this long-term forecast is consistent with (15.4.2).
2. Prove that the variance of $\hat{y}_{T+h}$ is $\text{Var}(\hat{y}_{T+h}) = \sigma^2\left[1/(2T+1) + (T+h)^2/2\sum_1^T i^2\right]$, as in Figure 15.1, where the forecast interval fans out as h increases.
3. Use the result on variance to construct 90% and 95% confidence intervals for $\hat{y}_{T+h}$.

15-B In the leading-indicators approach to forecasting, certain variables lead other variables over time, in that they turn upward or downward before these other variables, as in (15.2.17). In terms of an econometric model, the only explanatory variables are lagged exogenous variables, so the reduced-form equation, which explicitly treats lagged as well as current exogenous variables, reduces to

$$\mathbf{y}_t = \mathbf{z}_{t-1}\mathbf{\Pi}_3 + \mathbf{u}_t,$$

where the z's lead the y's.

1. Obtain short- and long-term forecasts using this model.
2. How would you use this model to predict turning points?

15-C Expert opinion has been interpreted in this chapter in terms of the selection of a specific value, or set of values, for the stochastic disturbance term. Another way to introduce such opinion is to use the Bayesian approach to the revision of probabilities, where the probabilities are forecast probabilities. State the Bayes theorem and interpret it in terms of expert opinion. Give a specific example of such an approach, for example, to forecasting the future unemployment rate.

15-D Obtain the long-term forecast using the final-form equations, where the iteration is carried back to the base-period vector of endogenous variables $\mathbf{y}_0$ rather than the current-period vector $\mathbf{y}_T$ in (15.4.2). When would this be used rather than (15.4.2)? What is the ex-post forecast for this case?

15-E Consider the distributed lag model for predicting future values of exogenous variables:

$$\hat{\mathbf{z}}_{t+1} = \sum_{j=0}^{\infty} \mathbf{z}_{t-j}\mathbf{F}_j,$$

where the $\mathbf{F}_j$ form a sequence of $k \times k$ matrices.

1. Obtain short- and long-run forecasts.
2. Obtain these forecasts in the special case of the Koyck distributed lag, as discussed in Section 6.8.

15-F Consider an econometric model that includes in its structural equations specific consideration of various lagged endogenous and exogenous variables:

$$\sum_{i=0}^{p} \mathbf{y}_{t-i}\mathbf{\Gamma}_i + \sum_{j=0}^{q} \mathbf{z}_{t-j}\mathbf{B}_j = \mathbf{u}_t,$$

where $\mathbf{\Gamma}_0, \mathbf{\Gamma}_1, \ldots, \mathbf{\Gamma}_p$ and $\mathbf{B}_0, \mathbf{B}_1, \ldots, \mathbf{B}_q$ are $p + q + 2$ matrices of constant terms.[57]

1. Find the reduced form and final form.
2. Obtain for this model both short- and long-term forecasts of all endogenous variables $\mathbf{y}$. Identify those factors upon which both forecasts are explicitly conditional.

15-G Suppose that two forecasts are available for y_{T+1}, given as $\hat{y}^1_{T+1}$ and $\hat{y}^2_{T+1}$. Assume further that if $\hat{e}^j_{T+1}$ is the error using forecast j, where

$$\hat{e}^j_{T+1} = y_{T+1} - \hat{y}^j_{T+1}, \qquad j = 1, 2,$$

then

$$E(\hat{e}^j_{T+1}) = 0, \qquad j = 1, 2,$$
$$\text{Var}(\hat{e}^j_{T+1}) = \sigma^2_j, \qquad j = 1, 2,$$
$$\text{Cov}(\hat{e}^1_{T+1}\, \hat{e}^2_{T+1}) = \rho\sigma_1\sigma_2.$$

Let $\hat{y}_{T+1}$ be a weighted average of the two forecasts:

$$\hat{y}_{T+1} = \alpha\hat{y}^1_{T+1} + (1-\alpha)\hat{y}^2_{T+1}$$

implying the forecast error:[58]

$$\hat{e}_{T+1} = y_{T+1} - \hat{y}_{T+1} = \alpha\hat{e}^1_{T+1} + (1-\alpha)\hat{e}^2_{T+1}.$$

1. Find the error variance for the average forecast, $\text{Var}(\hat{y}_{T+1})$.
2. Find the weight α that minimizes $\text{Var}(\hat{y}_{T+1})$ and show that, using this,
$$\text{Var}(\hat{e}_{T+1}) \leqslant \min[\text{Var}(\hat{e}^1_{T+1}),\ \text{Var}(\hat{e}^2_{T+1})].$$
Under what conditions will equality hold?
3. Show that the weight α can be negative, and provide an interpretation for a negative α.

15-H Consider a loss function reflecting the cost of an incorrect decision stemming from an error in a forecast. A general form for the loss function for the short-term forecast at period T is:

$$L_T = L(y_{T+1} - \hat{y}_{T+1}) = L(\hat{e}_{T+1}),$$

where y_{T+1} is the actual value, $\hat{y}_{T+1}$ is the forecast value, and the forecast error is:

$$\hat{e}_{T+1} = y_{T+1} - \hat{y}_{T+1}.$$

Generally, it is assumed that the loss function $L(\cdot)$ satisfies:

$$L(0) = 0,$$
$$L' > 0,\ \hat{e}_{T+1} > 0,$$
$$L(\hat{e}_{T+1}) = L(-\hat{e}_{T+1}).$$

1. Show that if $L(\cdot)$ is based on the absolute value function:
$$L^{(1)}_T = a\,|\,\hat{e}_{T+1}\,|, \qquad a > 0,$$
an appropriate measure of the inaccuracy of N forecasts is the mean absolute error:
$$\text{MAE} = \frac{1}{N}\sum_{T+1}^{T+N} |\,\hat{e}_{T+i}\,|.$$
2. Show that if $L(\cdot)$ is quadratic,
$$L^{(2)}_T = a\hat{e}^2_{T+1}, \qquad a > 0,$$

[57] See Klein (1971b, 1983).

[58] See Granger and Newbold (1986).

an appropriate measure of the inaccuracy of N forecasts is the mean squared error:

$$\text{MSE} = \frac{1}{N}\sum_{T+1}^{T+N} \hat{e}_{T+i}^2.$$

3. Generalize to the loss function:

$$L_T^{(k)} = a\,|\,\hat{e}_{T+1}\,|^k, \qquad a > 0,$$

which includes $L_T^{(1)}$ and $L_T^{(2)}$ as special cases corresponding to $k = 1$ and $k = 2$, respectively.[59]

15-I One approach to trend extrapolation uses the *logistic curve*:

$$y(t) = \frac{c}{1 + ae^{-bt}}, \qquad a,\ b,\ c > 0, \quad t \geqslant 0,$$

a curve that, starting from $c/(1 + a)$, rises at first at an increasing rate, then at a decreasing rate, asymptotically approaching the value of c.

1. At what time does the logistic reach an inflection point? Draw the curve.
2. At what time does the logistic reach 90% of c?
3. Show that the logistic curve satisfies the differential equation:

$$\frac{1}{y}\frac{dy}{dt} = b\left(1 - \frac{y}{c}\right).$$

15-J The *adaptive expectations* approach to forecasting changes the forecast from one period to the next by an amount proportional to the most recently observed forecast error, as in:[60]

$$\hat{y}_{T+1} - \hat{y}_T = \eta(y_T - \hat{y}_T).$$

1. Show that the solution to this difference equation in $\hat{y}_T$ is:

$$\hat{y}_{T+1} = \eta \sum_{j=0}^{\infty} (1 - \eta)^j y_{T-j},$$

which is a distributed lag of the Koyck type.

2. What do the model and its solution reduce to when $\eta = 1$? When $\eta = 0$?

15-K In Price's study of the effect of World War II on science in the United States, he found that if $A(t)$ is the number of abstracts in the physics journals at time t, then A was increasing exponentially at the rate α in the years prior to 1941:

$$A = A_0 e^{\alpha t} \quad \text{or} \quad \frac{\dot{A}}{A} = \alpha \qquad \text{for } t < 1941.$$

During the war years the rate fell to:

$$\frac{\dot{A}}{A} = \beta < \alpha \qquad \text{for } 1941 \leqslant t \leqslant 1945,$$

and after the war, the rate went back to the prewar rate:

$$\frac{\dot{A}}{A} = \alpha \qquad \text{for } t > 1945.$$

1. Show in diagrams A as a function of time and $\ln A$ as a function of time.
2. Find an expression for the number of abstracts in the postwar period.
3. What is the gap between the actual number of physics abstracts and the number there would have been if the prewar rate had continued throughout?
4. At what time will the gap exceed a prespecified number of abstracts $\bar{A}$?

[59]See Sims (1967).

[60]See Cagan (1956) and Nerlove (1958).

15-L Using the estimated Klein interwar model from Section 12.2 and data from the *Statistical Abstract of the United States*, forecast total output for the 1940s and 1950s. Plot your results on a diagram as in Figure 15.2 and discuss your findings.

15-M Consider the following variant of the inequality coefficient (15.5.12):[61]

$$\overline{U}^2 = \frac{\sum (F_t - A_t)^2}{\sum (A_t - A_{t-1})^2}.$$

1. To what naive forecast does this inequality coefficient compare the forecast?
2. Decompose $\overline{U}^2$ into constituent elements, as in (15.5.16).
3. Letting $A_t = F_t + \varepsilon_t$, where ε_t is the forecast error, relate the reciprocal of $\overline{U}$ to the Durbin–Watson statistic of Section 5.5.

15-N Starting with equation set (14.6.1) of Chapter 14, show how one-period-ahead forecasts for a vector of endogenous variables $\mathbf{y}_{T+1}$ could be produced, analogously to the step between (15.3.1) and (15.3.2).

1. What information must one have in this nonlinear case? In particular, is it any greater than what one must have in the linear case of Section 15.3?
2. Explain how in the nonlinear case one might produce forecasts of the vector $\mathbf{y}$ h periods into the future. Again, state the information required and compare it to that needed in the case of linear econometric models.

BIBLIOGRAPHY

ALEXANDER, S. S. (1958). "Rate of Change Approaches to Forecasting: Diffusion Indexes and First Differences." *Economic Journal*, 68: 288–301.

ALEXANDER, S. S., and H. O. STEKLER (1959). "Forecasting Industrial Production: Leading Series versus Autoregression." *Journal of Political Economy*, 67: 402–409.

ASHLEY, R. (1988). "On the Relative Worth of Recent Macroeconomic Forecasts." *International Journal of Forecasting*, 4: 363–376.

AUERBACH, A. J. (1982). "The Index of Leading Indicators: 'Measurement without Theory' Thirty-Five Years Later." *Review of Economics and Statistics*, 64: 589–595.

BATES, J. M., and C. W. J. GRANGER (1969). "The Combination of Forecasts." *Operational Research Quarterly*, 20: 451–468.

BIANCHI, C., and G. CALZOLARI (1980). "The One-Period Forecasts in Nonlinear Econometric Models." *International Economic Review*, 21: 201–208.

BODKIN, R. G., V. CANO-LAMY, E. CHOW, J. FORTIN, L. GUNARATNE, J. KUIPER, and C. SERRURIER (1979). "Ex Ante Forecasting of the Canadian Economy." *Journal of Post Keynesian Economics*, 1: 16–40.

BOX, G. E. P., and G. M. JENKINS (1970). *Time Series Analysis; Forecasting and Control*. San Francisco: Holden-Day, Inc. (Revised Edition, 1976).

CAGAN, P. (1956). "The Monetary Dynamics of Hyperinflation," in M. Friedman, Ed., *Studies in the Quantity Theory of Money*. Chicago: University of Chicago Press.

CHAMBERS, J. C., S. K. MULLICH, and D. D. SMITH (1971). "How to Choose the Right Forecasting Technique." *Harvard Business Review*, July/August, 49: 45–74.

CHRIST, C. (1951). "A Test of an Econometric Model for the U.S. 1921–1947." *Conference on Business Cycles*. New York: National Bureau of Economic Research.

[61]See Theil (1966).

Christ, C. (1956). "Aggregate Econometric Models: A Review Article." *American Economic Review*, 46: 385–408.

Christ, C. F. (1975). "Judging the Performance of Econometric Models of the U.S. Economy." *International Economic Review*, 16: 54–74.

Cootner, P., Ed. (1964). *The Random Character of Stock Market Prices*. Cambridge, Mass.: MIT Press.

Corrado, C., and M. Greene (1988). "Reducing Uncertainty in Short-Term Projections: Linkage of Monthly and Quarterly Models." *Journal of Forecasting*, 7: 77–102.

Dalkey, N. C., et al. (1972). *Studies in the Quality of Life; Delphi and Decision-Making*. Lexington, Mass.: Lexington Books.

Daub, M. (1987). *Canadian Economic Forecasting: In a World Where All's Unsure*. Kingston, Ontario, and Montreal: McGill–Queen's University Press.

Evans, M. K., Y. Haitovsky, and G. I. Treyz (1972). "An Analysis of the Forecasting Properties of U.S. Econometric Models," in B. G. Hickman, Ed., *Econometric Models of Cyclical Behavior*. National Bureau of Economic Research. New York: Columbia University Press.

Evans, M. K., L. R. Klein, and M. Saito (1972). "Short-Run Prediction and Long-Run Simulation of the Wharton Model," in B. G. Hickman, Ed., *Econometric Models of Cyclical Behavior*. National Bureau of Economic Research. New York: Columbia University Press.

Fair, R. C. (1974). "An Evaluation of a Short-Run Forecasting Model." *International Economic Review*, 15: 285–303.

Fair, R. C. (1980). "Estimating the Predictive Accuracy of Econometric Models." *International Economic Review*, 21: 355–378.

Fair, R. C. (1984). *Specification, Estimation, and Analysis of Macroeconometric Models*. Cambridge, Mass.: Harvard University Press.

Fair, R. C., and R. J. Shiller (1990). "Comparing Information in Forecasts from Econometric Models." *American Economic Review*, 80: 375–389.

Fama, E. F. (1971). "Efficient Capital Markets: A Review of Theory and Empirical Work," in M. D. Intriligator, Ed., *Frontiers of Quantitative Economics*. Amsterdam: North-Holland Publishing Company.

Ferber, R. (1958). *Employers' Forecasts of Manpower Requirements: A Case Study*. Bureau of Economic and Business Research: University of Illinois.

Friedman, M. (1953). "The Methodology of Positive Economics," in *Essays in Positive Economics*. Chicago: University of Chicago Press.

Friedman, M., and A. Schwartz (1963). *A Monetary History of the United States, 1867–1960*. Princeton, N.J.: Princeton University Press.

Fromm, G., and L. R. Klein (1973). "A Comparison of Eleven Econometric Models of the United States." *American Economic Review*, 63: 385–393.

Fromm, G., and L. R. Klein (1976). "The NBER/NSF Model Comparison Seminar: An Analysis of Results." *Annals of Economic and Social Measurement*, 5: 1–28.

Fromm, G. S., L. R. Klein, and G. R. Schink (1972). "Short- and Long-Term Simulations with the Brookings Model." in B. G. Hickman, Ed., *Econometric Models of Cyclical Behavior*. National Bureau of Economic Research. New York: Columbia University Press.

Fromm, G., and G. R. Schink (1973). "Aggregation and Econometric Models." *International Economic Review*, 14: 1–32.

Goldberger, A. S., A. L. Nagar, and H. S. Odeh (1961). "The Covariance Matrices of Reduced-Form Coefficients and of Forecasts for a Structural Econometric Model." *Econometrica*, 29: 556–573.

GRANGER, C. W. J. (1989). *Forecasting in Business and Economics*, 2nd ed. San Diego: Academic Press, Inc.

GRANGER, C. W. J., and O. MORGENSTERN (1970). *Predictability of Stock Market Prices*. Lexington, Mass.: Heath Lexington Books.

GRANGER, C. W. J., and P. NEWBOLD (1986). *Forecasting Economic Time Series*, 2nd ed. Orlando, FL: Academic Press, Inc.

GRANGER, C. W. J., and R. RAMANATHAN (1984). "Improved Methods of Combining Forecasts." *Journal of Forecasting*, 3: 197–204.

GRILICHES, Z. (1986). "Economic Data Issues," in Z. Griliches and M. D. Intriligator, Eds., *Handbook of Econometrics*, Vol. 3. Amsterdam: North-Holland Publishing Company.

HAITOVSKY, Y., and G. TREYZ (1972). "Forecasts with Quarterly Econometric Models: Equation Adjustments and Benchmark Predictions: The U.S. Experience." *Review of Economics and Statistics*, 44: 317–325.

HAITOVSKY, Y., G. TREYZ, and V. SU (1974). *Forecasts with Quarterly Macroeconometric Models*. National Bureau of Economic Research. New York: Columbia University Press.

HELMER, O. (1966). *Social Technology*. New York: Basic Books.

HOLDEN, K., D. A. PEEL, and J. L. THOMPSON (1990). *Economic Forecasting: An Introduction*. Cambridge: Cambridge University Press.

HOWREY, E. P. (1991). "New Methods for Using Monthly Data to Improve Forecast Accuracy," in L. R. Klein, Ed., *Comparative Performance of U.S. Econometric Models*. New York: Oxford University Press.

HYMANS, S. H. (1973). "On the Use of Leading Indicators to Predict Cyclical Turning Points." *Brookings Papers on Economic Activity*, 2: 339–375.

KLEIN, L. R. (1971a). *An Essay on the Theory of Economic Prediction*. Chicago: Markham Publishing Co.

KLEIN, L. R. (1971b). "Forecasting and Policy Evaluation Using Large Scale Econometric Models: The State of the Art," in M. D. Intriligator, Ed., *Frontiers of Quantitative Economics*. Amsterdam: North-Holland Publishing Company.

KLEIN, L. R. (1983). *Lectures in Econometrics*. Amsterdam: North-Holland Publishing Company.

KLEIN, P. A., and G. H. MOORE (1983). "The Leading Indicator Approach to Economic Forecasting: Prospect and Retrospect." *Journal of Forecasting*, 2: 119–137.

LITTERMAN, R. B. (1986). "Forecasting with Bayesian Vector Autoregressions: Five Years of Experience." *Journal of Business and Economic Statistics*, 4: 25–38.

LIU, T. C., and E. C. HWA (1974). "A Monthly Econometric Model of the U.S. Economy." *International Economic Review*, 15: 328–365.

MALKIEL, B. G. (1973). *A Random Walk down Wall Street*. New York: W.W. Norton Publishing Co. (Fifth edition, 1990).

MCNEES, S. K. (1973). "The Predictive Accuracy of Econometric Forecasts." *New England Economic Review*, September/October: 3–27.

MCNEES, S. K. (1975). "How Accurate are Economic Forecasts?" *New England Economic Review*, November/December: 2–39.

MCNEES, S. K. (1979). "The Forecasting Record for the 1970s." *New England Economic Review*, September/October: 33–53.

MCNEES, S. K. (1986a). "Forecasting Accuracy of Alternative Techniques: A Comparison of U.S. Macroeconomic Forecasts." *Journal of Business and Economic Statistics*, 4: 5–23 (including "Comments" by C. W. J. Granger, R. B. Litterman, and W. A. Spivey, and "Reply" by McNees).

MCNEES, S. K. (1986b). "The Accuracy of Two Forecasting Techniques: Some Evidence and an Interpretation." *New England Economic Review*, March/April: 20–31.

McNEES, S. K. (1988a). "How Accurate are Macroeconomic Forecasts?" *New England Economic Review*, July/August: 15–36.

McNEES, S. K. (1988b). "On the Future of Macroeconomic Forecasting." *International Journal of Forecasting*, 4: 359–362.

McNEES, S. K. (1990). "The Role of Judgment in Macroeconomic Forecasting Accuracy." *International Journal of Forecasting*, 6: 287–299.

McNEES, S. K. (1992). "The Uses and Abuses of 'Consensus' Forecasts." *Journal of Forecasting*, 11: 703–710.

MINCER, J., Ed. (1969). *Economic Forecasts and Expectations: Analyses of Forecasting Behavior and Performance*. National Bureau of Economic Research. New York: Columbia University Press.

MINCER, J., and V. ZARNOWITZ (1969). "The Evaluation of Economic Forecasts," in Mincer (1969).

MOORE, G. H., Ed. (1961). *Business Cycle Indicators*. National Bureau of Economic Research. Princeton, N.J.: Princeton University Press.

MOORE, G. H. (1969). "Forecasting Short-Term Economic Changes." *Journal of the American Statistical Association*, 64: 1–22.

MOORE, G. H. (1983). *Business Cycles, Inflation and Forecasting*, 2nd ed. Cambridge Mass.: Ballinger Publishing Co.

MOORE, G. H., and J. SHISKIN (1967). *Indicators of Business Expansions and Contractions*. New York: National Bureau of Economic Research.

MORGENSTERN, O. (1963). *On the Accuracy of Economic Observations*, 2nd ed. Princeton, N.J.: Princeton University Press.

NELSON, C. R. (1972). "The Prediction Performance of the FRB-MIT-PENN Model of the U.S. Economy." *American Economic Review*, 62: 902–917.

NELSON, C. R. (1984). "A Benchmark for the Accuracy of Econometric Forecasts." *Business Economics*, April: 52–58.

NERLOVE, M. (1958). "Adaptive Expectations and Cobweb Phenomena." *Quarterly Journal of Economics*, 73: 227–240.

NORTH, H. Q., and D. L. PYKE (1969). " 'Probes' of the Technological Future." *Harvard Business Review*, May/June 47: 68.

OKUN, A. M. (1962). "The Predictive Value of Surveys of Business Intentions." *American Economic Review, Papers and Proceedings*, 52: 218–225.

PALM, F. C., and A. ZELLNER (1992). "To Combine or Not to Combine? Issues of Combining Forecasts." *Journal of Forecasting*, 11: 687–701.

PARENTE, F. J., and J. K. ANDERSON-PARENTE (1987). "Delphi Inquiry Systems," in G. Wright and P. Ayton, Eds., *Judgmental Forecasting*. New York: John Wiley & Sons, Inc.

PINDYCK, R. S., and D. L. RUBINFELD (1991). *Econometric Models and Economic Forecasts*, 3rd ed. New York: McGraw-Hill Book Company.

SHISKIN, J. (1967). "Reverse Trend Adjustment of Leading Indicators." *Review of Economics and Statistics*, 49: 45–49.

SIMS, C. A. (1967). "Evaluating Short-Term Macroeconomic Forecasts: The Dutch Performance." *Review of Economics and Statistics*, 49: 225–236.

STEKLER, H. O. (1966). "Forecasting and Analysis with an Econometric Model: Comment." *American Economic Review*, 56: 1241–1248.

STEKLER, H. O. (1970). *Economic Forecasting*. New York: Praeger Publishers.

STOCK, J. H. and M. W. WATSON, (1993). "A Procedure for Predicting Recessions with Leading Indicators: Econometric Issues and Recent Experience," in J. H. Stock and M. W. Watson, Eds.,

Business Cycles, Indicators, and Forecasting, National Bureau of Economic Research, Vol. 28 of *Studies in Business Cycles*. Chicago: University of Chicago Press.

SU, V., and J. SU (1975). "An Evaluation of the ASA/NBER Business Outlook Survey Forecasts." *Explorations in Economic Research*, 2: 588–618.

SUITS, D. B. (1962). "Forecasting and Analysis with an Econometric Model." *American Economic Review*, 52: 104–132.

SUITS, D. B. (1967). "Applied Econometric Forecasting and Policy Analysis," in H. O. Wold, G. H. Orcutt, E. A. Robinson, D. B. Suits, and P. de Wolff, Eds., *Forecasting on a Scientific Basis*, Proceedings of an International Summer Institute. Lisbon: The Gulbenkian Foundation.

TAYLOR, J. B. (1993). "The Use of the New Macroeconometrics for Policy Formulation." *American Economic Review, Papers and Proceedings*, 83: 300–305.

THEIL, H. (1961). *Economic Forecasts and Policy*, 2nd rev. ed. Amsterdam: North-Holland Publishing Company.

THEIL, H. (1966). *Applied Economic Forecasting*. Amsterdam: North-Holland Publishing Company.

WALLIS, K. F. (1989). "Macroeconomic Forecasting: A Survey." *Economic Journal*, 99: 28–61.

ZARNOWITZ, V. (1967). *An Appraisal of Short-Term Economic Forecasts*. National Bureau of Economic Research, Occasional Paper 104. New York: Columbia University Press.

ZARNOWITZ, V. (1969). "The New ASA-NBER Survey of Forecasts by Economic Statisticians." *The American Statistician*, 23: 12–16.

ZARNOWITZ, V. (1972). "Forecasting Economic Conditions. The Record and the Prospect," in V. Zarnowitz, Ed., *The Business Cycle Today*. New York: National Bureau of Economic Research.

ZARNOWITZ, V. (1979). "An Analysis of Annual and Multiperiod Quarterly Forecasts of Aggregate Income, Output, and the Price Level." *Journal of Business*, 52: 1–33.

ZARNOWITZ, V., and P. BRAUN (1993). "Twenty-two Years of NBER-ASA Quarterly Economic Outlook Surveys: Aspects and Comparisons of Forecasting Performance," in J. H. Stock and M. W. Watson, Eds., *Business Cycles, Indicators, and Forecasting*. National Bureau of Economic Research, Vol. 28 of *Studies in Business Cycles*. Chicago: University of Chicago Press.

16

POLICY EVALUATION

16.1 THE NATURE OF POLICY EVALUATION

The final objective of econometrics, and perhaps its most important potential use, is that of *policy evaluation*. This objective refers to a situation in which a decision maker must choose one policy, called a "plan," from a given set of alternative policies. An important example is national macroeconomic planning, in which government decision makers must choose among alternative fiscal, monetary, and other policies that affect the national economy. Another example is corporate capital planning, in which corporate decision makers must choose among alternative investment projects. An example at the international level would be an international development fund, the officials of which must choose among alternative development projects.

Policy evaluation is closely related to forecasting and, just as in the case of forecasting, it will be assumed here that the policy choice is quantitative, explicit, and unambiguous. In fact, forecasting and policy evaluation are interrelated in a feedback system: A forecast must be based, in part, on assumptions concerning the actions of the relevant decision makers. Conversely, policy evaluation must be based, in part, on forecasts of the effects of policy choices. The forecaster and decision maker are indeed often combined in the same person (or agency or office), responsible for both forecasting and policy evaluation.

Just as the forecasting use of econometrics distinguishes between short- and long-term forecasts, the policy evaluation use also distinguishes between short- and long-term policy. In general, short-term policy is concerned, for macroeconometric models, with stabilization of the economy within a period of one or two years. Long-term policy, by contrast, is concerned with the pattern of growth over longer periods. A basic issue in policy evaluation, in fact, is the *time horizon* of the plan—the issue of how far ahead policy is to be formulated and how far ahead the effects of various policies are to be studied in order to evaluate the plan.[1] As in Chapter 15, the relevant time unit depends on the subject matter. For example, in some contexts an annual period is reasonable, while in others a quarter would be a more appropriate unit.

The type of policy evaluation to be stressed here is that of short-term policy evaluation, namely that of choosing a policy at time T given the course of events up to and including time $T-1$. The analysis can, however, be generalized to long-term policy, which is the choice of a policy for times $T, T+1, T+2, \ldots, T+h$, where $h+1$ is the time horizon of the plan.

Assuming the vector of variables $\mathbf{r}$ summarizes the policy variables to be chosen by the decision maker, the problem of policy evaluation in the short run is that of choosing optimal values for these variables during the current period T, *the short-term optimal policy*:

$$\mathbf{r}_T^* . \qquad *(16.1.1)$$

A *long-term optimal policy* would be summarized by the sequence of current and future values of policy variables:

$$\mathbf{r}_T^*, \mathbf{r}_{T+1}^*, \ldots, \mathbf{r}_{T+h}^*, \qquad *(16.1.2)$$

where $h+1$ is the time horizon of the plan.

While the methodologies to be presented here can be applied to any problem of policy evaluation, whether at the corporate, regional, national, or international level, they are most frequently applied to the evaluation of national economic policy. Some of the policy variables in this area, including fiscal, monetary, and other policy variables, are summarized in Table 16.1. These policy variables together with the (endogenous) variables of Table 12.1 and appropriate nonpolicy exogenous variables (e.g., demographic variables) constitute the variables of a relevant macroeconometric model for national economic policy evaluation, such as those of Chapter 12.

16.2 ALTERNATIVE APPROACHES TO POLICY EVALUATION

In Chapter 15 we explored several different approaches to forecasting, and corresponding approaches exist for policy evaluation. Furthermore, just as Chapter 15 showed that the econometric approach includes several of these approaches as special cases, so too in the area of policy evaluation the various approaches can be considered special cases of the econometric approach.

Expert opinion is the traditional approach to forecasting and it is also the traditional approach to policy evaluation. Indeed, in most areas of policy, the responsibility for selection of a particular policy alternative is assigned to particular people selected on the basis of their expertise. Thus national fiscal policy decisions in the United States are the responsibility of the executive and legislative branches. The president is advised by an Office of Management and Budget, and the Congress is advised by the Congressional Budget Office. The staff members of these organizations are chosen on the basis of their expertise, and their judgments influence,

[1]A related basic issue is the *frequency* of the plan (i.e., how often the plan is revised). The traditional annual plan revised annually has been replaced in many corporations by a three- to five-year plan revised either annually or every six months. Some macroeconometric forecasts (and corresponding policies) extend over six to eight quarters and are revised each quarter. Such a plan is called a *rolling plan*. See Intriligator and Sheshinski (1986).

TABLE 16.1 Policy Variables for the National Economy

Fiscal policy:
Nondefense purchases
Defense purchases
Transfer payments
Effective individual income tax rate
Value of the standard deduction in the individual income tax
Effective corporate tax rate
Investment tax credits
Depreciation tax lives
Social insurance tax rates
Social insurance taxable bases
Excise tax rates
Grants in aid to local authorities
Government employment
Monetary policy:
Unborrowed reserves
Required reserve ratio on demand and time deposits
Discount rate
Ceiling rates on certain types of deposits
Other policy:
Minimum wage rates
Government wage rates
Regulation of certain prices (e.g., certain natural resources, transportation)
Import quotas
Antitrust policy

Note See Table 12.1 for corresponding endogenous variables for the national economy.

to a significant extent, the fiscal policy of the nation. Policy decisions in other areas are also based on expert opinion. Thus major corporations, municipalities, and nonprofit organizations frequently have planning departments staffed by experts responsible for policy evaluation.

The *Delphi method* can be employed for policy evaluation, using an approach similar to that used for forecasting.[2] Opinions of a panel of experts can be merged to obtain a consensus on policy choices. In fact this method is similar to the approach that delegates responsibility for policy to a committee, the principal difference being that the Delphi method involves no face-to-face contact.[3]

Persistence forecasting also has an analog in the area of policy evaluation—that of continuation of the status quo with certain gradual changes, an approach sometimes referred to as *disjointed incrementalism*.[4] Decision makers using this approach analyze marginal

[2]See the discussion of the Delphi method in Section 15.2. A detailed discussion of the *Policy Delphi*, in particular of the manner in which it differs from the ordinary Delphi method, may be found in Turoff (1975). A study using this technique is Buck et al. (1993), where the authors used the Policy Delphi to study differences among interested parties in the values surrounding and approaches to vocational rehabilitation of handicapped persons; the four groups studied were government officials, academics, directors of centers for rehabilitation, and the staff of such centers.

[3]*Indicative planning*, as utilized in France, can be interpreted as a type of Delphi approach to policy. In this approach to planning, individual enterprises submit their plans to a ministry, which formulates a consistent set of estimates for the future course of the economy. These estimates are transmitted back to the individual enterprises, which modify their plans accordingly. The "self-fulfilling prophecy" element in indicative planning is similar to the iteration toward a consensus in the Delphi approach. On French-type planning, see Hickman, Ed. (1965).

[4]See Braybrooke and Lindblom (1963) and Lindblom (1968).

changes rather than global ones. An example of this approach is budgeting.[5] Under disjointed incrementalism decision makers do not decide on an entirely new budget each year. Rather, small changes are made from budget levels of the previous year, with only certain items being closely scrutinized. This approach to policy exemplifies *satisficing*, as opposed to optimizing, behavior. Rather than overall optimizing (e.g., creating an entire budget each year *de novo*), decision makers "satisfice," recognizing the inherent limitations on their capabilities in complex situations. The decision makers do not examine all possible courses of action but rather they search out satisfactory courses that attain certain aspiration levels.[6]

16.3 POLICY EVALUATION USING AN ECONOMETRIC MODEL

In the econometric approach to policy evaluation an estimated econometric model is combined with explicit or implicit information on objectives of policy to evaluate policy alternatives.[7] As shown in Figure 1.1, this evaluation aids in the selection of a desired policy. The chosen policy, together with external events, some of which are inherently stochastic, determines the outcomes, which become the facts to be utilized in future econometric analyses.

Several alternative ways in which an estimated econometric model can be used for policy evaluation are discussed in this chapter. This section develops a framework for treating policy evaluation. This framework and the various approaches to policy evaluation can be perhaps most readily understood in the case of a macroeconometric model, but they are, in fact, applicable to any econometric model that includes policy decisions as predetermined variables.

Consider the structural form of the econometric model as formulated in Section 14.1, but in which the policy variables are shown explicitly:

$$\underset{1\times g}{\mathbf{y}_t}\underset{g\times g}{\boldsymbol{\Gamma}} + \underset{1\times g}{\mathbf{y}_{t-1}}\underset{g\times g}{\mathbf{B}_1} + \underset{1\times k}{\mathbf{z}_t}\underset{k\times g}{\mathbf{B}_2} + \underset{1\times l}{\mathbf{r}_{t-1}}\underset{l\times g}{\mathbf{A}} = \underset{1\times g}{\boldsymbol{\varepsilon}_t}, \qquad t = 1, 2, \ldots, \qquad {*}(16.3.1)$$

Here $\mathbf{y}_t$ is a vector of g endogenous variables, $\mathbf{y}_{t-1}$ is a vector of g lagged endogenous variables, $\mathbf{z}_t$ is a vector of k exogenous variables, and $\boldsymbol{\varepsilon}_t$ is a vector of g stochastic disturbance terms, as before. The vector $\mathbf{r}_{t-1}$ represents l added exogenous variables that are subject to the control of the policymaker. Values of such variables at time $t-1$ influence the system at time t, as shown in the structural form (16.3.1).[8] The policy variables in $\mathbf{r}_{t-1}$ are also called *instruments*, and Table 16.1 summarizes some of these variables for macroeconometric models. The current endogenous variables in $\mathbf{y}_t$ are also called *targets*, for which the policymaker has certain goals, and Table 12.1 summarizes some of these variables for macroeconometric models.[9]

5See Davis, Dempster, and Wildavsky (1966) and Wildavsky (1964).

6See Simon (1955, 1959) and March and Simon (1958).

7Basic references on policy evaluation using an econometric model are Theil (1964), Hickman, Ed. (1965), Fox, Sengupta, and Thorbecke (1966), Klein (1971, 1983), Naylor (1971), Powell and Williams (1973), and Eckstein (1976). See also Greenberger, Crenson, and Crissey (1976), and Bodkin, Klein, Marwah (1991).

8Allowing for a lag in the influence of policy variables is convenient but not essential in this formulation.

9For a discussion of specific instruments and targets (goals) of economic policy in nine Western countries, see Kirschen and Morrisens (1965). Targets include full employment, price stability, an improved balance of payments, and expansion of production, while instruments include public finance, money and credit, exchange rate policy, direct controls, and institutional framework policies. Thus, in a practical case, the target variables will almost always be a proper subset of the group of current endogenous variables, particularly when this group is numerous.

The structural form can be solved for the values of the current endogenous variables if the $\mathbf{\Gamma}$ matrix is nonsingular. The resulting reduced form is:

$$\mathbf{y}_t = -\mathbf{y}_{t-1}\mathbf{B}_1\mathbf{\Gamma}^{-1} - \mathbf{z}_t\mathbf{B}_2\mathbf{\Gamma}^{-1} - \mathbf{r}_{t-1}\mathbf{A}\mathbf{\Gamma}^{-1} + \boldsymbol{\varepsilon}_t\mathbf{\Gamma}^{-1} \tag{16.3.2}$$

determining the endogenous variables as functions of lagged values, noncontrollable exogenous variables, policy variables, and stochastic disturbance terms.

Given this formulation of the econometric model, there are at least three alternative approaches to evaluating policy: the *instrument-targets approach*, the *social-welfare-function approach*, and the *simulation approach*, developed in the next three sections. For all three approaches it is assumed that the coefficients have been estimated to be $\hat{\mathbf{\Gamma}}$, $\hat{\mathbf{B}}_1$, $\hat{\mathbf{B}}_2$, and $\hat{\mathbf{A}}$. It is also assumed that the exogenous variables at the future time $T+1$ have been estimated to be $\hat{\mathbf{z}}_{T+1}$ by some mechanism other than that of the model itself, such as those discussed in Chapter 15. Finally, it is assumed that the stochastic disturbance terms take certain values $\hat{\boldsymbol{\varepsilon}}_{T+1}$, based on information and judgment about factors not explicitly included in the model, as in the case of add factors discussed in Chapter 15. The resulting structural form is:

$$\mathbf{y}_{T+1}\hat{\mathbf{\Gamma}} + \mathbf{y}_T\hat{\mathbf{B}}_1 + \hat{\mathbf{z}}_{T+1}\hat{\mathbf{B}}_2 + \mathbf{r}_T\hat{\mathbf{A}} = \hat{\boldsymbol{\varepsilon}}_{T+1} \qquad *(16.3.3)$$

and the corresponding reduced form is:

$$\mathbf{y}_{T+1} = -\mathbf{y}_T\hat{\mathbf{B}}_1\hat{\mathbf{\Gamma}}^{-1} - \hat{\mathbf{z}}_{T+1}\hat{\mathbf{B}}_2\hat{\mathbf{\Gamma}}^{-1} - \mathbf{r}_T\hat{\mathbf{A}}\hat{\mathbf{\Gamma}}^{-1} + \hat{\boldsymbol{\varepsilon}}_{T+1}\hat{\mathbf{\Gamma}}^{-1} \qquad *(16.3.4)$$

These two systems of equations are basic to the econometric approach to policy evaluation.

A simple specific example is again the prototype macro model, in which the reduced-form equation for national income can be written:

$$Y_t = \Pi_1 Y_{t-1} + \Pi_2 G_t + \Pi_3 + u_t. \tag{16.3.5}$$

Treating government spending G as a policy variable, and assuming that G_{T+1} is related to G_T (e.g., via trend extrapolation), the equation can be written for period $T+1$, using estimates $\hat{\Pi}_1, \hat{\Pi}_2, \hat{\Pi}_3$, and $\hat{u}_{T+1}$, as:

$$Y_{T+1} = \hat{\Pi}_1 Y_T + \hat{\Pi}_2' G_T + \hat{\Pi}_3 + \hat{u}_{T+1}, \qquad *(16.3.6)$$

where Π_2' is related to Π_2 in a simple manner. This is a simple example of the reduced form in (16.3.4)—the endogenous variable being a linear function of its lagged value and the one policy variable.

16.4 THE INSTRUMENTS-TARGETS APPROACH

A first approach to policy evaluation using an estimated econometric model is the *instruments-targets* approach, developed by Tinbergen.[10] This approach is based on two assumptions. The first is that there exist certain desired levels for each of the endogenous variables of the model (16.3.3), given as:

$$\mathbf{y}^0_{T+1}. \qquad *(16.4.1)$$

These are the fixed "targets" of policy. The second assumption is that there are enough policy variables, in particular that the number of policy variables, called "instruments," exceeds or equals the number of endogenous variables:

[10]See Tinbergen (1952, 1954, 1956); see also Hansen (1958).

$$l \geq g. \tag*{*(16.4.2)}$$

The difference $l - g$ is then called the *policy degrees of freedom.*

Consider first the problem with zero policy degrees of freedom, for which $l = g$, so $\mathbf{A}$ in (16.3.1) is a square matrix. Assume further that the estimated coefficient matrix $\hat{\mathbf{A}}$ is nonsingular, so that its inverse $\hat{\mathbf{A}}^{-1}$ exists. Postmultiplying the estimated structural form (16.3.3) by $\hat{\mathbf{A}}^{-1}$ and solving for the optimal values of policy instruments yields:

$$\mathbf{r}_T^* = -\mathbf{y}_{T+1}^0\hat{\mathbf{\Gamma}}\hat{\mathbf{A}}^{-1} - \mathbf{y}_T\hat{\mathbf{B}}_1\hat{\mathbf{A}}^{-1} - \hat{\mathbf{z}}_{T+1}\hat{\mathbf{B}}_2\hat{\mathbf{A}}^{-1} + \hat{\boldsymbol{\varepsilon}}_{T+1}\hat{\mathbf{A}}^{-1}. \tag*{*(16.4.3)}$$

This equation gives optimal values for the instruments $\mathbf{r}_T^*$ as linear functions of the desired values of target variables $\mathbf{y}_{T+1}^0$ (and also of the current values of target variables $\mathbf{y}_T$, the forecasted values of exogenous variables $\hat{\mathbf{z}}_{T+1}$, and the values of the stochastic disturbance terms $\hat{\boldsymbol{\varepsilon}}_{T+1}$). This equation indicates the basic interdependence of policies and objectives. In general, optimal values for each instrument depend on values of all target variables. Only in special circumstances will one instrument correspond to one target variable.[11]

From (16.4.3), the sensitivities of the optimal values of each of the variables to the desired values of each of the target variables can be readily determined. These sensitivities are summarized by:

$$\frac{\partial \mathbf{r}_T^*}{\partial \mathbf{y}_{T+1}^0} = -\hat{\mathbf{\Gamma}}\hat{\mathbf{A}}^{-1}, \tag{16.4.4}$$

which gives the impact of a change in any $\mathbf{y}_{T+1}^0$ on any $\mathbf{r}_T^*$.[12] Similarly, the impacts of $\mathbf{y}_T$, $\hat{\mathbf{z}}_{T+1}$, and $\hat{\boldsymbol{\varepsilon}}_{T+1}$ on $\mathbf{r}_T^*$ can be determined from (16.4.3).

In the case of a problem with positive policy degrees of freedom, a similar approach can be utilized. In such a case $l - g$ of the policy variables can be specified a priori at convenient levels, taking care that the reduced-form square coefficient matrix associated with the instruments having "free" values remains nonsingular. The remaining problem is then one with zero policy degrees of freedom, which can be solved as in (16.4.3).

In the case of the prototype macro model $l = g = 1$, so given a desired target value for the endogenous variable Y_{T+1}^0 the implied optimal value for the instrument variable G_T^* is given by solving (16.3.6) for G_T:

$$G_T^* = \frac{Y_{T+1}^0 - \hat{\Pi}_1 Y_T - \hat{\Pi}_3 - \hat{u}_{T+1}}{\hat{\Pi}_2'}. \tag{16.4.5}$$

Thus

$$\frac{\partial G_T^*}{\partial Y_{T+1}^0} = \frac{1}{\hat{\Pi}_2'}, \tag{16.4.6}$$

showing how a change in desired national income is translated into a change in the optimal level of government expenditure.[13]

[11]See Problem 16-B. Problem 16-D asks the reader to redo the algebra for the special case in which the target variables are a proper subset of the current endogenous variables.

[12]Do not confuse the elements of (16.4.4) with multipliers. Multipliers usually give the multiple effect of policy variables on endogenous variables, whereas the elements of (16.4.4) give the sensitivities of optimal policy variables to changes in the target endogenous variables. See Section 16.6 for a further discussion of policy multipliers.

[13]As in footnote 12, do not confuse this partial derivative with the multiplier $\partial Y_T/\partial G_T$, showing the effect of government expenditure on the level of national income.

The instruments-targets approach to policy evaluation has been utilized in modified form in the Netherlands by the Central Planning Bureau. Short-term stabilization policy has been formulated on the basis of an estimated econometric model and target values of endogenous variables.[14] Another example of use of the instruments-targets approach is the setting of target growth rates by international development funds of the UN and other organizations. In this case, capital transfers, treated as the instruments, can be computed on the basis of the target growth rates.

The instruments-targets approach has four serious difficulties. One is that it assumes there are no trade-offs among the targets, but rather specifies fixed values for each. The second is that it is doubtful that policymakers would or perhaps even could reveal specific target choices. The third is that of a shortage of independent instruments. The fourth difficulty is that the target chosen may be infeasible. For example, in a linear system this difficulty would become evident in having a solution value for at least one of the instruments that takes an impossible negative value. The first and fourth difficulties, but not the other two, are overcome by the social-welfare-function approach discussed in the next section. Finally, this approach is subject to all the other difficulties inherent in the use of econometric models, namely data errors, imperfect parameter estimation, misspecification, and structural change.

16.5 THE SOCIAL-WELFARE-FUNCTION APPROACH; OPTIMAL CONTROL

A second approach to policy evaluation using an estimated econometric model such as (16.3.3) is via a *social welfare function*, as developed by Theil.[15] This approach relaxes the assumptions of the instruments-targets approach. Rather than assuming specific desired targets for each endogenous variable, as in (16.4.1), it assumes the existence of a social welfare function, determining a scalar measure of performance on the basis of both endogenous and policy variables:[16]

$$W = W(\mathbf{y}_{T+1}, \mathbf{r}_T). \qquad *(16.5.1)$$

The endogenous variables $\mathbf{y}_{T+1}$ affect welfare directly, while the policy variables $\mathbf{r}_T$ can affect welfare if, for example, there are costs associated with use of such variables. With this approach it is not necessary to make the policy degrees-of-freedom assumption of the instruments-targets approach.

The social welfare function can incorporate information about trade-offs in objectives that the target levels in (16.4.1) do not allow. Thus holding welfare constant and taking a total differential yields

$$dW = \sum_{g'=1}^{g} \frac{\partial W}{\partial y_{g',T+1}} dy_{g',T+1} + \sum_{l'=1}^{l} \frac{\partial W}{\partial r_{l',T}} dr_{l',T} = 0, \qquad (16.5.2)$$

[14]See Hickman, Ed. (1965).

[15]See Theil (1961, 1964, 1965).

[16]Do not confuse this Theil social welfare function, a function of levels of endogenous and policy variables, with a Bergson-type social welfare function, a function of individual levels of utility. The approach here makes no explicit reference to or connection with individual utility functions.

indicating joint changes in the current endogenous variables and policy variables for which welfare does not change. In particular, if only $y_{1,T+1}$ and $y_{2,T+1}$ change, it follows that:

$$\left.\frac{dy_{1,T+1}}{dy_{2,T+1}}\right|_{W=\text{constant}} = -\frac{\partial W/\partial y_{2,T+1}}{\partial W/\partial y_{1,T+1}}. \tag{16.5.3}$$

This expression gives the trade-off between the first and second endogenous variables. If they change according to (16.5.3), welfare W does not change.

The social welfare function may or may not be based on the existence of certain desired values of endogenous (and policy) variables. If such desired values do exist, given by $\mathbf{y}^0_{T+1}$ and $\mathbf{r}^0_T$, respectively, the social welfare function is often assumed to be quadratic, of the form:

$$W = -\tfrac{1}{2}(\mathbf{y}_{T+1} - \mathbf{y}^0_{T+1})\mathbf{E}(\mathbf{y}_{T+1} - \mathbf{y}^0_{T+1})' - \tfrac{1}{2}(\mathbf{r}_T - \mathbf{r}^0_T)\mathbf{F}(\mathbf{r}_T - \mathbf{r}^0_T)', \qquad *(16.5.4)$$

where $\mathbf{E}$ and $\mathbf{F}$ are given constant positive-definite symmetric matrices.[17] In this case the maximum value of W is attained when the variables are at their desired levels:

$$\mathbf{y}_{T+1} = \mathbf{y}^0_{T+1}, \qquad \mathbf{r}_T = \mathbf{r}^0_T, \tag{16.5.5}$$

in which case $W = 0$.

Returning to the general welfare function of (16.5.1), the social-welfare-function approach to policy evaluation involves the choice of policy variables $\mathbf{r}_T$ so as to maximize the value of social welfare subject to the constraints of the basic estimated econometric model—that is,

$$\max_{\mathbf{r}_T} W(\mathbf{y}_{T+1}, \mathbf{r}_T) \quad \text{subject to} \quad \mathbf{y}_{T+1}\hat{\mathbf{\Gamma}} + \mathbf{y}_T\hat{\mathbf{B}}_1 + \hat{\mathbf{z}}_{T+1}\hat{\mathbf{B}}_2 + \mathbf{r}_T\hat{\mathbf{A}} = \hat{\boldsymbol{\varepsilon}}_{T+1}. \qquad *(16.5.6)$$

If $\hat{\mathbf{\Gamma}}$ is nonsingular, so the reduced form of the econometric model is:

$$\mathbf{y}_{T+1} = -\mathbf{y}_T\hat{\mathbf{B}}_1\hat{\mathbf{\Gamma}}^{-1} - \hat{\mathbf{z}}_{T+1}\hat{\mathbf{B}}_2\hat{\mathbf{\Gamma}}^{-1} - \mathbf{r}_T\hat{\mathbf{A}}\hat{\mathbf{\Gamma}}^{-1} + \hat{\boldsymbol{\varepsilon}}_{T+1}\hat{\mathbf{\Gamma}}^{-1}, \tag{16.5.7}$$

then this problem, which is one of classical programming, can be solved by the method of substitution.[18] Solving for $\mathbf{y}_{T+1}$ from the constraint, and inserting this value in the social welfare function, the problem becomes that of the unconstrained maximization of

$$W = W\left(-\mathbf{y}_T\hat{\mathbf{B}}_1\hat{\mathbf{\Gamma}}^{-1} - \hat{\mathbf{z}}_{T+1}\hat{\mathbf{B}}_2\hat{\mathbf{\Gamma}}^{-1} - \mathbf{r}_T\hat{\mathbf{A}}\hat{\mathbf{\Gamma}}^{-1} + \hat{\boldsymbol{\varepsilon}}_{T+1}\hat{\mathbf{\Gamma}}^{-1}, \mathbf{r}_T\right). \tag{16.5.8}$$

Using the chain rule, maximizing by choice of $\mathbf{r}_T$ requires that:

$$\left(\frac{\partial W}{\partial \mathbf{r}_T}\right)' = \hat{\mathbf{A}}\hat{\mathbf{\Gamma}}^{-1}\left(\frac{\partial W}{\partial \mathbf{y}_{T+1}}\right)'. \qquad *(16.5.9)$$

These are the first-order necessary conditions for maximizing the social welfare function subject to the constraints of the estimated econometric model.

In the quadratic case with certain desired levels of both endogenous and policy variables, for which the social welfare function is given in (16.5.4), the first-order necessary conditions (16.5.9) require that:

[17] The $\frac{1}{2}$ factors are included here simply for the sake of convenience. In differentiating the quadratic form the factors of 2 cancel the factors of $\frac{1}{2}$. It might be noted that the quadratic form is a convenient one that may be a reasonable approximation in a limited range around the values under consideration. In some instances, however, particularly away from the values under consideration, it may be inappropriate. Sometimes piecewise quadratic forms, each relevant in a particular range, are used to overcome this problem (see Friedman, 1975).

[18] See Intriligator (1971) for a discussion of classical programming.

$$\mathbf{F}(\mathbf{r}_T - \mathbf{r}_T^0)' = \hat{\mathbf{A}}\hat{\mathbf{\Gamma}}^{-1}\mathbf{E}(\mathbf{y}_{T+1} - \mathbf{y}_{T+1}^0)'. \tag{16.5.10}$$

Solving for $\mathbf{r}_T$ yields, since $\mathbf{E}$ and $\mathbf{F}$ are symmetric matrices and $\mathbf{F}$ is nonsingular (as it is positive definite), the optimal values of the policy variables:

$$\mathbf{r}_T^* = \mathbf{r}_T^0 + (\mathbf{y}_{T+1} - \mathbf{y}_{T+1}^0)\mathbf{E}(\hat{\mathbf{\Gamma}}')^{-1}\hat{\mathbf{A}}'\mathbf{F}^{-1}. \qquad *(16.5.11)$$

Thus the policy variables are optimally determined by starting at the desired levels and adjusting according to the deviations of the endogenous variables from their desired levels. This result is referred to as a *linear decision rule*, since it gives the optimal values for the policy variables as linear functions of the endogenous variables of the problem. A linear decision rule always results from maximizing a quadratic (social welfare) function subject to a linear (econometric) model.[19]

In the case of the prototype macro model, the social-welfare-function approach problem becomes:

$$\max_{G_T} W(Y_{T+1}, G_T) \quad \text{subject to} \quad Y_{T+1} = \hat{\Pi}_1 Y_T + \hat{\Pi}_2' G_T + \hat{\Pi}_3 + \hat{u}_{T+1}. \tag{16.5.12}$$

Assuming, for example, a quadratic welfare function, where Y_{T+1}^0 is the desired level of national income and G_T^0 is the desired level of government expenditure, of the form:

$$W = -\tfrac{1}{2}e(Y_{T+1} - Y_{T+1}^0)^2 - \tfrac{1}{2}f(G_T - G_T^0)^2, \tag{16.5.13}$$

the optimal government expenditure is given as:

$$G_T^* = G_T^0 - \frac{e}{f}\hat{\Pi}_2'(Y_{T+1} - Y_{T+1}^0). \tag{16.5.14}$$

Thus the optimal policy adjusts the desired level of government expenditure by a linear function of the difference between actual and desired national income. This type of policy, for which the corrective action is proportional to and of opposite sign to the error, here given as $Y_{T+1} - Y_{T+1}^0$, is called *proportional stabilization policy*.[20]

Van den Bogaard and Theil used the social-welfare-function approach in order to study policies that the United States might have pursued in the Great Depression.[21] The econo-

[19]See van Eijk and Sandee (1959), Holt et al. (1960), Holt (1962), and Theil (1964). In addition to a linear decision rule, problems involving a quadratic objective function and linear constraints generally exhibit *certainty equivalence*, in that the solution to the problem of maximizing expected welfare can be obtained by replacing random variables by their expected values. This result provides a justification for replacing the stochastic disturbance terms in the basic econometric model by their expected values of zero.

[20]See Phillips (1954, 1957) for a comparison of three types of policy, *proportional stabilization policy*, for which:

$$A(t) = -kE(t),$$

where A is the action at time t, E is the error (actual level less desired level), and k is a constant; *derivative stabilization policy*, for which:

$$A(t) = -k\frac{dE(t)}{dt};$$

and *integral stabilization policy*, for which:

$$A(t) = -k\int_{t_0}^{t} E(\tau)\,d\tau.$$

[21]See van den Bogaard and Theil (1959). Other examples of the use of the social welfare function appear in van Eijk and Sandee (1959), Fromm and Taubman (1968), and Fromm (1969a,b).

metric model they employed was the Klein interwar model, introduced in Section 12.2. Their objective function was of the quadratic type:

$$W = -\tfrac{1}{2}\left(\mathbf{y}_{T+1} - \mathbf{y}^0_{T+1}\right)\left(\mathbf{y}_{T+1} - \mathbf{y}^0_{T+1}\right)' - \tfrac{1}{2}\left(\mathbf{r}_T - \mathbf{r}^0_T\right)\left(\mathbf{r}_T - \mathbf{r}^0_T\right)', \qquad (16.5.15)$$

as in (16.5.4), where here the **E** and **F** matrices of (16.5.4) are both identity matrices. The endogenous variables $\mathbf{y}_{T+1}$ were consumption per capita, investment per capita, and a distribution variable giving the relation of profits to private wages. The target values of these variables $\mathbf{y}^0_{T+1}$ were their 1929 levels, the intent being to bring the depression to an end by restoring these endogenous variables to their predepression levels. The policy (instrument) variables $\mathbf{r}_T$ were (total) government wages, business taxes, and government expenditure on goods and services.[22] The target values of these variables $\mathbf{r}^0_T$ were obtained by simple extrapolation of time trends established over the period 1920–1932. The period under consideration was the first administration of President Franklin Roosevelt, extending from 1933 to 1936, and the objective function minimizes the expected value of the sum of the squares of the deviations of endogenous variables and policy variables from desired or target levels over the entire four-year period.

Van den Bogaard and Theil solved for the optimal behavior of the instruments given the objective function and the estimated model. They found the largest deviations between optimal and actual values for government expenditure on goods and services. For example, government expenditure should have been approximately \$14 billion in 1933, approximately \$5 billion higher than its actual value, and \$13 billion in 1936, \$3 billion higher than its actual value, all money magnitudes being in dollars of 1934 purchasing power. While optimal levels of business taxes were higher than actual levels, in part because of the inclusion of a target for the distribution of income, optimal national income exhibits an even greater deviation from realized levels, so tax *rates* are optimally *reduced*. Government wages are optimally somewhat higher than actual levels in 1933 but lower in the later years, optimal government wages being over \$1 billion *lower* than the realized figure of approximately \$7 billion for 1936.

The social-welfare-function approach can be extended to the determination of long-term optimal policy over the time period from T to $T+h$, as in (16.1.2), via *optimal control*.[23] In this approach an objective function for the entire time period is chosen and maximized by choice of time paths for the policy instruments subject to the constraint of the estimated econometric model in each period. An example of such an objective function, to be maximized by choice of $\mathbf{r}_T, \mathbf{r}_{T+1}, \ldots, \mathbf{r}_{T+h}$, is:

$$W = -\tfrac{1}{2} \sum_{t=T+1}^{T+h+1} \left[w_u\left(u_t - u^0_t\right)^2 + w_i\left(i_t - i^0_t\right)^2\right], \qquad (16.5.16)$$

[22]It might be noted that monetary variables, which Friedman and Schwartz (1963) found to be of crucial importance in explaining the Great Depression, were ignored here. Note that the group of endogenous variables that enter the social welfare function here is not the totality of endogenous variables of the model, but rather, a proper subset. This is often true, particularly for very large econometric models, as individual components may generally be of importance only as part of a larger total.

[23]See Pindyck (1973) and Klein (1983). For the mathematical theory of optimal control over continuous time, see Intriligator (1971).

where u_t is the rate of unemployment at time t, u_t^0 the target rate of unemployment, i_t the rate of inflation at time t, and i_t^0 the target rate of inflation.[24] The weights w_u and w_i determine the importance of the unemployment goal relative to the inflation goal. Optimal policies for this example might include time paths for monetary policy variables, fiscal policy variables, and other policy variables, as in Table 16.1. This approach determines the optimal timing as well as the optimal level for such policy variables.

A major problem with the social-welfare-function approach, whether of the short-run form, as in (16.5.1), or of the long-run optimal control form, as in (16.5.16), is that the parameters and even the specific form of the objective function are not known and cannot be elicited from policymakers in any practical way. (This is in addition to standard qualifications relating to the use of an estimated econometric model.) Thus alternative approaches that do not rely upon the specification of an explicit objective function (or explicit targets) would be useful. One such approach is that of policy simulation, described in the next section.

16.6 THE SIMULATION APPROACH

A third approach to policy evaluation using an estimated econometric model is *simulation*.[25] This approach avoids the necessity of assuming either the existence of desired levels of endogenous variables, as in the instruments-targets approach, or the existence of a well-defined objective function to be maximized, as in the social-welfare-function approach.

In general, *simulation* refers to the determination of the behavior of a system via the calculation of values from an estimated model of the system.[26] The model is assumed to be sufficiently explicit so that it can be programmed for numerical study, typically using a computer. The system's numerical behavior is then determined (simulated) under different assumptions in order to analyze its response to a variety of alternative inputs. Each simulation run is an experiment performed on the model, determining values of endogenous variables for alternative assumptions regarding the policy variables, other exogenous variables, stochastic disturbance terms, and values of parameters.[27]

In a *simulation run*, data on the values of the policy and other exogenous variables, together with estimated values of parameters and stochastic disturbance terms, are used to calculate the values of the endogenous variables from the equations of the model. The simulation run can, in fact, take several forms. A *historical simulation* refers to the computa-

[24]Note that the sum in (16.5.16) ranges from $T+1$ to $T+h+1$ because of the one-period lag in the effect of policy variables, which range from T to $T+h$. The short-run single-period case here corresponds to $h=0$. Also note that (16.5.16) gives each period equal weight, which was also the case in the study of van den Bogaard and Theil. Alternative weights might be treated (e.g., discounting future periods). The choice of a social rate of discount is indeed one of the most important, as well as one of the most subtle, choices that must be made in a *working* study of optimal economic policy.

[25]See Fromm and Taubman (1968), Naylor, Wertz, and Wonnacott (1968), Fromm (1969a,b), Naylor (1971), Howrey and Kelejian (1971), Duggal (1975), Eckstein (1976, 1983), and Klein (1983).

[26]See Orcutt (1960), Shubik (1960), Clarkson and Simon (1960), Orcutt et al. (1961), Naylor et al. (1968), and Naylor (1971).

[27]The stochastic disturbance terms can be either specified a priori at given levels (e.g., their expected values of zero) or chosen via random drawings from a distribution with the appropriate characteristics (here, the means and covariances). The latter case is that of *Monte Carlo analysis*. Section 10.9 used this type of analysis to study small-sample properties of estimators, but it can also be applied, as here, to the study of alternative policy choices in an estimated stochastic model.

tion of estimated values of endogenous variables for the sample actually observed, using historical values of exogenous variables (as in ex-post forecasts) and estimated parameters. These simulated values can then be compared to actual values in order to determine whether the model accurately "tracks" the historical period. A failure to "track" should suggest that the model be reformulated.[28] A second type of simulation is a *projection*, which forecasts values of endogenous variables beyond the sample, as discussed in the last chapter. The third type of simulation, the one emphasized here, is a *policy simulation*, which determines values of the endogenous variables for alternative assumed sets of values of policy variables, corresponding to the alternative policies that are under consideration.

For purposes of policy simulation with a linear model, it is most convenient to use the reduced form, as in (16.3.4):

$$\mathbf{y}_{T+1} = -\mathbf{r}_T\hat{\mathbf{A}}\hat{\mathbf{\Gamma}}^{-1} - \mathbf{y}_T\hat{\mathbf{B}}_1\hat{\mathbf{\Gamma}}^{-1} - \hat{\mathbf{z}}_{T+1}\hat{\mathbf{B}}_2\hat{\mathbf{\Gamma}}^{-1} + \hat{\boldsymbol{\varepsilon}}_{T+1}\hat{\mathbf{\Gamma}}^{-1}, \tag{16.6.1}$$

which expresses the future values of endogenous variables as linear functions of current policy variables, current endogenous variables, future exogenous variables, and future stochastic disturbance terms.[29] Specific estimated values are assumed: for the coefficient matrices $\hat{\mathbf{A}}$, $\hat{\mathbf{B}}_1$, $\hat{\mathbf{B}}_2$ $\hat{\mathbf{\Gamma}}$; for the future exogenous variables $\hat{\mathbf{z}}_{T+1}$; and for stochastic disturbance terms $\hat{\boldsymbol{\varepsilon}}_{T+1}$. The values assumed for the coefficient matrices are based on estimates of the system, while the future values assumed for the exogenous variables and stochastic disturbance terms are based on results of other models, on extrapolations of trends, or on judgment.

The simulation approach uses this estimated reduced-form system to provide policymakers with a "menu" of alternatives from which they can pick a desired alternative. The "menu" can be presented as in Table 16.2, where the option numbers simply index the set of alternative policies.[30] The policymakers would then select a particular alternative $\mathbf{r}_T^*$, $\mathbf{y}_{T+1}^*$ according to their preferences, which may depend on both the policy variables and the endogenous variables.[31] Conceptually, the result is similar to that of the earlier approaches,

TABLE 16.2 Simulated Effects of Alternative Policy Options

Option Number	Current Policy	Future Endogenous Variables
1	$\mathbf{r}_T^1$	$\mathbf{y}_{T+1}^1$
2	$\mathbf{r}_T^2$	$\mathbf{y}_{T+1}^2$
3	$\mathbf{r}_T^3$	$\mathbf{y}_{T+1}^3$
.	.	.
.	.	.
.	.	.

[28]Various measures of accuracy can be employed, some of which have been discussed in Chapter 15 (see especially Section 15.5).

[29]If the model is nonlinear, the solution for the endogenous variables is usually obtained using an iterative solution technique, such as the Gauss–Seidel algorithm. The Brookings, Wharton, and MPS models discussed in Chapter 12 all use this approach (see Klein, 1983; Section 14.6; and footnote 66 of Chapter 12).

[30]The table can be extended to consider entire time paths for both policy and endogenous variables (e.g., $\mathbf{r}_T^1$, $\mathbf{r}_{T+1}^1$, $\mathbf{r}_{T+2}^1$, . . . , and $\mathbf{y}_{T+1}^1$, $\mathbf{y}_{T+2}^1$, $\mathbf{y}_{T+3}^1$, . . . for option 1).

[31]Alternative simulations could, in fact, be developed depending on alternative assumptions as to the predicted future values of exogenous variables $\hat{\mathbf{z}}_{T+1}$. For example, different contingencies can be assumed for consumer or investment behavior in simulating a macroeconometric model. Such alternative simulations represent a substitute for explicit probabilistic forecasts.

but operationally it is quite different. The difference arises from the fact that it does not require the policymaker to state either specific targets or an entire social welfare function; rather, it requires only that he or she choose a policy, given the implications of each alternative policy option.

One way to interpret the simulation approach is that of experimentation within the model system. Rather than "trying out" alternative policies in the real world, the simulation approach "tries out" these alternatives within the model system. The results of these experiments, specifically the implied future values of endogenous variables, indicate to the policymaker the implications of each alternative policy. In this interpretation the estimated econometric model serves as a type of "laboratory" for policy alternatives. Just as a wind tunnel is used to test alternative configurations of aerodynamic bodies, an estimated econometric model is used to test alternative configurations of policy choices.[32] The alternative outcomes can each be regarded as a type of controlled experiment in the model system, where controlled experimentation in the real-world system is virtually impossible.

The method of policy simulation frequently uses *policy multipliers*. For the linear model (16.6.1) the policy multipliers can be obtained as:

$$\frac{\partial \mathbf{y}_{T+1}}{\partial \mathbf{r}_T} = -\hat{\mathbf{A}}\hat{\mathbf{\Gamma}}^{-1}, \tag{16.6.2}$$

giving the effect on each of the endogenous variables of a change in any of the policy variables. The total effect on the endogenous variable g of a change in each of the l policy variables can then be obtained by summing the separate effects of each of the policy variables, as in:

$$\Delta y_{g',T+1} = \sum_{l'=1}^{l} \frac{\partial y_{g',T+1}}{\partial r_{l',T}} \Delta r_{l',T}. \tag{16.6.3}$$

If the model is large, so the computation of $\hat{\mathbf{\Gamma}}^{-1}$ in (16.6.2) is cumbersome, or, as in Section 14.6, if the model is nonlinear, the policy multipliers can be obtained from the computation of two dynamic simulations. One is a "base run" using anticipated or status quo values of all exogenous variables and all policy variables. The other uses the same values for all exogenous variables and all policy variables, except that one policy variable is augmented by a unit amount. The differences in the resulting values for the endogenous variables for the two simulations can then be attributed to the particular policy variable that was changed. These differences can be interpreted as the policy multipliers, showing the effects on the endogenous variables, over time, of unit policy changes.[33] The overall effects of a set of policy changes can then be obtained by summing the separate effects of each, where each effect is the product of the corresponding change in the policy variable and the relevant policy multiplier, as in (16.6.3), provided that the model is at least approximately linear.

In the case of the prototype macro model, the simulation approach would be based on solving:

[32]Some have referred to this approach as "nondestructive testing" of economic policies, in contrast to the destructive testing in quality control problems or, more seriously, the "testing" of an ill-advised economic policy on an actual economy. Simulation can be based, as here, on an estimated econometric model. It can, however, also be used in other contexts, such as the system dynamics models of Forrester, cited in Chapter 2. For an application to a regional analysis, see Hamilton et al. (1969).

[33]See Fromm and Taubman (1968), Christ (1975), Fromm and Klein (1976), and Adams and Klein (1991).

$$Y_{T+1} = \hat{\Pi}_1 Y_T + \hat{\Pi}_2' G_T + \hat{\Pi}_3 + \hat{u}_{T+1} \tag{16.6.4}$$

for Y_{T+1}, future national income, given alternative values of government expenditure G_T and perhaps also alternative values of Y_T and $\hat{u}_{T+1}$ and alternative assumptions regarding the coefficients $\hat{\Pi}_1$, $\hat{\Pi}_2'$, and $\hat{\Pi}_3$. The single policy multiplier in this case is:

$$\frac{\partial Y_{T+1}}{\partial G_T} = \hat{\Pi}_2'. \tag{16.6.5}$$

Of course, this example is highly simplified. Simulation becomes relatively more valuable as an approach when the system is large, complex, and nonlinear.

One advantage of the simulation approach is that it facilitates a synthesis of subjective judgmental factors on the part of decision makers and objective analysis using an estimated econometric model, as in the add factors of the last chapter. Subjective considerations enter at several points in the simulation approach. First, the particular set of alternative policies to be investigated is chosen largely on the basis of subjective factors. Second, the simulation itself includes add factors to take account of expert judgment, as represented by $\hat{\boldsymbol{\varepsilon}}_{T+1}$, the values taken by the stochastic disturbance terms. Finally, the choice of a specific policy based on the various simulated results of alternative policies involves subjective judgments, which need not be made explicit, concerning the objectives of policy.

Of course, it should not be considered that the simulation approach represents a panacea, the solution to all the model builder's (or model user's) problems. There always exist the standard problems with an estimated econometric model, such as data errors, imperfect parameter estimation, a whole host of econometric problems (of which misspecification of the model is probably the most serious), and possible structural change between the period of estimation and the period of use. Most of these problems were mentioned at the end of Section 16.4. In addition, there are some inherent limitations to the simulation technique as well. No matter how many simulations the model specialist runs for the decision maker, there is no guarantee that the crucial simulation, yielding a much higher level of satisfaction for the decision maker, might not have been achieved on a simulation that the model specialist failed to run. This is unfortunate, but it is inherent in the use of a framework in which optimization is not carried out explicitly.

Three examples of the simulation approach involved use of the Brookings model of the U.S. economy to study fiscal and monetary policy. Klein analyzed the income tax cut of 1964, Fromm and Taubman analyzed the excise tax cut of 1965, and Fromm analyzed monetary and fiscal policy.[34] Klein solved the Brookings model for time paths of endogenous variables both with the tax rates prevailing in 1963 (the status quo) and with the new tax rates after the 1964 cut. These two solutions were then compared to determine the various impacts of the tax cut. Fromm and Taubman used the Brookings model to compare the situation that would have prevailed without the excise tax cut of 1965 to the situation with the tax cut. Excise taxes were considered in the context of taxes on broad commodity classes, and alternative assumptions were made as to how much of the tax cut was "absorbed" by producers and how much was "passed on" to consumers. Fromm used the Brookings model to analyze two fiscal policies (government purchase of durables and

[34]See Klein (1969), Fromm and Taubman (1968), and Fromm (1969a). For an econometric analysis of the 1968 tax surcharge using the Wharton model, see Klein (1974).

changes in federal personal income tax rates) and four monetary policies (changes in the discount rate, in the demand deposit reserve ratio, in the time deposit reserve ratio, and in unborrowed reserves). All three analyses were useful retrospective studies of how monetary and fiscal policies affect the economy.[35] While these studies were not used to *plan* policy, a similar methodology has been employed to determine the impacts of alternative policies *prior* to the choice of a particular policy. In fact, policy simulations conducted in and out of government have been a principal method of deriving and testing economic policies.

16.7 THE OPTIONS FOR CANADIAN POLICYMAKERS AT THE BEGINNING OF THE 1980S AND TWO OTHER EXAMPLES

Another example of the use of econometric models to consider policy alternatives is that of the CANDIDE model of the Canadian economy, described briefly in Section 12.8. Over the 15-year period 1972–1987, the CANDIDE model was used to make medium-term projections of the Canadian economy, usually under a variety of alternative hypotheses concerning the evolution of the exogenous variables. As some of these exogenous variables were, in fact, policy instruments of the type listed in Table 16.1, the users of the CANDIDE model at the Economic Council of Canada were able to generate a variety of alternative policy scenarios for their various *Annual Reviews*, which reviewed the macroeconomic performance of the Canadian economy.[36]

As an example of the use of the CANDIDE model to evaluate macroeconomic policy alternatives, consider the *Sixteenth Annual Review*, published in Autumn 1979, with the ironic subtitle, *Two Cheers for the Eighties*. To review the situation at the time, the Canadian economy had just entered the recession of 1979–1980, with the unemployment rate approaching 8% of the labor force and inflation, as measured by the annual change in the consumer price index, above 8%. Oil prices were rising dramatically, both in Canada and especially on the international scene, as the world price of oil had risen from \$12 (U.S.) to \$30 a barrel. The Canadian dollar was weakening in relation to the U.S. dollar, and the federal government deficit was just starting to become a problem. A larger recession in 1981–1982 was to follow shortly, but, of course, that was not known with certainty at that

[35] A related historical type of study uses simulation to analyze how various alternative policies might have affected the economy. Klein (1971), for example, reports on two studies of the 1929–1933 era involving simulation of alternative monetary and fiscal policies in the Great Depression. These studies indicated that simple monetary and fiscal policies could have substantially mitigated the Great Depression, a finding consistent with those of van den Bogaard and Theil (1959) discussed in Section 16.5. Klein also mentions studies of disarmament and currency revaluation using estimated econometric models.

[36] This series of studies began with the *Ninth Annual Review*, also entitled *The Years to 1980*, in which a number of policy alternatives were studied to return the Canadian economy, starting in 1971, to a "full-employment" growth path in which the rate of unemployment would average 4% of the labor force, in contrast to the 5.8% rate recorded during the 1969–1970 recession. It was also hoped that the model would be useful in constructing some "performance indicators," which were viewed as intermediate targets of economic performance that would be useful to business and public decision makers, along the lines of French indicative planning. As it turned out, the *Ninth Annual Review* projections proved to be overly optimistic, while the decentralized nature of the Canadian politico-economic system meant that the social gains from the exchange of information were relatively small.

time. The newly elected Conservative government had a number of options, which can be summarized as five possible courses of action.

The reference solution (number 3) was a middle-of-the-road set of policies in which fiscal policy was basically left neutral and monetary policy was geared to increasing the supply of money annually by 9%, policies consistent with the Bank of Canada's "monetarist" approach at that time. Solution 1, termed the "highly stimulative" one, involved an investment tax credit, a cut in corporate income tax rates, and a cut in personal income tax rates, carrying a fiscal cost of approximately $6 billion, spread roughly equally among these three components. Solution 2, termed the "stimulative" one, involved two of the three elements of solution 1, but omitted the personal income tax cut. Solution 4, termed "stimulative with offset," provided the investment tax credit and the cut in corporate income tax rates, but included an increase in personal income tax rates, designed to recoup the revenue losses from these two programs and indeed to add a modest amount to deficit reduction. Finally, solution 5, termed the one with "restraint" or, less formally, with a "cold shower," entailed only the personal income tax rate increases of solution 4, but no investment tax credit and no cut in corporate income tax rates and with the rate of growth of the money supply cut from 9% to 6% annually.

The medium-term results of these policy alternatives, as applied in late 1979 and held through the period to 1985, are shown in Table 16.3 and their implications for the trade-offs between inflation and unemployment are illustrated in Figure 16.1 None of these alternatives provided a reasonably satisfactory outcome for the Canadian economy over the period 1983–1985 and, in fact, the actual outcome was considerably different from any of these, due in part to the pronounced recession of 1981–1982, which, of course, was imperfectly foreseen at the time. Nevertheless, these simulations, perhaps augmented by some unconventional policy alternatives to improve the inflation–unemployment trade-off, could have been used to guide Canadian policymakers at the beginning of the 1980s.[37]

A contemporaneous study that used the LINK system of macroeconometric models (also summarized in Section 12.8) to study a simultaneous easing of monetary policy in 17 leading economies of the world is that of Klein, Simes, and Voisin.[38] The basic idea was

TABLE 16.3 Average Rate of Growth (Percent) of Real National Product, Consumer Price Level, and Average Rate of Unemployment, under Various Policy Settings, 1983–1985

Policy Setting	Averate Rate of Growth of Real GNP, 1983–1985	Average Rate of Change of CPI, 1983–1985	Average Rate of Unemployment, 1983–1985
1. Highly stimulative	3.6	9.25	4.1
2. Stimulative	3.57	9.07	4.3
3. Reference	3.3	8.77	4.87
4. Stimulative with offset	3.17	8.6	4.9
5. Restraint	2.87	8.1	5.47

Sources Bodkin (1982) and Preston et al. (1979).

[37]For more details, see the Economic Council of Canada (1979), Preston et al. (1979), and Bodkin (1982).

[38]See Klein, Simes, and Voisin (1981). These leading economies were Australia, Austria, Belgium, Canada, Denmark, Finland, France, Germany, Greece, Italy, Japan, the Netherlands, Norway, Sweden, Switzerland, the United Kingdom, and the United States.

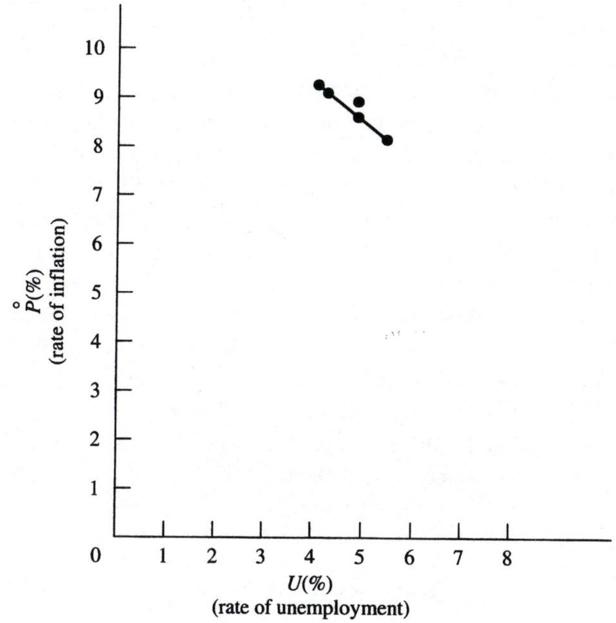

Figure 16.1 Medium-Term Trade-off Curve for the Canadian Economy, 1983–1985, CANDIDE Simulations
Source Table 16.3.

that while an independent easing of monetary policy in one country ran the risk of either capital outflows (due to lowered domestic interest rates) or of increased inflation (due, in part, to a weakened currency or a depreciated exchange rate), a simultaneous approach to easier monetary policy by the leading industrial economies of the world should obviate these dangers. Although the techniques of monetary easing varied according to individual models,[39] Klein, Simes, and Voisin simulated the effects of such coordinated ease in monetary policy over the four years 1980–1983. In the event, the results were most gratifying. For the typical industrial country, real domestic (or national) product and output per worker rose above control levels, while unemployment rates eased, often considerably. By contrast, price pressures from a more stimulative approach to macroeconomic policy were modest, according to the model simulations, and the coordinated approach to stabilization policy apparently prevented major problems with the individual countries' balance of payments. Finally, the authors noted that the effects for the less developed countries included in the LINK system appeared to be beneficial, also.[40]

[39]In some cases the money supply was increased above control levels, and in other cases a key interest rate under the control of the central bank was eased. In a few cases where the financial sector was judged inadequately developed, private domestic investment was increased by the use of an add factor.

[40]More recent simulations of macroeconomic policy in an international context may be found in Bryant, Hooper, and Mann (1993). In particular, these authors conclude (subject to a number of qualifications) that nominal income targeting (or focusing on the sum of the inflation rate and the rate of growth of real income) is for a variety of countries and under a number of circumstances, a better approach in general than maintaining a constant rate of growth of the money supply or targeting the exchange rate.

The final example of this section is the study by Taylor of a *credible* reduction of the U.S. budget deficit, in which a decline in U.S. government purchases of 3% of GDP was announced in 1993 but phased in for the five-year period 1994–1998.[41] The results of the simulations, which were carried out for the period 1993–2000, were quite different from the standard Keynesian analysis. The initial effects of such changes were *increases* in real GDP; only in the fifth year (1997) of the simulations did real GDP finally fall, relative of course to the control simulation. (The estimated effect for the entire simulation period was approximately neutral; it decreased in the final half of the period, roughly offsetting increases in the first half.) However, the other effects of such a policy change were overwhelmingly favorable. After some temporary (and small) increases, interest rates (short and long term) fell relative to control levels. Despite some temporary increases in 1994 and 1995, the dominant effect on price levels was also in the downward direction. Finally, the unambiguous effect on exchange rates (which occurs throughout the simulation period) was a depreciation of the U.S. dollar of approximately 17%, thus "crowding in" (augmenting) net exports. Of course, as Taylor notes, the critical issue in all these simulations was that of the "credibility" of the announced policy changes; the simulation results would not follow if economic agents did not believe the policymakers from the outset.

16.8 THE ECONOMETRIC APPROACH TO POLICY EVALUATION

Estimated econometric models, particularly large, disaggregated, and dynamic models, may in the future be of considerable importance in the formulation and evaluation of policy.[42] As the basic ingredients of econometrics—data and models—are further developed and improved, and as econometric techniques are further refined, there will become available estimated econometric models encompassing many of the areas in which policy choices must be made. Such areas include not only the traditional macroeconomic phenomena of Tables 12.1 and 16.1 but also important sectors such as transportation, housing, and health.

The particular way in which the econometric models can aid in formulating and evaluating alternative policies will probably involve a mixture of some or all of the elements of policy evaluation treated in previous sections of this chapter. To the extent that specific goals and policy variables can be identified, the instruments-targets approach would be useful. To the extent that some explicit objective function can be determined or elicited from policymakers, the social welfare function or optimal-control approach would be useful. To the extent that policymakers seek answers to "what if" type questions, the simulation approach would be useful. Expert opinion on goals, parameters, and forecasts of related variables would be useful. The approach therefore will probably be an eclectic one, involving both objective and subjective factors. Nevertheless, as suggested in the preceding sections, the simulation approach would appear to be the most important one by far.

[41] See Taylor (1993a,b). Taylor's quarterly model of the U.S. economy, which incorporates the hypothesis of rational expectations, is embedded in a multicountry macroeconometric framework. (In this context, "rational expectations" means that the expectations of the economic agents turn out to be consistent with the results generated by the macroeconometric model itself.)

[42] See Holt (1965), Kuh (1965), and Klein (1983, 1991).

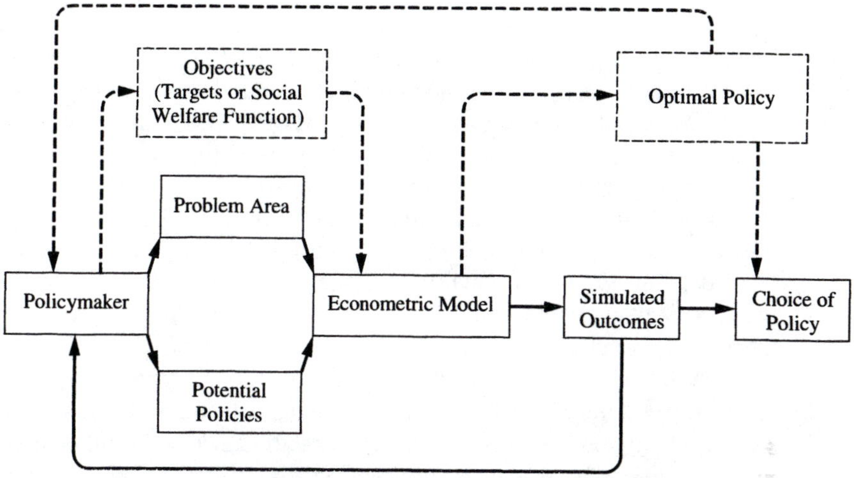

Figure 16.2 Econometric Approach to Policy Evaluation

The econometric approach to policy evaluation is indicated in a highly idealized fashion in Figure 16.2. The process might begin with a policymaker—for example, a government official. The policymaker (with staff assistance) would identify a particular issue or problem area that is both of concern and subject to influence by policy. Some potential policies bearing on the problem area would also be identified.

The problem area and policy alternatives would then be considered within the structure of an econometric model. The estimated model would be used to obtain simulated outcomes, typically in the form of a series of time paths for relevant variables, each of which is conditional on a particular choice of policy. A status quo simulation would project the likely course of relevant variables in the event no action is taken, and the other simulations would each employ one of the possible policy alternatives. The series of simulations would indicate both the likely effects of alternative policy choices and the sensitivity of the system to the various policy alternatives, as measured, for example, by multipliers or elasticities.[43] The simulations, if based on a sufficiently comprehensive model, would indicate not only the direct and immediate consequences of alternative policies, but also their indirect effects in other areas and their long-term consequences.

The simulated outcomes would be communicated to the policymaker, who might, in their light, revise either the problem area or the potential policies. If so, the process would be iterated. Eventually, guided by the simulated outcomes, the policymaker would choose a specific policy alternative. For example, after identifying the outcome that appears most desirable, the policy that led to this outcome might be adopted. Of course, actually carrying out a specific policy usually entails a complex process of implementation.

The dashed paths indicate that if the policymaker were able to formulate objectives in the form either of targets or of a social welfare function, the econometric model could be used to determine optimal policy for these objectives. Here also the process could be iterated, with the policymaker eventually choosing a specific policy, guided by the optimal policy implied by the objectives and model. The possibilities that are illustrated using dashed paths are of lesser importance because of the difficulties of defining objectives and of identifying optimal policy.

[43]See Klein (1983) and Eckstein (1976).

A few specific examples will illustrate this approach. In the first, a policymaker responsible for health is concerned with the problem of access to medical care. Various potential policies, in the form of alternative systems of health insurance, additional medical school enrollments, neighborhood health centers, and so on, are under consideration. Each can be evaluated using an econometric model of the health care system, such as presented in Section 13.5, to determine simulated outcomes—in particular, the access of various groups classified by income, region, and so on, to medical care. In fact, alternative features of various health insurance systems, such as coinsurance, deductibles, and alternative plans to expand medical school enrollments, can be separately treated and the simulated outcomes of each determined. Various "hybrid" schemes, involving different features of different systems, as well as other programs, can then be evaluated in order to help the policymaker choose an overall policy in this area.

A second example is the analysis of alternative energy policies, including various taxes on energy use, import and export duties, pricing policies, direct controls, and development of new energy sources. An estimated econometric model with sufficient detail as to energy demand and supply could be used to simulate the impacts of alternative policies, both singly and in various combined programs.[44] The resulting simulations could aid policy planners in selecting among alternative policy combinations.

The econometric approach of Figure 16.2 might also be applied in other areas of policy, such as transportation, education, housing, criminal justice, disarmament, economic development (of less developed countries), and the environment, where policies have traditionally been chosen with little or no understanding of their potential impacts, particularly secondary and long-run impacts. In these and in several other areas, an estimated econometric model might play a significant role in aiding and improving policy choices. Clearly, as has already been suggested, such an approach would encounter many problems of data collection, specification of relationships, estimation, structural change, implementation, and the like. If, however, these problems can be overcome, then the future of policy evaluation could very well be based on simulation or optimization using an estimated econometric model, with close links being formed between policymakers and econometricians as model builders.

PROBLEMS

16-A Formulate long-term optimal policy, as in (16.1.2), using the instruments-targets approach of Section 16.4. Obtain the sensitivities:

$$\frac{\partial r^*_{T+h'}}{\partial y^0_{T+h''}}, \qquad h', h'' = 1, 2, \ldots, h,$$

comparable to those of (16.4.4).

16-B In general, optimal instruments in the instruments-targets approach depend on *all* targets. Under what conditions will one instrument (or a subset of instruments) be determined entirely on the basis of one target (or a subset of targets)? Construct a macroeconometric model that yields "matching" behavior, in which fiscal policy is used for an employment objective and monetary policy is used for a price stability objective.

[44] See, for example, MacAvoy and Pindyck (1975), Jorgenson (1976), and Eckstein (1983).

16-C Consider the instruments-targets approach in each of the following cases. For each describe the nature of the optimal policy.

1. $\hat{\boldsymbol{\Gamma}}$ and $\hat{\mathbf{A}}$ are diagonal.
2. $\hat{\boldsymbol{\Gamma}}$ and $\hat{\mathbf{A}}$ are triangular.
3. $\hat{\boldsymbol{\Gamma}}$ and $\hat{\mathbf{A}}$ are block diagonal.
4. $\hat{\boldsymbol{\Gamma}}$ and $\hat{\mathbf{A}}$ are block triangular.

16-D Work out results comparable to those of Section 16.4 for the instruments-targets approach to policymaking if the target variables are a *proper subset* of the group of current endogenous variables.

16-E Generalize the developments of the instruments-targets, social-welfare-function, and simulation approaches to the case of an econometric model containing lagged endogenous variables with lags up to and including those of order p. [*Hint*: See Klein (1983). Pages 152 through 161 are particularly relevant.]

16-F Consider in the estimated Klein interwar model in equations (12.2.1)–(12.2.6) that G, W, and T are policy variables.

1. Assuming there are three target variables, Y, C, and W_p, illustrate the targets-instruments approach.
2. Assuming a quadratic objective function in output and private wages, illustrate the social-welfare-function approach.
3. Use the model to simulate the effects of alternative policy choices.

16-G For the problem of maximizing the social welfare function (16.5.12) in the case of the prototype macro model, show that the second-order condition for maximization does indeed hold (i.e., that the relevant second derivative is indeed negative), so the solution of (16.5.14) does indeed give a proper maximum.

BIBLIOGRAPHY

ADAMS, F. G., and L. R. KLEIN (1991). "Performance of Quarterly Econometric Models of the United States: A New Round of Model Comparisons," in Klein, Ed. (1991).

BODKIN, R. G. (1982). "Stability or Instability of the Canadian Trade-Off Curve: An Econometric Analysis." *Prévision et analyse économique* (Cahiers du GAMA), 3: 27–37 (published in mid-1987).

BODKIN, R. G., L. R. KLEIN, K. MARWAH (1991). *A History of Macroeconometric Model-Building*. Aldershot, Hants, England: Edward Elgar Publishing Ltd.

BRAYBROOKE, D., and C. E. LINDBLOM (1963). *A Strategy of Decision*. New York: Free Press.

BRYANT, R., P. HOOPER, and C. L. MANN, Eds. (1993). *Evaluating Policy Regimes: New Research in Empirical Macroeconomics*. Washington, D.C.: The Brookings Institution.

BUCK, A. J., M. GROSS, S. HAKIM, and T. WEINBLATT (1993). "Using the Delphi Process to Analyze Social Policy Implementation: A Post Hoc Case from Vocational Rehabilitation." *Policy Sciences*, 26: 271–288.

CHRIST, C. F. (1975). "Judging the Performance of Econometric Models of the U.S. Economy." *International Economic Review*, 16: 54–74.

CLARKSON, G. P. E., and H. A. SIMON (1960). "Simulation of Individual and Group Behavior." *American Economic Review*, 50: 920–932.

DAVIS, O. A., M. A. H. DEMPSTER, and A. WILDAVSKY (1966). "A Theory of the Budgetary Process." *American Political Science Review*, 60: 529–547.

DUGGAL, V. (1975). "Fiscal Policy and Economic Stabilization," in G. Fromm and L. R. Klein, Eds., *The Brookings Model: Perspective and Recent Developments*. Amsterdam: North-Holland Publishing Company.

ECKSTEIN, O., Ed. (1976). *Parameters and Policies in the U.S. Economy*. Amsterdam: North-Holland Publishing Company.

ECKSTEIN, O. (1983). *The DRI Model of the U.S. Economy*. New York: McGraw-Hill Book Company.

ECONOMIC COUNCIL OF CANADA (1972). *The Years to 1980*. Ninth Annual Review. Ottawa: Information Canada.

ECONOMIC COUNCIL OF CANADA (1979). *Two Cheers for the Eighties*. Sixteenth Annual Review. Ottawa: Department of Supply and Services of the Government of Canada.

FOX, K. A., J. K. SENGUPTA, and E. THORBECKE (1966). *The Theory of Quantitative Economic Policy, with Applications to Economic Growth and Stabilization*. Amsterdam: North-Holland Publishing Company; Chicago: Rand McNally & Company.

FRIEDMAN, B. M. (1975). *Economic Stabilization Policy: Methods in Optimization*. Amsterdam: North-Holland Publishing Company.

FRIEDMAN, M., and A. SCHWARTZ (1963). *A Monetary History of the United States, 1867–1960*. Princeton, N.J.: Princeton University Press.

FROMM, G. (1969a). "An Evaluation of Monetary Policy Instruments." in J. S. Duesenberry et al., Eds., *The Brookings Model: Some Further Results*. Amsterdam: North-Holland Publishing Company; Chicago: Rand McNally & Company.

FROMM, G. (1969b). "Utility Theory and the Analysis of Simulation Output Data," in T. H. Naylor, Ed., *The Design of Computer Simulation Experiments*. Durham, N.C.: Duke University Press.

FROMM, G., and L. R. KLEIN (1976). "The NBER/NSF Model Comparison Seminar: An Analysis of Results." *Annals of Economic and Social Measurement*, 5: 1–28.

FROMM, G., and P. TAUBMAN (1968). *Policy Simulations with an Econometric Model*. Amsterdam: North-Holland Publishing Company.

GREENBERGER, M., M. CRENSON, and B. CRISSEY (1976). *Models in the Policy Process*. New York: Russell Sage Foundation.

HAMILTON, H. R., et al. (1969). *Systems Simulation for Regional Analysis*. Cambridge, Mass.: MIT Press.

HANSEN, B. (1958). *The Economic Theory of Fiscal Policy*. London: George Allen & Unwin, Ltd. (originally published in Swedish in 1955).

HICKMAN, B. G., Ed. (1965). *Quantitative Planning of Economic Policy*. Washington, D.C.: The Brookings Institution.

HOLT, C. C. (1962). "Linear Decision Rules for Economic Stabilization and Growth." *Quarterly Journal of Economics*, 76: 20–45.

HOLT, C. C. (1965). "Quantitative Decision Analysis and National Policy: How Can We Bridge the Gap?" in Hickman, Ed. (1965).

HOLT, C. C., F. MODIGLIANI, J. F. MUTH, and H. SIMON (1960). *Planning Production, Inventories, and Work Force*. Englewood Cliffs, N.J.: Prentice Hall.

HOWREY, E. P., and H. H. KELEJIAN (1971). "Simulation versus Analytical Solution: the Case of Econometric Models," in Naylor, Ed. (1971).

INTRILIGATOR, M. D. (1971). *Mathematical Optimization and Economic Theory*. Englewood Cliffs, N.J.: Prentice Hall.

INTRILIGATOR, M. D., and E. SHESHINSKI (1986). "Toward a Theory of Planning," in W. Heller, R. Starr, and D. Starrett, Eds. *Essays in Honor of Kenneth J. Arrow*. New York: Cambridge University Press.

JORGENSON, D. W., Ed. (1976). *Econometric Studies of U.S. Energy Policy*. Amsterdam: North-Holland Publishing Company.

KIRSCHEN, E. S., and L. MORRISENS (1965). "The Objectives and Instruments of Economic Policy," in Hickman, Ed. (1965).

KLEIN, L. R. (1969). "An Econometric Analysis of the Tax Cut of 1964," in J. S. Duesenberry et al., Eds., *The Brookings Model: Some Further Results*. Amsterdam: North-Holland Publishing Company; Chicago: Rand McNally & Company.

KLEIN, L. R. (1971). "Forecasting and Policy Evaluation Using Large Scale Econometric Models: The State of the Art," in M. D. Intriligator, Ed., *Frontiers of Quantitative Economics*. Amsterdam: North-Holland Publishing Company.

KLEIN, L. R. (1974). "An Econometric Analysis of the Revenue and Expenditure Control Act of 1968–1969," in W. L. Smith and J. M. Culbertson, Eds., *Public Finance and Stabilization Policy*. Amsterdam: North-Holland Publishing Company.

KLEIN, L. R. (1983). *Lectures in Econometrics*. Amsterdam: North-Holland Publishing Company.

KLEIN, L. R., Ed. (1991). *Comparative Performance of U.S. Econometric Models*. New York: Oxford University Press.

KLEIN, L. R., R. SIMES, and P. VOISIN (1981). "Coordinated Monetary Policy and the World Economy." *Prévision et analyse économique* (Cahiers du GAMA), 2: 75–105.

KUH, E. (1965). "Econometric Models: Is a New Age Dawning?" *American Economic Review, Papers and Proceedings*, 55: 362–369.

LINDBLOM, C. E. (1968). *The Policy-Making Process*. Englewood Cliffs, N.J.: Prentice Hall.

MACAVOY, P. W., and R. S. PINDYCK (1975). *The Economics of the Natural Gas Shortage (1960–1980)*. Amsterdam: North-Holland Publishing Company.

MARCH, J. G., and H. SIMON (1958). *Organizations*. New York: John Wiley & Sons, Inc.

NAYLOR, T. H. (1971). "Policy Simulation Experiments with Macroeconometric Models: The State of the Art," in M. D. Intriligator, Ed., *Frontiers of Quantitative Economics*. Amsterdam: North-Holland Publishing Company.

NAYLOR, T. H., Ed. (1971). *Computer Simulation Experiments with Models of Economic Systems*. New York: John Wiley & Sons, Inc.

NAYLOR, T. H., J. L. BALINTFY, D. S. BURDICK, and K. CHU (1968). *Computer Simulation Techniques*. New York: John Wiley & Sons, Inc.

NAYLOR, T. H., K. WERTZ, and T. H. WONNACOTT (1968). "Methods for Evaluating the Effects of Economic Policies Using Simulation Experiments." *Review of the International Statistical Institute*, 36: 184–200.

ORCUTT, G. H. (1960). "Simulation of Economic Systems." *American Economic Review*, 50: 893–907.

ORCUTT, G. H., M. GREENBURGER, J. KORBEL, and A. M. RIVLIN (1961). *Microanalysis of Socioeconomic Systems: A Simulation Study*. New York: Harper & Row, Publishers, Inc.

PHILLIPS, A. W. (1954). "Stabilization Policy in a Closed Economy." *Economic Journal*, 64: 290–323.

PHILLIPS, A. W. (1957). "Stabilization Policy and the Time-Forms of Lagged Responses." *Economic Journal*, 67: 265–277.

PINDYCK, R. (1973). *Optimal Planning for Economic Stabilization*. Amsterdam: North-Holland Publishing Company.

POWELL, A. A., and R. A. WILLIAMS, Eds. (1973). *Econometric Studies of Macro and Monetary Relations*. Amsterdam: North-Holland Publishing Company.

PRESTON, R. S., C. BRAITHWAITE, B. CAIN, D. DESAULNIERS, B. L. EYFORD, S. GILBY, B. K. LODH, P. NEVIN, J. E. RAMIN, P. S. RAO, H. M. SAIYED, T. T. SCHWEITZER, and M. WILLIS (1979). "Sixteenth

Annual Review of Background Simulations and Policy Alternatives." Economic Council of Canada Research Document (mimeographed).

SHUBIK, M. (1960). "Simulation of the Industry and the Firm." *American Economic Review*, 50: 908–919.

SIMON, H. (1955). "A Behavioral Model of Rational Choice." *Quarterly Journal of Economics*, 69: 99–118.

SIMON, H. (1959). "Theories of Decision Making in Economics and Behavioral Science." *American Economic Review*, 49: 253–283.

TAYLOR, J. B. (1993a). "The Use of the New Macroeconomics for Policy Formulation." *American Economic Review, Papers and Proceedings*, 83: 300–305.

TAYLOR, J. B. (1993b). *Macroeconomic Policy in a World Economy: From Econometric Design to Practical Operation*. New York: W.W. Norton & Company, Inc.

THEIL, H. (1961). *Economic Forecasts and Policy*, 2nd rev. ed. Amsterdam: North-Holland Publishing Company.

THEIL, H. (1964). *Optimal Decision Rules for Government and Industry*. Chicago: Rand McNally & Company; Amsterdam: North-Holland Publishing Company.

THEIL, H. (1965). "Linear Decision Rules for Macrodynamic Policy Problems," in Hickman, Ed. (1965).

TINBERGEN, J. (1952). *On the Theory of Economic Policy*. Amsterdam: North-Holland Publishing Company.

TINBERGEN, J. (1954). *Centralization and Decentralization in Economic Policy*. Amsterdam: North-Holland Publishing Company.

TINBERGEN, J. (1956). *Economic Policy: Principles and Design*. Amsterdam: North-Holland Publishing Company.

TUROFF, M. (1975). "The Policy Delphi," in H. A. Linstone and M. Turoff, Eds., *The Delphi Method: Techniques and Applications*. Reading, Mass.: Addison-Wesley Publishing Company, Inc.

VAN DEN BOGAARD, P. J. M., and H. THEIL (1959). "Macrodynamic Policy-Making: An Application of Strategy and Certainty Equivalence to the Economy of the United States, 1933–36." *Metroeconomica*, 11: 149–167; reprinted in A. Zellner, Ed., *Readings in Economic Statistics and Econometrics*. Boston: Little, Brown and Company.

VAN EIJK, C. J., and J. SANDEE (1959). "Quantitative Determination of an Optimum Economic Policy." *Econometrica*, 27: 1–13.

WILDAVSKY, A. (1964). *The Politics of the Budgetary Process*. Boston: Little, Brown and Company. (Fourth edition, 1984.)

17

VALIDATION OF ECONOMETRIC MODELS AND MANAGERIAL ASPECTS OF THE USES OF ECONOMETRIC MODELS

17.1 INTRODUCTION

In this chapter we discuss problems of model maintenance and improvement after the model has been built. From the discussion in Chapter 2 it will be recalled that *all* models are imperfect representations of the phenomenon of being modeled, as the essence of fruitful simplification is to leave out many aspects of the "real world," and occasionally, these neglected aspects of the problem may turn out to be important. Hence no model can be built and then used indefinitely without ongoing model maintenance. In this section we look at various aspects of such a process, then in the next sections discuss the *statistical* (or narrowly, econometric) validation of already constructed econometric models, focusing on various formal and informal tests for judging how well the predictions of the model (including its *ex-post* forecasts for already known data) conform to the facts under study. This aspect of validating a model is very much akin to what an auditor (a special kind of accountant) does when she or he examines the books of an enterprise, attempting to judge whether the accounting records document the financial circumstances of this organization in a reasonably accurate fashion.

But an econometrician or investigator must be more than a mere record keeper. A project is a full-scale enterprise; accordingly, such a scholar must be also a manager, a person capable of exercising independent judgment. The final sections cover the role of judgment explicitly and some of the other broader aspects of the managerial function of the leader of an econometric model project. Case studies, generally drawn from macroeconometric model projects, demonstrate the great importance of gathering suitable, timely, and reasonably accurate data. As well, the great importance of reducing human error (as far as is *humanly* possible) is stressed. Of course, a number of aspects of these discussions will be pertinent to students when writing their own research papers.

17.2 ARE THE A PRIORI CONSTRAINTS RESPECTED?

The first question to ask in evaluating a model is the issue of what a priori constraints exist in a model and, if these do exist, whether they have been respected. Typically, this question will arise with regard to the accounting identities, although more complicated constraints may also be present, as the final paragraph of this section indicates. It can be argued, as Brainard and Tobin (1968) did very forcefully, that although respecting accounting identities will not necessarily produce an accurate model, a model that violates its own accounting identities cannot possibly be correct. Some examples may illustrate these propositions.

In their classic paper, Brainard and Tobin (1968) argued that many previous models of the financial sector were deficient because they did not respect the condition that desired demands for the various assets less desired levels of possible liabilities should be held equal to total wealth (net worth), a variable introduced as one of the arguments of these portfolio demand equations. Brainard and Tobin asserted that many current portfolio demand models either ignored this condition or violated it in a gross or subtle manner.[1] Brainard and Tobin termed this the "pitfalls" problem, which may also be called the problem of additive consistency.

Consider in slightly greater detail the very similar question studied by Bodkin (1974) with regard to the various categories of consumption demand. Of course, it is obvious that the sum of the various categories of consumption expenditures (including personal savings) should equal the generating value of personal disposable income (Y_d). In this study, six categories (or uses) of disposable income were distinguished: expenditures on consumer durables (C_d), expenditures on nondurables (C_n), expenditures on housing services (C_h), expenditures on other services (C_{os}),[2] consumer interest payments (C_i), and personal saving (S). Thus, in terms of the national income accounting identity, we have:

$$Y_d = C_d + C_n + C_h + C_{os} + C_i + S. \tag{17.2.1}$$

Deflating for the general level of consumer prices (P)[3] and dividing by the value of population at midyear in order to get the expenditure relationships slightly closer to the demand functions of standard microeconomic theory, the accounting relationship becomes:

$$\frac{Y_d}{PN} = \frac{C_d}{PN} + \frac{C_n}{PN} + \frac{C_h}{PN} + \frac{C_{os}}{PN} + \frac{C_i}{PN} + \frac{S}{PN}. \tag{17.2.2}$$

[1]If this constraint were ignored, the n portfolio demand equations will simply be estimated as though they are independent, when in fact they are connected by this accounting identity. The result will be a group of equations whose predicted values will agree with the accounting identity only by chance and certainly not for all sets of values of the various explanatory variables. However, this problem might be circumvented by having a "residual" asset or liability, a category whose demand relationship is not estimated explicitly. Then it becomes true that there is no gross violation of the accounting identity, but the implicit functional representation of the demand for the omitted category becomes a hodgepodge of the explanatory variables of *all* the remaining relationships, of a sort that would never be estimated initially if this relationship were to be specified directly rather than implicitly. On these points, see Brainard and Tobin (1968) and Smith (1975).

[2]The U.S. Department of Commerce distinguished another use of personal disposable income during this period: personal transfers to nonresidents. In this study, this category was placed in other services, on the grounds that it partially represented payments that were implicit compensation of services such as childrearing years ago on the part of an aged parent in the country of origin.

[3]Each category of expenditures might have employed its own deflator, to be closer to the notion of "real" quantities consumed. However, this would have destroyed the accounting identity that this study was intended to illustrate! Whether this alternative approach is in fact better depends, in large measure, on the importance one attaches to respecting identities and additive consistency.

The objective was to fit category consumption functions to these categories, with the property that the sum of the predicted levels of consumption of the six categories (including real personal savings per capita) should identically equal the generating value of real per capita disposable income. It may easily be proved (Problem 17-A) that this will be the case provided that the sum of the coefficients on real per capita disposable income (the category MPCs) is unity while the sum of the coefficients for all other explanatory variables is zero. Moreover, this condition, while clearly sufficient, is also necessary, at least if this property is to hold identically for *all* choices of the explanatory variables. (This condition implies that a nontrivial explanatory variable, other than income, must appear in at least two category regressions, if it appears at all.) However, one of the simplest ways to ensure that this will be the case is to include all of the explanatory variables judged relevant for at least one category in all the category regressions. To sketch a proof of this result, write the typical category relationship in vector-matrix notation as:

$$\mathbf{C}_m = \mathbf{X}\boldsymbol{\beta}_m + \mathbf{u}_m, \qquad m = 1, 2, \ldots, M, \tag{17.2.3}$$

where $\mathbf{C}_m$ is a column vector of n observations on the mth category of consumption expenditures, $\boldsymbol{\beta}_m$ is a column vector of k parameters associated with this category relationship, $\mathbf{X}$ is a design (or data) matrix of dimension $n \times k$ (which is common to all the category regressions), and $\mathbf{u}_m$ is a column vector of category relationship residuals, where there are M category relationships. The least squares estimates of the $\boldsymbol{\beta}_m$ parameters are given by:

$$\hat{\boldsymbol{\beta}}_m = (\mathbf{X}'\mathbf{X})^{-1}\mathbf{X}'\mathbf{C}_m. \tag{17.2.4}$$

Consider now the sum of the fitted regression coefficients across categories:

$$\begin{aligned}\sum_i^M \hat{\boldsymbol{\beta}}_m = \sum_i^M (\mathbf{X}'\mathbf{X})^{-1}\mathbf{X}'\mathbf{C}_m &= (\mathbf{X}'\mathbf{X})^{-1}\mathbf{X}'\sum_i^M \mathbf{C}_m \\ &= (\mathbf{X}'\mathbf{X})^{-1}\mathbf{X}'\mathbf{X}_k,\end{aligned} \tag{17.2.5}$$

where $\mathbf{X}_k$ is the final explanatory variable of the category relationships, assumed to be the sum total (disposable income) of these categories. The reader can finish the proof as an exercise (Problem 17-B).[4]

Consider now the results obtained in this study. The explanatory variables finally employed, after some preliminary experimentation (principally to consider the most appropriate way to incorporate the relative price variables) were real per capita disposable income (of course); real wealth (net worth) of the personal sector per capita at the beginning of the period (We_{-1}/PN); the real per capita stock of consumer durables at the beginning of the period (Dur_{-1}/PN)[5]; two relative price variables, namely the ratios of the implicit deflators of consumer durables expenditures and consumer nondurables expenditures (P_d and P_n, respectively) to the implicit deflator of all consumption expenditures; and a constant term. The basic idea was to develop a theory of expenditures on the various categories of consumption and wealth accumulation that would be loosely consistent with both the neoclas-

[4]This property is also true when the estimates of the category relationships are obtained by two-stage least squares rather than by ordinary least squares (Problem 17-C).

[5]There was no need, from the point of view of additivity considerations, to deflate the nominal value of the stock of consumer durables by the general implicit deflator for all consumption expenditures because the implicit deflator of durable goods expenditures would have served just as well. In point of fact, preliminary experimentation suggested that the general deflator performed slightly better, so this deflator was retained for this explanatory variable.

sical theory of utility maximization and the major theories of aggregate consumption behavior. The major results of this study are presented in Table 17.1.

This technique appears to work satisfactorily in this application, as the results are intuitively plausible and appealing. (If one wanted a more formal justification of this criterion, it might be termed "informal Bayesianism"; see Section 4.11.) For instance, the implied marginal propensity to spend out of wealth is 0.03 if expenditures on consumer durables are included and 0.054 if this category is excluded. Note also that the magnitude of the stock of consumer durables has exactly the appropriate portfolio adjustment effects: it favors conventionally measured savings (acquisition of financial, business, or housing assets) but discourages further accumulation of consumer durables.[6] The conditions for retaining an explanatory variable in this context are rather undefined; because of the interrelated nature of the regressions, it was argued that each explanatory variable should be strongly significant (i.e., significant at the 1% level or better) in at least one regression and reasonably significant (i.e., significant at the 5% level or better) in at least one other regression. The explanatory variables of Table 17.1 all meet this criterion. Accordingly, this study was regarded as successful, as it showed that modules of an econometric model meeting the criterion for additive consistency (or the "pitfalls" criterion) could be constructed. Of course, such a property would obviously be quite useful in the context of forecasting or policy applications of an econometric model.

To conclude this section, observe that this principle, that the estimators should respect a priori constraints, may be applied to more complicated constraints as well, in the context of the simultaneous-equations model. Zellner (1972) states some fairly general conditions under which bounds on the values of parameters in the simultaneous-equations model may be derived, based on information employed in specifying the model. Zellner goes on to show that such bounds, which are analogous to those obtained in the errors-in-variables model (Section 5.8), may be estimated consistently. Genberg (1972) applies this principle to the simple two-equation Haavelmo macroeconometric model (similar to the prototype macro model of Section 2.6 but with exogenous private investment) in order to generate an upper bound on the investment multiplier, which he then proceeds to estimate consistently. It is satisfying to observe that the data employed to illustrate this example generate a point estimate of the actual investment multiplier that respects this upper bound.

17.3 PARAMETRIC TESTS PRIOR TO THE RELEASE OF THE MODEL

Prior to the release of a model (which in ordinary language means making the model available to people who are not members of the research team or publication), the investigator will have made a number of standard t and F tests of the sort developed in Chapters 4 and 5. In most cases these tests may be quite simple, such as checking that a theoretically important variable has a statistically significant coefficient whose sign is in the expected direction. In general, these simple tests are among the most important ones that are employed an overwhelming majority of the time. In addition, some rather sophisticated diagnostic

[6]For a more detailed analysis of these results, consult the original study (Bodkin, 1974).

TABLE 17.1 Consumption Category Regressions Illustrating the Additivity Property, U.S. Data, 1949–1963, Ordinary Least Squares Regressions

Dependent Variable	Constant Term	$\frac{Y_d}{PN}$	$\frac{We_{-1}}{PN}$	$\frac{Dur_{-1}}{PN}$	$\frac{P_d}{P}$	$\frac{P_n}{P}$	R^2	$\bar{S}_u$	d
$\frac{C_d}{PN}$		0.3477	–0.02468	–0.2273	153.8	–625.4			
	$494.0	(3.33)	(1.73)	(3.04)	(0.60)	(1.31)	0.8152	10.35	2.42
$\frac{C_n}{PN}$		0.1592	0.01580	0.0072	5.6	673.2			
	–300.7	(5.88)	(4.28)	(0.37)	(0.08)	(5.44)	0.9855	2.679	2.40
$\frac{C_h}{PN}$		0.0868	0.00503	0.0797	–305.8	–70.0			
	329.8	(3.36)	(1.42)	(4.30)	(4.82)	(0.59)	0.9968	2.561	1.43
$\frac{C_{os}}{PN}$		0.1376	0.03329	–0.0883	–225.4	–409.1			
	597.4	(1.47)	(2.60)	(1.31)	(0.98)	(0.95)	0.9822	9.298	1.88
$\frac{C_i}{PN}$		0.0318	0.00037	0.0112	–39.3	–80.2			
	81.0	(4.46)	(0.38)	(2.20)	(2.24)	(2.46)	0.9961	0.7065	2.54
$\frac{S}{PN}$	0.2369	–0.02981	0.2174	411.1	511.5				
	–1201.6	(2.63)	(2.42)	(3.37)	(1.86)	(1.24)	0.7764	8.917	2.09
SUM	0	1.0000	0	0	0	0	—	—	—

Note For regression coefficients, t statistics (shown in parentheses) are given for all variables, except the constant term. R^2 is the coefficient of multiple determination, $\bar{S}_u$ is the estimated standard deviation of the residuals, and d is the Durbin–Watson test statistic.

tests have been developed by theoretical econometricians, and these specialized tests can be quite helpful on occasion.[7]

While it was recommended to check the sign of a coefficient against its theoretically expected value, some applied econometricians would argue that a regression coefficient whose numerical value contradicts expectations is statistically insignificant regardless of how high the *t* ratio (the absolute ratio of the fitted regression coefficient to its estimated standard error) may be. This is a reasonable point of view, reflecting the Dhrymes et al. (1972) recommendation that practicing econometricians move some distance in the Bayesian direction, becoming "informal Bayesians" in taking account of prior beliefs.

Another interesting issue treated in Dhrymes et al. (1972) is whether one should save a small part of the sample (in the limit one observation) for additional pretesting before the release of a model. The idea is a very simple one. Since any estimated model inevitably entails some forcing of the fit, it is desirable to have a completely independent observation available for a critical test before releasing the model. Dhrymes et al. (1972) outline test procedures, analogous to those concerning the standard error of forecast developed in Section 4.7, to test whether the final observation may reasonably be said to come from the same universe as that which generated the data from which the calculated model has been fitted. This suggestion is not recommended in general for several reasons. First, most studies suffer from a paucity of reliable data, and usually it is just too "expensive" (in terms of the reliability of the estimators) to give away any pertinent information. Second, often such a test will not be very powerful, in the sense that a model that will ultimately have to be rejected may still pass such a test. Finally, the investigator should test and retest a model that is to be released, with data that are genuinely independent.[8] Nevertheless, this is one of the issues about which specialists can well disagree, as it is obviously desirable to pretest a model as fully as possible before its release.

17.4 PARAMETRIC TESTS AFTER RELEASE

Subsequent to a model's release, the investigator should be testing and retesting the structure of the model to confirm that the model remains a useful representation of the underlying phenomena being modeled. Most of these subsequent checks will be nonparametric (which are discussed in the following section), but one group of tests will be introduced here. If the number of additional observations is large, the fitted relationship under examination can be reestimated for the postsample period. The estimated parameters for the two subperiods (the original sample period and the postsample period) can then be compared under classical assumptions (with the critical additional hypothesis that the estimated variance of the residuals remains the same in the two periods). An *F* test for the absence of a break in structure [the Chow (1960) test] can be formulated, as explained in Section 4.6. As noted earlier, it is not necessary that the number of additional observations exceed (or equal)

[7]See the review by Dhrymes et al. (1972), especially the references to papers by Ramsey and others. These papers, which test for various violations of the classical linear regression model, give very useful tests.

[8]In fact, it is very hard to put one observation aside in a drawer (literally or figuratively), as the nature of this observation may still be "at the back of" one's mind. By contrast, observations that nature generates after a model has been released are genuinely independent of the modeling procedure.

the number of parameters to be estimated (or reestimated), since a perfectly good F test can be formulated even when there are fewer additional observations. In the limit, one can test with one additional observation, as in the discussion of the standard error of forecast in Section 4.7. The "common sense" of this remark is the observation that with classical assumptions, the estimated residual can be used to decide whether this additional observation could "reasonably" (i.e., with a satisfactory probability of a Type I error) have come from the same universe as the sample observations.

Suppose that the statistical test does show a break in structure. Before drastic action is taken, it may well be worthwhile to verify the data. (For someone employing secondary data, this could be as simple as verifying that no copying error has been committed.) Sometimes in applied statistics it may be better to reject the data rather than the hypothesis maintained. An example of this occurs in macroeconometric modeling, where some relationships may possibly be called into question on the basis of preliminary data, whereas further testing with final national account estimates does in fact indicate no break in structure. This point has particular pertinence for well-established, long-standing relationships of macroeconomic theory such as the consumption function or the demand for money relationship. The first step, then, in the process of a post-release model "audit" is to be as sure as is humanly possible that the data employed are reliable.

Suppose that after such a check, the break in structure is indeed confirmed. What should the investigator do? Although it may be obvious that the model must be reformulated, in general it may not be clear how this should be done. This is where the art of model management enters. At times the offending relationship must be replaced by a whole new relationship,[9] while at other times some simple modification of the original structural relationship will suffice. If the postsample period is long enough that an independent subregression could be fitted to this set of data, the comparison of the two subregressions (in the context of a failed Chow test) may give valuable clues as to the variable (or variables or constant term) whose influence is so apparently different during this later period. But even if the postsample period is short enough that such direct probing is precluded, some judicious investigation may still indicate the apparent cause of the problem. The break in structure can then be "patched up" until a more intellectually satisfying solution to the problem can be constructed.[10] Thus a simple addition of a dummy variable for the postsample period to the constant term may suffice (as illustrated below), or perhaps one (or more) of the slope coefficients may be changed to allow for the operation of different underlying factors during this later period.

[9]It is sometimes possible that the researcher will be aided in this tack by the development of some new theoretical relationships. Moreover, it is just possible that these new relationships will fit the entire period (original sample period, together with the postsample period) much better than will the original theory. In cases such as these, it is truly possible to speak of progress in model building.

[10]In this connection, it has been the policy of Fair (1974, 1984) to reestimate the parameters of his (relatively small-scale) model every time new data became available, regardless of whether or not diagnostic tests indicated that the model was in need of reformulation. Such a procedure is equivalent to a sliding adjustment of the constant term and of all the slope coefficients, whether or not the outside evidence suggests that such a modification of the model is needed. While such a procedure gets the maximum use out of the data available to the researcher, it may at least be questioned whether this procedure represents the most efficient use of all the resources available. In addition, in cases where there is (or would be) evidence of a break in structure, such a procedure does not allow a concentration on the reestimation of the structural parameters that have been the subject of such a break in structure.

17.5 NONPARAMETRIC TESTS OF AN ECONOMETRIC MODEL

In this section we discuss nonparametric evaluation of an econometric model. No distinction is made between such tests carried out prior to or after the release of a model, as this event does not really influence the nonparametric testing that should be carried out more or less continually after the first phase of the building of the model has been completed. Of course, there may be phases when this sort of (nonparametric) testing is carried out more intensively, such as just prior to the release of the model or just before the researcher (or the group of researchers) releases a major forecast.

Nonparametric testing of a model is very much an art form rather than a strict scientific procedure. Dhrymes et al. (1972) speak of the researcher's role in such an effort being like that of "an econometric Sherlock Holmes"[11]; the investigator must take incomplete clues and perhaps contradictory bits of evidence and on the basis of a total picture (for which the parts may not always be in harmony) decide whether the model promises to be (or to remain) serviceable. Furthermore, validation, especially on the basis of the nonparametric testing, is generally problem dependent. For example, a model that is perfectly adequate for forecasting GNP and/or its major aggregates may be inadequate for federal budget planning, perhaps due to weakness in several minor (from the point of view of the overall economy) components of the federal budget. Thus the judgment of the researcher regarding the various strengths and weaknesses of the model is fundamentally critical.

A basic test is the adequacy of the model's "historical tracking," that is, the precision with which the model reproduces the "major" endogenous variables over which the sample has been fitted, or into the immediate postsample period. Thus full-model simulations (as described in Section 14.6) are of critical importance, as this signals how well the model functions as a system. (By contrast, most of the parametric tests discussed above apply only to a single equation and hence are of limited usefulness in gauging the performance of the model *as a system.*) This is not to say that simulations of smaller portions of the model, individual equations or subgroups (blocks) of individual equations, cannot be useful on occasion, for this is definitely the case. Nevertheless, for a "feel" for the model as a total system, it is necessary to use a full-system simulation.[12]

To gauge the acceptability of a set of model simulations, in general, note that model simulations are really a set of *ex-post* forecasts, so all the measures discussed in Chapter 15 can be employed. Thus relative measures such as the *Theil inequality coefficient*, or absolute measures such as the *root-mean-square error*, can be applied to an endogenous variable of particular interest. (Some researchers prefer the average absolute error as a measure of dispersion, feeling that it is less influenced by a few large, unrepresentative errors.) Tracking measures, such as the number of turning point errors and the magnitude of such errors, are very important, and it is reasonable to trade goodness of fit in general (low root-mean-square

[11]Interestingly, Leamer (1983b) also uses this analogy in his discussion of model choice and specification analysis. Leamer discusses in some detail some of the intricacies of model selection when the researcher does not have perfect knowledge.

[12]Although block simulations were not explained explicitly in Chapter 14, they are similar to simulations of complete models with one exception: all endogenous variables outside a particular block of equations are temporarily taken as exogenous (or "exogenized"). Thus, in the limit, the projections of a single regression equation can be taken as a block simulation, with that particular equation considered as a block in itself.

error or low Theil inequality coefficient) for a model that neither misses turning points nor signals falsely a turning point that is not found in the data. In addition, there are many tests that can be performed on the results of *ex-post* simulations of an econometric model as a system. A subset of the residuals of a key relationship can be studied to see whether the model has been overpredicting or underpredicting this variable in recent experience. (Such a test is often performed just before a major forecast, to judge whether the model remains "in tune" for this particular key endogenous variable.) In particular, an analysis of the largest residuals may be carried out to see whether these might be reduced by a consideration of other explanatory variables that are not currently included in the model (see also the first example of Section 17.8). Various tests of the randomness of particular sets of residuals, such as the numbers of runs of positive or negative residuals, or the simultaneous-equations counterpart of the Durbin–Watson test statistic, can also be performed, and this will help in arriving at a judgment about the quality of the model as a whole. At times a decomposition of the errors in the simulation, particularly a study of error transmission within the model, may help the investigator arrive at a judgment of either the model as a whole or the quality of a particular block of equations.[13]

Indeed, evaluation of the quality of the fit in a full model simulation does not proceed in a vacuum. At times a *comparative* measure of such quality may be desirable, as suggested in Section 15.6. While the more natural thing to do may be to pit one econometric model against another, it is often more instructive to gauge the goodness of fit of the full model simulation against another simple alternative. One such alternative is a naive model, as explained in Section 15.2. In recent years, econometricians have become rather sophisticated with their "naive" models, using ARIMA processes and the like to generate these, as explained in Chapter 6. A rough criterion for a successful full model simulation is that it should outperform in terms of forecasting ability the naive model (including such a time-series variant), by a considerable margin; after all, the naive model can be constructed at considerably lower cost. Some writers (e.g., Christ, 1975) have suggested noneconometric forecasts based principally on informed judgment as another benchmark for gauging comparative performance.

Still another criterion is the behavior of the model in standard multiplier simulations, of the sort discussed in Chapter 14. As an example, for macroeconometric models it would appear that a reasonable model of this type should display the familiar inverted "U" as the time pattern for the dynamic multipliers.[14] More generally, a study of the pattern of the dynamic multipliers generated by an econometric model can serve as another aspect of the nonparametric evaluation of a model, provided that some prior knowledge in this domain already exists.

Dhrymes et al. (1972) suggested that stochastic simulations[15] were another important aspect of the nonparametric evaluation of econometric models, particularly nonlinear econo-

[13]For further discussion of this point, see Fair (1980, 1993).

[14]The "dynamic multiplier" means the interim or medium-term multiplier discussed in Chapter 14. For example, as noted in Section 14.10, in the case of the Canadian macroeconometric model simulation, the deviant multiplier performance of one model (the University of Toronto's QFM model) was used to call into question the accuracy of this model as then formulated, with the result that the model was drastically respecified shortly afterward (see Helliwell et al., 1979).

[15]Stochastic simulations of econometric models are simulations in which the error terms of the behavioral equations are not fixed in advance, but rather, are drawn from some preexisting probability distribution (such as that estimated for the model's structure). Usually, a number of such simulations are studied, with the results generally presented in the form of some averages over the entire set of simulations that have been calculated.

metric models. In a nonlinear model the expected value of the stochastic simulations will not, in general, be equivalent to simulations setting the stochastic disturbances equal to their expected values (zero, in the usual case). Although this may be true, in practice the cost and effort entailed in extensive stochastic simulations means that this technique of model "auditing" has been used sparingly in recent years, as often researchers have judged that the gain in terms of the sharpness of model evaluation has not offset its total cost.[16] Helliwell et al. (1979) report attempting to use this technique for evaluation in their comparative study of macroeconometric models, without, however, obtaining much of value for this rather high-cost activity.

17.6 THE MODEL AS A SYSTEM OR GESTALT

Econometric models should reasonably be validated as entities or systems, rather than piecemeal. A good word to describe this approach, borrowed from experimental psychology, is the German word *gestalt* (which could be translated as "form," "shape," or "figure"). In particular, this approach would give relatively little weight to single-equation tests and even less weight to single-coefficient tests. Instead, the emphasis would be put on dynamic simulations of the full model.[17]

However, there is still more that can be done. Before making a model and its results publicly available, one can test all of the important policy levers, the instrumental variables of Chapter 16. These pre-release policy simulations should give reasonable results. This is not to say that a counterintuitive result is necessarily wrong (after all, this is generally the way in which progress is made in science), but such counterintuitive results must be clearly understood in the context of the functioning of the model, and at least a plausible case must be made that the "real world" does indeed behave in this manner. Other important features of the structure of a model should also be tested. Thus, in the context of a macroeconometric model of an open economy, one might wish to test the model's implied behavior for such critical phenomena as foreign exchange effects, the path of potential output, income shares, the rate of personal saving, the rate of productivity growth, and perhaps other phenomena. Again, counterintuitive results, although not necessarily absolutely disqualifying, may serve as a warning that the researcher may wish to take into account. In this context, note that simulations into the future (or at least beyond the sample period) may be very useful in validating an econometric model, in the sense of giving the model builder confidence that the model will hold up in a variety of contexts. In particular, again in the context of a macroeconometric model, Eckstein (1983) suggests that the model be the subject of *ex-ante* simulations under a fairly regular development of the exogenous variables to see whether the model will indeed generate balanced growth paths of the endogenous variables into the future. The rationale for this test is that most economists would argue that with regular development of the exogenous variables and in the absence of random perturbations, the macroeconomy should indeed settle into a path of balanced growth for the major endogenous variables.

Finally, another example of the testing of the model as a system or *gestalt* is to subject it to extreme pressures, to see whether the response of the system is reasonable. (It is

[16]See, however, the volume by Bryant et al. (1993), where the basis for the overall study is one of stochastic simulation. See also Mariano and Brown (1991), who place considerable emphasis on this technique.

[17]See Eckstein (1983) for an exposition of this position.

also obviously much better for the welfare of the economic agents to subject the model, rather than the economy itself, to such extreme pressures.) Again using the example of a macroeconometric model, can strong shocks (positive or negative, as the case may be) produce a hyperinflation or a major depression, respectively, as we believe the likely response of the real-world economy would be? Behavior at the extremes may well reveal much about the functioning of an econometric model in general, and thus either reinforce our confidence in it or lead us to replace at least its weakly functioning sectors or subsectors.

Thus the challenges to model builders have varied over the years, with full-system testing having become much more important in recent years. In some respects this makes perfect sense, as a model is a system, representing a whole entity, and thus much different from a simple collection of its individual parts. For example, a particular structural relationship may be quite adequate on the basis of single-equation criteria, yet this relationship may perturb greatly an otherwise well-functioning system. Accordingly, in validating an econometric model, it is very sensible to put the emphasis on the functioning of the system as a whole.

17.7 THE PROBLEM OF A POSSIBLE BREAK IN STRUCTURE; THE "LUCAS CRITIQUE"

The Chow test (discussed in Sections 4.6 and 17.4) is one possible method for testing for a break in structure. A break in structure is always a serious matter because it implies that *none* of the statistical techniques (hypothesis testing, confidence intervals, etc.) is valid any longer. Moreover, the substantive conclusions about the system being modeled that one might wish to draw are also vitiated, to a greater or smaller extent. Consider an important instance, much discussed in current macroeconometric literature, where this problem of a break in structure comes to the fore.

An important *possibility* of a break in structure is the "Lucas critique" (1976) of macroeconometric model building, discussed in Chapter 1. According to this view, the structural parameters of the macroeconomy (and hence those of the macroeconometric model attempting to represent this structural model) depend upon the nature of the policy regime that is in operation at a particular moment in time. In this view, every time the policy regime changes (or, indeed, every time the policymakers operate discretionary policy variables at a different setting) the structural parameters of the system (or at least some of them) *will change*![18] If this criticism were both true *and* an important source of changes in the structural parameters of a model, this objection would appear to be fatal to the estimation of econometric models, as well as their uses for policy purposes, as described in Chapter 16. However, Eckstein (1983) and Klein (1983) argue that this question is principally an empirical issue: Are these (possible) sources of disturbance or shock to the structural parameters sufficiently large in magnitude that previous techniques are indeed vitiated, or can regime changes from this source simply be absorbed into the disturbance terms included in each of the structural equations? Eckstein (1983) made an extensive attempt to answer this question, based on a survey of the forecasting errors in the DRI model of the U.S. economy. His

[18] Such an assertion need not always favor a monetarist approach, although it would appear to favor a noninterventionist approach. In the face of ignorance, better not to intervene, especially if the existing situation is deemed to be relatively optimal (or close to such an optimum).

major conclusion, after a thorough review of the forecasting errors of this model, was that shifts in policy regimes did not appear to be the major source of forecasting errors during the period studied. Instead, the major sources of forecasting errors appeared to be misguesses with regard to the realized values of the exogenous values of the model and also "autonomous" shocks coming from wars, strikes, embargoes, and so on, which affected the behavioral relationships of the system.

17.8 MANAGERIAL ASPECTS OF MODEL USES: FOUR EXAMPLES

To illustrate the working out in practice of some of these principles, consider four examples: model projects for the U.S., Canadian, and U.K. economies, and one that details the result of the U.S. economy to the state of California. The first modeling project is the Data Resources Incorporated (DRI) model of the U.S. economy.[19] Eckstein (1976) notes that the DRI model at that time contained roughly 900 endogenous variables and roughly 450 exogenous variables, but the organization maintained (at the time of writing) a data base of over 20,000 series. In other words, statistical information is regarded as the core of the service that DRI provides its subscribers, and the DRI macroeconometric model is, from one perspective, only a device for the organization of a minority subset (admittedly, an important minority subset) of this information. In particular, an enormous amount of working time goes into the collection, storage, accuracy maintenance, and retrieval of statistical information. Particular stress may be laid on the accuracy checks of statistical data; the possibility of human error due to fatigue, inattention, or other human failings has not been neglected by the DRI managers, and a fair number of accuracy checks have been built into their system for managing the data. As suggested above, in one view a macroeconometric model is simply an information system, which one attempts to render as accurate as possible. Thus the DRI personnel calculate after-the-fact postmortems of their *ex-ante* forecasts on a regular basis. Such internal evaluations help to point up possible trouble spots and make the internal audits of the model as useful as possible.

Many of the same lessons have emerged from the experience of Informetrica Limited, a modeling and software consulting group in Ottawa, Canada. Informetrica has produced a model with the acronym *TIM* (The Informetrica Model), a lineal descendent of the CANDIDE model reviewed in Chapter 12. As a recent version of TIM had roughly 6000 endogenous variables and 1100 exogenous variables, it is immediately apparent that a great deal of time must be spent on data management. Indeed, Informetrica duplicates DRI's experience of devoting a majority of its resources to the various aspects of data management. [In Informetrica's case, this is particularly true, because another important portion of the modeling effort is *RIM* (Regional Informetrica Model), which is a collection of 10 submodels of the economies of the 10 provinces of Canada, driven by a top-down spin-off from the national model, TIM. The data requirements to operate this system are obviously immense, and in some cases Informetrica has had to undertake to collect the data directly from primary sources.] Two other lessons that have emerged from the Informetrica experience are the importance of refining the model almost continually in order to learn from the mistakes of the past, and the importance of doing internal "audits" on the accuracy of past *ex-*

[19]Chapter 12 includes an overview of the DRI model.

ante forecasts.[20] Perhaps a critical final lesson is that economic theory and econometric theory are two essential but not sufficient elements in the construction of a successful macroeconometric model, a lesson undoubtedly experienced by other model builders also.

Another successful modeling project has been the UCLA model of California.[21] This project has been in operation for a long time, with the focus being short-run and medium-term projections of the economy of the state of California in general, with some specialization to the Los Angeles metropolitan region in particular. The projections are run from satellite models of these specific regions, driven by a model of the U.S. national economy. Again, lessons of model management and model validation have been experienced. At a regional level, the problem of data management is even more critical than at the national level, as in the case of Informetrica's experience. Second, *ex-post* evaluations of *ex-ante* forecasts can be a valuable instrument of management control, suggesting weaknesses in the existing model and leading to useful respecifications. Third, economic forecasts are not value-free, particularly of political values; at times, economic forecasts of a region as politically unified as a state can be very emotionally laden to politicians who regard themselves as judged by such forecasts![22] Finally, judgment of all sorts is very important in the art of model building and model maintenance. Not only is judgment useful for selecting the value of the add factors, where in some cases the appropriate course is far from obvious, but judgment enters in, in critical ways, when it becomes necessary to respecify the model. Of course, the question of when the existing model can no longer be patched but must be respecified and reestimated is itself a critical matter of judgment.

The final example is that of ESRC (Economic and Social Research Council), the macroeconomic modeling bureau for macroeconometric models of the U.K. economy, established at the University of Warwick in 1983.[23] This organization was established by a competition to provide a central bureau for the evaluation of macroeconometric models, following the sentiment that the then existing econometric models of the U.K. economy were both inadequate for precise policy advice and differed sufficiently among themselves that comparative analysis among the models and their forecasts could be quite useful. This bureau has maintained for some time a portfolio of models in which all stages of model management (design, execution, and analysis, including forecasts) have been examined. The fact that almost all major model builders in the United Kingdom are dependent on public money has been a nontrivial factor compelling adherence to membership in this cooperative endeavor. However, private modeling enterprises are not excluded, and Wallis (1993) reports that in recent years the bureau's portfolio has included one private-sector organization.

[20]In recent years, Informetrica Limited has served as the host for a field trip for Bodkin's class in economic models and policy applications, providing valuable field experience to supplement the materials that can be taught more naturally in the classroom.

[21]See the UCLA Business Forecasting Project (1991–).

[22]Thus, on one occasion, when the UCLA model suggested that the predicted national recession would very likely be even more severe in the state of California, a high official of the state government suggested that perhaps the funding for UCLA might not be independent of the forecasts of the model project. Although it seems extremely unlikely that such a threat would be carried out given the traditions of American academic freedom, the basic point remains: forecasts of all sorts, such as those generated by an econometric modeling project, can be extremely threatening on occasion.

[23]See Wallis (1988, 1993) and Wallis et al. (1987).

Many valuable lessons have been learned from this endeavor, including the importance of a continuing secretariat to monitor the lessons learned from comparative experience. Another lesson is that of slow, steady progress in model building rather than quantum leaps or major breakthroughs (as a general rule). Still another lesson is the importance of a variety of tests, as Hendry (1980) has stressed in a variety of contexts, in order to produce relationships that are reliable in policy analysis. In particular, this models-comparison project (and some of the work with the Wharton and DRI projects) suggests that macroeconomic theory and econometric theory have aided macroeconometric modeling in recent years. Finally, Wallis (1988) has argued that the "Lucas critique" (as discussed above and explained in Section 1.7) need not be disabling for macroeconometric modelers and users, as the system can be run with "model-consistent" expectations, and estimation theory can be developed that takes this complication into account.

17.9 MODEL MANAGEMENT AND THE ROLE OF JUDGMENT

A model-building enterprise is a complex organization, often with delicate problems of management. As with other organizations, management involves the human factor. With model building, data—raw data, partially processed data, and/or refined data—are the lifeblood of the enterprise. Since data errors tend to creep into the system, one characteristic of good management is that procedures will be instituted to keep data errors to an absolute minimum, as in the case of examples of the preceding section.

In terms of the model itself, which is the object of the organization's productive efforts, a number of approaches have been discussed for "validating" an econometric model, which is to say attempting to render the model *sufficiently* accurate for the purposes at hand. From the discussion of Chapter 2 it may be recalled that no model is ever a completely accurate reproduction of the phenomenon being modeled. Indeed, a completely faithful reproduction would probably be the entity itself being modeled, and that would be useless.[24] Nevertheless, it is desirable to have models that are quite good reproductions. Thus a number of formal tests, both of individual equations of the model and of the system as a whole, have been suggested. These tests represent the "scientific" aspect of the process of validating a model, although, even in this regard, judgment will enter when the investigator or model manager has to combine the results of several formal statistical or econometric tests in an informal manner, which ideally will be tempered by good judgment. In this area, as in many other domains, a great deal of relevant experience is a powerful aid to good judgment.

Despite the impressive number of formal techniques for evaluating the validity of an econometric model, the role of judgment in such a process should not be underestimated. At times, the decision process will have to be one in which the judgment of the investigator or researcher becomes an important, if not critical, element. In other words, the disci-

[24]A story from the early 1960s illustrates this point beautifully. It appeared that a student of the late Professor E. Kuh had become very excited because he had obtained an equation for national accounts capital consumption allowances in the United States with an R^2 value of 0.999. Professor Kuh was (correctly) suspicious and called a contact at the Department of Commerce. It turned out that the student had inadvertently reproduced the equation by which the Department of Commerce itself estimated this national accounts concept. The story also illustrates the danger of an overreliance on the coefficient of multiple determination in the selection of models; it will be recalled that this criterion was *not* recommended (nor even mentioned) in Section 17.4.

pline of model building is still largely an art form rather than an exercise in pure science, and this should always be borne in mind by the investigator. Thus it is rare that some criterion function can make a critical decision; judgment will generally have to play a role at the decision stage.

An example from Leamer (1983a) has the charming title, "Let's Take the Con out of Econometrics." Leamer's article quotes several amusing aphorisms pertaining to econometrics, such as "If you torture the data long enough, Nature will confess"; "There are two things that you are better off not watching in the making: sausages and econometric estimates"[25]; and "Econometricians, like artists, tend to fall in love with their models." Leamer illustrates these aphorisms with statistics from the states of the United States on the crime of murder. Leamer shows that the sample in question is very ambiguous with regard to the critical question of whether a death penalty does or does not deter homicide. Indeed, the data are ambiguous enough that the conclusion appears to depend critically on how the regression equation is specified, which in turn will be related to the underlying theoretical framework (prejudices?) of the investigator. Leamer uses this example to make two important points, which, in turn, are closely related to the Bayesian critique of classical econometrics.[26] First, many of the conclusions of the scholarly community are fragile, in the sense that they are not strongly supported by the empirical evidence or are not robust to alternative specifications. Second, the beliefs that drive model specification are often whimsical, in that they rest on strong theoretical or even emotional preconceptions. Thus, in many cases, nothing at all can be concluded from a strictly scientific point of view. Nevertheless, in many cases a tentative conclusion may be possible and even necessary, if only because an immediate policy decision is required. Thus, in the example used by Leamer, state legislators have to decide whether to retain, to reintroduce, or to abolish the death penalty, even though obviously its possible deterrent effect is only one of the relevant considerations. This is where *judgment* enters, for which formal test criteria are ultimately no substitute. The researcher should be open in admitting the basis (and biases) of the model and should ideally consider alternative specifications.

Another way to express this point of view is that in the present state of the discipline, econometric model building (and model maintenance and management) is essentially an art, not applied science. It is, to be sure, an art form constrained in important ways by a number of rules of scientific procedure that have been carefully built up by the discipline of econometrics (theoretical and applied) over a long period of time. As with any art, the aspiring student will learn deeply only by doing, and that is why the student reader should work carefully through Appendix A, "An Econometric Project," by formulating, estimating, and interpreting her or his own original econometric project.

PROBLEMS

17-A Show that in the context of the consumption category relationships of Section 17.2, a necessary and sufficient condition for the sum of the predicted levels of real category consumption per capita to be identically equal to the generating level of real per capita disposable income (the property of ad-

[25]This saying itself is obviously a variation of Bismarck's aphorism that there are two things that one is better off not observing in the making: sausages and legislation.

[26]Two sources for the Bayesian point of view are Zellner (1971) and Leamer (1980).

ditive consistency) is that the sum of the category MPCs should be unity, while the sum across categories for all other explanatory variables (including the constant term) should be zero.

17-B Finish the sketch of the proof, begun in Section 17.2, that least squares estimators of the category relationships do indeed satisfy the property of additive consistency. (*Hint*: Consider the interpretation of the sum of the category regression coefficient estimators as the result of a least squares regression of $\mathbf{X}_k$ on the entire set of explanatory variables. Are these estimators unique? Why or why not? In particular, what is one obvious set of regression coefficient estimators that will set the sum of the residuals of this artificial regression always equal to zero? Now apply Problem 17-A.)

17-C Show that the property of additive consistency for the consumption category coefficient estimators also holds if these estimators are obtained from a two-stage least squares process where all predetermined variables are included in the first-stage regressions. [*Hint*: Show that nothing essential is changed if $\mathbf{X}_k$ is interpreted as the first-stage estimator of real disposable income per capita rather than the measured values of this variable itself, so the only minimizing choice for the artificial regression under consideration is a vector equal to (0, 0, 0, . . . , 1), as before.]

BIBLIOGRAPHY

BODKIN, R. G. (1974). "Additively Consistent Relationships for Personal Savings and the Categories of Consumption Expenditures, U.S.A., 1949–1963." *Eastern Economic Journal*, 1: 20–51.

BRAINARD, W. C., and J. TOBIN (1968). "Pitfalls in Financial Model Building." *American Economic Review, Papers and Proceedings*, 58: 99–122.

BRYANT, R., P. HOOPER, and C. L. MANN, Eds. (1993). *Evaluating Policy Regimes: New Research in Empirical Macroeconomics*. Washington, D.C.: The Brookings Institution.

CHOW, G. (1960). "Tests of Equality between Sets of Coefficients in Two Linear Regressions." *Econometrica*, 28: 591–605.

CHRIST, C. F. (1975). "Judging the Performance of Econometric Models of the U.S. Economy." *International Economic Review*, 16: 54–74.

DHRYMES, P. J., E. P. HOWREY, S. HYMANS, J. KMENTA, E. E. LEAMER, R. E. QUANDT, J. B. RAMSEY, H. T. SHAPIRO, and V. ZARNOWITZ (1972). "Criteria for the Evaluation of Econometric Models." *Annals of Economic and Social Measurement*, 1: 291–324.

ECKSTEIN, O. (1976). "Econometric Models and Business Expectations." *Economic Impact*, 16: 44–51.

ECKSTEIN, O. (1983). *The DRI Model of the U.S. Economy*. New York: McGraw-Hill Book Company.

FAIR, R. C. (1974). "An Evaluation of a Short-Run Forecasting Model." *International Economic Review*, 15: 285–303.

FAIR, R. C. (1980). "Estimating the Expected Predictive Accuracy of Econometric Models." *International Economic Review*, 21: 355–378.

FAIR, R. C. (1984). *Specification, Estimation and Analysis of Macroeconometric Models*. Cambridge, Mass.: Harvard University Press.

FAIR, R. C. (1993). "Testing Macroeconometric Models." *American Economic Review, Papers and Proceedings*, 83: 287–293.

GENBERG, H. (1972). "Constraints on the Parameters in Two Simple Simultaneous Equation Models." *Econometrica*, 40: 855–865.

HELLIWELL, J. F., T. MAXWELL, and H. E. L. WASLANDER (1979). "Comparing the Dynamics of Canadian Macromodels." *Canadian Journal of Economics*, 12: 181–194.

HENDRY, D. F. (1980). "Econometrics—Alchemy or Science?" *Economica*, N.S., 47: 387–406.

KLEIN, L. R. (1983). *Lectures in Econometrics*. Amsterdam: North-Holland Publishing Company.

KLEIN, L. R., Ed. (1991). *Comparative Performance of U.S. Econometric Models*. New York: Oxford University Press.

LEAMER, E. E. (1978). *Specification Searches: Ad Hoc Inference with Nonexperimental Data*. New York: John Wiley & Sons, Inc.

LEAMER, E. E. (1983a). "Let's Take the Con out of Econometrics." *American Economic Review*, 73: 31–43.

LEAMER, E. E. (1983b). "Model Choice and Specification Analysis," in Z. Griliches and M. D. Intriligator, Eds., *Handbook of Econometrics*, Vol. 1. Amsterdam: North-Holland Publishing Company.

LUCAS, R. E., JR. (1976). "Econometric Policy Evaluation: A Critique," in K. Brunner and A. H. Meltzer, Eds., *The Phillips Curve and Labor Markets*, Vol. 1 of Carnegie-Rochester Conference Series on Public Policy. Amsterdam: North-Holland Publishing Company. Reprinted in R. E. Lucas, Jr., *Studies in Business-Cycle Theory*. Cambridge, Mass.: MIT Press, 1981.

MARIANO, R. S., and B. W. BROWN (1991). "Stochastic-Simulation Tests of Nonlinear Econometric Models," in Klein, Ed. (1991).

SMITH, G. (1975). "Pitfalls in Financial Model Building: A Clarification." *American Economic Review*, 65: 510–516.

UCLA BUSINESS FORECASTING PROJECT (1991–). *The UCLA Business Forecast for the Nation*. Los Angeles: John E. Anderson Graduate School of Management at UCLA, quarterly.

WALLIS, K. F. (1988). "Comments [on 'A Survey of Non-Dutch European Macroeconometric Models: Some International Perspective']," in W. Driehuis, M. M. G. Fase, and H. den Hartog, Eds., *Challenges for Macroeconomic Modelling*. Amsterdam: North-Holland Publishing Company.

WALLIS, K. F. (1993). "Comparing Macroeconometric Models: A Review Article." *Economica*, 60: 225–237.

WALLIS, K. F., P. G. FISHER, J. A. LONGBOTTOM, D. S. TURNER, and J. D. WHITLEY (1987). *Models of the UK Economy: A Fourth Review by the Macroeconomic Modelling Bureau*. Oxford: Oxford University Press.

ZELLNER, A. (1971). *An Introduction to Bayesian Inference in Econometrics*. New York: John Wiley & Sons, Inc.

ZELLNER, A. (1972). "Constraints Often Overlooked in Analyses of Simultaneous Equation Models." *Econometrica*, 40: 849–853.

APPENDIX A

AN ECONOMETRIC PROJECT

A.1 THE NATURE OF THE ECONOMETRIC PROJECT

A basic purpose of this book is to prepare its readers to carry out their own econometric study. The econometric project is a case study in formulating an original econometric model, collecting data relevant to the model, using econometric techniques to estimate the model, and interpreting the results obtained. It is strongly suggested that all readers, but especially students, actually carry out such a study. As noted in the Preface, econometrics, to a large extent, is best learned by actually doing an econometric study. Only then will the "uninitiated" learn the power as well as the pitfalls of the econometric approach. This appendix will guide the student in carrying out an econometric project.

As in any econometric study the "raw materials" are a model and a relevant set of data. These are the topics of the next two sections. Section A.4 treats estimation of the model, and in Section A.5 we summarize what to include in the write-up of the paper, which is most clearly and succinctly expressed in the style of an article in a scholarly journal.

A.2 THE MODEL

The model and the data are the starting points of an econometric project. The first step in formulating a model is to select a topic of interest and to consider the model's scope and purpose. In particular thought should be given to the objectives of the study, what boundaries to place on the topic, what hypotheses might be tested, what variables might be predicted, and what policies might be evaluated. Close attention must be paid, however, to the availability of adequate data: it is all too easy to design an ambitious project that fails for lack of data. In particular the model must involve *causal* relations among *measurable* variables. The most useful type of model in this context is typically a simultaneous-equations model, as discussed in Sections 2.8 to 2.10 and treated extensively in Chapters 9 and 10.

The topic selected can be either economic or noneconomic. It could be a particular market (e.g., the market for aerospace engineers, the market for pharmacists, the onion market, the markets for professional football seats and players), a process (economic development, political development, inflation), demographic phenomena (birth rates, death rates), environmental phenomena (water quality, air quality), political phenomena (elections, voting behavior of legislatures), some combination of these, or some other topic. Some topics that have been studied in student econometric papers are:[1]

Age at First Marriage: An Econometric Study of Becker's Theory of Marriage
Air Pollution and Population
Airline Deregulation
Bank Profitability
Baseball Performance and Attendance
Beer Consumption
Credit Card Delinquency Rate
Death in Motor Vehicle Accidents
Demand for and Supply of Higher Education
Demand for and Supply of Life Insurance
Demographic and Policy Evaluation of Divorce
Determinants of Hospital Wages
Determination of the Prime Rate: Comparison of the Policies of Various Chairmen of the Federal Reserve Board
Differential Growth of U.S. Cities
Discrimination in Retail Food Markets
Drug Use in the Elderly
Economic and Social Determinants of Infant Mortality in the United States
Effects of the Increase in the Minimum Drinking Age on Alcohol-Related Traffic Accidents
Elections and Money
Exports, Growth, and Import Substitution in Developing Economies
Factors Affecting Abortions
Female Participation in the Labor Force
Hypertension, Smoking, Personal Income, and Their Effects on the Onset of Heart Disease
Industry Profit Rates
Medical School Applications

[1]For applied econometric studies on various topics, see the bibliography for this appendix. See also the bibliographies for Chapters 7, 8, 12, and 13 for more "standard" econometric studies of demand, production and cost, macroeconomics, and other areas.

Mental Health Hospitals in the United States
Minority Enrollment in Higher Education
Mortality Rate Due to Coronary Heart Disease
Mutual Fund Performance
Negative Human Impact on Species Survival Rates
Police Expenditures and the Deterrence of Crime
Price and Quantity of Soybeans
The Price of Gold
Rates of Natural Increase in African Nations
The Recreational Vehicle Market
Religious Participation in the United States
Residential Water Use and Pricing
Salary and Performance of Major League Baseball Players
Social and Economic Factors Affecting Mortality
Supply of and Demand for Women in the Labor Force
Teen Pregnancies in the United States
Third World Competition and De-industrialization in Advanced Economies
Unemployment and Crime
Unemployment and the Suicide Rate
Unionization and Strike Activity
Youth Unemployment and High School Dropouts

Perhaps the best choice of a topic is one that the student has prior experience in or knowledge of, for example, one that may have been the subject of another course or that otherwise has been of previous interest. Of course, the previous literature on the subject should be identified and studied. Good sources are library catalogs and various indexes of the periodic literature.[2] The relevant literature should indicate, or at least suggest, a model and also hypotheses to be tested, variables to be forecast, and policies to be evaluated. It can also be a useful guide to relevant data.

All variables of the model should be defined, and the student should indicate for each whether it is being treated as endogenous or exogenous. If possible, these assumptions should be justified. To ensure that the model is both interesting and manageable it should contain at least two or three endogenous variables, three or four exogenous variables, and, if time-series data are used, one lagged endogenous variable. For purposes of this project, however, the number of variables should probably be limited to no more than, say, three endogenous and eight exogenous variables. The model should then be formulated as a set of algebraic, linear, stochastic equations and a corresponding verbal statement of the meaning of each equation. If appropriate, all identities, equilibrium conditions, definitions, and other non-

[2]For the general social science literature since 1973 see the *Social Sciences Citation Index*, which not only classifies articles by subject but also lists them by cited author. This index is extremely useful in identifying articles, given only the names of any individual author(s) who has (have) worked on the topic.

stochastic equations might then be eliminated. The resulting structural equations should be expressed as a matrix equation. From this structural form, the reduced form and, if appropriate, the final form should be determined and presented, both as sets of equations and as matrix equations.[3] This development of the model can follow that of Sections 2.5 and 2.6 on the prototype micro model and prototype macro model, respectively.

The expected signs of all structural and reduced-form coefficients should be given, and they should be utilized to analyze the comparative statics properties of the model, as in Figure 2.5. All relevant multipliers, short-run and long-run, should also be identified and discussed.

The last step in the development of the model is to investigate its identification. Both order and rank conditions of identification should be checked for each structural equation, and the model adjusted, if necessary, so as to ensure that all equations are either exactly identified or overidentified.[4] For all exactly identified equations it should be shown explicitly how the structural parameters can be inferred from reduced-form parameters, as in equations (2.10.5) for the prototype micro model.

A.3 THE DATA

Data form an essential ingredient in any econometric study, and obtaining an adequate and relevant set of data is an important and often critical part of the econometric project. Data should be available for all variables of the model, both endogenous and exogenous.

Good starting points for the acquisition of relevant data are the various national and international statistical abstracts or yearbooks. National *Statistical Abstracts, Statistical Yearbooks*, or *Statistical Handbooks*, published annually by the United States, Canada, the United Kingdom, and many other countries, provide both summary statistics and references to primary sources. The United Nations *Statistical Yearbook* provides a wealth of data on member countries, as do statistical yearbooks of other international organizations. Various almanacs and other reference works also abound in statistics. These sources contain data on so many topics that they may suggest a topic for the econometric project; to this end, Tables A.1 and A.2 summarize the contents of recent issues of the *Statistical Abstract of the United States* and the United Nations *Statistical Yearbook*, respectively. Table 3.5 in Chapter 3 provides an overall summary of sources of data.

Data can be either time-series or cross-section. For this project it is probably best not to pool data of the two types. Also it is best to avoid too-small data sets (e.g., fewer than, say, 15 observations).

The data should be examined and, if necessary, refined to make them suitable for the purposes of the model. For time-series data it may be necessary to use seasonal adjustment or perhaps to eliminate certain trends. For both time-series and cross-section data consideration should be given to whether to divide the data or perhaps exclude certain observations. Thus in time-series data it may (or may not) be appropriate to exclude war years or

[3]The reduced form should generally be a system of equations different from the structural form. If it is the same, not enough interactions among endogenous variables have been incorporated in the model, which should be reformulated to allow for such interactions.

[4]This adjustment is necessary, since the estimation technique to be employed, two-stage least squares, requires that all structural equations be exactly identified or overidentified.

TABLE A.1 Contents of a Recent *Statistical Abstract of the United States*

Section	
1. Population	18. Communications
2. Vital Statistics, Health, and Nutrition	19. Energy
3. Immigration and Naturalization	20. Science
4. Education	21. Transportation—Land
5. Law Enforcement, Federal Courts, and Prisons	22. Transportation—Air and Water
6. Geography and Environment	23. Agriculture
7. Public Lands, Parks, Recreation, and Travel	24. Forests and Forest Products
8. Federal Government Finances and Employment	25. Fisheries
9. State and Local Government Finances and Employment	26. Mining and Mineral Products
10. Social Insurance and Welfare Services	27. Construction and Housing
11. National Defense and Veterans Affairs	28. Manufactures
12. Labor Force, Employment, and Earnings	29. Distribution and Services
13. Income, Expenditures, and Wealth	30. Foreign Commerce and Aid
14. Prices	31. Outlying Areas under the Jurisdiction of the United States
15. Elections	32. Comparative International Statistics
16. Banking, Finance, and Insurance	33. Federal Administrative Regions and States
17. Business Enterprise	34. Metropolitan Area Statistics

TABLE A.2 Contents of a Recent United Nations *Statistical Yearbook*

Section	
World Summary	Transport
Population	Communications
Manpower	Consumption
Agriculture	Balance of Payments
Forestry	Wages and Prices
Fishing	National Accounts
Industrial Production	Finance
Mining, Quarrying	Public Finance
Manufacturing	Development Assistance
Construction	Health
Energy	Housing
Internal Trade	Education
External Trade	Science and Technology

years of recession. In a cross section of nations it may be inappropriate in an economic study to include all countries that are UN members; rather, the developed countries might be treated as one group and the developing countries as another. Dividing the data this way into subsamples not only leads to more homogeneous data sets but also facilitates the study by allowing comparative analyses. Thus, for a study using the UN data, a comparison of results for developed and developing countries would facilitate structural analysis (e.g., finding the greatest differences between the results from the two subsamples), forecasting (e.g., using current information on developed countries as proxies or predictions for future values of variables in developing countries), and policy evaluation (e.g., mapping out policies for developing countries that would enable them to follow the lead—or avoid the mistakes—of the developed countries).

A.4 ESTIMATION OF THE MODEL

After both model and data have been developed the next step is to utilize econometric techniques to estimate the model. Since the model utilizes several equations to determine values of several endogenous variables, the appropriate technique is one of simultaneous-equations estimation. Among these techniques, one of the most widely used is that of two-stage least squares (2SLS), as discussed in Section 10.5, which is recommended unless there are reasons for using another technique.

The model is most conveniently, quickly, and inexpensively estimated using a computer, and virtually all computers have library source programs for multiple linear regression.[5] Such a source program makes computer programming unnecessary, and typically the only cards that must be prepared are the control cards and the data cards, in the appropriate format.

To use a library multiple linear regression program to perform 2SLS, each of the two stages is estimated separately. In the first stage each of the reduced-form equations is estimated. The resulting estimates of the reduced form are used in the second stage. They are also of interest in their own right: they are quantitative estimates of the comparative statics of the model, giving for each endogenous variable the magnitudes of change associated with changes in each of the exogenous and lagged endogenous variables.

To prepare for the second stage, the estimated parameters of the reduced form are used to determine calculated values of endogenous variables from the reduced form. Some programs provide these estimates, but with a relatively small model and data set this calculation can be done easily with a small calculator.

The second stage is then completed by using the library source program for multiple linear regression once again to estimate each of the structural equations, replacing actual values of explanatory endogenous variables by their calculated values.[6]

The outputs of this estimation thus include both estimated reduced-form equations (as in Section 4.9) and estimated structural equations.

A.5 WHAT TO INCLUDE IN THE WRITE-UP

Unless there are reasons for doing otherwise, the best style to use in the final write-up of the econometric project is that of an article in a scholarly journal, a style that is both clear and succinct.[7] It should include the following:

[5]Examples of library source programs useful for applied econometric studies are those in RATS, SAS, SHAZAM, and STATA. Some of these library source programs also include 2SLS, but they generally do not print the results of the first state, namely the estimated reduced-form equations. For this reason, use might be made of both the 2SLS source program for the structural-form equations and the ordinary multiple linear regression source program for the reduced-form equations.

[6]This approach will yield the 2SLS estimates of the structural-form equations but it will not yield the correct standard errors or t-values, since the estimate of the variance of the stochastic disturbance term is based on the sum of squares of the $\hat{v}_1$ from (10.5.15) rather than the correct sum of squares of the $\hat{\varepsilon}_1$ from (10.5.14), as in (10.6.35) (see Problem 10-K). To obtain the standard errors and t-values requires either correcting the $\hat{v}_1$, using (10.5.16), or using a 2SLS source program, as in footnote 5.

[7]For examples of such articles, which might be considered models for econometric papers, see the articles in journals such as the *American Economic Review*, *Econometrica*, the *International Economic Review*, the *Journal of Econometrics*, and the *Review of Economics and Statistics*. See, in particular, the articles cited in Chapters 7, 8, 12, and 13, as well as the bibliography of this appendix.

1. A *title page*, including a descriptive title and names of all authors (students may gain more from a collaborative paper, involving two or three authors, than from a singly authored paper).
2. A *one-page abstract*, including a brief description of the topic; a summary of the variables and of the model; a discussion of the type of data used and the data sources; statements of the estimated equation; a summary of the uses of the estimated model for structural analysis, forecasting, and policy evaluation; and the most important conclusions.
3. An *introductory section*, stating the nature and objectives of the study; a general description of the scope and nature of the model; and what will be done with the estimated model in terms of structural analysis (including hypotheses to be tested), forecasting (identifying the variables to be forecast and over what periods), and policy evaluation (indicating the relevant decision maker, the policy variables, and the method to be used in obtaining values for these variables).
4. A section on the *previous literature*, summarizing the most important articles or books presenting the theory of the subject and those presenting empirical or econometric work on the topic, comparing their theory and model, data, and results to those of the study.
5. A section on the *model*, including definitions and discussion of each of the variables of the study; an indication as to which is endogenous and which is exogenous (discussing what theory or prior study justifies each as endogenous or exogenous); a formulation of the structural form, the reduced form, and (where relevant) the final form of the model; a discussion of the expected signs of coefficients and the comparative statics of the model; a summary of the stochastic and other assumptions being made concerning the model; and a discussion of how the model relates, if possible, to a standard model (e.g., the prototype micro model of demand/supply, the prototype macro model, consumer behavior, producer behavior, cost functions, portfolio theory).
6. A section on the *data*, including a table summarizing all data used, a complete description of their nature, their sources, refinements used, and their possible biases or other weaknesses. Include data on both endogenous and exogenous variables, and put data on a consistent basis (e.g., per capita or total), rescaling if necessary to measure variables in convenient units.
7. A section on the *estimated model*, including estimates of the reduced-form and structural-form parameters; related statistics, including standard errors and t statistics, and a discussion of which coefficients are significant at the 0.05 and 0.01 levels; R^2, F, and Durbin–Watson statistics for each equation and a discussion of their implications; and discussions of possible problems and their treatment, including multicollinearity, serial correlation, and heteroskedasticity. If possible, estimate the model for two different data sets, and compare the results (e.g., divide the sample into two subsamples, estimate each separately, and compare the two estimates). (This approach is preferable to the use of dummy variables, as it allows the slope coefficients as well as the intercept to be affected).
8. A section on the *uses of the estimated model*: its explicit and quantitative uses for structural analysis (including hypotheses tested and conclusions reached with regard to signs, values of coefficients, multipliers, and elasticities, comparing them to prior

studies); forecasting [including specific ex-ante or ex-post forecasts for periods (e.g., years) or units (e.g., countries) not in the sample, indicating how values for exogenous variables and add factors were obtained, and comparing forecasted and actual values]; and policy evaluation (including a discussion of the policy variables of the model, the approach used to determine optimal policy, and specific values for policy variables and their trade-offs).

9. A section on *overall conclusions*, including major findings, comparisons to the results of other studies, and suggestions for future studies.
10. A *bibliography*, including complete citations of all items referred to in the paper. Use the *Social Science Citation Index* to identify prior studies.

A.6 A BIBLIOGRAPHY OF ECONOMETRIC APPLICATIONS

From the following bibliography of the literature using econometric methods, the reader will see how extensive use is made of econometrics in all fields of economics and to various areas of social concern. This bibliography should be especially helpful to students doing research papers both in suggesting topics for such papers and in providing references that could be the basis for finding related publications on any of the topics covered (e.g., using these references as the starting point in a search in the *Social Science Citation Index*). See also the references in Chapters 7, 8, 12, and 13 for applications to the household, the firm, macroeconomics, and other areas of economics, respectively.

Commodity or Industry Models

ADAMS, F. G. (1977). "Primary Commodity Markets in a World Model System," in F. G. Adams and S. Klein, Eds., *Stabilizing World Commodity Markets*. Lexington, Mass.: D.C. Heath and Company.

CUMMINS, J. D. (1975). *An Econometric Model of the Life Insurance Sector of the U.S. Economy*. Lexington, Mass.: Lexington Books.

FISHER, F. M., P. H. COOTNER, and M. N. BAILY (1972). "An Econometric Model of the World Copper Industry." *Bell Journal of Economics and Management*, 3: 568–609.

HOROWITZ, I. (1963). "An Econometric Analysis of Supply and Demand in the Synthetic Rubber Industry." *International Economic Review*, 4: 325–345.

L'ESPERANCE, W. L. (1964). "A Case Study in Prediction: The Market for Watermelons." *Econometrica*, 32: 163–173.

ZUSMAN, P. (1962). "An Investigation of the Dynamic Stability and Stationary States of the United States Potato Market, 1930–1958." *Econometrica*, 30: 522–547.

Crime

EHRLICH, I. (1973). "Participation in Illegitimate Activities: A Theoretical and Empirical Investigation." *Journal of Political Economy*, 81: 521–565.

EHRLICH, I. (1975). "The Deterrent Effect of Capital Punishment: A Question of Life and Death." *American Economic Review*, 65: 397–417.

LEAMER, E. E. (1983). "Let's Take the Con out of Economics." *American Economic Review*, 73: 31–43.

MCPHETERS, L., and W. S. STRONG (1974). "Law Enforcement Expenditures and Urban Crime." *National Tax Journal*, 27: 633–644.

PHILLIPS, L., and H. L. VOTEY, JR. (1972). "An Economic Analysis of the Deterrent Effect of Law Enforcement on Criminal Activities." *Journal of Criminal Law, Criminology, and Policy Science*, 63: 336–342.

PHILLIPS, L., H. L. VOTEY, JR., and D. E. MAXWELL (1972). "Crime, Youth, and the Labor Market." *Journal of Political Economy*, 80: 491–504.

H. L. VOTEY, JR., and L. PHILLIPS (1972). "Police Effectiveness and the Production Function for Law Enforcement." *Journal of Legal Studies*, 1: 423–436.

Development Economics

BEHRMAN, J. R. (1972a). "Sectorial Investment Determination in a Developing Economy." *American Economic Review*, 62: 825–841.

BEHRMAN, J. R. (1972b). "Short-Run Flexibility in a Developing Economy." *Journal of Political Economy*, 80: 292–313.

CHENERY, H., and T. N. SRINIVASAN, Eds. (1988, 1989). *Handbook of Development Economics*, Vols. 1 and 2. Amsterdam: North-Holland Publishing Company.

YOTOPOULOS, P. A., and J. B. NUGENT (1976). *Economics of Development: Empirical Investigations*. New York: Harper & Row, Publishers, Inc.

Discrimination

AIGNER, D. J., and G. G. CAIN (1977). "Statistical Theories of Discrimination in Labor Markets." *Industrial and Labor Relations Review*, 30: 175–187.

ASHENFELTER, O., and A. REES, Eds. (1973). *Discrimination in Labor Markets*, Princeton, N.J.: Princeton University Press.

BLINDER, A. S. (1973). "Wage Discrimination: Reduced Form and Structural Estimates." *Journal of Human Resources*, 18: 436–455.

BLOOM, D. E., and M. R. KILLINGSWORTH (1982). "Pay Discrimination Research and Litigation: The Use of Regression Analysis." *Industrial Relations*, 21: 318–339.

CAIN, G. G. (1986). "The Economic Analysis of Labor Market Discrimination: A Survey," in O. Ashenfelter and R. Layard, Eds., *Handbook of Labor Economics*, Vol. 1. Amsterdam: North-Holland Publishing Company.

GOLDBERGER, A. S. (1984). "Reverse Regression and Salary Discrimination." *Journal of Human Resources*, 19: 293–318.

NEUMARK, D. (1988). "Employer Discriminatory Behavior and the Estimation of Wage Discrimination." *Journal of Human Resources*, 23: 279–295.

OAXACA, R. (1973). "Male–Female Wage Differentials in Urban Labor Markets." *International Economic Review*, 14: 693–709.

SMITH, J. P., and F. R. WELCH (1989). "Black Economic Progress after Myrdal." *Journal of Economic Literature*, 27: 519–564.

Economic Growth

BARRO, R. J. (1990). "Government Spending in a Simple Model of Economic Growth." *Journal of Political Economy*, 98: S103–S125.

BARRO, R. J. (1991). "Economic Growth in a Cross Section of Countries." *Quarterly Journal of Economics*, 106: 407–443.

JORGENSON, D. W., and K. Y. YUN (1990). "Tax Reform and U.S. Economic Growth." *Journal of Political Economy*, 98: S151–S193.

KORMENDI, R. C., and P. G. MEGUIRE (1985). "Macroeconomic Determinants of Growth: Cross-Country Evidence." *Journal of Monetary Economics*, 16: 141–163.

LANDAU, D. L. (1983). "Government Expenditure and Economic Growth: A Cross-Country Study." *Southern Economic Journal*, 49: 783–792.

Education

BECKER, G. S. (1964). *Human Capital*. New York: National Bureau of Economic Research.

BECKER, G. S., K. M. MURPHY, and R. TAMURA (1990). "Human Capital, Fertility and Economic Growth." *Journal of Political Economy*, 98: 12–37.

CAMPBELL, R., and B. N. SIEGEL (1967). "The Demand for Higher Education in the United Sates, 1919–1964." *American Economic Review*, 57: 482–494.

GRILICHES, Z. (1977). "Estimating the Returns to Schooling: Some Econometric Problems." *Econometrica*, 45: 1–22.

HANUSHEK, E. A. (1986). "The Economics of Schooling." *Journal of Economic Literature*, 24: 1141–1177.

MINCER, J. (1974). *Schooling, Experience and Earnings*. New York: Columbia University Press.

PSACHAROPOULOS, G. (1985). "Returns to Education: A Further International Update and Implications." *Journal of Human Resources*, 20: 583–604.

WILLIS, R. J. (1986). "Wage Determinants: A Survey and Reinterpretation of Human Capital Earnings Functions," in O. Ashenfelter and R. Layard, Eds., *Handbook of Labor Economics*, Vols. 1 and 2. Amsterdam: North-Holland Publishing Company.

Energy Economics

BALESTRA, P. (1967). *The Demand for Natural Gas in the United States*. Amsterdam: North-Holland Publishing Company.

FISHER, F. M. (1964). *Supply and Costs in the U.S. Petroleum Industry*. Baltimore: Johns Hopkins University Press.

JORGENSON, D. W., Ed. (1976). *Econometric Studies of U.S. Energy Policy*. Amsterdam: North-Holland Publishing Company.

KNEESE, A. V., and J. L. SWEENEY, Eds. (1985, 1992). *Handbook of Natural Resource and Energy Economics*. Vols. 1–3. Amsterdam: North-Holland Publishing Company.

Family Economics

BECKER, G. S. (1981). *A Treatise on the Family*. Cambridge, Mass.: Harvard University Press.

BECKER, G. S. (1988). "Family Economics and Macro Behavior." *American Economic Review*, 78: 1–13.

ROSENZWEIG, M. A., and O. STARK, Eds. (1994). *Handbook of Population and Family Economics*. Amsterdam: North-Holland Publishing Company.

Finance

BLACK, F., M. C. JENSEN, and M. SCHOLES (1972). "The Capital Asset Pricing Model: Some Empirical Tests," in M. C. Jensen, Ed., *Studies in the Theory of Capital Markets*. New York: Praeger Publishers.

FAMA, E. F. (1976). *Foundations of Finance*. New York: Basic Books, Inc.

HUANG, C.-F., and R. H. LITZENBERGER (1988). *Foundations for Financial Economics*. Amsterdam: North-Holland Publishing Company.

ROLL, R., and S. A. ROSS (1980). "An Empirical Investigation of the Arbitrage Pricing Theory." *Journal of Finance*, 35: 1073–1103.

Housing

GRANFIELD, M. (1975). *An Econometric Model of Residential Location*. Cambridge, Mass.: Ballinger Publishing Co.

OLSON, E. O. (1972). "An Econometric Analysis of Rent Control." *Journal of Political Economy*, 80: 1081–1100.

Industrial Organization

SCHMALENSEE, R., and R. WILLIG, Eds. (1989). *Handbook of Industrial Organization*, Vols. 1 and 2. Amsterdam: North-Holland Publishing Company.

Inflation

ASKIN, A. B., and J. KRAFT (1974). *Econometric Wage and Price Models*. Lexington, Mass.: Lexington Books.

BODKIN, R. G., F. CHABOT-PLANTE, and M. A. SHEIKH (1977). "Canadian Experience with Recent Inflation as Viewed through CANDIDE," in J. Popkin, Ed., *Analysis of Inflation: 1965–1974*. Cambridge, Mass.: Ballinger Publishing Co.

ECKSTEIN, O., Ed. (1972). *The Econometrics of Price Determination Conference*. Washington, D.C.: Board of Governors of the Federal Reserve System.

MCCALLUM, B. T. (1990). "Inflation: Theory and Evidence," in B. M. Friedman and F. H. Hahn, Eds., *Handbook of Monetary Economics*, Vol. 2. Amsterdam: North-Holland Publishing Company.

MELTZER, A. H. (1969). "Money, Intermediation, and Growth." *Journal of Economic Literature*, 7: 27–56.

ORPHANIDES, A., and R. M. SOLOW (1990). "Money, Inflation, and Growth," in B. M. Friedman and F. H. Hahn, Eds., *Handbook of Monetary Economics*, Vol. 1. Amsterdam: North-Holland Publishing Company.

POPKIN, J., Ed. (1977). *Analysis of Inflation: 1965–1974*. Cambridge, Mass.: Ballinger Publishing Co. (for the National Bureau of Economic Research, Conference on Research in Income and Wealth).

WOODFORD, M. (1990). "The Optimum Quantity of Money," in B. M. Friedman and F. H. Hahn, Eds., *Handbook of Monetary Economics*, Vol. 2. Amsterdam: North-Holland Publishing Company.

International Economics

JONES, R. W., and P. B. KENEN, Eds. (1984, 1985). *Handbook of International Economics*, Vols. 1 and 2. Amsterdam: North-Holland Publishing Company.

LEAMER, E. E., and R. M. STERN (1970). *Quantitative International Economics*. New York: Allyn and Bacon, Inc.

LINNEMANN, H. (1966). *An Econometric Study of International Trade Flows*. Amsterdam: North-Holland Publishing Company.

Labor Economics

ASHENFELTER, O., and R. LAYARD, Eds. (1986). *Handbook of Labor Economics*, Vols. 1 and 2. Amsterdam: North-Holland Publishing Company.

HECKMAN, J. J., and T. E. MACURDY (1981). "New Methods for Estimating Labor Supply Functions: A Survey," in R. Ehrenberg, Ed., *Research in Labor Economics*. London: JAI Press Ltd.

HECKMAN, J. J., and T. E. MACURDY (1986). "Labor Econometrics," in Z. Griliches and M. D. Intriligator, Eds., *Handbook of Econometrics*, Vol. 3. Amsterdam: North-Holland Publishing Company.

PENCAVEL, J. (1986). "Labor Supply of Men: A Survey," in O. Ashenfelter and R. Layard, Eds., *Handbook of Labor Economics*, Vol. 1. Amsterdam: North-Holland Publishing Company.

Monetary Economics

FRIEDMAN, B. M., and F. H. HAHN, Eds. (1990). *Handbook of Monetary Economics*, Vols. 1 and 2. Amsterdam: North-Holland Publishing Company.

FRIEDMAN, B. M., and K. K. KUTTNER (1992). "Money, Income, Prices, and Interest Rates." *American Economic Review*, 82: 472–491.

FRIEDMAN, M., and A. J. SCHWARTZ (1963). *A Monetary History of the United States, 1867–1960*. Princeton, N.J.: Princeton University Press.

FRIEDMAN, M., and A. J. SCHWARTZ (1970). *Monetary Statistics of the United States: Estimates, Sources, Methods*. New York: Columbia University Press.

GOLDFELD, S. (1973). "The Demand for Money Revisited." *Brookings Papers on Economic Activity*, 3: 577–638.

HOFFMAN, D. L., and R. H. RASCHE (1991). "Long-Run Income and Interest Elasticities of Money Demand in the U.S." *Review of Economics and Statistics*, 78: 665–674.

KING, R., C. I. PLOSSER, J. H. STOCK, and M. W. WATSON (1991). "Stochastic Trends and Economic Fluctuations." *American Economic Review*, 81: 819–840.

LUCAS, R. E. (1988). "Money Demand in the United States: A Quantitative Review." *Carnegie-Rochester Conference Series on Public Policy*, 29: 137–168.

Natural Resource Economics

KNEESE, A. V., and J. L. SWEENEY, Eds. (1985, 1992). *Handbook of Natural Resource and Energy Economics*, Vols. 1–3. Amsterdam: North-Holland Publishing Company.

Population

ADELMAN, I. (1963). "An Econometric Analysis of Population Growth." *American Economic Review*, 53: 314–339.

GREGORY, P. R., J. M. CAMPBELL, and B. S. CHENG (1972). "A Simultaneous Equation Model of Birth Rates in the U.S." *Review of Economics and Statistics*, 54: 374–380.

PHILLIPS, L., H. L. VOTEY, JR., and D. E. MAXWELL (1969). "A Synthesis of the Economic and Demographic Models of Fertility." *Review of Economics and Statistics*, 51: 298–308.

ROSENZWEIG, M. A., and O. STARK, Eds. (1994). *Handbook of Population and Family Economics*. Amsterdam: North-Holland Publishing Company.

Public Economics

AUERBACH, A. J., and M. FELDSTEIN, Eds. (1985, 1987). *Handbook of Public Economics*, Vols. 1 and 2. Amsterdam: North-Holland Publishing Company.

Regional Economics

NIJKAMP, P., and E. S. MILLS, Eds. (1987). *Handbook of Regional and Urban Economics*, Vols. 1 and 2. Amsterdam: North-Holland Publishing Company.

Transportation

FISHER, F. M., and G. KRAFT (1971). "The Effect of the Removal of the Fireman on Railroad Accidents, 1962–1967." *Bell Journal of Economics and Management Science*, 2: 470–494.

GRILICHES, Z. (1972). "Cost Allocation in Railroad Regulation." *Bell Journal of Economics and Management Science*, 3: 26–41.

Urban Economics

NIJKAMP, P., and E. S. MILLS, Eds. (1987). *Handbook of Regional and Urban Economics*, Vols. 1 and 2. Amsterdam: North-Holland Publishing Company.

APPENDIX B

MATRICES[1]

B.1 BASIC DEFINITIONS AND EXAMPLES

A *matrix* is a rectangular array of real numbers.[2] The size of the array, called the *order* of the matrix, is indicated by the number of rows and columns. The matrix **A** is of order $m \times n$ if

$$\underset{m\times n}{\mathbf{A}} = \begin{pmatrix} a_{11} & a_{12} & \cdots & a_{1n} \\ a_{21} & a_{22} & \cdots & a_{2n} \\ \vdots & & & \\ a_{m1} & a_{m2} & \cdots & a_{mn} \end{pmatrix} = (a_{ij}), \qquad *(\text{B.1.1})$$

so the matrix has m rows and n columns and contains mn *elements*. Here i is an index of the rows ($i = 1, 2, \ldots, m$), j is an index of the columns ($j = 1, 2, \ldots, n$), and a_{ij} is the typical element of the matrix. If $m = n = 1$, the matrix reduces to a *scalar* (an ordinary real number). If m or n equals unity, then the matrix is a *vector*, a $1 \times n$ *row vector* if $m = 1$ and an $m \times 1$ *column vector* if $n = 1$. Generally, scalars are represented by lower case letters (e.g., k), vectors are represented by boldface lowercase letters (e.g., $\mathbf{x}$), and matrices are repre-

[1]This appendix summarizes relevant definitions, examples, and properties of matrices for those who already have some familiarity with matrices. It is *not* intended as a way to learn matrices but rather as a review of concepts. Good introductions to matrices are Hadley (1961), Horst (1963), Graybill (1969), and Dhrymes (1978). Sections of this appendix not generally covered in standard texts or courses are the Kronecker product of matrices (B.3.21)–(B.3.24); the generalized inverse of a matrix, (B.5.9)–(B.5.12); least squares fits to systems of equations, (B.6.10)–(B.6.21); matrix derivatives, (B.9.1)–(B.9.4); and the theory of mathematical programming using matrices, (B.10.1)–(B.10.26). The format of this appendix is similar to one in Intriligator (1971). A further discussion, in slightly more detail, of most of the topics of this appendix may be found in Theil (1983).

[2]All matrices here are composed of real numbers. In other disciplines, such as physics, matrices with complex numbers are also used.

sented by boldface capital letters (e.g., **A**). If $m = n$, so that the number of rows equals the number of columns, the matrix is *square*, in which case the elements for which $i = j$, starting with the upper left (1, 1) element and ending with the lower right (n, n) element, are the elements of the *principal diagonal.*

Some examples of vectors and matrices used in econometrics are the column vector **y** of n observed values of a dependent variable:

$$\underset{n\times 1}{\mathbf{y}} = \begin{pmatrix} y_1 \\ y_2 \\ \vdots \\ y_n \end{pmatrix} = (y_i), \qquad i = 1, 2, \ldots, n, \tag{B.1.2}$$

the column vector $\boldsymbol{\beta}$ of k coefficients of explanatory variables:

$$\underset{k\times 1}{\boldsymbol{\beta}} = \begin{pmatrix} \beta_1 \\ \beta_2 \\ \vdots \\ \beta_k \end{pmatrix} = (\beta_j), \qquad j = 1, 2, \ldots, k, \tag{B.1.3}$$

the design matrix **X** of n observed values of each of k explanatory variables:

$$\begin{aligned} \underset{n\times k}{\mathbf{X}} &= \begin{pmatrix} x_{11} & x_{12} & \cdots & x_{1k} \\ x_{21} & x_{22} & \cdots & x_{2k} \\ \vdots & & & \\ x_{n1} & x_{n2} & \cdots & x_{nk} \end{pmatrix} \\ &= (\mathbf{x}_i) = (x_{ij}), \qquad i = 1, 2, \ldots, n;\ j = 1, 2, \ldots, k, \end{aligned} \tag{B.1.4}$$

where $\mathbf{x}_i$ is the row vector of values taken by each of the k variables at observation i:

$$\underset{1\times k}{\mathbf{x}_i} = (x_{i1} \quad x_{i2} \quad \cdots \quad x_{ik}), \qquad i = 1, 2, \ldots, n, \tag{B.1.5}$$

and the square matrix $\boldsymbol{\Omega}$ of covariances of stochastic disturbance terms:

$$\underset{n\times n}{\boldsymbol{\Omega}} = \begin{pmatrix} \omega_{11} & \omega_{12} & \cdots & \omega_{1n} \\ \omega_{21} & \omega_{22} & \cdots & \omega_{2n} \\ \vdots & & & \\ \omega_{n1} & \omega_{n2} & \cdots & \omega_{nn} \end{pmatrix} = (\omega_{ii'}), \qquad i, i' = 1, 2, \ldots, n, \tag{B.1.6}$$

where $\omega_{ii'}$ is the ii' covariance and ω_{ii} is the ith variance (see Appendix C for definitions of variance and covariance).

B.2 SOME SPECIAL MATRICES

The *zero matrix* is a matrix for which all elements are zero:

$$\underset{m\times n}{\mathbf{0}} = (a_{ij}) \quad \text{where} \quad a_{ij} = 0,\ i = 1, 2, \ldots, m; \quad j = 1, 2, \ldots, n. \tag{B.2.1}$$

For example,

$$(0), \qquad (0 \quad 0), \qquad \begin{pmatrix} 0 & 0 \\ 0 & 0 \end{pmatrix}$$

are all zero matrices. A zero matrix need not be square.

The *identity matrix* is a square matrix for which all elements along the principal diagonal are unity, and all other (off-diagonal) elements are zero:

$$\underset{n\times n}{\mathbf{I}} = (\delta_{ij}) \quad \text{where} \quad \delta_{ij} = \begin{Bmatrix} 1 \\ 0 \end{Bmatrix} \quad \text{if} \quad i \begin{Bmatrix} = \\ \neq \end{Bmatrix} j, \qquad i, j = 1, 2, \ldots, n, \quad \text{(B.2.2)}$$

and where δ_{ij} is called the *Kronecker delta*. For example,

$$(1), \quad \begin{pmatrix} 1 & 0 \\ 0 & 1 \end{pmatrix}, \quad \begin{pmatrix} 1 & 0 & 0 \\ 0 & 1 & 0 \\ 0 & 0 & 1 \end{pmatrix}$$

are all identity matrices. The columns of the identity matrix are *unit column vectors*, where

$$\mathbf{e}_1 = \begin{pmatrix} 1 \\ 0 \\ 0 \\ \vdots \\ 0 \end{pmatrix}, \quad \mathbf{e}_2 = \begin{pmatrix} 0 \\ 1 \\ 0 \\ \vdots \\ 0 \end{pmatrix}, \quad \text{etc.} \qquad \text{(B.2.3)}$$

are all unit vectors.

A *unity column vector* is a vector, all elements of which are unity:

$$\underset{n\times 1}{\mathbf{i}} = \begin{pmatrix} 1 \\ 1 \\ \vdots \\ 1 \end{pmatrix}. \qquad \text{(B.2.4)}$$

A *diagonal matrix* is a square matrix for which all elements off the principal diagonal are zero.

$$\underset{n\times n}{\mathbf{D}} = (d_{ij}) \quad \text{where} \quad d_{ij} = 0 \quad \text{if} \quad i \neq j, \quad i, j = 1, 2, \ldots, n. \qquad \text{(B.2.5)}$$

For example,

$$\begin{pmatrix} 2 & 0 \\ 0 & -3 \end{pmatrix}$$

and any identity matrix are diagonal matrices. If all elements on the diagonal matrix are equal, the matrix is a *scalar matrix*.

A *triangular matrix* is a square matrix for which all elements on one side of the principal diagonal are zero:

$$\underset{n\times n}{\mathbf{T}} = (t_{ij}) \quad \text{where} \quad t_{ij} = 0 \quad \text{if} \quad i > j \quad \text{or if} \quad i < j, \qquad i, j = 1, 2, \ldots, n. \quad \text{(B.2.6)}$$

For example,

$$\begin{pmatrix} 6 & -1 \\ 0 & 8 \end{pmatrix}$$

and any diagonal matrix are triangular matrices.

A *permutation matrix* is a square matrix for which each row and each column contain a one, all other elements being zero. For example,

$$\begin{pmatrix} 1 & 0 \\ 0 & 1 \end{pmatrix}, \quad \begin{pmatrix} 0 & 1 \\ 1 & 0 \end{pmatrix}, \quad \begin{pmatrix} 0 & 1 & 0 \\ 1 & 0 & 0 \\ 0 & 0 & 1 \end{pmatrix}$$

are permutation matrices, as are all the identity matrices. Altogether there are $n! = n(n-1)(n-2)\cdots(2)(1)$ permutation matrices of order n, of which one is an identity matrix.

A *partitioned matrix* is one that has been divided into submatrices of appropriate orders. For example,

$$\underset{m\times n}{\mathbf{A}} = \left(\begin{array}{c|c} \mathbf{A}_{11} & \mathbf{A}_{12} \\ \hline \mathbf{A}_{21} & \mathbf{A}_{22} \end{array}\right)\begin{array}{l} m_1 \\ \\ m-m_1 \end{array}, \qquad \begin{array}{c|c} n_1 & n-n_1 \end{array} \tag{B.2.7}$$

where $\mathbf{A}_{11}$ is an $m_1 \times n_1$ matrix, $\mathbf{A}_{12}$ is an $m_1 \times (n-n_1)$ matrix, and so on, is a partitioned matrix.

A *block diagonal matrix* can be partitioned in such a way that the only nonzero submatrices form a "principal diagonal" of square submatrices. Thus

$$\mathbf{A} = \left(\begin{array}{c|c|c|c} \mathbf{A}_{11} & \mathbf{0} & & \mathbf{0} \\ \hline \mathbf{0} & \mathbf{A}_{22} & & \mathbf{0} \\ \hline & & & \\ \hline \mathbf{0} & \mathbf{0} & & \mathbf{A}_{qq} \end{array}\right), \tag{B.2.8}$$

where each of the q submatrices $\mathbf{A}_{11}, \mathbf{A}_{22}, \ldots, \mathbf{A}_{qq}$ is square (but not necessarily of the same order), is a block diagonal matrix.

A *block triangular matrix* can be partitioned in such a way that only zero elements lie above or below a "principal diagonal" of submatrices. For example, both a triangular matrix and a block diagonal matrix are block triangular matrices.

B.3 MATRIX RELATIONS AND OPERATIONS

Two matrices are *equal* iff they are of the same order and corresponding elements are equal:[3]

$$\mathbf{A} = \mathbf{B} \quad \text{iff} \quad a_{ij} = b_{ij}, \qquad i = 1, 2, \ldots, m; \quad j = 1, 2, \ldots, n. \qquad *(\text{B.3.1})$$

Similarly, two matrices can satisfy various forms of *inequalities* if they are of the same order and if all corresponding elements satisfy the inequality. Thus

$$\mathbf{A} \leqslant \mathbf{B} \quad \text{iff} \quad a_{ij} \leqslant b_{ij}, \qquad i = 1, 2, \ldots, m; \quad j = 1, 2, \ldots, n. \tag{B.3.2}$$

For example,

$$(2 \quad 6) \leqslant (5 \quad 8).$$

The *addition of two matrices* of the same order involves adding corresponding elements:

$$\mathbf{A} + \mathbf{B} = \mathbf{C} \quad \text{iff} \quad c_{ij} = a_{ij} + b_{ij}, \qquad i = 1, 2, \ldots, m; \quad j = 1, 2, \ldots, n. \qquad *(\text{B.3.3})$$

[3] The expression "iff" means "if and only if," signifying a definition or an equivalence.

For example,

$$\begin{pmatrix} 2 & 0 \\ 1 & 3 \end{pmatrix} + \begin{pmatrix} 8 & 2 \\ -1 & 0 \end{pmatrix} = \begin{pmatrix} 10 & 2 \\ 0 & 3 \end{pmatrix}.$$

Properties of matrix addition include:[4]

$$\begin{aligned} &\text{(i)}\ \mathbf{A} + \mathbf{B} = \mathbf{B} + \mathbf{A} \\ &\text{(ii)}\ \mathbf{A} + (\mathbf{B} + \mathbf{C}) = (\mathbf{A} + \mathbf{B}) + \mathbf{C} \\ &\text{(iii)}\ \mathbf{A} + \mathbf{0} = \mathbf{0} + \mathbf{A} = \mathbf{A}. \end{aligned} \qquad *(\text{B.3.4})$$

The *multiplication of a matrix by a scalar* involves multiplying all elements of the matrix by the scalar:

$$k\mathbf{A} = \mathbf{B} \quad \text{iff} \quad b_{ij} = ka_{ij}, \qquad i = 1, 2, \ldots, m; \ j = 1, 2, \ldots, n. \qquad *(\text{B.3.5})$$

For example,

$$6\begin{pmatrix} 1 & 0 \\ 2 & -1 \end{pmatrix} = \begin{pmatrix} 6 & 0 \\ 12 & -6 \end{pmatrix}.$$

Properties of scalar multiplication include:

$$\begin{aligned} &\text{(i)}\ k\mathbf{A} = \mathbf{A}k \\ &\text{(ii)}\ k(\mathbf{A} + \mathbf{B}) = k\mathbf{A} + k\mathbf{B} \\ &\text{(iii)}\ (k + l)\mathbf{A} = k\mathbf{A} + l\mathbf{A} \\ &\text{(iv)}\ (kl)\mathbf{A} = k(l\mathbf{A}) \\ &\text{(v)}\ (-1)\mathbf{A} = -\mathbf{A} \quad (\textit{negative of a matrix}) \\ &\text{(vi)}\ \mathbf{A} + (-1)\mathbf{B} = \mathbf{A} - \mathbf{B} \quad (\textit{matrix subtraction}). \end{aligned} \qquad *(\text{B.3.6})$$

The *multiplication of two matrices* requires that the number of columns of the matrix on the left equal the number of rows of the matrix on the right. Elements of the product are then obtained by multiplying elements of a row of the left matrix by corresponding elements of a column of the right matrix and adding all such products:

$$\underset{m\times r}{\mathbf{A}}\ \underset{r\times n}{\mathbf{B}} = \underset{m\times n}{\mathbf{C}} \quad \text{iff} \quad c_{ij} = \sum_{k=1}^{r} a_{ik}b_{kj}, \qquad i = 1, 2, \ldots, m; \ j = 1, 2, \ldots, n. \qquad *(\text{B.3.7})$$

For example,

$$\begin{pmatrix} a_{11} & a_{12} \end{pmatrix} \begin{pmatrix} b_{11} & b_{12} \\ b_{21} & b_{22} \end{pmatrix} = \begin{pmatrix} a_{11}b_{11} + a_{12}b_{21} & a_{11}b_{12} + a_{12}b_{22} \end{pmatrix}$$

$$\begin{pmatrix} 2 & 1 \\ 0 & 5 \end{pmatrix} \begin{pmatrix} 8 & -1 \\ 2 & 3 \end{pmatrix} = \begin{pmatrix} 18 & 1 \\ 10 & 15 \end{pmatrix}, \qquad \begin{pmatrix} 8 & -1 \\ 2 & 3 \end{pmatrix} \begin{pmatrix} 2 & 1 \\ 0 & 5 \end{pmatrix} = \begin{pmatrix} 16 & 3 \\ 4 & 17 \end{pmatrix}$$

In general, **AB** does *not* equal **BA**, even if both are defined, so matrix multiplication is generally noncommutative. It is therefore essential to indicate the intended order of multiplication, using the concepts of *premultiplication* (i.e., multiplication on the left) and *postmultiplication* (multiplication on the right). Thus the matrix product **AB** means **A** is postmultiplied by **B** or, equivalently, **B** is premultiplied by **A**.

[4] Most of the important theorems on matrices are summarized by these "properties" statements containing subentries (i), (ii), and so on, such as (B.3.4), (B.3.6), and (B.3.8). The reader might test his or her understanding of this material by proving these properties. For help in the proofs, see Hadley (1961).

Properties of matrix multiplication include:

$$\begin{aligned}
&\text{(i)}\quad \mathbf{A}(\mathbf{B}+\mathbf{C}) = \mathbf{AB}+\mathbf{AC}\\
&\text{(ii)}\quad (\mathbf{A}+\mathbf{B})\mathbf{C} = \mathbf{AC}+\mathbf{BC}\\
&\text{(iii)}\quad \mathbf{A}(\mathbf{BC}) = (\mathbf{AB})\mathbf{C}\\
&\text{(iv)}\quad k(\mathbf{AB}) = \mathbf{A}(k\mathbf{B})\\
&\text{(v)}\quad \mathbf{A0} = \mathbf{0A} = \mathbf{0}\\
&\text{(vi)}\quad \mathbf{AI} = \mathbf{IA} = \mathbf{A}\\
&\text{(vii)}\quad \mathbf{I\,I} = \mathbf{I}\\
&\text{(viii)}\quad \mathbf{00} = \mathbf{0}.
\end{aligned} \qquad *(\text{B.3.8})$$

Premultiplication by a permutation matrix permutes the rows of a matrix, while postmultiplication by a permutation matrix permutes the columns of a matrix. For example,

$$\begin{pmatrix} 0 & 1 \\ 1 & 0 \end{pmatrix}\begin{pmatrix} 2 & 4 \\ 6 & 1 \end{pmatrix} = \begin{pmatrix} 6 & 1 \\ 2 & 4 \end{pmatrix},$$

$$\begin{pmatrix} 2 & 4 \\ 6 & 1 \end{pmatrix}\begin{pmatrix} 0 & 1 \\ 1 & 0 \end{pmatrix} = \begin{pmatrix} 4 & 2 \\ 1 & 6 \end{pmatrix}.$$

Powers of a matrix are obtained by repeated multiplication:

$$\mathbf{A}^t = \mathbf{A}\mathbf{A}^{t-1}, \qquad t = 1, 2, \ldots. \qquad *(\text{B.3.9})$$

Properties of powers of a matrix include:

$$\begin{aligned}
&\text{(i)}\quad \mathbf{A}^0 = \mathbf{I}\\
&\text{(ii)}\quad \mathbf{A}^t\mathbf{A}^s = \mathbf{A}^{t+s}\\
&\text{(iii)}\quad (\mathbf{A}^t)^s = \mathbf{A}^{ts}\\
&\text{(iv)}\quad \mathbf{I}^t = \mathbf{I}.
\end{aligned} \qquad *(\text{B.3.10})$$

The matrix **A** is *idempotent* iff

$$\mathbf{A}^2 = \mathbf{A}. \qquad *(\text{B.3.11})$$

Examples of idempotent matrices are:

$$\begin{pmatrix} 6 & 10 \\ -3 & -5 \end{pmatrix},$$

any identity matrix, and any square zero matrix [see (B.3.8) (vii) and (viii)]. If **A** is idempotent, then

$$\mathbf{A}^t = \mathbf{A} \qquad \text{for all } t \geqslant 1. \qquad (\text{B.3.12})$$

An *inner product* (or *scalar product, dot product*) of two vectors is a row vector times a column vector, yielding a scalar:

$$\underset{1\times n}{\mathbf{w}}\ \underset{n\times 1}{\mathbf{x}} = \sum_{j=1}^{n} w_j x_j. \qquad *(\text{B.3.13})$$

For example,

$$(1 \quad 3)\begin{pmatrix} 2 \\ -1 \end{pmatrix} = -1.$$

In fact, all the elements of the product of two matrices, as defined in (B.3.7), are inner products of the appropriate row vector of the left-hand matrix times the appropriate column vector of the right-hand matrix. If the inner product of the two vectors vanishes, the vectors are *orthogonal*. For example,

$$(4 \quad 6) \quad \text{and} \quad \begin{pmatrix} 3 \\ -2 \end{pmatrix}$$

are orthogonal.

An *outer product* of two vectors is a column vector times a row vector, yielding a matrix:

$$\underset{n\times 1}{\mathbf{x}}\ \underset{1\times n}{\mathbf{w}} = \begin{pmatrix} x_1 w_1 & \cdots & x_1 w_n \\ \vdots & & \vdots \\ x_n w_1 & \cdots & x_n w_n \end{pmatrix}. \tag{B.3.14}$$

The *transpose* $\mathbf{A}'$ of a matrix $\mathbf{A}$ is obtained by interchanging rows and columns. Thus

$$\underset{n\times m}{\mathbf{A}'} = (a_{ji}) \quad \text{iff} \quad \underset{m\times n}{\mathbf{A}} = (a_{ij}), \qquad i = 1, 2, \ldots, m; \quad j = 1, 2, \ldots, n. \qquad \text{*(B.3.15)}$$

For example,

$$\begin{pmatrix} 4 & 2 & 3 \\ 8 & 0 & -1 \end{pmatrix}' = \begin{pmatrix} 4 & 8 \\ 2 & 0 \\ 3 & -1 \end{pmatrix}.$$

Properties of the transpose include:

$$\begin{aligned} &\text{(i)} \ (\mathbf{A}')' = \mathbf{A} \\ &\text{(ii)} \ (k\mathbf{A})' = k\mathbf{A}' \\ &\text{(iii)} \ (\mathbf{A} + \mathbf{B})' = \mathbf{A}' + \mathbf{B}' \\ &\text{(iv)} \ (\mathbf{AB})' = \mathbf{B}'\mathbf{A}' \\ &\text{(v)} \ \mathbf{A}'\mathbf{A} = \mathbf{0} \text{ implies that } \mathbf{A} = \mathbf{0}. \end{aligned} \tag{B.3.16}$$

The square matrix $\mathbf{A}$ is *symmetric* iff $\mathbf{A} = \mathbf{A}'$. For example,

$$\begin{pmatrix} 8 & 2 \\ 2 & -6 \end{pmatrix},$$

any diagonal matrix, and the covariance matrix $\mathbf{\Omega}$ in (B.1.6) are all symmetric matrices. If $\mathbf{A}$ is symmetric of order n, then it contains $n(n+1)/2$ independent elements. The square matrix $\mathbf{A}$ is *skew-symmetric* iff $\mathbf{A} = -\mathbf{A}'$. For example,

$$\begin{pmatrix} 0 & 5 \\ -5 & 0 \end{pmatrix}$$

is skew-symmetric. If $\mathbf{A}$ is skew-symmetric of order n, then it contains $n(n-1)/2$ independent elements, since all elements on the principal diagonal must be zero.

Given the $n \times 1$ column vector $\mathbf{x}$, the *sum of squares* is the inner product of the vector with itself:

$$\mathbf{x}'\mathbf{x} = \sum_{j=1}^{n} \mathbf{x}_j^2 = \|\mathbf{x}\|^2. \tag{B.3.17}$$

Here $\| \mathbf{x} \|$, the square root of the sum of squares, is the *norm* of **x**, a measure of the "length" of the vector. The vector **x** is *normalized* iff $\| \mathbf{x} \| = 1$. The *scatter matrix* is the outer product of the vector with itself:

$$\mathbf{xx}' = \begin{pmatrix} x_1^2 & x_1x_2 & \cdots & x_1x_n \\ \vdots & & & \\ x_nx_1 & & \cdots & x_n^2 \end{pmatrix}, \qquad \text{(B.3.18)}$$

which is a symmetric matrix. For example, if $\mathbf{x} = \begin{pmatrix} 3 \\ 1 \end{pmatrix}$, then

$$\mathbf{x}'\mathbf{x} = 10, \quad \|\mathbf{x}\| = \sqrt{10}, \quad \text{and} \quad \mathbf{xx}' = \begin{pmatrix} 9 & 3 \\ 3 & 1 \end{pmatrix}.$$

The elements on the principal diagonal of the scatter matrix are the squares of the elements of the vector, while elements off the principal diagonal are cross products of elements of the vector.

The square matrix **A** is *orthogonal* iff each column (row) vector of **A** is normalized and orthogonal to any other column (row) vector, so that

$$\mathbf{AA}' = \mathbf{A}'\mathbf{A} = \mathbf{I}. \qquad \text{(B.3.19)}$$

Examples of orthogonal matrices include any permutation matrix and the matrix:

$$\begin{pmatrix} \dfrac{3}{\sqrt{10}} & \dfrac{2}{\sqrt{40}} \\ \dfrac{1}{\sqrt{10}} & \dfrac{-6}{\sqrt{40}} \end{pmatrix}.$$

The square matrix **A** is *decomposable* iff there exists a permutation matrix **P** such that:

$$\mathbf{P}'\mathbf{AP} = \left(\begin{array}{c|c} \mathbf{A}_{11} & \mathbf{A}_{12} \\ \hline \mathbf{0} & \mathbf{A}_{22} \end{array}\right), \qquad \text{(B.3.20)}$$

where $\mathbf{A}_{11}$ and $\mathbf{A}_{22}$ are square matrices. For example,

$$\begin{pmatrix} 0 & 2 & 0 \\ 0 & -8 & 0 \\ 1 & 3 & 5 \end{pmatrix}$$

is decomposable into

$$\left(\begin{array}{c|cc} 5 & 1 & 3 \\ \hline 0 & 0 & 2 \\ 0 & 0 & -8 \end{array}\right),$$

using the permutation matrix:

$$\begin{pmatrix} 0 & 1 & 0 \\ 0 & 0 & 1 \\ 1 & 0 & 0 \end{pmatrix}.$$

A matrix that is not decomposable is *indecomposable* (or *connected*). The $n \times n$ matrix $\mathbf{A}$ is indecomposable iff for every pair of indices (i, j) there exists a set of indices $j_1, j_2, \ldots, j_l$ such that:

$$a_{ij_1} a_{j_1 j_2} \cdots a_{j_l j} \neq 0, \qquad i, j = 1, 2, \ldots, n.$$

The *Kronecker product* of a matrix with a matrix involves multiplying each element of the matrix on the left by the entire matrix on the right, using the rule (B.3.5) for multiplying a matrix by a scalar.[5] Thus

$$\underset{m\times n}{\mathbf{A}} \otimes \underset{p\times q}{\mathbf{B}} = \underset{mp \times nq}{\left(\begin{array}{c|c|c|c} a_{11}\mathbf{B} & a_{12}\mathbf{B} & \cdots & a_{1n}\mathbf{B} \\ \hline a_{21}\mathbf{B} & a_{22}\mathbf{B} & \cdots & a_{2n}\mathbf{B} \\ \hline \vdots & & & \\ \hline a_{m1}\mathbf{B} & a_{m2}\mathbf{B} & \cdots & a_{mn}\mathbf{B} \end{array}\right)}. \tag{B.3.21}$$

For example, if $\mathbf{A}$ is the identity matrix of order 2 and $\mathbf{B}$ is a 2×2 matrix with elements (b_{ij}), then

$$\mathbf{I} \otimes \mathbf{B} = \left(\begin{array}{cc|cc} b_{11} & b_{12} & \multicolumn{2}{c}{\mathbf{0}} \\ b_{21} & b_{22} & & \\ \hline \multicolumn{2}{c|}{\mathbf{0}} & b_{11} & b_{12} \\ & & b_{21} & b_{22} \end{array}\right), \tag{B.3.22}$$

while if $\mathbf{A}$ is a 2×2 matrix with elements (a_{ij}) and $\mathbf{B}$ is the identity matrix of order 2, then

$$\mathbf{A} \otimes \mathbf{I} = \left(\begin{array}{cc|cc} a_{11} & 0 & a_{12} & 0 \\ 0 & a_{11} & 0 & a_{12} \\ \hline a_{21} & 0 & a_{22} & 0 \\ 0 & a_{21} & 0 & a_{22} \end{array}\right). \tag{B.3.23}$$

Properties of the Kronecker product of two matrices include:

$$\begin{aligned} &\text{(i)} \ (\mathbf{A} + \mathbf{B}) \otimes \mathbf{C} = \mathbf{A} \otimes \mathbf{C} + \mathbf{B} \otimes \mathbf{C} \\ &\text{(ii)} \ \mathbf{A} \otimes (\mathbf{B} + \mathbf{C}) = \mathbf{A} \otimes \mathbf{B} + \mathbf{A} \otimes \mathbf{C} \\ &\text{(iii)} \ \mathbf{A} \otimes (\mathbf{B} \otimes \mathbf{C}) = (\mathbf{A} \otimes \mathbf{B}) \otimes \mathbf{C} \\ &\text{(iv)} \ (\mathbf{A} \otimes \mathbf{B})' = \mathbf{A}' \otimes \mathbf{B}' \\ &\text{(v)} \ (\mathbf{A} \otimes \mathbf{B})(\mathbf{C} \otimes \mathbf{D}) = \mathbf{AC} \otimes \mathbf{BD}, \end{aligned} \tag{B.3.24}$$

assuming that all matrix sums and products are defined.

B.4 SCALAR-VALUED FUNCTIONS DEFINED ON MATRICES

The *trace* of a square matrix of order n is the sum of the n elements on its principal diagonal:

$$\operatorname{tr}(\mathbf{A}) = \sum_{i=1}^{n} a_{ii}. \tag{B.4.1}$$

[5]See Theil (1971, Sec. 7.2).

For example,

$$\mathrm{tr}\begin{pmatrix} 2 & 1 \\ 3 & 8 \end{pmatrix} = 10$$

and the trace of the scatter matrix (B.3.18) is the sum of squares (B.3.17).

Properties of the trace of a square matrix include:

(i) $\mathrm{tr}(\mathbf{I}) = n, \mathrm{tr}(\mathbf{0}) = 0.$

(ii) $\mathrm{tr}(\mathbf{A}') = \mathrm{tr}(\mathbf{A}).$

(iii) $\mathrm{tr}(\mathbf{AA}') = \mathrm{tr}(\mathbf{A}'\mathbf{A}) = \sum_{i=1}^{m}\sum_{j=1}^{n} a_{ij}^2$ (here **A** need not be square).

(iv) $\mathrm{tr}(k\mathbf{A}) = k\,\mathrm{tr}(\mathbf{A}).$

(v) If **A** and **B** are of the same order, $\mathrm{tr}(\mathbf{A}+\mathbf{B}) = \mathrm{tr}(\mathbf{A}) + \mathrm{tr}(\mathbf{B}).$ *(B.4.2)

(vi) If **AB** and **BA** are both defined, $\mathrm{tr}(\mathbf{AB}) = \mathrm{tr}(\mathbf{BA}).$

(vii) If **ABC**, **BCA**, and **CAB** are all defined, $\mathrm{tr}(\mathbf{ABC}) = \mathrm{tr}(\mathbf{BCA}) = \mathrm{tr}(\mathbf{CAB}).$

(viii) $\mathrm{tr}(\mathbf{A} \otimes \mathbf{B}) = \mathrm{tr}(\mathbf{A})\,\mathrm{tr}(\mathbf{B}).$

The *determinant* of a square matrix of order n is the sum of the $n!$ signed terms, each of which is the product of n elements of the matrix—one from each row and one from each column:

$$|\mathbf{A}| = \det(\mathbf{A}) = \sum_{\substack{\text{all } n! \\ \text{permutations} \\ (i_1, \ldots, i_n)}} \mathrm{sgn}(i_1, \ldots, i_n) a_{1i_1} a_{2i_2} \cdots a_{ni_n}, \qquad \text{*(B.4.3)}$$

where $\mathrm{sgn}(i_1, \ldots, i_n)$ is $\begin{Bmatrix} +1 \\ -1 \end{Bmatrix}$ if the permutation $(i_1, \ldots, i_n)$ is $\begin{Bmatrix} \text{even} \\ \text{odd} \end{Bmatrix}$; that is, obtained by an $\begin{Bmatrix} \text{even} \\ \text{odd} \end{Bmatrix}$ number of interchanges from $(1, 2, \ldots, n)$. For example, if $n = 2$, since sgn $(1, 2) = 1$ and $\mathrm{sgn}(2, 1) = -1$,

$$\begin{vmatrix} a_{11} & a_{12} \\ a_{21} & a_{22} \end{vmatrix} = a_{11}a_{22} - a_{12}a_{21}.$$

Properties of the determinant include:

(i) $|\mathbf{I}| = 1, |\mathbf{0}| = 0.$

(ii) $|\mathbf{A}| = |\mathbf{A}'| = (-1)^n |-\mathbf{A}| = (\lambda)^{-n} |\lambda \mathbf{A}|.$

(iii) If **A** and **B** are square and of the same order, $|\mathbf{AB}| = |\mathbf{A}|\,|\mathbf{B}|$, and $|\mathbf{AB}| = |\mathbf{BA}|.$

(iv) If **A** is diagonal or triangular, $|\mathbf{A}| = a_{11}a_{22} \cdots a_{nn}.$

(v) If **A** is orthogonal, then $|\mathbf{A}| = \pm 1.$

(vi) If any row (column) of **A** is a nontrivial linear combination of all the other rows (columns) of **A**, then $|\mathbf{A}| = 0$. [In particular, if two rows (or columns) of **A** are identical, or a row (or column) contains only zero, then $|\mathbf{A}| = 0$.] *(B.4.4)

(vii) If **B** results from **A** by interchanging two rows (or columns), then $|\mathbf{B}| = -|\mathbf{A}|.$

(viii) If $\mathbf{B}$ results from $\mathbf{A}$ by multiplying one row (or column) by k, then $|\mathbf{B}| = k|\mathbf{A}|$.

(ix) $|\mathbf{A} \otimes \mathbf{B}| = |\mathbf{A}|^n |\mathbf{B}|^m$ if $\mathbf{A}$ is square of order m and $\mathbf{B}$ is square of order n.

The *kth-order leading principal minor* of the square matrix $\mathbf{A}$ is the determinant of the $k \times k$ matrix consisting of the first k rows and columns of $\mathbf{A}$:

$$M_k = \begin{vmatrix} a_{11} & \cdots & a_{1k} \\ \vdots & & \vdots \\ a_{k1} & \cdots & a_{kk} \end{vmatrix} \tag{B.4.5}$$

A *kth-order principal minor* of the square matrix $\mathbf{A}$ of order n is the kth-order leading principal minor of $\mathbf{P'AP}$, where $\mathbf{P}$ is a permutation matrix; and the *kth-order trace*, α_k, is the sum of all $n!/[k!(n-k)!]$ possible kth-order principal minors. Thus,

$$\begin{aligned} \alpha_1 &= a_{11} + a_{22} + \cdots + a_{nn} = \mathrm{tr}(\mathbf{A}), \\ \alpha_2 &= \begin{vmatrix} a_{11} & a_{12} \\ a_{21} & a_{22} \end{vmatrix} + \begin{vmatrix} a_{11} & a_{13} \\ a_{31} & a_{33} \end{vmatrix} + \ldots, \\ &\vdots \\ \alpha_n &= |\mathbf{A}|. \end{aligned} \tag{B.4.6}$$

The *i, j minor* of a square matrix is the determinant of the $(n-1) \times (n-1)$ matrix obtained by deleting the ith row and jth column of $\mathbf{A}$:

$$M_{ij} = \begin{vmatrix} a_{11} & \cdots & a_{1j} & \cdots & a_{1n} \\ \vdots & & & & \vdots \\ a_{i1} & \cdots & a_{ij} & \cdots & a_{in} \\ \vdots & & & & \vdots \\ a_{n1} & \cdots & a_{nj} & \cdots & a_{nn} \end{vmatrix}. \tag{B.4.7}$$

The *i, j cofactor* of a square matrix is the same as the i, j minor if $i + j$ is even and the negative of the i, j minor if $i + j$ is odd:

$$C_{ij} = (-1)^{1+j} M_{ij}, \qquad i = 1, 2, \ldots, n; \quad j = 1, 2, \ldots, n. \tag{B.4.8}$$

The cofactors can be used to evaluate a determinant via the *expansion by cofactors*:

$$\begin{aligned} |\mathbf{A}| &= \sum_{i=1}^{n} a_{ij} C_{ij}, \quad \text{any } j, \quad j = 1, 2, \ldots, n \text{ (any column)}, \\ |\mathbf{A}| &= \sum_{j=1}^{n} a_{ij} C_{ij}, \quad \text{any } i, \quad i = 1, 2, \ldots, n \text{ (any row)}. \end{aligned} \tag{B.4.9}$$

The *rank* of any matrix $\mathbf{A}$, written rank($\mathbf{A}$), is the size of the largest nonvanishing determinant contained in $\mathbf{A}$.[6] For example,

[6]Equivalently, the rank is the (maximum) number of linearly independent rows (or columns) of $\mathbf{A}$, where $\mathbf{a}_1, \mathbf{a}_2, \ldots, \mathbf{a}_n$ is a set of *linearly independent* vectors iff

$$\sum_{j=1}^{n} k_j \mathbf{a}_j = 0 \quad \text{implies} \quad k_1 = k_2 = \cdots = k_n = 0.$$

See Hadley (1961) for a discussion of linear independence and other topics in linear algebra.

$$\text{rank}\begin{pmatrix} 2 & 3 \\ 8 & 6 \end{pmatrix} = 2, \qquad \text{rank}\begin{pmatrix} 3 & 6 \\ 2 & 4 \end{pmatrix} = 1.$$

Properties of the rank of a matrix include:

(i) $0 \leqslant \text{rank}(\mathbf{A}) = \text{integer} \leqslant \min(m, n)$, where $\mathbf{A}$ is an $m \times n$ matrix.
(ii) $\text{rank}(\mathbf{I}) = n$, $\text{rank}(\mathbf{A}) = n$, $\text{rank}(\mathbf{0}) = 0$, $\text{rank}(\mathbf{P}) = n$, where $\mathbf{A}$ is an orthogonal matrix.
(iii) $\text{rank}(\mathbf{A}) = \text{rank}(\mathbf{A}') = \text{rank}(\mathbf{A}'\mathbf{A}) = \text{rank}(\mathbf{A}\mathbf{A}')$.
(iv) If $\mathbf{A}$ and $\mathbf{B}$ are of the same order, $\text{rank}(\mathbf{A} + \mathbf{B}) \leqslant \text{rank}(\mathbf{A}) + \text{rank}(\mathbf{B})$.
(v) If $\mathbf{AB}$ is defined, $\text{rank}(\mathbf{AB}) \leqslant \min[\text{rank}(\mathbf{A}), \text{rank}(\mathbf{B})]$. *(B.4.10)
(vi) If $\mathbf{A}$ is diagonal, $\text{rank}(\mathbf{A})$ = number of nonzero elements.
(vii) If $\mathbf{A}$ is idempotent, $\text{rank}(\mathbf{A}) = \text{tr}(\mathbf{A})$.
(viii) The rank of a matrix is not changed if one row (column) is multiplied by a nonzero constant or if such a multiple of one row (column) is added to another row (column).
(ix) $\text{rank}(\mathbf{A} \otimes \mathbf{B}) = \text{rank}(\mathbf{A})\,\text{rank}(\mathbf{B})$ if $\mathbf{A}$ and $\mathbf{B}$ are square.

A square matrix of order n is *nonsingular* iff it is of full rank:

$$\text{rank}(\mathbf{A}) = n \quad \text{or equivalently} \quad |\mathbf{A}| \neq 0. \tag{B.4.11}$$

Otherwise, it is singular ($|\mathbf{A}| = 0$). The rank of a matrix is unchanged by premultiplying or postmultiplying by a nonsingular matrix. Thus if there are nonsingular matrices $\mathbf{E}$ and $\mathbf{F}$ for which

$$\mathbf{EAF} = \left(\begin{array}{c|c} \mathbf{I} & \mathbf{0} \\ \hline \mathbf{0} & \mathbf{0} \end{array}\right), \tag{B.4.12}$$

where $\mathbf{I}$ is the identity matrix of order k, then $\text{rank}(\mathbf{A}) = k$.

B.5 INVERSE AND GENERALIZED INVERSE MATRICES

If $\mathbf{A}$ is a square, nonsingular matrix of order n, a unique inverse matrix $\mathbf{A}^{-1}$ of order n exists, where

$$\mathbf{A}\mathbf{A}^{-1} = \mathbf{A}^{-1}\mathbf{A} = \mathbf{I}. \tag{*B.5.1}$$

The inverse matrix can be computed as:

$$\mathbf{A}^{-1} = \frac{(C_{ij})'}{|\mathbf{A}|} = \frac{\left((-1)^{i+j} M_{ji}\right)}{|\mathbf{A}|}, \tag{B.5.2}$$

where (C_{ij}) is the matrix of cofactors, and its transpose $(C_{ij})'$ is called the *adjoint matrix*. For example, if

$$\mathbf{A} = \begin{pmatrix} 2 & 3 \\ 1 & 3 \end{pmatrix},$$

then

$$\mathbf{A}^{-1} = \frac{1}{3}\begin{pmatrix} 3 & -1 \\ -3 & 2 \end{pmatrix}' = \begin{pmatrix} 1 & -1 \\ -\frac{1}{3} & \frac{2}{3} \end{pmatrix}.$$

Properties of the inverse matrix include:

(i) $\mathbf{I}^{-1} = \mathbf{I}$.
(ii) $(\mathbf{A}^{-1})^{-1} = \mathbf{A}$, $(\mathbf{A}')^{-1} = (\mathbf{A}^{-1})'$, $|\mathbf{A}^{-1}| = |\mathbf{A}|^{-1} = 1/|\mathbf{A}|$.
(iii) $(\mathbf{AB})^{-1} = \mathbf{B}^{-1}\mathbf{A}^{-1}$, assuming that both $\mathbf{A}$ and $\mathbf{B}$ are nonsingular and of the same order.
(iv) $\mathbf{A}^{-1} = \mathbf{A}'$ iff $\mathbf{A}$ is orthogonal, in which case $\mathbf{A}^{-1}$ and $\mathbf{A}'$ are also orthogonal. *(B.5.3)
(v) Given the diagonal matrix $\mathbf{D} = (d_j\delta_{ij})$, $\mathbf{D}^{-1} = (d_j^{-1}\delta_{ij})$, where δ_{ij} is the Kronecker delta of (B.2.2) and the d_j's are all nonzero.
(vi) If $\mathbf{A}$ is nonsingular and symmetric, so is $\mathbf{A}^{-1}$.
(vii) $(\mathbf{A} \otimes \mathbf{B})^{-1} = \mathbf{A}^{-1} \otimes \mathbf{B}^{-1}$ if $\mathbf{A}$ and $\mathbf{B}$ are square and nonsingular.

For the partitioned matrix:

$$\mathbf{A} = \left(\begin{array}{c|c} \mathbf{A}_{11} & \mathbf{A}_{12} \\ \hline \mathbf{A}_{21} & \mathbf{A}_{22} \end{array}\right), \qquad \text{(B.5.4)}$$

assuming that $\mathbf{A}_{22}$ and $\mathbf{B} = \mathbf{A}_{11} - \mathbf{A}_{12}\mathbf{A}_{22}^{-1}\mathbf{A}_{21}$ are nonsingular,

$$\mathbf{A}^{-1} = \left(\begin{array}{c|c} \mathbf{B}^{-1} & -\mathbf{B}^{-1}\mathbf{A}_{12}\mathbf{A}_{22}^{-1} \\ \hline -\mathbf{A}_{22}^{-1}\mathbf{A}_{21}\mathbf{B}^{-1} & \mathbf{A}_{22}^{-1}(\mathbf{I} + \mathbf{A}_{21}\mathbf{B}^{-1}\mathbf{A}_{12}\mathbf{A}_{22}^{-1}) \end{array}\right). \qquad \text{(B.5.5)}$$

In particular, the inverse of a (nonsingular) block diagonal matrix is also block diagonal.

If $\mathbf{A}$ is a nonnegative square matrix, then $(\mathbf{I} - \mathbf{A})$ has a nonnegative inverse iff all principal minors of $(\mathbf{I} - \mathbf{A})$ are positive. Then the inverse of $(\mathbf{I} - \mathbf{A})$ can be written as the expansion:

$$(\mathbf{I} - \mathbf{A})^{-1} = \mathbf{I} + \mathbf{A} + \mathbf{A}^2 + \cdots. \qquad \text{(B.5.6)}$$

Two square matrices of the same order, $\mathbf{A}$ and $\mathbf{B}$, are *similar* iff there exists a nonsingular matrix $\mathbf{M}$ such that:

$$\mathbf{B} = \mathbf{M}^{-1}\mathbf{A}\mathbf{M}. \qquad \text{*(B.5.7)}$$

Properties of similar matrices $\mathbf{A}$ and $\mathbf{B}$ include:

(i) $\text{tr}(\mathbf{A}) = \text{tr}(\mathbf{B})$.
(ii) $|\mathbf{A}| = |\mathbf{B}|$.
(iii) $\text{rank}(\mathbf{A}) = \text{rank}(\mathbf{B})$. *(B.5.8)
(iv) $\mathbf{B}^t = \mathbf{M}^{-1}\mathbf{A}^t\mathbf{M}$, where $\mathbf{B}^t$ is the tth power of $\mathbf{B}$ as in (B.3.9).

Given the square or nonsquare matrix $\mathbf{A}$ of order $m \times n$, the *generalized inverse matrix* $\mathbf{A}^+$ of order $n \times m$ is the matrix satisfying the properties:[7]

[7]See Theil (1971, Sec. 6.6; 1983, Sec. 10).

$$\begin{aligned} \mathbf{AA^+A} &= \mathbf{A}, \\ \mathbf{A^+AA^+} &= \mathbf{A^+}, \\ \mathbf{AA^+} &= (\mathbf{AA^+})', \quad \text{that is,} \quad \mathbf{AA^+} \text{ is symmetric}, \\ \mathbf{A^+A} &= (\mathbf{A^+A})', \quad \text{that is,} \quad \mathbf{A^+A} \text{ is symmetric}. \end{aligned} \tag{*B.5.9}$$

If $\mathbf{A}$ is square and nonsingular, $\mathbf{A^+}$ is unique and is given by $\mathbf{A}^{-1}$, so $\mathbf{A^+}$ is, indeed, a generalization of the concept of an inverse matrix. If $\mathbf{A}$ is square but singular, there is no inverse matrix, but a generalized inverse exists. If $\mathbf{A}$ is not square, a unique generalized inverse also exists. For example,

$$\mathbf{0}^+ = \mathbf{0}',$$

$$(\mathbf{B} \quad \mathbf{0})^+ = \begin{pmatrix} \mathbf{B}^{-1} \\ \mathbf{0} \end{pmatrix} \qquad \text{if } \mathbf{B} \text{ is square and nonsingular},$$

$$\left(\begin{array}{c|c} \mathbf{B} & \mathbf{0} \\ \hline \mathbf{0} & \mathbf{0} \end{array}\right)^+ = \left(\begin{array}{c|c} \mathbf{B}^{-1} & \mathbf{0} \\ \hline \mathbf{0} & \mathbf{0} \end{array}\right) \qquad \text{if } \mathbf{B} \text{ is square and nonsingular}.$$

Properties of the generalized inverse include:

(i) $\mathbf{A^{++}} = \mathbf{A}$.
(ii) $(\mathbf{A^+})' = (\mathbf{A}')^+$.
(iii) $\mathbf{AA^+}, \mathbf{A^+A}, \mathbf{I} - \mathbf{AA^+}, \mathbf{I} - \mathbf{A^+A}$ are all idempotent matrices. *(B.5.10)
(iv) $\text{rank}(\mathbf{A^+}) = \text{rank}(\mathbf{A})$.
(v) $\mathbf{A} = \mathbf{A^+}$ if $\mathbf{A}$ is idempotent and symmetric.

If $\mathbf{A}$ is $m \times n$, where $m > n$ and $\text{rank}(\mathbf{A}) = n$, then

$$\mathbf{A^+} = (\mathbf{A'A})^{-1}\mathbf{A}', \tag{*B.5.11}$$

where the inverse exists by reason of (B.4.10) (iii). In this case, using (B.5.10)(iii),

$$\mathbf{I} - \mathbf{AA^+} = \mathbf{I} - \mathbf{A}(\mathbf{A'A})^{-1}\mathbf{A}' \tag{*B.5.12}$$

is an idempotent matrix.

B.6 SYSTEMS OF LINEAR EQUATIONS; SOLUTIONS AND LEAST SQUARES FITS

The system of m linear equations in n unknowns

$$\begin{aligned} a_{11}x_1 + a_{12}x_2 + \cdots + a_{1n}x_n &= b_1, \\ a_{21}x_1 + a_{22}x_2 + \cdots + a_{2n}x_n &= b_2, \\ &\cdots \\ a_{m1}x_1 + a_{m2}x_2 + \cdots + a_{mn}x_n &= b_m, \end{aligned} \tag{B.6.1}$$

is summarized by the matrix equation:

$$\underset{m\times n}{\mathbf{A}}\ \underset{n\times 1}{\mathbf{x}} = \underset{m\times 1}{\mathbf{b}}, \tag{*B.6.2}$$

where $\mathbf{A} = (a_{ij})$ is the $m \times n$ coefficient matrix, $\mathbf{x} = (x_j)$ is the column vector of variables, and $\mathbf{b} = (b_i)$ is the column vector of constants, $i = 1, 2 \ldots, m; j = 1, 2, \ldots, n$. The system can also be written in summation notation as:

$$\sum_{j=1}^{n} a_{ij}x_j = b_i, \qquad i = 1, \ldots, m. \tag{B.6.3}$$

An example of such a system is:

$$2x_1 + 3x_2 = 7$$
$$x_1 + 4x_2 = 6,$$

which can be summarized by the matrix equation:

$$\begin{pmatrix} 2 & 3 \\ 1 & 4 \end{pmatrix}\begin{pmatrix} x_1 \\ x_2 \end{pmatrix} = \begin{pmatrix} 7 \\ 6 \end{pmatrix}.$$

The system of linear equations can have a unique solution, a nonunique solution, or no solution. A solution exists iff

$$\text{rank}(\mathbf{A}) = \text{rank}(\mathbf{A} \mid \mathbf{b}) = r, \tag*{*(B.6.4)}$$

and if a solution exists, it is unique iff $r = n$. If a solution exists but $r < n$, then $n - r$ of the variables can be assigned arbitrary values, with the remaining r variables then being uniquely determined.

If the coefficient matrix is square (the number of equations equals the number of unknowns) and nonsingular (the equations are independent), so that

$$m = n = \text{rank}(\mathbf{A}), \tag*{*(B.6.5)}$$

the solution is unique. The solution can be obtained in this case by premultiplying the matrix equation by the inverse matrix as:

$$\mathbf{x} = \mathbf{A}^{-1}\mathbf{b}. \tag*{*(B.6.6)}$$

For example, the solution to the equation above is:

$$\begin{pmatrix} x_1 \\ x_2 \end{pmatrix} = \begin{pmatrix} 2 & 3 \\ 1 & 4 \end{pmatrix}^{-1}\begin{pmatrix} 7 \\ 6 \end{pmatrix} = \begin{pmatrix} 2 \\ 1 \end{pmatrix}.$$

The solution can also be obtained from *Cramer's rule*:

$$x_j = \frac{|\mathbf{A}_j|}{|\mathbf{A}|}, \qquad j = 1, 2, \ldots, n, \tag{B.6.7}$$

where $\mathbf{A}_j$ is obtained from $\mathbf{A}$ by replacing the jth column of $\mathbf{A}$ by $\mathbf{b}$. In the example above the unique solutions are:

$$x_1 = \frac{\begin{vmatrix} 7 & 3 \\ 6 & 4 \end{vmatrix}}{\begin{vmatrix} 2 & 3 \\ 1 & 4 \end{vmatrix}} = 2, \qquad x_2 = \frac{\begin{vmatrix} 2 & 7 \\ 1 & 6 \end{vmatrix}}{\begin{vmatrix} 2 & 3 \\ 1 & 4 \end{vmatrix}} = 1.$$

Unique solutions can exist, however, even if $m \neq n$. For example, if

$$\begin{pmatrix} 2 \\ 8 \end{pmatrix} x_1 = \begin{pmatrix} 6 \\ 24 \end{pmatrix},$$

then $x_1 = 3$.

A case in which solutions exist but are nonunique is the *homogeneous* case in which the vector of constants is zero. For this case a necessary and sufficient condition for nontrivial solutions to exist is that the coefficient matrix be of less than full column rank. In this case, therefore, from (B.6.4)

$$\mathbf{b} = \mathbf{0} \text{ and } \operatorname{rank}(\mathbf{A}) = r < n. \qquad *(\text{B.6.8})$$

The solution is nonunique in that $n - r$ of the variables can be assigned arbitrary values. An example is:

$$\begin{pmatrix} 2 & 4 \\ 3 & 6 \end{pmatrix}\begin{pmatrix} x_1 \\ x_2 \end{pmatrix} = \mathbf{0},$$

where $n - r = 1$. Setting x_1 equal to the arbitary value c, all solutions are of the form:

$$\begin{pmatrix} x_1 \\ x_2 \end{pmatrix} = \begin{pmatrix} c \\ -c/2 \end{pmatrix}.$$

In general, in this homogeneous case, if $\operatorname{rank}(\mathbf{A}) = n - 1$, the solution is unique up to a factor of proportionality. Since $\operatorname{rank}(\mathbf{A}) \leqslant \min(m, n)$, another case in which nonunique solutions exist is that in which the number of equations is less than the number of unknowns and the rank condition is satisfied, so that $m < n$, but $\operatorname{rank}(\mathbf{A}) = \operatorname{rank}(\mathbf{A} \mid \mathbf{b})$. For example, if

$$\begin{pmatrix} 2 & -3 & 1 \\ 8 & 2 & 0 \end{pmatrix}\begin{pmatrix} x_1 \\ x_2 \\ x_3 \end{pmatrix} = \begin{pmatrix} 2 \\ 4 \end{pmatrix},$$

then, setting x_1 equal to the arbitrary value c, all solutions are of the form:

$$\begin{pmatrix} x_1 \\ x_2 \\ x_3 \end{pmatrix} = \begin{pmatrix} c \\ 2 - 4c \\ 8 - 14c \end{pmatrix}.$$

No solutions exist if $\operatorname{rank}(\mathbf{A}) < \operatorname{rank}(\mathbf{A} \mid \mathbf{b})$. Some examples are

$$\begin{pmatrix} 2 \\ 3 \end{pmatrix} x_1 = \begin{pmatrix} 6 \\ -1 \end{pmatrix}, \quad \begin{pmatrix} 2 & 4 \\ 3 & 6 \end{pmatrix}\begin{pmatrix} x_1 \\ x_2 \end{pmatrix} = \begin{pmatrix} 6 \\ 10 \end{pmatrix}, \quad \begin{pmatrix} 1 & 2 & -3 \\ 2 & 4 & -6 \end{pmatrix}\begin{pmatrix} x_1 \\ x_2 \\ x_3 \end{pmatrix} = \begin{pmatrix} 4 \\ 6 \end{pmatrix},$$

where $m > n$, $m = n$, and $m < n$, respectively.

Geometrically, each linear equation represents a hyperplane in Euclidean n-space, E^n, the space of all n-tuples of real numbers. If all m hyperplanes intersect at a point, then this point is the unique solution to the system of linear equations. If they intersect to form a line (plane, etc.), then all points on this line (plane, etc.) are solutions, and one (two, more) of the variables can be assigned arbitrary values. If they do not intersect (e.g., parallel lines in the plane E^2), no solution exists. A homogeneous equation represents a hyperplane passing through the origin, so, unless nonunique solutions exist, the only solution is the unique but trivial solution at the origin.

When there are more equations than unknowns, the system of linear equations is rewritten as:

$$\underset{n \times 1}{\mathbf{y}} = \underset{n \times k}{\mathbf{X}}\ \underset{k \times 1}{\boldsymbol{\beta}}, \qquad *(\text{B.6.9})$$

where $\mathbf{X}$ is an $n \times k$ coefficient matrix, $\boldsymbol{\beta}$ is a $k \times 1$ vector of unknowns, and $\mathbf{y}$ is an $n \times 1$ vector of constants.[8] It is assumed that n, the number of equations, exceeds k, the number

[8]This switch in notation will ensure that the notation here is consistent with that in the text, particularly Chapter 4. The switch replaces $\mathbf{A}$ by $\mathbf{X}$, $\mathbf{x}$ by $\boldsymbol{\beta}$, and $\mathbf{b}$ by $\mathbf{y}$, so $\mathbf{Ax} = \mathbf{b}$ is replaced by $\mathbf{X}\boldsymbol{\beta} = \mathbf{y}$.

of unknowns. One approach to "solving" this system is that of *least squares fit*. This approach minimizes the sum of squared deviations between elements of $\mathbf{y}$ and elements of $\mathbf{X}\boldsymbol{\beta}$, given as:[9]

$$S = \|\mathbf{y} - \mathbf{X}\boldsymbol{\beta}\|^2 = (\mathbf{y} - \mathbf{X}\boldsymbol{\beta})'(\mathbf{y} - \mathbf{X}\boldsymbol{\beta}) = \text{tr}(\mathbf{y} - \mathbf{X}\boldsymbol{\beta})(\mathbf{y} - \mathbf{X}\boldsymbol{\beta})'. \quad {}^*(\text{B.6.10})$$

The solution for $\boldsymbol{\beta}$ to the problem of minimizing S is:

$$\hat{\boldsymbol{\beta}} = \mathbf{X}^+\mathbf{y}, \quad {}^*(\text{B.6.11})$$

where $\mathbf{X}^+$ is the generalized inverse matrix defined in (B.5.9). If the $\mathbf{X}$ matrix has maximal rank, then, from (B.5.11),

$$\mathbf{X}^+ = (\mathbf{X}'\mathbf{X})^{-1}\mathbf{X}' \qquad [\text{when rank}(\mathbf{X}) = k]. \quad {}^*(\text{B.6.12})$$

In this case

$$\hat{\boldsymbol{\beta}} = (\mathbf{X}'\mathbf{X})^{-1}\mathbf{X}'\mathbf{y}. \quad {}^*(\text{B.6.13})$$

Both the solution in (B.6.11) and the solution in the special case in (B.6.13) corresponding to a coefficient matrix of maximal rank are called the *least squares estimators* of $\boldsymbol{\beta}$.

In the maximal-rank case, since

$$\mathbf{y} - \mathbf{X}\hat{\boldsymbol{\beta}} = \mathbf{y} - \mathbf{X}(\mathbf{X}'\mathbf{X})^{-1}\mathbf{X}'\mathbf{y} = \left[\mathbf{I} - \mathbf{X}(\mathbf{X}'\mathbf{X})^{-1}\mathbf{X}'\right]\mathbf{y}, \quad {}^*(\text{B.6.14})$$

where $\mathbf{I} - \mathbf{X}(\mathbf{X}'\mathbf{X})^{-1}\mathbf{X}'$ is a symmetric and idempotent matrix, the sum of squares S in (B.6.10) can be written:

$$S = (\mathbf{y} - \mathbf{X}\hat{\boldsymbol{\beta}})'(\mathbf{y} - \mathbf{X}\hat{\boldsymbol{\beta}}) = \mathbf{y}'\left[\mathbf{I} - \mathbf{X}(\mathbf{X}'\mathbf{X})^{-1}\mathbf{X}'\right]\mathbf{y} = \mathbf{y}'\mathbf{M}\mathbf{y}. \quad {}^*(\text{B.6.15})$$

The $\mathbf{M}$ matrix, here defined as $[\mathbf{I} - \mathbf{X}(\mathbf{X}'\mathbf{X})^{-1}\mathbf{X}']$, is the *fundamental idempotent matrix of least squares*. It satisfies the properties:

$$\begin{aligned} &\text{(i)} \ \ \mathbf{M} = \mathbf{M}', \\ &\text{(ii)} \ \ \mathbf{M} = \mathbf{M}^2, \\ &\text{(iii)} \ \ \rho(\mathbf{M}) = \text{tr}(\mathbf{M}) = n - k, \\ &\text{(iv)} \ \ \mathbf{M}\mathbf{X} = \mathbf{0}. \end{aligned} \quad {}^*(\text{B.6.16})$$

More generally, consider the *weighted* sum of squared deviations, $S(\mathbf{W})$, defined as:

$$S(\mathbf{W}) = (\mathbf{y} - \mathbf{X}\boldsymbol{\beta})'\mathbf{W}(\mathbf{y} - \mathbf{X}\boldsymbol{\beta}), \quad (\text{B.6.17})$$

where $\mathbf{W}$ is a symmetric nonsingular matrix of weights.[10] Then the *weighted least squares estimator* is given as:

$$\hat{\boldsymbol{\beta}} = (\mathbf{P}\mathbf{X})^+\mathbf{P}\mathbf{y}, \quad (\text{B.6.18})$$

where $\mathbf{P}$ is a nonsingular matrix that satisfies:[11]

$$\mathbf{P}'\mathbf{P} = \mathbf{W}. \quad (\text{B.6.19})$$

In particular, if $\mathbf{P}\mathbf{X}$ is of full rank, then

$$\hat{\boldsymbol{\beta}} = [(\mathbf{P}\mathbf{X})'(\mathbf{P}\mathbf{X})]^{-1}(\mathbf{P}\mathbf{X})'\mathbf{P}\mathbf{y}, \quad (\text{B.6.20})$$

[9]See (B.4.2)(iii).

[10]The matrix $\mathbf{W}$ is usually assumed to be positive definite, a property defined below in Section B.8. The weighted sum of squares in (B.8.1) is a quadratic form, as defined in (B.8.1).

[11]From (B.8.2)(vii) below, if $\mathbf{W}$ is positive definite, such a matrix always exists.

leading to:

$$\hat{\boldsymbol{\beta}} = [\mathbf{X}'\mathbf{W}\mathbf{X}]^{-1}\mathbf{X}'\mathbf{W}\mathbf{y}, \tag{B.6.21}$$

which is the weighted least squares estimator under the full-rank condition.

B.7 LINEAR TRANSFORMATIONS AND CHARACTERISTIC ROOTS AND VECTORS

Any $m \times n$ matrix $\mathbf{A}$ represents a linear transformation from Euclidean n-space to Euclidean m-space in that, given any vector $\mathbf{x} \in E^n$, there exists a unique vector $\mathbf{y} \in E^m$ such that:[12]

$$\mathbf{y} = \mathbf{A}\mathbf{x} = \mathbf{A}(\mathbf{x}). \qquad \text{*(B.7.1)}$$

The transformation is linear, since

$$\mathbf{A}(\mathbf{x}^1 + \mathbf{x}^2) = \mathbf{A}\mathbf{x}^1 + \mathbf{A}\mathbf{x}^2 \qquad \text{*(B.7.2)}$$

$$\mathbf{A}(k\mathbf{x}^1) = k\mathbf{A}(\mathbf{x}^1), \qquad \text{*(B.7.3)}$$

where $\mathbf{x}^1$ and $\mathbf{x}^2$ are vectors in E^n and k is any scalar. A property of such linear transformations is:

$$\mathbf{A}(\mathbf{0}) = \mathbf{0}. \tag{B.7.4}$$

A *characteristic vector* (or *eigenvector*) for a square matrix, $\mathbf{A}$, is a nonzero vector $\mathbf{x}$, which, when transformed by $\mathbf{A}$, yields the same vector except for a scale factor

$$\mathbf{A}\mathbf{x} = \lambda\mathbf{x}, \tag{B.7.5}$$

where the scale factor λ is a *characteristic root* (or *eigenvalue*) of $\mathbf{A}$. Since the equation above can be written:

$$(\mathbf{A} - \lambda\mathbf{I})\mathbf{x} = \mathbf{0}, \tag{B.7.6}$$

which is a homogeneous system of equations, a necessary condition for nontrivial solutions, from (B.6.8), is that the coefficient matrix be of less than full rank, so:

$$|\mathbf{A} - \lambda\mathbf{I}| = 0. \tag{B.7.7}$$

The resulting equation for λ is the *characteristic equation.* If $\mathbf{A}$ is an $n \times n$ matrix, the characteristic equation is an nth-order polynomial equation in λ:

$$|\mathbf{A} - \lambda\mathbf{I}| = (-\lambda)^n + \alpha_1(-\lambda)^{n-1} + \cdots + \alpha_{n-1}(-\lambda) + \alpha_n = 0, \tag{B.7.8}$$

where α_k is the kth-order trace of $\mathbf{A}$, $k = 1, \ldots, n$, as in (B.4.6). For example, in the 2×2 case,

$$\begin{aligned} |\mathbf{A} - \lambda\mathbf{I}| &= \begin{vmatrix} a_{11} - \lambda & a_{12} \\ a_{21} & a_{22} - \lambda \end{vmatrix} \\ &= \lambda^2 - (a_{11} + a_{22})\lambda + (a_{11}a_{22} - a_{12}a_{21}) \\ &= 0. \end{aligned} \tag{B.7.9}$$

The solution to the characteristic equation consists of n roots, $\lambda_1, \lambda_2, \ldots, \lambda_n$, which are not necessarily all distinct or real. To each of these characteristic roots there corresponds a characteristic vector that is determined up to a constant. For example, if

[12] E^n is Euclidean n-space, the space of all n-tuples of real numbers, here treated as the space of all n-dimensional column vectors.

$$\mathbf{A} = \begin{pmatrix} 6 & 10 \\ -2 & -3 \end{pmatrix},$$

the characteristic equation is $\lambda^2 - 3\lambda + 2 = 0$, yielding $\lambda_1 = 1, \lambda_2 = 2$. The characteristic vector corresponding to λ_1 is

$$\mathbf{x}^1 = \begin{pmatrix} c \\ -c/2 \end{pmatrix},$$

while that corresponding to λ_2 is

$$\mathbf{x}^2 = \begin{pmatrix} c \\ -\frac{2}{5}c \end{pmatrix},$$

where c is any constant. Constants are often eliminated by normalizing the vectors, and the normalized characteristic vectors for this example are, respectively:

$$\begin{pmatrix} 2/\sqrt{5} \\ -1/\sqrt{5} \end{pmatrix} \quad \text{and} \quad \begin{pmatrix} 5/\sqrt{29} \\ -2/\sqrt{29} \end{pmatrix}.$$

Properties of characteristic roots $\lambda_1, \lambda_2, \ldots, \lambda_n$ of any square matrix $\mathbf{A}$ include:

(i) $\sum_{j=1}^{n} \lambda_j = \text{tr}(\mathbf{A}) = \alpha_1$.

(ii) $\prod_{j=1}^{n} \lambda_j = |\mathbf{A}| = \alpha_n$.

(iii) $\lambda_j = d_j$ if $\mathbf{A}$ is the diagonal matrix $(d_j \delta_{ij})$.

(iv) $\lambda_j = 1$ or -1 if $\mathbf{A}$ is orthogonal.

(v) $\lambda_j = 1$ or 0 and $\text{rank}(\mathbf{A}) = \Sigma \lambda_j$ if $\mathbf{A}$ is an idempotent matrix.

(vi) If $\mathbf{A}$ and $\mathbf{B}$ are similar matrices, then they have the same characteristic roots. *(B.7.10)

(vii) λ_j^t are the characteristic roots of $\mathbf{A}^t$ if λ_j are the (nonzero) characteristic roots of $\mathbf{A}$ and t is any positive integer (or any integer if $\mathbf{A}$ is nonsingular).

(viii) If $\mathbf{x}_j$ is a normalized characteristic vector of $\mathbf{A}$ corresponding to the characteristic root λ_j, then $\mathbf{x}_j'\mathbf{A}\mathbf{x}_j = \lambda_j$.

Properties of the characteristic roots $\lambda_1, \lambda_2, \ldots, \lambda_n$ and vectors for any *symmetric* matrix $\mathbf{A}$ include:

(i) $\text{rank}(\mathbf{A})$ = the number of nonzero characteristic roots.

(ii) The characteristic roots λ_j are all real.

(iii) Any two characteristic vectors $\mathbf{x}_j$ and $\mathbf{x}_{j'}$ corresponding to distinct characteristic roots λ_j and $\lambda_{j'}$ are orthogonal, so $\mathbf{x}_j'\mathbf{x}_{j'} = 0$. (B.7.11)

(iv) $\mathbf{A}$ is similar to a diagonal matrix $\mathbf{\Lambda}$, the diagonal elements of which are the characteristic roots of $\mathbf{A}$, so $\mathbf{M}^{-1}\mathbf{A}\mathbf{M} = \mathbf{M}'\mathbf{A}\mathbf{M} = \mathbf{\Lambda}$. Here $\mathbf{M}$ is the *modal matrix*, an orthogonal matrix the columns of which are the normalized characteristic vectors of $\mathbf{A}$.

To give an example, if

$$\mathbf{A} = \begin{pmatrix} 6 & 2 \\ 2 & 3 \end{pmatrix}, \text{ then } \lambda_1 = 7, \ \lambda_2 = 2, \text{ and } \mathbf{M} = \frac{1}{\sqrt{5}}\begin{pmatrix} 2 & 1 \\ 1 & -2 \end{pmatrix},$$

where $\mathbf{M'AM} = \begin{pmatrix} 7 & 0 \\ 0 & 2 \end{pmatrix} = \mathbf{\Lambda}$.

B.8 QUADRATIC FORMS

Given a square symmetric matrix **A** and a column vector **x**, the *quadratic form* of **A** is:[13]

$$\begin{aligned} Q_{\mathbf{A}}(\mathbf{x}) &= \mathbf{x'Ax} \\ &= \sum_{i=1}^{n}\sum_{j=1}^{n} a_{ij}x_i x_j \\ &= a_{11}x_1^2 + a_{22}x_2^2 + \cdots + a_{nn}x_n^2 + 2a_{12}x_1x_2 + 2a_{13}x_1x_3 \\ &\quad + \cdots + 2a_{n-1,n}x_{n-1}x_n. \end{aligned} \qquad *(\text{B.8.1})$$

For example, if

$$\mathbf{A} = \begin{pmatrix} 1 & 3 \\ 3 & 4 \end{pmatrix}, \quad \text{then } Q_{\mathbf{A}}(\mathbf{x}) = x_1^2 + 4x_2^2 + 6x_1x_2,$$

while if **D** is the diagonal matrix $(d_j\delta_{ij})$, then $Q_{\mathbf{D}}(\mathbf{x})$ is

$$\sum_{j=1}^{n} d_j x_j^2,$$

the weighted sum of squares.

The quadratic form $Q_{\mathbf{A}}(\mathbf{x})$ is *positive definite* iff $Q_{\mathbf{A}}(\mathbf{x}) > 0$ for all $\mathbf{x} \neq \mathbf{0}$; is *negative definite* iff $Q_{\mathbf{A}}(\mathbf{x}) < 0$ for all $\mathbf{x} \neq \mathbf{0}$; is *positive semidefinite* iff $Q_{\mathbf{A}}(\mathbf{x}) \geqslant 0$ for all **x** and $Q_{\mathbf{A}}(\mathbf{x}) = 0$ for some $\mathbf{x} \neq \mathbf{0}$; is *negative semidefinite* iff $Q_{\mathbf{A}}(\mathbf{x}) \leqslant 0$ for all **x** and $Q_{\mathbf{A}}(\mathbf{x}) = 0$ for some $\mathbf{x} \neq \mathbf{0}$; and otherwise is *indefinite*. Sometimes the related matrix **A** is described as positive definite (etc.) if $Q_{\mathbf{A}}(\mathbf{x})$ is positive definite (etc.). For example, a diagonal matrix the diagonal elements of which are all positive (negative) is a positive (negative) definite matrix. If, for the diagonal matrix, all diagonal elements are nonnegative (nonpositive) and at least one is zero, then the matrix is positive (negative) semidefinite. Another example is an idempotent matrix, which must be either positive semidefinite or positive definite.

Properties of quadratic forms for the symmetric matrix **A** include:

(i) **A** is positive definite iff all characteristic roots of **A** are positive or, equivalently, iff all leading principal minors of **A** are positive.

[13]The assumption that **A** is symmetric is not restrictive, since

$$Q_{\mathbf{A}}(\mathbf{x}) = \mathbf{x'Ax} = \sum\sum a_{ij}x_ix_j = \sum\sum \tfrac{1}{2}\left(a_{ij} + a_{ji}\right)x_ix_j.$$

It will always be assumed that the matrix of the quadratic form is symmetric.

(ii) **A** is negative definite iff all characteristic roots of **A** are negative or, equivalently, iff all leading principal minors of **A** alternate in sign from negative to positive.

(iii) **A** is positive (semi) definite iff –**A** is negative (semi) definite.

(iv) If **A** is positive (negative) definite, then **A** is nonsingular, $\mathbf{A}^{-1}$ exists, and $\mathbf{A}^{-1}$ is positive (negative) definite.

(v) If **A** is positive (negative) definite and **P** is nonsingular, then $\mathbf{P'AP}$ is positive (negative) definite. *(B.8.2)

(vi) If **A** is of order $m \times n$ and rank(**A**) $= n < m$, then $\mathbf{A'A}$ is positive definite (and nonsingular), while $\mathbf{AA'}$ is positive semidefinite.

(vii) If **A** is a positive definite matrix, there exists a nonsingular matrix **P** such that $\mathbf{P'P} = \mathbf{A}$ and $\mathbf{PA}^{-1}\mathbf{P'} = \mathbf{I}$. There is also a unique (lower) triangular matrix **T** such that $\mathbf{A} = \mathbf{TT'}$.

(viii) If $\mathbf{x} = \mathbf{My}$, where **M** is the modal matrix of (B.7.11)(iv), then from the diagonalization of a symmetric matrix:

$$Q_{\mathbf{A}}(\mathbf{x}) = \mathbf{x'Ax} = \mathbf{y'}\Lambda\mathbf{y} = \sum_{j=1}^{n} \lambda_j y_j^2$$

so the quadratic form can always be written as a weighted sum of squares, the weights being the characteristic roots.

B.9 MATRIX DERIVATIVES

It is possible to differentiate matrices or to differentiate with respect to matrices. Differentiating a vector or matrix with respect to a scalar yields a vector or matrix of derivatives. Thus

(i) If $\mathbf{x} = (x_1, x_2, \ldots, x_n)'$, then

$$\frac{d\mathbf{x}}{dt} = \left(\frac{dx_1}{dt}, \frac{dx_2}{dt}, \ldots, \frac{dx_n}{dt}\right)'.$$

(ii) If $\mathbf{A} = (a_{ij})$, then

$$\frac{d\mathbf{A}}{dt} = \left(\frac{da_{ij}}{dt}\right).$$

(iii) $\dfrac{\partial \mathbf{AB}}{\partial t} = \mathbf{A}\dfrac{\partial \mathbf{B}}{\partial t} + \dfrac{\partial \mathbf{A}}{\partial t}\mathbf{B}.$

(iv) $\dfrac{\partial \mathbf{A}^{-1}}{\partial t} = -\mathbf{A}^{-1}\dfrac{\partial \mathbf{A}}{\partial t}\mathbf{A}^{-1}$. In particular, letting $\mathbf{A}^{-1} = (a^{gh})$,

$$\frac{\partial a^{gh}}{\partial a_{ij}} = \left(-a^{gi}a^{jh}\right), \qquad \text{*(B.9.1)}$$

where, in all cases, t is a scalar on which some or all of the elements of the vector or matrix depend.

Differentiating a scalar with respect to a column (row) vector yields a row (column) vector.[14] Examples of such derivatives include:

(i) If $y = f(\mathbf{x})$, where $\mathbf{x} = (x_1, x_2, \ldots, x_n)'$, then

$$\frac{\partial y}{\partial \mathbf{x}} = \left(\frac{\partial f}{\partial x_1}, \frac{\partial f}{\partial x_2}, \ldots, \frac{\partial f}{\partial x_n}\right),$$

which is the *gradient vector* $\partial f(\mathbf{x})/\partial \mathbf{x}$.

(ii) Given the linear form (inner product) **cx**,

$$\frac{\partial \mathbf{cx}}{\partial \mathbf{x}} = \mathbf{c}.$$

(iii) Given the quadratic form **x′Ax**,

$$\frac{\partial \mathbf{x'Ax}}{\partial \mathbf{x}} = 2\mathbf{x'A}. \quad \text{*(B.9.2)}$$

(iv) Given the bilinear form **wAx**,

$$\frac{\partial \mathbf{wAx}}{\partial \mathbf{w}} = \mathbf{Ax}, \qquad \frac{\partial \mathbf{wAx}}{\partial \mathbf{x}} = \mathbf{wA}.$$

Differentiating a scalar with respect to an $m \times n$ matrix yields an $n \times m$ matrix. Examples of such derivatives include:

(i) Given the quadratic form **x′Ax**,

$$\frac{\partial \mathbf{x'Ax}}{\partial \mathbf{A}} = \mathbf{xx'}.$$

(ii) Given the bilinear form **wAx**,

$$\frac{\partial \mathbf{wAx}}{\partial \mathbf{A}} = \mathbf{xw}.$$

(iii) Given the bilinear form **wAx**, where **A** is square and nonsingular and where $\mathbf{C} = \mathbf{A}^{-1}$, *(B.9.3)

$$\frac{\partial \mathbf{wC}^{-1}\mathbf{x}}{\partial \mathbf{C}} = -\mathbf{C}^{-1}\mathbf{xwC}^{-1}.$$

(iv) If $\mathrm{tr}(\mathbf{A})$ = trace of **A**, then

$$\frac{\partial\, \mathrm{tr}(\mathbf{A})}{\partial \mathbf{A}} = \mathbf{I}.$$

(v) If $|\mathbf{A}|$ = determinant of **A**, then

$$\frac{\partial |\mathbf{A}|}{\partial \mathbf{A}} = (C_{ji}) = |\mathbf{A}|\mathbf{A}^{-1} \quad \text{(if } \mathbf{A} \text{ is nonsingular)},$$

$$\frac{\partial \ln |\mathbf{A}|}{\partial \mathbf{A}} = \mathbf{A}^{-1} \quad \text{(assuming that } |\mathbf{A}| > 0).$$

Differentiating a vector with respect to a vector yields a matrix. Examples of such derivatives include:

[14]This convention follows Intriligator (1971, App. B).

(i) $\partial \mathbf{Ax}/\partial \mathbf{x} = \mathbf{A}$.

(ii) If $(\partial f/\partial \mathbf{x})$ is the gradient vector, then

$$\frac{\partial}{\partial \mathbf{x}}\left(\frac{\partial f}{\partial \mathbf{x}}\right) = \frac{\partial^2 f}{\partial \mathbf{x}^2} = \frac{\partial^2 f}{\partial x_i\, \partial x_j}, \qquad *(\text{B.9.4})$$

which is the *Hessian matrix* (a symmetric matrix).

(iii) If $\mathbf{g} = \mathbf{g}(\mathbf{x}) = [g_1(\mathbf{x}), g_2(\mathbf{x}), \ldots, g_m(\mathbf{x})]'$, where $\mathbf{x} = (x_1, x_2, \ldots, x_n)'$, then

$$\frac{\partial \mathbf{g}}{\partial \mathbf{x}}(\mathbf{x}) = \left(\frac{\partial g_i}{\partial x_j}\right),$$

which is the *Jacobian matrix*.

B.10 MATHEMATICAL PROGRAMMING[15]

The problem of mathematical programming is that of choosing the column vector $\mathbf{x} = (x_1, x_2, \ldots, x_n)'$ within the set X in Euclidean n-space E^n so as to

$$\max_{\mathbf{x}} F(\mathbf{x}) \quad \text{subject to} \quad \mathbf{x} \in X \subset E^n. \qquad *(\text{B.10.1})$$

A problem of minimization, e.g., that of minimizing $G(\mathbf{x})$, can be formulated as one of maximizing $-G(\mathbf{x})$.

A global maximum is defined as a point $\mathbf{x}^0$ for which

$$\mathbf{x}^0 \in X \quad \text{and} \quad F(\mathbf{x}^0) \geqslant F(\mathbf{x}) \qquad \text{for all } \mathbf{x} \in X. \qquad *(\text{B.10.2})$$

Such a global maximum always exists, by the Weierstrass theorem, if the function $F(\cdot)$ is continuous and the set X is closed and bounded. A local maximum is defined as $\mathbf{x}^0$ for which

$$\mathbf{x}^0 \in X \quad \text{and} \quad F(\mathbf{x}^0) \geqslant F(x) \quad \text{for all } \mathbf{x} \in X, \text{ where } \mathbf{x} \in N_\varepsilon(\mathbf{x}^0), \qquad *(\text{B.10.3})$$

and where $N_\varepsilon(\mathbf{x}^0)$ is an ε-neighborhood of $\mathbf{x}^0$. A local maximum is thus a maximum relative to "nearby" points. Clearly, a global maximum is a local maximum, but not necessarily vice versa.

In the unconstrained case, when the set X is the entire space E^n, so the problem is

$$\max_{\mathbf{x}} F(\mathbf{x}), \qquad *(\text{B.10.4})$$

a first-order necessary condition for $\mathbf{x}^0$ to be a local maximum of $F(\mathbf{x})$ is that the gradient vector defined in (B.9.2)(i) vanish:

$$\frac{\partial F}{\partial \mathbf{x}}(\mathbf{x}^0) = \mathbf{0}, \qquad *(\text{B.10.5})$$

so that the point is a *stationary point* at which all first-order partial derivatives vanish. A second-order necessary condition is that the Hessian matrix defined in (B.9.4)(ii), evaluated at this point, be negative definite or negative semidefinite:

$$\frac{\partial^2 F}{\partial \mathbf{x}^2}(\mathbf{x}^0) \text{ negative definite or negative semidefinite.} \qquad *(\text{B.10.6})$$

[15]See Intriligator (1971), especially Chapters 2 and 3, and Intriligator (1981, 1987).

Sufficient conditions for $\mathbf{x}^0$ to be a local maximum are:

$$\frac{\partial F}{\partial \mathbf{x}}(\mathbf{x}^0) = \mathbf{0},$$
$$\frac{\partial^2 F}{\partial \mathbf{x}^2}(\mathbf{x}^0) \text{ negative definite.} \qquad *(B.10.7)$$

An example is the problem of least squares, as in (B.6.10), where the problem is one of minimizing the sum of squares. The problem is:

$$\max_{\boldsymbol{\beta}} - S(\boldsymbol{\beta}) = -(\mathbf{y} - \mathbf{X}\boldsymbol{\beta})'(\mathbf{y} - \mathbf{X}\boldsymbol{\beta}) = -\mathbf{y}'\mathbf{y} + 2\boldsymbol{\beta}'\mathbf{X}'\mathbf{y} - \boldsymbol{\beta}'\mathbf{X}'\mathbf{X}\boldsymbol{\beta} \qquad (B.10.8)$$

and the first-order conditions state that:

$$\frac{\partial S}{\partial \boldsymbol{\beta}'} = 2\mathbf{X}'\mathbf{y} - 2(\mathbf{X}'\mathbf{X})\boldsymbol{\beta} = \mathbf{0}. \qquad (B.10.9)$$

The second-order sufficiency condition is met, since assuming that rank($\mathbf{X}$) = k,

$$\frac{\partial^2 S}{\partial \boldsymbol{\beta}'^2} = -2(\mathbf{X}'\mathbf{X}) \text{ negative definite.} \qquad (B.10.10)$$

Solving for the vector $\boldsymbol{\beta}$ that minimizes $S(\boldsymbol{\beta})$ from (B.10.9) yields:

$$\hat{\boldsymbol{\beta}} = (\mathbf{X}'\mathbf{X})^{-1}\mathbf{X}'\mathbf{y}, \qquad (B.10.11)$$

as in (B.6.13).

In the classically constrained case the set X is defined by a set of m equality constraints, so

$$X = \{\mathbf{x} \mid \mathbf{g}(\mathbf{x}) = \mathbf{b}\}. \qquad (B.10.12)$$

Here

$$\mathbf{g}(\mathbf{x}) = \begin{pmatrix} g_1(x_1, x_2, \ldots, x_n) \\ g_2(x_1, x_2, \ldots, x_n) \\ \vdots \\ g_m(x_1, x_2, \ldots, x_n) \end{pmatrix}, \qquad \mathbf{b} = \begin{pmatrix} b_1 \\ b_2 \\ \vdots \\ b_m \end{pmatrix} \qquad (B.10.13)$$

and $n > m$; that is, there are more variables to choose than there are constraints. Thus the problem can be stated:[16]

$$\max_{\mathbf{x}} F(\mathbf{x}) \quad \text{subject to} \quad \mathbf{g}(\mathbf{x}) = \mathbf{b}. \qquad *(B.10.14)$$

A classical approach to solving this problem is the *method of Lagrange multipliers*. It utilizes a row vector of m additional new variables,

$$\boldsymbol{\lambda} = (\lambda_1 \lambda_2 \cdots \lambda_m), \qquad (B.10.15)$$

one for each constraint. These variables are called *Lagrange multipliers* and they are used to define a Lagrangian function

$$L(\mathbf{x}, \boldsymbol{\lambda}) = F(\mathbf{x}) + \boldsymbol{\lambda}[\mathbf{b} - \mathbf{g}(\mathbf{x})], \qquad *(B.10.16)$$

where the last term is the inner product of a row vector and a column vector. The necessary first-order conditions for solving (B.10.4) are then the $n + m$ conditions[17]

[16]It is assumed that the constraints are independent in that rank($\partial\mathbf{g}/\partial\mathbf{x}$) = m, where $\partial\mathbf{g}/\partial\mathbf{x}$ is the Jacobian matrix of (B.9.4)(iii).

[17]For a discussion of the second-order conditions, see Intriligator (1971).

$$\frac{\partial L}{\partial \mathbf{x}} = \frac{\partial F}{\partial \mathbf{x}} - \lambda \frac{\partial \mathbf{g}}{\partial \mathbf{x}} = \mathbf{0} \qquad (n \text{ conditions})$$
$$\frac{\partial L}{\partial \boldsymbol{\lambda}} = \mathbf{b} - \mathbf{g}(\mathbf{x}) = \mathbf{0} \qquad (m \text{ conditions}). \tag{B.10.17}$$

Thus, at the solution $\mathbf{x}^0$ the constraint $\mathbf{g}(\mathbf{x}^0) = \mathbf{b}$ is met and, in addition,

$$\frac{\partial F}{\partial \mathbf{x}}(\mathbf{x}^0) = \boldsymbol{\lambda} \frac{\partial \mathbf{g}}{\partial \mathbf{x}}(\mathbf{x}^0). \tag{B.10.18}$$

As an example, suppose that the sum of squares $S(\boldsymbol{\beta})$ in (B.10.8) is to be minimized subject to the m linear constraints[18]

$$\mathbf{A}\boldsymbol{\beta} = \mathbf{c}, \tag{B.10.19}$$

where $\mathbf{A}$ is a given $m \times k$ matrix of rank m and $\mathbf{c}$ is a given $m \times 1$ vector. The Lagrangian for this problem of least squares subject to linear constraints is:

$$L = -\mathbf{y}'\mathbf{y} + 2\boldsymbol{\beta}'\mathbf{X}'\mathbf{y} - \boldsymbol{\beta}'\mathbf{X}'\mathbf{X}\boldsymbol{\beta} + \boldsymbol{\lambda}(\mathbf{c} - \mathbf{A}\boldsymbol{\beta}). \tag{B.10.20}$$

Using the conditions in (B.10.17),

$$\frac{\partial L}{\partial \boldsymbol{\beta}'} = 2\mathbf{X}'\mathbf{y} - 2\mathbf{X}'\mathbf{X}\boldsymbol{\beta} - \mathbf{A}'\boldsymbol{\lambda}' = \mathbf{0} \qquad (k \text{ conditions}),$$
$$\frac{\partial L}{\partial \boldsymbol{\lambda}} = \mathbf{c} - \mathbf{A}\boldsymbol{\beta} = \mathbf{0} \qquad (m \text{ conditions}). \tag{B.10.21}$$

From the first set of conditions:

$$\boldsymbol{\beta} = (\mathbf{X}'\mathbf{X})^{-1}(\mathbf{X}'\mathbf{y} - \tfrac{1}{2}\mathbf{A}'\boldsymbol{\lambda}'), \tag{B.10.22}$$

so, using the constraint:

$$\mathbf{A}(\mathbf{X}'\mathbf{X})^{-1}\mathbf{X}'\mathbf{y} - \tfrac{1}{2}\mathbf{A}(\mathbf{X}'\mathbf{X})^{-1}\mathbf{A}'\boldsymbol{\lambda}' = \mathbf{c}, \tag{B.10.23}$$

this equation may be solved for $\boldsymbol{\lambda}'$ as:

$$\boldsymbol{\lambda}' = 2\left[\mathbf{A}(\mathbf{X}'\mathbf{X})^{-1}\mathbf{A}'\right]^{-1}\left[\mathbf{A}(\mathbf{X}'\mathbf{X})^{-1}\mathbf{X}'\mathbf{y} - \mathbf{c}\right]. \tag{B.10.24}$$

Finally, inserting this value in (B.10.22) yields:

$$\hat{\hat{\boldsymbol{\beta}}} = (\mathbf{X}'\mathbf{X})^{-1}\mathbf{X}'\mathbf{y} - (\mathbf{X}'\mathbf{X})^{-1}\mathbf{A}'\left[\mathbf{A}(\mathbf{X}'\mathbf{X})^{-1}\mathbf{A}'\right]^{-1}\left[\mathbf{A}(\mathbf{X}'\mathbf{X})^{-1}\mathbf{X}'\mathbf{y} - \mathbf{c}\right]. \tag{B.10.25}$$

This is the least squares estimator subject to the additional linear constraints that $\mathbf{A}\boldsymbol{\beta} = \mathbf{c}$. In terms of the ordinary estimator $\hat{\boldsymbol{\beta}}$ in (B.10.11),

$$\hat{\hat{\boldsymbol{\beta}}} = \hat{\boldsymbol{\beta}} - (\mathbf{X}'\mathbf{X})^{-1}\mathbf{A}'\left[\mathbf{A}(\mathbf{X}'\mathbf{X})^{-1}\mathbf{A}'\right]^{-1}\left[\mathbf{A}\hat{\boldsymbol{\beta}} - \mathbf{c}\right]. \tag{B.10.26}$$

If $\hat{\boldsymbol{\beta}}$ satisfies the constraints, then $\hat{\hat{\boldsymbol{\beta}}} = \hat{\boldsymbol{\beta}}$. More generally, the difference between the estimators $\hat{\hat{\boldsymbol{\beta}}} - \hat{\boldsymbol{\beta}}$ is a linear function of the amounts by which the ordinary estimator fails to satisfy the constraints, $\mathbf{A}\hat{\boldsymbol{\beta}} - \mathbf{c}$.

[18]See Theil (1971).

BIBLIOGRAPHY

DHRYMES, P. J. (1978). *Mathematics for Econometrics*. New York: Springer-Verlag New York, Inc. (Second edition, 1984.)

GRAYBILL, F. A. (1969). *Introduction to Matrices with Applications in Statistics*. Belmont, Calif.: Wadsworth Publishing Co., Inc.

HADLEY, G. (1961). *Linear Algebra*. Reading, Mass.: Addison-Wesley Publishing Company, Inc.

HORST, P. (1963). *Matrix Algebra for Social Scientists*. New York: Holt, Rinehart, & Winston.

INTRILIGATOR, M. D. (1971). *Mathematical Optimization and Economic Theory*. Englewood Cliffs, N.J.: Prentice Hall.

INTRILIGATOR, M. D. (1981). "Mathematical Programming, with Applications to Economics," in K. J. Arrow and M. D. Intriligator, Eds., *Handbook of Mathematical Economics*, Vol. 1. Amsterdam: North-Holland Publishing Company.

INTRILIGATOR, M. D. (1987). "Nonlinear Programming," in J. Eatwell, M. Milgate, and P. Newman, Eds., *The New Palgrave: A Dictionary of Economic Theory and Doctrine*. London: Macmillan.

THEIL, H. (1971). *Principles of Econometrics*. New York: John Wiley & Sons, Inc.

THEIL, H. (1983). "Linear Algebra and Matrix Methods in Econometrics," in Z. Griliches and M. D. Intriligator, Eds., *Handbook of Econometrics*, Vol. 1. Amsterdam: North-Holland Publishing Company.

APPENDIX C

PROBABILITY AND STATISTICS[1]

C.1 PROBABILITY

The concept of probability underlies the whole field of statistics and thus also econometrics, which is based upon statistical foundations.[2] Consider the *sample space* S, the set of all possible outcomes of a (conceptual) experiment, and let the subsets $A, B, \ldots$ of S represent possible *events*. The *probability* of an event is defined as a real-valued function mapping the subsets of S into the closed interval $[0, 1]$ on the real line, where $P(A)$ is the probability of event A. The probabilities, which can be interpreted either as the real-valued function or values taken by this function, satisfy the following three axioms:

$$0 \leq P(A) \leq 1, \qquad *(\text{C.1.1})$$

$$P(\emptyset) = 0, \quad P(S) = 1, \qquad *(\text{C.1.2})$$

$$P(A \cup B) = P(A) + P(B) - P(AB). \qquad *(\text{C.1.3})$$

The first fundamental axiom (C.1.1) states that the probability of any event is a nonnegative real number not larger than unity. A probability of zero means the event is essentially impossible, while a probability of one means the event is essentially certain. The second axiom (C.1.2) states that the empty set $\emptyset$ is impossible and that the entire set S is certain in that some event must occur and S includes all possible events. The third axiom (C.1.3) states that the probability of a union of two events is the sum of the probabilities of each taken individually less the probability of the joint event that both occur, where $P(AB) = P(A \cap B)$. Thus, in particular, if the two events are disjoint ($A \cap B = \emptyset$), the probability of the union of the two events is the sum of the probabilities of the separate events.[3]

[1]Basic references on statistics are Cramer (1946), Wilks (1962), Fisz (1963), and Rao (1973). Good introductory books are Fraser (1958), Hoel (1984), and Mood, Graybill, and Boes (1974). A more advanced survey of this material, along with a discussion of elementary statistical applications, may be found in Zellner (1983).

[2]Basic references on probability are Fisz (1963) and Feller (1968).

There are several possible interpretations of probability. The classical examples of coin tossing or rolling dice suggest a *relative-frequency* interpretation, where

$$P(A) = \frac{\text{number of times } A \text{ occurs}}{\text{total number of trials}} = \frac{N(A)}{N}. \qquad *(\text{C.1.4})$$

This relative-frequency interpretation is meaningful and real. It usually, however, makes sense only in the context of rather stylized experiments of the sort described and utilized almost exclusively by statisticians, such as tossing coins, rolling dice, or selecting colored balls out of urns. For the purposes of social science research, and particularly econometrics, a more reasonable interpretation of probability is that of *limiting relative frequency*, where, using the notation of (C.1.4),

$$P(A) = \lim_{N \to \infty} \frac{N(A)}{N}. \qquad *(\text{C.1.5})$$

One therefore imagines a whole series of experiments in which the limiting (asymptotic) ratio of the number of times A occurs to the total number of trials is the probability of A. To give an example, a statement such as "The probability that GNP will be between \$7400 and \$7700 billion next year is 0.9" means that if all the conditions for the next year could be replicated many times and GNP were calculated for each replication, 90% of the replications would involve a level of GNP between \$7400 and \$7700 billion.

A third interpretation of probability, which has been used in social science and even in econometrics, is that of *subjective degree of belief*. Under this interpretation each individual forms his or her own assessment of the likelihood of events, and the probability is a measure of this assessment.[4] Thus a higher probability of an event means a greater belief that the event will occur. Economic forecasts are sometimes based on such probabilities. With this interpretation the statement "The probability that GNP will be between \$1400 and \$1700 billion next year is 0.9" means that the individual making the statement would be indifferent between betting that GNP next year will fall in this range or betting that a randomly selected digit in a table of random digits will be a number other than zero.

Given a set of probabilities, under any of the interpretations given here there is defined a *calculus of probabilities*. For example, *conditional probabilities* are defined as:

$$P(A \mid B) = \frac{P(AB)}{P(B)}. \qquad *(\text{C.1.6})$$

Since

$$P(AB) = P(A \mid B)P(B) = P(B \mid A)P(A), \qquad (\text{C.1.7})$$

it follows that

$$P(B \mid A) = \frac{P(B)P(A \mid B)}{P(A)}. \qquad (\text{C.1.8})$$

[3]More generally, given a finite or infinite sequence of disjoint subsets A_i of S,

$$P\left(\bigcup_{i=1}^{n} A_i\right) = \sum_{i=1}^{n} P(A_i), \quad \text{where } A_i \cap A_j = \emptyset \text{ for } i \neq j.$$

[4]See Savage (1954), Raiffa (1968), and De Groot (1969).

If the events $B_1, B_2, \ldots, B_n$ form a mutually exclusive and exhaustive set of events—that is,

$$P(B_iB_j) = 0 \qquad \text{for } i \neq j, \tag{C.1.9}$$

$$P\left(\bigcup_{i=1}^{n} B_i\right) = 1, \tag{C.1.10}$$

then it follows that:

$$P(A) = \sum_{i=1}^{n} P(B_i)P(A|B_i). \tag{C.1.11}$$

Thus (C.1.8) implies that:

$$P(B_i|A) = \frac{P(B_i)P(A|B_i)}{\sum P(B_i)P(A|B_i)}. \tag*{*(C.1.12)}$$

This result, known as *Bayes' theorem*, forms the foundation of Bayesian statistics, which involves yet another interpretation of probabilities.[5] Interpret $P(B_i \mid A)$ in (C.1.12) as the probability of the ith hypothesis B_i, given the observation, event A. According to Bayes' theorem this probability is obtained as the product of the *prior probability* of the hypothesis $P(B_i)$ times the *likelihood* of the observation A, given the hypothesis, $P(A \mid B_i)$, normalized by dividing by the sum of all such products of likelihoods and prior probabilities. The result is the *posterior probability* $P(B_i \mid A)$—that is, the probability after observing the event A. Bayes' theorem thus represents a rule for generating posterior probabilities from prior probabilities and likelihoods. If the prior probability is interpreted as a subjective degree of belief, the posterior probability combines this subjective belief with objective information on an observed event, A, to determine a hybrid subjective-objective probability. The rule can be used again and again, however, at each stage taking account of the prior probability, which has taken the past observations into account, and the current observations. The limit of this process is an objective probability, independent of the initial subjective degree of belief (unless the prior belief is held with certainty). It can be interpreted as a limiting relative frequency as in (C.1.5). Thus Bayes' theorem (C.1.12) represents a bridge between two interpretations of probability.

C.2 RANDOM VARIABLES; DISTRIBUTION AND DENSITY FUNCTIONS

A *random variable* is a real-valued function defined on a sample space. If S is the sample space, the space of all possible events, the random variable X is a mapping from S into the real line:

$$X : S \to E. \tag*{*(C.2.1)}$$

For example, if S consists of the events heads (H) and tails (T) obtained by tossing a coin, one possible random variable defined on this sample space would be

$$X(H) = 1, \qquad X(T) = 0, \tag{C.2.2}$$

[5]For a discussion of the Bayesian approach to econometrics, see Section 4.11.

but, of course, many other random variables could be defined on this sample space. Usually the problem suggests a convenient choice of random variable. Thus, if the sample space consists of all possible values of GNP, the random variable may be defined simply as the value taken by GNP. Thus, for example, for a GNP of \$7500 billion,

$$X(\$7500 \text{ billion}) = 7500. \tag{C.2.3}$$

The term *random variable* can apply to either the function, as in (C.2.1), or the values taken by the function. In the latter interpretation the random variable can be finite or countable. Thus the head–tail example of (C.2.2) defines a finite random variable, while the GNP example defines a countable random variable, since the values assumed by the random variable include all the positive integers. Continuous random variables are also possible, where the values assumed by the random variable define a continuum of points on the real line. In fact, the emphasis below, corresponding to that in econometrics, will be on continuous random variables.[6]

Given a random variable X, the *distribution function* $F(x)$ is defined as:

$$F(x) = P(-\infty < X \leqslant x), \qquad *(\text{C.2.4})$$

that is, as the probability that the values assumed by the random variable are less than or equal to the value x. For example, for the random variable defined by (C.2.2), if the coin is a fair coin,

$$F(x) = \begin{Bmatrix} 0 \\ \frac{1}{2} \\ 1 \end{Bmatrix} \text{ for } \begin{Bmatrix} x < 0 \\ 0 \leqslant x < 1 \\ 1 \leqslant x \end{Bmatrix}. \tag{C.2.5}$$

Since $F(x)$ is a probability, it must satisfy:

$$0 \leqslant F(x) \leqslant 1, \quad \text{all } x, \tag{C.2.6}$$

where, taking limits,

$$\lim_{x \to -\infty} F(x) = F(-\infty) = 0, \qquad \lim_{x \to \infty} F(x) = F(\infty) = 1. \tag{C.2.7}$$

The distribution function is nondecreasing in that

$$F(x) \geqslant F(x') \text{ if } x \geqslant x', \tag{C.2.8}$$

so assuming that the random variable is continuous and $F(x)$ is a differentiable function:

$$\frac{dF(x)}{dx} \geqslant 0, \qquad -\infty < x < \infty. \tag{C.2.9}$$

Geometrically, then, the distribution function is a curve that is nonnegative, "starting" at zero and "ending" at unity, nowhere falling in value.

Given a differentiable distribution function $F(x)$, the *density function* $f(x)$ is defined as the derivative of $F(x)$ evaluated at x:

$$f(x) = \lim_{\Delta x \to 0} \frac{F(x + \Delta x) - F(x)}{\Delta x} = \frac{dF(x)}{dx} \geqslant 0, \qquad -\infty < x < \infty. \qquad *(\text{C.2.10})$$

The *probability element* is defined as:

$$dF(x) = f(x)\, dx = P(x < X \leqslant x + dx) \geqslant 0. \qquad *(\text{C.2.11})$$

Integrating the probability element from a to b, where $a < b$,[7]

[6]For discussions of discrete statistics, see the basic references of footnote 1; see also footnote 7.

[7]Integrals are used here and below because of the emphasis on *continuous* rather than discrete distributions. In the discrete case the integrals would be replaced by summation signs with appropriate limits.

$$\int_a^b dF(x) = \int_a^b f(x)\, dx = F(b) - F(a) = P(a < X \leqslant b), \qquad *(\text{C.2.12})$$

so the definite integral of the density function has the interpretation of a probability. Taking the limit as $a \to -\infty$,

$$\int_{-\infty}^{b} f(x)\, dx = F(b) = P(-\infty < X \leqslant x) \quad \text{so} \quad \int_{-\infty}^{x} f(\xi)\, d\xi = F(x), \qquad *(\text{C.2.13})$$

expressing the relation between the distribution and density function in integral form, the relation having been expressed previously in differential form in (C.2.10). Taking the limit as $b \to \infty$, using (C.2.7),

$$\int_{-\infty}^{\infty} f(\xi)\, d\xi = 1. \qquad (\text{C.2.14})$$

Geometrically, then, the density function is a curve that is nonnegative, can rise above unity, can fall in value, but has "under" it a unit area. Any function $f(x)$ satisfying these conditions can be interpreted as a density function. The relation between distribution and density function is illustrated in Figure C.1. When $F(x)$ is "flat," $f(x)$ is zero, and when $F(x)$ reaches an inflection point, $f(x)$ is at a maximum. The total shaded area "under" $f(x)$ is unity. Note that $f(x)$ is *not* a probability, even though $f(x)\, dx$, the probability element, is.

The correspondence between the distribution function and the axioms of probability should be clear. Thus (C.2.6) corresponds to (C.1.1), and (C.2.7) corresponds to (C.1.2). Finally, by the definition of the definite integral,

$$\begin{aligned} F(x) &= \int_{-\infty}^{y} f(\xi)\, d\xi + \int_{y}^{x} f(\xi)\, d\xi \\ &= P(X \leqslant y) + P(y < X \leqslant x) = P(X \leqslant x), \end{aligned} \qquad (\text{C.2.15})$$

corresponding to (C.1.3).

The concepts introduced thus far refer to a *single* random variable, the *univariate* case. They can be extended readily, however, to the *multivariate* case. In the multivariate case there are m real-valued functions defined on the sample space, so

$$\mathbf{X} : S \to E^m. \qquad *(\text{C.2.16})$$

Thus the *m-dimensional random variable* (or m-vector valued random variable) $\mathbf{X}$ maps the sample space S into Euclidean m-space, the space of all m-tuples of real numbers.[8] The random variable is summarized by the column vector:

$$\underset{m\times 1}{\mathbf{X}} = \begin{pmatrix} X_1 \\ X_2 \\ \vdots \\ X_m \end{pmatrix} = (X_1 \quad X_2 \quad \cdots \quad X_m)', \qquad (\text{C.2.17})$$

where X_j is the jth random variable, $j = 1, 2, \ldots, m$. The *distribution function* is then:

$$\begin{aligned} F(x) &= F(x_1, x_2, \ldots, x_m) \\ &= P(-\infty < X_1 \leqslant x_1, -\infty < X_2 \leqslant x_2, \ldots, -\infty < X_m \leqslant x_m), \end{aligned} \qquad *(\text{C.2.18})$$

that is, the probability that each of the m random variables is less than the corresponding given value. This definition reduces to (C.2.4) in the *univariate case*, the special case in which $m = 1$; and the *bivariate case* is that for which $m = 2$. As before, since $F(x)$ is a probability,

[8]For discussions of *multivariate statistics*, the study of multivariate random variables, see Anderson (1984), Kendall and Stuart (1983), Graybill (1961), and Rao (1973), and see also Scheffé (1959) and Searle (1971).

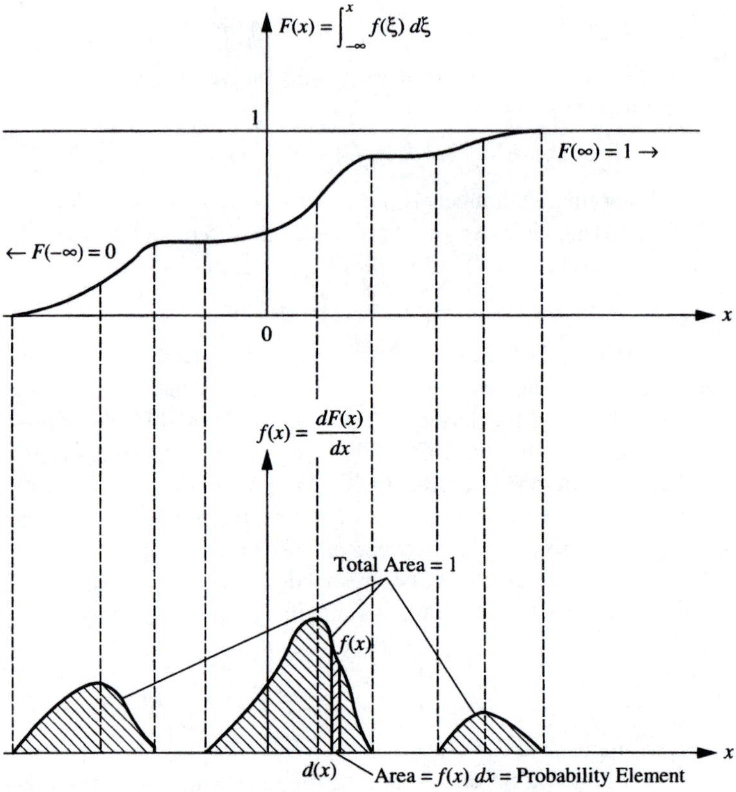

Figure C.1 Distribution and Density Functions

$$0 \leqslant F(\mathbf{x}) \leqslant 1. \tag{C.2.19}$$

Generalizing (C.2.7),

$$F(x_1, x_2, \ldots, x_m) = 0 \qquad \text{if any } x_j = -\infty, \qquad j = 1, 2, \ldots, m, \tag{C.2.20}$$

$$F(x_1, x_2, \ldots, x_m) = 1 \qquad \text{if all } x_j = +\infty, \qquad j = 1, 2, \ldots, m. \tag{C.2.21}$$

Assuming differentiability of $F(x)$, generalizing (C.2.9),

$$\frac{\partial F}{\partial x_j}(\mathbf{x}) \geqslant 0, \qquad j = 1, 2, \ldots, m. \tag{C.2.22}$$

The *density function* is $f(\mathbf{x})$, defined as:

$$f(\mathbf{x}) = \frac{\partial^m F}{\partial x_1 \ \partial x_2 \ \cdots \ \partial x_m}(\mathbf{x}) \geqslant 0, \tag*{*(C.2.23)}$$

so the *probability element* is:

$$\begin{aligned} dF(\mathbf{x}) &= f(x_1, x_2, \ldots, x_m)\, dx_1\, dx_2 \cdots dx_m \\ &= P(x_j < X_j < x_j + dx_j,\ j = 1, 2, \ldots, m) \geqslant 0. \end{aligned} \tag*{*(C.2.24)}$$

Integrating the probability element,

$$\int_{-\infty}^{b_m} \cdots \int_{-\infty}^{b_1} f(x_1, x_2, \ldots, x_m)\, dx_1\, dx_2 \cdots dx_m = F(b_1, b_2, \ldots, b_m). \qquad *(\text{C.2.25})$$

Thus the relation between the density function and the distribution function can be written in integral form:

$$\int_{-\infty}^{x_m} \cdots \int_{-\infty}^{x_1} f(\xi_1, \xi_2, \ldots, \xi_m)\, d\xi_1\, d\xi_2 \cdots d\xi_m = F(x_1, x_2, \ldots, x_m), \qquad *(\text{C.2.26})$$

an alternative form to the differential form of (C.2.23). From (C.2.21),

$$\int_{-\infty}^{\infty} \cdots \int_{-\infty}^{\infty} f(\xi_1, \xi_2, \ldots, \xi_m)\, d\xi_1\, d\xi_2 \cdots d\xi_m = F(\infty, \infty, \ldots, \infty) = 1. \qquad (\text{C.2.27})$$

Furthermore, from the definition of the probability element (C.2.24),

$$\begin{aligned}\int_{a_m}^{b_m} \cdots \int_{a_1}^{b_1} & f(\xi_1, \xi_2, \ldots, \xi_m)\, d\xi_1\, d\xi_2 \cdots d\xi_m \\ &= F(b_1, b_2, \ldots, b_m) - F(a_1, a_2, \ldots, a_m) \qquad *(\text{C.2.28}) \\ &= P(a_j < X_j < b_j, j = 1, 2, \ldots, m).\end{aligned}$$

Geometrically, the multivariate case can be illustrated in the bivariate case $m = 2$, as the three-dimensional density function surface $f(x_1, x_2)$. This surface has, at any point (x_1, x_2), a nonnegative value, and the total volume enclosed by the surface is unity, i.e.,

$$f(x_1, x_2) \geqslant 0, \qquad \int_{-\infty}^{\infty} \int_{-\infty}^{\infty} f(\xi_1, \xi_2)\, d\xi_1\, d\xi_2 = 1. \qquad (\text{C.2.29})$$

Given a partition of the random variable $\mathbf{X}$ as:

$$\mathbf{X} = \begin{pmatrix} \mathbf{X}_1 \\ ---- \\ \mathbf{X}_2 \end{pmatrix} \begin{matrix} p \\ m - p \end{matrix}, \qquad (\text{C.2.30})$$

where $\mathbf{X}_1$ is a column vector of p elements and $\mathbf{X}_2$ is a column vector of $m - p$ elements $(p < m)$, the *marginal distribution function* of $\mathbf{X}_1$ is defined as:

$$F_1(\mathbf{x}_1) = F_1(x_1, x_2, \ldots, x_p) = F(x_1, x_2, \ldots, x_p, \infty, \infty, \ldots, \infty), \qquad (\text{C.2.31})$$

and the *marginal density function* of $\mathbf{X}_1$ is defined as:

$$f_1(\mathbf{x}_1) = f_1(x_1, x_2, \ldots, x_p) = \frac{\partial^p F_1(x_1, x_2, \ldots, x_p)}{\partial x_1\, \partial x_2 \cdots \partial x_p}. \qquad (\text{C.2.32})$$

The set of random variables $\mathbf{X}_1$ is *statistically independent* of the set $\mathbf{X}_2$ if

$$F(\mathbf{x}) = F(\mathbf{x}_1, \mathbf{x}_2) = F_1(\mathbf{x}_1)F_2(\mathbf{x}_2) \quad \text{so} \quad f(\mathbf{x}) = f_1(\mathbf{x}_1)f_2(\mathbf{x}_2). \qquad (\text{C.2.33})$$

In particular, the set $X_1, X_2, \ldots, X_m$ is *mutually independent* if

$$F(x_1, x_2, \ldots, x_m) = F_1(x_1)F_2(x_2) \cdots F_m(x_m), \qquad (\text{C.2.34})$$

where $F_j(x_j)$ is the marginal distribution function of X_j. The *conditional density* of $\mathbf{X}_1$ given $\mathbf{X}_2$ is:

$$f(\mathbf{x}_1 | \mathbf{x}_2) = \frac{f(x_1, x_2, \ldots, x_m)}{f_2(x_{p+1} x_{p+2} \cdots x_m)} = \frac{f(\mathbf{x})}{f_2(\mathbf{x}_2)}. \qquad (\text{C.2.35})$$

If $\mathbf{X}_1$ and $\mathbf{X}_2$ are statistically independent, then

$$f(\mathbf{x}) = f_1(\mathbf{x}_1)f_2(\mathbf{x}_2) \quad \text{so} \quad f(\mathbf{x}_1 | \mathbf{x}_2) = f_1(\mathbf{x}_1). \qquad (\text{C.2.36})$$

C.3 MEAN, VARIANCE, COVARIANCE, AND OTHER MOMENTS; SAMPLE MEASURES

Given a univariate random variable, the mean of the random variable is defined as:

$$\mu = \int_{-\infty}^{\infty} xf(x)\,dx. \qquad *(\text{C.3.1})$$

This definition may be motivated by noting that the mean is obtained by taking any value x, "weighting" it by the probability element $f(x)\,dx$, and adding (integrating) over all such x. Geometrically, the mean is the center of gravity of the density function $f(x)$, the point where a template cut out in the shape of $f(x)$ "just balances." It is a measure of central tendency. In the multivariate case the *jth mean* of $\mathbf{X}$ is defined as:

$$\mu_j = \int_{-\infty}^{\infty} \cdots \int_{-\infty}^{\infty} x_j f(x_1, x_2, \ldots, x_m)\,dx_1\,dx_2 \cdots dx_m, \quad j = 1, 2, \ldots, m \qquad *(\text{C.3.2})$$

and $\boldsymbol{\mu}$ is the column vector of all m of these means:

$$\underset{m\times 1}{\boldsymbol{\mu}} = (\mu_1, \mu_2, \ldots, \mu_m)'. \qquad (\text{C.3.3})$$

Geometrically, the mean $\boldsymbol{\mu}$ is the center of gravity of the density function $f(x_1, x_2, \ldots, x_m)$, located where the surface defined by this function "just balances."

Returning to the univariate case, the *variance* of the random variable is defined as:

$$\text{Var}(x) = \sigma^2 = \int_{-\infty}^{\infty} (x - \mu)^2 f(x)\,dx \geqslant 0. \qquad *(\text{C.3.4})$$

Here deviations of x from the mean μ are squared to eliminate the sign, weighted by the probability element, and summed over all possible x values. The variance is a measure of the dispersion of the distribution. In the multivariate case the *jth variance* of $\mathbf{X}$ is:

$$\begin{aligned} \text{Var}(x_j) &= \sigma_j^2 = \sigma_{jj} \\ &= \int_{-\infty}^{\infty} \cdots \int_{-\infty}^{\infty} (x_j - \mu_j)^2 f(x_1, x_2, \ldots, x_m)\,dx_1\,dx_2 \cdots dx_m \geqslant 0, \qquad *(\text{C.3.5}) \\ &\qquad j = 1, 2, \ldots, m \end{aligned}$$

so there are m such variances, measuring the dispersion in each coordinate direction. The jj' covariance of $\mathbf{X}$ is defined in this case as

$$\begin{aligned} \text{Cov}(x_j x_{j'}) &= \sigma_{jj'} \\ &= \int_{-\infty}^{\infty} \cdots \int_{-\infty}^{\infty} (x_j - \mu_j)(x_{j'} - \mu_{j'}) f(x_1, x_2, \ldots, x_m) \qquad *(\text{C.3.6}) \\ &\qquad \cdot dx_1\,dx_2 \cdots dx_m, \qquad j, j' = 1, 2, \cdots, m, \end{aligned}$$

so the variance is the special case corresponding to $j = j'$—that is, $\sigma_{jj} = \sigma_j^2$. The matrix of all variances and covariances is the *covariance matrix* of $\mathbf{X}$:

$$\underset{m\times m}{\text{Cov}(\mathbf{x})} = \boldsymbol{\Sigma} = \begin{pmatrix} \sigma_{11} & \sigma_{12} & \cdots & \sigma_{1m} \\ \sigma_{21} & \sigma_{22} & \cdots & \sigma_{2m} \\ \vdots & & & \\ \sigma_{m1} & \sigma_{m2} & \cdots & \sigma_{mm} \end{pmatrix} = \begin{pmatrix} \sigma_1^2 & \sigma_{12} & \cdots & \sigma_{1m} \\ \sigma_{21} & \sigma_2^2 & \cdots & \sigma_{2m} \\ \vdots & & & \\ \sigma_{m1} & \sigma_{m2} & \cdots & \sigma_m^2 \end{pmatrix}, \qquad *(\text{C.3.7})$$

where the elements along the principal diagonal are the m variances and the other elements are the covariances proper. Clearly, from the definition (C.3.6)

$$\sigma_{jj'} = \sigma_{j'j}, \qquad j, j' = 1, 2, \ldots, m, \qquad (\text{C.3.8})$$

so the covariance matrix is a symmetric matrix. It is also a positive-semidefinite matrix.[9] It contains m variances and $m(m-1)/2$ independent covariances, thus containing altogether $m(m+1)/2$ independent elements. For example, if $m = 2$, the three elements:

$$\begin{pmatrix} \sigma_1^2 & \sigma_{12} \\ & \sigma_2^2 \end{pmatrix} \qquad \text{(C.3.9)}$$

define the covariance matrix, the missing element equaling σ_{12}.

The definitions introduced thus far can be expressed in terms of *expectations*, where in the multivariate case the expectation of a given function of **X**, say $\varphi(\mathbf{x})$, is defined as:

$$E[\varphi(\mathbf{x})] = \int_{-\infty}^{\infty} \cdots \int_{-\infty}^{\infty} \varphi(x_1, x_2, \ldots, x_m) f(x_1, x_2, \ldots, x_m)\, dx_1\, dx_2 \cdots dx_m. \qquad \text{*(C.3.10)}$$

The jth mean of X is then given as:

$$\mu_j = E(x_j), \qquad j = 1, 2, \ldots, m, \qquad \text{*(C.3.11)}$$

so in vector notation the column vector of means (C.3.3) is:

$$\boldsymbol{\mu} = (\mu_1 \ \ \mu_2 \ \ \cdots \ \ \mu_m)' = E(\mathbf{x}). \qquad \text{*(C.3.12)}$$

The *jth variance* of **X** is:

$$\text{Var}(x_j) = \sigma_j^2 = E(x_j - \mu_j)^2 = \sigma_{jj}, \qquad j = 1, 2, \ldots, m, \qquad \text{*(C.3.13)}$$

and the *jj′ covariance* of **X** is:

$$\text{Cov}(x_j x_{j'}) = \sigma_{jj'} = E(x_j - \mu_j)(x_{j'} - \mu_{j'}), \qquad j, j' = 1, 2, \ldots, m. \qquad \text{*(C.3.14)}$$

Thus the *covariance matrix* can be expressed in matrix notation as:

$$\Sigma = E(\mathbf{x} - \boldsymbol{\mu})(\mathbf{x} - \boldsymbol{\mu})' = \text{Cov}(\mathbf{x}) = (\sigma_{jj'}), \qquad \text{*(C.3.15)}$$

where $(\mathbf{x} - \boldsymbol{\mu})'$ is the row vector obtained by transposing the column vector $(\mathbf{x} - \boldsymbol{\mu})$.

The expectation operator $E(\cdot)$ defined by (C.3.10) satisfies the linearity property that for any given $(r \times 1)$-column vector **a** and any given $r \times m$ matrix **B**:

$$E(\mathbf{a} + \mathbf{B}\mathbf{x}) = \mathbf{a} + \mathbf{B}E(\mathbf{x}) = \mathbf{a} + \mathbf{B}\boldsymbol{\mu}. \qquad \text{*(C.3.16)}$$

In particular, the expectation of a weighted sum of random variables $E(\mathbf{bx})$, where **b** is a given row vector of weights, is the weighted sum of the expectations $\mathbf{b}E(\mathbf{x})$—that is, $\mathbf{b}\boldsymbol{\mu}$. By contrast the covariance operator of (C.3.15) satisfies:

$$\text{Cov}(\mathbf{a} + \mathbf{B}\mathbf{x}) = \mathbf{B}\,\text{Cov}(\mathbf{x})\mathbf{B}' = \mathbf{B}\,\Sigma\,\mathbf{B}\boldsymbol{\mu}, \qquad \text{*(C.3.17)}$$

so $\text{Cov}(\cdot)$ is not a linear operator. In particular the variance of a weighted sum of random variables $\text{Var}(\mathbf{bx})$ is the quadratic form $\mathbf{b}\,\text{Cov}(\mathbf{x})\mathbf{b}'$—that is, $\mathbf{b}\Sigma\mathbf{b}'$.[10] In the univariate case the variance of a linear function of the random variables, $\text{Var}(a + bx)$, is given by $b^2\,\text{Var}(x)$.

If X_j and $X_{j'}$ are statistically independent, as in (C.2.33), then

$$E(x_j x_{j'}) = E(x_j)E(x_{j'}) \quad \text{and} \quad \sigma_{jj'} = 0. \qquad \text{(C.3.18)}$$

Thus if the random variables $X_1, X_2, \ldots, X_m$ are mutually independent, as in (C.2.34), then the covariance matrix $\text{Cov}(\mathbf{x})$ is a diagonal matrix, since then $\sigma_{jj'} = 0$ for $j \neq j'$. While independence implies zero covariance, the converse is *not* true: zero covariance does not nec-

[9]For the definition of "positive semidefinite," see Appendix B, Section B.8.

[10]For the definition of "quadratic form," see Appendix B, Section B.8.

essarily imply that random variables are statistically independent. Variables with a zero covariance are *uncorrelated*, and statistical independence is sufficient but not necessary for variables to be uncorrelated.

The j, j' *correlation coefficient* of $\mathbf{X}$ is:

$$\rho_{jj'} = \frac{\sigma_{jj'}}{\sigma_j \sigma_{j'}}, \qquad -1 \leqslant \rho_{jj'} \leqslant 1, \quad j, j' = 1, 2, \ldots, m. \tag{C.3.19}$$

If the random variables X_j and $X_{j'}$ are uncorrelated, then $\rho_{jj'} = 0$, since then $\sigma_{jj'} = 0$.

Moments can be defined in terms of expectations. The $(h_1, h_2, \ldots, h_m)$ moment about the point x^0 is defined as:

$$\begin{aligned} &E\left(x_1 - x_1^0\right)^{h_1}\left(x_2 - x_2^0\right)^{h_2} \cdots \left(x_m - x_m^0\right)^{h_m} \\ &= \int_{-\infty}^{\infty} \cdots \int_{-\infty}^{\infty} \left(x_1 - x_1^0\right)^{h_1} \cdots \left(x_m - x_m^0\right)^{h_m} f(x_1 \cdots x_m) dx_1 \cdots dx_m. \end{aligned} \tag*{*(C.3.20)}$$

The first mean μ_1 is then the $(1, 0, \ldots, 0)$ moment about the origin, and, in general, the jth mean is the $(0, 0 \ldots, 1, \ldots, 0)$ moment about the origin. The first variance is the $(2, 0, \ldots, 0)$ moment about the mean, and the $(1, 2)$ covariance is the $(1, 1, 0, \ldots, 0)$ moment about the mean. Given a density function $f(x_1 \cdots x_m) = f(\mathbf{x})$, all the moments are defined; conversely, given all the moments, the density function is defined. Sometimes *statistics* is defined as simply the study of moments. The moments are convenient ways of summarizing a distribution (e.g., means provide measures of central tendency, variances measure dispersion, covariances measure the degree to which variables move together, etc.). There is, in fact, a one-to-one unique correspondence between a probability density function and a moment generating function, where the *moment generating function* is defined as:

$$\begin{aligned} M_{\mathbf{X}}(\mathbf{t}) &= E\left(e^{t_1 x_1 + \cdots + t_m x_m}\right) \\ &= \int_{-\infty}^{\infty} \cdots \int_{-\infty}^{\infty} e^{t_1 x_1 + \cdots + t_m x_m} f(x_1 \cdots x_m) dx_1 \cdots dx_m, \end{aligned} \tag{C.3.21}$$

assuming that the integral converges. This function "generates" moments in that, for example,

$$\left.\frac{\partial M_{\mathbf{X}}(\mathbf{t})}{\partial t_j}\right|_{\mathbf{t}=\mathbf{0}} = E\left(x_j\right) = \mu_j. \tag{C.3.22}$$

The one-to-one correspondence implies that a distribution is completely characterized by its moments. In particular, if two random variables $\mathbf{X}$ and $\mathbf{Y}$ have the same moment generating functions:

$$M_{\mathbf{X}}(\mathbf{t}) = M_{\mathbf{Y}}(\mathbf{t}) \qquad \text{for all } \mathbf{t}, \tag{C.3.23}$$

then $\mathbf{X}$ and $\mathbf{Y}$ have the same distribution.

Sample measures can be defined in terms of data points. Assuming a sample of n observations of the form $\mathbf{x}_1, \mathbf{x}_2, \ldots, \mathbf{x}_n$, where each sample point is an $m \times 1$ vector, these data can be expressed as the *data matrix* (termed a *design matrix* in the text):

$$\underset{n \times m}{\mathbf{X}} = \begin{pmatrix} \mathbf{x}_1' \\ \mathbf{x}_2' \\ \vdots \\ \mathbf{x}_n' \end{pmatrix} = \left(x_{ij}\right), \qquad i = 1, 2, \ldots, n; \; j = 1, 2, \ldots, m, \tag{C.3.24}$$

where j is an index of the variable and i is an index of the data point. Each sample point is a row of the data matrix. The jth *sample mean* is defined as:

$$\bar{x}_j = \frac{1}{n}\sum_{i=1}^{n} x_{ij} \tag{C.3.25}$$

and the *sample mean vector* is:

$$\bar{\mathbf{x}} = (\bar{x}_1, \bar{x}_2, \ldots, \bar{x}_m). \tag{C.3.26}$$

The *j*th *sample variance* is:

$$s_j^2 = \frac{1}{n}\sum_{i=1}^{n} (x_{ij} - \bar{x}_j)^2 = s_{ij}, \tag{C.3.27}$$

and the j, j' *sample covariance* is:

$$s_{jj'} = \frac{1}{n}\sum_{i=1}^{n} (x_{ij} - \bar{x}_j)(x_{ij'} - \bar{x}_{j'}). \tag{C.3.28}$$

The *sample covariance matrix* is then

$$\mathbf{S} = \begin{pmatrix} s_1^2 & s_{12} & \cdots & s_{1m} \\ s_{21} & s_2^2 & \cdots & s_{2m} \\ \vdots & & & \\ s_{m1} & s_{m2} & \cdots & s_m^2 \end{pmatrix} = (s_{jj'}), \tag{C.3.29}$$

the j, j' *sample correlation coefficient* is:

$$r_{jj'} = \frac{s_{jj'}}{s_j s_{j'}}, \tag{C.3.30}$$

and the *sample correlation matrix* is:

$$\mathbf{R} = (r_{jj'}). \tag{C.3.31}$$

C.4 SOME SPECIFIC DISTRIBUTIONS

This section treats some specific distributions that are used in econometrics, including the normal, lognormal, multivariate normal, χ^2, t, and F distributions.

One of the most widely used distributions is the *normal distribution*. The univariate random variable X is distributed as the normal distribution with mean μ and variance σ^2, written:

$$X \sim N(\mu, \sigma^2) \tag*{*(C.4.1)}$$

if the density function is of the form[11]

$$f(x) = \frac{1}{\sqrt{2\pi}\sigma}\exp\left(-\frac{1}{2}\frac{(x-\mu)^2}{\sigma^2}\right), \qquad -\infty < x < \infty. \tag*{*(C.4.2)}$$

The familiar smooth symmetric bell shape of this continuous distribution is illustrated in Figure C.2. The mean of the distribution is μ and the variance is σ^2, and these two parameters:

$$E(x) = \mu, \qquad \mathrm{Var}(x) = \sigma^2 \tag*{*(C.4.3)}$$

completely characterize the normal distribution. For the *standard normal distribution* $X \sim N(0, 1)$; that is, the mean is zero and the variance is unity.

[11]The expression "exp(z)" means e^z, where e is the base of the natural logarithms.

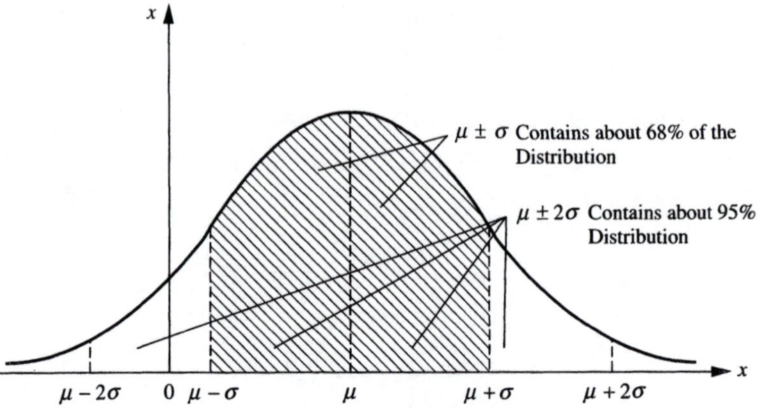

Figure C.2 Normal Density Function

An important justification for the wide use of the normal distribution is the *central limit theorem.* According to this theorem, whenever the outcome of an event depends on the superposition of many independent random variables, the distribution of outcomes converges stochastically to the normal distribution; that is, as the number of independent random variables increases without limit, the probability of observing any arbitrary deviation from normality approaches zero. More specifically, if $[X_i]$ form a sequence of independent random variables distributed identically with mean μ and finite variance σ^2, then the sample mean converges to the normal distribution defined by these parameters; that is,[12]

$$\overline{X}(r) = \frac{1}{r}\sum_{i=1}^{r} x_i \rightarrow N\left(\mu, \frac{\sigma^2}{r}\right) \qquad \text{as } r \rightarrow \infty. \qquad *(\text{C.4.4})$$

Note that the limiting expectation of $\overline{X}(r)$ is μ, the mean of the random variable.[13]

A random variable, the logarithm of which is normally distributed, is said to have the *lognormal distribution:*

$$\log X \sim N(\mu, \sigma^2). \qquad (\text{C.4.5})$$

The density function for the lognormal distribution, unlike that for the normal distribution, is asymmetric, exhibiting a long tail in the positive direction. It is defined only for positive values of X. A justification for the lognormal distribution is provided by the central limit theorem, according to which the geometric mean of independent identically distributed positive random variables converges stochastically to the lognormal distribution.

A multivariate generalization of the normal distribution is the *multivariate normal distribution.* The m-dimensional (column vector) random variable $\mathbf{X}$ is distributed as the multivariate normal with mean vector $\boldsymbol{\mu}$ and covariance matrix $\boldsymbol{\Sigma}$ (where $\boldsymbol{\Sigma}$ is symmetric and positive definite), written:

[12]The theorem can be generalized to allow each observation to come from a different probability distribution, provided the random variables are independent and have variances that are approximately equal. This result is useful in econometrics, since it provides a justification for normally distributed stochastic disturbance terms, assuming that they represent the superposition of many independent stochastic terms.

[13]This result is consistent with the law of large numbers, which states that plim $\overline{X}(r) = \mu$ that is, for any $\varepsilon > 0$, $\lim_{r\to\infty} P(|\overline{X}(r) - \mu| < \varepsilon) = 1$.

$$\mathbf{X} \sim \mathbf{N}(\boldsymbol{\mu}, \boldsymbol{\Sigma}), \tag{*C.4.6}$$

if the density function is of the form:

$$f(\mathbf{x}) = (2\pi)^{-m/2} |\boldsymbol{\Sigma}|^{-1/2} \exp\left[-\tfrac{1}{2}(\mathbf{x} - \boldsymbol{\mu}'\boldsymbol{\Sigma}^{-1}(x - \boldsymbol{\mu})\right], \tag{*C.4.7}$$

where $|\boldsymbol{\Sigma}|$ is the determinant of the covariance matrix and $\boldsymbol{\Sigma}^{-1}$ is the inverse of this matrix, known as the *precision matrix.*[14] Here

$$E(\mathbf{x}) = \boldsymbol{\mu}, \qquad \text{Cov}(\mathbf{x}) = \boldsymbol{\Sigma}, \tag{*C.4.8}$$

which generalize (C.4.3), where the $m + [m(m + 1)/2]$ independent parameters in $\boldsymbol{\mu}$ and $\boldsymbol{\Sigma}$ completely characterize this distribution. The set of all vectors $\mathbf{x}$ such that $(\mathbf{x} - \boldsymbol{\mu})'\boldsymbol{\Sigma}^{-1}(\mathbf{x} - \boldsymbol{\mu})$ = constant is the *ellipsoid of concentration* centered at $\boldsymbol{\mu}$. In the two-variable case (m = 2), the bivariate normal density function is of the form:

$$f(x_1, x_2) = \frac{1}{2\pi\sqrt{\sigma_1^2\sigma_2^2 - \sigma_{12}^2}} \exp\left\{\frac{-1}{2(\sigma_1^2\sigma_2^2 - \sigma_{12}^2)}\left[\sigma_2^2(x_1 - \mu_1)^2 - 2\sigma_{12}(x_1 - \mu_1)(x_2 - \mu_2) + \sigma_1^2(x_2 - \mu_2)^2\right]\right\}$$

$$f(x_1, x_2) = \frac{1}{2\pi\sigma_1\sigma_2\sqrt{1 - \rho_{12}^2}} \exp\left\{\frac{-1}{2(1 - \rho_{12}^2)}\left[\left(\frac{x_1 - \mu_1}{\sigma_1}\right)^2 - 2\rho_{12}\left(\frac{x_1 - \mu_1}{\sigma_1}\right)\left(\frac{x_2 - \mu_2}{\sigma_2}\right) + \left(\frac{x_2 - \mu_2}{\sigma_2}\right)^2\right]\right\}. \tag{C.4.9}$$

Here the five parameters defining the distribution are the means (μ_1, μ_2), the variances (σ_1^2, σ_2^2), and the covariance (σ_{12}). In the second formulation σ_{12} is replaced by ρ_{12}, the correlation coefficient, given as $\sigma_{12}/\sigma_1\,\sigma_2$, as in (C.3.19).

If $\mathbf{X}$ is distributed as the multivariate normal distribution and the random variables X_1, $X_2, \ldots, X_m$ are mutually independent, then

$$f(x_1x_2 \cdots x_m) = f_1(x_1)f_2(x_2) \cdots f_m(x_m), \tag{C.4.10}$$

where $f_j(x_j)$ is the scalar normal distribution as in (C.4.2). The multivariate normal distribution reduces to this case if the covariance matrix $\boldsymbol{\Sigma}$ is a diagonal matrix, in which case:

$$f(\mathbf{x}) = \prod_{j=1}^{m} \frac{1}{\sqrt{2\pi}\sigma_j} \exp\left[-\frac{1}{2}\frac{(x_j - \mu_j)^2}{\sigma_j^2}\right], \tag{C.4.11}$$

so the multivariate normal distribution (C.4.7) reduces to a product of univariate normal distributions. Thus, for the normal distribution a diagonal covariance matrix guarantees independence, so zero covariance is equivalent to independence. This property does *not* hold, however, for any arbitary distribution, as discussed after (C.3.18).

If $\mathbf{X} \sim \mathbf{N}(\boldsymbol{\mu}, \boldsymbol{\Sigma})$, then if $\mathbf{a}$ is a given $r \times 1$ column vector and $\mathbf{B}$ is a given $r \times m$ matrix,

$$\mathbf{a} + \mathbf{B}\mathbf{X} \sim \mathbf{N}(\mathbf{a} + \mathbf{B}\boldsymbol{\mu}, \mathbf{B}\boldsymbol{\Sigma}\mathbf{B}'). \tag{*C.4.12}$$

That is, any linear function of multivariate normally distributed random variables is itself multivariate normally distributed. In particular, there exists a triangular matrix $\mathbf{C}$ such that:

[14]Note that the term in the exponential function is, other than the factor $-\frac{1}{2}$, a quadratic form in the precision matrix $\boldsymbol{\Sigma}^{-1}$. See Appendix B for a discussion of matrices, including quadratic forms and inverse matrices.

$$\mathbf{C}(\mathbf{X} - \boldsymbol{\mu}) \sim \mathbf{N}(\mathbf{0}, \mathbf{I}), \tag{C.4.13}$$

where $\boldsymbol{\Sigma}^{-1} = \mathbf{C}'\mathbf{C}$. Here $\mathbf{N}(\mathbf{0}, \mathbf{I})$ is the standard *multivariate normal distribution*, with zero means, unit variances, and zero covariances. This standard distribution is, in the univariate case of (C.4.1), a normal distribution with zero mean and unit variance.

Furthermore, the marginal distribution of any set of components of $\mathbf{X}$ is normal with means, variances, and covariances obtained by taking the corresponding components of $\boldsymbol{\mu}$ and $\boldsymbol{\Sigma}$, respectively. The conditional distribution of any q components of $\mathbf{X}$, say $\mathbf{X}^{(1)}$, given any other $m - q$ components, say $\mathbf{X}^{(2)} = \mathbf{x}^{(2)}$, is also normal with mean:

$$\boldsymbol{\mu}^{(1)} + \boldsymbol{\Sigma}_{12}\boldsymbol{\Sigma}_{22}^{-1}(\mathbf{x}^{(2)} - \boldsymbol{\mu}^{(2)})$$

and covariance matrix $\boldsymbol{\Sigma}_{11} - \boldsymbol{\Sigma}_{12}\boldsymbol{\Sigma}_{22}^{-1}\boldsymbol{\Sigma}_{21}$, where $\boldsymbol{\mu}^{(1)}$, $\boldsymbol{\mu}^{(2)}$ are the means of $\mathbf{X}^{(1)}$ and $\mathbf{X}^{(2)}$, respectively, and $\boldsymbol{\Sigma}_{11}$, $\boldsymbol{\Sigma}_{12}$, $\boldsymbol{\Sigma}_{22}$ are the covariance matrices of $\mathbf{X}^{(1)}$, of $\mathbf{X}^{(1)}$ and $\mathbf{X}^{(2)}$, and of $\mathbf{X}^{(2)}$, respectively (see, e.g., Anderson, 1984).

According to the *Lindeberg–Levy central limit theorem,* the average of independent identically distributed random m vectors converges stochastically to the multivariate normal distribution. More specifically, if $\{\mathbf{X}_i\}$ form a sequence of independent n-dimensional random variables distributed identically with mean vector $\boldsymbol{\mu}$ and covariance matrix $\boldsymbol{\Sigma}$, then

$$\frac{1}{\sqrt{r}}\sum_{i=1}^{r}(\mathbf{X}_i - \boldsymbol{\mu}) \rightarrow \mathbf{N}(\mathbf{0}, \boldsymbol{\Sigma}) \qquad \text{as } r \rightarrow \infty, \tag{C.4.14}$$

so the limiting distribution is multivariate normal.

Consider a set of r independent random variables $Z_1, Z_2, \ldots, Z_r$, each of which is distributed as a univariate standardized normal distribution—with zero mean and unit variance. The random variable consisting of the sum of squares of these random variables is distributed as the χ^2 *(chi-square) distribution* with r degrees of freedom:

$$\chi^2 = \sum_{i=1}^{r} Z_i^2 \sim \chi^2(r). \tag*{*(C.4.15)}$$

For example, assuming a parent normal population, if s^2 is the sample variance, defined in (C.3.27), then $\frac{ns^2}{\sigma^2}$ is distributed as χ^2 with $n - 1$ degrees of freedom (since it sums only $n - 1$ independent terms). The χ^2 distribution is a positively skewed distribution defined over nonnegative values. The mean is r, the number of degrees of freedom, and the variance is $2r$. From the central limit theorem, as r increases, the distribution of $\chi^2(r)$ approaches that of the normal distribution. Furthermore, from (C.4.13), if $\mathbf{X} \sim \mathbf{N}(\boldsymbol{\mu}, \boldsymbol{\Sigma})$ is an r-dimensional vector distributed as the multivariate normal with mean $\boldsymbol{\mu}$ and covariance matrix $\boldsymbol{\Sigma}$, then

$$(\mathbf{X} - \boldsymbol{\mu})'\boldsymbol{\Sigma}^{-1}(\mathbf{X} - \boldsymbol{\mu}) \sim \chi^2(r). \tag{C.4.16}$$

The sum of a finite number of independent χ^2 distributions is also distributed as χ^2, with the number of degrees of freedom equal to the sum of the degrees of freedom of the underlying distributions.

If Z is distributed as a standardized normal with zero mean and unit variance $N(0, 1)$, and $\chi^2(r)$ is independently distributed as the chi-square distribution with r degrees of freedom, then the ratio of Z to the (positive) square root of $\chi^2(r)$, deflated by r, is distributed as the *t distribution* with r degrees of freedom:

$$t = \frac{Z}{\sqrt{\chi^2(r)/r}} \sim t(r). \tag*{*(C.4.17)}$$

For example, again assuming a parent normal population, if $\bar{x}$ is the sample mean, defined in (C.3.25), and s^2 is the sample variance, defined in (C.3.27), then $(\bar{x} - \mu)/(s/\sqrt{n-1})$ is distributed as the t distribution with $n - 1$ degrees of freedom. The t distribution is a symmetric distribution for which the mean is zero and the variance is $r/(r-2)$ (for $r > 2$). The distribution has wider tails than the normal distribution, but it approaches the normal distribution $N(0, 1)$ as $r \to \infty$. In fact, for $r > 30$ the t distribution does not differ appreciably from the normal distribution.

If $\chi^2(r)$ is distributed as the chi-square distribution with r degrees of freedom and $\chi^2(s)$ is distributed independently as the chi-square distribution with s degrees of freedom, then the ratio of these two, after deflating each for the number of degrees of freedom, is distributed as the *F distribution* with r and s degrees of freedom:

$$F = \frac{\chi^2(r)/r}{\chi^2(s)/s} \sim F(r, s). \qquad *(C.4.18)$$

For example, yet again assuming a parent normal population, if s_i^2 is the variance from a sample of size n_i, then the ratio $\frac{n_1 s_1^2}{n_1 - 1} \Big/ \frac{n_2 s_2^2}{n_2 - 1}$ is distributed as the F distribution with $(n_1 - 1)$ and $(n_2 - 1)$ degrees of freedom. The F and t distributions are related by:

$$\sqrt{F(1, s)} = \frac{|Z|}{\sqrt{\chi^2(s)/s}} = |t(s)|, \qquad *(C.4.19)$$

which is the t distribution with s degrees of freedom. The F distribution is a positively skewed distribution defined over nonnegative values. As $s \to \infty$, the ratio $\chi^2(s)/s$ approaches unity in the probability limit, so $F(r, s)$ approaches $\chi^2(r)/r$. As both r and $s \to \infty$, $F(r, s)$ approaches unity in the probability limit.

C.5 ADDITIONAL RESULTS ON DISTRIBUTION THEORY

THEOREM C.1. *If* $\mathbf{B}$ *is a* $g \times p$ *matrix,* $\mathbf{A}$ *is a* $p \times p$ *matrix, and* $\mathbf{Y}$ *is distributed* $N(\mathbf{0}, \sigma^2\mathbf{I})$, *the linear forms* $\mathbf{BY}$ *are independent of the quadratic form* $\mathbf{Y'AY}$ *if and only if* $\mathbf{BA} = \mathbf{0}$.

THEOREM C.2. *If* $\mathbf{Y} \sim N(\mathbf{0}, \mathbf{I})$, *the two positive semidefinite quadratic forms* $\mathbf{Y'AY}$ *and* $\mathbf{Y'BY}$ *are independent if and only if* $\mathbf{AB} = \mathbf{0}$.

THEOREM C.3. *Suppose that* $\mathbf{M}, \mathbf{N}$ *are* $n \times n$ *idempotent matrices of rank r, s respectively, and suppose that* $\mathbf{MN} = \mathbf{0}$. *Suppose that* $\mathbf{Y} \sim N(\mathbf{0}, \mathbf{I}_n)$. *Then* $\mathbf{Y'MY}$ *and* $\mathbf{Y'NY}$ *are independently* χ^2*-distributed with r and s degrees of freedom, respectively.*

The proof of these theorems can be found in Plackett (1960) or in Theil (1971).

BIBLIOGRAPHY

ANDERSON, T. W. (1984). *An Introduction to Multivariate Statistical Analysis*, 2nd ed. New York: John Wiley & Sons, Inc.

CRAMER, H. (1946). *Mathematical Methods of Statistics*. Princeton, N.J.: Princeton University Press.

DE GROOT, M. H. (1969). *Optimal Statistical Decisions*. New York: McGraw-Hill Book Company.

FELLER, W. (1968). *An Introduction to Probability Theory and Its Applications*, 3rd ed. New York: John Wiley & Sons, Inc.

FISZ, M. (1963). *Probability Theory and Mathematical Statistics*, 3rd ed. New York: John Wiley & Sons, Inc.

FRASER, D. A. S. (1958). *Statistics: An Introduction*. New York: John Wiley & Sons, Inc.

GRAYBILL, F. A. (1961). *An Introduction to Linear Statistical Models*. New York: McGraw-Hill Book Company.

HOEL, P. G. (1984). *Introduction to Mathematical Statistics*, 5th ed. New York: John Wiley & Sons, Inc.

KENDALL, M. G., and A. STUART (1983). *The Advanced Theory of Statistics*, 4th ed. New York: Hafner Publishing Co.

MOOD, A. M., F. A. GRAYBILL, and D. C. BOES (1974). *Introduction to the Theory of Statistics*, 3rd ed. New York: McGraw-Hill Book Company.

PLACKETT, R. L. (1960). *Principles of Regression Analysis*. London: Oxford University Press.

RAIFFA, H. C. (1968). *Decision Analysis*. Reading, Mass.: Addison-Wesley Publishing Company, Inc.

RAO, C. R. (1973). *Linear Statistical Inference and Its Applications*, 2nd ed. New York: John Wiley & Sons, Inc.

SAVAGE, L. J. (1954). *The Foundations of Statistics*. New York: John Wiley & Sons, Inc.

SCHEFFÉ, H. (1959). *The Analysis of Variance*. New York: John Wiley & Sons, Inc.

SEARLE, S. R. (1971). *Linear Models*. New York: John Wiley & Sons, Inc.

THEIL, H. (1971). *Principles of Econometrics*. New York: John Wiley & Sons, Inc.

WILKS, S. S. (1962). *Mathematical Statistics*. New York: John Wiley & Sons, Inc.

ZELLNER, A. (1983). "Statistical Theory and Econometrics," in Z. Griliches and M. D. Intriligator, Eds., *Handbook of Econometrics*, Vol. 1. Amsterdam: North-Holland Publishing Company.

INDEX

NAME INDEX

Adams, F.G., 430*f*, 440*f*, 441*f*, 442*f*, 443*f*, 447*f*, 450*f*, 451*f*, 452, 453, 460, 507, 512, 557*f*, 565, 593
Adelman, F., 437, 460
Adelman, I., 437, 460, 597
Aigner, D.J., 156*f*, 180, 594
Aitcheson, J., 94, 122
Akaike, H., 109, 122
Alexander, L.S., 450*f*, 462
Alexander, S.S., 518*f*, 540
Allen, R.G.D., 249, 263*f*, 273
Almon, S., 229, 235
Amemiya, T., 90*f*, 94, 108, 122, 125*f*, 138, 159*f*, 160, 162, 163, 164*f*, 165*f*, 180, 360*f*, 366*f*, 374*f*, 390–392, 396, 458*f*, 460
Andersen, L.C., 450*f*, 460
Anderson, R.L., 204, 235
Anderson, T.W., 59*f*, 68, 187*f*, 208, 209, 212, 235, 386*f*, 420, 426, 629*f*, 638, 639
Anderson-Parente, J.K., 516*f*, 543
Ando, A., 345, 441*f*, 442*f*, 460
Andrews, D.K., 419, 426
Andrews, W.H., 290*f*, 316
Angrist, J.D., 157*f*, 180
Ansley, C.F., 207, 236
Apostol, T.M., 84*f*, 122, 384*f*, 396
Arrow, K.J., 1*f*, 2*f*, 11, 286*f*, 293*f*, 296, 307*f*, 313
Ashenfelter, O., 474, 475*f*, 487, 594, 597
Ashenfelter, P., 146*f*, 147, 180
Ashley, R., 529*f*, 531*f*, 533*f*, 540
Askin, A.B., 596
Atkinson, A.C., 105, 122
Auerbach, A.J., 518*f*, 540, 598
Aukrust, O., 307, 313
Aydelotte, W.O., 483*f*, 488
Baily, M.N., 306*f*, 308*f*, 313, 593
Bain, J.S., 470*f*, 486
Balestra, P., 595
Balintfy, J.L., 567
Ball, R.J., 19*f*, 47
Barro, R.J., 594, 595
Barten, A.P., 239*f*, 254*f*, 255*f*, 257*f*, 273, 497, 512
Bartlett, M.S., 201, 225, 236
Basmann, R.L., 360*f*, 386*f*, 389*f*, 396, 397, 449*f*, 460
Bates, J.M., 535*f*, 540
Baumol, W.J., 275*f*, 313
Beach, E.F., 19*f*, 47
Becker, G.S., 595
Beckwith, N., 146*f*, 180
Behrman, J.R., 594
Belsley, D.A., 49, 128, 129, 132, 180
Bera, C.M., 154, 174, 183
Bergstrom, A.R., 19*f*, 47
Berkson, J., 163, 180, 181
Berndt, E.R., 96, 122, 293*f*, 301*f*, 305*f*, 313
Berner, R., 374*f*, 397
Bianchi, C., 522*f*, 540
Bickel, P.J., 168, 181
Bierans, H., 146, 154, 174, 181, 214, 236
Bismarck (Otto von), 583*f*
Black, F., 596
Blattberg, R.C., 167, 181
Blinder, A.S., 594
Bliss, C., 296*f*, 313
Bloom, D.E., 594
Bodkin, R.G., 19*f*, 33*f*, 47, 98*f*, 122, 159, 181, 288*f*, 313, 430*f*, 431*f*, 436*f*, 447*f*, 449*f*, 450*f*, 453*f*, 455*f*, 457*f*, 460, 532*f*, 540, 548*f*, 560*f*, 565, 570, 572*f*, 581*f*, 584, 596
Boes, D.C., 625*f*, 640
Bogue, A.G., 483*f*, 488
Böhm, V., 239*f*, 273
Bollerslev, T., 147, 181
Boot, J.C.G., 40*f*, 49, 423, 429, 433*f*, 435*f*, 464
Borus, M.E., 146, 181
Bos, H.C., 46*f*, 49
Boskin, M., 306*f*, 308, 309*f*, 314
Bowden, R., 157*f*, 181, 323*f*, 345
Bowley, A.L., 249
Box, G.E.P., 61*f*, 68, 111, 112, 113*f*, 122, 144, 174, 181, 187*f*, 198, 199, 201–204, 207, 212, 223–225, 236, 237, 400, 402, 404–407, 423, 426, 429, 517*f*, 540
Brainard, W.C., 570, 584
Braithwaite, C., 567
Bratton, W.K., 69
Braun, P., 516*f*, 532*f*, 544
Braybrooke, D., 537*f*, 565
Breusch, T.S., 139, 174, 181
Brinner, R.E., 443*f*, 460, 509*f*, 512
Brown, B.W., 341, 345, 393, 397, 398, 578*f*, 585
Brown, M., 284*f*, 293*f*, 296*f*, 306*f*, 307, 314
Brown, R.G., 59*f*, 68
Brown, T.M., 19*f*, 47
Brundy, J.M., 369*f*, 374*f*, 397
Brunner, K., 468*f*, 486
Bryant, R., 454*f*, 461, 561*f*, 565, 578*f*, 584
Buck, A.J., 547*f*, 565
Burdick, D.S., 567
Cagan, P., 539*f*, 540
Cain, B., 567
Cain, C.G., 57*f*, 68, 594
Caines, P.E., 410*f*, 426

Calzolari, G., 522*f*, 540
Campbell, J.M., 597
Campbell, R., 595
Cannan, Edwin, 49
Cano-Lamy, V., 540
Carlson, K.M., 450*f*, 460
Carroll, R.J., 168, 172, 181
Carter, H.O., 297*f*, 315
Carter, R.A.L., 389*f*, 397
Caves, R.E., 471*f*, 486
Chabot-Plante, F., 596
Chamberlain, G., 138, 181
Chambers, J.C., 513*f*, 540
Chan, C.W., 410*f*, 426
Chan, K.H., 210*f*, 236
Chan, N.H., 212*f*, 236, 417, 426
Chenery, H.B., 293*f*, 312*f*, 313, 314, 594
Cheng, S., 597
Chou, R.Y., 147, 181
Chow, E., 540
Chow, G.C., 97, 122, 174, 181, 265, 266, 272, 273, 382*f*, 397, 574, 584
Christ, C., 19*f*, 47, 49, 347*f*, 432*f*, 436*f*, 447*f*, 461, 506, 512, 521*f*, 529, 532*f*, 533*f*, 540, 541, 557*f*, 565, 577, 584
Christensen, L.R., 283*f*, 298*f*, 314
Chu, K., 567
Clark, P.G., 293*f*, 314
Clark, P.K., 431*f*, 461
Clarkson, G.P.E., 555*f*, 565
Clements, K.W., 254*f*, 274
Cockenboo, L.J., 313*f*, 314
Coen, R.M., 450*f*, 461, 462
Comanor, W.S., 470*f*, 471*f*, 487
Committee on Econometric Methods, 35*f*, 47
Connolly, R.A., 471*f*, 487
Conrad, A.H., 483*f*, 488
Cooper, J.P., 468*f*, 486
Cooper, R.L., 189, 236
Cootner, P.H., 23*f*, 47, 522*f*, 541, 593
Corrado, C., 536, 537, 541
Cox, D.R., 105, 106, 123, 162, 181
Cragg, J.G., 138, 181, 386*f*, 397
Cramer, H., 625*f*, 639
Cramer, J.S., 291*f*, 314
Crenson, M., 548*f*, 566
Crissey, B., 548*f*, 566
Cummins, D., 373*f*, 396
Cummins, J.D., 593
Dalkey, N.C., 516*f*, 541
Data Resources, Inc., 64*f*, 68, 443, 444, 461
Daub, M., 532, 541
David, P.A., 307*f*, 314
Davidson, R., 106, 107, 123, 125*f*, 181
Davies, N., 201, 236
Davis, O.A., 548*f*, 565
De Angelo, H., 471*f*, 487
Deaton, A.S., 238*f*, 239*f*, 247*f*, 254*f*, 257*f*, 261*f*, 273, 431*f*, 461
de Bever, L., 507*f*, 512
de Cani, J.S., 293*f*, 296*f*, 314
De Groot, M.H., 626*f*, 635
Deistler, M., 402, 427
de Leeuw, F., 441*f*, 461
Dempster, A.H., 548*f*, 565
Denton, F.T., 388*f*, 397
Desaulniers, D., 567
Dhrymes, P.J., 61*f*, 68, 226*f*, 236, 296*f*, 297, 314, 347*f*, 366*f*, 374*f*, 397, 574, 576, 577, 584, 599*f*, 624
Dickey, D.A., 212–215, 236
Diebold, F.X., 212*f*, 236
Dielman, T., 146*f*, 181
Diewert, W.E., 247*f*, 273, 302*f*, 314
Dillon, J.L., 287*f*, 297*f*, 315
Doksum, K., 168, 181
Domar, E.D., 46, 48
Donihue, M.R., 462, 512
Douglas, P.H., 287*f*, 291, 307, 314
Drabek, L.J., 477*f*, 488
Draper, N.R., 159*f*, 181
Drèze, J., 290*f*, 317, 347*f*, 397
Duesenberry, J.S., 35*f*, 48, 447*f*, 449*f*, 461
Duggal, V.G., 440*f*, 460, 461, 495, 512, 555*f*, 565
Duncan, O.D., 35*f*, 48
Dunsmuir, W., 401, 427
Durbin, J., 142, 143, 157*f*, 181, 182, 232, 236
Durlauf, S.N., 210*f*, 236
Duru, G., 476*f*, 487
Dutta, M., 374*f*, 397
Eckstein, O., 17*f*, 48, 64*f*, 68, 305*f*, 317, 443*f*, 447*f*, 457*f*, 461, 502*f*, 509, 548*f*, 555*f*, 563*f*, 564*f*, 566, 578–580, 584, 596
Economic Council of Canada, 455, 456, 461, 508, 559, 560*f*, 566
Edwards, J.B., 34*f*, 48
Ehrlich, I., 593
Eicker, F., 137, 182
Eisenpress, H., 382*f*, 397
Engerman, S.L., 483*f*, 484*f*, 489
Engle, R., 72, 96, 123, 145, 173, 174, 182, 415, 416, 418, 421, 426, 427
Enke, S., 16*f*, 48
Ericsson, N.R., 173, 183
Erlat, H., 374*f*, 397
Evans, G.B.A., 212*f*, 236
Evans, M.K., 438*f*, 458*f*, 459, 461, 463, 521*f*, 526*f*, 531*f*, 541
Eyford, B.L., 567
Fair, J., 57*f*, 68
Fair, R.C., 305*f*, 314, 374*f*, 397, 451, 461, 462, 466*f*, 498*f*, 512, 521*f*, 531*f*, 532*f*, 541, 575*f*, 577*f*, 584
Fama, E.F., 522*f*, 541, 596
Federal Reserve Board, 441, 442*f*, 452
Feldstein, M., 598
Feller, W., 625*f*, 640
Ferber, R., 57*f*, 58*f*, 68, 517*f*, 541
Ferguson, C.E., 284*f*, 296, 297*f*, 314
Ferguson, T.S., 163, 182
Fischer, J., 430*f*, 447*f*, 453, 464
Fisher, F.M., 151*f*, 182, 323*f*, 326*f*, 332*f*, 334*f*, 340, 345, 346, 366*f*, 374*f*, 397, 399, 457*f*, 462, 593, 595, 598
Fisher, G.R., 105*f*, 106, 123
Fisher, P.G., 513, 585
Fishman, G.S., 61*f*, 68
Fisk, P.R., 382*f*, 397
Fisz, M., 625*f*, 640
Fletcher, L.B., 298*f*, 316
Fogel, R.W., 483*f*, 484*f*, 488, 489
Foot, D.K., 512
Forrester, 17*f*, 48, 557*f*
Fortin, J., 540
Fox, K.A., 259, 260, 273, 437*f*, 462, 548*f*, 566
Franklin, Benjamin, 9
Fraser, D.A.S., 626*f*, 641
Fraumeni, B.M., 306*f*, 308*f*, 315
Friedman, B.M., 552*f*, 566, 597
Friedman, M., 156*f*, 175, 182, 515*f*, 518*f*, 541, 554*f*, 566, 597
Frisch, R., 269*f*, 273, 284*f*, 310*f*, 314
Fromm, G., 48, 447*f*, 449*f*, 450*f*, 457*f*, 458*f*, 461, 462, 506*f*, 512, 521*f*, 531*f*, 533*f*, 534*f*, 541, 553*f*, 555*f*, 557*f*, 558, 566
Fuchs, V.R., 296, 314, 476*f*, 487
Fuller, W.A., 212–215, 236, 237, 416, 427
Fuss, M., 283*f*, 301*f*, 314
Gallant, R.A., 392, 398
Gamaletsos, T., 256, 273
Genberg, H., 572, 584
Geroski, P.A., 471*f*, 487
Gibson, W.E., 468*f*, 486
Gilby, S., 567
Godfrey, L., 107, 123
Gold, B., 299*f*, 314
Goldberger, A.S., 35*f*, 48, 131*f*, 182, 185, 230, 237, 256, 273, 432*f*, 436*f*, 437*f*, 462, 463, 502, 504, 505, 512, 513, 521*f*, 541, 594
Goldfeld, S.M., 125*f*, 151*f*, 160, 182, 340*f*, 346, 466*f*, 467, 484, 486, 597
Goldin, C., 483*f*, 489
Goldsmith, R.W., 58*f*, 68
Gollop, F.M., 306*f*, 308*f*, 315
Gonodes, N.J., 167, 181
Gorbet, F.W., 462
Grabowski, H., 471*f*, 487
Gramlich, E.M., 441*f*, 461
Granfield, M., 596
Granger, C.W.J., 59*f*, 68, 173, 182, 187*f*, 207, 236, 407, 409, 410, 412, 415, 416, 418, 426, 427, 513*f*, 516*f*, 522*f*, 535, 538*f*, 540, 542
Graybill, F.A., 599*f*, 624, 625*f*, 629*f*, 640
Green, E.W., 443*f*, 457*f*, 461
Green, G.R., 450*f*, 462, 463
Green, H.A.J., 261*f*, 273, 291*f*, 314
Green, R.J., 450*f*, 461, 494, 512
Greenberger, M., 69, 546*f*, 566, 567
Greene, M., 536, 537, 541
Greene, W.H., 125*f*, 182
Greenstadt, J., 382*f*, 397
Gregory, P.R., 597
Griffiths, W., 184
Griliches, Z., 50*f*, 62*f*, 63, 68, 124, 155*f*, 157*f*, 175, 182, 226*f*, 236, 290*f*, 293*f*, 296*f*, 297*f*, 298*f*, 308*f*, 314, 315, 523*f*, 542, 595, 598
Grimm, B.T., 450*f*, 462
Gross, M., 565
Grossman, 476*f*, 488
Gunaratne, L., 540
Guntmacher, F.R., 421, 427
Guo, S., 214, 236
Haavelmo, T., 354*f*, 398, 447*f*, 572
Hadley, G., 599*f*, 603*f*, 609*f*, 624
Hahn, F., 597
Haitovsky, Y., 520*f*, 526*f*, 531*f*, 541, 542
Hakim, S., 565

Haldi, J., 312*f*, 315
Halter, A.N., 297*f*, 315
Hamilton, H.R., 4*f*, 11, 557*f*, 566
Hamilton, J.D., 187*f*, 236
Hammersley, J.M., 387*f*, 398
Handscomb, 387*f*, 398
Hannan, E.J., 402–404, 427
Hansen, B.E., 214, 236, 418, 428, 549*f*, 566
Hansen, L.P., 86, 123
Hanushek, E.A., 595
Harberger, A., 264*f*, 273
Harkema, R., 347*f*, 398
Hartley, H.O., 161, 182
Harvey, A.C., 59*f*, 68, 187*f*, 237
Harvey, J.M., 65, 66
Hatanaka, M., 229, 237, 374*f*, 402, 427
Haugh, L.D., 410, 411, 427, 428
Hausman, J.A., 164, 182, 174, 347*f*, 382*f*, 411, 427
Hay, D.A., 470*f*, 487
Hayya, J.C., 210*f*, 236
Heady, E.O., 287*f*, 297*f*, 315
Heckman, J.J., 164, 166, 182, 474, 475*f*, 487, 597
Helliwell, J.F., 430*f*, 442*f*, 462, 498*f*, 507*f*, 508*f*, 512, 577*f*, 578, 584
Helmer, O., 513*f*, 542
Henderson, R.D., 461
Hendry, D.F., 10, 11, 59*f*, 68, 72, 123, 144*f*, 173–175, 182, 183, 387*f*, 398, 403, 415, 427, 582, 584
Hickman, B.G., 437*f*, 451*f*, 454, 461, 462, 512, 547*f*, 548*f*, 551*f*, 566
Hildebrand, G.H., 284*f*, 290*f*, 299*f*, 315
Hildenbrand, W., 1*f*, 11
Hill, R., 184
Hirsch, A.A., 443*f*, 450*f*, 460, 462, 463, 509*f*, 512
Hirsch, W.Z., 57*f*, 58*f*, 68
Hirschey, M., 471*f*, 487
Hocking, J.G., 297*f*, 315
Hoel, P.G., 625*f*, 640
Hoffman, D.L., 597
Hoffman, K., 384*f*, 398
Hoffman, R.F., 298*f*, 316
Holden, K., 513*f*, 535*f*, 542
Holt, C.C., 553*f*, 562*f*, 566
Holtham, G., 461
Hooper, P., 461, 561*f*, 565, 584
Horowitz, I., 593
Horst, P., 599*f*, 624
Horwitz, S.J., 16*f*, 48
Hoskin, J.R.M., 407, 427
Houthakker, H.S., 136*f*, 184, 250–252, 253*f*, 254, 266, 267, 268*f*, 273, 274, 291*f*, 315, 498*f*, 512
Howrey, E.P., 452*f*, 462, 510*f*, 512, 536, 537, 542, 557*f*, 566, 584
Hsiao, C., 131*f*, 147*f*, 150, 156*f*, 164, 165, 173, 180, 183, 184, 326*f*, 332*f*, 340, 346, 402, 404, 411, 421, 427
Huang, C.-F., 596
Huang, D.S., 135*f*, 186
Huber, P.J., 168, 183
Hum, D., 57*f*, 68
Hurd, M.D., 450*f*, 462
Hurwicz, L., 231, 237
Hwa, E.C., 452, 463, 542
Hymans, S.H., 451, 462, 463, 510*f*, 512, 518*f*, 542, 584
Intriligator, M.D., 1*f*, 11, 19*f*, 33*f*, 48, 87*f*, 124, 239*f*, 244*f*, 273, 275*f*, 276*f*, 281*f*, 293*f*, 308*f*, 310*f*, 315, 471*f*, 477, 479*f*, 487, 488, 492*f*, 513, 546*f*, 552*f*, 554*f*, 566, 599*f*, 620*f*, 621*f*, 622*f*, 624
ISI (Institute of Scientific Information, Incorporated), 11
Izenman, A.J., 169, 183
Jarque, A.K., 154, 174, 183
Jeffreys, H., 113*f*, 123, 167, 183
Jenkins, G.M., 61*f*, 68, 187*f*, 198, 199, 201–204, 207, 212, 224, 225, 236, 402, 423, 426, 517*f*, 540
Jensen, M.C., 596
Johansen, L., 284*f*, 291*f*, 296*f*, 310*f*, 315
Johansen, S., 417–421, 427, 428
Johnson, K., 455*f*, 463
Johnston, J., 125*f*, 184, 299*f*, 315
Jones, R.W., 596
Jordon, J.L., 450*f*, 460
Jorgenson, D.W., 223, 237, 257, 273, 283*f*, 298*f*, 301*f*, 306*f*, 308*f*, 314, 315, 369*f*, 374*f*, 382*f*, 390, 398, 431*f*, 463, 564*f*, 566, 595
Judd, J.P., 466*f*, 486
Judge, G., 125*f*, 184
Jump, G.V., 512
Jureen, L., 238, 269*f*, 274
Juselius, K., 417, 418, 428
Kadane, J.B., 386*f*, 398
Kaldor, N., 46, 48
Kalman, P.J., 492*f*, 513
Kang, H., 210*f*, 237
Kapteyn, A., 180
Kelejian, H.H., 360*f*, 398, 555*f*, 566
Kendall, M.G., 19*f*, 48, 629*f*, 640
Kenen, P.B., 596
Kennedy, C., 306*f*, 315
Kershaw, D., 57*f*, 68
Killingsworth, M.R., 594
Kimbell, L.J., 292, 311, 315, 477, 488, 529, 531*f*
Kindahl, J.K., 63*f*, 69
King, R., 414, 428, 597
Kirschen, E.S., 548*f*, 567
Klein, B., 467, 486
Klein, L.R., 4*f*, 11, 19*f*, 33, 47, 48, 159, 181, 288*f*, 366*f*, 385*f*, 389*f*, 398, 402, 428, 430*f*, 432, 436*f*, 437*f*, 438*f*, 440*f*, 442*f*, 443*f*, 447*f*, 449*f*, 450*f*, 451*f*, 452–454, 455*f*, 457*f*, 458*f*, 460–463, 495, 502*f*, 504*f*, 506*f*, 507, 512, 513, 513*f*, 515*f*, 517*f*, 519*f*, 520*f*, 521*f*, 531*f*, 533*f*, 534*f*, 538*f*, 541, 542, 548*f*, 554*f*, 555*f*, 556*f*, 557*f*, 558*f*, 559, 560, 562*f*, 563*f*, 565–567, 579, 584, 585
Klein, P.A., 518*f*, 542
Klep, P.M.M., 483*f*, 489
Kloek, T., 366*f*, 398
Kmenta, J., 290*f*, 296*f*, 297*f*, 315, 317, 584
Kneese, A.V., 595, 597
Koenker, R., 168*f*, 184
Konijn, H.S., 156*f*, 184
Korbel, J., 69, 567
Kormendi, R.C., 595
Koyck, L.M., 228, 237
Kraft, G., 598
Kraft, J., 596
Kreps, 239*f*, 247*f*, 273, 275*f*, 315
Kresge, D.T., 457*f*, 463
Kroner, K.F., 147, 181
Kuh, E., 48, 49, 56*f*, 69, 128, 131*f*, 180, 184, 305*f*, 315, 461, 562*f*, 567, 582*f*
Kuiper, J., 388*f*, 397, 540
Kuttner, K.K., 597
Kuznets, S., 56*f*, 69
Laffont, J.J., 382*f*, 390, 398
Laidler, D.E.W., 466*f*, 486
Landau, D.L., 595
Lau, L.J., 257*f*, 273, 283*f*, 298*f*, 306*f*, 308, 309*f*, 314, 315
Layard, R., 474*f*, 487, 597
Leamer, E.E., 10*f*, 11, 111, 113*f*, 123, 175, 184, 576*f*, 583–585, 594, 596
Lee, T., 184
Leenders, C.T., 383*f*, 385*f*, 399
Leontief, W.W., 35, 48, 62*f*, 69, 293*f*, 315
L'esperance, W.L., 593
Li, W.K., 407, 428
Liebenberg, M., 450*f*, 462, 463
Lindblom, C.E., 547*f*, 565, 567
Linnemann, H., 597
Litterman, R.B., 517, 530, 531, 533*f*, 542
Litzenberger, 596
Liu, T.C., 173, 184, 284*f*, 290*f*, 299*f*, 315, 404, 428, 448*f*, 452, 463, 542
Ljung, G.M., 204, 237
Lluch, C., 256*f*, 273
Lodh, B.K., 567
Longbottom, J.A., 513, 585
Lorant, J., 292, 311, 315
Loretan, M., 417*f*, 428
Lovell, C.A.K., 298*f*, 316
Lu, Y., 298*f*, 316
Lucas, R.E., Jr., 10, 11, 585, 597
Lütkepohl, H., 184
Lyttkens, E., 374*f*, 397, 398
MacAvoy, P., 483, 489, 564*f*, 567
MacDuffee, C.C., 402, 428
MacKinnon, J.G., 105–107, 123, 125*f*, 181
MaCurdy, T., 474*f*, 487, 597
Madansky, A., 138*f*, 184, 347*f*, 369*f*, 375*f*, 382*f*, 383*f*, 398
Maddala, G.S., 125*f*, 131*f*, 149, 184
Malinvaud, E., 125*f*, 184, 275*f*, 316, 347*f*, 366*f*, 370*f*, 373*f*, 382*f*, 398, 431*f*, 463
Malkiel, B.G., 522*f*, 542
Mallows, C.L., 109, 123
Mann, C.L., 561*f*, 565, 584
Manski, C.F., 172, 184
March, J.G., 548*f*, 567
Mariano, R.S., 393, 397, 398, 578*f*, 585
Marquardt, D.W., 160, 184
Marschak, J., 290*f*, 316
Martin, S., 471*f*, 487
Marwah, K., 19*f*, 33*f*, 47, 430*f*, 447*f*, 449*f*, 450*f*, 453*f*, 460, 548*f*, 565
Maxwell, D.E., 594, 598
Maxwell, T., 507*f*, 508*f*, 512, 584
Mayor, T.H., 296*f*, 316
McAleer, M., 106, 123
McAnulty, J.C., 16*f*, 49
McCallum, B.T., 596
McCarthy, M.D., 440*f*, 461, 463, 495, 512
McCracken, M.C., 455*f*, 457*f*, 463

McFadden, D., 247f, 273, 283f, 301f, 314, 391f, 398
McLeod, A.I., 407, 428
McNees, S.K., 513f, 515f, 529–531, 532f, 533f, 534, 535f, 542, 543
McPheters, L., 594
Meguire, P.G., 595
Melmon, K., 146f, 185
Meltzer, A.H., 468f, 486, 596
Mennes, L.B.M., 366f, 398
Merz, J., 34f, 48
Meyer, J., 56f, 69, 131f, 184
Meyer, Lawrence, 453f, 507f
Mikhail, W.W., 386f, 399
Milhøj, A., 146, 184
Mills, E.S., 598
Mincer, J., 513f, 517f, 526f, 543, 595
Minhas, B.S., 293f, 313, 316
Mitchell, B., 366f, 374f, 399
Mizon, G., 107f, 123, 173f, 183
Modigliani, F., 441f, 442f, 460, 464, 468f, 486, 566
Monahan, J.C., 419, 426
Mood, A.M., 626f, 641
Moore, F.T., 312f, 316
Moore, G.H., 518f, 529f, 532f, 542, 543
Morales, J.A., 347f, 399
Morehouse, N.F., 16f, 48
Morganstern, O., 50f, 62f, 63, 69, 522f, 523f, 542, 543
Morishima, M., 307f, 316, 449f, 464
Morris, D.J., 470f, 487
Morrisens, L., 548f, 567
Mosbaek, E.J., 389f, 399
Mountain, D., 173, 184
Muellbauer, J., 238f, 247f, 254f, 257f, 261f, 273, 431f, 461
Mueller, D.C., 471f, 487
Mullich, S.K., 514f, 540
Mundlak, Y., 150, 184
Murphy, K.M., 595
Muth, J.F., 566
Nadiri, M.I., 275f, 286f, 293f, 302f, 305f, 306f, 316
Nagar, A.L., 144f, 185, 386f, 399, 521f, 541
Naines, J.B., Jr., 16f, 49
Nantell, T., 146f, 181
Narasimham, G.L.V., 450f, 462
Naylor, T.H., 17f, 48, 387f, 399, 548f, 555f, 567
Neenan, W.B., 476f, 488
Nelson, C.R., 59f, 69, 189, 210f, 237, 529, 530, 535f, 543
Nerlove, M., 61f, 69, 212f, 228, 236, 237, 264f, 271, 273, 284f, 287f, 289f, 293f, 297f, 298f, 301f, 316, 529f, 543
Neumark, D., 594
Nevin, P. 567
Newbold, P., 187f, 201, 207, 235, 236, 407, 416, 427, 535f, 538f, 542
Newey, W.K., 154, 184, 391, 399
Newhouse, J.P., 476, 477f, 478f, 488
Neyman, J., 163, 184
Nicholls, D.F., 403, 428
North, H.Q., 516f, 543
Nugent, J.B., 594
Nukamp, P., 598
Oaxaca, R., 594
Odeh, H.S., 521f, 541
Okun, A.M., 517f, 543
Orcutt, G.H., 34, 48, 57f, 69, 555f, 567
Ord, J.K., 210f, 236
Olson, E.O., 596
Ornstein, S., 479f, 488
Orphanides, A., 596
Paelinck, J.H.P., 476f, 487
Pagan, A.R., 59f, 68, 139, 174, 181, 403, 414, 427, 428
Palm, F., 215–218, 237, 422, 429, 536f, 543
Pantula, S.G., 216, 236
Papademos, L., 468f, 486
Parente, F.J., 513, 516f
Park, J.Y., 214, 237, 417, 418, 428
Parnes, H.S., 57f, 69
Peel, D.A., 513f, 535f, 542
Pencavel, J., 597
Perlman, M., 476f, 488
Pesaran, M.H., 105, 107, 123
Phelps, C.D., 476, 477f, 478f, 488
Phelps, E.S., 4f, 11, 308f, 316
Phillips, A.W., 4f, 553f, 567
Phillips, L., 594, 598
Phillips, P.C.B., 210f, 214, 236, 237, 386f, 399, 414, 416–418, 426, 428
Phlips, L., 238f, 239f, 247f, 253f, 254f, 265f, 266f, 274
Pierce, D.A., 144, 174, 181, 204, 236, 410, 428
Piggott, J., 34f, 48
Pindyck, R.S., 536, 543, 554f, 564f, 567
Plackett, R.L., 639, 640
Plosser, C.I., 428, 597
Poirier, D.J., 117f, 123, 231, 237
Pollak, R.A., 266f, 273
Popkin, J., 437f, 450f, 463, 596
Porter, M.E., 471f, 486
Powell, A.A., 238f, 254f, 256f, 273, 274, 548f, 567
Prais, S.J., 136f, 184, 250, 251f, 253f, 254, 274
Preston, R.S., 440f, 464, 560f, 567
Price, D.J. de Solla, 7f, 11, 99, 513f, 539
Psacharopoulos, G., 595
Pyke, D.L., 516f, 543
Quandt, R.E., 125f, 151f, 159f, 160, 182, 184, 340f, 346, 584
Quinke, H., 34f, 48
Quliaris, S., 416, 428
Raiffa, H.C., 112, 123, 626f, 640
Ramanathan, R., 535f, 542
Ramin, J.E., 567
Ramsey, J.B., 146, 153, 154, 174, 185, 574f, 584
Ransom, R.L., 483f, 489
Rao, C.R., 95, 123, 382f, 399, 625f, 629f, 640
Rao, P.S., 567
Rasche, R.H., 441f, 460, 464, 468f, 486, 597
Rees, A., 594
Revankar, N., 297f, 298f, 316, 317
Richard, J.F., 72, 107f, 123, 173f, 174, 175, 182, 183, 347f, 397
Ringstad, V., 290f, 296f, 297f, 298f, 314, 316
Rivlin, A.M., 69, 567
Robinson, P.M., 49, 169–172, 185
Rockoff, H., 483f, 489
Roll, R., 596
Rose, R.L., 172, 185
Rosen, S., 305f, 316
Rosenberg, B., 146f, 185
Rosenzweig, M.A., 595, 598
Ross, A., 596
Rossett, R.N., 476f, 488
Rothenberg, T.J., 49, 117f, 123, 323f, 326f, 346, 382f, 383f, 385f, 386f, 399
Rowe, D.A., 264f, 265f, 266f, 274
Roy, A.D., 167, 185
Rubinfeld, D.L., 536, 543
Rudin, W., 384f, 399
Ruggles, N.D., 63f, 69
Saito, M., 307f, 316, 449f, 464, 521f, 541
Saiyed, H.M., 567
Salehi, H., 479f, 488
Samuelson, P.A., 28f, 48, 275f, 283f, 287f, 310f, 316
Sandee, J., 553f, 568
Sargan, J.D., 59f, 68, 369, 374f, 375f, 382f, 383f, 385f, 386f, 399, 403, 415, 427, 428
Sato, K., 255f, 274, 284f, 291f, 298f, 316
Sato, R., 298f, 316
Savage, L.J., 626f, 640
Savin, N.E., 96, 122, 212f, 236
Sawa, T., 386f, 396
Sawyer, J.A., 512
Scadding, J.L., 466f, 486
Scarf, H.E., 34f, 49
Scheffé, H., 629f, 640
Scherer, F.M., 312f, 317, 470f, 487
Schink, G.R., 521f, 534f, 541
Schlaiffer, R., 112, 123
Schmalensee, R., 470f, 471f, 487, 596
Schmidt, P., 323f, 346, 347f, 399
Scholes, M., 596
Schultz, H., 249, 250, 260, 272, 274
Schultze, C.L., 306f, 308f, 313
Schwartz, A.J., 175, 182, 518f, 541, 554f, 566, 597
Schweitzer, S., 479f, 488
Schweitzer, T.T., 567
Searle, S.R., 629f, 640
Sengupta, J.K., 548f, 566
Serrurier, C., 540
Sewell, W.P., 119f, 123
Shapiro, H.T., 441f, 451f, 463, 464, 584
Sheikh, M.A., 596
Sheiner, L., 146f, 185
Shephard, R., 283f, 299f, 317
Sheshinski, E., 546f, 566
Shiller, R.J., 230, 237, 507f, 513, 531f, 541
Shinkai, Y., 457f, 462
Shiskin, J., 518f, 543
Shoven, J.B., 34f, 49
Shubik, M., 555f, 567
Sichel, D.E., 466f, 467, 484, 486
Siegel, B.N., 595
Silberston, A., 312f, 317
Silvey, S.D., 95, 122, 123, 131, 185
Simes, R., 560, 561, 567
Simon, H., 275f, 317, 345, 548f, 555, 565–568
Simpson, W., 57f, 68
Sims, C.A., 10f, 11, 42f, 49, 173, 185, 226f, 237, 404, 410, 417, 428, 539f, 543
Sinai, A., 443f, 453, 457f, 461, 464, 507f
Smith, Adam, 15, 49
Smith, D.D., 513f, 540

Smith, G., 570*f*, 585
Smith, H., 159*f*, 181
Smith, J.P., 594
Smith, V.K., 386*f*, 389*f*, 399
Smith, V.L., 58*f*, 69, 312*f*, 317
Smithies, A., 46, 49
Solari, L., 2*f*, 12, 34, 49
Solon, G., 146*f*, 147, 180
Solow, R.M., 284*f*, 285*f*, 306*f*, 307, 308*f*, 313, 317, 596
Sonnenschein, H., 1*f*, 11
Spanos, A., 173, 185
Sparks, G.R., 462
Spence, A.M., 471*f*, 486
Srinivasan, T.N., 594
Stark, O., 595, 598
Statistics Canada, 58*f*, 66, 69, 455*f*
Stekler, H.O., 513*f*, 518*f*, 524*f*, 532*f*, 540, 543
Stern, R.M., 596
Stewart, I.A., 462
Stigler, G.J., 63*f*, 69
Stock, J.H., 414, 416–418, 428, 429, 518*f*, 543, 597
Stoker, T., 257*f*, 273
Stone, C.J., 172, 185, 391*f*, 392, 399
Stone, R. (or J.R.N.), 2*f*, 6, 7, 12, 131*f*, 185, 238, 252, 253*f*, 254*f*, 264*f*, 265*f*, 266*f*, 274, 497
Strong, W.S., 594
Strotz, R.H., 16*f*, 48, 49
Stuart, A., 629*f*, 640
Su, J., 516*f*, 544
Su, V., 516*f*, 520*f*, 532*f*, 542, 544
Suits, D.B., 19*f*, 49, 265, 266, 274, 342, 346, 448, 464, 502–505, 511, 524*f*, 532*f*, 534, 544
Sutch, R., 483*f*, 489
Sweeney, J.L., 595, 597
Symansky, S., 461
Tamura, R., 595
Tanny, S., 455*f*, 457*f*, 460
Taubman, P., 450*f*, 462, 553*f*, 555*f*, 557*f*, 558, 566
Taylor, J.B., 430*f*, 452, 453, 454*f*, 464, 507*f*, 513*f*, 544, 562*f*, 568
Taylor, L.D., 266, 267, 268*f*, 273
Teigen, R., 468–470, 486
Temin, P., 483, 484, 489
Terrell, R.D., 403, 427, 428
Theil, H., 40*f*, 49, 90*f*, 107–109, 123, 125*f*, 131*f*, 135*f*, 144*f*, 151*f*, 153, 167*f*, 185, 230, 235, 237, 254*f*, 257*f*, 261*f*, 274, 360*f*, 368*f*, 369*f*, 373*f*, 375*f*, 377*f*, 382*f*, 399, 423, 429, 432*f*, 433*f*, 435*f*, 436*f*, 437*f*, 464, 511, 512, 513*f*, 519*f*, 525*f*, 526*f*, 540*f*, 544, 548*f*, 551, 553, 554, 555*f*, 559*f*, 568, 576, 577, 599*f*, 607*f*, 611*f*, 623*f*, 624, 639, 640
Thirwall, A.P., 306*f*, 315
Thompson, J.L., 513*f*, 535*f*, 542
Thorbecke, E., 548*f*, 566
Tiao, G.C., 111, 112, 113*f*, 122, 223, 236, 400, 404–407, 429
Tinbergen, Jan, 33, 46*f*, 447, 454, 464, 549, 568
Tobin, J., 131*f*, 164, 185, 570, 584
Toda, H., 426, 428
Toro-Vizcarrondo, C., 88, 123
Treyz, G., 520*f*, 526*f*, 532*f*, 541, 542
Tsay, R.S., 407, 429
Tsukahara, T., Jr., 476*f*, 488
Tukey, J.W., 167, 185
Turkington, D., 157*f*, 181
Turner, D.S., 513, 585
Turoff, M., 547*f*, 568
Tustin, A., 16*f*, 49
UCLA Business Forecasting Project, 581*f*, 585
Uebe, G., 430*f*, 447*f*, 453*f*, 464
U.S. Bureau of the Census, 62*f*, 64, 65
U.S. Department of Commerce, 64, 65
Valavanis, S., 447*f*, 464
van de Klundert, T., 307*f*, 314
van den Bogaard, P.J.M., 436*f*, 464, 553, 554, 555*f*, 559*f*, 568
Van der Gaag, 476*f*, 488
van der Wee, H., 483*f*, 489
van Eijk, C.J., 553*f*, 568
Vannoni, M.G., 69
Varian, H., 239*f*, 247*f*, 274, 275*f*, 283*f*, 317
Visco, I., 507*f*, 513
Voisin, 560, 561, 567
von Ungern-Sternberg, T., 415, 427
Votey, H.L., Jr., 594, 598
Vuong, Q., 109*f*, 124
Waelbroeck, J.L., 454*f*, 464
Wagstaff, A., 476, 488
Wald, A., 157*f*, 185
Wallace, T.D., 88, 123, 124
Wallis, K.F., 10*f*, 12, 216–219, 237, 508*f*, 513, 531, 532, 544, 581, 582, 585
Walters, A.A., 284*f*, 287*f*, 289*f*, 291*f*, 299*f*, 317
Walton, G.M., 483*f*, 489
Wansbeek, T., 180
Waslander, H.E.L., 507*f*, 508*f*, 512, 584
Waterson, M., 470*f*, 487
Watson, G.S., 143, 174, 182
Watson, M.W., 59*f*, 68, 414, 417, 428, 429, 518*f*, 543, 597
Watts, H.W., 34*f*, 48, 57*f*, 68
Waud, R.N., 304, 317
Wei, C.Z., 212*f*, 236, 417, 426
Weinblatt, T., 565
Weiss, L.W., 470, 487
Welch, F.R., 594
Welsh, R.E., 128, 180
Wertz, K., 17*f*, 48, 555*f*, 567
Weston, J.F., 471*f*, 487
Whalley, J., 34*f*, 48
Whitcomb, D., 312*f*, 315
White, H., 137–139, 174, 179, 185, 186
White, J.S., 212, 237
Whitley, J.D., 513, 585
Wickens, M.R., 414, 428
Wiener, Norbert, 63*f*
Wildavsky, A., 548*f*, 565, 568
Wiles, P., 299*f*, 317
Wilks, S.S., 625*f*, 640
Williams, A., 476*f*, 488
Williams, A.W., 69
Williams, R.A., 548*f*, 567
Williamson, O.E., 275*f*, 317
Willig, R., 596
Willis, M., 567
Willis, R.J., 595
Wilson, T.A., 305*f*, 317, 470*f*, 471*f*, 487
Wise, D.A., 164, 182
Wold, H., 193*f*, 237, 238, 269*f*, 274, 336*f*, 346, 389*f*
Wonnacott, T., 17*f*, 48, 555*f*, 567
Wood, D.O., 305*f*, 313
Woodford, M., 596
Wright, G., 483*f*, 489
Wright, R., 146*f*, 181
Wu, D.M., 174, 186, 411, 429
Yett, D.E., 477, 488
Yoo, B. Sam, 421, 427–429
Yotopoulos, P.A., 594
Yun, K.Y., 595
Zarembka, P., 296*f*, 317
Zarnowitz, V., 516*f*, 517*f*, 526*f*, 529, 532*f*, 543, 544, 584
Zellner, A., 19*f*, 49, 111, 112, 113*f*, 117*f*, 124, 135*f*, 186, 215–218, 237, 290*f*, 297*f*, 317, 347*f*, 375*f*, 399, 422, 429, 536*f*, 543, 572, 583*f*, 585, 625*f*, 640
Zusman, P., 593

SUBJECT INDEX

Accuracy of data (*See* Data, accuracy of)
Adaptation (in the context of semiparametric estimation), 172
Add factors, 440, 442, 451, 520–523, 526, 528, 529, 532–534, 536, 549, 558, 575, 581, 593
"Adding-up theorem" (*See* Euler's theorem)
Additive consistency, 570, 572, 573, 583, 584
Advertising, effect on supply-demand analysis, 480–482
Aggregation, 23, 34, 57*f*, 261, 262, 271, 290*f*, 291*f*, 311
aggregation conditions, 245, 246, 262, 271
Agricultural price formation, 259, 260, 272, 342, 343, 483, 484
(*See also* Cobweb model)
Akaike information criterion, 109, 204, 219, 411, 412
Aitken estimators (*See* Generalized least squares [GLS])
Alcoholism, simultaneous equations of, 479–482
Almon distributed lag, 190, 229, 230, 236, 439, 445
Almost ideal demand system (AIDS), 257, 272
American Economic Association, 67, 99
Analysis of variance (ANOVA), for a regression, 94, 104
Anticipations (of future events), 440, 446, 515, 516, 522
A posteriori information (*See* Information, *a posteriori*)
A priori information (*See* Information, *a priori*)
Arc elasticity, 5–6
Asymptotic distribution, 90, 90*f*, 168, 169, 173, 369*f*, 373, 382*f*, 383, 391, 392, 394, 395, 417–419, 421, 426, 636, 638, 639

Asymptotic relative efficiency (ARE), 167*f*
Asymptotic unbiasedness (*See* Estimators, asymptotic unbiasedness)
Augmented Dickey–Fuller test statistic (*See* Dickey-Fuller test statistic, augmented)
Autocorrelation, 57–59, 73, 133, 139–146, 148, 171, 177, 192, 225, 231, 232, 236, 347, 374, 377, 401, 402, 418, 419, 519, 592
  tests for, 142–145, 174, 176, 179, 469
  (*See also* Stationary processes, autocorrelations)
Automobile demand (in DRI model), 445, 446, 448, 451
  in Suits model, 534
Autoregressive conditional heteroskedasticity (ARCH), 145, 146, 174
Autoregressive integrated moving average (ARIMA) process, 209–212, 222, 422, 423, 517*f*, 529, 530, 536, 577
Autoregressive moving average (ARMA) process, 197–200, 202, 204 206–210, 212, 215, 221–223, 226, 402, 404–409, 421, 422, 425, 426
  characteristic (or determinantal) equation, 209, 422
  explosive, 208, 209
  use in forecasting, 202
Autoregressive process, first-order, 140–142, 159, 171, 195, 212, 213, 220, 231, 232, 236, 252, 267*f*, 272, 407, 451
Autoregressive (AR) process, general, 194–197, 200, 204, 207, 213, 220, 231, 232, 402, 405–407, 411, 412, 421–423, 520*f*, 522
  characteristic equation, 194–197, 404
  stationarity condition, 195, 197, 404
  vector (*See* Vector autoregressive process)
Average absolute error, 576
Bandwith parameter, 169, 419
Bartlett's formula, 201
Basic linear regression model, 70–109, 125, 179, 188, 208, 348, 353, 535, 536, 591
  assumptions of, 72–73, 139
  Bayesian analysis, 109–117
  degrees of freedom of, 82
  multiple linear regression, example of, 102–104
  simple linear regression, example of, 99–102
  unbiased estimator of the variance of the disturbance term, 82, 213
Bayesian approach to econometrics, 9–10, 70, 109–117, 131*f*, 173, 537, 572, 574, 583, 627*f*
  forecasting, 115–117, 521, 531, 536*f*, 537
  interval estimation, 115
  point estimate, 114, 115
Bayesian vector autoregressive method (*See* Vector autoregressive process)
Bayes risk, 114, 115
Bayes' theorem, 109, 110, 117
Behavioral relations, 34
Bergson social welfare function, 551
Best linear unbiased estimator (BLUE), 81, 119–120, 125, 140, 148 167, 179, 322 (*See also* Gauss–Markov theorem)
Best linear unbiased predictor, 98, 141, 142
Best unbiased estimator, 167
Bias:
  in general, 360, 365, 387, 388, 389, 393, 394, 426, 524, 535
  least squares, 354–356, 358
Black box modeling (as opposed to white box), 14, 15
Box–Jenkins analysis of time series, 189, 198–207, 223–225, 228, 403, 404, 407–409, 421, 423, 517*f*
  diagnostic checks, 199, 203, 204, 207, 225, 404, 407
  estimation, 199, 201–203, 207, 225, 404
  example, 215–219
  identification, 199–201, 203, 207, 225, 404, 407
  multiplicity (of model), 199, 204
  overfitting, 204
  parsimony, principle of, 198, 199
Box–Pierce Q statistic, 144, 174, 204, 218, 225
Brookings model (*See* Models, Brookings)
Brownian motion, 417, 522*f*
Budget constraint (*See* Household, theory of)
Budget shares (*See* Household, theory of)
Business cycles, econometric model approach to, 437–439, 447, 449, 453
Cambridge *k*, 466, 467
Canadian economy, 442*f*, 452, 453*f*, 454–456, 498, 502, 503, 508, 532, 559–561, 577*f*, 580, 589
Capacity utilization rate, 285*f*
  Wharton index of, 285*f*, 438
Cauchy distribution, 215
Censored regression models (*See* Models, censored regression)
Central limit theorem, 21, 22*f*, 373 (*See also* Probability and statistics, central limit theorem)
Central Planning Bureau (of the Netherlands), 551
Chase econometric model (*See* Models, Chase econometric)
Chi-squared distribution, 89, 94, 96, 139, 154, 204, 393, 411, 418, 638, 639
Chow test, 97, 174, 574, 575, 579, 592
"Classical" approach to econometrics (*See* Bayesian approach to econometrics *and* Econometrics, classical approach to)
Cliometrics, 3*f*, 483, 484
Cobb–Douglas production function, 20, 86, 87, 271, 287–293, 295–298, 301–308, 310, 311, 342, 438, 449, 450, 452, 491, 492, 497
Cobweb model (of agricultural price formation), 224, 225, 263, 264, 272, 343, 345, 352
Cochrane–Orcutt transformation (*See* Pseudo differences)
Coefficient of determination (*See* R^2)
Cointegration, 403*f*, 409, 412–421, 423, 425, 426
  cointegration rank, 413, 416, 417, 420, 423
Column kernel, 334*f*
Common stochastic trends test, 417
Common trends (*See* Trends, common)
Comparative statics, 27, 28, 28*f*, 40, 492–495, 589, 592
Complements, 252–254
Completeness (of a system of equations), 35
Computer (electronic), 16, 17*f*, 456, 457
Concentration, 470, 474
Concentration ratio, 470–473, 485
Conditional distribution (*See* Probability and statistics, conditional density)
Conditional moment tests, 154
Confidence interval(s), 22, 91, 92, 98, 99, 110
Conjugate prior, 111–113
Consistency (*See* Estimators, consistency)
Constant elasticity demand functions (*See* Household, theory of, demand functions)
Constant elasticity of substitution (CES) production function, 159, 271, 293–297, 302, 303*f*, 307*f*, 310, 312, 339, 452, 491
Consumption function, 6–8, 18, 19–21, 29, 136–138, 156, 157, 350–352, 355, 356, 358–360, 367, 370, 371, 430, 431*f*, 432–434, 448, 458, 459, 494, 511, 571, 575, 583, 584
Continuous work history sample (CWHS), 147
Correlation coefficient, 634, 635
Correlogram, 193, 201
Cost curve, 278–280, 282, 284, 299–301, 309, 312 (*See also* Firm)
  cubic, 299, 309
Cost function, 281*f*, 283, 284, 299*f*, 301, 302, 305, 309, 312, 592
  Cobb–Douglas, 301, 302, 312
  generalized Leontief, 302, 305, 313
  translog, 258, 298*f*, 302, 305, 313
Council of Economic Advisers, 450, 451
Covariance matrix, 80, 81, 103, 136, 137, 139, 158, 166, 179, 202, 203, 231, 319–325, 332, 336–338, 341, 344, 347, 348, 352, 364*f*, 372–375, 377, 379–385, 387, 388, 390–395, 403, 409, 411, 418, 419, 421, 449*f*, 483*f*, 493, 600, 605, 632, 633, 635–638
Covariance transformation (in context of error components model), 148
Cramer–Rao lower bound, 84, 167*f*, 382*f*, 383*f*, 411
Cramer's rule, 613
Credibility (of fiscal policy), 562
Crime, econometrics of, 583, 587, 593, 594
Cross-correlation coefficients, 223–225, 377–379, 389, 395, 404, 406, 407, 409, 411
Cross-covariance coefficients, 223–225, 404, 405
Cross-section data (*See* Data, cross-section)
"Crowding out," 502, 506, 512
Current Population Survey, 147
Data, 1, 3, 50–64, 174, 175, 582, 588–590, 592
  accuracy of, 62–64, 569, 592
  admissibility, 174
  banks, 443*f*, 450, 580
  computerized, 443*f*
  cross-section, 33, 54–57, 71, 131, 136, 139, 146, 147, 295, 296, 589
  experimental, 57–58
  extrapolation, 60, 209
  grouped, 157*f*
  interpolation, 59, 60, 209
  longitudinal (*See* Data, panel)
  macro, 57, 64, 262, 290, 291
  management, 580, 582, 583
  massaging (*See* Data, refined or "massaged")
  matrix (*See* Design matrix)
  measurement errors (*See* Errors in variables)
  micro, 57, 64
  monthly, 452, 536
  multicollinearity, 131, 132
  nonexperimental, 57–58
  panel, 56, 57, 146, 147
  points, 388, 634
  pooled, 55–57, 71, 589
  problems with, 58, 59
  qualitative, 51–54
  quantitative, 51, 52
  quarterly (vs. annual), 438, 439, 442, 449, 451, 467, 468, 529, 530, 536
  refined or "massaged," 3, 51, 59–62, 592
  revisions, 446, 533
  smoothing, 61, 62

sources of, 64–66, 592
splicing, 60
time series, 54–57, 71, 136, 139, 147, 188, 189, 290, 291, 296*f*, 589 (*See also* Time series analysis)
Data-generating process (DGP), 173
Data Resources–McGraw-Hill, Inc. (DRI), 64, 443
Decomposition of time series (*See* Time series decomposition)
Definitional relationships, 34
Degrees of freedom, 57, 59, 153, 175, 189, 228, 366*f*, 373*f*, 449, 638, 639
Delphi method (*See* Forecasts and forecasting *and* Policy evaluation)
Demand curves and functions (*See* Household, theory of)
Demographics, 447, 451, 455, 479
Depreciation rate (of a capital stock), 265
Design matrix, 71, 75, 102, 122, 128–130, 321, 348–351, 363, 370, 371, 381, 387, 388, 600, 634
singular values, 128–130
Determination, coefficient of (*See* R^2)
Dickey–Fuller test statistic, 212–214, 416
augmented, 213, 214
Difference operator, 209–212, 215, 217, 225, 252, 266, 267, 403*f*, 412, 414, 425, 448
Diffuse prior, 111, 113, 115
Diffusion index, 518*f*
Disaggregation, 438, 449, 450, 451, 455
Discrete response models (*See* Models, discrete response)
Disjointed incrementalism, 547, 548
Distributed lag models, 190, 223, 225–231, 265, 439, 452, 468, 519, 537
linear, 226
Shiller, 230
spline, 230, 231
(*See also* Almon distributed lag, Koyck distributed lag, Rational distributed lag)
Disturbance term (*See* Stochastic disturbance term)
Divisia indexes, 257
Division of labor, 15
DRI model, 443–448, 457*f*, 459, 506, 507*f*, 509, 510, 529, 534, 579, 580, 582
Duesenberry–Eckstein–Fromm model, 443,447, 448
Dummy variable, 51–54, 125, 205, 223, 265, 266, 439, 446, 448, 469*f*, 476, 477*f*, 575, 592
Durable and non-durable goods, 164, 264–268, 571, 572
Durbin *h* statistic, 232
Durbin-Watson test statistic (d), 143, 144, 146, 174, 176, 179, 304, 469, 540, 577, 592
Econometric model, 1, 2, 3, 14*f*, 19–24, 35, 151, 189, 303, 305*f*, 311, 318–341, 347–351, 374, 375, 393, 465*f*, 493, 519, 520, 548–564, 586–588
"audit" (*See* Econometric model, managerial aspects)
dynamic aspects, 400–403, 421–425, 562
evaluation of (*see* Econometric model, managerial aspects)
linear, 19–21, 24, 35–40, 318–339, 490, 491, 493, 498–500, 519, 521, 523, 557
macroeconometric, 33, 33*f*, 46, 430–458, 468*f*, 495, 502, 510, 519, 527, 529, 546, 548, 551, 556*f*, 562, 564, 569, 572, 575, 577–582
managerial aspects, 4, 457*f*, 459, 498*f*, 569–583
nonlinear, 382*f*, 390–393, 500–502, 522*f*, 523, 540, 556*f*, 557, 558, 577, 578
optimal scale of, 456, 457, 459, 534, 562
role of judgment, 569, 581–583
surveys, 432–456, 466–484
Econometrics:
classical approach to, 116, 117, 173–175
definition, 1, 3
purposes, 2, 4, 238
student studies (*See* Student studies)
techniques, 1, 2, 3, 10, 569, 580–583
Economic and Social Research Council (of the United Kingdom), 581
Economic history, 483, 484, 597
cotton price fluctuations, 483, 484
railway rates, 483
Economic statistics (different from econometrics), 1, 2
Economies of scale (*See* Firm, theory of, returns to scale)
Elasticity (in general), 282, 303–305, 446, 469, 484, 491, 495–498, 563, 592
constant, 395, 496–498
Elasticity of cost, 300–302, 310, 312, 313
Elasticity of demand:
cross price, 243, 250, 252–254, 269, 270, 480, 482
in general, 241, 242, 246, 250, 251, 266, 267*f*, 481
income, 242, 243, 250–254, 260, 265–270, 445, 467, 469, 472, 476, 478, 480, 497, 498, 510
own price, 5–7, 242, 243, 249–254, 260, 265–271, 472, 476, 478, 480–482
Elasticity of production (or output), 286*f*, 287, 288, 291–293, 297, 301*f*, 302, 307, 308, 310, 449
Elasticity of substitution, 286, 287, 294–298, 309, 475
constant, 293–297, 310, 311, 491, 492
Endogenous variables (*See* Variables, endogenous)
Energy economics (*See* Policy evaluation, energy policy)
Engel curve (*See* Household, theory of)
Engel's Law, 241–243, 252, 269, 498, 510
Entropy (as a measure of concentration), 485, 486
Error:
mean squared, 80 (*See also* Mean squared error)
mean squared matrix, 80
Error components, 146–150
Error correction model, 414–419
Errors in variables, 23, 24, 59, 151, 155–158, 177, 323*f*, 389, 520, 523, 551, 558, 572, 575, 582
treatment of, 157, 158
Estimating techniques, comparison of, 386–389
Estimation:
constrained, 86–88, 572
full information approach (*See* Full information approach)
by instrumental variables (*See* Instrumental variables)
limited information approach, 351, 352, 356, 358, 360, 368, 369*f*, 381, 389
mixed, 131*f*
naive approach (*See* Naive approach)
of simultaneous equations, 288, 290, 347–396, 437*f*, 447, 449, 451, 572, 574, 582, 591
Estimators:
asymptotic unbiasedness, 83, 84, 86, 170, 354, 418
consistency, 82–84, 86, 119, 148, 153, 160, 165, 170, 172, 173, 231, 290*f*, 322, 323, 336, 341, 352, 354, 356, 358, 360, 364–366, 368, 372–375, 378, 380–383, 386, 388–390, 392, 393, 394, 403, 418, 471*f*, 572
distribution of, 389*f*, 523, 551, 558
efficiency, 80, 81, 119, 136, 153, 160, 170, 172, 173, 322*f*, 356, 358*f*, 369*f*, 373*f*, 375, 379, 380, 382, 383, 386, 391, 392, 393, 395, 403, 418
extraneous, 131
instrumental variables, 352, 366, 368*f*, 369–374, 381, 382, 388, 392, 394, 395
k-class, 352, 360, 366, 368, 369*f*, 372, 373, 375*f*, 388, 389, 394, 395
linearity, 79
maximum likelihood (*See* Maximum likelihood estimation)
nonlinear (simultaneous equations estimators), 360*f*
residuals (other than least squares), 373
small sample properties of, 353, 356, 369*f*, 374, 386–389
unbiasedness, 79–81, 86, 153, 164, 165, 173, 231, 232, 290*f*, 291, 292, 322, 323, 336, 341, 352, 354, 356, 358, 360, 364, 365, 374, 378, 386, 393, 523, 524
Euclidean n-space, 614
Euler's theorem, 244, 282, 286
Exchange rate (*See* Rate of foreign exchange)
Exogeneity, weak, 72
Exogenous variables (*See* Variables, exogenous)
Expansion path, 277, 278
Expectations:
adaptive, 234, 271, 272, 539
extrapolative, 453
mathematical (*See* Probability and statistics, expectations)
model-consistent, 10*f*, 451, 453, 562*f*, 582
rational, 10, 10*f*, 451–453, 562*f*
Experimental data (*See* Data, experimental)
Experimentation, social, 50, 57, 58, 147, 164
Expert opinion (*See* Forecasts and forecasting, expert opinion, *and* Policy evaluation, judgment)
Explanatory variable (*See* Variable, explanatory)
Extraneous estimator, 131, 175, 255, 256
Extrapolation (*See* Data, extrapolation)
F probability distribution, 93, 639
F statistic, 93, 97, 146, 153, 592
Factor demand equations: estimation of, 284, 302–305, 434
Factor demand functions, 280–284, 298*f*, 302–305, 312, 313, 452
labor requirements approach, 304, 305, 437, 450, 452, 458
Factor price frontier, 298*f*, 310
Factor shares, 288, 289, 291, 292, 302, 311, 313, 449
"Facts" (in general), 2–4
Fair model, 451, 507*f*, 532*f*
Federal Reserve System, 441, 450, 469, 509
Final form (equations), 31, 32, 40–42, 345, 423, 491, 500, 523, 537, 538, 592
Financial innovation, 468, 470
Finite distributed lag (*See* Distributed lag models)
Finite length polynomial lag (*See* Almon distributed lag)
Firm, theory of, 275–309, 592, 593
capital, difficulty of measurement, 285, 288, 291*f*, 300*f*, 305, 308
complementary inputs, 281
cost minimization, 284, 299
costs, 277–280, 299–302, 312

Firm, theory of (*cont.*)
duality approach, 283, 284, 301
expansion path, 277–280
factor demand functions (*See* Factor demand functions)
factor shares (*See* Factor shares)
factors of production, 275, 276, 280, 284, 285, 288, 295, 298, 299, 300*f*, 301, 303–306, 308, 309, 311, 313
fixed factors of production (or fixed costs), 278, 279, 300,
imperfect competition, 310
inferior inputs, 282
isocosts, 277, 278
isoquants, 277, 278, 285, 287, 293, 294, 306, 311, 313
marginal products, 276, 277, 282*f*, 285, 287–290, 295, 311
marginal rate of technical substitution, 276–278, 286, 313
minimum efficient scale, 300, 301
output supply curve, 281–283
output supply function, 259, 280–282, 309, 312, 479, 587, 588
price function, 283*f*
product curve, 311
production function (*See* Production functions)
profit function, 275, 276, 281, 283, 284, 309
profit maximization, 275, 276, 280, 281, 282, 286–290, 293, 295, 300, 303, 312
reswitching, 291*f*
returns to scale, 283*f*, 285, 286, 289–293, 296, 301, 302, 307–310, 312, 449
sign conditions, 281
substitutability of inputs, 276, 286, 294, 295, 296*f*, 298, 306
substitute inputs, 281
symmetry conditions, 281, 302
tangency point solution, 277, 278
technical change, 291*f*, 306–309, 449, 452
disembodied, 306, 449
embodied, 308
(Hicks) neutral, 306–308, 449
Fiscal policy, 447, 449*f*, 450–453, 503–505, 509, 510*f*, 511, 545, 548, 548*f*, 551, 553–555, 558–560, 562, 564, 598
Fixed effects (in context of error components models), 148–150
Flexible functional form, 257, 258, 298
Flow diagram, 29–30, 36–37
Flow-of-funds, 441
Forecasts and forecasting:
accuracy, 515, 520, 522–527, 530–533, 535–537
big vs. medium-sized models, 530*f*, 533, 534
geometrical interpretation, 525, 526
inequality coefficient, 526, 527, 540, 576, 577
add factors (*See* Add factors)
anticipations surveys, 515, 516, 517*f*, 519, 520, 522
autoregressive model, 134, 135, 140–142, 516, 517, 520*f*
backcasting, 513*f*, 517, 518
Bayesian approach to, 115–117, 521, 531, 536*f*, 537
best linear unbiased predictor (BLUP), 141, 142, 219, 220–222
BMARK forecasts (of Charles Nelson), 530, 531
Brownian motion (*See* Brownian motion)
business forecasting, 513*f*
combination of forecasts and forecasting methods, 535–538
cone of underestimation of change, 525
conservative bias of, 526
Delphi method, 516, 547
deterministic, 524, 527, 528
diffusion index, 518*f*
econometric approach, 393, 434–436, 438–440, 442, 446, 448, 451, 452, 455, 456, 476, 515, 516*f*, 518–523, 527–530, 532–534, 536, 537, 546*f*
errors of, 219–222, 410, 515, 521*f*, 522*f*, 523, 524, 526, 530, 531, 535, 579, 580, 593
ex ante, 520, 521, 524, 528, 529, 532*f*, 533*f*, 578, 580, 581, 593
expert opinion, 515, 516, 520, 522, 532–534, 537, 546
ex post, 520–523, 529, 537, 576, 593
in general, 4, 10*f*, 28, 33, 34, 238, 513–537, 545, 546, 549, 556, 572, 577, 581, 588, 590, 593
horizon, 514, 517, 523, 529, 533, 536, 537, 540
industrial organization approach, 532
interval, 514, 515, 521, 523, 537
judgmental (informal), 516*f*, 521, 522, 532*f*, 533
leading indicators, 518, 522, 537
least squares predictors, 76, 98, 99
line of perfect forecasts, 525
long-term, 456, 515, 523, 524, 528, 529, 533, 537, 538
macroeconomic, 513, 516*f*, 517*f*, 519, 523, 527–537, 540, 546*f*
mean squared prediction error, 108, 109
medium-term, 456, 533, 581
model accuracy, as a test of, 175, 515, 577
persistence forecasting, 516, 522, 547
point, 514–516, 523, 528
prediction error (*See* Forecasting, errors of)
probability, 514, 515, 521, 556*f*
residual-based predictor (nonlinear simultaneous equations model), 393
reverse forecasting (*See* Forecasts and forecasting, backcasting)
short-term, 515, 518–524, 528, 532*f*, 533, 536–538, 540, 581
status quo, 516, 522, 526, 527
stochastic, 521, 523
time series methods, 189, 418*f*, 522, 531
time series models, 219–222, 408, 421, 418*f*, 529, 530, 532*f*
trend extrapolation, 209, 211, 421, 517, 520, 522, 537, 539, 554
turning point errors, 518*f*, 525, 526*f*, 527, 529, 576, 577
underestimation of changes, causes of, 525, 526, 534
Frequency domain approach, 403
Full information approach, 351–353, 373*f*, 375, 381, 389
Full information maximum likelihood (FIML) estimation, 353, 374, 382–386, 388, 389, 392, 393, 395, 433
asymptotic covariance matrix, 383, 385
change of variables, 383, 384
linearized version, 385*f*
Monte Carlo studies, 388, 389
ordinary least squares, and, 386
recursive case, 385, 386
three-stage least squares, and, 383, 385
Fundamental idempotent matrices of least squares estimation, 76, 119, 153, 322, 362, 363, 368*f*, 615
Gauss–Markov theorem, 79–81, 98, 152, 322, 354, 358*f*, 388
assumptions, 72, 73, 136, 176
in context of generalized least squares, 133, 134, 176
proof, 81
Gauss–Newton iterative formula, 159, 160, 203, 403
Gauss–Seidel algorithm, 458*f*, 556*f*
Generalized inverse (*See* Matrices, generalized inverse)
Generalized least squares (GLS), 133–136, 148, 149
autocorrelation, application to, 141, 142, 232
best linear unbiased estimators (BLUE), 133, 134
feasible estimator, 134, 135, 138, 142, 144, 146, 149, 232
heteroskedasticity, application to, 137, 138, 179
mixed regression, 230
ordinary least squares, relation to, 133
panel data, application to, 147–149
partially generalized least squares, 138, 139
seemingly unrelated regressions, relation to, 135, 136
simultaneous equations context, 342, 371, 372, 375, 379, 380
weighted least squares, relation to, 138
Geometric mean, 289*f*
Gestalt, 578, 579
"Giffen factor," 282
Giffen good, 25, 246, 268, 282
Gradient vector (*See* Matrices, gradient vector)
Granger causality, 409–412, 422, 424–426
Granger representation theorem, 415, 416, 418
Great Depression, 432, 436, 553, 554, 555*f*, 559*f*
Gresham's Law, 485
Growth of science, 7–9, 539
Habit formation, 266–268, 459
Hausman specification test, 411
Health economics, 292, 293, 311, 475–479, 587, 588
Herfindahl index, 485
Heteroskedasticity, 136–139, 140, 161, 171, 172, 176, 288–290, 419, 592
autoregressive conditional (*See* Autoregressive conditional heteroskedasticity [ARCH])
tests for, 139, 174
Hicksian demand functions, 247
Homogeneity (of production functions), 283, 286, 288, 301, 310
Homogeneity conditions, 244, 246, 248, 271, 282, 484
Homogeneity of factor demand equations, 282
Homoskedasticity, 73, 133, 179, 347, 377
Homotheticity, 286
Hospital stays, determinants of, 476, 477
Hotelling's lemma, 283, 309
Household, theory of, 234–268, 592, 593
aggregation, 258, 261, 262, 271
aggregation conditions, 245, 246, 262, 271
budget constraint, 239, 240, 243, 246, 248
budget shares, 243–246, 269, 270
complements (*See* Complements)
demand analysis, dynamic, 258, 263–268
changes in variables (rather than levels), 265, 266
cobweb model, 263–264
distributed lag, 264
habit formation, 266, 267
time trend, 249, 251–254, 268
demand curves, 241, 242, 268
demand equations, identification (*See* Identification)

demand equations, systems of, 248, 254–258
demand functions, 239–241, 247–258, 270, 271, 479, 587, 588
constant elasticity (*See* demand functions, log-linear)
linear, 249, 254, 261, 262, 264, 266, 267*f*, 268, 270
log-linear, 250–254, 256*f*, 259, 263, 268, 270, 271, 287 479, 480, 496, 497
semilogarithmic, 250, 268
duality approach, 247, 269
economies of scale, 251
elasticities of demand (*See* Elasticity of demand)
Engel curve, 241, 243, 246, 248–251, 255, 258, 262, 268, 271
Engel's Law, 241–243, 252, 269
expenditure function, 247
Giffen good, 25, 246, 268
habit formation, 266–268
homogeneity conditions (*See* Homogeneity conditions)
income-consumption path, 241, 243
indifference curve, 239, 240
indirect utility function, 247, 255*f*, 257, 258
inferior good, 242, 246, 250, 254, 268, 270
marginal rate of substitution, 240
money illusion, lack of, 244*f*
negativity conditions, 244, 248
normal good, 246, 268, 475
ordinal utility, 239*f*
price-consumption path, 241, 242
Slutsky conditions, 244–246, 269, 475*f*
substitute goods, 252–254
substitution effects, 244*f*, 245*f*, 475
superior good, 25, 246, 268
symmetry condition, 245, 269, 475
tangency point solution, 239, 240
Törnquist–Engel curves, 269
utility maximization, 239, 240, 247, 255, 258, 269, 572
Houthakker–Taylor model, 266–268, 272
Human capital, 474, 595
Hypothesis testing, regression analysis, in general, 88–98, 173–175, 208, 426, 572, 574, 575, 578, 579, 582, 592
all parameters, 93–94, 574, 575, 592
autocorrelation, 142–145
Box–Jenkins analysis, in context of, 204
heteroskedasticity, 139
linear restrictions on parameters, 92–96
nonnested, 104–107, 109*f*
simultaneous-equations context, 374, 382, 393
single regression coefficient, 90–92, 208, 426, 574, 578, 592
structural break, 96–99
unit roots (in time series analysis), 211–215
Identification, 41–43, 161*f*, 258–261, 272, 318, 323–345, 352, 485
Box–Jenkins analysis, in context of, 199–201, 203, 207, 225 404, 407
demand-supply model, in context of, 258–261
by equality restrictions, 325, 332, 333, 335, 336, 342
in general, 6*f*, 10*f*, 348, 404, 411, 412, 425
by general linear restrictions, 325, 326, 332–336, 340, 344, 348, 352, 356, 358, 366*f*, 368*f*, 374*f*, 389*f*
general order condition, 328–331, 334, 335, 343, 345, 363, 401, 402, 485, 589
general rank condition, 327–331, 333–335, 341, 343, 345, 351, 401, 402, 589
just identified case, 42–44, 259, 323, 328, 330, 331, 335, 336, 343, 351, 356–358, 360, 363, 364, 366, 367, 369*f*, 370, 375, 379, 389*f*, 394, 395, 589
money, demand for and supply of, 396
nonlinear case, 339–341
overidentified case, 42, 44, 323, 328, 336, 343, 344, 351, 356, 360, 363, 366, 367, 369*f*, 375, 395, 589
under permanent income hypothesis, 156, 177, 323*f*, 335
recursive systems, in context of, 326, 337–339, 344
by relative variances, 260, 261, 271, 325, 326
restrictions on coefficient and covariance matrices, 325, 326, 344
underidentified case, 42–44, 328, 335, 336, 363
by zero restrictions, 36, 42*f*, 43, 258, 259, 325–331, 335, 337, 348–350, 468
(*See also* Indirect least squares [ILS])
Implicit function theorem, 492*f*, 493*f*
Income elasticity of demand (*See* Elasticity of demand, income)
Index model, 171
Indicative planning (*See* Policy evaluation, indicative planning)
Indifference curves (*See* Household, theory of, indifference curve)
Indirect least squares, 331, 336, 338, 339, 352, 356–360, 361*f*, 364, 366, 367, 369*f*, 370, 371, 394–396
Indirect translog system of demand equations, 257, 258
Industrial organization, 470–474, 587, 593, 596
advertising, 470, 472, 474
bias of previous studies, 474
inflation, 470
result of study, 470, 473, 474
simultaneous estimation of relationships, 471–474, 485
structure-conduct-performance (SCP) hypothesis, 470–472
(*See also* Concentration)
Inferior good, 242, 246, 250, 254, 268, 270, 497
Inferior inputs (*See* Firm, theory of, inferior inputs)
Information:
a posteriori, 325, 326, 333, 533, 627
a priori, 325, 326, 332, 333, 383, 385, 425, 471*f*, 499, 533, 572, 580
Information criterion (*See* Akaike information criterion)
Information matrix, 84, 203, 236
Information set, 409, 410
Informetrica Limited, 580, 581
Input-output (system or production functions), 33, 35, 293–295, 302, 305, 311, 313, 440, 441, 443, 453*f*, 455, 457, 491
Institutional relationships, 34
Instrumental variables, 157, 158, 229, 369, 370–374, 379–382, 391, 392, 471*f*
Instrumental variables estimator (*See* Estimators)
Instruments (of policy), 34, 211, 344, 435, 436, 438–442, 450, 452, 480, 510, 546–559, 578, 593
Integrated processes, 208–212, 412, 413, 421
Interdependence, 336*f*
Interpolation (*See* Data, interpolation)
Invariance property (for probability limits), 83
Inverted gamma (probability distribution), 112
Invertibility condition (of a time series process), 198, 200, 219, 404, 410, 414
Investment function, 431, 432, 434, 437, 458, 459, 494, 512, 529
Investment tax credit (of the United States), 53–54, 121
"Invisible hand," 15–16
IS-LM analysis, 495
Isocosts (*See* Firm, theory of)
Isoquants (*See* Firm, theory of)
Iterative instrumental variables (IIV) estimator, 374
Jacobian (*See* Matrices, Jacobian matrix)
Judgment in econometrics, role of 10*f*, 582, 583 (*See also* Econometric model, role of judgment)
Just identified case (*See* Identification)
k-class estimator (*See* Estimator)
Kernel estimate (nonparametric estimation), 169, 170, 419
Klein–Goldberger model, 436–438, 447, 448, 504, 505, 529, 534
Klein interwar model, 432–436, 459, 510, 529, 534, 540, 554, 565
Koyck distributed lag, 190, 228, 229, 234, 265, 267, 272, 437, 459, 484, 537, 539
Kronecker delta, 269, 601, 611
Kronecker product (*See* Matrices, Kronecker product)
Labor economics, 474, 475
earnings and individual characteristics, 475
Lagged variables (including lagged dependent variables), 102, 144*f*, 179, 213, 214, 225, 226, 228, 231, 232, 263, 401, 437, 452, 467–469, 500, 533, 548*f*, 549
Lag operator, 189, 190, 202, 203, 206, 209, 211, 219–223, 228, 400–404, 407, 408, 410, 411, 413–415, 421–425
Lagrange multipliers, 87*f*, 88, 94–96, 134*f*
Lagrange multiplier test, 94–96, 139
Latent continuous random variable crossing threshold, 161
Leading indicators, 408, 518
composite index, 518*f*
diffusion index, 518*f*
League of Nations, 454
Least squares dummy variable estimator (in context of error components model), 148, 149
Least squares estimation, 70, 74–79, 136, 137, 140, 148, 149, 151–153, 167, 168, 202, 203, 212, 215, 229, 231, 256, 295, 299, 352, 353, 363, 366, 371, 416, 418, 419, 426, 615
and additive consistency, 571–573, 584
in censored regression models, 164–166
consistency of, 83–84, 358
constrained, 87–88
with errors in variables, 155–157
fundamental idempotent matrix of (*See* Fundamental idempotent matrices of least squares estimation)
geometric interpretation of, 76–78, 122
indirect (*See* Indirect least squares)
as an instrumental variable estimator, 158
lagged dependent variables, with, 231, 232
nonlinear, 159, 160, 165, 203, 209, 217, 225, 390
ordinary (*See* Ordinary least squares)
predictor, 98
reduced forms, 322, 341, 356–359, 361–364, 366, 368, 372, 374, 375

Least squares estimation (*cont.*)
residuals, 76–78, 143, 153, 154, 322, 362, 363, 365, 366, 367*f*, 368, 372, 380, 390, 418, 584
three-stage (*See* Three-stage least squares)
two-stage (*See* Two-stage least squares)
weighted regression (as an alternative), 168
Least variance ratio (LVR) estimator, 369*f*
Less developed countries (LDCs), application of macroeconometric and CGE models to, 33, 34*f*, 453*f*
Likelihood function, 84–86, 97, 112, 117, 150, 162, 164, 165, 201–203, 345, 368*f*, 383–386, 420
Likelihood ratio test, 94–96, 417, 420
Limited dependent variable, 160–166
Limited information approach (*See* Estimation)
Limited information maximum likelihood (LIML) estimator, 352, 353, 368*f*, 369*f*, 373*f*, 392, 393, 437
Limited information single equation (LISE) estimator, 369*f*
Limiting distribution (*See* Asymptotic distribution)
Linear decision rule (*See* Policy evaluation)
Linear difference equations 190, 191
boundary conditions, 190
determinantal equation, 190–191, 263, 264
non-homogeneous form, 191, 263
stationary condition, 191, 263
Linear expenditure system, 254–256, 263, 270, 271
base quantities, 255, 256
estimation, 255, 256, 258
marginal budget shares, 255, 256
supernumerary income, 255, 256
Linear filter, 222
Linear independence of vectors (*See* Matrices)
Linearity (contrasted to nonlinearity), 47, 171, 172, 209, 441, 457, 458, 493, 498, 500, 511, 540, 588
Linear production function, 294, 295
Linear restrictions on regression coefficients, 86–88, 92, 93, 131*f*, 231
Linear transformations, 616, 633
LINK (*See* Project LINK)
Linked systems (*See* Models, multicountry)
Logarithmic transformation, 20, 24*f*, 47
Logistic curve, 209, 539
Log likelihood ratio statistic, 105, 107
Log-linear form (and log-linear functions), 448
Lognormal probability distribution, 636
Loss function, 114, 116, 538, 539
Lucas critique, 10, 579 580, 582
Marginalization (in context of analyzing economic data), 173
Marginal products (*See* Firm, theory of, marginal products)
Marginal propensity to consume, 7, 20*f*, 33, 157, 350, 351, 355, 356, 359, 370, 371, 394, 433, 459, 494, 496, 511, 571–573, 584
Markov process (*See* Autoregressive process, first-order)
Marshallian demand functions, 247
Mathematical economics (different from econometrics), 1, 2
Mathematical programming (*See* Matrices)
Matrices, 26–27, 36*f*, 37, 319*f*, 589, 599–623, 634, 637–639
addition, 602, 603, 607
adjoint matrix, 422, 610
bilinear forms, and, 620
block diagonal, 345, 376, 378, 379, 391, 565, 602, 611
block triangular, 345, 384, 565, 602
characteristic equation, 616, 617
characteristic root, 420, 500*f*, 616–619
characteristic vector, 420, 616, 617
co-factor, 609, 610
covariance (*See* Covariance matrix)
Cramer's rule, and (*See* Cramer's rule)
decomposable, 606, 607
derivatives, 565, 599*f*, 619–623
determinants, 422, 608, 609, 611, 617, 620, 637
diagonal matrix, 336, 337, 344, 375, 377, 379, 380, 385, 386, 402, 403, 421, 449*f*, 483*f*, 565, 601, 605, 608, 610, 611, 617, 618, 633, 637
eigenvalue (*See* Matrices, characteristic root)
eigenvector (*See* Matrices, characteristic vector)
elements, 599
equality, 602
fundamental idempotent matrix (*See* Fundamental idempotent
matrices of least squares regression)
generalized inverse, 392, 599*f*, 611, 612, 615
gradient vector, 620, 621
Hessian matrix, 285, 621
homogeneous linear equations, 328*f*, 333, 335*f*, 613, 614, 616
trivial solution, 328*f*, 333, 614, 616
idempotent matrix, 363, 604, 610, 612, 615, 618, 639
identity matrix, 402, 601, 602, 607, 610, 619
indecomposable (or connected) matrix, 607
indefiniteness (of quadratic forms), 618
inequality, 602
information (*See* Information matrix)
inner product (or dot product or scalar product), 604, 605
inverse, 27, 27*f*, 160, 421*f*, 610–613, 619, 620, 637
inverse as a series expansion, 611
Jacobian matrix, 85, 340, 383, 384, 492*f*, 621, 622*f*
Kronecker product, 377–380, 382, 384, 385, 390, 599*f*, 607, 610
k-th order trace, 609, 616
Lagrange multipliers, and, 622, 623
leading principal minor, 609, 618, 619
least squares fit, and, 599*f*, 615, 616, 622, 623
under linear constraints, 623
weighted least squares fit, 615, 616
linear equations (*See* Matrices, systems of linear equations)
linear form (or inner product), 620, 639
linearly independent vectors, 412, 413, 424, 425, 609*f*
linear transformations, and (*See* Linear transformations)
mathematical programming (optimization), and, 553, 554, 566, 599*f*, 621–623
minor, 609
modal matrix, 617–619
multiplication, matrix, 603–605, 607
multiplication, scalar, 603, 607
negative (of a matrix), 603
negative definiteness of, 618, 619, 621, 622
negative semidefiniteness of, 81, 244, 285, 381, 383*f*, 618, 619, 621
nonsingular, 320, 324*f*, 363, 364 365, 373, 380, 391*f*, 493*f*, 500*f*, 550, 551, 553, 554, 610–613, 615, 617, 619, 620
normalized vector, 606, 617
norm of vector, 606, 615
null space, 413
order, 599, 610, 611, 619
orthogonal matrix, 606, 608, 610, 611, 617
orthogonal vectors, 605, 606, 617
outer product, 605
partitioned, 153*f*, 333, 357, 359, 362–364, 366*f*, 368, 369, 372, 376, 378, 379, 384, 602, 611, 612, 631
permutation matrix, 601, 602, 604, 606, 609
polynomials, and, 401, 403, 404, 421*f*, 422, 423, 616
positive definiteness, 114, 320, 347, 393, 552, 553, 615*f*, 618, 619, 636
positive semidefiniteness, 391*f*, 393, 618, 619, 633, 639
postmultiplication, 603, 604, 610
powers of, 604, 611, 617
premultiplication, 603, 604, 610, 612
principal diagonal, 600, 602, 605, 606, 632
principal minor, 609, 611
quadratic forms, 552*f*, 553, 554, 615*f*, 618–620, 633, 637*f*, 639
rank (*See* Rank [of a matrix])
scalar, 599, 619, 620
scalar matrix, 601
scatter matrix, 606, 608
similar matrices, 611, 617
singular matrix, 610, 612
skew-symmetric matrix, 605
solutions (to systems of linear equations), 613
unique, 613, 614
square matrix, 600, 608–613, 616, 618, 620
stationary point, 621
submatrices, 602, 606, 607, 610–612
subtraction, 603
sum of squares, 605, 606, 615, 623
symmetric matrix, 244, 363, 605, 606, 611, 612, 615, 617, 618, 633, 636
systems of linear equations, 328*f*, 612–615, 622, 623
geometric interpretation, 614
trace of, 82*f*, 89, 607–609, 611, 615, 617, 620
transpose, 605
triangular matrix, 336, 337, 344, 385, 386, 449*f*, 565, 601, 608, 619, 637, 638
unit vectors, 601
unity vectors, 601
vectors, 599, 600, 605, 613, 614, 618–621, 632–634, 636–638
weighted sum of squares, 615, 619
zero matrix, 600
Maximum likelihood estimation, 70, 84–86, 95, 119, 148, 154, 160, 162, 163, 165, 166, 168, 172, 180, 201–203, 207, 217, 229, 342, 353, 358*f*, 383–386, 407, 419, 420
Mean, arithmetic (*See* Probability and statistics, mean [universe] *and* Probability and statistics, sample mean)
Mean squared error, 80, 81, 219, 220, 388, 389, 535, 539
Measurement errors (*See* Errors in variables)
Method of moments, 70, 86
Method of scoring, 163
Minimum chi-square estimator, 163
Minimum drinking age, 480–482
Misspecification (*See* Specification error)
Models:
AERIC, 532*f*
algebraic, 17–19, 24, 465, 588

analytical, 14–15
black box, 14
Boston Company Economic Advisors (BCEA), 453, 507*f*
Brookings, 35*f*, 443, 448–450, 457*f*, 506, 556*f*, 558
Bureau of Economic Analysis (BEA), 443*f*, 450, 451, 506*f*, 507*f*, 529
CANDIDE, 35*f*, 455, 456, 457*f*, 508, 532*f*, 559, 561
censored regression, 164–166, 171, 172, 177
Chase econometric, 443*f*, 529, 534
choice of, 45, 70, 107–109, 173–175
cobweb (*See* Cobweb model)
computable general equilibrium (CGE), 34*f*, 35
constraints within, 570
decision, 34
definition of, 13–15
descriptive, 14
deterministic, 21, 23*f*
discrete response, 160–164
DRI (*See* DRI model)
dynamic, 23, 24
econometric (*See* Econometric model)
Economic Planning Agency (EPA), 35*f*
error components (*See* Error components)
error correction (*See* Error correction model)
Fair (*See* Fair model)
Federal Reserve Board (new), 442*f*, 507*f*
FOCUS (University of Toronto), 508*f*
forecasting (*See* Forecasts and forecasting)
in general, 2, 3, 13, 14, 582, 592
generalized gravity, 47
geometric, 16–18, 465
Georgia State University, 529
growth, 447, 448, 451, 452
Harrod–Domar (of economic growth), 46
Hickman–Coen, 451, 452, 495, 506
index, 171, 172
Indiana University Center for Econometric Research, 453*f*, 495, 507*f*
intervention, 223
Kaldor (of trade cycle), 46
Kent Economic and Development Institute (KEDI), 529
Klein postwar quarterly, 437*f*
linear probability, 161, 162, 178
Liu, 448, 452
Liu–Hwa, 448, 452, 536*f*
logit, 162, 163*f*, 164, 171, 178
Michigan Quarterly (MQEM), 448, 450, 495, 506*f*, 507*f*, 510*f*, 529, 536*f*
microanalytic simulation (*See* Simulation models, microanalytic)
MPS (FMP), 441, 442, 451, 468*f*, 506*f*, 507*f*, 530*f*, 536*f*, 557*f*
multicountry, 452, 454, 455, 457
naive, 529, 530, 532*f*, 577
Office of Business Economics (OBE) (*See* Models, Bureau of Economic Analysis)
partial adjustment, 228, 234, 235, 264, 265, 272, 305, 467–469, 484, 485
peripheral (*See* Models, satellite)
physical, 16
policy, 34
probit, 161–164, 166, 171, 177
prototype macro, 24, 29–33, 39, 42, 44, 50, 53, 55, 102, 225, 325, 350, 352, 360, 370, 371, 393, 420, 430, 432–434, 494–496, 498, 499, 511, 527, 528, 549, 550, 553, 557, 558, 565, 572, 589, 592
prototype micro, 16, 24–29, 39, 43, 50–52, 121, 122, 258, 259, 326, 330, 331, 394, 510, 589, 592
putty-clay (of technology), 296*f*
Quarterly Forecasting Model (QFM), University of Toronto, 508, 532*f*
RDX2, 508
RIM (Regional Informetrica Model), 580
satellite, 519, 582
seasonal (*See* Seasonality)
selection (*See* Model, choice of)
simultaneous equations (*See* Econometric model, linear)
Smithies (multiplier-accelerator), 46
static, 23, 24, 29
stochastic, 19, 21–23, 23*f*, 24
stock adjustment (*See* Model, partial adjustment)
structural equations model (*See* Econometric model, linear)
Suits, 448, 451, 503, 524*f*, 534
Taylor, 452, 453, 507*f*, 562*f*
TIM (The Informetrica Model), 579
TRACE (University of Toronto), 508
truncated regression (*See* Models, censored regression)
UCLA, 529, 581
Valavanis (*See* Valavanis model)
verbal/logical, 15
vintage, 308
Washington University Macro Model (WUMM), 453*f*, 507*f*
Working's, 257
Moments (*See* Probability and statistics, moments [universe])
Monetarism, 442*f*, 443, 450, 506, 560
Money:
active balances, 467
asset demand, 467, 470
"liquidity trap," 469
models of supply and demand, 45, 395, 396, 441*f*, 450, 458, 466–470, 484, 485, 575
monetary policy, 211, 441, 448, 449*f*, 450, 452, 453, 509, 510, 545, 548*f*, 551, 555, 559–561, 587
monetary sector, 438, 440–443, 452, 453, 554*f*, 558–560, 564, 588, 592, 595–597
motives for holding, 466
passive balances, 467
precautionary motive, 466
speculative (or portfolio) motive, 466
time-series models, 425
transactions demand, 466, 467
velocity, 467, 485
Monte Carlo studies, 168, 212, 213, 215, 369*f*, 374, 386–389, 393, 416, 421, 521, 555*f*
Morishima–Saito model, 448, 449
Moving average (MA) process (time-series), 194–198, 200, 202, 204, 207, 221, 402, 406, 410, 411, 422
MPS model (*See* Models, MPS)
Multicollinearity, 58, 59, 104 126–133, 153, 175, 189, 228, 258, 288–291, 386, 389, 481, 592
condition index of, 128, 129
imperfect, 127–130
perfect, 126, 127, 392
remedies for, 131, 132
variance decomposition proportions, measure of, 128–130
Multiple correlation coefficient, 79
Multiple linear regression (*See* Basic linear regression model)
Multiplier:
comparative, 502, 506–508, 509*f*, 577*f*
in general, 18, 19, 20*f*, 358*f*, 446, 449*f*, 453, 491, 498–510, 550*f*, 563, 572, 577, 592
impact, 31, 32, 33, 104, 494, 496, 498, 500, 502, 504, 505, 508–512
interim, 32, 450, 451, 452*f*, 453*f*, 499–503, 505–511, 577
long-term, 32, 33, 42, 104, 435, 499–502, 504, 507, 508, 510, 511, 589
short-term, 31, 33, 42, 511, 589
t-period, 32, 499
Naive approach, 351, 352, 388, 540 (*See also* Models, naive)
National Bureau of Economic Research, 64, 438, 517*f*, 529, 532*f*, 535
National Longitudinal Surveys (NLS) of Labor Market Experience, 146
Nearest neighbors (in context of nonparametric estimation), 170, 391, 392
Negativity conditions (*See* Household, theory of, negativity conditions)
Nerlove–Ringstad production function, 298, 310
Neumann expansion, 500*f*
New Keynesianism, 452, 453
Newton–Raphson method, 159, 160, 162, 165, 403
"Noise" (in a time series) (*See* Stochastic disturbance term)
Nonlinear least squares (*See* Least squares estimation, nonlinear)
Nonnested hypothesis testing, 104–107, 109*f*
Nonparametric estimation, 168–171, 391
Nonparametric testing, 576–578
Nonstationary time series, 207–215
Normal equations (of least squares estimation), 75, 82, 158, 369
Normal goods (*See* Household, theory of)
Normalization rule, 38, 319, 325, 327, 328*f*, 331, 333, 335, 337, 339, 348, 350, 369*f*, 383, 385, 412–414, 416, 420
Normal probability distribution, 22, 154, 174, 212, 320, 321, 342, 369*f*, 373, 382*f*, 383, 392, 393, 411, 419, 635–638, 639
multivariate normal distribution, 636–639
Nuisance parameters (*See* Parameters, nuisance)
Observational equivalence, 324, 325
Office of Business Economics/Bureau of Economic Analysis (OBE/BEA) econometric model (*See* Models, Bureau of Economic Analysis)
Optimal control (*See* Policy evaluation)
Optimization (*See* Matrices, mathematical programming)
Ordinal utility, 239*f*
Ordinary least squares (OLS), as a simultaneous equations estimator, 323, 336, 352–356, 358, 363, 364, 366, 368–370, 372, 373, 377, 378, 381, 386, 388, 389, 393–396, 437*f*, 439, 440, 445, 448, 472–474, 483, 571*f*
Orthogonal (matrices or vectors) (*See* Matrices)
Overidentified case (*See* Identification)
Panel data (*See* Data, panel)
Panel Study of Income Dynamics, 146
Paradigm, 15, 465
Parameters, 3, 10, 19, 20, 25, 35, 43, 71, 175, 198, 199, 203, 209, 294, 323–325, 336–339, 343, 348, 350, 351, 352, 368, 373*f*, 374, 384, 385, 387, 390, 402, 407, 409, 442, 449, 451, 492–497, 500, 511, 512, 549, 550, 556, 558, 571, 637
bogus, 324, 325, 336, 345, 352, 401
nuisance, 171, 172, 418

Pareto distribution, 167
Partial adjustment model (*See* Models, partial adjustment)
Partial autoregressive matrix, 405–407
Partial equilibrium analysis, 241, 248, 303
Partially generalized least squares, 138, 139
Performance indicators, 559*f*
Period (of a seasonal pattern), 205
Period functions (*See* Seasonality)
Permanent income hypothesis, 156, 157, 467, 484
Phillips Curve, 4, 4*f*, 339, 439, 451, 561
Physician visits, demand for, 476–479
Pierce and Haugh test, 410, 411
"Pitfalls" model (*See* Additive consistency)
Policy evaluation, 4, 10, 28, 33, 238, 440, 446–449, 452, 476, 470, 481, 482, 514, 516*f*, 545–565, 572, 581*f*, 582, 588, 590, 593
  certainty equivalence, 553*f*
  decision variables (instruments) (*See* Instruments [of policy])
  Delphi method, 517*f*, 547
  derivative stabilization policy, 553*f*
  disjointed incrementalism, 547, 548
  econometric approach, 436, 440, 442*f*, 546*f*, 548–564
  energy policy, 564, 595
  expert opinion, 546, 547, 562
  feasibility (of objectives), 551
  frequency of revision, 546*f*
  horizon, 545, 546, 554, 555*f*
  indicative planning, 547*f*, 559*f*
  instruments-targets approach, 548–551, 555, 557, 562–565
  integral stabilization policy, 553*f*
  judgment, role of, 546, 547, 558
  linear decision rule, 553
  long-term, 545, 546, 555, 564
  macroeconomic (*See* Fiscal policy *and* Money, monetary policy)
  "menu" of alternatives, 556, 557
  optimal control, 554, 555, 562
  optimal policy, 546, 550, 552–554, 558, 563–565, 593
  policy degrees of freedom, 550, 551
  policy multipliers, 557, 558, 564
  proportional stabilization policy, 553
  rolling plan, 546*f*
  short-term, 545, 546, 555
  simulation approach, 549, 555–565
  social rate of discount, 555*f*
  social-welfare-function approach, 549, 551–555, 557, 562, 563, 565
  trade-offs (among policy objectives), 551, 552, 560, 593
Policy regime, 579, 580
Policy simulation (*See* Simulation, policy *and* Policy evaluation, simulation approach)
Polynomial distributed lag (*See* Almon distributed lag)
Posterior distribution, 110–114
Posterior odds, 116, 117
Potential output (or GNP), 450, 451, 578
Predetermined variables (*See* Variables, predetermined)
Prediction (*see* Forecasts and forecasting)
Prediction criterion, 108, 109
Price system, 15–16
Principal components, 366*f*
Prior distribution, 110, 112, 117
Probability and statistics, 625–639
  Bayes theorem, 627
  calculus of probabilities, 626, 630
  central limit theorem, 636, 638 (*See also* Central limit theorem)
  chi-squared (X^2) distribution (*See* Chi-squared distribution)
  conditional density, 631, 638
  conditional probability, 626, 627
  correlation coefficient (universe), 634, 637
  covariance (universe), 632, 633, 637, 638
  covariance matrix (*See* Covariance matrix)
  density functions, 340, 628–632, 635–637
  distribution function, 628–631, 634, 636, 637
  ellipsoid of concentration, 637
  events, 625
  expectations (mathematical), 360, 365, 633
  F distribution (*See F* probability distribution)
  law of large numbers, 636*f*
  limiting relative-frequency definition of probability, 626
  Lindeberg–Levy central limit theorem (*See* Probability and statistics, central limit theorem)
  lognormal distribution (*See* Lognormal probability distribution)
  marginal density function, 631, 638
  marginal distribution function, 631, 638
  mean (universe), 632, 635–639
  moment generating function, 634
  moments (universe), 634
  multivariate statistics, 629*f*
  normal probability distribution (*See* Normal probability distribution)
  "objective" probability, 627
  posterior probability, 627
  precision matrix, 637
  prior probability, 627
  probability, axiomatic definition of, 625, 626
  probability element, 628–632
  random variable (*See* Random variable)
  relative-frequency interpretation of probability, 626
  sample correlation coefficient, 635
  sample covariance, 635
  sample mean, 634–636, 639
  sample space, 625, 627, 628
  sample variance, 635, 638, 639
  skewed distribution, 636, 638, 639
  statistical (mutual) independence, 631, 633, 634, 636–639
  statistics (definition), 634
  subjective degree of belief (interpretation of probability), 626, 627
  t distribution (*See* Student *t* probability distribution) variance (universe), 632, 633, 635–639
Probability limit, 82–84, 155, 157, 158, 231, 232, 354–356, 358, 360, 361, 364, 365, 368, 369, 372–374, 380–382, 394, 411, 636, 639
Production functions (in general), 20, 21, 35, 150, 275, 276, 284–299, 304, 306, 437, 448
  engineering, 312, 313
  intensive form, 289, 290
Project LINK, 454, 455, 560, 561
Protectionism, 454, 455
Pseudo differences (in context of autocorrelation), 141, 402
Quadratic forms (*See* Matrices, quadratic forms)
Qualitative dependent variable, 161–164
Quantity theory of money, 467
R^2, 78–79, 121, 366, 367*f*, 389, 481, 483, 519, 582, 592
  adjusted for degrees of freedom, 107, 108
Random effects (in context of error components models), 148, 150
Random numbers, 387
Random shocks 437, 438
Random variable, 71, 72, 421, 422, 524, 553*f*, 627–638
  bivariate case, 629, 631
  continuous, 628
  countable, 628
  finite (discrete), 628
  m-dimensional, 629, 631–634, 637, 638
  uncorrelated random variables, 633, 634, 637
Random walk, 23*f*, 216, 408, 414, 522*f*
Rank (of a matrix), 73, 126, 153, 322, 328*f*, 329, 330, 334, 335, 340, 341, 344, 351, 363, 390, 401, 413–415, 417, 420, 423, 609–617, 619, 622, 623
Rate of foreign exchange, 440, 443, 444, 451, 453, 454, 510*f*, 532, 548*f*, 561, 562, 578
Rational distributed lag, 223, 236
Rationing, 238
Recursive systems, 326, 336–339, 344, 345, 354*f*, 385, 386, 388, 389, 394, 449*f*, 483*f*
  block recursive system, 345, 449*f*
Reduced form:
  coefficients, 27, 43, 320–331, 333, 336–339, 341, 343, 356–359, 361, 364, 375, 387, 491, 498, 519–524, 528
  equations, 27, 30, 31, 39, 41, 42, 43, 50, 102, 260, 320–323, 326, 333, 336–339, 341, 342, 345, 356, 357, 359, 361, 363, 366, 380, 387, 423, 435, 437*f*, 458, 480, 481, 491, 493, 494, 499, 504, 511, 518–520, 522*f*, 523, 528, 538, 549, 552, 556, 589, 591, 592
Redundancy (in dynamic econometric models), 401, 402
Regression:
  analysis, 74
  origin of term, 117
  simple examples, 99–104
RESET test, 146, 153, 154
Residual-based tests, 416
Residuals, analysis of, 577
Reswitching (*See* Firm, theory of, technical change)
Robust methods, 167, 168
Root mean square error, 388*f*, 533*f*, 576, 577
Rotterdam system (of demand equations), 257, 272
Roy's identity, 247, 269
St. Louis model (*See also* Monetarism) 450, 451, 506, 507, 534
Sample size, 170, 385*f*, 386, 389, 392, 403, 437*f*, 589
Sample space (*See* Probability and statistics, sample space)
Satisficing, 275*f*, 548
Saturation level, 268
Savings function (*See* Consumption function)
Scale elasticity (*See* Elasticity of production)
Scatter matrix, 390
Score test, 95
Seasonal adjustment, 206, 207, 211, 589
Seasonality, 205–207, 211, 216
Seemingly unrelated regressions, 135, 136, 177, 317*f*, 375, 379, 403
Selection bias, 164
Semiparametric estimation, 171–173
Sensitivity analysis, 175
Serial correlation (*See* Autocorrelation)
Series approximation (in context of nonparametric estimation), 391, 392
Shephard's lemma, 247, 269, 284, 302, 305, 309, 313

"Signal" (of a time series), 61
Sign conditions, 281, 282
Sims test, 410
Simulation, 17*f*, 387*f*, 499*f*, 500, 501, 507*f*, 509*f*, 521, 557
  block, 576
  historical, 555, 556, 576, 577
  policy, 556, 562, 578
  projection, 556, 561, 578
  stochastic, 521, 555*f*, 577, 578
Simulation models, microanalytic, 34, 35, 57*f*
Simultaneous equations estimation (*See* Estimation)
Simultaneous equations model (*See* Econometric model *and* Econometric model, linear)
Slutsky conditions (*See* Household, theory of)
Slutsky equation, 244*f*, 245*f*, 269, 475*f*
Small sample properties (*See* Estimators)
Smoothing parameter, 169
Social Science Citation Index, 11, 588*f*, 593
Social welfare function (Bergson-type) (*See* Bergson social welfare function)
Specification (of a model), 3, 45, 189, 204, 218, 219, 389*f*
Specification bias, 152, 208
Specification error, 24*f*, 132, 144, 145, 150–155, 177, 208, 356, 389, 431, 523, 551, 558
Spectral analysis, 61*f*, 419
Spherical disturbances (*See* Stochastic disturbance term, spherical)
Speed of convergence, 90
Stage-of-processing prices submodel, 441, 443
Standard error of prediction, 98, 99, 421, 514*f*, 521, 537, 574, 575
Standard errors (of regression coefficients), 82, 90, 170, 217, 218, 406, 407, 469, 470, 472, 477*f*, 497, 591*f*, 592
  asymptotic, 364*f*, 374
Stationary processes (time series), 191–198, 200, 211, 212–219, 225, 403, 404, 412–416, 418, 421, 424
  autocorrelations, 192, 197, 199–201, 203, 204, 207, 215–222
  autocovariances, 192, 197–200, 202, 405
  generating functions, 192–194, 197, 198, 202
  partial autocorrelation functions, 199–201, 203, 207, 215–219
  strict stationarity, 192, 193, 196
  weak stationarity, 192–194, 196
Statistical discrepancy, 62, 450
Statistical significance (*See* Hypothesis testing)
Stochastic disturbance term, 22–26, 29, 37, 40, 41, 61, 71, 72, 208, 226, 231, 232, 248, 252, 260–262, 267*f*, 288–290, 295, 302, 303, 319, 320, 322, 336–339, 347, 350, 351, 354, 357, 361, 364–370, 372, 373*f*, 374–379, 381, 382*f*, 383, 386, 387, 390, 392, 393, 401–403, 410, 411, 413, 415, 416, 431, 440, 442, 444, 458, 475, 480, 483*f*, 490, 491, 493, 500, 501, 520, 521, 524, 526, 528, 532, 534, 536, 549, 550, 553*f*, 555, 556, 558, 578, 579, 588, 591*f*, 600, 636*f*
  spherical, 72, 73, 133, 188 (*See also* White noise)
Stochastic simulation (*See* Simulation, stochastic)
Stock adjustment (in Houthakker-Taylor model), 267, 268
Stock adjustment model (*See* Models, partial adjustment)
Stock market prices, 23*f*, 425, 442, 444, 447, 453, 518, 522*f*
Stone–Geary (Klein–Rubin) utility function, 255*f*, 270
Structural analysis, 10, 28, 33, 238, 435, 446, 448, 449, 476, 490–510, 590
Structural change 59, 62, 96, 97, 131*f*, 174, 436, 469*f*, 551, 558, 575, 579, 580
Structural coefficients, 27, 43, 323–332, 336, 338, 339, 343, 356–359, 366, 374, 375, 387, 388, 490, 491, 493, 495, 499
Structural equation(s), 19, 25, 27, 36, 42, 260, 318, 319, 323, 326, 332, 336–339, 343, 355, 361, 366, 375, 380, 389, 430, 432, 433, 444, 445, 453, 519, 579, 580, 589, 591
Structural equations model (*See* Econometric model *and* Econometric model, linear)
Structural form, 25, 26, 30, 36, 38, 40–41, 50,
  260, 326, 332, 345, 358, 361, 383, 458,
  481, 490, 493, 499, 519, 548, 549, 550, 591*f*, 592
Structure-conduct-performance (SCP) hypothesis (or paradigm) (*See* Industrial organization)
Student studies, 11, 14*f*, 569, 583, 586–593
Student *t* probability distribution, 113, 115, 146, 167, 212–214, 476*f*, 477*f*, 591*f*, 592, 638, 639
Substitutes (*See* Household, theory of and Firm, theory of)
Substitution, ex ante, 296*f*
Substitution, ex post, 296*f*
Substitution, marginal rate of technical (*See* Firm, theory of)
Suits model (*See* Models, Suits)
Summation operator, 210
Supercomputer, 454
Superior good, 25, 246, 268
Supply function (*See* Firm, theory of output supply function)
Symmetry condition (*See* Household, theory of *and* Firm, theory of)
"System dynamics," 17*f*
Systems of linear equations (*See* Matrices)
Tangency point solution, 240, 277
Taylor's series expansion, 21, 159, 160, 249*f*, 257, 258, 297, 302
Technical change (*See* Firm, theory of, technical change)
Technical coefficients (of input-output production function), 293
Technical relations, 34, 302
Teigen model, 468–470, 485
Theil inequality coefficient (*See* Forecasts and forecasting, accuracy, inequality coefficient)
Theil-Nagar test statistic (for first order autocorrelation), 144*f*
Three-stage least squares (3SLS), 353, 373*f*, 374–383, 385, 388–395, 475
Time-series analysis, 187–189, 210, 465
  multiple, 403–425, 518*f*
Time-series decomposition, 61, 188
Time-series processes, 188, 207–222, 225 (*See also* Stationary processes)
Tinbergen model, 447
Tobit models (*See* Models, censored regression)
Törnquist–Engel curves, 269
t probability distribution (*See* Student *t* probability distribution)
Trade-off curve (*See* Phillips Curve)
Transcendental production function, 297, 310, 311
Transfer function models, 222–225, 228, 423 (*See also* Distributed lag models)
Translog cost function (*see* Cost function, translog)
Translog production function, 298, 302, 308, 310
Trends, 7–9, 99–102, 207–209, 211, 213, 537
  common 414, 416
  polynomial, 208–210
  removal, 392, 589
Trigonometric functions (to represent periodicity), 206
Two-stage least squares (2SLS) estimator, 352, 353, 360–368, 369*f*, 370–375, 377–382, 388–390, 392–396, 439, 448, 469, 472–474, 571*n*, 584, 589*f*, 591
Unbiasedness (*See* Estimators, unbiasedness)
Underidentified case (*See* Identification)
Unique inverse relationship, 339, 340
Unit root (of determinantal equation of ARMA process), 208–215, 231, 416–418, 421
Utility function, indirect (*See* Household, theory of, indirect utility function)
Utility maximization (*See* Household, theory of, utility maximization)
Valavanis model, 447
Variable-elasticity-of-substitution (VES) production function, 298, 299
Variables:
  dummy (*See* Dummy variable)
  endogenous, 19, 24, 26, 29, 30, 35, 37, 40, 41, 51, 70, 160–166, 226, 288, 289, 295, 318, 319, 323, 326, 327, 331, 335–339, 345, 347–354, 357, 361, 362, 364–366, 369–372, 375, 376, 378, 379, 383, 388–391, 409, 418, 422, 423, 433–436, 439, 440, 441, 443–445, 447, 449, 458, 469, 471, 472, 475, 478–480, 490, 493, 495, 498–504, 507*f*, 510, 511, 518–523, 537, 540, 546, 548–557, 565, 576, 578, 580, 591, 592, 600
  exogenous, 18, 19, 24, 26, 29, 30, 35, 40, 41, 51, 70, 175, 226, 291*f*, 295, 318, 339, 345, 349, 350, 352, 353, 357, 359, 361, 362, 364–366, 368*f*, 369–372, 378–380, 387, 388, 390, 409, 411, 418, 422–425, 433–436, 438–444, 447–449, 453, 456, 458, 469, 471, 472, 475, 479, 480, 490, 491, 493, 495, 498–501, 503, 504, 507*f*, 510, 518–524, 526, 528, 534, 546, 548–550, 555–557, 559, 576*f*, 578, 580, 588, 591–593
  explanatory, 70–72, 158, 295, 323, 331, 337, 345, 349, 350, 352, 353, 357, 361, 362, 364–366, 369–372, 374–376, 378, 388, 449, 480, 571, 572, 600
  instrumental (*See* Instrumental variables)
  lagged endogenous, 29, 30, 34, 35, 40, 41, 51, 318, 349*f*, 351, 352, 374, 386, 423, 433–435, 437*f*, 442, 490, 491, 493, 495, 518, 522, 528, 548, 565, 588, 591
  predetermined, 30, 35, 37, 40, 231, 318, 319, 327, 331, 337, 347, 348, 349*f*, 351, 352, 402, 437*f*, 455*f*, 490, 491, 504, 511, 518, 548
  random (*See* Random variable)
Variance (in Monte Carlo studies), 387, 388
Variance of disturbance term, estimator of, 82, 86, 134, 158, 213, 322, 364*f*, 373, 374, 394, 408, 591*f*